DRAMATISTS

Great Writers of the English Language

Poets

Novelists and Prose Writers

Dramatists

GREAT WRITERS OF THE ENGLISH LANGUAGE

DRAMATISTS

EDITOR
JAMES VINSON

ASSOCIATE EDITOR
D. L. KIRKPATRICK

ST. MARTIN'S PRESS
NEW YORK

All rights reserved. For information write:
ST. MARTIN'S PRESS
175 Fifth Avenue
New York, New York 10010

ISBN 0–312–34570–4
Library of Congress Catalog Card Number 78–78303

Typeset by Computacomp (UK) Ltd.,
Fort William, Scotland

CONTENTS

EDITOR'S NOTE

The selection of writers included in this book is based on the recommendations of the advisers listed on page ix.

The entry for each writer consists of a biography, a complete list of his published books, a selected list of published bibliographies and critical studies on the writer, and a signed critical essay on his work.

In the biographies, details of education, military service, and marriage(s) are generally given before the usual chronological summary of the life of the writer; awards and honours are given last.

The Publications section is meant to include all book publications, though as a rule broadsheets, single sermons and lectures, minor pamphlets, exhibition catalogues, etc. are omitted. Under the heading Collections, we have listed the most recent collections of the complete works and those of individual genres (verse, plays, novels, stories, and letters); only those collections which have some editorial authority and were issued after the writer's death are listed; on-going editions are indicated by a dash after the date of publication; often a general selection from the writer's works or a selection from the works in the individual genres listed above is included.

Titles are given in modern spelling, though the essayists were allowed to use original spelling for titles and quotations; often the titles are "short." The date given is that of the first book publication, which often followed the first periodical or anthology publication by some time; we have listed the actual year of publication, often different from that given on the title-page. No attempt has been made to indicate which works were published anonymously or pseudonymously, or which works of fiction were published in more than one volume. We have listed plays which were produced but not published, but only since 1700; librettos and musical plays are listed along with the other plays; no attempt has been made to list lost or unverified plays. Reprints of books (including facsimile editions) and revivals of plays are not listed unless a revision or change of title is involved. The most recent edited version of individual works is included if it supersedes the collected edition cited.

In the essays, short references to critical remarks refer to items cited in the Publications section or in the Reading List. Introductions, memoirs, editorial matter, etc. in works cited in the Publications section are not repeated in the Reading List.

We would like to thank the advisers and contributors for their patience and help.

ADVISERS

Walter Allen
F. W. Bateson
Bernard Bergonzi
Earle Birney
Ruby Cohn
Allen Curnow
Warren French
John C. Gerber
Roma Gill
Daniel Hoffman
C. Hugh Holman
Louis James
A. Norman Jeffares
Lewis Leary
David Lodge

W. H. New
Roy Harvey Pearce
George Perkins
John M. Reilly
H. Winston Rhodes
Pat Rogers
Gāmini Salgādo
C. K. Stead
James Sutherland
Derek A. Traversi
Gerald Weales
Margaret Willy
James Woodress
Judith Wright

CONTRIBUTORS

Leonard R. N. Ashley
Paula R. Backscheider
Martin C. Battestin
R. W. Bevis
Walter Bode
Laurel Brake
Alan Brissenden
Ian Campbell
D. D. C. Chambers
Ruby Cohn
Saros Cowasjee
T. W. Craik
Eugene Current-Garcia
Tish Dace
Daniel DeMatteis
Charles Doyle
Victor A. Doyno
John Drakakis
Rhodes Dunlap
Geoffrey Dutton
Ian Fletcher
Joseph M. Flora
Margaret Forey
G. S. Fraser
Warren French
A. M. Gibbs
Roma Gill
Ian A. Gordon
Dorothy Green
Roger Lancelyn Green

Andrew Gurr
Robert Hogan
Leo Hughes
A. Norman Jeffares
Robert K. Johnson
Nancy C. Joyner
Zoë Coralnik Kaplan
Richard Kelly
Malcolm Kelsall
Burton Kendle
Kimball King
John G. Kuhn
Chirantan Kulshrestha
Don Kunz
G. A. Lester
Peter Lewis
Maurice Lindsay
Frederick M. Link
Bruce A. Lohof
John Lucas
E. D. Mackerness
James S. Malek
W. J. McCormack
Howard McNaughton
Walter J. Meserve
Jordan Y. Miller
Earl Miner
Margery Morgan
J. E. Morpurgo
L. J. Morrissey

Alastair Niven
B. C. Oliver-Morden
Barbara M. Perkins
Kirsten Holst Petersen
Helen Houser Popovich
Pat Rogers
James E. Ruoff
Ann Saddlemyer
Gāmini Salgādo
Arthur H. Scouten
Raymond C. Shady
J. N. Sharma
Stan Smith
Harry M. Solomon
Christopher Spencer
Louis Charles Stagg

Jane W. Stedman
Thomas B. Stroup
Peter A. Tasch
Ned Thomas
Peter Thomson
Ralph R. Thornton
E. W. F. Tomlin
Derek A. Traversi
Simon Trussler
William M. Tydeman
Raymond B. Waddington
Richard Walser
Harold H. Watts
Gerald Weales
Margaret Willy
Kenneth Young

DRAMATISTS

Edward Albee
Maxwell Anderson
John Arden
W. H. Auden

Enid Bagnold
Joanna Baillie
John Bale
John Banks
Harley Granville-Barker
James Nelson Barker
J. M. Barrie
Philip Barry
Clifford Bax
James K. Baxter
Francis Beaumont
Samuel Beckett
Brendan Behan
Aphra Behn
S. N. Behrman
David Belasco
Isaac Bickerstaff
Robert Montgomery Bird
George Henry Boker
Edward Bond
Gordon Bottomley
Dion Boucicault
James Bridie
Harold Brighouse
Richard Brome
Henry Brooke
George Villiers, Duke of Buckingham
John Baldwin Buckstone
Ed Bullins
John Burgoyne
H. J. Byron

Henry Carey
William Cartwright
Susanna Centlivre
George Chapman
Paddy Chayefsky
Henry Chettle
Colley Cibber
George M. Cohan
Sir Aston Cokayne
George Colman, the Elder
George Colman, the Younger
William Congreve
Mark Connelly
Noël Coward
Hannah Cowley
Rachel Crothers
John Crowne

Richard Cumberland

Augustin Daly
Clemence Dane
Sir William Davenant
John Day
Thomas Dekker
John Dennis
Charles Dibdin
Robert Dodsley
John Drinkwater
John Dryden
Ronald Duncan
William Dunlap
Lord Dunsany
Thomas D'Urfey

T. S. Eliot
St. John Ervine
Sir George Etherege

George Farquhar
Nathan Field
Henry Fielding
Clyde Fitch
Edward Fitzball
George Fitzmaurice
John Fletcher
Samuel Foote
John Ford
Christopher Fry
Athol Fugard

John Galsworthy
David Garrick
John Gay
W. S. Gilbert
William Gillette
Henry Glapthorne
Susan Glaspell
Oliver Goldsmith
Simon Gray
Paul Green
Lady Gregory

St. John Hankin
Lorraine Hansberry
Edward Harrigan
Moss Hart
Ben Hecht
Lillian Hellman
James A. Herne
John Heywood
Thomas Heywood

Aaron Hill
John Home
William Douglas Home
William Stanley Houghton
Laurence Housman
Bronson Howard
Sir Robert Howard
Sidney Howard
John Hughes
N. C. Hunter

William Inge

Douglas William Jerrold
Denis Johnston
Henry Arthur Jones
LeRoi Jones
Ben Jonson

George S. Kaufman
George Kelly
Hugh Kelly
Thomas Killigrew
Sidney Kingsley
James Sheridan Knowles
Arthur Kopit
Thomas Kyd

Arthur Laurents
Ray Lawler
John Howard Lawson
Nathaniel Lee
George Lillo
Frederick Lonsdale
John Lyly

Charles MacArthur
Percy MacKaye
Charles Macklin
Archibald MacLeish
Christopher Marlowe
Shakerley Marmion
John Marston
Edward Martyn
Bruce Mason
Philip Massinger
W. Somerset Maugham
Thomas May
Jasper Mayne
Henry Medwall
David Mercer
Thomas Middleton
Arthur Miller
Langdon Mitchell

William Thomas Moncrieff
William Vaughn Moody
Edward Moore
John Mortimer
Thomas Morton
Anna Cora Mowatt
Anthony Munday
Arthur Murphy

Thomas Nabbes
Thomas Norton

Sean O'Casey
Clifford Odets
John O'Keeffe
Eugene O'Neill
Joe Orton
John Osborne
Thomas Otway

John Howard Payne
George Peele
Stephen Phillips
Arthur Wing Pinero
Harold Pinter
James Robinson Planché
John Poole
J. B. Priestley

Thomas Randolph
John Rastell
Terence Rattigan
Edward Ravenscroft
James Reaney
Elmer Rice
Thomas William Robertson
Nicholas Rowe
William Rowley

Thomas Sackville
William Saroyan
Elkanah Settle
Thomas Shadwell
Peter Shaffer
William Shakespeare
George Bernard Shaw
Sam Shepard
Richard Brinsley Sheridan
R. C. Sherriff
Robert E. Sherwood
James Shirley
N. F. Simpson
Thomas Southerne
Wole Soyinka

Sir Richard Steele
Douglas Stewart
Tom Stoppard
David Storey
Alfred Sutro
J. M. Synge

Nahum Tate
John Tatham
Tom Taylor
Augustus Thomas
Cyril Tourneur
Ben Travers
Royall Tyler

Nicholas Udall
Peter Ustinov

Sir John Vanbrugh

John van Druten

Wakefield Master
Derek Walcott
Mercy Warren
John Webster
Arnold Wesker
Patrick White
William Whitehead
John Whiting
Oscar Wilde
Thornton Wilder
Emlyn Williams
Tennessee Williams
John Wilson
Robert Wilson
William Wycherley

William Butler Yeats

ALBEE, Edward (Franklin, III).   American.   Born in Washington, D.C., 12 March 1928. Educated at Lawrenceville School; Valley Forge Military Academy, Pennsylvania; Choate School, Connecticut, graduated 1946; Trinity College, Hartford, Connecticut, 1946–47. Served in the United States Army. Worked as a radio writer, WNYC, office boy, Warwick and Legler, record salesman, Bloomingdale's, book salesman, G. Schirmer, counterman, Manhattan Towers Hotel, messenger, Western Union, 1955–58, all in New York. Producer, with Richard Barr and Clinton Wilder, New Playwrights Unit Workshop, later Albarwild Theatre Arts, and Albar Productions, New York; also a stage director. Founder, William Flanagan Center for Creative Persons, Montauk, Long Island, New York, 1971. United States Cultural Exchange Visitor to Russia. Recipient: Berlin Festival Award, 1959, 1961; Vernon Rice Award, 1960; Obie Award, 1960; Argentine Critics Award, 1961; Lola D'Annunzio Award, 1961; New York Drama Critics Circle Award, 1964; Outer Circle Award, 1964; Antoinette Perry Award, 1964; Margo Jones Award, 1965; Pulitzer Prize, 1967, 1975. Litt.D.: Trinity College, 1974. Member, National Institute of Arts and Letters, 1966. Lives in Montauk, New York.

PUBLICATIONS

Plays

> *The Zoo Story* (produced 1959).   In *The Zoo Story, The Death of Bessie Smith, The Sandbox,* 1960.
> *The Sandbox* (produced 1960).   In *The Zoo Story, The Death of Bessie Smith, The Sandbox,* 1960.
> *The Death of Bessie Smith* (produced 1960).   In *The Zoo Story, The Death of Bessie Smith, The Sandbox,* 1960.
> *The Zoo Story, The Death of Bessie Smith, The Sandbox: Three Plays.*   1960; as *The Zoo Story and Other Plays,* 1962.
> *Fam and Yam* (produced 1960).   1961.
> *The American Dream* (produced 1961).   1961.
> *Bartleby,* with James Hinton, Jr., music by William Flanagan, from the story by Melville (produced 1961).
> *Who's Afraid of Virginia Woolf?* (produced 1962).   1962.
> *The Ballad of the Sad Café,* from the story by Carson McCullers (produced 1963).   1963.
> *Tiny Alice* (produced 1964).   1965.
> *Malcolm,* from the novel by James Purdy (produced 1966).   1966.
> *A Delicate Balance* (produced 1966).   1966.
> *Breakfast at Tiffany's,* music by Bob Merrill, from the story by Truman Capote (produced 1966).
> *Everything in the Garden,* from the play by Giles Cooper (produced 1967).   1968.
> *Box and Quotations from Chairman Mao Tse-Tung: Two Inter-Related Plays* (as *Box-Mao-Box,* produced 1968; as *Box and Quotations from Chairman Mao Tse-Tung,* produced 1968).   1969.
> *All Over* (produced 1971).   1971.
> *Seascape* (produced 1975).   1975.
> *Listening* (broadcast 1976; produced 1977).   In *Two Plays,* 1977.
> *Counting the Ways* (produced 1976).   In *Two Plays,* 1977.
> *Two Plays.*   1977.
> *The Lady from Dubuque.*   1978.

Radio Play: *Listening,* 1976.

Bibliography: *Albee at Home and Abroad: A Bibliography, 1958–June 1968* by Richard E. Amacher and Margaret Rule, 1970.

Reading List: *Albee* by Ruby Cohn, 1969; *Albee* by Richard E. Amacher, 1969; *Albee* by C. W. E. Bigsby, 1969, and *Albee: A Collection of Critical Essays* edited by Bigsby, 1975; *Albee* by Ronald Hayman, 1971; *From Tension to Tonic: The Plays of Albee* by Anne Paolucci, 1972; *Albee: The Poet of Loss* by Anita M. Stenz, 1978.

*   *   *

At age fifty, after two decades of playwriting, Edward Albee remains the most controversial playwright of the United States. Critics are divided as to whether he is a realist or absurdist. Critics and public are divided as to the quality of his writing after *Who's Afraid of Virginia Woolf?* Actors and directors are divided as to whether he is wise to direct his own plays. Never one to soar above the battle, Albee wittily attacks his attackers. More importantly, he continues to write plays in his own restless search for new dramatic forms.

The Zoo Story, completed in 1958 when he was thirty years old, played in New York City on the same bill as Beckett's *Krapp's Last Tape*, and Albee was immediately pigeonholed as absurdist. Rather than dramatize a metaphysical impasse, however, Albee creates a protagonist who is a martyr to brotherly love and cultural vigor. In arousing smug Peter to enact a zoo story, Jerry strikes hard at complacent conformity, and Albee strikes hard at conventional theater.

Albee's next few plays in the next few years are more traditionally satiric. *The Death of Bessie Smith* lacerates white racism; *The American Dream* and *The Sandbox* ridicule American materialism and mindlessness. *Fam and Yam*, a slight piece which Albee continues to direct, confronts an old established playwright with a bright young novice.

For all the energetic idiom of *The Zoo Story* and the satiric verve of his other short plays, Albee remained a fringe playwright until his very full evening of theater, *Who's Afraid of Virginia Woolf?* The play has been misunderstood as a marital problem play, a campus satire, or veiled homosexuality, but, even misunderstood, its verbal pyrotechnics attracted audiences. Slowly, its symbolic import has seeped through an apparently realistic surface. George and Martha, ostensibly an American academic couple but related by name to the father (and mother) of the United States, have based their union on the illusion of a child. On the eve of the child's twenty-first birthday, the fantasy parents return home from a campus party. Drinking heavily, the older couple uses a younger couple for "flagellation." As in O'Neill's *Long Day's Journey into Night* alcohol proves confessional and penitential for all four characters. In the play's third act "Exorcism" George kills their imaginary son. The middle-aged couple, alone at daybreak, has to learn to live with naked reality.

A direct challenge to O'Neill's *The Iceman Cometh*, *Who's Afraid of Virginia Woolf?* is a noteworthy contribution to American dramatic preoccupation with illusion, in the lineage of Williams's *Streetcar Named Desire* and Miller's *Death of a Salesman*. In this big four O'Neill and Williams are the romantics, Miller and Albee the realists, and yet *Virginia Woolf* reveals hints of nostalgia for illusion. Moreover, with time, the play's verbal vitriol seems diluted, clarifying the theatricalization of a crisis in Western culture.

All Albee's subsequent plays hinge on this theme, for which he finds new forms. He continues the corruscating dialogue of *Virginia Woolf* into the first scene of *Tiny Alice* but then shifts to slower rhythms of mystery – both murder and metaphysics. As in *Zoo Story* and *Virginia Woolf*, the protagonist of *Tiny Alice* seeks the reality beneath the surface, and the surface glitters theatrically with such devices as a model castle, a Cardinal who keeps caged cardinal-birds, a beautiful woman disguised as an old crone, an operatic staircase, and visual reminders of the Pietà and Crucifixion. Brother Julian claims to be "dedicated to the reality of things, rather than the appearance." Abandoned on his wedding day by his bride Alice and her entourage, literally shot into reality, Julian finally lies in cruciform posture, clinging to illusion as he really dies.

A Delicate Balance returns to a more realistic surface; as in *Virginia Woolf* a love relationship in one couple is explored through the impact of another couple. In Friday's Act I terrorized friends seek refuge with Tobias and Agnes; in Saturday's Act II Tobias welcomes them, but his daughter Julia reacts hysterically. In Sunday's Act III the friends know they are not welcome, know that they would not have welcomed, and they leave. The passion leads not to resurrection but restitution of a delicate family balance.

After two related and exploratory plays, *Box-Mao-Box*, Albee returns in *All Over* to the upper middle-class American milieu that he stylizes deftly. He brings to the center of this play a theme at the periphery of his other plays – the existential impact of death. In spite of the title, "all" is not quite "over," for a once powerful man is dying behind a stage screen. Waiting for his death are his wife, mistress, best friend, son, and daughter, whose mannered conversation traces the man's presence everywhere or "all over." Death precariously joins these people, only to sunder them again, as each is suffused in his/her own unhappiness.

Between *A Delicate Balance* and *All Over*, upper middle-class plays in credible settings, Albee wrote "two inter-related" and experimental plays, *Box* and *Quotations from Chairman Mao Tse-Tung*. In *Box*, "a parenthesis around *Mao*," a brightly lit cube usurps the whole stage while the audience hears nearby an associational monologue of a middle-aged woman. Apparently rambling, the speech is carefully structured: "When art hurts. That is what to remember." *Quotations* theatricalizes art hurting. Within the cube appears a steamship deck with four characters on it – a silent minister, Chairman Mao speaking only in the titular quotations, a shabby old woman speaking only doggerel verse of Will Carleton, and a middle-class, middle-aged, long-winded lady whose discourse further develops the themes of art and suffering. Skillfully and movingly counterpointed, the three voices dramatize the frailty of art – how it is nourished by suffering and how it suffers.

After the jejune lapse of *Seascape* Albee created another two short experimental plays, *Listening* and *Counting the Ways*. *Listening*, "a chamber play" translated from radio, resembles a chamber quartet in its blend of four voices – a recorded voice announcing the twenty scenes, a fifty-year old man, a fifty-year old woman, and a twenty-five year old "girl." Grouped about a fountain pool, the three visible characters engage in non-linear dialogue through which certain themes recur, particularly the girl's charge: "You don't listen....Pay attention, rather, is what you don't do." Though the characters seem to speak in a limbo beyond life, the play is climaxed by a shocking suicide and a last reiteration of the girl's charge countered by the fifty-year old woman: "*I* listen." Less resonant but nevertheless witty and inventive is the two-character *Counting the Ways*, "A Vaudeville" in twenty-one scenes varying the moods of a love affair as Bergman does that of a marriage.

The corpus of Albee's work shows more stylistic variety and closer attention to the nuances of language than the work of any American playwright, living or dead, Rarely facile, never clumsy, recently mannered, Albee continues to dramatize deep themes in distinctive theatrical forms.

—Ruby Cohn

ANDERSON, Maxwell. American. Born in Atlantic, Pennsylvania, 15 December 1888; grew up in North Dakota. Educated at Jamestown High School, North Dakota, graduated 1908; University of North Dakota, Grand Forks, 1908–11, B.A. 1911; Stanford University, California, 1913–14, M.A. 1914. Married 1) Margaret C. Haskett in 1911 (died, 1931), three sons; 2) Gertrude Maynard in 1933 (died, 1953), one daughter; 3) Gilda Oakleaf in 1954. Teacher, Minnewaukan High School, North Dakota, 1911–13, and Polytechnic High School,

San Francisco, 1914–17; Professor and Head of the English Department, Whittier College, California, 1917–18; Staff Member, *New Republic* magazine, New York, 1918–19, New York *Evening Globe*, 1919–21, and New York *World*, 1921–24; Founder-Editor, with Frank Ernest Hill, *Measure* magazine, New York, 1921; Founder, with Robert E. Sherwood, Elmer Rice, S. N. Behrman, Sidney Howard, and John F. Wharton, Playwrights Company, 1938. Recipient: Pulitzer Prize, 1933; New York Drama Critics Circle Award, 1936, 1937; American Academy of Arts and Letters Gold Medal, 1954. *Died 28 February 1959.*

PUBLICATIONS

Collections

    Dramatist in America: Letters 1912–1958, edited by Laurence G. Avery.   1977.

Plays

    White Desert (produced 1923).
    What Price Glory?, with Laurence Stallings (produced 1924).   In *Three American Plays*, 1926.
    First Flight, with Laurence Stallings (produced 1925).   In *Three American Plays*, 1926.
    The Buccaneer, with Laurence Stallings (produced 1925).   In *Three American Plays*, 1926.
    The Feud.   1925.
    Outside Looking In, from the novel *Beggars of Life* by Jim Tully (produced 1925).   With *Gods of the Lightning*, 1929.
    Forfeits (produced 1926).
    Saturday's Children (produced 1927).   1926.
    Gypsy (produced 1929).   Shortened version in *The Best Plays of 1928–29*, edited by Burns Mantle, 1929.
    Gods of the Lightning, with Harold Hickerson (produced 1928).   1929.
    Elizabeth the Queen (produced 1930).   1930.
    Night over Taos (produced 1932).   1932.
    Sea-Wife (produced 1932).
    Both Your Houses (produced 1933).   1933.
    Mary of Scotland (produced 1933).   1934.
    Valley Forge (produced 1934).   1934.
    Winterset (produced 1935).   1935.
    The Masque of Kings (produced 1937).   1936.
    The Wingless Victory (produced 1936).   1936.
    High Tor (produced 1937).   1937.
    The Feast of Ortolans (broadcast 1937; produced 1938).   1938.
    The Star-Wagon (produced 1937).   1937.
    Knickerbocker Holiday, music by Kurt Weill (produced 1938).   1938.
    Second Overture (produced 1940).   1938.
    Key Largo (produced 1939).   1939.
    Journey to Jerusalem (produced 1940).   1940.
    The Miracle of the Danube (broadcast 1941).   In *The Free Company Presents*, edited by James Boyd, 1941.
    Candle in the Wind (produced 1941).   1941.
    The Eve of St. Mark (produced 1942).   1942.

Your Navy, in *This Is War!* 1942.
Letter to Jackie, in *The Best One-Act Plays of 1943,* edited by Margaret Mayorga. 1944.
Storm Operation (produced 1944). 1944.
Joan of Lorraine (produced 1946). 1947.
Truckline Cafe (produced 1946).
Anne of the Thousand Days (produced 1948). 1948.
Joan of Arc (screenplay, with Andrew Solt). 1948.
Lost in the Stars, music by Kurt Weill, from the novel *Cry the Beloved Country* by Alan Paton (produced 1949). 1950.
Barefoot in Athens (produced 1951). 1951.
The Bad Seed, from the novel by William March (produced 1954). 1955.
A Christmas Carol, music by Bernard Heermann, from the story by Dickens (televised 1954). 1955.
The Masque of Pedagogues, in *North Dakota Quarterly,* Spring 1957.
The Day the Money Stopped, from the novel by Brendan Gill (produced 1958).
The Golden Six (produced 1958).

Radio Plays: *The Feast of Ortolans,* 1937; *The Bastion Saint-Gervais,* 1938; *The Miracle of the Danube,* 1941; *The Greeks Remember Marathon,* 1944.

Television Play: *A Christmas Carol,* 1955.

Screenplays: *All Quiet on the Western Front,* with others, 1930; *We Live Again,* with others, 1934; *So Red the Rose,* 1935; *Joan of Arc,* with Andrew Solt, 1948; *The Wrong Man,* with Angus MacPhail, 1957.

Verse

You Who Have Dreams. 1925.
Notes on a Dream, edited by Laurence G. Avery. 1971.

Other

The Essence of Tragedy and Other Footnotes and Papers. 1939.
The Bases of Artistic Creation: Essays, with Rhys Carpenter and Roy Harris, 1942.
Off Broadway: Essays about the Theatre. 1947.

Bibliography: *A Catalogue of the Anderson Collection* by Laurence G. Avery, 1968; *Anderson and S. N. Behrman: A Reference Guide* by William Klink, 1977.

Reading List: *Anderson: The Man and His Plays* by Barrett H. Clark, 1933; *Anderson: The Playwright as Prophet* by Mabel Driscoll Bailey, 1957; *Life among the Playwright's Producing Company* by John F. Wharton, 1974; *Anderson* by Alfred S. Shivers, 1976.

*   *   *

Maxwell Anderson became a playwright by accident, but once committed to a career in the theater, he set out to base his work on carefully wrought principles of composition. His dramatic theories were based on the practices of ancient Greece and the Elizabethan period, and he was fiercely dedicated to the ideal of the theater as the democratic cultural institution.

11

He reintroduced the idea of poetic tragedy and attracted large audiences to his historical verse plays though there are few striking passages of poetry in his work.

For Anderson the theater was both a spiritual experience and a commercial medium. While he agreed with Aristotle that the audience should be led by the playwright to experience strong emotions, he was sure that the proper mark of success was ticket sales. He accepted the maxim that no playwright deserves or will get posthumous adulation who has not attracted an enthusiastic audience during his lifetime. He attacked the New York critics for short-circuiting the gleaning process with their first-night reviews, but was personally willing to accept the audience's spontaneous judgment. He rejected the notion of government subsidization because he thought it would interfere with the natural selection process and resisted the lure of off-Broadway production on the grounds that only the more rigorous Broadway circuit was an ample test. Anderson successfully countered the commercial forces of Broadway for more than a quarter of a century and dominated American theater in the 1930's.

Anderson believed in theater of ideas. In an essay called "Keeping the Faith" he enunciated as rule number one the necessity of having a central idea or conviction which cannot be excised without killing the play. His *Joan of Lorraine* dramatizes the process of making concessions to the realities of play production while trying to protect the central core of the play's integrity. Though his convictions changed markedly during his career, his use of the stage to express them did not. He attacked big government, defended democracy, preached pacifism, and urged commitment to war. As his ideas about war, for instance, changed from the cynicism of *What Price Glory?* (written with Laurence Stallings) to the patriotic fervor of *The Eve of St. Mark* and *Storm Operation*, he presented each new certainty with as much strength as the one before.

Anderson's overriding theme is the spiritual victory of humanity. In his essay "Off Broadway" he defined theater as "a religious institution devoted entirely to the exaltation of the spirit of man." He tried through the disillusionment of the 1920's, the depression of the 1930's, and the global war of the 1940's to present the triumphant human spirit. He has been accused of being a pessimist, but his view is essentially that of an optimistic humanist. He emphasized the importance of individual choice and the necessity of commitment. King McCloud of *Key Largo*, for instance, having failed to make a stand in the last days of the Spanish Civil War, finds it hard to stop running. His spirit triumphs only when he finds something for which he is willing to die. Mio of *Winterset*, emotionally crippled by lust for revenge, becomes a complete person only when he accepts love.

In many plays Anderson used the lives of historical characters to illumine broad questions of power and choice. He wrote plays about Christ, Socrates, Elizabeth I, Mary Stuart, George Washington, and Peter Stuyvesant. A comparison of *Elizabeth the Queen* with *Masque of Kings* illustrates the major problem in Anderson's method of historical tragedy. He is able to delineate Elizabeth's choice to have her lover Essex beheaded as a triumph of wise government over personal weakness, but Rudolph's suicide will not fit into such a neat pattern. As a result the third act of *Masque of Kings* takes a different direction from the one we might reasonably expect after the recognition scene of Act II, and the ending is weak and inappropriate.

The high seriousness of his subject matter is often a mistake. It is unfortunate that he did not leaven his work with comedy more often. In *High Tor* and *Knickerbocker Holiday* (music by Kurt Weill) he demonstrated a rich gift for humor. *Both Your Houses*, a play about Congressional corruption, makes excellent use of satire and was highly praised by critics.

Anderson's deficiencies as a playwright seem to be related to conflicts between his intellectual approach to form and his spontaneous ideas for content. He wanted to emphasize the primacy of individual choice, for instance, but Aristotelian tragedy, which he chose to emulate, best communicates the powerful forces that neutralize free will. He wanted to write plays constructed around a second act recognition scene followed by spiritual triumph in physical defeat, but some of the historical characters he chose do not fit this pattern. He wanted to show the triumph of the human spirit, but one of his most successful plays, *The*

Bad Seed, demonstrates the victory of congenital evil. He wanted to treat universal themes, but in plays such as *Gods of the Lightning* and *Wingless Victory* he got bogged down in heavy social commentary.

Anderson has been criticized for lack of innovation, and that is a fair criticism. His approach and subject matter are quite traditional. Echoes of *Medea* are clear in the plot of *Wingless Victory*, and the parallels between *Winterset* and *Romeo and Juliet* are obvious. His concern is less with striking out into new territories than with re-vitalizing the old. The actors in *Elizabeth the Queen* actually use Shakespeare's lines, for instance, but the effect is to illuminate the Queen's character and judgment.

Anderson was a prolific writer whose work attracted audiences and made money; by his own criteria he was a success. In comparison with his fellow writers in the American theater he must also be rated a success; only O'Neill outshone him in his time. Anderson did not always overcome the problems posed by his own methods, but he did illuminate the mazes of power, freedom, and faith he set out to explore. For over a quarter of a century, especially with works such as *Elizabeth the Queen*, *High Tor*, and *Winterset*, he dramatized the human condition in some striking scenes and created some high moments in American theater.

—Barbara M. Perkins

ARDEN, John. English. Born in Barnsley, Yorkshire, 26 October 1930. Educated at Sedbergh School, Yorkshire; King's College, Cambridge, B.A. 1953; Edinburgh College of Art, diploma in architecture, 1955. Served as a Lance-Corporal in the British Army Intelligence Corps, 1949–50. Married the actress Margaretta Ruth D'Arcy in 1957; has four sons. Architectural Assistant, London, 1955–57; Fellow in Playwriting, University of Bristol, 1959–60; Visiting Lecturer in Politics and Drama, New York University, 1967; Regents Lecturer, University of California at Davis, 1973; Writer-in-Residence, University of New England, Armidale, New South Wales, 1975. Co-Founder, Corrandulla Arts Centre, County Galway, Ireland, 1973. Recipient: BBC Northern Region Prize, 1957; *Evening Standard* award, 1959; Trieste Festival Award, 1961; Vernon Rice Award, 1966; Arts Council award, 1973. Lives in County Galway, Ireland.

PUBLICATIONS

Plays

> *All Fall Down* (produced 1955).
> *The Waters of Babylon* (produced 1957). In *Three Plays*, 1964.
> *When Is a Door Not a Door?* (produced 1958). In *Soldier, Soldier and Other Plays*, 1967.
> *Live Like Pigs* (produced 1958). In *Three Plays*, 1964.
> *Serjeant Musgrave's Dance: An Unhistorical Parable* (produced 1959). 1960; revised version (produced 1972).
> *The Happy Haven*, with Margaretta D'Arcy (produced 1960). In *Three Plays*, 1964.
> *Soldier, Soldier* (televised 1960). In *Soldier, Soldier and Other Plays*, 1967.

The Business of Good Government: A Christmas Play, with Margaretta D'Arcy
(produced, as *A Christmas Play*, 1960). 1963.

Wet Fish (televised 1961). In *Soldier, Soldier and Other Plays*, 1967.

Ironhand, from a play by Goethe (produced 1963). 1965.

The Workhouse Donkey: A Vulgar Melodrama (produced 1963). 1964.

Three Plays. 1964.

Armstrong's Last Goodnight: An Exercise in Diplomacy (produced 1964). 1965.

Ars Longa, Vita Brevis, with Margaretta D'Arcy (produced 1964). 1965.

Fidelio, from a libretto by Joseph Sonnleithner and Friedrich Treitschke, music by
Beethoven (produced 1965).

Left-Handed Liberty: A Play about Magna Carta (produced 1965). 1965.

Friday's Hiding, with Margaretta D'Arcy (produced 1966). In *Soldier, Soldier and
Other Plays*, 1967.

The Royal Pardon: or, The Soldier Who Became an Actor, with Margaretta D'Arcy
(produced 1966). 1966.

Soldier, Soldier and Other Plays. 1967.

The True History of Squire Jonathan and His Unfortunate Treasure (produced
1968). In *Two Autobiographical Plays*, 1971.

The Hero Rises Up: A Romantic Melodrama, with Margaretta D'Arcy (produced
1968). 1969.

The Soldier's Tale, from a libretto by Ramuz, music by Stravinsky (produced 1968).

Harold Muggins Is a Martyr, with Margaretta D'Arcy and the Cartoon Archetypical
Slogan Theatre (produced 1968).

The Bagman; or, The Impromptu of Muswell Hill (broadcast 1970). In *Two
Autobiographical Plays*, 1971.

Two Autobiographical Plays. 1971.

The Ballygombeen Bequest, with Margaretta D'Arcy (produced 1972). In *Scripts 9*,
September 1972.

The Island of the Mighty: A Play on a Traditional British Theme, with Margaretta
D'Arcy (produced 1972). 1974; section, as *A Handful of Watercress* (produced
1976).

The Non-Stop Connolly Show: A Dramatic Cycle of Continuous Struggle in Six Parts,
with Margaretta D'Arcy (produced 1975). 3 vols., 1978 (first four parts).

Radio Plays: *The Life of Man*, 1956; *The Bagman*, 1970; *Pearl*, 1978.

Television Plays: *Soldier, Soldier*, 1960; *Sean O'Casey* (documentary), with Margaretta
D'Arcy, 1973.

Other

To Present the Pretence: Essays on the Theatre and Its Public. 1978.

Reading List: *Arden* by Ronald Hayman, 1968; *Theatre Language: A Study of Arden,
Osborne, Pinter, and Wesker* by John Russell Brown, 1972; *Arden* by Simon Trussler, 1973;
Arden: A Study of His Plays by Albert Hunt, 1974; *Arden* by Gloria Leeming, 1974; *Anger
and Detachment: A Study of Arden, Osborne, and Pinter* by Michael Anderson, 1976.

*   *   *

A consciousness of society and politics as well as the individual informs John Arden's work as a playwright, critic, and actor. In almost any context one attempts to place him he appears, to his credit, abrasive and anomalous. Loosely implicated in the "angry young men" group of the 1950's, he countered the commitment of their work with a resolute disengagement; as the universities have expanded to include modern drama in the syllabus of the academy, he observes the tyranny of the "literary" text of the play and the mistaken valuation of the "objective"; and as state subsidies have created a secure and, some might say, "entrenched" British theatre, Arden criticises a system where selection and production of plays are determined by a director-administrator whose policies are administrative rather than artistic. In an age where writers of all kind accept their isolation even when they do not prize it, Arden stresses collaboration – with other playwrights, and of playwrights with directors, actors, and production workers.

In an article reprinted in *To Present the Pretence*, Arden acknowledges a debt to Jonson rather than Shakespeare, distinguishing between Jonson's concrete and Shakespeare's impressionist language. But in its energy, catholicity, and virtuosity the achievement of Arden's plays is Shakespearian, while the richness of the worlds of his plays reveals a more general influence of Renaissance drama as a whole. Arden's own descriptions of this richness of content and form indicate other of its contexts: in the Preface to *The Workhouse Donkey* he calls for "the old essential attributes of Dionysus" which include noise, disorder, generosity, corruption, fertility, and ease; and in *The Hero Rises Up* (about Nelson) he and Margaretta D'Arcy unfavourably contrast the rectilinear Romans with the curvilinear natives of ancient Britain who endearingly "muddle through"; both the Dionysiac and the curvilinear point to his marked preoccupation with natural man, and the modes of popular, and Brechtian, theatre.

Although the plays before 1970 share a similar kind of disengagement, and the plays after evident commitment, and though they all include prose and verse, there is no other single common language or style, as one finds in Pinter for example. A prodigious range of class, education, region, and historical period is manifest in the language of the plays. In the comedies set in the present, such as *The Waters of Babylon*, *Live Like Pigs*, and *The Workhouse Donkey*, the verse is balladic, the prose colloquial, and the mode at times melodrama, but in some of the British history plays, such as *Left-Handed Liberty* (on Magna Carta) and *Armstrong's Last Goodnight*, both the verse and prose are more poetic and in a high, literary style which is in part due to the strangeness to Arden's audience of medieval English and sixteenth-century Scots respectively. The fables, too, such as *Serjeant Musgrave's Dance* and *The Bagman*, share this poetic quality of language, which is conceived so as to be taken in on first hearing rather than only when read.

In several of his prefaces to the plays Arden links them to contemporary political situations (*Armstrong* with the Congo and *Musgrave* with Cyprus), in the way that Arthur Miller treats McCarthyism in *The Crucible*, but Arden's distance from all his characters in the earlier plays forces the audience to tolerate the more culpable characters along with the more innocent so that complete identification of the audience with the "good" is prevented; at the same time Arden provides a certain sympathy and room for imperfect men who verge on the repugnant such as Musgrave; and through this technique two recurring, rather sordid characters, Charlie Butterthwaite and Krank, take on Falstaffian proportions and complexity. But overall Arden curtails our interest in individual character and forces us to see the archetype, and the social and political implications of his characters' decisions.

The preface to *The Bagman* and the play itself chart the immediate circumstances of Arden's move from detachment to commitment in his life and work. Not surprisingly, however, even plays after this shift, *The Island of the Mighty* (on the Arthurian legends) and *The Ballygombeen Bequest* (on absentee landlordism and exploitation in Ireland) attest to Arden's virtuosity, the first being an epic of three very complex and poetic plays, and the latter a melodramatic but documented treatise.

In addition to these works, Arden has written several plays for children, opera libretti, drama for television and radio, and fascinating criticism – in the often ample prefaces to the plays and in *To Present the Pretence*. He is prolific, and his work is original, independent, ambitious, and memorable, if somewhat uneven. With Samuel Beckett, he appears as one of the principal innovators on the contemporary British scene.

—Laurel Brake

AUDEN, W(ystan) H(ugh). American. Born in York, England, 21 February 1907; emigrated to the United States in 1938; naturalized, 1946. Educated at St. Edmund's School, Grayshott, Surrey; Gresham's School, Holt, Norfolk; Christ Church, Oxford (exhibitioner), 1925–28. Served with the Loyalists in the Spanish Civil War; with the Strategic Bombing Survey of the United States Army in Germany during World War II. Married Erika Mann in 1935. Schoolmaster, Larchfield Academy, Helensburgh, Scotland, and Downs School, Colwall, near Malvern, Worcestershire, 1930–35. Co-Founder of the Group Theatre, 1932; worked with the G.P.O. Film Unit, 1935. Travelled extensively in the 1930's, in Europe, Iceland, and China. Taught at St. Mar's School, Southborough, Massachusetts, 1939–40; American Writers League School, 1939; New School for Social Research, New York, 1940–41, 1946–47; University of Michigan, Ann Arbor, 1941–42; Swarthmore College, Pennsylvania, 1942–45; Bryn Mawr College, Pennsylvania, 1943–45; Bennington College, Vermont, 1946; Barnard College, New York, 1947; Neilson Research Professor, Smith College, Northampton, Massachusetts, 1953; Professor of Poetry, Oxford University, 1956–61. Editor, Yale Series of Younger Poets, 1947–62. Member of the Editorial Board, *Decision* magazine, 1940–41, and *Delos* magazine, 1968; The Readers' Subscription book club, 1951–59, and The Mid-Century Book Club, 1959–62. Recipient: King's Gold Medal for Poetry, 1936; Guggenheim Fellowship, 1942; American Academy of Arts and Letters Award of Merit Medal, 1945, Gold Medal, 1968; Pulitzer Prize, 1948; Bollingen Prize, 1954; National Book Award, 1956; Feltrinelli Prize, 1957; Guinness Award, 1959; Poetry Society of America's Droutskoy Gold Medal, 1959; National Endowment for the Arts grant, 1966; National Book Committee's National Medal for Literature, 1967. D.Litt.: Swarthmore College, 1964. Member, American Academy of Arts and Letters, 1954; Honorary Student, Christ Church, 1962, and in residence, 1972–73. *Died 28 September 1973.*

PUBLICATIONS

Collections

    The Collected Poems, edited by Edward Mendelson. 1976.

Plays

    The Dance of Death (produced 1934; as *Come Out into the Sun*, produced 1935). 1933.
    The Dog Beneath the Skin; or, Where Is Francis?, with Christopher Isherwood (produced 1936; revised version, produced 1947). 1935.
    No More Peace! A Thoughtful Comedy, with Edward Crankshaw, from the play by Ernst Toller (produced 1936). 1937.

The Ascent of F6, with Christopher Isherwood (produced 1937). 1936; revised edition, 1937.

On the Frontier, with Christopher Isherwood (produced 1938). 1938.

The Dark Valley (broadcast, 1940). In *Best Broadcasts of 1939–40,* edited by Max Wylie, 1940.

Paul Bunyan, music by Benjamin Britten (produced 1941). 1976.

The Duchess of Malfi, music by Benjamin Britten, from the play by John Webster (produced 1946).

The Knights of the Round Table, from the work by Jean Cocteau (broadcast, 1951; produced 1954). In *The Infernal Machine and Other Plays,* by Jean Cocteau, 1964.

The Rake's Progress, with Chester Kallman, music by Igor Stravinsky (produced 1951). 1951.

Delia; or, A Masque of Night, with Chester Kallman (libretto), in *Botteghe Oscure XII.* 1953.

The Punch Revue (lyrics only) (produced 1955).

The Magic Flute, with Chester Kallman, from the libretto by Schikaneder and Giesecke, music by Mozart (televised, 1956). 1956.

The Play of Daniel (narration only) (produced 1958). Editor, with Noah Greenberg, 1959.

The Seven Deadly Sins of the Lower Middle Class, with Chester Kallman, from the work by Brecht, music by Kurt Weill (produced 1959). In *Tulane Drama Review,* September 1961.

Don Giovanni, with Chester Kallman, from the libretto by Lorenzo da Ponte, music by Mozart (televised, 1960). 1961.

The Caucasian Chalk Circle (lyrics only), with James and Tania Stern, from the play by Brecht (produced 1962). In *Plays,* by Brecht, 1960.

Elegy for Young Lovers, with Chester Kallman, music by Hans Werner Henze (produced 1961). 1961.

Arcifanfarlo, King of Fools; or, It's Always Too Late to Learn, with Chester Kallman, from the libretto by Goldoni, music by Dittersdorf (produced 1965).

Die Bassariden (The Bassarids), with Chester Kallman, music by Hans Werner Henze (produced 1966). 1966.

Moralities: Three Scenic Plays from Fables by Aesop, music by Hans Werner Henze. 1969.

The Ballad of Barnaby, music by Wykeham Rise School Students realized by Charles Turner (produced 1970).

Love's Labour's Lost, with Chester Kallman, music by Nicholas Nabokov, from the play by Shakespeare (produced 1973).

The Entertainment of the Senses, with Chester Kallman, music by John Gardner, (produced 1974). In *Thank You, Fog,* 1974.

The Rise and Fall of the City of Mahagonny, with Chester Kallman, from the opera by Brecht. 1976.

Screenplays (documentaries, in verse): *Night Mail,* 1936; *Coal Face,* 1936; *The Londoners,* 1938.

Radio Writing: *Hadrian's Wall,* 1937 (UK); *the Dark Valley,* 1940 (USA); *The Rocking-Horse Winner,* with James Stern, from the story by D. H. Lawrence, 1941 (USA); *The Knights of the Round Table,* from a work by Jean Cocteau, 1951 (UK).

Television Writing (with Chester Kallman): *The Magic Flute,* 1956 (USA); *Don Giovanni,* 1960 (USA).

17

Verse

Poems. 1928.
Poems. 1930; revised edition, 1933.
The Orators: An English Study. 1932; revised edition, 1934, 1966.
Poems (includes *The Orators* and *The Dance of Death*). 1934.
Look, Stranger! 1936; as *On This Island*, 1937.
Spain. 1937.
Letters from Iceland, with Louis MacNeice. 1937.
Selected Poems. 1938.
Journey to a War, with Christopher Isherwood. 1939; revised edition, 1973.
*Ephithalamion Commemorating the Marriage of Giuseppe Antonio Borghese and
    Elisabeth Mann.* 1939.
Another Time: Poems (includes *Spain*). 1940.
Some Poems. 1940.
The Double Man. 1941; as *New Year Letter*, 1941.
Three Songs for St. Cecilia's Day. 1941.
For the Time Being. 1944.
The Collected Poetry. 1945.
Litany and Anthem for St. Matthew's Day. 1946.
The Age of Anxiety: A Baroque Eclogue (produced 1954). 1947.
Collected Shorter Poems 1930–1944. 1950.
Nones. 1951.
The Shield of Achilles. 1955.
The Old Man's Road. 1956.
Reflections on a Forest. 1957.
Goodbye to the Mezzogiorno (bilingual edition). 1958.
Auden: A Selection by the Author. 1958; as *Selected Poetry*, 1959.
Homage to Clio. 1960.
Auden: A Selection, edited by Richard Hoggart. 1961.
Elegy for J.F.K., music by Igor Stravinsky. 1964.
The Common Life (in German, translated by Dieter Leisegang). 1964.
The Cave of Making (in German, translated by Dieter Leisegang). 1965.
Half-Way. 1965.
About the House. 1965.
The Twelve, music by William Walton. 1966.
Marginalia. 1966.
Collected Shorter Poems, 1927–1957. 1966.
River Profile. 1967.
Selected Poems. 1968.
Collected Longer Poems. 1968.
Two Songs. 1968.
A New Year Greeting, with *The Dance of the Solids*, by John Updike. 1969.
City Without Walls and Other Poems. 1969.
Academic Graffiti. 1971.
Epistle to a Godson and Other Poems. 1972.
Auden/Moore: Poems and Lithographs, edited by John Russell. 1974.
Poems, lithographs by Henry Moore, edited by Vera Lindsay. 1974.
Thank You, Fog: Last Poems. 1974.

Other

Education Today – and Tomorrow, with T. C. Worsley. 1939.

The Intent of the Critic, with others, edited by Donald A. Stauffer. 1941.

Poets at Work: Essays Based on the Modern Poetry Collection at the Lockwood Memorial Library, University of Buffalo, with others, edited by Charles D. Abbott. 1948.

The Enchafèd Flood; or, The Romantic Iconography of the Sea. 1950.

The Dyer's Hand and Other Essays. 1962.

Selected Essays. 1964.

Secondary Worlds. 1968.

A Certain World: A Commonplace Book. 1970.

Forewords and Afterwords (essays), edited by Edward Mendelson. 1973.

The English Auden: Poems, Essays, and Dramatic Writings, 1927–1939, edited by Edward Mendelson. 1977.

Editor, with Charles Plumb, *Oxford Poetry 1926.* 1926.

Editor, with C. Day Lewis, *Oxford Poetry 1927.* 1927.

Editor, with John Garrett, *The Poet's Tongue: An Anthology.* 2 vols., 1935.

Editor, *The Oxford Book of Light Verse.* 1938.

Editor, *A Selection from the Poems of Alfred, Lord Tennyson.* 1944; as *Tennyson: An Introduction and a Selection*, 1946.

Editor, *The American Scene, Together with Three Essays from "Portraits of Places,"* by Henry James. 1946.

Editor, *Slick But Not Streamlined: Poems and Short Pieces*, by John Betjeman. 1947.

Editor, *The Portable Greek Reader.* 1948.

Editor, with Norman Holmes Pearson, *Poets of the English Language.* 5 vols., 1950.

Editor, *Selected Prose and Poetry*, by Edgar Allan Poe. 1950; revised edition, 1955.

Editor, *The Living Thoughts of Kierkegaard.* 1952; as *Kierkegaard*, 1955.

Editor, with Marianne Moore and Karl Shapiro, *Riverside Poetry 1953: Poems by Students in Colleges and Universities in New York City.* 1953.

Editor, with Chester Kallman and Noah Greenberg, *An Elizabethan Song Book: Lute Songs, Madrigals, and Rounds.* 1955.

Editor, *The Faber Book of Modern American Verse.* 1956; as *The Criterion Book of Modern American Verse*, 1956.

Editor, *Selected Writings of Sydney Smith.* 1956.

Editor, *Van Gogh: A Self-Portrait: Letters Revealing His Life as a Painter.* 1961.

Editor, with Louis Kronenberger, *The Viking Book of Aphorisms: A Personal Selection.* 1962; as *The Faber Book of Aphorisms*, 1964.

Editor, *A Choice of de la Mare's Verse.* 1963.

Editor, *The Pied Piper and Other Fairy Tales*, by Joseph Jacobs. 1963.

Editor, *Selected Poems*, by Louis MacNeice. 1964.

Editor, with John Lawlor, *To Nevill Coghill from Friends.* 1966.

Editor, *Selected Poetry and Prose*, by Byron. 1966.

Editor, *Nineteenth Century British Minor Poets.* 1966; as *Nineteenth Century Minor Poets*, 1967.

Editor, *G. K. Chesterton: A Selection from His Non-Fiction Prose.* 1970.

Editor, *A Choice of Dryden's Verse.* 1973.

Editor, *George Herbert.* 1973.

Editor, *Selected Songs of Thomas Campion.* 1974.

Translator, with Elizabeth Mayer, *Italian Journey 1786–1788*, by Goethe. 1962.

Translator, with Leif Sjöberg, *Markings*, by Dag Hammarskjöld. 1964.

Translator, with Paul B. Taylor, *Völupsá: The Song of the Sybil*, with an Icelandic Text edited by Peter H. Salus and Paul B. Taylor. 1968.

Translator, *The Elder Edda: A Selection.* 1969.

Translator, with Elizabeth Mayer and Louise Bogan, *The Sorrows of Young Werther, and Novella*, by Goethe. 1971.

Translator, with Leif Sjöberg, *Evening Land/Aftonland,* by Pär Lagerkvist.   1975.

Bibliography: *Auden: A Bibliography 1924–1969* by Barry C. Bloomfield and Edward Mendelson, 1972.

Reading List: *The Poetry of Auden: The Disenchanted Island* by Monroe K. Spears, 1963, and *Auden: A Collection of Critical Essays* edited by Spears, 1964; *Auden's Poetry* by Justin Replogle, 1969; *Changes of Heart: A Study of the Poetry of Auden* by Gerald Nelson, 1969; *A Reader's Guide to Auden* by John Fuller, 1970; *Auden* by Dennis Davison, 1970; *The Later Auden* by George W. Bahlke, 1970; *Auden as a Social Poet* by Frederick H. Buell, 1973; *Man's Place: An Essay on Auden* by Richard Johnson, 1973; *Auden: A Tribute* edited by Stephen Spender, 1975.

*   *   *

One of the most recurrent features of W. H. Auden's poetry is the *paysage moralisé* (an early poem is actually called this) in which the landscape becomes the emblematic topography of a spiritual condition. Auden, whose earliest reading was in geology and mining and who first thought of becoming an engineer, has always believed that the way we locate ourselves in space, in a specific landscape we alter and adapt to, both determines and reveals our moral being, our sense of personal destiny and collective responsibility. Thus, in those fine "Horatian" *Bucolics* from the 1950's he can playfully link our neuroses with our choice of locale, as in "Mountains" –

> And it is curious how often in steep places
>   You meet someone short who frowns,
> A type you catch beheading daisies with a stick

– or prescribe the curative powers of "Lakes" (which always recall the "amniotic mere" of the womb): "Moraine, pot, oxbow, glint, sink, crater, piedmont, dimple ...?/Just reeling off their names is ever so comfy." While in "Plains" he can express his aversion to those flats "where all elsewheres are equal," "nothing points," and the tax-collector's writ is unchallengable ("where roads run level,/How swift to the point of protest strides the crown./ It hangs, it flogs, it fines, it goes"). "In Praise of Limestone" (1948) sets the tone for much of this later work, making a limestone landscape symbol of both our yearning for stability and our actual transience, beginning

> If it form the one landscape that we, the inconstant ones,
>   Are consistently homesick for, this is chiefly
> Because it dissolves in water

and ending with a wistful confession:

> Dear, I know nothing of
> Either, but when I try to imagine a faultless love
>   Or the life to come, what I hear is the murmur
> Of underground streams, what I see is a limestone landscape.

The tone is more relaxed in these post-war poems, but the technique is the same as that employed in those poems of quest, pursuit, and flight which dominate his earlier writings, poems whose terrain is best described by Caliban in *The Sea and the Mirror,* that extended commentary in verse and prose on Shakespeare's *Tempest* which enables Auden to dramatize his views on the relation between life and art. Caliban, spokesman of the carnal and material, of "history," speaks with sympathy of the spirit Ariel's obligation to deliver us from "the terrible mess that this particularized life, which we have so futilely attempted to tidy, sullenly insists on leaving behind," translating "all the phenomena of an empirically ordinary world" into "elements in an allegorical landscape":

> a nightmare which has all the wealth of exciting action and all the emotional poverty of an adventure story for boys, a state of perpetual emergency and everlasting improvisation where all is need and change.

Certainly, John Buchan seems as much an influence as Marx or Nietzsche on those early poems in which the young, proud inheritor finds himself unexpectedly turned into an outsider, as in "The Watershed," "frustrate and vexed" in face of an abandoned, derelict landscape racked by depression and unemployment, "already comatose,/Yet sparsely living"; one who "must migrate" ("Missing") to become a leader, turn into a "trained spy" ("The Secret Agent"), and ("Our Hunting Fathers") "hunger, work illegally,/And be anonymous" in a world of suspicion, insecurity and betrayal, as "all the while/Conjectures on our maps grow stranger/And threaten danger" ("No Change of Place"). The Auden of these early poems, walking a dangerous tightrope between "Always" and "Never" ("Between Adventure") saw his personal anxieties bodied forth in the world at large, and found a refuge for his public-school hauteur and élitism in a communism which rationalized his contempt for an age of mediocrity, impotence and defeat. In "Family Ghosts," for example, he sees "the assaulted city" surrounded by "the watchfires of a stronger army," and it isn't possible to decide whether this is a personal allegory of love or a political poem which looks towards class-struggle as release from the "Massive and taciturn years, the Age of Ice." Christopher Isherwood, Auden's collaborator in the verse-plays *The Dog Beneath the Skin*, *The Ascent of F6*, and *On the Frontier*, wrote of him in these terms in 1937, speaking of Auden's love for the Norse sagas: "The saga world is a schoolboy world, with its feuds, its practical jokes, its dark threats conveyed in puns and riddles and understatements"; in *Paid on Both Sides*, Auden's early, expressionist charade, he adds, "the two worlds are so inextricably confused that it is impossible to say whether the characters are really epic heroes or only members of a school O.T.C." Stephen Spender, also one of Auden's "Gang" during this period, has written of the "schoolboy ruthlessness" and latent fascism of *The Orators*, and the once-popular plays in which Auden and Isherwood tried to explore the contemporary crisis in the terms of Ruritanian allegory, knockabout, and morality-play which rob it of all urgency, are dismissed by Spender as virtuoso exercises, "a hash of the revolutionary and pacifist thought of the 1930s, reduced to their least convincing terms," which "provide considerable evidence that one aspect of the 1930s was a rackety exploitation of literary fashions."

Letter to Lord Byron perhaps best sums up the ambivalence of Auden's mood in the 1930's. Written in a skilful pastiche of Byron's own insouciant rhythms and rhymes, it expresses an aristocratic, Byronic disdain for the cant and hypocrisy of the "well-to-do" Home Counties, with their bland, self-deceiving smugness, against which Auden sets the urgencies of a more desolate world:

> To those who live in Warrington or Wigan,
> It's not a white lie, it's a whacking big 'un.
> There on the old historic battlefield,
>   The cold ferocity of human wills,
> The scars of struggle are as yet unhealed;
>   Slattern the tenements on sombre hills,
>   And gaunt in valleys the square-windowed mills
> That since the Georgian house, in my conjecture
> Remain our finest native architecture.

21

Yet that shift in the last couplet from moral outrage to sober aesthetic appreciation, together with the easy abstraction and the typecast imagery, reveals Auden's basic remoteness from his subject; indeed, a stanza later he can confess openly to his twentieth-century delight in that landscape: "Tramlines and slagheaps, pieces of machinery,/That was, and still is, my ideal scenery."

"Journey to Iceland" (1936) explains the rationale of Auden's travelogues: "North means to all *Reject*"; but such rejection also brought with it a new perspective that extended his control of his material and made possible a larger, clearer vision, revealed in that mythic conspectus of human evolution "Sonnets from China," originally included in the travel book *Journey to a War*. After the claustrophobic, cryptic, furtive atmosphere of the earlier poems, Auden here perfected the new straightforwardness already evinced in "Spain 1937," where "the menacing shapes of our fever/Are precise and alive." Significantly, the latter's explicit commitment to communism led a censorious later Auden to excise it from the canon (those patriarchal, castrating imagos, the Censor and the Scissor Man, have made themselves felt again and again in his poetic career). His reasons are interesting. Of the last stanza of "Spain" –

> The stars are dead. The animals will not look.
> We are left alone with our day, and the time is short, and
> > History to the defeated
> May say alas but cannot help or pardon

– he has said: "To say this is to equate goodness with success. It would have been bad enough if I had ever held this wicked doctrine, but that I should have stated it simply because it sounded to me rhetorically effective is quite inexcusable." But what the poem in fact stresses is the openness of human choice and the tragic discrepancy between history and morality (success may involve "The conscious acceptance of guilt in the necessary murder"), between – in Pascal's terms – Nature and Justice.There is nothing here which belies Auden's later conversion to Kierkegaard's Christian existentialism: the belief that man is responsible for his acts, and must make his leap of faith in fear and trembling, knowing that it may be a wrong and corrosive choice.

That faith is best expressed in *For the Time Being*, a "Christmas Oratorio" which recreates the Christian myth in contemporary terms (casting Herod, for example, as a well-intentioned liberal statesman whose massacre of the innocents is for the public good). History is now for Auden seen in the perspective of eternity:

> To those who have seen
> The Child, however dimly, however incredulously
> The Time Being is, in a sense, the most trying time of all.
> For the innocent children who whispered so excitedly
> Outside the locked door where they knew the presents to be
> Grew up when it opened. Now, recollecting that moment
> We can repress the joy, but the guilt remains conscious.

For Auden, who had originally identified with "Voltaire at Ferney" (1939), perennial oedipal rebel –

> Cajoling, scolding, scheming, cleverest of them all,
> He'd led the other children in a holy war
> Against the infamous grownups

– this "growing up" expressed, in terms of traditional theology, his final transfer of allegiance from the Son to the Father, effected, ironically enough, through the advent of that Child to a world at war. The transfer can be seen occurring in his fine poem "In Memory of Sigmund

Freud" (1939), where that liberating discoverer of the unconscious is seen both as wide-eyed child and benevolent father who

> showed us what evil is, not, as we thought,
> deeds that must be punished, but our lack of faith,
> our dishonest mood of denial,
> the concupiscence of the oppressor.

The same affirmation animates "In Memory of Ernst Toller," acknowledging the great gift of both Freud and Marx to human self-understanding: the disclosure of those unconscious determinations of our identity – whether biological or socio-economic, each shaping the other – which constrain our existential freedom only when unrecognized:

> We are lived by powers we pretend to understand:
> They arrange our loves; it is they who direct at the end
> The enemy bullet, the sickness, or even our hand.
> It is their tomorrow hangs over the earth of the living
> And all that we wish for our friends: but existence is believing
> We know for whom we mourn and who is grieving.

For the later, Anglican, Auden, finally expatriate in an alien and yet familiar America, acknowledgment of our guilt is the ground of freedom. Rosetta, one of the four "displaced persons" lining a wartime bar in New York in *The Age of Anxiety*, at a time when "Many have perished, more will," daydreams of

> one of those landscapes familiar to all readers of English detective stories, those lovely innocent countrysides inhabited by charming eccentrics with independent means and amusing hobbies to whom, until the sudden intrusion of a horrid corpse onto the tennis court or into the greenhouse, work and law and guilt are just literary words.

As the 1936 poem "Detective Story" and the essay "The Guilty Vicarage" make clear, this landscape is Auden's own peculiar version of the myth of the Fall: to live in history is to accept complicity, and to accept complicity is the beginning of grace: "But time is always guilty. Someone must pay for/Our loss of happiness, our happiness itself." Each of the "travellers through time" of *The Age of Anxiety* sets out "in quest of his own/Absconded self yet scared to find it" (for it will turn out to be the culprit). In *New Year Letter* Auden resolves, in his own person, to accept responsibility for his fallen condition. History is the middle way, that Purgatory where, "Consenting parties to our lives," we may "win/Truth out of Time. In Time we sin./But Time is sin and can forgive"; in Time too we learn "To what conditions we must bow/In building the Just City now." But the world remains one in which "Aloneness is man's real condition."

What underlies all Auden's poetry, in fact, early and late, is this tension between aristocratic disdain and a humble and, at times, humiliating love for the things of this world. It is there in his love poetry, whether in the early and beautiful "Lullaby" ("Lay your sleeping head, my love,/Human on my faithless arm") or the innocuous narcissism of the last poem in his *Collected Poems* (1976), also called "A Lullaby" – "now you fondle/your almost feminine flesh/with mettled satisfaction" – but with its last line, "Sleep, Big Baby, sleep your fill," almost an epitaph. The explicit homosexual lust of "Three Posthumous Poems" suggests that translation of *Eros* into *Agape*, of sensual into spiritual love, was no more difficult for Auden than it was for the Sufi poets. His perennial movement between renouncing and embracing, *askesis* and indulgence, is embodied in his very language, which at once delights in the rich multiplicity of an abundant world and yet keeps it at bay with a deliberate, distancing artificiality that defamiliarizes the accustomed, or calls attention to the medium itself through nonce-words and neologisms, arcane or archaic usages, portentous polysyllables cut short by sudden racy slang, magpie gauds and macaronics. By turns demotic and hieratic, shifting peremptorily in rhythm, tone, and register, skittish, hoydenish, and haughty, polyglot and jargonish, ruminative and aphoristic, shocking and coy, Auden's language corresponds in its variety to a frame of mind, to that master of disguises (Sherlock Holmes was always a hero) his poems expose from first to last. If his later poetry is more domestic and muted, full of thanksgivings and valedictions, elegies and reminiscences, it can still rise to pyrotechnic heroisms of language. But perhaps the best of these later volumes is *Homage to Clio*, a series of poems dedicated to Auden's first and last love, the matronly Muse of History:

> Madonna of silences, to whom we turn
>
> When we have lost control, your eyes, Clio, into which
>   We look for recognition after
> We have been found out....
>
>   I have seen
> Your photo, I think, in the papers, nursing
>   A baby or mourning a corpse: each time
>
> You had nothing to say and did not, one could see,
>   Observe where you were, Muse of the unique
> Historical fact, defending with silence
>   Some world of your beholding....

With this one poem alone Auden could establish his claim to be a serious and a major poet, fulfilling that specifically human vocation, the ability "with a rhythm or a rhyme" to "Assume ... responsibility for time."

—Stan Smith

BAGNOLD, Enid. English. Born in Rochester, Kent, 27 October 1899. Educated at Prior's Field, Godalming, Surrey, and in Marburg, Germany, and at the Villa Leona, Paris; studied painting with Walter Sickert. Married Sir Roderick Jones in 1920 (died, 1962); three sons and one daughter. Served as a driver with the French Army during World War I. Recipient: Arts Theatre Prize, 1951; American Academy of Arts and Letters Award of Merit, 1956. C.B.E. (Commander, Order of the British Empire), 1976. Lives in Rottingdean, Sussex.

PUBLICATIONS

Plays

    Lottie Dundass (produced 1942). 1943.
    National Velvet, from her own novel (produced 1945). 1961.
    Poor Judas (produced 1946). In *Two Plays,* 1951.
    Two Plays (includes *Lottie Dundass* and *Poor Judas*). 1951.
    Gertie (produced 1952; as *Little Idiot,* produced 1953).
    The Chalk Garden (produced 1955). 1956.
    The Last Joke (produced 1960). In *Four Plays,* 1970.
    The Chinese Prime Minister (produced 1964). 1964.
    Call Me Jacky (produced 1967). In *Four Plays,* 1970; (revised version, as *A Matter of Gravity,* produced 1975).
    Four Plays (includes *The Chalk Garden, The Last Joke, The Chinese Prime Minister, Call Me Jacky*). 1970.

Fiction

    The Happy Foreigner. 1920.
    Serena Blandish; or, The Difficulty of Getting Married. 1924.
    National Velvet. 1935.
    The Squire. 1938; as *The Door of Life,* 1938.
    The Loved and Envied. 1951.
    The Girl's Journey: Containing The Happy Foreigner and The Squire. 1954.

Verse

    The Sailing Ships and Other Poems. 1918.

Other

    A Diary Without Dates. 1918.
    Alice and Thomas and Jane (juvenile). 1930.
    Autobiography: From 1889. 1969.

    Translator, *Alexander of Asia,* by Princess Marthe Bibesco. 1935.

*   *   *

The title of Enid Bagnold's first novel proclaims a preoccupation with a character type that has dominated most of her work: *The Happy Foreigner* concerns, in Katherine Mansfield's words, "an unknown young woman, secret, folded within herself." Gradually, the young woman has become older, and the non-fictional substructure indicated in the autobiographical *Diary Without Dates* has become less obvious. *The Squire*, for example, offers the vision of a lady literally "folded within herself" by pregnancy, and isolated from her family and household by her social status; this may be seen as the prototype of Bagnold's dramatic protagonists, almost all of whom find human relationships impossible or illusory.

Though her novel *Serena Blandish* was dramatised by S. N. Behrman in 1929, it was only after *The Squire* that Miss Bagnold turned seriously to drama, and initially she appears to have been unable to reconcile the objectivity of stage presentation with the characteristically introverted nature of her human material. The stage version of *National Velvet* lacks both the semi-documentary impact of her novel and, more importantly, the subjectivity which has given the novel an identification appeal for two generations of youngsters. Plays like *Lottie Dundass* and *Poor Judas* retain a degree of power through their convincing presentation of unpleasant characters, but all of these early plays reveal an uncertain handling of a somewhat fanciful story-line which would be more easily acceptable in prose form.

The Chalk Garden is Miss Bagnold's most famous play, celebrated for its spectacular stage successes, for the response of critics like Tynan, and for its Chekhovian parallel between human and vegetable life. But it also marks the playwright's most complex essay in the relationships among variously abrasive and isolated characters, with the action developing easily from the depth of female characterisation in a way that is lacking in the somewhat self-indulgent perspective of the three later plays. *The Last Joke* is based on an episode in Miss Bagnold's *Autobiography*, and appears to have been limited dramaturgically by fidelity to this extraordinary source material. The play includes a character who may be seen as somewhat authorial but who remains towards the periphery of the action. In *The Chinese Prime Minister* and *Call Me Jacky*, however, such a character is at the core of the play, so that the action emanates largely from the whims of a leisurely and eccentric lady without the effective counterweight of other characters such as those in *The Chalk Garden*.

Enid Bagnold's reputation as a playwright may be gauged by the number of celebrated actors and actresses who have appeared in her works, but none of her plays is in any sense merely a vehicle for a performer. Indeed, though most of them pose formidable casting problems, their literary sophistication has ensured a popularity in the library to plays which have failed on the stage, so that *Call Me Jacky* is as satisfying reading as mature novels like *The Loved and Envied*.

—Howard McNaughton

BAILLIE, Joanna. Scottish. Born at the Manse of Bothwell, Lanarkshire, 11 September 1762. Educated at schools in Glasgow. Settled with her family in London, 1783; lived with her sister, in Hampstead, 1806 until her death. *Died 23 February 1851.*

PUBLICATIONS

Plays

A Series of Plays in Which It Is Attempted to Delineate the Stronger Passions of the Mind

(includes *Count Basil, The Trial, De Monfort, The Election, Ethwald, The Second Marriage, Orra, The Dream, The Siege, The Beacon*).   3 vols., 1798–1812.
De Monfort (produced 1800).   In *A Series of Plays 1*, 1798.
The Election, music by Charles Edward Horn (produced 1817).   In *A Series of Plays 2*, 1802.
Miscellaneous Plays (includes *Rayner, The Country Inn, Constantine, Paleologus*).   1804.
The Family Legend (produced 1810).   1810.
The Beacon (produced 1815).   In *A Series of Plays 3*, 1812.
The Martyr.   1826.
The Bride.   1828.
Dramas (includes *The Martyr, Romiero, The Alienated Manor, Henriquez, The Separation, The Stripling, The Phantom, Enthusiasm, Witchcraft, The Homicide, The Bride, The Match*).   3 vols., 1836.
Henriquez (produced 1836).   In *Dramas*, 1836.
The Separation (produced 1836).   In *Dramas*, 1836.

Verse

Fugitive Verses.   1790(?); revised edition, 1840.
Metrical Legends of Exalted Characters.   1821.
Complete Poetical Works.   1832.
Ahalya Baee.   1849.

Other

A View of the General Tenor of the New Testament Regarding the Nature and Dignity of Jesus Christ.   1831.
Dramatic and Poetical Works.   1851.

Editor, *A Collection of Poems from Living Authors*.   1823.

Reading List: *The Life and Works of Baillie* by Margaret S. Carhart, 1923 (includes bibliography); "The Plays of Baillie" by M. Norton, in *Review of English Studies*, 1947.

*   *   *

The long-lived Joanna Baillie as a young girl won Burns's admiration for her substantially original revision of the folk-song "Saw ye Johnie Comin'?," which Burns called "unparalleled ... for genuine humour in the verses, and lively originality in the air." She scored a similar success with her versions of other folk-songs, notably "The Weary Pund o' Tow," "Tam o' the Linn," and "Woo'd and Married an' a'." As it was thought unseemly for ladies who, like herself, came from an old Scottish family to acknowledge authorship, both her *Fugitive Verses* and the first two volumes of her "Plays on the Passions" appeared anonymously.

So wide was the spread of Burns's genius, and so great the shade it cast, that few seedlings grew up in its vicinity. Joanna Baillie, however, did achieve one original lyric in Scots, "A Scottish Song," unaided by echoes from the common stock:

> The gowan glitters on the sward,
>   The lav'rock's in the sky,
> And Collie on my plaid keeps ward,
>   And time is passing by.
>   Oh no! sad an' slow
> And lengthen'd on the ground
>   The shadow of our trysting bush,
> It wears so slowly round.

The themes of her plays were historical. She scored a success with *De Monfort* in London in 1809, mainly because of the acting of John Kemble and Mrs. Siddons. By then, however, she enjoyed the support of Scott, who did much to promote the enthusiastic success of her Highland drama *Family Legend* in Edinburgh the following year, again starring Kemble and Mrs. Siddons, with a prologue by Scott and an epilogue by Henry Mackenzie. In spite of Scott's praise, reinforced by that of David Hume and Robert Blair, the success was not repeated. The fustian, pseudo-Shakespearean blank verse seems dead to us today, and all that retains life is an occasional lively song, like "The Chough and the Crow" from *Orra*.

Joanna Baillie won the lifelong friendship of Scott, whose "Halidon Hill" was written at her request, and who salutes and eulogises her in the introduction to Canto iii of *Marmion* in the passage beginning "When she, the bold enchantress, came/ With fearless hand and heart on flame...." She lived into her ninetieth year, at the centre of an admiring literary circle in her Hampstead cottage.

—Maurice Lindsay

BALE, John. English. Born in Cove, near Dunwich, Suffolk, 21 November 1495. Entered the Carmelite Monastery, Norwich: educated there, and at Jesus College, Cambridge; converted to Protestantism by the teaching of Lord Wentworth, and renounced his monastic vows. Married to Dorothy Bale; several children. Rector of Thornden, Suffolk; also in the service of Thomas Cromwell: led an acting troupe at Cromwell's behest, 1537–40, and wrote propaganda for him; after Cromwell's death, lived in Germany, 1540 until the accession of Edward VI, 1547; appointed Rector of Bishopstoke, Hampshire; Vicar of Swaffham, 1551; Bishop of Ossory in Ireland, 1552–53; after the accession of Mary, lived on the Continent, 1553 until the accession of Elizabeth, 1558; returned to England: Prebendary at Canterbury, 1560–63. *Died in November 1563.*

PUBLICATIONS

Collections

Select Works, edited by Henry Christmas.   1849.
Dramatic Writings, edited by John S. Farmer.   1907.

Plays

> *King John* (produced ?). 1538; edited by William A. Armstrong, in *English History Plays*, 1965.
> *The Chief Promises of God unto Man* (produced ?). 1545(?); edited by Ernest Rhys, in *Everyman and Other Interludes*, 1909.
> *The Temptation of Our Lord* (produced ?). 1548(?); edited by P. Schwemmer, 1919.
> *Three Laws, of Nature, Moses, and Christ, Corrupted by Sodomites, Pharisees, and Papists* (produced ?). 1548(?).
> *John Baptist* (produced ?). In *Harleian Miscellany 1*, 1774.

Verse

> *An Answer to a Papistical Exhortation.* 1548(?); edited by H. Hugh, in *Fugitive Tracts in Verse 1*, 1875.

Other

> *A Brief Chronicle Concerning Sir John Oldcastle, the Lord Cobham.* 1544.
> *The Acts of English Votaries.* 1546; revised edition, 1548.
> *The Examination of Anne Askewe.* 2 vols., 1546–47.
> *The Image of Both Churches after the Revelation of St. John.* 1548(?).
> *Illustrium Majoris Britanniae Scriptorum Summarium.* 1548; revised edition, as *Scriptorum Illustrium Majoris Britanniae Catalogus*, 2 vols., 1557–59; notebook edited by R. L. Poole and M. Bateson, as *Index Britanniae Scriptorum*, 1902.
> *The Apology of Bale Against a Rank Papist.* 1555(?).
> *Acta Romanorum Pontificum.* 1558.
> *A Declaration Concerning the Clergy of London.* 1561.

> Editor, *A Treatise unto Henry VIII*, by John Lambert. 1548(?).

> Translator, *The True History of the Christian Departing of Martin Luther*, by Justus Jonas. 1546.

Bibliography: *A Bibliography of Bale* by William T. Davies, 1947.

Reading List: *Bale: A Study in the Minor Literature of the Reformation* by Jesse W. Harris, 1940; *Bale, Dramatist and Antiquary* by Honor MacCusker, 1942; *The Plays of Bale* by Thora B. Blatt, 1968; *Mittelälterliche Tradition und Reformatorische Polemik in den Spielen Bales* by Klaus Sperk, 1973; *Bale, Mythmaker for the English Reformation* by Leslie P. Fairfield, 1976.

*   *   *

John Bale, Bishop of Ossory, was the first English writer to use the drama for polemical purposes, inveighing against the "heap of adders of Antichrist's generation" (*King John*) and urging his audiences, as he urged congregations, to turn away from the practices of Roman Catholicism and towards an orthodoxy that recognized the king as God's deputy on earth and sole representative of the Amighty as head of His church. No Christian doctrine was infallible, he taught, unless it was grounded in Holy Scripture.

Of some twenty-one dramas that Bale is believed to have written, only five survive; and these five, one alone, *King John*, is readily available and of interest to students of the drama both for its intrinsic merit and for its unique position mid-way between the Morality Play and the historical dramas of the Elizabethans. The spur for Bale's writing of *King John* may have been provided by a remark of William Tyndale's in his *Obedience of a Christian Man* (1528); Tyndale invited his readers to "Consider the story of King John, where I doubt not but they [the Catholic historians] have put the best and fairest for themselves, and the worst for King John." Bale repeats the charge in his play:

> You priests are the cause that chronicles doth defame
> So many princes and men of notable name;
> For you take upon you to write them evermore;
> And, therefore, King John is like to rue it sore.

The play shows John at his most protestant, defending Widow England against the powers of Sedition, Private Wealth, Cardinal Pandulphus, and the Pope. England is widowed, she tells the king, because "These vile popish swine" have driven her husband into exile; her husband is no less than "God himself, the spouse of every sort/That seek him in faith to the soul's health and comfort." Although John has the authority of the Bible for all his actions, he is nevertheless forced to capitulate to Rome; but he does so with the resignation of a martyr:

> As God shall judge me, I do not this of cowardness,
> But of compassion in this extreme heaviness.
> Shall my people shed their blood in such habundance?
> Nay! I shall rather give up my whole governance.

King John dies of poison, administered by Simon of Swinsett; but the play does not end here. In a final scene Verity addresses Clergy, Nobility, and Civil Order, pointing out their failings and the king's virtues until, in the presence of Imperial Majesty, she exacts a new declaration of faith and intent: "We detest the Pope, and abhor him to the fiend." Imperial Majesty is then advised how best to maintain supreme power, and the play ends with a hymn of praise. Bale probably wrote his first version c. 1538, but revised and added to it throughout his life; it may well have been performed on the occasion of Queen Elizabeth's visit to Ipswich in 1561.

In the figures of King John himself, Stephen Langton, and Cardinal Pandulphus, Bale is presenting individuals, their characteristics supplied by the chronicles (although adapted, when necessary, to suit the dramatist's didactic purpose). But the unashamed abstractions of Clergy, Private Wealth, Dissimulation, and Nobility set the play securely in the Morality tradition. Sedition is the Morality's Vice, at best a comic nuisance and at worst the devil's advocate. Impartial satire is vested in the Vice: Sedition, although he claims to support the pope, is an eloquent exponent of the Roman church's false relics:

> Here is first a bone of the blessed Trinity,
> A dram of the turd of sweet Saint Barnaby.
> Here is a feather of good Saint Michael's wing,
> A tooth of Saint Twyde, a piece of David's harp string,
> The good blood of Hales, and our blessed Lady's milk;
> A louse of Saint Francis in this same crimson silk.

With this combination of the real and the allegorical in his *dramatis personae*, Bale shows himself a master of theatricality. He has arranged his dialogue so that nineteen speaking parts can be performed by nine actors – a necessity often forced upon the small travelling companies who acted the Morality Plays. But Bale extracts a virtue from this necessity: the real and the allegorical fuse – as in this stage direction: "Here go out Usurped Power and Private Wealth and Sedition: Usurped Power shall dress for the Pope: Private Wealth for a Cardinal; and Sedition for a Monk." That the transformations were intended to be noticed by the audience is clear from King John's observation when Sedition enters, this time dressed as the bishop, Stephen Langton: "Methink[s] this bishop resembleth much Sedition."

The language of *King John* is simple, but Bale achieves a variety of tones, from the moving pleas of Widow England to the dignified oratory of Imperial Majesty. Most notable of all is the racy colloquialism, contained within the blank verse line, of the speeches of Sedition; here Bale shows himself to be not only the inheritor of the Morality tradition and its Vice, but also the precursor of the Elizabethan history play with its Falstaff.

—Roma Gill

BANKS, John.   English.   Very little is known about his life: flourished 1677–96. Studied law; a member of the society of the New Inn.

PUBLICATIONS

Plays

>   *The Rival Kings; or, The Loves of Oroondates and Statira* (produced 1677).   1677.
>   *The Destruction of Troy* (produced 1678).   1679.
>   *The Unhappy Favourite; or, The Earl of Essex* (produced 1681).   1682; edited by James
>   Sutherland, in *Restoration Tragedies*, 1976.
>   *Virtue Betrayed; or, Anna Bullen* (produced 1682).   1682.
>   *The Island Queens; or, The Death of Mary, Queen of Scotland.*   1684; revised version,
>   as *The Albion Queens* (produced 1704), 1704.
>   *The Innocent Usurper; or, The Death of the Lady Jane Gray.*   1694.
>   *Cyrus the Great; or, The Tragedy of Love* (produced 1695).   1696.

Reading List: Introduction by Thomas M. H. Blair to *The Unhappy Favourite*, 1939; *Banks: Eine Studie* by Hans Hochuli, 1952.

*   *   *

John Banks is certainly one of the weakest playwrights in the long history of English drama and he was not even considered a poet by his later contemporaries. Yet he was responsible for a major change in tragedy and he was an innovator in turning to recent English history as subject matter for his most popular plays. In making a woman the central character, he brought about a sweeping change in the nature of English tragedy. The prevailing pattern of earlier drama showed the fall of a strong hero – Faustus, Richard III, Bussy d'Ambois, Lear, Coriolanus; the current mode of the heroic play had its Almanzors and Montezumas; Banks offered, instead, a heroine in distress. In fact, in two of his most popular plays both the heroine and the villain are women. Critics sneered and termed his plays "she-tragedies," but the dramatists fell in line – Otway, Southerne, Congreve, especially Nicholas Rowe – to follow this major shift in tragic structure.

A basic characteristic of the contemporary heroic drama was its distant s action was often set at a remote time. Banks showed considerable initiative in choosing his material for historical events in the lifetime of Queen Elizabeth I. Deficient as he was in attempting verse, he had no difficulty in recognizing tragic episodes from history: the plight of Anne Boleyn, the ordeal of decision by Queen Elizabeth on the Earl of Essex and Mary, Queen of Scots. Some of these events were scarcely a century old, it will be recalled. This fact, together with the native setting, probably created a strong sense of realism for Restoration audiences, and provided a striking contrast to the purposeful artificiality of the heroic drama. The subject matter of "real" versus "usurping" rulers and the deposition and execution of queens led of course to many of the plays being banned from the stage.

—Arthur H. Scouten

BARAKA, Amiri.   See **JONES, LeRoi.**

BARKER, Harley Granville -.   English.   Born in London, 25 November 1877. Served in the Red Cross and the British Army Intelligence during World War I. Married 1) the actress Lillah McCarthy in 1906 (divorced, 1917); 2) Helen Huntington Gates in 1918. Worked as child entertainer with his mother, then as a stage actor: London debut in 1892; acted and directed for the Stage Society, London 1900–04; campaigned for a National Theatre, and successfully ran a pilot scheme for such a theatre at the Court Theatre, London, 1904–07; established Shaw's reputation as a dramatist; in management, with Lillah McCarthy, at the Little, Kingsway, St. James's, and Savoy theatres before 1914; toured America, 1915; ceased to work in the theatre, except intermittently, after his second marriage, and began to hyphenate his name; lived in Paris after 1930. Clark Lecturer, Cambridge, 1930; Romanes Lecturer, Oxford, 1937; Director of the British Institute of the University of Paris, 1937–39; Visiting Professor, Yale University, New Haven, Connecticut, 1940, and Harvard University, Cambridge, Massachusetts, 1941–42, 1944–45. Member of the Executive Committee of the Fabian Society, 1907–12; Chairman of the British Drama League, 1919–32. LL.D.: University of Edinburgh, 1930; Litt.D.: University of Reading, 1937; D. Litt.: Oxford University, 1937. Fellow, and Member of the Academic Committee, Royal Society of Literature. *Died 31 August 1946.*

PUBLICATIONS

Collections

   Collected Plays.   1967 (one volume only published).
   Three Plays (includes *The Marrying of Ann Leete, The Voysey Inheritance, Waste*), edited by Margery Morgan.   1977.

Plays

The Weather-Hen, with Berte Thomas (produced 1899).

The Marrying of Ann Leete (produced 1902).   1909; in *Three Plays*, 1977.

Prunella; or, Love in a Dutch Garden, with Laurence Housman (produced 1904).   1906; revised version, 1930.

The Voysey Inheritance (produced 1905).   1909; revised version, 1913, 1934; in *Three Plays*, 1977.

Waste (produced 1907).   1909; revised version (produced 1936), 1926; in *Three Plays*, 1977.

A Miracle (produced 1907).

The Madras House (produced 1910).   1910; revised version, 1925.

Rococo (produced 1911).   In *Rococo* ..., 1917.

Anatol (includes *Ask No Questions and You'll Hear No Stories, The Wedding Morning, A Christmas Present, An Episode, Keepsakes*), from plays by Schnitzler (produced 1911).   1911 (includes also the play *A Farewell Supper*, translated by Edith A. Browne and Alix Grein); edited by Eric Bentley, in *From the Modern Repertory 3*, 1956.

Das Märchen, with C. E. Wheeler, from the play by Schnitzler (produced 1912).

The Morris Dance, from the novel *The Wrong Box* by Robert Louis Stevenson and Lloyd Osbourne (produced 1913).

The Harlequinade: An Excursion, with D. C. Calthrop (produced 1913).   1918.

The Dynasts, from the play by Hardy (produced 1914).

Vote by Ballot (produced 1917).   In *Rococo* ..., 1917.

Rococo, Vote by Ballot, Farewell to the Theatre.   1917; as *Three Short Plays*, 1917.

Deburau, from a play by Sacha Guitry (produced 1920).   1921.

The Romantic Young Lady, with Helen Granville Barker, from a play by G. Martinez Sierra (produced 1920).   In *The Plays of Martinez Sierra*, 1923.

The Two Shepherds, with Helen Granville Barker, from a play by G. Martinez Sierra (produced 1921).   In *The Plays of Martinez Sierra*, 1923.

The Kingdom of God, with Helen Granville Barker, from a play by G. Martinez Sierra (produced 1923).   In *The Plays of Martinez Sierra*, 1923.

Wife to a Famous Man, with Helen Granville Barker, from a play by G. Martinez Sierra (produced 1924).   In *The Plays of Martinez Sierra*, 1923.

The Secret Life.   1923.

Doctor Knock, from a play by Jules Romains (produced 1926).   1925; edited by Eric Bentley, in *From the Modern Repertory 3*, 1956.

Six Gentlemen in a Row, from a play by Jules Romain (produced 1927).   1927.

Four Plays, with Helen Granville Barker, from plays by S. and J. Alvarez Quintero (includes *A Hundred Years Old, Fortunato, The Lady from Alfaqueque, The Women Have Their Way*, produced 1928).   1927.

His Majesty.   1928.

Take Two from One, with Helen Granville Barker, from a play by G. Martinez Sierra.   1931.

Four Comedies (includes *Love Passes By, Don Abel Wrote a Tragedy, Peace and Quiet, Doña Clarines*), with Helen Granville Barker, from plays by S. and J. Alvarez Quintero.   1932.

Fiction

Souls on Fifth (stories).   1916.

Other

> *Scheme and Estimates for a National Theatre,* with William Archer.   1904; revised
> edition, 1907.
> *The Red Cross in France.*   1916.
> *The Exemplary Theatre.*   1922.
> *Prefaces to Shakespeare.*   5 vols., 1927–47; revised edition, 2 vols., 1946–47; *More*
> *Prefaces to Shakespeare,* edited by Edward M. Moore, 1974.
> *A National Theatre.*   1930.
> *On Dramatic Method* (lectures).   1931.
> *The Use of the Drama.*   1945; revised edition, 1946.

> Editor, *The Players Shakespeare.*   7 vols., 1923–27 (prefaces also published separately).
> Editor, *The Eighteen-Seventies.*   1929.
> Editor, with G. B. Harrison, *A Companion to Shakespeare Studies.*   1934.
> Editor, *Eight Letters from T. E. Lawrence.*   1939.

Reading List: *The Court Theatre 1904–07* by Desmond MacCarthy, 1907, edited by Stanley
Weintraub, 1966; "Granville Barker: Some Particulars" by G. B. Shaw in *Drama,* Winter
1946; *The Lost Leader* by W. Bridges Adams, 1954; *Granville Barker, Man of the Theatre,*
Dramatist, and Scholar by C. B. Purdom, 1955 (includes bibliography by Frederick May and
Margery Morgan), and *Bernard Shaw's Letters to Granville Barker* edited by Purdom, 1956;
A Drama of Political Man: A Study in the Plays of Granville Barker by Margery Morgan,
1961.

*   *   *

Harley Granville-Barker wrote his first plays as a young actor, and his mature drama was
one aspect of his total effort to carve out the model of an English national theatre. His various
books and articles advocating such a theatre and discussing the art of acting (e.g., *A National*
Theatre, The Exemplary Theatre, "The Heritage of the Actor") are matched by the public
themes and challenging techniques of his plays. These demand large casts of experienced
actors and prolonged, intensive rehearsal. The unusual degree of intelligence and imagination
needed for their presentation has to call out like qualities from an attentive audience. Barker's
early retirement from active stage work meant that he did not break theatrical ground for the
two plays he wrote in the 1920's (*The Secret Life* and *His Majesty*), and in the lengthy interval
before the growth of civic theatre after the World War II most of his other work was
neglected and forgotten. The simplest piece, *The Voysey Inheritance,* has had regular revivals,
but otherwise Barker has had to wait for the 1970's, and conditions in the major subsidised
theatres approximate to what he sought for the theatre as a whole, for any measure of rediscovery.

His close professional and personal association with G. B. Shaw has delayed recognition of
the individuality of Barker's drama. Comparison of *The Marrying of Ann Leete* with his later
plays can establish precisely what additions to his dramatic resources he drew from Shaw.
First among these is a greater explicitness, accessory to the occasional use of broader styles of
comic characterisation (e.g., Booth Voysey and Major Thomas and Eustace Perrin State in
The Madras House), the rhetorically constructed monologue (as given to Constantine in Act
III of *The Madras House* or to Lord Clumbermere in *The Secret Life*), and the orchestrated
debate, or discussion, among a stageful of characters focussing on the themes of the play (e.g.,
Waste, Act III; *The Madras House,* Act III; *The Secret Life,* Act III, scene ii); the
introduction of elements of fantasy into a predominently naturalistic context (e.g., the
Moorish Room and the mannequins in *The Madras House*) was partly anticipated in the
grotesque wedding scene of *Ann Leete,* an animated Hogarth caricature. Certainly Shaw and

Barker stimulated each other's thinking, and whole groups of their plays are interlinked by common themes and images, but the two minds had opposite tendencies, Barker's being introspective, questing, exact, and sensitively alert. The structure of thought in his plays is close and continuous, and in place of Shaw's galvanic energy he offers dramatic concentration and a more finely turned, subtle style of dialogue.

Most of his early unpublished plays which survive were written, to varying degree, in collaboration with an older actor, Berte Thomas. They are concerned with aspects of the emancipation of women and the moral transformation it entails. After this phase, the lessons of Ibsen are most evident in the extensions of naturalism Barker practises. His use of the idiom of evangelical Christianity ("salvation" and "soul" are key terms) dates the plays, though it is not dogmatic religion he is interested in, but the difficult search for values, vision, and a far-reaching purpose beyond self-interest facing those who (like Trebell in *Waste*) "grew up in the late nineteenth-century, neo-Polytechnic belief that you couldn't take God seriously and be an F.R.S." For the far regions of experience he wanted to explore, he relied largely on the trained ability of actors to bring out meanings implicit in the text and between its lines, as indicated in his essay "The Coming of Ibsen." To this end he writes a loaded but deliberately fractured dialogue, and incidentally anticipates Harold Pinter's technique of scoring the text. The loading is achieved by devices learnt mainly from Shakespeare: verbal repetition, running imagery, puns, multi-faceted lines open to delivery with varying patterns of stress and inflection, when the actor's awareness of the discarded possibilities may inform the reading he chooses. Fully developed, in his later plays and the revised version of *Waste*, these techniques emerge as a symphonic structure reinforcing, or virtually replacing, the more obvious line of dramatic action.

Although these features are embryonic in *The Marrying of Ann Leete*, the spareness and astringency of the writing help establish this play as a fable of late nineteenth-century consciousness in late eighteenth-century guise. In *The Voysey Inheritance* and *The Madras House*, the move towards surrogate musical composition allows Barker to subdue narrative interest, as happens in the modernist novel, while combining a novelistic richness of detail with plot-forms better suited to documenting and discussing the condition of contemporary England. Barker's socialism is most directly active in his satiric treatment of middle-class capitalist society in *The Voysey Inheritance* and the more impressive survey of economic imperialism and the relations of the sexes, interlocked into a single system and its supporting mental structures, in *The Madras House*. But he is not primarily a polemical, let alone propagandist, writer, and it is the trapped anti-hero, conscious of his own impotence, who brings each of these plays home. Faced by the trivialisation of politics in Edwardian England, the central character in *Waste* is more heroic, and his ultimate suicide shows his potent refusal to be assimilated. Undoubtedly Barker's personal dilemmas and reflections on leaving the theatre have informed the meditative, lyrical elements in his two last plays, perhaps to a morbid extent in *The Secret Life*, but there is no narrowing of relevance. War-devastated Europe is the implied background to both these plays: *The Secret Life*, concerned with the unstrung will, integrity, and commitment in political life; and *His Majesty*, in which realism is intermeshed with Ruritanian fable, and the mystique of leadership and authority is examined in the context of rising fascism.

The wit and elegance of Barker's naturalistic dialogue distinguish his English versions of foreign plays, including the translations from the Spanish in collaboration with his second wife. His interest in theatrical tradition, his practical theatre-craft, and a dry-eyed, slightly bitter quality seem to have been his contributions to the plays written in collaboration with Laurence Housman and D. C. Calthrop. The *Prefaces to Shakespeare* remain the outstanding example of academic criticism combined with full awareness of the practical theatre.

—Margery Morgan

BARKER, James Nelson. American. Born in Philadelphia, Pennsylvania, 17 June 1784; son of General George Barker. Educated in schools in Philadelphia. Commissioned Captain in the 2nd United States Artillery, 1812; served as Assistant Adjutant-General of the United States Army, rising to the rank of Major, 1814–17. Married Mary Rogers in 1811; one daughter. Began writing for the stage, Philadelphia, 1804–08; lived in Washington, D.C., studying government, 1809–10; returned to Philadelphia, and resumed writing for the stage, 1812; contributed series of articles on "The Drama" to *Dramatic Press,* 1816–17; Alderman of Philadelphia, 1817–29; Mayor, 1819–21; Collector of the Port of Philadelphia, 1829–38; Controller of the United States Department of the Treasury, Washington, 1838–41, and subsequently served various administrations as Clerk in the office of the Chief Clerk of the Treasury, 1841 until his death. *Died 9 March 1858.*

PUBLICATIONS

Plays

> *Tears and Smiles* (produced 1807). 1808; edited by Paul H. Musser, in *Barker,* 1929.
> *The Embargo; or, What News?* (produced 1808).
> *Travellers; or, Music's Fascination,* from a work by Andrew Cherry (produced 1808).
> *The Indian Princess; or, La Belle Sauvage,* music by John Bray (produced 1808). 1808; revised version, as *Pocahontas* (produced 1820).
> *Marmion; or, The Battle of Flodden Field,* from the poem by Scott (produced 1812). 1816.
> *The Armourer's Escape; or, Three Years at Nootka Sound* (produced 1817).
> *How to Try a Lover* (as *A Court of Love,* produced 1836). 1817.
> *Superstition; or, The Fanatic Father* (produced 1824). 1826.

Other

> *Delaplaine's Repository of the Lives and Portraits of Distinguished American Characters,* vol. 1, part 2. 1817.
> *Sketches of the Primitive Settlements on the River Delaware.* 1827.

Reading List: *Barker* by Paul H. Musser, 1929 (includes bibliography).

*   *   *

James Nelson Barker, Democratic mayor of Federalist Philadelphia and amateur historian, wrote for the Chestnut Street Theatre. The craft of his research and allegorical verse fed best into his politics and plays. His critical articles examined "Tragedy of Character," the problems of adapting and performance, and the social function of drama. Barker intended his earliest, unproduced "mask" (*America,* with "Liberty" singing) to conclude an unfinished dramatization of John Smith's 1624 history of Virginia. Instead, his popular but comically melodramatic opera *The Indian Princess* (John Bray's music) introduced the frequently repeated Pocahontas figure to the stage.

The stage for Barker addressed and shaped the partisan energies that preceded the War of 1812. *Tears and Smiles,* his clever sentimental comedy, marshalled early Yankee types, a patriotic sailor, fops, an Irishman, and mysterious European fugitives to question commercial aristocracy and praise domestic products in fashions, morals, and persons. *The Embargo* supported a comedian's benefit and Jefferson's controversial ban on trade with Britain or France. After the war, Barker's "melo-dramatic sketch" *The Armourer's Escape* let the Indian-captured sailor Jewitt play himself, to capitalize on 1817 interest in the Oregon boundary dispute.

How to Try a Lover, a singularly unpolitical gem in prose, was produced as *A Court of Love*. It celebrates blinding love, from insatiable lust to its most courtly and impractical idealism. Love's confusing possibilities are drawn, with literary parodies ("Almanzor" as hero-lover's pseudonym; conventional allegories of love/honor), through the neoclassically comic dance of a picaresque plot, while carefully described settings develop from dark gothic vault toward brilliant court. Movements and situations belie spoken words. Barker's balancings of characters and antithetical dialogue intensify the skeptical-romantic counterpoint in this "only dream" that "satisfied" him as artist.

Barker's verse tragedies explore what politicians considered resolved. *Marmion* and *Superstition* are historical tragedies of personal and national character. "*The* American playwright" (New York review) and best adaptor of Scott's poem (London critic) re-examined Scott's sources, tightened artistic structure, alternated scenes for deeper psychological effect, and rallied sentiment for war against Britain – though in 1811–12 victory seemed unlikely. *Marmion* poses determining destiny against individual responsibility. In *Superstition* manifest destiny and liberty are susceptible to public hysteria. The inspired leadership of the Puritan Unknown (a fugitive regicide) saves a New England community from Indian attack; but the perverting religious fervor of witch-hunts and narrow-mindedness, part of the colonial heritage, leave a Columbia-figure and the young lovers of a New World dead. Spying courtiers supply objectifying comedy. Behind the play's action loom the New England fathers and the war for independence from the mother country, as well as the current themes of Greek and South American independence, Philadelphia's epidemics and religious riots, and Barker's campaigning for Andrew Jackson (Hero of the People) against New England's Adams ("John the Second"). Though Barker as politician honored "The People," *Superstition* questions their readiness for genuine democracy and implies a vision of rational, tolerant, effective, and affective leadership, fatalistic action, and individual heroism. Allegory becomes symbolic and moving in these tragedies, the finest of early America.

—John G. Kuhn

BARRIE, Sir J(ames) M(atthew). Scottish. Born in Kirriemuir, Forfarshire, now Angus, Scotland, 9 May 1860. Educated at Glasgow Academy, 1868–70; Forfar Academy, 1870–71; Dumfries Academy, 1873–78; University of Edinburgh, 1878–82, M.A. 1882. Married the actress Mary Ansell in 1894 (divorced, 1909). Drama and Book Critic, *Edinburgh Courant*, 1879–82; Leader Writer, *Nottingham Journal*, 1883–84. Lived in London after 1885: worked as a journalist, contributing to the *St. James's Gazette* and *British Weekly*, 1885–90; wrote for the theatre from 1890. President, Society of Authors, 1928–37, and Dramatists' Club, 1934–37. LL.D.: University of St. Andrews, 1898; University of Edinburgh, 1909; D.Litt.: Oxford University; Cambridge University. Rector, University of St. Andrews, 1919–22; Chancellor, University of Edinburgh, 1930–37. Created Baronet, 1913; Order of Merit, 1922. *Died 19 June 1937.*

Collections

Letters, edited by Viola Meynell.   1942.
Plays and Stories, edited by Roger Lancelyn Green.   1962.

Plays

Caught Napping.   1883.
Ibsen's Ghost; or, Toole Up-to-Date (produced 1891).
Richard Savage, with H. B. Marriott Watson (produced 1891).   1891.
Walker, London (as *The Houseboat,* produced 1892).   1907.
The Professor's Love Story (produced 1892).   In *Plays,* 1942.
Becky Sharp (produced 1893).
Jane Annie; or, The Good Conduct Prize, with Arthur Conan Doyle, music by Ernest
    Ford (produced 1893).   1893.
The Little Minister, from his own novel (produced 1897; as *Little Mary,* produced
    1903).   In *Plays,* 1942.
A Platonic Friendship (produced 1898).
The Wedding Guest (produced 1900).   1900.
The Admirable Crichton (produced 1902).   1914.
Quality Street (produced 1902).   1913.
Peter Pan; or, The Boy Who Wouldn't Grow Up (produced 1904; revised version,
    produced 1905).   In *Plays,* 1928.
Pantaloon (produced 1905).   In *Half Hours,* 1914.
Alice Sit-by-the-Fire (produced 1905).   1919.
Josephine (produced 1906).
Punch (produced 1906).
When Wendy Grew Up: An Afterthought (produced 1908).   1957.
What Every Woman Knows (produced 1908).   1918.
Old Friends (produced 1910).   In *Plays,* 1928.
A Slice of Life (produced 1910).
The Twelve-Pound Look (produced 1910).   In *Half Hours,* 1914.
Rosalind (produced 1912).   In *Half Hours,* 1914.
The Dramatists Get What They Want (produced 1912; as *The Censor and the Dramatists,*
    produced 1913).
The Will (produced 1913).   In *Half Hours,* 1914.
The Adored One: A Legend of the Old Bailey (produced 1913; as *The Legend of Leonora,*
    produced 1914; shortened version, as *Seven Women,* produced 1917).   *Seven
    Women* included in *Plays,* 1928.
Half an Hour (produced 1913).   In *Plays,* 1928.
Half Hours.   1914.
Der Tag (produced 1914; as *Der Tag; or, The Tragic Man,* produced 1914).   1914.
Rosy Rapture; or , The Pride of the Beauty Chorus, music by H. Darewski and Jerome
    Kern (produced 1915).
The Fatal Typist (produced 1915).
The New Word (produced 1915).   In *Echoes of the War,* 1918.
The Real Thing at Last (produced 1916).
Irene Vanbrugh's Pantomime (produced 1916).
Shakespeare's Legacy (produced 1916).   1916.
A Kiss for Cinderella (produced 1916).   1920.

The Old Lady Shows Her Medals (produced 1917).   In *Echoes of the War*, 1918.
Reconstructing the Crime (produced 1917).
Dear Brutus (produced 1917).   1922.
La Politesse (produced 1918).
A Well-Remembered Voice (produced 1918).   In *Echoes of the War*, 1918.
Echoes of the War.   1918.
Barbara's Wedding (produced 1927).   In *Echoes of the War*, 1918.
The Truth about the Russian Dancers (ballet), music by Arnold Bax (produced 1920).   1962.
Mary Rose (produced 1920).   1924.
Shall We Join the Ladies? (produced 1921).   In *Plays*, 1928.
Neil and Tinntinabulum.   1925.
Representative Plays (includes *Quality Street, The Admirable Crichton, What Every Woman Knows, Dear Brutus, The Twelve-Pound Look, The Old Lady Shows Her Medals*).   1926.
The Plays of Barrie (includes *Peter Pan, The Admirable Crichton, Alice Sit-by-the-Fire, What Every Woman Knows, A Kiss for Cinderella, Dear Brutus, Mary Rose, Pantaloon, Half an Hour, Seven Women, Old Friends, Rosalind, The Twelve-Pound Look, The New Word, A Well-Remembered Voice, Barbara's Wedding, The Old Lady Shows Her Medals, Shall We Join the Ladies?*).   1928; augmented edition, edited by A. E. Wilson (includes *Walker, London; The Professor's Love Story; The Little Minister; The Wedding Guest; The Boy David*), 1942.
The Boy David (produced 1936).   1938.

Screenplay: *As You Like It*, with Robert Cullen, 1936.

Fiction

Better Dead.   1887.
When a Man's Single: A Tale of Literary Life.   1888.
The Little Minister.   1891.
Sentimental Tommy: The Story of His Boyhood.   1896.
Tommy and Grizel.   1900.
The Boy Castaways of Black Lake Island.   1901.
The Little White Bird.   1902; as *The Little White Bird; or, Adventures in Kensington Gardens*, 1902; revised material for children, as *Peter Pan in Kensington Gardens*, 1906.
Peter and Wendy.   1911; as *Peter Pan and Wendy*, 1921.
Farewell Miss Julie Logan: A Wintry Tale.   1931.

Verse

Scotland's Lament: A Poem on the Death of Robert Louis Stevenson.   1895.

Other

The New Amphion.   1886.
Auld Licht Idylls.   1888.
A Window in Thrums.   1889.
An Edinburgh Eleven: Pencil Portraits from College Life.   1889.
My Lady Nicotine.   1890.

Allahakbarries C. C. (on cricket).   1893.
Margaret Ogilvy, by Her Son.   1896.
The Allahakbarrie Book of Broadway Cricket for 1899.   1899.
George Meredith 1909.   1909; as *Neither Dorking nor the Abbey,* 1910.
The Works (Kirriemuir Edition).   10 vols., 1913.
Charles Frohman: A Tribute.   1915.
Who Was Sarah Findley? by Mark Twain, with a Suggested Solution of the Mystery.   1917.
The Works.   10 vols., 1918.
The Works (Peter Pan edition).   14 vols., 1929–31.
The Greenwood Hat, Being a Memoir of James Anon, 1885–1887.   1930; revised edition, 1937.
M'Connachie and J. M. B.: Speeches.   1938.

Bibliography: *Barrie: A Bibliography* by B. D. Cutler, 1931.

Reading List: *Barrie* by F. J. Harvey Darton, 1929; *Barrie* by Denis Mackail, 1941; *Barrie* by Roger Lancelyn Green, 1960; *Barrie: The Man Behind the Image* by Janet Dunbar, 1970; *Barrie* by Harry M. Geduld, 1971; *Barrie* by Allen Wright, 1976; *Barrie and the Lost Boys* by Andrew Birkin, 1978.

*   *   *

J. M. Barrie, wrote a critic at the time of his death, was "a romantic who could suddenly turn round and write the realists off the stage. It is customary nowadays to make fun of his excursions into fairyland. That he made greater excursions elsewhere is too easily forgotten."

The irony of Barrie's career is that his most famous and most frequently performed play, *Peter Pan*, probably the greatest children's play ever written, has prevented him from being taken seriously as a major dramatist. Yet even *Peter Pan* has its undertones of tragedy, certainly for the adult play-goer or reader – and for them the true ending is Peter's last despairing glance through the closed window of the Darling nursery: "He had ecstasies innumerable that other children can never know; but he was looking through the window at the one joy from which he must be for ever barred."

Although Barrie had already written in his novels *Sentimental Tommy* and *Tommy and Grizel* of "the boy who could not grow up," it is unsafe to treat Tommy Sandys as a complete self-portrait, though the grim pessimism of the second follows his own part-predicament mercilessly to its probable conclusion if that predicament had been complete. At the date of writing this predicament could not be followed in absolute detail – only hinted at by Grizel: "He did not love her. 'Not as I love him,' she said to herself, 'Not as married people ought to love, but in the other way he loves me dearly.' By the other way she meant that he loved her as he loved Elspeth [his sister], and loved them both just as he had loved them when all three played in the den. He was a boy who could not grow up." Barrie's personal predicament, that he was nearly though not quite impotent, brought about the break up of his marriage ten years later, but by then he had finished with novel writing as his triumph in the theatre became complete.

His novels and short stories are most unduly neglected: Conan Doyle lamented that the theatre had "diverted from literature the man with the purest style of his age," and Stevenson had greeted his most popular novel, *The Little Minister*, as holding the promise of real genius. But the theatre was already claiming Barrie in 1891–2 when the one-act parody, *Ibsen's Ghost*, and the full-length farce, *Walker, London,* both achieved long runs and high acclaim.

Barrie was still, however, known for his "Thrums" novels and stories, and his next play, *The Professor's Love Story,* was an amusing and charming triviality set in his native Kirriemuir. Real success came with the dramatised version of *The Little Minister*. His attempt at the problem play in the new Ibsen tradition which Shaw and Pinero were bringing into fashion (*The Wedding Guest*) was less successful, and he wisely turned to his own individual kind of play with *Quality Street* and *The Admirable Crichton*.

With these he entered truly into his kingdom. They are plays of charm, fancy, even at times whimsy, which hide a real problem, social and personal, that might easily have been the subject of tragedy. Yet the treatment sends the audience away with the conscious joy of escape and the, perhaps unconscious, feeling also of having been posed with a problem as potentially "real" as anything in Ibsen or Galsworthy or Granville-Barker, and as thought-provoking as Shaw at his best. When Captain Brown comes back from the wars and finds his first love, Phoebe Throssell, old and tired in her working clothes teaching her school in Quality Street, he turns from her to her niece who seems all that Phoebe had been before he went away. That the niece turns out to be Phoebe herself making her one desperate bid to win back his love – and succeeds – does not take away from the "problem," and the possibility of a tragic ending.

The basic idea for *The Admirable Crichton* was a remark by Conan Doyle that "if a King and an able seaman were wrecked together on a desert island for the rest of their lives, the sailor would end as King and the monarch as his servant." From this grew Barrie's parable of the Earl of Loam and his party, cast away on their island and helpless in this new setting until Crichton, the butler, who in the first act has been the perfect servant in an aristocratic household, takes control and shows himself to be the natural master in the given circumstances. By the end of the third act the situation is approaching its remorselessly logical conclusion, with Crichton, as undisputed king, about to choose the Earl's eldest daughter as his bride, when the rescue party reaches the island – summoned by Crichton who fires the beacon at the supreme moment, though he knows what the result will be. In the last act Crichton is once more the butler in Lord Loam's Mayfair house, while all the party have slipped back almost into their original characters, and their reactions to their island experience point the moral and underline the quiet satire on the values of civilisation.

Peter Pan followed, between two lesser plays, and then came *What Every Woman Knows*, which remains the best-known and most frequently revived after *Peter Pan* itself. Here again we have Barrie's unique mixture of romance and realism as Maggie saves her husband's career and their marriage without him realising that both depend on her superior courage, wit, and understanding.

His next outstanding play, *Dear Brutus*, employed fantasy as well as realism, and is held by many to be Barrie's greatest play; it has been revived many times.

Its theme is contained in the quotation from *Julius Caesar*: "The fault, dear Brutus, is not in our stars, but in ourselves": guests at a house party, after revealing their characters and blaming various chance mistakes for their failures, go out in Lob's magic wood at the end of act one. In the wood we see most of them throwing away their second chances in the same way as their first; and in act three they return and wake to a far deeper understanding of their own characters, though only one couple, the Dearths, are given real hope of a lasting change. "Barrie with a plot," wrote Denis Mackail, "and Barrie expressing a philosophy on which he had mused for years and in its own mood and convention, as near as almost nothing to a flawless play." *Mary Rose*, with a greater use of fantasy, was even more popular in its early years, but has not worn so well.

Barrie was also a master of the one-act play. The best known are *The Twelve-Pound Look*, *The Will*, *The Old Lady Shows Her Medals*, and *Shall We Join the Ladies?*, which is the first act of a thriller which for various reasons Barrie did not finish – though not, as is often said, because he was unable to complete the plot.

Towards the close of his life he turned back to the Scottish scenes of his youth with the short-story *Farewell Miss Julie Logan*, and to his early journalistic days in *The Greenwood Hat*, both more enjoyable for the modern reader than his early Auld Licht sketches and journalism.

Barrie has been out of favour with critics for a longer time than usually follows an author's death. But recent revivals have delighted audiences and shown Barrie's supreme skill in the basic mechanics of the dramatist's art. Some at least of his plays, besides *Peter Pan*, may confidently be claimed for immortality.

—Roger Lancelyn Green

BARRY, Philip. American. Born in Rochester, New York, 18 June 1896. Educated in public schools in Rochester; Yale University, New Haven, Connecticut (Editor, *Yale Review*), A.B. 1919; studied with George Pierce Baker at Harvard University, Cambridge, Massachusetts, 1919–22. Worked in the Code Department of the U.S. Embassy, London, 1918–19. Married Ellen Semple in 1922; two sons. Professional playwright from 1922; wrote for M.G.M., Hollywood, from 1934; lived in France, 1938–39. Member, National Institute of Arts and Letters. *Died 3 December 1949.*

PUBLICATIONS

Collections

    States of Grace: Eight Plays, edited by Brendan Gill. 1975.

Plays

    A Punch for Judy (produced 1921). 1922.
    You and I (produced 1922). 1923.
    God Bless Our Home. 1924.
    The Youngest (produced 1924). 1925.
    In a Garden (produced 1925). 1926.
    White Wings (produced 1926). 1927; revised version, music by Douglas Moore (produced 1935).
    John (produced 1927). 1929.
    Paris Bound (produced 1927). 1929.
    Cock Robin, with Elmer Rice (produced 1928). 1929.
    Holiday (produced 1928). 1929.
    Hotel Universe (produced 1930). 1930.
    Tomorrow and Tomorrow (produced 1931). 1931.
    The Animal Kingdom (produced 1932). 1932.
    The Joyous Season (produced 1934). 1934.
    Bright Star (produced 1935).
    Spring Dance, from a play by Eleanor Golden and Eloise Barrangon (produced 1936). 1936.
    Here Come the Clowns (produced 1938). 1939.
    The Philadelphia Story (produced 1939). 1939.
    Liberty Jones (produced 1941). 1941.
    Without Love (produced 1943). 1943.

Foolish Notion (produced 1945).   Abridged version in *The Best Plays of 1944–45*, edited
by Burns Mantle, 1945.
Second Threshold, completed by Robert E. Sherwood (produced 1951).   1951.

Fiction

War in Heaven.   1938.

Reading List: *The Drama of Barry* by Gerald Hamm, 1948; *Barry* by Joseph Roppolo, 1965.

*   *   *

American theater has never been particularly congenial to that honorable but somewhat amorphous genre *high comedy.* Philip Barry is one of the very few American playwrights who is a celebrated practitioner of the form. In plays like *Paris Bound, The Animal Kingdom, Without Love,* and – most famously – *Holiday* and *The Philadelphia Story,* he places articulate and well-to-do people in well-appointed homes and forces them to face domestic crises – usually a marriage in danger – with an equanimity that might be called courage and a wit which demands – but does not always get – audiences willing to listen for the precise meaning of lines which will direct them to the seriousness which lies at the heart of all the plays. That Barry is not simply an elegant entertainer can be seen in the variety of work in his canon – in which the successful comedies share space with a satirical extravaganza (*White Wings*), a Biblical play more concerned with theology than anecdote (*John*), a mood play in which characters find spiritual regeneration through psychodrama (*Hotel Universe*), a parable of good and evil among vaudevillians (*Here Come the Clowns*, based on Barry's own novel *War in Heaven*), a symbolic political drama (*Liberty Jones*), and a mixture of the real and the imaginary (*Foolish Notion*).

The comedies tend to be more effective than the overtly earnest plays, in which art sometimes loses out to exposition. But the important thing about Barry as a serious playwright is that, light or heavy, his work is informed by a major theme. Most of his plays, from *You and I* to *Second Threshold*, deal with man's need to be faithful to himself and his possibilities, personal and professional. The Barry protagonists have to escape the rigidities dictated by family (*The Youngest*), convention (*The Animal Kingdom*), society (*Holiday*). Sometimes, as with John and Herodias in *John*, the characters are trapped by their own preconceptions, and the luckier among them learn to live by discovering that, however benign their intentions, they too are manipulators (Nancy in *The Youngest*, Linda in *Holiday*) or by accepting their own imperfect, human condition (Tracy Lord in *The Philadelphia Story*). Barry's central concern is supported by recurrent minor themes – marriage as a bond of love, not a legal or religious ritual; work as a self-fulfilling activity, not a social imposition – and by the implicit religious assumptions that mark him even at his most secular. That *Holiday* and *The Philadelphia Story* are likely to remain Barry's most popular plays should not hide the fact that a number of the others – particularly the neglected *In a Garden* – deserve a place in the working American repertory.

—Gerald Weales

BAX, Clifford.   English.   Born in London, 13 July 1886; brother of the composer Sir

Arnold Bax. Educated privately; studied art at the Slade School, London. Married 1) Gwendolen Bishop Smith in 1910 (died, 1926), one daughter; 2) Vera May Young in 1927. Lived in Germany, Belgium, and Italy; returned to England and gave up painting to concentrate on literary and dramatic work: Editor, *Orpheus* magazine, 1909–14, and the Orpheus series of books, 1909–17. Chairman, Incorporated Stage Society, 1929. Fellow, Royal Society of Literature, and Society of Antiquaries. *Died 18 November 1962.*

PUBLICATIONS

Plays

The Poetasters of Ispahan (produced 1912).   In *Antique Pageantry,* 1921.
The Masque of the Planets, in *Orpheus 17,* 1912.
The Game of Death, in *Orpheus 23,* 1913.
The Marriage of the Soul (produced 1913).
The Sneezing Charm (produced 1918).
Square Pegs (produced 1919).   1920.
Antique Pageantry: A Book of Verse Plays (includes *The Poetasters of Ispahan, The Apricot Tree, The Summit, Aucassin and Nicolette*).   1921.
The Apricot Tree (produced 1922).   In *Antique Pageantry,* 1921.
Old King Cole.   1921.
Shakespeare, with Harold F. Rubenstein.   1921.
The Impresario from Smyrna, in *Four Comedies by Goldoni.*   1922.
Mine Hostess, from a play by Goldoni (produced 1924).   In *Four Comedies by Goldoni,* 1922.
Polite Satires (includes *The Unknown Hand, The Volcanic Island, Square Pegs*).   1922.
The Unknown Hand (produced 1926).   In *Polite Satires,* 1922.
Polly, music by Frederic Austin, from the play *The Beggar's Opera* by John Gay (produced 1922).   1923.
And So Ad Infinitum (The Life of the Insects), with Nigel Playfair, from a translation by Percy Selver of a play by Karel Capek (as *The World We Live In,* produced 1922; as *The Insect Play,* produced 1923).   1923.
Up Stream (produced 1925).   1922.
The Cloak (produced 1923).   1924.
Midsummer Madness, music by Armstrong Gibbs (produced 1924).   1923.
Nocturne in Palermo.   1924.
Prelude and Fugue (produced 1927).   1924.
Studio Plays (includes *Prelude and Fugue, The Rose and the Cross, The Cloak*).   1924.
Mr. Pepys: A Ballad-Opera, music by Martin Shaw (produced 1926).   1926.
Rasputin, from a work by A. N. Tolstoy and P. E. Shchegolev (produced 1929).
Socrates (produced 1930).   1930.
The Chronicles of Cupid, Being a Masque of Love Throughout the Ages, with Geoffrey Dearmer.   1931.
The Venetian (produced 1931).   In *Valiant Ladies,* 1931.
The Immortal Lady (produced 1931).   In *Valiant Ladies,* 1931.
The Rose Without a Thorn (produced 1932).   In *Valiant Ladies,* 1931.
Valiant Ladies.   1931.
Twelve Short Plays, Serious and Comic.   1932.
April in August (produced 1934).   1934.
The Quaker's Cello.   1934.
Tragic Nesta.   1934.

The House of Borgia (produced 1935).   1937.
Battles Long Ago, in *Eight One-Act Plays of 1936,* edited by William Armstrong.   1937.
Hemlock for Eight, with Leon M. Lion (broadcast 1943).   1946.
Golden Eagle (produced 1946).   1946.
The Buddha: A Radio Version of His Life and Ideas (broadcast 1947).   1947.
The Play of St. Lawrence: A Pageant Play.   1947.
Circe (as *A Day, A Night, and a Morrow,* produced 1948).   1949.

Radio Plays: *Mr. Williams of Hamburg,* 1943; *Hemlock for Eight,* with Leon M. Lion, 1943; *Out of His Senses,* 1943; *The Buddha,* 1947; *The Shrouded Candle,* 1948; *The Life That I Gave Him,* from a play by Pirandello, 1951.

Fiction

Many a Green Isle.   1927.
Time with a Gift of Tears: A Modern Romance.   1943.

Verse

Twenty Chinese Poems Paraphrased.   1910; augmented edition, as *Twenty-Five Chinese Poems,* 1916.
Poems Dramatic and Lyrical.   1911.
Japanese Impromptus, with Daphne Bax.   1914.
A House of Words.   1920.
The Traveller's Tale.   1921.
Farewell, My Muse.   1932.

Other

Friendship.   1913.
Inland Far: A Book of Thoughts and Impressions.   1925.
Bianca Capello (biography).   1927.
Leonardo da Vinci.   1932.
Pretty Witty Nell: An Account of Nell Gwynn and Her Environment.   1932.
That Immortal Sea: A Meditation upon the Future of Religion and Sexual Morality.   1933.
Ideas and People.   1936.
Highways and Byways in Essex.   1939.
The Life of the White Devil (on Vittoria Orsini).   1940.
Evenings in Albany.   1942.
Whither the Theatre −? A Letter to a Young Playwright.   1945.
The Beauty of Women.   1946.
Rosemary for Remembrance (autobiography).   1948.
Some I Knew Well.   1951.
W. G. Grace (biography).   1952.
Who's Who in Heaven: A Sketch.   1954.

Editor, *Four Comedies by Goldoni,* translated by Bax, Marguerite Tracy, and Eleanor and Herbert Farjeon.   1922.
Editor, *Letters,* by Florence Farr, Bernard Shaw, and W. B. Yeats.   1941.
Editor, *Never Again!*   1942.

Editor, *Vintage Verse.* 1945.

Editor, *The Silver Casket, Being Love Letters and Love Poems Attributed to Mary Stuart.* 1946.

Editor, *All the World's a Stage: Theatrical Portraits.* 1946.

Editor, *The Poetry of the Brownings.* 1947.

Editor, with Meum Stewart, *The Distaff Muse.* 1948.

Translator, *Initiation and Its Results,* by Rudolf Steiner. 1909.

Translator, *The Age of Gold: A Chorus Translated Out of Tasso's L'Aminta.* 1944.

*   *   *

Clifford Bax's background was affluent and cultured (the composer Arnold Bax was his eldest brother), and he began his career as a student of art at the Slade School, combining this training with an interest in the occult which led him to the Theosophical Society. In the 1920's and 1930's he was associated with such noncommercial theatrical organizations as the Incorporated Stage Society, the Phoenix Society, and the Three Hundred Club, and collaborated with Nigel Playfair in several ventures at the Lyric, Hammersmith. His view of the stage was set forth in a pamphlet, *Whither the Theatre* −?

Although Bax produced a range of works encompassing poetry, translations from Capek and Goldoni, a biography of the cricketer W. G. Grace, several volumes of reminiscences, and a romantic novel chronicling the inter-war years, his reputation chiefly rests on his stage adaptations and original plays. His unexacting light entertainments were an attractive contribution to the London theatre of their day, but when he essayed the handling of strong situations or significant themes, certain deficiencies were apparent beneath the professional gloss. Thus in the novelettish *Up Stream,* a drama of conflict and emotion set in the Amazonian jungle, clumsy exposition, stilted dialogue, and implausible behaviour vitiate the plot's latent possibilities.

After 1925 Bax wisely chose to write primarily "costume plays" on historical and literary subjects, although *Socrates,* arguably the best of these, is unlike any other "period" drama of its time. Its episodes are largely skilful adaptations of Plato's dialogues, which when staged can prove unduly static, but a sympathetic yet unsentimentalized portrait of Socrates emerges. Bax avoids a total dissipation of theatrical interest by sensibly focusing on the successful campaign to destroy the philosopher. His more romantic treatments of historical materials, if livelier, were less satisfactory, depending on incident rather than insight for their success: hence, because of the lightweight psychological motivation of its protagonists, *The Venetian,* a spirited attempt at an Italianate drama of love-intrigue on Jacobean lines, fails to build to the required climax. *The Immortal Lady,* a tribute to the Countess of Nithsdale who rescued her Jacobite husband from the Tower in 1716, is accomplished and entertaining, yet contrives to present the escape with only the seriousness and suspense appropriate to a schoolgirls' escapade, while the highly popular *The Rose Without a Thorn,* in seeking to demythologize and humanize Henry VIII, comes dangerously close to trivializing him. Again, there is a basic lack of conviction in the reasons for the characters' conduct (most notably Katheryn Howard), and the contemporary idiom in which the Queen and her lovers converse is fatally defective in Tudor resonance. Although this was part of the author's deliberate intention, Bax was not the only twentieth-century playwright to discover that the themes of historical high romance blended unhappily with characters, situations, and diction drawn from modern Mayfair. While Bax enjoyed some well-deserved celebrity during his working life, it must be admitted that there is a certain facile quality about all but his best plays, and that even these do not satisfy now at a very deep or permanent level.

—William M. Tydeman

BAXTER, James K(eir). New Zealander. Born in Dunedin, 29 June 1926; son of the writer Archibald Baxter. Educated at Quaker schools in New Zealand and England; Otago University, Dunedin; Victoria University, Wellington, B.A. 1952. Married Jacqueline Sturm in 1948; two children. Worked as a labourer, journalist, and school-teacher. Editor, *Numbers* magazine, Wellington, 1954–60. Spent 5 months in India studying school publications, 1958; started commune in Jerusalem (a Maori community on the Wanganui River), 1969. Recipient: Unesco grant, 1958; Robert Burns Fellowship, Otago University, 1966, 1967. *Died 22 October 1972.*

PUBLICATIONS

Plays

> *Jack Winter's Dream* (broadcast, 1958). In *The Wide Open Cage and Jack Winter's Dream,* 1959.
> *The Wide Open Cage* (produced 1959). In *The Wide Open Cage and Jack Winter's Dream,* 1959.
> *The Wide Open Cage and Jack Winter's Dream: Two Plays.* 1959.
> *The Spots of the Leopard* (produced 1963).
> *The Band Rotunda* (produced 1967). In *The Devil and Mr. Mulcahy and The Band Rotunda,* 1971.
> *The Sore-Footed Man,* based on *Philoctetes* by Euripides (produced 1967). In *The Sore-Footed Man and The Temptations of Oedipus,* 1971.
> *The Bureaucrat* (produced 1967).
> *The Devil and Mr. Mulcahy* (produced 1967). In *The Devil and Mr. Mulcahy and The Band Rotunda,* 1971.
> *Mr. O'Dwyer's Dancing Party* (produced 1968).
> *The Day Flanagan Died* (produced 1969).
> *The Temptations of Oedipus* (produced 1970). In *The Sore-Footed Man and The Temptations of Oedipus,* 1971.
> *The Devil and Mr. Mulcahy and The Band Rotunda.* 1971.
> *The Sore-Footed Man and The Temptations of Oedipus.* 1971.

Radio Play: *Jack Winter's Dream,* 1958.

Verse

> *Beyond the Palisade: Poems.* 1944.
> *Blow, Wind of Fruitfulness.* 1948.
> *Hart Crane.* 1948.
> *Rapunzel: A Fantasia for Six Voices.* 1948.
> *Charm for Hilary.* 1949.
> *Poems Unpleasant,* with Louis Johnson and Anton Vogt. 1952.
> *The Fallen House: Poems.* 1953.
> *Lament for Barney Flanagan.* 1954.
> *Traveller's Litany.* 1955.
> *The Night Shift: Poems of Aspects of Love,* with others. 1957.
> *The Iron Breadboard: Studies in New Zealand Writing* (verse parodies). 1957.
> *In Fires of No Return: Poems.* 1958.
> *Chosen Poems, 1958.* 1958.

Ballad of Calvary Street. 1960.
Howrah Bridge and Other Poems. 1961.
Poems. 1964.
Pig Island Letters. 1966.
A Death Song for M. Mouldybroke. 1967.
*A Small Ode on Mixed Flatting: Elicited by the Decision of the Otago University
    Authorities to Forbid This Practice among Students.* 1967.
The Lion Skin: Poems. 1967.
*A Bucket of Blood for a Dollar: A Conversation Between Uncle Sam and the Rt. Hon.
    Keith Holyoake, Prime Minister of New Zealand.* 1968.
The Rock Woman: Selected Poems. 1969.
Ballad of the Stonegut Sugar Works. 1969.
Jerusalem Sonnets: Poems for Colin Durning. 1970.
The Junkies and the Fuzz. 1970.
Jerusalem Daybook (poetry and prose journal). 1971.
Jerusalem Blues (2). 1971.
Autumn Testament (poetry and prose journal). 1972.
Four God Songs. 1972.
Letter to Peter Olds. 1972.
Runes. 1973.
The Labyrinth: Some Uncollected Poems, 1944–1972. 1974.
The Bone Chanter: Unpublished Poems 1945–1972. 1977.
*The Holy Life and Death of Concrete Grady: Various Uncollected and Unpublished
    Poems,* edited by J. E. Weir. 1977.

Other

Recent Trends in New Zealand Poetry. 1951.
The Fire and the Anvil: Notes on Modern Poetry. 1955; revised edition, 1960.
Oil (primary school bulletin). 1957.
The Coaster (primary school bulletin). 1959.
The Trawler (primary school bulletin). 1961.
New Zealand in Colour, photographs by Kenneth and Jean Bigwood. 1961.
The Old Earth Closet: A Tribute to Regional Poetry. 1965.
Aspects of Poetry in New Zealand. 1967.
The Man on the Horse (lectures). 1967.
The Flowering Cross: Pastoral Articles. 1969.
The Six Faces of Love: Lenten Lectures. 1972.
A Walking Stick for an Old Man. 1972.

Reading List: *The Poetry of Baxter* by J. E. Weir, 1970; *Baxter* by Charles Doyle, 1976;
Baxter by Vincent O'Sullivan, 1976.

*   *   *

At his best one of the finest English-language poets of the past thirty years, James K. Baxter
is the one New Zealand poet of undeniable international reputation. Although he died in his
mid-forties, his literary career lasted for over thirty years. Its fruits were many volumes of
poems, a number of plays, works of literary commentary or criticism, essays on religious
topics, and a small amount of fiction (he was a fine exponent of the parable).

With publication of his first book, *Beyond the Palisade,* when he was eighteen, Baxter at
once became a figure of note in New Zealand letters. Within a few years, he already occupied

a central position in the literary scene, so that his booklet, *Recent Trends in New Zealand Poetry*, a beautifully condensed commentary, was from the first accepted as authoritative. Alongside his literary reputation, Baxter quickly began to build one as a maverick and a bohemian. When, late in the 1940's, he moved to Wellington and began his long friendship and collaboration with Louis Johnson, they became the focus of the "romantic" element in New Zealand writing, which found its centre in Wellington for the next dozen years or so.

Throughout the 1950's Baxter produced a prolific variety of poems, plays, stories, and criticism, work which ranged from makeshift to brilliant. With Johnson and Charles Doyle (and, latterly, others) he edited the characteristically erratic periodical *Numbers*, then the only alternative to the few "establishment" periodicals such as *Landfall*.

1958 was a crucial moment in Baxter's career. Until then, his adult life had been a strange compound of Christian concern and rip-roaring bohemianism. That year he stayed for a long spell in the Trappist monastery at Kopua, Hawke's Bay, and was converted to Roman Catholicism. At the same time, his superb collection *In Fires of No Return* drew upon the work of his whole career to that point. *Howrah Bridge and Other Poems* followed in 1961 and was composed of new poems plus fine pieces ranging back to the 1940's; but Baxter's talent as a poet for a time seemed to lose focus. It was typical of Baxter that he made little or no effort to become known outside his own country; untypical as he was, he was very deeply a New Zealander, though anguished at his country's unspiritual puritanism.

After a low-energy period, Baxter's career gathered momentum again when he was awarded a Burns Fellowship at the University of Otago. Writing in the *Dominion* on 23 October 1965, Louis Johnson suggested that "the Burns scholarship may well mark a turning-point in his career" and this proved to be the case in remarkable ways. First, it produced what many consider to be Baxter's best verse collection, *Pig Island Letters*, a book in which he learned from, and transcended, the unlikely twin influences of Lawrence Durrell and Robert Lowell. Besides the critical-autobiographical pieces of *The Man on the Horse* and *Aspects of Poetry in New Zealand*, those years in Dunedin witnessed the flowering of Baxter's career as a playwright. During 1967 and 1968, Patric Carey at the Globe Theatre produced seven Baxter plays, including all the most important. Although secondary to the poetry, those plays make it a reasonable claim that, besides being the country's foremost poet, Baxter is the most productive and interesting New Zealand playwright up to the present.

The Dunedin years also led him more deeply into religious and social concerns. After a period of catechetical work in the city, he went into solitude for some months at Jerusalem (Hiruharama), a tiny religious settlement on the Wanganui River. Later he founded a commune there for troubled youths and social drop-outs, and he was also the moving spirit in setting up doss-houses in both Auckland and Wellington. These ventures, pursued in a Franciscan spirit, including a vow of poverty, took much of his energy, but the commitment also carried over into his vocation as poet and this period witnessed a further remarkable shift in the development of his writing, especially in the Jerusalem writings, *Jerusalem Sonnets*, *Jerusalem Daybook*, and *Autumn Testament*. He developed a very personal "sonnet" form, in fluid pentameter couplets, and, particularly in *Jerusalem Daybook*, made effective use of an amalgam of prose and verse.

Baxter was also important in his community as a man. His best poems have a natural incandescence which partly derives from his being permeated from boyhood with the finest poetry of the British tradition, but which also comes from a human commitment based on religion. New Zealand is a relatively successful social welfare state, secular in spirit. Baxter, notably, brought to it a strong religious consciousness. A literary talent with a touch of genius was deepened and strengthened by the religious element in his character. That this did not escape the notice of his fellow-countrymen is evident from the crowds which thronged to his funeral and memorial services. Baxter's legacy to his country is a double one, a substantial amount of first-rate writing, especially poems, and the example of a man able to carry the spiritual life as far as it can go.

—Charles Doyle

BEAUMONT, Francis. English. Born in Gracedieu, Leicestershire, in 1584 or 1585; brother of the poet Sir John Beaumont. Educated at Broadgates Hall, now Pembroke College, Oxford, 1597–98, left without taking a degree; entered Inner Temple, London, 1600, but never practised law. Married Ursula Isley in 1613; two daughters. Lived in London from 1600; a friend of Drayton and Ben Jonson; met John Fletcher in 1605, and thereafter collaborated with him in writing for the theatre until his retirement at the time of his marriage. *Died 6 March 1616.*

PUBLICATIONS

Collections

> *Comedies and Tragedies,* with Fletcher and others. 1647; revised edition, 1679.
> *The Dramatic Works in the Beaumont and Fletcher Canon,* edited by Fredson Bowers. 3 vols (of 10), 1966–76.

Plays

> *The Woman's Prize,* with Fletcher (produced after 1604). In *Comedies and Tragedies,* 1647.
> *The Woman Hater* (produced 1605). 1607; edited by George Walton Williams, in *Dramatic Works 1,* 1966.
> *The Knight of the Burning Pestle* (produced 1607). 1613; edited by Andrew Gurr, 1968.
> *Philaster; or, Love Lies A-Bleeding,* with Fletcher (produced before 1610). 1620; edited by Dora Jean Ashe, 1974.
> *The Maid's Tragedy,* with Fletcher (produced before 1611). 1619; edited by Robert K. Turner, Jr., in *Dramatic Works 2,* 1970.
> *A King and No King,* with Fletcher (produced 1611). 1619; edited by George Walton Williams, in *Dramatic Works 2,* 1970.
> *Cupid's Revenge,* with Fletcher (produced before 1612). 1615; edited by Fredson Bowers, in *Dramatic Works 2,* 1970.
> *The Coxcomb,* with Fletcher (produced 1612). In *Comedies and Tragedies,* 1647; edited by Irby B. Cauthen, Jr., in *Dramatic Works 1,* 1966.
> *The Masque of the Inner Temple and Gray's Inn* (produced 1613). 1613; edited by Fredson Bowers, in *Dramatic Works 1,* 1966.
> *The Scornful Lady,* with Fletcher (produced 1613–17?). 1616; edited by Cyrus Hoy, in *Dramatic Works 2,* 1970.
> *The Captain,* with Fletcher (produced 1613). In *Comedies and Tragedies,* 1647; edited by L. A. Beaurline, in *Dramatic Works 1,* 1966.
> *Love's Pilgrimage,* with Fletcher (produced 1616?). In *Comedies and Tragedies,* 1647; edited by L. A. Beaurline, in *Dramatic Works 2,* 1970.
> *The Wild Goose Chase,* with Fletcher (produced 1621?). 1652.
> *The Noble Gentleman,* with Fletcher (produced 1625–26?). In *Comedies and Tragedies,* 1647; edited by L. A. Beaurline, in *Dramatic Works 3,* 1976.

Verse

> *Salmacis and Hermaphroditus.* 1602; edited by N. Alexander, in *Elizabethan Narrative Verse,* 1968.

Poems.   1640; revised edition, 1653, 1660.
Songs and Lyrics from the Plays of Beaumont and Fletcher, edited by E. H.
Fellowes.   1928.

Bibliography: *Beaumont and Fletcher: A Concise Bibliography* by S. A. Tannenbaum, 1938;
supplement, 1946; supplement in *Elizabethan Bibliographies Supplements 8* by C. A. Pennell
and W. P. Williams, 1968.

Reading List: *Beaumont, Fletcher, and Company: Entertainers to the Jacobean Gentry* by L.
B. Wallis, 1947; *The Pattern of Tragicomedy in Beaumont and Fletcher* by Eugene Waith,
1952; *Beaumont and Fletcher: A Critical Study* by W. W. Appleton, 1956; *Beaumont and
Fletcher* by Ian Fletcher, 1967.

*   *   *

Francis Beaumont's career was almost a parody of the aspirations of a minor literary
figure. A younger son of rural gentry, he gained notice as a poet and fame and fortune as a
playwright on the London stage. At 16 he was living in London and studying law at an Inn of
Court. A burlesque lecture on grammar which he gave for his fellow students at the Inner
Temple survives, and he fairly certainly wrote *Salmacis and Hermaphroditus,* published in
1602. It is a fluent but routine piece of sub-erotic versifying of a story from Ovid in the
fashion made popular by Shakespeare and Marlowe in the 1590's and often practised by law
students. His masque, written for the Inner Temple and Gray's Inn as a contribution to the
celebrations of the Palatine marriage in 1613, is a similar piece of fashionable versifying.

His lack of an inclination to study law, his preference for writing, and perhaps a need for
money are indicated by the performance of his prose comedy *The Woman Hater,* by the boy
company of St. Paul's. Its complex plot and strenuous wit-play owe an obvious debt to Ben
Jonson's early comedies. The other boy company of the time produced his comic
masterpiece, *The Knight of the Burning Pestle.* Its first performance, however, was a flop, and
all of Beaumont's subsequent playwriting was in collaboration with John Fletcher, a man in a
similar position and with similar ambitions. They were both members of the so-called "tribe
of Ben," friends and followers of Jonson. Both Beaumont and Fletcher wrote commendatory
verses for the publication of *Volpone* in 1607. Beaumont's most famous poem is his verse
letter to Jonson celebrating their meetings at the Mermaid tavern, a poem which encapsulates
Beaumont's vision of literary life in London in 1607.

His own greatest fame arrived when he started his collaboration with Fletcher as founder
member of a writing partnership which in the end produced more than fifty plays; these
works share with Shakespeare's and Jonson's the distinction of being the only corpus of
Jacobean drama thought worthy of being collected in folio. Beaumont actually shared in the
writing of only a few, but three of these, *Philaster, The Maid's Tragedy,* and *A King and No
King,* established the distinctive style and reputation of the partnership. From 1609 they
appear to have taken over Shakespeare's duties of providing his company with one serious
play and one comedy each year. Beaumont retired from the partnership in 1613 when he
married an heiress.

Beaumont's chief claim to artistic standing is *The Knight of the Burning Pestle.* As John
Doebler notes in *Studies in English Literature* (1965), it burlesques the Prodigal Son theme of
the popular merchant and apprentice plays with the story of a prodigal father, celebrating
mirth above money. A witty mixture of plays within plays satirising citizen tastes and
unsophisticated audiences, and laced with both popular ballads and composers' songs, it is
one of the few wholly successful Jacobean comedies outside Shakespeare.

The antithesis of this sophisticated mockery of popular inanities appeared with *Philaster,*
the first play written by the partnership for Shakespeare's company, and its first success.
Closely related to *Cymbeline* in the time of its writing and in its genre as a tragi-comedy or

romance, it was evidently designed as a vehicle for a new taste in theatrical fashion. Its ambience is the courtly world of Sidney's *Arcadia*, where honour and virtue are tested and examined in a variety of arduous situations, as J. F. Danby (*Elizabethan and Jacobean Poets*, 1952) has demonstrated. It was a taste which caught on rapidly, and the fifty or more plays which the Beaumont and Fletcher canon eventually grew into testify to its massive dominance on the Jacobean stage.

The tragicomedy which was developed as a distinctive genre in *Philaster* can be seen at its best in some of the plays written by Fletcher after Beaumont retired. Its "romance" flavour also appeared in tragedies, however, notably *The Maid's Tragedy*, the most powerful of the plays in which Beaumont had a hand. It is a tragedy in that most of its leading characters die by the end, but it shares the chief qualities of the tragi-comedies. Character is less important than moral qualities, situations are contrived to test ethics, the verse is a simple and economic vehicle for the testing situations. *The Maid's Tragedy*, for instance, canvasses the possibilities of two alternative courses of conduct when honour is at risk. A king has a secret mistress; for appearance's sake he marries her to a young man. The husband finds his honour is stained on his wedding night, but holds back from revenge because the adulterer is his king. The woman's brother, a soldier, has no such hesitation and contrives the king's death. The young husband kills himself on realising how much destruction has followed his hesitation, while the soldier lives on "accurst." This sort of patterning through parallels and contrasts is a conspicuous feature of the design of all the "Beaumont and Fletcher" plays, and a clear acknowledgement of their literary model, Sidney's *Arcadia*, as a guide to courtly ethics. The taste they created lasted on the English stage for more than a century.

—Andrew Gurr

BECKETT, Samuel (Barclay). Irish. Born in Foxrock, County Dublin, 13 April 1906. Educated at Portora Royal School, Enniskillen, County Fermanagh; Trinity College, Dublin, B.A. in French and Italian 1927, M.A. 1931. Worked at the Irish Red Cross Hospital, St. Lô, France, 1945. Married Suzanne Dechevaux-Dumesnil in 1948. Lecturer in English, Ecole Normale Supérieure, Paris, 1928–30; Lecturer in French, Trinity College, Dublin, 1930–32. Closely associated with James Joyce in Paris in the late 1920's and 1930's. Settled in Paris in 1937, and has written chiefly in French since 1945; translates his own work into English. Recipient: *Evening Standard* award, 1955; Obie Award, 1958, 1960, 1962, 1964; Italia Prize, 1959; Prix Formentor, 1959; International Publishers Prize, 1961; Prix Filmcritice, 1965; Tours Film Prize, 1966; Nobel Prize for Literature, 1969. D.Litt.: University of Dublin, 1959. Member, American Academy of Arts and Letters, 1968. Lives in Paris.

PUBLICATIONS

Plays

Le Kid, with Georges Pelorson (produced 1931).
En Attendant Godot (produced 1953). 1952; as *Waiting for Godot: Tragicomedy* (produced 1955), 1954.
Fin de Partie, Suivi de Acte sans Paroles (produced 1957). 1957; as *Endgame, Followed*

by Act Without Words (*Endgame* produced 1958, *Act Without Words* produced 1960), 1958.

All That Fall (broadcast 1957). 1957.

Krapp's Last Tape (produced 1958). With *Embers,* 1959.

Embers (broadcast 1959). With *Krapp's Last Tape,* 1959.

Act Without Words II (produced 1959). In *Krapp's Last Tape and Other Dramatic Pieces,* 1960.

Happy Days (produced 1961). 1961; bilingual edition edited by James Knowlson, 1978.

Words and Music (broadcast 1962). In *Play,* 1964.

Cascando (in French, broadcast 1963). 1963; in English (broadcast 1964; produced on stage 1970), in *Play,* 1964.

Play (produced 1963). 1964.

Eh Joe (televised 1966). In *Eh Joe and Other Writings,* 1967.

Come and Go: Dramaticule (produced 1966). 1967.

Film. 1969.

Breath (produced 1970). In *Breath and Other Shorts,* 1971.

Not I (produced 1972). 1973.

That Time (produced 1976). 1976.

Footfalls (produced 1976). 1976.

Tryst (televised 1976). In *Ends and Odd,* 1976.

Ends and Odd: Dramatic Pieces. 1976.

Screenplay: *Film,* 1965.

Radio Plays: *All That Fall,* 1957; *Embers,* 1959; *The Old Tune,* 1960; *Words and Music,* 1962; *Cascando,* 1963.

Television Plays: *Eh Joe,* 1966; *Tryst,* 1976; *Shades (Ghost Trio, Not I, … But the Clouds …),* 1977.

Fiction and Texts

More Pricks Than Kicks (stories). 1934.

Murphy. 1938.

Molloy (in French). 1951; translated by the author and Patrick Bowles, 1955.

Malone Meurt. 1951; as *Malone Dies,* 1956.

L'Innommable. 1953; as *The Unnamable,* 1958.

Watt (in English). 1953.

Nouvelles et Textes pour Rien. 1955; as *Stories and Texts for Nothing,* 1967.

From an Abandoned Work. 1958.

Comment C'Est. 1961; as *How It Is,* 1961.

Imagination Morte Imaginez. 1965; as *Imagination Dead Imagine,* 1965.

Assez. 1966; as *Enough,* in *No's Knife,* 1967.

Bing. 1966; as *Ping,* in *No's Knife,* 1967.

No's Knife: Selected Shorter Prose 1945–1966. 1967.

L'Issue. 1968.

Sans. 1969; as *Lessness,* 1971.

Mercier et Camier. 1970; as *Mercier and Camier,* 1974.

Séjour. 1970.

Premier Amour. 1970; as *First Love,* 1973.

Le Depeupleur. 1971; as *The Lost Ones,* 1972.

The North. 1973.

First Love and Other Shorts. 1974.
Fizzles. 1976.
For to End Yet Again and Other Fizzles. 1977.
Four Novellas. 1977.
Residua. 1978.

Verse

Whoroscope. 1930.
Echo's Bones and Other Precipitates. 1935.
Gedichte (collected poems in English and French, with German translations) 1959.
Poems in English. 1961.
Collected Poems in English and French. 1977.

Other

Proust. 1931; with *Three Dialogues with Georges Duthuit,* 1965.
Bram van Welde, with Georges Duthuit and J. Putman. 1958.
A Beckett Reader. 1967.
I Can't Go On: A Selection from the Work of Beckett, edited by Richard W. Seaver. 1976.

Translator, *Anthology of Mexican Poetry,* edited by Octavio Paz. 1958.
Translator, *La Manivelle/The Old Tune,* by Robert Pinget. 1960.
Translator, *Zone,* by Guillaume Apollinaire. 1960.
Translator, *Drunken Boat,* by Arthur Rimbaud, edited by James Knowlson and Felix Leakey. 1977.

Bibliography: *Beckett: His Work and His Critics: An Essay in Bibliography* by Raymond Felderman and John Fletcher, 1970.

Reading List: "Beckett Issue" of *Perspective 11,* 1959, and of *Modern Drama 9,* 1966, both edited by Ruby Cohn, and *Beckett: The Comic Gamut,* 1962, and *Back to Beckett,* 1973, both by Cohn; *Beckett: A Critical Study,* 1961, revised edition, 1968, and *A Reader's Guide to Beckett,* 1973, both by Hugh Kenner; *Beckett* by William York Tindall, 1964; *The Novels of Beckett* by John Fletcher, 1964; *Beckett: A Collection of Critical Essays* edited by Martin Esslin, 1965; *Beckett at Sixty: A Festschrift,* 1967; *Beckett* by Ronald Hayman, 1968; *Beckett/Beckett: The Truth of Contradictories* by Vivian Mercier, 1977; *Beckett: A Biography* by Deirdre Bair, 1978.

*   *   *

No living author in English or French has molded words so skillfully in fiction and drama, 'le paradoxically protesting his own failure. Better appreciated as a playwright, Beckett 'f has taken deepest pains with his fiction – most of it originally written in French but 'lated into his native English. Most of his drama, in contrast, was translated into 'n English. "English is a good theatre language," he has said, "because of its its close relationship between thing and vocable." Two languages and two 'indelibly marked by Beckett's vision – a reaching toward human essence or

print in 1929 with a piece on *Finnegans Wake,* written at Joyce's request, with a pastiche dialogue on contraception in Ireland, with a cryptic short story "Assumption." Supercilious mannerism mars the three pieces, and yet they predict Beckett's generic variety. From 1929 to 1977 no year has passed without his contribution to some literary or theatre genre. Nearly half a century of creative activity, however his characters may yearn for indolence.

In the early 1930's, in English, Beckett wavered between obscure verse and satiric short fiction, publishing a volume of each. At about the time he settled in Paris, he published his first English novel, *Murphy* − traditional in its coherence and comic omniscience. It was perceptively reviewed by Dylan Thomas: "[*Murphy*] is serious because it is, mainly, the study of a complex and oddly tragic character who cannot reconcile the unreality of the seen world with the reality of the unseen, and who, through scorn and neglect of 'normal' society, drifts into the society of the certified abnormal in his search for 'a little world.' " The sentence also describes Beckett's next very untraditional novel, *Watt*, and it is relevant too to Beckett's French fiction, where "the seen world" recedes toward a vanishing point.

Watt is a less finished but more important novel than *Murphy* because it predicts the anarchic immediacy of most of the French fiction. Watt carries the Beckettian burden of solitude, attracted and rejected as he is by the inscrutable Mr. Knott. A would-be Cartesian, Watt thinks in order to try to be, but his French successors, adopting the language of Descartes, will try *not* to think in order to be. Beckett revised *Watt* several times during a four-year period in which he fled from his Paris home to a Free French farm. Back in Paris, forty years old when World War II ended, Beckett wrote with prolific zest, producing four long stories, four novels, and two plays. He has never again attained such fluidity.

The French fiction, considered by many to be his most important work, is a shifting soulscape painted by a narrating "I." But "I" 's identity changes in the stories, in the novels, and in the works that grow out of them − *Texts for Nothing* and *How It Is*. The story narrators are nameless social outcasts, old and ill, inventing their ways of survival. Conflict and climax do not structure these alogical cumulations of passionate language. But common to all of them is the overriding sense that they are stories.

The reach toward formal fiction is inherited by the novel heroes Molloy, Moran, Malone, and the Unnamable − four narrators of three books that Beckett himself calls a trilogy. Molloy seeks his mother, and Moran seeks Molloy; both write an account of a fruitless search. Malone writes so as to fill the time of his dying. The Unnamable disowns the written for the spoken discourse, whosoever the voice that speaks it. Even more aural is *How It Is*, whose narrator/narrated tries to order chaos through a few images, many numbers, and skeletal story remnants rising from ubiquitous mud. Probably the most difficult sustained work in the Beckett canon, *How It Is* invents a language rhythmically if not lexically, a language that conveys the body's movements through its mud and the mind's movements through its mud. After *How It Is* Beckett discards first-person fiction and assumes resolute objectivity for the short rending fictions of the late 1960's.

It is a critical convenience to discuss Beckett's fiction and drama as though each had an independent development, but this is inaccurate. Not only did Beckett zigzag from drama to fiction and back (from 1948 to 1971, at any rate), but he frequently translated in the one genre while producing original work in the other. He himself has stated that drama is a relaxation for him: "You have a definite space and people in this space. That's relaxing." In relaxation he has created a spate of works in dramatic form; the list of those published and/or produced includes fourteen plays for the stage, six for radio, three for television, two mime plays, and one film script.

The stage images are at once visually arresting and metaphysically meaningful: two frayed comedians by a tree, a throned and shabby ruler with two ashbins, a prattling blonde buried in the ground, an unkempt old man bent over a tape recorder, three grey faces atop three grey urns, three stately faceless women, a mouth adrift in the dark, a whitehaired head turned up to the light, "a faint tangle of pale grey tatters." The radio plays introduce a rare verbal music to the medium. The television plays are at once paintings through the camera eye and soul searches beyond the camera's power.

Though Beckett does not speak of a stage trilogy, one might so view his three full-evening plays, *Waiting for Godot, Endgame, Happy Days*. All three are plays in which the main action is waiting; all three are plays in which the stage day is ending without quite coming to an end. Rather than follow the plays chronologically, however, a Beckett baptism might well begin with simpler pieces. In *Breath* a faint cry signals an increase of light and breath to a maximum in about ten seconds, holds for five seconds, and fades to the cry "*as before.*" Vagitus and death-rattle are barely distinguishable in the black depths of eternity. This Beckett obsession is dramatized far more memorably in the plays of the 1970's. *Not I* embraces an asyntactical incantation of a life from premature birth to compulsive speech at age seventy, that biblical terminus. *That Time* looks back on three ages of man, finally giving to dust the pronouncement of human brevity. *Footfalls* paces through human pain, unable to escape it even beyond the grave, but always and forever revolving it all in the mind.

Brief as human life may be, Beckett theatricalizes it. The mime plays do this in almost allegorical fashion, the first teaching its arotagonist what Beckett in *Proust* calls the "oblation of desire," and the second demonstrating the repetitive futility of contrasting life-processes. *Come and Go*, less absolute than *Breath*, links childhood and age in a beautifully regular pattern; it is the first of several Beckett stage plays to dramatize the mystery at the heart of being. With the exception of *Not I*, Beckett's stage plays end in a stasis that confirms mystery.

Though Beckett's recent plays hover at death's threshold, he is more widely known for the theater trilogy that is absorbed in life. *Happy Days* implies courage even as Winnie sinks ever deeper into that old extinguisher, the earth. *Endgame*'s four characters reflect on each expiring moment. Liveliest of all Beckett's plays, and living on many stages in many languages is that contemporary classic, *Waiting for Godot*.

The impact of *Godot* is immediate; the impact of *Godot* is inexhaustible. Vaudeville turns are threaded on philosophic nihilism and a classico-Christian tradition. The seed of *Godot* is Luke's account of the crucifixion, as summarized by St. Augustine: "Do not despair: one of the thieves was saved. Do not presume: one of the thieves was damned." The two thieves are Vladimir and Estragon; the two thieves are Pozzo and Lucky; the two thieves are Godot's boy and his brother. On the stage, characters divide into two inseparable couples; action divides into two repetitive acts. The two friends are conscientious about trying to live through each disappointing evening, for Godot may always come tomorrow. In the meantime they volley routines with Wimbledon finesse. In their dogged invention lies the delight of *Godot*. Each act ends: "Well, shall we go?" "Yes, let's go," but the friends "*do not move.*" They do not move, but they have moved audiences and readers the world over.

—Ruby Cohn

BEHAN, Brendan (Francis). Irish. Born in Dublin, 9 February 1923. Educated at the French Sisters of Charity School, Dublin. Married Beatrice ffrench-Salkeld in 1955; one daughter. Joined the Irish Republican Army, 1937; sent to a British borstal (correctional school) for attempting to blow up a Liverpool shipyard, 1939; sentenced to 14 years for the attempted murder of two detectives, 1942; released in general amnesty, 1946; in prison, Manchester, 1947, deported, 1952; worked as housepainter and journalist. Recipient: Obie Award, 1958; Paris Festival Award, 1958; French Critics' Award, 1962. *Died 20 March 1964.*

PUBLICATIONS

Collections

The Wit of Behan, edited by Sean McCann.   1968.
The Complete Plays.   1978.

Plays

The Quare Fellow (produced 1954).   1956.
The Hostage (produced 1958).   1958; revised version, 1962.
The Big House (broadcast 1957; produced 1963). In *Evergreen Review,*
    September–October 1961.
Moving Out, and A Garden Party, edited by Robert Hogan.   1967.
Richard's Cork Leg, edited and completed by Alan Simpson (produced 1972).   1973.
Time for a Gargle (produced 1973).

Radio Play: *The Big House,* 1957.

Fiction

The Scarperer.   1964.

Verse

Life Styles: Poems, with Nine Translations from the Irish of Brendan Behan, translated by
    Ulick O'Connor.   1973.

Other

Borstal Boy (autobiography).   1958.
Behan's Ireland: An Irish Sketch-Book.   1962.
Hold Your Hour and Have Another (articles).   1963.
Behan's New York.   1964.
Confessions of an Irish Rebel.   1965.

Reading List: *My Brother Brendan Behan* by Dominic Behan, 1965; *The World of Behan,* edited by Sean McCann, 1965; *Behan, Man and Showman* by Rae Jeffs, 1966; *Behan* by Ted E. Boyle, 1969; *Behan* by Ulick O'Connor, 1970; *The Major Works of Behan* by Peter Gerdes, 1973; *My Life with Brendan* by Beatrice Behan, Des Hickey, and Gus Smith, 1974.

*   *   *

Brendan Behan's fame within his own lifetime, and his abiding reputation, depends on his merits as a dramatist. The two internationally successful plays, *The Quare Fellow* and *The Hostage,* share a theme which is central to all his work – the paradox of man's urge towards love and fellowship on the one hand and his persistent practice of inhumanity on the other. Imprisonment – which the playwright had himself experienced – concentrates these complementary features, providing a graphic account of institutional violence and degradation, and the incidental redeeming evidence of individual human kindness and sympathy. In *The Quare Fellow* the emotional atmosphere of a prison on the eve of an execution is sustained with subtle and humorous control; in *The Hostage*, on the other hand, sentiment intrudes to falsify the real strength of the play. Why should two plays, written within a few years of each other differ so markedly; why should the second fall short so distressingly?

The Quare Fellow impresses with the inhuman logic of inevitable death, whereas *The Hostage* (in which an English soldier is held in Dublin by republican subversives) is based on uncertainty, chance, flux. The "quare fellow" (who is tantalisingly kept off stage) is finally murdered by law, whereas the Tommy in *The Hostage* is accidentally shot in a raid by police trying to rescue him. But beyond this elementary explanation there lies a more significant one. In *The Quare Fellow* Behan's satirical humour is directed very exactly against specific social conditions – the tyranny of officials, the hypocrisy of respectable folk, and the cruelty of faceless law. Each of these is present in the play in concrete and individual characters. *The Hostage*, in contrast, tackles a larger and more abstract problem – the discovery of a basic humanity in people of different nationalities and cultures. And the didacticism of the later play is reflected in the new role adopted by song; in *The Quare Fellow* song had provided mood in a manner which integrated the various levels of society implicated in the drama, in *The Hostage* it adds a neat commentary – nothing more. A third play, *Richard's Cork Leg* (posthumously prepared for the stage) contributes little to Behan's reputation as a serious dramatist.

Of the prose works, *Borstal Boy* is outstanding, with its attention to imprisonment as the epitome of human perversity. It belongs to a sub-genre which has been for many years important in Irish writing – the fictionalised autobiography. And significantly, it proved successful when adapted for the stage. Much of the remainder of Behan's work rises only occasionally above the level of good, original journalism. Behan gives the appearance, consequently, of being an untutored sporadic genius for whom literary tradition meant nothing. In fact, he had a lively (if unconventional) appreciation of literature: the influence of Oscar Wilde, André Gide, and Sean O'Casey can be readily charted. In addition, he wrote occasionally in Gaelic, and was affected by the peculiar power of folk literature both urban and rural. To appreciate his best work one must read it in conjunction with the essays and tape-recorded fragments, the ballads and the wonderfully disrespectful gossip with which he spiced his Spoken Arts record.

—W. J. McCormack

BEHN, Aphra (Johnson). English. Born, probably in Harbledown, Kent, baptized 14 December 1640. Probably married a Mr. Behn c. 1664 (died before 1666). Lived in Surinam, Dutch Guiana, c. 1663–64; employed by the English as a spy in Antwerp in 1666; imprisoned for debt in late 1660's; professional writer. *Died 16 April 1689.*

PUBLICATIONS

Collections

Works, edited by Montague Summers.   6 vols., 1915.

Selected Writings, edited by Robert Phelps.   1950.

Plays

The Forced Marriage; or, The Jealous Bridegroom (produced 1670).   1671.
The Amorous Prince; or, The Curious Husband (produced 1671).   1671.
The Dutch Lover (produced 1673).   1673.
Abdelazar; or, The Moor's Revenge, from the play *Lust's Dominion* (produced 1676).   1677.
The Town Fop; or, Sir Timothy Tawdrey (produced 1676).   1677.
The Debauchee; or, The Credulous Cuckold, from the play *A Mad Couple Well Matched* by Richard Brome (produced 1677).   1677.
The Rover; or, The Banished Cavaliers (produced 1677).   1677; edited by Frederick M. Link, 1967.
Sir Patient Fancy (produced 1678).   1678.
The Feigned Courtesans; or, A Night's Intrigue (produced 1679).   1679.
The Young King; or, The Mistake (produced 1679).   1683.
The Revenge; or, A Match in Newgate, from the play *The Dutch Courtesan* by Marston (produced 1680).   1680.
The Second Part of The Rover (produced 1681).   1681.
The Roundheads; or, The Good Old Cause, from the play *The Rump* by John Tatham (produced 1681).   1682.
The False Count; or, A New Way to Play an Old Game (produced 1681).   1682.
The City Heiress; or, Sir Timothy Treat-All, from the play *A Mad World, My Masters* by Middleton (produced 1682).   1682.
The Lucky Chance; or, An Alderman's Bargain (produced 1686).   1687; edited by A. Norman Jeffares, in *Restoration Comedy*, 1974.
The Emperor of the Moon (produced 1687).   1687; edited by Leo Hughes and Arthur H. Scouten, in *Ten English Farces*, 1948.
The Widow Ranter; or, The History of Bacon in Virginia (produced 1689).   1690.
The Younger Brother; or, The Amorous Jilt (produced 1696).   1696.

Fiction

Love Letters Between A Nobleman and His Sister.   3 vols., 1683–87.
The Fair Jilt; or, The History of Prince Tarquin and Miranda.   1688.
Oroonoko; or, The Royal Slave.   1688.
The History of the Nun; or, The Fair Vow-Breaker.   1689.
The Lucky Mistake.   1689.
Histories and Novels.   1696; revised edition, 1697, 1700.

Verse

Poems upon Several Occasions, with a Voyage to the Island of Love.   1684.
A Pindaric on the Death of Our Late Sovereign.   1685.
A Pindaric Poem on the Happy Coronation of His Sacred Majesty James II and His Illustrious Consort Queen Mary.   1685.
A Poem to Catherine, Queen Dowager.   1685.
To Christopher, Duke of Albemarle, on His Voyage to Jamaica: A Pindaric.   1687.
To the Memory of George, Duke of Buckingham.   1687.
A Poem to Sir Roger L'Estrange.   1688.

A Congratulatory Poem to Her Majesty. 1688.
A Congratulatory Poem to the King's Most Sacred Majesty. 1688.
To Poet Bavius. 1688.
Lycidus; or, The Lover in Fashion, Together with a Miscellany of New Poems by Several Hands, with others. 1688.
A Congratulatory Poem to Her Sacred Majesty Queen Mary, upon Her Arrival in England. 1689.
A Pindaric Poem to the Rev. Dr. [Thomas] Burnet. 1689.

Other

Editor, *Convent Garden Drollery.* 1672; edited by G. Thorn-Drury, 1928.
Editor, *Miscellany, Being a Collection of Poems by Several Hands* (includes Behn's translation of La Rochefoucauld). 1685.

Translator, *La Montre; or, The Lover's Watch,* by Balthasar de Bonnecorse. 1686.
Translator, *The Fatal Beauty of Agnes de Castro,* by J. B. de Brillac. 1688.
Translator, *A Discovery of New Worlds,* by Fontennelle. 1688; as *The Theory of New Worlds,* 1700.
Translator, *The History of Oracles, and the Cheats of the Pagan Priests,* by Fontennelle. 1688.
Translator, with others, *Cowley's Six Books of Plants.* 1689.

Reading List: *Behn* by V. Sackville-West, 1927; *The Incomparable Aphra* by George Woodcock, 1948; *New Light on Behn* by W. J. Cameron, 1961; *Behn* by Frederick M. Link, 1968 (includes bibliography); *The Passionate Shepherdess: Behn* by Maureen Duffy, 1977.

*   *   *

Aphra Behn began her literary career as a dramatist. Her early plays are undistinguished imitations of the romantic tragi-comedy deriving from Beaumont and Fletcher; *Abdelazar,* for instance, is a successful but conventional tragedy of blood and lust. Her first good play is *The Town Fop,* a racy London comedy combining complex intrigue, farce, and expert dialogue. This formula, often augmented by a pair of witty lovers, she repeats in later plays like *The Rover, Sir Patient Fancy, The Feigned Courtesans, The Second Part of The Rover,* and *The Lucky Chance. The False Count* is a romantic farce in the traditional manner; *The Emperor of the Moon* a fine farce in the new *commedia dell' arte* style. *The Roundheads* is clumsy Tory propaganda, but Behn's other political play, *The City Heiress,* is coherent and witty enough to rank with her best work. Two plays were produced posthumously; three others are usually attributed to her, *The Revenge* with near certainty.

Behn's comedies are action-focused. At their best, they show sure craft, an accurate ear for speech rhythms, considerable wit, and mastery of stagecraft. Most of them borrow from earlier European or English sources; a play wholly original, like *The Feigned Courtesans,* is unusual. Some works, like *The Lucky Chance,* make minor use of sources. Others, like *Sir Patient Fancy, The City Heiress,* and *The Emperor of the Moon,* borrow both plot suggestions and the outline of characters. *The Town Fop* and *The Rover* are among Behn's adaptations of earlier plays which are in every case better than the originals. What she borrows she makes her own; plot ideas may come from Killigrew or Molière, but dialogue, pace, organization, most detail, and stagecraft are nearly always original. Her themes sometimes go beyond the conventional, especially in her emphasis on mature relationships between the sexes and on the evils of marriages made for money instead of love, and many of her characters (Hellena in *The Rover,* for example) have a vitality that transcends the stereotypes of the period.

Behn's poetry is occasional. The elegies and panegyrics are inconsequential and often clumsy; the prologues, epilogues, and songs for the plays are generally successful and often excellent. Several forgettable translations of French and Latin works belong to her later years when she was desperate for money; even so, her version of La Rochefoucauld is better than one might expect. Her short fiction has been overrated. *The Fair Jilt*, a study of the *femme fatale*, and *The Wandering Beauty*, a pastoral fairy tale, are worth reading, but *Oroonoko*, which contrasts the nobility of a savage with the baseness of supposedly civilized Englishmen in Surinam, is the only piece comparable to her best comedies. The majority of these were stage successes; indeed, *The Rover* and *The Emperor of the Moon* survived nearly a century. Taken together, they rank Aphra Behn with Dryden, Etherege, Wycherley, and Shadwell among the comic dramatists of her day – no mean achievement for the first Englishwoman to make her living by her pen.

—Frederick M. Link

BEHRMAN, S(amuel) N(athaniel).   American.   Born in Worcester, Massachusetts, 9 June 1893. Educated at Clark College, now Clark University, Worcester, 1912–14; Harvard University, Cambridge, Massachusetts, B.A. 1916 (Phi Beta Kappa); Columbia University, New York, M.A. 1918. Married Elza Heifetz in 1936; one son, two step-children. Book Reviewer for the *New Republic*, New York, and the *New York Times*; Columnist, *The New Yorker*. Founder, with Robert E. Sherwood, Elmer Rice, Maxwell Anderson, Sidney Howard, and John F. Wharton, Playwrights Company, 1938. Trustee, Clark University. Recipient: American Academy of Arts and Letters grant, 1943; New York Drama Critics Circle Award, 1944; Brandeis University Creative Arts Award, 1962. LL.D.: Clark University, 1949. Member, National Institute of Arts and Letters, and American Academy of Arts and Sciences. *Died 9 September 1973.*

PUBLICATIONS

Plays

> *Bedside Manners: A Comedy of Convalescence* with J. Kenyon Nicholson (produced 1923).   1924.
> *A Night's Work*, with J. Kenyon Nicholson (produced 1924).   1926.
> *The Man Who Forgot*, with Owen Davis (produced 1926).
> *The Second Man* (produced 1927).   1927.
> *Love Is Like That*, with J. Kenyon Nicholson (produced 1927).
> *Serena Blandish*, from the novel by Enid Bagnold (produced 1929).   In *Three Plays*, 1934.
> *Meteor* (produced 1929).   1930.
> *Brief Moment* (produced 1931).   1931.
> *Biography* (produced 1932).   1933.
> *Love Story* (produced 1934).
> *Three Plays: Serena Blandish, Meteor, The Second Man.*   1934.
> *Rain from Heaven* (produced 1935).   1935.

End of Summer (produced 1936).   1936.
Amphitryon 38, with Roger Gellert, from a play by Jean Giraudoux (produced 1937).   1938.
Wine of Choice (produced 1938).   1938.
No Time for Comedy (produced 1939).   1939.
The Talley Method (produced 1941).   1941.
The Pirate, from a work by Ludwig Fulda (produced 1942).   1943.
Jacobowsky and the Colonel, with Franz Werfel (produced 1944).   1944.
Dunnigan's Daughter (produced 1945).   1946.
Jane, from a story by W. Somerset Maugham (produced 1946; as *The Foreign Language*, produced 1951).   1952.
I Know My Love, from a play by Marcel Achard (produced 1949).   1952.
Let Me Hear the Melody (produced 1951).
Fanny, with Joshua Logan, music by Harold Rome, from a trilogy by Marcel Pagnol (produced 1954).   1955.
Four Plays: The Second Man, Biography, Rain from Heaven, End of Summer.   1955.
The Cold Wind and the Warm (produced 1958).   1959.
The Beauty Part (produced 1962).
Lord Pengo: A Period Comedy, based on his book *Duveen* (produced 1962).   1963.
But for Whom Charlie (produced 1964).   1964.

Screenplays: *Liliom*, with Sonya Levien, 1930; *Lightnin'*, with Sonya Levien, 1930; *The Sea Wolf*, with Ralph Block, 1930; *The Brat*, with others, 1931; *Surrender*, with Sonya Levien, 1931; *Daddy Long Legs*, with Sonya Levien, 1931; *Rebecca of Sunnybrook Farm*, with Sonya Levien, 1932; *Tess of the Storm Country*, with others, 1932; *Brief Moment*, 1933; *Queen Christina*, 1933; *Cavalcade*, 1933; *Hallelujah, I'm a Bum*, 1933; *My Lips Betray*, 1933; *Biography of a Bachelor Girl*, 1934; *As Husbands Go*, with Sonya Levien, 1934; *The Scarlet Pimpernel*, with others, 1934; *A Tale of Two Cities*, with W. P. Lipscomb, 1935; *Conquest*, with others, 1937; *Parnell*, with John Van Druten, 1937; *The Cowboy and the Lady*, with others, 1937; *The Cowboy and the Lady*, with Sonya Levien, 1938; *No Time for Comedy*, 1940; *Waterloo Bridge*, with others, 1940; *Two-Faced Woman*, with others, 1941; *Quo Vadis*, with others, 1951; *Me and the Colonel*, with George Froeschel, 1958; *Fanny*, with Joshua Logan, 1961.

Fiction

The Burning-Glass.   1968.

Other

Duveen.   1952.
The Worcester Account (*New Yorker* sketches).   1954.
Portrait of Max: An Intimate Memoir of Sir Max Beerbohm.   1960; as *Conversation with Max*, 1960.
The Suspended Drawing Room.   1965.
People in a Diary: A Memoir.   1972; as *Tribulations and Laughter: A Memoir*, 1972.

Bibliography: *Maxwell Anderson and Behrman: A Reference Guide* by William Klink, 1977.

Reading List: "Behrman: The Quandary of the Comic Spirit" by Charles Kaplan, in *College English 9*, 1950.

It is now 50 years since S. N. Behrman's *The Second Man* was produced by the Theatre Guild and made him famous. Even by the 1950's the material was old-hat, and writers of comedies of manners (even better ones, such as Philip Barry) are now quite out of date. Behrman's work after the 1930's was fairly unimportant, largely adaptations. His sophisticated comedy belongs to an earlier generation. A recent revival of *The Second Man* looked very old-fashioned. It, of course, lacked the Lunts, who created roles in it (and Noël Coward and Raymond Massey, who played it in London), and it needed them.

In his time Behrman also had the assistance of stars like Greta Garbo, Ina Claire, Katherine Cornell, and Laurence Olivier. He, like the blasé and aphoristic writer Clark Storey in *The Second Man*, said "(*Seriously*) Life is sad. I know it's sad. But I think it's gallant to pretend that it isn't." In the 1930's this approach made him an American Noël Coward and gave him "perhaps the most considerable reputation" among young playwrights (A. H. Quinn). But soon proletarian and "socially significant drama" was to render inoperable the approach of the heroine of *Biography*, which was to laugh at injustice because nothing could be done about it, and the hero of *No Time for Comedy*, who chose to write light comedy instead of propagandist melodrama. The depression and World War II wiped out Behrman's impassive, indifferent, intellectual sophisticates who gracefully soared above reality. In *Rain from Heaven*, even though it revolves around Fascists and German refugees, the sophisticates are still doing arabesques on the thin ice of political problems.

Behrman wrote a number of screenplays, including such movies as *Queen Christina* and *Anna Karenina*, both with Garbo, *Waterloo Bridge*, and *Quo Vadis*. For the *New Yorker* he wrote the sketches that became *Duveen* (about the art dealer who became Lord Millbank) and *The Worcester Account* (about his boyhood in Worcester, Massachusetts). These, I think, surpass his original comedies of manners, his adaptation of Giraudoux (*Amphytrion 38*) or his collaboration with Franz Werfel (*Jacobowsky and the Colonel*), his dramatization of stories by Enid Bagnold (*Serena Blandish*) and W. Somerset Maugham (*Jane*), all his theatre work, and his cinema writing. It is unfortunate that he did not find time in his 80 years to write a work for the stage about the sort of people who enliven *The Worcester Account*. His cosmopolitan intellectuals may be well observed for a "Brief Moment" (as a 1931 play of his was called), but they are seen by a stranger, however clever. The people of Providence Street in Worcester, Behrman knew.

—Leonard R. N. Ashley

BELASCO, David. American. Born in San Francisco, California, 25 July 1853; moved with his family to Victoria, British Columbia, 1858. Educated at a monastery in Victoria, 1858–62; in various schools in San Francisco, where his family returned in 1865; Lincoln College, California, 1875. Married Cecilia Loverich in 1873; two daughters. Worked as an actor in repertory, touring California; acted at Piper's Opera House in Virginia City, where he was employed briefly by Dion Boucicault as a secretary, 1873; Stage Manager, Maguire's Theatre, San Francisco, 1874; Assistant to the Manager, 1875–78, and Stage Manager, 1878–82, Lucky Baldwin's Academy of Music, San Francisco; began writing for the stage in the late 1870's; Lighting Manager, then Stage Manager, Madison Square Theatre, New York, 1882–86; Manager, with David Frohman, Lyceum Theatre, New York, 1886–90; Independent Actor/Manager, New York, 1890–1906; Owner, Stuyvesant Theatre, later Belasco Theatre, New York, 1906 until his death. Produced over 350 plays for Broadway and stock companies. *Died 14 May 1931.*

Collections

> *The Plays of Henry C. DeMille and Belasco* (includes *The Senator's Wife, Lord Chumley, The Charity Ball, Men and Women*), edited by Robert Hamilton Ball. 1941.
> *The Heart of Maryland and Other Plays* (includes *The Stranglers of Paris, La Belle Russe, The Girl I Left Behind Me, Naughty Anthony*), edited by Glenn Hughes and George Savage. 1941.

Plays

> *The Doll Master* (produced 1874–75?).
> *Sylvia's Lovers* (produced 1875?).
> *The Creole*, from a play by Adolphe Belot (produced 1876–77?).
> *Olivia*, from the novel *The Vicar of Wakefield* by Goldsmith (produced 1878).
> *Proof Positive* (produced 1878).
> *Within an Inch of His Life*, with James A. Herne, from a play by Emile Gaboriau (produced 1879). Edited by Arthur Hobson Quinn, in *The Early Plays of Herne*, 1940.
> *A Fast Family*, from a play by Sardou (produced 1879).
> *The Millionaire's Daughter* (produced 1879).
> *Marriage by Moonlight*, with James A. Herne, from the play *Camilla's Husband* by Watt Philips (produced 1879).
> *Drink*, from a novel by Zola (produced 1879).
> *Hearts of Oak*, with James A. Herne (as *Chums*, produced 1879; as *Hearts of Oak*, produced 1879). Edited by Mrs. James A. Herne, in *Shore Acres and Other Plays*, by Herne, 1928.
> *Paul Arniff; or, The Love of a Serf* (produced 1880).
> *True to the Core*, from the play by A. R. Slous (produced 1880).
> *La Belle Russe*, from the plays *Forget-Me-Not* and *New Magdalen* (produced 1881). 1914; in *The Heart of Maryland and Other Plays*, 1941.
> *The Stranglers of Paris*, from a novel by Adolphe Belot (produced 1881). In *The Heart of Maryland and Other Plays*, 1941.
> *The Curse of Cain*, with Peter Robinson (produced 1882).
> *American Born*, from the play *British Born* (produced 1882).
> *Valerie*, from a play by Sardou (produced 1886).
> *The Highest Bidder*, from the play *Trade* by John Maddison Morton and Robert Reece (produced 1887).
> *Baron Rudolph*, with Bronson Howard, revised version (produced 1887). Edited by Allan H. Halline, in *The Banker's Daughter and Other Plays*, by Howard, 1941.
> *Pawn Ticket 210*, with Clay M. Greene (produced 1887).
> *The Senator's Wife*, with Henry C. DeMille (as *The Wife*, produced 1887; as *The Senator's Wife*, produced 1892). In *The Plays of DeMille and Belasco*, 1941.
> *Lord Chumley*, with Henry C. DeMille (produced 1888). In *The Plays of DeMille and Belasco*, 1941.
> *The Charity Ball*, with Henry C. DeMille (produced 1889). In *The Plays of DeMille and Belasco*, 1941.
> *The Marquis*, from a play by Sardou (produced 1889).
> *Men and Women*, with Henry C. DeMille (produced 1890). In *The Plays of DeMille and Belasco*, 1941.
> *Miss Helyett*, from a play by Maxime Boucheron (produced 1891).

The Girl I Left Behind Me; or, The Country Ball, with Franklin Fyles (produced 1893). In *The Heart of Maryland and Other Plays*, 1941.

The Younger Son, from a play by O. Vischer (produced 1893).

The Heart of Maryland (produced 1895). In *The Heart of Maryland and Other Plays*, 1941.

Under the Polar Star, with Clay M. Greene (produced 1896).

Zaza, from a play by Pierre Berton and Charles Simon (produced 1898).

Naughty Anthony (produced 1899). In *The Heart of Maryland and Other Plays*, 1941.

Madame Butterfly, from the story by John Luther Long (produced 1900). In *Six Plays*, 1928.

Du Barry (produced 1901). In *Six Plays*, 1928.

The Darling of the Gods, with John Luther Long (produced 1902). In *Six Plays*, 1928.

Sweet Kitty Bellairs, from the novel *The Bath Comedy* by Agnes and Egerton Castle (produced 1903).

Adrea, with John Luther Long (produced 1904). In *Six Plays*, 1928.

The Girl of the Golden West (produced 1905). In *Six Plays*, 1928.

The Rose of the Rancho, from the play *Juanita* by Richard Walton Tully (produced 1906). 1936.

A Grand Army Man, with Pauline Phelps and Marion Short (produced 1907).

The Lily, from a play by Pierre Wolff and Gaston Leroux (produced 1909).

The Return of Peter Grimm (produced 1911). In *Six Plays*, 1928.

The Governor's Lady, with Alice Bradley (produced 1912).

The Secret, from a work by Henri Bernstein (produced 1913).

Van Der Decken: A Legendary Play of the Sea (produced 1915).

The Son-Daughter, with George Scarborough (produced 1919).

Timothy Shaft, with W. J. Hurlbut (produced 1921).

Kiki, from the play by André Picard (produced 1921).

The Merchant of Venice, from the play by Shakespeare (produced 1922). 1922.

The Comedian, from a play by Sacha Guitry (produced 1923).

Laugh, Clown, Laugh!, with Tom Cushing, from a play by Fausto Martini (produced 1923).

Salvage. 1925.

Fanny, with Willard Mack (produced 1926).

Mima, from a play by Molnar (produced 1928).

Six Plays (includes *Madame Butterfly, Du Barry, The Darling of the Gods, Adrea, The Girl of The Golden West, The Return of Peter Grimm*). 1928.

Other

My Life's Story. 2 vols., 1915.

The Theatre Through Its Stage Door, edited by Louis V. Defoe. 1919.

A Souvenir of Shakespeare's Merchant of Venice. 1923.

Plays Produced under the Stage Direction of David Belasco. 1925.

Editor, with Charles A. Byrne, *Fairy Tales Told by Seven Travellers at the Red Lion Inn*. 1906.

Reading List: *The Life of Belasco* by William Winter, 2 vols., 1918; *The Life and Work of Belasco, The Bishop of Broadway* by Craig Timberlake, 1954; *Belasco: Naturalism in the American Theatre* by Lise-Lone Marker, 1974.

*   *   *

The parents of David Belasco came to San Francisco from England during the Gold Rush, and his early theatrical experience was gained entirely in the American and Canadian west. Humphrey Abraham Belasco was a harlequin turned shopkeeper, and his son at the age of eleven played the Duke of York to Charles Kean's Richard III. At twelve, he wrote and produced his first melodrama. He supered, prompted, played Hamlet, Uncle Tom, and Armand on tour, and in 1876 was secretary to Dion Boucicault, whose "sensation dramas" heavily influenced the would-be playwright.

While stage manager at Baldwin's Academy of Music, Belasco began to experiment with spectacle and stage lighting as well as adapting and collaborating on several plays, one of which, *La Belle Russe* was a success in New York. Its derivative plot involves a woman's impersonation of her virtuous twin sister, even to the sister's titled husband. Here Belasco began treating "strong," sometimes demonic, always sexual female characters and tense situations. The sketchy good twin also foreshadows Belasco's virtuous, suffering heroines such as Adrea and Cho-Cho-San.

In 1882 Belasco came east, where he was at times associated with the Frohmans, and in the late 1880's collaborated with Henry C. DeMille on four very popular but immemorable plays. Belasco's real success as a playwright began with *The Heart of Maryland* in 1895, in which Mrs. Leslie Carter swung on the clapper of a bell to save her soldier-sweetheart, Belasco having been inspired by the Civil War and "Curfew Shall Not Ring Tonight!" Mrs. Carter, the star of a scandalous divorce trial, was taught to act by Belasco, who later wrote *Zaza, Du Barry*, and *Adrea* for her. Too high in voice and too low in stature to be effective on stage himself, he acted through the players he coached and in his own off-stage character as the silver-haired, clerical-collared "Bishop of Broadway."

In 1900 Belasco collaborated with John Luther Long on *Madame Butterfly*, from which Puccini derived his opera, and when the same composer set Belasco's *The Girl of the Golden West*, the playwright directed Caruso and the Metropolitan Opera cast for its 1910 premiere. Belasco's later work was largely as director and deviser of scenic effects, and the plays he dealt with were inconsequential except for his productions of Sacha Guitry's *Deburau*, *The Merchant of Venice* with David Warfield as Shylock, and Molnar's *Mima* – unsuccessful but stupendous.

It is doubtful that David Belasco did anything which could be called truly original, but he improved all he touched and he touched almost everything in the theatre of his day. A master of the exciting plot, he developed from the physical sensationalism of Boucicault to the emotional sensationalism of Sardou. In *The Girl I Left Behind Me*, for example, he used elements of Boucicault's *Defense of Lucknow* for a situation which John Ford would adapt for his film *Stage Coach*. Belasco heroines such as Du Barry, Minnie, and Yo-San face Tosca's dilemma of proscribed lover and lascivious authority, while *Adrea* with its blind princess, wicked sister, exotic kingdom, disloyal lover, and tower of death recalls the extravagant costume dramas Sardou created for Sarah Bernhardt. Yet Belasco could also devise plays of quiet sentiment such as *The Return of Peter Grimm* with its affectionate ghost *ex machina* (and its only partly-acknowledged debt to the young Cecil B. DeMille). As Belasco explained in *The Theatre Through Its Stage Door*, his plays appealed because he tried "to tug at the hearts of my audience." He also made those heart-strings zing with excitement, part of which arose from his extraordinary scenic effects.

Dion Boucicault had blown up steamboats on stage; David Belasco created battlefields. Later, working in the tradition of realistic *mise en scène* introduced by Tom Robertson, Belasco used a real switchboard and telephone booths in his production of William C. DeMille's *The Woman* and re-created the interior of a Childs' Restaurant on stage in *The Governor's Lady* by Alice Bradley. The theatres which he built (the Belasco and the Stuyvesant) contained the most sophisticated stage equipment of their day, and he experimented endlessly with electricity, first used by W. S. Gilbert at the Savoy Theatre.

Belasco believed that color and light could "communicate to audiences the underlying symbolism of a play." Cho-Cho-San's pathetic vigil was accompanied by fourteen minutes of mood lighting in which twilight darkened to night, stars appeared, lamps were lighted and flickered out one by one, and dawn broke. The River of Souls in *The Darling of the Gods* was composed of shadowy spirits "floating across and disappearing," an anticipation of back projection. For *The Girl of the Golden West*, Belasco spent three months designing a sunset, only to reject it – "It was a good sunset, but it was not Californian."

Although Belasco's meticulous realism is no longer fashionable, it is still significant in the *verismo* operas which Puccini based on his plays and productions. Moreover, like his predecessors Robertson and Gilbert, Belasco played a part in turning the stage from a star-dominated playhouse to a director's theatre. Finally, the exciting motifs which he developed or adapted are still part of the vocabulary of American melodrama.

—Jane W. Stedman

BICKERSTAFF, Isaac. Irish. Born in Dublin, 26 September 1733. Soldier: Page to Lord Chesterfield, Lord Lieutenant of Ireland, 1745; commissioned Ensign in the Fifth Regiment of Foot, 1745, and 2nd Lieutenant, 1746 until he resigned, 1755; 2nd Lieutenant, 91st Company, Plymouth Marine Corps, 1758–63. Wrote for the stage, 1756–71; fled England to avoid arrest as a homosexual, 1772, and spent the remainder of his life in exile abroad. *Died c. 1808.*

PUBLICATIONS

Plays

> *Thomas and Sally; or, The Sailor's Return*, music by Thomas Arne (produced 1760). 1761; revised edition, 1780.
> *Judith* (oratorio), music by Thomas Arne (produced 1761). 1761.
> *Love in a Village*, music by Thomas Arne and others (produced 1762). 1763.
> *The Maid of the Mill*, music by Samuel Arnold and others (produced 1765). 1765.
> *Daphne and Amintor*, from a work by Saint-Foix (produced 1765). 1765.
> *The Plain Dealer*, from the play by Wycherley (produced 1765). 1766.
> *Love in the City*, music by Charles Dibdin and others (produced 1767). 1767; shortened version, as *The Romp* (produced 1774), 1786.
> *Lionel and Clarissa*, music by Charles Dibdin (produced 1768). 1768; revised version, as *The School for Fathers* (produced 1770), 1770.
> *The Absent Man* (produced 1768). 1768.
> *The Padlock*, music by Charles Dibdin (produced 1768). 1768.
> *The Royal Garland*, music by Samuel Arnold (produced 1768). 1768.
> *Queen Mab* (cantata), music by Charles Dibdin (produced 1768). 1768.
> *The Hypocrite*, from the play *The Non-Juror* by Cibber (produced 1768). 1769.
> *Doctor Last in His Chariot*, from a play by Molière (produced 1769). 1769.
> *The Captive*, music by Charles Dibdin, from the play *Don Sebastian* by Dryden (produced 1769). 1769.
> *The Ephesian Matron; or, The Widow's Tears*, music by Charles Dibdin (produced 1769). 1769.
> *Tis Well It's No Worse*, from a play by Calderón (produced 1770). 1770.

The Recruiting Serjeant, music by Charles Dibdin (produced 1770).   1770.

He Would If He Could; or, An Old Fool Worse Than Any, music by Charles Dibdin, from
a play by G. A. Federico (as *The Maid the Mistress,* produced 1770; as *He Would If He
Could,* produced 1771).   1771.

The Sultan; or, A Peep into the Seraglio, from a play by C. S. Favart, music by Charles
Dibdin and others (produced 1775).   1780.

Fiction

The Life and Adventures of Ambrose Gwinnet.   1768.

Verse

Leucothoë: A Dramatic Poem.   1756.

Reading List: *The Dramatic Cobbler: The Life and Works of Bickerstaff* by Peter A. Tasch,
1971; *English Theatre Music in the Eighteenth Century* by Roger Fiske, 1973.

*   *   *

Between 1760 and 1772, Isaac Bickerstaff was the dramatist primarily responsible for
originating English comic opera and making it fashionably popular. His plots were not new –
he adapted and borrowed from English and French plays more than he ever acknowledged –
but he paired music, much of it by continental composers, and only some of it commissioned
for his operas, with often witty and always singable lyrics.

Love in a Village is by critical assent the first English comic opera and the most popular in
the eighteenth century. Thomas Arne composed the music specifically for five of the forty-
two songs and used thirteen of his earlier melodies. Bickerstaff borrowed from Wycherley's
The Gentleman's Dancing Master and plundered Charles Johnson's *The Village Opera.*
Despite harsh criticism of his plagiarism, the comic opera was an overwhelming success (37
performances at Covent Garden during its first season). Bickerstaff repeated his success with
The Maid of the Mill in which Charles Dibdin, who became his composer two years later,
played the comic role of Ralph.

As successful as Bickerstaff and Dibdin were to be, their first superb effort, *Love in the City,*
failed because its satire was too apposite for the London audience. Profiting from their
mistake, they returned to pastoral plots for their next comic opera, *Lionel and Clarissa.* In the
four comic operas which Bickerstaff wrote during the 1760's for Covent Garden, he
developed the form of musical comedy which lasted until the time of Gilbert and Sullivan a
hundred years later.

Unable to compete with Covent Garden, Garrick hired Bickerstaff and Dibdin, but their
only full-length opera for Drury Lane was their revised *Lionel and Clarissa, School for
Fathers.* However, Bickerstaff did write the musical farce, *The Padlock,* with Dibdin's music;
and Dibdin played the comic servant Mungo in blackface – the first such occurrence on the
London stage. Bickerstaff also adapted comedies like Wycherley's *The Plain Dealer* for
Garrick. Although his most popular comedy, *The Hypocrite,* was based on Cibber's *Non-
Juror,* Bickerstaff's character Maw-worm was original and kept the play alive well into the
nineteenth century.

Bickerstaff's and Dibdin's most interesting musical works were two serenatas for Ranelagh
House: *The Ephesian Matron* and *The Recruiting Serjeant.* These short Italianate light operas
(similar in style to *La Serva Padrona*) might have led the two men to new musical dramatic
forms, but in 1772 Bickerstaff's career ended when he fled to France to avoid arrest as a

homosexual. Despite his short career, Bickerstaff is important to English drama because to it he contributed comic opera.

—Peter A. Tasch

BIRD, Robert Montgomery. American. Born in New Castle, Delaware, 5 February 1806. Educated at Germantown Academy, Philadelphia; University of Pennsylvania, Philadelphia, 1824–27, M.D. 1827. Married Mary Mayer in 1837; one son. Practised as a physician in Philadelphia for one year, then gave up medicine to devote himself to writing; wrote plays for the actor-producer Edwin Forrest, 1831–34, then turned to writing novels, 1835–40; suffered a breakdown and retired to a farm in Maryland, where he subsequently recovered, 1840; Professor of the Institutes of Medicine and Materia Medica, Pennsylvania Medical College, Philadelphia, 1841–43; Literary Editor and Part-Owner, *North American*, Philadelphia, 1847–54. Honorary Member, English Dramatic Authors Society. *Died 23 January 1854.*

PUBLICATIONS

Collections

    The Life and Dramatic Works (includes *Pelopidas, The Gladiator, Oralloossa*), edited by Clement E. Foust. 1919.
    The Cowled Lover and Other Plays (includes *Calidorf; or, The Avenger; News of the Night; or, A Trip to Niagara; 'Twas All for the Best; or 'Tis All a Notion*), edited by Edward O'Neill. 1941.

Plays

    The Gladiator (produced 1831; also produced as *Spartacus*). In *The Life and Dramatic Works*, 1919.
    Oralloossa (produced 1832). In *The Life and Dramatic Works*, 1919.
    The Broker of Bogota (produced 1834). Edited by Arthur Hobson Quinn, in *Representative American Plays*, 1917.
    News of the Night; or, A Trip to Niagara (produced 1929). In *The Cowled Lover and Other Plays*, 1941.
    The City Looking Glass: A Philadelphia Comedy, edited by Arthur Hobson Quinn (produced 1933). 1933.

Fiction

    Calavar; or, The Knight of the Conquest. 1834; as *Abdalla the Moor and the Spanish Knight*, 1835.
    The Infidel; or, The Fall of Mexico. 1835; as *Cortez*, 1835; as *The Infidel's Doom*, 1840.

The Hawks of Hawk-Hollow: A Tradition of Pennsylvania. 1835.
Sheppard Lee. 1836.
Nick of the Woods; or, The Jibbenainosay: A Tale of Kentucky. 1837; edited by Cecil B. Williams, 1939.
Peter Pilgrim; or, A Rambler's Recollections. 1838.
The Adventures of Robin Day. 1839.

Bibliography: in *Bibliography of American Literature* by Jacob Blanck, 1955.

Reading List: *Life of Bird* by Mary Mayer Bird, edited by C. Seymour Thompson, 1945; *Bird* by Curtis Dahl, 1963.

*   *   *

One of the truly remarkable men of his time, Robert Montgomery Bird boasted sufficiently varied interests and equally responsive talents to lead his active mind through the fields of medicine, science, music, art, history, politics, pedagogy, and literature. Early in life he outlined a literary career in which he would begin with poetry and drama, turn next to novels, and finally write history. A scholarly man, widely read in the classics, he was also very much a product of and a part of the Romantic tradition which was being revealed in the idealism of Emerson and Thoreau, the Gothic qualities in Hawthorne and Poe, and the concern for nature which distinguished the novels of Cooper, John P. Kennedy and William G. Simms. Indeed, Bird was a significant force in bringing Romanticism to American literature, particularly the drama.

For his career as a dramatist Bird projected at least fifty-five plays, and in response to the play contests which Edwin Forrest established in 1828 he began to write in earnest. Four of Forrest's nine prize plays were written by Bird – *Pelopidas, The Gladiator, Oralloossa,* and *The Broker of Bogota* – but it did not prove to be a completely happy arrangement. For his efforts Bird received $1,000 for each play; Forrest, on the other hand, made hundreds of thousands of dollars. When Bird realized that plays such as *The Gladiator* and *The Broker of Bogota* would become permanent in Forrest's repertory, he complained, received no satisfaction, and stopped writing for the stage. "What a fool I was to think of writing plays!" he confided in his *Secret Records.* In all he completed only nine of his projected plays.

As a consequence of the events surrounding his relations with Forrest, Bird turned to politics, journalism, and novels. Two of his most popular novels are *The Hawks of Hawk-Hollow* and *Nick of the Woods.* Bird's loss to American drama, however, must be considered significant. An imaginative man, keenly aware of the forces working upon his culture, he espoused theories of dramaturgy which not only reflected the Romanticism of his day but were ideally suited to the style of acting currently popular. The idealized hero was the central force in his plays. All other dramatic elements – the plot, the dramatic incidents and spectacle, the poetic speech, the passions of the characters, the theme of the play – contributed to the creation of the hero and led to the climax of the play. Bird obviously had the energy and the skill to write good romantic melodrama. An early play, *The City Looking Glass* (written in 1828), also showed considerable potentiality for comedy. Unfortunately, all of this talent was shelved when his indignation was righteously ignited, and the help that copyright laws might have provided was years in the future.

—Walter J. Meserve

BOKER, George Henry. American. Born in Philadelphia, Pennsylvania, 6 October 1823. Educated at the College of New Jersey, now Princeton University (one of the founders of the *Nassau Monthly*, 1842), graduated 1842; also studied law. Married Julia Mandeville Riggs in 1844; one son. Devoted himself to writing from 1845, and to writing for the stage from 1848; Founding Member, 1862, Secretary, 1862–71, and President, 1879, Union Club, later Union League, Philadelphia; United States Ambassador to Turkey, 1871–75, and to Russia, 1875–78; President, Fairmount Park Commission, Philadelphia, 1886 until his death. President, Philadelphia Club, 1878. *Died 2 January 1890.*

PUBLICATIONS

Collections

    Glaucus and Other Plays (includes *The World a Mask, The Bankrupt*), edited by Sculley Bradley. 1940.

Plays

    Calaynos (produced 1849). 1848.
    Anne Boleyn (produced 1850). 1850.
    The Betrothal (produced 1850). In *Plays and Poems*, 1856.
    The World a Mask (produced 1851). 1856; in *Glaucus and Other Plays*, 1940.
    The Widow's Marriage (produced 1852). In *Plays and Poems*, 1856.
    Leonor de Guzman (produced 1853). In *Plays and Poems*, 1856.
    Francesca da Rimini (produced 1855). In *Plays and Poems*, 1856.
    The Bankrupt (produced 1855). In *Glaucus and Other Plays*, 1940.
    Nydia, edited by Sculley Bradley. 1929; revised version, as *Glaucus*, in *Glaucus and Other Plays*, 1940.

Verse

    The Lesson of Life and Other Poems. 1848.
    The Podesta's Daughter and Other Miscellaneous Poems. 1852.
    Poems of the War. 1864.
    Our Heroic Themes. 1865.
    Königsmark: The Legend of the Hounds and Other Poems. 1869.
    The Book of the Dead: Poems. 1882.
    Sonnets: A Sequence on Profane Love, edited by Sculley Bradley. 1929.

Other

    Plays and Poems. 2 vols., 1856.

Bibliography: in *Bibliography of American Literature* by Jacob Blanck, 1955.

Reading List: *Boker, Poet and Patriot* by Sculley Bradley, 1927.

*   *   *

In keeping with his aspiration to live the life of the poet, George Henry Boker's first publication, *The Lesson of Life*, was a book of verse. The scion of a wealthy and aristocratic family who was classically educated at what would become Princeton University, Boker followed this first book with poems on public affairs, with patriotic verse, and with sonnets – a form with which he enjoyed particular felicity – on love and statesmanship. He subsequently collected many of these pieces into *Plays and Poems*, whose two volumes have been reprinted many times and are today the most accessible source of Boker's verse. Despite his love for poetry, however, Boker is remembered primarily as a dramatist, having written nearly a dozen plays between his first, *Calaynos*, a tragedy in blank verse, and his last, *Nydia*, which he rewrote as *Glaucus* in 1886.

Surely the most famous of Boker's plays is *Francesca da Rimini*, completed in 1853 and first produced in New York two years later. Based on the tragic love story of thirteenth-century Italy which Dante celebrated in *The Inferno* and which had been reworked by so many other authors, Boker's *Francesca* consists of more than 3,500 lines of neo-Elizabethan verse, so befitting its author's poetic urges as well as the day's theatrical tastes. In these lines Boker chronicled once again the unhappy triangle of Francesca, a noblewoman of Ravenna, Paolo, a nobleman of Rimini to whom she had given her heart, and Lanciotto, Paolo's equally noble but sadly deformed brother to whom she had given her hand in marriage. A stirring success, *Francesca* ran on the New York and Philadelphia stage in 1855, and was reproduced for longer runs in 1882–83 and again in 1901–02.

As the corpus of his work reveals, George Henry Boker was a playwright whose sense of the literary matched his sense of the theatrical. Understandably, then, he is among the best remembered of America's nineteenth-century dramatists.

—Bruce A. Lohof

BOND, Edward. English. Born in London, 18 July 1934. Educated in state schools to age 14. Served in the British Army for two years. Married Elisabeth Pablé in 1971. Member of the Writers Group of the Royal Court Theatre, London. Recipient: George Devine Award, 1968; John Whiting Award, 1969.

PUBLICATIONS

Plays

The Pope's Wedding (produced 1962).   In *The Pope's Wedding and Other Plays*, 1971.
Saved (produced 1965).   1966.
The Three Sisters, from a play by Chekhov (produced 1967).
Narrow Road to the Deep North (produced 1968).   1968; revised version, as *The Bundle* (produced 1978), 1978.
Early Morning (produced 1968).   1968.
Black Mass (produced 1970).   In *The Pope's Wedding and Other Plays*, 1971.
Passion (produced 1971).   In *Plays: Two*, 1978.
Lear (produced 1971).   1972.
The Pope's Wedding and Other Plays (includes *Mr. Dog, The King with Golden Eyes, Sharpville Sequence, Black Mass*).   1971.

The Sea (produced 1973). 1973.
Bingo: Scenes of Money and Death (and Passion) (produced 1973). 1974.
Spring Awakening, from a play by Frank Wedekind (produced 1974).
The Fool: Scenes of Bread and Love (produced 1975). In *The Fool, and We Come to the River*, 1976.
We Come to the River: Actions for Music, music by Hans Werner Henze (produced 1976). 1976.
A-A-America: Grandma Faust, and The Swing (produced 1976). In *Stone, and A-A-America*, 1976.
The White Devil, from the play by Webster (produced 1976).
Stone (produced 1976). In *Stone, and A-A-America*, 1976.
The Fool, and We Come to the River. 1976.
Stone, and A-A-America. 1976.
The Woman: Scenes of War and Freedom (produced 1978).

Screenplays: *Blow-Up*, with Michelangelo Antonioni and Tonino Guerra, 1967; *Laughter in the Dark*, 1969; *The Lady of Monza* (English dialogue), 1970; *Walkabout*, 1971.

Radio Play: *Badger by Owl-Light*, 1975.

Verse

Theatre Poems and Songs. 1978.

Reading List: *Bond* by Simon Trussler, 1976; *The Plays of Bond* by Richard Scharine, 1977; *The Plays of Bond* by Tony Coult, 1978.

*   *   *

In a relatively brief dramatic career, and little over half-a-dozen full-length plays, Edward Bond has emerged as a distinctive yet wholly representative voice in the British theatre – representative not of a school of dramatists, but of that growing concern for ecological values which became widespread in the early 1970's, and of which Bond emerged as an early prophet. Not that he engages in the immediacies of the debate: but from the first his plays have had to do with the "quality of life," in a sense far wider than would have been understood by dramatists a generation earlier. He is concerned with the effects an increasingly technological society has had upon the relations between man and man, and between man and his environment, while recognising that there can be no return to the superficially attractive values of a rustic past.

In the earliest plays, *The Pope's Wedding* and *Saved*, these issues were presented through a direct reflection of two contrasting but contemporary social settings – respectively, deprived rural and urban working-class communities, in East Anglia and South London. Primarily, however, both plays held a compelling narrative line: whether in the slow, hermit-like withdrawal of a once braggardly country youth in *The Pope's Wedding*, or the slender hope represented in *Saved* by the survival of one man's inarticulate sense of goodness amidst moral and social lethargy, they sustained the interest on the simple level of event succeeding event. And, of course, both contained an element of violence which for some has given a misleading emphasis to Bond's work: for the dramatist himself, the violence is a consequence of the state of society and (more to the point dramatically) it is also consequential.

These early plays were already assured in their self-developing episodic structures, precise in their very different but distinctive verbal idioms, and, incidentally, often very funny

73

indeed. In all his later work Bond has abandoned contemporary for semi-historical – and sometimes fully mythic – settings. Although *Early Morning*, his third play, is apparently identifiable with a precise historical period, the mid-Victorian age, its surreal combination of anachronism and total moral anarchy quickly (too quickly) lifts it to a symbolic level. Its nightmarish sequence of plots and counter-plots involving many Victorian archetypes (and not a few of Bond's own) has its compulsive quality, but *Early Morning* remains the only one of Bond's plays where the lack of moral co-ordinates blurs the impact of the statements he is making.

It is thus in marked contrast to *Narrow Road to the Deep North* – whose setting in "seventeenth, eighteenth, or nineteenth century" Japan is also anachronistic, but here for the purpose of establishing a clear counterpoint between oriental and western values. The poet Basho seeks ivory-towered enlightenment as the balance of power shifts between home-grown and imported modes of oppression: yet while Christian imperialism is lampooned, the alternative is in no way romanticised, and the stylised slaughter by the Japanese tyrant Shogo of the children of a mission school is a remarkable theatrical moment, incongruous yet immensely moving. The play is structured throughout with an austere fluidity, and marked a further progression in Bond's sure feeling for formal propriety.

His next work moved from the quasi-historical to the truly mythic. And, fine as some of his more recent plays have been, *Lear* must stand as his highest artistic achievement to date. The play had its beginnings in Bond's dissatisfaction with various elements in Shakespeare's version, but it stands entirely in its own right in its vision of the once authoritarian, dispossessed Lear travelling a lonely road of self-discovery as his daughters do battle for his kingdom, and the revolutionary leader Cordelia perpetuates Lear's mistakes. He dies in a futile attempt to dismantle the wall into whose "defensive" construction he had diverted the energies of his kingdom.

Lear is a very personal achievement, yet persuades one of its dramatic rightness, and impels with its moral force. The ghost who has to die a second time is a recurrent figure in Bond's plays – yet here it is no idiosyncratic ingredient, but an entirely appropriate embodiment of an insidiously attractive way of living in which Lear once found refuge, but which ultimately, like the ghost, must be allowed to die. On paper, the symbolism may intrude: but Bond writes for the stage, and the increasingly skeletal visual image is perhaps the only possible "companion" for Lear on his lonely journey.

In *The Sea*, Bond apparently transposes Chekhov to an English seaside resort, evoking an atmosphere of Edwardian self-assurance overshadowed by tidings of war and social unrest. An accidental drowning brings together a young man and woman, and gives focus to a convergence of local eccentrics, a sort of gauntlet for the couple to run – the aristocratic Mrs. Rafi, the ur-fascist shopkeeper Hatch, the seashore hermit Evens, and many lesser grotesques who merge with everyday elements to form a vision that is, again, fully self-sufficient, yet wholly individual.

This is less true, however, of *Bingo*, in which Shakespeare's historical complicity in the Welcombe enclosures is seen as a betrayal of his art. Perhaps because the incidental events and characters here *seem* incidental to the dramatist's self-determined death, the play lacks the integration of *The Sea* – as it also denies its central character the redemption of *Lear*. *The Fool* is a much more satisfying recreation of a poet's relationship to his society: in this case the poet is John Clare, and he too is caught in the upheavals of an age of enclosures. Here, the environment is fully realized, as is Clare's withdrawal into madness, and a complex balance of sympathies is struck. An opening mumming scene, a boxing match in Hyde Park, the final scene in the madhouse – all bear witness alike to Bond's vividly *theatrical* vision, and to his ability to weave such disparate threads into a unified work of dramatic art. In the blending of satisfaction with an artistic experience and dissatisfaction with the society it has evoked, Bond comes closer to Brecht than any other writer in the modern British theatre.

—Simon Trussler

BOTTOMLEY, Gordon. English. Born in Keighley, Yorkshire, 20 February 1874. Educated at Keighley Grammar School. Married Emily Burton in 1905 (died, 1947). President, Scottish Community Drama Association; Vice-President, British Drama League. Recipient: Femina-Vie Heureuse Prize, 1923; Royal Society of Literature Benson Medal, 1928. LL.D: University of Aberdeen, 1930; D.Litt.: University of Durham, 1940; Litt.D.: University of Leeds, 1944. Fellow, Royal Society of Literature, 1926. *Died 25 August 1948.*

PUBLICATIONS

Collections

Poems and Plays, edited by Claude Colleer Abbott. 1953.

Plays

The Crier by Night (produced 1916). 1902.
Midsummer Eve (produced 1930). 1905.
Laodice and Danaë (produced 1930). 1909.
The Riding to Lithend (produced 1928). 1909.
King Lear's Wife (produced 1915). 1920.
Britain's Daughter (produced 1922). With *Gruach,* 1921.
Gruach (produced 1923). 1921.
A Parting, and The Return. 1928.
Scenes and Plays (includes *A Parting, The Return, The Sisters, The Widow, Towie Castle, Merlin's Grave, Ardvorlich's Wife, The Singing Sands*). 1929.
Lyric Plays (includes *Marsaili's Weeping, Culbin Sands, The Bower of Wandel, Suilven and the Eagle, Kirkconnel Lea, The Women from the Voe*). 1932.
The Acts of Saint Peter: A Cathedral Festival Play (produced 1933). 1933.
The White Widow (produced 1936). In *Scottish One-Act Plays,* edited by J. M. Reid, 1935.
The Falconer's Lassie (as *The Falconer's Daughter,* produced 1938). In *Choric Plays,* 1939.
Ealasaid (produced 1939). In *50 One-Act Plays,* second series, edited by Constance M. Martin, 1940.
Choric Plays and a Comedy (includes *Fire at Calbart, The Falconer's Lassie, Dunaverty*). 1939.
Fire at Calbart (produced 1944). In *Choric Plays,* 1939.
Deirdre, from works by Alexander Carmichael. 1944.
Kate Kennedy (produced 1944). 1945.
Maids of Athens. 1945.
Crookback's Crown. 1947.

Verse

The Mickle Drede and Other Verses. 1896.
Poems at White-Nights. 1899.
The Gate of Smaragdus. 1904.
Chambers of Imagery. 2 vols., 1907–12.

A Vision of Giorgione: Three Variations on Venetian Themes.   1910; revised edition, 1922.
Poems of Thirty Years.   1925.
Frescoes from Buried Temples, drawings by James Guthrie.   1927.
Festival Preludes.   1930.

Other

A Note on Poetry and the Stage.   1944(?).
A Stage for Poetry: My Purposes with My Plays.   1948.
Poet and Painter, Being the Correspondence Between Bottomley and Paul Nash 1910–46, edited by Claude Colleer Abbott and Anthony Bertram.   1955.

Editor, *Poems,* by Isaac Rosenberg.   1922; revised edition, with D. Harding, as *Collected Poems,* 1949.
Editor, with D. Harding, *The Collected Works of Isaac Rosenberg.*   1937.
Editor, *Essays by Divers Hands.*   1944.
Editor, *The Madness of Merlin,* by Laurence Binyon.   1947.

Reading List: "Bottomley" by A. J. Farmer, in *Etudes Anglaises 9,* 1956; *The Christian Tradition in Modern British Drama* by William V. Spanos, 1967.

*   *   *

The outstanding playwright among Georgian poets, Gordon Bottomley may be ranked as one of the most accomplished verse dramatists of the twentieth century after Yeats and Eliot. Never a popular writer, his reputation has not noticeably revived since his death, although his grave, polished poems recall Edward Thomas's ability to convey a complex sensibility through simple statement, a talent far removed from the *faux naïf* manner and thinness of texture commonly associated with Georgianism. That his work was largely insulated from modern life was perhaps inevitable: forced by illness to dwell remote from cities and find solace in contemplation and meditation, he was also led to reject everyday subjects by influences which included Rossetti and Morris. He maintained a wide circle of correspondents, notably Thomas and the painter Paul Nash, whose published exchanges with the poet contain valuable comments on art, literature, and drama.

It was with his plays that Bottomley discovered a public voice and gained such measure of public attention as was accorded him. The earliest dramas preserve a strong literary element, but the firm control, concentrated psychological interest, narrative tension, and interplay of forceful personalities indicate a true dramatist rather than a mere lyrical decorator. A powerful example is *The Crier by Night,* in which sexual rivalry between a farmer's sadistic wife and a proud Irish bondmaid is resolved by a supernatural water-spirit who draws husband and girl to their deaths in Lake Windermere. Comparable images of physical cruelty are found in *King Lear's Wife,* which, given pride of place in Marsh's second anthology of *Georgian Poetry,* was adversely criticized for its calculated brutality: the play offers a prologue to Shakespeare postulating an adulterous love-affair between the king and an attendant at Lear's wife's death-bed; Goneril, on discovering their clandestine relationship, kills the girl as the queen's body is prepared for burial. In summary the action sounds intolerably crude, but Bottomley invests the dialogue with the required degree of primitive splendour, and the boldly drawn figures are something more than feebly grandiloquent replicas of their Jacobean counterparts. The less sensational *Gruach,* which describes the swift courtship of the Macbeths, is an equally daring and assured performance in a more minor key. By contrast, *Britain's Daughter* is theatrical and over-wrought.

Bottomley's plays were always concerned with far-off periods and regions; in his later plays he turned to esoteric forms, choosing to work with private and amateur groups. Under the influence of Yeats's *Plays for Dancers*, from which he adopted the devices of masks, choric figures, and the concealment of the stage by unfolding a cloth, he composed a number of plays dramatizing incidents from Celtic folklore and history, in which the diction is leaner and less overtly lyrical than formerly. Of these the best are found in *Lyric Plays*, among which are *Marsaili's Weeping*, which recreates a sixteenth-century Highland tragedy, and *The Woman from the Voe*, a beautiful adaptation of a Shetland legend in which a Seal-Woman marries a mortal. *A Stage for Poetry* sets out Bottomley's views on drama, and forms an admirable record of his achievements.

—William M. Tydeman

BOUCICAULT, Dion.   Irish.   Born Dionysius Lardner Bourcicault in Dublin, probably in December 1820. Educated at schools in Dublin; Thomas Wright Hill's school at Bruce Castle, Tottenham, London; possibly University of London. Married 1) Anne Guiot in 1845 (died, 1848); 2) the actress Agnes Robertson in 1853 (separated, 1885; divorced, 1888), six children; 3) eloped with the actress Louise Thorndyke in 1885, married, 1888, two children. Actor and playwright from 1838; achieved first success in 1841; appeared frequently in New York from 1853; Temporary Manager of Drury Lane theatre, London, 1862; Manager of Astley's, London, 1863; retired to America, 1875. *Died 18 September 1890.*

PUBLICATIONS

Collections

Forbidden Fruit and Other Plays (includes *Louis XI, Dot, Robert Emmett, Flying Scud, Mercy Dodd*), edited by Allardyce Nicoll and F. T. Clark.   1940.
The Dolmen Boucicault (includes *The Colleen Bawn, Arragh-na-Pogue, The Shaughraun*), edited by David Krause.   1964.

Plays

A Legend of the Devil's Dyke (produced 1838).   1898.
Lodgings to Let (produced 1839).
Jack Sheppard (produced 1839).
London Assurance (produced 1841).   1841; edited by Ronald Eyre, 1971.
The Old Guard (produced 1842).   1900(?).
The Irish Heiress (produced 1842).   1842.
A Lover by Proxy (produced 1842).   1845(?).
Alma Mater; or, A Cure for Coquettes (produced 1842).   1842(?).
Curiosities of Literature (produced 1842).   1842(?).
The Bastille (produced 1842).
Woman (produced 1843).
Victor and Hortense; or, False Pride (produced 1843).
Laying a Ghost (produced 1843).

Sharp's the Word (produced 1843).

Old Heads and Young Hearts (produced 1844). 1845.

Used Up, with Charles Matthews, from a play by F. A. Duvert and A. T. de Lauzanne de Vauxroussel (produced 1844). 1848(?).

Judith; or, The Maid of Geneva (produced 1844).

The Fox and the Goose; or, The Widow's Husband, with Ben Webster, music by Ambroise Thomas (produced 1844). 1844.

Don Caesar de Bazan; or, Love and Honour, with Ben Webster, from a play by P. F. Dumanoir and Adolph Dennery (produced 1844). 1844.

Lolah; or, The Wreck Light (produced 1844).

Love in a Sack (produced 1844).

Mother and Son (produced 1844).

A Soldier of Fortune; or, The Irish Settler, with Ben Webster (produced 1845).

Enquire Within (produced 1845).

Up the Flue; or, What's in the Wind, with Charles Kenney (produced 1846; also produced as *Who Did It?*).

The Old School (produced 1846).

Mr. Peter Piper; or, Found Out at Last (produced 1846).

The Wonderful Water Cure, with Ben Webster (produced 1846). N.d.

Shakespeare in London (produced 1846).

The School for Scheming (produced 1847). 1847(?).

A Confidence (produced 1848).

The Knight of Arva (produced 1848). 1868(?).

The Willow Copse, with Charles Kenney, from a play by Frederic Soulie (produced 1849). 1856(?).

A Radical Cure (produced 1850).

La Garde Nationale (produced 1850).

Giralda; or, The Invisible Husband, from a play by Scribe (produced 1850); revised version, as *A Dark Night's Work* (produced 1870).

L'Abbaye de Castro (produced 1851).

Sixtus V; or, The Broken Vow, with John Bridgeman, from a play by Dinaux and Lemoine (produced 1851). 1851; as *The Pope of Rome*, n.d.

Love in a Maze (produced 1851). 1851.

The Dame of Spades, from a play by Scribe (as *The Queen of Spades*, produced 1851). 1851.

O'Flannigan and the Fairies (produced 1851).

The Corsican Brothers; or, The Vendetta, from a play by Dumas père (produced 1852). 1852; edited by Michael Booth, in *English Plays of the Nineteenth Century 2*, 1969.

The Phantom, from a play by Carmouche, de Jouffrey, and Charles Nodier (as *The Vampire*, produced 1852; as *The Phantom*, produced 1862). 1852(?).

The Prima Donna (produced 1852). 1852(?).

The Fox Hunt; or, Don Quixote II (produced 1853; as *The Fox Chase*, produced 1864).

The Sentinel, music by Stöpel (produced 1853).

Genevieve; or, The Reign of Terror, from a play by Dumas père and Auguste Maquet (produced 1853).

The Young Actress, from the work *The Manager's Daughter* by Edward Lancaster (produced 1853).

Faust and Marguerite, from a play by Michel Carré (produced 1854). 1854.

Janet Pride (produced 1854).

Andy Blake; or, The Irish Diamond, from a play by Bayard and Vanderburch (produced 1854). 1884.

The Devil's in It, from a play by Scribe (produced 1854).

The Fairy Star (produced 1854).

Apollo in New York (produced 1854).

Pierre the Foundling, from a play by Mme. Dudevant (produced 1854).

Eugénie; or, A Sister's Vow (produced 1855).

Louis XI, King of France, from a play by Casimir Delavigne (produced 1855).   1855; in *Forbidden Fruit and Other Plays,* 1940.

Agnes Robertson at Home (produced 1855).

There's Nothing in It (produced 1855).

Grimaldi; or, Scenes in the Life of an Actress, from a play by Anicet-Bourgeois and Théodore Barrière (produced 1855; as *Violet,* produced 1856).   1856.

The Cat Changed into a Woman, from a play by Scribe (produced 1855).

Rachel Is Coming (produced 1855).

The Chameleon (produced 1855).

Azael; or, The Prodigal, from a play by Scribe (produced 1856).

Una (produced 1856).

Blue Belle, from a play by Adolphe de Leuven and Mazilier, music by Adolphe Adam (produced 1856).

The Streets of New York, from a play by Brisebarre and Nus (as *The Streets of London,* produced 1857; as *The Poor of Liverpool,* produced 1864; as *The Poor of New York,* produced 1864).   1857(?).

George Darville (produced 1857).

Wanted a Widow, with Immediate Possession, with Charles Seymour, from a play by Theanlon and Choquart (produced 1857).   N.d.

Jessie Brown; or, The Relief of Lucknow (produced 1858).   1858.

Pauvrette, from a play by Desnoyer and Adolph Dennery (produced 1858; also produced as *The Snow Flower*).   1858(?).

The Octoroon; or, Life in Louisiana (produced 1859).   1859.

Dot, from the story *The Cricket and the Hearth* by Dickens (produced 1859; as *A Christmas Story,* produced 1870).   In *Forbidden Fruit and Other Plays,* 1940.

Chamooni III, from a play by Scribe (produced 1859).

Smike; or, Scenes from Nicholas Nickleby, from the novel by Dickens (produced 1859).

The Colleen Bawn; or, The Brides of Garryowen, from the novel *The Collegians* by Gerald Griffin (produced 1860).   1860(?); in *The Dolmen Boucicault,* 1964; revised version, as *The Lily of Killarney,* with John Oxenford, music by Jules Benedict (produced 1862), 1863.

Vanity Fair (produced 1860).

The Trial of Effie Deans; or, The Heart of Midlothian, from the novel by Scott (produced 1860).

Lady Bird; or, Harlequin Lord Dundreary (produced 1862).

How She Loves Him! (produced 1863).   1868.

Omoo; or, The Sea of Ice, from a play by Adolph Dennery and Dugue (produced 1864).

Arrah-na-Pogue; or, The Wicklow Wedding (produced 1864).   1865; in *The Dolmen Boucicault,* 1964.

Rip Van Winkle, from the play by Joe Jefferson based on the story by Washington Irving (produced 1865).   Edited by Arthur Hobson Quinn, in *Representative American Plays,* 1917.

The Two Lives of Mary Leigh (produced 1866; as *Hunted Down,* produced 1866).

The Parish Clerk (produced 1866).

The Long Strike (produced 1866).   1870(?); as *The Strike* (produced 1896).

Flying Scud; or, A Four Legged Fortune (produced 1866).   In *Forbidden Fruit and Other Plays,* 1940.

Wild Goose, with Lester Wallack, from the work *Rosedale* by Wallack (produced 1867).

Foul Play, with Charles Reade (produced 1868; revised version, produced 1868).   1868; revised version, as *Our Seamen* (produced 1874); as *The Scuttled Ship* (produced 1877).

After Dark: A Tale of London Life (produced 1868). N.d.; edited by J. O. Bailey, in *British Plays of the Nineteenth Century,* 1966.

Presumptive Evidence, from a play by Moreau, Siraudin, and Delacour (produced 1869; as *Mercy Dodd,* produced 1874). In *Forbidden Fruit and Other Plays,* 1940.

Seraphine; or, A Devotee, from a play by Sardou (produced 1869).

Formosa; or, The Railroad to Ruin (produced 1869). 1869; revised version (produced 1891).

Lost at Sea: A London Story, with H. J. Byron (produced 1869).

Paul La Farge; or, Self Made (produced 1870).

The Rapparee; or, The Treaty of Limerick (produced 1870). N.d.

Jezebel; or, The Dead Reckoning, from a play by Anicet-Bourgeois and Michel Masson (produced 1870). 1870.

Dreams, from the play *My Lady Clara* by T. W. Robertson (produced 1870).

Elfie; or, The Cherry-Tree Inn (produced 1871). N.d.

Night and Morning, from a play by Emile de Girardin (produced 1871). N.d.; revised version, as *Kerry* (produced 1893).

John Bull; or, The Gentleman's Fireside, from the play by George Colman the Younger (produced 1872).

Babil and Bijou; or, The Lost Regalia, songs by J. R. Planché (produced 1872).

Led Astray, from a play by Octave Feuillet (produced 1873). 1873(?).

Mora; or, The Golden Fetters (produced 1873).

A Man of Honor, from a play by Dumas fils (produced 1873).

The O'Dowd; or, Life in Galway, from a play by Cormon and Grange (produced 1873; as *Daddy O'Dowd,* produced 1880; also produced as *Suil-a-mor).* 1909.

Mimi, from a play by Théodore Barrière and Henry Murger (produced 1873).

The Shaughraun (produced 1874). 1880; in *The Dolmen Boucicault,* 1964.

Boucicault in California (produced 1874).

Venice Preserved, from the play by Otway (produced 1874).

Belle Lamar (produced 1874; as *Fin Maccoul,* produced 1887). Edited by Garrett H. Leverton, in *Plays for the College Theatre,* 1932.

Forbidden Fruit (produced 1876). In *Forbidden Fruit and Other Plays,* 1940.

A Bridal Tour (produced 1877; as *Marriage,* produced 1880).

Norah's Vows (produced 1878).

Clarissa Harlowe, from the novel by Richardson (produced 1878).

Spell-Bound (produced 1879).

Rescued; or, A Girl's Romance (produced 1879).

Contempt of Court (produced 1879).

Vice Versa, from a play by Duru and Chivot (produced 1883).

The Amadan (produced 1883).

Robert Emmett, from a work by Frank Marshall (produced 1884). In *Forbidden Fruit and Other Plays,* 1940.

The Jilt (produced 1885). 1904.

Phryne; or, The Romance of a Young Wife (produced 1887).

Captain Swift, from a play by Haddon Chambers (produced 1888).

The Spae Wife, from the novel *Guy Mannering* by Scott (produced 1888; also produced as *Cuishla Ma Chree).*

Jimmy Watt (produced 1890; as *The Tale of a Coat,* produced 1890).

Lend Me Your Wife, from a play by Maurice Desvallières (produced 1890).

99 (produced 1891).

Fiction

Foul Play, with Charles Reade. 1868.

Other

The Story of Ireland. 1881.
The Art of Acting. 1926.

Reading List: *The Career of Boucicault* by Townsend Walsh, 1915; *Boucicault* by Julius H. Tolson, unpublished dissertation, University of Pennsylvania, 1951; *Boucicault* by Robert Hogan, 1969.

*   *   *

Extraordinarily clever and precocious, the young Dion Boucicault played leading roles in his teens in the English provinces; and his first major work, the comedy of *London Assurance*, was the great London success of the 1841 season. A comedy of manners, the play reflected palely but truly the great comedies of the eighteenth century and the Restoration. It was one of the most performed English plays in the last half of the nineteenth century, and even now in occasional revivals has not quite outlived its effectiveness. With a handful of other comedies and farces from the 1840's − particularly *Old Heads and Young Hearts* − Boucicault has a secure place among the minor English dramatists; and the breezy flipness of his dialogue seems thin only in comparison to the wit of such predecessors as Congreve, Vanbrugh, Goldsmith, and Sheridan, and of such successors as Wilde and Shaw.

In the 1850's, because of the much poorer royalties playwrights were receiving for new and original work, Boucicault began churning out a long succession of potboilers and adaptations. In such plays, he incorporated a dash of comedy, of pathos, of romance, and of melodrama, as well as depictions of recent historical events, illustrations of new scientific discoveries, and sensational scenes involving avalanches, burning tenements, subway trains, and racing horses. His plots were now melodramatic, his characters stereotypical, and his themes exaggeratedly heroic and sentimental. Nevertheless, he always retained a superb sense of what worked in the theatre and a fine flair for comic situations and glib dialogue. The most memorable of his many stage entertainments were his Irish comic-melodramas, particularly *The Colleen Bawn*, *Arrah-na-Pogue*, and *The Shaughraun*. In these plays he exploited the stage-Irishman as a genial, whimsical, lovable scamp rather than as a crude Hibernian lout; and his acting of these roles was thought to rank among the best comic work of the day. His adaptation of *Rip Van Winkle* for Joe Jefferson was little more − but nothing less − than a fine American equivalent.

Boucicault wrote more (perhaps many more) than 125 plays, and was one of the leading actors and managers of the late nineteenth-century theatre. He divided his time mainly between England and America, but travelled as far afield as Australia. His personal life was sometimes stormy and often marred by scandal; and, after amassing and spending several fortunes, he died in somewhat reduced circumstances in New York City in 1890. His contemporaries remembered him with both delight and loathing; and his work and personality retain more fascination and demand more tolerance than perhaps any other stage personality of his time.

—Robert Hogan

BRIDIE, James.   Pseudonym for Osborne Henry Mavor.   Scottish.   Born in Glasgow, 3

January 1888. Educated at Glasgow Academy; Glasgow High School; University of Glasgow (Editor, *University Magazine*); qualified as a physician; Fellow of the Royal Faculty of Physicians and Surgeons, Glasgow. Served with the Royal Army Medical Corps, 1914–19, 1939–42. Married Rona Bremner; two sons. Professor of Medicine, Anderson College, Glasgow; Honorary Consulting Physician, and Governor, Victoria Infirmary, Glasgow. Founder, with Paul Vincent Carroll, Glasgow Citizen's Theatre, 1943; Founder, Glasgow College of Drama, 1950. Member of the Council, League of Dramatists; Scottish Chairman, Arts Council of Great Britain. LL.D.: University of Glasgow, 1939. Fellow, Royal Society of Literature. C.B.E. (Commander, Order of the British Empire), 1946. *Died 29 January 1951.*

PUBLICATIONS

Plays

> *The Jackals of Lone Pine Gulch* (produced 1918).
> *The Sunlight Sonata; or, To Meet the Seven Deadly Sins* (produced 1928). In *The Switchback* ..., 1930.
> *The Switchback* (produced 1929). In *The Switchback* ..., 1930; revised version (produced 1931).
> *What It Is to Be Young* (produced 1929). In *Colonel Wotherspoon and Other Plays*, 1934.
> *The Anatomist: A Lamentable Comedy of Know, Burke, and Hare, and the West Port Murders* (produced 1930). In *The Anatomist and Other Plays*, 1931.
> *The Girl Who Did Not Want to Go to Kuala Lumpur* (produced 1930). In *Colonel Wotherspoon and Other Plays*, 1934.
> *Tobias and the Angel* (produced 1930). In *The Anatomist and Other Plays*, 1931.
> *The Switchback, The Pardoner's Tale, The Sunlight Sonata.* 1930.
> *The Dancing Bear* (produced 1931). In *Colonel Wotherspoon and Other Plays*, 1934.
> *The Anatomist and Other Plays* (includes *Tobias and the Angel* and *The Amazed Evangelist*). 1931.
> *The Amazed Evangelist* (produced 1932). In *The Anatomist and Other Plays*, 1931.
> *Jonah and the Whale: A Morality* (produced 1932). 1932; revised version, as *The Sign of the Prophet Jonah* (broadcast, 1942), in *Plays for Plain People*, 1944.
> *A Sleeping Clergyman* (produced 1933). 1933.
> *Marriage Is No Joke* (produced 1934). 1934.
> *Colonel Wotherspoon; or, The Fourth Way of Greatness* (produced 1934). In *Colonel Wotherspoon and Other Plays*, 1934.
> *Mary Read*, with Claud Gurney (produced 1934). 1935.
> *Colonel Wotherspoon and Other Plays* (includes *What It Is to Be Young, The Dancing Bear, The Girl Who Did Not Want to Go to Kuala Lumpur*). 1934.
> *The Black Eye* (produced 1935). 1935.
> *Mrs. Waterbury's Millennium.* 1935.
> *The Tragic Muse*, in *Scottish One-Act Plays*, edited by J. M. Reid. 1935.
> *Storm in a Teacup*, from a play by Bruno Frank (produced 1936; as *Storm over Patsy*, produced 1937). 1936.
> *Susannah and the Elders* (produced 1937). In *Susannah and the Elders and Other Plays*, 1940.
> *Roger – Not So-Jolly*, with Ronald Mavor. 1937.
> *The King of Nowhere* (produced 1938). In *The King of Nowhere and Other Plays*, 1938.
> *Babes in the Wood* (produced 1938). 1938.
> *The Last Trump* (produced 1938). In *The King of Nowhere and Other Plays*, 1938.

The Kitchen Comedy (broadcast 1938). In *Susannah and the Elders and Other Plays,* 1940.

The King of Nowhere and Other Plays (includes *The Last Trump* and *Babes in the Wood*). 1938.

The Letter-Box Rattles. 1938.

The Golden Legend of Shults (produced 1939). In *Susannah and the Elders and Other Plays,* 1940.

What Say They? (produced 1939). 1939.

Susannah and the Elders and Other Plays (includes *What Say They?, The Golden Legend of Shults, The Kitchen Comedy*). 1940.

The Niece of the Hermit Abraham (produced 1942; revised version, as *The Dragon and the Dove; or, How the Hermit Abraham Bought the Devil for his Niece,* produced 1943).

Jonah 3 (produced 1942). In *Plays for Plain People,* 1944.

Holy Isle (produced 1942). In *Plays for Plain People,* 1944.

A Change for the Worse (produced 1943). In *Tedious and Brief,* 1944.

Mr. Bolfry (produced 1943). In *Plays for Plain People,* 1944.

It Depends What You Mean: An Improvisation for the Glockenspiel (produced 1944). 1948.

The Forrigan Reel (produced 1944; revised version, produced 1945). In *John Knox and Other Plays,* 1949.

Plays for Plain People (includes *Lancelot, Holy Isle, Mr. Bolfry, Jonah 3, The Sign of the Prophet Jonah, The Dragon and the Dove*). 1944.

Lancelot (produced 1945). In *Plays for Plain People,* 1944.

The Pyrate's Den (produced 1946).

The Wild Duck, from a play by Ibsen (produced 1946–47?).

Dr. Angelus (produced 1947). In *John Knox and Other Plays,* 1949.

Gog and Magog (produced 1948).

Daphne Laureola (produced 1949). 1949.

John Knox and Other Plays (includes *Dr. Angelus, It Depends What You Mean, The Forrigan Reel*). 1949.

The Tintock Cup, with George Munro (produced 1949).

Mr. Gillie (produced 1950). 1950.

Red Riding Hood, with others (produced 1950).

The Baikie Charivari; or, The Seven Prophets (produced 1952). 1953.

Meeting at Night, edited by Archibald Batty (produced 1954). 1956.

Screenplays: *Under Capricorn,* with Hume Cronyn, 1949; *Stage Fright,* with Alma Reville and Whitfield Cook, 1950.

Fiction

The Christmas Card (story). 1949.

Other

Some Talk of Alexander: A Revue with Interludes in the Antique Mode. 1926.

The Perilous Adventures of Sir Bingo Walker of Alpaca Square (juvenile). 1931.

Alphabet for Little Glasgow Highbrows (essays). 1934.

One Way of Living (autobiography). 1939.

Tedious and Brief (miscellany). 1944.

The British Drama. 1945.

A Small Stir: Letters on the English, with M. McLaren.   1949.

Reading List: *Bridie and His Theatre: A Study of Bridie's Personality, His Stage Plays, and His Work for the Foundation of a Scottish National Theatre* by Winifred Bannister, 1955; *Bridie: Clown and Philosopher* by Helen L. Luybem, 1965.

*   *   *

O.H. Mavor (James Bridie) is an elusive man: unlike some of his contemporaries who shunned publicity and deliberately kept their private lives private (one could cite Edwin Muir), he appears to have enjoyed public life, yet to have cultivated an impish sense of humour to disconcert would-be critics and reviewers. This is especially obvious in his scintillating autobiographical sketch *One Way of Living,* which gives the picture of a clever medical student and practising doctor with a preference for literature, but the need for a more profitable source of income. Bridie's output was prodigious, its quality inevitably uneven, but at his best he is a notable figure in modern British drama and some of his work stands up to revival exceptionally well.

The theatre in Scotland for which Bridie worked inherited neither a strong corps of Scottish-born actors of first talent, nor a tradition of Scottish dramatic writing. For many years frowned on by civic and religious authority, the theatre in Scotland was a late developer. Bridie found it difficult to have his plays performed to his satisfaction, despite some very fortunate choices of actors, but eventually he conquered London's West End, and by the time of his death was a widely-accepted household name.

Comparison with Barrie is impossible to avoid. Barrie aimed openly for London and big-time success, and his plays are professional in appealing to a wide audience and, particularly in his fantasy plays, in achieving a state of emotional involvement on the part of the audience which suspends disbelief. Barrie's great contemporary is quite opposite: Bridie is a confirmed satirist (though always a serious playwright), a man in whose work reality intrudes painfully. Impatient and brusque with those whose ideologies or religious orthodoxies are second-hand or uncritical, like Mr. McCrimmon in *Mr. Bolfry,* iconoclastic – to the medical profession in *The Anatomist* and *A Sleeping Clergyman,* to educationists in *Mr. Gillie,* and to the Old Testament in the delightful skit *Tobias and the Angel* – Bridie is out to startle and to challenge rather than to achieve Barrie's successes simply by imitation. The parallel can be carried too far: Bridie uses his Scottish backgrounds when it suits him to establish an identifiable atmosphere and control the emotional response in consequence (he does this in *Mr. Gillie* shamelessly), and Barrie, of course, has moments of tough self-analysis, particularly in his fiction. Yet the main point emerges strongly that Bridie is a masterful manipulator of dialogue and comic effect, clearly indebted to Shaw in the mischievous puncturing of affectation and arrogance, and the neatness with which he does it. He knows his stage well – he handles the crowds of *The Anatomist* or *Tobias* excellently; he masterfully makes the Devil's umbrella walk off-stage at the end of *Mr. Bolfry,* when the characters are convincing themselves they had not seen the Devil, but merely had a nightmare; he very neatly uses the sleeping clergyman (who takes no part in the action) as a frame for several generations of family interaction and at the same time as comment on the slumbering moral guardians of an age. His moral range encompasses the passionate inhuman ambitions of Dr. Knox in *The Anatomist,* the cool angel who guides Tobias, the devil-may-care Dr. Cameron who scorns his doctor's etiquette yet develops the serum to save the world from plague, the emptiness of the failed teacher in *Mr. Gillie* who sees his creature move away from the dreams he had planned for him. There are odd moments of anticipation, of Muriel Spark's Miss Brodie, of Edward Albee's handling of disembodied characters as spectators of their own deaths. The form of the enclosed stage is stretched as far as it can go, the comment on society as wide as possible.

The variety of his achievement, often touching on sensitive moral issues, is easy to overlook because of the genial humour which never deserts him, and which expresses itself in light and well-handled humorous dialogue. But the satirist is always waiting in the wings, and the simplest speeches have currents of irony. The man who wrote "Some generalisations, even if they are made about women, are true. At least, they are what are called facts" can never be taken at face value.

In his preface to *Colonel Wotherspoon and Other Plays* Bridie confessed himself a professional playwright, and acknowledged his indebtedness to actors and producers, and he disclaimed writing either an overtly moral play, or what he mockingly called "the first Great Scottish Play." "The truth is that Scotland does not yet deserve a great play.... She is due, however, a little amusement; and the only Scottish dramatist who has reached the very first rank (if we except Ben Jonson) doesn't bother himself much with morals or greatness. Indeed, if we dive for a moral in any one of the plays of Sir James Barrie, we are running the risk of a very horrid surprise." Such a man neatly defies simple description, yet such was the character of the dramatist who has so far dominated the Scottish stage in the present century.

—Ian Campbell

BRIGHOUSE, Harold. Pseudonym, with John Walton: Olive Conway. English. Born in Eccles, Lancashire, 26 July 1882. Educated at Manchester Grammar School. Served in the Royal Air Force, attached to the Intelligence Staff, Air Ministry, during World War I. Associated with Gilbert Cannan and Stanley Houghton in the repertory theatre movement in England; director of a Manchester cotton mill; Drama Critic, Manchester *Guardian*. Chairman of the Dramatic Committee, Author's Society, 1930–31. *Died 25 July 1958*.

PUBLICATIONS

Plays

> *The Doorway* (produced 1909). 1913.
> *Dealing in Futures* (produced 1909). 1913.
> *The Price of Coal* (produced 1909). 1911.
> *Graft* (as *The Polygon*, produced 1911). 1913.
> *Lonesome-Like* (produced 1911). 1914.
> *Spring in Bloomsbury* (produced 1911). 1913.
> *The Oak Settle* (produced 1911). 1911.
> *The Scaring Off of Teddy Dawson* (produced 1911). 1911.
> *The Odd Man Out* (produced 1912). 1912.
> *Little Red Shoes* (produced 1912). 1925.
> *The Game* (produced 1913). In *Three Lancashire Plays*, 1920.
> *Garside's Career* (produced 1914). 1914.
> *The Northerners* (produced 1914). In *Three Lancashire Plays*, 1920.
> *Followers: A "Cranford" Sketch* (produced 1915). 1922.
> *The Hillarys*, with Stanley Houghton (produced 1915).
> *Converts* (produced 1915). 1920.
> *Hobson's Choice* (produced 1915). 1916; edited by E. R. Wood, 1964.
> *The Road to Raebury* (produced 1915). 1921.

Zack: A Character Comedy (produced 1916).   In *Three Lancashire Plays*, 1920.

The Clock Goes Round (produced 1916).

Maid of France (produced 1917).   1917.

The Bantam V.C. (produced 1919).   1925.

Other Times (produced 1920).

The Starlight Widow, with John Walton.   1920.

Plays for the Meadow and Plays for the Lawn (includes *Maypole Morning, The Paris Doctor, The Prince Who Was a Piper, The Man about the Place*).   1921.

Once a Hero (produced 1922).   1922.

The Happy Hangman: A Grotesque (produced 1925).   1922.

Once a Year (produced 1923).

The Apple Tree; or, Why Misery Never Dies.   1923.

The Happy Man.   1923.

A Marrying Man (produced 1924).   1924.

Mary's John (produced 1924).   1925.

Becky Sharp, with John Walton, from the novel *Vanity Fair* by Thackeray (produced 1924).   1924.

Open Air Plays (includes *The Laughing Mind, The Oracles of Apollo, The Rational Princess, The Ghosts of Windsor Park, How the Weather Is Made*).   1926.

Costume Plays, with John Walton (includes *Becky Sharp, Mimi, Prudence Corner, The King's Waistcoat*).   1927.

What's Bred in the Bone (produced 1927).   1927.

The Little Liberty.   1927.

Fossie for Short, from his own novel.   1927.

The Might of "Mr. H.": A Charles Lamb Pastiche.   1927.

When Did They Meet Again?   1927.

The Witch's Daughter, in *One-Act Plays for Stage and Study 4.*   1928.

It's a Gamble (produced 1928).

Safe Amongst the Pigs (produced 1929).   1930.

Behind the Throne.   1929.

Coincidence.   1929.

The Sort-of-a-Prince.   1929.

The Stoker.   1929.

Four Fantasies for the Open Air (includes *The Exiled Princess, The Ghost in the Garden, The Romany Road, Cupid and Psyche*).   1931; augmented edition, as *Six Fantasies* (includes *The Ghosts of Windsor Park* and *The Oracles of Apollo*), 1931.

A Bit of War.   1933.

Smoke-Screens.   1933.

Exhibit C., in *Best One-Act Plays of 1933*, edited by J. W. Marriott.   1934.

Tip and Run, in Three Sections, with John Walton, in *The One-Act Theatre 1.*   1934.

The Dye-Hard, in *One-Act Plays of Today 6*, edited by J. W. Marriott.   1934.

The Great Dark, from a play by Don Totheroh.   1934.

The Boy: What Will He Become?, in *Best One-Act Plays of 1934*, edited by J. W. Marriott.   1935.

The Friendly King.   1935.

Back to Adam: A Glimpse of Three Periods.   1936.

The Wish Shop.   1936.

Mr. Somebody, from a play by Molnar (produced 1936).

Modern Plays in One Act, with John Walton (includes *One of Those Letters, Dux, When the Bells Rang, The Bureaucrats, The Desperationist, Wireless Can't Lie, Women Do Things Like That*).   1937.

Below Ground, in *Eight One-Act Plays of 1936*, edited by William Armstrong.   1937.

New Leisure, in *The Best One-Act Plays of 1936*, edited by J. W. Marriott.   1937.

Passport to Romance.   1937.

Under the Pylon, in *One-Act Plays for Stage and Study 9.* 1938.
The Funk-Hole: A Farce of the Crisis. 1939.
British Passport. 1939.
The Man Who Ignored the War. 1940.
The Golden Ray: An Idealistic Melodrama. 1941.
London Front. 1941.
Hallowed Ground, in *The Best One-Act Plays of 1941,* edited by J. W. Marriott. 1942.
Sporting Rights. 1943.
Albert Gate. 1945.
The Inner Man. 1945.
Let's Live in England, in *The Best One-Act Plays of 1944–45,* edited by J. W. Marriott. 1946.
Alison's Island, in *The Best One-Act Plays of 1946–47,* edited by J. W. Marriott. 1948.
Above Rubies, in *The Best One-Act Plays of 1952–53,* edited by H. Miller. 1954.

Fiction

Fossie for Short. 1917.
Hobson's, with Charles Forrest. 1917.
The Silver Lining. 1918.
The Marbeck Inn. 1920.
Hepplestall's. 1922.
Captain Shapely. 1923.
The Wrong Shadow: A Romantic Comedy. 1923.
Hindle Wakes. 1927.

Other

What I Have Had: Chapters in Autobiography. 1953.

Editor, *The Works of Stanley Houghton.* 3 vols., 1914.

*   *   *

It is understandable that in the public mind Harold Brighouse should be associated with the "Manchester School" of playwrights nurtured by Miss Annie Elizabeth Horniman, but unfortunate that his reputation should derive almost exclusively from a lone play, *Hobson's Choice.* His achievements were far more varied both in range and content than such a narrow view suggests. Born in Eccles, educated at Manchester Grammar School where Stanley Houghton, Ben Iden Payne, and James Agate were contemporaries, and then entering the cotton business, Brighouse was only discovered as a playwright with the opening of the Gaiety Theatre, Manchester, for repertory drama in 1908, and with Miss Horniman's determined encouragement for new authors who would supply her with plays reflecting life in the local community. His indigenous experience made him the ideal Lancastrian dramatist, but, in fact, many of his plays did not receive their premieres at the Gaiety, but at other repertory theatres in Britain; nonetheless it was to Miss Horniman that Brighouse recorded his gratitude for the opportunity to learn his craft.

It was in the demanding field of the one-act play that he first revealed his ability to handle working-class situations and characters with sensitivity and restraint, combining a tenderness which never degenerates into sentimentality with an eye for humorous quirks of personality and an ear for the turns of regional dialect. While his early full-length plays such as *Dealing in Futures, The Polygon,* and even *Garside's Career* tend to blend psychological observation and social criticism somewhat uneasily, *The Doorway*, *The Price of Coal*, and *Lonesome-Like* are masterly in their economy of construction and ease of dialogue, and in their subtle shifts of mood. Yet Brighouse's dramatic range is far from negligible: of his four full-length plays staged between 1912 and 1914, *The Odd Man Out* was a witty farce, *Garside's Career* a Lancashire comedy with education as its theme, *The Game* a spirited but somewhat improbable comedy with a professional footballing background, and *The Northerners* a grim drama based on the Luddite riots of the 1820's, somewhat hampered by its indebtedness to Victorian melodramatic conventions. And there are features in *Zack* and his post-war dramas to command interest and respect. In a number of collections, published from 1921 onwards, Brighouse's talent for charming fantasy was especially evident, although the temptation to substitute whimsy for fantasy was not always resisted. After about 1930 he tended to concentrate almost entirely on the short play and continued to enjoy success with this form.

Yet the fact remains that Brighouse never quite equalled the success of his comedy of Lancastrian manners, *Hobson's Choice*, and its perennial appeal is not hard to explain: it contains almost text-book examples of comic reversal in the "taming" of the bullying Hobson and the regeneration of the downtrodden Will Mossop by the Shavian yet humane heroine, while its essentially gentle view of lower-middle-class marriage contrasts with that presented in the plays of D. H. Lawrence written at roughly the same time. It is a beautifully structured play, full of quietly observant humour, and, while it points a moral, it does so kindly and without malice. Its place in the modern repertory seems assured.

—William M. Tydeman

BROME, Richard. English. Born in England c. 1590. Little is known about his life except that he was a servant to Ben Jonson c. 1614, and was afterwards Jonson's friend and protégé. *Died in 1652.*

PUBLICATIONS

Collections

Dramatic Works, edited by R. H. Shepherd. 3 vols., 1873.

Plays

The Northern Lass (produced 1629).   1632.
The Queen's Exchange (produced 1629–30?).   1657; as *The Royal Exchange*, 1661.
The City Wit; or, The Woman Wears the Breeches (produced 1630–31?).   In *Five New Plays*, 1653.
The Novella (produced 1632).   In *Five New Plays*, 1653.
The Weeding of Covent Garden; or, The Middlesex Justice of Peace (produced 1632?).   In *Five New Plays*, 1653.
The Love-Sick Court; or, The Ambitious Politique (produced 1633–34?).   In *Five New Plays*, 1658.

The Late Lancashire Witches, with Thomas Heywood (produced 1634). 1634.
The Sparagus Garden (produced 1635). 1640.
The New Academy; or, The New Exchange (produced 1635?). In *Five New Plays*, 1658.
The Queen and the Concubine (produced 1635–36?). In *Five New Plays*, 1658.
The English Moor; or, The Mock Marriage (produced 1637). In *Five New Plays*, 1658.
The Antipodes (produced 1638). 1640; edited by Ann Haaker, 1966.
The Damoiselle; or, The New Ordinary (produced 1638?). In *Five New Plays*, 1653.
A Mad Couple Well Matched (produced 1639?). In *Five New Plays*, 1653; edited by A.
   S. Knowland, in *Six Caroline Plays*, 1962.
The Court Beggar (produced 1640). In *Five New Plays*, 1653.
A Jovial Crew; or, The Merry Beggars (produced 1641). 1652; edited by Ann Haaker,
   1966.
Five New Plays. 1653.
Five New Plays, edited by Alexander Brome. 1658.

Other

Editor, *Monsieur Thomas*, by John Fletcher. 1639.
Editor, *Lachrymae Musarum: The Tears of the Muses* (elegies on the death of Henry,
   Lord Hastings). 1649.

Reading List: *A Study of the Comedies of Brome, Especially as Representative of Dramatic Decadence* by Herbert F. Allen, 1912; *Brome: A Study of His Life and Works* by Clarence E. Andrews, 1913; *Brome, Caroline Playwright* by R. J. Kaufmann, 1961.

*   *   *

The tradition of Jonsonian satirical comedy survived until the closing of the theatres in 1642 chiefly in the plays of Richard Brome, whom Jonson himself twice described as his servant. Between 1623, the date of his first recorded play, *A Fault of Friendship* (not extant), and 1642, when he revised a play written ten years earlier, *The Weeding of Covent Garden*, Brome was responsible for some twenty surviving plays and several others now lost. He combined a talent for satirical comedy in the Jonsonian manner with a real feeling for the more romantic comic drama of Heywood and Dekker. His two best plays, *The Northern Lass* and *A Jovial Crew*, show Brome's dramatic gifts at their happiest. Both the savage eye for the grotesque and the linguistic vitality of Jonson are lacking here, but both plays show a good deal of cheerful wit and ingenuity of plot. Another aspect of Brome's dramatic talent is displayed in *The Late Lancashire Witches*, a spirited melodrama based on topical events which he wrote in collaboration with Heywood. Among his other plays, *The Love-Sick Court* is of interest as Brome's variant on the heroic drama which held the stage in the 1630's. It is difficult to judge how far Brome intended the play as a satire on the heroic mode.

Decidedly a minor dramatist, Brome has a place in the history of English drama that is small but secure by virtue of a refreshing directness of feeling and adroitness of construction. He is the "Son of Ben" in drama to the same degree that Herrick is in lyric poetry.

—Gãmini Salgãdo

BROOKE, Henry. Irish. Born in Rantavan, County Cavan, c. 1703. Educated at Trinity College, Dublin, 1720; The Temple, London. Married his cousin Catherine Meares; 22 children. From c. 1725 divided his time between London and Dublin; became involved in English politics: because of difficulties caused by his championing the Prince of Wales against George II returned to Dublin and settled there, 1740: appointed Barrack-Master, Dublin, c. 1745; in later years suffered from mental debility. *Died 10 October 1783.*

PUBLICATIONS

Collections

Poetical Works, edited by Charlotte Brooke. 4 vols., 1792.

Plays

Gustavus Vasa, The Deliverer of His Country (as *The Patriot,* produced 1744; as *Gustavus Vasa,* produced 1805). 1739.
The Female Officer (produced 1740). In *A Collection of Plays and Poems,* 1778.
The Earl of Westmorland (as *The Betrayer of His Country,* produced 1742; as *Injured Honour,* produced 1754). In *A Collection of Plays and Poems,* 1778.
The Triumph of Hibernia, music by Niccolo Pasquali (produced 1748).
Little John and the Giants (as *Jack the Giant Queller,* produced 1749). In *A Collection of Plays and Poems,* 1778.
The Earl of Essex (produced 1750). 1761.
The Victims of Love and Honour (produced 1762). In *A Collection of Plays and Poems,* 1778.

Fiction

The Fool of Quality; or, The History of Henry, Earl of Moreland. 5 vols., 1764–70; edited by E. A. Baker, 1902.
Juliet Grenville; or, The History of the Human Heart. 1774.

Verse

Universal Beauty. 1735.
Constantia; or, The Man of Law's Tale, in *The Canterbury Tales Modernised,* edited by George Ogle. 1741.
Fables for the Female Sex, with Edward Moore. 1744.
New Fables. 1749.
A Description of the College Green Club: A Satire. 1753.
Redemption. 1772.

Other

The Farmer's Six Letters to the Protestants of Ireland. 1745; as *Essays Against Popery,* 1750.

The Secret History and Memoirs of the Barracks of Ireland.   1745.
A New Collection of Fairy Tales.   1750.
The Spirit of Party.   2 vols., 1753–54.
The Interests of Ireland Considered.   1759.
The Case of the Roman Catholics of Ireland.   1760.
Trial of the Cause of the Roman Catholics.   1761.
A Proposal for the Restoration of Public Wealth and Credit.   1762(?).
A Collection of Plays and Poems (includes, besides the plays listed above, *The Vestal Virgin, The Marriage Contract, Montezuma, The Imposter, The Contending Brother, The Charitable Association, Cymbeline, Antony and Cleopatra*).   4 vols., 1778.

Translator, *Tasso's Jerusalem Delivered* (books 1–2).   1738.
Translator, *A New System of Fairy; or, A Collection of Fairy Tales,* by Comte de Caylus.   2 vols., 1750.

Reading List: *Brookiana: Anecdotes of Brooke* by C. H. Wilson, 2 vols., 1804; *Memoirs of Brooke* by Isaac D'Olier, 1816; *Brooke* by H. Wright, 1927.

*   *   *

The eighteenth century so abounds in truly great novelists that excellent or eccentric second-raters are ignored. John Wesley hailed *The Fool of Quality* as "one of the most beautiful pictures that ever was drawn in the world; the strokes are so fine, the touches so easy, natural, and affecting, that I know not who can survey it with tearless eyes, unless he has a heart of stone." Now it may win only a notice in some learned discussion of William Law's *A Serious Call to the Devout and Holy Life* or of Shaftesbury's sentimental philosophy. In fact, Brooke's sentimental and discursive picaresque novel, with its variety, vivacity, and breeziness, ought to be linked with the "free fantasia" school of fiction in Sterne's wake, and with an eye to the influence of Rousseau.

Brooke's tragedy *Gustavus Vasa* (banned in London as revolutionary but produced in Dublin as *The Patriot*), is better know than *The Fool of Quality*. It deals with the Job-like tribulations of the Nordic giant who in the years following 1521 strove to unify and strengthen the kingdom of Sweden. Strindberg's play of the same name centers on the man himself; Brooke centers on the manipulations of the plot, and ends with fustian bombast. Brooke's *Earl of Essex* escaped the "bow-wow" attack of Dr. Johnson on *Gustavus Vasa*, but is inferior to it.

Brooke's verse is of interest for two reasons. "Conrade," purporting to be a fragment of old Celtic saga, fits into the poetic revival of Irish poetry exemplified by the Ossian controversy. Pope is said to have assisted Brooke in *Universal Beauty*, and the poem was highly praised in its day. Bonamy Dobrée (in *English Literature in the Early Eighteenth Century*) says that Brooke "most nearly made a real poem out of science"; like Erasmus Darwin's *Temple of Love*, it repays investigation. Brooke was also a sincere and articulate political writer, especially on the Jacobite tendencies of the Irish Catholics and the notorious penal laws.

—Leonard R. N. Ashley

BUCKINGHAM, 2nd Duke of; George Villiers.   English.   Born in Westminster, London,

30 January 1628; succeeded to the dukedom, 1628; raised by King Charles I with his own children. Educated at Trinity College, Cambridge M.A. 1642. At the beginning of the Civil War joined the King at Oxford and served under Prince Rupert at the storming of Lichfield Close, 1643; later committed to the care of the Earl of Northumberland; sent on a Continental tour, lived in Florence and Rome; served under the Earl of Holland, in Surrey, during the second civil war, 1648; after defeat of the Royalists, escaped to France; appointed by Charles II a Member of the Order of the Garter, 1649, and Privy Councillor, 1650; appointed General of the Eastern Association of Forces, 1650, also commissioned to raise forces for the King on the Continent; Commander-in-Chief of the English royalists in Scotland, 1651; lands sequestered, 1651; accompanied Charles II on his expedition to England, quarrelled with the King, and returned to exile in Holland, 1651; returned to England, 1657; imprisoned in the Tower of London, 1658–59; served with the forces of Lord Fairfax, 1660. Married Mary Fairfax in 1657; later associated with the Countess of Shrewsbury, by whom he had a son. Recovered his estates at the Restoration; became gentleman of the king's bedchamber, 1660, and Privy Councillor, 1662; Lord Lieutenant of the West Riding of Yorkshire, 1661–67; briefly imprisoned and stripped of office for opposition to government policies, 1667; served as the King's principal minister in the "Cabal" administration, 1667–69; appointed master of the horse, 1668; replaced by Arlington in the King's confidence and kept ignorant of private negotiations with the French King, 1669, 1670; negotiated treaties with France for attack upon Holland, 1670, 1672; appointed Lieutenant General, 1673; quarrelled openly with Arlington, whom the King supported, 1673, and censured by Parliament for the French treaties, and deprived of his offices by the King, 1674; joined the Country Party, and thereafter acted as a leader of the opposition in the House of Lords, working for the establishment of a Whig parliament; admitted Freeman of the City of London, 1681; after the accession of James II abandoned public career and retired to Yorkshire. *Died 16 April 1687.*

PUBLICATIONS

Collections

> *Works*, edited by Tom Brown. 1704; revised edition, 2 vols., 1715.
> *Works*, edited by T. Percy. 1806(?).

Plays

> *The Chances*, from the play by Fletcher (produced 1667). 1682.
> *The Rehearsal* (produced 1671). 1672; revised version, 1675; edited by D. E. L. Crane, 1976.
> *The Militant Couple, The Belgic Hero Unmasked,* and *The Battle,* in *Works.* 1704.
> *The Country Gentleman,* with Robert Howard, edited by Arthur H. Scouten and Robert D. Hume. 1976.

Other

> *A Letter to Sir Thomas Osborn upon the Reading of a Book Called The Present Interest of England.* 1672.
> *A Short Discourse upon the Reasonableness of Men's Having a Religion.* 1685.

Reading List: *Plays about the Theatre* by Dane F. Smith, 1936; *Great Villiers* by Hester W. Chapman, 1949; *The Burlesque Tradition in the English Theatre after 1660* by V. C. Clinton-Baddeley, 1952; *A Rake and His Times* by John H. Wilson, 1954; "*The Rehearsal*: A Study of Its Satirical Methods" by Peter Lewis, in *Durham University Journal*, March 1970.

*　　*　　*

Just as *Don Quixote* and *The Dunciad* have outlived the hack writing they parodied, so Buckingham's *The Rehearsal* survives as an eminently stageworthy play, while the heroic tragedies it burlesqued are studied more often for the theories justifying their form than for their intrinsic interest. *The Rehearsal* was Buckingham's single major contribution to the drama (though his adaptation of Fletcher's *The Chances* is still occasionally preferred to its original), for he was, as Dryden claimed in *Absalom and Achitophel*, "everything by starts, and nothing long," a man of curious vice, and considerable virtuosity.

Though first drafted in the mid-1660's, *The Rehearsal* did not reach the stage till 1671, by which time the heroic dramas of Davenant, Boyle, Dryden, Stapylton, and the Howards had successfully caught and held the public taste. In the following year, Dryden, recently created laureate, could still claim that heroic verse was "in possession of the stage," and that "very few tragedies, in this age, shall be received without it." That he himself shortly afterwards abandoned the form for good was in no small part due to the success of *The Rehearsal*, in which he is caricatured as the mock-dramatist Bayes.

The play anticipates many of the techniques perfected in the great age of burlesque, the early eighteenth century, in its rehearsal framework, and in its employment of "bathos," as re-defined by Pope. Its "plot" — the attempted usurpation of the two-seater throne of the Kingdom of Brentford — is bedecked with ludicrous imagery, absurd discoveries (a banquet appears out of a coffin), and contrived twists and turns in the action. Moreover, the framework permits Bayes to make a fool of himself in his own annotations to his play. Heroic drama could withstand charges of unreality (it was, after all, concerned with elevated behaviour): but Buckingham made it appear downright absurd, and so hastened its end.

—Simon Trussler

BUCKSTONE, John Baldwin. English. Born in Hoxton, London, 14 September 1802. Educated at schools in London; briefly employed on a man-of-war, then returned to school; later articled to a solicitor. Married; one daughter. Actor-comedian: appeared on the provincial stage, 1820–23; made his London debut, 1823, and thereafter appeared at numerous London theatres; member of the Coburg Company, 1824–27, and of the Terry Company at the Adelphi Theatre, 1827–40; also appeared in his own plays at the Haymarket Theatre, summers 1833–39; visited America, 1840–42; on his return to England joined the Haymarket Theatre: Actor/Manager of the Haymarket, 1853–76. *Died 31 December 1879.*

PUBLICATIONS

Plays

The Bear Hunters; or, The Fatal Ravine (produced 1825). 1825(?).

Curiosity Cured; or, Powder for Peeping (produced 1825).

The Death Fetch; or, The Student of Gottingen (produced 1826). 1887.

Luke the Labourer; or, The Lost Son (produced 1826). 1826; edited by A. E. Morgan, in *English Plays 1660–1820*, 1935.

John Street, Adelphi (as *A Card! 23 John Street, Adelphi*, produced 1826). 1835(?).

The Dead Shot (produced 1827). 1850.

Presumptive Evidence; or, Murder Will Out (produced 1828). 1829.

The Snake King; or, Harlequin and the Fairy of the Coral Branch (produced 1828).

The Boyne Water; or, Oonagh of the Broken Heart (produced 1828). 1886.

Theodore the Brigand; or, The Corsican Conscript (produced 1828). 1830(?).

A New Don Juan (produced 1828). 1828.

Mischief-Making (produced 1828). 1828(?).

The Absent Son (produced 1828).

Wanted a Partner; or, A Bill Due Sept. 29th (produced 1828).

The May Queen; or, Sampson the Serjeant (produced 1828). 1834.

The Young Quaker (produced 1829).

Peter Bell the Waggoner; or, The Murderers of Massiac! (produced 1829). 1835(?).

Vidocq the French Police Spy (produced 1829).

The Happiest Day of My Life (produced 1829). 1835(?).

Billy Taylor; or, The Gay Young Fellow (produced 1829). 1829(?).

Snakes in the Grass (produced 1829). 1835(?).

Popping the Question (produced 1830). 1840(?).

Grimalkin the Great; or, Harlequin and the King of the Cats (produced 1830).

The Pilot; or, A Tale of the Thames (produced 1830).

Don Juan (produced 1830). 1887.

A Husband at Sight, from a play by A. H. J. Duveyrier and P. F. A. Carmouche (produced 1830). 1840(?).

The Wreck Ashore; or, A Bridegroom from the Sea (produced 1830). 1840(?).

The Cab-Driver (produced 1830). 1887.

The King of the Alps; or, The Misanthrope (produced 1831). 1852.

The Ice Witch; or, The Frozen Hand, music by Tom Cooke (produced 1831). 1845(?).

Hyder Ali; or, The Lions of Mysore, music by Tom Cooke (produced 1831).

Moments of Mystery; or, The Widow Bewitched (produced 1831).

The Little Corporal; or, The School of Brienne (produced 1831).

Number One! or, The Hackney Coachman (produced 1831).

John Jones (produced 1831). 1856.

The Sea Serpent; or, The Wizard and the Winds, with Edward Fitzball (produced 1831).

Victorine; or, I'll Sleep on It (produced 1831). 1840(?).

Damon and Pythias (produced 1831). 1831(?).

Robert le Diable; or, The Devil's Son, with Edward Fitzball, from an opera by Scribe and Casimir Delavigne, music by Meyerbeer (produced 1832).

The Best of Husbands (produced 1832).

The Forgery; or, The Reading of the Will (produced 1832). 1887.

Second Thoughts (produced 1832). 1835.

The Little Red Man; or, The Witch of the Water Snakes (produced 1832).

Henriette the Forsaken (produced 1832). 1840(?).

Jacopo the Bravo: A Story of Venice, from the novel *The Bravo* by Cooper (as *The Bravo*, produced 1833). 1887.

The Pet of the Petticoats (produced 1833). 1887.

Open House; or, The Twin Sisters (produced 1833). 1845(?).

Ellen Wareham (produced 1833). 1887.

Nicholas Flam, Attorney-at-Law (produced 1833). 1887.

Uncle John (produced 1833). 1833.

The Rake and His Pupil; or, Folly, Love, and Marriage (produced 1833). 1833.

Isabelle; or, Woman's Life (produced 1834; also produced as *Thirty Years of a Woman's Life*).   1840(?).

Married Life (produced 1834).   1834.

The Kitchen Sylph (produced 1834).

Rural Felicity (produced 1834).   1870(?).

The Christening (produced 1834).   With *John Jones*, 1887(?).

Agnes de Vere; or, The Wife's Revenge (produced 1834).   1836.

The Last Days of Pompeii; or, Seventeen Hundred Years Ago, from the novel by Bulwer-Lytton (produced 1834).   1887.

Popular Dramas.   2 vols., 1834–36.

Good Husbands Make Good Wives (produced 1835).   1887.

The Scholar (produced 1835).   1887.

The Two Queens; or, Politics in Petticoats (produced 1835).   1837.

The Dream at Sea (produced 1835).   1835.

Rienzi, The Last of the Tribunes (produced 1836).

Harlequin and Georgy Barnwell; or, The London Prentice (produced 1836).

The Doom of Morana; or, The Spirit of Good and Evil, from a play by Dumas père (produced 1836).   1887.

The Duchess de la Vaubalière, from a play by M. N. Balisson de Rougemont (produced 1837).   1837.

Abelard and Heloise (produced 1837).   1837.

Love and Murder; or, The School for Sympathy (produced 1837).   1886.

Shocking Events (produced 1838).   1838.

Sinbad the Sailor; or, The Valley of Diamonds (produced 1838).

Our Mary Anne (produced 1838).   1838.

Weak Points (produced 1838).   1838.

The Irish Lion (produced 1838).   1838(?).

A Lesson for Ladies (produced 1838).   1838.

I Will Be a Duchess (produced 1839).

Single Life (produced 1839).   1840(?).

Brother Tom; or, My Dear Relations (produced 1839).   With *The Irish Lion*, 1887(?).

Jack Sheppard (produced 1839).   1840(?).

Poor Jack; or, A Sailor's Wife (produced 1840).   1887(?).

The Devil in London; or, Sketches in 1840, with R. B. Peake (produced 1840).   N.d.

Harlequin and Poor Richard; or, Old Father Time and the Almanac Maker (produced 1840).

A Kiss in the Dark (produced 1840).   1852.

The Snapping Turtles; or, Matrimonial Masquerading (produced 1842).   1866.

Harlequin and the Sleeping Beauty (produced 1843).

My Old Woman; or, Love and Wambles (produced 1843).

Josephine, The Child of the Regiment; or, The Fortune of War (produced 1844).   1856.

The Thimble Rig! (produced 1844).   1844(?).

The Green Bushes; or, A Hundred Years Ago (produced 1845).   1865(?).

The Maid with the Milking Pail (produced 1846).   1853.

The Flowers of the Forest: A Gipsy Story (produced 1847).   1847(?).

Nine Too Many (produced 1847).   With *The Wigwam*, by Shirley Brooks, 1890.

A Rough Diamond (produced 1847).   1855.

An Alarming Sacrifice (produced 1849).   1849.

Leap Year; or, The Ladies' Privilege (produced 1850).   1850.

Good for Nothing (produced 1851).   1855.

Grandmother Grizzle (produced 1851).

The Foundlings (produced 1852).

Harlequin and the Three Bears; or, Little Silver Hair and the Fairies, music by Edward Fitzwilliam (produced 1853).

Little Bo-Peep; or, Harlequin and the Girl Who Lost Her Sheep (produced 1854). 1854.
Married for Money (produced 1857).
The Sleeping Beauty in the Wood (produced 1857).
Undine; or, Harlequin and the Spirit of the Waters (produced 1858).
Valentine's Day; or, Harlequin and the Fairy of the True Lover's Knot (produced 1859).
Little Miss Muffett and Little Boy Blue; or, Harlequin and Old Daddy Long Legs, with Frederick Buckstone (produced 1861). 1861.
The Little Treasure (produced 1862).
The Trafalgar Medal (produced 1863).
Brother Sam, with E. A. Sothern and John Oxenford (produced 1865).
The Beggar Boy of Brussels. 1887.
The Maid of Athens. 1887.

*   *   *

In his brief study *Melodrama*, John D. Jump notes that "after scenes of heavy pathos, the funny man comes on and entertains the audience with a selection of side-splitting jokes. Melodrama finds no incongruity in this sudden whirligig of emotions." After describing Buckstone's *The Green Bushes*, Jump concludes, "Often the comic provides a vulgar commentary on the main plot." So the irrepressible, genial comedian Buckstone fell right into place with popular theatre in its heyday of gore, Gothicism, and gorgeosity, and rose to be not only a famous actor and manager of the Haymarket Theatre for 25 years, but a prolific author of farces as well.

His first important play, *Luke the Labourer*, was something of a milestone in the development of domestic melodrama. Other writers were concentrating on spectre-haunted castles and cataracts of the Ganges, "burning down" the sets of *Sardanapalus*, but Buckstone hit on something less exotic but not a bit less effective: tear-jerking sentimentality and rib-tickling fun in a simple, rustic setting. The audience cheered the ruined farmer, and hissed the nameless, indeed archetypical, evil squire. There were a noble tar, a seducing landlord, and a vulnerable virgin who cried "Unhand me, sir, or I will call for help." There were sensationalism and morality (H. B. Baker called the heroes "oppressively virtuous"). It was a formula for success, and Buckstone exploited it to the full with a huge number of successful farces, musicals, and pantomimes. Although Planché's "dramatic revues" attacked this approach, the audiences loved Buckstone's confections, and it must be remembered that this was the era of the dominance of the lowest common denominator in dramatic taste, the era of the audience Dickens described in "Two Views of a Cheap Theatre" (in *The Uncommercial Traveller*): "Besides prowlers and idlers, we were all mechanics, clock-labourers, costermongers, petty tradesmen, small clerks, milliners, stay-makers, shoe-binders, slop workers, poor workers in a hundred highways and byeways ... all come together ... to enjoy an evening's entertainment in common."

Buckstone would not have suffered gladly Eliot's comment, "When I see a play and understand it the first time, then I know it can't be much good." He was a comedian and master of the *coup de théâtre*. His justification was that "they loved it," and it brought him immense satisfaction during a long and active life in the commercial theatre.

—Leonard R. N. Ashley

BULLINS, Ed. American. Born in Philadelphia, Pennsylvania, 2 July 1935. Educated in

Philadelphia public schools; William Penn Business Institute, Philadelphia; Los Angeles City College; San Francisco State College. Served in the United States Navy. Playwright-in-Residence, 1967–71, and since 1967, Associate Director, The New Lafayette Theatre, Harlem, New York. Editor, *Black Theatre* magazine, Harlem, 1969–74, Recipient: Rockefeller grant, 1968; Vernon Rice Award, 1968; American Place grant, 1968; Obie Award, 1971; Guggenheim grant, 1971; National Endowment for the Arts grant, 1974; New York Drama Critics Circle Award, 1975, 1977. D.L.: Columbia College, Chicago, 1976. Lives in Brooklyn, New York.

PUBLICATIONS

Plays

    Clara's Ole Man (produced 1965). In *Five Plays*, 1969.

    How Do You Do: A Nonsense Drama (produced 1969). 1965.

    Dialect Determinism (produced 1965). In *Spontaneous Combustion: Eight New American Plays*, edited by Rochelle Owens, 1972.

    In New England Winter (produced 1967). In *New Plays from the Black Theatre*, edited by Bullins, 1969.

    In the Wine Time (produced 1968). In *Five Plays*, 1969.

    A Son, Come Home (produced 1968). In *Five Plays*, 1969.

    The Electronic Nigger (produced 1968). In *Five Plays*, 1969.

    Goin' a Buffalo: A Tragifantasy (produced 1968). In *Five Plays*, 1969.

    The Gentleman Caller (produced 1969). In *Illuminations 5*, 1968.

    Five Plays. 1969; as *The Electronic Nigger and Other Plays*, 1970.

    The Game of Adam and Eve, with Shirley Tarbell (produced 1969).

    It Has No Choice (produced 1969).

    The Corner (produced 1969). In *Black Drama Anthology*, edited by Woodie King and Ron Milner, 1972.

    Street Sounds (produced 1970).

    The Fabulous Miss Marie (produced 1970). In *The New Lafayette Theatre Presents*, edited by Bullins, 1974.

    It Bees Dat Way (produced 1970). In *Four Dynamite Plays*, 1971.

    The Pig Pen (produced 1970). In *Four Dynamite Plays*, 1971.

    Death List (produced 1970). In *Four Dynamite Plays*, 1971.

    State Office Building Curse, in *The Drama Review*, September 1970.

    The Duplex: A Black Love Fable in Four Movements (produced 1970). 1971.

    The Devil Catchers (produced 1971).

    Night of the Beast (screenplay), in *Four Dynamite Plays*, 1971.

    Four Dynamite Plays (includes *It Bees Dat Way*, *Death List*, *The Pig Pen*, *Night of the Beast*). 1971.

    The Psychic Pretenders (produced 1972).

    You Gonna Let Me Take You Out Tonight, Baby (produced 1972).

    House Party, music by Pat Patrick, lyrics by Bullins (produced 1973).

    The Taking of Miss Janie (produced 1975).

    The Mystery of Phyllis Wheatley (produced 1976).

    Jo Anne!!! (produced 1976).

    Home Boy, music by Aaron Bell, lyrics by Bullins (produced 1976).

    Michael (produced 1978).

Screenplays: *Night of the Beast*, 1971; *The Ritual Masters*, 1972.

Fiction

The Hungered One: Early Writings (stories). 1971.
The Reluctant Rapist. 1973.

Verse

To Raise the Dead and Foretell the Future. 1971.

Other

Editor, *New Plays from the Black Theatre.* 1969.
Editor, *The New Lafayette Theatre Presents: Plays with Aesthetic Comments by 6 Black Playwrights.* 1974.

Bibliography: in *Black Image on the American Stage* by James V. Hatch, 1970.

Reading List: "The Polished Reality: Aesthetics and the Black Writer" in *Contact Magazine,* 1962; "The Theatre of Reality" in *Black World,* 1966; "Up from Politics" in *Performance,* 1972.

*   *   *

Ed Bullins is the most original and prolific playwright of the American Black Theatre movement. To quote him: "To make an open secret more public: in the area of playwrighting, Ed Bullins, at this moment in time, is almost without peer in America – black, white or imported." Written in 1973, the statement exaggerates little. Included in a volume *The Theme Is Blackness,* Bullins's title polemically reduces his actual thematic range; he dramatizes many relationships of black people – family, friendship, business, the business of crime. From urban black ghettos Bullins draws characters who speak with humor, obscenity, and sophistication. Whereas Langston Hughes had to strain to capture underworld idiom in Harlem, Bullins modulates a language that ignores the black as the white middle-class.

As ambitious as O'Neill, Bullins has embarked on a Twentieth Century Cycle of twenty plays, to depict the lives of certain Afro-Americans between 1900 and 1999. Five of these plays have been completed to date (1977), very loosely tracing the experiences of the Dawson – it would be inaccurate to call them a family, since the men found households, abandon them, disappear, reappear. Even incomplete, the cycle stresses the necessarily fragmentary nature of relationships of black urban males in twentieth-century America. Each of the plays focuses on a complete action, free in dramatic form, often embellished with song and dance, rich in rhythmic speech and terse imagery which Bullins crafts so beautifully. Indefatigable, Bullins has also written agit-prop Dynamite Plays, in which his anti-white rage is indistinguishable from that of LeRoi Jones. Other extra-cycle plays resemble Chekhov in their evocation of a dying class, e.g., *Clara's Ole Man* and *Goin' a Buffalo.* Like Chekhov, Bullins dramatizes the foibles of his people, endearing them to us through a poignant humor.

—Ruby Cohn

BURGOYNE, John. English. Born at Sutton Park, Bedfordshire, in 1722. Educated at Westminster School, London. Married Lady Charlotte Stanley in 1743 (died, 1776); had four children by Susan Caulfield. Soldier: cornet, 1740, lieutenant, 1741, and captain, 1744, in the 13th Light Dragoons; sold his commission and lived in France to escape his creditors, 1749–55; returned to England, obtained captaincy in the 11th Dragoons, 1756, and exchanged that commission for captaincy and lieutenant-colonelcy in the Coldstream Guards, 1758; served in expeditions to Cherbourg and St. Malo, 1758, 1759; devised schemes for creation of the King's Light Dragoons and Queen's Light Dragoons, 1759; sent to Portugal as Brigadier-General to assist the Portuguese against Spain: captured Valencia de Alcantara, 1762; Tory Member of Parliament for Midhurst, 1762–68, and for Preston, 1768–74; appointed Governor of Fort William, Scotland, 1769; Major-General, 1772; sent to the American colonies to reinforce General Gage's forces, 1774; during the Revolutionary War, Commander of the British attack of the United States from Canada: captured Ticonderoga and Fort Ward, and promoted to Lieutenant-General, then defeated by, and surrendered to, General Gates at Saratoga, 1777; on his return to England condemned for his actions by the House of Commons and the press, and deprived by the king of his commands and the governorship of Fort William; supported by the opposition and on return of Whigs to power appointed Commander-in-Chief in Ireland, 1782–83; thereafter devoted himself to writing. *Died 4 June 1792.*

PUBLICATIONS

Collections

    Dramatic and Poetical Works. 2 vols., 1808.

Plays

    The Maid of the Oaks, music by F. H. Barthelemon (produced 1774; revised version, produced 1774). 1774.
    The Lord of the Manor, music by William Jackson, from a play by Jean-François Marmontel (produced 1780). 1781.
    The Heiress (produced 1786). 1786.
    Richard Coeur de Lion, music by Thomas Linley, from an opera by Michel Jean Sedaine, music by Grétry (produced 1786). 1786.

Other

    A Letter to His Constituents upon His Late Resignation. 1779.
    A State of the Expedition from Canada. 1780; supplement, 1780.
    Political and Military Episodes Derived from the Life and Correspondence, by E. B. de Fonblanque. 1786.
    The Orderly Book from His Entry in the State of New York until His Surrender at Saratoga, edited by E. B. O'Callaghan. 1860.

Reading List: *Gentleman Johnny Burgoyne* by Francis J. Hudleston, 1927; *The Man Who Lost America* by Paul Lewis, 1973.

*   *   *

At Saratoga in 1777 General John Burgoyne lost an army. The fault was not his and the American commander who forced the surrender owed less to his own skill than to the complacency of the British Government and to the indolence of Burgoyne's superiors in North America. But Saratoga, the first battle-honour of the United States Army, spelt for Burgoyne the end of a long, gallant, and thoughtful career as a soldier. The fifteen years that were left to him Burgoyne used energetically and not often wisely. In Parliament as M.P. for Preston he was always ready to intervene on behalf of the Army and particularly of its private soldiers and non-commissioned officers, but his speeches were muddled and prolix and he was, not unnaturally, testy about his own military reputation. He wenched, he gambled, he roistered. But he also wrote, and the honours that had been denied him in his prime profession came his way eventually by way of the theatre.

His first dramatic piece, *The Maid of the Oaks* had been staged at Drury Lane before the American Revolution. It was damned by Horace Walpole (who damned almost everything that Burgoyne attempted whether in the Army, in Parliament, or for the stage), but David Garrick, better-qualified then Walpole to judge an entertainment, proclaimed it "a great success," and the play survived in the repertory for several months and, in book form, enjoyed a considerable vogue for many years. But it is in truth a heavy-handed and stylised piece, remarkable only for its mawkishness and portentous morality so utterly out of keeping with the author's personal inclinations and activities.

In *The Lord of the Manor* Burgoyne abandoned the ludicrously inappropriate pastoral idyll and took to the world he knew. Sergeant Sash, Corporal Dill, and Corporal Snip are caricatures only in the sense that they are exaggerations of reality, and Burgoyne understood the reality that is the British soldier. An eighteenth-century audience was never averse to a resounding platitude and Burgoyne gave them many to applaud, most of them from the lips of his *alter ego* hero, Trumore. *The Lord of the Manor* was written as a libretto, for the music of William Jackson of Exeter. Most of its faults are the faults of the operatic genre but they are as nothing when compared to the faults of Burgoyne's second attempt at opera, his adaptation of a serious French libretto, *Richard Coeur de Lion*.

The Heiress is a different matter. The plot is thin and moved forward in a flurry of coincidences. The characterisation is simplistic and is moulded almost entirely by the names of the participants (Lord Gayville; Mr. Rightly, the honest lawyer, and Mr. Alscrip, his devious colleague; Chignon, the prissy French hairdresser; the social climbers, Mr. and Mrs. Blandish) but the play has pace, the wit is sharp, and the social comment incisive.

With *The Heiress* Burgoyne made only £200 but he won the affection of the theatre-going public, of the critics, not only in England but also in France and Germany, and even of Horace Walpole: "Burgoyne's battles and speeches will be forgotten, but his delightful comedy *The Heiress* will continue the delight of the stage and one of the most pleasing domestic compositions."

—J. E. Morpurgo

BYRON, H(enry) J(ames).   English.   Born in Manchester in January 1834. Apprenticed to a surgeon in Manchester, and later to his grandfather, Dr. Bradley, in Buxton; disliked medicine, and joined a provincial company of actors; Manager, Alexandra Theatre, Liverpool, and later also the Theatre Royal and Amphitheatre, Liverpool, 1857; entered the Middle Temple, London, 1858, to study law, but left to write for the stage. Settled in London: wrote burlesques for the Strand Theatre, 1858–65; Manager, with Marie Wilton, Prince of Wales's Theatre, 1865–67; first Editor, *Fun* weekly, and Founder, *Comic Times*; made

London debut as an actor, 1869, and thereafter appeared in the London productions of his own comedies; Manager, Criterion Theatre, 1874; Editor, *Mirth*, 1877. *Died 11 April 1884.*

PUBLICATIONS

Plays

Richard of the Lion Heart (produced 1857).

The Lady of Lyons; or, Twopenny Pride and Penny-tence (produced 1858).   1858.

Fra Diavolo; or, The Beauty and the Brigands (produced 1858).   1858.

The Bride of Abydos; or, The Prince, The Pirate, and the Pearl (produced 1858).   1858.

The Maid and the Magpie; or, The Fatal Spoon (produced 1858).   1859.

The Very Latest Edition of The Lady of Lyons (produced 1859).   N.d.

The Babes in the Wood! And the Good Little Fairy Birds! (produced 1859).   1859.

Jack the Giant Killer; or, Harlequin King Arthur and ye Knights of ye Round Table (produced 1859).   1859.

Mazeppa (produced 1859).   1865.

The Nymph of the Lurleyburg; or, The Knight and the Naiads (produced 1859).   1859.

The Pilgrim of Love! (produced 1860).   1860.

The Miller and His Men, with Francis Talfound (produced 1860).   1860.

The Garibaldi Excursionists (produced 1860).   1861.

Blue Beard! From a New Point of Hue (produced 1860).   1861.

Cinderella; or, The Lover, The Lackey, and the Little Glass Slipper (produced 1860).   1861.

Robinson Crusoe; or, Harlequin Friday and the King of the Caribee Islands, music by W. H. Montgomery (produced 1860).   1861.

The Rival Othellos (produced 1860).

Aladdin; or, The Wonderful Scamp! (produced 1861).   1861.

The Old Story! (produced 1861).   1861.

Esmeralda; or, The "Sensation" Goat! (produced 1861).   1862.

Miss Eily O'Connor (produced 1861).   1862; as *The Colleen Bawn* (produced 1870).

Puss in a New Pair of Boots, music by F. Musgrave (produced 1861).   1862.

Whittington and His Cat; or, Harlequin King Kollywobbol and the Genius of Good Humour, music by W. H. Montgomery (produced 1861).   1862.

Goldenhair the Good (produced 1862).

Beauty and the Beast; or, The Gnome Queen and the Good Fairy (produced 1862).   1862.

George de Barnwell; or, Harlequin Folly in the Realms of Fancy (produced 1862).   1863.

Ivanhoe, in Accordance with the Spirit of the Times, music by F. Musgrave (produced 1862).   1864.

Ali Baba; or, The Thirty Nine Thieves, in Accordance with the Author's Habit of Taking One Off! (produced 1863).   1864.

Beautiful Haidée; or, The Sea Nymph and the Sallee Rovers (produced 1863).   1863.

Ill-Treated Il Trovatore; or, The Mother, The Maiden, and the Musicianer (produced 1863).   1863(?).

The Motto: I Am "All There" (produced 1863).   1864.

The Rosebud of Stingingnettle Farm; or, The Villainous Squire and the Virtuous Villager (produced 1863).   1867.

Harlequin St. George and the Dragon; or, The Seven Champions and the Beautiful Princess (produced 1863).   1863.

Lady Belle Belle; or, Fortunio and His Seven Magicians (produced 1863). 1864.

Orpheus and Eurydice; or, The Young Gentleman Who Charmed the Rocks (produced 1863). 1864; revised version, as *Eurydice* (produced 1871), 1872; revised version, as *Pluto* (produced 1881).

1863; or, The Sensations of the Past Season (produced 1863). 1864.

Mazourka; or, The Stick, The Pole, and the Tartar (produced 1864). 1865.

Timothy to the Rescue (produced 1864). 1865.

Sensation Dramas for the Back Drawing Room. 1864.

Lord Dundreary Married and Done For (produced 1864).

The "Grin" Bushes; or, The "Mrs." Brown of the "Missis"-sippi (produced 1864). 1865.

The Lion and the Unicorn (produced 1864). 1864.

Princess Spring-Time; or, The Envoy Who Stole the King's Daughter (produced 1864). 1866.

Pan; or, The Loves of Echo and Narcissus (produced 1865). 1866.

La! Sonnabula! or, The Supper, The Sleeper, and the Merry Swiss Boy (produced 1865). 1866.

War to the Knife (produced 1865). 1866.

Lucia di Lammermoor; or, The Laird, The Lady, and the Lover (produced 1865). 1867.

Little Don Giovanni; or, Leporello and the Stone Statue (produced 1865). 1867.

A Hundred Thousand Pounds (produced 1866). 1868.

Der Freischutz; or, The Bill! the Belle!! and the Bullet!!! (produced 1866). 1869.

Pandora's Box; or, The Young Spark and the Old Flame (produced 1866). 1875.

Harlequin Blue Beard (produced 1866).

Little Dick Whittington, Thrice Lord Mayor of London; or, Harlequin Hot Pot and the Fairies of the Elfin Grot (produced 1866).

The Wonderful Travels of Gulliver (produced 1867). 1867.

Robinson Crusoe; or, The Injun Bride and the Injured Wife, with others (produced 1867).

William Tell, with a Vengeance! or, The Pet, The Patriot, and the Pippin (produced 1867). 1868.

The Lancashire Lass; or, Tempted, Tried, and True (produced 1867). 1879.

Dearer Than Life (produced 1867).

Blow for Blow (produced 1868). 1875.

Lucrezia Borgia, M.D.; or, La Grande Doctresse (produced 1868). 1871.

Cyril's Success (produced 1868). 1870.

Not Such a Fool as He Looks (produced 1868). 1884.

Robinson Crusoe; or, Friday and the Fairies (produced 1868). 1868.

Lost at Sea: A London Story, with Dion Boucicault (produced 1869).

Minnie; or, Leonard's Love (produced 1869).

The Corsican "Bothers"; or, The Troublesome Twins (produced 1869). 1871.

Uncle Dick's Darling (produced 1869). 1907.

Lord Bateman; or, The Proud Young Porter and the Fair Sophia (produced 1869). 1871.

The Yellow Dwarf; or, Harlequin Cupid and the King of the Gold Mines (produced 1869). 1869.

The Prompter's Box: A Story of the Footlights and the Fireside (produced 1870; as *Two Stars,* produced 1872; as *The Crushed Tragedian,* produced 1878). 1884.

Robert Macaire; or, The Roadside Inn Turned Inside Out (produced 1870). 1872.

The Enchanted Wood; or, The Three Transformed Princes (produced 1870). 1874.

An English Gentleman; or, The Squire's Last Shilling (produced 1870). 1887.

Wait and Hope (produced 1871).

Daisy Farm (produced 1871). 1879.

The Orange Tree and the Humble Bee; or, The Little Princess Who Was Lost at Sea (produced 1871). 1872.

Not If I Know It (produced 1871).

Giselle; or, The Sirens of the Lotus Lake (produced 1871). 1872.

Partners for Life (produced 1871). 1878.

Camaralzaman and the Fair Badoura; or, The Bad Djinn and the Good Spirit (produced 1871). 1872.

Blue Beard (produced 1871). 1871.

Haunted Houses; or, Labyrinths of Life: A Story of London and the Bush (produced 1872).

The Spur of the Moment (produced 1872).

Time's Triumph (produced 1872).

Good News (produced 1872).

The Lady of the Lane (produced 1872).

Mabel's Life; or, A Bitter Bargain (produced 1872).

Old Soldiers (produced 1873). 1879.

Fine Feathers (produced 1873). 1884.

Chained to the Oar (produced 1873).

A Wife for a Day (produced 1873).

La Fille de Mme. Angot, from the opera by L.F. N. Clairville, P. Siraudin, and V. Koning, music by A. C. Lecocq (produced 1873).

Sour Grapes (produced 1873). 1887.

Don Juan (produced 1873).

Blackmail (produced 1873; as *The Thumbscrew,* produced 1874).

Guy Fawkes (produced 1874).

An American Lady (produced 1874).

Normandy Pippins (produced 1874).

The Pretty Perfumeress, from an opera by H. Crimieux and E. Blum, music by Offenbach (produced 1874).

The Demon's Bride, music by Georges Jacobi (produced 1874).

Old Sailors (produced 1874). 1880.

Oil and Vinegar (produced 1874).

Our Boys (produced 1875). 1880.

Weak Women (produced 1875). 1878.

Married in Haste (produced 1875). 1879.

Tottles (produced 1875).

Wrinkles: A Tale of Time (produced 1876). 1879.

£20 a Year − All Found (produced 1876). 1880.

Little Don Caesar de Bazan (produced 1876).

Widow and Wife (produced 1876).

Old Chums (produced 1876).

Pampered Menials. 1876.

The Bohemian G'yurl and the Unapproachable Pole (produced 1877).

Guinea Gold; or, Lights and Shadows of London Life (produced 1877).

Little Doctor Faust (produced 1877).

Bits of Burlesque. 1877.

A Fool and His Money (produced 1878).

Ali Baba and the Forty Thieves, with others (produced 1878).

Il Sonnambula and the Lively Little Alessio (produced 1878).

A Hornet's Nest (produced 1878).

Conscience Money (produced 1878).

Uncle (produced 1878). 1880.

Young Fra Diavolo, The Terror of Terracina (produced 1878).

Jack the Giant Killer (produced 1878).

Pretty Esmeralda and Captain Phoebus of Ours (produced 1879).

Handsome Hernani; or, The Fatal Penny Whistle (produced 1879).

Courtship; or, The Three Caskets (produced 1879).   1884.
The Gaiety Gulliver (as *Gulliver's Travels,* produced 1879).   1880.
The Girls (as *Our Girls,* produced 1879).   1887.
The Upper Crust (produced 1880).
Il Trovatore; or, Larks with a Libretto (produced 1880).
Without a Home (produced 1880).
Bow Bells (produced 1880).   1881.
The Light Fantastic (produced 1880).
Michael Strogoff (produced 1881).
Punch (produced 1881).   1887.
New Brooms (produced 1881).
Fourteen Days (produced 1882).
Auntie (produced 1882).
Frolique, with H. B. Farnie (produced 1882).
Open House (produced 1885).
The Shuttlecock, completed by J. A. Sterry (produced 1885).

Fiction

Paid in Full.   1865.

Other

The Slang Dictionary, with W. C. Hazlitt.   1864.

*   *   *

   H. J. Byron's first success as a writer came in 1858 with his burlesque version of *Fra Diavolo.* This was also the first triumph for the Swanboroughs in their management of the Strand Theatre. Until his move to the Prince of Wales's Theatre in 1865, Byron was the chief provider of the burlesque extravaganzas for which the Strand was famous. These lacked the narrative vigour of Planché's earlier extravaganzas, preferring to rely on relentless punning and the elaboration of comic incidentals. Byron's move into joint-management with Marie Wilton of the Prince of Wales's coincided with a decline in his appetite for the writing of burlesque. Even so, he was surprised by the firmness of Marie Wilton's preference for comedy. *War to the Knife* and *A Hundred Thousand Pounds* were his only contributions in that genre to the repertory of his new theatre, and they are perfunctory pieces. His departure from the Prince of Wales's is evidence of a loss of heart, a recognition that Tom Robertson was better able to provide Marie Wilton with quality plays than he was.
   Blow for Blow, an early example of Byron's compromise with the kind of domestic melodrama he loved to ridicule, is characteristically short of conviction in the final act. It is then that the failure to suit character to story is most obvious. Even Joseph Knight, a friendly critic, complains of Byron's making his characters his shuttlecocks, and observes, after watching *Married in Haste,* that "Mr. Byron's comedies are like fruit trees growing on espaliers. The slightest possible amount of fabric serves to support the utmost obtainable quantity of product." The plain truth is that Byron wrote too much. *Blow for Blow* was one of five pieces staged in 1868 (*Cyril's Success,* perhaps his most admired play, was another), and that was a less than usually productive year. Nicoll records 143 pieces in a career of under thirty years. What needs to be said is that Byron spans and represents the popular drama of his time more completely than any other writer. The phenomenal success of *Our Boys,* which

ran for over four year at the Vaudeville, is evidence of the sureness of his familiarity with his audience. Despite a crudely defective final act, this is probably his best play – but he had learned by then the dangers of aiming too high.

—Peter Thomson

CAREY, Henry. English. Born, probably in Yorkshire, c. 1687; believed by some scholars to have been the natural son of Henry Savile, Marquis of Halifax. Studied music with Olaus Linnert, Roseingrave, and Geminiani. Married in 1708; four children. Taught music in various boarding schools; settled in London, 1710; a member of Addison's circle; produced the magazine *The Records of Love*, 1710; wrote farces and songs for the London stage, 1715–39. *Died* (by suicide) *4 October 1743.*

PUBLICATIONS

Collections

Poems, edited by Frederick T. Wood. 1930.

Plays

The Contrivances; or, More Ways Than One (produced 1715). 1715; revised version, music by the author (produced 1729), 1729.
Hanging and Marriage; or, The Dead-Man's Wedding (produced 1722). 1722; revised version, as *Betty; or, The Country Bumpkins,* music by the author (produced 1732), songs published 1732.
Amelia, music by J. F. Lampe (produced 1732). 1732.
Teraminta, music by J. C. Smith (produced 1732). 1732.
The Happy Nuptials, music by the author (produced 1733). Extracts in *Gentleman's Magazine,* November 1733; revised version, as *Britannia; or, The Royal Lovers* (produced 1734).
The Tragedy of Chrononhotonthologos, music by the author (produced 1734). 1734.
The Honest Yorkshireman, music by the author (produced 1735). 1736; pirated version, as *A Wonder,* 1735.
The Dragon of Wantley, music by J. F. Lampe (produced 1737). 1737.
Margery; or, A Worse Plague Than the Dragon, music by J. F. Lampe (produced 1738). 1738.
Nancy; or, The Parting Lovers, music by the author (produced 1739). 1739.
Dramatic Works. 1743.

Verse

Poems on Several Occasions. 1713; revised edition, 1720, 1729.
Works (songs and cantatas, with music by Carey). 1724; revised edition, 1726.
Of Stage Tyrants: An Epistle. 1735.
The Musical Century (songs). 2 vols., 1737; revised edition, 1740, 1743.
An Ode to Mankind, Addressed to the Prince of Wales. 1741.

Other

A Learned Dissertation on Dumpling. 1726.
Pudding and Dumpling Burnt to Pot; or, A Complete Key to the Dissertation on Dumpling. 1727.
Cupid and Hymen: A Voyage to the Islands of Love and Matrimony, with others. 1748.

Reading List: *English Comic Drama 1700–1750* by F. W. Bateson, 1929; *The Burlesque Tradition in the English Theatre after 1660* by V. C. Clinton-Baddeley, 1952; "Carey's *Chrononhotonthologos*: A Plea" by Samuel L. Macey, in *Lock Haven Review,* 1969; "Carey's *Chrononhotonthologos*" by Peter Lewis, in *Yearbook of English Studies,* 1974.

*   *   *

Henry Carey thought himself a musician who wrote poetry for diversion. Posterity remembers him, if at all, for "Sally in Our Alley" and – debatably – for "God Save the King." Contemporaries knew him as a writer of popular songs, ballad operas, and burlesques. His poetic gift was meager; the classical imitations, moralistic and satiric pieces, and the heavier amatory verses are pedestrian at best. His only good poems are parodies like "Namby-Pamby," popular ballads like "Sally" and "The Town Spark and the Country Lass," and the lighter songs in his plays – "Oh, London Is a Dainty Place," from *The Honest Yorkshireman*, for example. Nor was Carey a well-trained musician. What he had was a knack for light rhymes and catchy tunes, and these together account for much of his success.

His first play, *The Contrivances*, was a smash hit after he turned if from farce to ballad opera; it was played nearly 200 times during the century. Carey also wrote both words and music for *Nancy; or, The Parting Lovers*, a short musical piece popular under several titles for decades. He supplied the music for a hit pantomime (*Harlequin Doctor Faustus*, 1723) and for a popular masque (*Cephalus and Procris*); much of the music for his ballad opera *The Honest Yorkshireman* is also original. *Amelia* and *Teraminta* show his interest in promoting English opera, but his librettos are flat and conventional; it was certainly J. F. Lampe's music which made *Amelia* a success.

Carey's real achievements, aside from *The Contrivances*, came late in his career. *Chrononhotonthologos* burlesques contemporary (and earlier) tragedy. No reader will easily forget the King of Queerumania and his court, or the opening lines of the play. Although not as directly parodic as *The Rehearsal*, it is delightful to read and stands comparison with *Tom Thumb*, its immediate predecessor. *The Dragon of Wantley*, a burlesque with music by Lampe, is even better, and was as popular for the rest of the century as *The Contrivances*. The plot, based on a laundered version of the ballad, is deliberately thin, and the burlesque of the Italian opera – evident in the music as well as the text – pointed and hilarious. So successful was the piece, indeed, that it nearly drove Italian opera off the English stage for a year or two. *Margery*, like most sequels, was less successful.

Carey is said to have heard his tunes everywhere he went. The modern reader is not so fortunate. No available edition of *The Dragon of Wantley*, for example, includes the music, yet it is as difficult to appreciate Carey's achievement without it as to judge *West Side Story* on its libretto. Like Isaac Bickerstaff and several other successful authors of the century, Carey remains largely inaccessible.

—Frederick M. Link

CARTWRIGHT, William. English. Born in Northway, near Tewkesbury, Gloucestershire, in September 1611. Educated at a free school in Cirencester; Westminster School, London (King's Scholar); Christ Church, Oxford, student 1628, M.A. 1635. Ordained, 1635, and became noted as an Oxford preacher; Reader in Metaphysic, Oxford University, 1642; appointed to the Council of War, 1642; Succentor of the Church in Salisbury, 1643; Junior Proctor of Oxford University, 1643. *Died 29 November 1643.*

PUBLICATIONS

Collections

Plays and Poems, edited by G. Blakemore Evans.   1951.

Plays

The Royal Slave (produced 1636).   1639.
The Ordinary (produced ?).   In *Comedies...,* 1651.
The Lady-Errant (produced ?).   In *Comedies...,* 1651.
The Siege; or, Love's Convert, in *Comedies....*   1651.
Comedies, Tragi-Comedies, with Other Poems.   1651.

Other

An Offspring of Mercy Issuing Out of the Womb of Cruelty (sermon).   1652.

Reading List: *The Life and Poems of Cartwright* by R. Cullis Goffin, 1918.

*   *   *

Even if William Cartwright's work had nothing else to commend it, it would provide an index to the mind and taste of Oxford in the time of Charles I. Cartwright's poetic range includes topical verse on university and court, witty songs, love lyrics (among which the ardent trochees of "A Song of Dalliance" are outstanding), deft translations and adaptations ("Lesbia on Her Sparrow" cleverly echoes both Catullus and Skelton), and choral texts on the Nativity, the Circumcision, and the Epiphany for use by the King's Music. Toward the end of his brief life he was to shine as a preacher; a surviving Passion Sermon, delivered at Christ Church, refers to the Redeemer in terms which might normally be applied to a devoted Cavalier.

Proudly claimed as a poetic "son" by Ben Jonson, he composed an Elegy on Jonson's death, and his single comedy, *The Ordinary,* is constructed on Jonsonian principles. Its array of humours, in a London setting, includes the antiquary Moth, who speaks only Chaucerian English. In *The Siege; or, Love's Convert,* a tragi-comedy based on a hint in Plutarch, a tyrant of Byzantium pursues a maid's virtue but reforms in the end ("His Flames are now as chaste, as erewhile foul"); for comic relief there is an unlovely widow who would welcome the tyrant's attentions. Another tragi-comedy, *The Lady-Errant,* which seems to have been privately produced on the occasion of a wedding, offers in the title-role a sort of female Hotspur, and there is an Aristophanic assembly of women who plan to banish all men from Cyprus; the serious plot elements involve idealized love and friendship. All these plays (even *The Siege,* which Cartwright says he would have destroyed in an early draft had it not been for the intercession of the King) show ingenuity and a sense for situation, if not much depth of thought or character.

But Cartwright's undoubted triumph is *The Royal Slave.* This tragi-comedy was presented in the hall of Christ Church before the King and Queen when they visited Oxford in 1636, and it would be hard to conceive a production better fitted to the occasion. In an action enlivened by music and dance, brilliantly mounted by Inigo Jones's stagecraft, and resounding with fine speeches, the noble Cratander is, in accordance with a Persian custom, made king for three days, after which he must be slain as a sacrifice to the Sun; during this period he manifests virtues which are proof against all temptation and wins not only the eloquently Platonic love of the Persian Queen but even the admiration of the Persian King. In a final spectacular episode he is saved by a solar eclipse, along with a fall of rain which puts out the sacrificial fires. So deeply pleased were King Charles and his Queen that they expressed a desire for another performance of the play at Hampton Court. "It was the day of St. Felix," remarked Archbishop Laud, "and all things went happy."

—Rhodes Dunlap

CENTLIVRE, Susanna. English. Born in or near Holbeach, Lincolnshire, 1669. Possibly married a nephew of Sir Stephen Fox, c. 1684, and an officer named Carroll, c. 1685; married Joseph Centlivre, principal cook to Queen Anne and George I, 1707. Actress in the provinces, often appearing in her own works, written under the name S. Carroll; devoted herself to writing from 1700; lived in London from 1712. *Died 1 December 1723.*

PUBLICATIONS

Collections

Works. 3 vols., 1760–61; as *Dramatic Works*, 1872.

Plays

The Perjured Husband; or, The Adventures of Venice (produced 1700). 1700.
The Beau's Duel; or, A Soldier for the Ladies (produced 1702). 1702.
The Stolen Heiress; or, The Salamanca Doctor Outplotted (as *The Heiress*, produced 1702). 1703.
Love's Contrivance; or, Le Medecin Malgré Lui (produced 1703). 1703.
The Gamester, from a play by J. F. Regnard (produced 1705). 1705.
The Basset-Table (produced 1705). 1706.
Love at a Venture (produced 1706?). 1706.
The Platonic Lady (produced 1706). 1707.
The Busy Body (produced 1709). 1709.
The Man's Bewitched; or, The Devil to Do about Her (produced 1709). 1710.
A Bickerstaff's Burying; or, Work for the Upholders (produced 1710). 1710; as *The Custom of the Country* (produced 1715).
Mar-Plot; or, The Second Part of the Busy Body (produced 1710). 1711.
The Perplexed Lovers (produced 1712). 1712.
The Wonder! A Woman Keeps a Secret (produced 1714). 1714.
The Gotham Election. 1715; as *The Humours of Election*, 1737.
A Wife Well Managed (produced 1724). 1715.
The Cruel Gift; or, The Royal Resentment (produced 1716). 1717.
A Bold Stroke for a Wife (produced 1718). In *A Collection of Plays 3*, 1719; edited by Thalia Stathas, 1967.

The Artifice (produced 1722). 1723.

Verse

A Trip to the Masquerade; or, A Journey to Somerset House. 1713.
A Poem to His Majesty upon His Accession to the Throne. 1715.
An Epistle to Mrs. Wallup, Now in the Train of the Princess of Wales. 1715.
A Woman's Case, in an Epistle to Charles Joye. 1720.

Bibliography: "Some Uncollected Authors 14" by Jane E. Norton, in *Book Collector*, 1957.

Reading List: *The Celebrated Mrs. Centlivre* by John W. Bowyer, 1952.

*　　*　　*

Mrs. Centlivre wrote seventeen comedies, including three short farces, and strayed once or twice into tragedy. (Her poems are unimportant, orthodox complimentary or epistolary effusions for the most part.) Few of the plays were outright flops, and at least four enjoyed considerable success. The least merited popularity, perhaps, was that attached to *The Gamester*, a sentimental comedy rebuking the age for its addiction to gambling. A sequel, *The Basset-Table*, met with a less favourable reception, but it displays more vivacity in places, as in the scenes involving the uxorious City drugster Sago and his extravagantly flighty wife.

Throughout the eighteenth and nineteenth centuries, the dramatist's name was kept alive by two comedies which held the boards for decade after decade and which each totted up many hundreds of performances across the English-speaking world. Probably the better play is the earlier, entitled *The Busie Body*, constructed around the "sly, cowardly, inquisitive fellow" Marplot, who frustrates all the schemes he attempts to abet. This was a true acting part, and Theophilus Cibber, Henry Woodward, and Garrick all enjoyed great success in the role. Equally well-known was *The Wonder! A Woman Keeps a Secret*, which introduced some of Mrs. Centlivre's favourite Latin lovers – in this case melodramatic Portuguese grandees. Both the male and female leads provide fine opportunities for an accomplished player, and Garrick, Kemble, Mrs. Yates, and Susanna Cibber at various times all made a striking impact in the play.

Mrs. Centlivre's outstanding comedy is probably *A Bold Stroke for a Wife*, which traces the attempts of Colonel Fainwell to obtain the hand of Mrs. Lovely, a spirited heiress. The hero has to overcome the objections of four guardians, and he adopts a succession of disguises to deceive each of these well-marked "humour" characters – an antiquated beau, a foolish virtuoso, a grasping stock-jobber, and a sanctimonious Quaker. The play clearly exhibits the author's talent for lively dialogue, energetic stage business, and vivid portrayal of eccentric traits. It is worth adding that the unacted farce called *A Gotham Election* was an unlucky victim of political censorship. It is short but exceedingly amusing. The principal characters are conventional in outline, but nicely realised: for example, the amorous Squire Tickup, a Tory and seemingly a Jacobite into the bargain, who is opposed by the pompous Whig Sir Roger Trusty, a ready orator with a mouthful of high-minded party rhetoric always at his disposal. Around the gentry there are placed a wide range of rustic wiseacres, apparently foolish peasants with a vein of peasant shrewdness. As some of the names indicate – Shallow, Sly, Gabble – there is an echo of the Shakespearian clown in their speech, which is compounded of strange Mummerzet dialect and brutally direct colloquialisms. It is a pity that Susanna Centlivre did not get the opportunity to develop this vein of comedy; the play shows her capable of a realistic dramatic idiom rarely encountered on the eighteenth-century stage.

—Pat Rogers

CHAPMAN, George. English. Born near Hitchin, Hertfordshire, c. 1560. Educated possibly at Cambridge University and Oxford University. Lived on the Continent, 1585–91, and served with the forces of Sir Francis Vere in the Low Countries; returned to London and wrote for Philip Henslowe until 1599, then for the Children of St. Paul's Chapel (later known as the Children of the Queen's Revels) until 1608, and thereafter devoted himself mainly to his translations; Server-in-Ordinary to Prince Henry, 1603–12; imprisoned in the Tower of London for satirical references to James I, 1605; in later life enjoyed patronage of the Earl of Somerset. *Died 12 May 1634.*

PUBLICATIONS

Collections

> *Tragedies, Comedies,* edited by T. M. Parrott.   2 vols., 1910–14.
> *Poems,* edited by Phyllis Brooks Bartlett.   1941.
> *Plays: The Comedies,* edited by Allan Holaday.   1970.

Plays

> *Fedele and Fortunio: The Deceits in Love,* with Munday and Stephen Gosson (produced 1584?).   1585; edited by P. Simpson, 1909.
> *The Blind Beggar of Alexandria* (produced 1596).   1598; edited by Lloyd E. Berry, in *Plays,* 1970.
> *An Humorous Day's Mirth* (produced 1597).   1599; edited by Allan Holaday, in *Plays,* 1970.
> *The Gentleman Usher* (produced 1602?).   1606; edited by Robert Ornstein, in *Plays,* 1970.
> *All Fools* (produced 1604).   1605; edited by G. Blakemore Evans, in *Plays,* 1970.
> *Monsieur D'Olive* (produced 1604).   1606; edited by Allan Holaday, in *Plays,* 1970.
> *Bussy D'Ambois* (produced 1604).   1607; edited by M. Evans, 1965.
> *Eastward Ho,* with Jonson and Marston (produced 1605).   1605; edited by C. G. Petter, 1973.
> *Sir Giles Goosecap, Knight* (produced ?).   1606; edited by W. Bang and R. Brotanek, 1909.
> *The Conspiracy and Tragedy of Charles, Duke of Byron, Marshal of France* (produced 1608).   1608; edited by W. L. Phelps, 1895.
> *May Day* (produced 1609).   1611; edited by Robert F. Welsh, in *Plays,* 1970.
> *The Widow's Tears* (produced before 1609).   1612; edited by Robert Ornstein, in *Plays,* 1970.
> *The Revenge of Bussy D'Ambois* (produced 1610?).   1613; edited by F. S. Boas, 1905.
> *The Memorable Masque of the Middle Temple and Lincoln's Inn* (produced 1613).   1613; edited by G. Blakemore Evans, in *Plays,* 1970.
> *The Wars of Caesar and Pompey* (produced 1613?).   1631.
> *Chabot, Admiral of France* (produced 1613?).   Version revised by Shirley, published 1639; edited by Ezra Lehman, 1906.

Verse

> *The Shadow of Night, Containing Two Poetical Hymns.*   1594.

Ovid's Banquet of Sense, a Coronet for His Mistress Philosophy, and His Amorous Zodiac. 1595; edited by Elizabeth Story Donno, in *Elizabethan Minor Epics*, 1963.

Seven Books of the Iliad of Homer. 1598; *Achilles' Shield*, 1598; *Twelve Books*, 1609(?); complete work, 1611.

Hero and Leander, Begun by Marlowe, Finished by Chapman. 1598; edited by Louis L. Martz, 1972.

Euthymiae Raptus; or, The Tears of Peace, with Interlocutions. 1609.

An Epicede or Funeral Song on the Death of Henry Prince of Wales. 1612.

Petrarch's Seven Penitential Psalms, Paraphrastically Translated with Other Philosophical Poems and a Hymn to Christ upon the Cross. 1612.

Andromeda Liberata; or, The Nuptials of Perseus and Andromeda. 1614.

Eugenia; or, True Nobility's Trance for the Death of William Lord Russell. 1614.

Homer's Odyssey, 12 books. 1614(?); complete work, 1615(?).

The Divine Poem of Musaeus. 1616; edited by Elizabeth Story Donno, in *Elizabethan Minor Epics*, 1963.

The Georgics of Hesiod. 1618.

Pro Vere Autumni Lachrymae, Inscribed to the Memory of Sir Horatio Vere. 1622.

The Crown of All Homer's Works, Batrachomyomachia, or, The Battle of Frogs and Mice, His Hymns and Epigrams. 1624(?).

A Justification of a Strange Action of Nero, Being the Fifth Satire of Juvenal Translated. 1629.

Chapman's Homer: The Iliad, The Odyssey, and the Lesser Homerica, edited by Allardyce Nicoll. 2 vols., 1956.

Other

A Free and Offenceless Justification of Andromeda Liberata. 1614.

Bibliography: *Chapman: A Concise Bibliography* by S. A. Tannenbaum, 1938; supplement, 1946.

Reading List: *Chapman: The Effect of Stoicism upon His Tragedies* by John W. Wieler, 1949; *Chapman: Sa Vie, Sa Poésie, Son Théâtre, Sa Pensée* by Jean Jacquot, 1951; *The Tragedies of Chapman: Renaissance Ethics in Action* by Ennis Rees, 1954; *Homeric Renaissance: The Odyssey of Chapman* by George de F. Lord, 1956; *Chapman: A Critical Study* by Millar MacLure, 1966; *Chapman* by C. Spivak, 1967; *An Index to the Figurative Language of Chapman's Tragedies* by L. C. Stagg, 1970; *The Mind's Empire: Myth and Form in Chapman's Narrative Poems* by Raymond B. Waddington, 1974; *Chapman: Action and Contemplation in His Tragedies* by Peter Bement, 1974.

*   *   *

George Chapman's activities as poet, dramatist, and translator place him second only to his friend and sometimes collaborator Ben Jonson as a man of letters. While the two men shared a devotion to learning and a sense of vocation as professional writers, in other respects the differences are large. To the clarity which is Jonson's stylistic ideal, Chapman retorts that oratorically plain poetry "were the plaine way to barbarisme." His own style is so notoriously difficult that – mistakenly – he has been associated with the Metaphysicals. Instead, Chapman wrote as a Platonic mystagogue, using meaningful obscurity to conceal his truth from the many and reveal it to the worthy few. He should be seen as one in the line of visionary poets extending from Spenser through Milton and Blake.

Chapman was influenced heavily by Marsilio Ficino; and Chapman's Platonism supplies the key to his thought and poetics, as his various theoretical statements make clear. Poetry is an epiphany of Truth, always associated with wisdom and learning, attained through divine inspiration. The vatic poet accommodates this Truth to human understanding through symbolic images, fables, and myths. Although few men will undertake the intellectual and spiritual discipline necessary to comprehend such poetry, for the "understanders" it will "turne blood to soule" and "heighten [man's] transition into God." Central to Chapman's poetics is his conception of *form*: this includes conventional literary form (genre) by which the poet announces his general intentions; the inner form of the myth, fable, or story (understood via the traditions of allegorical commentary); and the indwelling form or "soul" of the Truth, a notion deriving from the Platonic Idea.

Chapman's most important poems were those published at the beginning of his career. *The Shadow of Night* consists of two hymns addressed to Night and to Cynthia, both revealed by the Orphic poet as religious mysteries, which anatomize man's condition and prescribe remedies. In the second, around the triune identity of the goddess as Cynthia – Diana – Hecate, Chapman interweaves a complex, three-level allegory – philosophical, political, and poetic. *Ovids Banquet of Sence*, an oblique riposte to the fashion of Ovidian erotic narratives, ironically presents Ovid as seducer, glibly misusing Platonic doctrine to achieve his end; deliberately ambiguous, the entire poem – as the title-page emblem suggests – is a *trompe l'oeil*, warning us not to trust our senses. Chapman's continuation of *Hero and Leander* "corrects" Marlowe's incomplete narrative (as does his editing of the Marlowe), restoring the moral balance and high seriousness in an Ovidian epic, written from the perspective of the allegorical commentaries upon *The Metamorphoses*. Of the Jacobean poems, two deserve mention: *The Teares of Peace*, oddly combining medieval dream-vision and Hermetic revelation, is Chapman's most sustained defense of learning; and *Andromeda Liberata* projects political allegory through mythological narrative in a manner reflecting the influence of court masques.

By 1598 Francis Meres could list Chapman among "the best Poets" for both comedy and tragedy; and theatrical writing in several dramatic genres dominated his activities for the next decade. M. C. Bradbrook credits *An Humorous Day's Mirth* with initiating the comedy of humours; and Jackson Cope had demonstrated that *The Gentleman Usher* and *The Widow's Tears* – tragi-comic romance and satiric comedy, respectively – are philosophic dramas, using mythic frameworks to explore positive and negative versions of the Platonic quest for absolute knowledge. In the tragedies Chapman obsessively rewrites the script of a flawed Titan, greater by far than the surrounding society, yet contaminated and eventually destroyed by his compromises with that society and by his own hubris. It is conventional to mark the shift from the Achillean active heroes, Bussy and Byron, to the passive, Stoic virtue of Clermont, Cato, and Chabot. But, just as Platonism always informs his poetics, so Stoicism is the foundation of his ethics throughout, a personal and eclectic Stoicism that is flexible enough to encompas both Achilles's justified wrath and the encomium of Clermont as "this Senecal man." *Bussy D'Ambois* "inwardly" measures its hero's greatness and failure against the myths of Hercules, Prometheus, and Christ; "outwardly" it is heroic tragedy and sensational melodrama. This combination of dimensions has earned its modern status as the single "anthology piece" among the tragedies. An age as receptive as ours to the drama of ideas, however, might well give more attention to the interiorized tragedies of *Byron* and *The Revenge of Bussy D'Ambois*. Although only *The Memorable Maske* survives as evidence of Chapman's skill at this new form, we have Jonson's testimony "That next himself only Fletcher and Chapman could make a Mask."

Chapman launched his Homer translation with *Seven Bookes of the Iliades* and *Achilles Shield* (1598); *The Teares of Peace* (1609) announces his visionary inspiration by Homer and his renewed dedication to the task. *The Iliads* was finished in 1611, the complete *Odyssey* in 1615, the two published together as *The Whole Works* the next year, and the lesser Homerica followed later. Despite his unfulfilled promise to present "my Poeme of the mysteries/ Reveal'd in Homer," Chapman does not encumber the epics with Platonic exegesis; rather, he sees "naked *Vlysses* clad in eternall Fiction" as totally mythic. Disdaining "word-for-word traductions," he regarded his job as *translation*, making the universal values of Homer comprehensible and therefore relevant to his own time and culture. His English systematically renders explicit the ethical and philosophical attitudes which he perceived as implicit in the text. Chapman's famous statement that the "Proposition" of each epic is contracted in the first word (*wrath* and *man*) itself epitomizes his approach to translation: "in one, the Bodie's fervour and fashion of outward Fortitude to all possible height of Heroicall Action; in the other, the Mind's inward, constant and unconquered Empire...." The adequacy of Chapman's Greek and the degree of fidelity to the original are much mooted questions which can distract attention from his very considerable achievement. Despite the hiatus in composition, Chapman's *Iliads* is generally viewed as more successful than his *Odyssey* in its consonance to the meaning of the Homer and in its unity. Certainly Chapman's *Iliads* is a splendid poem. His other literary accomplishments notwithstanding, his description of the Homer translations as "The Worke that I was borne to doe" is one to which most readers give assent.

—Raymond B. Waddington

CHAYEFSKY, Paddy. American. Born Sidney Chayefsky in the Bronx, New York, 29 January 1923. Educated at DeWitt Clinton High School, Bronx, graduated 1939; City College of New York, B.S. 1943. Served as a Private First Class in the United States Army, 1943–45; Purple Heart. Married Susan Sackler in 1949; one son. President, Sudan Productions, New York, 1956, and Carnegie Productions, New York, 1957. Since 1959, President of S.P.D. Productions; since 1967, President of Sidney Productions; since 1971, President of Simcha Productions – all New York. Since 1962, Member of the Council of the Dramatists Guild. Recipient: Screen Writers Guild Best Screenplay Award, 1954, 1971; Academy Award, 1955, 1972; New York Film Critics Award, 1956, 1971; Cannes Film Festival Award, 1955; Brussels, Venice and Edinburgh film festivals awards, 1958. Lives in New York City.

PUBLICATIONS

Plays

    Printer's Measure (televised 1953). In *Television Plays*, 1955.
    Middle of the Night (televised 1954; revised version, produced 1956). 1957.
    Televison Plays (includes *The Bachelor Party, The Big Deal, Holiday Song, Marty, The Mother*, and *Printer's Measure*). 1955.
    The Bachelor Party (screenplay). 1957.
    The Goddess (screenplay; stage version produced 1971). 1958.
    The Tenth Man (produced 1959). 1960.
    Gideon (produced 1961). 1962.
    The Passion of Josef D (produced 1964). 1964.
    The Latent Heterosexual (produced 1968). 1967.

    Screenplays: *As Young as You Feel*, with Lamar Trotti, 1951; *Marty*, 1955; *The*

Bachelor Party, 1957; *The Goddess,* 1958; *Middle of the Night,* 1959; *The Americanization of Emily,* with Alan Jay Lerner, 1964; *Paint Your Wagon,* 1969; *The Hospital,* 1971; *Network,* 1975.

Television Plays: *Holiday Song,* 1952; *The Reluctant Citizen,* 1953; *Printer's Measure,* 1953; *Marty,* 1953; *The Big Deal,* 1953; *The Bachelor Party,* 1953; *The Sixth Year,* 1953; *Catch My Boy on Sunday,* 1953; *The Mother,* 1954; *Middle of the Night,* 1954; *The Catered Affair,* 1955.

Fiction

Altered States. 1978.

*   *   *

Paddy Chayefsky was nurtured in television. There, he says, he learned to concentrate on "small moments in people's lives" and no more than "four people at the same time. TV drama cannot expand in breadth, so it must expand in depth." His first TV drama, *Holiday Song,* was set in a synagogue and based on a *Reader's Digest* story. The next year he was even more successful with *Marty:* the *New Yorker* described it as the story of "a shy, portly, and homely butcher of thirty-four, whose chief problem in life is to find a girl" (calling the plot "not only simple but even outlandish"). But Chayefsky, as he said, was "determined to shatter the shallow and destructive illusions ... that love is simply a matter of physical attraction."

Harriet Van Horne, TV critic for the *New York World Telegram and Sun,* thought Chayefsky "as important to television drama in the 1950's as was Ibsen to the stage in the 1890's. He has broken new ground, introduced a new realism, and resolutely turned his back on some of the old, constricting conventions" (27 July 1955). The famous "tape-recorder" ear for dialogue helped a great deal to make Chayefsky's reputation, but it was nothing new. It was Bronx Odets without quite so much pretension, and was familiar from Arthur Laurents's *Home of the Brave* (1946). Walter Kerr commented in his pointed *How Not to Write a Play* (1955): "He is on the side of the angels; so am I. He is going to develop his argument along certain lines; I know them. He is going to complete his charge to the jury in a burst of warm rhetoric; I can recite it in my sleep."

More recently, in films like *Hospital* and *Network,* Chayefsky has adopted still another device which connects him with television, the commercial, and indeed the television commercial. The larger screen has enabled him, in several ways, to turn up the volume.

The still minor art of television drama derived much benefit from this minor playwright. That he works long and hard and deftly with inarticulate characters and semi-hysterical situations is interesting. But what increasingly emerges is that he has really very little to say.

—Leonard R. N. Ashley

———————

CHETTLE, Henry. English. Born in London c. 1560. Married; one daughter. Apprenticed to Thomas East, printer, 1577–84; Member of the Stationer's Company, 1584. Partner, with John Danter and William Hoskins, in a printing firm, 1589–91; imprisoned for debt in Marshalsea Prison, 1598–99; wrote for Philip Henslowe, 1598–1603; contracted to write for the Earl of Nottingham's Players from 1602. *Died c. 1607.*

PUBLICATIONS

Plays

> *The Downfall of Robert, Earl of Huntingdon,* with Anthony Munday (produced 1598). 1601; edited by J. C. Meagher, 1965.
> *The Death of Robert, Earl of Huntingdon,* with Anthony Munday (produced 1598). 1601; edited by J. C. Meagher, 1967.
> *Patient Grissel,* with William Haughton and Thomas Dekker (produced 1600). 1603; edited by Fredson Bowers, in *Dramatic Works of Dekker,* 1953.
> *The Blind Beggar of Bethnal Green,* with John Day (produced 1600). 1659; edited by W. Bang, 1902.
> *Hoffman; or, A Revenge for a Father* (produced after 1602). 1631; edited by H. Jenkins and C. J. Sisson, 1951.

Fiction

> *Kind-Heart's Dream.* 1593; edited by G. B. Harrison, 1923.
> *Piers Plainness' Seven-Years' Prenticeship.* 1595; edited by James Winny in *The Descent of Euphues,* 1957.

Other

> *England's Mourning Garment in Memory of Elizabeth.* 1603; edited by C. M. Ingleby, in *Shakspere Allusion-Books,* part 1, 1874.

> Editor, *Greene's Groatsworth of Wit, Bought with a Million of Repentance.* 1592.

Reading List: *The Life and Work of Chettle* by Harold Jenkins, 1934.

*   *   *

Henry Chettle, along with so many other playwrights of Shakespeare's time, has suffered from a series of disadvantages: not only is he a "candle in the sun," but also he has been badly treated by posterity (which has lost most of his work) and by fate and finances (which teamed him up with more distinguished writers and compelled him to churn out hack work for a voracious theatre). When he died in obscurity, he had already retired from a career which involved about 50 plays for the Lord Admiral's Men and Worcester's Men.

Hoffman; or, A Revenge for a Father is the only extant play he wrote unaided. It is interesting in the light of the *ur-Hamlet* and Shakespeare's own *Hamlet,* and fits into the revenge tradition by having an Ophelia character and a determined revenger. Two plays written with Munday are perhaps his best work, centering on the Earl of Huntingdon and the Robin Hood legend. Other workman-like plays were written with Haughton and Dekker (*Patient Grissel*) and with Day (*The Blind Beggar of Bethnal Green*). A play written with Dekker (*Troilus and Cressida*) does not survive, but the "plot" is described in British Museum

Add. MS 10449. The titles of his other works are so varied that he was possibly a play doctor of his day, much as George Abbott is in our time.

Fate has been kinder to his non-dramatic work. Chettle was a friend of Greene, and edited his *Groatsworth of Wit* though, in the prefatory matter to *Kind Heart's Dream*, he politely dissociated himself from the wit's waspish attack on the actors ("antics garnished in our colors") and Shakespeare ("upstart crow, beautified with our feathers"). *Kind Heart's Dream* itself is a satirical dream fable; *Piers Plainness' Seven-Years' Prenticeship* is a picaresque pastoral narrative; *England's Mourning Garment* is a charming account of the end of the spacious days of Elizabeth I.

—Leonard R. N. Ashley

CIBBER, Colley. English. Born in London, 6 November 1671. Educated at the Free School, Grantham, Lincolnshire, 1682–87. Joined the Earl of Devonshire's Volunteers, 1688, and remained in the service of the Earl of Devonshire, 1688–90. Married Katherine Shore in 1693; ten children. Actor in the Drury Lane Company, London, 1691–1706, and Adviser to the Manager after 1700, and Actor at the Haymarket, London, 1706 until the two theatres consolidated, 1708; Co-Owner/Manager of the Drury Lane Company, 1708–32; retired officially as an actor in 1733, but occasionally appeared on the stage until 1745. Poet Laureate, 1730 until his death. *Died 11 December 1757.*

PUBLICATIONS

Collections

> *Dramatic Works.* 4 vols., 1760; 5 vols., 1777.
> *Three Sentimental Comedies* (includes *Love's Last Shift, The Careless Husband, The Lady's Last Stake*), edited by Maureen Sullivan. 1973.

Plays

> *Love's Last Shift; or, The Fool in Fashion* (produced 1696). 1696; in *Three Sentimental Comedies,* 1973.
> *Woman's Wit; or, The Lady in Fashion* (produced 1697). 1697.
> *Xerxes* (produced 1699). 1699.
> *King Richard III,* from the play by Shakespeare (produced 1700). 1700; edited by Christopher Spencer, in *Five Restoration Adaptations of Shakespeare,* 1965.
> *Love Makes a Man; or, The Fop's Fortune* (produced 1700). 1701.
> *She Would and She Would Not; or, The Kind Imposter* (produced 1702). 1703.
> *The Schoolboy; or, The Comical Rival,* from his own play *Woman's Wit* (produced 1703). 1707.
> *The Careless Husband* (produced 1704). 1705; in *Three Sentimental Comedies,* 1973.
> *Perolla and Izadora* (produced 1705). 1706.

The Comical Lovers (produced 1707).   1707; as *Marriage a la Mode* (produced 1707; as *Court Gallantry*, produced 1715).

The Double Gallant; or, The Sick Lady's Cure (produced 1707).   1707.

The Lady's Last Stake; or, The Wife's Resentment (produced 1707).   1708; in *Three Sentimental Comedies*, 1973.

The Rival Fools (produced 1709).   1709.

The Rival Queens (produced 1710).   1729; edited by William M. Peterson, 1965.

Hob; or, The Country Wake, from the play *The Country Wake* by Thomas Dogget (produced 1710).   1715.

Ximena; or, The Heroic Daughter, from a play by Corneille (produced 1712).   1719.

Bulls and Bears (produced 1715).

Myrtillo, music by J. C. Pepusch (produced 1715).   1715.

Venus and Adonis, music by J. C. Pepusch (produced 1715).   1715.

The Non-Juror, from a play by Molière (produced 1717).   1718.

Plays.   2 vols., 1721.

The Refusal; or, The Ladies' Philosophy, from a play by Molière (produced 1721).   1721.

Caesar in Egypt (produced 1724).   1724.

The Provoked Husband; or, A Journey to London, from a play by Vanbrugh (produced 1728).   1728; edited by Peter Dixon, 1975.

Love in a Riddle (produced 1729).   1729; shortened version, as *Damon and Phillida* (produced 1729), 1729; revised version, 1730.

Polypheme, from an opera by Paul Rolli, music by Nicholas Porpora (produced 1734).

Dramatic Works.   5 vols., 1736.

Papal Tyranny in the Reign of King John, from the play *King John* by Shakespeare (produced 1745).   1745.

Verse

A Poem on the Death of Queen Mary.   1695.

The Sacred History of Arlus and Odolphus.   1714.

An Ode to His Majesty for the New Year.   1731.

An Ode for His Majesty's Birthday.   1731.

A Rhapsody upon the Marvellous Arising from the First Odes of Horace and Pindar.   1751.

Verses to the Memory of Mr. Pelham.   1754.

Other

An Apology for the Life of Mr. Colley Cibber, Comedian.   1740; revised edition, 1750, 1756; edited by B. R. S. Fone, 1968.

A Letter to Mr. Pope.   1742; *Second Letter*, 1743; *Another Letter*, 1744.

The Egoist; or, Colley upon Cibber.   1743.

The Character and Conduct of Cicero Considered.   1747.

The Lady's Lecture: A Theatrical Dialogue Between Sir Charles Easy and His Marriageable Daughter.   1748.

Bibliography: by Leonard R. N. Ashley, in *Restoration and 18th-Century Theatre Research* 6, 1967.

Reading List: *Mr. Cibber of Drury Lane* by R. H. Barker, 1939; *Cibber* by Leonard R. N.

Ashley, 1965; "Cibber's *Love's Last Shift* and Sentimental Comedy" by B. R. S. Fone, in *Restoration and Eighteenth Century Theatre Research 7*, May 1968.

*   *   *

Colley Cibber was a superb actor. In a career which lasted from 1691 (when he acted in a bit part in *Sir Anthony Love* by Thomas Southerne) till 1745 (when he starred in ten performances of his own *Papal Tyranny in the Reign of King John*) he created an army of coxcombs ("first in all foppery") and sneering villains (including his adaptation of *Richard III*). In all he played about 130 different parts. He was also one of the most important actor-managers in the history of the English stage. With others, he ran, for decades, the Theatre Royal in Drury Lane, and though he was sometimes criticized for his treatment of authors and inevitably made mistakes, he had a long and generally favorable influence on the stage.

He told the story of his public life in a brilliant autobiography, *An Apology for the Life of Mr. Colley Cibber, Comedian*. The real Cibber much resembles the striking, colored bust by Roubillac in London's National Portrait Gallery: a cheerful, shrewd, frank, ruddy face, the humorous expression of the rather thin lips suggesting that they might speak, probably with some self-satisfied vanity and with more than a little determination, some wisdom and more wit. The *Apology* covers 40 years of the London stage from the pen of a man who had a chief part in shaping its goals and achievements. The writer's style is conversational, his prejudices betrayed (or clearly stated), his friends defended, his enemies attacked, but this is a discussion of his professional, not his private, life. There is little here of Cibber the family man, the gambler, the *beau garçon*. His versatility and vitality dazzle us, his talent and tenacity win our admiration, and his very flaws and frailties endear him to us, for he is a true original (as Edward Young would say) even when he comes to us like an eastern potentate bedecked in light feathers.

Cibber aroused even more opposition than the *Apology* stimulated by gaining the appointment as Poet Laureate, though Gay was at pains to point out that a better man would not have accepted the job and a worse one could not have held it. Bad as he was, Cibber was, after all, the best Poet Laureate since Dryden, and it must be admitted that the odes which Joseph Knight recklessly called "the most contemptible things of literature" do not look so bad alongside those which Masefield (and more recent) laureates have perpetrated. Pope was biased but right to say Cibber's poetry was "prose on stilts," but Dr. Johnson was right too: "Colley Cibber, Sir, was by no means a blockhead."

Cibber's true worth was in his plays. His first play, *Love's Last Shift*, he wrote out of his "own raw uncultivated Head" and it was so good his enemies later swore it must have been stolen. It was a landmark in the history of English drama and launched the long vogue of sentimental comedy. For that (and the follow-up in this genre, *The Careless Husband*) Cibber's name must be featured in every history of the drama. Even his enemy John Dennis described it as having "a just Design, distinguished Characters, and a proper Dialogue." It's a good comedy. And *The Careless Husband* is a better one.

Cibber's tragedies are, on the whole, inferior to his comedies, though he has a deft hand with melodrama, and it must be noted that his version of *Richard III* replaced Shakespeare on the stage for about 125 years. The most famous of Cibber's *rifacimenti*, however, was Molière's *Tartuffe* adapted as *The Non-Juror*; and the best-loved of Cibber's plays in his own time (second only to Shakespeare in popularity) was the comedy *The Provok'd Husband*. All of these are still worth attention.

Thus let us put Cibber down as Laureate and regret his odes, read his *Apology* and declare it too smug, praise his brilliant portrayals of the fop onstage and regret some of his private life offstage, criticize some of his comedic carpentry but recognize his occasional excellences and his undoubted place in the history of the drama, and accept Pope's diatribe in the *Dunciad* (which, after all, immortalized Cibber) while balancing it against Warburton's judicious estimate: "Cibber, with a great stock of levity, vanity, and affectation, had sense, and wit, and humor."

Leonard R. N. Ashley

COHAN, George M(ichael).   American.   Born in Providence, Rhode Island, 3 July 1878; son of the vaudevillians Jerry and Helen Cohan. Briefly attended two elementary schools in Providence; received no formal education after age 8. Married 1) Ethelia Fowler (the actress Ethel Levey) in 1899, one daughter; 2) Agnes Nolan in 1907, two daughters and one son. Travelled with his parents as a child, and made his stage debut with them in 1887; thereafter regularly appeared with his parents and sister as The Four Cohans; appeared as an actor in *Peck's Bad Boy*, in New York, 1890; toured America, with The Four Cohans, throughout the 1890's, and was appearing with them in leading vaudeville houses in New York and Chicago by the turn of the century; produced first musical for the New York stage, starring The Four Cohans and his wife, in 1901; formed producing partnership with Sam Harris, 1904, and wrote, presented, and starred in number of musical hits on Broadway; presented plays, with Harris, at the New Gaiety Theatre, New York, 1908–10, and at the George M. Cohan Theatre, New York, 1910–20; lived in semi-retirement after 1920, occasionally appearing on the New York stage. Produced 150 plays, and wrote more than 500 songs. Recipient: United States Congress gold medal, 1940. *Died 5 November 1942.*

PUBLICATIONS

Plays

   The Governor's Son (produced 1901).   Songs published 1901(?).
   Running for Office (produced 1903); revised version, as *The Honeymooners* (produced 1907).
   Little Johnny Jones (produced 1904).
   Popularity (produced 1906).
   Forty-Five Minutes from Broadway (produced 1906).
   George Washington, Jr. (produced 1906).
   Fifty Miles from Boston (produced 1907).
   The Talk of New York (produced 1907).
   The American Idea (produced 1908).   1909.
   The Yankee Prince (produced 1908).
   The Man Who Owns Broadway (produced 1909).   Songs published 1909(?).
   Get-Rich-Quick Wallingford, from a story by George Randolph Chester (produced 1910).
   The Little Millionaire (produced 1911).   1911.
   Broadway Jones (produced 1912).   1923; revised version, music by the author, as *The Two of Us* (as *Billie*, produced 1928), 1928.
   Seven Keys to Baldpate, from the novel by Earl Derr Biggers (produced 1913).   1914.
   The Miracle Man, from a story by Frank L. Packard (produced 1914).

Hello, Broadway!, music by the author (produced 1914).
What Advertising Brings, with L. Grant (produced 1915).
Hit-the-Trail Holliday (produced 1915).   1916.
The Cohan Revue 1916 (produced 1916).
Honest John O'Brien (produced 1916).
The Cohan Revue 1918 (produced 1918).
The Voice of McConnell (produced 1918).
The Fireman's Picnic. 1918.
A Prince There Was, from the novel *Enchanted Hearts* by Darragh Aldrich (produced 1918).   1927.
The Royal Vagabond, with Stephen Ivor-Szinny and William Cary Duncan, music by Anselm Goetzl (produced 1919).   1919.
The Farrell Case: A One Act Mystery (produced 1919).
Madeleine and the Movies (produced 1922).
Little Nelly Kelly (produced 1922).
The Song and Dance Man (produced 1923).
The Rise of Rosie O'Reilly (produced 1923).   Songs published 1923(?).
American Born (produced 1925).
The Home-Towners (produced 1926).
The Baby Cyclone (produced 1927).   1929.
The Merry Malones (produced 1927).
Whispering Friends (produced 1928).
Gambling (produced 1929).
Friendship (produced 1931).
Confidential Service.   1932.
Pigeons and People (produced 1933).   1941.
Dear Old Darling (produced 1935).
Fulton of Oak Falls, from a story by Parker Fennelly (produced 1936).
The Return of the Vagabond (produced 1940).   1940.

Verse

Songs of Yesteryear.   1924.

Other

Twenty Years on Broadway, and the Years It Took to Get There.   1925.

*   *   *

Cohan the dramatist? Surely not. Cohan the Yankee Doodle Dandy, the song and dance man, the song writer (not only "Yankee Doodle Dandy" but also "Mary's a Grand Old Name" and "Give My Regards to Broadway"). But Cohan the playwright is as unknown today as Cohan the vaudevillean and Cohan the movie star. The only play of his that is still remembered is probably *Seven Keys to Baldpate*, a comedy-thriller filmed five times.

In his own time, however, Cohan was significant not only as an actor but as a playwright. As Alan S. Downer puts it (in *Fifty Years of American Drama,* 1951), "Out of the variety houses and into the legitimate theatre came George M. Cohan, the apostle of rampant Americanism. With a sharp ear for the colloquial speech of New York ... , with his single-minded devotion to the color combination in Old Glory, he created a wise-cracking, quick-footed, dashing young hero who could instantaneously declare and prove his superiority to all lesser mortals, 'reubens' or 'limeys' or both." From his success derive plays such as those of Winchell Smith and George Kelly, the tough talk of the 1930's films, the snappy wisecracks of Kaufman and Dorothy Parker.

The best of the plays are probably *Little Johnny Jones*, *Forty-Five Minutes from Broadway*, *Get-Rich-Quick Wallingford*, *Seven Keys to Baldpate*, *The Miracle Man*, and *Gambling*. Cohan learned his craft in the 1880's and 1890's and seldom went beyond what he learned. He used theatrical tricks in many of the plays, shocked the audience by putting Billy Sunday on the stage in *Hit-the-Trail Holliday*, kept the title character offstage in *The Miracle Man*, had no intermission in *Pigeons and People*, revealed the identity of the robber in the first act of *Confidential Service*, always with an eye on theatrical effect. His one rule was to "wow them." When he died, he had long outlasted his time as a personality and writer.

— Leonard R. N. Ashley

COKAYNE, Sir Aston. English. Born in Elvaston, Derbyshire, baptized 20 December 1608. Educated at Chenies School, Buckinghamshire; Trinity College, Cambridge (fellow commoner); entered one of the Inns of Court, London; created M.A. at Oxford c. 1642. Married Mary Knyveton c. 1633 (died, 1683); one son and two daughters. Toured France and Italy, 1632; succeeded to Pooley Hall, Warwickshire, 1638, and the family estate at Ashbourne, Derbyshire, 1664; received baronet's patent, 1642; dissipated his wealth in extravagant living and in the service of the king and church: forced to sell Ashbourne, 1671, and Pooley, 1683, and died in poverty. *Died 13 February 1684.*

PUBLICATIONS

Collections

> *Dramatic Works*, edited by James Maidment and W. H. Logan.   1874.
> *Poems*, edited by A. E. Cockayne.   1877.
> *Dramen*, edited by H. Spaemann.   1923.

Plays

> *A Masque Presented at Bretbie in Derbyshire on Twelfth Night 1639* (produced 1639).   In *Small Poems*, 1658.
> *The Obstinate Lady.*   1657.
> *Trappolin Creduto Principe; or, Trappolin Supposed a Prince* (produced ?).   In *Small Poems*, 1658.
> *The Tragedy of Ovid*, in *Poems.*   1662.

Verse

> *Small Poems of Divers Sorts.*   1658; as *A Chain of Golden Poems*, 1658; revised edition, as *Poems*, 1662.

Translator, *Dianea*, by Giovanni F. Loredano.   1654.

*   *   *

Aston Cokayne owes his place in the annals of English drama less to his creative efforts than to his services to literary detectives. In *A Chain of Golden Poems*, an otherwise undistinguished collection of occasional verses, he revealed the existence of collaboration in the Beaumont and Fletcher canon on a much wider scale than would otherwise have been supposed. He reproached the publishers of the 1647 Folio:

> In the large book of Playes you late did print
> (In *Beaumonts* and in *Fletchers* name) why in't
> Did you not justice? give to each his due?
> For *Beaumont* (of those many) writ in few:
> And *Massinger* in other few.

The work of disintegration is still not complete, but no scholar can embark upon the study of a "Fletcher" play without being mindful of Cokayne.

In other poems in the collection, Cokayne refers to his friendships with contemporary dramatists, and no doubt these friendships urged him to emulation. He had little talent. His best-known play, *The Obstinate Lady*, shows Fletcher's influence taken to absurd extremes. A fondness for the woman-page disguise is not restricted to the young girl who is in love with her "master." Cleanthe dresses as a lad, calling herself Anclethe, to wait upon Carionil, who thinks he is in love with Lucora; the situation is similar to that in Fletcher's *Philaster*, but Cokayne also introduces Rosinda, wife of Polidacre, who has reported herself to be dead and disguised herself as a man (Tandorix) in order to test her husband's fidelity:

> to know if he
> Would keep his promise to me, which with oaths
> He oft hath made, that never, if he should
> Survive me, he would take another wife.

Perhaps a touch of Marston's *The Malcontent* enters here.

The "obstinate lady" is Lucora, who first vows herself to chastity and who is then offered in marriage (by her father) to Carionil's friend, Falorus. Naturally Falorus esteems friendship with Carionil more than love for any woman, and refuses to fight: "I do not wear a weapon for such a quarrel" (I, ii; p. 36). But since Carionil cannot win Lucora's love in his own shape, he disguises himself as a negro because, as Falorus advises him, "She that cannot love a man of a better complexion,/On one of them may settle her affection." Sure enough, Lucora forgets her vow of chastity and prepares to elope with the "negro," Tucapelo. Whilst he is waiting below her window, however, Tucapelo (or Carionil) has a flash of insight into his situation: "have I cause to love/A lady that hath so neglected me/That she preferr'd a negro?" With this, he resumes his own shape, consigns Lucora to Falorus, and receives Cleanthe into his affections. Other equally confused actions complicate the plot, and the readiness of every character to assume an alias makes the play still more difficult to read; there is no evidence that it was ever performed.

Giving an account of Cokayne's life and works, Gerard Langbaine (in *An Account of the English Dramatick Poets*, 1691) reported that he was "very much addicted to Books, and the study of Poetry; spending most of his time in the Muses company." His works show every sign of this preoccupation with art − indulged, one feels, at the expense of experience of life.

—Roma Gill

COLMAN, George, the Elder. English. Born in Florence, Italy, where his father was envoy at court, in April 1732; returned to London, 1733. Educated at Westminster School, London, 1746–51; Christ Church, Oxford, matriculated 1751, B.A. 1755, M.A. 1758; Lincoln's Inn, London, 1755–57; called to the Bar, 1757. Married the actress Miss Ford (died, 1771); children include George Colman the Younger, *q.v.* Founding Editor, with Bonnell Thornton, *Connoisseur*, 1754–56; practised law on the Oxford circuit, 1759–64; left an income by his patron, the Earl of Bath, which allowed him to abandon the law, 1764; purchased one-quarter of the Covent Garden Theatre, 1767: Manager, 1767–74; retired to Bath; contributed to the *London Packet*, 1775; bought the Little Theatre, Haymarket, and managed it, 1777–89: paralysed by a stroke, 1785, and thereafter became increasingly feeble-minded; succeeded at the Haymarket by his son, 1789. *Died 14 August 1794.*

PUBLICATIONS

Plays

Polly Honeycombe: A Dramatic Novel (produced 1760). 1760; edited by Richard Bevis, in *Eighteenth Century Drama: Afterpieces*, 1970.
The Jealous Wife, from the novel *Tom Jones* by Fielding (produced 1761). 1761; edited by Allardyce Nicoll, 1925.
The Musical Lady (produced 1762). 1762.
Philaster, from the play by Beaumont and Fletcher (produced 1763). 1763.
The Deuce Is in Him (produced 1763). 1763.
A Fairy Tale, from the play *A Midsummer Night's Dream* by Shakespeare (produced 1763). 1763.
The Clandestine Marriage, with David Garrick (produced 1766). 1766.
The English Merchant, from a play by Voltaire (produced 1767). 1767.
The Oxonion in Town (produced 1767). 1769.
King Lear, from the play by Shakespeare (produced 1768). 1768.
Man and Wife; or, The Shakespeare Jubilee (produced 1769). 1770.
The Portrait, music by Samuel Arnold, from a play by Louis Anseaume, music by Grétry (produced 1770). 1770.
Mother Skipton, music by Samuel Arnold (produced 1770). Songs published 1771.
The Fairy Prince, music by Thomas Arne, from the masque *Oberon* by Jonson (produced 1771). 1771.
Comus, music by Thomas Arne, from the masque by Milton (produced 1773). 1772.
An Occasional Prelude (produced 1772). 1776.
Achilles in Petticoats, music by Thomas Arne, from a work by John Gay (produced 1773). 1774.
The Man of Business (produced 1774). 1774.
The Spleen; or, Islington Spa (produced 1776). 1776.
Epicoene; or, The Silent Woman, from the play by Jonson (produced 1776). 1776.
New Brooms! An Occasional Prelude, with David Garrick (produced 1776). 1776.
Polly, from the play by John Gay (produced 1777). 1777.
The Sheep Shearing, music by Thomas Arne and others, from the play *A Winter's Tale* by Shakespeare (produced 1777). 1777.
The Spanish Barber; or, The Fruitless Precaution, music by Samuel Arnold, from a play by Beaumarchais (produced 1777).
The Distressed Wife (produced 1777).
Dramatic Works. 4 vols., 1777.

The Female Chevalier, from the play *The Artful Wife* by William Taverner (produced 1778).
The Suicide (produced 1778).
Bonduca, music by Samuel Arnold, from the play by Fletcher (produced 1778). 1778.
The Separate Maintenance (produced 1779).
The Manager in Distress (produced 1780). 1790.
The Genius of Nonsense, music by Samuel Arnold (produced 1780). Songs published 1781.
Preludio to The Beggar's Opera (produced 1781).
Harlequin Teague; or, The Giant's Causeway, with John O'Keeffe (produced 1782). Songs published 1782.
Fatal Curiosity, from the play by Lillo (produced 1782). 1783.
The Election of the Managers (produced 1784).
Tit for Tat; or, The Mutual Deception, from a work by Marivaux (produced 1786). 1788.
Ut Pictura Poesis! or, The Enraged Musicians: A Musical Entertainment Founded on Hogarth, music by Samuel Arnold (produced 1789). 1789.

Verse

Two Odes, with Robert Lloyd. 1760.
Poems on Several Occasions. 3 vols., 1787.

Other

The Connoisseur, with Bonnell Thornton. 4 vols., 1757.
A Letter of Abuse to D—d G—k. 1757.
A True State of the Differences (on Covent Garden Theatre). 1768.
An Epistle to Dr. Kenrick. 1768.
T. Harris Dissected. 1768.
Prose on Several Occasions. 3 vols., 1787.
Some Particulars of the Life of George Colman, Written by Himself. 1795.

Editor, with Bonnell Thornton, *Poems by Eminent Ladies*. 2 vols., 1755.
Editor, *The Works of Beaumont and Fletcher*. 10 vols., 1778.

Translator, *The Comedies of Terence*. 1765; revised edition, 1766.
Translator, *The Merchant*, in *Comedies of Plautus*. 1769.
Translator, *Epistola de Arte Poetica*, by Horace. 1783.

Reading List: *Memoirs of the Colman Family, Including Their Correspondence* by Richard B. Peake, 2 vols., 1841; *Colman the Elder* by Eugene R. Page, 1935; "Bickerstaff, Colman, and the Bourgeois Audience" by Peter A. Tasch, in *Restoration and 18th Century Theatre Research 9*, May 1970.

*   *   *

The work of the many-faceted George Colman the Elder – lawyer, essayist, editor, translator, playwright, and theatre manager – is divisible into two phases: before and after 1764. In that year his uncle and patron, William Pulteney, Earl of Bath, died without fulfilling his nephew's great expectations, and this rude jolt sent a number of aftershocks through Colman's life and consciousness, as may be seen in his plays. Prior to 1764 he thought he was merely amusing himself at the bar and in the theatre until he could be made "easy," and his early dramatic efforts are commensurately light-hearted. *Polly Honeycombe*, "A Dramatick Novel of One Act," was an auspicious beginning; with strong acting by such comedians as Yates, King, and Miss Pope, who played the titular heroine on whom Sheridan modelled Lydia Languish, it pleased the town and gained a place in the repertory, giving Colman a quick reputation as a bright young man and a promising new comic voice. He followed this up the next season – with some editorial help from Garrick, according to tradition – by adapting *Tom Jones* for the stage as *The Jealous Wife*, his first full-length comedy and another success. *The Musical Lady* and *The Deuce Is in Him* kept his name before the public in the next two years without adding to his lustre or altering his "image"; both are two-act afterpieces.

What is notable about these first four plays – especially in view of his later work – is their general antipathy to sentiment, supposedly the prevailing taste at the time. *Polly* is a spirited attack on the sentimental novel (first cousin to the sentimental comedy), *The Deuce Is in Him* on one species of sentimentalist (the Tortuous Tester of Motives; compare Sheridan's Faulkland). *The Musical Lady*, supposedly culled from the overlong first draft of *Jealous Wife* but reminiscent of *Polly* in plot, is a thin wisp of manners satire. *The Jealous Wife* is mellower – as audiences expected a *main*piece to be – and has one rather sentimental reform scene, but is basically what Goldsmith later called a "laughing comedy." In these early plays Colman clearly feels that he is witty and amusing, and that he is free to choose his satiric targets without considering which of the drama's patrons might be in the line of fire.

The discovery that he was not to be a gentleman of leisure altered Colman's whole intellectual and emotional orientation from the free-wheeling to the careful; if he must "live to please," he "must please to live." After 1764 his tone changed rather suddenly from that of Foote to that of Garrick, and his mind kept reverting – understandably – to the simple but enormous difference between bourgeois and aristocrat. *The Clandestine Marriage*, co-authored with Garrick, tells the story of a poor young clerk who secretly marries his rich boss's daughter and then has to watch her being wooed by noblemen until the truth is revealed in act five. It is a very class-conscious play – at times almost an essay in sociology – that strikes a rough balance between laughter and sentiment, ridicule and sympathy, which made it quite popular with audiences of the time and gave Colman his greatest success. The 1975 London production survived by making Lord Ogleby, a comically senile rake probably created by Garrick, the centre of the play, leaving the distressed lovers to take care of themselves.

In 1767 Colman became manager of Covent Garden Theatre. His biggest coup in that position was producing *She Stoops to Conquer* in 1773 after Garrick had rejected it; otherwise his stewardship of Covent Garden (and later the Haymarket) was undistinguished. Presumably it was the demands of his managerial duties that made his subsequent efforts at dramatic authorship diffuse and relatively disappointing. He essayed most of the genres then current, but with a marked preference for the shorter, lighter and easier forms: farces, burlettas, spectacles, alterations. *The English Merchant*, adapted from Voltaire, is notable as Colman's most sentimental comedy, perhaps his only real one; both it and *The Man of Business* reveal his continuing preoccupation with the problems of the bourgeois, but their heaviness mars their gestures at social significance in a comic framework. Of his afterpieces in these years, *The Oxonian in Town* and *Man and Wife*, a gibe at Garrick's Shakespeare Jubilee in Stratford, have some entertainment value, while *New Brooms!* makes some interesting comments on theatrical taste and managerial dilemmas at the end of the Garrick era, when Sheridan took over Drury Lane.

Colman worked at a time when traditional tragedy and comedy were breaking down into new genres; perhaps he is best remembered as one of the first English writers of the *drame* or problem play. *The Man of Business* might be called a "comedy of fiscal responsibility," yet is also kin to the domestic tragedy of Lillo. It is filled with improving epigrams ("Regularity and punctuality are the life of business") and home questions ("What has a man of business to do with men of pleasure? Why is a young banker to live with young noblemen?") that the middle-class audience found piquant and relevant, and to which Colman himself could not have been oblivious. *The Suicide* returns to the theme of a young bourgeois toying with aristocratic vices, but in a bolder, darker, and more interesting way; it deserves more attention than it has ever received. Some of Colman's best writing is in the opening scene, of revellers returning at dawn to a London household just beginning to stir, and in the black comedy of the pseudo-suicide itself. His late play *The Separate Maintenance*, while less original, again shows Colman immersed in a contemporary social problem of genuine concern to his audience. Although he never decided exactly *what* point he wanted to make about the relationship between the bourgeoisie and the aristocracy, Colman's persistence in bringing living issues onto the London stage, at a time when most comedy was escapist, is significant on the eve of the French Revolution.

—R. W. Bevis

COLMAN, George, the Younger. English. Born in London, 21 October 1762; son of George Colman the Elder, *q.v.* Educated at a school in Marylebone, London, until 1771; Westminster School, London, 1772–79; Christ Church, Oxford, 1779–81; King's College, Aberdeen, 1781–82; Lincoln's Inn, London. Married 1) Clara Morris in 1784 (died); 2) the actress Mrs. Gibbs. Took over management of his father's Haymarket Theatre, 1789–1813 (purchased the Haymarket patent, 1794; disposed of all of his shares to his partner by 1820); appointed Lieutenant of the Yeoman of the Guard by George IV, 1820; Examiner of Plays, 1824 until his death. *Died 17 October 1836.*

PUBLICATIONS

Collections

    Poetical Works. 1840.
    Broad Grins, My Night-Gown and Slippers, and Other Humorous Works, edited by G. B.
        Buckstone. 1872.

Plays

    The Female Dramatist, from the novel *Roderick Random* by Smollett (produced 1782).
    Two to One, music by Samuel Arnold (produced 1785). 1784.
    Turk and No Turk, music by Samuel Arnold (produced 1785). Songs published 1785.
    Inkle and Yarico, music by Samuel Arnold (produced 1787). 1787.
    Ways and Means; or, A Trip to Dover (produced 1788). 1788.
    The Battle of Hexham, music by Samuel Arnold (produced 1789). 1790.
    The Surrender of Calais, music by Samuel Arnold (produced 1791). 1792.
    Poor Old Haymarket; or, Two Sides of the Gutter (produced 1792). 1792.
    The Mountaineers, music by Samuel Arnold (produced 1793). 1794.

New Hay at the Old Market (produced 1795). 1795; revised version, as *Sylvester Daggerwood* (produced 1796), 1808.

The Iron Chest, music by Stephen Storace, from the novel *Caleb Williams* by William Godwin (produced 1796). 1796; edited by Michael R. Booth, in *Eighteenth Century Tragedy,* 1965.

The Heir at Law (produced 1797). 1800.

Blue Beard; or, Female Curiosity! A Dramatic Romance, music by Michael Kelly, from a play by Michel Jean Sedaine (produced 1798). 1798.

Blue Devils, from a play by Patrat (produced 1798). 1808.

The Castle of Sorrento, with Henry Heartwell, music by Thomas Attwood, from a French play (produced 1799). 1799.

Feudal Times; or, The Banquet-Gallery, music by Michael Kelly (produced 1799). 1799.

The Review; or, The Wags of Windsor, music by Samuel Arnold (produced 1800). 1801.

The Poor Gentleman (produced 1801). 1802.

John Bull; or, An Englishman's Fireside (produced 1803). 1803.

Love Laughs at Locksmiths, music by Michael Kelly, from a play by J. N. Bouilly (produced 1803). 1803.

The Gay Deceivers; or, More Laugh Than Love, music by Michael Kelly, from a play by Theodore Hell (produced 1804). 1808.

The Children in the Wood (produced 1805?). 1805.

Who Wants a Guinea? (produced 1805). 1805.

We Fly by Night; or, Long Stories (produced 1806). 1808.

The Forty Thieves, with Sheridan, music by Michael Kelly (produced 1806). 1808; as *Ali Baba,* 1814.

The Africans; or, War, Love, and Duty, music by Michael Kelly (produced 1808). 1808.

X.Y.Z. (produced 1810). 1820.

The Quadrupeds of Quedlinburgh; or, The Rovers of Weimar (produced 1811).

Doctor Hocus Pocus; or, Harlequin Washed White (produced 1814).

The Actor of All Work; or, First and Second Floor (produced 1817).

The Law of Java, music by Henry Bishop (produced 1822). 1822.

Stella and Leatherlungs; or, A Star and a Stroller (produced 1823).

Dramatic Works. 4 vols., 1827.

Verse

My Nightgown and Slippers; or, Tales in Verse. 1797; revised edition, as *Broad Grins,* 1802.

Poetical Vagaries. 1812.

Vagaries Vindicated; or, Hypocrite Hypercritics. 1813.

Eccentricities for Edinburgh. 1816.

Other

Random Records (autobiography). 2 vols., 1830.

Editor, *Posthumous Letters Addressed to Francis Colman and George Colman the Elder.* 1820.

Reading List: *Colman the Younger* by Jeremy F. Bagster-Collins, 1946; "The Early Career of Colman" by Peter Thomson, in *Essays on Nineteenth-Century British Theatre* edited by Kenneth Richards and Thomson, 1971.

*   *   *

The younger George Colman was a shrewd judge of the theatrical public's taste. As such, he earned for himself a reputation as a superior writer without ever achieving anything more than popularity. His dramatic work was of four main kinds. Firstly, he was the originator of a new kind of play (his contemporary, James Boaden, writes of "a sort of Colman drama of three acts"), in which Elizabethan blank verse and a serious theme are lightened by frequent songs and imported comic characters. *The Battle of Hexham*, *The Surrender of Calais*, *The Mountaineers*, and *The Iron Chest* are all in this style, and Colman was still ready to exploit it in 1822, when he wrote *The Law of Java*. They are plays that eased the important passage of traditional tragedy into nineteenth-century melodrama. Secondly, he wrote comedies that were generally saved by his sense of humour from conceding too much to the contemporary vogue for sentimentality. *Inkle and Yarico*, his first striking success and still an interesting piece to stage, is a comedy with songs, *Ways and Means* an imitative comedy of manners, and *The Heir at Law* shows some ingenuity in the creation of Pangloss and an ability to handle the full five-act form. *The Poor Gentleman* is too much in the mawkish shadow of Cumberland's *The West Indian*, but Colman's finest comedy, *John Bull*, merits more attention than it has received. It is robust and not at all mealy-mouthed. Thirdly, there are the ephemeral theatre-pieces, *Doctor Hocus Pocus*, a pantomime, *Blue Beard*, a spectacular, *Love Laughs at Locksmiths*, a farce, and many others. Finally, there are pieces that grew out of his work as a theatre-manager. *Poor Old Haymarket* was a prelude to the new season at the small summer theatre which he had inherited from his ailing father. It reveals a fondness for the Haymarket, and a felt sense of the difference between it and the vast patent houses. *New Hay at the Old Market* exhibits Colman's familiarity with the contemporary theatre, and furnishes us with a lot of information about it.

His autobiographical *Random Records* is honest to its title. It tells regrettably little about his final years as Examiner of Plays. He was much abused for his strictness, not least because his own light verse has prurient edges; but abuse is an inevitable concomitant of the office. Colman's Examinership was unimpressive but not malicious. The submerged tradition that he was the author of *Don Leon*, a witty and obscene poem in heroic couplets proposing an explanation of the collapse of Lord Byron's marriage, may owe its currency to a contemporary delight in taxing with immorality the official guardian of theatrical morals.

—Peter Thomson

CONGREVE, William. English. Born in Bardsey, Yorkshire, baptized 10 February 1670; moved with his family to Ireland, 1674. Educated at school in Kilkenny, 1681–85; Trinity College, Dublin; Middle Temple, London, 1691. Involved with Henrietta, Duchess of Marlborough, who bore him a daughter. Manager, Lincoln's Inn Theatre, London, 1697–1705; wrote little for the stage after failure of *The Way of the World*, 1700; associated with Vanbrugh in managing the Queen's Theatre, London, 1705; retired from the theatre, 1706, and thereafter, at the intercession of friends, held various minor government posts, including Commissioner of Wine Licenses, Undersearcher of Customs, and Secretary for Jamaica. *Died 19 January 1729.*

PUBLICATIONS

Collections

Complete Works, edited by Montague Summers.   4 vols., 1923.
Works, edited by F. W. Bateson.   1930.
Letters and Documents, edited by John C. Hodges.   1964.
Complete Plays, edited by Herbert J. Davis.   2 vols., 1967.
The Comedies, edited by Anthony G. Henderson.   1977.

Plays

The Old Bachelor (produced 1693).   1693.
The Double-Dealer (produced 1693).   1694.
Love for Love (produced 1695).   1695.
The Mourning Bride (produced 1697).   1697.
The Way of the World (produced 1700).   1700.
The Judgement of Paris (produced 1701).   1701.
Semele, in *Works.*   1710.
Squire Trelooby, with Vanbrugh and William Walsh, from a play by Molière (produced
    1704).   Revised version by James Ralph published as *The Cornish Squire,* 1734.

Fiction

Incognita; or, Love and Duty Reconciled.   1692; edited by A. Norman Jeffares, with
    The Way of the World, 1966.
An Impossible Thing: A Tale.   1720.

Other

Amendments of Mr. Collier's False and Imperfect Citations.   1698.
Works.   3 vols., 1710.
A Letter to the Viscount Cobham.   1729.
Last Will and Testament.   1729.

Editor, *The Dramatic Works of Dryden.*   6 vols., 1717.

Reading List: *Congreve* by D. Crane Taylor, 1931; *Congreve the Man: A Biography* by John
C. Hodges, 1941; *A Congreve Gallery* by Kathleen M. Lynch, 1951; *Congreve* by Bonamy
Dobrée, 1963; *The Cultivated Stance: The Designs of Congreve's Plays* by W. Van Voris,
1966; *Congreve* by Maximillian E. Novak, 1971 (includes bibliography); *Congreve: A
Collection of Critical Studies,* edited by Brian Morris, 1972.

*   *   *

William Congreve is now largely read for his plays; his poems, some of which had made
his name in London by 1692, are polished and epigrammatic; he wrote translations, short
lyrics, and occasional poems as well as ballads, his neat songs being perhaps his best
contribution. But his first literary work of note is *Incognita,* a novel largely influenced by

stage techniques. Congreve wrote it, he tells us in his *Preface*, in a fortnight; he decided to imitate dramatic writing in the plot. This is a double one with two pairs of lovers. Mistaken identities, the lovers unaware their elders have already arranged the marriages as they themselves would wish them, family feuds ultimately settled by the marriages – all of it echoes polite society and permits romantic feeling. It is finely controlled, and the comic situations bring out the sophistication with which Congreve wrote this elegant, flowing story. He told the story with obvious enjoyment and embellished it with somewhat cynical comments.

His first play was *The Old Batchelor*, a light comedy full of witty conversation, yet with undertones of reality in the character of Heartwell, the surly old bachelor who prides himself on speaking truth. He is different from the stock characters of Restoration comedy, the rakes and fops; and, of course, he is entrapped and then exposed. The situation is comic, the flippancy of Bellmour and Vainlove matched by the mockery of Belinda. And the whole play moves quickly, with a liveliness that probably owed much to Congreve's careful study of Plautus, Terence and Juvenal, as well as of Ben Jonson and the Restoration playwrights.

The Double-Dealer followed, a sombre play indeed, which verges upon the tragic, although it has its lively songs, its coxcombs and coquettes and its wit. Maskwell is Iago-like in his machinations and Lady Touchwood's fate, after her infamy is exposed, is hardly the stuff of comedy, however much Congreve thought comedy should expose the follies of vicious people. By making them ashamed of these faults, he remarked, it should instruct them, while delighting good people "who are at once both warn'd and diverted at the expense of the Vicious." The comedy was too black for its time, however much the reader can admire the classical skill Congreve showed in its construction, its unity of time – a few hours in one evening – and place – for the action takes place in the long gallery of Lord Touchwood's house (except for two episodes in a room opening off it). The absurdity of Mr. Brisk and Lord Froth, pert and solemn coxcombs respectively, Lady Froth, the coquette who pretends to poetry, wit, and learning, and Sir Paul Plyant, an uxorious old fool, all relieve the play's starkness, and indeed we realise Cynthia and Mellefont are convincingly in love, however she may doubt the merits of marriage. The comedy centres upon Maskwell's continuous capacity for intrigue, and the passion displayed not only by the Touchwoods but by Mellefont suggests that Congreve's concept of comedy was dominated in writing this play by satiric ambitions.

His next play, *Love for Love*, rightly brought him back to public favour. This is his best acting play; it has a clear plot, abundant absurdity, humorous characterisation, and satire in plenty. Here are the stock ingredients of the comedy of manners: youth and age in conflict, contrasts between city and country ways, questions of debts and inheritances, conversations between master and servant, intrigues and marriages, deceits and .witty conversations. Foresight, with his passion for astrology, his hypochondria, and his credulity, is Jonsonian; Sir Sampson Legend, authoritarian father and self-deluding lover, matches him in comic characterisation, and is akin to one of Molière's creations.

Miss Prue, the wilful ingenue, is matched by the bluff young sailor Ben, another Jonsonian character whose "humour" is marked out by his nautical language. Scandal's affair with Mrs. Foresight follows the conventional pattern of comedy which recognises the relationship of rakes and cynical married women who enjoy intrigue; Mrs. Frail, wanting to marry Valentine for his money, is tricked into marriage with Tattle whom she despises, and Valentine marries Angelica. But he has to live down his past; she is enigmatic in her response to him until he renounces his inheritance and so proves he is not primarily interested in her wealth. The "humour, plot and satire" claimed in the Prologue are all there, but this relationship between Valentine and Angelica moves a little from Restoration conventions; a touch of idealism suddenly penetrates the cynicism of Restoration comic conventions. Wit and gallantry, Angelica argues at the end of the play, are not enough. And the idealism is, perhaps, founded upon disillusion, and upon a certain fastidiousness.

In *The Mourning Bride* Congreve tried his hand at the heroic play, that strange genre which flourished in Charles the Second's age and is somewhat baffling to us. Here we have the classical use of rhetoric and music, exalted verse, and a lively plot. Congreve exhibits his dramatic sense in welding together two themes – the love of Alphonso and Almeira, and the passion of Zara, her murder of Selim, and her suicide – against a broad background of a popular resistance movement against a tyrant. For the play is violently dramatic and arresting, its language exalted yet affective.

Congreve, who had written "An Essay Concerning Humour in Comedy" in 1695 which, as well as distinguishing between wit and humour, offers us an excellent defence of English eccentricity, was now forced into a situation where he had, in effect, to defend humour on the stage. Jeremy Collier's attack on the immorality and profanity of the English stage prompted Congreve's *Amendments of Mr. Collier's False and Imperfect Citations*. It is an example of how not to reply in anger; but it shows us something more of Congreve's attitudes to comedy: that the satirical portrayal of well bred people was justifiable if their manners were ridiculous, that the author's own ideas must not be thought the same as those of the foolish people he exposed on the stage, that passages from those plays should not be taken out of context.

There followed Congreve's most brilliant comedy, *The Way of the World*, virtually his last work for the stage. (He subsequently wrote a masque, *The Judgement of Paris*, and an "Ode for St. Cecilia's Day.") This is a complex play, revolving around marriage and money, in which information is slowly revealed, and things turn out not to be what they seem. Lady Wishfort, gullible and gulled, is finally forced to allow Mirabell and Millamant to marry, Fainall is exposed, Mrs. Marwood and Mrs. Fainall suffer. The minor characters, Sir Wilfull Witwoud the buffoon, Petulant and Witwoud the fops, the servants Foible, Mincing, and Waitwell, are all brilliantly drawn, differentiated, from their first appearance on stage, by their language and attitudes. And Mirabell and Millamant mark a new refinement; they foreshadow a new sensibility, a humane quality. And they are witty, polished, epigrammatic in speech. The whole play is sparkling and lively, it brings order out of chaos, and shows Congreve was fundamentally serious, moral, idealistic. This is an impression confirmed by the few letters of his which survive. In these his warmth of heart balances his astuteness, his taste and delicacy show why his contemporaries looked upon him with – in Steele's words – "the greatest affection and veneration."

—A. Norman Jeffares

CONNELLY, Marc(us Cook). American. Born in McKeesport, Pennsylvania, 13 December 1890. Educated at Trinity Hall, Washington, Pennsylvania, 1902–07. Married Madeline Hurlock in 1930 (divorced, 1935). Reporter and Drama Critic for the Pittsburgh *Press* and *Gazette-Times*, 1908–15; moved to New York, 1915: free-lance writer and actor, 1915–33; Reporter, New York *Morning Telegraph*, 1918–21; associated with *The New Yorker* in the 1920's; wrote screenplays and directed in Hollywood, 1933–44; Professor of Playwriting, Yale University Drama School, New Haven, Connecticut, 1947–52. United States Commissioner to UNESCO, 1951; Adviser, Equity Theatre Library, 1960. Since 1920, Member of the Council of the Dramatists Guild; Member, Executive Committee, United States National Committe for UNESCO. Recipient: Pulitzer Prize, 1930; O. Henry Award, for short story, 1930. Litt.D.: Bowdoin College, Brunswick, Maine, 1952; Baldwin-Wallace College, Berea, Ohio, 1962. Past President, Authors League of America; President, National Institute of Arts and Letters, 1953–56. Lives in New York City.

PUBLICATIONS

Plays

$2.50 (produced 1913).
The Lady of Luzon (lyrics only; produced 1914).
Follow the Girl (lyrics only, uncredited; produced 1915).
The Amber Express, music by Zoel Joseph Parenteau (produced 1916).
Dulcy, with George S. Kaufman (produced 1921).   1921.
Erminie, revised version of the play by Henry Paulton (produced 1921).
To the Ladies!, with George S. Kaufman (produced 1922).   1923.
No, Sirree!, with George S. Kaufman (produced 1922).
The 49ers, with George S. Kaufman (produced 1922).
West of Pittsburgh, with George S. Kaufman (produced 1922; revised version, as *The Deep Tangled Wildwood,* produced 1923).
Merton of the Movies, with George S. Kaufman, from the story by Harry Leon Wilson (produced 1922).   1925.
A Christmas Carol, with George S. Kaufman, from the story by Dickens, in *Bookman,* December 1922.
Helen of Troy, N.Y., with George S. Kaufman, music and lyrics by Harry Ruby and Bert Kalmar (produced 1923).
Beggar on Horseback, with George S. Kaufman, music by Deems Taylor, from a play by Paul Apel (produced 1924).   1925.
Be Yourself, with George S. Kaufman (produced 1924).
The Wisdom Tooth: A Fantastic Comedy (produced 1925).   1927.
The Wild Man of Borneo, with Herman J. Mankiewicz (produced 1927).
How's the King? (produced 1927).
The Green Pastures: A Fable Suggested by Roark Bradford's Southern Sketches "Ol' Man Adam an' His Chillun" (produced 1930).   1929.
The Survey (skit), in *New Yorker,* 1934.
The Farmer Takes A Wife, with Frank B. Elser, adaptation of the novel *Rome Haul* by Walter D. Edmonds (produced 1934).   Abridgement in *Best Plays of 1934–1935,* edited by Burns Mantle, 1935.
Little David: An Unproduced Scene from "The Green Pastures."   1937.
Everywhere I Roam, with Arnold Sundgaard (produced 1938).
The Traveler.   1939.
The Mole on Lincoln's Cheek (broadcast 1941).   In *The Free Company Presents,* edited by James Boyd, 1941.
The Flowers of Virtue (produced 1942).
The Good Earth, with others, in *Twenty Best Film Plays,* edited by John Gassner and Dudley Nichols.   1943.
A Story for Strangers (produced 1948).
Hunter's Moon (produced 1958).
The Portable Yenberry (produced 1962).

Screenplays: *Whispers,* 1920; *Exit Smiling,* with others, 1926; *The Bridegroom, The Burglar, The Suitor,* and *The Uncle* (film shorts), 1929; *The Unemployed Ghost* (film short), 1931; *The Cradle Song,* 1933; *The Little Duchess* (film short), 1934; *The Green Pastures,* 1936; *The Farmer Takes a Wife,* 1937; *Captains Courageous,* 1937; *The Good Earth,* with others, 1937; *I Married a Witch,* 1942; *Reunion (Reunion in France),* 1942; *The Imposter* (additional dialogue), 1944; *Fabiola* (English dialogue), 1951; *Crowded Paradise* (additional scenes), 1956.

Radio Play: *The Mole on Lincoln's Cheek,* 1941.

Fiction

A Souvenir from Qam. 1965.

Other

Voices Off-Stage: A Book of Memoirs. 1968.

Reading List: *Connelly* by Paul T. Nolan, 1969.

* * *

Born to parents who had both had stage careers, Marc Connelly early became dedicated to the theatre. As a young child, he says in his memoirs, he got the "feeling that going to the theater is like going to an unusual church, where the spirit is nourished in mystical ways, and pure magic may occur at any moment." Connelly has spent his life as a man of the theatre seeking to produce that pure magic – as actor, director, and playwright.

Convinced that there was much to be enjoyed in life, Connelly as a young man fell in naturally with the famed "Round Table" of the 1920's at New York's Algonquin Hotel. His first New York stage venture had been the lyrics for the musical *The Amber Express* (1916), but success did not come until the collaborations with George S. Kaufman. In 1921 their *Dulcy,* a mixture of gentle satire and fun, helped to set the standard for the Broadway comedy of the 1920's. They collaborated on six other plays. Their *Merton of the Movies,* based on the story by Harry Leon Wilson, inaugurated an era of Broadway satires on Hollywood. The play's success was marked by Hollywood's turning it into a movie.

The most important play of the Kaufman-Connelly collaboration was *Beggar on Horseback,* a masterpiece of American expressionism and a fitting symbol of the *joie de vivre* the collaborators consistently sought to bring to the stage. The play is based on Paul Apel's *Hans Sonnestössers Höllenfahrt,* but it is no slavish copy of the German play – the expressionism has been completely Americanized in technique and in its satiric ends. Framed by scenes of comic realism, the visual and audial effects of the expressionism, helped by cinematic techniques, are more varied than those of Elmer Rice's *The Adding Machine* (1923).

After the success of *Beggar on Horseback,* the collaborators decided to pursue their careers apart. Connelly wrote musicals and plays (most successfully *The Wisdom Tooth*) and wrote short stories for *The New Yorker* (he was on the editorial board of the struggling new magazine), but it was not until he read Roark Bradford's *Ol' Man Adam an' His Chillun* that he wrote the play that insured his unique position in twentieth-century drama. In Bradford's rendering of Old Testament stories from the viewpoint of uneducated Louisiana Negroes, Connelly immediately perceived the basis of a drama where pure magic might nourish the human spirit. The result was *The Green Pastures,* a work which, while it contained much of the fun of Bradford, gave it a greater dignity and a greater vision. Connelly's Lawd is a growing protagonist; his play's action concerns man's search for God and God's search for man. Connelly enhanced his episodically structured play through the use of Negro spirituals, suggesting other aspects of the folk longings. By framing the play with a children's Sunday School, Connelly conveyed the value of his material: unless one becomes as a little child, the play's vision would be beyond him. Broadway had long been without a religious play, and an all-Negro cast was also unusual. Connelly had difficulty getting backing for the play, but the production (directed by himself) proved the sceptics wrong. The play ran for five years, totalling 1642 performances.

Connelly was in Hollywood often in the 1930's, writing screenplays (some of the best of the period) and directing. (He would later act in *Our Town* and in other plays.) While he wrote some scripts and other plays, none has matched his earlier successes. He published *A Souvenir from Qam*, his only novel, in 1965. He reminisced about his many years on the stage and in the movies in *Voices Off-Stage*, which gives brief glimpses of famous contemporaries but is most valuable in its story of *The Green Pastures*.

—Joseph M. Flora

COWARD, Sir Noël (Pierce). English. Born in Teddington, Middlesex, 16 December 1899. Educated at Chapel Road School, Clapham, London, and privately; studied acting at the Italia Conti Academy, Liverpool. Served in the Artists' Rifles, British Army, 1918; in the British Information Service, 1939–40; entertained troops during the Second World War. Actor, producer and director: made London debut in 1911, and thereafter appeared on the London and New York stage, often in productions of his own works; also composer, lyricist, night-club entertainer, and film actor. President, Actors Orphanage, 1934–56. Recipient: New York Drama Critics Circle Award, 1942. D.Litt.: University of Sussex, Brighton, 1972. Fellow, Royal Society of Literature. Knighted, 1970. *Died 26 March 1973*.

PUBLICATIONS

Collections

Cowardy Custard: The World of Coward, edited by John Hadfield. 1973.

Plays

Ida Collaborates, with Esme Wynne (produced 1917).
Woman and Whisky, with Esme Wynne (produced 1917).
Sketches in *Tails Up!* (produced 1918).
I'll Leave It to You (produced 1920). 1920.
Bottles and Bones (produced 1921).
The Better Half (produced 1922).
Sketches in *The Co-Optimists: A Pierrotic Entertainment* (produced 1922; revised version, produced 1924).
The Young Idea: A Comedy of Youth (produced 1922). 1922.
London Calling!, with Ronald Jeans (revue; produced 1923; revised versions produced 1923, 1924). Some items in *The Collected Sketches and Lyrics*, 1931, and *The Noël Coward Song-Book*, 1953.
The Vortex (produced 1924). 1925.
Sketches in *Charlot's London Revue of 1924* (produced 1924).
The Rat Trap (produced 1926). 1924.

Sketches in *Yoicks!* (produced 1924).

Sketches in *Charlot's Revue of 1926* (produced 1925).

On with the Dance, music by Philip Braham (revue; produced 1925). Some items in *The Collected Sketches and Lyrics*, 1931, and *The Noël Coward Song-Book*, 1953.

Hay Fever (produced 1925). 1925.

Fallen Angels (produced 1925; revised version, produced 1967). 1925.

Easy Virtue (produced 1925). 1926.

Three Plays: The Rat Trap, The Vortex, Fallen Angels, With the Author's Reply to His Critics. 1925.

The Queen Was in the Parlour (produced 1926). 1926.

This Was a Man (produced 1926). 1926.

The Marquise (produced 1927). 1927.

Home Chat (produced 1927). 1927.

Sirocco (produced 1927). 1927.

Sketches in *White Birds* (produced 1927).

This Year of Grace! (revue; produced 1928). In *Play Parade II*, 1939.

Bitter-Sweet, music by the author (produced 1929). 1929.

Private Lives: An Intimate Comedy (produced 1930). 1930.

Sketches in *Charles B. Cochran's 1931 Revue* (produced 1931).

Sketches in *The Third Little Show* (produced 1931). 1931.

Post-Mortem. 1931.

The Collected Sketches and Lyrics. 1931.

Cavalcade (produced 1931). 1932.

Weatherwise (produced 1932). In *The Collected Sketches and Lyrics*, 1931.

Words and Music (revue; produced 1932; revised version, as *Set to Music*, produced 1938). In *Play Parade II*, 1939.

Design for Living (produced 1933). 1933.

Play Parade:
    I. *Cavalcade, Bitter-Sweet, The Vortex, Hay Fever, Design for Living, Private Lives, Post-Mortem.* 1933.
    II. *This Year of Grace!, Words and Music, Operette, Conversation Piece.* 1939; augmented edition including *Fallen Angels* and *Easy Virtue*, 1950.
    III. *The Queen Was in the Parlour, I'll Leave It to You, The Young Idea, The Rat Trap, Sirocco, This Was a Man, Home Chat, The Marquise.* 1950.
    IV. *Tonight at 8:30, Present Laughter, This Happy Breed.* 1954.
    V. *Pacific 1860, Peace in Our Time, Relative Values, Quadrille, Blithe Spirit.* 1958.
    VI. *Point Valaine, South Sea Bubble, Ace of Clubs, Nude with Violin, Waiting in the Wings.* 1962.

Conversation Piece (produced 1934). 1934.

Point Valaine (produced 1934). 1935.

Tonight at 8:30 (includes *We Were Dancing, The Astonished Heart, Red Peppers: An Interlude with Music, Hands Across the Sea, Fumed Oak: An Unpleasant Comedy, Shadow Play, Family Album: A Victorian Comedy with Music, Star Chamber, Ways and Means, Still Life*) (produced in three programmes 1935). 3 vols., 1936 (*Star Chamber* unpublished).

Operette, music by the author (produced 1938). 1938.

Sketches in *All Clear* (produced 1939).

Blithe Spirit: An Improbable Farce (produced 1941). 1941.

Present Laughter (produced 1942). 1943.

This Happy Breed (produced 1942). 1943.

Sigh No More (revue; produced 1945). Some items in *The Noël Coward Song-Book*, 1953.

Pacific 1860: A Musical Romance, music by the author (produced 1946). In *Play Parade V*, 1958.

Peace in Our Time (produced 1947).   1947.

Brief Encounter, in *Three British Screen Plays,* edited by Roger Manvell.   1950.

Ace of Clubs, music by the author (produced 1950).   In *Play Parade VI,* 1962.

Relative Values (produced 1951).   1954.

Sketches in *The Lyric Revue* (produced 1951).

South Sea Bubble (as *Island Fling,* produced 1951; as *South Sea Bubble,* produced
    1956).   1954.

Quadrille (produced 1952).   1952.

Sketches in *The Globe Revue* (produced 1952).

After the Ball, music by the author, from the play *Lady Windermere's Fan* by Wilde
    (produced 1954).   1954.

Nude with Violin (produced 1956).   1957.

Look after Lulu, from a play by Feydeau (produced 1959).   1959.

Waiting in the Wings (produced 1960).   1960.

Sail Away, music by the author (produced 1961).

The Girl Who Came to Supper (composer and lyricist only; produced 1963).

*Suite in Three Keys: A Song at Twilight, Shadows of the Evening, Come into the Garden
    Maud* (produced in two programmes, 1966).   1966.

Semi-Monde (produced 1977).

Screenplays: *In Which We Serve* 1942; *This Happy Breed,* 1944; *Blithe Spirit,* 1945;
Brief Encounter, with others, 1946; *The Astonished Heart,* with others, 1950; *Meet Me
Tonight,* 1952.

Radio Play: *The Kindness of Mrs. Redcliffe,* 1951.

Ballet Scenario: *London Morning* (also composer), 1959.

Fiction

To Step Aside: Seven Short Stories.   1939.

Star Quality: Six Stories.   1951.

Pomp and Circumstance.   1960.

The Collected Short Stories.   1962.

Seven Stories.   1963.

Pretty Polly Barlow and Other Stories.   1964; as *Pretty Polly and Other Stories,* 1965.

Bon Voyage and Other Stories.   1967.

Verse

Poems by Hernia Whittlebot.   1923.

Chelsea Buns (as Hernia Whittlebot).   1925.

Spangled Unicorn: An Anthology.   1932.

The Coward Song-Book.   1953.

The Lyrics of Coward.   1965.

Not Yet the Dodo and Other Verses.   1967.

Other

A Withered Nosegay: Imaginary Biographies.   1922; augmented edition, as *Terribly
Intimate Portraits,* 1922.

Present Indicative (autobiography). 1937.
Australian Broadcast. 1941; as *Australia Visited 1940,* 1941.
Middle East Diary, July to October 1943. 1944.
Future Indefinite (autobiography). 1954.
Short Stories, Short Plays, and Songs, edited by Gilbert Millstein. 1955.
The Wit of Coward, edited by D. Richards. 1968.

Editor, *The Last Bassoon: From the Diaries of Fred Bason.* 1960.

Bibliography: *Theatrical Companion to Coward: A Pictorial Record of the First Performances of the Theatrical Works of Coward* by Raymond Mander and Joe Mitchenson, 1957.

Reading List: *The Art of Coward* by Robert Greacen, 1953; *Coward* by Milton Levin, 1968; *A Talent to Amuse: A Biography of Coward* by Sheridan Morley, 1969; *Noël* by Charles Castle, 1972; *The Life of Coward* by Cole Lesley, 1976, as *Remembered Laughter,* 1976.

*   *   *

Noël Coward was an actor, a nightclub performer, a singer who managed to overcome the lack of a good voice, a director, a producer, a screenwriter, a lyricist and composer, a raconteur and bon vivant, a short-story writer and occasional poet, the author of a couple of autobiographies, a man who gave a style to a whole era, and a dramatist. I must have left out a lot.

His work is essentially moralistic, for all its shock in the 1920's. He was, as St. John Ervine noted (in *Essays by Divers Hands,* 1935), "a Savanarola in evening dress." He is often nostalgic and sentimental but a native cynicism keeps the effect from being cloying. He is one of the great masters of drawing-room comedy and the well-made play but equally at home in revue and musical comedy and the cinema. John Bowen (in *Contemporary Dramatists,* 1973) wrote of him: "Coward is like Mozart – graceful, decorative, logical, witty and above all a craftsman." It is probably this craftsmanship, the finish, the polish, evident in everything from *The Lyrics of Noël Coward* to *The Collected Short Stories* to the forgotten novel and verse, not to mention his sparkling comedies and his acting and singing (marked with a peculiarly refreshing precision of enunciation, said to be due to coping with his mother's deafness, but probably deriving from a determination to do everything definitively) – this *professionalism* that is Coward's hallmark. Mander and Mitchenson's *Theatrical Companion to Coward* is a pictorial record of a career, whatever its ups and downs, of a multi-talented and joyful perfectionist.

His "serious" plays show him as hardworking as ever but perhaps not at the top of his form. *The Rat Trap* ("my first really serious attempt at psychological conflict") of 1926 cannot compare to the dazzling comedies of 1925: *Fallen Angels* and *Hay Fever. The Vortex* (1924) was a deft problem play which established him on the theatrical scene, but it was with comedies of the 1930's (such as *Private Lives*) and the 1940's (such as *Blithe Spirit*) that he built a lasting fame. I like *Easy Virtue* (1926), and see in it more real sympathy with his characters than in *A Song at Twilight* (1966), though in the latter play the aged homosexual writer is drawn with great skill. The basic patriotism of Coward is better seen in that "big play on a big scale" *Cavalcade* (1931) than in the England-between-the wars of *This Happy Breed* (1942) or England-after-the-war (as if Hitler had won) in *Peace in Our Time* (1947). The sentimental Englishness is best when tempered by wry humor, as in songs like "There Are Bad Times Just Around the Corner," "Mad Dogs and Englishmen," "Let's Not Be Beastly to the Germans," and raucous music-hall airs ("Saturday Night at the Rose and Crown"). "London Pride" and "London at Night" are a whit less witty, therefore a smidgen more schmaltzy. But in the end it is only fair that he loved his country. It loved him. Only a Lady Mayoress in New Zealand thought "The Stately Homes of England," Coward reported, "let down the British Empire." The Empire is now gone. The melody lingers on....

"The whole Edwardian era," wrote Coward, "was saturated with operetta and musical comedy. In addition to the foreign imprintations, our own native music was of a quality never equalled in this country since.... I was born into a generation whose parents still took light musicals seriously." Coward's contribution to it has been immense and may well prove to be his most lasting memorial. Waltzes such as "I'll See You Again," "Ziguener," "Some Day I'll Find You" and "I'll Follow My Secret Heart" sing in everyone's memory. And the comic songs! No wonder Benny Green has nominated him as "the best British composer of the last fifty years ... the best lyricist this country has produced, certainly since Wodehouse, perhaps since Gilbert."

Coward embodied a whole era. His boyhood friend Micheál Mac Liammóir said on a BBC series on "The Master" that "Noël Coward invented the 20's, just as Oscar Wilde invented the 90's."

The lifestyle presented in *Hay Fever, Design for Living, Private Lives* and *Blithe Spirit* is somewhat more acceptable now than it was in Coward's day, but the plays can never be either controversial or dated. Coward emphasized entertainment, not message, and the principal appeal of these scintillating comedies arises from their bantering dialogue (with just a touch of malice and cynicism) and their amusing situations (with just a touch of sexual spice). The artificiality of both is part of their charm. The carefully wrought machine runs on jewels of wit, and charming little figures parade before us at the appropriate times with striking effect. That it also indicates The Times is almost incidental, but useful.

In *Hay Fever* Judith Bliss, a retired actress, runs through a few of her favorite roles (glamorous star, neglected wife, self-sacrificing mother, flirt) during one hectic weekend. In *Design for Living* we have a *ménage à trois* and *la vie de Bohème* among the artists: "Otto who loved Gilda, Leo who loved Gilda, Otto who loved Leo, Leo who loved Otto, and Gilda who loved them both." *Private Lives* does something to illustrate Coward's personal credo that "the fewer illusions that I have about me or the world around me, the better company I am for myself."

Coward himself said of *Bitter-Sweet*: "disdaining archness and false modesty, I knew it was witty, I knew it was well constructed, and I also knew it would be a success." That description can suffice for a great many Coward plays (and other achievements) and makes the main points. That comedy, and not tragedy, should have been his *métier* may convince the injudicious that he is brittle and trivial – but neither the chic nor the wise can trouble themselves about people like that.

—Leonard R. N. Ashley

COWLEY, Hannah (née Parkhouse). English. Born in Tiverton, Devon, in 1743. Privately educated. Married Captain Thomas Cowley c. 1768 (died, 1797); one son and one daughter. Wrote for the stage, 1776–95; as Anna Matilda engaged in poetical correspondence with Robert Merry ("Della Crusca") in *World*, 1787. *Died 11 March 1809.*

PUBLICATIONS

Collections

Works: Dramas and Poems.   3 vols., 1813.

Plays

The Runaway (produced 1776). 1776.
Who's the Dupe? (produced 1779). 1779.
Albina, Countess Raimond (produced 1779). 1779.
The Belle's Stratagem (produced 1780). 1781; edited by T. H. Lacy, 1867.
The School of Eloquence (produced 1780).
The World as It Goes; or, A Party at Montpellier (produced 1781); as *Second Thoughts Are Best* (produced 1781).
Which Is the Man? (produced 1783). 1782.
A Bold Stroke for a Husband (produced 1783). 1784.
More Ways Than One (produced 1783). 1784; as *New Ways to Catch Hearts* (produced 1783).
A School for Greybeards; or, The Mourning Bride, from the play *The Lucky Chance* by Behn (produced 1786). 1786.
The Fate of Sparta; or, The Rival Kings (produced 1788). 1788.
A Day in Turkey; or, The Russian Slaves (produced 1791). 1792.
The Town Before You (produced 1794). 1795.

Verse

The Maid of Aragon: A Tale. 1780.
The Scottish Village; or, Pitcairne Greene. 1786.
The Poetry of Anna Matilda. 1788.
The Siege of Acre: An Epic Poem. 1801; revised edition, 1810.

Bibliography: "Some Uncollected Authors 16: Cowley" by J. E. Norton, and "Cowley" by William B. Todd, in *Book Collector 7*, 1958.

*　　*　　*

Hannah Cowley's first play, *The Runaway*, was a country-house comedy dedicated to Garrick, who "nourished" and "embellished" it. According to *The Gentleman's Magazine* for 1809, the play was written in a fortnight; if so, Cowley wrote fluently, for it is an unusually good first effort and lasted ten seasons on the stage. Her second work, *Who's the Dupe?*, a two-act farce, became one of the most popular afterpieces of the period. Later plays, including the comic opera *A Day in Turkey*, are five-act mainpieces. The two tragedies were fairly successful – *Albina, Countess Raimond* ran for seven nights and *The Fate of Sparta* for nine – but their plots are hackneyed and their language and characters dull.

The comedies, however, are among the best of their day. *The Belle's Stratagem* was the fourth most popular mainpiece written between 1776 and 1800 and was revived as late as 1913. It mixes fast-paced comic intrigue with witty dialogue and sets off a sparkling heroine and her lover in the main plot against a more sentimental pair in the sub-plot. This pattern is often repeated in later successes like *Which Is the Man?* and *More Ways Than One*. In the latter, for example, Miss Archer recalls Letitia Hardy of *The Belle's Stratagem* and Arabella parallels Lady Touchwood; in each case, the witty heroine better reflects the tone of the play than the sober one. Occasionally the blocking action opposes a father to a daughter or ward; more often, the obstacle is the attitude of one of the principals, in which cases Cowley has the other use some "stratagem" to assure the comic resolution. These comedies and *The Town Before You*, Cowley's last play, often suggest the gaiety of earlier comedy, particularly in their dialogue and heroines. Intrigue is nevertheless prominent and sometimes central, as in *A School for Greybeards*, based on Aphra Behn's *The Lucky Chance*; it sometimes sinks into farce and sometimes produces developed characters like Lord Sparkle in *Which Is the Man?*

Cowley is a mediocre poetess. *The Maid of Aragon*, *The Scottish Village*, "Edwina," and *The Siege of Acre* are included in her collected works but will not bear rereading. The last-named is interesting as an epic by a woman, but Cowley's patriotism cannot excuse her couplets. As a comic dramatist she deserves to be better known. Most of her mainpieces are fresh enough in language to play successfully today. Though she draws her characters and comic situations from the large pool used by all the dramatists of the century, she chooses and combines these elements well and is usually able to vivify the stereotype. Her best characters, especially, are memorable creations.

—Frederick M. Link

CROTHERS, Rachel.   American.   Born in Bloomington, Illinois, 12 December 1878. Educated at Illinois State Normal School, Bloomington, graduated 1892; Wheatcroft School of Acting, New York, 1893. Acted with an amateur dramatic society in Bloomington; with Felix Morris's Company; directed and staged all her own plays. Founder and First President, American Theatre Wing. Recipient: Megrue Prize, 1933; Chi Omega National Achievement Award, 1939. *Died in 1958.*

PUBLICATIONS

Plays

> *Nora* (produced 1903).
> *The Point of View* (produced 1904).
> *Criss Cross.*   1904.
> *The Rector.*   1905.
> *The Three of Us* (produced 1906).   1916.
> *The Coming of Mrs. Patrick* (produced 1907).
> *Myself, Bettina* (produced 1908).
> *Kiddie.*   1909.
> *A Man's World* (produced 1910).   1915.
> *He and She* (as *The Herfords*, produced 1912; as *He and She*, produced 1920).   1932.
> *Young Wisdom* (produced 1914).   1913.
> *Ourselves* (produced 1913).
> *The Heart of Paddy Whack* (produced 1914).   1925.
> *Old Lady 31*, from the novel by Louise Forsslund (produced 1916).   In *Mary the Third* ..., 1923.
> *Mother Carey's Chickens*, with Kate Douglas Wiggin, from the novel by Wiggin (produced 1917).   1925.
> *Once upon a Time* (produced 1918).   1925.
> *39 East* (produced 1919).   In *Expressing Willie* ..., 1924.
> *Everyday* (produced 1921).   1930.
> *Nice People* (produced 1921).   In *Expressing Willie* ..., 1924.
> *Mary the Third* (produced 1923).   In *Mary the Third* ..., 1923.

Mary the Third, Old Lady 31, A Little Journey: Three Plays. 1923.
Expressing Willie (produced 1924). In *Expressing Willie ...*, 1924.
Expressing Willie, Nice People, 39 East: Three Plays. 1924.
Six One-Act Plays (includes *The Importance of Being Clothed, The Importance of Being Nice, The Importance of Being Married, The Importance of Being a Woman, What They Think, Peggy).* 1925.
A Lady's Virtue (produced 1925). 1925.
Venus (produced 1927). 1927.
Let Us Be Gay (produced 1929). 1929.
As Husbands Go (produced 1931). 1931.
Caught Wet (produced 1931). 1932.
When Ladies Meet (produced 1932). 1932.
The Valiant One. 1937.
Susan and God (produced 1937). 1938.

*   *   *

Rachel Crothers was that rarity, a total woman of the theatre. Not since the Duke of Saxe-Meiningen and André Antoine in the last quarter of the 19th century had such a complexity of personal supervision over an entire theatrical production been seen. She was even more commanding than these two estimable and influential gentlemen since this complete control was exercised over her *own* plays which were generally directed, and occasionally even acted in, by her. Most extraordinary was the fact that it was a woman who had such a multi-leveled theatrical success and over so long a period of time. Altogether, the career of Rachel Crothers was unparalleled.

As a writer, she was a playwright and a playwright only, and the singlemindedness of her literary style also became the singlemindedness of her essential theme, that of woman emerging from the oppressions of society. Her "problem comedies" – which were notable for their witty and natural dialogue – dealt with such themes as career versus marriage (*He and She*), the "liberated" girl of the 1920's (*Nice People*), the generation gap (*Mary the Third*), divorce (*Let Us Be Gay*), adultery (*When Ladies Meet*), and emotional-cum-spiritual restlessness (*Susan and God*).

Miss Crothers was critically and popularly acclaimed as America's foremost woman playwright for over thirty years. Always concerned with human dignity, Miss Crothers organized war relief committees in both world wars. This patriotism carried into her work, for, in addition to her depiction of her theme of the feminine view of life in many variations, she was a very endemically American playwright. Speaking of her play on love firmly rooted in Yankee soil (*Old Lady 31*), a *New York Times* article of 9 February 1919 compared her to Booth Tarkington, saying "Rachel Crothers must be admitted to the small and select group of those who tend to reveal America to the Americans."

In her time she was enormously successful, and perhaps the wholesomeness of her approach and the sound common sense and decency of spirit underlying all her plays (which stand up theatrically because of their timely situations and excellent dialogue) are the essential reasons behind this resounding success. Her interest in the "balanced or everyday life" was epitomized in her work: it is her plea for "sanity in all art," as she herself termed it, which her plays so ably exemplify.

—Zoë Coralnik Kaplan

CROWNE, John. English. Born, probably in Shropshire, c. 1640; emigrated with his family to Nova Scotia, where they were granted territory by Cromwell, 1656; returned to England after the Restoration when the French seized the land, 1660. Early in the reign of Charles II worked as a gentleman-usher to a lady in London; began writing in 1665; wrote for the theatre from 1671. *Died in April 1712.*

PUBLICATIONS

Collections

Dramatic Works, edited by James Maidment and W. H. Logan. 4 vols., 1872–74.

Plays

Juliana; or, The Princess of Poland (produced 1671). 1671.
The History of Charles the Eighth of France; or, The Invasion of Naples by the French (produced 1671). 1672.
Andromache, from a play by Racine (produced 1674). 1675.
The Prologue to Calisto, with Choruses Between the Acts. 1675
Calisto; or, The Chaste Nymph, music by Nicholas Staggins (produced 1675). 1675.
The Country Wit (produced 1676). 1675.
The Destruction of Jerusalem by Titus Vespasian, 2 parts (produced 1677). 1677; part 1 edited by Bonamy Dobrée, in *Five Heroic Plays,* 1960.
The Ambitious Statesman; or, The Loyal Favourite (produced 1679). 1679.
The Misery of Civil War, from a play by Shakespeare (produced 1680). 1680; as *Henry the Sixth,* part 2, 1681.
Thyestes (produced 1680). 1681.
Henry the Sixth, part 1, from the play by Shakespeare (produced 1681). 1681.
City Politics (produced 1683). 1683; edited by John H. Wilson, 1967.
Sir Courtly Nice; or, It Cannot Be (produced 1685). 1685; edited by A. Norman Jeffares, in *Restoration Comedy,* 1974.
Darius, King of Persia (produced 1688). 1688.
The English Friar; or, The Town Sparks (produced 1690). 1690.
Regulus (produced 1692). 1694.
The Married Beau; or, The Curious Impertinent (produced 1694). 1694.
Caligula (produced 1698). 1698.

Fiction

Pandion and Amphigenia; or, The History of the Coy Lady of Thessalis. 1665.

Verse

A Poem on the Death of King Charles the II. 1685.
Daeneids; or, The Noble Labours of the Great Dean of Notre-Dame in Paris: An Heroic Poem, from a poem by Boileau. 1692.
The History of the Love Between a Parisian Lady and a Young Singing Man: An Heroic Poem. 1692.

Other

Notes and Observations on The Empress of Morocco by Settle, with Dryden and Shadwell. 1674.

Bibliography: *The First Harvard Playwright: A Bibliography of Crowne* by George P. Winship, 1922.

Reading List: *Crowne: His Life and Dramatic Works* by Arthur F. White, 1922; *The Restoration Court Stage, with a Particular Account of the Production of Calisto* by Eleanore Boswell, 1932; Introduction by Charlotte B. Hughes to *Sir Courtly Nice,* 1966.

*   *   *

John Crowne's strengths are his sharp characterizations and a sense of the stage as medium. A competent and successful dramatist, Crowne combined an understanding of contemporary taste with consistent ethical principles. His tragedies reflect the shifting forms and politics of his age, and his comedies the growing demand for sentimental reform. His contempt for political and religious faction, for fanaticism, and for tyranny of all sorts underlies much of his work.

Although Sir Courtly Nice is Crowne's best known character, his Sir Mannerly Shallow, Ramble, and the Molierian servant girl Isabella in *The Country Wit* and Young Ranter and Father Finical in *The English Friar* are well drawn satiric figures. Each represents a familiar London type and benefits from the tradition of humours characters while bearing wider implications. Ranter, for example, is a rake and a bully, a farcical rowdy, yet his father and society's tolerance contribute to his immorality. The characterizations benefit from lively dialogue often sprinkled with witty conceits, idiomatic phrases, and graceful sentences. Crowne writes far better than most of his peers and individualizes almost every character. Bartoline lisps, Artall delights in his wit, and Florio pretends piety in *City Politiques*. A number of characters refer to Adam, Eve, Eden, and the serpent in *The Married Beau*, and their words ("we are sons of Adam/And he ne'er got much honour by his sons") suit their morals. Although Crowne's tragedies have more conventional characters, some of them are notable. The Constable of France in *The Ambitious Statesman*, Caligula, and Atreus are merciless tyrants: Phraartes, the rational opponent of religion in *The Destruction of Jerusalem*, and Memnon, the son of the Amazon in *Darius*, are original heroes. Crowne is particularly good at pairing characters. The courageous, honorable Valerius contrasts to the posturing, mad Caligula: *The History of Charles the Eighth of France* has three heroes; Airy and Laura represent two types of irresponsibility in *The English Friar*.

Crowne's comic plots are rich in intrigue, discoveries, stage business, and satire. Laura chases Young Ranter with a sword: Surly smudges and belches upon the fastidious Sir Courtly Nice, and Florio and Artall anticipate Wycherley's Horner in feigning illness in order to gain access to other men's wives. Crowne's tragedies abound with virtuous maidens, wronged queens, noble warriors, tyrants, conspirators, and ghosts in plots familiar to any student of the heroic play. Within the conventions, however, Crowne produces some well-plotted, effective plays. He arranges Antigone's visit to her imprisoned mother immediately before the scene in which her lover finds his exiled father in a cave (*Thyestes*); he portrays Phraartes's frenzied reaction to Cleonora's death just before Titus Vespasian renounces Berenice in the interest of Titus's duty to Rome. Crowne, however, is capable of extravagant language and excessive violence. The Constable of France racks his own son on stage; Atreus serves Thyestes his son's blood and then the butchered body is displayed; Darius's ghost appears and gloats over the mangled bodies of his murderers.

In addition to his tragedies and comedies, Crowne wrote a court masque, *Calisto*, an adaptation of Racine's *Andromache*, two adaptations of Shakespearian plays, and a tragi-comedy, *Juliana*.

—Paula R. Backscheider

CUMBERLAND, Richard. English. Born in Cambridge, 19 February 1732. Educated at a school in Bury St. Edmunds, Suffolk; Westminster School, London, 1744–47; Trinity College, Cambridge, 1747–51, B.A. 1751. Married Elizabeth Ridge in 1759; 4 sons and 3 daughters. Fellow of Trinity College, 1752; Private Secretary to Lord Halifax in the 1750's, and Ulster Secretary under Halifax, 1761–62; Clerk of Reports, 1762–75, and Secretary, 1775–80, Board of Trade; retired to Tunbridge Wells, Kent. D.C.L.: University of Dublin, 1771. *Died 7 May 1811.*

PUBLICATIONS

Plays

    The Banishment of Cicero. 1761.
    The Summer's Tale, music by Thomas Arne (produced 1765). 1765; revised version, as *Amelia* (produced 1768), 1768; revised version, music by Charles Dibdin (produced 1771), 1771.
    The Brothers (produced 1769). 1770.
    The West Indian (produced 1771). 1771.
    Timon of Athens, from the play by Shakespeare (produced 1771). 1771.
    The Fashionable Lover (produced 1772). 1772.
    The Squire's Return (produced 1772).
    The Note of Hand; or, The Trip to Newmarket (produced 1774). 1774.
    The Choleric Man (produced 1774). 1775.
    The Princess of Parma (produced 1778).
    The Election (produced 1778).
    Calypson: A Masque, in *Miscellaneous Poems.* 1778; revised version, music by Thomas Butler (produced 1779), 1779.
    The Bondman, from the play by Massinger (produced 1779).
    The Duke of Milan, from the play by Massinger (produced 1779).
    The Widow of Delphi; or, The Descent of the Deities, music by Thomas Butler (produced 1780). Songs published 1780.
    The Walloons (produced 1782). In *Posthumous Dramatic Works*, 1813.
    The Mysterious Husband (produced 1783). 1783.
    The Carmelite (produced 1784). 1784.
    The Natural Son (produced 1784). 1785; revised version (produced 1794).
    Alcanor (as *The Arab*, produced 1786). In *Posthumous Dramatic Works*, 1813.
    The Country Attorney (produced 1787; as *The School for Widows*, produced 1789).
    The Imposters (produced 1789). 1789.
    An Occasional Prelude (produced 1792).

The Clouds, from the play by Aristophanes. 1792.
The Armourer (produced 1793). Songs published 1793.
The Box-Lobby Challenge (produced 1794). 1794.
The Jew (produced 1794). 1794.
The Wheel of Fortune (produced 1795). 1795.
First Love (produced 1795). 1795.
The Defendant (produced 1795).
The Days of Yore (produced 1796). 1796.
Don Pedro (produced 1796). In *Posthumous Dramatic Works,* 1813.
The Last of the Family (produced 1797). In *Posthumous Dramatic Works,* 1813.
The Village Fete (produced 1797).
False Impressions (produced 1797). 1797.
The Eccentric Lover (produced 1798). In *Posthumous Dramatic Works,* 1813.
The Passive Husband (as *A Word for Nature,* produced 1798). In *Posthumous Dramatic Works,* 1813.
Joanna of Montfaucon, music by Thomas Busby, from a work by Kotzebue (produced 1800). 1800.
Lover's Resolutions (produced 1802). In *Posthumous Dramatic Works,* 1813.
The Sailor's Daughter (produced 1804). 1804.
The Death and Victory of Lord Nelson (produced 1805). 1805.
A Hint to Husbands (produced 1806). 1806.
The Jew of Mogadore, music by Michael Kelly (produced 1808). 1808.
The Robber (produced 1809).
The Widow's Only Son (produced 1810).
Posthumous Dramatic Works (includes the unproduced plays *The Confession, Torrendal, Tiberius in Capreae, The False Demetrius*). 2 vols., 1813.
The Sybil; or, The Elder Brutus (produced 1818). In *Posthumous Dramatic Works,* 1813.

Fiction

Arundel. 1789.
Henry. 1795.
John de Lancaster. 1809.

Verse

An Elegy Written on Saint Mark's Eve. 1754.
Odes. 1776.
Miscellaneous Poems. 1778.
Calvary; or, The Death of Christ. 1792.
A Poetical Version of Certain Psalms of David. 1801.
The Exodiad, with J. B. Burges. 1801.
Retrospective: A Poem in Familiar Verse. 1811.

Other

A Letter to the Bishop of O—d. 1767.
Anecdotes of Eminent Painters in Spain During the 16th and 17th Centuries. 2 vols., 1782.
A Letter to Richard, Lord Bishop of Llandaff. 1783.

Character of the Late Viscount Sackville. 1785.
An Accurate Catalogue of the Paintings in the King of Spain's Palace at Madrid. 1787.
The Observer. 5 vols., 1788; edited by A. Chalmers, in *British Essayists*, 1817.
A Few Plain Reasons Why We Should Believe in Christ. 1801; as *The Anti Carlile*, 1826.
Memoirs. 2 vols., 1806–07; edited by Henry Flanders, 1856.

Editor, *Pharsalia*, by Lucan. 1760.
Editor, *The London Review.* 2 vols., 1809.
Editor, *The British Drama.* 14 vols., 1817.

Reading List: *Cumberland: His Life and Dramatic Works* by Stanley T. Williams, 1917 (includes bibliography); *Dramatic Character in the English Romantic Age* by Joseph Donohue, 1970; *Cumberland* by Richard J. Dircks, 1976.

*   *   *

Richard Cumberland is better remembered as the original of Sir Fretful Plagiary in Sheridan's *The Critic* than for his own prolific output, although *The West Indian* gets a mention in most theatrical histories as an archetype of sentimental comedy. Yet Cumberland was the author of around fifty plays in most contemporary forms, including a new version of *Timon of Athens* and, in *The Jew*, an enlightened plea for its time on behalf of a persecuted people. Sensitive to criticism though Cumberland was (and as his own *Memoirs* affirms), Sheridan's satire did nothing to discourage a dramatic career which began with *The Banishment of Cicero* in 1761 and ended with *The Widow's Only Son* just a year before his death, fifty years later.

Goldsmith, in his posthumous *Retaliation*, describes him as: "A flattering painter who made it his care/To draw men as they ought to be, not as they are." And it is true that his comedies too often tended to be the "bastard tragedies" Goldsmith elsewhere dubbed them. Yet Cumberland's first play was a true tragedy, and he also tried his hand at comic opera before attempting his first comedy, *The Brothers*, in 1769. Presumably it was the relatively favourable reception accorded this play that encouraged him to continue in this vein with *The West Indian*, whose titular hero, Belcour, blunders his good-natured but untutored way through London society, a sort of diluted, colonial version of Tom Jones.

The plot of the play is convoluted even by the standards of its time, and few of the characters do more than exemplify their required vice or virtue: but Belcour himself is strong enough to sustain a certain interest through the twists and turns of the plotting, and the Irish Major O'Flaherty, an honest soldier of fortune, serves occasionally to deflate the more sententious exchanges. If Cumberland lacked much originality, his work remains nevertheless an interesting link between sentimental comedy and melodrama, and the moral code enshrined in the one is often expressed in the exclamatory style of the other in his later work.

—Simon Trussler

DALY, (John) Augustin. American. Born in Plymouth, North Carolina, 20 July 1838; grew up in New York City. Educated in local schools. Married Mary Dolores Duff in 1869. Drama Critic for the *Sunday Courier*, and writer for the *Times*, *Sun*, and *Express*, New York, 1859–68; professional playwright from 1862; Manager of the Fifth Avenue Theatre, New York, where he established his own company of actors, 1869 until the theatre burned down in 1873; took over the New York Theatre and reopened it as Daly's Fifth Avenue Theatre, 1873; also formed the first professional organization of theatrical managers in New York, 1873; managed the Grand Opera House, New York, 1873, and the New Fifth Avenue Theatre, 1873–77; visited England, 1878–79; returned to New York and converted the Old Broadway Theatre into Daly's Theatre, where he assembled a new company of actors, and subsequently became internationally known for his productions of Shakespeare: managed the theatre and company, 1879 until his death; toured London, 1884, 1886, 1888, and Paris, 1888, 1891; opened Daly's Theatre, London, 1893. *Died 7 June 1899.*

PUBLICATIONS

Collections

> *Man and Wife and Other Plays* (includes *Divorce*, *The Big Bonanza*, *Pique*, *Needles and Pins*), edited by Catherine Sturtevant. 1942.

Plays

> *Leah the Forsaken*, from a play by S. H. von Mosenthal (produced 1862). 1886.
> *Taming a Butterfly*, with Frank Wood, from a play by Sardou (produced 1864). 1867; revised version, as *Delmonico's; or, Larks up the Hudson* (produced 1871).
> *Lorlie's Wedding*, from a play by C. Birchpfeiffer (produced 1864).
> *Judith, The Daughter of Merari*, with Paul Nicholson (produced 1864).
> *The Sorceress* (produced 1864).
> *Griffith Gaunt; or, Jealousy*, from the novel by Charles Reade (produced 1866). 1868.
> *Hazardous Ground*, from a play by Sardou (produced 1867). 1868.
> *Under the Gaslight; or, Life and Death in These Times* (produced 1867). 1867; revised version (produced 1881); edited by Michael Booth, in *Hiss the Villain: Six English and American Melodramas*, 1964.
> *A Legend of "Norwood"; or, Village Life in New England*, with Joseph W. Howard, from the novel *Norwood* by H. W. Beecher (produced 1867). 1867.
> *Pickwick Papers*, from the novel by Dickens (produced 1868).
> *A Flash of Lightning*, from a play by Sardou (produced 1868). 1885.
> *The Red Scarf; or, Scenes in Aroostock* (produced 1868).
> *Fernanda*, with Hart Jackson, from a play by Sardou (produced 1870).
> *Man and Wife*, from the novel by Wilkie Collins (produced 1870). 1885; in *Man and Wife and Other Plays*, 1942.
> *The Red Ribbon* (produced 1870).
> *Frou Frou*, from a play by Henri Meilhac and Ludovic Halévy (produced 1870). 1870(?).
> *Come Here; or, The Debutante's Test*, from a play by F. von Elsholtz (produced 1870).
> *Divorce*, from the novel *He Knew He Was Right* by Anthony Trollope (produced 1871). 1884; in *Man and Wife and Other Plays*, 1942.
> *Horizon* (produced 1871). 1885.
> *No Name*, from the novel by Wilkie Collins (produced 1871).

Article 47, from a play by Adolphe Belot (produced 1872).

King Carrot, from a play by Sardou, music by Offenbach (produced 1872).

Round the Clock (produced 1872).

Alixe, from a play by Théodore Barrière and A. Régnauld de Prébois (produced 1873).

Roughing It (produced 1873).

Uncle Sam; or, The Flirtation, from a play by Sardou (produced 1873).

Madelaine Morel, from a play by S. H. von Mosenthal (produced 1873).   1884.

The Parricide, from a play by Adolphe Belot (produced 1873).

Folline, from a play by Sardou (produced 1874).

Monsieur Alphonse, from a play by Dumas fils (produced 1874).   1886.

What Should She Do? or, Jealousy, from a novel by E. About (produced 1874).

The Two Widows, from a play by F. Mallefille (produced 1874).

The Critic, from the play by Sheridan (produced 1874; as *Rehearsing the Tragedy*, produced 1888).   1889.

Yorick, from a play by M. Tamayo y Baus (produced 1874).

The Big Bonanza; or, Riches and Matches, from a play by Gustav von Moser (produced 1875).   1884; in *Man and Wife and Other Plays*, 1942.

Pique (produced 1875; as *Only a Woman*, produced 1882; as *Her Own Enemy*, produced 1884).   1884; in *Man and Wife and Other Plays*, 1942.

The School for Scandal, from the play by Sheridan (produced 1874).   1891.

Life (produced 1876).

The American, from a play by Dumas fils (produced 1876).

Lemons; or, Wedlock for Seven, from a play by Julius Rosen (produced 1877).   1877.

Blue Glass, from a play by J. B. von Schweitzer (produced 1877).

The Princess Royal, from a play by J. Adenis and J. Rostaing (produced 1877).

Vesta, from a play by D. A. Parodi (produced 1877).

The Dark City! and Its Bright Side, from a play by T. Cogniard and L. F. Nicolaïe (produced 1877).

The Assommoir, from a novel by Zola (produced 1879).

Love's Young Dream, from a French play (produced 1879).   In *Three Preludes to the Play*, n.d.

An Arabian Night; or, Haroun Al Raschid and His Mother-in-Law, from a play by Gustav von Moser (produced 1879).   1884.

Needles and Pins, from a play by Julius Rosen (produced 1880).   1884; in *Man and Wife and Other Plays*, 1942.

The Royal Middy, with Frederick Williams, from an opera by F. Zell, music by R. Genée (produced 1880).

The Way We Live, from a play by A. L'Arronge (produced 1880).

Tiote; or, A Young Girl's Heart, from a translation by Frederick Williams of a play by M. Drach (produced 1880).

Zanina; or, The Rover of Cambaye, from an opera by A. West and F. Zell, music by R. Genée (produced 1881).

Quits; or, A Game of Tit for Tat (produced 1881).

Royal Youth, from a play by Dumas père and fils (produced 1881).

The Passing Regiment, from a play by Gustav von Moser and Franz von Schönthan (produced 1881).   1884.

Odette, from a play by Sardou (produced 1882).

Mankind, from the play by P. Merritt and G. Conquest (produced 1882).

Our English Friend, from a play by Gustav von Moser (produced 1882).   1884.

She Would and She Would Not, from the play by Colley Cibber (produced 1883).   1884.

Serge Panine, from a play by G. Ohnet (produced 1883).

Seven-Twenty-Eight; or, Casting the Boomerang, from a play by Franz von Schönthan (produced 1883).   1886.

Dollars and Sense; or, The Heedless Ones, from a play by A. L'Arronge (produced 1883). 1885.

The Country Girl, from Garrick's adaptation of the play *The Country Wife* by Wycherley (produced 1884). 1898.

Red Letter Nights; or, Catching a Croesus, from a play by E. Jacobson (produced 1884).

A Woman Won't, from a play by M. Röttinger (produced 1884).

A Wooden Spoon; or, Perdita's Penates, from a play by Franz von Schönthan (produced 1884).

Love on Crutches, from a play by H. Strobitzer (produced 1884). 1885.

Nancy and Company, from a play by Julius Rosen (produced 1886). 1884.

A Night Off; or, A Page from Balzac, from a play by Franz von Schönthan (produced 1885). 1887.

The Recruiting Officer, from the play by Farquhar (produced 1885). 1885.

Denise, from a play by Dumas fils (produced 1885).

Living for Show, from a German play (produced 1885).

The Merry Wives of Windsor, from the play by Shakespeare (produced 1886). 1886.

A Wet Blanket, from a play by P. Bilhaud and J. Lévy (produced 1886). In *Three Preludes to the Play*, n.d.

A Sudden Shower, from a play by F. Beissier (produced 1886). In *Three Preludes to the Play*, n.d.

After Business Hours, from a play by Oscar Blumenthal (produced 1886). 1886.

Love in Harnass; or, Hints to Hymen, from a play by Albin Valabrègue (produced 1886). 1887.

The Taming of the Shrew, from the play by Shakespeare (produced 1887). 1887.

The Railroad of Love, from a play by Franz von Schönthan and G. Kadelburg (produced 1887). 1887.

A Midsummer Night's Dream, from the play by Shakespeare (produced 1888). 1888.

The Lottery of Love, from a play by A. Bisson and A. Mars (produced 1888). 1889.

The Under Current (produced 1888).

The Inconstant; or, The Way to Win Him, from the play by Farquhar (produced 1889). 1889.

An International Match, from a play by Franz von Schönthan (produced 1889). 1890.

Samson and Delilah, from a play by A. Bisson and J. Moineaux (produced 1889).

The Golden Widow, from a play by Sardou (produced 1889).

Roger la Honte; or, A Man's Shadow, from the play by R. Buchanan (produced 1889).

The Great Unknown, from a play by Franz von Schönthan and G. Kadelburg (produced 1889). 1890.

As You Like It, from the play by Shakespeare (produced 1889). 1890.

Miss Hoyden's Husband, from the play *A Trip to Scarborough* by Sheridan (produced 1890).

The Last Word, from a play by Franz von Schönthan (produced 1890). 1891.

The Prodigal Son, from a play by M. Carré, music by A. Wormser (produced 1891).

Love's Labour's Lost, from the play by Shakespeare (produced 1891). 1891.

Love in Tandem, from a play by H. Bocage and C. de Courcy (produced 1892). 1892.

Little Miss Million, from a play by Oscar Blumenthal (produced 1892). 1893.

A Test Case; or, Grass Versus Granite, from a play by Oscar Blumenthal and G. Kadelburg (produced 1892). 1893.

The Hunchback, from the play by J. S. Knowles (produced 1892). 1893.

The Belle's Strategem, from the play by Hannah Cowley (produced 1893). 1892.

Twelfth Night, from the play by Shakespeare (produced 1893). 1893.

The Orient Express, from a play by Oscar Blumenthal and G. Kadelburg (produced 1895).

The Two Gentlemen of Verona, from the play by Shakespeare (produced 1895). 1895.

A Bundle of Lies, from a play by K. Laufs and W. Jacoby (produced 1895).

The Transit of Leo, from a play by B. Köhler and Oscar Blumenthal (produced 1895).
The Countess Gucki, from a play by Franz von Schönthan and F. Koppel-Ellfeld (produced 1896). 1895.
Much Ado about Nothing, from the play by Shakespeare (produced 1896). 1897.
The Wonder! A Woman Keeps a Secret, from the play by Susanna Centlivre (produced 1897). In *Two Old Comedies*, 1897.
The Tempest, from the play by Shakespeare (produced 1897). 1897.
Number Nine; or, The Lady of Ostend, with F. C. Burnand, from a play by Oscar Blumenthal and G. Kadelburg (produced 1897).
Cyrano de Bergerac, from a translation by G. Thomas and M. F. Guillemard of a play by Rostand (produced 1898).
The Merchant of Venice, from the play by Shakespeare (produced 1898). 1898.

Other

Woffington: A Tribute to the Actress and the Woman. 1888.

Reading List: *The Life of Daly* by Joseph F. Daly, 1917; *Daly's: The Biography of a Theatre* by D. F. Winslow, 1944.

*   *   *

The career of Augustin Daly is particularly difficult to capsulize. A man of tremendous energies and almost total dedication to the theatre, he became the most powerful man in American theatre during his lifetime. A drama critic, theatre manager, playwright, and adapter of foreign plays, he was also the manager of a company of actors that successfully performed Shakespearean drama in England and Europe. In the modern sense of the term he was the first stage director in America, and the strict control he exercised over all aspects of a theatrical production, even the lives of his actors, suggests both his tyranny and his devotion.

The two most important trends in late nineteenth-century American drama were an interest in social comedy and realism. Daly contributed to both, while illustrating in his plays that he was living in the age of spectacular melodrama as well as the rise of realism. Both *Divorce* and *Pique* suggest the slowly developing social comedy. *Under the Gaslight* was his first successful melodrama and boasted such realistic scenes as the Blue Room at Delmonico's, the New York pier, and the famous railroad scene in which the heroine switches the train and saves the life of the hero who is tied to the tracks. His other spectacular melodramas included *A Flash of Lightning* with its water and fire thrills, and *The Red Scarf*, in which the hero was tied to a log and sent to the saw mill.

A strong-minded impresario, Daly was primarily interested in giving audiences what they wanted. Although he tried to encourage playwriting, even tried to work with Mark Twain and William Dean Howells, he was not an innovator. Realism was spectacle to him, not a theory of living and writing. Plays by Shaw and Ibsen were never produced on his stages, and his encouragement to playwrights always involved the limitations which he felt the public dictated. As for his own plays, either original or adaptations, there is still some mystery concerning the part that his brother Joseph Daly contributed to their writing. Because he understood the requirements of the theatre he was able to inject the right ingredients into his plays and meet the demands of commercial theatre. But for this same reason he did not contribute markedly to the development of American drama and, in some ways, considering the force of his standing in theatrical circles, was a negative influence. Mainly he was a contriver of effects, a bold and ingenious creator of theatrical magic from his position as a *regisseur.* But in his best commercial successes, in both the manner of production and the material dramatized, he suggested certain truths about the society that melodrama may reflect.

—Walter J. Meserve

DANE, Clemence. Pseudonym for Winifred Ashton. English. Born in Blackheath, London, in 1887. Educated at various private schools, and at the Slade School of Art, London, 1904–06; also studied art in Dresden, 1906–07. Taught French in Geneva, 1903, and in Ireland, from 1907; left teaching for the stage, 1913: actress, as Diana Portis, 1913–18; playwright from 1921. President, Society of Women Journalists, 1941. C.B.E. (Commander, Order of the British Empire), 1953. *Died 28 March 1965.*

PUBLICATIONS

Plays

A Bill of Divorcement (produced 1921).   1921.
The Terror (produced 1921).
Will Shakespeare: An Invention (produced 1921).   1921.
The Way Things Happen: A Story, from her own novel *Legend* (produced 1923).   1924.
Shivering Shocks; or, The Hiding Place: A Play for Boys.   1923.
Naboth's Vineyard.   1925.
Granite (produced 1926).   1927.
Mariners (produced 1927).   1927.
Mr. Fox: A Play for Boys.   1927.
A Traveller Returns.   1927.
Adam's Opera, music by Richard Addinsell (produced 1928).   1928.
Gooseberry Fool (produced 1929).
Wild Decembers (produced 1933).   1932.
Come of Age, music by Richard Addinsell (produced 1934).   1933.
L'Aiglon, music by Richard Addinsell, from the play by Rostand (produced 1934).   1934.
Moonlight Is Silver (produced 1934).   1934.
The Happy Hypocrite, from the story by Max Beerbohm (produced 1936).
Herod and Mariamne, from the play by Hebbel (produced 1938).   1938.
England's Darling.   1940.
Cousin Muriel (produced 1940).   1940.
The Saviours: Seven Plays on One Theme (broadcast 1940–41).   1942.
The Golden Reign of Queen Elizabeth (produced 1941).   1941.
Alice's Adventures in Wonderland and Through the Looking-Glass, music by Richard Addinsell, from the novels by Lewis Carroll (produced 1943).   1948.
The Lion and the Unicorn.   1943.
Call Home the Heart (produced 1947).   1947.
Scandal at Coventry (broadcast 1958).   In *Collected Plays,* 1961.

Eighty in the Shade (produced 1958). 1959.
Till Time Shall End (televised 1958). In *Collected Plays*, 1961.
Collected Plays 1 (all published). 1961.
The Godson: A Fantasy. 1964.

Screenplays: *The Tunnel* (*Transatlantic Tunnel*), with Kurt Siodmak, and L. DuGarde Peach, 1935; *Anna Karenina*, 1935; *The Amateur Gentleman*, with Edward Knoblock, 1936; *Farewell Again* (*Troopship*), with Patrick Kirwan, 1937; *Fire over England*, with Sergei Nolbandov, 1937; *St. Martin's Lane* (*Sidewalks of London*), 1938; *Salute John Citizen*, with Elizabeth Baron, 1942; *Perfect Strangers* (*Vacation from Marriage*), with Anthony Pelissier, 1945; *Bonnie Prince Charlie*, 1948; *Bride of Vengeance*, with Cyril Hume and Michael Hogan, 1949; *The Angel with the Trumpet*, with Karl Hartl and Franz Tassie, 1950.

Radio Plays: *The Scoop* (serial), with others, 1931; *The Saviours* (7 plays), 1940–41; *Henry VIII*, from the play by Shakespeare, 1954; *Don Carlos*, from the play by Schiller, 1955; *Scandal at Coventry*, 1958.

Television Play: *Till Time Shall End*, 1958.

Fiction

Regiment of Women. 1917.
First the Blade: A Comedy of Growth. 1918.
Legend. 1919.
Wandering Stars, with The Lover. 1924.
The Dearly Beloved of Benjamin Cobb. 1927.
The Babyons: A Family Chronicle. 1928.
Enter Sir John, with Helen Simpson. 1928.
The King Waits. 1929.
Printer's Devil, with Helen Simpson. 1930; as *Author Unknown*, 1930.
Broome Stages. 1931.
Re-Enter Sir John, with Helen Simpson. 1932.
Fate Cries Out: Nine Tales. 1935.
The Moon Is Feminine. 1938.
The Arrogant History of White Ben. 1939.
He Brings Great News. 1944.
The Flower Girls. 1954.

Verse

Trafalgar Day 1940. 1940.

Other

The Woman's Side. 1926.
Tradition and Hugh Walpole. 1929.
Recapture (miscellany). 1932.
London Has a Garden. 1964.

Editor, *A Hundred Enchanted Tales.* 1937.

Editor, *The Shelter Book.* 1940.
Editor, *The Nelson Touch: An Anthology of Nelson Letters.* 1942.

Reading List: *Some Modern Authors* by S. P. B. Mais, 1923; *Some Contemporary Dramatists* by G. Sutton, 1924.

*　　*　　*

Clemence Dane was one of the lesser luminaries among a group of talented women writers of middle-class origin who, emerging during or shortly after the First World War, formed an important feature of the English literary scene until the 1950's. Lacking the ironic wit of a Rose Macaulay or the intuitive sensibility of a Rosamond Lehmann or an Elizabeth Bowen, she had the most vigorous talent of them all, being the author of some dozen popular novels, several collections of essays and short stories, and a large number of successful West-End dramas. Educated in England and abroad, trained at the Slade School of Art, Clemence Dane was herself on the stage for some time, acting under the name Diana Portis, before gaining celebrity as a writer. A large, generous, and energetic personality, and a distinguished sculptor and painter, her real name was Winifred Ashton, her pseudonym being adapted from St. Clement Danes church in London.

Her first novel, *Regiment of Women*, is a story of life (and especially emotional life) in a girls' boarding school, where a close relationship between two teachers is impaired by the death of a pupil and by the younger teacher's love affair, while *Legend* satirizes effectively if mildly the London literary jungle, where the bickering intimates of a young woman novelist unfeelingly dissect her life and work on the night of her death. With *The Babyons* Clemence Dane turned to the familiar romantic family chronicle, and her strong sense of historical continuity was further exploited in two lengthy, highly-acclaimed novels with theatrical backgrounds, *Broome Stages*, which charts the fortunes of a stage dynasty through seven generations, and *The Flower Girls*. While the sense of period is not very highly developed in these works, they possess a good deal of authenticity alongside their somewhat contrived "charm."

But it is primarily as a playwright that Clemence Dane is remembered. Her first play, *A Bill of Divorcement*, presenting sympathetically the case for the annulment of marriage on the grounds of insanity, is simply an updating of the topical late-Victorian "problem play" of Jones and Pinero, with a similarly unlikely, sentimental resolution of the moral dilemma. But *Will Shakespeare*, a highly-fictionalized "Invention" principally concerning the dramatist's relations with Anne Hathaway, Mary Fitton, Marlowe, and his queen, is a courageous venture into the dangers of sham-Tudor blank-verse and prose, and its style, in adorning simple sentiments in colourful language, couples a genuine beauty and bravura with un-Elizabethan decorousness. *The Way Things Happen* and *Mariners* were plays in the contemporary drawing-room convention, but *Granite*, a powerful tragedy of marital cruelty, adulterous desires, and primitive jealousies culminating in murder, set on Lundy Island in the 1810's, is perhaps Clemence Dane's finest single achievement, its skilfully constructed plot rich in ironies unfortunately unmatched by the dialogue. She returned to literary subjects with the Brontës in *Wild Decembers* and Thomas Chatterton in *Come of Age*, while historical figures are central to *England's Darling* (Alfred), *Scandal at Coventry* (Godiva) and *Till Time Shall End* (Elizabeth I). Her last stage play, *Eighty in the Shade*, took place in an Old People's Home, and starred Sybil Thorndike and Lewis Casson, who had both appeared in *Granite* in 1926.

—William M. Tydeman

DAVENANT, Sir William. English. Born in Oxford in February 1606. Educated at Oxford Grammar School; Lincoln College, Oxford, left without taking a degree. Married 1) Mary c. 1624, two children; 2) Dame Anne Cademan in 1652 (died, 1655); 3) Henrietta Maria du Tremblay in 1655. Page to the Duchess of Richmond, then entered the household of Fulke Greville, Lord Brooke, until Brooke's death in 1628; began writing for the stage in the 1620's, presented masques at court, and succeeded Ben Jonson as Poet Laureate, 1638; managed the Cockpit Theatre in Drury Lane, 1639 until the Puritans closed the theatres; fought for the Royalists at the siege of Gloucester, and knighted by the king, 1643; negotiated numerous royal missions in the Netherlands and France, 1643–49; joined the court in exile in Paris, 1650, and was appointed Lieutenant Governor of Maryland: led a colonizing expedition to America, 1650, intercepted by the Puritans, interned at Cowes, then in the Tower of Lodon, 1651; released, 1652; pardoned by Cromwell, 1654; gave theatrical productions (which he styled as "operas" to avoid Puritan restrictions) at Rutland House, 1656, and transferred to the Cockpit Theatre, 1658; after the Restoration patented by Charles II to open the Lincoln's Inn Fields Theatre. *Died 7 April 1688.*

PUBLICATIONS

Collections

> *Plays,* edited by James Maidment and W. H. Logan.   5 vols., 1872–74.
> *Selected Poems,* edited by Douglas Bush.   1943.

Plays

> *The Cruel Brother* (produced 1627).   1630.
> *The Siege* (as *The Colonel,* produced 1629?).   In *Works,* 1673.
> *Albovine, King of the Lombards.*   1629.
> *The Just Italian* (produced 1629).   1630.
> *The Wits* (produced 1634).   1636.
> *Love and Honour* (produced 1634).   1649; edited by Harold Reinoehl Walley and J. H.
>   Wilson, in *Early Seventeenth-Century Plays,* 1930.
> *The Platonic Lovers* (produced 1635).   1636.
> *The Temple of Love* (produced 1635).   1635.
> *News from Plymouth* (produced 1635).   In *Works,* 1673.
> *The Triumphs of the Prince d'Amour,* music by William Lawes (produced 1636).   1636.
> *The Fair Favourite* (produced 1638).   In *Works,* 1673.
> *Britannia Triumphans* (produced 1638).   1638.
> *The Unfortunate Lovers* (produced 1638).   1643.
> *Luminalia; or, The Festival of Light* (produced 1638).   1638; edited by Alexander B.
>   Grosart, in *Miscellanies of the Fuller Worthies' Library,* 1876.
> *Salmacida Spolia,* music by Lewis Richard (produced 1640).   1640; edited by Terence
>   J. B. Spencer, in *A Book of Masques in Honor of Allardyce Nicoll,* 1967.
> *The Siege of Rhodes,* music by Henry Lawes and others (produced 1656).   1656;
>   revised version (produced 1658), 1663; edited by Ann-Mari Hedbäck, 1973.
> *The First Day's Entertainment at Rutland House* (produced 1656).   1657.
> *The Preparation of the Athenians for the Reception of Phocion.*   1657.
> *The Cruelty of the Spaniards in Peru* (produced 1658).   1658.
> *The History of Sir Francis Drake* (produced 1658).   1659.

Hamlet, from the play by Shakespeare (produced 1661). 1676 (possibly by the actor
  Betterton).
The Law Against Lovers (produced 1662). In *Works*, 1673.
The Play House to Be Let (produced 1663). In *Works*, 1673.
The Rivals, from the play *The Two Noble Kinsmen* by Fletcher and Shakespeare
  (produced 1664). 1668.
The Tempest; or, The Enchanted Island, with Dryden, from the play by Shakespeare
  (produced 1667). 1670; edited by Vivian Summers, 1974.
The Man's the Master, from a play by Scarron (produced 1668). 1669.
Macbeth, from the play by Shakespeare (produced 1673). 1674; edited by Christopher
  Spencer, 1961.
The Distresses, in *Works*. 1673.
Julius Caesar, with Dryden, from the play by Shakespeare (produced before 1676). In
  A Collection of Plays by Eminent Hands, 1719.

Verse

Madagascar, with Other Poems. 1638.
London, King Charles His Augusta or City Royal. 1648.
Gondibert: An Heroic Poem. 1651; *Seventh and Last Canto*, 1685; edited by David F.
  Gladish, 1971.
Poem upon His Majesty's Return. 1660.
Poem to the King's Most Sacred Majesty. 1663.
Shorter Poems and Songs from the Plays and Masques, edited by Anthony M.
  Gibbs. 1972.

Other

A Discourse upon Gondibert. 1650; edited by J. E. Spingarn, in *Seventeenth-Century
  Critical Essays*, 1908.
Works. 1673.

Reading List: *Davenant, Poet, Venturer* by Alfred Harbage, 1935 (includes bibliography);
Davenant, Poet Laureate and Playwright-Manager by Arthur H. Nethercot, 1938, revised
edition, 1967; *Der Stilwandel im Dramatischen Werk Davenants* by Lothar Hoennighausen,
1965; *The Comedy of Davenant* by Howard S. Collins, 1967.

*   *   *

Davenant's dramatic works provide a strikingly diverse and comprehensive reflection of
changing theatrical tastes in the middle years of the seventeenth century, from the reign of
Charles I to the early years of the Restoration. He was an exuberant and entertaining writer
whose work was both imitative and innovative. His early work was strongly influenced by
Shakespeare, Jonson, Fletcher and others, but Davenant also made original contributions to
the theatrical tradition of his age. He played a major part in the development of English opera
and in the creation of the heroic drama, and was a lively early experimenter in burlesque and
other comic forms which became popular in the Restoration period. Lurid incident and
frequently strained and bombastic language mark his largely unsuccessful early attempts at
tragedy, such as *Albovine, King of the Lombards* and *The Cruel Brother*, written in the
manner of late Jacobean tragedies of sexual intrigue and violence in courtly settings. *The Just
Italian*, with its comic ending and markedly sentimental ingredients, shows the break-up of

the Jacobean tradition of tragedy and also anticipates the Restoration comedy of manners. With *The Platonic Lovers*, *News from Plimouth*, and, especially, *The Wits*, all written in the 1630's, Davenant brought to maturity his considerable gift for comedy. Set in London, *The Wits*, his most successful and popular play, combines adroit handling of comic situation with vivacious and amusing dialogue, while *Love and Honour*, written directly afterwards and concerned with lofty themes of self-sacrificing love and manly valour, is Davenant's first essay in heroic drama. The several court masques which he produced in collaboration with Inigo Jones in the 1630's, though tediously complimentary at times, contain spirited and skilful writing in the songs and choruses.

As the first playwright to gain official approval for the staging of theatrical entertainments in the last years of the Puritan regime, Davenant produced a series of works which owe their irregular character partly to the fact that the authorities would have frowned upon the production of ordinary stage plays. *The First Day's Entertainment at Rutland House* was a presentation comprising dialogue about the opera and about the relative merits of London and Paris interspersed with songs and consort music composed by Henry Lawes and others. *The Siege of Rhodes* is a landmark in the establishment both of English opera and the heroic drama. The "heroical" story of the work, designed "to advance the characters of vertue in the shapes of valour and conjugal love," is based primarily on the account of the siege of Christian Rhodes given by Richard Knolles in his *Historie of the Turkes* (1603). The play is divided into Entries instead of Acts, and its rhymed dialogue in "stilo recitativo" and frequent songs and choruses give the work much of the character of opera. Other "operatic" works of this period were *The Cruelty of the Spaniards in Peru* and *The History of Sir Francis Drake*, in the latter of which there occur passages of dialogue in song. In the Restoration period Davenant's main energies were directed towards translation (the principal work being *The Man's the Master*, a translation, popular in the theatre for many years, of Scarron's *Le Maitre Valet*) and his notorious, but to contemporaries greatly diverting, adaptations of Shakespeare.

In non-dramatic writing Davenant's major work is the unfinished romance-epic, *Gondibert*, a poem in heroic quatrains which incorporates many of the themes and motifs of the love-and-honour drama. He was highly talented as a writer of lyrical and occasional poems, among the best of which are "The lark now leaves his watery nest," "The philosopher and the lover," "The Soldier going to the field," "For the lady, Olivia Porter," and "To the Queen, entertained at night by the Countess of Anglesey." His delightful comic songs and poems include "Wake all the dead!," "My lodging it is on the cold ground," "The long vacation in London," and "The plots."

—A. M. Gibbs

DAY, John. English. Born in Cawston, Norfolk, in 1574. Educated at a school in Ely; Caius College, Cambridge, 1592–93. Playwright in London for Philip Henslowe, 1598–1603, and for Worcester's Company, 1602–03. *Died in 1640.*

PUBLICATIONS

Collections

Works, edited by A. H. Bullen.   2 vols., 1881.

Plays

> *The Blind Beggar of Bethnal Green*, with Henry Chettle (produced 1600).   1659; edited
> by W. Bang, 1902.
> *Law Tricks; or, Who Would Have Thought It* (produced 1604).   1608; edited by J.
> Crow and W. W. Greg, 1950.
> *The Isle of Gulls*, from the work *Arcadia* by Sidney (produced 1606).   1606; edited by
> G. B. Harrison, 1936.
> *The Travels of the Three English Brothers, Sir Thomas, Sir Anthony, Mr. Robert Shirley*,
> with William Rowley and George Wilkins (produced 1607).   1607.
> *Humour Out of Breath* (produced 1608?).   1608; edited by Arthur Symons, in *Nero and
> Other Plays*, 1888.

Verse

> *The Parliament of Bees, with Their Proper Characters* (pastoral dialogues).   1641;
> edited by Arthur Symons, in *Nero and Other Plays*, 1888.

Other

> *Peregrinatio Scholastica; or, Learning's Pilgrimage*, in *Works*.   1881.

*   *   *

John Day is one of the most neglected dramatists of the Elizabethan period, a distinction which is, for the most part, justified. His dramatic talents do not include the strong lines and "supernatural music" of Marlowe, Middleton, or Webster; and he rarely matches the dramatic craftsmanship of Dekker or Heywood. While his surviving plays exhibit a considerable diversity in subject matter, he pays little attention to the delineation of his characters, who with a few exceptions remain conventional or superficial. Day's dramatic verse is memorable for its stylistic regularity and euphuistic extravagance, though at moments it possesses a lyrical grace and delicacy that rival the poetry of his better-known contemporaries.

Day collaborated with at least half a dozen of Henslowe's writers on twenty-two plays between 1598 and 1603, though only two survive: *The Blind-Beggar of Bednal-Green*, with its haphazard plot construction, still maintains what Swinburne saw as "some good simple fun"; and *The Travailes of the Three English Brothers* is a topical romantic adventure similar to the early plays of Heywood. The remainder of Day's surviving plays were written for the more sophisticated audience of the private theatres. *The Ile of Guls*, according to the Prologue, is "a little spring ... drawne fro the full streame of the right worthy Gentleman Sir *Phillip Sydneys* well known Archadea." The play contains some of the best of Day's verse dialogue, but the "gulling" satire is as limp as the characterization. *Law Trickes; or, Who Would Have Thought It* reveals Day's indebtedness to Marston for elements of his comic satire. The result is an often strained but not displeasing comedy in which even the Epilogue queries, "Who would have thought such strange euents should fall/ Into a course so smooth and comicall?" The influence of Lyly and Shakespeare can be seen in *Humour Out of Breath*, a play which shows Day at his best as a dramatic poet. The character of his heroine, Florimell, outshines any other figure in his works, and resembles to a lesser degree Shakespeare's Rosalind. At the same time, this well-constructed comedy contains several notable passages of lyrical value.

The Parliament of Bees, generally regarded as Day's finest work, is a series of twelve colloquies most likely based on the *Georgics* of Virgil and the plethora of verse satires written in the 1590's. The characters of the individual bees are less memorable than the abundance of pure poetry and high flights of fancy in such musical, rhymed verse as:

> When of the sudaine, listning, you shall heare
> A noise of Hornes and hunting, which shall bring
> *Acteon* to *Diana* in the spring.

Many years after his dramatic floruit, Day wrote an interesting and capable allegorical prose tract, *Peregrinatio Scholastica or Learneinges Pillgrimage*, which is divided into twenty "morall Tractates." The dedication to this piece provides an illuminating autobiographical note: Day acknowledges that he has been passed over by the "Credit" and "Opinion" bestowed on his luckier contemporaries, and yet he writes, "The day may come when *Nos quoque floruimus* may be there motto as well as myne: in the mean time, being becalmde in a fogg of necessity, I am content to ly at Anchor before the Ilands *Meliora Speramus*."

Day's neglect, then, goes back to his own lifetime, as he presumably finished his career in "a fogg of necessity." As a hack writer in good earnest for Henslowe and the private companies, he saw moderate success on the stage, but Day will ultimately be remembered for his airy and melodious lyrics.

—Raymond C. Shady

DEKKER, Thomas. English. Born in London c. 1570. Nothing is known for certain about his parentage, education, or marriage(s). Playwright for Philip Henslowe, c. 1598–1602; mentioned in documents as having worked on 50 plays; after 1602 divided his time between playwriting and writing pamphlets; lived in extreme poverty: saved from debtor's prison by Henslowe, 1598, 1599; imprisoned for debt in the King's Bench Prison, London, 1613–19. *Died* (buried) *25 August 1632.*

PUBLICATIONS

Collections

Non-Dramatic Works, edited by A. B. Grosart.   5 vols., 1884–86.
Dramatic Works, edited by Fredson Bowers.   4 vols., 1953–61.
Selected Writings (prose), edited by E. D. Pendry.   1968.

Plays

Old Fortunatus (produced 1599).   1600.
The Shoemaker's Holiday; or, The Gentle Craft (produced 1599).   1600; edited by R. L. Smallwood and Stanley Wells, 1978.
Patient Grissel, with Henry Chettle and William Haughton (produced 1600).   1603.
Lust's Dominion; or, The Lascivious Queen (as *The Spanish Moor's Tragedy,* produced 1600).   1657.

Satiromastix; or, The Untrussing of the Humorous Poet (produced 1601).   1602.
Sir Thomas Wyatt, with Thomas Heywood and Webster (produced 1602–07?).   1607.
King James His Royal and Magnificent Entertainment, with Jonson (produced 1603).   With *Entertainment of the Queen and Prince at Althorp*, by Jonson, 1604.
The Honest Whore, with Middleton (produced 1604).   1604; as *The Converted Courtesan*, 1604.
Westward Ho, with Webster (produced 1604).   1607.
The Roaring Girl; or, Moll Cut-Purse, with Middleton (produced 1604–10?).   1611; edited by Andor Gomme, 1976.
Northward Ho, with Webster (produced 1605).   1607.
The Honest Whore, part 2 (produced 1605?).   1630.
The Whore of Babylon (produced 1605–07?).   1607.
If This Be Not Good the Devil Is in It (produced 1610–12?).   1612.
Match Me in London (produced 1611–13?).   1631.
Troia-Nova Triumphans, London Triumphing (produced 1612).   1612.
The Virgin Martyr, with Massinger (produced 1620).   1622.
The Witch of Edmonton, with William Rowley and John Ford (produced 1621).   1658.
The Noble Soldier; or, A Contract Broken, Justly Revenged (as *The Noble Spanish Soldier*, produced 1622–31?).   1634.
The Wonder of a Kingdon (produced 1623–31?).   1636.
The Welsh Ambassador, with Ford (produced 1623).   Edited by H. Littledale and W. W. Greg, 1920.
The Sun's Darling: A Moral Masque, with Ford (produced 1624).   1656.
Britannia's Honour (produced 1628).   1628.
London's Tempe; or, The Field of Happiness (produced 1629).   1629.

Fiction and Prose

The Wonderful Year, Wherein Is Shown the Picture of London Lying Sick of the Plague.   1603; in *Selected Writings*, 1968.
News from Gravesend, Sent to Nobody.   1604; edited by F. P. Wilson, in *Plague Pamphlets*, 1925.
The Meeting of Gallants at an Ordinary; or, The Walks in Paul's.   1604; edited by F. P. Wilson, in *Plague Pamphlets*, 1925.
The Double PP: A Papist Encountered by the Protestant.   1606.
News from Hell.   1606; revised edition, as *A Knight's Conjuring, Done in Earnest, Discovered in Jest*, 1607; edited by Larry M. Robbins, 1974.
The Seven Deadly Sins of London.   1606; edited by H. F. B. Brett-Smith, 1922.
Jests to Make You Merry, with George Wilkins.   1607.
The Dead Term; or, Westminster's Complaint for Long Vacations and Short Terms.   1608.
The Bellman of London, Bringing to Light the Most Notorious Villainies.   1608; edited by O. Smeaton, 1904.
Lantern and Candle-Light; or, The Bellman's Second Night's Walk.   1608; revised edition, 1609; as *O Per Se O; or, A New Crier of Lantern and Candle-Light*, 1612; revised edition, as *Villainies Discovered by Lantern and Candle-Light*, 1616, 1620; revised edition, as *English Villainies*, 1638, 1648; in *Selected Writings*, 1968.
Four Birds of Noah's Ark.   1609; edited by F. P. Wilson, 1924.
The Gull's Horn-Book.   1609; in *Selected Writings*, 1968.
The Raven's Almanac Foretelling of a Plague, Famine, and Civil War.   1609.
Work for Armourers; or, The Peace Is Broken.   1609.
A Strange Horse Race.   1613.
Dekker His Dream.   1620; edited by J. O. Halliwell, 1860.

A Rod for Runaways. 1625; revised edition, 1625; edited by F. P. Wilson, in *Plague Pamphlets*, 1925.

The Black Rod and the White Rod, Justice and Mercy, Striking and Sparing London. 1630; edited by F. P. Wilson, in *Plague Pamphlets*, 1925.

Penny-Wise Pound-Foolish; or, A Bristow Diamond Set in Two Rings and Both Cracked. 1631; in *Selected Writings*, 1968.

Verse

The Artillery Garden. 1616; edited by F. P. Wilson, 1952.
Wars, Wars, Wars. 1628.

Bibliography: *Dekker: A Concise Bibliography* by S. A. Tannenbaum, 1939; supplement, 1945; supplement in *Elizabethan Bibliographies Supplements 2* by D. G. Donovan, 1967; *Dekker: A Bibliographical Catalogue (to 1700)* by Antony F. Allison, 1972.

Reading List: *Dekker: A Study in Economic and Social Backgrounds* by K. L. Gregg, 1924; *The Base String: The Underworld in Elizabethan Drama* by N. Berlin, 1968; *Dekker* by George R. Price, 1969; *Dekker: An Analysis of Dramatic Structure* by James H. Conover, 1969; *Rhetoric in the Plays of Dekker* by Suzanne K. Blow, 1972; *Serious and Tragic Elements in the Comedy of Dekker* by Peggy F. Shirley, 1975.

*   *   *

Like his predecessor Robert Greene, Thomas Dekker was both a playwright and a writer of popular didactic pamphlets. To Ben Jonson, he was merely a "dresser of plays," a debt-ridden hack in Philip Henslowe's staple of play doctors who wrote, often in collaboration, any type of play required by the Lord Admiral's Men – romantic comedy, comedy of manners, satire, tragi-comedy, or tragedy. Dekker's earliest success, performed at court by the Lord Admiral's Men in 1599, was *Old Fortunatus*, an old-fashioned play in the style of Greene and George Peele. Derived from an ancient German folk tale, it relates a rambling story of the misfortunes of an old beggar and his sons who foolishly choose riches when offered a choice of any of the world's benefits by the goddess Fortune. It represents every romantic excess the newer dramatists like Chapman and Jonson scorned: allegorical characters from the old morality plays, action that moves from Cyprus to England, farce and sentimentality, and sermonizing on the vanity of human wishes. In a fresher, more sophisticated mode is Dekker's greatest comedy, *The Shoemaker's Holiday*, also performed at court by the Lord Admiral's Men. This sprightly London Comedy Dekker based in part on Thomas Deloney's highly popular prose tale *The Gentle Craft*, the story of how a simple cobbler rose to become lord mayor of London, and on the Cinderella-like courtship in Greene's *Friar Bacon and Friar Bungay*. Like Shakespeare's Henriad plays, which were on the stage of the Globe at about the same time, *The Shoemaker's Holiday* portrays London and its environs amid the stir of Henry V's French wars, but Dekker's concerns, unlike Shakespeare's, are neither historical nor political. His story is the simple one of how Lacey, a noble's son, woos the beautiful commoner Rose in the disguise of a Dutch apprentice in the employ of the madcap shoemaker Simon Eyre and his biosterous journeymen. The comedy has all of Dekker's distinctive dramatic qualities: a tender romantic love story accompanied by a sub-plot of farce occasionally touched with realism; lyrical love scenes of unabashed sentiment contrasted with vivid colloquial prose; sweet love songs and raucous tradesmen's choruses and morris dances. *The Shoemaker's Holiday* is Dekker's sole masterpiece; in his later plays he was never able to equal this superb integration of farce, realism, and romance.

After *The Shoemaker's Holiday*, plot construction became Dekker's salient weakness, possibly because poverty compelled him to write rapidly and in collaboration with others. *Satiromastix; or, The Untrussing of the Humorous Poet* in part retaliates against Jonson for his satire against Dekker and Marston in *The Poetaster*. The rest of *Satiromastix* combines satire with tragicomedy and romanticized chronicle (England around 1100 A.D.). This indifference to form is equally evident in *Westward Ho* and *Northward Ho*, both comedies in collaboration with John Webster. Dekker worked with Thomas Middleton on Part I of *The Honest Whore* in 1604, then wrote Part II by himself the following year. Without Middleton's clever plot designing and lively characterizations, Part II is markedly inferior to Part I. Dekker collaborated with Middleton again on *The Roaring Girl*, a comedy based on the real-life story of Mary Frith, alias Moll Cutpurse, whom Dekker portrays as a tender-hearted rogue aiding lovers in distress. The characterization is typical of Dekker, who often showed bluff monarchs, stern fathers, or threatening employers to be essentially good-humored and benevolent. Never a cynic, Dekker sought out the best in human beings, and his rare moral indignation is reserved for deliberate cruelty, never simple weakness. In *The Witch of Edmonton*, written with William Rowley and John Ford, Dekker wrote those portions of the play most sympathetic to the old witch Elizabeth Sawyer, whom Dekker portrays as an ignorant and helpless woman driven to witchcraft by the persecution of her cruel neighbors.

This moral conscience, occasionally implicit in the plays, is expressed consistently and overtly in the prose pamphlets Dekker wrote during the period 1603–10, beginning with *The Wonderful Year* which opens as a commemoration of James I's succession and develops into a vivid description of the terrible sufferings of the 1602 plague. *The Seven Deadly Sins of London* excoriates contemporary economic frauds, whereas *The Bellman of London* and *Lantern and Candle-Light* resemble Robert Greene's coney-catching pamphlets in exposing the sharp practices of the Elizabethan underworld. In these and other pamphlets Dekker employs a plain, unadorned style, more didactic and exhortatory than informative. As a writer of pamphlet literature, he is far less fictive and mythic than Greene, less learned and witty than Thomas Nashe, but his occasional descriptive passages and bursts of dialogue and anecdote serve to envigorate his otherwise drab, sermonizing prose. A notable exception is *The Gull's Horn-Book*, a brilliant satire describing a typical day in the life of a London gull, or fop. Of especial interest is the chapter "How a Gull Should Conduct Himself in the Popular Playhouse," a wildly funny invective that throws considerable light on the incredibly informal and intimate theatrical conditions at public playhouses like the Globe or the Swan, where a gallant like Dekker's could sit on the stage and twit the players and playwright, and quite possibly be pulled down and beaten by the audience.

Dekker's career extends from the golden age of 1590's to the decline of the popular theatres in the 1630's, when the aged dramatist tried unsuccessfully to tailor his plays to the new, jaded tastes of the Caroline court and its coterie. What characterizes his plays and prose pamphlets throughout that lengthy period is a certain ingenuous vitality and affection for humanity, a frequent gaiety, and an occasional touch of compassion and sorrow.

—James E. Ruoff

DENNIS, John. English. Born in London in 1657. Educated at Harrow School, 1670–75; Caius College, Cambridge, 1675–79, B.A. 1679; awarded M.A. at Trinity Hall, Cambridge, 1683. Fellow of Trinity Hall, 1679–80, then settled in London: noted early in his career as a political pamphleteer, subsequently as a playwright, and later, most notably, as a literary critic; enjoyed patronage of the Duke of Marlborough; "royal waiter" in the Port of London, 1705–20; involved in a literary feud with Alexander Pope from 1711; lived in great poverty at the end of his life. *Died 6 January 1734.*

PUBLICATIONS

Plays

A Plot and No Plot (produced 1697).   1697.
Rinaldo and Armida (produced 1698).   1699.
Iphigenia (produced 1699).   1700.
The Comical Gallant; or, The Amours of Sir John Falstaff, from the play The Merry
    Wives of Windsor by Shakespeare (produced 1702).   1702.
Liberty Asserted (produced 1704).   1704.
Gibraltar; or, The Spanish Adventure (produced 1705).   1705.
Orpheus and Eurydice.   1707.
Appius and Virginia (produced 1709).   1709.
The Invader of His Country; or, The Fatal Resentment, from the play Coriolanus by
    Shakespeare (produced 1719).   1720.

Verse

Poems in Burlesque.   1692.
Poems and Letters upon Several Occasions.   1692.
The Passion of Byblis, from Ovid.   1692.
Miscellanies in Verse and Prose.   1693; as Miscellany Poems, 1697.
The Court of Death: A Pindaric Poem to the Memory of Queen Mary.   1695.
The Nuptials of Britain's Genius and Fame: A Pindaric Poem on the Peace.   1697.
The Monument: A Poem to the Memory of William the Third.   1702.
Britannia Triumphans.   1704.
The Battle of Ramillia.   1706.
A Poem upon the Death of Queen Anne and the Accession of King George.   1714.

Other

The Impartial Critic; or, Some Observations upon "A Short View of Tragedy" by
    Rymer.   1693.
Remarks on a Book Entitled King Arthur.   1696.
Letters upon Several Occasions.   1696.
The Usefulness of the Stage.   1698.
The Seamen's Case.   1700(?).
The Advancement and Reformation of Modern Poetry: A Critical Discourse.   1701.
The Danger of Priestcraft to Religion and Government.   1702.
An Essay on the Navy.   1702.
A Proposal for Putting a Speedy End to the War.   1703.
The Person of Quality's Answer to Mr. Collier's Letter.   1704.
The Grounds of Criticism in Poetry.   1704.
An Essay on the Operas after the Italian Manner.   1706.
An Essay upon Public Spirit, Being a Satire in Prose upon the Manners and Luxury of the
    Times.   1711.
Reflections Critical and Satirical upon a Late Rhapsody Called "An Essay upon
    Criticism."   1711.
An Essay upon the Genius and Writings of Shakespeare.   1712.
Priestcraft Distinguished from Christianity.   1715.
A True Character of Mr. Pope and His Writings.   1716.

Reflections upon Mr. Pope's Translation of Homer, with Two Letters Concerning "Windsor Forest" and "The Temple of Fame." 1717.
Select Works. 2 vols., 1718; revised edition, 1718–21.
The Characters and Conduct of Sir John Edgar and His Three Deputy Governors. 1720; *Third and Fourth Letter,* 1720.
Original Letters, Familiar, Moral, and Critical. 2 vols., 1721.
A Defense of Sir Fopling Flutter. 1722.
Julius Caesar Acquitted and His Murderers Condemned. 1722.
Remarks upon a Play Called "The Conscious Lovers." 1723.
Vice and Luxury Public Mischiefs; or, Remarks on a Book Entitled "The Fable of the Bees." 1724.
The Stage Defended from Scripture, Reason, Experience, and the Common Sense of Mankind. 1726.
Miscellaneous Tracts, vol. 1. 1727.
Remarks upon Mr. Pope's "Rape of the Lock," in Several Letters to a Friend. 1728.
Remarks upon Several Passages in the Preliminaries to "The Dunciad," and in Pope's Preface to His Translation of Homer's Iliad. 1729.
Critical Works, edited by Edward N. Hooker. 2 vols., 1939–43.

Translator, with others, *The Annals and History of Tacitus,* vol. 3. 1698.
Translator, *The Faith and Duties of Christians,* by Thomas Burnet. 1728.
Translator, *A Treatise Concerning the State of Departed Souls,* by Thomas Burnet. 1730.

Reading List: *Dennis: His Life and Criticism* by Harry G. Paul, 1911; *The Word "Sublime" and Its Context 1650–1760* by Theodore E. B. Wood, 1972.

*   *   *

John Dennis attained greater stature as a critic than as a playwright, and it is on his criticism, chiefly, that his reputation as an arch-classicist rests. According to Pope (*Essay on Criticism*), Don Quixote (in the Georgian continuation)

> Discours'd in Terms as just, with Looks as Sage,
> As e'er cou'd *Dennis,* of the *Grecian* Stage;
> Concluding all were desp'rate Sots and Fools,
> Who durst depart from *Aristotle*'s Rules.

If the second couplet is aimed at Dennis it misses the mark. Throughout his career, Dennis (like Pope) did regard Aristotle, Horace, and other ancients as the clear, unchanging universal light of "methodiz'd" Nature in which contemporary literature should be examined; his classicism is particularly evident in the cogent attacks on *The Conscious Lovers* as a misunderstanding of traditional comedy. But – as Edward N. Hooker writes in the indispensable introduction to the *Critical Works* – Dennis was an "intelligent classicist," a man alive to the power of passion in life and art, not the dry expounder of dead rules that Pope satirized. He knew and approved Longinus on the sublime; he felt, and admitted that he felt, the sublimity of the Alps and of Shakespeare. The latter, indeed, gave him difficulties, but also brought out his critical honesty: he testified to Shakespeare's greatness as well as to his disregard of the "Rules of dramatick Composition" which Dennis espoused, and then followed his logic beyond the point where angels and prudence bad him stop. Shakespeare would have written even better had he possessed "Learning and the Poetical Art," and his plays could now be improved by remedying these defects. Dennis proceeded to "regularize"

The Merry Wives of Windsor as *The Comical Gallant*, and *Coriolanus* ("Where Master-strokes in wild Confusion lye") as *The Invader of His Country*. Both failed.

Whenever he turned from theory to practice, in fact, Dennis struggled as if in an alien medium. He could not contrive to embody his ideas in dramatic form so as to move spectators or readers, though he tried everything, even abandoning his own critical precepts; Dennis's plays were much more hospitable to "romantic" influences such as the heroic drama than his relevant critical prose would lead one to expect. The Preface to *Rinaldo and Armida* announces a *telos* of Sophoclean terror, but the text itself is a rather entertaining hodge-podge of masque, opera, and tragi-comedy with debts to Tasso, Spenser, Dryden, and Milton ("perhaps the greatest genius" in 1700 years). It contains a song with the deathless couplet – "All around venereal Turtles/Cooing, billing, on the Myrtles" – which gives some idea of the distance between Dennis and a neoclassicist such as Addison. *Iphigenia* indulged in spectacular costumes and a mighty tempest that later occasioned Dennis's only contribution to English idiom: "They've stolen my thunder!" *Liberty Asserted*, set in Canada, features a half-breed noble savage and exhibits a fondness for rant: "These are Events surpassing all Examples;/These are th'amazing Miracles of Fate!" His few comic pieces are quite unclassical.

It is easy to see why critics and audiences did not like Dennis's plays: bombast, uncertain plotting, awkward exposition, a certain laborious lifelessness. Unfortunately the repeated failures brought out a captious streak in Dennis that allowed Pope to liken him to Appius, the irascible tyrant of one of his own tragedies.

In one overlong preface after another Dennis blamed his woes on audiences, managers, theatres, the acting, the weather, or a combination thereof, and his strictures on successful playwrights such as Steele became suspect. Dennis could not accept the verdict of theatrical audiences – whom he considered ignorant, mercantile, and debased – as final, appealing instead to the reading public, to posterity; but posterity has so far seen no reason to overturn the original decision against his plays, though it has sometimes endorsed his criticism.

—R. W. Bevis

DIBDIN, Charles. English. Born in Southampton, Hampshire, baptized 4 March 1745. Chorister, Winchester Cathedral, Hampshire, 1756–60. Married c. 1764, but later left his wife; associated with the actress Harriet Pitt, 1767–74: had three children by her, including the playwrights Charles Isaac Mungo Dibdin and Thomas Dibdin; later married Anne Wylde, four children. Settled in London, 1760; singer and actor from 1762, and appeared in theatres in London and the provinces; playwright and composer: wrote some 1400 songs; contract composer at Drury Lane, London, 1769–76; lived in France, 1776–78; returned to Drury Lane, 1778–81; Joint Manager of the Royal Circus, later called the Surrey, 1782–85; proprietor of the periodicals *The Devil*, 1786–87, and *The Bystander: or, Universal Weekly Expositor*, 1789–90; solo performer of "entertainments" from 1787, and had his own theatre, the Sans Souci, 1796–1805. Granted Civil List pension, 1803. *Died 25 July 1814.*

PUBLICATIONS

Plays

The Shepherd's Artifice, music by the author (produced 1764). 1765.
The Mischance, music by the author (produced 1773).

The Ladle, music by the author, from the poem by Prior (produced 1773).   1773.

The Wedding Ring, music by the author, from a play by Goldoni (produced 1773).   Songs published 1773.

La Zingara; or, The Gipsy, music by F. H. Barthélémon, from a play by Mme. Favart (produced 1773).

The Deserter, music by the author, from a play by Michel Jean Sedaine, music by P. A. Monsigny and F. A. Philidor (produced 1773).   1773.

The Waterman; or, The First of August, music by the author (produced 1774).   1774.

The Cobbler; or, A Wife of Ten Thousand, music by the author, from a play by Michel Jean Sedaine (produced 1774).   1774.

The Quaker, music by the author (produced 1775).   1777.

The Comic Mirror, music by the author (produced 1775).

The Metamorphoses, music by the author, from plays by Molière (produced 1775).   1776.

The Seraglio, with E. Thompson, music by the author (produced 1776).   1776.

Poor Vulcan, music by the author, from a play by P. A. Motteux (produced 1778).   1778.

She Is Mad for a Husband, music by the author (produced 1778).

The Gipsies, music by Samuel Arnold, from a play by Mme. Favart (produced 1778).   1778.

Rose and Colin, music by the author, from a play by Michel Jean Sedaine (produced 1778).   1778.

The Wives Revenged, music by the author, from a play by Michel Jean Sedaine (produced 1778).   1778.

Annette and Lubin, music by the author, from a play by Santerre and Mme. Favart (produced 1778).   1778.

The Chelsea Pensioner, music by the author (produced 1779).   1779.

The Touchstone; or, Harlequin Traveller, music by the author (produced 1779).   Songs published 1779.

The Mirror; or, Harlequin Everywhere, music by the author (produced 1779).   1779.

The Shepherdess of the Alps, music by the author, from an opera by J. F. Marmontel, music by Joseph Kohaut (produced 1780).   1780.

The Islanders, music by the author, from plays by Saint-Foix and Framéry (produced 1780).   Songs published 1780; revised version, as *The Marriage Act* (produced 1781), 1781.

Harlequin Freemason, with J. Messink, music by the author (produced 1780).

Jupiter and Alcmena, music by the author, from the play *Amphitryon* by Dryden (produced 1781).

None So Blind as Those Who Won't See, music by Samuel Arnold, from a play by Dorvigny (produced 1782).

The Graces, music by the author (produced 1782).   1782.

The Passions, music by the author (produced 1783).

The Regions of Accomplishment, music by the author (produced 1783).

The Cestus, music by the author (produced 1783).   1783.

Harlequin Phantom of a Day, music by the author (produced 1783).   1783.

The Lancashire Witches; or, The Distress of Harlequin, music by the author (produced 1783).

The Talisman of Orosmanes, music by the author (produced 1783).   1783(?).

The Long Odds, music by the author (produced 1783).   1783.

The Milkmaid, music by the author (produced 1783).

The Saloon, music by the author (produced 1784).

The Statue; or, The Bower of Confidence, music by the author (produced 1785).

Life, Death, and Renovation of Tom Thumb, music by the author (produced 1785).   1785(?).

Clump and Cudden; or, The Review, music by the author (produced 1785).   1785.
Liberty Hall; or, A Test of Good Fellowship, music by the author (produced 1785).   1785.
Harvest Home, music by the author (produced 1787).   1787.
The Fortune Hunters; or, You May Say That, music by the author (produced 1789).
A Cure for a Coxcomb; or, The Beau Bedevilled, music by the author and John Collins (produced 1792).
A Loyal Effusion, music by the author (produced 1794).
A Pennyworth of Wit; or, The Wife and the Mistress, music by John Davy (produced 1796).
First Come, First Served, music by the author (produced 1797).
Hannah Hewit; or, The Female Crusoe, music by the author, from his own novel (produced 1798).   Songs published in *Chorus of Melody*, n.d.
The Broken Gold, music by the author (produced 1806).
The Round Robin (produced 1811).

Other plays and entertainments: *The False Dervise, The Land of Simplicity, Pandora, The Refusal of Harlequin, The Razor-Grinder, England Against Italy, The Imposter, The Old Woman of Eighty;* performer in *The Whim of the Moment* and *The Oddities,* 1789, and *The Wags,* 1790 – performances continued until 1809.

Fiction

Hannah Hewit; or, The Female Crusoe.   1792.
The Younger Brother.   1793.
Henry Hooka.   1807.

Verse

The Harmonic Preceptor.   1804.
The Lion and the Water-Wagtail.   1809.
The Songs, edited by George Hogarth.   2 vols., 1842.

Other

The Musical Tour (autobiography).   1778.
Royal Circus Epitomized.   1784.
A Letter on Music Education.   1791.
A Complete History of the English Stage.   5 vols., 1800.
Observations on a Tour Through England and Scotland.   2 vols., 1801–02.
The Professional Life of Dibdin, Written by Himself, with the Words of 600 Songs.   4 vols., 1803; revised edition, 6 vols., 1809.
Music Epitomized.   1808.
The English Pythagoras; or, Every Man His Own Music Master.   1808.

Bibliography: *A Dibdin Bibliography* by Edward R. Dibdin, 1937.

Reading List: *A Brief Memoir of Dibdin* by William Kitchiner, 1884; *English Theatre Music in the 18th Century* by Roger Fiske, 1973.

*   *   *

Despite his prodigious outpouring of songs, operas, entertainments, stage histories, didactic poetry, satires, novels, and autobiography, for most of his career Charles Dibdin was a Sullivan without an appropriate Gilbert. His first and best partner and librettist was Isaac Bickerstaff with whom, from 1765 to 1772, Dibdin collaborated on about eight musical pieces for the London theatres and for Garrick's Shakespeare Jubilees (1769). He wrote all the music for the popular afterpiece, *The Padlock* (1768), and in it played the servant Mungo in blackface – the first foretaste of the nineteenth-century minstrel shows. Two of Bickerstaff's and Dibdin's musical entertainments or serenatas for Ranelagh House, *The Ephesian Matron* (1769) and *The Recruiting Serjeant* (1770), are witty, short pieces modelled after the form of *La Serva Padrona* and are still occasionally performed.

After Bickerstaff exiled himself, although Dibdin continued to write for Garrick (whom he detested) until 1776, he turned out thirty pantomimes and musical dialogues between 1772 and 1782 for Thomas King at Sadler's Wells. Dibdin's often-produced ballad opera, *The Waterman; or, The First of August*, was first played at the Little Theatre in the Haymarket. A comic opera, *The Quaker*, had one performance sloppily produced at Drury Lane in 1775, but it was not until 1777, when Dibdin was in France avoiding creditors, that the opera was successfully staged. Perpetually in debt, always quarreling with theatre managers and collaborators, constantly flirting with, but not exploring, new forms of popular entertainment, Dibdin shifted from one theatre to another. He even became a partner in a new theatre, the Royal Circus, later named the Surrey, in 1782, for which he wrote upwards of sixty works, but ended up in debtor's prison for his efforts. In 1785 he wrote the comic opera *Liberty Hall* which is remembered (if at all) for three songs: "The Highmettled Racer," "Jock Ratlin," and "The Bells of Aberdovey." Two years later he toured the country with his own one-man show to raise money for an aborted voyage to India. Typical of Dibdin's energy was his *The Whim of the Moment* (1789), one of about thirty "table entertainments" for which he was manager, author, composer, narrator, singer, and accompanist. Renamed *The Oddities* and produced at the Lyceum, it includes Dibdin's most famous song, "Tom Bowling."

At his own theatre, the Sans Souci, Dibdin introduced many of his popular, uplifting, patriotic sea songs. In all he wrote about 1,400 songs and a huge number of stage productions from puppet shows and brief musical dialogues to comic operas. Although he was awarded a £200 pension in 1803 for celebrating the bravery and loyalty of the British sailor, Dibdin's creative energies were most fully realized when he collaborated early in his career with Bickerstaff.

—Peter A. Tasch

DODSLEY, Robert. English. Born near Mansfield, Nottinghamshire, 13 February 1703. Apprenticed to a stocking weaver in Mansfield, from whom he ran away. Married; his wife died in 1754. Became a footman to the Hon. Mrs. Lowther in London, who encouraged him in his writing and secured him other patrons, including Alexander Pope; set up as a bookseller, at "Tully's Head" in Pall Mall, 1735, and subsequently published works by Johnson, Pope, and others; suggested to Johnson the scheme of an English dictionary, 1746, and was one of the publishers of the first edition, 1755; started various journals, *The Publick Register*, 1741, *The Museum*, 1746–47, *The Preceptor*, 1748, and *The World*, 1753–56; founded *the Annual Register*, initially edited by Edmund Burke, 1758; retired from bookselling and publishing, 1759. *Died 23 December 1764.*

PUBLICATIONS

Collections

Works of the English Poets 15, edited by A. Chalmers. 1810.

Plays

An Entertainment for Her Majesty's Birthday. 1732.
An Entertainment for the Wedding of Governor Lowther. 1732.
The Toy-Shop (produced 1735). 1735; with *Epistles and Poems on Several Occasions,* 1737.
The King and the Miller of Mansfield (produced 1737). 1737.
Sir John Cockle at Court, Being the Sequel to The King and the Miller (produced 1738). 1738.
The Blind Beggar of Bethnal Green, from the play by John Day and Henry Chettle (produced 1741). 1741.
Rex and Pontifex, in *Trifles.* 1745.
The Triumph of Peace, music by Thomas Arne (produced 1749). 1749.
Cleone (produced 1758). 1758.

Verse

Servitude. 1729; as *The Footman's Friendly Advice,* 1731.
An Epistle from a Footman to Stephen Duck. 1731.
A Sketch of the Miseries of Poverty. 1731.
A Muse in Livery; or, The Footman's Miscellany. 1732.
The Modern Reasoners: An Epistle to a Friend. 1734.
An Epistle to Mr. Pope, Occasioned by His Essay on Man. 1734.
Beauty; or, The Art of Charming. 1735.
The Art of Preaching, in Imitation of Horace's Art of Poetry. 1738.
Colin's Kisses, Being Twelve New Songs. 1742.
Pain and Patience. 1742.
Public Virtue, book 1: Agriculture. 1753.
Melpomene; or, The Regions of Terror and Pity. 1757.

Other

The Chronicle of the Kings of England, Written in the Manner of the Ancient Jewish Historians. 2 vols., 1740–41.
Trifles. 2 vols., 1745–77.
The Oeconomy of Human Life, Translated from an Indian Manuscript. 1751.

Editor, *A Select Collection of Old Plays.* 12 vols., 1744; edited by W. C. Hazlitt, 15 vols., 1874–76.
Editor, *A Collection of Poems by Several Hands.* 3 vols., 1748; revised edition, 6 vols., 1748–58; edited by I. Reed, 6 vols., 1782.
Editor, *Select Fables of Aesop and Other Fabulists.* 1761.
Editor, *Fugitive Pieces on Various Subjects.* 2 vols., 1761.
Editor, *The Works of William Shenstone.* 2 vols., 1764.

Reading List: *Dodsley, Poet, Publisher, and Playwright* by Ralph Straus, 1910 (includes bibliography).

*   *   *

Footman, poet, and playwright, Robert Dodsley was the most important publisher of the eighteenth century both in terms of the men whose works he issued – Pope, Young, Akenside, Gray, Johnson, Burke, Shenstone, Sterne, among others – and in terms of the works he edited or initiated. His *Collection of Poems by Several Hands* rescued from pamphlet obscurity many of the best and most representative poems of the mid-century. *A Select Collection of Old Plays* did the same for the lesser Elizabethan dramatists. His enormously successful society periodical *The World* is second in quality only to *The Spectator*; and *The Annual Register*, which he astutely contracted Burke to edit, established a tradition of excellence in assembling the best of each year's poetry and prose. A labor of love, his popular *Select Fables* included the first comprehensive, orginal study of that genre of English.

Although he is not an important poet, many of Dodsley's verses are better than his amusingly ill-considered lines "To the Honourable Lady Howe, Upon the Death of Her Husband": "But let this thought alleviate/The sorrows of your mind:/He's gone – but he is gone so late/You can't be long behind." If, in its celebration "of various Manures" and its delineation of sheep diseases, there is a turgid frivolity to the blank verse of his ambitious georgic *Agriculture*, the couplets of *The Art of Preaching*, a satire on abuses of the clergy, show facility and cleverness. The more ephemeral the subject, the surer Dodsley's touch. A few of his epigrams are excellent. "An Epistle to Stephen Duck" ingratiatingly compares Dodsley, the aspiring footman, to the thresher poet, newly called to eminence by the Queen. "Colin's Kisses," variations on a pastoral theme, are always melodious and often charming. Dodsley's one success in a more august mode – *Melpomene; or, the Regions of Terrour and Pity* – was applauded as sublime by his contemporaries, and even today the stanza and imagery of this homostrophic ode effectively present the various tragic tableaux.

Three of Dodsley's plays deserve particular mention. The plotless but good-humored *Toy-Shop* offers a satiric merchant who philosophizes over every sale. *The King and the Miller of Mansfield*, the democratically biased tale of a monarch lost in Sherwood Forest who is entertained incognito by an honest tradesman, was a theatrical triumph, establishing Dodsley as the most important sentimentalist of the 1730's. A disappointing sequel, *Sir John Cockle at Court*, reverses the premise of the original play by taking the blunt miller to London. Dodsley's greatest success and the play in which he comes closest to "the sentiment sublime, the language of the heart" which he recommends in *Melpomene* is *Cleone*, a domestic drama of traduction, murder, and madness which avoids the stilted heroics usual in mid-century tragedies. Although psychologically unconvincing, the play does achieve by flashes an authentic tragic tone worthy of Otway, to whose work Johnson compared it. Eighteenth-century audiences found the pathetic madness and death of Cleone so emotionally disturbing that Sarah Siddons had to discontinue the role.

—Harry M. Solomon

DRINKWATER, John.   English.   Born in Leytonstone, Essex, 1 June 1882. Educated at the City of Oxford High School. Married 1) Kathleen Walpole in 1906 (divorced, 1924); 2) Daisy Kennedy in 1924, one daughter. Worked for the Northern Assurance Company in Nottingham, 1897–1901, and in Birmingham, 1901–09. Co-Founder with Sir Barry Jackson,

Pilgrim Players, later Birmingham Repertory Theatre, 1907, and Manager of the theatre from 1910; also, Editor, Pilgrim Players *Scallop Shell* magazine, 1911. Ph.D.: University of Athens; M.A.: University of Birmingham. *Died 25 March 1937.*

PUBLICATIONS

Plays

    Ser Taldo's Bride, with B. V. Jackson (produced 1911).
    Cophetua (produced 1911).   1911.
    An English Medley, music by Rutland Boughton (produced 1911).   1911.
    Puss in Boots (produced 1911; revised version, produced 1916, 1926).   1911.
    The Pied Piper: A Tale of Hamelin City, music by F. W. Sylvester (produced 1912).   1912.
    The Only Legend: A Masque of the Scarlet Pierrot (produced 1913).   1913.
    Rebellion (produced 1914).   1914.
    Robin Hood and the Pedlar, music by James Brier (produced 1914).   1914.
    The Storm (produced 1915).   1915.
    The God of Quiet (produced 1916).   1916.
    The Wounded, with R. De Smet (produced 1917).
    X = O: A Night of the Trojan War (produced 1917).   1917.
    Pawns: Three Poetic Plays.   1917.
    Abraham Lincoln (produced 1918).   1918.
    Mary Stuart (produced 1921).   1921.
    Oliver Cromwell (produced 1923).   1921.
    Robert E. Lee (produced 1923).   1923.
    Collected Plays.   2 vols., 1925.
    Robert Burns.   1925.
    The Mayor of Casterbridge, from the novel by Hardy (produced 1926).
    Bird in Hand (produced 1927).   1927.
    John Bull Calling: A Political Parable (produced 1928).   1928.
    Holiness (produced 1928).
    Napoleon: The Hundred Days, from a play by Benito Mussólini and Giovacchino Forzano (produced 1932).   1932.
    Midsummer Eve (broadcast 1932).   1932.
    Laying the Devil (produced 1933).   1933.
    A Man's House (produced 1934).   1934.
    Garibaldi.   1936.

Screenplays: *The King of Paris,* with W. P. Lipscomb and Paul Gangelin, 1934; *Blossom Time (April Romance),* with others, 1934; *Pagliacci (A Clown Must Laugh),* with others, 1936; *The King's People,* 1937; *The Mill on the Floss,* with others, 1937.

Radio Play: *Midsummer Eve,* 1932.

Fiction

    Robinson of England.   1937.

Verse

Poems. 1903.
The Death of Leander and Other Poems. 1906.
Lyrical and Other Poems. 1908.
Poems of Men and Hours. 1911.
Poems of Love and Earth. 1912.
Cromwell and Other Poems. 1913.
Swords and Ploughshares. 1915.
Olton Pools. 1916.
Poems 1908–1914. 1917.
Tides. 1917; revised edition, 1917.
Loyalties. 1918.
Poems 1908–1919. 1919.
Seeds of Time. 1921.
Cotswold Characters. 1921.
Preludes 1921–1922. 1922.
Selected Poems. 1922.
Collected Poems. 3 vols., 1923–27.
From an Unknown Isle. 1924.
From the German: Verses Written from the German Poets. 1924.
New Poems. 1925.
All about Me: Poems for a Child. 1928.
Poems (selection). 1928.
More about Me: Poems for a Child. 1929.
American Vignettes 1860–65. 1931.
Christmas Poems. 1931.
Summer Harvest: Poems 1924–1933. 1933.

Other

William Morris: A Critical Study. 1912.
Swinburne: An Estimate. 1913.
The Lyric. 1915.
Rupert Brooke: An Essay. 1916.
Prose Papers. 1917.
Lincoln, The World Emancipator. 1920.
Claud Lovat Fraser: A Memoir, with Albert Rutherston. 1923.
Victorian Poetry. 1923.
Patriotism in Literature. 1924.
The Muse in Council. 1925.
The Pilgrim of Eternity: Byron: A Conflict. 1925.
A Book for Bookmen. 1926.
Mr. Charles, King of England. 1926.
Cromwell: A Character Study. 1927.
The Gentle Art of Theatre-Going. 1927; as *The Art of Theatre-Going*, 1927.
Charles James Fox. 1928.
The World's Lincoln. 1928.
Story-Folk (juvenile), with E. Terriss. 4 vols., 1929.
Pepys: His Life and Character. 1930.
Inheritance, Discovery (autobiography). 2 vols., 1931–32.
The Life and Adventures of Carl Laemmle. 1931.
John Hampden's England. 1933.

Shakespeare. 1933.
This Troubled World. 1933.
The King's Reign: A Commentary in Prose and Pictures. 1935.
English Poetry: An Unfinished History. 1938.

Editor, *Poems, Letters, and Prose Fragments,* by Henry Kirke White. 1907.
Editor, *The Poems of Sidney.* 1910.
Editor, *The Way of Poetry* (juvenile). 1920.
Editor, *The Outline of Literature.* 26 vols., 1923–24.
Editor, *Select Poems of Lord De Tabley.* 1924.
Editor, *An Anthology of English Verse.* 1924.
Editor, *The Way of Prose* (juvenile). 4 vols., 1924.
Editor, *Little Nineteenth Century Classics.* 3 vols., 1925.
Editor, with William Rose Benét and Henry Seidel Canby, *Twentieth-Century Poetry.* 1929.
Editor, *The Eighteen-Sixties.* 1932.
Editor, *A Pageant of English Life.* 1934.

Bibliography: *Drinkwater: Catalogue of an Exhibition,* 1962; "Drinkwater: An Annotated Bibliography of Writings about Him" by Peter Berven, in *English Literature in Transition 21,* 1978.

Reading List: *The Poetry of Drinkwater* by Godfrey W. Matthews, 1925; *Drinkwater and His Historical Plays* by C. Ghidelli, 1937.

*   *   *

John Drinkwater first gained attention as a poet in the first decade of the present century and between 1910 and 1930 added to this a considerable reputation as author of plays in verse and prose, many of them composed for performance at the Birmingham Repertory Theatre, in which Drinkwater served as (in his own words) "actor, producer, manager, and odd-job man." His father, Alfred, had made a career on the stage after an Oxford education and some years of school-teaching, and Drinkwater was brought up by his grandfather in Oxford, attending the High School and spending summers with farming relations in the local countryside. After leaving school, he spent twelve years in the Northern and other assurance companies in Nottingham and Birmingham, writing verse after office hours and helping to found the Pilgrim Players, an amateur dramatic society, with Barry Jackson in 1907, becoming their full-time manager in 1910. He was a contributor to all five volumes of Sir Edward Marsh's *Georgian Poetry* between 1912 and 1922, and a prolific writer of literary and historical biographies, studies, and sketches. Two volumes of rather tame autobiography appeared in 1931 and 1932.

As a poet Drinkwater displays the typical virtues and deficiencies of the Georgian school as a whole: his lyrics and poems in blank verse are often successful in celebrating predictable aspects of the rural scene or human relationships, but in a calculatedly unsophisticated, self-consciously timeless, and frequently ponderous vein, contriving to be simultaneously simple in diction and imprecise in meaning. He is inspired to poetry by the carefully observed beauty of natural objects, by a delighted consciousness of historical continuity, by rustic encounters and strong but restrained sexual emotion, and by national crisis, but his tendency to choose the readiest and most conventional image in preference to the most telling one results in mere confirmation of the reader's own perceptions and responses rather than their extension or controversion. Drinkwater's highly-developed sense of poetic decorum, his air of "talking down" to his audience, his taste for extracting profound sentiments from commonplace experiences, have all served to obscure his human sensitivity, his poetic sincerity, and his complete devotion to his craft.

His plays are a curiously mixed collection, the earliest compositions being mainly short experimental verse-dramas such as *Cophetua*, *The Storm*, *The God of Quiet*, and *X = O*, all of which may be more accurately described as dramatic poems rather than true dramas. However, with *Abraham Lincoln* (1918) Drinkwater embarked on a more satisfactory sequence of historical plays, unromanticized, semi-documentary, episodic presentations of the problems of leadership encountered by Lincoln, Cromwell, and Robert E. Lee. Despite the author's declared intention of retaining "something of the enthusiasm and poignancy of verse" in these plays, they are actually in slightly stiff but workmanlike modern prose; if they are a little dry and circumspect, they remain absorbing theatre, hampered slightly by their earnest didactic tone. With them may be linked the more sentimentalized portrayal of Mary Stuart, itself in total contrast to Drinkwater's last significant play, *Bird in Hand*, a cheerful but conventional love-comedy unlike anything he had attempted before.

—William M. Tydeman

DRYDEN, John.   English.   Born in Aldwinckle All Saints, Northamptonshire, 19 August 1631. Educated at Westminster School, London (King's Scholar), 1646–50; Trinity College, Cambridge (pensioner), 1650–54, B.A. 1654. Married Lady Elizabeth Howard in 1663. Remained in Cambridge, 1654–57; settled in London, 1657, and possibly held a minor post in Cromwell's government; thereafter supported himself mainly by writing plays. Appointed Poet Laureate, 1668, and Historiographer Royal, 1669; converted to Roman Catholicism, c. 1685, and lost his royal offices at the accession of William and Mary, 1689. Member, Royal Society, 1660. *Died 1 May 1700.*

PUBLICATIONS

Collections

> *The Works*, edited by Sir Walter Scott.   18 vols., 1808; revised edition edited by George Saintsbury, 1882–92.
> *Dramatic Works*, edited by Montague Summers.   6 vols., 1931–32.
> *Letters*, edited by Charles E. Ward.   1942.
> *Works*, edited by Edward N. Hooker and H. T. Swedenberg, Jr.   1956 –
> *Poems*, edited by James Kinsley.   4 vols., 1958.
> *Four Comedies, Four Tragedies* (includes *Secret Love, Sir Martin Mar-All, An Evening's Love, Marriage A-la-Mode, The Indian Emperor, Aureng-Zebe, All for Love, Don Sebastian*), edited by L. A. Beaurline and Fredson Bowers.   2 vols., 1967.
> *A Selection*, edited by John Conaghan.   1978.

Plays

> *The Wild Gallant* (produced 1663).   1669; in *Works 8*, 1962.

The Indian Queen, with Sir Robert Howard (produced 1664). In *Four New Plays*, by Howard, 1665.

The Rival Ladies (produced 1664). 1664; in *Works 8*, 1962.

The Indian Emperor; or, The Conquest of Mexico by the Spaniards, Being the Sequel of The Indian Queen (produced 1665). 1667; in *Works 9*, 1966.

Secret Love; or, The Maiden Queen (produced 1667). 1668; in *Works 9*, 1966.

Sir Martin Mar-All; or, The Feigned Innocence, from a translation by William Cavendish of a play by Molière (produced 1667). 1668; in *Works 9*, 1966.

The Tempest; or, The Enchanted Island, with William Davenant, from the play by Shakespeare (produced 1667). 1670; edited by Vivian Summers, 1974.

An Evening's Love; or, The Mock Astrologer (produced 1668). 1671; in *Works 10*, 1970.

Tyrannic Love; or, The Royal Martyr (produced 1669). 1670; in *Works 10*, 1970.

The Conquest of Granada by the Spaniards, 2 parts (produced 1670, 1671). 1672; in *Works 2*, 1978.

Marriage A-la-Mode (produced 1672). 1673; in *Works 2*, 1978.

The Assignation; or, Love in a Nunnery (produced 1672). 1673; in *Works 2*, 1978.

Amboyna (produced 1673). 1673.

Aureng-Zebe (produced 1675). 1676; edited by Frederick M. Link, 1971.

The State of Innocence and Fall of Man. 1677.

All for Love; or, The World Well Lost, from the play *Antony and Cleopatra* by Shakespeare (produced 1677). 1678; edited by David M. Vieth, 1974.

The Kind Keeper; or, Mr. Limberham (produced 1678). 1680; edited by A. Norman Jeffares, in *Restoration Comedy*, 1974.

Oedipus, with Nathaniel Lee (produced 1678). 1679.

Troilus and Cressida; or, Truth Found Too Late, from the play by Shakespeare (produced 1679). 1679.

The Spanish Friar; or, The Double Discovery (produced 1680). 1681.

The Duke of Guise, with Nathaniel Lee (produced 1682). 1683.

Albion and Albanius, music by Lewis Grabu (produced 1685). 1685.

Don Sebastian, King of Portugal (produced 1689). 1690; in *Four Tragedies*, 1967.

Amphitryon; or, The Two Socias (produced 1690). 1690.

King Arthur; or, The British Worthy, music by Henry Purcell (produced 1691). 1691.

Cleomenes, The Spartan Hero (produced 1692). 1692.

Love Triumphant; or, Nature Will Prevail (produced 1694). 1694.

The Secular Masque, in *The Pilgrim*, by Vanbrugh (produced 1700). 1700.

Comedies, Tragedies, and Operas. 2 vols., 1701.

Verse

Heroic Stanzas to the Memory of Oliver, Late Lord Protector, in *Three Poems upon the Death of His Late Highness Oliver, Lord Protector*, with Waller and Sprat. 1659.

Astraea Redux: A Poem on the Happy Restoration and Return of His Sacred Majesty Charles the Second. 1660.

To His Sacred Majesty: A Panegyric on His Coronation. 1661.

To My Lord Chancellor, Presented on New Year's Day. 1662.

Annus Mirabilis, The Year of Wonders 1666: An Historical Poem. 1667.

Ovid's Epistles, with others. 1680.

Absalom and Achitophel. 1681; *Second Part*, with Nahum Tate, 1682; edited by James and Helen Kinsley, 1961.

The Medal: A Satire Against Sedition. 1682.

Mac Flecknoe; or, A Satire upon the True-Blue-Protestant Poet T[homas] S[hadwell]. 1682.

Religio Laici; or, A Layman's Faith. 1682.

Miscellany Poems. 1684; *Sylvae; or, The Second Part,* 1685; *Examen Poeticum, Being the Third Part,* 1693; *The Annual Miscellany, Being the Fourth Part,* 1694; *Fifth Part,* 1704; *Sixth Part,* 1709.

Threnodia Augustalis: A Funeral-Pindaric Poem Sacred to the Happy Memory of King Charles II. 1685.

The Hind and the Panther. 1687.

A Song for St. Cecilia's Day 1687. 1687.

Britannia Rediviva: A Poem on the Birth of the Prince. 1688.

Eleonora: A Panegyrical Poem Dedicated to the Memory of the Late Countess of Abingdon. 1692.

The Satires of Juvenal, with others, *Together with the Satires of Persius.* 1693.

An Ode on the Death of Henry Purcell. 1696.

The Works of Virgil, Containing His Pastorals, Georgics, and Aeneis. 1697; edited by James Kinsley, 1961.

Alexander's Feast; or, The Power of Music: An Ode in Honour of St. Cecilia's Day. 1697.

Fables Ancient and Modern. 1700.

Ovid's Art of Love, Book 1, translated. 1709.

Hymns Attributed to Dryden, edited by George Rapall and George Reuben Potter. 1937.

Prologues and Epilogues, edited by William B. Gardner. 1951.

Other

Of Dramatic Poesy: An Essay. 1668; revised edition 1684; edited by George Watson, in *Of Dramatic Poesy and Other Critical Essays,* 1962.

Notes and Observations on The Empress of Morocco, with John Crowne and Thomas Shadwell. 1674.

His Majesty's Declaration Defended. 1681.

The Vindication. 1683.

A Defence of An Essay of Dramatic Poesy. 1688.

Works. 4 vols., 1695.

Critical and Miscellaneous Prose Works, edited by Edmond Malone. 4 vols., 1800.

Essays, edited by W. P. Ker. 2 vols., 1900.

Literary Criticism, edited by A. C. Kirsch. 1966.

Editor, *The Art of Poetry,* by Nicolas Boileau, translated by William Soames, revised edition. 1683.

Translator, *The History of the League,* by Louis Maimbourg. 1684.

Translator, *The Life of St. Francis Xavier,* by Dominique Bouhours. 1688.

Translator, with Knightly Chetwood, *Miscellaneous Essays,* by Saint-Evremond. 1692.

Translator, with others, *The Annals and History of Tacitus.* 3 vols., 1698.

Bibliography: *Dryden: A Bibliography of Early Editions and of Drydeniana* by Hugh Macdonald, 1939; *Dryden: A Survey and Bibliography of Critical Studies 1895–1974* by David J. Latt and Samuel J. Monk, 1976.

Reading List: *The Poetry of Dryden* by Mark Van Doren, 1920, revised edition, 1931; *Dryden: Some Biographical Facts and Problems* by J. M. Osborn, 1940, revised edition, 1965;

Dryden and the Conservative Myth by B. N. Schilling, 1961; *Life of Dryden* by Charles E. Ward, 1961; *Dryden's Imagery* by Arthur W. Hoffman, 1962; *Essential Articles for the Study of Dryden* edited by H. T. Swedenberg, Jr., 1966; *Dryden's Major Plays* by Bruce King, 1966; *Dryden's Poetry* by Earl Miner, 1967; *Contexts of Dryden's Thought* by Philip Harth, 1968; *Dryden: The Critical Heritage* edited by James and Helen Kinsley, 1971; *Dryden* by William Myers, 1973; *Dryden and the Development of Panegyric* by James Dale Garrison, 1975; *Dryden, The Public Writer 1660–1685* by George McFadden, 1978.

*   *   *

John Dryden's life is largely obscure until he commences as author. He was born on 19 August 1631 at Aldwinckle All Saints in Northamptonshire, and about 1646 he entered, as a King's Scholar, Westminster School under the famous master Richard Busby. Much later he recalled that about 1648 he had translated Persius's third satire as a Thursday night exercise for the school. His first published poem, "Upon the Lord Hastings," appeared in 1649; on 18 May of the following year he was admitted as pensioner to Trinity College, Cambridge, proceeding B.A. in 1654. The next years are yet more obscure. Some color is given to the tradition he served the Protectorate by the publication in 1659 of the *Heroique Stanza's* on Cromwell's death.

His career may be said to begin, however, with the Restoration, and its first period to run from 1660–1680. Early in these years he published poems on the new order, bringing together historical, political, religious, and heroic elements. Although such a poem as *Astraea Redux* is inferior to the poem on Cromwell, it is more ambitious. Somewhat of the new effort succeeds in *Annus Mirabilis*, whose year of wonders (1666) included the second naval war with Holland and the Great Fire of London. Dryden seeks too hard to connect these diverse events, and his execution is uneven. But it has bounding energy and is his sole fully narrative poem till far later. His talents were being recognized – in 1668 he succeeded Davenant as poet laureate, and in 1669 Howell as historiographer royal. By the end of this period he had completed but not published his first poetic masterpiece, *Mac Flecknoe*. If Elkanah Settle was its first dunce hero, Thomas Shadwell finally gained the honor. The poem assesses good and bad art, using a mock coronation skit. Father Flecknoe abdicates for his son (Shadwell). Art, politics, and religious matters combine with paternal love to assess both the dunces and true drama. Flecknoe is "King by Office" and "Priest by Trade." He passes to his son *Love's Kingdom*, his own dull play, as "Sceptre." From "this righteous Lore" comes Shadwell's soul, his opera *Psyche*. Humor and allusion combine to establish the true canons of drama and to fix Shadwell immemorially.

Mac Flecknoe shows that Dryden's chief interest in these decades is the stage. After a first comedy, he turned to the rhymed heroic play, rising to the high astounding terms of the two-part *Conquest of Granada*. He approached earth thereafter. *Marriage A-la-mode* consists of a mingling of serious and comic plots especially congenial to him, and a favorite still. In the Prologue to his heroic play *Aureng-Zebe*, he professes himself "weary" of rhyme, and in *All for Love* he wrote a blank verse tragedy on Antony and Cleopatra, thought by many his finest play. His collaboration with Nathaniel Lee for *Oedipus* altered his smooth earlier blank verse style to a harsher, more various medium that appears again in his adaptation of *Troilus and Cressida*. After his enormously popular *Spanish Fryar* (1680), he wrote no plays single-handedly till 1689.

The next period, 1680–1685, is dominated by engagement with the tumultuous times. In the state of near revolution over the Popish Plot and efforts to seize power from Charles II, Dryden published *Absalom and Achitophel*, his poem most admired today. Using the biblical parallel of the plot against David (Charles), Dryden creates an epic-historic-satiric blend for the machinations of Achitophel (Earl of Shaftesbury) and his dupe Absalom (Duke of Monmouth). The Chaucer-like portraits of individuals and the personal statement on government (ll. 751–810) show Dryden in full command of a public poetry.

1682 brought Dryden further attention. *Mac Flecknoe* now first appeared in print, pirated.

When Shaftesbury was released from prison by a Whig jury in November 1681, a triumphant medal was struck. Next March Dryden's one bitter poem, *The Medall*, appeared. Perhaps his anger was feigned. His usual composure is evident in *Religio Laici*, his first religious poem, which curiously begins with rich imagery and progresses to a direct, non-metaphorical style unique in his poetry. In 1684 he published one of his poems most popular today, "To the Memory of Mr. Oldham," on a young poet recently dead. In that year and the next he joined the bookseller Jacob Tonson in putting out the first two of a series of "Dryden miscellanies," collections of poetry by various hands. Charles II died, and James acceded, in 1685. Dryden celebrated these events in *Threnodia Augustalis*, his first pindaric ode after one of his finest poems, the translation of Horace, *Odes*, III, xxix.

The next period, 1685–1688, coincides with the brief rule by James II. Probably about the summer of 1685 Dryden became a Roman Catholic, and in 1687 published his second religious poem, *The Hind and the Panther*, whose 2592 lines make it his longest poem apart from translations. Its style is as complex as that of *Religio Laici* had been simple. Using sacred zoögraphy (the Hind represents Catholicism, the Panther Anglicanism, etc.), fables, myth, allusion, allegory, and the slightest of plots, Dryden sets forth a timeless version of the times, including the recent and distant past (Part I), present contentions (II), and the ecclesiastical as well as national future (III). Each part has a moving personal passage and those who have most opposed Dryden's doctrine or his fable have often called the style of this poem his finest. The poetic and personal confidence thereby implied finds expression in the ode, so praised by Dr. Johnson, on Anne Killigrew, whose small poetic abilities nonetheless may represent the artist's high vocation. Music is an equally confidently used metaphor in *A Song for Cecilia's Day*, which enacts history from Creation to Judgment.

When James fled late in 1688, and when William and Mary were invited as sovereigns by Parliament, Dryden entered into the most difficult period of his career, 1688–1694. Stripped of offices and denied full engagement with his times, he turned again to "the ungrateful stage." Two plays that now seem his greatest resulted: *Don Sebastian*, concerned with tragic fate, and *Amphitryon*, a very bleak comedy. Both deal with human identity in a hostile world. In 1691 he enjoyed a fortunate collaboration with Henry Purcell on *King Authur*, an opera. In 1694, his last play, *Love Triumphant*, featured a happy ending engineered by an unconvincing change of heart. Such doubts and sputters in these years had fullest exercise in the *Satires* of 1693 (translating Juvenal and Persius) and the Preface to *Examen Poeticum*, the third miscellany.

In the last period, 1694–1700, Dryden worked through his problems. If he could not address all his contemporaries, he could focus on individuals. In 1694 two of his finest poetic addresses appear: "To my Dear Friend Mr. Congreve" and "To Sir Godfrey Kneller." Gloom remains in both, but the gloomier "Kneller" shows chastened faith even in "these Inferiour Times." The "Congreve" bears uncanny resemblance in motif to *Mac Flecknoe*. Drama is again the topic, with comparisons again settling values. Now Dryden must abdicate and Congreve have legitimate succession, even if a usurper should sneak in for a time. The "son" merits, however, and the "father" loves.

Addresses lacked the capaciousness to adjust new strains to old hopes. Such scale was achieved in the 1697 *Virgil*. Although it and his comedies most require re-assessment, it does seem that he darkens the second half of his *Aeneis* (as if the military and the public worlds do not quite merge), and that he renders the *Georgics* even more heroically and sympathetically than Virgil to show the terms on which hope remained. His real epic was to come in cento, *Fables Ancient and Modern* (1700). It combines seventeen poems made over from Ovid, Boccaccio, Chaucer, and Homer with four solely Dryden's: those two handsome ones to the Duchess of Ormonde and to John Dryden of Chesterton toward the beginning, as also *Alexander's Feast* and "The Monument of a Fair Maiden Lady" toward the end. In redoing the *Metamorphoses* as Milton had redone the *Aeneid* in *Paradise Lost*, Dryden relates his poems by links, themes, motifs, and central subject – the human search for the good life. A serene wisdom shows that such a life can finally be gained only on Christian terms. Yet the vain and sinful race continues to endear itself to the old poet. *Fables* is once again becoming a favorite of readers as it had been for the Romantics and Dryden's own contemporaries. He died on May Day 1700 of degenerative diseases, yet calm of mind to the end.

The limitations of such periodizing are represented by its failure to allow for his constant writing in "the other harmony of prose" (Preface to *Fables*). He was by no means the modern stylist some claim. He writes in numerous styles and sometimes shows no more knowledge than Milton of modern paragraph and sentence writing. In his styles, however, he established English criticism, struggling like others before him to create the critical essay. As early as *The Rival Ladies* (1664) he found his way in use of the preface, employing a method inquisitive, devoted to current issues, and yet enough assured to deal with general principles. *Of Dramatick Poesy. An Essay* is really a dialogue, his most elaborate criticism, a semi-fiction, offering heroic debate on the proper character of drama. In the "Parallel Betwixt Poetry and Painting" (a preface to *De Arte Graphica* in 1695) we see most clearly his attempt to unite neo-Aristotelian mimesis with neo-Horatian affectivism. Once more he asserted the poet's right to heighten – to take a better or worse "likeness" and remain true, or to deal with the best "nature," unlike the scientist. In a way prescient for his career, the "Account" prefixed to *Annus Mirabilis* (1667) had placed historical poetry and panegyric (by implication satire also) under the aegis of epic. These prefaces, the *Dramatick Poesy*, and his poems as well dealt with the concept of hope for human progress, which was relatively new in England, and also introduced critical and historical principles. The element most neglected by historians of criticism was his historical understanding, which permitted him to compare and differentiate and evolve a historical relativism that would later undermine mimetic presumptions. To him we owe the concept of a historical age or period possessing its own temper or Zeitgeist, with all that such assumptions have meant to subsequent thought about literature.

Such diversity – there are over thirty plays, operas, and cantatas alone – yields to no easy summary. We can observe what joins him to, or differentiates him from, his great contemporaries – or the next century. Like Marvell, Dryden was a gifted lyric poet, although in odes rather than ruminative lyrics. Like Butler, he was a learned satirist, but where Butler degrades Dryden exalts. Like Milton, he excelled in varieties of narrative and drama, just as both also overcame crises toward the end of their lives. Dryden had what Milton lacked – wit, humor, and generosity. But his extraordinary intellectual power to liken and assimilate was incapable of Milton's higher fusion of all into a single intense reality. And where Milton, like Spenser, created an artistic language spoken by no one, Dryden like Donne and Jonson created a more natural language founded on actual speech. Born early enough to remember the outbreak of civil war (1642) and to live through four different national constitutions, Dryden wrote of subjects that poets no longer treat directly – the most momentous events of their times. For all that, his powers took on greatness only in the second half of his life, developing to the end. He practiced every literary kind except the novel, never repeating himself except in songs for plays. He is a rare example of a writer whose finest work comes at the end of a lifetime, of a century, and of a distinct period of literature. The next equivalent of *Fables* is not heroic poetry but the novel.

—Earl Miner

DUNCAN, Ronald (Frederick Henry).   English.   Born in Salisbury, Rhodesia, 6 August 1914. Educated in Switzerland and at Downing College, Cambridge, M.A. 1936. Married Rose Marie Theresa Hansom in 1941; one son and one daughter. Farmer in Devon since 1939. Poetry Editor, *The Townsman*, London, 1938–46; Columnist ("Jan's Journal"), *Evening Standard*, London, 1946–56. Founder, Devon Festival of the Arts, Bideford, 1953; Co-Founder, English Stage Company at the Royal Court Theatre, London, 1955.

Plays

Birth (produced 1937).
The Dull Ass's Hoof (includes *The Unburied Dead: Pimp, Skunk and Profiteer; Ora Pro Nobis*). 1940.
This Way to the Tomb: A Masque and Anti-Masque, music by Benjamin Britten (produced 1945). 1946.
The Eagle Has Two Heads, from a play by Jean Cocteau (produced 1946). 1948.
The Rape of Lucretia, music by Benjamin Britten, from a play by André Obey (produced 1946). 1946; augmented edition, 1948.
Amo Ergo Sum (cantata), music by Benjamin Britten (produced 1948).
The Typewriter, from a play by Jean Cocteau (produced 1950). 1948.
Stratton, music by Benjamin Britten (produced 1949). 1950.
St. Spiv (as *Nothing up My Sleeve,* produced 1950; revised version, as *St. 'Orace,* music by Jerry Wayne, produced 1964). In *Collected Plays,* 1971.
Our Lady's Tumbler, music by Arthur Oldham (produced 1950). 1951.
Don Juan (produced 1953). 1954.
The Death of Satan (produced 1954). 1955.
A Man Named Judas, from a play by C. A. Puget and Pierre Bost (produced 1956).
The Cardinal, with Hans Keuls, from a play by Harald Bratt (produced 1957).
The Apollo de Bellac, from a play by Jean Giraudoux (produced 1957). 1958.
The Catalyst (produced 1958; revised version, as *Ménage à Trois,* produced 1963). 1964.
Christopher Sly, music by Thomas Eastwood (produced 1960).
Abélard and Héloise: A Correspondence for the Stage (produced 1960). 1961.
The Rabbit Race, from a play by Martin Walser (produced 1963). In *Plays, vol. I* by Walser, 1963.
O-B-A-F-G: A Play in One Act in Stereophonic Sound (produced 1964). 1964.
The Trojan Women, from a play by Jean-Paul Sartre based on the play by Euripides (produced 1967). 1967.
The Seven Deadly Virtues: A Contemporary Immorality Play (produced 1968). In *Collected Plays,* 1971.
The Gift (produced 1968). In *Collected Plays,* 1971.
The Rehearsal (as *Still Life,* televised 1970). In *Collected Plays.* 1971.
Collected Plays (includes *This Way to the Tomb, St. Spiv, Our Lady's Tumbler, The Rehearsal, The Seven Deadly Virtues, O-B-A-F-G, The Gift*). 1971.

Screenplay: *Girl on a Motorcycle,* 1968.

Television Plays: *The Portrait,* 1954; *The Janitor,* 1955; *Preface to America,* 1959; *Not All the Dead Are Buried,* 1960; *The Rebel,* music by Thomas Eastwood, 1969; *Still Life,* 1970; *Mandala,* 1972.

Fiction

The Last Adam. 1952.
Saint Spiv. 1961.
The Perfect Mistress and Other Stories. 1969.
A Kettle of Fish (stories). 1971.
The Tale of Tails: Ten Fables. 1977.

Verse

> *Postcards to Pulcinella.* 1941.
> *The Mongrel and Other Poems.* 1950.
> *The Solitudes.* 1960.
> *Judas.* 1960.
> *Unpopular Poems.* 1969.
> *Man,* parts 1–5. 4 vols., 1970–74.
> *For the Few.* 1977.

Other

> *The Complete Pacifist.* 1937.
> *The Rexist Party Manifesto.* 1937.
> *Strategy in War.* 1937.
> *Journal of a Husbandman.* 1944.
> *Home-Made Home* (on architecture). 1947.
> *Jan's Journal 1–2.* 2 vols., 1949–54.
> *Tobacco Cultivation in England.* 1951.
> *The Blue Fox* (newspaper articles). 1951.
> *Jan at the Blue Fox* (newspaper articles). 1952.
> *Where I Live.* 1953.
> *All Men Are Islands: An Autobiography.* 1964.
> *Devon and Cornwall.* 1966.
> *How to Make Enemies* (autobiography). 1968.
> *Obsessed: A Third Volume of Autobiography.* 1977.

> Editor, *Songs and Satires of John Wilmot, 2nd Earl of Rochester.* 1948.
> Editor, *Selected Poems,* by Ben Jonson. 1949.
> Editor, *Selected Writings of Mahatma Gandhi.* 1951.
> Editor, with the Countess of Harewood, *Classical Songs for Children.* 1965.
> Editor, with Marion Harewood, *The Penguin Book of Accompanied Songs.* 1973.
> Editor, with Miranda Weston-Smith, *The Encyclopedia of Ignorance.* 2 vols., 1977.

> Translator, *Diary of a Film: La Belle et le Bête,* by Jean Cocteau. 1950.

Reading List: *Duncan* by Max Walter Haueter, 1969 (includes bibliography); *A Lone Wolf Howling: The Thematic Content of Duncan's Plays,* 1973, and *Duncan Interviewed,* 1973, both by William B. Wahl; *Tribute to Duncan* by Lord Harewood and others, 1974.

*   *   *

Despite its variety, Ronald Duncan's work has shown a marked consistency and steadfastness of purpose. His first love was poetry, and significantly the fruit of his late middle-age was the epic *Man,* one of the longest poems in the English language. Uniting the wisdom of the humanities with the knowledge and insight gained by science, this five-part work is paralleled, at least in content, only by Lucretius's *De Rerum Natura,* Victor Hugo's *La Légende des Siècles,* and, among modern productions, Alfred Noyes's *The Torch-Bearers.* As it remains virtually "undiscovered," its literary merits have still to be debated. Better known to the public, and of admitted dramatic merit, are the plays, especially *This Way to the Tomb,* which brought Duncan fame, *The Death of Satan,* and *The Catalyst,* which have been performed throughout the world. The fact that most of his best dramatic works are in verse (and this includes *The Catalyst*) bears out his steadfastness, since the vogue for verse-drama has waned. Duncan has also written several volumes of short stories, some sketches of rural life of great charm, and three volumes of controversial and unfinished autobiography.

Ezra Pound, a lifelong friend and a powerful influence, called Duncan "the lone wolf of English letters." The description is apt: for Duncan continued to write in studied poetic forms when his contemporaries were experimenting in obscurity and incoherence; to pursue traditional dramatic form when others were cultivating "the absurd"; and to broaden his scope by composing 63 cantos when his fellows were convinced that the epic was long dead. Moreover, Duncan specialized in both adaptation and translation – once a respectable literary art – in *The Eagle Has Two Heads*, when he brought Cocteau to the English stage; in *Our Lady's Tumbler*, and in the highly effective dialogue, *Abélard and Héloise*. He also wrote opera librettos, the best known being that for Britten's opera *The Rape of Lucretia*.

It must not be forgotten that Duncan was a farmer as well as a writer, and that his knowledge of the land and his empathic understanding of animals (he once worked with pit ponies) was fed into his writing. The following is from *This Way to the Tomb*:

> And look, there by the brook
> A hot-blooded mare
> Has lost her leggy foal,
> Watch how her head's thrust back,
> On her neck's great muscles;
> And the white panic of her eyes.
> Her nostrils dilate, she calls, and the furious engine stamps the earth.

Indeed, his non-literary experiences often afforded him insight into the nature of writing techniques. In his revulsion against free verse, he sought a more exact form of expression which should nevertheless avoid being "poetic." "It was an incident in my garden which solved this technical problem for me. I was watering the vegetable garden. I observed that the intensity of the jet of water was governed by restricting the outlet. Though obvious to me, this was a revelation; I realized that intensity in language can only be achieved by running it against a defined form, otherwise you get a dribble and not a jet" (Introduction to *Collected Plays*). At their best, Duncan's verse and prose show, besides wit, a capacity for the direct and illuminating *aperçu*.

—E. W. F. Tomlin

DUNLAP, William. American. Born in Perth Amboy, New Jersey, 19 February 1766. Educated in local schools until his family moved to New York in 1777; thereafter studied painting with a New York artist. Married Elizabeth Woolsey in 1789; one son and one daughter. Set up as a portraitist in New York, 1782–84; studied art with Benjamin West in London, 1784–86; returned to New York and abandoned painting to write for the New York stage; became a partner in his father's china importing business, c. 1790; Manager and Part-Owner, Old American Company, at the John Street Theatre, later at the Park Theatre, New York, presenting his own plays as well as current French and German plays in translation, 1796 until he went bankrupt, 1805; travelling miniaturist, 1805–06; General Assistant to the new manager of the Park Theatre, 1806–11; established the *Monthly Recorder*, New York, 1813; Assistant Paymaster-General, New York Militia, 1814–16; resumed painting as a livelihood, 1816 until his death. One of the founders, 1826, and Vice-President, 1831–38, of the National Academy of Design. *Died 28 September 1839.*

PUBLICATIONS

Plays

The Father; or, American Shandy-ism (produced 1789). 1789; revised version, as *The Father of an Only Child,* in *Dramatic Works,* 1806.

Darby's Return (produced 1789). 1789; edited by Walter J. Meserve and William R. Reardon, in *Satiric Comedies,* 1969.

The Miser's Wedding (produced 1793).

Leicester (as *The Fatal Deception; or, The Progress of Guilt,* produced 1794). In *Dramatic Works,* 1806.

Shelty's Travels (produced 1794).

Fountainville Abbey (produced 1795). In *Dramatic Works,* 1806.

The Archers; or, Mountaineers of Switzerland, music by Benjamin Carr (produced 1796). 1796.

Ribbemont; or, The Feudal Baron (as *The Mysterious Monk,* produced 1796). 1803.

The Knight's Adventure (produced 1797). 1807.

The Man of Fortitude, with John Hodgkinson (produced 1797). 1807.

Tell Truth and Shame the Devil, from a play by A. L. B. Robineau (produced 1797). 1797.

The Stranger, from a play by Kotzebue (produced 1798). 1798.

André (produced 1798). 1798.

False Shame; or, The American Orphan in Germany, from a play by Kotzebue (produced 1798). Edited by Oral Sumner Coad, with *Thirty Years,* 1940.

The Natural Daughter (produced 1799).

The Temple of Independence (produced 1799).

Don Carlos, from the play by Schiller (produced 1799).

Indians in England, from a play by Kotzebue (produced 1799).

The School for Soldiers, from a play by L. S. Mercier (produced 1799).

The Robbery, from a play by Boutet de Monval (produced 1799).

The Italian Father, from the play *The Honest Whore* by Dekker (produced 1799). 1800.

Graf Benyowsky, from a play by Kotzebue (produced 1799).

Sterne's Maria; or, The Vintage (produced 1799).

Lovers' Vows, from a play by Kotzebue (produced 1799). 1814.

The Force of Calumny, from a play by Kotzebue (produced 1800).

The Stranger's Birthday, from a play by Kotzebue (produced 1800).

The Knight of Guadalquiver (produced 1800).

The Wild-Goose Chase, from a play by Kotzebue (produced 1800). 1800.

The Virgin of the Sun, from a play by Kotzebue (produced 1800). 1800.

Pizarro in Peru; or, The Death of Rolla, from a play by Kotzebue and the version by Sheridan (produced 1800). 1800.

Fraternal Discord, from a play by Kotzebue (produced 1800). 1809.

The Soldier of '76 (produced 1801).

Abbe de l'Epee, from a play by Jean Bouilly (produced 1801).

Where Is He?, from a German play (produced 1801).

Abaelline, The Great Bandit, from a play by J. H. D. Zschokke (produced 1801). 1802.

The Merry Gardener, from a French play (produced 1802).

The Retrospect; or, The American Rovolution (produced 1802).
Peter the Great; or, The Russian Mother, from a play by J. M. Babo (produced 1802). 1814.
The Good Neighbors: An Interlude, from a work by A. W. Iffland (produced 1803). 1814.
Blue Beard: A Dramatic Romance, from the play by George Colman the Younger. 1803.
The Voice of Nature, from a play by L. C. Caigniez (produced 1803). 1803.
The Blind Boy, from a play by Kotzebue (produced 1803).
Bonaparte in England (produced 1803).
The Proverb; or, Conceit Can Cure, Conceit Can Kill (produced 1804).
Lewis of Monte Blanco; or, The Transplanted Irishman (produced 1804).
Nina, from a play by Joseph Marsollier (produced 1804).
Chains of the Heart; or, The Slave of Choice, from a play by Prince Hoare (produced ?). 1804.
The Wife of Two Husbands, from a play by Pixérécourt (produced 1804). 1804.
The Shipwreck, from a play by Samuel James Arnold (produced ?). 1805.
Dramatic Works. 3 vols., 1806–16.
Alberto Albertini; or, The Robber King (produced 1811).
Yankee Chronology; or, Huzza for the Constitution! (produced 1812). 1812.
The Glory of Columbia: Her Yeomanry! (produced 1813). 1817.
The Flying Dutchman (produced 1827).
A Trip to Niagara; or, Travellers in America (produced 1828). 1830.
Thirty Years; or, The Gambler's Fate, from a play by Prosper Goubaux and Victor Ducange (produced 1828). Edited by Oral Sumner Coad, with *False Shame*, 1940.

Other

Memoirs of the Life of George Frederick Cooke. 2 vols., 1813; revised edition, as *The Life of Cooke*, 1815.
A Record, Literary and Political, of Five Months in the Year 1813, with others. 1813.
The Life of the Most Noble Arthur, Marquis and Earl of Wellington, with Francis L. Clarke. 1814.
A Narrative of the Events Which Followed Bonaparte's Campaign in Russia. 1814.
The Life of Charles Brockden Brown, with Selections. 2 vols., 1815; as *Memoirs of Charles Brockden Brown*, 1822.
A History of the American Theatre. 1832.
A History of the Rise and Progress of the Arts of Design in the United States. 2 vols., 1834; revised edition, edited by Alexander Wyckoff, 1965.
Thirty Years Ago; or, The Memoirs of a Water Drinker. 2 vols., 1836.
A History of New York, for Schools. 2 vols., 1837.
History of the New Netherlands, Province of New York, and the State of New York. 2 vols., 1840.
Diary: The Memoirs of a Dramatist, Theatrical Manager, Painter, Critic, Novelist, and Historian, edited by Dorothy C. Barck. 3 vols., 1930.

Bibliography: in *False Shame, and Thirty Years*, edited by Oral Sumner Coad, 1940.

Reading List: *Dunlap: A Study of His Life and Works and of His Place in Contemporary Culture* by Oral Sumner Coad, 1917; *Arts of the Young Republic: The Age of Dunlap* by Harold E. Dickson, 1968.

*   *   *

"The American Vasari" and "Father of American Theatre" are phrases which honor William Dunlap as the first historian of United States arts. But his *Rise and Progress of the Arts*, though richly anecdotal, is a moralistic, opinionated source of biographical sketches. His *American Theatre* concentrates on 1787 to 1811 when Dunlap, as playwright and manager, knew everyone in the business and contributed to its growth from a British "provincial" company to a theatre bragging of native-born stars and playwrights. Dunlap proposed federal subsidization, questioned the star-system, and despised the new Scribean play-factories – despite having translated the lurid *Gambler's Fate*.

The democratic abolitionist and artist saw himself as an anti-partisan reconciler. Because the best European models required an indefinable purification of "old world vices," Dunlap was left without dependable aesthetic grounds for resisting commercial standardization. He became the compromiser who packaged the acceptable best. Over half of his plays introduced fashionable continental dramatists into the American repertory. After successfully adapting *The Stranger*, Dunlap depended particularly upon the popularity of Kotzebue's plays (twelve translations) with their affecting sentimentality coupled with, admittedly, "false philosophy and unsound morals." *False Shame* typically puts all major characters through set-piece confessions of "false shame" before redeeming them by intermarriage or discovering family relationships. It conforms in kind to Dunlap's own sentimental comedies.

Dunlap's first produced play, *The Father*, uses the stock comic doctor and country maidservant to give some savor to its purposeful actions: an American patriot's reunion with his son, an English officer; the redemption of a mildly rakish husband; a pallid literary borrowing from Sterne. Art, politics, and business "now in Virtue's cause engage/And rear that glorious thing, a *Moral Stage*." For stars' benefits or historical occasions Dunlap framed narrative songs. In *Yankee Chronology* a sailor returns to tell and sing of the 1812 victory of the (parable-pun) U.S.S. Constitution. Contradicting the travel-writers, *A Trip to Niagara* frames a moving diorama with interesting American (and British) types to persuade an English snob of some American virtues.

Only an unsophisticated audience could tolerate the ghastliness, disguises, and mistaken identities of the gothic *Mysterious Monk* and the romantic *Fatal Deception* – harmlessly abstract figures justified by much talk in verse about honor. But idea and theme, finally, make *André* a substantial and significant tragedy. General Washington and Major André are its heroic figures, while young Bland tries to be Otway's Pierre. Captain Bland and the other American officers play out their neoclassic alternatives of mind or heart, and the poetic drama gathers relevant force in their debate of the modes, moralities, and reconciliations necessary for an independent country in 1780, or in 1798 (the year of production).

Dunlap refashioned his controversial, unpopular, but finest play into a popular celebration. Incoherent and delightful, *The Glory of Columbia: Her Yeomanry!* wraps pieces of *André* with a despicable Benedict Arnold, some honest Yankee soldiers who capture André, a singing sister Sal in uniform, and a canny Irishman. He changes sides for a final victory pageant at Yorktown and a chorale to "Columbia's Son, Immortal Washington!"

—John G. Kuhn

DUNSANY, Lord; Edward John Moreton Drax Plunkett, 18th Baron Dunsany. Irish. Born in London, 24 July 1878; succeeded to the barony, 1899. Educated at Cheam School, Surrey; Eton College; Sandhurst. Served as 2nd Lieutenant in the Coldstream Guards in the Boer War, 1899–1902; Captain in the Royal Inniskilling Fusiliers in World War I; wounded, 1916. Associated with Yeats in the Irish theatre movement,

Dublin; Byron Professor of English Literature, University of Athens, 1940–41. President, Kent County Chess Association. Recipient: Harmsworth Literary Award. Follow, Royal Society of Literature, and Royal Geographical Society; Member, Irish Academy of Letters; Honorary Member, Institut Historique et Heraldique de France. *Died 25 October 1957.*

PUBLICATIONS

Plays

The Glittering Gate (produced 1909). In *Five Plays,* 1914.
The Gods of the Mountain (produced 1911). In *Five Plays,* 1914.
King Argimines and the Unknown Warrior (produced 1911). In *Five Plays,* 1914.
The Sphinx at Gizeh, in *Tripod,* May 1912.
The Golden Doom (produced 1912). In *Five Plays,* 1914.
The Lost Silk Hat (produced 1913). In *Five Plays,* 1914.
Five Plays. 1914.
The Tents of the Arabs (produced 1914). In *Plays of Gods and Men,* 1917.
A Night at an Inn (produced 1916). 1916.
The Queen's Enemies (produced 1916). In *Plays of Gods and Men,* 1917.
Plays of Gods and Men. 1917.
The Laughter of the Gods (produced 1919). In *Plays of Gods and Men,* 1917.
The Murderers (produced 1919).
The Prince of Stamboul (produced 1919?).
If (produced 1921). 1921.
Cheezo (produced 1921). In *Plays of Near and Far,* 1922.
Plays of Near and Far (includes *The Compromise of the King of the Golden Isles, The Flight of the Queen, Cheezo, A Good Bargain, If Shakespeare Lived Today, Fame and the Poet*). 1922.
Fame and the Poet (produced 1924). In *Plays of Near and Far,* 1922.
Lord Adrian (produced 1923). 1933.
Alexander and Three Small Plays (includes *The Old King's Tale, The Evil Kettle, The Amusement of Khan Kharuda*). 1925.
Alexander (produced 1938). 1925.
His Sainted Grandmother (produced 1926). In *Seven Modern Comedies,* 1928.
Mr. Faithful (produced 1927). 1939.
Seven Modern Comedies (includes *Atalanta in Wimbledon, The Raffle, The Journey of the Soul, In Holy Russia, His Sainted Grandmother, The Hopeless Passion of Mr. Bunyon, The Jest of Hahalaba*). 1928.
The Old Folks of the Centuries. 1930.
Plays for Earth and Air (includes *Fame Comes Late, A Matter of Honour, Mr. Sliggen's Hour, The Pumpkin, The Use of Man, The Bureau de Change, The Seventh Symphony, Golden Dragon City, Time's Joke, Atmospherics*). 1937.
The Strange Lover. 1939.

Fiction

The Gods of Pegāna. 1905.
Time and the Gods. 1906.
The Sword of Welleran and Other Stories. 1908.
A Dreamer's Tales. 1910.

The Book of Wonder: A Chronicle of Little Adventures at the Edge of the World. 1912.
Fifty-One Tales. 1915.
Tales of Wonder. 1916; as *The Last Book of Wonder,* 1916.
Tales of War. 1918.
Tales of Three Hemispheres. 1919.
The Chronicles of Rodriguez. 1922; as *Don Rodriguez: Chronicles of Shadow Valley,* 1922.
The King of Elfland's Daughter. 1924.
The Old Woman's Tale. 1925.
The Charwoman's Shadow. 1926.
The Blessing of Pan. 1927.
The Travel Tales of Mr. Joseph Jorkens. 1931.
The Curse of the Wise Woman. 1933.
Mr. Jorkens Remembers Africa. 1934.
Mr. Faithful. 1935.
Up in the Hills. 1935.
Rory and Bran. 1936.
The Story of Mona Sheehy. 1939.
Jorkens Has a Large Whisky (stories). 1940.
Guerilla. 1944.
The Fourth Book of Jorkens. 1948.
The Man Who Ate the Phoenix. 1949.
The Strange Journeys of Colonel Polders. 1950.
His Fellow Men. 1952.
The Little Tales of Smethers. 1952.
Jorkens Borrows Another Whisky. 1954.

Verse

Fifty Poems. 1929.
Mirage Water. 1938.
War Poems. 1941.
A Journey. 1943.
Wandering Songs. 1943.
The Year. 1946.
To Awaken Pegasus and Other Poems. 1949.

Other

Selections. 1912.
Nowadays. 1918.
Unhappy Far-Off Things. 1919.
If I Were Dictator. 1934.
My Talks with Dean Spanley. 1936.
My Ireland. 1937.
Patches of Sunlight (autobiography). 1938.
The Donellan Lectures 1943. 1945.
While the Sirens Slept (autobiography). 1944.
A Glimpse from a Watchtower: A Series of Essays. 1945.
The Sirens Wake (autobiography). 1945.
The Last Revolution. 1951.

Translator, *The Odes of Horace.* 1947.

Bibliography: *Bibliographies of Modern Authors 1,* by H. Danielson, 1925.

Reading List: *Dunsany the Dramatist* by Edward H. Bierstadt, 1917; *Lord Dunsany, King of Dreams: A Personal Portrait* by Hazel Smith, 1959.

*   *   *

Lord Dunsany, poet, novelist, essayist, and dramatist, began his theatrical career at The Abbey Theatre with *The Glittering Gate*, featuring two dead burglars who break into heaven, only to find a glittering void and much laughter. Dunsany, whose first literary heroes were the brothers Grimm, Andersen, and the Greek Olympians, achieves his crushingly ironic, frequently terrifying effects by quiet, witty, concise understatement and "free-swinging fantasy," especially in his best plays. *King Argimines and the Unknown Warrior* features a deposed monarch who, through discovery of a mystical sword in the slave fields, regains his kingdom because Darniak's profligate court ignores the prophet's Old-Testament hellfire-and-brimstone warnings. Darniak's god is broken into seven pieces, as the tear song of the downtrodden overwhelms the wine song of royalty at orgy, in a play asking what is majesty, what is nobility. A better play is *The Gods of the Mountain*, which displays the fatalism and hubris of Greek tragedy. It presents a group of beggars impersonating the gods of the mountain (to obtain the good life), being challenged by the worshipping public, then to their terror being turned to stone by the enraged gods, moving the populace to tears for having killed them through their doubts, and begging their forgiveness for having doubted them. *A Night at an Inn* is an eerie study of horrible vengeance by an angry oriental god and its priests who methodically destroy the helpless jewel thieves, in an increasingly crushing, terrifying display of perfect dramatic form, dialogue, and suspense. All three are plays which act as well now as they ever have.

Dunsany's mythological world seen in the plays and tales is wild, grotesque, primitive, suggestive of William Blake's universe; his prose style is admittedly influenced by Herodotus, the King James Bible, and William Morris. One must expend intellectual energy (well worth the effort) to grasp the symbolic meaning underlying Dunsany's frequently stormy gods and hopeless-looking mortals. Edwin Bjorkman (in his introduction to *Five Plays*, 1914) finds the weird beauty, the exuberant imagination based on solid observation, and the exquisite fantasy, characteristic of the poetic rebirth of Ireland. The characters in this beautiful, dreamlike world of cosmic, universal gods, where mortals may indeed be measured against monsters, fairies, and gods (and where Dunsany may be highly interested in ideas), though living at the edge of the world, are as familiar as if they were on an Irish or English street.

Dunsany's fiction continues to enthrall us (we read, dream, then enter into the worlds created) whether it be the story of the beginnings of the world in which creator Mana-Yood-Sushai sleeps (don't pray to him), Fate and Chance play their mist-shrouded game, Mung "signs" mortals to oblivion, Limpang-tung takes his music to the grass and winds and ocean, or Yoharnath-Lahai gives the cities peaceful sleep at night, while Skarl drums incessantly to keep Mana-Yood-Sushai asleep lest the world and the gods be forced to enter their golden galleons and glide down to the sea (*The Gods of Pegāna*); or whether the great spirits of Merimna's warriors inspire Rold to activate the spirit and sword of Welleran to save the city, or whether we weep with the little wild thing giving back her soul because self-centered, materialistic Christians made it impossible to worship God in perfect joy (*The Sword of Welleran*); or whether we "sail" with the bad ship *Desperate Lark* across the Sahara Desert (on wheels) to escape jail for piracy on the high seas and a massacre by the desert Arabs ("A Story of Land and Sea," *The Book of Wonder*).

—Louis Charles Stagg

D'URFEY, Thomas. English. Born in Exeter, Devon, in 1653. Settled in London; an intimate of Charles II and of James II; wrote for the stage from 1676; also composed numerous songs; Editor, *Momus Ridens; or, Comical Remarks on the Public Reports*, weekly, 1690–91. *Died 26 February 1723.*

PUBLICATIONS

Plays

The Siege of Memphis; or, The Ambitious Queen (produced 1676). 1676.
Madame Fickle; or, The Witty False One, from the play *A Match at Midnight* by William
    Rowley (produced 1676). 1677; edited by A. Norman Jeffares, in *Restoration
    Comedy,* 1974.
The Fool Turned Critic (produced 1676). 1678.
A Fond Husband; or, The Plotting Sisters (produced 1677). 1677.
Trick for Trick; or, The Debauched Hypocrite, from the play *Monsieur Thomas* by
    Fletcher (produced 1678). 1678.
Squire Oldsapp; or, The Night-Adventurers (produced 1678). 1679.
The Virtuous Wife; or, Good Luck at Last (produced 1679). 1680.
Sir Barnaby Whigg; or, No Wit Like a Woman's (produced 1681). 1681.
The Royalist (produced 1682). 1682.
The Injured Princess; or, The Fatal Wager, from the play *Cymbeline* by Shakespeare
    (produced 1682). 1682.
A Commonwealth of Women, from the play *The Sea Voyage* by Fletcher and Massinger
    (produced 1685). 1686.
The Banditti; or, A Lady's Distress (produced 1686). 1686.
A Fool's Preferment; or, The Three Dukes of Dunstable, from the play *The Noble
    Gentleman* by Beaumont and Fletcher (produced 1688). 1688.
Love for Money; or, The Boarding School (produced 1691). 1691.
Bussy D'Ambois; or, The Husband's Revenge, from the play by Chapman (produced
    1691). 1691.
The Marriage-Hater Matched (produced 1692). 1692.
The Richmond Heiress; or, A Woman Once in the Right (produced 1693). 1693.
The Comical History of Don Quixote, 3 parts (produced 1694–95). 3 vols., 1694–96.
Cinthia and Endimion; or, The Loves of the Deities (produced 1696). 1697.
The Intrigues at Versailles; or, A Jilt in All Humours (produced 1697). 1697.
The Campaigners; or, The Pleasant Adventures at Brussels (produced 1698). 1698.
The Rise and Fall of Massaniello, 2 parts (produced 1699). 1699–1700.
The Bath; or, The Western Lass (produced 1701). 1701.
The Old Mode and the New; or, Country Miss with Her Furbeloe (produced
    1703). 1703.
Wonders in the Sun; or, The Kingdom of the Birds (produced 1706). 1706.
The Modern Prophet; or, New Wit for a Husband (produced 1709). 1709.
New Operas, with Comical Stories and Poems (includes *The Two Queens of Brentford, or,
    Bayes No Poetaster; The Grecian Heroine, or, The Fate of Tyranny; Ariadne, or, The
    Triumph of Bacchus*). 1721.

Fiction

Tales Tragical and Comical. 1704.
Stories Moral and Comical. 1707.

Verse

Archery Revived; or, The Bow-Man's Excellence: An Heroic Poem, with Robert Shotterel. 1676.
The Progress of Honesty; or, A View of Court and City: A Pindaric Poem. 1681.
Butler's Ghost; or, Hudibras, The Fourth Part. 1682.
Scandalum Magnatum; or, Potapski's Case: A Satire Against Polish Oppression. 1682.
A New Collection of Songs and Poems. 1683.
Choice New Songs. 1684.
Several New Songs. 1684.
A Third Collection of New Songs. 1685.
An Elegy upon the Late Blessed King Charles II, and Two Panegyrics upon Their Present Sacred Majesties King James and Queen Mary. 1685.
A Complete Collection of Songs and Odes, and *A New Collection of Songs and Poems.* 2 vols., 1687.
A Poem Congratulatory on the Birth of the Young Prince. 1688.
New Poems, Consisting of Satires, Elegies, and Odes. 1690.
Collin's Walk Through London and Westminster: A Poem in Burlesque. 1690.
A Pindaric Ode on New Year's Day. 1691.
A Pindaric Poem on the Royal Navy. 1691.
The Moralist; or, A Satire upon the Sects. 1691.
The Triennial Mayor; or, The New Raparees. 1691.
The Weasels: A Satirical Fable. 1691.
The Weasel Trapped. 1691.
A Pindaric Ode upon the Fleet. 1692.
Gloriana: A Funeral Pindaric Poem Sacred to the Memory of Queen Mary. 1695.
Albion's Blessings: A Poem Panegyrical on His Sacred Majesty King William the III. 1698.
A Choice Collection of New Songs and Ballads. 1699.
An Ode for the Anniversary Feast Made in Honour of St. Cecilia. 1700.
The Trophies; or, Augusta's Glory: A Triumphant Ode. 1707.
Honor and Opes; or, The British Merchant's Glory. 1708.
Musa et Musica; or, Honour and Music. 1710.
Songs, edited by Cyrus L. Day. 1933.

Other

The Canonical Statesman's Grand Argument Discussed. 1693.

Editor, *Songs Complete, Pleasant, and Divertive.* 5 vols., 1719; revised edition, as *Wit and Mirth; or, Pills to Purge Melancholy,* 6 vols., 1719–20.

Reading List: *A Study of the Plays of D'Urfey* by Robert S. Forsythe, 2 vols., 1916–17; *Dates and Performances of D'Urfey's Plays* by Cyrus L. Day, 1950.

*   *   *

Thomas D'Urfey is probably best-known today for his delightful and influential collection of ballads and songs, *Pills to Purge Melancholy.* However, he was a dramatist of some consequence in his day, contributing about 30 comedies, tragedies, and operas between 1676 and 1709. He is a useful author for the literary historian, as he participated in the successive trends of contemporary drama; nevertheless, his real merit lies in the distinct individuality he achieved within his otherwise imitative productions.

With *A Fond Husband*, D'Urfey followed the influential vogue of sex-intrigue comedy established by Wycherley and Etherege, yet he peoples his landscape with grotesque "humours" characters designed for the low comedians James Nokes and Anthony Leigh. D'Urfey experienced the undoubted satisfaction of seeing Charles II in attendance at three of the first five performances of this comedy.

When Ravenscroft led the way toward farce, D'Urfey quickly turned in this direction with several plays, but in one of them, *The Virtuous Wife*, he inserted a serious presentation of female virtue, introduced by a hilarious "induction" scene in which the profligate and immoral actress Elizabeth Barry announced her refusal to play the role of a virtuous woman. Again, James Nokes scored a triumph as the elderly Lady Beardly in a farcical part.

To the phase of political satires, D'Urfey offered *Sir Barnaby Whigg* and *The Royalist*. When this vogue ended, Shadwell began experimenting with exemplary drama, to which D'Urfey contributed the two works which entitle him to a place in the history of English drama: *Love for Money* and *The Richmond Heiress*. In the former, he introduced a vulgar and realistic account of a girls' boarding school for the functional purpose of securing atmosphere by means of "local colour." The main plot-line shows a distressed heroine, who speaks in the high pathetic style, and a hero who is a "man of sense" rather than the customary town rake we associate with Restoration comedy. This hero tests the heroine and seeks dominance over her, not for sentimental reasons but for future financial security. I doubt that Stendhal would have disclaimed this play, so carefully has D'Urfey built his various ironic patterns. In *The Richmond Heiress*, D'Urfey presented several innovations. The action deals with fortune hunters, all of whom are severely ridiculed, and the play ends without a marriage of the principal characters. Also, the serious treatment of the morality of the characters and the emphasis on "The Papers" (showing legal control of the estate) suggest plays of a century later.

With the three-part *Comical History of Don Quixote*, D'Urfey followed the vogue of the bawdy which led to the famous attack by Jeremy Collier. Indecent language and incident are presented with verve and vitality. The best invention is Sancho's low-life daughter, Mary the Buxom, whose rough, coarse speeches carry vividly.

Originality appears in the two-part drama *Massaniello*, in which D'Urfey chooses prose as the language of tragedy. The harsh, realistic portrayal of a bestial mob raised to power well illustrates D'Urfey's creative skill. His plays became longer and longer, containing multiple plots, and hence can be viewed as a precursor of the coming genre of the novel.

—Arthur H. Scouten

ELIOT, T(homas) S(tearns).   English.   Born in St. Louis, Missouri, U.S.A., 26 September 1888; naturalized, 1927. Educated at Smith Academy, St. Louis, 1898–1905; Milton Academy, Massachusetts, 1905–06; Harvard University, Cambridge, Massachusetts (Editor, *Harvard Advocate*, 1909–10; Sheldon Fellowship, for study in Munich, 1914), 1906–10, 1911–14, B.A. 1909, M.A. 1910; the Sorbonne, Paris, 1910–11; Merton College, Oxford, 1914–15. Married 1) Vivienne Haigh-Wood in 1915 (died, 1947); 2) Esmé Valerie Fletcher, 1957. Teacher, High Wycombe Grammar School, Buckinghamshire, and Highgate School, London, 1915–17; Clerk, Lloyds Bank, London, 1917–25; Editor, later Director, Faber and Gwyer, later Faber and Faber, publishers, London, 1926–65. Assistant Editor, *The Egoist*, London, 1917–19; Founding Editor, *The Criterion*, London, 1922–39. Clark Lecturer, Trinity College, Cambridge, 1926; Charles Eliot Norton Professor of Poetry, Harvard University, 1932–33; Page-Barbour Lecturer, University of Virginia, Charlottesville, 1933; Theodore Spencer Memorial Lecturer, Harvard University, 1950. President, Classical Association, 1941, Virgil Society, 1943, and Books Across the Sea, 1943–46. Resident, Institute for Advanced Study, Princeton University, New Jersey, 1950; Honorary Fellow, Merton College, Oxford, and Magdalene College, Cambridge. Recipient: Nobel Prize for Literature, 1948; New York Drama Critics Circle Award, 1950; Hanseatic Goethe Prize, 1954; Dante Gold Medal, Florence, 1959; Order of Merit, Bonn, 1959; American Academy of Arts and Sciences Emerson-Thoreau Medal, 1960. Litt.D.: Columbia University, New York, 1933; Cambridge University, 1938; University of Bristol, 1938; University of Leeds, 1939; Harvard University, 1947; Princeton University, 1947; Yale University, New Haven, Connecticut, 1947; Washington University, St. Louis, 1953; University of Rome, 1958; University of Sheffield, 1959; LL.D.: University of Edinburgh, 1937; University of St. Andrews, 1953; D.Litt.: Oxford University, 1948; D.Lit.: University of London, 1950; Docteur-ès-Lettres, University of Aix-Marseille, 1959; University of Rennes, 1959; D.Phil.: University of Munich, 1959. Officer, Legion of Honor; Honorary Member, American Academy of Arts and Letters; Foreign Member, Accademia dei Lincei, Rome, and Akademie der Schönen Künste. Order of Merit, 1948. *Died 4 January 1965.*

PUBLICATIONS

Collections

Selected Prose, edited by Frank Kermode.   1975.

Plays

The Rock: A Pageant Play (produced 1934).   1934.
Murder in the Cathedral (produced 1935).   1935; revised version, as *The Film of Murder in the Cathedral,* 1952.
The Family Reunion (produced 1939).   1939.
The Cocktail Party (produced 1949).   1950; revised version, 1950.
The Confidential Clerk (produced 1953).   1954.
The Elder Statesman (produced 1958).   1959.
Collected Plays: Murder in the Cathedral, The Family Reunion, The Cocktail Party, The Confidential Clerk, The Elder Statesman.   1962; as *The Complete Plays,* 1969.

Verse

Prufrock and Other Observations.   1917.

Poems. 1919.
Ara Vos Prec. 1920; as *Poems,* 1920.
The Waste Land. 1922; *A Facsimile and Transcripts of the Original Drafts Including the Annotations of Ezra Pound,* edited by Valerie Eliot, 1971.
Poems 1909–1925. 1925.
Ash-Wednesday. 1930.
Sweeney Agonistes: Fragments of an Aristophanic Melodrama. 1932.
Collected Poems 1909–1935. 1936.
Old Possum's Book of Practical Cats. 1939.
The Waste Land and Other Poems. 1940.
East Coker. 1940.
Later Poems 1925–1935. 1941.
The Dry Salvages. 1941.
Little Gidding. 1942.
Four Quartets. 1943.
A Practical Possum. 1947.
Selected Poems. 1948.
The Undergraduate Poems of T. S. Eliot. 1949.
Poems Written in Early Youth, edited by John Hayward. 1950.
Collected Poems 1909–1962. 1963.

Other

Ezra Pound: His Metric and Poetry. 1917.
The Sacred Wood: Essays on Poetry and Criticism. 1920.
Homage to John Dryden: Three Essays on Poetry in the Seventeenth Century. 1924.
For Lancelot Andrewes: Essays on Style and Order. 1928.
Dante. 1929.
Thoughts after Lambeth. 1931.
Selected Essays 1917–1932. 1932; revised edition, 1950.
John Dryden: The Poet, The Dramatist, The Critic. 1932.
The Use of Poetry and the Use of Criticism: Studies in the Relation of Criticism to Poetry in England. 1933.
After Strange Gods: A Primer of Modern Heresy. 1934.
Elizabethan Essays. 1934; as *Elizabethan Dramatists,* 1963.
Essays Ancient and Modern. 1936.
The Idea of a Christian Society. 1939.
Points of View, edited by John Hayward. 1941.
Reunion by Destruction: Reflections on a Scheme for Church Unity in South India Addressed to the Laity. 1943.
Notes Towards the Definition of Culture. 1948.
The Complete Poems and Plays. 1952.
Selected Prose, edited by John Hayward. 1953.
On Poetry and Poets. 1957.
George Herbert. 1962.
Knowledge and Experience in the Philosophy of F. H. Bradley (doctoral dissertation). 1964.
To Criticize the Critic and Other Writings. 1965.
The Literary Criticism of Eliot: New Essays, edited by David Newton de-Molina. 1977.

Editor, *Selected Poems,* by Ezra Pound. 1928; revised edition, 1949.
Editor, *A Choice of Kipling's Verse.* 1941.
Editor, *Introducing James Joyce.* 1942.

Editor, *Literary Essays of Ezra Pound.*   1954.
Editor, *The Criterion 1922–1939.*   18 vols., 1967.

Translator, *Anabasis: A Poem,* by St.-John Perse.   1930; revised edition, 1938, 1949, 1959.

Bibliography: *Eliot: A Bibliography* by Donald Gallup, 1952, revised edition, 1969; *The Merrill Checklist of Eliot* by B. Gunter, 1970.

Reading List: *The Achievement of Eliot: An Essay on the Nature of Poetry* by F. O. Matthiessen, 1935, revised edition, 1947, with additional material by C. L. Barber, 1958; *Four Quartets Rehearsed* by R. Preston, 1946; *Eliot: The Design of His Poetry* by Elizabeth Drew, 1949; *The Art of Eliot* by Helen Gardner, 1949; *The Poetry of Eliot* by D. E. S. Maxwell, 1952; *Eliot's Poetry and Plays: A Study in Sources and Meaning* by Grover Smith, 1956, revised edition, 1975; *The Invisible Poet: Eliot* by Hugh Kenner 1959; *Eliot: A Collection of Critical Essays* edited by Hugh Kenner, 1962; *Eliot's Dramatic Theory and Practice* by Carol H. Smith, 1963; *Eliot* by Northrop Frye, 1963; *Eliot: Movements and Patterns* by Leonard Unger, 1966; *Eliot* by Bernard Bergonzi, 1972; *Eliot in His Time: Essays on the Occasion of the Fiftieth Anniversary of the Waste Land* edited by A. Walton Litz, 1973; *Eliot: The Longer Poems* by Derek A. Traversi, 1976.

*   *   *

T. S. Eliot's influence was predominant in English poetry in the period between the two World Wars. His first small volume of poems, *Prufrock and Other Observations,* appeared in 1917. The title is significant. Eliot's earliest verse is composed of *observations,* detached, ironic, and alternately disillusioned and nostalgic in tone. The prevailing influence is that of French poetry, and in particular of Jules Laforgue; the mood is one of reaction against the comfortable certainties of "Georgian" poetry, the projection of a world which presented itself to the poet and his generation as disconcerting, uncertain, and very possibly heading for destruction.

The longest poem in the volume, "The Love Song of J. Alfred Prufrock," shows these qualities, but goes beyond them. The speaker is a kind of modern Hamlet, a man who after a life passed in devotion to the trivial has awakened to a sense of his own futility and to that of the world around him. He feels that some decisive act of commitment is needed to break the meaningless flow of events which his life offers. The question, however, is whether he really dares to reverse the entire course of his existence by a decision the nature of which eludes him:

> And indeed there will be time
> To wonder, "Do I dare?" and, "Do I dare?"
> Time to turn back and descend the stair,
> With a bald spot in the middle of my hair …
> Do I dare
> Disturb the universe?

The answer, for Prufrock, is negative. Dominated by his fear of life, misunderstood when he tries to express his sense of a possible revelation, Prufrock concludes "No! I am not Prince Hamlet, nor was meant to be," refuses to accept the role which life for a moment seemed to have thrust upon him, and returns to the stagnation which his vision of reality imposes.

After a second small volume, published in 1919, which shows, more especially in its most impressive poem, "Gerontion," a notable deepening into tragedy, the publication in 1922 of *The Waste Land* burst upon its readers with the effect of a literary revolution. Many of its first readers found the poem arid and incomprehensible, though it was in fact neither. The poet tells us that he is working through "a heap of broken images." He does this because it is a world of dissociated fragments that he is describing; but his aim, like that of any artist, is not merely an evocation of chaos. The poem is built on the interweaving of two great themes: the broken pieces of the present, as it presents itself to a disillusioned contemporary understanding, and the significant continuity of tradition. These two strains begin apart, like two separate themes in a musical composition, but the poem is animated by the hope, the *method*, that at the end they will converge into some kind of unity. Some critics, reading it in the light of Eliot's later development, have tried to find in the poem a specifically "religious" content, which however is not there. At best, there is a suggestion at the close that such a content, were it available, might provide a way out of the "waste land" situation, that the life-giving rain *may* be on the point of relieving the intolerable drought; but the poet cannot honestly propose such a resolution and the step which might have affirmed it is never rendered actual.

For some years after 1922, Eliot wrote little poetry and the greater part of his effort went into critical prose, much of it published in *The Criterion*, the literary quarterly which he edited until 1939. Eliot's criticism, which profoundly affected the literary taste of his generation, contributed to the revaluation of certain writers – the lesser Elizabethan dramatists, Donne, Marvell, Dryden – and, more controversially, to the depreciation of others, such as Milton (concerning whom, however, Eliot later modified his views) and some of the Romantic poets. It was the work of a poet whose interest in other writers was largely conditioned by the search for solutions to the problems raised by his own art; and, as such, it was marked by the idiosyncrasies which constitute at once its strength and its limitation.

In 1928, in his preface to the collection of essays *For Lancelot Andrewes*, Eliot declared himself Anglo-Catholic in religion, royalist in politics, classicist in literature: a typically enigmatic statement which indicated the direction he was to give to the work of his later years. 1930 saw the publication of *Ash-Wednesday*, his first considerable poem of explicitly Christian inspiration: a work at once religious in content and modern in inspiration, personal yet without concession to sentiment. The main theme is an acceptance of conversion as a necessary and irretrievable act. The answer to the question posed by Prufrock – "Do I dare/ Disturb the universe?" – is seen, in the translation of the first line of the Italian poet Guido Cavalcanti's ballad, "Because I do not hope to turn again," as an embarkation, dangerous but decisive, upon the adventure of faith.

The consequences of this development were explored in the last and in some respects the most ambitious of Eliot's poetic efforts: the sequence of poems initiated in 1935 and finally published, in 1943, under the title of *Four Quartets*. The series opens, in *Burnt Norton*, with an exploration of the *possible* significance of certain moments which seem to penetrate, briefly and elusively, a reality beyond that of normal temporal experience. "To be conscious," the poem suggests, "is not to be in time": only to balance that possibility with the counter-assertion that "Only through time time is conquered." The first step towards an understanding of the problems raised in the *Quartets* is a recognition that time, though inseparable from our human experience, is not the whole of it. If we consider time as an ultimate reality, our spiritual intuitions are turned into an illusion: whereas if we seek to deny the reality of time, our experience becomes impossible. The two elements – the temporal and the timeless – need to be woven together in an embracing pattern of experience which is, in fact, the end to which the entire sequence points.

The later "quartets" build upon this provisional foundation in the light of the poet's experience as artist and human being. The impulse to create in words reflects another, still more fundamental, impulse which prompts men to seek *form*, coherence, and meaning in the broken intuitions which their experience offers them. The nature of the search is such that it can never be complete in time. The true value of our actions only begins to emerge when we abstract ourselves from the temporal sequence – "time before and time after" – in which they were realized; and the final sense of our experience only reveals itself when the pattern is completed, at the moment of death. This moment, indeed, is not properly speaking a single final point, but a reality which covers the whole course of our existence.

These reflections lead the poet, in the last two poems of the series, *The Dry Salvages* and *Little Gidding*, to acceptance and even to a certain optimism. The end of the journey becomes the key to its beginning, and this in turn an invitation to confidence: "Not fare well,/But fare forward, voyagers." The doctrine of detachment explored in the second poem, *East Coker*, becomes an "expanding" one of "love beyond desire." The conclusion stresses the continuity between the "birth" and "death" which are simultaneously present in each moment, in each individual life, and in the history of the human race. It is true, as the closing section of *Little Gidding* puts it, that "we die with the dying"; but it is equally true, as it also goes on to say, that "we are born with the dead." We die, in other words, as part of the tragedy which the fact of our humanity implies, but we are born again when, having understood the temporal process in its true light, we are ready to accept our present position within a still-living and continually unfolding tradition.

Eliot's poetic output was relatively small and intensely concentrated: a fact which at once confirms its value and constitutes, in some sense, a limiting factor. It should be mentioned that in his later years he devoted himself to the writing of verse plays, in an attempt to create a contemporary mode of poetic drama. The earlier plays, *Murder in the Cathedral* and *The Family Reunion*, which are also the best, take up the themes which were being explored at the same time in his poetry and develop them in ways that are often interesting. *The Cocktail Party*, though still a skilful work, shows some decline in conception and execution, and the later plays – *The Confidential Clerk* and *The Elder Statesman* – can safely be said to add little to Eliot's achievement.

—Derek A. Traversi

ERVINE, St. John (Greer).   Irish.   Born in Belfast, Northern Ireland, 28 December 1883. Served as a Lieutenant in the Royal Dublin Fusiliers in France during World War I; wounded, 1918. Married Leonora Mary Davis in 1911. Drama Critic for *The Labour Leader*, 1910, *The Daily Citizen*, 1911, and *The Weekly Despatch*, 1912, all in Dublin; associated with the Abbey Theatre, Dublin: Manager, 1915–16; settled in London after World War I: Drama Critic for *The Observer*, 1919–23, *The Morning Post*, 1925, and *The Daily Express*, 1929; also, Guest Critic, *New York World*, 1928–29; critic/commentator with the BBC from 1932; Professor of Dramatic Literature for the Royal Society of Literature, 1933–36. President, Critics' Circle, 1929. LL.D.: University of St. Andrews. Fellow of the Royal Society of Literature; Member of the Irish Academy. *Died 24 January 1971.*

PUBLICATIONS

Plays

Mixed Marriage (produced 1911).   1911.
Compensation (produced 1911).
The Magnanimous Lover (produced 1912).   1912.
The Orangeman (produced 1913).   In Four Irish Plays.   1914.
Jane Clegg (produced 1913).   1914.

The Critics; or, A New Play at the Abbey Theatre (produced 1913).   In Four Irish Plays, 1914.
Four Irish Plays (includes The Magnanimous Lover, Mixed Marriage, The Critics, The Orangeman). 1914.
John Ferguson (produced 1915).   1915.
The Island of Saints, and How to Get Out of It (produced 1920).
The Wonderful Visit, with H. G. Wells, from the novel by Wells (produced 1921).
The Ship (produced 1922).   1922.
Progress (produced 1922).   In Four One-Act Plays, 1928.
Mary, Mary, Quite Contrary (produced 1923).   1923.
The Lady of Belmont (produced 1924).   1923.
Anthony and Anna (produced 1926).   1925; revised version, 1930.
Ole George Comes to Tea (produced 1927).   In Four One-Act Plays, 1928.
She Was No Lady (produced 1927).   In Four One-Act Plays, 1928.
Four One-Act Plays (includes Ole George Comes to Tea, Progress, She Was No Lady, The Magnanimous Lover).   1928.
The First Mrs. Fraser (produced 1929).   1929.
People of Our Class (produced 1937).   1936.
Boyd's Shop (produced 1936).   1936.
Robert's Wife (produced 1937).   1938.
William John Mawhinney (produced 1940).
Friends and Relations (produced 1941).   1947.
Private Enterprise (produced 1947).   1948.
The Christies (produced 1947; revised version, produced 1948).   1949.
My Brother Tom (produced 1952).   1952.

Fiction

Mrs. Martin's Man.   1914.
Alice and the Family: A Story of South London.   1915.
Changing Winds.   1917.
The Foolish Lovers.   1920.
The Wayward Man.   1927.
The Mountain and Other Stories.   1928.
The First Mrs. Fraser.   1931.
Sophia.   1941.

Other

Francis Place, The Tailor of Charing Cross.   1912.
Eight O'Clock and Other Studies.   1913.
Sir Edward Carson and the Ulster Movement.   1915.
Some Impressions of My Elders.   1922.
The Organized Theatre: A Plea in Civics.   1924.
Parnell.   1925.
How to Write a Play.   1928.
The Theatre in My Time.   1933.
The Future of the Press.   1933.
God's Soldier: General William Booth.   2 vols., 1934.
If I Were Dictator.   1934.
A Journey to Jerusalem.   1936.
Is Liberty Lost?   1941.

Craigavon, Ulsterman. 1949.
Oscar Wilde: A Present Time Appraisal. 1951.
Bernard Shaw: His Life, Work, and Friends. 1956.

*   *   *

St. John Ervine's early work is nearly all in the socio-realistic mode in vogue in Britain until the First World War, employing settings from the writer's native Ulster as well as his adopted London where he arrived to work as an insurance clerk in 1900. Of his novels, *Mrs. Martin's Man* was praised by H. G. Wells, and *Alice and a Family: A Story of South London* was considered by *The Daily News* to be the work of "one of our wisest and most brilliant young novelists." But it was as a dramatist that Ervine made his principal impact. His first play, staged at the Abbey Theatre in 1911, was *Mixed Marriage*, in which the precarious alliance between a Belfast Protestant and a Catholic is shattered when the Orangeman's son proposes to marry a Catholic girl, the father's subsequent inflammatory speeches causing riots and the fiancée's death. Ervine's next major success came with *Jane Clegg*, excellently presented at the Gaiety, Manchester, with Sybil Thorndike as the wife who, after loyally condoning her worthless commercial traveller husband's infidelities and financial irresponsibility, finally breaks with him. With *John Ferguson*, another fine Abbey Theatre play, Ervine returned to an Irish Protestant setting, his powerful presentation of unquenchable religious faith and stoicism in adversity somewhat weakened by the melodramatic elements in the plot.

After World War I, Ervine discovered a forte for light comedy, although *The Ship* is a strong, Ibsenesque portrayal of conflict between a materialistic shipbuilder and his rebellious son. Audiences of the inter-war years, however, preferred such well-groomed Knightsbridge ephemera as *The First Mrs. Fraser*, in which a charming, ruthless divorcée detaches her former husband from his youthful second wife with the help of a little blackmail, or humorous depictions of Ulster country life, as in *Boyd's Shop*, which centres on an old-fashioned village shop, and rivalries for the hand of the shopkeeper's daughter. A better play than these is *Robert's Wife*, a somewhat wordy piece that is slow to develop, but which contains much character interest and presents an engrossing theme: in it the birth-control clinic run by the doctor-wife of the popular local parson becomes the subject of much controversy, especially when the Vicar is offered a Deanery and his pacifist stepson is imprisoned for sedition. Ervine's most intriguing post-war play was perhaps *The Christies*, which turns on an embezzler's release from gaol and its impact on his family, particularly his wife now grown independent of him, and his pious mother who is shocked to find him unrepentant.

Novelist, critic, playwright, theatre manager, biographer, and polemicist, Ervine combined a long life with a remarkably varied literary output which incorporated a volume on writing a successful play, a topical study entitled *If I Were Dictator*, a sequel to *The Merchant of Venice*, and a life of the founder of the Salvation Army. To this medley may be added short stories, essays, reminiscences, as well as pungent reviews contributed to *The Observer* and *The Morning Post*, and innumerable prefaces and introductions, Irish political studies of Carson, Parnell, and Lord Craigavon, a trenchant critical biography of Oscar Wilde, and an immensely long and laudatory one of Shaw.

—William M. Tydeman

ETHEREGE, Sir George.   English.   Born, probably at Maidenhead, Berkshire, c 1635.

Little is known of his early life: may have studied at Cambridge University, and at the Inns of Court, London, and may have spent many years abroad: unknown when his first play was produced in 1664. Had one daughter by the actress Mrs. Barry; married Mary Arnold c. 1680. Prominent figure in Restoration London, in the circle of Sedley and the Earl of Rochester; also served the court as a diplomat: Secretary to the Ambassador to Constantinople, Sir Daniel Harvey, 1668–71; on diplomatic assignment in The Hague, 1671; Ambassador to the Imperial Court at Ratisbon (Regensburg), Bavaria, 1685–89; possibly served in Paris, 1691. Knighted c. 1685. *Died in 1691.*

PUBLICATIONS

Collections

Works, edited by H. F. B. Brett-Smith.   2 vols. (of 3), 1927.
Poems, edited by James Thorpe.   1963.
Letters, edited by Frederick Bracher.   1974.

Plays

The Comical Revenge; or, Love in a Tub (produced 1664).   1664.
She Would If She Could (produced 1668).   1668; edited by Charlene M. Taylor, 1971.
The Man of Mode; or, Sir Fopling Flutter (produced 1676).   1676; edited by John Conaghan, 1973.

Other

The Letterbook, edited by Sybil M. Rosenfeld.   1928.

Reading List: *Etherege: Sein Leben, Seine Zeit, und Seine Dramen* by V. Meindl, 1901; *Etherege: A Study in Restoration Comedy* by Frances S. McCamic, 1931; *Etherege and the 17th-Century Comedy of Manners* by Dale Underwood, 1957.

*   *   *

Although Sir George Etherege wrote only three plays, he exerted enormous influence on his successors and is usually regarded as the originator of the Restoration comedy of manners. All of his plays contain the wit and satire that characterize this kind of comedy, but it was his last and best play, *The Man of Mode,* that provided the characters, values, and language that became models for later dramatists.

Etherege's plays depict the sophisticated, fashionable world of courtier-rakes and coquettes, and satirize the affectations and foibles of a society Etherege knew intimately. The appeal of Etheregean comedy, which is chiefly based on brilliant wit and polished dialogue, is usually intellectual, although occasional farcical elements are present, while plot complications derive from sexual and romantic intrigue.

Each of Etherege's plays affirms a unique and complex set of values which carefully defines a hierarchy of characters and modes of behavior, and by which each character and event is measured. The action in each play centers around a battle of wits between hero and heroine. The hero, who has not seriously considered marriage, is captured by a heroine who

199

is the only character who fully understands the hero. The hero and heroine are contrasted with minor characters whose activities help delineate the characters of the hero and heroine. Each hero is superior to the other men in his play in that he exhibits greater knowledge of self and environment, is able to determine the proper balance between convention and nature, can manipulate his fellow-creatures to his advantage, and follows the most "reasonable" course of action circumstances allow. Each heroine is able to meet and outmaneuver the hero on his own ground, recognizes her unique limitations, comprehends the difficulty and implications of the problem she faces, and makes the hero feel that marriage is the most desirable course of action. Etherege's heroes and heroines are always evenly matched, and because they seldom face problems imposed by the external world, happiness is achieved when they overcome obstacles resulting from their own characters.

Despite these broad similarities, Etherege's plays differ significantly in structure and quality. Etherege steadily refined his art until he produced, in *The Man of Mode*, one of the most brilliant comedies in the English language.

The Comical Revenge contains four largely separate plots, each of which provides implicit commentary on the others. The main plot is a battle between evenly matched and resourceful lovers, Sir Frederick Frollick and Widow Rich. Comedy derives from their verbal and tactical adeptness in trying to force each other into confessions of love. The "heroic" plot is written in couplets, contains long speeches on courtly love and honor, and depicts the adventures of four lovers and a faithful friend. The two remaining "low" plots deal with the nearly successful duping of a country booby, Sir Nicholas Cully, and the imprisonment of Sir Frederick's servant, Dufoy, in a tub.

Sir Frederick and Widow Rich constitute a mean between the heroic and low plots. Love is depicted as an honorable passion, free from lust and based on purity, in the heroic plot, a conception burlesqued by Sir Frederick's continual understatement, and as a "disease" whose end-product is literally venereal disease in the Dufoy plot. Sir Frederick's concept of love is both "natural," in that it is not opposed to physical appetite and freedom, and "reasonable," in that it takes practical considerations into account. Like later Etherege heroes, Sir Frederick is able to manipulate others and to dissemble, and is generally in control of events, except those involving Widow Rich, whose self-sufficiency and resourcefulness he underestimates.

Many of the minor characters in *The Comical Revenge* are not differentiated from one another, nor is the Sir Frederick–Widow Rich plot developed as fully as the main plots in Etherege's later plays. Moreover, much of the play's humor depends on farce and burlesque, and it is not always easy to see the relationship of individual parts to one another or to the whole.

There is no heroic plot in *She Would If She Could*, but there are two sets of heroes and heroines. Characters who are able to recognize the proper relationship between social decorum and honesty are contrasted with characters entirely ruled by custom. The older, unsympathetic characters return to the country, always an undesirable place in Etheregean comedy, with the same mistaken notions they brought to town. Although minor distinctions among the four sympathetic lovers are made, the hierarchy of values is not nearly as complex as in *The Man of Mode*.

Like *She Would If She Could*, *The Man of Mode* contrasts characters who do not recognize the necessity for occasional plain-dealing with those who do, but it also contrasts those who do not understand the importance of social conventions with those who do. Characters of all shades inhabit the ground between the extremes in *The Man of Mode*. Instead of two sets of lovers, Harriet and Dorimant dominate the action of the play and regulate our response to the other characters. Dorimant is contrasted with each of the other male characters, from the completely affected Sir Fopling Flutter to such near-misses as Young Bellair, who, despite good breeding, lacks Dorimant's wit. Dorimant is acquainted with and able to profit from all fashionable modes of behavior, but is still able to maintain his identity. His only match in the play is Harriet, who is contrasted with all other women in the play, from Loveit, who sacrifices all necessary conventional restraints to emotion, to Bellinda, who, though attractive and witty, is unable to control Dorimant. Harriet's intellect, beauty, wealth, familiarity with the world, understanding of self and others, and powers of manipulation enable her to make Dorimant desire marriage. Their union represents an Etheregean ideal in which both retain individuality, freedom, and the excitement of the chase, and in which no fundamental character changes occur.

The Etheregean hero and heroine become progressively more refined in each play. Sir Frederick's drunken rowdiness is replaced by Dorimant's polished wit and naturally easy sense of propriety, much as Widow Rich's occasional coarseness gives way to Harriet's restraint and quiet aggressiveness. Sir Frederick is closer than Dorimant to the good-natured hero of sentimental comedy; in *The Man of Mode*, "good nature" can be feigned, but is not a necessary virtue.

Language is a more important source of pleasure in each successive play. In *The Comical Revenge*, language is important primarily because the sections written in couplets contrast with the prose parts; in *The Man of Mode*, Harriet and Dorimant demonstrate their superiority partially through mastery of language, and much intellectual pleasure derives from extended metaphors. In general, wit changes from frankly physical allusions to complex sexual puns and sophisticated dialogue.

The differences between *The Comical Revenge* and *The Man of Mode* illustrate Etherege's growth as a playwright. In the former, the reader is sometimes puzzled by scenes that have little relationship to preceding and following scenes, interest is divided among four plots, and our feelings about the hero and heroine are sometimes ambivalent when Etherege clearly wishes them to be positive. In the latter, plot elements are unified, our sympathies are wholly engaged by the Harriet–Dorimant relationship, and interest is fully maintained throughout by Etherege's varied and complex portrait of Restoration society.

—James S. Malek

FARQUHAR, George.   Irish.   Born in Londonderry, Northern Ireland, c. 1677. Educated at a school in Londonderry; Trinity College, Dublin (sizar), 1694–95. Married Margaret Pemell in 1703; two daughters. Corrector for the press of a Dublin bookseller, 1696; actor at the Smock Alley Theatre, Dublin, 1696–97, but gave up acting after accidentally wounding a fellow-actor; settled in London, 1697, and began writing for the stage; also an army officer: commissioned Lieutenant in the Militia, and served in Holland, 1700; Lieutenant in the Grenadiers, 1704, engaged in recruiting in Lichfield and Shrewsbury, 1705–06. *Died 29 April 1707.*

PUBLICATIONS

Collections

   Complete Works, edited by Charles Stonehill.   2 vols., 1930.

Plays

   Love and a Bottle (produced 1698).   1699.
   The Constant Couple; or, A Trip to the Jubilee (produced 1699).   1700; edited by A.
      Norman Jeffares, in *Restoration Comedy,* 1974.
   Sir Harry Wildair, Being the Sequel of The Trip to the Jubilee (produced 1701).   1701.
   The Inconstant; or, The Way to Win Him, from the play *The Wild Goose Chase* by
      Fletcher (produced 1702).   1702.
   The Twin-Rivals (produced 1702).   1703.
   The Stage Coach, from a play by Jean de la Chapelle (produced 1704).   1704.
   The Recruiting Officer (produced 1706).   1706; edited by John Ross, 1978.
   The Beaux' Strategem (produced 1707).   1707; edited by Charles N. Fifer, 1977.

Verse

   *Love and Business in a Collection of Occasionary Verse and Epistolary Prose, A Discourse
      Likewise upon Comedy in Reference to the English Stage.*   1702.
   Barcelona; or, The Spanish Expedition.   1710.

Fiction

   The Adventures of Covent Garden.   1698.

Reading List: *Young George Farquhar: The Restoration Drama at Twilight* by W. Connely, 1949; *Farquhar* by Albert J. Farmer, 1966; *Farquhar* by Eric Rothstein, 1967; *The Development of Farquhar as a Comic Dramatist* by Eugene N. James, 1972.

*   *   *

   Of the many comic writers who have emerged from Ireland, George Farquhar is among the very best, keeping company with such fellow-dramatists as Goldsmith and Wilde. During his short life (he died at about age thirty), he wrote eight plays (all comedies), an interesting critical essay entitled "A Discourse upon Comedy in reference to the English Stage," and some much less important miscellaneous poetry and prose. Farquhar is usually regarded as the last major dramatist writing "Restoration" comedy, but it is important to distinguish him from both his predecessors, notably Etherege and Wycherley, and his contemporaries, such as Vanbrugh and Congreve.

Farquhar's theatrical career spans the years from 1698 to 1707, which belong to a period of transition in comic drama, partly in response to increasing demands during the 1690's and early eighteenth century for more decorum and positive moral standards on the stage. The preoccupation with sexual licence, bawdry, and satire of the early Restoration playwrights, especially in the 1670's, gradually gave way to a more genteel and morally exemplary conception of comedy, culminating in eighteenth-century "sentimental" comedy. Although Farquhar's plays look back to the first masters of "wit" or "manners" comedy and are certainly not lacking in bawdy, they do exhibit features characteristic of this new tendency towards greater propriety. Most of Farquhar's heroes, for example, prove to be much less rakish in their conduct than their witty speech suggests, and they seem benevolent, good-hearted, and almost chaste in comparison to such calculating cynics and sexual athletes as Wycherley's Horner in *The Country Wife* and Etherege's Dorimant in *The Man of Mode*. Consequently critics have argued that Farquhar is more wholesome, humane, and morally nutrient as well as being emotionally softer than most Restoration dramatists. Yet this does not mean that he sacrifices comic liveliness to sentiment and sententiousness. On the contrary, there is more low comedy in Farquhar, especially in his two masterpieces, *The Recruiting Officer* and *The Beaux' Stratagem*, than in the stylistically refined though sexually squalid world of much contemporary "manners" comedy. *The Recruiting Officer* is built around an army recruiting campaign in Shrewsbury, and *The Beaux' Stratagem*, set in Lichfield, features a gang of highwaymen, prefiguring another great play of the century, Gay's *The Beggar's Opera*. Farquhar's great innovation in these, his last two plays, was to breathe new life into the conventions of Restoration comedy, which were becoming stale and outworn by the time he was writing, and he achieved this mainly by setting the actions in the provinces, not in London like most of his previous plays, and by drawing heavily on his personal experience of provincial life. The Restoration comedy of manners is virtually synonymous with London and with a small section of London Society at that, the beau monde. Characters from the provinces are almost invariably laughing-stocks because of their boorish country habits, crude speech, and ignorance of the ways of the fashionable world, and are contrasted unfavourably with modish city wits. By breaking out of the claustrophobic confines of London high society to include a much wider social spectrum, and by departing from Restoration stereotypes, Farquhar let more than a draught of fresh air into comic drama. By placing his characters in the world of small-town justices, innkeepers, tradesmen, soldiers, military recruits, highwaymen, and country wenches, Farquhar necessarily put the emphasis on humour rather than on wit, and opened up new possibilities for comedy; sadly these were not much exploited by subsequent dramatists in England, although one of the three or four great plays of the eighteenth century not by Farquhar, Goldsmith's *She Stoops to Conquer*, is certainly indebted to his example. Farquhar's real successor in this respect is the Fielding of *Joseph Andrews* and *Tom Jones*. Farquhar did, however, exert a strong influence on the development of German drama in the eighteenth century, mainly as a result of Lessing's enthusiasm for him, and even in the twentieth century he has had some impact on the German theatre; he, like his younger contemporary John Gay, was one of the British dramatists who influenced Brecht.

Farquhar's first play, *Love and a Bottle*, is an entertaining but overloaded ragbag of traditional comic devices and conventions, including mistaken identities, multiple disguises, and a complex intrigue plot. His next play, *The Constant Couple; or, A Trip to the Jubilee*, is a considerable advance, and is cleverly plotted, inventive, and full of well-drawn comic characters, yet tinged with sentimentalism. It was a great theatrical success in its first season and remained a favourite with audiences throughout the eighteenth century. Much of its popularity was due to the appealing central character, Sir Harry Wildair, who superficially resembles the rakes and libertines of Restoration comedy but differs from them in that beneath his affectation of fast-living and profligacy he is really good-natured and well-intentioned. He is unconventional, impulsive, and imprudent rather than corrupt or debauched. Encouraged by the public response to *The Constant Couple*, Farquhar wrote a sequel featuring the same principal characters, *Sir Harry Wildair*, which is even more inferior to its predecessor than most sequels. Two of his next three plays are adaptations of other plays. *The Inconstant*, based on Fletcher's *The Wild-Goose Chase* but with substantial changes, is full of broad humour and lively action. The other adaptation is the much slighter *The Stage-Coach*, a popular farcical afterpiece taken from a contemporary French play. Between these two adaptations came an original, serious, and morally explicit play upholding strict poetic justice, *The Twin-Rivals*, which differs from his previous work in its pervasive sentimentalism. In form it is a comedy, but, with its virtuous heroes and heroines, its licentious rake who is finally redeemed at a stroke, and its deformed villain, as well as its exposé of vice and evil in society, it approximates to a *drame* and falls uneasily between comedy and social-problem play.

It was after completing *The Stage-Coach* that Farquhar, now in the Army, spent some time in the provinces as a recruiting officer, visiting both Shrewsbury and Lichfield. His experiences on this mission were crucial to his artistic development, and in *The Recruiting Officer* and *The Beaux' Stratagem* he transmuted these experiences into excellent drama, at the same time revitalising the conventions of comedy. *The Recruiting Officer* contains plenty of boisterous humour, especially in the scenes satirizing corrupt recruiting methods and involving the ingenious and roguish Sergeant Kite, but at its centre is the perennial theme of comedy, love and its problems. The recruiting officer himself and the romantic hero, Captain Plume, is a descendant of Sir Harry Wildair and proves to be a man of sensibility for all his dashing military qualities, while the resourceful and practical heroine, Silvia, recalls Rosalind in *As You Like It* and Viola in *Twelfth Night*, and like them spends part of the play disguised as a young man. The triumph of romantic love over all obstacles is also a major theme of *The Beaux' Stratagem*, in which two fashionable young men-about-town, short of money and attempting to recoup their losses in the provinces, meet two country ladies and eventually fall in love with them after initially trying to trick them. Partly because the two men are mistaken for both highwaymen and Jesuits, the plot is full of comic misunderstandings and complications that give the play much of its theatrical dynamism. Both of these plays, which celebrate human vitality and variety in an almost Shakespearean way, were immediately recognised to be outstanding contributions to the genre of comedy, and time has certainly not withered their vitality and variety.

—Peter Lewis

FIELD, Nathan. English. Born in Cripplegate, London, baptized 17 October 1587. Educated at St. Paul's School, London. Married to Anne Field; had several children. Actor with the Children of the Queen's Revels from c. 1600, with Lady Elizabeth's Players, and with the King's Men from c. 1615. *Died in 1619 or 1620.*

PUBLICATIONS

Collections

> *Plays* (includes *A Woman Is a Weathercock* and *Amends for Ladies*), edited by William Peery. 1950.

Plays

Four Plays or Moral Representations in One, with Fletcher (produced 1608–13?).   In
    Comedies and Tragedies, by Beaumont and Fletcher, 1647.
A Woman Is a Weather-Cock (produced 1609–10?).   1612.
Amends for Ladies (produced 1610–11?).   1618.
The Honest Man's Fortune, with Fletcher (produced 1613).   In *Comedies and
    Tragedies*, by Beaumont and Fletcher, 1647; edited by J. Gerritsen, 1952.
The Queen of Corinth, with Fletcher and Massinger (produced 1616–17?).   In *Comedies
    and Tragedies*, by Beaumont and Fletcher, 1647.
The Knight of Malta, with Fletcher and Massinger (produced 1616–19?).   In *Comedies
    and Tragedies*, by Beaumont and Fletcher, 1647.
The Fatal Dowry, with Massinger (produced 1616–19?).   1632; edited by T. A. Dunn,
    1969.

Reading List: *Field, The Actor-Playwright* by R. F. Brinkley, 1928.

*   *   *

Considering that his father was a Puritan clergyman in the days when all Puritans regarded the theatre as the sink of sin, it is remarkable that Nathan Field became such a famous actor and playwright.

It began about 1600 when young Field became one of the little eyeases of whom Shakespeare complained: one of the Children of the Queen's Chapel. It may have been a fairly ordinary move for a lad educated at St. Paul's School but it meant that the chorister would also be an actor. He made a career of performing. He became one of the six principal child actors of the Queen's Revels. As a boy he starred in *Cynthia's Revels*, *The Poetaster*, and *Epicoene*, and in *Bartholomew Fair* his mentor Ben Jonson hailed him (with Richard Burbage) as the best in his profession. He stayed in the theatre as he grew up and was the leading man in Lady Elizabeth's Players when the Queen's zookeeper turned a bear-baiting pit into The Hope Theatre. When the Globe, which had burned down, reopened, Freedley and Reeves guess, he "doubtless joined with Ben Jonson, Fletcher, Massinger and others who identified themselves with the King's Men, the old Lord Chamberlain's company." So he played Shakespeare and Jonson and Beaumont and Fletcher and the leading role in *Bussy D'Ambois* with what Dryden called "grace of action" and romantic panache. In an age when competition was fierce, he was among the very greatest stars of the stage. In his day Field brought a thorough knowledge of the practical theatre when he turned his hand to plays, whether in collaboration or alone, and he made them if nothing else eminently actable. W. Bridges-Adams (*The Irresistible Theatre*) comments on this quality in the two plays Field seems to have written as vehicles for his own acting talent, *A Woman Is a Weathercocke* and *Amends for Ladies*, describing the first as "farcical comedy, salacious and second-rate but, as we should expect from Field, excellent actor's stuff."

Field also worked, as did so many other dramatists of his period, in collaboration and he had the good fortune to contribute his stage-sense to the work of more famous men. His two humour comedies were very much in the style of Jonson but his collaborations were with Beaumont, Fletcher, and Massinger. R. F. Brinkley's 1928 book and Peery's edition will give the scholar detailed information about these collaborations and related matters. Brinkley's was a fine book for its time, but after half a century Field deserves a complete modern critical study. There is more to be said than Tucker Brooke and Shaaber's terse comment in Baugh's *Literary History*: "Field naturally knew the stage, and he moulded his structure, though not his moral philosophy, upon Jonson's. He is adept at bright dialogue, brisk action, and clever disguise. His prose is lively and idiomatic; but his humour characters, though very varied, are superficial, and his verse is uninspired."

—Leonard R. N. Ashley

FIELDING, Henry. English. Born in Sharpham Park, Glastonbury, Somerset, 22 April 1707; brother of Sarah Fielding. Educated at Eton College; studied literature at the University of Leyden, 1728–29; entered the Middle Temple, London, 1737; called to the Bar, 1740. Married 1) Charlotte Craddock in 1734 (died, 1742); 2) Mary Daniel in 1747. Settled in London, 1727; successful playwright, in London, 1728–37; Author/Manager, Little Theatre, Haymarket, 1737 (theatre closed as a result of Licensing Act); Editor, with James Rolph, *The Champion*, 1739–41; lawyer and novelist from 1740, also writer/editor for *The True Patriot*, 1745–46, *The Jacobite's Journal*, 1747–48, and the *Convent Garden Journal*, 1752; Principal Justice of the Peace for Middlesex and Westminster, 1748; Chairman, Westminster Quarter Sessions, 1749–53. *Died 8 October 1754.*

PUBLICATIONS

Collections

> *Complete Works*, edited by W. E. Henley. 16 vols., 1903.
> *Works* (Wesleyan Edition), edited by W. B. Coley. 1967–.

Plays

> *Love in Several Masques* (produced 1728). 1728.
> *The Temple Beau* (produced 1730). 1730.
> *The Author's Farce, and The Pleasures of the Town* (produced 1730). 1730; revised version (produced 1734), 1750; 1730 version edited by Charles B. Woods, 1966.
> *Tom Thumb* (produced 1730). 1730; revised version, as *The Tragedy of Tragedies; or, The Life and Death of Tom Thumb the Great* (produced 1731), 1731; edited by LeRoy J. Morrissey, 1973.
> *Rape upon Rape; or, The Justice Caught in His Own Trap* (produced 1730). 1730; revised version, as *The Coffee-House Politician* (produced 1730), 1730.
> *The Letter-Writers; or, A New Way to Keep a Wife at Home* (produced 1731). 1731.
> *The Welsh Opera; or, The Grey Mare the Better Horse* (produced 1731). 1731; as *The Genuine Grub Street Opera*, 1731; edited by LeRoy J. Morrissey, 1973.
> *The Lottery* (produced 1732). 1732.
> *The Modern Husband* (produced 1732). 1732.
> *The Covent Garden Tragedy* (produced 1732). 1732.
> *The Old Debauchees* (produced 1732). 1732; as *The Debauchees; or, The Jesuit Caught*, 1745.
> *The Mock Doctor; or, The Dumb Lady Cured*, from a play by Molière (produced 1732). 1732; edited by J. Hampden, 1931.

The Miser, from a play by Molière (produced 1733).   1733.
Deborah; or, A Wife for You All (produced 1733).
The Intriguing Chambermaid, from a play by J. F. Regnard (produced 1734).   1734.
Don Quixote in England (produced 1734).   1734.
An Old Man Taught Wisdom; or, The Virgin Unmasked (produced 1735).   1735.
The Universal Gallant; or, The Different Husbands (produced 1735).   1735.
Pasquin: A Dramatic Satire on the Times, Being the Rehearsal of Two Plays, Viz a Comedy Called The Election and a Tragedy Called The Life and Death of Common Sense (produced 1736).   1736; edited by O. M. Brack, Jr., and others, 1973.
Tumble-Down Dick; or, Phaeton in the Suds (produced 1736).   1736.
Eurydice (produced 1737).   In *Miscellanies*, 1743.
The Historical Register for the Year 1736 (produced 1737).   With *Eurydice Hissed*, 1737; revised version, 1737; edited by William W. Appleton, 1967.
Eurydice Hissed; or, A Word to the Wise (produced 1737).   With *The Historical Register*, 1737; revised version, 1737; edited by William W. Appleton, 1967.
Plautus, The God of Riches, with W. Young, from a play by Aristophanes.   1742.
Miss Lucy in Town: A Sequel to The Virgin Unmasqued, music by Thomas Arne (produced 1742).   1742.
The Wedding Day (produced 1743).   In *Miscellanies*, 1743.
Dramatic Works.   2 vols., 1745.
The Fathers; or, The Good-Natured Man (produced 1778).   1778.

Fiction

An Apology for the Life of Mrs. Shamela Andrews.   1741; edited by A. R. Humphreys, with *Joseph Andrews*, 1973.
The History of the Adventures of Joseph Andrews and of His Friend Mr. Abraham Adams.   1742; revised edition, 1742; edited by Martin C. Battestin, in *Works*, 1967.
The Life of Mr. Jonathan Wild the Great, in *Miscellanies*.   1743.
The History of Tom Jones, A Foundling.   1749; revised edition, 1749, 1750; edited by Fredson Bowers and Martin C. Battestin, in *Works*, 2 vols., 1975.
Amelia.   1752; revised edition, in *Works*, 1762.

Verse

The Masquerade.   1728; edited by C. E. Jones, in *The Female Husband and Other Writings*, 1960.
The Vernon-iad.   1741.

Other

Of True Greatness: An Epistle to George Dodington, Esq.   1741.
The Champion; or, The British Mercury.   2 vols., 1741; excerpt edited by S. J. Sackett, as *The Voyages of Mr. Job Vinegar*, 1958.
The Opposition: A Vision.   1742.
A Full Vindication of the Duchess Dowager of Marlborough.   1742.
Some Papers Proper to Be Read Before the Royal Society.   1743.
Miscellanies.   3 vols., 1743; vol. 1 edited by Henry Knight Miller, in *Works*, 1972.
An Attempt Toward a Natural History of the Hanover Rat.   1744.
The Charge to the Jury.   1745.
The History of the Present Rebellion in Scotland.   1745.

A Serious Address to the People of Great Britain, in Which the Certain Consequences of the Present Rebellion Are Fully Demonstrated. 1745.

A Dialogue Between the Devil, The Pope, and the Pretender. 1745.

The Female Husband; or, The Surprising History of Mrs. Mary, Alias Mr. George Hamilton, Taken from Her Own Mouth since Her Confinement. 1746; edited by C. E. Jones, in *The Female Husband and Other Writings,* 1960.

A Dialogue Between a Gentleman of London, Agent for Two Court Candidates, and an Honest Alderman of the Country Party. 1747.

Ovid's Art of Love, Adapted to the Present Times. 1747; as *The Lover's Assistant,* 1759.

A Proper Answer to a Late Scurrilous Libel, Entitled An Apology for the Conduct of a Late Celebrated Second-Rate Minister. 1747.

A Charge Delivered to the Grand Jury. 1749.

A True State of the Case of Bosavern Penlez, Who Suffered on Account of the Late Riot in the Strand. 1749.

An Enquiry into the Causes of the Late Increase of Robbers. 1751.

A Plan of the Universal Register Office, with John Fielding. 1752.

Examples of the Interposition of Providence in the Detection and Punishment of Murder. 1752.

A Proposal for Making an Effectual Provision for the Poor. 1753.

A Clear State of the Case of Elizabeth Canning. 1753.

The Journal of a Voyage to Lisbon. 1755; edited by H. E. Pagliaro, 1963.

The Covent Garden Journal, edited by G. E. Jensen. 1915.

The True Patriot, and the History of Our Own Times, edited by M. A. Locke. 1964.

Criticism, edited by Ioan Williams. 1970.

The Jacobite's Journal, edited by W. B. Coley, in *Works.* 1974.

Translator, *The Military History of Charles XII, King of Sweden,* by M. Gustavus Alderfeld. 3 vols., 1840.

Bibliography: by Martin C. Battestin, in *The English Novel* edited by A. E. Dyson, 1973.

Reading List: *The History of Fielding* by Wilbur L. Cross, 3 vols., 1918; *Fielding the Novelist: A Study in Historical Criticism* by Frederic T. Blanchard, 1926; *Fielding: His Life, Works, and Times* by F. Homes Dudden, 2 vols., 1952; *Fielding* by John Butt, 1954, revised edition, 1959; *The Moral Basis of Fielding's Art* by Martin C. Battestin, 1959; *Essays on Fielding's "Miscellanies"* by Henry Knight Miller, 1961; *Fielding's Social Pamphlets* by Marvin R. Zinker, Jr., 1966; *Fielding and the Language of Irony* by Glenn W. Hatfield, 1968; *Fielding and the Nature of the Novel* by Robert Alter, 1968; *Fielding and the Augustan Ideal under Stress* by Claude J. Rawson, 1972; *Fielding: A Critical Anthology* edited by Claude J. Rawson, 1973; *Fielding's "Tom Jones": The Novelist as Moral Philosopher* by Bernard Harrison, 1975; *Occasional Form: Fielding and the Chains of Circumstance* by J. Paul Hunter, 1975.

*   *   *

Though Henry Fielding is remembered chiefly as a novelist – as, indeed, along with Defoe and Richardson, one of the founders of the modern novel and as the author of one of the dozen or so greatest novels in English, *Tom Jones* – he began his literary career as a poet and a dramatist. A young man of twenty, without much money but with strong family connections to the Whig establishment, he came to London from the West Country in 1727 determined to make his mark as a wit and to solicit the patronage of the Court at a time when, because of the uncertain political climate following the death of George I, a talented writer might expect that his services would be appreciated by the prime minister, Sir Robert Walpole. Contrary to the usual view of Fielding as a staunch and unswerving opponent of Walpole and the Court, his earliest poems and plays reveal that when he was not actively seeking the king's and Walpole's favors he prudently adopted a neutral attitude in politics: to judge from the title of his first published work, *The Coronation: A Poem, and An Ode on the Birthday* (issued in November 1727 but now lost), he began, even in a Cibberian vein, by openly declaring his loyalty to George II; and beside several other poems soliciting Walpole's patronage in 1729–31, he dedicated to the prime minister his most ambitious, if unsuccessful, comedy, *The Modern Husband*. Indeed, as B. L. Goldgar persuasively argues in *Walpole and the Wits* (1976), of the fifteen comedies and farces which Fielding produced between 1728 – when his first play, *Love in Several Masques*, was acted at Drury Lane – and 1734 all but one were calculated shrewdly to amuse the widest possible audience without offending the Court; only in *The Welsh Opera* (1731) – a transparent political allegory satirizing not only Walpole and the leader of the Opposition, but the royal family itself – did he abandon this cautious policy, the result being, predictably, that the play was first withdrawn for revision and then suppressed.

These were the years in which Fielding established himself as London's most popular living playwright. With the exception of *The Modern Husband*, which treats rather too earnestly the disturbing theme of adultery and marital prostitution in high life, his more conventional comedies are entertaining and skillful, but by inviting comparison with the greater works of Congreve and Molière they have suffered the condescension of historians of the drama. No other critic, certainly, has endorsed Shaw's declaration that Fielding was "the greatest practising dramatist, with the single exception of Shakespeare, produced by England between the Middle Ages and the nineteenth century...." Where Fielding did shine was in the lesser modes of farce, burlesque, and satire – in *The Tragedy of Tragedies*, for example, an hilarious travesty of heroic drama, or in *The Author's Farce*, a delightful adaption of the "rehearsal play" concluding with a satiric "puppet show" performed by live actors, a work which in fact anticipates the expressionism of modern experimental drama.

Despite his reputation as the theatrical gadfly of the Court, it was only in the final three years (1734–37) of his dramatic career that Fielding moved, rather hesitantly, into the camp of the Opposition. Though he dedicated *Don Quixote in England* to Chesterfield, who had recently joined their ranks, the political satire in this play – as indeed even in *Pasquin*, which is usually said to be vehemently antiministerial – is in fact directed at the venality and incompetence of both parties. Only with *The Historical Register* and its after-piece *Eurydice Hiss'd* did he at last drop the mask of impartiality and, by ridiculing Walpole all too effectively, help to precipitate the Theatrical Licensing Act of 1737, which terminated his career as a playwright.

Forced by an Act of Parliament to abandon the stage, Fielding began preparing for the bar and, to supplement the meager income he would earn as a barrister, enlisted as a hackney author in the Opposition's campaign against Walpole. In this latter capacity, during his editorship of *The Champion* (1739–41), he almost certainly drafted his first work of fiction, *The Life of Jonathan Wild the Great*, a mock biography of an infamous real-life criminal whom he ironically praises for the very qualities of unscrupulous self-aggrandisement by which the prime minister himself had achieved "greatness." This work, however, which Walpole appears to have paid Fielding to suppress, was withheld from publication until 1743, a year after the Great Man's fall from power, when it was issued as part of the *Miscellanies*; by this time Fielding presumably had revised the novel substantially, generalizing the political satire and perhaps expanding the narrative to accommodate the more positive, contrasting element of Wild's relationship with the good-natured Heartfrees. Also included in the *Miscellanies* was *A Journey from This World to the Next*, a satirical fiction done in brisk imitation of Lucian.

It was not politics, however, but a quite remarkable literary event that provoked Fielding into finding his true voice as a novelist. Amused and not a little exasperated by the extraordinary success of Richardson's *Pamela* (1740), Fielding responded first by parodying the novel, hilariously, in *Shamela* (1741) and then by offering in *Joseph Andrews* (1742) his own alternative conception of the art of fiction. Though Fielding's improbably virtuous hero is meant to continue the ridicule of Richardson's indomitable virgin, *Joseph Andrews* is much more than merely another travesty of *Pamela*. Modelled in some respects on Cervantes' masterpiece, it yet enacts Fielding's own original theory of the "comic epic-poem in prose," whose subject is "the true ridiculous" in human nature, exposed in all its variety as Joseph and the amiable quixote Parson Abraham Adams journey homeward through the heart of England. In contrast to the brooding, claustrophobic world evoked in the letters of Richardson's beleaguered maidens, Fielding's is cheerful and expansive, presided over by a genial, omniscient narrator who seems a proper surrogate of that beneficent Providence celebrated by Pope in *An Essay on Man* (1733–34).

In *Joseph Andrews* Fielding founded, as he put it, a "new province of writing." *Tom Jones*, his masterpiece, fulfilled the promise of that ambitious, splendid beginning. Generations of readers have delighted in the comic adventures and nearly disastrous indiscretions of the lusty foundling boy who grows to maturity, discovers the identity of his parents, and marries the beautiful girl he has always loved – a story simple enough in outline, but crowded with entertaining characters, enlivened by the wit and humanity of the narrator, and complicated by the intricacies of an ingenious plot which Coleridge called one of the most perfect in all literature. Like most great books, moreover, *Tom Jones* offers us more than superficial pleasures: it is the realization of its author's profoundest philosophy of life, an artfully constructed model of a world abundant, orderly, and ultimately benign, as the Christian humanist tradition conceived it to be. Thus Fielding declares his subject to be "human nature" and his book to be nothing less than "a great creation of our own." His foundling hero stands for all of us: like the protagonists of romance, he is a kind of wayfaring Everyman who, having been expelled from "Paradise Hall," must through hard experience gain that knowledge of himself which will enable him to be united with the girl, Sophia, whose name signifies Wisdom. *Tom Jones* is, as few books have managed to be, the consummate expression of a particular form and conception of literary art.

With the publication of *Tom Jones* Fielding's life and work entered a new phase. As a reward for his services as publicist for the Pelham administration, he was appointed to the magistracy, an office which he exercised with an energy and diligence that shortened his life. His new role as a public figure, working actively to preserve the peace and to improve the wretched condition of the poor, affected his art in interesting, but most critics would say regrettable, ways. *Amelia*, his last novel, is a very different book from *Tom Jones*: Fielding's tone has become darker, more monitory, in keeping with his subject – no longer the follies of men, but their errors and cupidities and the doubtful efficacy of those institutions, the law and the church, meant to preserve the social order; his narrator less frequently appears upon the stage, and his voice, wavering between anger and a maudlin sentimentality, no longer inspires confidence. Though his ostensible focus is the domestic tribulations of the feckless Captain Booth and his long-suffering wife, Fielding's true intentions are all too patently didactic: scene after scene is calculated to expose the imperfections of the penal laws, the destructiveness of infidelity, the injustices of the patronage system, and the immoralities of an effete and pleasure-loving society. To be sure, *Amelia* is less fun to read than any of Fielding's other novels, but in the starkness and candor of its social commentary it is compelling none the less. It is in fact the first true novel of social protest and reform in England, sounding themes that would not be resumed until the next century.

—Martin C. Battestin

FITCH, (William) Clyde. American. Born in Elmira, New York, 2 May 1865; moved with his family to Schenectady, New York, 1869. Educated at a high school in Hartford, Connecticut, and at a college preparatory school in Holderness, New Hampshire; Amherst College, Massachusetts, 1882–86 (Editor, *Student*), B.A. 1886, M.A. 1902. Settled in New York, 1886; wrote for *Life* and *Puck*, and worked as a tutor; visited Paris and London, and met various writers of the aesthetic movement, 1888; returned to New York, and supported himself by writing children's stories for the *Churchman*, *Independent*, and other magazines; began writing for the stage: full-time playwright and producer/director of his own plays from 1898. *Died 4 September 1909.*

PUBLICATIONS

Collections

> *Plays* (includes *Beau Brummell, Lovers' Lane, Nathan Hale, Barbara Frietchie, Captain Jinks of the Horse Marines, The Climbers, The Stubbornness of Geraldine, The Girl with the Green Eyes, Her Own Way, The Woman in the Case, The Truth, The City*), edited by Montrose Moses and Virginia Gerson. 4 vols., 1915.

Plays

> *Beau Brummell* (produced 1890). 1908; in *Plays*, 1915.
> *Frédéric Lemaitre* (produced 1890). Edited by Oscar Cargill, in *The Social Revolt*, 1933.
> *Betty's Finish* (produced 1890).
> *Pamela's Prodigy* (produced 1891). 1893.
> *A Modern Match* (produced 1892; as *Marriage*, produced 1892).
> *The Masked Ball*, from a play by A. Bisson (produced 1892).
> *The Moth and the Flame* (as *The Harvest*, produced 1893; revised version, as *The Moth and the Flame*, produced 1898). 1908; edited by Montrose Moses, in *Representative Plays*, 1921.
> *April Weather* (produced 1893).
> *A Shattered Idol*, from a novel by Balzac (produced 1893).
> *The Social Swim*, from a play by Sardou (produced 1893).
> *An American Duchess*, from a play by Henri Lavedan (produced 1893).
> *Mrs. Grundy, Jr.*, from a French play (produced 1893).
> *His Grace de Grammont* (produced 1894).
> *Gossip*, with Leo Ditrichstein, from a play by Jules Claretie (produced 1895).
> *Mistress Betty* (produced 1895; revised version, as *The Toast of the Town*, produced 1905).
> *Bohemia*, from a play by Théodore Barrière (produced 1896).
> *The Liar*, from a play by A. Bisson (produced 1896).
> *A Superfluous Husband*, with Leo Ditrichstein, from a play by Ludwig Fulda (produced 1897).
> *The Head of the Family*, with Leo Ditrichstein, from a play by A. L'Arronge (produced 1898).
> *Nathan Hale* (produced 1898). 1899; in *Plays*, 1915.
> *The Merry-Go-Round*, with F. Kinsey Peile (produced 1898).
> *The Cowboy and the Lady* (produced 1899). 1908.
> *Barbara Frietchie, The Frederick Girl* (produced 1899). 1900; in *Plays*, 1915.

Sapho, from the play by Daudet and Belot, based on the story by Daudet (produced 1899).

Captain Jinks of the Horse Marines (produced 1901). 1902; in *Plays,* 1915.

The Climbers (produced 1901). 1905; in *Plays,* 1915.

Lovers' Lane (produced 1901). In *Plays,* 1915.

The Marriage Game, from a play by Emile Augier (produced 1901).

The Last of the Dandies (produced 1901).

The Way of the World (produced 1901).

The Girl and the Judge (produced 1901).

The Stubbornness of Geraldine (produced 1902). 1906; in *Plays,* 1915.

The Girl with the Green Eyes (produced 1902). 1905; in *Plays,* 1915.

The Bird in the Cage, from a play by E. von Wildenbruch (produced 1903).

The Frisky Mrs. Johnson, from a play by Paul Gavault and Georges Beer (produced 1903). 1906.

Her Own Way (produced 1903). 1907; in *Plays,* 1915.

Algy (produced 1903).

Major André (produced 1903).

Glad of It (produced 1903).

The Coronet of a Duchess (produced 1904).

Granny, from a play by Georges Michel (produced 1904).

Cousin Billy, from a play by Labiche and Martin (produced 1905).

The Woman in the Case (produced 1905). In *Plays,* 1915.

Her Great Match (produced 1905). Edited by A. H. Quinn, in *Representative American Plays,* 1917.

Wolfville, with Willis Steell, from a novel by Alfred Henry Lewis (produced 1905).

Toddles, from a play by Godferneaux and Bernard (produced 1906).

The House of Mirth, with Edith Wharton, from the novel by Wharton (produced 1906).

The Girl Who Has Everything (produced 1906).

The Straight Road (produced 1906).

The Truth (produced 1907). 1909; in *Plays,* 1915.

Miss McCobb, Manicurist (produced 1907).

Her Sister, with Cosmo Gordon-Lennox (produced 1907).

The Honor of the Family, from a play by A. Fabre based on a novel by Balzac (produced 1908).

Girls, from a play by Alexander Engel and Julius Horst (produced 1908).

The Blue Mouse, from a play by Alexander Engel and Julius Horst (produced 1908).

A Happy Marriage (produced 1909).

The Bachelor (produced 1909).

The City: A Modern Play of American Life (produced 1909). In *Plays,* 1915.

Fiction

The Knighting of the Twins and Ten Other Tales (juvenile). 1891.

A Wave of Life. 1909.

Other

Some Correspondence and Six Conversations. 1896.

The Smart Set: Correspondence and Conversations. 1897.

Clyde Fitch and His Letters, edited by Montrose Moses and Virginia Gerson. 1924.

*   *   *

No playwright in the history of American drama has been able to match the commercial success of Clyde Fitch and at the same time achieve the international reputation that his work brought him. Many have written better plays; probably some have made more money; but none has equalled his accumulative successes. Clearly aided by the copyright law of 1891 and his membership in the "Syndicate School," Fitch produced a considerable body of work (more than 50 plays, including many adaptations of foreign works), became the first millionaire dramatist in America, and showed himself to be not just an extremely colorful man of the theatre but a dramatist of some sensitivity whose plays were produced in several countries.

His theory of playwriting reflected the prevailing nineteenth-century attitudes toward literature and art. "Try to be truthful," Fitch explained, true to the details of life and environment which he saw, true to every emotion, every motive, every occupation, every class. Fitch himself was most successful in portraying the upper levels of society which in a few plays occasionally reflected the realistic and truthful detail of noteworthy drama. In most instances, however, his concern for truth lacked the necessary perspective, and he simply imitated the popular melodramatic caricature of life with an excess of what became recognized as "Fitchian detail."

As a flamboyant man-about-town Fitch enjoyed the places frequented by New York society. The problems of married life, the peculiarities of individuals, the faults and foibles of a rapidly changing society – these were the aspects of life which appealed to Fitch and which he tried to picture truthfully in his plays. His first full-length social drama was *A Modern Match*, concerned with a selfish woman who refused to assume the responsibilities of marriage. *The Climbers* is one of his better social melodramas, ridiculing the hypocrisy and materialism of New York society. *The Stubbornness of Geraldine* and *Her Great Match* reflect the international social scene. In *The Truth*, concerned with a pathological liar, and *The Girl with the Green Eyes*, which dramatized what he termed an "inherited" jealousy, Fitch was at his melodramatic best, using the particular personal insight which distinguished the plays. In his final play, *The City*, he attempted to present a serious view of city life disintegrating under a weight of moral, economic, and political problems, but the lighter and satiric view of high society was his proper métier.

As one who prepared the way for an established social comedy in America Fitch deserves attention. He was above all a man of that society, and a craftsman of the commercial theatre whose interest in truthfulness in drama helped him create some believable characters and memorable social scenes against a background of melodrama.

—Walter J. Meserve

FITZBALL, Edward. English. Born in Burwell, near Mildenhall, Cambridgeshire, in 1793. Educated at Albertus Parr's school at Newmarket; apprentice in a printing house in Norwich, 1809–12. Married Adelaide Fitzball in 1814; one daughter. Founded a printing house and magazine in Norwich, which subsequently failed; thereafter wrote for the theatre, first in Norwich, and from 1821 in London, where he wrote numerous melodramas for minor theatres; wrote for the more important London theatres from 1828: Resident Dramatist and Reader at Covent Garden, 1835–38; Reader at Drury Lane from 1838. *Died 27 October 1873.*

Plays

Edwin, Heir of Cressingham, from the novel *The Scottish Chiefs* by Jane Porter
(produced 1817).
Bertha; or, The Assassins of Istria (produced 1819).   1819.
The Ruffian Boy (produced 1819; also produced as *Giraldi*).
Edda (produced 1820).
Antigone; or, The Theban Sister (produced 1821).
Alonza and Imogene (produced 1821).
The Innkeeper of Abbeville; or, The Hostler and the Robber (produced 1822).   1822.
The Fortunes of Nigel; or, King James I and His Times, from the novel by Scott
(produced 1822; as *George Heriot,* produced 1823).   1830(?).
Joan of Arc; or, The Maid of Orleans (produced 1822).   1823.
The Barber; or, The Mill of Bagdad (produced 1822).   1822.
Peveril of the Peak; or, The Days of King Charles II, from the novel by Scott (produced
1823).   1823.
Iwan; or, The Mines of Ischinski (produced 1823).
Laurette; or, The Forest of Unterwald (produced 1823).
Nerestan, Prince of Persia; or, The Demon of the Flood (produced 1823).
The Three Hunchbacks; or, The Sabre Grinders of Damascus (produced 1823).   1823.
Thalaba the Destroyer; or, The Burning Sword (produced 1823).   1826.
Waverley, music by George Rodwell, from the novel by Scott (produced 1824).   1824.
The Fire-Worshippers; or, The Paradise of the Peris (produced 1824).
The Floating Beacon; or, The Norwegian Wreckers (produced 1824).   1824.
William the Conqueror; or, The Days of the Curfew Bell (produced 1824).
The Koeuba; or, The Indian Pirate's Vessel (produced 1824).   1836(?).
The Burning Bridge; or, The Spectre of the Lake (produced 1824).
Der Freischutz; or, The Demon of the Wolf's Glen and the Seven Charmed Bullets
(produced 1824).
Wardock Kennilson; or, The Outcast Mother and Her Son (produced 1824).   1835(?).
Omala; or, Settlers in America (produced 1825).   1826.
Hans of Iceland; or, The Iron Casket (produced 1825).
Father and Son; or, The Rock of La Charbonniere (produced 1825).   N.d.
Cupid in Disguise (produced 1825).
The Pilot; or, A Tale of the Sea, from the novel by Cooper (produced 1825).   1825.
The Betrothed (produced 1826).
The Flying Dutchman; or, The Phantom Ship, music by George Rodwell (produced
1827).   1829(?).
The Libertine's Lesson (produced 1827).   N.d.
Nelson; or, The Life of a Sailor (produced 1827).   1886.
Antoine the Savage; or, The Outcast (produced 1828).
The Inchcape Bell (produced 1828).   1828(?).
The Earthquake; or, The Spectre of the Nile, music by George Rodwell (produced
1828).   1829(?).
The Red Rover; or, The Mutiny of the Dolphin, from the novel by Cooper (produced
1829).   1831(?).
The Devil's Elixir; or, The Shadowless Man, music by George Rodwell (produced
1829).   1829(?).
The Rauberbraut; or, The Robber's Bride, music by Ferdinand Ries (produced 1829).
The Night Before the Wedding, music by Henry Bishop, from a play by Scribe and J. N.
Bouilly, music by Adrien Boieldieu (produced 1829).

Mr. Chairman (produced 1829).

Ninetta; or, The Maid of Palaiseau, music by Henry Bishop, from an opera by G. Gherardini, music by Rossini (produced 1830).   1830; revised version, as *The Maid of Palaiseau* (produced 1838), 1838.

The Maid of the Oaks (produced 1830).

The Black Vulture; or, The Wheel of Death (produced 1830).

Adelaide; or, The Royal William (produced 1830; as *William and Adelaide,* produced 1830).

The Libertine of Poland; or, The Colonel of Hussars (produced 1830).

Hofer, The Tell of the Tyrol, music by Henry Bishop, from an opera by de Jouy and others, music by Rossini (produced 1830; as *Andreas Hofer,* produced 1830).   1832(?).

The Haunted Hulk (produced 1831).

The Sorceress, music by Ferdinand Ries (produced 1831).

The Sea Serpent; or, The Wizard and the Winds, with J. B. Buckstone (produced 1831).

Robert le Diable; or, The Devil's Son, with J. B. Buckstone, from an opera by Scribe and Casimir Delavigne, music by Meyerbeer (produced 1832).

The Alchymist (songs only), libretto by T. H. Bayly, music by Henry Bishop, from an opera by K. Pfeiffer, music by Spohr (produced 1832).

Nina, The Bride of the Galley Slave (produced 1832).

The Dillosk Gatherer; or, The Eagle's Nest (produced 1832).

The Bottle of Champagne, music by Henry Bishop (produced 1832).

The Sedan Chair (produced 1832).

The Maid of Cashmere, music by Henry Bishop, from an opera by Scribe, music by Auber (produced 1833).   Songs published 1833.

Margaret's Ghost; or, The Libertine's Ship (produced 1833).   1833(?).

The Felon of New York (produced 1833).

The Soldier's Widow; or, The Ruins of the Mill (produced 1833).

Jonathan Bradford; or, The Murder at the Roadside Inn, music by Jolly (produced 1833).   1833(?).

Mary Glastonbury (produced 1833).   1833(?).

Walter Brand; or, The Duel in the Mist (produced 1833).   1834(?).

Esmeralda; or, The Deformed of Notre Dame, from the novel by Hugo (produced 1834).   1855(?).

Tom Cringle; or, The Man with the Iron Hand (produced 1834).   1834(?).

The Lord of the Isles; or, The Gathering of the Clan, music by George Rodwell, from the novel by Scott (produced 1834).

The Young Courier; or, The Miser of Walden (produced 1834).

The Black Hand; or, The Dervise and the Peri (produced 1834).

The Last Days of Pompeii; or, The Blind Girl of Tessaly, from the novel by Bulwer-Lytton (produced 1835).

The Note Forger (produced 1835).   1835(?).

Carmilhan; or, The Drowned Crew (produced 1835).   1835(?).

Paul Clifford, music by George Rodwell, from the novel by Bulwer-Lytton (produced 1835).   1835(?).

The Siege of Rochelle, music by Michael Balfe, from a novel by the Countess de Genlis (produced 1835).   1843(?).

Inheritance; or, The Unwelcome Guest, from the novel by Susan Ferrier (produced 1835).

The Carmelites; or, The Convent Belles, from a French play (produced 1835).   1836.

The Bronze Horse; or, The Spell of the Cloud King, music by George Rodwell, from an opera by Scribe, music by Auber (produced 1835).   1836(?).

Quasimodo; or, The Gipsy Girl of Notre Dame, from the novel by Hugo (produced 1836).   1836.

Za-Ze-Zi-Zo-Zu; or, Dominoes! Chess!! and Cards!!!, from a French play (produced 1836).   1836(?).

The Assurance Company; or, The Boarding School of Montesque (produced 1836).

The Wood Devil (produced 1836).

The Rose of the Alhambra; or, The Enchanted Lute, from an opera with music by de Pinna (produced 1836).

The Sexton of Cologne; or, The Burgomaster's Daughter, music by George Rodwell (produced 1836).

The Hindoo Robber (produced 1836).

Mutual Expense; or, A Female Travelling Companion (produced 1836).

False Colours! or, The Free Trader! (produced 1837).   1837(?).

The Eagle's Haunt (produced 1837).

Walter Tyrrel (produced 1837).   1837.

Zohrab the Hostage; or, The Storming of Mezanderan (produced 1837).

Joan of Arc, music by Michael Balfe (produced 1837).

The Negro of Wapping; or, The Boat-Builder's Hovel (produced 1838).   1838(?).

Diadeste; or, The Veiled Lady, music by Michael Balfe (produced 1838).   Songs published 1838.

Oconesto; or, The Mohawk Chief (produced 1838).

The King of the Mist; or, The Miller of the Hartz Mountains, music by G. F. Stansbury (produced 1839).   1839(?).

Scaramuccia; or, The Villagers of San Quintino, music by Luigi Ricci (produced 1839).   Songs published 1839.

Këolanthe; or, The Unearthly Bride, music by Michael Balfe (produced 1841).

The April Fool (produced 1841).

The Robber's Sister; or, The Forge in the Forest (produced 1841).

Charlotte Hanwell; or, Sorrow and Crime (produced 1842).

Ombra; or, The Spirit of the Reclining Stone (produced 1842).

The Trooper's Horn; or, The Goblin of the Chest (produced 1842).

Jane Paul; or, The Victim of Unmerited Persecution (produced 1842).

The Miller's Wife (produced 1842).

The Owl Sisters; or, The Haunted Abbey Ruin (produced 1842).

Mary Melvyn; or, The Marriage of Interest (produced 1843).   1843.

The Queen of the Thames; or, The Anglers, music by John Hatton (produced 1843).   1843.

The Ranger's Daughter (produced 1843).

Ondine; or, The Naid, from a play by Pixérécourt (produced 1843).   N.d.

The Favorite, from an opera by Gustave Vaez and Alphonse Roger, music by Donizetti (produced 1843).

Madelaine; or, The Daughter of the Regiment, music by J. H. Tully, from an opera by J. H. V. de Saint-Georges and J. F. A. Bayard, music by Donizetti (produced 1843).   1844(?); revised version (produced 1847), 1886.

Ben Bradshaw; or, A Man Without a Head (produced 1844).

The Momentous Question (produced 1844).   1844(?).

Home Again! or, The Lieutenant's Daughters (produced 1844).   1845(?).

Maritana, music by Vincent Wallace, from a play by A. P. d'Ennery and P. F. Dumanoir (produced 1845).   1845.

The Crown Jewels, music by J. H. Tully, from an opera by Scribe and J. H. V. de Saint-Georges, music by Auber (produced 1846).   1846.

The Desert; or, The Imann's Daughter, music by J. H. Tully, from an opera by Auguste Colin, music by Felicien David (produced 1847).

The Wreck and the Reef (produced 1847).

The Traveller's Room (produced 1847).   1847(?).

The Maid of Honour, music by Michael Balfe (produced 1847).

The Lancashire Witches: A Romance of Pendle Forest (produced 1848). 1897(?).

The Crock of Gold! or, The Murder at the Hall (produced 1848). 1848(?).

Marmion; or, The Battle of Flodden Field, from the poem by Scott (produced 1848). 1848(?).

Quentin Durward, music by H. R. Laurent, from the novel by Scott (produced 1848). 1848.

Corasco; or, The Warrior's Steed (produced 1849).

The White Maiden of California (produced 1849).

Alhamar the Moor; or, The Brother of Valencia (produced 1849).

The Prophet, from an opera by Scribe, music by Meyerbeer (produced 1849).

Harlequin and Humpty Dumpty; or, Robin de Bobbin and the First Lord Mayor of London (produced 1850). 1851.

The Four Sons of Aymon; or, The Days of Charlemagne (produced 1850).

Alonzo the Brave and the Fair Imogene; or, Harlequin and the Baron All Covered with Spangles and Gold (produced 1850).

The Cadi's Daughter, music by Sydney Nelson (produced 1851).

Azael the Prodigal, music by H. R. Laurent, from an opera by Scribe, music by Auber (produced 1851). 1851(?).

Hans von Stein; or, The Robber Knight (produced 1851). 1851(?).

Vin Willoughby; or, The Mutiny of the Isis (produced 1851).

The Greek Slave; or, The Spectre Gambler (produced 1851). 1851(?).

The Last of the Fairies (produced 1852). 1852(?).

The Secret Pass; or, The Khan's Daughter (produced 1852).

Alice May; or, The Last Appeal (produced 1852). 1852(?).

Peter the Great (produced 1852). 1898(?).

The Field of Terror; or, The Devil's Diggings (produced 1852).

Uncle Tom's Cabin; or, The Horrors of Slavery (produced 1852). N.d.

The Rising of the Tide (produced 1853).

Amakosa; or, Kaffir Warfare (produced 1853).

The Miller of Derwent Water (produced 1853). 1853.

Raymond and Agnes, music by Edward Loder (produced 1855). N.d.

Nitocris; or, The Ethiop's Revenge (produced 1855).

The Children of the Castle (produced 1857). 1858(?).

The Husband's Vengeance; or, The Knight of Wharley (produced 1857).

Pierette; or, The Village Rivals, music by W. H. Montgomery (produced 1858). 1858(?).

Auld Robin Gray, music by A. Lee (produced 1858).

The Lancashire Witches; or, The Knight, The Giant, and the Castle of Manchester (produced 1858).

The Widow's Wedding (produced 1859). 1859.

Lurline, music by Vincent Wallace (produced 1860). 1860.

Christmas Eve; or, A Duel in the Snow (produced 1860). 1860.

Robin Hood; or, The Merry Outlaws of Sherwood (produced 1860). 1861(?).

She Stoops to Conquer, music by George Macfarren, from the play by Goldsmith (produced 1864). 1864.

The Magic Pearl, music by T. Pede (produced 1873).

A Sailor's Legacy; or, The Child of a Tar. With *A Soldier and a Sailor, A Tinker and a Tailor,* by William Rogers, 1888(?).

Fiction

The Idiot Boy. 1815.

The Black Robber. 1819.

The Sibyl's Warning. 1822.
Michael Schwartz; or, The Two Runaway Apprentices. 1858.

Verse

Serena of Oakwood; or, Trials of the Heart, and Other Poems. 1815.
The Revenge of Taran. 1821.
The House to Let, with Other Poems. 1857.
Bhanavar; The Story of Fadleen. 1858.
The Wee Craft. 1866.
My Pretty Jane. 1891.

Other

Thirty-Five Years of a Dramatic Author's Life (autobiography). 2 vols., 1859.

*   *   *

Edward Fitzball really has more connection with the early swashbucklers and spectaculars of the cinema than with what we have come to think of as the modern drama. He lives in the tradition of "shake and bake" movie epics (*Earthquake* and *The Towering Inferno*) rather than on the stage, but he was in his long and varied career one of the busiest and most influential popular dramatists, a master of nautical and spectacular melodrama.

To the English stage Fitzball brought the devices of such French playwrights as Pixérécourt, and his theatrically effective pieces were in turn the source of many later melodramas. He knew how to package and present material which could fill the cavernous theatres of his time, and he borrowed widely. He could wring the thrills out of Southey's poem *Thalaba the Destroyer* as well as extract every drop of sensationalism from *Uncle Tom's Cabin*. His adaptations of James Fenimore Cooper have less art but more vitality than the originals: *Red Rover* has a typically Fitzball conclusion: " 'I am slain and will perish with my ship.' *Red fire to burn at the side wing.* CURTAIN FALLS." In *The Pilot*, Fitzball contrived to make Cooper's Americans look silly and the British admirable. From *Edwin, Heir of Cressingham*, based on Jane Porter's *The Scottish Chiefs*, to the libretto for Goldsmith's *She Stoops to Conquer*, his career is practically a summary of the topics and techniques that galvanized the gallery; the accursed Vanderdecken (in *The Flying Dutchman*), appearing and disappearing in bursts of red and blue fire, so captured the theatre-goers' attention that he was still being revived decades later as a vehicle for Sir Henry Irving. Just as the fires and other stage effects were *real*, so were his heroes the genuine melodramatic article: "one that hates cruelty, and defies oppression − one that fears no death like the death of dishonour" (*The Earthquake*) or "my hand is free from bloodshed − I have never wronged, but always defended that unfortunate" (*Paul Clifford*).

His work is much better than some of these examples might suggest, and it influenced writers like Tom Taylor and Dion Boucicault as well as film-makers like Griffith and De Mille. Equally interesting are his technical innovations on stage, of which the four rooms in the inn seen simultaneously (in *Jonathan Bradford*) is the best-known example.

—Leonard R. N. Ashley

FITZMAURICE, George. Irish. Born in Listowel, County Kerry, 28 January 1877. Served in the British Army during World War I. Clerk in the Irish Civil Service, Dublin. Contributed sketches of Kerry peasant life to the popular press, 1900–07; wrote for the stage from 1907. *Died 12 May 1963.*

<small>PUBLICATIONS</small>

Collections

  Plays.   3 vols., 1967–70.

Plays

  The Country Dressmaker (produced 1907).   In *Five Plays,* 1914.
  The Pie-Dish (produced 1908).   In *Five Plays,* 1914.
  The Magic Glasses (produced 1913).   In *Five Plays,* 1914.
  Five Plays (includes *The Country Dressmaker, The Moonlighter, The Pie-Dish, The Magic Glasses, The Dandy Dolls*).   1914.
  The Moonlighter (produced 1948).   In *Five Plays,* 1914.
  The Dandy Dolls (produced 1969).   In *Five Plays,* 1914.
  'Twixt the Giltinans and the Carmodys (produced 1923).   In *Plays 3,* 1970.
  One Evening Gleam (produced 1952).   In *Plays 3,* 1970.
  There Are Tragedies and Tragedies (produced 1952).   In *Plays 2,* 1970.
  The Ointment Blue; or, The King of the Barna Men (as *The King of the Barna Men,* produced 1967).   In *Plays 2,* 1970.
  The Linnaun Shee, The Green Stone, The Enchanted Land, The Waves of the Sea, The Terrible Baisht, The Toothache, The Simple Hanrahans, and *The Coming of Ewn Andzale,* in *Plays.*   1967–70.

Fiction

  The Crows of Mephistopheles and Other Stories.   1970.

Reading List: *Fitzmaurice and His Enchanted Land* by Howard K. Slaughter, 1972 (includes bibliography); *Fitzmaurice* by Arthur E. McGuinness, 1974.

*   *   *

George Fitzmaurice was born in County Kerry, Ireland, the son of a Protestant clergyman and a Catholic mother. This, for that time, quite unusual union may partly explain his eccentric habits and rather reclusive life. Fitzmaurice's comedies, whether nominally realistic or grotesquely fanciful, are almost all about Kerry peasants, but his birth prevented him from knowing them intimately, as his personal diffidence prevented him from participating in the literary life of Dublin. His early writings were broad comic sketches of the Kerry peasant and appeared in the popular press from about 1900 to 1907. Ten of these stories have so far come to light, and none is of great literary value, but they do prefigure the content of some of his early plays.

Fitzmaurice's first produced play, the comedy *The Country Dressmaker,* was done at the

Abbey Theatre in 1907, where it was quite successful and remained for years a staple of the theatre's repertory. This quite broad comedy, like some of Synge's and many of Lady Gregory's, did not so much celebrate as exaggerate the Irish peasant. That exaggeration became even more queerly pronounced in Fitzmaurice's finest work – *The Dandy Dolls, The Enchanted Land,* and *The Ointment Blue; or, The King of the Barna Men.* In such plays, Fitzmaurice did not proceed ever further into broad quaintness as did many popular Abbey dramatists. Rather, he transformed Kerry in these plays into an inimitably personal landscape that owed more to his own fantastic imagination than it did to sociology or geography. Also, these plays have a rather mature dourness of theme that is startlingly counter-pointed against a gaily playful, if sometimes over-embroidered dialogue. One other fault of some of the plays is an awkwardly handled plot structure which emphasises exposition at the expense of dramatisation. However, Fitzmaurice's work is of a consistently high level, and scarcely poorer than the above-mentioned plays are the sombre four-act tragedy, *The Moonlighter;* several grotesque farces, such as *The Simple Hanrahans, The Terrible Baisht,* and *The Green Stone;* and the two extraordinary one-act tragi-comedies *The Pie-Dish* and *The Magic Glasses.*

In the early 1920's, Fitzmaurice withdrew his plays from the Abbey Theatre, and in the last forty years of his life received only a handful of productions. Indeed, he actually resisted production of his work. His friend, Seumas O'Sullivan, the poet and editor, did persuade him to allow several plays to be published in *The Dublin Magazine;* nevertheless, when Fitzmaurice died in Dublin in 1963, he was virtually forgotten. The posthumous publication of his seventeen plays in a collected edition revived interest in his work, and since the late 1960's there have been several productions of his plays at the Abbey Theatre. Fitzmaurice is probably now regarded not so much as a follower of Synge, as, indeed, almost an equal. His view of Ireland is as individual as was that of Synge, or of James Stephens, or of Flann O'Brien. Like them, he did not so much report Ireland in his work, as transform it.

—Robert Hogan

FLETCHER, John. English. Born in Rye, Sussex, in December 1579. Educated at Benet College, now Corpus Christi College, Cambridge. Met Francis Beaumont in 1605, and collaborated with him in writing for the theatre until Beaumont retired c. 1613; thereafter wrote for the King's Men, on his own and in collaboration with others, particularly Massinger and Shakespeare. *Died* (buried) *29 August 1625.*

PUBLICATIONS

Collections

    Comedies and Tragedies, with Beaumont and others, 1647; revised edition, 1679.
    Works of Beaumont and Fletcher, edited by A. Glover and A. R. Waller. 10 vols., 1905–12.
    Variorum Edition, edited by A. H. Bullen. 4 vols. (incomplete), 1904–12.
    The Dramatic Works in the Beaumont and Fletcher Canon, edited by Fredson Bowers. 3 vols. (of 10), 1966–76.

Plays

The Woman's Prize; or, The Tamer Tamed, with Beaumont (produced after 1604).   In
    Comedies and Tragedies, 1647.
The Woman Hater (produced 1606).   1607; edited by George Walton Williams, in
    Dramatic Works 1, 1966.
The Faithful Shepherdess (produced 1608–09?).   1609(?); edited by Cyrus Hoy, in
    Dramatic Works 3, 1976.
Four Plays or Moral Representations in One, with Nathan Field (produced
    1608–13?).   In *Comedies and Tragedies*, 1647.
Bonduca (produced 1609–14?).   In *Comedies and Tragedies*, 1647; edited by W. W.
    Greg, 1951.
Philaster; or, Love Lies A-Bleeding, with Beaumont (produced before 1610).   1620;
    edited by Dora Jean Ashe, 1974.
Valentinian (produced 1610–14?).   In *Comedies and Tragedies*, 1647; edited by R. G.
    Martin, in *Variorum Edition 4*, 1912.
Monsieur Thomas (produced 1610–16?).   Edited by Richard Brome, 1639; as *Father's
    Own Son*, 1661(?); edited by R. G. Martin, in *Variorum Edition 4*, 1912.
The Maid's Tragedy, with Beaumont (produced before 1611).   1619; edited by Robert
    K. Turner, Jr., in *Dramatic Works 2*, 1970.
A King and No King, with Beaumont (produced 1611).   1619; edited by George Walton
    Williams, in *Dramatic Works 2*, 1970.
Cupid's Revenge, with Beaumont (produced before 1612).   1615; edited by Fredson
    Bowers, in *Dramatic Works 2*, 1970.
The Coxcomb, with Beaumont (produced 1612).   In *Comedies and Tragedies*, 1647;
    edited by Irby B. Cauthen, Jr., in *Dramatic Works 1*, 1966.
Henry VIII, with Shakespeare (produced 1613).   In *Comedies, Histories, and Tragedies
    by Shakespeare*, 1623; edited by Louis B. Wright and V. A. LaMar, 1968 (Fletcher's
    collaboration is questionable).
The Two Noble Kinsmen, with Shakespeare (produced 1613).   1634; edited by G. R.
    Proudfoot, 1970.
The Captain, with Beaumont (produced 1613).   In *Comedies and Tragedies*, 1647;
    edited by L. A. Beaurline, in *Dramatic Works 1*, 1966.
The Honest Man's Fortune, with Nathan Field (produced 1613).   In *Comedies and
    Tragedies*, 1647; edited by J. Gerritsen, 1952.
The Scornful Lady, with Beaumont (produced 1613–17?).   1616; edited by Cyrus Hoy,
    in *Dramatic Works 2*, 1970.
Wit Without Money (produced 1614?).   1639; edited by R. B. McKerrow, in *Variorum
    Edition 2*, 1905.
The Nice Valour; or, The Passionate Madman, with Middleton (produced before
    1616).   In *Comedies and Tragedies*, 1647.
Love's Pilgrimage, with Beaumont (produced 1616?).   In *Comedies and Tragedies*,
    1647; edited by L. A. Beaurline, in *Dramatic Works 2*, 1970.
The Mad Lover (produced 1616?).   In *Comedies and Tragedies*, 1647.
The Queen of Corinth, with Nathan Field and Massinger (produced 1616–17?).   In
    Comedies and Tragedies, 1647.
The Knight of Malta, with Nathan Field and Massinger (produced 1616–19?).   In
    Comedies and Tragedies, 1647.
The Chances (produced 1617?).   In *Comedies and Tragedies*, 1647.
The Loyal Subject; or, The Faithful General (produced 1618).   In *Comedies and
    Tragedies*, 1647.
The Laws of Candy (produced 1619?).   In *Comedies and Tragedies*, 1647.
The Humorous Lieutenant; or, Generous Enemies (produced 1619?).   In *Comedies and
    Tragedies*, 1647; edited by M. Cook and F. P. Wilson, 1951.

Sir John Van Olden Barnevelt, with Massinger (produced 1619). Edited by A. H. Bullen, in *A Collection of Old English Plays*, vol. 2, 1883; edited by W. P. Frijlinck, 1922.

The Custom of the Country, with Massinger (produced 1619–20?). In *Comedies and Tragedies*, 1647.

The Island Princess (produced 1619–21?). In *Comedies and Tragedies*, 1647.

Women Pleased (produced 1619–23?). In *Comedies and Tragedies*, 1647.

The Little French Lawyer, with Massinger (produced 1619–23?). In *Comedies and Tragedies*, 1647.

The False One, with Massinger (produced 1620?). In *Comedies and Tragedies*, 1647.

Thierry, King of France, and His Brother Theodoret, with Massinger (produced ?). 1621; edited by Robert K. Turner, Jr., in *Dramatic Works 3*, 1976.

The Pilgrim (produced 1621?). In *Comedies and Tragedies*, 1647.

The Wild Goose Chase, with Beaumont (produced 1621?). 1652.

The Double Marriage, with Massinger (produced 1621?). In *Comedies and Tragedies*, 1647.

The Spanish Curate, with Massinger (produced 1622?). In *Comedies and Tragedies*, 1647.

The Prophetess, with Massinger (produced 1622). In *Comedies and Tragedies* 1647.

The Sea Voyage, with Massinger (produced 1622). In *Comedies and Tragedies*, 1647.

The Beggars' Bush, with Massinger (produced 1622). In *Comedies and Tragedies*, 1647; edited by Fredson Bowers, in *Dramatic Works 3*, 1976.

The Lovers' Progress (produced 1623). Revised version by Massinger published in *Comedies and Tragedies*, 1647.

The Maid in the Mill, with Rowley (produced 1623). In *Comedies and Tragedies*, 1647.

Rule a Wife and Have a Wife (produced 1624). 1640.

A Wife for a Month (produced 1624). In *Comedies and Tragedies*, 1647.

The Elder Brother, with Massinger (produced 1625?). 1637; edited by W. H. Draper, 1916.

The Fair Maid of the Inn, with Massinger (produced 1625–26?). In *Comedies and Tragedies*, 1647.

The Noble Gentleman, with Beaumont (produced 1625–26?). In *Comedies and Tragedies*, 1647; edited by L. A. Beaurline, in *Dramatic Works 3*, 1976.

A Very Woman, with Massinger (produced 1634). In *Three New Plays*, by Massinger, 1655.

The Night Walker; or, The Little Thief (produced ?). 1640.

Love's Cure; or, The Martial Maid, with Massinger (produced ?). In *Comedies and Tragedies*, 1647; edited by George Walton Williams, in *Dramatic Works 3*, 1976.

Wit at Several Weapons, with Middleton and Rowley (produced ?). In *Comedies and Tragedies*, 1647.

Bibliography: *Beaumont and Fletcher: A Concise Bibliography* by S. A. Tannenbaum, 1938; supplement, 1946; supplement in *Elizabethan Bibliographies Supplements 8*, by C. A. Pennell and W. P. Williams, 1968.

Reading List: *Beaumont, Fletcher, and Company: Entertainers to the Jacobean Gentry* by L. B. Wallis, 1947; *The Pattern of Tragicomedy in Beaumont and Fletcher* by E. M. Smith, 1952; *Beaumont and Fletcher: A Critical Study* by W. W. Appleton, 1956; *Beaumont and Fletcher* by Ian Fletcher, 1967.

*   *   *

After Jonson and Shakespeare, John Fletcher was the most gifted and influential of the

Elizabethan and Stuart dramatists. His mastery is most notable in two dramatic types, tragi-comedy and comedy of manners, both of which exerted a pervasive influence on dramatists in the reign of Charles I and during the Restoration.

A characteristically heroic tragi-comedy is *The Island Princess*, based on a recent Spanish history, Bartomé Leonardo de Argensola's *La Conquist de las Isles Maluces* (1609). The setting is exotic and remote (the Moluccan island of Tidore); the plot tangled and swift-moving; the theme love and honor; the language both coarse and lyrical; the characters aristocratic and refined, and given over to sudden, inexplicable changes of moods and motives. As usual, Fletcher begins with a contrived, melodramatic situation: the beautiful pagan princess Quisara's father has been imprisoned by a ruthless tyrant, and, although she is in love with the Portuguese commander Ruy Dias, she offers to marry the suitor who frees her father. When this is accomplished by another young Portuguese, Armusia, she plots with Ruy Dias to murder him rather than fulfill her promise. Armusia conducts himself so nobly, however, that Ruy Dias repents of his treachery and magnanimously rescues Armusia from execution, whereupon Quisara, equally inspired by Armusia's resplendent virtues, is converted to Christianity and marries him. In the end, of course, her father is restored to his throne and the tyrant is exiled. Thus the characters simply alter their behavior to avert the many disasters ingeniously prepared for them by the author. The heroes are paradigms of cavalier virtues with almost perverse obsessions for making excruciatingly fine distinctions between love and honor; the heroine is a garrulous *précieuse* straight out of the French and Spanish heroic romances. The setting is not the bustling world of Jonson and Shakespeare, but the artificial landscape of Sidney's *Arcadia*, where action and dialogue serve to express certain aristocratic ideas about love and honor.

Fletcher had written a similar type of tragi-comedy in 1608 with his *Faithful Shepherdess*, an imitation of Guarini's pastoral drama *Il Pastor Fido*, but this effort to adapt the conventions of the formal pastoral love debate to the popular stage failed utterly. A year earlier Francis Beaumont's satiric comedy *The Knight of the Burning Pestle* had met with a similar fate, perhaps for similar reasons, and the two dramatists decided to combine their talents. In retrospect, the famous collaboration of Beaumont and Fletcher would appear almost inevitable. They were ardent disciples of Jonson, shared quarters on the Bankside, had written a number of plays for the boys' company at St. Paul's, and were shifting over to the King's Men, who, in turn, were contracting for plays more suitable to the genteel taste of the private theatres. No doubt the King's Men, in catering to the refined audience at the Blackfriars, felt they could trust the social instincts of Beaumont, scion of a distinguished Leicestershire family, and Fletcher, a bishop's son. In any event, their collaboration, extending from 1608 until Beaumont's retirement from the stage around 1613, produced a string of successes: *Cupid's Revenge*, *The Coxcomb*, *The Scornful Lady*, *Philaster*, *The Maid's Tragedy*, and *A King and No King*. The 1647 folio of their plays included thirty-four; the second edition of 1679 fifty-two. Most of these are now believed to have been by Fletcher, many in collaboration with dramatists other than Beaumont.

Beaumont and Fletcher's first notable success on behalf of Shakespeare's company came around 1610 with *Philaster; or, Love Lies A-Bleeding*, a flamboyant tragi-comedy that became the prototype of the cavalier dramas of the 1630's and the heroic plays of Dryden and Orrery in the Restoration. The similarities of *Philaster* and Shakespeare's *Cymbeline*, both written about the same time, have often been noted; but most resemblances derive from common appropriation of fairly conventional romantic situations, such as a virtuous heroine disguised as a page and falsely accused of treachery. Shakespeare's romance, set in ancient Britain, lacks the courtly rhetoric and idealized characterizations of Beaumont and Fletcher's tragi-comedy, which owes less to robust folklore or legend than to delicate sentiments and ritualistic deportment portrayed in French heroic pastorals and Sidney's *Arcadia*. In *Cymbeline* Shakespeare tells a wondrous, adventurous tale; in *Philaster* Beaumont and Fletcher depict niceties of courtly conduct and sentiments. Philaster's tortuous sensitivity and brooding melancholy, which prohibit any forthright action, are not maladies but aristocratic traits setting him apart from ordinary mortals. Hence, although apotheosized in testimony as "god-like" and "divine," he is ineffectual and "lily-livered," a kind of ranting Cambises more concerned with his lady-love's unaccountable petulances than with the rigors of war. As in many of Fletcher's tragi-comedies, beginning with his *Faithful Shepherdess*, the characters in *Philaster* are created to suggest various concepts of love in a manner resembling that of the French pastorals, the *Arcadia*, and *The Faerie Queene*, Book III. The noble Philaster and his virtuous Arethusa, appropriately long-suffering, are contrasted to the base, sensual Pharamond and his lascivious courtesan Megra, whereas "Bellario" (ethereal Euphrasia disguised as a page in the hero's service) represents Fletcher's flirtation with the idea of Platonic love, a theme seized upon and developed even less intellectually by Fletcher's imitators in the Caroline period.

In a play like *Philaster*, it is difficult to distinguish Beaumont's contributions from Fletcher's. Beaumont is credited with having been a more confident master of total plot construction, of deeper characterizations, of a firm, regular verse with frequent run-on lines. Fletcher was a skillful contriver of sensational, heart-rending individual scenes, a superb rhetorician in dialogue with a loose-flowing style of verse that melts into rhythmic prose with numerous feminine endings and end-stopped lines. Judging from those plays written by Fletcher alone, a critic surmises that he, rather than Beaumont, had a keen perception of the changing tastes of the times. This last quality is most apparent in Fletcher's comedy of manners *The Wild-Goose Chase* (revised in 1702 by George Farquhar as *The Inconstant*), which anticipates the urbane, cynical Restoration comedies of Wycherley, Etherege, and Congreve. In *The Wild-Goose Chase*, as in many of Fletcher's comedies of manners, he adopts his master Ben Jonson's technique of presenting a fixed comic situation with a variety of "humorous" characters. A prodigal young rake and his sportive companions, much to the chagrin of their wealthy, indulgent parents, seek to outmaneuver a covey of vivacious girls bent on matrimony. Thus Fletcher combines the themes of the battle of the sexes and the alienation of generations, but, unlike Jonson, he deals with these in a relaxed, amoral way totally pleasing to his sophisticated audience. The characters are drawn from the familiar background of Jonson's and Middleton's London comedies – madcap rakes, stodgy bourgeois fathers, confused matrons, nubile lasses and dotty "fantastics" – all given renewed vitality by Fletcher's single-minded concern with pure entertainment rather than moral exploration or didacticism.

Fletcher collaborated with a dozen dramatists (including Shakespeare in *Two Noble Kinsmen* and *Henry VIII*) in addition to Beaumont, and he succeeded Shakespeare as master dramatist of the King's Men, providing that company with three or four plays a year. In spite of his limitations of loose plot construction, careless versification, and indifference to any high seriousness, Fletcher's achievements and influence were immense. After Shakespeare and Jonson, he alone provided the stage with a large number of variegated plays unparalleled for their ingenuity and vitality.

—James E. Ruoff

FOOTE. Samuel. English. Born in Truro, Cornwall, baptized 27 January 1720. Educated at Truro Grammar School; Worcester College, Oxford, 1737–40, left without taking a degree; entered the Temple, London, 1740. Married Mary Hickes in 1741; two sons. Jailed for debt, Fleet Prison, London, 1742–43; actor in London and Dublin from 1744; began writing for the stage in the 1740's; operated an unlicensed "lecture" theatre, London, 1762–66; lost a leg in a riding accident, 1766; granted a patent to erect a theatre: built and ran the Haymarket Theatre, London, 1766–77. *Died 21 October 1777.*

Collections

Dramatic Works, edited by John Badcock.   3 vols., 1830.

Plays

The Auction of Pictures (produced 1748).
The Knights (produced 1749; revised version, produced 1754).   1754.
Taste (produced 1752).   1752; revised version, as *The Diversions of the Morning* (produced 1758, and regularly thereafter), in *Dramatic Works*, 1830.
The Englishman in Paris (produced 1753).   1753.
The Englishman Returned from Paris (produced 1756).   1756.
The Author (produced 1757).   1757.
The Minor (produced 1760; revised version, produced 1760).   1760.
Tragedy a la Mode, from the play *Fatal Constancy* by William Whitehead (as *Modern Tragedy*, produced 1761).   In *The Wandering Patentee* by Tate Wilkinson, 1795; as *Lindamira*, in *Thespian Gleanings* by Thomas Matthews, 1805.
The Liar, from a play by Molière (produced 1762).   1764.
The Orators (produced 1762).   1762.
The Young Hypocrite, from a French play, in *The Comic Theatre*.   1762.
The Mayor of Garret (produced 1763).   1764.
The Trial of Samuel Foote for a Libel on Peter Paragraph (produced 1763).   In *The Wandering Patentee* by Tate Wilkinson, 1795.
The Patron (produced 1764).   1764.
The Commissary (produced 1765).   1765; edited by R. W. Bevis, in *Eighteenth Century Drama: Afterpieces*, 1970.
The Tailors: A Tragedy for Warm Weather, revised by Colman the Elder (produced 1767).   1778.
An Occasional Prelude (produced 1767).   In *Memoirs of Foote* by William Cooke, 1805.
The Devil upon Two Sticks (produced 1768).   1778.
The Lame Lover (produced 1770).   1770.
The Maid of Bath (produced 1771).   1771; revised version, 1778.
The Nabob (produced 1772).   1778.
Piety in Pattens (produced 1773).   Edited by Samuel N. Bogorad and Robert G. Noyes, in *Theatre Survey*, Fall 1973.
The Bankrupt (produced 1773).   1776.
The Cozeners (produced 1774).   1778.
A Trip to Calais (as *The Capuchin*, produced 1776).   1778.

Other entertainments: *A Writ of Inquiry; Comic Lectures; Morning Lectures*.

Other

A Treatise on the Passions, So Far as They Regard the Stage.   1747.
The Roman and English Comedy Considered and Compared, with Remarks on The Suspicious Husband.   1747.
A Letter to the Author of The Remarks Critical and Christian on The Minor.   1760.
Apology for The Minor, in a Letter to Mr. Baine.   1771.

Editor, *The Comic Theatre* (French plays).   5 vols., 1762.

Reading List: *Foote: A Biography* by Percy H. Fitzgerald, 1910; *The Dramatic Work of Foote* by Mary M. Belden, 1929 (includes bibliography); *The Life and Works of Foote* by John W. Wilkinson, 1936; *Foote, Comedian* by Simon Trefman, 1971.

*   *   *

If Samuel Foote possessed the "wit of escape," as Dr. Johnson said, "in an eminent degree," he often had to employ it to escape from situations created by his wit in the first place. For most of his thirty years on the London stage Foote was something of a dramatic outlaw, "wanted" by the Lord Chamberlain's office either for evasion of the Licensing Act or slander and libel. When he emerged as a mimic in the 1740's the issue was his right to perform at all. Having no patent, Foote would invite his friends to "Tea" or "Chocolate," or (as the Examiner of Plays caught up with each name) "Diversions" or an "Auction," for which admission was charged, and then provide "free entertainment": such topical skits as a night-club comedian might devise today. Eventually this satirical pot-pourri became *Taste*. Foote was a man of many dodges, and in the end the law came over to him, so to speak: in 1766, after he had lost a leg in a riding accident, his friends procured him a summer patent at the Haymarket as a kind of disability pension. For the next few years he wrote plays around crippled heroes (*The Lame Lover, The Devil upon Two Sticks*). Long before that, however, the issue had become the angry protests of the victims of his take-offs. Virtually every one of Foote's twenty-odd plays mimicked a living individual (including George Whitefield, Thomas Sheridan, and Thomas Arne) or satirized an influential group (Methodists, nabobs, war profiteers). Usually Foote's wit extricated him from the scrape – the nabobs who came to chastise him were so charmed they stayed to dinner – or else he converted the outcry into profitable publicity; but his portrait of the Duchess of Kingston as Lady Kitty Crocodile in *A Trip to Calais* was a fatal mistake. She had the play banned, and her deputy harried Foote out of the theatre on a sodomy charge. Though acquitted, he died the following year.

Foote's extreme topicality also brought critical disapproval: only general satire of human types should be admissible and would survive, he was warned, whereas the individual eccentricities he so cruelly mimicked were by their nature ephemeral and would deservedly perish. The playwright's unfailing response was to wave the banner of Old Comedy (his favourite of many nicknames was "the English Aristophanes"). If Socrates could be spoofed on the classical Athenian stage, asked Foote, why should a modern nuisance not be pilloried likewise? He liked to think of himself as a dramatic magistrate or watchman, and of his plays as quasi-legal instruments "for the correction of individuals." Foote insisted, moreover, on calling his plays "comedies," though his contemporaries (and later critics) slighted them as "farces" and "sketches." If they are thought of as Aristophanic or *old* comedy the perfunctory and truncated plots seem less damaging, since they were merely vehicles for the main cargo of satire.

For the theatre historian Foote was an important (though not quite respectable) influence on the drama of his time. Taking up the satirical afterpiece where Fielding left off, he developed it considerably in range and style over the next three decades. Several of his long-forgotten playlets contributed stock plots and characters to Georgian comedy; Sheridan, for example, was indebted to *The Minor* and *The Author*. And perhaps the most obscure of them all was once the most influential: *Piety in Pattens*, a shrewd and amusing send-up of sentimentalism, was credited by several writers with bringing the Muse of the Woeful Countenance into disrepute just days before the première of *She Stoops to Conquer*.

To the general reader unmoved by such *arcana*, Foote can still appeal by virtue of his delight in language: not the periods of Johnson, or the wit of Sheridan, but the spoken language of the kingdom in his day. The "genius for mimicry" to which his contemporaries testified comes across now as a good ear for colloquial speech, of which Foote was a student. Although he did not hold the mirror up to nature or man, he did create a remarkably sensitive, albeit primitive, recording device, on which the voices of the men and women of Georgian England can yet be heard. The dialogue of *The Patron* and *The Commissary* remains vivid after two centuries: its tones as brash, its distortion as poignant, as an old vaudeville record.

—R. W. Bevis

————————————

FORD, John. English. Born in Islington, Devon, baptized 17 April 1586. Educated at Exeter College, Oxford, 1601–02; Middle Temple, London, 1602–05, 1608–17, but probably never practised law. Very little is known about his life: probably retired from London to Devon c. 1638. *Died c. 1640.*

PUBLICATIONS

Collections

>   *Works,* edited by William Gifford, revised by A. Dyce.   3 vols., 1869.
>   *Dramatic Works,* edited by W. Bang and Henry de Vocht.   2 vols., 1908–27.

Plays

>   *The Witch of Edmonton,* with Rowley and Dekker (produced 1621).   1658; edited by Fredson Bowers, in *Dramatic Works of Dekker,* 1953–61.
>   *Perkin Warbeck: A Strange Truth* (produced 1622–32?).   1634; edited by Peter Ure, 1968.
>   *The Welsh Ambassador,* with Dekker (produced 1623).   Edited by H. Littledale and W. W. Greg, 1920.
>   *The Sun's Darling: A Moral Masque,* with Dekker (produced 1624).   1656.
>   *The Broken Heart* (produced 1627–31?).   1633; edited by Donald K. Anderson, Jr., 1968.
>   *The Lover's Melancholy* (produced 1628).   1629.
>   *'Tis Pity She's a Whore* (produced 1629–33?).   1633; edited by Brian Morris, 1969.
>   *Love's Sacrifice* (produced 1632?).   1633.
>   *The Fancies, Chaste and Noble* (produced 1635–36?).   1638.
>   *The Lady's Trial* (produced 1638).   1639.
>   *The Queen; or, The Excellency of Her Sex* (produced ?).   1653.

Verse

>   *Fame's Memorial; or, The Earl of Devonshire Deceased.*   1606; edited by S. E. Brydges, 1810.
>   *Christ's Bloody Sweat.*   1613.

Other

>   *Honour Triumphant; or, The Peers' Challenge.*   1606.

The Golden Mean. 1613; revised edition, 1614, 1638.
A Line of Life, Pointing at the Immortality of a Virtuous Name. 1620.

Bibliography: *Ford: A Concise Bibliography* by S. A. Tannenbaum, 1941; supplement in *Elizabethan Bibliographies Supplements 8* by C. A. Pennell and W. P. Williams, 1968.

Reading List: *Ford* by M. J. Sargeaunt, 1935; *Burtonian Melancholy in the Plays of Ford* by S. Blaine Ewing, 1940; *The Tragic Muse of Ford* by George F. Sensabaugh, 1944; *The Problem of Ford* by H. J. Oliver, 1955; *Ford and the Drama of His Time* by Clifford Leech, 1957; *Ford and the Traditional Moral Order* by Mark Stavig, 1968; *Ford* by Donald K. Anderson, Jr., 1972; *The Tragic Vision of Ford* by Tucker Orbison, 1974.

*   *   *

John Ford's dramatic career begins in 1621 with *The Witch of Edmonton*, a tragedy based on a contemporary event involving accusations of witchcraft. The main plot is the work of Thomas Dekker and William Rowley; Ford's contribution consists of the sub-plot which deals with a star-crossed youth and his progress towards murder.

Fifteen years earlier Ford had produced two non-dramatic works which, in their different ways, are characteristic of the temperament we sense behind the plays. *Fame's Memorial* is an elegy on the death of Charles Blount, Earl of Devonshire and second husband of Sidney's Stella. Typically, Ford chose to eulogise a courtier who was, at the time of his death, out of favour at court. In *Honour Triumphant; or, The Peers' Challenge*, four young gallants conduct a highly mannered debate on certain vaguely paradoxical topics, such as that beautiful women are necessarily virtuous. This penchant for ethical paradox is also a feature of Ford's plays.

The first play written entirely by Ford was probably *The Lover's Melancholy*, performed in 1628. The hothouse atmosphere of self-generated emotion characteristic of all Ford's work is evident in this story of a father driven mad and a lover on the edge of despair because of the death of a daughter and mistress respectively. Ford's almost obsessive interest in abnormal psychology is very much a feature of his first independent play, and is a direct result of the influence on him of that compendious psychological treatise, Robert Burton's *The Anatomy of Melancholy*.

It was four years later that Ford's next play *Love's Sacrifice* was performed. Here too there is a good deal of emotion which seems to exist for its own sake, as in the scene where the Duchess, who had earlier spurned the advances of her husband's friend Fernando, presents herself to him in his chambers, swearing the while to kill herself after she has lost her honor. For all its emotional self-indulgence, this play is notable for the character of the villainous D'Avolos; Shakespeare's Iago influences but does not overwhelm Ford in his creation of this character.

Ford's interest in the psychology of individuals in emotional extremity and his fondness for ethical paradox find their most striking dramatic embodiment in his next two plays, *'Tis Pity She's a Whore* and *The Broken Heart*. The first of these is undoubtedly his finest play, in which the theme of incest is treated with an honesty and a sensitiveness which are in marked contrast to the evasiveness with which the same theme is handled by Beaumont and Fletcher in *A King and No King*. The superficial impression we gain that Giovanni, the incestuous brother, is the only honourable character in the play is, however, only apparently paradoxical. By contrast with his sister Annabella, he is finally revealed as totally lacking in self-discipline and therefore morally defective. It is doubtful, however, whether Ford is seriously interested in the moral predicament of his chief characters; their psychological states and the predictable reactions of the pillars of church and state around them are probably more important to him.

In *The Broken Heart* the tragic situation is more diffuse than it is in *'Tis Pity*, and, because the dramatist seems not to be fully in control of it, the general effect is orgiastic rather than tragic, a welter of torture and death rather than a truly tragic climax. A beautiful young girl who deliberately starves herself to death rather than endure marriage with an ancient and possessive husband, and the murder of her brother by her erstwhile lover – these events have all the trappings of melodrama. But Ford's gift for subtle psychological analysis redeems the play, and the final act, where Calantha continues dancing while she hears of the successive deaths of those near and dear to her until she falls down dead, is more than a mere theatrical coup.

Ford's other important play is rather different in style and scope from those already mentioned. Taking Bacon's history of Henry VII and Thomas Gainsford's *True and Wonderful History of Perkin Warbeck* as his sources, Ford produced his own highly individual version of that moribund genre, the chronicle play, *Perkin Warbeck*. The characterization of the hero is especially effective, and the whole play has an energy which recalls, if not Shakespeare, at least the Marlowe of *Edward II*.

Two inconsiderable romantic comedies, *The Fancies Chaste and Noble* and *The Lady's Trial*, bring Ford's dramatic career to its close. But it is on *'Tis Pity*, *The Broken Heart*, and *Perkin Warbeck* that his claim to be the finest dramatist of the years immediately preceding the closing of the theatres depends.

—Gāmini Salgādo

FRY, Christopher. English. Born in Bristol, 18 December 1907. Educated at the Bedford Modern School, 1918–26. Served in the Non-Combatant Corps, 1940–44. Married Phyllis Marjorie Hart in 1936; one son. Teacher, Bedford Froebel Kindergarten, 1926–27; Actor and Office Worker, Citizen House, Bath, 1927; Schoolmaster, Hazelwood School, Limpsfield, Surrey, 1928–31; Secretary to H. Rodney Bennett, 1931–32; Founding Director, Tunbridge Wells Repertory Players, Kent, 1932–35; Lecturer and editor of schools magazine, Dr. Barnardo's Homes, 1934–39; Director, 1939–40, and Visiting Director, 1945–46, Oxford Playhouse; Visiting Director, 1946, and Staff Dramatist, 1947, Arts Theatre Club, London. Recipient: Shaw Prize Fund Award, 1948; Foyle Poetry Prize, 1951; New York Drama Critics Circle Award, 1951, 1952, 1956; Queen's Gold Medal for Poetry, 1962; Heinemann Award, 1962. Fellow, Royal Society of Literature, 1962. Lives in Sussex.

PUBLICATIONS

Plays

    Youth and the Peregrines (produced 1934).
    To Sea in a Sieve (produced 1935).
    She Shall Have Music, with F. Eyton and M. Crick (produced 1935).
    Open Door (produced 1936). N.d.
    The Boy with a Cart: Cuthman, Saint of Sussex (produed 1938). 1939.
    The Tower (pageant; produced 1939).
    Thursday's Child: A Pageant, music by Martin Shaw (produced 1939). 1939.
    A Phoenix Too Frequent (produced 1946). 1946.

The Firstborn (broadcast 1947; produced 1948). 1946; revised version (produced 1952). 1952, 1958.
The Lady's Not for Burning (produced 1948). 1949; revised version, 1950, 1958.
Thor, With Angels (produced 1948). 1948.
Venus Observed (produced 1950). 1950.
Ring round the Moon: A Charade with Music, from a play by Jean Anouilh (produced 1950). 1950.
A Sleep of Prisoners (produced 1951). 1951.
The Dark Is Light Enough: A Winter Comedy (produced 1954). 1954.
The Lark, from a play by Jean Anouilh (produced 1955). 1955.
Tiger at the Gates, from a play by Jean Giraudoux (produced 1955). 1955.
Duel of Angels, from a play by Jean Giraudoux (produced 1958). 1958.
Curtmantle (produced 1961). 1961.
Judith, from a play by Jean Giraudoux (produced 1962). 1962.
The Bible: Original Screenplay, assisted by Jonathan Griffin. 1966.
Peer Gynt, from the play by Ibsen (produced 1970). 1970.
A Yard of Sun: A Summer Comedy (produced 1970). 1970.
The Brontës of Haworth (televised 1973). 2 vols., 1975.
Cyrano de Bergerac, from the play by Edmond Rostand (produced 1975). 1975.

Screenplays: The Beggar's Opera, with Denis Cannan, 1953; *The Queen Is Crowned* (documentary), 1953; *Ben Hur,* 1959; *Barabbas,* 1962; *The Bible: In the Beginning,* 1966.

Radio Plays: *The Tall Hill,* 1939; for *Children's Hour* series, 1939–40; *The Firstborn,* 1947; *Rhineland Journey,* 1948.

Television Plays: *The Canary,* 1950; *The Tenant of Wildfell Hall,* 1968; *The Brontës of Haworth* (four plays), 1973; *The Best of Enemies,* 1976; *Sister Dora,* from work by Jo Manton, 1977.

Verse

Root and Sky: Poetry from the Plays of Fry. 1975.

Other

An Experience of Critics, with *The Approach to Dramatic Criticism* by W. A. Darlington and others. 1952.
The Boat That Mooed (juvenile). 1966.
Can You Find Me: A Family History. 1978.

Translator, *The Boy and the Magic,* by Colette. 1964.

Bibliography: "A Bibliography of Fry" by B. L. Schear and E. G. Prater, in *Tulane Drama Review 4,* March 1960.

Reading List: *Fry* by Derek Stanford, 1954, revised edition, 1962; *The Drama of Comedy: Victim and Victor* by Nelson Vos, 1965; *Creed and Drama* by W. M. Merchant, 1965; *The Christian Tradition in Modern Verse Drama* by William V. Spanos, 1967; *Fry* by Emil Roy, 1968; *Fry: A Critical Essay* by Stanley M. Wiersma, 1970.

Familiar with every aspect of stage technique, and with poetry in his plays sounding like poetry, not prose, Christopher Fry burst upon the Bristol theatrical scene in 1946 as a major poetic dramatist with *A Phoenix Too Frequent*, one of the best comedies of manners since the Restoration, a creation with marvelous merits in language as well as drama. Haunting beauty of verse, epigram, and symbolism marks his dialogue as distinctly poetic and his own. At no time did he try to compete with Shakespeare in style, romance, or characterization, as did others at this period, but he preferred developing what has been called "mature contemporary poetry," which took him into the experimental realm, yet which did not hinder his dramatic effects. Fry was concerned about the beauty of life and spiritual validity apart from materialistic reality (his "principle of mystery" according to Derek Stanford), no matter how much Dynamene protested she wanted to die (a rebirth cycle lasting 30 minutes rather than the traditional 500 years), where the rescuer was named Chromis for the color he brought into Dynamene's drab life within the depths of her deceased husband's tomb. Reality, easily identifiable here as Chromis helps life triumph, is not always so easily detected, however.

Fry's first major success, *The Lady's Not for Burning*, won the Shaw Prize and boosted his career throughout the English-speaking theatre world. Fry was intensely concerned about the beauty of life, no matter how often Mendip demanded to be hanged. The poetic drama carries well, as a whole, but the longer, more earnest dialogues and speeches can seem heavy. Fry has abandoned rigid forms and probabilities for the symbolic, and seems at times far from reality, but produced exciting, gripping incidents to create suspense, not only in *The Lady's Not for Burning* but also in *A Phoenix Too Frequent*, *Venus Observed*, and *A Sleep of Prisoners*. Jennet Jourdemayne would confess to nothing concerning being a witch, and Thomas Mendip wouldn't stop confessing to reasons as to why he should die. Jennet, who vowed that facts and facts alone should rule her life, suddenly had to face the prospect that Thomas, trying to protect her by claiming he had murdered the man she was supposed to have turned into a dog, had fallen in love with her. Finally faced with the prospect of having to live, when the "murder victim" turned up alive – of having to face life with the beautiful Jennet, who now would accept him – he stole away into the night with her.

Venus Observed is much more than a mere gathering of the Duke's mistresses to see the eclipse and to review his past life; it is an analysis of the autumn of life, Fry tells us, as *A Phoenix Too Frequent* was of summer, *The Lady's Not for Burning* spring, and *The Dark Is Light Enough* winter. *Venus Observed*, considering the Duke's declining years, is like a musical composition keyed to the slow fading out of life, a definite autumnal mood, dialogue describing the autumn wind in the leaves, and entire scenes (like the first one in the Temple of the Ancient Verities) proclaiming it, in addition to the Duke's description of the planet called Venus as it rises, but Lucifer as it sets, going from goddess to demon. The Duke's telescope hangs ominously over the heads of his guests, cutting him off from a meaningful relationship with his mistresses. The essence of reality is as hard to pinpoint here as it is in the strange event when Pebbleman and the Duke safely escape down the stairs previously consumed by flames.

Fry's major appeal is to the ear, so the action is at times suspended in favor of vigorous clashes of ideas, which are as fierce as anyone's swords, yet there are intensely dramatic moments when the incendiary Rosabel determines to destroy the Duke's astronomy laboratory and when, in *Thor, With Angels*, the Christian waits to be sacrificed if the missionaries fail to persuade his Norse captors to save his life. Intensity concerning the plagues and what they will do to or for the Hebrews, and for the relationship between Moses and Rameses, develops in *The Firstborn*. Fry said that this play featured the movement of Moses to maturity, "towards a balancing of life within the mystery, where the conflicts and dilemmas are the trembling of the balance." The death of Rameses, the firstborn, he suggested, gave the Hebrews freedom and created Moses a great leader. Rameses's qualities of innocence, humanity, vigour, and worth (on the enemy's side) failed to alter the justice of or the need for Moses's cause but asked deep questions about the relationship between the ways of God and the ways of men, as the very dramatic ending shattered the audience.

Significant among his later works is *A Sleep of Prisoners*, a psychological reincarnation of the medieval mystery cycle episodes, set in the dreams of four prisoners in a German-occupied cathedral in France during World War II: with Cain and Abel in the first murder; King David, Joab, and Absalom, in Absalom's rebellion; the Abraham-Isaac story; and the adventure of the three Hebrews – Shadrac, Meshac, and Abednego – in Nebuchadnezzar's fiery furnace. One prisoner "stars" in each of the first three dreams, but all four participate in the last. Also notable are the additional songs and lyrics Fry wrote for the filming of *The Beggar's Opera* and his adaptation of Giraudoux's *La Guerre de Troie n'aura pas lieu* (*Tiger at the Gates*), a view of Helen and the Trojan War debunking the "kidnapped" theory, among other things.

—Louis Charles Stagg

FUGARD, Athol. South African. Born in Middleburg, Cape Province, 11 June 1932. Educated at Port Elizabeth Technical College; Cape Town University, 1950–53. Married Sheila Meiring in 1955; one daughter. Worked as a seaman, journalist, and stage manager; since 1959, actor, director, playwright; Director, Serpent Players, Port Elizabeth, since 1965; Co-Founder, The Space experimental theatre, Cape Town, 1972. Recipient: Obie Award, 1971. Lives in Port Elizabeth.

PUBLICATIONS

Plays

Nongogo (produced 1957).   In *Dimetos and Two Early Plays*, 1977.
No-Good Friday (produced 1958).   In *Dimetos and Two Early Plays*, 1977.
The Blood Knot (produced 1961).   1963.
Hello and Goodbye (produced 1965).   1966.
People Are Living There (produced 1968).   1969.
The Occupation, in *Ten One Act Plays*, edited by Cosmo Pieterse.   1968.
Boesman and Lena (produced 1969).   1969.
Statements after an Arrest under the Immorality Act (produced 1972).   In *Statements*, 1974.
Sizwe Bansi Is Dead, with John Kani and Winston Ntshona (produced 1972).   In *Statements*, 1974.
The Coat, with *The Third Degree* by Don MacLennan.   1973.
The Island, with John Kani and Winston Ntshona (produced 1974).   In *Statements*, 1974.
Statements: Two Workshop Productions Devised by Fugard, John Kani and Winston Ntshona, Sizwe Bansi Is Dead and The Island, and a New Play, Statments after an Arrest under the Immorality Act.   1974.
Dimetos (produced 1975).   In *Dimetos and Two Early Plays*, 1977.
Botticelli (produced 1976).
Dimetos and Two Early Plays.   1977.
The Guest (screenplay).   1977.

Screenplays: *Boesman and Lena*, 1972; *The Guest at Steenkampskraal*, 1977.

Television Play: *Mille Miglia*, 1968.

         *   *   *

Athol Fugard has emerged as the major South African dramatist. His particular strength lies in a unique combination of a specific social protest and a universal concern with the human condition. Each of his plays deals with one or several aspects of apartheid, and they all carry a strong condemnation of its inhumanity – *Statements after an Arrest under the Immorality Act* is concerned with the immorality act and *The Island* with prison conditions on Robben Island. To that extent his plays fall under the heading of protest literature, but the protest is in each case widened out to include comments and reflections on aspects of human nature, in particular on the problem of identity.

In this as well as in his use of the Open Space theatre technique (theatre of the mind) Fugard owes much to Samuel Beckett. This is most obvious in *Boesman and Lena*, which has strong overtones of *Waiting for Godot*. The set of apartheid laws dealt with in this play are the ones designed to prevent squatting on South African-owned land by homeless migratory workers. Thus the coloured couple Boesman and Lena wake up one morning to find that bulldozers have arrived to destroy their shack, and they wander off in search of somewhere to sleep for the night. Boesman takes his frustrations out on Lena and beats her. In his excessive emotional cruelty he is a convincing psychological portrait of a victim of a cruel society. Lena on the other hand is beset by the problem of her identity. Stranded on featureless mudflats where they spend the night she is disorientated in time and space and she sees the clue to her identity in recognition by others, "Another pair of eyes," to acknowledge her existence. She establishes a relationship with a dog and a dying old African, but even this meagre contact is destroyed by Boesman who chases the dog away and kills the old man, thus forcing them to flee from the law, the system, and themselves.

In *Sizwe Bansi Is Dead* the problem of identity is further exacerbated by the pass laws. A black migratory worker Robert Swelinzima is "endorsed out" of Johannesburg, i.e., sent back to his homeland because his passbook is out of order. He is naive and honest, and therefore helpless in the maze of South African pass laws, but his smart city friend persuades him to steal the identity-card from the body of a dead man they find lying in the street. Robert thus changes his identity and becomes Sizwe Bansi. This creates great confusion in his mind, and he makes a bid to maintain his name because to him it carries his dignity and human worth mainly in his role as a husband and father. He is, however, persuaded to change his mind by his cynical friend who has become totally disillusioned: he has realized that as black men in South Africa they have no dignity to preserve, and the struggle to simply maintain life must take priority over concerns with dignity and identity.

These problems are, however, not confined to the blacks in South Africa; in *Hello and Goodbye* Fugard explores the effect of Calvinism and the resulting Boer morality on the poor section of the white community. Hester and her brother Johnnie search through their late father's belongings looking for a sum of money they think he has received as compensation for the loss of his leg while working on the railway. They are both prisoners of their society; Hester is a prostitute, and her brother is drawing near to madness as a result of the loneliness he feels as a result of the father's death. The search for the compensation becomes a search for a memory of just one act of love or kindness to compensate for the coldness and sterility of their Boer upbringing. Needless to say they do not find it: Hester returns to her life as a prostitute devoid of all illusions of love, and Johnnie takes the final step into madness and assumes the father's identity because it provides him with a past and thereby an identity. "I'm a man with a story," he says. Thus their attempts to establish an identity through memory are thwarted.

The Blood Knot explores what in the world of today can only be termed a myth – that all men are brothers, we are all descendants of Adam and share a universal mother. Morrie and

233

Zachariah share the same mother but not father: Zachariah is black, and Morrie light enough to pass for a white. The entire action of the play takes place in a one-room shack in the Non-White location of Korsten, near Port Elizabeth. On the realistic level it is Zach's home which is now being shared by Morrie, while on the symbolic level it is a microcosm of South Africa. Zach, who is illiterate, has acquired a penpal whom Morrie writes to; from her letters it becomes obvious that she is white, and this polarizes them into black and white attitudes. Prompted by this event they explore their roles in a series of games. They leave behind their identities and in suspended time act out the archetypal roles of black and white, forcing each other into extreme caricature. The play acting is stopped by the ringing of an alarm clock, bringing them back to time, history, and reality. The games they play perform a psychological function. Insofar as they force each other into their stereotyped roles and compel each other to see themselves as black or white society sees them, they are in effect acting as Freudian analysts on each other, exposing their neuroses and hopefully, through exposure, curing them. Fugard does not, however, offer this as a solution to the South African problem. He is merely reflecting on the situation, and his preoccupation with role playing and identity problems is a logical result of a situation where — in his own words — "people have lost their faces and have become just literally the colour of their skins."

—Kirsten Holst Petersen

GALSWORTHY, John. English. Born in Combe, Surrey, 14 August 1867. Educated at the Sangeen School, Bournemouth, 1876; Harrow School, Middlesex, 1881–86; New College, Oxford, 1886–89; entered Lincoln's Inn, London, 1889: called to the Bar, 1890. Married Ada Cooper in 1905. Travelled in the United States, Canada, Australia, New Zealand, and the South Seas, then briefly practised law until 1895; thereafter a full-time writer. President, P.E.N. Club, 1921. Recipient: Nobel Prize for Literature, 1932. D.Litt.: Oxford University, 1931. Honorary Fellow, New College, Oxford. Honorary Member, American Academy of Arts and Sciences, 1931. Order of Merit, 1929. *Died 31 January 1933.*

PUBLICATIONS

Collections

The Galsworthy Reader, edited by Anthony West.   1967.

Plays

The Silver Box (produced 1906).   1909; edited by John Hampden, 1964.
Joy: A Play on the Letter I (produced 1907).   1909.
Strife (produced 1909).   1909.
Justice (produced 1910).   1910; edited by John Hampden, 1964.
The Little Dream: An Allegory (produced 1911).   1911; revised edition, 1912.
The Pigeon: A Fantasy (produced 1912).   1912.
The Eldest Son: A Domestic Drama (produced 1912).   1912.
The Fugitive (produced 1913).   1913.
The Mob (produced 1914).   1914.
The Little Man (produced 1915).   In *Six Short Plays,* 1921.
A Bit o' Love (produced 1915).   1915.
The Foundations: An Extravagant Play (produced 1917).   1920.
The Skin Game (produced 1920).   1920.
The Defeat (produced 1920).   In *Six Short Plays,* 1921.
A Family Man (produced 1921).   1922.
The First and the Last (produced 1921).   In *Six Short Plays,* 1921.
Six Short Plays (includes *The First and the Last, The Little Man, Hallmarked, Defeat, The Sun, Punch and Go*).   1921.
The Sun (produced 1922).   In *Six Short Plays,* 1921.
Punch and Go (produced 1924).   In *Six Short Plays,* 1921.
Loyalties (produced 1922).   1922.
Windows: A Comedy for Idealists and Others (produced 1922).   1922.
The Forest, from his own story "A Stoic" (produced 1924).   1924.
Old English (produced 1924).   1924.
The Show (produced 1925).   1925.
Escape: An Episodic Play (produced 1926).   1926; edited by John Hampden, 1964.
Plays.   1928.
Exiled: An Evolutionary Comedy (produced 1929).   1929.
The Roof (produced 1929).   1929.
Carmen, with Ada Galsworthy, from the opera by Henri Meilhac and Ludovic Halévy, music by Bizet.   1932.
The Winter Garden: Four Dramatic Pieces (includes *Escape – Episode VII, The Golden Eggs, Similes, The Winter Garden*).   1935.

Fiction

From the Four Winds (stories).   1897.
Jocelyn.   1898.
Villa Rubein.   1900; revised edition, 1909.
A Man of Devon.   1901; revised edition, with *Villa Rubein*, 1909.
The Island Pharisees.   1904; revised edition, 1908.
The Man of Property.   1906; *In Chancery,* 1920; *Awakening,* 1920; *To Let,* 1921;
     complete version as *The Forsyte Saga,* 1922.
The Country House.   1907.
Fraternity.   1909.
The Patrician.   1911.
The Dark Flower.   1913.
The Freelands.   1915.
Beyond.   1917.
Five Tales.   1918; as *The First and the Last,* and *The Stoic,* 2 vols., 1920; as *The Apple
     Tree and Other Tales,* 1965.
The Burning Spear, Being the Adventures of Mr. John Lavender in Time of War.   1919.
Saint's Progress.   1919.
Tatterdemalion (stories).   1920.
Captures (stories).   1923.
The White Monkey.   1924; *The Silver Spoon,* 1926; *Swan Song,* 1928; complete
     version as *A Modern Comedy,* 1929.
Caravan: The Assembled Tales.   1925.
Two Forsyte Interludes.   1927.
On Forsyte 'change.   1930.
Soames and Flag.   1930.
Maid in Waiting.   1931; *Flowering Wilderness,* 1932; *Over the River,* 1933 (as *One
     More River,* 1933); complete version as *End of the Chapter,* 1934.
Corduroys.   1937.
The Rocks.   1937.
'Nyasha.   1939.

Verse

Moods, Songs and Doggerels.   1912.
Five Poems.   1919.
Verses New and Old.   1926.
Collected Poems, edited by Ada Galsworthy.   1934.

Other

A Commentary.   1908.
A Justification of the Censorship of Plays.   1909.
A Motley.   1910.
The Inn of Tranquillity: Studies and Essays.   1912.
The Little Man and Other Satires.   1915; as *Abracadabra and Other Satires,* 1924.
A Sheaf.   1916.
The Land: A Plea.   1917.
Addresses in America.   1919.
Another Sheaf.   1919.
Memorable Days.   1924.

Castles in Spain and Other Screeds. 1927.
Works. 26 vols., 1927–34.
Two Essays on Conrad. 1930.
Author and Critic. 1935.
Glimpses and Reflections. 1937.
Forsytes, Pendyces, and Others, edited by Ada Galsworthy. 1935.
Autobiographical Letters: A Correspondence with Frank Harris. 1933.
Letters 1900–1932, edited by Edward Garnett. 1934.
My Galsworthy Story (letters), by Margaret Morris. 1967.

Editor, with Ada Galsworthy, *Ex Libris John Galsworthy.* 1933.

Bibliography: *A Bibliography of the Works of Galsworthy* by H. V. Marrot, 1928; *Galsworthy: His First Editions* by G. H. Fabes, 1932; "Galsworthy: An Annotated Bibliography of Writings about Him" by H. E. Gerber, with continuation by E. E. Stevens, in *English Literature in Transition 1* and *7,* 1958, 1967; *Galsworthy the Dramatist: A Bibliography of Criticism* by E. H. Mikhail, 1971.

Reading List: *The Life and Letters of Galsworthy* by H. V. Marrot, 1935; *Galsworthy* by Ralph H. Mottram, 1953; *The Man of Principle: A View of Galsworthy,* by Dudley Barker, 1963; *Galsworthy* by David Holloway, 1968; *Galsworthy: A Biography* by Catherine Dupré, 1976.

*   *   *

As is the fate of many writers', Galsworthy's reputation fell steeply in the twenty years after his death, partly for the purely snobbish reason that he was not born working-class. Today it has greatly recovered, and he is recognized as standing no less high than such of his near-contemporaries as Wells, Ford, and Bennett, and in the theatrical field not so far below the mighty Shaw. Galsworthy's recovery of reputation is in part due to the immensely successful television dramatization of *The Forsyte Saga* which went – and is probably still going – round the world. In addition, there has recently been a more sober reassessment of writers of Galsworthy's heyday. The former glib dismissals of him as genteel, a moralising humanitarian, a man too aware of the "claims of niceness" will not do for those who have been reawakened to *The Forsyte Saga,* or who have seen some of the splendid revivals of his plays.

The Forsyte Saga itself and its pendants (two trilogies and additional single works) gradually written and assembled over more than twenty years, is far from consistent in tone and style. Its early volumes picture a largely departed way of life – of the upper business and professional classes in late Victorian and early Edwardian times – and its later books are a unique evocation of the lives of those same classes in the 1920's. But today's fashionable interest in Victoriana, and nostalgia generally – including perhaps a bit of envy among middle-class readers in the picture of a spacious and expansive world – are not enough to explain the interest in Galsworthy's novels. The books are full of interesting characters in a changing and developing time, resulting in an almost documentary view of the period. There are strong dramatic situations, with a highly rich series of plots. And though Galsworthy is short on humour, he is strong on irony. Even outside the strongly focused story of *The Forsyte Saga* itself (*The Man of Property, In Chancery, Awakening,* and *To Let*), the story of the family and its acquaintances and relations continue in later volumes far from negligible as fiction.

His plays have made an even greater come-back in the 1960's and 1970's, largely based on successes on the stage. Young critics acclaim his dramatic talent, his rich and subtle realism and, as Gareth Lloyd Evans in *The Language of Modern Drama* says, "a quality of associativeness in the language." Evans notes that he is a great master of the pause in dialogue, in creating *tableaux vivants*, and in stage directions which are both evocative and of great practical help to the actor.

Often his plays take a theme of the day, almost from a newspaper account, and present it as a problem, but with a wide imaginative and intellectual breadth. The treatment sometimes attains something approaching poetry, and one may detect the cadences of Synge. In this, in fact, he has been compared to Pinter. Galsworthy himself points out in an essay in the collection *Candelabra* (in *Works*, 1932) that though he sets problems in many of his best plays — *Strife*, *Justice*, *The Silver Box*, and *The Skin Game* — he does not try to solve them or to effect direct reform; he seeks only "to present truth and, gripping with it his readers or his audience, to produce in them a sort of mental and moral fermenting, whereby vision may be enlarged, imagination livened, and understanding promoted." Like Shaw, Galsworthy shows society to itself. "He was perhaps," writes Gareth Lloyd Evans, "the last prose dramatist of undoubted importance who realized that prose itself need not be the servant alone of the world of public man but can minister to matters more deeply interfused and less palpable."

—Kenneth Young

GARRICK, David. English. Born in Hereford, 19 February 1717. Educated at Lichfield Grammar School, Staffordshire; Samuel Johnson's Academy at Edial, Staffordshire, 1736–37. Married Eva Marie Violetti in 1749. Moved to London with Samuel Johnson, 1737; wine merchant, with his brother, in London, 1738–42; appeared on the stage from 1741, and came to be regarded as the greatest actor of his age, noted for his portrayal of tragic heroes; Joint Manager, with Sheridan, Theatre Royal, Dublin, 1745–46; Joint Owner/Manager, with James Lacy, 1747–73, and Sole Owner/Manager, 1773 until he retired, 1776, Drury Lane Theatre, London. *Died 20 January 1779.*

PUBLICATIONS

Collections

> *Poetical Works.* 2 vols., 1785.
> *Dramatic Works.* 3 vols., 1798.
> *Three Farces* (includes *The Lying Valet, A Peep Behind the Curtain, Bon Ton*), edited by Louise B. Osborn. 1925.
> *Three Plays* (includes *The Meeting of the Company, Harlequin's Invasion, Shakespeare's Garland*), edited by E. P. Stein. 1926.
> *Letters*, edited by David M. Little and George R. Kahrl. 3 vols., 1963.

Plays

> *Lethe; or, Aesop in the Shades*, from the play *An Hospital for Fools* by James Miller (produced 1740). 1745; revised version, 1757.
> *The Lying Valet*, from the play *All Without Money* by Peter Motteux (produced 1741). 1741; in *Three Farces*, 1925.

Miss in Her Teens; or, The Medley of Lovers, from a play by F. C. Dancourt (produced 1747). 1747; edited by Richard Bevis, in *Eighteenth Century Drama: Afterpieces,* 1970.

Albumazar, from the play by Thomas Tonkis (produced 1747; revised version, produced 1773). 1773.

Romeo and Juliet, from the play by Shakespeare (produced 1748). 1750.

Every Man in His Humour, from the play by Jonson (produced 1751). 1752.

The Chances, from the play by Fletcher (produced 1754). 1773.

The Fairies, from the play *A Midsummer Night's Dream* by Shakespeare (produced 1755). 1755.

Catharine and Petruchio, from the play *The Taming of the Shrew* by Shakespeare (produced 1756). 1756.

King Lear, from the play by Shakespeare (produced 1756). In *Bell's Shakespeare,* 1786.

Florizel and Perdita; or, The Winter's Tale, from the play by Shakespeare (produced 1756). 1758.

Lilliput (produced 1756). 1757.

The Tempest, music by J. C. Smith, from the play by Shakespeare (produced 1756). 1756.

The Male Coquette; or, Seventeen Hundred Fifty Seven (as *The Modern Fine Gentleman,* produced 1757). 1757.

Isabella; or, The Fatal Marriage, from the play by Thomas Southerne (produced 1757). 1757.

The Gamesters, from the play *The Gamester* by Shirley (produced 1757). 1758.

Antony and Cleopatra, with Edward Capell, from the play by Shakespeare (produced 1759). 1758.

The Guardian, from a play by B. C. Fagan (produced 1759). 1759.

Harlequin's Invasion: A Christmas Gambol (produced 1759). In *Three Plays,* 1926.

The Enchanter; or, Love and Magic, music by J. C. Smith (produced 1760). 1760.

Cymbeline, from the play by Shakespeare (produced 1761). 1762.

The Farmer's Return from London (produced 1762). 1762.

A Midsummer Night's Dream, from the play by Sheakespeare (produced 1763). 1763.

The Clandestine Marriage, with Colman the Elder (produced 1766). 1766.

Neck or Nothing, from a play by Le Sage (produced 1766). 1766.

The Country Girl, from the play *The Country Wife* by Wycherley (produced 1766). 1766.

Cymon: A Dramatic Romance, music by Michael Arne (produced 1767). 1767.

Linco's Travels, music by Michael Arne (produced 1767).

A Peep Behind the Curtain; or, The New Rehearsal (produced 1767). 1767; in *Three Farces,* 1925.

The Elopement (produced 1767).

Dramatic Works. 3 vols., 1768.

The Jubilee, music by Charles Dibdin (produced 1769). 1769; revised version, as *Shakespeare's Garland; or, The Warwickshire Jubilee,* music by Dibdin and others (produced 1769), 1769; in *Three Plays,* 1926.

King Arthur; or, The British Worthy, music by Thomas Arne, from the play by Dryden, music by Purcell (produced 1770). 1770; as *Arthur and Emmeline,* 1784.

The Institution of the Garter; or, Arthur's Round Table Restored, music by Charles Dibdin, from the poem by Gilbert West (produced 1771). 1771.

The Irish Widow (produced 1772). 1772.

Hamlet, from the play by Shakespeare (produced 1772).

A Christmas Tale, music by Charles Dibdin, from a play by C. S. Favart(?) (produced 1773). 1774; revised version, 1776.

The Alchemist, from the play by Jonson (produced 1774?). 1777.

The Meeting of the Company; or, Bayes's Art of Acting (produced 1774). In *Three Plays*, 1926.
Bon Ton; or, High Life above Stairs (produced 1775). 1775; in *Three Farces*, 1925.
The Theatrical Candidates, music by William Bates (produced 1775). With *May Day*, 1775.
May Day; or, The Little Gipsy, music by Thomas Arne (produced 1775). 1775.

Verse

An Ode on the Death of Mr. Pelham. 1754.
The Fribbleriad. 1761.
An Ode upon Dedicating a Building and Erecting a Statue to Shakespeare at Stratford upon Avon. 1769.

Other

Mr. Garrick's Answer to Mr. Macklin's Case. 1743.
An Essay on Acting. 1744.
Reasons Why David Garrick Should Not Appear on the Stage. 1759.
The Diary of Garrick, Being a Record of His Memorable Trip to Paris in 1751, edited by R. C. Alexander. 1928.
The Journal of Garrick Describing His Visit to France and Italy in 1763, edited by G. W. Stone. 1939.
Letters of Garrick and Georgiana Countess Spencer 1759–1779, edited by Earl Spencer and Christopher Dobson. 1960.

Bibliography: *A Checklist of Verse by Garrick* by Mary E. Knapp, 1955; "Garrick: An Annotated Bibliography" by Gerald M. Berkowitz, in *Restoration and Eighteenth-Century Theatre Research 11*, 1972.

Reading List: *Memoirs of the Life of Garrick* by Thomas Davies, 1780; *The Life of Garrick* by Arthur Murphy, 2 vols., 1801; *Garrick, Dramatist* by E. P. Stein, 1938; *Garrick* by Carola Oman, 1958; *Garrick, Director* by Kalman A. Burnim, 1961; *Garrick and Stratford*, 1962, and *Garrick's Jubilee*, 1964, both by Martha England; *Theatre in the Age of Garrick* by Cecil Price, 1973; *A Splendid Occasion: The Stratford Jubilee of 1769* by Levi Fox, 1973.

*   *   *

Although David Garrick was the author of poems, prologues, epilogues, and plays, he is remembered for his complete mastery of the British stage. His style of acting – comparatively natural contrasted to the earlier bombast of Quin and other tragedians – broke with the old way and began a tradition which with inevitable changes still continues. "If this young fellow be right," Quin exclaimed, "then we have been all wrong." His success at Drury Lane proved him right and forced his competitors at Covent Garden and the theatres in Dublin and the provinces to follow his example of acting style and dramatic repertory. Only comic opera, successful at Covent Garden in the early 1760's, escaped Garrick's management for a few years until he augmented his company by inviting Covent Garden's major composer and author to work for him. Under Garrick's and James Lacy's management, Drury Lane prospered; when Garrick died his estate was estimated at up to £100,000.

As a patentee of Drury Lane, and director, manager, author, and actor, Garrick tilted the balance to a theatre dominated by the performer rather than by the author. The names associated with the "Age of Garrick" are most likely to be those of his fellow actresses and actors: Clive, Abington, Shuter, Woffington, Moody, King. But despite contemporary satires which portrayed Garrick discouraging talented dramatists (as in Smollett's *Roderick Random*), Garrick helped authors to rewrite their plays for a demanding but frivolous audience. As George Winchester Stone, Jr. points out (in *The London Stage*, Part 4), Garrick produced 63 new mainpieces and 107 new afterpieces during his 29-year reign. If his worst missteps were to reject John Home's *Douglas* (which succeeded at Covent Garden) and support Hugh Kelly's *False Delicacy* over Goldsmith's *Good Natur'd Man*, they are covered by the great strides Drury Lane took in stagecraft and prestige under his management.

Of the 212 different mainpieces produced by Garrick from 1747 to 1776, Stone shows that the first three of the ten most frequently performed tragedies were by Shakespeare. Of the 15 most popular comedies, three were Shakespeare's and two were by Jonson. Almost 20% of the total performances were plays by Shakespeare. Following custom, Garrick altered plays by Jonson and Shakespeare, among others, to make them vehicles for his own acting and for his repertory company, and entertaining for eighteenth-century audiences. Thus, though he did not treat *The Alchemist* or *Hamlet*, for instance, as literature, he recognized that drama must be performed if it is to be preserved. His most ambitious venture was the Shakespeare Jubilee at Stratford-on-Avon in 1769, an elaborate self-congratulatory celebration which attracted most of London's fashionable artists and their admirers. Though itself a failure, the Jubilee — at which nothing by Shakespeare was performed — can be considered one of the beginnings of Shakespearean idolatry.

Garrick's adaptations of comedies and his original farces like *The Lying Valet* and *Bon Ton; or, High Life above Stairs* amused; but *The Clandestine Marriage*, most of which was by George Colman the Elder, is an accomplished comedy unfairly overshadowed by Goldsmith's plays. Its Epilogue, a miniature comic opera by Garrick, satirizes fashionable playgoers and their infatuation with comic opera; it epitomizes Garrick's skill at light verse and bantering dialogue.

Of the over ninety roles which Garrick performed, among his most famous were Ranger (*Suspicious Husband*, Hoadly), Abel Drugger (*Alchemist*, Jonson), Hamlet and Lear, Benedick (*Much Ado*, Shakespeare), Archer and Scrub (*Beaux' Stratagem*, Farquhar), Don Felix (*The Wonder*, Centlivre), and Bayes (*The Rehearsal*, Villiers). On stage, departing from tradition, Garrick remained in character even when other performers spoke. Whatever the role, Frederick Grimm wrote in 1765, Garrick "abandons his own personality, and puts himself in the situation of him he has to represent ... he ceases to be Garrick." Of "middle stature, small rather than big," Garrick's "vivacity is extreme." Unlike many other actors, Garrick could switch from tragedy to comedy; but whether he was Richard III or Sir John Brute in Vanbrugh's *Provok'd Wife*, Garrick's "negative capability" enabled him to convince his audience that he had become that person.

Now, when actors have been knighted and performers are often associated with American politics, it might be easy to minimize Garrick's importance. But like Samuel Johnson, Garrick was an arbiter of taste. Sterne turned to him for early approval of *Tristram Shandy*, as well he should have since Garrick held shares in two London newspapers, *St. James Chronicle* (which he helped found with the elder Colman and others) and the *Public Advertiser*; his enemies accused him of being a censor-general of London's press. Artists like Reynolds and Hogarth caught his naturalness on canvas, and Goldsmith, Burke, and others of the Literary Club counted him a member. "In his time," concluded one of his early biographers, Arthur Murphy, "the theatre engrossed the minds of men to such a degree that it may now be said there existed in England a *fourth estate*, King, Lords, and Commons, and *Drury-Lane play-house*." His funeral was magnificent; appropriately, Garrick was buried in the Poets' Corner at the foot of Shakespeare's monument. Summarizing Garrick's career, Burke wrote, "He raised the character of his profession to the rank of a liberal art."

—Peter A. Tasch

GAY, John. English. Born in Barnstaple, Devon, baptized 16 September 1685. Educated at the free grammar school in Barnstaple; apprenticed to a silk mercer in London. Secretary to the household of the Duchess of Monmouth, 1712–14; Secretary to the Earl of Clarendon on his diplomatic mission to Hanover, 1714; accompanied William Pulteney, later Earl of Bath, to Aix, 1717; lived at Lord Harcourt's estate in Oxfordshire, 1718; earned considerable income from publication of his collected poems, 1720, and made and lost a fortune in South Sea funds speculation; Commissioner for the Public Lottery, 1722–31; recovered much of his fortune from the success of the *Beggar's Opera*, 1728; lived with his patrons the Duke and Duchess of Queensberry, 1728–32. *Died 4 December 1732.*

PUBLICATIONS

Collections

    Poetical, Dramatic, and Miscellaneous Works. 6 vols., 1795.
    Plays. 2 vols., 1923.
    Poetical Works, edited by G. C. Faber. 1926.
    Letters, edited by Chester F. Burgess. 1966.
    Poetry and Prose, edited by Vinton A. Dearing and Charles Beckwith. 2 vols., 1974.
    Selected Works, edited by Samuel Joseloff. 1976.

Plays

    The Mohocks. 1712.
    The Wife of Bath (produced 1713). 1713; revised version (produced 1730), 1730.
    The What D'ye Call It (produced 1715). 1715.
    Three Hours after Marriage, with Pope and Arbuthnot (produced 1717). 1717; revised version, in *Supplement to the Works of Pope*, 1757; 1717 edition edited by Richard Morton and William Peterson, 1961.
    Acis and Galatea, music by Handel (produced 1719). 1732.
    Dione, in *Poems on Several Occasions.* 1720.
    The Captives (produced 1724). 1724.
    The Beggar's Opera (produced 1728). 1728; edited by Peter Lewis, 1973.
    Polly, Being the 2nd Part of The Beggar's Opera (version revised by Colman the Elder produced 1777). 1729; in *Poetical Works*, 1926.
    Achilles (produced 1733). 1733.
    The Distressed Wife (produced 1734). 1743; as *The Modern Wife* (produced 1771).
    The Rehearsal at Goatham. 1754.

Verse

    Wine. 1708.
    Rural Sports. 1713; revised edition, 1720; edited by O. Culbertson, 1930.
    The Fan. 1714.
    The Shepherd's Week. 1714.
    A Letter to a Lady. 1714.
    Two Epistles, One to the Earl of Burlington, The Other to a Lady. 1715(?).
    Trivia; or, The Art of Walking the Streets of London. 1716.
    Horace, epode iv, Imitated. 1717(?).

The Poor Shepherd.   1720(?).
Poems on Several Occasions.   2 vols., 1720.
A Panegyrical Epistle to Mr. Thomas Snow.   1721.
An Epistle to Her Grace Henrietta Duchess of Marlborough.   1722.
A Poem Addressed to the Quidnunc's.   1724.
Blueskin's Ballad.   1725.
To a Lady on Her Passion for Old China.   1725.
Daphnis and Cloe.   1725(?).
Molly Mog.   1726.
Fables.   2 vols., 1727–38; edited by Vinton A. Dearing, 1967.
Some Unpublished Translations from Ariosto, edited by J. D. Bruce.   1910.

Other

The Present State of Wit.   1711.
*An Argument Proving That the Present Mohocks and Hawkubites Are the Gog and Magog
    Mentioned in the Revelations.*   1712.

Bibliography: in *Poetical Works,* 1926; *Gay: An Annotated Checklist of Criticism* by Julie T. Klein, 1973.

Reading List: *Gay, Favorite of the Wits* by William H. Irving, 1940; *Gay, Social Critic* by Sven M. Armens, 1954; *Gay* by Oliver Warner, 1964; *Gay* by Patricia M. Spacks, 1965.

*   *   *

Although John Gay was one of the most talented English writers in the first third of the eighteenth century, he is overshadowed by his two close friends and fellow-members of the Scriblerus Club, Swift and Pope. Comparisons with the two literary giants of the period are therefore inevitable and usually to Gay's detriment, which is unfortunate since his gifts are significantly different from theirs. It is unfair to think of Gay as a lesser Swift or a lesser Pope. Gay certainly lacks the emotional intensity, intellectual power, and penetrating insight of Swift's great satires, and rarely equals Pope in refined verbal wit, imaginative inventiveness, and incisive irony. The all-embracing cultural survey of *Gulliver's Travels* or even the moral breadth of Pope's *Moral Essays* and *Imitations of Horace* were beyond Gay, as were the gloomy visionary quality and sustained mock-heroic elaboration of *The Dunciad.* Gay's mature work does not seem to stem from a firm ideological foundation of inter-connected philosophical ideas, political convictions and moral values in the way that Swift's and Pope's do. Nevertheless Swift and Pope are not the measure of all Augustan writers as they are sometimes thought to be, and Gay, although influenced by his two friends, usually followed his own creative impulses and did not attempt to do what they were doing. As a result he acquired a distinctive literary voice, less relentless and angry than Swift's, less acerbic and barbed than Pope's, more genial, warm-hearted and gentle than both. His satirical and burlesque works, for example, are less single-minded than theirs, so that his ridicule is often tempered with sentiment, producing a bitter-sweet amalgam that is very much Gay's own and that is particularly evident in his masterpiece, *The Beggar's Opera.* Furthermore Gay, with his less fixed intellectual commitment, was much more chameleon-like than his friends, which helps to explain the extraordinary diversity of his output.

In addition to being a versatile poet, he was a fairly prolific playwright in both verse and prose, and the only member of the Scriblerus Club to devote himself to drama. Indeed it is as the author of *The Beggar's Opera* that he is best remembered today. As a dramatist he did not restrict himself to the "regular" and neoclassically respectable genres of tragedy and comedy but attempted most of the theatrical forms of the period; and with *The Beggar's Opera* he actually invented the ballad opera, which became very popular in the eighteenth century and is the precursor of English comic opera and of the modern musical, as well as being an important influence on Brecht. Gay began his dramatic career with a short farce, *The Mohocks*, and followed this with an undistinguished comedy based on Chaucer, *The Wife of Bath*, before turning his hand to two very different satirical plays. The popular *The What D'Ye Call It* is a fine burlesque of contemporary tragedy, especially "pathetic" plays, that succeeds in transcending burlesque, while the controversial *Three Hours after Marriage*, written as a Scriblerian enterprise with Pope and Arbuthnot, is a lively and frequently farcical dramatic satire attacking a number of well-known contemporary intellectuals and artists. Not long after this he provided Handel with a libretto for his pastoral opera *Acis and Galatea* and then made two not particularly successful attempts at tragedy, *Dione*, written in couplets and in a pastoral and sentimental vein, and *The Captives*, a blank-verse tragedy in a more heroic manner that ends happily with virtue rewarded and poetic justice established. Next came by far his greatest theatrical success, *The Beggar's Opera*, a truly original work of genius and one of the very few eighteenth-century plays to hold the stage until the present day. By using a mixture of speech and song and by providing his own words for well-known tunes, Gay created a new kind of music theatre, the ballad opera, while simultaneously burlesquing Italian opera, which was enjoying a vogue in England. In addition *The Beggar's Opera*, set in the London underworld, is a most unusual love story, both romantic and anti-romantic, as well as a pungently ironic social and political satire. Amazingly enough, Gay was able to weld these diverse elements together into a unified work of art that manages to be both highly topical and universal. After the unprecedented commercial success of *The Beggar's Opera*, Gay wrote an inferior sequel, *Polly*, which was banned from the stage by the Government, offended by the scathing political ridicule of its predecessor. None of his three posthumous plays, *Achilles*, a farcical treatment of a classical legend in ballad-opera form, and the two satirical comedies, *The Distress'd Wife* and *The Rehearsal at Goatham*, adds much to his dramatic achievement.

The range and variety of his dramatic work is matched by that of his poetry, although the quality is again decidedly uneven. He wrote mock-heroic poetry, notably *The Fan*, which is indebted to *The Rape of the Lock*; an extended georgic in the manner of Virgil, *Rural Sports*; a group of pastoral poems, *The Shepherd's Week*, which burlesque Ambrose Philips's *Pastorals* yet are much more than burlesque; a long mock-georgic about London life, laced with acute social observations, guide-book advice and moral precepts, *Trivia; or, The Art of Walking the Streets of London*; a number of urbane verse *Epistles* to friends on various topics; a set of ironic Eclogues, mainly Town Eclogues about fashionable women and love; two series of *Fables* in the manner of Aesop and La Fontaine; various narrative poems, including bawdy tales inspired by Chaucer's *fabliaux*; a few meditative poems such as "A Contemplation on Night" (1714); some lyrics and ballads including the well-known "Sweet William's Farewell to Black-ey'd Susan" (1720); and translations of Ovid and Ariosto. Although much of his poetry is written in decasyllabic couplets, the standard form of the time, Gay is again more varied than many of his contemporaries since he uses the lighter and racier octosyllabic couplets for the *Fables* and some of the tales, blank verse for his early mock-heroic *Wine*, ottava rima for one of his Epistles, "Mr. Pope's Welcome from Greece," and a variety of stanza forms for his songs and ballads. His finest poetic achievement is the first series of *Fables*, ostensibly written to entertain a young member of the Royal Family but, as in the case of earlier fable literature, having a much wider moral, social, and political significance than the apparently innocuous subject-matter suggests. Gay's *Fables* are not of the supreme quality of La Fontaine's, but they remain the best examples of their kind in English since Henryson's admirable adaptations of Aesop into Middle Scots. *Trivia*, which has been claimed to be the finest poem about London in the language, is also a genuinely individual work revealing some of his best qualities: his observant eye for detail, his great sympathy for ordinary humanity, his down-to-earth good sense, his sturdy versification, and plain, unfussy diction. *The Shepherd's Week* is probably the most important Augustan contribution to the genre of pastoral. Much of Gay's work is now of interest only to the specialist, but in a few cases, notably the *Fables* and above all *The Beggar's Opera*, he transcends his own time and must therefore rank as a major Augustan writer.

—Peter Lewis

GILBERT, Sir W(illiam) S(chwenck).   English.   Born in London, 18 November 1836. Educated at a school in Boulogne, 1843–46; Western Grammar School, Brompton, London, 1846–50; Great Ealing School, London, 1850–55; King's College, London, 1855–57, B.A. 1857; Inner Temple, London, from 1855; called to the Bar, 1863. Commissioned in the militia in the 3rd Battalion of the Gordon Highlanders, 1857; Captain, 1867; retired with the rank of Major, 1883. Married Lucy Agnes Turner in 1867. Clerk in the Education Department of the Privy Council Office, London, 1857–61; regular contributor, as author and artist, to *Fun*, London, 1861–71; practised law in London and on the northern circuit, 1864–68; began writing for the stage in the 1860's, and in partnership with the composer Arthur Sullivan, 1871–96: wrote operas with Sullivan for Richard D'Oyly Carte at the Royalty Theatre from 1875 (transferred to the Savoy, a new theatre specially built for them by D'Oyly Carte, 1881); after 1896 resumed his separate career as a playwright; built the Garrick Theatre, London, 1889; purchased the estate of Grims Dyke, Middlesex, 1890; Justice of the Peace and Deputy-Lieutenant of Middlesex, 1891–1911. Knighted, 1907. *Died 29 May 1911.*

PUBLICATIONS

Collections

New and Original Extravaganzas (includes *Dulcamara, La Vivandière, The Merry Zingara, Robert the Devil, The Pretty Druidess*), edited by Isaac Goldberg.   1931.
The First Night Gilbert and Sullivan, edited by Reginald Allen.   1958.
The Savoy Operas.   2 vols., 1962.
Gilbert Before Sullivan: Six Comic Plays (includes *No Cards, Ages Ago, Our Island Home, A Sensation Novel, Happy Arcadia, Eyes and No Eyes*), edited by Jane W. Stedman.   1967.
The Bab Ballads, edited by James Ellis.   1970.

Plays

Uncle Baby (produced 1863).   Edited by Terence Rees, 1968.
Ruy Blas, in *Warne's Christmas Annual*.   1866.
Dulcamara; or, The Little Duck and the Great Quack (produced 1866).   1866; in *New and Original Extravaganzas*, 1931.
Hush-a-Bye Baby on the Tree Top, with Charles Millward (produced 1866).

Le Vivandière; or, True to the Corps, from a work by Donizetti (produced 1867). 1867; in *New and Original Extravaganzas,* 1931.

Robinson Crusoe; or, The Injured Bride and the Injured Wife, with others (produced 1867).

Harlequin Cock-Robin, and Jenny Wren (produced 1867). 1867.

Allow Me to Explain (produced 1867).

Highly Improbable (produced 1867).

The Merry Zingara; or, The Tipsy Gipsy and the Pipsy Wipsy: A Whimsical Parody on The Bohemian Girl (produced 1868). 1868; in *New and Original Extravaganzas,* 1931.

Robert the Devil; or, The Nun, The Dun, and the Son of a Gun (produced 1868). 1868; in *New and Original Extravaganzas,* 1931.

No Cards, music by L. Elliott (produced 1869). 1869; in *Gilbert Before Sullivan,* 1967.

The Pretty Druidess; or, The Mother, The Maid, and the Mistletoe Bough (produced 1869). 1869; in *New and Original Extravaganzas,* 1931.

An Old Score (produced 1869). 1869(?).

Ages Ago: A Ghost Story, music by Fred Clay (produced 1869). 1869; in *Gilbert Before Sullivan,* 1967.

The Princess: A Whimsical Allegory, Being a Respectful Perversion of Tennyson's Poem (produced 1870). 1870.

The Gentleman in Black, music by Fred Clay (produced 1870). 1870.

Our Island Home, music by German Reed (produced 1870). In *Gilbert Before Sullivan,* 1967.

The Palace of Truth (produced 1870). 1870(?).

A Medical Man (produced 1872). In *Drawing-Room Plays and Parlour Pantomimes,* edited by C. W. Scott, 1870.

Randall's Thumb (produced 1871). 1871.

A Sensation Novel, in Three Volumes, music by German Reed (produced 1871). 1871; in *Gilbert Before Sullivan,* 1967.

Creatures of Impulse, music by Alberto Randegger (produced 1871). 1871.

The Brigands, from a work by Meilhac and Halévy, music by Offenbach (produced 1889). 1871.

Great Expectations, from the novel by Dickens (produced 1871).

On Guard (produced 1871). 1871.

Pygmalion and Galatea (produced 1871). 1872.

Thespis; or, The Gods Grown Old: A Grotesque Opera, music by Arthur Sullivan (produced 1871). 1871.

Happy Arcadia, music by Fred Clay (produced 1872). 1872; in *Gilbert Before Sullivan,* 1967.

The Wicked World (produced 1873). 1873.

The Happy Land, with Gilbert à Beckett (produed 1873). 1873.

The Wedding March: An Eccentricity, from a play by Eugène Labiche and Marc-Michel (produced 1873). 1873; revised version, music by George Grossmith, Jr., as *Haste to the Wedding* (produced 1892), 1892.

The Realm of Joy (produced 1873). Edited by Terence Rees, 1969.

Ought We to Visit Her?, from the novel by Annie Edwardes (produced 1874). 1874.

The Blue-Legged Lady (produced 1874). Edited by Jane W. Stedman, in *Nineteenth Century Theatre Research,* Spring 1975.

Charity (produced 1874). 1874.

Topsy-Turvydom (produced 1874). 1931.

Sweethearts (produced (1874). 1874.

On Bail, from a play by Meilhac and Halévy (as *Committed for Trial,* produced 1874; revised version, as *On Bail,* produced 1877). 1877.

Trial by Jury, music by Arthur Sullivan (produced 1875). 1875.

Tom Cobb; or, Fortune's Toy (produced 1875). 1875.

Eyes and No Eyes; or, The Art of Seeing, music by German Reed (produced 1875). 1875; in *Gilbert Before Sullivan,* 1967.

Broken Hearts (produced 1875). 1875.

Princess Toto, music by Fred Clay (produced 1876). 1876.

Dan'l Druce, Blacksmith (produced 1875). 1876.

Original Plays. 4 vols., 1876–1911; revised edition, 1920.

Engaged (produced 1877). 1877.

The Sorcerer, music by Arthur Sullivan, from the story "An Elixir of Love" by Gilbert (produced 1877). 1877; revised version (produced 1884), 1884.

The Forty Thieves, with others (produced 1878). 1878.

The Ne'er-Do-Weel (produced 1878). 1878; revised version, as *The Vagabond* (produced 1878).

H.M.S. Pinafore; or, The Lass That Loved a Sailor, music by Arthur Sullivan (produced 1878). 1878.

Gretchen (produced 1879). 1879.

The Pirates of Penzance; or, The Slave of Duty, music by Arthur Sullivan (produced 1879). 1879.

The Martyr of Antioch, music by Arthur Sullivan, from the poem by Henry Hart Milman (produced 1880).

Patience; or, Bunthorne's Bride!, music by Arthur Sullivan (produced 1881). 1881.

Foggerty's Fairy, from his own story (produced 1881). 1881.

Iolanthe; or, The Peer and the Peri, music by Arthur Sullivan (produced 1882). 1882.

Princess Ida; or, Castle Adamant, music by Arthur Sullivan, from the poem *The Princess* by Gilbert, based on the poem by Tennyson (produced 1884). 1884.

Comedy and Tragedy (produced 1884). 1884.

The Mikado; or, The Town of Titipu, music by Arthur Sullivan (produced 1885). 1885.

Ruddigore; or, The Witch's Curse!, music by Arthur Sullivan (as *Ruddygore,* produced 1887). 1887.

The Yeoman of the Guard; or, The Merryman and His Maid, music by Arthur Sullivan (produced 1888). 1888.

Brantinghame Hall (produced 1888). 1888.

The Gondoliers; or, The King of Barataria, music by Arthur Sullivan (produced 1889). 1889.

A Stage Play. 1890.

Rosencrantz and Guildenstern (produced 1891). 1892.

The Mountebanks, music by Alfred Cellier (produced 1892). 1892.

Utopia (Limited); or, The Flowers of Progress, music by Arthur Sullivan (produced 1893). 1893.

His Excellency, music by Osmond Carr (produced 1894). 1894.

The Grand Duke; or, The Statutory Duel, music by Arthur Sullivan (produced 1896). 1896.

The Fortune Hunter (produced 1897). 1897.

The Fairy's Dilemma, from his own story (produced 1904). 1911.

Fallen Fairies; or, The Wicked World, music by Edward German (produced 1909). 1909.

The Hooligan (produced 1911). In *Century Illustrated Magazine,* November 1911.

Trying a Dramatist. 1911.

A Colossal Idea. 1932.

Fiction

Foggerty's Fairy and Other Tales. 1890.

Verse

The "Bab" Ballads: Much Sound and Little Sense, illustrated by the author. 1869.
More "Bab" Ballads, illustrated by the author. 1873.
Fifty "Bab" Ballads. 1877.
Songs of a Savoyard, illustrated by the author. 1890.
Songs of Two Savoyards. 1892.
Lost Bab Ballads, edited by T. Searle. 1932.

Other

The Pinafore Picture Book: The Story of H.M.S. Pinafore. 1908.
The Story of The Mikado. 1921.

Bibliography: *A Bibliography of Gilbert* by T. Searle, 1931; *Gilbert: An Anniversary Survey and Exhibition Checklist*, 1963.

Reading List: *Gilbert: His Life and Letters* by Sidney Dark and Rowland Greay, 1923; *The Story of Gilbert and Sullivan* by Isaac Goldberg, 1928; *The Gilbert and Sullivan Book* by Leslie W. A. Bailey, 1952, revised edition, 1956; *Gilbert and Sullivan Opera* by Aubrey Williamson, 1953; *Gilbert: His Life and Strife* by Hesketh Pearson, 1957; *Thespis: A Gilbert and Sullivan Enigma* by Terence Rees, 1964; *Gilbert: A Century of Scholarship and Commentary* edited by John Bush Jones, 1970; *Gilbert and Sullivan Papers* edited by James Helyar, 1970; *Gilbert* by Max Sutton, 1975; *Gilbert and Sullivan and Their Victorian World* by Christopher Hibbert, 1976; *Gilbert, Stage Director* by William Cox-Ife, 1978.

*   *   *

When W. S. Gilbert began his collaboration with Arthur Sullivan, he was already well-known as the most important new dramatist of his day and as the author of the *Bab Ballads*, a series of nonsense verses published in *Fun*, the comic magazine that for a few brilliant years rivalled *Punch*. Having been a government clerk and an almost briefless barrister, Gilbert turned to journalism and the stage, where he was at once recognized as a reformer and innovator. In amusingly parodistic reviews he attacked exaggerated acting, slovenly enunciation, anachronistic costumes and props, and sprawling dramatic construction. At the same time, he defended the theatre against attacks by the rigidly righteous, a defense which he continued in such plays as *Ought We to Visit Her?*

Gilbert's nonsense verse, like that of Carroll and Lear, combines technical ingenuity and complex regularity of form with wildly inventive, sometimes violent content. In his ballads, as in many of his libretti, the plot is worked out in terms of strict logic operating relentlessly from absurd or impossible premises. Captain Cleggs, for instance, visits the mermaids, and the mermen cut off his legs and replace them with a tail, whereupon the Admiralty deprives him of his command, saying that as half a captain, he will only get half-pay. A shipwrecked ancient mariner, having devoured his companions, believes himself to be simultaneously "a cook and a captain bold,/And the mate of the *Nancy* brig,/And a bo'sun tight, and a midshipmite,/And the crew of the captain's gig." The plots of the *Bab Ballads* use many melodramatic incidents such as last-minute rescues and revelations of identity, and, like Carroll's "The Walrus and the Carpenter," Gilbert's verses often attack self-interestedness and hypocrisy. In "Gentle Alice Brown," for instance, a robber's daughter murders a baby and forges a check, but only when she becomes interested in a respectable young man does her family priest object, lest she reform and he lose the profit from her confessions. In a serious ballad, "The Pantomime 'Super' to His Mask," the player and his grotesque mask engage in a dialogue as to whether the mask imposes its deformity upon the man or whether the man may not be the disfigured mask of something within himself. This double, sometimes multiple identity is a device which Gilbert carried over into many of his plays and libretti, using it for satiric and comic effects and as a plot element. In fact, Victorian critics immediately noted that the *Bab Ballads* contributed heavily to the Gilbert and Sullivan operas.

Gilbert also wrote short stories and critical articles, his fiction often Dickensian in tone, his criticism directed toward improving the stage by freeing it from censorship and by giving the dramatist, not the actor, complete control over performance. Gilbert himself exercised increasing authority over the productions of his dramatic works, which include almost all the genres known to the Victorian stage. His early burlesques of grand opera were praised for their wit and construction, and in his "respectful perversion" of Tennyson's poem *The Princess* Gilbert experimented with what he described as "a blank verse burlesque in which a picturesque story should be told in a strain of mock-heroic seriousness." He was also writing "entertainments," mini-libretti, set to music by Fred Clay and others. Of these, *Ages Ago* ran longer than any other Victorian "entertainment" and anticipated both *Iolanthe* and *Ruddigore*. In such plays for the Gallery of Illustration and others written for other theatres, Gilbert continued to perfect his technique, experimenting further with what are now familiar Gilbertian elements, including multiple personalities for each character, arbitrary manipulations of "reality," logical absurdity, strong contralto characters, a satiric view of human nature, and lyrics which are integral to the action. Gilbert's satire against a society which talked in terms of love and duty while it acted in terms of money and prestige continued throughout his career, often causing reviewers to describe him as "cynical" and "heartless," terms especially applied to his eccentric comedy *Engaged*.

In 1870 Gilbert began a series of "fairy plays" in verse, ranging from the broad comedy of *The Palace of Truth* to the deep pathos of *Broken Hearts*. Fairies do not appear as characters in these plays, but the plot of each is directed by some supernatural force or magic object. In *Pygmalion and Galatea*, the most popular of the group, the innocent frankness of the animated statue characteristically upsets human relationships until, disillusioned, she returns to stone. These "fairy comedies" were generally considered the most innovative and successful verse dramas of their day. Gilbert himself burlesqued one of them anonymously, changing *The Wicked World* to *The Happy Land* and the object of his satire from the effects of sexual love to the principles of politicians, notably Gladstone. *The Happy Land* was temporarily banned, whereupon Gilbert adapted *The Realm of Joy* (from the French) as a satire on censorship.

During these years (1870–75), he also wrote two problem plays, one of which, *Charity*, depicts a "fallen woman" as more admirable than her accusers and is a forerunner of the New Drama of the 1890's. Gilbert began to collaborate with Sullivan, first in *Thespis* at the Gaiety Theatre, then in *Trial by Jury* at the Royalty Theatre, managed by Richard D'Oyly Carte, a theatrical agent-musician-impresario. The "triumvirate" of Gilbert, Sullivan, and D'Oyly Carte continued for more than twenty years to produce the Savoy Operas, named after the Savoy Theatre which D'Oyly Carte built for them. In them, Gilbert perfected the comic technique he had developed through many stages, while his metrical sophistication and parodistic play were matched by comparable qualities in Sullivan, whose musicianship far surpassed that of other light opera composers. These works continued Gilbert's satiric view of human nature, being peopled with characters who openly reveal their stupidity, vanity, greed,incompetence, and cowardice as a matter of course. Even the romantic heroines, like Yum-Yum, really know their worth and, like Rose Maybud, are motivated by the main chance. Gilbert still satirized his favourite target – hypocrisy, as well as the Army, the Navy, the Church, Monarchy, popular melodramatic morality, aesthetic poseurs, and eventually, in *Utopia (Limited)*, all British institutions, political and financial. He also satirized the audience themselves, who, charmed by Sullivan's ameliorating music, seldom took Gilbert's criticism to heart.

Having learned the principles of stage-management from Tom Robertson, who introduced domestic realism to the English stage, Gilbert directed his own works, staged them meticulously, often designing sets and costumes himself, and trained his company to act in a high comic style exactly suited to the formality of his dialogue.

Although the last two Savoy operas were much less popular than their predecessors, the D'Oyly Carte Opera Company revived earlier successes even after the deaths of the triumvirate, and has continued to perform the operas for more than a century, a unique theatrical run. During the 1890's, Gilbert collaborated with other musicians in light operas which, although well-received at the time, have not endured, partly because of less attractive scores, partly because Gilbert increased his *dramatis personae* and loosened his plots, partly because these late works did not have an on-going company to support them.

Gilbert also wrote several prose dramas, among them *Sweethearts*, a gently amusing piece, frequently revived; *Dan'l Druce, Blacksmith*, suggested by an episode in *Silas Marner*; and *Comedy and Tragedy*, a display piece for the virtuoso acting of Mary Anderson. A recurrent theme in several of his works is the effect of environment in creating "sinners" and criminals. His last play, *The Hooligan*, is set in a condemned cell during the last moments of a feeble-minded coster boy who has killed his unfaithful girl. Critics said that Gilbert had met Galsworthy on his own ground and surpassed him in social realism.

As a writer, however, Gilbert did not have a wide range. Although he worked in a variety of genres, he transferred many of the same elements and devices from form to form, which eventually made his plots seem mechanical and his characters familiar. He preferred to polish rather than to improvise. Neither he nor Sullivan could depict passion successfully, although in *The Wicked World* he dealt with the destructive elements of sexuality.

Nevertheless, Gilbert's influence on the development of the comedy of ideas is significant, especially in Wilde's *The Importance of Being Earnest*, which drew heavily on Gilbert's plays, and in the social satire of George Bernard Shaw. Gilbert's treatment of reality looks forward to Tom Stoppard's *Rosencrantz and Guildenstern Are Dead* and his treatment of logic to the so-called "absurd" plays of Eugene Ionesco. As a stage director, he was important in turning the theatre from domination by the actor to domination by the director. As a satirist Gilbert upheld a golden mean and an increased self-knowledge, which, however, he saw man as unlikely to achieve.

—Jane W. Stedman

GILLETTE, William (Hooker).   American.   Born in Hartford, Connecticut, 24 July 1853. Educated at Hartford High School; Trinity College, Hartford, left without taking a degree. Married Helen Nickles in 1882 (died, 1888). Debut as an actor, New Orleans, later New York and Boston, 1875; appeared with Bernard Macauley's company in Cincinnati and Louisville, 1876–77; returned to New York and from 1881 was one of the most prominent actors of the New York and London stage; appeared in nine of his own plays: especially noted for his portrayal of Sherlock Holmes; retired in 1919 to an estate in Connecticut, but later came out of retirement to appear in various of his early roles in New York and on tour throughout America; retired again in 1936. Awarded honorary degrees by Yale University, New Haven, Connecticut, Columbia University, New York, and Trinity College, all in 1930. Member, American Academy of Arts and Letters, 1913. *Died 29 April 1937.*

Plays

Esmeralda, with Frances Hodgson Burnett (produced 1881; as *Young Folks' Ways*, produced 1883). 1882.
The Professor (produced 1881; as *The Professor's Wooing*, produced 1881).
Held by the Enemy (produced 1886). 1898.
A Legal Wreck (produced 1888).
All the Comforts of Home, with H. C. Duckworth, from a German play (produced 1890). 1897.
Mr. Wilkinson's Widows, from a play by Alexandre Bisson (produced in the 1890's ?).
Too Much Johnson (produced 1894). 1912.
Secret Service (produced 1895). 1898.
Sherlock Holmes, with A. Conan Doyle, from works by Doyle (produced 1899). 1922.
The Painful Predicament of Sherlock Holmes (produced 1905). 1955.
Clarice (produced 1905).
Among Thieves (produced 1909; as *The Robber*, produced 1909). In *One-Act Plays for Stage and Study 2*, 1925.
Electricity (produced 1910). 1913.
The Dream Maker, with Howard E. Morton (produced 1921).
The Red Owl. 1924.
How Well George Does It! 1936.

Fiction

A Legal Wreck. 1888.
The Astounding Crime on Torrington Road. 1927.

Other

The Illusion of the First Time in Acting. 1915.

Editor, *How to Write a Play: Letters from Augier, Banville, Dennery, Dumas, Gondinet, Labiche, Legouvé, Pailleron, Sardou, and Zola*, translated by Dudley Miles. 1916.

Reading List: *Sherlock Holmes and Much More* by Doris E. Cook, 1970.

*   *   *

William Gillette's first performance, with an assist from Mark Twain, was in *Faint Heart Ne'er Won Fair Lady* in 1875. He appeared in several stock companies before opening his own play, *The Professor*, at Madison Square Garden in 1881. Thereafter he appeared chiefly in his own plays, except for roles in *Samson, The Admirable Crichton, A Successful Calamity*, and *Dear Brutus*. Frequently he was at his best in portraying the "cool man of action," whether it was the title role in his own *Sherlock Holmes* (he played the part for 30 years) or Brant in his own *Held by the Enemy* (a melodrama but also the first successful play about the American Civil War). Notable among his other plays are *A Legal Wreck* (about a coastal New England town), *Secret Service* (his most popular American Civil War play), and *The Painful Predicament of Sherlock Holmes*. The last is an hysterically funny mini-play sequel to

Sherlock Holmes featuring a bumbling, loquacious, accident-prone escapee from the nearby mental hospital, who, while she appeals for help to the always silent Holmes, accidentally destroys his violin, violin bow, lamp, cocaine pot, crime case notes, and photographs, before Holmes's servant can summon sanitorium assistance.

Gillette's best claim to fame today lies in his *Sherlock Holmes*, written in collaboration with Sir Arthur Conan Doyle, and revived to great acclaim in 1975. Gillette's play bends Doyle's stories "A Scandal in Bohemia" and "The Final Problem," and not only demonstrates Holmes's great skill against Moriarity, the Napoleon of Crime, but also shows him falling in love with the heroine, Alice Faulkner, though one sometimes wonders whether he will shoot Moriarity or cocaine. Gillette judiciously and skillfully lifts dialogue directly from Doyle's stories, along with the most dramatic moments, though the melodramatic tension is Gillette's. A good script editor can easily keep the play's many complicated dramatic turns from becoming too intricate, and its melodramatic turns from becoming maudlin. Holmes quickly solves the mystery, foils the thugs, recovers the blackmail papers (50% honestly), and jails Moriarity. Holmes besottedly in love could have provided a deadly melodramatic element, especially when coupled with Alice's innocence and naivety; but, to the audience's delight, the romance spurs interest in the triumph of good, and Alice falls ecstatically into Holmes's arms at the final curtain.

—Louis Charles Stagg

GLAPTHORNE, Henry. English. Born in Whittlesey, Cambridgeshire, 28 July 1610. Very little is known about his life: educated at Corpus Christi College, Cambridge; probably enjoyed the patronage of a lord; presumed to be a Royalist and probably died in the Civil War. *Died in 1644.*

PUBLICATIONS

Collections

Plays and Poems, edited by R. H. Shepherd. 2 vols., 1874.

Plays

Argalus and Parthenia (produced 1632–38?). 1639.
The Lady's Privilege (produced 1632–40?). 1640.
Albertus Wallenstein (produced 1634–39?). 1639.
The Lady Mother (produced 1635). Edited by A. H. Bullen, in *A Collection of Old English Plays,* 1883; edited by Arthur Brown, 1959.
The Hollander (produced 1636). 1640.
Wit in a Constable (produced ?). 1640.
Revenge for Honour (produced 1640?). 1654.

Verse

Poems. 1639.
Whitehall, with Elegies and An Anniversary. 1643.

Other

His Majesty's Gracious Answer to the Message Sent from the Honourable City of London Concerning Peace. 1643.

Editor, *Poems, Divine and Humane,* by Thomas Beedome. 1641.

Reading List: *Glapthorne* by M. Zwickert, 1881; *The Sons of Ben: Jonsonian Comedy in Caroline England* by J. L. Davis, 1967.

*   *   *

Henry Glapthorne is an obscure English dramatist who wrote for the popular theatre during the last half of the reign of Charles I. He is perhaps best known for a play which in fact he may not have written, *Revenge for Honour.* For although the Stationers' Register for 1653 lists Glapthorne as author, Chapman's name appears on the title page. Certainly he wrote no other play in the Eastern heroic vein. During a short theatrical career of less than ten years, Glapthorne set his hand to pastoral, tragedy, comedy, and tragi-comedy, producing no play totally in a single theatrical mode. This is a generic eclecticism common to much Caroline drama. For example, the Fletcherian pastoral, *Argalus and Parthenia*, is based on an incident from Sidney's revision of his *Arcadia.* Although in Glapthorne's play Argalus still dies for honour and Parthenia for love, thus preserving the high heroics of Sidney's romantic epic, the suitor Demagorgas is reduced to a *miles gloriosus*, and the tragic main plot is filled out with a comic sub-plot of some proportion and with the masque-like pleasantries of pastoral song and dance. The tragedy *Albertus Wallenstein* concerns both the politics of the rebellion of Wallenstein from the German Emperor Ferdinand the Second and the romance of Albertus, Wallenstein's son, with Isabella, one of his mother's ladies-in-waiting. And *The Hollander* can't decide whether it is romantic comedy, the subject of the main plot, satire against the affectations of the "Galland naturaliz'd Dutchman" Sconce, the subject of its title, or simply farce.

Glapthorne's plays are interesting primarily for historical rather than for artistic reasons. Glapthorne seems to grasp at successful theatrical ideas from many earlier English Renaissance dramatists. Most noticeably, he looks back to Jonson for his comedies, especially for the ubiquitous humour characters, and back to Shirley, Fletcher, or Lyly for the florid surface and decorated pathos of his style. Yet the comedies adumbrate weakly the glittering intelligence of Restoration drama. Such a play is *Wit in a Constable*, a comedy of some vitality set in London and in fact revived, although perhaps unsuccessfully, in 1662. Two sets of suitors vie for the hands of the young cousins, Grace and Clare. The would-be's, Sir Timothy Shallowit and Jeremy Holdfast, have come to London, the one from the country and the other from Cambridge. Both pretend to the true wit needed to win the ladies, but Jeremy's flights into pedantry are matched by Sir Timothy's lapses into boorishness. The successful suitors are Thorowgood and Valentine, young gentlemen as well as friends. However, the lovers' difficulties are resolved not by their gentle intelligence but by Constable Busie and his common-sense wit. As the title suggests *Wit in a Constable* has a "citizen" bias, despite the more elevated status of the main characters.

The language of Glapthorne's plays is their major fault. The style is too often poetic, not dramatic. Glapthorne's plots have much theatrical possibility, his sense of the scene division is intelligent, and the threads of his sub-plots are interwoven ingeniously enough to provide variety and interest. But his characters do not talk; they recite. Too often Glapthorne clothes his simple thoughts in stiff and ill-fitting conceits, especially in those drawn from nature experienced through books.

The same stultifying inventiveness mars his poems. The subjects and forms of the poems – love poems to an imaginary mistress Lucinda, elegies or epistles to his friends – suggest an interest in the matter and manner of Latin literature common to many cavalier poets, including Glapthorne's "noble Friend and Gossip, Captaine Richard Lovelace." The Royalist sympathies which this dedication implies are also indicated by the curious poem "White-Hall," which employs the palace itself as narrator of the royal history of Tudor and Stuart England. The building itself is personified as the abandoned wife of Charles I, then in battle against his subjects, soon to be beheaded.

—Daniel DeMatteis

GLASPELL, Susan (Keating).   American. Born in Davenport, Iowa, 1 July 1882. Educated at Drake University, Des Moines, Iowa, 1897–99, Ph.B. 1899; did graduate work at the University of Chicago, 1903. Married 1) the writer George Cram Cook in 1913 (died, 1923); 2) the writer Norman Matson in 1925 (divorced 1931). State House and Legislative Reporter, *Daily News* and *The Capital*, Des Moines, 1899–1901; returned to Davenport, 1901, to concentrate on writing: supported himself by writing stories for *Harper's*, the *American*, and other magazines; moved to Provincetown, Massachusetts, 1911; with her husband helped found the Provincetown Players, 1915, and wrote for the company, in Provincetown and New York, 1916–22; lived in Greece, 1922–24. Recipient: Pulitzer Prize, 1931. *Died 27 July 1948.*

PUBLICATIONS

Plays

> *Suppressed Desires*, with George Cram Cook (produced 1915).   1916.
> *Trifles* (produced 1916).   1916.
> *The People* (produced 1917).   1918.
> *Close the Book* (produced 1917).   With *The People*, 1918.
> *The Outside* (produced 1917).   In *Plays*, 1920.
> *Woman's Honor* (produced 1918).   In *Plays*, 1920.
> *Tickless Time*, with George Cram Cook (produced 1918).   In *Plays*, 1920.
> *Bernice* (produced 1919).   In *Plays*, 1920.
> *Plays*.   1920; as *Trifles and Other Short Plays*, 1926.
> *Inheritors* (produced 1921).   1921.
> *The Verge* (produced 1921).   1922.
> *Chains of Dew* (produced 1922).
> *The Comic Artist*, with Norman Matson (produced 1928).   1927.
> *Alison's House* (produced 1930).   1930.

Fiction

> *The Glory of the Conquered.*   1909.
> *The Visioning.*   1911.
> *Lifted Masks: Stories.*   1912.
> *Fidelity.*   1915.
> *A Jury of Her Peers* (stories).   1927.
> *Brook Evans.*   1928; as *The Right to Love,* 1930.
> *The Fugitive's Return.*   1929.
> *Ambrose Holt and Family.*   1931.
> *The Morning Is near Us.*   1939.
> *Cherished and Shared of Old.*   1940.
> *Norma Ashe.*   1942.
> *Judd Rankin's Daughter.*   1945; as *Prodigal Giver,* 1946.

Other

> *The Road to the Temple* (on George Cram Cook).   1927.

> Editor, *Greek Coins* (verse), by George Cram Cook.   1925.

Reading List: *Glaspell* by Arthur E. Waterman, 1966.

*   *   *

When the Provincetown Players opened a subscription theatre in Greenwich Village in 1916, their two major playwrights were Eugene O'Neill and Susan Glaspell. With her husband, George Cram "Jig" Cook, Glaspell was a founder of the Provincetown Players and, before his dissatisfaction with the direction the theatre was taking and their departure for Greece in 1922, she was a substantial contributor to the success of the group. Although she lacked O'Neill's theatricality, at this time, she was much closer to O'Neill in his concern for intense, meaningful drama than any of their contemporaries.

An intelligent and perceptive person, confident in her art and the values she found meaningful, she was most impressive in her thoughtful and theatrically effective one-act plays. *Suppressed Desires* (written with Cook) is a clever satire on the idea of complete freedom in self-expression. *Trifles* combines mystery with a penetrating understanding of a woman's character in a single tense scene. Other one-act plays performed by the Provincetown Players were *The People, The Outside,* and *Woman's Honor.*

Her full-length plays, all of which reveal a liberal woman's approach with force and dignity, never quite reached the quality she seemed destined to produce. *Bernice,* although too conversational and contrived, shows the power and thoughtful ingenuity of a loving wife to effect a dramatic and sustaining change upon her husband after her death. One of her most popular plays from this period is *Inheritors,* which dramatizes the problems of a mid-western college in carrying on the liberal ideas of its founder over the conservatism of its present Board of Trustees. It is mainly in *The Verge* that Glaspell approached the emotional struggles that determined O'Neill's playwriting. Searching for an understanding of herself, the heroine is on the "verge" both of insanity and that answer which eludes her. In language and idea the play suggests a power which was never completely dramatized.

After her husband's death in Greece, Glaspell wrote a moving and interesting biography-autobiography of their work together in theatre and his last years – *The Road to the Temple.* She also produced a number of short stories and novels which did little for her reputation as a writer. Her single outstanding work of this later period was the Pulitzer Prize-winning

Alison's House, a thought-provoking and beautifully expressed play based on Emily Dickinson's life. Her major contribution to American drama and theatre, however, rests almost entirely on those years of the Provincetown Players, an extremely important time in the growth of American drama.

—Walter J. Meserve

GOLDSMITH, Oliver. Irish. Born in Pallas, near Ballymahon, Longford, 10 November 1728. Educated at the village school in Lissoy, West Meath, 1734–37; Elphin School, 1738; a school in Athlone, 1739–41, and in Edgeworthstown, Longford, 1741–44; Trinity College, Dublin (sizar), 1745–49 (Smyth exhibitioner, 1747), B.A. 1749; studied medicine at the University of Edinburgh, 1752–53; travelled on the Continent, in Switzerland, Italy, and France, 1753–56, and may have obtained a medical degree. Settled in London, 1756; tried unsuccessfully to support himself as a physician in Southwark; worked as an usher in Dr. Milner's classical academy in Peckham, 1756, and as a writer for Ralph Griffiths, proprietor of the *Monthly Review*, 1757–58; Editor, *The Bee*, 1759; contributed to the *British Magazine*, 1760; Editor, *The Lady's Magazine*, 1761; also worked for the publisher Edward Newbery: worked as a proof-reader and preface writer, contributed to the *Public Ledger*, 1760, and prepared a *Compendium of Biography*, 7 volumes, 1762; after 1763 earned increasingly substantial sums from his own writing; one of the founder members of Samuel Johnson's Literary Club, 1764. *Died 4 April 1774.*

PUBLICATIONS

Collections

> *Collected Letters*, edited by Katharine C. Balderston. 1928.
> *Collected Works*, edited by Arthur Friedman. 5 vols., 1966.
> *Poems and Plays*, edited by Tom Davis. 1975.

Plays

> *The Good Natured Man* (produced 1768). 1768.
> *The Grumbler*, from a translation by Charles Sedley of a work of Brueys (produced 1773). Edited by Alice I. P. Wood, 1931.
> *She Stoops to Conquer; or, The Mistakes of a Night* (produced 1773). 1773; edited by Arthur Friedman, 1968.
> *Threnodia Augustalis, Sacred to the Memory of the Princess Dowager of Wales*, music by Mattia Vento (produced 1772). 1772.
> *The Captivity* (oratorio), in *Miscellaneous Works*. 1820.

Fiction

> *The Vicar of Wakefield.* 1766; edited by Arthur Friedman, 1974.

Verse

The Traveller; or, A Prospect of Society. 1764.
Poems for Young Ladies in Three Parts, Devotional, Moral, and Entertaining. 1767.
The Deserted Village. 1770.
Retaliation. 1774.
The Haunch of Venison: A Poetical Epistle to Lord Clare. 1776.

Other

An Enquiry into the Present State of Polite Learning in Europe. 1759.
The Bee. 1759.
The Mystery Revealed. 1762.
The Citizen of the World; or, Letters from a Chinese Philosopher Residing in London to His Friends in the East. 2 vols., 1762.
The Life of Richard Nash of Bath. 1762.
An History of England in a Series of Letters from a Nobleman to His Son. 2 vols., 1764.
An History of the Martyrs and Primitive Fathers of the Church. 1764.
Essays. 1765; revised edition, 1766.
The Present State of the British Empire in Europe, America, Africa, and Asia. 1768.
The Roman History, from the Foundation of the City of Rome to the Destruction of the Western Empire. 2 vols., 1769; abridged edition, 1772.
The Life of Thomas Parnell. 1770.
The Life of Henry St. John, Lord Viscount Bolingbroke. 1770.
The History of England, from the Earliest Times to the Death of George II. 4 vols., 1771; abridged edition, 1774.
The Grecian History, from the Earliest State to the Death of Alexander the Great. 2 vols., 1774.
An History of the Earth and Animated Nature. 8 vols., 1774.
A Survey of Experimental Philosophy, Considered in Its Present State of Improvement. 2 vols., 1776.

Editor, The Beauties of English Poesy. 2 vols., 1767.

Translator, The Memoirs of a Protestant, by J. Marteilhe. 2 vols., 1758; edited by A. Dobson, 1895.
Translator, Plutarch's Lives. 4 vols., 1762.
Translator, A Concise History of Philosophy and Philosophers, by M. Formey. 1766.
Translator, The Comic Romance of Scarron. 2 vols., 1775.

Bibliography: Goldsmith Bibliographically and Biographically Considered by Temple Scott, 1928.

Reading List: Goldsmith by Ralph Wardle, 1957; Goldsmith by Clara M. Kirk, 1967; Goldsmith: A Georgian Study by Ricardo Quintana, 1967; Life of Goldsmith by Henry A. Dobson, 1972; Goldsmith by A. Lytton Sells, 1974; Goldsmith: The Critical Heritage, edited by George S. Rousseau, 1974; The Notable Man: The Life and Times of Goldsmith by John Ginger, 1977.

*   *   *

Oliver Goldsmith's reputation is made up of paradox. His blundering, improvident nature nevertheless won him the loyalty and friendship of figures like Dr. Johnson, Sir Joshua Reynolds, and Edmund Burke. While in society he was a buffoon, his writing testifies to personal charm and an ironic awareness of his own and others' absurdity. Critical opinion of his work similarly varies from acceptance of Goldsmith as the sensitive apologist for past values to appraisal of him as an accomplished social and literary satirist. Indeed, his work can operate on both levels, a fact perhaps recognised by the young Jane Austen in her *Juvenilia* when she took Goldsmith's abridgements of history for young persons as a model for her own exercise in irony.

Drifting into authorship after a mis-spent youth (as Macaulay notes in his disapproving *Life*), Goldsmith turned to hack writing, contributing articles to the *Monthly* and *Critical Reviews* from 1757. His more ambitious *Inquiry into the Present State of Polite Learning* of 1759 won him the reputation of a man of learning and elegant expression. In this last essay he reveals his fundamental dislike of the contemporary cult of sensibility which was to generate not only his own "laughing" form of comedy in the drama but also *The Vicar of Wakefield*. Meeting Smollett, then editor of the *British Magazine*, Goldsmith was encouraged to expand his contributions to literary journalism. He produced the weekly periodical *The Bee*; many papers collected and published in 1765 and 1766 as *Essays*; and, most important, the "Chinese Letters" of 1760–61 collected as *The Citizen of the World*.

The "citizen" is, of course, an Oriental traveller, observing the fashions and foibles of the *bon ton* in London with wide-eyed innocence that carries within it implicit comment and criticism not unmixed with humour. The device was borrowed from the French, notably Montesquieu's *Lettres Persanes* (1721). In each essay the absurdities of behaviour are marked, the whole inter-woven by continuing narratives around the Man in Black, Beau Tibbs, the story of Hingo and Zelis, for instance. In many ways the ironies, improbabilities, and apparent innocence of the Chinese letters prefigure the extended prose romance of *The Vicar of Wakefield*.

This could be seen as Goldsmith's answer to Sterne's *Tristram Shandy* (1759). He had attacked Sterne's sentimental fiction as "obscene and pert" in *The Citizen*; in many ways *The Vicar* parodies Sterne's novel but with such a light hand that it has been taken on face value for many generations as the tale indeed of a family "generous, credulous, simple, and inoffensive." However, Goldsmith early establishes for the observant the manifest danger of complacency in such apparent virtues. His Yorkshire parson displays the moral duplicity of a feeling heart, for Goldsmith's approach to life and art is the opposite of Sterne's relativism and dilettante values.

Goldsmith's moral seriousness (while softened by genial good humour) dominates that other work now considered "classic," *The Deserted Village*. His earlier sortie in the genre of topographical/philosophical verse, *The Traveller*, did much to establish his reputation. It is an accomplished use of convention, where the poet climbs an eminence only to have his mind expanded into contemplation of universal questions. In *The Deserted Village*, however, the poet comes to terms with a particular social problem in a particular landscape as opposed to former abstract musings above imaginary solitudes. "Sweet Auburn" can be identified closely with the village of Nuneham Courtenay, where the local land-owner had recently moved the whole community out in order to extend and improve his landscape park. The fact becomes a catalyst for Goldsmith in a consideration of where aesthetic values and irresponsible wealth lead: a symbol taken from life and not from poetic convention.

Goldsmith's rhymed couplets have grace and ease, particularly when his verse is unlaboured, as in the prologues and epilogues to his own and others' plays. The charm and humour of these can be observed in his later poem *Retaliation*, which has a pointed raciness born out of the settling of personal scores. Always the butt of jokes in the group known as The Club, here he gets his own back with a series of comic epitaphs for the other members. Notable is that for Garrick – "On the stage he was natural, simple, affecting;/Twas only that when he was off he was acting" – but he labels himself the "gooseberry fool."

As a dramatist, Goldsmith exploited both verbal dexterity and the comedy of situation, looking back to Shakespeare in the rejection of the so-called genteel comedy of Hugh Kelly or

Richard Cumberland. Affected and strained in tone and action, the drama of sentiment offered to Goldsmith nothing of the "nature and humour" that he saw as the first principle of theatre. However he might despise the sentimental school, he cannot avoid using some of its conventions, the good-natured hero, of course, and the device of paired lovers, but the way these are treated is particular to himself. Together with Sheridan, Goldsmith exploits the theatrical unreality of comedy, using the stage as a separate world of experience with its own laws and therefore demanding the suspension of disbelief in order that farcical unreality might unmask farcical reality. His character Honeydew in *The Good Natured Man* has something in common with Charles Surface in *School for Scandal*, but the tone of Goldsmith's comedy is less brittle than that of Sheridan. This mellow tone, a fundamental wholesomeness, is magnificently encapsulated in *She Stoops to Conquer*.

Goldsmith's first play met with a poor response, as being too "low" in its matter (especially the bailiffs scene), and, though *She Stoops to Conquer* was open to similar criticism, its riotous humour overcame prejudice. In short, it was good theatre and this is testified by its continuing popularity in production. Characters like Tony Lumpkin, Mrs. Hardcastle, and the old Squire have become literary personalities, while the pivot of the plot, Marlow's loss of diffidence in apparently more relaxed circumstances, holds true to human nature. The character of Kate is a liberated heroine in the Shakespearean style, contrasted as in the older comedy with a foil. One is able to relate Goldsmith's "laughing" comedy to that of Shakespeare in many ways, for the Lord of Misrule dominates both.

The range of Goldsmith's work is touched by this same humour and sensitivity, the good heart that is so easily squandered as he himself acknowledged in *The Good Natured Man*, but is just as easily extended with purpose to the reader. As Walter Scott observed, no man contrived "so well to reconcile us to human nature."

—B. C. Oliver-Morden

GRANVILLE-BARKER, Harley. See **BARKER, Harley Granville-.**

GRAY, Simon. English. Born on Hayling Island, Hampshire, 21 October 1936. Educated at Westminster School, London; Dalhousie University, Halifax, Nova Scotia, Canada, 1954–57, B.A. (honours) in English 1957; Trinity College, Cambridge, 1958–61, B.A. (honours) in English 1961. Married Beryl Mary Kevern in 1965; one son and one daughter. Harper-Wood Student, St. John's College, Cambridge, 1961–62; Research Student, Trinity College, Cambridge, 1962–63; Lecturer in English, University of British Columbia, Vancouver, 1963–64; Supervisor in English, Trinity College, Cambridge, 1964–66. Since 1966, Lecturer in English, Queen Mary College, London. Since 1964, Editor of *Delta* magazine, Cambridge. Recipient: *Evening Standard* award, 1972, 1976; New York Drama Critics Circle Award, 1977. Lives in London.

PUBLICATIONS

Plays

Molly (as *Death of a Teddy Bear*, televised 1967; revised version, as *Molly*, produced
   1977).   In *The Rear Column and Other Plays*, 1978.
Wise Child (produced 1967).   1968.
Sleeping Dog (televised 1967).   1968.
Spoiled (televised 1968; produced 1970).   1971.
Dutch Uncle (produced 1969).   1969.
The Idiot, from a novel by Dostoevsky (produced 1970).   1971.
Butley (produced 1971).   1971.
Man in a Side-Car (televised 1971).   In *The Rear Column and Others Plays*, 1978.
Dog Days (produced 1975).   1976.
Otherwise Engaged (produced 1975).   1975.
Plaintiffs and Defendants (televised 1975).   In *Otherwise Engaged and Other Plays*,
   1976.
Two Sundays (televised 1975).   In *Otherwise Engaged and Other Plays*, 1976.
Otherwise Engaged and Other Plays.   1976.
The Rear Column (produced 1978).   In *The Rear Column and Other Plays*, 1978.
The Rear Column and Other Plays.   1978.

Screenplay: *Butley*, 1975.

Television Plays: *The Caramel Crisis*, 1966; *Death of a Teddy Bear*, 1967; *A Way with
the Ladies*, 1967; *Sleeping Dog*, 1967; *Spoiled*, 1968; *Pig in a Poke*, 1969; *The Dirt on
Lucy Lane*, 1969; *Style of the Countess*, 1970; *The Princess*, 1970; *Man in a Side-Car*,
1971; *Plaintiffs and Defendants*, 1975; *Two Sundays*, 1975.

Fiction

Colmain.   1963.
Simple People.   1965.
Little Portia.   1967.
A Comeback for Stark.   1969.

Other

Editor, with Keith Walker, *Selected English Prose*.   1967.

*   *   *

> Beth: In other words, you do know.
> Simon: In other words, can't we confine
> ourselves to the other words.

   Simon Gray's characters wear literal disguises or play witty verbal games to hide their
unexpressed frustrations; they convey their unhappiness with the current state of England by
a nostalgia for the past; and, though often married, they lead unconventional sex lives. *Wise*

Child, Gray's first play, depicted a heterosexual criminal wearing female garb to elude the police, while his young associate's wigs and games revealed a desire to revert to childhood and make the criminal his "Mum." Murder and a sexual tangle like a grim parody of *As You Like It* reinforce the ciminal's indictment of the English ("the beggars of Europe as we are now"), however skewed his perspective. In this play and his next, *Dutch Uncle*, Gray's wit seems forced from unsophisticated characters, and he uneasily mixes cartoon-like farce with grotesque comedy. *Dutch Uncle* focuses on the impotent Mr. Godboy, who has miscast himself as a literal lady-killer. Again, Godboy seems an ironical spokesman for the strength of the English past: "Five years ago there wasn't a man in this country wouldn't have laid his life down for Winnie, and glad to do it."

Gray turned to more literate characters in his dramatization of Dostoevsky's *The Idiot*, but eliminated much of their loquacious philosophizing that gave the plot meaning. Characteristically he translates Dostoevsky's young radicals into the students who suggest a bleak present and bleaker future in many of Gray's works: "Louts, Madame! That is to say, students." His next play, *Spoiled*, confronts what the stage directions call "the comfortable, middle-class, intellectual" world of his best plays. The married protagonist, a French teacher, tutors a working-class youth while courting him obliquely with verses from Mallarmé in Gray's funniest, most complex writing thus far. The teacher's Pygmalion-like role foreshadows Ben Butley's shaping the taste of his former male student Joey, while the soured vulnerability of middle-class marriage prefigures the heterosexual Simon Hench's adventures with young girls in *Otherwise Engaged*.

The dazzling wit of Butley, a university literature teacher, gives the illusion of order to the messy reality of his life and hides his confused sexuality. He forgets names, continually and insultingly fusing Joey's new lover Reg with his predecessor Ted, presumably to deny Reg any meaning in Joey's life. Though both Joey and the audience get caught up in Ben's power to transform reality, ultimately reality triumphs: Reg makes Joey move from both Ben's office and flat. And despite Ben's Wildean "After all, a man's bound to be judged by his wife's husband," Ben's wife will marry "the most boring man in London," whose novel will be published by Reg, while Ben's own book on T. S. Eliot remains unfinished. Thus, the other characters occasionally best Ben, who hides behind his "marriage," probably non-sexual: "Reg: ... our Joey will be moving out of figures of speech into matters of fact. Ours will be too much like a marriage to be a metaphor." Helped immeasurably by the warmth of Alan Bates's acting, both Ben and Simon Hench (in *Otherwise Engaged*) tricked the audience into equating wit with strength, until the action forces a re-evaluation of the characters. Ben finally refuses to repeat the Joey pattern with a new student: "You're not what I mean at all, not what I mean at all. I'm too old for the likes of you." But this echo of Eliot reinforces Ben's domination by the English tradition.

Simon Hench prefers to ignore his wife's infidelity, though even his epigrammatic wit cannot disguise her pregnancy. Like Ben, he pounces on verbal ambiguities to trivialize or over-complicate real problems like the loss of his wife. He acknowledges romantic passion only through a new recording of *Parsifal*; he spends the entire play trying to hear the music, and when, just before the final curtain, the opening bars "fill the theatre," they mock his reduction of disorderly passion to the artistic statement of someone else. The audience shares Simon's ridicule of the unhygienic, uneducated student Dave, but it becomes clear that Simon's concern with elegant surfaces allows too little attention to the moral content of anything (Simon, like other Gray adulterers, washes off the "stench" of his affairs with quick showers at his club). Since a character is writing a book on British sadism in colonial Africa (the subject of Gray's play *The Rear Column*), Simon may no longer be able to retreat behind a belief in the English past or European art.

Dog Days shares themes and characters with *Otherwise Engaged* and the television plays *Plaintiffs and Defendants* and *Two Sundays*. The wit of an adulterous publisher hides familiar middle-aged terrors; he impresses his monogamous brother with tales of seducing the daughters of Gide and Cocteau, but fails in his one attempt at infidelity. Though Gray's wit cuts as deep as ever, the play is a bit thin; there are too few characters to provide the social and psychological interplay of *Butley* and *Otherwise Engaged*, and the protagonist is exposed beyond future exploration.

The homosexuality in Gray's plays provides a realistic index to the sophisticated London-Oxbridge world they chronicle, but homosexuality pervades the obviously non-U *Wise Child* as well. The theme is crucially linked to Gray's disguise motif: Joey and his lover apparently fool Reg's family and friends in the hearty masculine world of Reg's hometown. That sexual identity can assume convincing disguises here and in *Wise Child* raises questions about its real nature, and about other forms of behavior or belief, like the obsession with England's past. Deeper even than his characters' habit of mockery, belief in this past, perhaps the final illusion Ben and Simon adopt, helps blot out their chaotic present. Gray, the chronicler of the clever and bitter publishers and teachers who shape England's current intellectual life and precariously support its values, has peopled his world with the most savagely witty characters on the contemporary stage.

—Burton Kendle

GREEN, Paul (Eliot).   American. Born in Lillington, North Carolina, 17 March 1894. Educated at Buies Creek Academy, North Carolina, graduated 1914; University of North Carolina, Chapel Hill, A.B. 1921, graduate study 1921–22; Cornell University, Ithaca, New York, 1922–23. Served in the United States Army Engineers, 1917–19: Lieutenant. Married Elizabeth Atkinson Lay in 1922; four children. Lecturer, then Associate Professor of Philosophy, 1923–39, Professor of Dramatic Arts, 1939–44, and Professor of Radio, Television, and Motion Pictures, 1962–63, University of North Carolina. Editor, *The Reviewer* magazine, Chapel Hill, 1925. President, National Folk Festival, 1934–35; President, National Theatre Conference, 1940–42; President, North Carolina State Literary and Historical Association, 1942–43; Member of the United States Executive Committee, and Member of the National Commission, UNESCO, 1950–53, and United States Delegate to the UNESCO Conference, Paris, 1951; Director, American National Theatre Company, 1959–61; Delegate to the International Conference on the Performing Arts, Athens, 1962. Recipient: Pulitzer Prize, 1927; Guggenheim Fellowship, 1928, 1929; Clare M. Senie Drama Study Award, 1939; Freedoms Foundation George Washington Medal, 1951, 1956, 1966; Susanne M. Davis Award, 1966. Litt.D.: Western Reserve University, Cleveland, 1941; Davidson College, North Carolina, 1948; University of North Carolina, 1956; Berea College, Kentucky, 1957; University of Louisville, Kentucky, 1957; Campbell College, Buies Creek, North Carolina, 1969; Moravian College, Bethlehem, Pennsylvania, 1976; D.F.A.: North Carolina School of the Arts, Winston-Salem, 1976. Member, National Institute of Arts and Letters, 1941. Lives in Chapel Hill, North Carolina.

PUBLICATIONS

Plays

   Surrender to the Enemy (produced 1917).
   The Last of the Lowries (produced 1920).   In *The Lord's Will and Other Carolina Plays*, 1925.
   The Long Night, in *Carolina Magazine*, 1920.

Granny Boling, in *Drama*, August–September 1921.

Old Wash Lucas (The Miser) (produced 1921). In *The Lord's Will and Other Carolina Plays*, 1925.

The Old Man of Edenton (produced 1921). In *The Lord's Will and Other Carolina Plays*, 1925.

The Lord's Will (produced 1922). In *The Lord's Will and Other Carolina Plays*, 1925.

Blackbeard, with Elizabeth Lay Green (produced 1922). In *The Lord's Will and Other Carolina Plays*, 1925.

White Dresses (produced 1923). In *Lonesome Road*, 1926.

Wrack P'int (produced 1923).

Sam Tucker, in *Poet Lore*, Summer 1923; revised version, as *Your Fiery Furnace*, in *Lonesome Road*, 1926.

Fixin's, with Erma Green (produced 1924). 1934.

The No 'Count Boy (produced 1925). In *The Lord's Will and Other Carolina Plays*, 1925; revised (white) version, 1953.

In Aunt Mahaly's Cabin: A Negro Melodrama (produced 1925). 1925.

The Lord's Will and Other Carolina Plays. 1925.

Quare Medicine (produced 1925). In *In the Valley and Other Carolina Plays*, 1928.

The Man Who Died at Twelve O'Clock (produced 1925). 1927.

In Abraham's Bosom (produced 1926). In *The Field God, and In Abraham's Bosom*, 1927.

Lonesome Road: Six Plays for the Negro Theatre (includes *In Abraham's Bosom*, one-act version; *White Dresses; The Hot Iron; The Prayer Meeting; The End of the Row; Your Fiery Furnace*). 1926.

The Hot Iron, in *Lonesome Road*. 1926; revised version, as *Lay This Body Down* (produced 1972), in *Wings for to Fly*, 1959.

The Field God (produced 1927). In *The Field God, and In Abraham's Bosom*, 1927.

The Field God, and In Abraham's Bosom. 1927.

Bread and Butter Come to Supper. 1928; as *Chair Endowed* (produced 1954).

In the Valley and Other Carolina Plays (includes *Quare Medicine, Supper for the Dead, Saturday Night, The Man Who Died at Twelve O'Clock, In Aunt Mahaly's Cabin, The No 'Count Boy, The Man on the House, The Picnic, Unto Such Glory, The Goodbye*). 1928.

Supper for the Dead (produced 1954). In *In the Valley and Other Carolina Plays*, 1928.

Unto Such Glory (produced 1936). In *In the Valley and Other Carolina Plays*, 1928.

The Goodbye (produced 1954). In *In the Valley and Other Carolina Plays*, 1928.

Blue Thunder; or, The Man Who Married a Snake, in *One Act Plays for Stage and Study*. 1928.

Old Christmas. 1928.

The House of Connelly (produced 1931). In *The House of Connelly and Other Plays*, 1931; revised version (produced 1959), in *Five Plays of the South*, 1963.

The House of Connelly and Other Plays. 1931.

Potter's Field (produced 1934). In *The House of Connelly and Other Plays*, 1931; revised version, as *Roll Sweet Chariot: A Symphonic Play of the Negro People*, music by Dolphe Martin (produced 1934), 1935.

Tread the Green Grass, music by Lamar Stringfield (produced 1932). In *The House of Connelly and Other Plays*, 1931.

Shroud My Body Down (produced 1934). 1935; revised version, as *The Honeycomb*, 1972.

The Enchanted Maze: The Story of a Modern Student in Dramatic Form (produced 1935). 1939.

Hymn to the Rising Sun (produced 1936). 1936.

Johnny Johnson: The Biography of a Common Man, music by Kurt Weill (produced 1936). 1937; revised version, 1972.

The Southern Cross (produced 1936).   1938.

The Lost Colony (produced 1937).   1937; revised version, 1939, 1946, 1954, 1962.

Alma Mater, in *The Best One-Act Plays of 1938,* edited by Margaret Mayorga.   1938.

Out of the South: The Life of a People in Dramatic Form (includes *The House of Connelly, The Field God, In Abraham's Bosom, Potter's Field, Johnny Johnson, The Lost Colony, The No 'Count Boy, Saturday Night, Quare Medicine, The Hot Iron, Unto Such Glory, Supper for the Dead, The Man Who Died at Twelve O'Clock, White Dresses, Hymn to the Rising Sun).* 1939.

The Critical Year: A One-Act Sketch of American History and the Beginning of the Constitution. 1939.

Franklin and the King. 1939.

The Highland Call: A Symphonic Play of American History (produced 1939).   1941.

Native Son (The Biography of a Young American), with Richard Wright, from the novel by Wright (produced 1941).   1941.

A Start in Life (broadcast 1941).   In *The Free Company Presents,* edited by James Boyd, 1941; as *Fine Wagon,* in *Wings for to Fly,* 1959.

The Common Glory: A Symphonic Drama of American History (produced 1947).   1948; revised version, 1975.

Faith of Our Fathers (produced 1950).

Peer Gynt, from the play by Ibsen (produced 1951).   1951.

The Seventeenth Star (produced 1953).

Serenata, with Josefina Niggli (produced 1953).

Carmen, from the libretto by H. Meilhac and L. Halévy, music by Bizet (produced 1954).

Salvation on a String (includes *The Goodbye, Chair Endowed, Supper for the Dead, The No 'Count Boy)* (produced 1954).

Wilderness Road: A Symphonic Outdoor Drama (produced 1955; revised version, produced 1972).   1956.

The Founders: A Symphonic Outdoor Drama (produced 1957).   1957.

The Confederacy: A Symphonic Outdoor Drama Based on the Life of General Robert E. Lee (produced 1958).   1959.

The Stephen Foster Story: A Symphonic Drama Based on the Life and Music of the Composer (produced 1959).   1960.

Wings for to Fly: Three Plays of Negro Life, Mostly for the Ear But Also for the Eye (includes *The Thirsting Heart, Lay This Body Down, Fine Wagon).* 1959.

The Thirsting Heart (produced 1971).   In *Wings for to Fly,* 1959.

Five Plays of the South (includes *The House of Connelly, In Abraham's Bosom, Johnny Johnson, Hymn to the Rising Sun, White Dresses).* 1963.

Cross and Sword: A Symphonic Drama of the Spanish Settlement of Florida (produced 1965).   1966.

The Sheltering Plaid. 1965.

Texas: A Symphonic Outdoor Drama of American Life (produced 1966).   1967.

Sing All a Green Willow (produced 1969).

Trumpet in the Land (produced 1970).   1972.

Drumbeats in Georgia: A Symphonic Drama of the Founding of Georgia by James Edward Oglethorpe (produced 1973).

Louisiana Cavalier: A Symphonic Drama of the 18th Century French and Spanish Struggle for the Settling of Louisiana (produced 1976).

We the People: A Symphonic Drama of George Washington and the Establishment of the United States Government (produced 1976).

Screenplays: *Cabin in the Cotton,* 1932; *State Fair,* 1933; *Dr. Bull,* 1933; *Voltaire,* 1933; *The Rosary,* 1933; *Carolina,* 1934; *David Harum,* 1934; *Time Out of Mind,* 1947; *Roseanna McCoy,* 1949; *Broken Soil,* 1949; *Red Shoes Run Faster,* 1949.

Radio Play: *A Start in Life*, 1941.

Fiction

Wide Fields (stories). 1928.
The Laughing Pioneer: A Sketch of Country Life. 1932.
This Body the Earth. 1935.
Salvation on a String and Other Tales of the South. 1946.
Dog on the Sun: A Volume of Stories. 1949.
Words and Ways: Stories and Incidents from My Cape Fear Valley Folklore Collection. 1968.
Home to My Valley (stories). 1970.
Land of Nod and Other Stories: A Volume of Black Stories. 1976.

Verse

The Lost Colony Song-Book. 1938.
The Highland Call Song-Book. 1941.
Song in the Wilderness. 1947.
The Common Glory Song-Book. 1951.
Texas Song-Book. 1967.
Texas Forever. 1967.

Other

Contemporary American Literature: A Study of Fourteen Outstanding American Writers, with Elizabeth Lay Green. 1925; revised edition, 1927.
The Hawthorn Tree: Some Papers and Letters on Life and the Theatre. 1943.
Forever Growing: Some Notes on a Credo for Teachers. 1945.
Dramatic Heritage (essays). 1953.
Drama and the Weather: Some Notes and Papers on Life and the Theatre. 1958.
Plough and Furrow: Some Essays and Papers on Life and the Theatre. 1963.

Reading List: *Green* by Barrett H. Clark, 1928; *Green of Chapel Hill* by Agatha Boyd Adams, 1951; *Green* by Walter S. Lazenby, 1970; *Green* by Vincent S. Kenny, 1971.

*   *   *

Paul Green's career as a playwright can be divided conveniently into four overlapping periods. Utilizing the history, dialect, superstitions, customs, and beliefs of both white and black inhabitants of his native region in eastern North Carolina, he began by writing short realistic folkplays, comedies as well as tragedies. Noticeable from the outset was a compassion for society's expendibles, those cast-offs who, though victims of social injustice, held within them the dreams and hopes common to all mankind. The full-length *In Abraham's Bosom*, its protagonist a luckless black schoolteacher, was an extended treatment of a one-act play. It was followed on Broadway by *The Field God*, dealing with the oppressive religious orthodoxy among back-country whites.

Tread the Green Grass, a deliberate experiment, turned from realism toward a mythic non-realistic folk drama, but retained the kind of rustic characters who were now his special province. Green's stylized blend of pantomime, dance, ritual, dream sequences, puppetlike movements, fantasy and legend, with music an integral part of the play as with the Greeks, expanded, he believed, the accepted concepts of time and space on the stage. For those plays by him synthesizing the theatrical arts – plays like *Roll Sweet Chariot* (earlier title, *Potter's Field*), *Shroud My Body Down*, and *Sing All a Green Willow* – Green coined the term "symphonic drama," intending apparently to devise an American *Gesamtkunstwerk*.

Meanwhile he did not abandon the commercial theater. *The House of Connelly*, a dramatization of the fluctuating conditions among aristocrats and "poor whites" in the post-Civil War South, conformed to Broadway standards of what a well-made play should be. The anti-war musical *Johnny Johnson* was a collaborative effort with Kurt Weill, and *Native Son* an adaptation of Richard Wright's tragic story of a black misfit in Chicago. For the New York stage he provided an English version of *Peer Gynt*, and for an opera theater in Colorado a translation of Carmen.

The fourth phase began in 1937 with *The Lost Colony*, an "outdoor symphonic drama" produced on the very spot where Sir Walter Ralegh's colonists landed in 1587. Applying the elements of his experimental plays, and superimposing upon an event in history a tightly drawn plot, Green was finally permitted, on the huge open-air stage, the freedom of sweeping folk dances, large choruses, and broad movements of men, women, and children. The throngs of unsophisticated ticket-buyers who attended *The Lost Colony* inspired him to establish away from Broadway a "theater of the people." In 1947 came *The Common Glory* for Virginia, then *Faith of Our Fathers* (Washington, D.C.), and other plays like *Wilderness Road* (Kentucky), *Cross and Sword* (Florida), *Texas*, and *Trumpets in the Land* (Ohio). Four decades after *The Lost Colony*, Green and his followers had used his "formula" for more than sixty similar works, spread out from the Atlantic coastline to California and Alaska. Never satisfied with his last versions, Green constantly revised the annual summertime repetitions of his outdoor plays.

—Richard Walser

GREGORY, Lady; Isabella Augusta Persse Gregory.   Irish.   Born in Roxborough, County Galway, 5 March 1852. Educated privately. Married Sir William Gregory in 1881 (died, 1892); one son. Co-Founder, with Edward Martyn and William Butler Yeats, Irish Literary Theatre, 1899, which became the Abbey Theatre, Dublin, 1904; Director, with Yeats, and with Synge (to 1909), until her death; toured the United States with the Abbey Players, 1911–13. Lived at Coole Park, County Galway. *Died 22 May 1932.*

PUBLICATIONS

Collections

Selected Plays, edited by Elizabeth Coxhead.   1962.
Works (Coole Edition), edited by T. R. Henn and Colin Smythe.   1970–
(Collected Plays) edited by Ann Saddlemyer, in *Works.*   4 vols., 1971.

Plays

The Twisting of the Rope (produced 1901).   In *Samhain,* October 1901.
A Losing Game.   1902; revised version, as *Twenty-Five* (produced 1903), in *Lost Plays*

266

of the Irish Renaissance, edited by Robert Hogan and J. F. Kilroy, 1970; revised version, as *On the Racecourse,* 1926.

The Lost Saint, in *Samhain,* October 1902.

Spreading the News (produced 1904).   In *Spreading the News ...,* 1906.

The Poorhouse, with Douglas Hyde (produced 1904).   In *Spreading the News ...,* 1906.

Kincora (produced 1905).   1905; revised version, in *Irish Folk-History Plays,* 1912.

The White Cockade (produced 1905).   1905.

Hyacinth Halvey (produced 1906).   1906.

The Rising of the Moon (produced 1906).   In *Spreading the News ...,* 1906.

Spreading the News, The Rising of the Moon, and The Poorhouse, with Douglas Hyde.   1906.

The Doctor in Spite of Himself, from a play by Molière (produced 1906).   In *The Kiltartan Molière,* 1910.

The Canavans (produced 1906).   In *Irish Folk-History Plays,* 1912.

The Gaol Gate (produced 1906).   In *Seven Short Plays,* 1909.

The Unicorn from the Stars, with W. B. Yeats, from the play *Where There Is Nothing* by Yeats (produced 1907).   In *The Unicorn from the Stars,* 1908.

The Jackdaw (produced 1907).   In *Seven Short Plays,* 1909.

Dervorgilla (produced 1907).   In *Irish Folk-History Plays,* 1912.

The Workhouse Ward (produced 1908).   In *Seven Short Plays,* 1909.

Teja, from a play by Sudermann (produced 1908).

The Rogueries of Scapin, from a play by Molière (produced 1908).   In *The Kiltartan Molière,* 1910.

The Miser, from a play by Molière (produced 1909).   In *The Kiltartan Molière,* 1910.

Seven Short Plays (includes *Spreading the News, Hyacinth Halvey, The Rising of the Moon, The Jackdaw, The Workhouse Ward, The Travelling Man, The Gaol Gate*).   1909.

The Travelling Man, with W. B. Yeats (produced 1910).   In *Seven Short Plays,* 1909.

The Image (produced 1909).   1910.

Mirandolina, from a play by Goldoni (produced 1910).   1924.

Coats (produced 1910).   In *New Comedies,* 1913.

The Full Moon (produced 1911).   1911.

The Nativity Play, from a play by Douglas Hyde (produced 1911).

The Deliverer (produced 1911).   In *Irish Folk-History Plays,* 1912.

Irish Folk-History Plays (includes *Grania, Kincora, Dervorgilla, The Canavans, The White Cockade, The Deliverer*).   2 vols., 1912.

The Bogie Man (produced 1912).   In *New Comedies,* 1913.

Damer's Gold (produced 1912).   In *New Comedies,* 1913.

McDonagh's Wife (produced 1912).   In *New Comedies,* 1913.

New Comedies (includes *The Bogie Man, The Full Moon, Coats, Damer's Gold, McDonagh's Wife*).   1913.

The Marriage, from a play by Douglas Hyde (produced 1913).

The Wrens (produced 1914).   In *The Image and Other Plays,* 1922.

Shanwalla (produced 1915).   In *The Image and Other Plays,* 1922.

The Golden Apple: A Play for Kiltartan Children (produced 1920).   1916.

Hanrahan's Oath (produced 1918).   1918.

The Dragon: A Wonder Play (produced 1919).   1920.

Aristotle's Bellows (produced 1921).   In *Three Wonder Plays,* 1922.

The Image and Other Plays (includes *The Wrens, Hanrahan's Oath, Shanwalla*).   1922.

Three Wonder Plays (includes *The Dragon, Aristotle's Bellows, The Jester*).   1922.

The Old Woman Remembers (produced 1923).

The Story Brought by Brigit: A Passion Play (produced 1924).   1924.

The Would-Be Gentleman, from a play by Molière (produced 1926).   In *Three Last Plays,* 1928.

Sancho's Master (produced 1927).   In *Three Last Plays,* 1928.
Dave (produced 1927).   In *Three Last Plays,* 1928.
Three Last Plays (includes *Sancho's Master, Dave, The Would-Be Gentleman*).   1928.
My First Play (Colman and Guaire).   1930.

Other

Arabi and His Household.   1882.
Poets and Dreamers: Studies and Translations from the Irish.   1903.
A Book of Saints and Wonders.   1906.
The Kiltartan History Book.   1909.
The Kiltartan Wonder Book.   1910.
Our Irish Theatre: A Chapter of Autobiography.   1913; revised edition, in *Works,* 1972.
Hugh Lane's Life and Achievement.   1921; as *Sir Hugh Lane: His Life and Legacy,* in *Works,* 1973.
Case for the Return of Sir Hugh Lane's Pictures to Dublin.   1926.
Coole.   1931; in *Works,* 1971.
Journals 1916–30, edited by Lennox Robinson.   1946; revised edition, in *Works,* 2 vols., 1978.
Seventy Years (1852–1922), edited by Colin Smythe.   1974.

Editor, *The Autobiography of Sir William Gregory.*   1894.
Editor, *Mr. Gregory's Letter Box 1813–30.*   1898.
Editor, *Ideals in Ireland.*   1901.
Editor, *Visions and Beliefs in the West of Ireland.*   2 vols., 1930; in *Works,* 1970.

Translator, *Cuchulain of Muirthemne: The Story of the Men of the Red Branch of Ulster.*   1902; in *Works,* 1970.
Translator, *Gods and Fighting Men: The Story of the Tuatha De Danaan and of the Fianna of Ireland.*   1904; in *Works,* 1970.
Translator, *The Kiltartan Poetry Book: Prose Translations from the Irish.*   1918.

Reading List: *Lady Gregory: A Literary Portrait,* 1961, and *Synge and Lady Gregory,* 1962, both by Elizabeth Coxhead; *In Defence of Lady Gregory, Playwright* by Ann Saddlemyer, 1966; *Me and Nu: Childhood at Coole* by Anne Gregory, 1970; *Lady Gregory* by Hazard Adams, 1973; *Interviews and Recollections* edited by E. H. Mikhail, 1977.

*   *   *

It is not easy to disentangle the role of doyenne of Coole from the prolific writer whose own publications include memoirs, biographies, political and economic pamphlets, editions of diaries and letters, poetry, essays, translations, and forty plays. Nor would Lady Gregory herself feel it was necessary, for to her the collaborations with Yeats and Douglas Hyde, the advice and sympathy offered to Synge, Joyce and O'Casey, the long struggle to bring back Hugh Lane's pictures to Ireland, the fund-raising, administration, stage management, translations and plays for the Abbey Theatre, the collecting of folklore and mythology – all were necessary aids to the restoration and reawakening of Ireland's ancient dignity and a preparation for political independence. The translation of epics and mythology, the creation of her folk-history plays, even her later children's wonder plays were conceived as educating her countrymen through simple entertainment. Even the delightful one-act comedies, written to accompany the more poetic dramas of her colleagues, reflect their creator's clear-eyed view of the universe and the judicious blending of apprenticeships both at home and abroad. In the spinning of fresh wonders by the daft, delightfully self-appraising but uncritical Cloonfolk of her early plays, she laid the foundation of all her work: simplicity of fable and action, balance and counterpoint of dialogue, easy transition from spare prose to music and poetry, delicacy of feeling interwoven with farcical horseplay, and, above all, a constant stripping away of easy sentiment. The result in all her writing is a blend of folk tradition with historical fact, inviting the listener to suspend disbelief while acknowledging the greater truth to human nature implicit in the fable. It is this unselfish sincerity of purpose which gives strength to all Lady Gregory's writing, and, on those few occasions when she wrote tragedy, even indeed in those painful evocations of Ireland's image-makers which she aptly labelled "tragic comedies," unflinching truth leads to some of her most moving work. Of the one-act tragedy *The Gaol Gate*, Frank O'Connor wrote in *The Saturday Review*, 10 December 1966, "It makes everything else written in Ireland in our time seem like the work of a foreigner."

Because of her close familiarity with the company and theatre for which she wrote, Lady Gregory's plays, if uneven in literary quality, are nearly always eminently playable; frequently, as in her Kiltartan adaptations from Molière, her experiments are more flexible and demanding than those of Yeats and Synge. Bernard Shaw once wrote of her natural gift for writing dialogue, and the fluency with which she wrote her plays and translations also provided an easy, readable style for her essays and journals. The biography of her nephew, Hugh Lane, is both dignified and simple; *Our Irish Theatre*, her account of the early years of the Abbey Theatre, including the battles she waged against censor (for Shaw's *Shewing-up of Blanco Posnet*) and militant patriot (for Synge's *Playboy of the Western World*), does author and movement credit; occasional articles, such as the description for *The Nation* of the outrages of the Black and Tans, are courageous in their outspoken honesty and accurate reporting.

She applied the same demanding code of standards to those about her, providing fine common-sense criticism and practical physical assistance not only for playwrights but for politicians, philosophers, artists, and players. But with typical generosity of spirit, she herself was proudest of the unbroken friendship and support of her life-long collaborator, W. B. Yeats, who in turn confided to his journal: "She has been to me mother, friend, sister and brother. I cannot realize the world without her – she brought to my wavering thoughts steadfast nobility." The life and the work are one.

—Ann Saddlemyer

HANKIN, St. John (Emile Clavering). English. Born in Southampton, Hampshire, 25 September 1869. Educated at Malvern College, Worcestershire (house and foundation scholar), 1883–86; Merton College, Oxford, 1886–90 (Ackroyd scholar), B.A. 1890. Married Florence Routledge in 1901. Journalist: began career as contributor to the *Saturday Review*, London, 1890–94; member of staff of the *Indian Daily News*, Calcutta, 1894–95; afterwards worked for *The Times*, London, and contributed drama criticism and miscellaneous articles to various London newspapers, and wrote two satiric essay-series for *Punch*, London; wrote for the stage from the 1890's; retired from journalism in 1905, settled in Campden, Gloucestershire, and thereafter devoted himself to writing for the stage. *Died* (by suicide) *15 June 1909.*

PUBLICATIONS

Collections

> *Dramatic Works.* 3 vols., 1912; revised edition, as *Plays*, 2 vols., 1923.

Plays

> *Andrew Patterson*, with N. Vynne (produced 1893).
> *Mr. Punch's Dramatic Sequels* (13 skits). 1901; as *Dramatic Sequels*, 1925.
> *The Two Mr. Wetherbys* (produced 1903). 1907(?).
> *The Three Daughters of M. Dupont*, from a play by Eugène Brieux (produced 1905). In *Three Plays*, by Brieux, 1911.
> *The Return of the Prodigal* (produced 1905). 1908.
> *The Charity That Began at Home* (produced 1906). 1908.
> *The Cassilis Engagement* (produced 1907). 1908.
> *The Burglar Who Failed* (produced 1908). In *Dramatic Works*, 1912.
> *The Last of the De Mullins* (produced 1908). 1909.
> *The Constant Lover* (produced 1912). 1912.
> *Thompson*, completed by George Calderon (produced 1913). 1913.

Verse

> *Lost Masterpieces and Other Verses.* 1904.

Reading List: Introduction by John Drinkwater to *Plays*, 1923; *Hankin als Dramatiker* by G. Engel, 1931 (includes bibliography); Introduction by St. John Ervine to *The Return of the Prodigal*, 1949.

*   *   *

St. John Hankin came to the theatre by way of dramatic criticism and some slight pastiche sequels to well-known plays, published in *Punch*, but little of this background is reflected in his major dramas. *The Two Mr. Wetherbys*, contrasting the marital attitudes and fortunes of two brothers, is the most tentative and least satisfying of these, but *The Return of the Prodigal* is a stylishly ironic treatment of the return to his ambitious *nouveau riche* family's bosom of Eustace, its feckless but astute black sheep, who proceeds to achieve a very comfortable accommodation with his pompous if respectable relations by means of social blackmail. In *The Charity That Began at Home* and *The Cassilis Engagement* the satire grows sharper but never grotesque, and it is accompanied by a keen compassion which extends even to the least prepossessing of the *dramatis personae*. The action in both plays involves a potentially disastrous marriage, averted in one case by the hero's recognition that the lives of pure altruism embraced by Lady Denison and her daughter Margery are full of pitfalls and only suit the chosen few, and in the other by the shrewd tactics of Mrs. Cassilis who subjects her son's unsuitable fiancée and her vulgar mother to ordeal by house-party in order to expose their inability to merge happily with their social superiors. Hankin is able to score equally off philanthropists and beneficiaries, and (more bitterly) off *parvenus* and snobs, without entirely alienating our sympathies from them, and the result is two confidently good-humoured comedies whose ethical bases still stimulate debate. Humour is virtually absent from *The Last of the De Mullins*, which explores the impact caused when Janet De Mullins, the liberated mother of an illegitimate son, returns briefly to her family home. Despite the topical indictment of patriarchal tyranny and ancestral tradition, the need for excessive recapitulation unbalances the slight plot development, and in many of Janet's ardent utterances the verbal slackness shows that even Hankin could be betrayed into substituting liberal and feminist clichés for originality of expression.

Three of Hankin's pieces were first presented by the Stage Society and two by the Vedrenne-Barker management at the Court Theatre, but it is doubtful if their author maintained an earnest belief in the social and moral function of the New Drama. However, like Shaw, he did replace the accepted romantically theatrical conventions of the previous age with the truthful presentation of the realities of actual human conduct and character. His work can perhaps be most helpfully viewed as a thorough-going extension of H. A. Jones's and Pinero's commentaries on upper- and middle-class hypocrisies and ruthlessness, unweakened in its unremittingly pragmatic conclusions by Pinero's evasive sentimentality or the complacent conservatism of Jones. Hankin was doubtless encouraged in his approach to drama by the naturalistic movement: his crises are seemingly casually motivated and credibly resolved, his characterisations are generally individualised and wrought with considerable subtlety, and his dialogue is rarely marred by the urge to engineer strongly emphasized dramatic climaxes. He rarely passed judgement: he was normally careful to preserve strict authorial control even while siding with the rebel, and his moral comments are conveyed only by implication. While not the work of a theatrical revolutionary, Hankin's plays deserve recognition as something other than mere muted renderings of Wilde's detached comedy of social observation.

—William M. Tydeman

HANSBERRY, Lorraine (Vivian).   American.   Born in Chicago, Illinois, 19 May 1930. Educated at the Art Institute, Chicago; University of Wisconsin, Madison, 1948. Married Robert Barron Nemiroff in 1953 (divorced, 1964). Worked as a journalist and editor. Recipient: New York Drama Critics Circle Award, 1959. *Died 12 January 1965.*

PUBLICATIONS

Collections

>Les Blancs: The Collected Last Plays (includes Les Blancs, The Drinking Gourd, What Use are Flowers?), edited by Robert Nemiroff. 1972.

Plays

>A Raisin in the Sun (produced 1959). 1959.
>The Sign in Sidney Brustein's Window (produced 1964). 1965.
>To Be Young, Gifted, and Black: A Portrait of Hansberry in Her Own Words, adapted by Robert Nemiroff (produced 1969). 1971.
>Les Blancs, edited by Robert Nemiroff (produced 1970). In Les Blancs (collection), 1972.

>Screenplay: A Raisin in the Sun, 1961.

Other

>The Movement: Documentary of a Struggle for Equality. 1964; as A Matter of Colour: Documentary of the Struggles for Racial Equality in the USA, 1965.
>To Be Young, Gifted, and Black: Hansberry in Her Own Words, adapted by Robert Nemiroff. 1969.

*　　*　　*

The importance of Lorraine Hansberry as an American dramatist rests with two plays, *A Raisin in the Sun* and *The Sign in Sidney Brustein's Window*, both produced during her tragically short life of thirty-four years. The first, by all measurements, was a major success. The second was a commercial failure, meeting only limited critical support. There were two posthumous productions, the effective but somewhat pasted-up collection presented as *To Be Young, Gifted, and Black* and *Les Blancs*, more or less complete but obviously still unfinished.

Lorraine Hansberry is an important, though minor, figure in American drama if for no more than the fact that she wrote an outstanding play of substantial popular and critical success as a Black writer contributing to an essentially white-oriented commercial theatre during a period when the Black identity in American letters was at a very delicate stage. It was a period when a strong pull existed between those Blacks who would prefer to stand on their achievements as artists, irrespective of race, and those who would prefer to take a stand, artistic as well as social or political, because of the very fact of their blackness. It is clear, as one encounters the opinions of critics who evaluate Lorraine Hansberry as a Black writer, that a dichotomy exists. While she herself was completely uncontroversial – she was indeed no LeRoi Jones nor Dick Gregory – and avoided the pointedly racial-political involvements associated with Black writers of her era, there is some controversy as to whether or not her two major plays were merely outstanding, relatively conventional, dramatic works of a fine young American playwright of promising talent who happened to be black, or were the works of a dedicated Black playwright treating subjects directly involved in the causes espoused by the writers overtly conscious of their race.

A Raisin in the Sun at first glance would suggest that Hansberry is squarely in the camp of those Black writers choosing to place onstage the social issue of the ghetto-trapped family.

The specifications are there from the exasperated young Black male, fumbling and frustrated in The Man's world, to the matriarch holding the fatherless family together. But Lorraine Hansberry has actually composed a solid, almost conventional "well-made" play, centering upon a theme which could have at one time as easily been Irish, Jewish, or Oriental, but which happens, given the time it was written and the knowledge of its creator, to be Black. True, the plight of the Youngers, a serious and prevalent American theme, exists almost entirely *because* they are black, but the confrontations, save for that with the rather pitiful Linder, who brings the outside forces briefly into the Youngers' living room, remain offstage or are postponed until after the curtain falls. Audience interest in the Youngers is in their human, not their racial, qualities.

The Sign in Sidney Brustein's Window is a sensitive comedy far removed in subject and intent from *Raisin*. The world of a white Jewish flat in Greenwich Village, visited by attractive, if not always "normal" characters and centered upon a strictly local political campaign, is not the usual subject associated with a Black writer intent on attacks against the social injustices of a racist society. Hansberry attacks petty individual prejudices, those against Black or sexual deviant, as well as personal selfishness which can be fatal to those one ought to love.

It is impossible to know where Lorraine Hansberry might have gone. Perhaps she would have become "radicalized," or perhaps she was already more radicalized than we recognize. It hardly matters. Judgment of her two important plays shows that she was a writer of singular promise, a very important voice in an uncertain historical and social period.

—Jordan Y. Miller

HARRIGAN, Edward. American. Born in New York City, 26 October 1844. Received little schooling; largely self-taught. Married Annie T. Braham in 1876; seven children. Left home for San Francisco, and appeared in vaudeville in the west, 1867–70; returned to New York, and appeared on stage, with Sam Rickey, as a vaudeville comic team, 1870; first appeared with Anthony J. Cannon (stage name: Tony Hart), as Harrigan and Hart, 1871, and with him managed and appeared at the Theatre Comique, New York, 1871 until the theatre was torn down, 1881: during this period wrote more than 80 sketches, music by David Braham, which developed into the complete plays of his later career in which he always acted the leading part; with Hart, opened the New Theatre Comique, 1881, and managed it until it was destroyed by fire, 1884; partnership with Hart ended in 1885; leased Harrigan's Park Theatre, 1884–88; built Harrigan's, later the Garrick, Theatre, 1891-95; retired from the stage in 1908. *Died 6 June 1911.*

PUBLICATIONS

Collections

The Famous Songs of Harrigan and Hart, edited by Edward B. Marks. 1938.

Plays and Sketches

The Mulcahy Twins (produced 1870).   Songs published 1872.

The Little Frauds (produced 1870).   Songs published 1870.

The Mulligan Guards (produced 1873).   Songs published 1873.

The Donovans (produced 1873).

Patrick's Day Parade (produced 1873; revised 1874 and thereafter).   Songs published 1884.

The Absent-Minded Couple (produced 1873).

The Skidmores (produced 1874).

The Invalid Corps (produced 1874).

Going Home Again (produced 1874).

The Night-Clerk's Troubles; or, The Fifth Avenue Hotel (produced 1875).   1875.

The Blue and the Gray (produced 1875).   1875.

Fee Gee (produced 1875).

King Calico's Body Guard (produced 1875).

The Two Awfuls (produced 1875).

Behind the Scenes (produced 1875).

Slavery Days (produced 1875).   Songs published 1875.

Down Broadway; or, From Central Park to the Battery (produced 1875).   Songs published 1878.

The Editor's Trouble (produced 1876).   1875.

Christmas Joys and Sorrows (produced 1876).   1877.

Lascaire (produced 1876).

The Telephone (produced 1876).

Ireland vs. Italy (produced 1876).

The Bradys (produced 1876).

The Italian Ballet Master (produced 1876).

Malone's Night Off (produced 1876).

The Bold Hibernian Boys (produced 1876).

S.O.T. (Sons of Temperance) (produced 1876).   Songs published 1876.

The Grand Duke Opera House (produced 1877).

Old Lavender (produced 1877; revised 1878, 1885).   1877.

My Wife's Mother.   1877

Callahan the Detective (produced 1877).

The Crushed Actors (produced 1877).

The Pillsbury Muddle (produced 1877).

Sullivan's Christmas (produced 1877).

The Irish Cousins (produced 1877).

Walking for Dat Cake (produced 1877).   Songs published 1877.

The Two Young Fellows and Her Majesty's Marines (produced 1877).

My Boy Dan (produced 1877).

The Terrible Example (produced 1877).

Love and Insurance (produced 1877).

The Celebrated Hard Case (produced 1878).   1878.

O'Brien, Counsellor-at-Law (produced 1878).

The Great In-Toe-Natural-Walking Match (produced 1878).

The Lorgaire (produced 1878; revised 1888).   1878.

The Mulligan Guard Picnic (produced 1878).   1880.

The Mulligan Guard Ball (produced 1879).   1879.

The Mulligan Guard Chowder (produced 1879).   1879.

The Mulligan Guards' Christmas (produced 1879).   1879.

The Mulligan Guard Nominee (produced 1880).   1880.

The Mulligan Guard Surprise (produced 1880).   1880.

The Major (produced 1881).   1881.
The Mulligans' Silver Wedding (produced 1881).   1881.
Squatter Sovereignty (produced 1882).   1881.
Mordecai Lyons (produced 1882).   1882.
McSorley's Inflation (produced 1882).   1882.
The Muddy Day (produced 1883).   Songs published 1883.
Cordelia's Aspirations (produced 1883).
Dan's Tribulations (produced 1884).   Songs published 1893.
Investigation (produced 1884).   Songs published 1884.
McAllistair's Legacy (produced 1885).
Are You Insured? (produced 1885).
The Grip (produced 1885).
The O'Reagans (produced 1886).
The Leather Patch (produced 1886).   Songs published 1886.
McNooney's Visit (produced 1887).
Pete (produced 1887).
Waddy Googan (produced 1888).   Songs published 1893.
Reilly and the Four Hundred (produced 1890).   Songs published 1890.
The Last of the Hogans (produced 1891; shortened version, as *Sargent Hickey*, produced
    1897).   Songs published 1891.
The Woolen Stocking (produced 1893).   Songs published 1893.
Notoriety (produced 1894).   Songs published 1894.
Marty Malone (produced 1896).
Under Cover (produced 1903).
The Simple Life (produced 1905).

Fiction

The Mulligans.   1901.

Verse

Songs for the Banjo.   1888.
Songs.   1893.

Other

Comique Joker, with Tony Hart.   1870(?).
Pictorial History of the Mulligan Guard Ball.   1879.

Reading List: *The Merry Partners: The Age of Harrigan and Hart* by E. J. Kahn, Jr., 1955.

*   *   *

The enthusiastic comparisons which critics applied to Edward Harrigan's plays would
seem to have assured him an international reputation. William Dean Howells (in *Harper's,*
July 1886) described him as the American Goldoni and a playwright who created "the spring
of a true American Comedy." Others compared him to Hogarth, Balzac, Zola, and Dickens.
At a time when American literature and art were firmly caught up in the rise of realism
Harrigan deserved this critical attention through his successful depiction of Lower East Side

275

New York life. As a comedian and a playwright he believed in "Holding the Mirror Up to Nature," as he explained it in an essay in *Pearson's Magazine* (November 1903), and providing a "series of photographs of life today in the Empire City" (*Harper's Weekly*, 2 February 1889). By using authentic scenes, character types, speech, dress, and gestures he provided realistic farce-comedy in which he infused his own belief in the kindness and good nature of the majority of people. As riotous fun, his plays and performances were both a reflection of the serious artistic and social movements of his generation and an antidote to the grimness which they frequently unveiled.

Harrigan, after several years in vaudeville, formed a comedy team with Anthony J. Cannon, who soon changed his name to Hart. As "Harriganandhart" they performed for fourteen years, and Harrigan began writing the sketches, with music by David Braham, that often developed into full-length plays. Many of the most memorable take place in Mulligan's Alley in New York's Sixth Ward. It was a part of New York that Harrigan researched and knew very well − a jumbled population of Germans, Italians, Chinese, Negroes, and Irish who took their ward politics seriously as well as their social activities which seemed always haunted by the "battle of the sexes." There was the Wee Drop Saloon run by Walfingham McSweeny, an Italian junk shop, a Chinese laundry-lodging combination, Lochmuller's butcher shop, and a Negro social club called the Full Moon Union. It was an international community which Harrigan brought to life with elaborate stage-business, meticulous attention to realistic detail, and a comedian's enthusiasm for the "general melee" which characterized his plays.

Harrigan's most famous plays involved the Mulligans − *The Mulligan Guards*, *The Mulligan Guard Ball*, *The Mulligan Guard Nominee*, and so on − through which he satirized contemporary military organization, social life on the Lower East Side, and politics. *Cordelia's Aspirations* and *Dan's Tribulations* also involve Dan Mulligan and his wife. His other important plays include *Old Lavender*, *Waddy Googan*, and *Reilly and the Four Hundred*. The people and their ideas were real if slight, and the spectators came to see something of themselves on stage. Trying always to be "truthful to the laws that govern society," Harrigan also confessed to being provincial and optimistic. Although he did not fulfill the potentiality that some critics saw or stimulate followers for his theory of American comedy, he was a major favorite for a generation or more of New York theatre-goers.

—Walter J. Meserve

HART, Moss.   American.   Born in New York City, 24 October 1904. Educated in New York public schools. Married the actress Kitty Carlisle in 1946; one son and one daughter. Worked with the Thalian Players, New York, then as a floor walker in a clothing store, and directed little theatre groups in Brooklyn and Newark, New Jersey; full-time playwright from 1930, often in collaboration with George S. Kaufman; later also produced and directed for the Broadway stage. Recipient: Megrue Prize, 1930; Pulitzer Prize, with George S. Kaufman, 1937; New York Drama Critics Circle Award, for direction, 1955; Antoinette Perry Award, for direction, 1957. *Died 20 December 1961.*

PUBLICATIONS

Plays

The Hold-Up Man (produced 1923).
Jonica, with Dorothy Heyward, music by Joseph Meyer, lyrics by William Moll (produced 1930).
No Retreat (produced 1930).
Once in a Lifetime, with George S. Kaufman (produced 1930).   1930.
Face the Music, music by Irving Berlin (produced 1932).
As Thousands Cheer, with Irving Berlin, music and lyrics by Edward Heyman and Richard Myers (produced 1933).
The Great Waltz, from a play by Ernst Marischka and others, music by Johann Strauss (produced 1934).
Merrily We Roll Along, with George S. Kaufman (produced 1934).   1934.
The Paperhanger, with George S. Kaufman.   1935(?).
Jubilee, music by Cole Porter (produced 1935).
The Show Is On (revue), with others (produced 1936).
You Can't Take It with You, with George S. Kaufman (produced 1936).   1937.
I'd Rather Be Right, with George S. Kaufman, music by Richard Rodgers, lyrics by Lorenz Hart (produced 1937).   1937.
The Fabulous Invalid, with George S. Kaufman (produced 1938).   1938.
The American Way, with George S. Kaufman, music by Oscar Levant (produced 1939).   1939.
The Man Who Came to Dinner, with George S. Kaufman (produced 1939).   1940.
George Washington Slept Here, with George S. Kaufman (produced 1940).   1940.
Lady in the Dark, music by Kurt Weill, lyrics by Ira Gershwin (produced 1941).   1941.
Winged Victory (produced 1943).   1943.
Christopher Blake (produced 1946).   1947.
Light Up the Sky (produced 1948).   1949.
The Climate of Eden, from the novel *Shadows Move among Them* by Edgar Mittelholzer (produced 1952).   1953.

Screenplays: *Winged Victory,* 1944; *Gentleman's Agreement,* 1947; *Hans Christian Andersen,* with Myles Connolly, 1952; *A Star Is Born,* 1954; *Prince of Players,* 1954.

Other

Act One (autobiography).   1959.

*   *   *

Moss Hart's first play, *The Hold-Up Man,* written at 19, folded in Chicago, but his *Once in a Lifetime* caught Sam Harris's eye, he was given George S. Kaufman as a collaborator (a story wittily told in Hart's autobiography, *Act One*), and the rest is history. Their play *Once in a Lifetime* was a success and the team continued with *Merrily We Roll Along,* the classic *You Can't Take It With You, The Man Who Came to Dinner,* and *George Washington Slept Here.*

Then Hart, never secure alone, sought other collaborators and produced important work. Having written *Face the Music* and *As Thousands Cheer* with Irving Berlin, *Jubilee* with Cole Porter, and *I'd Rather Be Right* with Kaufman and Rodgers and Lorenz Hart, he carried on his musical success in 1941 with Kurt Weill and Ira Gershwin: *Lady in the Dark.* This was probably the highlight of his own musical work though he directed such hits by others as

Irving Berlin's *Miss Liberty* (1949) and the Lerner and Loewe blockbusters *My Fair Lady* (1956) and *Camelot* (1960). In 1943 he created a "spectacle in two acts and seventeen scenes" for the USAF called *Winged Victory*, starring 300 servicemen, including Red Buttons and Lee J. Cobb. "The Army Emergency Relief Fund needs the money," was Lewis Nichols' review in *The Times*, but he patriotically if not critically added that it was "a wonderful show." After World War II Hart gave us *Christopher Blake* (1946) – which can be forgotten. *Light Up the Sky*, however, is one of my favorite plays about theatre folk – slick, sentimental, simplistic, and very funny. It is a delightful expansion of real life. In *The Climate of Eden*, "Eden" turns out to be the British Guiana mission of Gregory Hawke's uncle, and there our hero, feeling guilty for his wife's death, is obsessed with various problems. More interesting are Hart's films such as *Gentleman's Agreement* and *A Star Is Born*.

Moss Hart was always the innovative sort of theatre man who could call for four revolving stages where no one had ever used more than two before – and the dependent sort of theatre man that leaned on collaborators but also got four times as much out of them, and himself, as had ever been obtained before. He was also the sort who could submit *Once in a Lifetime* to six managers (all of whom accepted it) and then sell it to Sam Harris with the understanding that Kaufman would collaborate.

That collaboration produced one of the best comedies of the American theatre, *The Man Who Came to Dinner*. Of course, "real life" made them a gift of the inimitable Alexander Woollcott, but *they* knew what to do with him. It also takes a crack at Noël Coward, one of the Marx Brothers, the Lizzie Borden story (which is rather ineptly worked in), and the Middle West, would-be writers, fussy nurses, "the most chic actress on the New York or London stage," etc. The plot (largely Hart's?) is carpentry, but the wisecracks (mostly Kaufman's) are pure gold. Add Monty Woolley (who, said Richard Severo in *The New York Herald Tribune* of 7 May 1963, "wore his beard with the aplomb of a Madison Ave. Santa Claus," brought from Yale some "class" Kaufman and Hart always lacked, and "reduced the nurse ... to the potency of a pound of wet Kleenex") and the audience was limp with laughter. Without him the play is inevitably much less, but is still runs beautifully.

—Leonard R. N. Ashley

HECHT, Ben. American. Born in New York City, 28 February 1894; moved with his family to Chicago, then to Racine, Wisconsin. Educated at Racine High School. Married 1) Marie Armstrong in 1915 (divorced, 1925), one daughter; 2) Rose Caylor in 1925. Journalist, *Chicago Journal*, 1910–14; Reporter, 1914–18, Correspondent in Berlin, 1918–19, and Columnist, 1919–23, *Chicago News*; Founding Editor and Publisher, *Chicago Literary Times*, 1923–25; thereafter a full-time writer for the stage, and for motion pictures from 1933; formed a production company with Charles MacArthur, 1934; Columnist ("1001 Afternoons in Manhattan") *PM* newspaper, Long Island, New York, 1940–41. Active Zionist from 1946: Co-Chairman, American League for a Free Palestine. Recipient: Academy Award, 1928, 1936. *Died 18 April 1964.*

PUBLICATIONS

Plays

> *The Wonder Hat: A Harlequinade,* with Kenneth Sawyer Goodman (produced 1916). 1920.

The Hero of Santa Maria, with Kenneth Sawyer Goodman (produced 1916–17?). 1920.

The Master Poisoner, with Maxwell Bodenheim, in *Minna and Myself*, by Bodenheim. 1918.

The Hand of Siva, with Kenneth Sawyer Goodman. 1920.

The Egoist (produced 1922).

The Wonder Hat and Other One-Act Plays (includes *The Two Lamps, An Idyll of the Shops, The Hand of Siva, The Hero of Santa Maria*), with Kenneth Sawyer Goodman. 1925.

The Stork, from a play by Laszlo Fodor (produced 1925).

Christmas Eve: A Morality Play. 1928.

The Front Page, with Charles MacArthur (produced 1928). 1928.

Twentieth Century, with Charles MacArthur (produced 1932). 1932.

The Great Magoo, with Gene Fowler (produced 1932). 1933.

Jumbo, with Charles MacArthur, music by Richard Rodgers, lyrics by Lorenz Hart (produced 1935). 1935.

To Quito and Back (produced 1937). 1937.

Ladies and Gentlemen, with Charles MacArthur, from a play by Ladislas Bush-Fekete (produced 1939). 1941.

Fun to Be Free: A Patriotic Pageant, with Charles MacArthur (produced 1941). 1941.

Lily of the Valley (produced 1942).

We Will Never Die (produced 1943). 1943.

Wuthering Heights (screenplay), with Charles MacArthur, in *Twenty Best Film Plays*, edited by John Gassner and Dudley Nichols. 1943.

A Tribute to Gallantry, in *The Best One-Act Plays of 1943*, edited by Margaret Mayorga. 1943.

Miracle of the Pullman (broadcast 1944). In *The Best One-Act Plays of 1944*, edited by Margaret Mayorga, 1945.

Swan Song, with Charles MacArthur, from a story by Ramon Romero and Harriett Hinsdale (produced 1946). In *Stage Works of MacArthur*, 1974.

A Flag Is Born, music by Kurt Weill (produced 1946).

Spellbound (screenplay), with Angus MacPhail, in *Best Film Plays 1945*, edited by John Gassner and Dudley Nichols. 1946.

Hazel Flagg, music by Jule Styne, lyrics by Bob Hilliard, from a story by James Street and the screenplay *Nothing Sacred* (produced 1953). 1953.

Winkelberg (produced 1958). 1958.

Screenplays: *Underworld*, with others, 1927; *The Big Noise*, with George Marion, Jr., and Tom J. Geraghty, 1928; *The Unholy Night*, with others, 1929; *Roadhouse Nights*, with Garrett Fort, 1930; *The Great Gabbo*, with Hugh Herbert, 1930; *The Front Page*, with Charles MacArthur, 1931; *Scarface, Shame of the Nation*, 1932; *Design for Living*, 1933; *Hallelujah, I'm a Bum*, 1933; *Topaze*, 1933; *Viva Villa!*, 1934; *Twentieth Century*, with Charles MacArthur, 1934; *Crime Without Passion*, with Charles MacArthur, 1934; *The Scoundrel*, with Charles MacArthur, 1935; *Barbary Coast*, with Charles MacArthur, 1935; *The Florentine Dagger*, 1935; *Once in a Blue Moon*, with Charles MacArthur, 1935; *Soak the Rich*, with Charles MacArthur, 1936; *Nothing Sacred*, 1937; *Goldwyn Follies*, with others, 1938; *Gunga Din*, with others, 1939; *Lady of the Tropics*, 1939; *Wuthering Heights*, with Charles MacArthur, 1939; *It's a Wonderful World*, with Herman J. Mankiewicz, 1939; *Let Freedom Ring*, 1939; *Until I Die*, with Charles MacArthur, 1940; *Angels over Broadway*, 1940; *Comrade X*, with Charles Lederer and Walter Reisch, 1940; *Lydia*, with others, 1941; *Tales of Manhattan*, with others, 1942; *The Black Swan*, with Seton I. Miller, 1942; *China Girl*, with Melville Crossman, 1942; *Spellbound*, with Angus MacPhail, 1945; *Specter of the Rose*, 1946; *Notorious*, 1946; *Her Husband's Affairs*, with Charles Lederer, 1947; *Kiss*

279

of Death, with Charles Lederer and Eleazar Lipsky, 1947; *Ride the Pink Horse*, with Charles Lederer, 1947; *The Miracle of the Bells*, with Quentin Reynolds, 1948; *Whirlpool*, with Andrew Solt, 1950; *Where the Sidewalk Ends*, with others, 1950; *Actors and Sin*, 1952; *The Indian Fighter*, with Frank Davis and Ben Kadish, 1955; *Ulysses*, with others, 1955; *Miracle in the Rain*, 1956; *The Iron Petticoat*, 1956; *Legend of the Lost*, with Robert Presnell, Jr., 1957; *A Farewell to Arms*, 1957; *Queen of Outer Space*, with Charles Beaumont, 1958; *Mutiny on the Bounty* (uncredited), with others, 1962; *Circus World*, with others, 1964; *Casino Royale* (uncredited), with others, 1967.

Radio Play: *Miracle of the Pullman*, 1944.

Fiction

Erik Dorn. 1921.
Fantazius Mallare: A Mysterious Oath. 1922.
A Thousand and One Afternoons in Chicago (stories). 1922.
Gargoyles. 1922.
The Florentine Dagger. 1923.
Humpty Dumpty. 1924.
The Kingdom of Evil: A Continuation of the Journal of Fantazius Mallare. 1924.
Cutie, A Warm Mamma, with Maxwell Bodenheim. 1924.
Broken Necks, Containing More 1001 Afternoons (stories). 1926.
Count Bruga. 1926.
A Jew in Love. 1931.
The Champion from Far Away (stories). 1931.
Actor's Blood (stories). 1936.
A Book of Miracles (stories). 1939.
1001 Afternoons in New York. 1941.
Miracle in the Rain. 1943.
I Hate Actors! 1944; as *Hollywood Mystery!*, 1946.
The Collected Stories. 1945.
Concerning a Woman of Sin and Other Stories. 1947.
The Cat That Jumped Out of the Story (juvenile). 1947.
The Sensualists. 1959.
In the Midst of Death. 1964.

Other

A Guide for the Bedevilled. 1944.
A Child of the Century (autobiography). 1954.
Charlie: The Improbable Life and Times of Charles MacArthur. 1957.
A Treasury of Ben Hecht. 1959.
Perfidy. 1961.
Gaily, Gaily (autobiography). 1963.
Letters from Bohemia. 1964.

*   *   *

Ben Hecht began his writing career before the "audience renaissance," a term he used in a 1963 *Theatre Arts* article for the evolution of "play lovers" into "play decipherers," a process which undermined the status of the theatre as "our most ancient bridgehead of lucidity." Hecht's earliest literary values, influenced by his career in journalism, taught him that "whatever confusions possessed the other arts, the art of the theatre remained basically that of a Western Union telegram – terse and informative." These principles were to govern most of his dramatic output, and partially explain why such a disciplined, intelligent, and prolific writer has only intermittently attracted critical attention.

The journalist's attention to incident and detail, the "katatonic armor" that shields him in daily contact with the extremes and eccentricities of life, and the pragmatism of shaping these into a "story" are all prominent factors in his plays. Hecht's most famous collaboration with Charles MacArthur, *The Front Page*, has often been dismissed as a romantic melodrama about journalism; however, it also generates a poignant dilemma between individual values and public significance, articulated with a vigorous realism that was all but unique on Broadway in 1928. *To Quito and Back*, considered by many to be the best play that Hecht wrote alone, also introduces a journalist as a secondary character to sift out a situation in Ecuador similar to that of the Spanish Civil War. However, the diversity of content and style in Hecht's drama is almost as great as in his screenplays. His early one-act plays (written 1914–18) show experimentation with various types of stylisation then fashionable in "art theatres," a tendency which declines after the death of his first collaborator, the more experienced playwright Kenneth Sawyer Goodman, in 1918. Working with MacArthur, Hecht produced the Hollywood satire *Twentieth Century*, the musical extravaganza *Jumbo*, and the murder melodrama *Swan Song*; with Gene Fowler, he wrote the "dramatic cartoon" *The Great Magoo*; with Kurt Weill, he collaborated in the pageant of Jewish history *A Flag Is Born*, which gave a starring part to the young Marlon Brando and netted nearly one million dollars for the Zionist cause in 1946. Several of Hecht's later plays are also graveyard dramas: *Lily of the Valley* is a purgatorial allegory, and his last play, *Winkelberg*, is a work of expressionistic nostalgia. This stylistic eclecticism of Hecht's drama is reflected in the range of collaborators with whom he proved compatible, but his claim to a place in American dramatic history must rest on his tough, anecdotal realism.

Antedating Hecht's "audience renaissance" was the "Chicago literary renaissance" to which he was a central contributor, and which provided the context of *Winkelberg*. Criticism of the "clever saccharinity" of the Chicago school is substantiated by a reading of his earliest prose fiction, from *Erik Dorn* to *Gargoyles*. Hecht's foundation editorship of the *Chicago Literary Times* (which he also printed, published, managed, proofed, and helped distribute) was a watershed in his career, and it was a much less pretentious Hecht who emerged to write *The Front Page*; his original purpose in that play was to reflect his "intellectual disdain of and superiority to the Newspaper," but a much more honest, frontal attitude to his writing developed, resulting in his finest novel, *A Jew in Love*, as well as the best of his short stories.

Ironically, it was only late in his career that Hecht found a commitment that would have given cohesive solidity to his central output. Jews and journalists abound in his early novels and plays, but it is only in his later autobiographical writings that he deliberately anatomises his own identity as an American Jew. However, the growth of this commitment during World War II resulted in one of his finest books: *A Guide for the Bedevilled* confronts anti-Semitism with a sense of stylistic strategy and a passionate urbanity that recall the best prose writing of Bernard Shaw.

—Howard McNaughton

HELLMAN, Lillian (Florence). American. Born in New Orleans, Louisiana, 20 June 1907. Educated at New York University, 1923–25; Columbia University, New York, 1926. Married the writer Arthur Kober in 1925 (divorced, 1932). Reader, Horace Liveright, publishers, New York, 1924–25; Reviewer, New York *Herald Tribune*, 1925–28; Theatrical Play Reader, 1927–30; Reader, MGM, 1930–32. Taught at Yale University, New Haven, Connecticut, 1966; and at Harvard University, Cambridge, Massachusetts; Massachusetts Institute of Technology, Cambridge; and the University of California, Berkeley. Recipient: New York Drama Critics Circle Award, 1941, 1960; Brandeis University Creative Arts Award, 1960; National Institute of Arts and Letters Gold Medal, 1964; Paul Robeson Award, 1976. M.A.: Tufts College, Medford, Massachusetts, 1940; LL.D.: Wheaton College, Norton, Massachusetts, 1961; Rutgers University, New Brunswick, New Jersey, 1963; Brandeis University, Waltham, Massachusetts, 1965; Yale University, 1974; Smith College, Northampton, Massachusetts, 1974; New York University, 1974; Franklin and Marshall College, Lancaster, Pennsylvania, 1975; Columbia University, 1976. Member, National Institute of Arts and Letters; American Academy of Arts and Sciences. Lives in New York City.

PUBLICATIONS

Plays

The Children's Hour (produced 1934).   1934.
Days to Come (produced 1936).   1936.
The Little Foxes (produced 1939).   1939.
Watch on the Rhine (produced 1941).   1941.
The North Star: A Motion Picture about Some Russian People.   1943.
The Searching Wind (produced 1944).   1944.
Watch on the Rhine (screenplay), with Dashiell Hammett, in *Best Film Plays of 1943–44,* edited by John Gassner and Dudley Nichols.   1945.
Another Part of the Forest (produced 1946).   1947.
Montserrat, from a play by Emmanuel Roblès (produced 1949)   1950.
Regina, music by Marc Blitzstein (produced 1949).
The Autumn Garden (produced 1951).   1951.
The Lark, from a play by Jean Anouilh (produced 1955).   1955.
Candide, music by Leonard Bernstein, lyrics by Richard Wilbur, John LaTouche and Dorothy Parker, from the novel by Voltaire (produced 1956).   1957.
Toys in the Attic (produced 1960).   1960.
My Mother, My Father and Me, from the novel *How Much?* by Burt Blechman (produced 1963).   1963.
The Collected Plays.   1972.

Screenplays: *The Dark Angel*, with Mordaunt Shairp, 1935; *These Three*, 1936; *Dead End*, 1937; *The Little Foxes*, with others, 1941; *Watch on the Rhine*, with Dashiell Hammett, 1943; *The North Star*, 1943; *The Searching Wind*, 1946; *The Children's Hour*, with John Michael Hayes, 1961; *The Chase*, 1966.

Other

An Unfinished Woman: A Memoir.   1969.
"Pentimento": A Book of Portraits.   1973.
Scoundrel Time.   1976.

Editor, *Selected Letters*, by Chekhov, translated by Sidonie Lederer.   1955.

Editor, *The Big Knockover: Selected Stories and Short Novels,* by Dashiell Hammett. 1966; as *The Dashiell Hammett Story Omnibus,* 1966.

Reading List: *Hellman, Playwright* by Richard Moody, 1971; *The Dramatic Works of Hellman* by Lorena R. Holmin, 1973; *Hellman* by Doris V. Falk, 1978.

*   *   *

Lillian Hellman is one of America's major dramatists. She entered a male-dominated field when she was nearly thirty and wrote some dozen plays in three decades. Her early model was Ibsen, and she shared his love of tightly knit plots and emphasis on sociological and psychological forces. Her best plays, like Ibsen's, are those in which a powerful character cuts loose and transcends the limitations of the play's rigid symmetry and plot contrivance. Along with Clifford Odets, the other significant writing talent of the 1930's, Hellman showed a keen interest in Marxist theory and explored the relationship between the nuclear family and capitalism. Hellman, more than Odets, held ambiguous views of man and society. Her antagonists are not wholly the products of environment but seem at times innately malicious. The quest for power fascinated the author and her characters became famous for their ruthlessness and cunning. Most of her plays verge on melodrama but are admired for their energetic protagonists and swift-moving plots.

In her first play, *The Children's Hour*, Hellman showed how the capricious wielding of power could ruin innocent people. Two young women at a girl's school are falsely accused of having a lesbian relationship by a disturbed child. They are brought to trial by outraged parents and eventually lose their case – and their school. One of the teachers commits suicide and, too late, the child's treachery is discovered. The homosexual motif, though discreetly handled, accounted for the play's notoriety in 1934; but the abuse of power by an arrogant elite is its enduring theme.

Usurping power is also the motivating force in Hellman's best-known play, *The Little Foxes*, at once a political statement and a complex study of family dynamics. The rapacious Hubbard family represents a new brand of Southern capitalist who subordinates all traditions and human values to the goal of acquiring wealth and property. The strength of the play lies in Hellman's implicit comparison of the Hubbard siblings' rivalries with the competitiveness of Americans in the free enterprise system. The role of Regina Hubbard, who withholds her dying husband's heart medicine and who outwits her equally greedy brothers in a major business coup, has become a favorite vehicle for American actresses.

At the beginning of World War II Hellman wrote *Watch on the Rhine* and *The Searching Wind* which both dealt with the fascist menace. The former play contains some witty repartee and suspenseful moments; but its solutions to the international crisis are simplistic, and it is better described as an adventure story than a thesis play.

When the war ended, Hellman returned to the easy-to-hate Hubbard family in *Another Part of the Forest*. Unfortunately the exaggerated spitefulness and hysteria of the characters and the unrelieved high-tension atmosphere of this play become nearly ludicrous. The concept of personal manipulation had become an obsession with the author, and a correlation seemed to have developed between her studies of social and societal exploitation and her own excessive control over plot characterization and stage effects. Perhaps the playwright realized this, because in her last plays she turned from Ibsen to Chekhov for inspiration. Both *The Autumn Garden* and *Toys in the Attic* recall the mood and ambiguous moral judgments of the great Russian dramatist. Neither of these plays has a truly pernicious villain, and most of the characters seem to be suffering from a Chekhovian paralysis of will. The atmosphere is deterministic and the plots are truer to life. What has changed is that all bids for personal power prove self-defeating – the predatory are caught in traps of their own making and hardly struggle before acknowledging defeat. Nevertheless these plays also include sharp, amusing verbal exchanges and the famous blackmail scenes associated with Hellman.

Blackmail, present in all of her plays, is Hellman's favorite metaphor for personal manipulation; but in the later works she uses blackmail and other devices with greater subtlety, and presents a somewhat blurred but more convincing vision of stumbling modern man and his society.

Hellman's dramatic mode, based on her adherence to continental models, is bound to an earlier era. Most of her experiments with film-writing proved frustrating. Her best recent works have been autobiographical sketches. In *An Unfinished Woman*, *Penitmento*, and *Scoundrel Time* she reveals her penetrating intelligence but tacitly acknowledges that her insights and talents are presently better suited to the historical memoir.

—Kimball King

HERNE, James A. American. Born James Ahern in Cohoes, New York, 1 February 1839. Educated in local schools until age 13; largely self-taught. Married 1) Helen Western in 1866 (divorced); 2) the actress Katherine Corcoran in 1878, three daughters. Debut as an actor, in repertory, Troy, New York, 1859; appeared with John Ford's company in Baltimore and Washington, D.C. during the Civil War; leading man in the Lucille Western Company, touring the United States, 1865–67; thereafter managed the Grand Opera House, New York; Stage Director of the Baldwin Theatre, San Francisco, 1875–80: began writing for the stage by collaborating with his associate David Belasco in 1879: starred in *Hearts of Oak* for the next seven years, a success which allowed him to retire to Dorchester, Massachusetts, and devote himself to writing full-time for the stage; dissipated his fortune on his next play: forced to move back to New York and work as a stage manager for Klaw and Erlanger, 1891; appeared in *Shore Acres*, 1892–98, the success of which restored his fortunes; retired to Southampton, Long Island. *Died 2 June 1901.*

PUBLICATIONS

Collections

>   *Shore Acres and Other Plays* (includes *Sag Harbor, Hearts of Oak*), edited by Mrs. James A. Herne. 1928.
>   *The Early Plays* (includes *The Minute Men of 1774–1775, Drifting Apart, The Reverend Griffith Davenport, Within an Inch of His Life*), edited by Arthur Hobson Quinn. 1940.

Plays

>   *Within an Inch of His Life* with David Belasco, from a play by Gaboriau (produced 1879). In *The Early Plays*, 1940.
>   *Marriage by Moonlight*, with David Belasco, from the play *Camilla's Husband* by Watts Phillips (produced 1879).
>   *Hearts of Oak*, with David Belasco (as *Chums*, produced 1879; as *Hearts of Oak*, produced 1879). In *Shore Acres and Other Plays*, 1928; revised version by Herne, as *Sag Harbor* (produced 1900), in *Shore Acres and Other Plays*, 1928.

The Minute Men of 1774–1775 (produced 1886).   In *The Early Plays,* 1940.

Drifting Apart (produced 1888).   In *The Early Plays,* 1940.

Margaret Fleming (produced 1890).   Edited by Myron Matlaw, in *The Black Crook and Other 19th-Century American Plays,* 1967.

My Colleen (produced 1892).

Shore Acres (produced 1893).   In *Shore Acres and Other Plays,* 1928.

The Reverend Griffith Davenport, from the novel *An Unofficial Patriot* by Helen H. Gardener (produced 1899).   In *The Early Plays,* 1940; Act III edited by Arthur Hobson Quinn, in *American Literature 24,* 1952.

Bibliography: "Selected Bibliography of Herne" by John Perry, in *Bulletin of Bibliography 31,* 1974.

Reading List: *Herne: The Rise of Realism in the American Drama* by Herbert J. Edwards and Julie A. Herne, 1964; *Herne, The American Ibsen* by John Perry, 1978.

*   *   *

Most of the plays by the accomplished actor, James A. Herne, remain in the limbo of strictly minor American drama. *The Minute Men of 1774–1775, Drifting Apart, My Colleen,* or *The Reverend Griffith Davenport,* and even those written in collaboration with David Belasco, including *Within an Inch of His Life, Marriage by Moonlight,* or *Hearts of Oak,* redone by Herne as *Sag Harbor,* are now so obscure as to be virtually unobtainable save in limited library collections. But with *Margaret Fleming* and *Shore Acres* Herne has survived as the most important pivotal American playwright of the late 19th century. In these two plays, particularly the former, Herne took the most significant steps of any American dramatist of his time away from the well-made artificialities of 19th-century romance and melodrama toward the development of effective dramatic realism.

Margaret Fleming abounds in 19th-century conventions and artifices: the wronged young girl who must bear her child in shame and die; the threatened vengeance of the shamed girl's sister, a servant in the home of the seducer; the angelic wife struck blind as she learns of her husband's faithlessness. But the play goes well beyond the surface clichés. The seducer is no caddish rogue, but a successful manufacturer, Philip Fleming, obviously well-respected within the community, and deeply in love with his wife. He is no villain, but neither is he a hero. He is in truth, a "fallen man," and it is his suffering and redemption which motivate a good part of the action, not the fate of the fallen woman who, in life and death, remains offstage, merely a point of reference. The problem of Philip Fleming's infidelity is strictly a domestic matter to be recognized and discussed by husband, wife, and family physician. Margaret Fleming, stunned by her husband's inadequately explained deed, refuses to be martyred and she survives through firmness and conviction evolving out of common sense and rational behavior. Her own behavior as an offended human being, not merely a stereotyped wronged woman, renders her far superior to her husband, whom she permits to return to her but only on her conditions. Reconciliation remains solely a dim hope in the indefinite future.

Thus Herne's skill in giving his central characters the strengths, weaknesses, and motivations of recognizable human individuals well developed within a recognizable contemporary society keeps *Margaret Fleming* from collapse into sentimental bathos. The last act, which survives today through Herne's daughter's reconstruction, refuses to tie up the threads in conventionally neat fashion. There will be a life together for Philip and Margaret Fleming, but the ending, rather than "happy," is believable and eminently satisfactory. The wall remains between husband and wife, but, as Herne acknowledges in this ending (he apparently experimented with several) so shocking to 19th-century audiences, men and women, do, in reality, survive such traumas. They continue their lives; the world does not end; the drama does not conclude with the descent of the final curtain. The "ever after," as in life, is uncertain, possibly dangerous, and even terrifying.

Shore Acres, a lesser play, has too many outdated melodramatics. Still, Herne permits no heroes, no heroines, and no villains. There are logic and sound reason behind the businessman who would foreclose and subdivide the homestead. The love affair and its complications, if we ignore the dark and stormy night syndrome, are understandable. Uncle Nat, the prime mover, talks and acts with reasonable believability. The minor characters, relatively well-developed, enter and depart with clear motivation. For all the frequent transparent arbitrariness, there is a realistic aura in setting, action, and language.

Neither play is a great work of dramatic art. Both, however, are significant. To criticize the creaks and groans of structure is to miss the point of their artistic advances. Though *Margaret Fleming* may have been quite literally driven from the stage by adverse reaction to its daring theme and shocking ending, the courage of the playwright in creating it is recognized for the exceptional deed that it was. The significance of the play, together in a lesser degree with *Shore Acres*, in providing the substantial push behind the American drama's movement toward full-fledged artistic participation in 20th-century world theatre is abundantly apparent.

—Jordan Y. Miller

HEYWOOD, John. English. Born, possibly in North Mimms, Hertfordshire, c. 1497. Educated at Oxford University. Married Eliza Rastell in the 1520's; two sons, including the writer Jasper Heywood. Associated with the court of Henry VIII, and with Sir Thomas More and his circle: court musician and music teacher to Princess Mary, from whom he afterwards received a pension; received court payments in 1519 and 1520 as a singer; admitted to the liberties of the City of London, 1523; Steward of the King's Chamber, later Queen's Chamber, 1528–58; involved in a plot to overthrow Cranmer, imprisoned and pardoned, 1544; left England for religious reasons in 1564, and lived in Belgium until his death. *Died in 1578.*

PUBLICATIONS

Collections

    Dramatic Writings, edited by J. S. Farmer.   1905.
    Works, and Miscellaneous Short Poems, edited by B. A. Milligan.   1956.

Plays

    John John, Tib, and Sir John.   1533; edited by J. S. Farmer, in *Two Tudor Shrew Plays*, 1908.
    The Pardoner and the Friar.   1533; edited by J. S. Farmer, 1906.
    A Play of Love.   1533; edited by K. W. Cameron, 1944.
    The Play of the Weather.   1533; edited by K. W. Cameron, 1944.

The Four P's. 1543(?); edited by F. S. Boas, in *Five Pre-Shakespearean Comedies,* 1934.
Witty and Witless, edited by F. W. Fairholt. 1846; edited by K. W. Cameron, 1941.

Verse

A Dialogue Containing All the Proverbs in the English Tongue. 1546; revised edition, 1561; edited by R. E. Habenicht, 1963.
An Hundred Epigrams. 1550; later editions add 500 more.
A Ballad Specifying the Marriage Between Our Sovereign Lord and Lady. 1554.
The Spider and the Fly. 1556; edited by A. W. Ward, 1894.
A Ballad Touching the Taking of Scarborough Castle. 1557.
A Ballad Against Slander and Detraction. 1562.
Works. 1562.
Of a Number of Rats. 1562 (?).

Reading List: *The Life and Works of Heywood* by R. W. Bolwell, 1921; "Heywood and His Friends" and "The Canon of Heywood's Plays," in *Early Tudor Drama* by A. W. Reed, 1926; *Heywood, Entertainer* by Rupert de la Bère, 1937; *French Farce and Heywood* by Ian C. M. Maxwell, 1946; *Heywood* by Robert Carl Johnson, 1970.

*   *   *

John Heywood is the best-known exponent of the Tudor interlude. The canon of his work has never been established, but he certainly wrote *Witty and Witless, A Play of Love, The Play of the Weather, The Four P's,* and probably also *John John, Tib and Sir John* and *The Pardoner and the Friar.*

Tudor interludes were secular dramatic entertainments performed mainly at banquets in private houses and at court. Short plays were therefore appropriate, and none of Heywood's is longer than about 1,500 lines. Because of the environment in which they were performed, there is a sense of intimacy and audience contact, particularly in *The Play of the Weather* in which the antics of the "Vice," Merry Report, resemble those of the Elizabethan Fool.

Thin in plot, Heywood's interludes sometimes come closer to debate than drama. *The Four P's,* for example, introduces a contrast between a Palmer, Pardoner, 'Pothecary, and Pedlar as to who can tell the best lie. In *The Play of the Weather* the characters lodge successive pleas to Jupiter to send the Weather which suits them best. *Witty and Witless* (the weakest and perhaps the earliest of Heywood's surviving plays) presents three characters debating ponderously the relative merits of ignorance and wisdom. *The Pardoner and the Friar* has some rudimentary dramatic action in that the characters eventually come to blows over the merits of their respective professions. But the real exception is *John John, Tib and Sir John,* which is modelled on a French farce. It presents the typical *fabliau* triangle of jealous husband, amorous wife, and priestly lover, and makes clever use of double entendre, the priest enjoying the wife's "pie" while the husband ineffectually tries to stop up a hole in a bucket with a piece of wax.

The plays are, in themselves, poor "theatre," being composed mainly in monotonous couplets, with entrances and exits unskillfully managed, but there is supplementary material in the form of songs, which reflect Heywood's interest in music as master of the royal choir school. Children probably acted alongside adults, and in *The Play of the Weather* there seems to be an awareness of the effective contrast between the adult characters and the boy, "the least [i.e., smallest] that can play," who comes to request a plentiful supply of snow for snowballing.

The characters mostly represent distinct social types, like Lover-Not-Loved and Loved-

Not-Loving who debate their relative unhappiness in *A Play of Love*. Heywood plagiarises the Prologue to Chaucer's *Pardoner's Tale* to provide an arresting beginning for his *The Pardoner and the Friar*, but the play rapidly deteriorates after this, and only in *John John* are the characters convincingly individualised.

Even the dullest of Heywood's interludes is not without its humour, though in all of them except *John John* it is of a verbal type which does not usually appeal to modern taste. Ribald antifeminism is common, and there is a strong element of frankly sexual innuendo.

Heywood was associated with Sir Thomas More and his circle, and suffered for his adherence to Catholicism. But concern with politics and moral issues is not noticeable in his work. However, his criticism of the abuses of the church, such as the activities of pardoners, is as vehement as Chaucer's. *The Play of the Weather*, perhaps the most successful of the plays, exposes society's self-interest and factionalism and there is nice irony in the fact that at the end everyone is deliriously happy to accept the varied weathers they are already receiving.

Heywood's abuse of women can be traced in his collection of 300 proverbs on marriage. He composed 600 epigrams, most of them lacking in pith, a verse parable called *The Spider and the Fly*, and a small number of ballads.

—G. A. Lester

HEYWOOD, Thomas. English. Born in Lincolnshire in 1573. Possibly educated at Cambridge University. Lived in London; wrote plays for Philip Henslowe from 1596; actor and possibly a shareholder in Henslowe's company, the Lord Admiral's Men, from 1598; later a member of other companies, including the Earl of Worcester's players; succeeded Dekker as writer of mayoral pageants for the City of London; claimed to have been involved in the writing of 220 plays, of which some 35 survive. *Died* (buried) *16 August 1641*.

PUBLICATIONS

Collections

Dramatic Works, edited by R. H. Shepherd. 6 vols., 1874.

Plays

The Four Prentices of London (produced 1592?). 1615.
King Edward the Fourth, 2 parts (produced before 1599). 1599; edited by S. de Ricci, 1922.
How a Man May Choose a Good Wife from a Bad (produced 1602?). 1602; edited by A. E. H. Swaen, 1912.
The Royal King and the Loyal Subject (produced 1602?). 1637; edited by K. W. Tibbals, 1906.
Sir Thomas Wyatt, with Dekker and Webster (produced 1602–07?). 1607; edited by Fredson Bowers, in *Dramatic Works* by Dekker, 1953–61.

A Woman Killed with Kindness (produced 1603). 1607; edited by R. Van Fossen, 1961.

The Rape of Lucrece (produced 1603–08?). 1608; edited by A. Holaday, 1950.

The Wise Woman of Hogsdon (produced 1604?). 1638.

If You Know Not Me, You Know Nobody; or, The Troubles of Queen Elizabeth (produced 1605). 1605; edited by Madeleine Doran, 1935.

The Second Part of If You Know Not Me, You Know Nobody (produced 1605). 1606; as *The Second Part of Queen Elizabeth's Troubles*, 1609; edited by Madeleine Doran, 1935.

Fortune by Land and Sea, with William Rowley (produced 1607?). 1655; edited by J. E. Walker, 1899.

The Miseries of Enforced Marriage, with George Wilkins (produced 1607). 1607; edited by G. H. Blayney, 1964.

Appius and Virginia, with Webster (produced 1608?). 1654; edited by F. L. Lucas, in *Works* by Webster, 1927.

The Fair Maid of the West; or, A Girl Worth Gold, part 1 (produced before 1610). 1631; edited by Brownell Salomon, 1975; *The Fair Maid of the West*, part 2 (produced 1630?), 1631; edited by R. K. Turner, with part 1, 1967.

The Golden Age (produced 1611?). 1611.

The Silver Age (produced 1612?). 1613.

The Brazen Age (produced 1613?). 1613.

The Iron Age, 2 parts (produced 1613). 1632.

The Martyred Soldier, with Henry Shirley (produced before 1619). 1638; edited by A. H. Bullen, in *A Collection of Old English Plays 1*, 1882.

The Captives; or, The Lost Recovered (produced 1624). Edited by A. H. Bullen, in *A Collection of Old English Plays*, 1885; edited by A. Brown, 1953.

A Maidenhead Well Lost (produced 1625–34?). 1634.

The English Traveller (produced 1627?). 1633.

Pleasant Dialogues and Dramas, from Lucian, Erasmus, Ovid (produced 1630–36?). 1637.

London's Jus Honorarium, Expressed in Sundry Triumphs, Pageants, and Shows (produced 1631). 1631.

Londini Artium et Scientiarum Scaturigo; or, London's Fountain of Arts and Sciences (produced 1632). 1632; edited by Arthur M. Clark, in *Theatre Miscellany*, 1953.

Londini Emporia; or, London's Mercatura (produced 1633). 1633; edited by Arthur M. Clark, in *Theatre Miscellany*, 1953.

The Late Lancashire Witches, with Richard Brome (produced 1634). 1634.

Love's Mistress; or, The Queen's Masque (produced 1634). 1636; edited by H. M. Blake, 1910.

A Challenge for Beauty (produced 1634–35?). 1636.

Londini Sinus Salutis; or, London's Harbour of Health and Happiness (produced 1635). 1635.

Londini Speculum; or, London's Mirror (produced 1637). 1637.

Porta Pietatis; or, The Port or Harbour of Piety (produced 1638). 1638.

Londini Status Pacatus; or, London's Peaceable Estate (produced 1639). 1639.

Verse

Oenone and Paris. 1594; edited by Elizabeth Story Donno, in *Elizabethan Minor Epics*, 1963.

Troia Britannica; or, Great Britain's Troy. 1609.

A Marriage Triumph. 1613; edited by E. M. Goldsmid, 1884.

A Funeral Elegy upon King James. 1625.

The Hierarchy of the Blessed Angels. 1635.

The Life and Death of Queen Elizabeth, in Heroical Verse. 1639.
Reader, Here You'll Plainly See Judgement Perverted by These Three: A Priest, A Judge, A Patentee. 1641.

Other

An Apology for Actors. 1612; as *The Actors' Vindication,* 1658; shortened version, edited by E. K. Chamber, in *The Elizabethan Stage,* 1923.
Nine Books of Various History Concerning Women. 1624; as *The General History of Women,* 1657.
England's Elizabeth: Her Life and Troubles During Her Minority. 1631.
Philocothonist; or, The Drunkard Opened, Dissected, and Anatomized. 1635.
The Wonder of This Age. 1635.
The New Year's Gift. 1636.
The Three Wonders of This Age. 1636.
A True Discourse of the Two Prophets, Richard Farnham, Weaver, and John Bull, Weaver. 1636.
A Curtain Lecture, As It Is Read by a Country Farmer's Wife to Her Good Man. 1637.
The Phoenix of These Times; or, The Life of Mr. Henry Welby. 1637.
A True Description of His Majesty's Royal Ship Built This Year 1637 at Woolwich in Kent. 1637; revised edition, 1638.
A True Relation of the Lives and Deaths of the Two Most Famous English Pirates, Purser and Clinton. 1639.
The Exemplary Lives and Memorable Acts of Nine of the Most Worthy Women of the World. 1640.
The Black Box of Rome Opened. 1641.
Brightman's Predictions and Prophecies. 1641.
A Dialogue Betwixt Mr. Alderman Abell and Richard Kilvert. 1641.
The Life of Merlin, Surnamed Ambrosius, His Prophecies and Predictions Interpreted. 1641.
Machiavel's Ghost. 1641; as *Machiavel, as He Lately Appeared,* 1641.
A New Plot Discovered. 1641.
The Rat Trap; or, The Jesuits Taken in Their Own Net. 1641.
A Revelation of Mr. Brightman's Revelation. 1641.
Sir Richard Whittington. 1656.

Translator, *De Arte Amandi; or, The Art of Love,* by Ovid. 1600(?).
Translator, *The Two Most Worthy and Notable Histories of Catiline and Jugurtha,* by Sallust. 1608.

Bibliography: *Heywood: A Concise Bibliography* by S. A. Tannenbaum, 1939, supplement in *Elizabethan Bibliographies Supplements 2* by Dennis Donovan, 1967.

Reading List: *The Bourgeois Elements in the Dramas of Heywood* by F. M. Velte, 1922, revised edition, 1966; *Heywood: A Study in the Elizabethan Drama of Everyday Life* by Otelia Cromwell, 1928; *Heywood, Playwright and Miscellanist* by Arthur M. Clark, 1931; *Heywood* by F. S. Boas, 1950; *An Index to the Figurative Language in Heywood's Tragedies* by Louis Charles Stagg, 1967; *Images of Women in the Work of Heywood* by Marilyn L. Johnson, 1974.

*   *   *

Thomas Heywood of Lincolnshire, Tucker Brooke's "drama bridge" between Marlowe and Jonson, eminent actor, non-dramatic poet, translator, critic, composer of Lord Mayor pageants and masques (notably *Love's Mistress*, in the Platonic love tradition), wrote his 220 plays (10% surviving) in the classical, English history, romance, and bourgeois realism traditions.

Heywood's classical plays include *The Rape of Lucrece*, a Roman tragedy from Livy, its tragic impact partly blunted by songs worthy of *The Beggar's Opera*, and a five-part study of Greek myth ranging from *The Golden Age*, dealing with the earliest legends of Greek gods, through the two-part *Iron Age*, dealing with the fates of warriors who fought at Troy, the vigor and variety sometimes suggesting Marlowe and Shakespeare.

"Bourgeois" "untrammeled Elizabethan" zest for life during Elizabeth's reign comes through well in Heywood's two-part English history, *If You Know Not Me, You Know Nobody*, especially part two, but nearly drowns in *King Edward the Fourth* because of the songs and the sentimentality of the Jane Shore plot. For example, Jane, the mistress of Edward, submits in a flood of tears and kisses to Edward's queen for chastisement, a scene in which Edward is present; such sentimentality is topped only by the finally reconciled Shores' death agonies, as they join hands across a grave and sing till they expire.

Heywood's masterpiece of romance, the two-part *Fair Maid of the West*, features true, simple, frank, chaste, loyal, English Bess's exotic adventures to rescue her lover, ranging from the Raleigh-Essex Island Voyage to the court of Mulisheg, Morocco, successful because of her honesty, courage, and beauty. Part two gets the two chief couples safely married and home. Heywood's absurd but entertaining chivalric romance set during the crusades, *The Four Prentices of London* (satirized in *The Knight of the Burning Pestle*), has the apprentices become kings and their sister marry an Italian prince.

A Woman Killed with Kindness, Heywood's masterpiece of bourgeois realism and domestic tragedy, abandons the romantic tradition in *Othello* so dominant in Spanish and English theatre, demanding the adulterous wife's death. Frankford "heaps coals of fire" upon the heads of the conscience-stricken lovers by offering Anne forgiveness, becoming as eloquent for forgiveness as Wendoll was for sin. Keeping his dignity as betrayed husband, Frankford creates a mood of pathetic sorrow, anguish, and consternation, mixed with some righteous indignation; he weeps with, not hates, the evil doers, persuading the audience to do likewise, experiencing only one outburst of rage during which he would have killed them had not an accident intervened. The plot unfolds against a very realistic background, but the imagery presents Frankford as God and Adam in Eden, then Christ (betrayed), St. Paul, and God (in judgment), while Wendoll is Satan, Cain, and Judas.

—Louis Charles Stagg

HILL, Aaron. English. Born in London, 10 February 1685. Educated at Barnstaple Grammar School, Devon; Westminster School, London. Married Miss Morris in 1710 (died, 1731); nine children. Visited his relative, Lord Paget, then Ambassador in Constantinople, and sent by Paget on a tour of the east, 1700–03; subsequently travelled as a tutor to Sir William Wentworth; settled in London: Manager of the Drury Lane Theatre, 1709–10, and the opera in the Haymarket, 1710–13; managed the Little Theatre, Haymarket, c. 1720–33; Editor, with William Bond, *The Plain-Dealer*, 1724–25; Editor, *The Prompter*, 1734–36; also involved in various unsuccessful business ventures, including extracting oil from beechmast, 1713, colonizing in Georgia, 1718, etc.; retired to Essex, 1738. *Died 8 February 1750.*

PUBLICATIONS

Collections

> *Works.* 4 vols., 1753.
> *Dramatic Works.* 2 vols., 1760.

Plays

> *Elfrid; or, The Fair Inconstant* (produced 1710). 1710; revised version, as *Athelwold* (produced 1731), 1732.
> *The Walking Statue; or, The Devil in the Wine Cellar* (produced 1710). With *Elfrid,* 1710.
> *Rinaldo,* music by Handel, from a play by Giacomo Rossi (produced 1711). 1711.
> *Il Pastor Fido, The Faithful Shepherd,* music by Handel, from a play by Giacomo Rossi (produced 1712). 1712.
> *The Fatal Vision; or, The Fall of Siam* (produced 1716). 1716.
> *The Fatal Extravagance,* with Joseph Mitchell (produced 1721). 1720; revised version (produced 1730), 1726.
> *King Henry the Fifth; or, The Conquest of France by the English,* from the play by Shakespeare (produced 1723). 1723.
> *The Tragedy of Zara,* from a work by Voltaire (produced 1735). 1736.
> *Alzira,* from a work by Voltaire (produced 1736). 1736.
> *Merope,* from a work by Voltaire (produced 1749). 1749.
> *The Roman Revenge,* from a work by Voltaire (produced 1753?). 1753.
> *The Insolvent; or, Filial Piety,* from the play *The Guiltless Adultress* by Davenant based on *The Fatal Dowry* by Massinger (produced 1758). 1758.
> *The Muses in Mourning, Merlin in Love, The Snake in the Grass, Saul,* and *Daraxes,* in *Dramatic Works.* 1760.

Verse

> *Camillus.* 1707.
> *The Invasion: A Poem to the Queen.* 1708.
> *The Dedication of the Beech Tree.* 1714.
> *The Northern Star.* 1718; revised edition, 1739.
> *The Creation: A Pindaric.* 1720.
> *The Judgment-Day.* 1721.
> *The Progress of Wit: A Caveat.* 1730.
> *Advice to the Poets.* 1731.
> *The Tears of the Muses.* 1737.
> *The Fanciad: An Heroic Poem.* 1743.
> *The Impartial: An Address Without Flattery.* 1744.
> *The Art of Acting.* 1744.
> *Free Thoughts on Faith; or, The Religion of Reason.* 1746.
> *Gideon; or, The Patriot: An Epic Poem.* 1749.

Other

> *A Full Account of the Present State of the Ottoman Empire.* 1709.

An Enquiry into the Merit of Assassination. 1738.
A Collection of Letters Between Hill, Pope, and Others. 1751.
Selections from The Prompter, edited by W. A. Appleton and K. A. Burnim. 1966.

Editor, *The Plain-Dealer* (periodical). 2 vols., 1730.

Translator, with Nahum Tate, *The Celebrated Speeches of Ajax and Ulysses,* by Ovid. 1708.

Reading List: *The Life and Works of Hill* by H. Ludwig, 1911; *Hill, Poet, Dramatist, Projector* by Dorothy Brewster, 1913.

*   *   *

Aaron Hill was a man of great ambition but very frequently a loser. As a teenager he visited Constantinople (where a relative, Lord Paget, was British ambassador) but his book on the Ottoman Empire was written too early in life and later he deprecated it. He addressed a poem to Lord Peterborough but failed to take the preferment it occasioned. He wrote another in honor of Peter the Great and was awarded a gold medal – which he never collected. He proposed the colonization of Georgia but then dropped the idea. He invented some gadgets and processes – he patented one for extracting oil from beechmast – but nothing came of it. He wrote the libretto for Handel's *Rinaldo* (1711) but did not benefit either from the subsequent popularity for opera or from the spate of parodies, ballad operas, and other reactions which followed the Italian fad. He was appointed by William Collier to manage the Theatre Royal in Drury Lane but the actors beat him up and rioted: for this Powell was dismissed and Booth, Bickerstaff, Keen and Leigh disciplined, but in the end Hill suffered most. He defended Shakespeare against the attacks of Voltaire when the French genius was temporarily touted over the native one and said some nasty things about Pope in *The Progress of Wit,* which gained him the notoriety of a mention in *The Dunciad.* He adapted several of Voltaire's plays for the English stage but Arthur Murphy rather upstaged him with *The Orphan of China* (1759). His version of Voltaire's *Merope* was commanded as a benefit performance by Frederick, Prince of Wales – but Hill died the night before the performance.

As a playwright, Hill was not notable, though his early farce *The Walking Statue* showed more promise than such poems as *Camillus* and *The Northern Star. Elfrid; or, The Fair Inconstant* betrayed some of the jejune quality in *A Full Account of the Ottoman Empire,* and, while rhodomontade might pass on the stage, when *Aethelwold* (the revised version of *Elfrid*) appeared in print it was greeted with well-deserved ridicule. I must confess that Voltaire's pseudo-classical plays leave me cold and that Hill's English *réchauffages* are no help. Even the poetry of Stephen Duck (1705–1756) is probably better than Hill's if one must have a Wiltshire bard of the time, though Hill retired to family farms in Wiltshire after London rejected him, while Duck committed suicide after his brief vogue. Hill's verse is more pompous than that of John Home's *Douglas* (1757) but far less impressive, and Hill's greatest contribution to poetry was (when he was self-importantly setting himself up as *censor elegantarium* in competition with Pope) in recognizing true talent in James Thomson's *Winter* (1726, brought to Hill's attention by Thomson's friend David Mallet) and generously publicizing it. One might add that Hill regarded Thomson's *Liberty* as "mighty work" and "the last stretched blaze of our expiring genius" – probably because Thomson was then the heir-apparent to Pope. In his controversy with Pope, Hill was lively but did not really emerge as well as Colley Cibber. In the end he made up with Pope and numbered him and Richardson and many other celebrities among his friends. He befriended Richard Savage and wrote about him in his newspaper.

It was his journalism and his letters that saved Hill from being "a bit of a bore." *The Plain-Dealer* (23 March 1724 to 7 May 1725), conducted with William Bond, "maintained a good philosophic literary level" (Bonamy Dobrée, *English Literature in the Early Eighteenth Century*, 1959), and *The Prompter* (12 November 1734 to 2 July 1736) is of interest to all students of the theatre, its 173 numbers full of good criticism. Moreover Hill's letters are "always in the centre of the literary scene" (Dobrée) and concern Pope and *The Dunciad*; projects involving real estate and potash; coffee, sugar, and the tax on Madeira; Drury Lane and actors like Barton Booth and Robert Wilks; an ill-fated attempt to run the opera at the Haymarket; advice to Thomson on the use of capitals and to actors about tone and delivery; a letter to Sir Robert Walpole on "the encouragement of able *writers*" and one to Lady Walpole on rock-gardens; praise of Richardson's *Pamela* and criticism of Mallet's *Euridice*; communications to celebrities as different as Peterborough and Voltaire. Perhaps Hill was, as Pope waspishly said, a "bad author" but he was a fascinating individual, and the letters do much to prove the truth of another judgment of the Wasp of Twickenham: that Aaron Hill was "not quite a swan, not wholly a goose." If only as the author of *The Prompter*, Hill deserves a more modern study than those of Brewster or Ludwig.

—Leonard R.N. Ashley

HOME, John.   Scottish.   Born in Leith, near Edinburgh, 21 September 1722. Educated at the grammar school in Leith; University of Edinburgh, graduated 1742. Fought on the Hanoverian side in the Edinburgh volunteers, subsequently as a Lieutenant in the Glasgow volunteers, 1745–46: taken prisoner at Falkirk, 1746. Married Mary Home in 1770. Licensed to preach by the presbytery of Edinburgh, 1745; Minister of Athelstaneford, East Lothian, 1747 until he resigned before he could be tried on charges of profanity in his play *Douglas*, 1757; Private Secretary to the Earl of Bute, and subsequently tutor to the Prince of Wales, from 1757: granted pension by George III on his accession, 1760; Conservator of Scots privileges at Campvere, Holland, from 1763; built a mansion in Kilduff, East Lothian, and lived there, 1770–79; settled in Edinburgh, 1779. *Died 5 September 1808.*

PUBLICATIONS

Collections

   Works.   3 vols., 1822.

Plays

   Douglas (produced 1756).   1757; edited by Gerald D. Parker, 1972.
   Agis, music by William Boyce (produced 1758).   1758.
   The Siege of Aquileia (produced 1760).   1760.
   Dramatic Works.   1760; revised edition, 2 vols., 1798.
   The Fatal Discovery (produced 1769).   1769.
   Alonzo (produced 1773).   1773.
   Alfred (produced 1778).   1778.

Other

The History of the Rebellion in the Year 1745.   1802.

Reading List: *The Works of Home* by Henry Mackenzie, 1822; *Home: A Study of His Life and Works* by Alice E. Gipson, 1917.

*   *   *

Although John Home wrote six tragedies, his reputation is based almost entirely on *Douglas,* the second of his plays in order of composition but the first to be performed. After Garrick declined the play at Drury Lane, *Douglas* was performed with great success in Edinburgh, which led to a remarkably heated controversy concerned chiefly with the impropriety of a minister contributing to "wicked" theatrical activity. *Douglas* was also an immediate success when performed at Covent Garden in London, quickly became standard repertory fare, and remained popular for over a century.

One of the eighteenth century's best blank-verse tragedies, *Douglas* deals with the untimely death of the valiant Douglas and the ensuing suicide of his mother, Lady Randolph, with whom he has been reunited after having been separated since infancy. The contrast between Lady Randolph's past suffering and current, though temporary, joy is central to the play, which seeks to evoke "celestial melancholy" by focusing on tragic irony and pity for Lady Randolph's frustrated maternal love. The play's popularity can also be attributed to its fervid language, highly romantic setting, and appeal to Scottish national pride.

Of Home's five other plays, *Agis, The Siege of Aquileia, The Fatal Discovery,* and *Alonzo* were moderately well-received on the eighteenth-century stage, while his last effort, *Alfred,* ran for only three nights. With the exception of *The Siege of Aquileia,* these plays also employ tragic irony, melancholy atmospheres, or romantic settings to evoke pathos, but are generally inferior to *Douglas.*

Agis, written before *Douglas,* deals with the assassination of a political hero who fails to recognize the treachery of his enemies. In *The Fatal Discovery,* based on one of James Macpherson's Ossianic fragments, the heroine, Rivine, commits suicide after placing love above personal honor. Rivine is made to appear an innocent victim of deception; hence emphasis is placed on the growing pathos of her situation as the play progresses. *Alonzo* is nearly identical to *Douglas* in plot conception and in stressing frustrated maternal affection; however, Lady Randolph's suicide is well-motivated and moving, whereas Ormisinda, in *Alonzo,* kills herself for no apparent reason at the moment when various misunderstandings could be corrected and disaster averted. *Alfred* is a melodrama that deserves to remain the most obscure of Home's plays. It consists of a series of schemes devised by Alfred to save his betrothed from Hinguar, the Danish king.

The best of these five plays is *The Siege of Aquileia,* in which Aemilius, a Roman consul and governor, must either sacrifice his sons or betray his country and personal honor. Home handles Aemilius's dilemma effectively, making the choice progressively more difficult. This is the only one of Home's plays in which the protagonist must choose between equally worthy, conflicting sets of values; hence it allows for more complex tragic effects than the pathos that remains uppermost in all of Home's other plays.

—James S. Malek

HOME, William Douglas. Scottish. Born in Edinburgh, 3 June 1912. Educated at Eton College; New College, Oxford, B.A. in history 1935; Royal Academy of Dramatic Art, London, 1935–37. Served in the Royal Armoured Corps, 1940–44: Captain. Married Rachel Brand in 1951; one son and three daughters. Progressive Independent candidate for Parliament, for the Cathcart division of Glasgow, April 1942, Windsor division of Berkshire, June 1942, and Clay Cross division of Derbyshire, April 1944; Liberal candidate for South Edinburgh, 1957. Lives in Hampshire.

PUBLICATIONS

Plays

 Great Possessions (produced 1937).
 Passing By (produced 1940).
 Now Barabbas ... (produced 1947). 1947.
 The Chiltern Hundreds (produced 1947). 1949; as *Yes, M'Lord* (produced 1949), 1949.
 Ambassador Extraordinary (produced 1948).
 Master of Arts (produced 1949). 1950.
 The Thistle and the Rose (produced 1949). In *The Plays*, 1958.
 Caro William (produced 1952).
 The Bad Samaritan (produced 1952). 1954.
 The Manor of Northstead (produced 1954). 1956.
 The Reluctant Debutante (produced 1955). 1956.
 The Iron Duchess (produced 1957). 1958.
 The Plays (includes *Now Barabbas ..., The Chiltern Hundreds, The Thistle and the Rose, The Bad Samaritan, The Reluctant Debutante).* 1958.
 Aunt Edwina (produced 1959). 1960.
 Up a Gum Tree (produced 1960).
 The Bad Soldier Smith (produced 1961). 1962.
 The Cigarette Girl (produced 1962).
 The Drawing Room Tragedy (produced 1963).
 The Reluctant Peer (produced 1964). 1964.
 Two Accounts Rendered: The Home Secretary and Lady J.P.2 (produced 1964).
 A Friend Indeed (produced 1965). 1966.
 Betzi (produced 1965).
 The Queen's Highland Servant (produced 1967).
 The Secretary Bird (produced 1968). 1968.
 The Grouse Moor Image (produced 1968).
 The Bishop and the Actress (televised 1968). 1969.
 Uncle Dick's Surprise (produced 1970).
 The Jockey Club Stakes (produced 1970). 1973.
 The Editor Regrets (televised 1970; produced 1978).
 The Douglas Cause (produced 1971).
 Lloyd George Knew My Father (as *Lady Boothroyd of the By-Pass*, produced 1972; as *Lloyd George Knew My Father*, produced 1972). 1973.
 The Bank Manager (produced 1972).
 At the End of the Day (produced 1973).
 The Dame of Sark (produced 1974).
 The Lord's Lieutenant (produced 1974).
 In the Red (produced 1977).
 The Kingfisher (produced 1977).

Rolls Hyphen Royce (produced 1977).
The Perch (produced 1977).

Screenplays: *Sleeping Car to Trieste,* with Allan Mackinnon, 1948; *For Them That Trespass,* with J. Lee-Thompson, 1949; *The Chiltern Hundreds (The Amazing Mr. Beecham),* with Patrick Kirwan, 1949; *Your Witness (Eye Witness),* with Hugo Butler and Ian Hunter, 1950; *Made in Heaven,* 1952; *The Colditz Story,* with others, 1955; *The Reluctant Debutante,* 1959; *Follow That Horse!,* with Howard Mason and Alfred Shaughnessy, 1960.

Television Plays: *The Bishop and the Actress,* 1968; *The Editor Regrets,* 1970; *On Such a Night,* 1974.

Verse

Home Truths. 1939.

Other

Half-Term Report: An Autobiography. 1954.

*   *   *

William Douglas Home is a dramatist of considerable range and variety. Whether he is writing a play that has an historical setting (e.g., *The Thistle and the Rose*) or one that is modern in setting and theme, Home displays a keen sense of what is telling on the stage. In fact, his comedies have often been the vehicles for actors of great distinction. It is this latter sort of play, rather than the rather episodic historical spectacles, which constitute Home's claim to attention. In general, Home's imagination moves with facility in the medium of upper-class British life; the plays suggest that he is a sympathetic and yet mildly critical observer of that life. The plays also suggest that Home has also looked with attention at the plays of Maugham and Lonsdale.

Sometimes Home indicates that the world he depicts best is changing, as in *The Chiltern Hundreds* and *The Jockey Club Stakes.* In the former play an election reminds upper-class persons that it is the middle of the twentieth century and change is imminent; butlers as well as masters aspire to political power. *The Jockey Club Stakes* shows the entrenched directors of a sporting club threatened by a parvenu; with a characteristic *coup de théâtre,* the upstart who challenges the closed circle discovers that his wife is as dishonest as the men he is confronting. The result, here and elsewhere in his plays, is a draw, if not a full return to the status quo. The same can be said of other plays. *Lloyd George Knew My Father* begins with a piquant situation: a noble lady threatens suicide if a freeway crosses her acres. Of course, she does not do away with herself. But her protests provide entertainment and a mild consideration of the costs of social change.

Sometimes only the former benefit – entertainment – marks a particular play. *The Reluctant Debutante* shows prosperous parents in London attempting to find a suitable mate for their daughter. And *The Secretary Bird* is a neat and diverting linkage of adultery and conventional morality. A clever husband brings his wife, his wife's lover, his own secretary, and himself together for a typical English stage weekend. By the time Monday morning comes, it is certain that the husband will keep his wife. After a great deal of brittle talk and suspect behavior, the characters – and the audience – exit by familiar doors.

In short, Home is a careful craftsman of the not quite obvious – a not quite obvious that resolves itself, by the end of a play, into shapes that have been long familiar.

—Harold H. Watts

HOUGHTON, (William) Stanley. English. Born in Ashton-upon-Mersey, Cheshire, 22 February 1881. Educated at Bowdon School; Stockport Grammar School; West Imslow Grammar School; Manchester Grammar School, 1896–97. Worked in his father's cotton business in Manchester, 1897–1912; Dramatic Critic, *Manchester City News*, 1905–06; Feature Writer and Literary/Dramatic Critic, *Manchester Guardian*, 1905–13; settled in Paris, 1913, then, because of illness, returned to Manchester. *Died 11 December 1913.*

PUBLICATIONS

Collections

Works, edited by Harold Brighouse. 3 vols., 1914.

Plays

The Intriguers, with Frank G. Naismith (produced 1906).
The Reckoning, with Frank G. Naismith (produced 1907; as *The Day of Reckoning*, produced 1912).
The Dear Departed (produced 1908). 1910.
Independent Means (produced 1909). 1911.
The Master of the House (produced 1910). 1913.
The Younger Generation (produced 1910). 1910.
Fancy Free (produced 1911). 1912; revised version, as *Partners* (produced 1915), in *Works 2*, 1914.
Hindle Wakes (produced 1912). 1912.
Phipps (produced 1912). 1913.
Pearls (produced 1912).
Trust the People (produced 1913).
The Fifth Commandment (produced 1913). 1913; revised version, as *The Perfect Cure* (produced 1913), in *Works 2*, 1914.
Ginger (produced 1913).
The Old Testament and the New (produced 1914). In *Works 3*, 1914.
Marriages in the Making, in *Works 1*. 1914.
The Hillarys, with Harold Brighouse (produced 1915).

Reading List: *Houghton: Eine Untersuchung Seiner Dramen* by Marcel Gaberthuel, 1973.

*   *   *

Stanley Houghton came to prominence with a series of neatly constructed, shrewd comedies of provincial life, written for Miss Horniman's pioneering repertory company at the Gaiety Theatre, Manchester, and, although his plays were indebted to the new "intellectual" iconoclastic drama of Shaw and Hankin, Houghton's affinities and insights were exclusively confined to the Lancastrian milieu, and he was ill-at-ease when portraying conditions elsewhere. His strength as a dramatist lay in his keen eye for human pretensions, hypocrisies, and evasions, his skilful depiction of psychological reactions to crises resulting from changing standards of morality and behaviour, and an ability to extract ironic resonances from domestic situations and dry humour from everyday dialogue. Admittedly he never exploited the richness of regional dialect, his dramatic expositions could lack subtlety, and his subject-matter was sometimes ephemeral, but his best plays transcended these blemishes, and Houghton is now regarded as one of the most interesting playwrights of his decade.

His first solo play to be staged, *The Dear Departed*, now has the status of a classic one-act comedy: the presumed death of an aged man permits the merciless exposure of the "departed" one's mercenary daughters, to whose predations their spineless husbands are compliant accessories. The "corpse's" subsequent discomfiture of the rival sisters provides a satisfying conclusion to a small masterpiece of economy and observation. *Independent Means*, Houghton's first full-length play, is unsatisfactory, being less securely rooted in accurate scrutiny of character and environment: its subject is bankruptcy in a well-to-do Manchester suburb, and part of its theme is women's rights, but there is an air of contrivance about the piece and the dialogue is flat to the point of banality. However, the independent-minded, resourceful girl, the shiftless son, and the dominating father recur to greater effect in *The Younger Generation* and *Hindle Wakes*, where their actions are less unconvincing and their creator's touch more assured. *The Younger Generation* presents youth rebelling in support of freedom from repressive parental restrictions, and its encouragement by the liberal-minded, expatriate brother of the chapel-going teetotaller Mr. Kennion: here the characterization is rounder, the humour riper, and the plot development less predictable, even if the theme is not uncommon.

But his major triumph is indubitably *Hindle Wakes*. This play attracted some notoriety for its daringly explicit sexual matter when first produced (Oxford students were banned from attending performances). It is an impeccably told story of a boldly self-reliant mill-girl who spends a hotel week-end with the spoiled son of her employer, and then successfully resists both families' efforts to force the couple into a face-saving marriage. It challenged traditional propriety by arguing that women too might have a voice in their own sexual activities and marital destinies, and that the "New Woman" was not found exclusively among the leisured and educated classes. Yet the play's message never dominates the dramatic narration, and the unforced quality of writing which rarely sinks to the melodramatic, coupled with Houghton's restraint, sincerity, and wry comic intelligence, makes *Hindle Wakes* an absorbing play of considerable power.

—William M. Tydeman

HOUSMAN, Laurence. English. Born in Bromsgrove, Worcestershire, 18 July 1865; brother of the poet A. E. Housman. Educated at Bromsgrove School; moved to London, 1883, and studied painting at Lambeth School of Art and the National Art Training College. Contributor, as author and illustrator, to the *Universal Review*, London; Art Critic for the *Manchester Guardian*, 1895–1911; began writing for the theatre c. 1900; lived in Somerset from 1924. Noted for espousal of liberal causes: member of the men's section of the

Women's Social and Political Union; pacifist; supporter of the League of Nations, on which he lectured in the United States. *Died 20 February 1959.*

PUBLICATIONS

Plays

> *Bethlehem: A Nativity Play,* music by Joseph Moorat (produced 1902). 1902; revised version, music by Rutland Boughton (produced 1923), 1927.
> *Prunella; or, Love in a Dutch Garden,* with Harley Granville-Barker (produced 1904). 1906; revised version, 1930.
> *The Vicar of Wakefield,* music by Liza Lehmann, from the novel by Goldsmith (produced 1906). 1906.
> *The Chinese Lantern: A Fairy Play,* music by Joseph Moorat (produced 1908). 1908.
> *A Likely Story* (produced 1910). 1916.
> *The Lord of the Harvest* (produced 1910). 1916.
> *Lysistrata,* from the play by Aristophanes (produced 1910). 1911.
> *Alice in Ganderland: A Political Skit* (produced 1911). 1911.
> *Pains and Penalties: The Defence of Queen Caroline* (produced 1911). 1911.
> *The Return of Alcestis.* 1916.
> *Nazareth.* 1916.
> *As Good as Gold.* 1916.
> *The Snow Man.* 1916.
> *Bird in Hand: A Fairy Play* (produced 1918). 1916.
> *The Wheel* (includes *Apollo in Hades, The Death of Alcestis, The Doom of Admetus*). 1919.
> *Angels and Ministers: Three Plays of Victorian Shade and Character* (includes *The Queen, God Bless Her!; His Favourite Flower; The Comforter*). 1921; augmented version (includes *Possession, The King-Maker, The Man of Business, The Instrument*), 1922.
> *The Queen, God Bless Her!* (produced 1929). In *Angels and Ministers,* 1921.
> *The Comforter* (as *Mr. Gladstone's Comforter,* produced 1929). In *Angels and Ministers,* 1921.
> *The House Fairy* (as *The Fairy,* produced 1921). In *False Premises,* 1922.
> *The Death of Orpheus.* 1921; revised version, 1925.
> *Possession: A Peep-Show in Paradise* (produced 1923). In *Angels and Ministers,* 1922.
> *Dethronements: Imaginary Portraits of Political Characters.* 1922.
> *False Premises: Five One-Act Plays* (includes *The Christmas Tree, The Torch of Time, Moonshine, A Fool and His Money, The House Fairy*). 1922.
> *Little Plays of St. Francis.* 1922; second series, 1931; augmented edition, 3 vols., 1935.
> *Echo de Paris: A Study from Life.* 1923.
> *Followers of St. Francis.* 1923.
> *The Death of Socrates.* 1925.
> *The Comments of Juniper.* 1926.
> *Ways and Means: Five One Act Plays of Village Characters.* 1928.
> *Cornered Poets: A Book of Dramatic Dialogues.* 1929.
> *The New Hangman.* 1930.
> *Palace Plays.* 1930; *The Queen's Progress,* 2nd series, 1932; *Victoria and Albert,* 3rd series, 1933; complete series, as *Victoria Regina* (produced 1937), 1934.
> *Ye Fearful Saints! Plays of Creed, Custom, and Credulity.* 1932.
> *Nunc Dimittis: An Epilogue to Little Plays of St. Francis.* 1933.

Four Plays of St. Clare.   1934.
Palace Scenes.   1937.
The Golden Sovereign.   1937.
Glorious Majesty.   1941.
Palestine Plays.   1942.
Samuel the Kingmaker.   1944.
Happy and Glorious (selected from *Victoria Regina, The Golden Sovereign,* and *Glorious Majesty).*   1945.
The Family Honour (produced 1948).   1950.
Old Testament Plays.   1950.

Fiction

All-Fellows: Seven Legends of Lower Redemption.   1896.
Gods and Their Makers.   1897.
An Englishwoman's Love-Letters.   1900.
Blind Love (story).   1901.
The Tale of a Nun, with L. Simons.   1901.
A Modern Antaeus.   1901.
Sabrina Warham: The Story of Her Youth.   1904.
The Blue Moon and Other Tales.   1904.
The Cloak of Friendship (story).   1905.
John of Jingalo: The Story of a Monarch in Difficulties.   1912; as *King John of Jingalo,* 1937.
The Royal Runaway and Jingalo in Revolution.   1914.
The Sheepfold: The Story of a Shepherdess and Her Sheep, and How She Lost Them.   1918.
The Wheel.   1919.
Trimblerigg: A Book of Revelation.   1924.
Odd Pairs: A Book of Tales.   1925.
Ironical Tales.   1926.
Uncle Tom Pudd: A Biographical Romance.   1927.
The Life of H.R.H. the Duke of Flamborough.   1928.
Hop-o'-Me-Heart: A Grown Up Fairy Tale.   1938.
What Next: Provocative Tales of Faith and Morals.   1938.
Strange Ends and Discoveries: Tales of This World and the Next.   1948.
The Kind and the Foolish: Short Tales of Myth, Magic, and Miracle.   1952.

Verse

Green Arras.   1896.
Spikenard: A Book of Devotional Love-Poems.   1898.
Rue.   1899.
The Little Land, with Songs from Its Four Rivers.   1899.
Mendicant Rhymes.   1906.
Selected Poems.   1908.
The Heart of Peace and Other Poems.   1918.
The Love Concealed.   1928.
Collected Poems.   1937.
Cynthia.   1947.

Other

A Farm in Fairyland (juvenile). 1894.
The House of Joy (juvenile). 1895.
The Field of Clover (juvenile). 1898.
The Story of the Seven Young Goslings (juvenile). 1899.
The Missing Answers to An Englishwoman's Love-Letters. 1901.
Stories from the Arabian Nights, Retold. 1907.
Articles of Faith in the Freedom of Women. 1910.
*The New Child's Guide to Knowledge: A Book of Poems and Moral Lessons for Old and
    Young.* 1911.
The Immoral Effects of Ignorance in Sex Relations. 1911.
The Bawling Brotherhood. 1913.
The "Physical Force" Fallacy. 1913.
The Law-Abiding. 1914.
Great Possessions. 1915.
The Winners. 1915.
Christianity a Danger to the State. 1916.
The Relation of Fellow-Feeling to Sex. 1917.
St. Francis Poverello. 1918.
Ploughshare and Pruning-Hook (lectures). 1919.
Moonshine and Clover (selections). 1922.
A Doorway in Fairyland (selections). 1922.
The New Humanism. 1923.
The Open Door (juvenile), with *Toffee Boy* by Mabel Marlowe. 1925.
Puss-in-Boots (juvenile). 1926.
A Thing to Be Explained (juvenile). 1926.
Wish to Goodness! (juvenile), with *The Dragon at Hide and Seek* by G. K.
    Chesterton. 1927.
The "Little Plays" Handbook. 1927.
Etheldrinda's Fairy (juvenile), with *The Tame Dragon* by A. V. Leaper. 1928.
The Religious Advance Toward Rationalism. 1929.
The Boiled Owl (juvenile). 1930.
Busybody's Land (juvenile). 1930.
Cotton-Woolleena (juvenile). 1930.
A Gander and His Geese (juvenile). 1930.
Little and Good (juvenile). 1930.
Turn Again Tales (juvenile). 1930.
A Clean Sweep: A Tale of a Cat and a Broomstick (juvenile). 1931.
Histories, Introductory to Marten and Carter's Histories, with C. H. K. Marten. 4 vols.,
    1931–32.
What O'Clock Tales (juvenile). 1932.
The Long Journey: The Tale of Our Past, with C. H. K. Marten. 1933.
The Unexpected Years (autobiography). 1937.
What Can We Believe? (correspondence with Dick Sheppard). 1939.
The Preparation of Peace. 1940.
Military Necessity in the Middle Ages. 1941.
Back Words and Fore Words: An Author's Year-Book 1893–1945 (miscellany). 1945.
What Price Salvation Now? 1949.
Moonlight and Fairyland (juvenile). 1978.

Editor, with W. Somerset Maugham, *Venture: An Annual of Art and Literature.* 2
    vols., 1903–05.
Editor, *War Letters of Fallen Englishmen.* 1930.

Editor, *A. E. Housman: Some Poems, Some Letters, and a Personal Memoir.* 1937.

Translator, *Of Aucassin and Nicolette, with Annabel and Amoris.* 1902.

Bibliography: *Housman: A Brief Catalogue of the Collection Presented to the Street [Somerset] Library* by Ivor Kemp, 1965.

Reading List: *Die Dichtung von Housman* by A. Rudolf, 1930.

*   *   *

Laurence Housman was an extremely prolific writer whose work spread itself over many categories. The abundance and versatility were paid for in the lack of real tension and conflict in most of his work. Known among his contemporaries as the most censored of dramatists, he brought this fate on himself not in his character as a sexual reformer, but through his presentation of sacred and royal personages on the stage. Apart from this violation of protocol in the days of the Lord Chamberlain's power over the theatre, *Bethlehem*, the medieval-style Christian play best remembered because Gordon Craig produced it, and *Pains and Penalties*, concerned with the public humiliation of Queen Caroline, were surely always innocuous enough.

If there is a consistency to be found throughout Housman's work, it is probably a matter of temperament, a bias towards the feminine and towards the domestic, combined with a rationalism that accommodates a desire for spiritual values. His early poetry has a ninetyish contrived simplicity about it and recalls aspects oi Rossetti's poetry; other influences are Matthew Arnold (evident in such verse plays as *The Death of Orpheus*) and, persistently, George Herbert. Although he wrote of it in his autobiography, *The Unexpected Years*, as work he was rather ashamed of, his anonymously published best-seller, *An Englishwoman's Love Letters*, remains of some interest for the skill with which the epistolary form is used to create a novel of temperament and emotion which almost entirely dispenses with plot and subsidiary characters. There is more to its febrile lyricism, also, than a response to Meredith's *Ordeal of Richard Feverel*. Its theme of love doomed to premature ending without fulfilment associates it with the largely autobiographical novel of childhood and youth ending in premature death, *A Modern Antaeus*. Housman's series of plays about the Royal Family, including the selection of episodes from the life of Queen Victoria which had considerable theatrical success under the title *Happy and Glorious*, when the ban on performance was lifted at the time of the silver jubilee of George V, is marked by indifference to historical accuracy, but concern to break through reverential mists to the truth of human personalities. In this series and his *Little Plays of St. Francis*, which became a favourite for amateur production, he followed a design since made very familiar through television: the series of short plays linked together by centring on the same character, or group of characters, which can be multiplied indefinitely. The artist and spiritual man combined to create the plays of Saint Francis, which are mildly pleasing and show the author's virtuosity in a tradition that has little to do with modern life or modern art forms. The Housman who embroiled himself in feminist and pacificist causes is more easily identified in the author of the political playlets published as *Dethronements* and the satirical novels *John of Jingalo* and *Trimblerigg*, a stinging satire on Lloyd George. *Echo de Paris* stands on its own, an effective and moving one-act play based on an actual meeting between Laurence Housman and a friend with Robert Ross and Oscar Wilde. *The Unexpected Years* refers to a number of plays that Housman worked on with Granville-Barker, but the delicate and bittersweet *commedia dell'arte* pastiche, *Prunella*, was the only one produced and published under both their names.

—Margery Morgan

HOWARD, Bronson (Crocker). American. Born in Detroit, Michigan, 7 October 1842. Educated at schools in Detroit, and at Russell's Institute, New Haven, Connecticut. Married Alice Wyndham in 1880. Member of the staff of the *Detroit Free Press*; began writing for the stage, 1864; moved to New York, 1865, and worked as a reporter for the *Evening Mail*, *Tribune*, and *Evening Post*, until his first dramatic success, 1870; thereafter a full-time playwright. Founder, 1891, and first President, American Dramatist's Club (later the Society of American Dramatists and Composers). *Died 4 August 1908.*

PUBLICATIONS

Collections

   The Banker's Daughter and Other Plays (includes *Old Love Letters, One of Our Girls, Hurricanes, Knave and Queen, Baron Rudolph*), edited by Allan G. Halline. 1941.

Plays

   Fantine (produced 1864).
   Saratoga; or, Pistols for Seven (produced 1870). 1870.
   Ingomar the Idiotic; or, The Miser, The Maid, and the Mangle, with Oswald Allen (produced 1871).
   Diamonds (produced 1872).
   The Banker's Daughter (as *Lilian's Lost Love,* produced 1873; revised version as *The Banker's Daughter,* produced 1878; as *The Old Love and the New,* produced 1879). 1878; in *The Banker's Daughter and Other Plays,* 1941.
   Moorcroft; or, The Double Wedding (produced 1874).
   Knave and Queen, with Charles L. Young (as *Ivers Dean,* produced 1877). In *The Banker's Daughter and Other Plays,* 1941.
   Old Love Letters (produced 1878). 1897; in *The Banker's Daughter and Other Plays,* 1941.
   Hurricanes (produced 1878; as *Truth,* produced 1878). In *The Banker's Daughter and Other Plays,* 1941.
   Wives, from a play by Molière (produced 1879).
   The Amateur Benefit. 1881.
   Baron Rudolph (produced 1881; revised version, with David Belasco, produced 1887). In *The Banker's Daughter and Other Plays,* 1941.
   Fun in a Green Room (produced 1882).
   Young Mrs. Winthrop (produced 1882). 1899.
   One of Our Girls (produced 1885; as *Cousin Kate,* produced 1889). 1897; in *The Banker's Daughter and Other Plays,* 1941.
   Camping Out (produced 1886).
   Met by Chance (produced 1887).
   The Henrietta (produced 1887). 1901; edited by Allan G. Halline, in *American Plays,* 1935.
   Shenandoah (produced 1888). 1897; edited by A. H. Quinn, in *Representative American Plays,* 1917.
   Aristocracy (produced 1892). 1898.
   Peter Stuyvesant, with Brander Matthews (produced 1899).

Fiction

Kate. 1906.

Other

The Autobiography of a Play (on *The Banker's Daughter*). 1914.

Reading List: *In Memoriam Bronson Howard* (addresses), 1910.

*   *   *

The contribution to American drama which inspired some critics to describe Bronson Howard as the "Dean of American Drama" derives largely from his ability to support himself as a dramatist, the first American to achieve this distinction. As a professional dramatist he founded the American Dramatist's Club in 1891, lectured at Harvard on what he termed "The Laws of Dramatic Composition," established himself firmly as the major playwright to deal with the American businessman, and brought to American drama the international social scene which was then being exploited in fiction with considerable success by Henry James and William Dean Howells.

The fact that Howard could make a career as a playwright suggests something about his abilities. As a good craftsman of the stage, he understood and accepted the commercially oriented conventions and limiting requirements of the late nineteenth-century American theatre. Although he was markedly more farsighted than his contemporaries in terms of his chosen themes and materials, he carefully adhered to his own outline of a well-constructed play which must be "satisfactory" to an audience and reach a properly moral and happy conclusion. Toward the end of his career he weakened his position as a man of independent thought by joining the stable of playwrights of the Theatrical Syndicate. He was always a man of the theatre, sometimes belligerently so, and it was never his intention to pull together the established rift in America between theatre and drama. Indeed, his expressed antagonism toward dramatic literature and literary people probably further delayed a developing American drama.

A major characteristic of his playwriting was the carefully crafted and commercially successful work which suggested a direction for future dramatists whose careers among theatre managers would be more secure after Howard's efforts. His first success was a play called *Saratoga,* for which he embroidered the usual farce action with better than average farce dialogue and used a favorite American resort as his scene. The fact that the play was transferred successfully to English circumstances by Frank Marshall as *Brighton* (1874) suggests something of his style. More significant are his business plays. *Young Mrs. Winthrop* showed the difficulties which the demands of the business world may bring to married life. *The Henrietta* satirized life on the New York Stock Exchange. *Aristocracy* combined Howard's interest in the American businessman and the socially intriguing international scene by revealing that the obvious route by which new wealth of the American west may unite with New York traditional society was through London aristocracy. In an earlier play, *One of Our Girls,* Howard contrasted American and French social conventions. His single play – a very successful one – which remains outside his usual society-oriented work is *Shenandoah,* a romantic tale of the Civil War.

Basically a transitional dramatist in American theatre, Howard helped to diminish the popularity of foreign plays on the American stage and give the American dramatist greater importance in the theatre. This is his real contribution. Otherwise, he was a generally skillful dramatist for his time who could write entertaining and sentimental social melodrama.

—Walter J. Meserve

HOWARD, Sir Robert. English.   Born in England in 1626; son of the Earl of Berkshire; brother-in-law of John Dryden, *q.v.* Probably educated at Magdalen College, Oxford. Married 1) Ann Kingsmill in 1645, one daughter; 2) Lady Honora O'Brien in 1665, one son; 3) Annabella Dives in 1692. Royalist: knighted for bravery at the second battle of Newbury, 1644; imprisoned during the Commonwealth at Windsor Castle; after the Restoration became Member of Parliament for Stockbridge, Hampshire, was made a Knight of the Bath, and became Secretary to the Commissioners of the Treasury; Auditor of the Exchequer, 1677 until his death; Member of Parliament for Castle Rising, Norfolk, 1678–98; Privy Councillor, 1688; commissioner to enquire into the state of the fleet, 1690; commander of the militia horse, 1690. *Died 3 September 1698.*

PUBLICATIONS

Plays

> *The Blind Lady*, in *Poems.* 1660.
> *The Surprisal* (produced 1662).   In *Four New Plays*, 1665.
> *The Committee; or, The Faithful Irishman* (produced 1662).   In *Four New Plays*, 1665; edited by Carryl N. Thurber, 1921.
> *The Indian Queen* (produced 1664).   In *Four New Plays*, 1665; revised version, music by Purcell (produced 1695); in *Works 8* by Dryden, 1962.
> *The Vestal Virgin; or, The Roman Ladies* (produced 1665).   In *Four New Plays*, 1665.
> *Four New Plays.* 1665; expanded edition, as *Five New Plays*, 1692; as *Dramatic Works*, 1722.
> *The Great Favourite; or, The Duke of Lerma* (produced 1668).   1668; edited by D. D. Arundell, in *Dryden and Howard*, 1929.
> *The Country Gentleman*, with George Villiers, edited by Arthur H. Scouten and Robert D. Hume.   1976.

Verse

> *Poems.* 1660.
> *The Duel of the Stags.*   1668.

Other

> *An Account of the State of His Majesty's Revenue.*   1680.
> *The Life and Reign of King Richard the Second.*   1680.
> *Historical Observations upon the Reigns of Edward I, II, III, and Richard II.*   1689.
> *A Letter to Mr. Samuel Johnson.*   1692.
> *The History of Religion.*   1694; as *An Account of the Growth of Deism*, 1709.

Reading List: *Howard: A Critical Biography* by Harold J. Oliver, 1963 (includes bibliography).

*   *   *

Sir Robert Howard was active in various aspects of the revival of drama upon the re-opening of the theatres in 1660, as he not only wrote comedies and one of the earliest heroic plays but also engaged in dramatic theory. A new kind of tragedy was emerging, and Harold J. Oliver calls Howard's first play, *The Blind Lady*, "half-way between Jacobean tragedy and Heroic drama." Howard then went all the way towards creating a new form in *The Indian Queen*. Here we find an epic hero, a conflict between the claims of Love and Honour, serious debates, and spectacular stage effects. The reception of this new type of drama led Howard into unprofitable literary controversies over the place of rhymed verse in tragedy and the validity of tragi-comedy.

Of his four comedies, *The Committee* was his great success, holding the stage into the nineteenth century. This vivacious work presents an implacable conflict between the puritans and the royalists toward the end of the Commonwealth period and contains an intrinsically comic figure in the Irish servant Teague. More important, however, in a critical analysis of Howard as a playwright is his achieving what strikes the reader as a genuine rather than an artificial portrayal of women in his imaginative creation of the heroine Ruth and the villain Mrs. Day, a former dairy maid who has risen to become the wife of the chairman of the sequestration committee. These two women are more than a match for the men throughout the play.

Similar psychological insight and emphasis on the role of women appear in *The Country Gentleman*, the long-lost political comedy by Howard and George Villiers, which was discovered in 1973. In the play, Howard experiments with the love game between the romantic couples, a technique which was to become standard practice in later sex-comedies of the Restoration. Yet Howard proceeds with sturdy independence to present an exemplary father (unheard of in this early period), to champion the country against the city, and to engage in satire which includes positive as well as negative examples. His neoclassical taste is revealed in the structure of this comedy, all of which is set in two rooms of one house, with the time of the action only slightly exceeding the actual time of the representation.

After a promising beginning as a playwright, Howard abandoned literature and turned to a full career in politics.

—Arthur H. Scouten

HOWARD, Sidney (Coe). American. Born in Oakland, California, 26 June 1891. Educated at the University of California, Berkeley, B.A. 1915; studied with George Pierce Baker at Harvard University, Cambridge, Massachusetts, 1915–16. Served in the American Ambulance Corps, and later in the United States Army Air Corps, in World War I: Captain. Married 1) the actress Clare Jenness Eames in 1922 (divorced, 1930), one daughter; 2) Leopoldine Blaine Damrosch in 1931, one daughter and one son. Member of the Editorial Staff, 1919–22, and Literary Editor, 1922, *Life* magazine, New York; Special Investigator and Feature Writer, *New Republic* and *Hearst's International Magazine*, New York, 1923; full-time playwright from 1923; Founder, with Robert E. Sherwood, Elmer Rice, Maxwell Anderson, S. N. Behrman, and John F. Wharton, Playwrights Company, 1938. Member, Board of Directors, American Civil Liberties Union; President, American Dramatists Guild. Recipient: Pulitzer Prize, 1925. Litt.D.: Washington and Jefferson College, Washington, Pennsylvania, 1935. Member, American Academy of Arts and Letters. *Died 23 August 1939.*

PUBLICATIONS

Plays

Swords (produced 1921). 1921.
Casanova, from a play by Lorenzo de Azertis (produced 1923). 1924.
Lexington (produced 1925). 1924.
They Knew What They Wanted (produced 1924). 1925.
Bewitched, with Edward Sheldon (produced 1924).
Lucky Sam McCarver (produced 1925). 1926.
Ned McCobb's Daughter (produced 1926). 1926.
The Silver Cord (produced 1926). 1927.
Salvation, with Charles MacArthur (produced 1928). In *Stage Works of MacArthur*, 1974.
Olympia, from a play by Molnar (produced 1928). 1928.
Half Gods (produced 1929). 1930.
Lute Song, with Will Irwin (as *Pi-Pa-Ki*, produced 1930); revised version, as *Lute Song*, music by Raymond Scott, lyrics by Bernard Hanighen (produced 1946). 1955.
The Late Christopher Bean, from a play by René Fauchois (produced 1932). 1933.
Alien Corn (produced 1933). 1933.
Ode to Liberty, from a play by Michel Duran (produced 1934).
Dodsworth, from the novel by Sinclair Lewis (produced 1934). 1934.
Yellow Jack, with Paul de Kruif, from a work by de Kruif (produced 1934). 1934.
Paths of Glory, from the novel by Humphrey Cobb (produced 1935). 1935.
The Ghost of Yankee Doodle (produced 1937). 1938.
Madam, Will You Walk? (produced 1953). 1955.

Screenplays: *Bulldog Drummond*, with Wallace Smith, 1929; *Condemned*, 1929; *A Lady to Love*, 1930; *Free Love*, 1930; *Raffles*, 1930; *Arrowsmith*, 1931; *One Heavenly Night*, 1931; *The Greeks Had a Word for It*, 1932; *Dodsworth*, 1936; *Gone with the Wind*, 1939; *Raffles*, with John Van Druten, 1939.

Fiction

Three Flights Up (stories). 1924.

Other

The Labor Spy: A Survey of Industrial Espionage. 1921; revised edition, 1924.
Professional Patriots, with John Hearley, edited by Norman Hapgood. 1927.

*   *   *

The first major writer of social drama after American drama approached the age of maturity following World War I, Howard mixed melodrama and comedy with the established mode of realism in literature to reflect a dominant social idea of the 1920's – *They Knew What They Wanted*. As the title of one of his best plays, it presented the positive individualism of his generation which other playwrights (Philip Barry, S. N. Behrman, Maxwell Anderson, Paul Green) soon emphasized. In contrast to some of his outstanding contemporaries, Howard was not an innovator in dramatic form nor a particularly profound writer. He readily admitted such shortcomings, if indeed, they were that. Instead, he was a substantial playwright of considerable theatrical skill and imagination who stepped into the ongoing stream of social drama in America and produced at least two major plays in that genre.

They Knew What They Wanted is a modern version of the Paolo-Francesca love story but with a modern twist that none of those who told the story from Dante to Wagner would have accepted. But Howard's intelligently expedient people, battling the exigencies of the modern world, know what they want, and his hero, Tony, can become, as Frank Loesser's musical adaptation made him, "The Most Happy Fella." In *The Silver Cord* Howard took advantage of ideas propounded by Strindberg and Freud. With a diabolic cunning worthy of Strindberg's Laura, Howard's protagonist fights for the control of her sons in an emotion-packed drama that remains one of America's best thesis plays. Emotion and spectacle are always major aspects of a Howard play. He wrote about people, frequently with a strong sense of irony, and all of his plays held at least one spectacular scene which he handled with a craftsmanship critics have admired. The best include *Lucky Sam McCarver*, *Ned McCobb's Daughter*, and *The Late Christopher Bean*; he also adapted Sinclair Lewis's *Dodsworth* to the stage.

During a life cut short by a farm accident in 1939 Howard wrote some twenty plays, most of them either adaptations or collaborations. But his reputation in American drama rests solidly upon the plays he wrote by himself, the best of which appeared during the 1920's. He seemed unable to relate successfully to the social atmosphere of the Depression years which followed.

—Walter J. Meserve

HUGHES, John. English. Born in Marlborough, Wiltshire, 29 January 1677; brother of the translator Jabez Hughes. Educated at a dissenting academy, probably in Little Britain, London. Worked in the Ordnance Office, London, and served as Secretary to various commissions for the purchase of lands for the royal dockyards; Secretary to the commissions of peace in the court of chancery, from 1717. *Died 17 February 1720.*

PUBLICATIONS

Collections

   Poems on Several Occasions, with Some Select Essays, edited by W. Duncombe. 2 vols., 1735.

Plays

   Six Cantatas, music by J. C. Pepusch (produced 1710). 1710.
   The Court of Neptune. 1699.
   The House of Nassau: A Pindaric Ode. 1702.
   An Ode in Praise of Music. 1703.
   An Ode to the Creator of the World, Occasioned by the Fragments of Orpheus. 1713.

An Ode for the Birthday of the Princess of Wales.   1716.
The Ecstasy: An Ode.   1720.

Verse

The Triumph of Peace.   1698.
Calypso and Telemachus, music by J. E. Galliard (produced 1712).   1712.
Apollo and Daphne: A Masque, music by J. C. Pepusch (produced 1716).   1716.
Orestes.   1717.
The Siege of Damascus (produced 1720).   1720.

Other

A Review of the Case of Ephraim and Judah.   1705.
The Lay-Monastery, Consisting of Essays, Discourses, etc., with Richard
   Blackmore.   1714.
A Layman's Thoughts on the Late Treatment of the Bishop of Bangor.   1717.
Charon; or, The Ferry-Boat: A Vision.   1719.
The Complicated Guilt of the Late Rebellion.   1745.
Letters of Several Eminent Persons Deceased, with others, edited by J.
   Duncombe.   1772; as *The Correspondence of Hughes and Several of His Friends,* 2
   vols., 1773.

Editor, *A Complete History of England,* vols. 1–2, by W. Kennett.   1706.
Editor, *Advice from Parnassus,* by Traiano Boccalini.   1706.
Editor, *The Works of Spenser.*   6 vols., 1715; commentary edited by Scott Elledge, in
   Eighteenth-Century Critical Essays, vol. 1, 1961.

Translator, *Fontenelle's Dialogues of the Dead, with Two Original Dialogues.*   1708.
Translator, *The History of the Revolutions in Portugal,* by the Abbot de Vertot.   1712.
Translator, *Letters of Abelard and Heloise, Extracted Chiefly from Bayle.*   1718 (3rd
   edition).

Reading List: "Some Sources for *The Siege of Damascus*" by John R. Moore, in *Huntington
Library Quarterly 21,* 1958.

*   *   *

Critics have been reluctant to pass favourable judgment on John Hughes. Eminent
contemporaries were less than generous towards his achievement, and Johnson's *Life* is non-
committal. Gibbon, on the other hand, praised *The Siege of Damascus* for its "rare merit of
blending nature and history...." As a playwright Hughes had some success in the sphere of
high tragedy; but his more ambitious poems such as *The House of Nassau* and the *Ode to the
Creator of the World* lack coherence, while his shorter verses are overburdened with
Augustan conventionalities. What redeems Hughes's considerable talent is his excellent
understanding of other authors' intentions (as in the "Essay on Allegorical Poetry" prefixed
to his 1715 edition of Spenser) and his discerning views on the potentialities of sung poetry.
   At a time when Italian vocal music was all the rage, Hughes aimed "to improve a sort of
(English) verse, in regular measures, purposely fitted for music ... which, of all the modern
kinds, seems to be the only one that can now properly be called lyrics." Rejecting Edmund
Waller's notion that "soft words with nothing in them make a song" and paying due respect

to the composer's demand for a congenial text, Hughes produced *Six Cantatas* (set by J. C. Pepusch) and other brief works in which the airs and recitatives employ suitably contrasting accentuations. On a more ambitious scale are several odes, also intended for music. The inventiveness they display is again evident in stage masques written as an alternative genre to Italianate music drama. A more resourceful composer than Pepusch might have created a minor masterpiece out of *Apollo and Daphne*; for his opera *Calypso and Telemachus* Hughes had collaborated with J. E. Galliard, for whose music Handel had a high regard. This work constituted an attempt to refute "a late Opinion among some, that *English* words are not proper for Musick" and bears out Hughes's contention that the alleged shortcomings of the English language need not deter an inventive librettist.

Hughes's prose writings include translations and periodical essays. His work as a whole reveals a wide knowledge of general literature; although overshadowed by Steele, Addison, and Pope his critical abilities place him well above the level of incorrigible mediocrity.

—E. D. Mackerness

HUNTER, N(orman) C(harles). English. Born in Derbyshire, 18 September 1908. Educated at Repton School; Royal Military College, Sandhurst. Commissioned in the Dragoon Guards, 1930; relinquished commission, 1933; served in the Royal Artillery during World War II. Married Germaine Marie Dachsbeck in 1933. Staff Member of the BBC, 1934–39. Lived in Montgomeryshire. *Died 19 April 1971.*

PUBLICATIONS

Plays

The Merciless Lady, with John Ferguson (produced 1934).
All Rights Reserved (produced 1935). 1935.
Ladies and Gentlemen (produced 1937).
Little Stranger, from a play by Katherine Hilliker and H. H. Caldwell (produced 1938).
A Party for Christmas (produced 1938). 1938.
Grouse in June (as *Galleon Gold,* produced 1939; as *Grouse in June,* produced 1939). 1939.
Smith in Arcady (produced 1947).
The Affair at Assino (produced 1950).
A Picture of Autumn (produced 1951). 1957.
Waters of the Moon (produced 1951). 1951.
Adam's Apple: A Victorian Fairy Tale (produced 1951; as *Now the Serpent,* produced 1951). 1953.
A Day by the Sea (produced 1953). 1954.
A Touch of the Sun (produced 1958). 1958.
A Piece of Silver (produced 1960). 1961.
The Tulip Tree (produced 1962). 1963.
The Excursion (produced 1964). 1964.
Adventures of Tom Random (produced 1967).

One Fair Daughter (produced 1970).

Screenplay: *Poison Pen,* with others, 1939.

Radio Plays: *The Coneen Ghost,* 1939; *The Phantom Island,* 1941; *The Clerk's Story,* 1958; *Henry of Navarre,* from book by Hesketh Pearson, 1966.

Fiction

Let's Fight till Six. 1933.
The Servitors. 1934; as *Marriage with Nina,* 1934.
Riot. 1935.
The Ascension of Mr. Judson. 1950.
The Romsea Romeo. 1950.
The Losing Hazard. 1951.

Other

Translator, *The Fight in the Forest,* by Victor Eloy. 1949.

*   *   *

N. C. Hunter came to prominence as a dramatist in the early 1950's after producing a number of unremarkable light comedies and novels, and achieved his greatest successes at a time when the dominant British theatrical form was still the well-made naturalistic play of middle-class life, featuring articulate and generally unextraordinary characters who conveyed their beliefs and attitudes through the vocabulary of bourgeois reticence and understatement. Hunter's distinction, however, lay in largely dispensing with incidents resulting from the conventional pressures exerted by a formal plot, so that his plays appeared more genuinely "true to life" than those of his contemporaries, especially when complemented by the seeming inconsequentiality of everyday conversations, and by an atmosphere of stoical endurance typical of the national mood during and after the Second World War. Hunter's elegies for the educated middle class in post-war decline are in a very attenuated sense reminiscent of Chekhov's presentation of the last days of the Russian aristocracy, and it was almost inevitable that his mature works with their note of autumnal sadness and their gallery of gentle eccentrics should have been accorded the epithet Chekhovian.

The first of this group, aptly entitled *A Picture of Autumn,* is set in a decaying Wiltshire manor, where, against a background of Edwardian recollections and reminders of the modern social revolution, the older and younger generations confront the abandonment of the ancestral residence with its mixture of memories and inconveniences. Next followed Hunter's major success, *Waters of the Moon,* performed by a distinguished cast in 1951, in which a wealthy but insensitive woman contrives to unsettle the shabby and disillusioned inmates of a snowbound hotel on Dartmoor by offering them a glimpse of a comfortable world to which they cannot return or aspire. The same air of resignation is evident in *A Day by the Sea,* which brings together an intense but arid diplomat and his childhood sweetheart defeated after two unsatisfactory marriages, only to frustrate a lasting reunion, but arguing that consolation lies in acceptance of one's own limitations and of life's continuity. *A Touch of the Sun* contrasts respectable and impecunious righteousness with affluent vulgarity, by charting the effect on a priggish, idealistic preparatory schoolmaster and his family of a Riviera holiday with his materialistic brother and rich American wife: again the playwright opts for moral courage and personal integrity as the best available lifelines in despair. In *The Tulip Tree* an estranged couple are shown gradually reconciling themselves to the death of a beloved son, to the inevitable onset of advancing age, and to each other, a further instance of Hunter's emphasis on honesty in human relationships, and the central importance of not evading unpalatable truths about oneself or one's dependents.

Any vogue for Hunter's plays has now declined, but such excellent examples of an outmoded dramatic form should not be judged by inappropriate criteria of more recent origin. A valid critical assessment must weigh Hunter's unquestioning preference for traditional liberal values and conventional models, and his plays' too-accurate reflection of the concerns of one social class at one period in history, against his careful characterisations and finely orchestrated dialogue, his immaculate control of exposition and *dénouement*, his overall craftsmanship. Hunter's work may yet receive that fuller appraisal its quality still merits.

—William M. Tydeman

INGE, William (Motter). American. Born in Independence, Kansas, 3 May 1913. Educated at the University of Kansas, Lawrence, A.B. 1935; Peabody Teachers College, Nashville, Tennessee, M.A. 1936; Yale University, New Haven, Connecticut, Summer 1940. Taught at Columbus High School, Kansas, 1937–38, and Stephens College, Columbia, Missouri, 1938–43; Art Critic, St. Louis *Star-Times*, 1943–46; taught at Washington University, St. Louis, 1946–49, University of North Carolina, Chapel Hill, 1969, and the University of California at Irvine, 1970. Recipient: George Jean Nathan Award, 1951; Pulitzer Prize, 1953; New York Drama Critics Circle Award, 1953; Donaldson Award, 1953; Academy Award, 1962. *Died 10 June 1973.*

PUBLICATIONS

Plays

The Dark at the Top of the Stairs (as *Farther Off from Heaven*, produced 1947; revised version, as *The Dark at the Top of the Stairs*, produced 1957). 1958.
Come Back, Little Sheba (produced 1950). 1950.
Picnic: A Summer Romance (produced 1953). 1953; revised version, as *Summer Brave* (produced 1962), in *Summer Brave and Eleven Short Plays*, 1962.
Bus Stop (produced 1955). 1955.
Glory in the Flower (produced 1959). In *24 Favorite One-Act Plays*, edited by Bennett Cerf and Van H. Cartmell, 1958.
The Tiny Closet (produced 1959). In *Summer Brave and Eleven Short Plays*, 1962.
A Loss of Roses (produced 1959). 1960.
Splendor in the Grass: A Screenplay. 1961.
Natural Affection (produced 1962). 1963.
Summer Brave and Eleven Short Plays (includes *To Bobolink, For Her Spirit; A Social Event; The Boy in the Basement; The Tiny Closet; Memory of Summer; The Rainy Afternoon; The Mall; An Incident at the Standish Arms; People in the Wind; Bus Riley's Back in Town; The Strains of Triumph*). 1962.
Where's Daddy? (as *Family Things Etc.*, produced 1965; as *Where's Daddy?*, produced 1966). 1966.
The Disposal (as *Don't Go Gentle*, produced 1967–68?; as *The Last Pad*, produced 1972). In *Best Short Plays of the World Theatre 1958–1967*, edited by Stanley Richards, 1968; revised version, as *The Disposal*, music by Anthony Caldarella, lyrics by Judith Gero (produced 1973).
Two Short Plays: The Call, and A Murder. 1968.
Midwestern Manic, in *Best Short Plays 1969*, edited by Stanley Richards. 1969.
Caesarian Operation (produced 1972).
Overnight (produced 1974).
Love Death Plays: Dialogue for Two Men, Midwestern Music, The Love Death, Venus and Adonis, The Wake, The Star (produced 1975).

Screenplays: *Splendor in the Grass*, 1961; *All Fall Down*, 1962.

Television Play: *On the Outskirts of Town*, 1964–65?

Fiction

Good Luck, Miss Wyckoff. 1971.

My Son Is a Splendid Driver.   1972.

Reading List: *Inge* by Robert B. Shuman, 1965.

*   *   *

William Inge remains an interesting phenomenon in American drama. His impact upon critic and public alike demands that he be included in any serious consideration of the post-war theatre, but in subject matter and in style he was so counter to the patterns of his contemporaries as to seem from quite another generation. Leaving behind a minimal impression upon the development of recent American drama, his name rapidly fading, he was nonetheless a major figure for almost a decade and wrote some of the most appealing dramatic pieces of the fifteen post-war years.

William Inge's place in American drama is limited to four plays: *Come Back, Little Sheba*, *Picnic, Bus Stop,* and *The Dark at the Top of the Stairs.* His first, *Farther Off from Heaven,* produced by Margo Jones in Dallas, got to New York only in a much-revised version. *A Loss of Roses* failed completely, as did *Natural Affection* and *Family Things, Etc.* His screenplays brought no added fame, and his prose fiction is limited in appeal.

While Tennessee Williams, Arthur Miller, and Eugene O'Neill dwelt upon the tragic nature of their often inauspicious characters, Inge chose to emphasize his characters' fundamentally pathetic and frequently comic nature. The tragic fates are nowhere in evidence. Inge's appeal lies in a compassionate understanding of and a great sensitivity toward his petty little people, as he conveys successfully to his audiences the universally amusing and simultaneously agonizing quality of ordinary human nature under very ordinary circumstances. Furthermore, at a time when his major contemporaries favored impressionistic stagings, stylized settings, politico-historical themes, and regional emphases, Inge remained consistently a writer of straightforward, single-set plays of Ibsenesque realism. His characters, straight from the unprepossessing streets and towns of the vast mid-section of contemporary America, moved within settings, both geographical and theatrical, remarkable for their unobtrusive, innocuous nature. Inge is one of the most regional of dramatists, but he is emphatically not a "regionalist"; that is, his chosen locale is so lacking in specific regional association and importance, and hence influence upon his characters, as to be virtually neutral. The importance of the surroundings into which Inge places his characters lies precisely in their lack of any importance at all.

Nor does Inge permit the many individual problems of his characters to become the central "problem" of the plays as a whole. His first success, *Come Back, Little Sheba*, is a fine case in point. For instance, we learn a great deal about A.A. and alcoholism, but it is not a play *about* alcoholism. Sexual restraints, taboos, and frustrations, past and present, cause serious personal problems for Doc and Lola, but the play is in no way *about* sex. The air of pessimistic hopelessness surrounding the Delaneys may be the strongest theme, but the play refuses to dwell upon the subject and, in fact, displays a considerable awareness of the positive aspect of human resilience *and* ultimate hope. *Come Back, Little Sheba* is, then, a play which sends out strong shock waves from all of these problems, permitting none of them to dominate the action. The audience finds itself attracted to these wholly undistinguished people in this undistinguished small town by bonds of mutual sympathy and understanding, together with an appreciation of Inge's outstanding ability to demonstrate what human love, patience, and endurance really mean to virtually all of us. Much has been lost by Doc and Lola in the course of the action, but much has been gained in return. Everybody, at the final curtain, is back at the beginning, more or less, and that, in the end, is far more the way of the world than otherwise. Inge's characters, here and elsewhere, will move no mountains in their lifetimes, but they are, as one critic has said, the salt of the earth, their importance lying almost entirely in the fact of their being human.

Picnic, as one opening night critic observed, is still "basic Inge." The sensation of the season, the play won a Pulitzer Prize and remains probably Inge's most famous play. Adding a few characters and moving them from kitchen to back yard, Inge proved that his formula for the dramatic impact of *Sheba* had been no fluke. "Affectionate, understanding, interesting, engagingly funny, emotionally touching, with fascinating characters" were the critical terms that greeted the play's portrayal of what happens on a Labor Day weekend in a Kansas back yard among a group of almost embarrassingly stock stage figures from clucking-hen mother to sexually frustrated old-maid schoolteacher. Highly emotional things happen in *Picnic*, as they do in *Sheba*, caused mainly by the intrusion of the handsome semi-clad drifter who causes a general loosening of assorted libidos, culminating in fornication, drunkenness, and elopement. But none of these things in themselves, any more than in *Sheba*, is the point. What matters is Inge's highly skilled and absolutely convincing portrayal of the driving human forces of underlying desires, frustrations, fears, and joys of these routinely bland people in an equally bland environment.

In *Bus Stop* Inge falls back on a device that worked for Shakespeare on Prospero's island, for Melville aboard the *Pequod*, and for James Jones in his pre-Pearl Harbor army. Into Grace's microcosmic lunchroom, driven by the unalterable force of a prairie blizzard, the playwright sends a group of individuals as stereotyped and undistinguished as anything he or many another artist has attempted. What emerges, for all that, is a wholly delightful human comedy with an underlying drama of deep human pathos. The pursuit and capture of the pitifully floozy "chantoosie" by the frantically infatuated, rambunctious but innocent cowboy is superbly comic, beautifully controlled. Simultaneously, the parallel affair of the decadent professor and the naive waitress, while ever on the edge of the pit of gratuitous sensation, carries the more serious theme with touching effectiveness. Before he is through with us, Inge has made us care a great deal about Bo, Cherie, Lyman, Elma, and Virgil. Normally we, as well as the rest of the world, would take little note of them, but Inge has shown us that they are highly important people to themselves and in many ways to each other. Cherie, hopelessly tarnished, artistically a fiasco, has stood her ground with dignity while vigorously defending her womanly honor against the onrushing Bo. He, in turn, literally forced to bow before her, has learned, to his wondering astonishment, that women are not calves to be bulldogged, hogtied, and subdued. Elma has come dangerously close to the total destruction of her innocence, but that very innocence has given the aging sensualist pause enough to permit both of them, for the time, to escape. By the time Inge returns all on stage to equilibrium and sends his bus on its journey, we have encountered a touching human experience of lasting impressiveness.

In his final and least noteworthy "success," *The Dark at the Top of the Stairs*, Inge unfortunately surrenders to artificialities of plot, less than subtle symbolism, gratuitous violence, and remarkably unconvincing characters. There is much of the "basic Inge" to be seen and, upon occasion, praised, but the strong human appeal of the first three plays is lost amid generally unsatisfactory handling of marital problems, racial prejudices, and parent–child relationships. We may still understand some of the reasons for Rubin Flood's infidelity and Sonny's mamma's boy behavior, as well as little Sammy's suicide, but, on the whole, there is too much of the trite and unimaginative to be as convincing as we would like.

The ultimate appeal of William Inge seems to lie in his ability to transform the lives and behavior of drab people in drab surroundings into a significant drama of human experience. Taking us inside and outside the houses most of us pass every day down the block and around the corner, he reveals some rather profound human truths, and he grips us in fascination as he does so.

—Jordan Y. Miller

JERROLD, Douglas William. English. Born in London, 3 January 1803; moved with his family to Sheerness where his father, an actor, had a lease on a theatre, 1807; appeared on stage on several occasions as a child. Attended Mr. Herbert's school in Sheerness; largely self-educated. Midshipman in the Royal Navy, 1813–15. Married Mary Swann in 1824; one son. Printer's apprentice in London, 1816–19; began writing for the theatre c. 1818; worked as a compositor for Mr. Bigg, printer of the *Sunday Monitor*, 1819, and afterwards contributed to the *Sunday Monitor*, *Weekly Times*, *The Ballot*, and other periodicals; employed as an adapter by Davidge, manager of the Coburg Theatre, 1825–29; Resident Dramatist at the Surrey Theatre, 1829; Co-Manager, with W. J. Hammond, Strand Theatre, 1836; after 1840 devoted himself increasingly to journalism: contributor to *Punch*, 1841 until his death; Editor, *Illuminated Magazine*, 1843–45; Founding Editor, *Douglas Jerrold's Shilling Magazine*, 1845–48; Owner and Editor, *Douglas Jerrold's Weekly Magazine*, 1846–48; Editor, *Lloyd's Weekly Magazine*, 1852 until his death. *Died 8 June 1857.*

PUBLICATIONS

Collections

> *Works.*   5 vols., 1863–64.
> *The Best of Mr. Punch: The Humorous Writings*, edited by Richard Kelly.   1970.

Plays

> *More Frightened Than Hurt* (produced 1821).   1888.
> *The Chieftains' Oath; or, The Rival Clans* (produced 1821).
> *The Gipsy of Derncleuch*, from the novel *Guy Mannering* by Scott (produced 1821).   N.d.
> *The Island; or, Christian and His Comrades*, from the poem by Byron (produced 1823).
> *Dolly and the Rat; or, The Brisket Family* (produced 1823).   N.d.
> *The Smoked Miser; or, The Benefit of Hanging* (produced 1823).   1823(?).
> *The Living Skeleton* (produced 1825).
> *London Characters: Puff! Puff!! Puff!!!* (produced 1825).
> *Popular Felons* (produced 1825).
> *Paul Pry*, from the play by John Poole (produced 1827).   N.d.
> *The Statue Lover* (produced 1828).   N.d.
> *Descart, The French Buccaneer* (produced 1828).   1830(?).
> *The Tower of Lochlain; or, The Idiot Son* (produced 1828).   N.d.
> *Wives by Advertisement; or, Courting in the Newspapers* (produced 1828).   With *Winning a Husband* by George Macfarren, 1888.
> *Ambrose Gwinett; or, A Sea-Side Story* (produced 1828).   1885.
> *Two Eyes Between Two; or, Pay Me for My Eye* (produced 1828).   1888.
> *Fifteen Years of a Drunkard's Life!* (produced 1828).   N.d.
> *Vidocq! The French Police Spy* (produced 1829).   N.d.
> *Bampfyde Moore Carew* (produced 1829).   N.d.
> *John Overy the Miser; or, The Southwark Ferry* (produced 1829).   N.d.
> *Law and Lions!* (produced 1829).   N.d.
> *Black-Eyed Susan; or, All in the Downs* (produced 1829).   1829; edited by George Rowell, in *Nineteenth-Century Plays*, 1953.
> *The Flying Dutchman* (produced 1829).   1829(?).
> *The Lonely Man of Shiraz* (produced 1829).

Thomas à Becket (produced 1829).   N.d.
The Witch-Finders (produced 1829).
Sally in Our Alley (produced 1830).   1888(?).
Gervaise Skinner; or, Penny Wise and Pound Foolish (produced 1830).
The Mutiny at the Nore; or, British Sailors in 1797 (produced 1830).   N.d.
The Press-Gang; or, Archibald of the Wreck (produced 1830).
The Devil's Ducat; or, The Gift of Mammon (produced 1830).   N.d.
Martha Willis the Servant Maid; or, Service in London (produced 1831).   N.d.
The Bride of Ludgate (produced 1831).   N.d.
The Lady Killer (produced 1831).
The Broken Heart; or, The Farmer's Daughter of the Severn Side (produced 1832).
The Rent Day (produced 1832).   1832.
The Golden Calf (produced 1832).   N.d.
The Factory Girl (produced 1832).
Nell Gwynne; or, The Prologue (produced 1833).   1833.
The Housekeeper; or, The White Rose (produced 1833).   1833.
Swamp Hall; or, The Friend of the Family (produced 1833).   1833.
The Wedding Gown (produced 1834).   1834.
Beau Nash, The King of Bath (produced 1834).   1834.
The Schoolfellows (produced 1835).   1835.
Birds of Paradise (produced 1835).
The Hazard of the Die (produced 1835).   1835.
Hearts and Diamonds (produced 1835).
The Man's an Ass (produced 1835).
Doves in a Cage (produced 1835).   N.d.
The Painter of Ghent (produced 1836).   N.d.
The Man for the Ladies (produced 1836).   1885.
The Bill-Sticker; or, An Old House in the City (produced 1836).
The Perils of Pippins; or, The Man Who "Couldn't Help It" (produced 1836).   N.d.
A Gallantee Showman; or, Mr. Peppercorn at Home (produced 1837).
The Mother (produced 1838).
The White Milliner (produced 1841).   N.d.
Bubbles of the Day (produced 1842).   1842.
The Prisoner of War (produced 1842).   1842.
Gertrude's Cherries; or, Waterloo in 1835 (produced 1842).   1842.
Time Works Wonders (produced 1845).   1845.
Mrs. Caudle's Curtain Lecture (produced 1845).   1846.
A Honeymoon Scruple (produced 1845).
The Spendthrift (produced 1850).
The Mother's Dream; or, The Gipsy's Revenge (produced 1850).
The Catspaw (produced 1850).   1850.
Retired from Business (produced 1851).   1851.
St. Cupid; or, Dorothy's Fortune (produced 1853).   1853.
The Heart of Gold (produced 1854).   1854.

Fiction

Men of Character.   1838.
The Story of a Feather.   1844.
The Chronicles of Clovernook, with Some Account of the Hermit of Bellyfull.   1846.
A Man Made of Money.   1849.
St. Giles and St. James, in *Writings*.   1852.
Cakes and Ale (tales and essays), in *Writings*.   1852.

Tales, edited by J. L. Robertson.   1891.

Other

Facts and Fancies.   1826.
The Hand-Book of Swindling.   1839.
Heads of the People, illustrated by Kenny Meadows.   2 vols., 1840–41.
Punch's Letters to His Son.   1843.
Punch's Complete Letter Writer.   1845.
Mrs. Caudle's Curtain Lectures.   1846; edited by Walter Jerrold, 1902.
Writings.   8 vols., 1851–54.
The Brownrigg Papers, edited by Blanchard Jerrold.   1860.
Other Times, with Blanchard Jerrold.   1868.
The Barber's Chair and the Hedgehog Letters, edited by Blanchard Jerrold.   1874.
Essays, edited by Walter Jerrold.   1903.

Reading List: *Jerrold and Punch*, 1910, and *Jerrold, Dramatist and Wit*, 2 vols., 1914, both by Walter Jerrold; *Jerrold* by Richard Kelly, 1972.

*   *   *

When one refers to the Great Exhibition of 1851 as the "Crystal Palace," he is indebted to the satirical imagination of Douglas William Jerrold, who coined the title to poke fun at the Victorians' self-importance. Jerrold was among the most popular and prolific dramatists of his day, the man most responsible for the early success of *Punch*, the author of numerous short stories, sketches, and essays, an editor of several newspapers and magazines, and a friend to many prominent Victorians, including Thackeray and Dickens. His most lasting contribution to literature, however, is his comic journalism, a medium he not only pioneered but one that he made respectable for serious artists.

Jerrold's ambition as a playwright was never very grand. Despite his prodigious output of journalism and fiction, he managed to write and have produced some seventy plays. Most of these works were either melodramas or farces, the two most successful being *Black-Eyed Susan* and *The Rent Day*. Although it is now fashionable to sneer at Victorian drama, its chief contribution to English and American popular culture – the melodrama – can be seen today in motion pictures and television.

The staying power of Jerrold's reputation in our own day, however, derives from his work as the star satirist of *Punch* during the 1840's. Queen Victoria, Prince Albert, Benjamin Disraeli, Sir Robert Peel, President James K. Polk, P. T. Barnum, and General Tom Thumb are among the many victims of Jerrold's bold ridicule. In his most famous serial for *Punch*, *Mrs. Caudle's Curtain Lectures*, he creates a woman of martial temperament whose nightly lectures to her husband Job provide an enduring literary monument to *Punch's* well-known "advertisement" – "Advice to persons about to marry; don't!" "The English in Little," another serial, satirizes the vulgarity and greed of Barnum and Tom Thumb while it scores the pompousness and gullibility of the English aristocracy. *Punch's Letters to His Son* and *Punch's Complete Letter Writer* poke fun at the political, social, and moral hypocrisy of the Victorians and parody Lord Chesterfield's *Letters to His Son*.

Jerrold's three novels – *The Story of a Feather*, *St. Giles and St. James*, and *A Man Made of Money* – were all aimed at underscoring the social and political unrest of the 1840's. Although read and admired by thousands of people, including Dickens, these works strike the modern reader as excessively didactic and sentimental.

In all of his writings – plays, stories, essays, serials, and novels – Jerrold's principal objectives were to entertain his readers and to win their sympathy for the poor and oppressed lower class of society. A moralist committed to the principle of equal justice for all people, Jerrold worked diligently at his craft in order to educate the imagination of a lethargic middle-class audience as a first step towards arousing its concern for the common man. Because he has created a believable "world" – especially in his serials for *Punch* – and peopled it with characters the modern reader can recognize, Jerrold's wit and humor have not lost their savor; furthermore, his social gospel has an uncanny relevance to the issues of the present day.

—Richard Kelly

JOHNSTON, (William) Denis. Irish. Born in Dublin, 18 June 1901. Educated at St. Andrew's College, Dublin; Merchiston Castle School, Edinburgh; Christ's College, Cambridge (President of the Union), 1921–23, M.A., LL.M. 1926; Harvard Law School, Cambridge, Massachusetts (Pugsley Scholar), 1923–24; Barrister, Inner Temple, London, and King's Inns, Dublin, 1925, and Northern Ireland, 1926. Married 1) Shelah Richards in 1928 (divorced), one son and one daughter, the novelist Jennifer Johnston; 2) Betty Chancellor in 1945, two sons. Producer, Dublin Drama League, and Abbey Theatre, Dublin, and the Dublin Gate Theatre, 1927–36, also a Member of the Board of Directors of the Dublin Gate Theatre, 1931–36; Features Producer, BBC, Belfast, 1936–38; Television Producer, BBC, London, 1938–39; BBC Correspondent, in the Middle East, Italy, France, and Germany, 1942–45: mentioned in despatches; O.B.E. (Officer, Order of the British Empire), 1946; Director of Television Programmes, BBC, London, 1945–47; Visiting Director, Kirby Memorial Theatre, Amherst, Massachusetts, 1950; Professor of English, Mount Holyoke College, South Hadley, Massachusetts, 1950–60; Chairman of the Department of Theatre and Speech, Smith College, Northampton, Massachusetts, 1960–66; Visiting Professor, Amherst College, Massachusetts, 1966–67, University of Iowa, Iowa City, 1967–68, and the University of California at Davis, 1970–71; Berg Professor, New York University, 1971–72; Arnold Professor, Whitman College, Walla Walla, Washington, 1972–73. Literary Editor, Abbey Theatre, Dublin, 1975. Recipient: Guggenheim Fellowship, 1954. Lives in County Dublin.

PUBLICATIONS

Plays

The Old Lady Says "No!" (produced 1929). In The Moon in the Yellow River and The Old Lady Says "No!," 1932.
The Moon in the Yellow River (produced 1931). 1931.
The Moon in the Yellow River and The Old Lady Says "No!": Two Plays. 1932.
A Bride for the Unicorn (produced 1933). In Storm Song and A Bride for the Unicorn, 1935.
Storm Song (produced 1934). In Storm Song and A Bride for the Unicorn. 1935.
Storm Song and A Bride for the Unicorn: Two Plays. 1935.
Blind Man's Buff, with Ernst Toller, from a play by Toller (produced 1936). 1938.
The Golden Cuckoo (produced 1938). In The Golden Cuckoo and Other Plays, 1954; revised version, 1971.

The Dreaming Dust (as *Weep for Polyphemus*, broadcast 1938; revised version, as *The Dreaming Dust*, produced 1940).   In *The Golden Cuckoo and Other Plays*, 1954.

A Fourth for Bridge (as *The Unthinking Lobster*, televised 1948).   In *The Golden Cuckoo and Other Plays*, 1954.

Six Characters in Search of an Author, from a play by Pirandello (produced 1950); revised version, music by Hugo Weisgall (produced 1956).   1957.

The Golden Cuckoo and Other Plays.   1954.

Strange Occurrence on Ireland's Eye (produced 1956).   In *Collected Plays II*, 1960.

Tain Bo Cuailgne (pageant; produced 1956).

The Scythe and the Sunset (produced 1958).   In *Collected Plays I*, 1960.

Ulysses in Nighttown, adaption of parts of *Ulysses* by James Joyce (produced 1958).

Finnegans Wake, from the novel by James Joyce (produced 1959).

Collected Plays I–II.   2 vols., 1960.

Nine Rivers from Jordan, music by Hugo Weisgall (produced 1969).   1969.

Dramatic Works 1.   1977.

Screenplays: *Guests of the Nation*, 1933; *River of Unrest*, 1937; *Ourselves Alone*, 1937.

Radio Plays: *Death at Newtownstewart*, 1937; *Lillibulero*, 1937; *Weep for Polyphemus*, 1938; *Multiple Studio Blues*, 1938; *Nansen of the "Fram,"* 1940; *The Gorgeous Lady Blessington*, 1941; *The Autobiography of Mark Twain*, 1941; *Abraham Lincoln*, 1941; *In the Train*, 1946; *Not One Returns to Tell*, 1946; *Verdict of the Court* series, 1960.

Television Plays: *The Last Voyage of Captain Grant*, 1938; *The Parnell Commission*, 1939; *Weep for the Cyclops*, 1946; *The Unthinking Lobster*, 1948; *The Call to Arms*, 1949; *Siege at Killyfaddy*, 1960.

Ballet: *The Indiscreet Goat*, Dublin, 1931.

Other

Dionysia.   1949.

Nine Rivers from Jordan: The Chronicle of a Journey and a Search (wartime autobiography).   1953.

In Search of Swift.   1959.

John Millington Synge.   1965.

The Brazen Horn (autobiographical).   1968; revised edition, 1976.

Reading List: *Johnston's Irish Theatre* by Harold Ferrar, 1975.

*   *   *

Denis Johnston was trained for the law at Cambridge and Harvard, but he found the drama a more absorbing pursuit, and became involved as actor and director with the Dublin Drama League and the new Dublin Gate Theatre of Hilton Edwards and Micheál Mac Liammóir. His subsequent career has been extraordinarily varied, and has embraced acting, directing, and writing for radio, films, and television. As a playwright, Johnston was much less influenced by the peasant drama of the Abbey Theatre than he was by the experimental drama of the continent. However, his restless search for form has militated against a recognisable "Johnston" play – as, for instance, there is the recognisable early O'Casey and late O'Casey. His plays were produced by both the Gate and the Abbey theatres, the Gate doing the more unconventional ones and the Abbey the seemingly more traditional.

His first play, *The Old Lady Says "No!,"* produced by the Gate, was a satiric expressionistic play about contemporary Ireland which stunningly used the technique of allusion that T. S. Eliot had popularised in poetry and James Joyce in fiction. For years the play seemed both too baffling and too Irish to travel well outside of Ireland, but in Ireland its sophisticated technique was wedded to such a broad theatricality that it remained an important item of the Gate's repertory for almost thirty years. The play's day may now have passed, for in a 1977 revival by the Abbey it seemed not only somewhat dated but, surprisingly, a bit superficial.

Johnston's keen satiric mind and enormous technical expertise have made even such nominally realistic plays as *The Moon in the Yellow River* and *The Scythe and the Sunset* as complex yet smooth as Chekhov, but as rarely produced as Turgenev or Granville-Barker. Although *The Moon in the Yellow River* is tied to the aftermath of the Irish Civil War and *The Scythe and the Sunset* to the 1916 Rising, both plays have a density of theme, a complexity of plot, a comic theatricality, and even intermittently a humanity that make them transcend their time and place.

The best of Johnston's minor work is almost as good as his very best, and would certainly include the symbolic fantasy *A Bride for the Unicorn*, the sardonic farce *The Golden Cuckoo*, and perhaps the best dramatic treatment yet of Jonathan Swift, *The Dreaming Dust*. His chief non-dramatic work includes a work on Swift, a war memoir, and a dubious philosophic treatise. Despite his bold experiments, he will probably be most remembered for the two social-political comedies which broadened the possibilities of realism, and which have not yet been assimilated by the modern theatre.

—Robert Hogan

JONES, Henry Arthur. English. Born in Grandborough, Buckinghamshire, 20 September 1851. Educated at John Grace's Commercial Academy in Winslow, Buckinghamshire, until age 12. Married Jane Eliza Seeley in 1875 (died, 1924); three sons and four daughters. Worked for his uncle, a draper in Ramsgate, Kent, 1864–67, and for another draper in Gravesend, Kent, 1867–69; commercial traveller in London, Bradford, and Exeter, 1869–79; full-time playwright from 1879. M.A.: Harvard University, Cambridge, Massachusetts, 1907. *Died 7 January 1929.*

PUBLICATIONS

Collections

Representative Plays, edited by Clayton Hamilton.   4 vols., 1926.

Plays

    Hearts of Oak; or, A Chip of the Old Block (produced 1879).   1879; as *Honour Bright,* 1879.
    Harmony (as *Harmony Restored,* produced 1879; as *It's Only round the Corner,* produced 1879; as *The Organist,* produced 1892).   1883.

Elopement (produced 1879). 1879.
A Clerical Error (produced 1879). 1879.
A Drive in June. 1879.
An Old Master (produced 1880). 1880.
A Garden Party. 1880.
Lady Caprice. 1880.
Humbug. 1881.
Home Again (produced 1881).
His Wife (produced 1881).
A Bed of Roses (produced 1882). 1882.
The Silver King, with Henry Herman (produced 1882). 1907; edited by J. O. Bailey, in *British Plays of the Nineteenth Century,* 1966.
The Wedding Guest. 1882.
Breaking a Butterfly, with Henry Herman, from a play by Ibsen (produced 1884). 1884.
Chatterton, with Henry Herman (produced 1884).
Saints and Sinners (produced 1884). 1891.
Hoodman Blind, with Wilson Barrett (produced 1885). N.d.
The Lord Harry, with Wilson Barrett (produced 1886).
The Noble Vagabond (produced 1886).
Hard Hit (produced 1887).
Heart of Hearts (produced 1887).
Sweet Will (produced 1887). 1893.
The Middleman (produced 1889). 1907.
Wealth (produced 1889).
Judah (produced 1890). 1894.
The Deacon (produced 1890). 1893.
The Dancing Girl (produced 1891). 1907.
The Crusaders (produced 1891). 1893.
The Bauble Shop (produced 1893). 1893.
The Tempter (produced 1893). 1898.
The Masqueraders (produced 1894). 1894; edited by J. O. Bailey, in *British Plays of the Nineteenth Century,* 1966.
The Case of Rebellious Susan (produced 1894). 1894.
The Triumph of the Philistines (produced 1895). 1895.
Grace Mary. 1895.
Michael and His Lost Angel (produced 1896). 1896.
The Rogue's Comedy (produced 1896). 1896.
The Physician (produced 1897). 1897.
The Liars (produced 1897). 1901; edited by George Rowell in *Late Nineteenth-Century Plays,* 1968.
The Goal (produced 1907). 1898.
The Manoeuvres of Jane (produced 1898). 1898.
Carnac Sahib (produced 1899). 1899.
The Lackey's Carnival (produced 1900). 1900.
Mrs. Dane's Defence (produced 1900). 1900; edited by Michael Booth, in *English Plays of the Nineteenth Century,* 1969.
James the Fogey. 1900.
The Princess's Nose (produced 1902). 1902.
Chance, The Idol (produced 1902). 1902.
Whitewashing Julia (produced 1903). 1903.
Joseph Entangled (produced 1904). 1904.
The Chevaleer (produced 1904). 1904.
Chrysold. 1904.

The Sword of Gideon. 1905.
The Heroic Stubbs (produced 1906). 1906.
The Hypocrites (produced 1907). 1906.
The Galilean's Victory (as *The Evangelist,* produced 1907). 1907.
Dolly Reforming Herself (produced 1908). 1908; shortened version, as *Dolly's Little Bills* (produced 1912), 1910.
The Knife (produced 1909).
Fall In, Rookie (produced 1910). 1910.
We Can't Be As Bad As All That! (produced 1910). 1910.
The Ogre (produced 1911).
Lydia Gilmore (produced 1912).
Mary Goes First (produced 1913). 1913.
The Divine Gift. 1913.
The Lie (produced 1914). 1915.
The Theatre of Ideas: A Burlesque Allegory and Three One-Act Plays: The Goal, Her Tongue, Grace Mary. 1915.
Cock o' the Walk (produced 1915).
The Pacifists (produced 1917). 1917.

Other

The Renascence of the English Drama: Essays, Lectures, and Fragments Relating to the Modern English Stage 1883–94. 1895.
The Foundations of a National Drama: Lectures, Essays, and Speeches 1896–1912. 1913.
Patriotism and Popular Education. 1919.
My Dear Wells: A Manual for the Haters of England. 1921.
What Is Capital? An Enquiry into the Meaning of the Words Capital and Labour. 1925.
The Shadow of Henry Irving. 1931.

Reading List: *The Life and Letters of Jones* by Doris Arthur Jones, 1930 (includes bibliography); *Jones and the Modern Drama* by Richard A. Cordell, 1932; *The Rise and Fall of the Well Made Play* by John Russell Taylor, 1967.

* * *

Henry Arthur Jones was above all a professional writer for the theatre, though curiously he had little practical experience of the stage in his younger years. He began his career with the standard melodrama of the late 19th century, and achieved success with *The Silver King.* The construction of his plays, though, tended to suffer from the prescribed four-act form; his sense of craftsmanship would not allow him to end a play ambiguously or with a character still in development; as a consequence, his fourth acts are often anti-climactic. Moreover, he reacted against the tableaux and picture-postcard act-conclusions. But, despite some powerful scenes, most of his plays did tend to the merely "theatrical"; the influence of melodrama remained with him for most of his career. None the less, the fact of his being brought up in a less comfortable environment than many of his middle-class colleagues gives real strength to his frequent satire on middle-class and working-class hypocrisy, particularly the religious narrowness he attacks in *Saints and Sinners,* based to some extent on personal experience.

Jones's most accomplished work – presaged by *Judah* and his own favourite, *Michael and His Lost Angel* – is to be found in social comedies such as *The Liars* and *Whitewashing Julia,* both of which would sustain revival. He could also achieve the powerful cross-examination scene that occupies Act 3 of *Mrs. Dane's Defence.* In spite of his lack of formal education,

Jones was an avid reader, and his prose style is often flexible and idiomatic, though not particularly paradoxical and rarely memorable. Individual lines such as "O God put back thy universe and give me yesterday," from *The Silver King*, have attained a kind of copper-plated immortality. Occasionally he pitched his literary ambitions too high and essayed dramatic poetry; the result was stilted rather than disastrous, but in the one-act play, uniquely in dialogue, *Grace Mary*, he achieves a quasi-tragic effect.

Jones matured late, and produced his most distinguished work between 1890 and 1905, by which time his popularity had begun to fail with the onset of the "new" dramatists Granville-Barker and Hankin and the rising prestige of Shaw. He always claimed that Ibsen had not influenced him, and indeed his social satire generally concludes with submission to "the way of the world," the world, it should be added, of the aristocracy. In spite of the small amount of his work that is alive, Jones deserves the occasional revival, and his muted fame as one of those who brought the theatre in England by precept and example into closer connection with literature and the current of ideas.

—Ian Fletcher

JONES, (Everett) LeRoi. Pseudonym: Amiri Baraka. American. Born in Newark, New Jersey, 7 October 1934. Educated at the Central Avenue School, and Barringer High School, Newark; Howard University, Washington, D.C. Served in the United States Air Force, 1954–56. Married 1) Hettie Cohen in 1958 (divorced, 1965), two daughters; 2) Sylvia Robinson (Bibi Amina Baraka) in 1966, five children. Taught at the New School for Social Research, 1961–64; State University of New York at Buffalo, Summer 1964; Columbia University, 1964; Visiting Professor, San Francisco State College, 1966–67. Founder, *Yugen* magazine and Totem Press, New York, 1958; Editor, with Diane di Prima, *Floating Bear* magazine, New York, 1961–63. Founding Director, Black Arts Repertory Theatre, Harlem, New York, 1964–66. Since 1966, Founding Director, Spirit House, Newark. Involved in Newark politics: Member of the United Brothers, 1967, and Committee for Unified Newark, 1968. Member of the International Coordinating Committee, Congress of African Peoples; Chairman, Congress of Afrikan People; Secretary-General, National Black Political Assembly. Recipient: Whitney Fellowship, 1961; Obie Award, 1964; Guggenheim Fellowship, 1965; Dakar Festival Prize, 1966; National Endowment for the Arts grant, 1966. Member, Black Academy of Arts and Letters. Lives in Newark, New Jersey.

PUBLICATIONS

Plays

A Good Girl is Hard to Find (produced 1958).
Dante (produced 1961; as *The 8th Ditch*, produced 1964). In *The System of Dante's Hell*, 1965.
The Toilet (produced 1962). In *The Baptism and The Toilet*, 1967.
Dutchman (produced 1964). In *Dutchman and The Slave*, 1964.
The Slave (produced 1964). In *Dutchman and The Slave*, 1964.
Dutchman, and The Slave. 1964.

The Baptism (produced 1964). In *The Baptism and The Toilet,* 1967.
Jello (produced 1965). 1970.
Experimental Death Unit No. 1 (produced 1965). In *Four Black Revolutionary Plays,* 1969.
A Black Mass (produced 1966). In *Four Black Revolutionary Plays,* 1969.
The Baptism and The Toilet. 1967.
Arm Yrself or Harm Yrself (produced 1967). 1967.
Slave Ship: A Historical Pageant (produced 1967). 1967.
Madheart (produced 1967). In *Four Black Revolutionary Plays,* 1969.
Home on the Range (produced 1968). In *Drama Review,* Summer 1968.
Police, in *Drama Review,* Summer 1968.
The Death of Malcolm X, in *New Plays from the Black Theatre,* edited by Ed Bullins. 1969.
Great Goodness of Life (A Coon Show) (produced 1969). In *Four Black Revolutionary Plays,* 1969.
Four Black Revolutionary Plays. 1969.
Junkies Are Full of (SHHH ...), and Bloodrites (produced 1970). In *Black Drama Anthology,* edited by Woodie King and Ron Milner, 1971.
BA-RA-KA, in *Spontaneous Combustion: Eight New American Plays,* edited by Rochelle Owens. 1972.
A Recent Killing (produced 1973).
Sidnee Poet Heroical (produced 1975).
S-1 (produced 1976). In *The Motion of History and Other Plays,* 1978.
The Motion of History (produced 1977). In *The Motion of History and Other Plays,* 1978.
The Motion of History and Other Plays (includes *S-1* and *Slave Ship*). 1978.

Other plays: *Columbia the Gem of the Ocean; Resurrection of Life.*

Screenplays: *Dutchman,* 1967; *A Fable,* 1971.

Fiction

The System of Dante's Hell. 1965.
Tales. 1967.

Verse

Preface to a Twenty Volume Suicide Note. 1961.
The Dead Lecturer. 1964.
Black Art. 1966.
Black Magic: Poetry 1961–1967. 1969.
It's Nation Time. 1970.
In Our Terribleness: Some Elements of Meaning in Black Style, with Billy Abernathy. 1970.
Spirit Reach. 1972.
Afrikan Revolution. 1973.
Hard Facts. 1976.

Other

Cuba Libre. 1961.

Blues People: Negro Music in White America. 1963.
Home: Social Essays. 1966.
Black Music. 1968.
A Black Value System. 1970.
Raise Race Rays Raze: Essays since 1965. 1971.
Strategy and Tactics of a Pan-African Nationalist Party. 1971.
The Creation of the New Ark. 1975.

Editor, *Four Young Lady Poets.* 1962.
Editor, *The Moderns: New Fiction in America.* 1964.
Editor, with Larry Neal, *Black Fire: An Anthology of Afro-American Writing.* 1968.
Editor, *African Congress: A Documentary of the First Modern Pan-African Congress.* 1972.
Editor, with Diane di Prima, *The Floating Bear: A Newsletter, Numbers 1–37.* 1974.

Bibliography: *Jones (Imamu Amiri Baraka): A Checklist of Works by and about Him* by Letitia Dace, 1971.

Reading List: *From LeRoi Jones to Amiri Baraka: The Literary Works* by Theodore R. Hudson, 1973; *Baraka: The Renegade and the Mask* by Kimberly W. Benston, 1976; *Baraka/Jones: The Quest for a "Populist Modernism"* by Werner Sollors, 1978.

*　　　*　　　*

LeRoi Jones − now known as Amiri Baraka − says he has "always tried to be a revolutionary." That is the consistent quality in a twenty-year career which has included writing in every literary genre and representing contradictory points of view.

The rebel in Jones led him in his youth to prefer running with the ghetto gangs to remaining in his respectable middle-class home. At Howard University, which he found distastefully bourgeois, it led him to quit college after his junior year to join the Air Force. In New York in the late 1950's, it prompted him to become a Greenwich Village bohemian and a disciple of Allen Ginsberg and Jack Kerouac, to turn out lyric poetry and surreal fiction expressing the romantic *angst* and waggish frivolity which permitted publication under titles such as *The System of Dante's Hell* and *Preface to a Twenty Volume Suicide Note*: "My wife is left-handed./which implies a fierce de-/termination. ITS WEIRD BABY./The way some folks are always trying to be/different. A sin & a shame."

Jones in the late 1950's and early 1960's possessed a boundless energy and an extraordinarily diverse talent. He was still speaking to white people and writing for a racially mixed audience. He founded periodicals with two white women, the magazine *Yugen* with his wife Hettie Cohen and the newsletter *The Floating Bear* − its title derived from an A. A. Milne Winnie the Pooh story − with the poet Diane di Prima. His saturation in the western literary tradition (William Carlos Williams, Whitman, Eliot, Yeats, Pound, and the Black Mountain poets) was clearly discernible in his poetry and novel. At that time Jones did not write specifically ethnic literature. Indeed, he alleged in 1959 that "Negro writing" can at best be folklore, for what is written out of racial consciousness cannot achieve literary status. In 1961 his poetry muses "Africa/is a foreign place. You are/as any other sad man here/american."

Yet even in the early work techniques analogous to black music − jazz and the blues − are evident, and Jones was also writing music criticism and essays expressing an increasingly inflammatory political consciousness. He was becoming politicized as early as 1960, when he visited Cuba and wrote the essay *Cuba Libre* in praise of Castro and that island's revolution. His verse became edgy, uneasy with his white life, and his essays and plays began to express an urgency which was turning, by 1964, to racial militancy.

Although a portion of his novel and the play *The Toilet* had been produced earlier, 1964 was the year that Baraka really won attention as a playwright. In March *The Eighth Ditch* (his *Dante* play) opened and was quickly closed by police on grounds of obscenity. Within a week *The Baptism*, an equally startling play, this one a religious satire which drew charges of both obscenity and blasphemy, jarred and amused its spectators. The very next day *Dutchman* opened, and later that year a double bill of *The Toilet* and *The Slave* further solidified Baraka's reputation. (A full-length play, *A Recent Killing*, which was written in this year but not produced until a decade later, dramatizes an inter-racial cooperation in which Jones was already losing faith.)

These plays are blistering in their dramatization of raw racial tensions on a realistic level, but they also function on an allegorical plane. *Dutchman*, in particular, is generally acknowledged to be his finest achievement. The Flying Dutchman constitutes one of the more obvious symbolic references in this play about a woman picking up a man on a New York City subway, but critical opinion has been divided over whether white Lula or black Clay embodies the legendary captain who is doomed to roam until his final peace can be purchased by a lover willing to die with him. Perhaps it is white racism, as exemplified by the murderous Lula, that won't die, or possibly the swallowing of pride and suppression of rage which the superficially assimilated Clay practices represents what Jones had in mind. Whatever the parallel, a double death does not occur, so the spectre of racism is not exorcised.

Dutchman can also be interpreted as a modernization of the Adam and Eve story in which Lula — who keeps eating and offering apples — is a corrupter of the innocent, natural man of Africa and the cause of his expulsion from the paradise of the American dream. Other religious parables which have been discerned include that of Clay as Christ and Lula as Satan (with the young man at the end representing the resurrection) and the idea that Clay is being baptized in hell-fire. *Dutchman* can therefore be viewed as a reference to disguise and the voluntary assumption of roles. Lula is an author creating a series of characters for herself. When Clay stops concealing his blackness behind white clothes, intellectual interests, and a courteous demeanor, Lula rewards his self-assertion with murder.

Equally playable and nearly equally subject to glosses (sometimes more arcane than illuminating), *The Toilet* and *The Slave* take somewhat different approaches to racial conflict. The earlier play, *The Toilet*, depicts interracial relations in a fashion which Jones later came to regard as more sentimental than realistic, for the black gang leader really loves the white boy who is beaten up in the lavatory, and he returns to comfort Karolis when the bullies have left. A major factor in the play's appeal is Jones's embodiment in his protagonist of a universal conflict between the gentle, nurturing, reflective aspect of the character (the "Ray" side of us) and the belligerent, aloof, authoritative aspect (the "Foots" side). The split in this particular temperament, of course, sets up a conflict between the assimilationist with aspirations to white goals (Ray, the good student who is attracted to Karolis) and the true black man (Foots, the natural leader).

Although *The Toilet* is milder than *Dutchman*, *The Slave* finds its protagonist has progressed beyond the birth of militance, which Clay barely reaches, to full leadership in a race war. Walker has left the insurgents just long enough to visit a white couple, his ex-wife and her new husband, the latter a college professor who represents the western culture to which Walker has bidden farewell. That he would pay such a call at all suggests that Walker is still something of a slave to the white liberal heritage, and the old slave whom Walker becomes in a long monologue reinforces that notion. Still, Walker is wiping out, literally, the old associations, and he, like Jones himself at this time of his life, sets a new, independent course.

Jones's drama had been by and large realistic and by and large addressed to a white or racially mixed audience. But the radical changes in his life — his departure in 1965 for Harlem and soon thereafter for the Newark ghetto, his divorce (subsequent to the prophetic *The Slave*) from the white wife (who now felt she was the enemy) and his remarriage to a black woman, his conversion to the Kawaida sect of Muslim and his adoption of an African name,

Amiri (prince) Baraka (blessedness), preceded for a time by the religious title Imamu (spiritual leader) – all reflect an ideological transformation which had a profound effect upon all his writing. The essays grew violent, the poetry took on the dialect of black speech, and the plays increasingly spoke only to blacks and were presented in segregated theatres. Realism was generally rejected in favor of a technique sometimes expressionistic and sometimes a montage of brief episodes, cinematic juxtapositions.

The first plays of this black militant period, including *Experimental Death Unit No. 1*, *Jello*, *A Black Mass*, and *Madheart*, explicitly proclaim the superiority of black to white, of black revolutionist to assimilationist, and of male to female. *Jello* is also a quite funny parody of Jack Benny's radio show in which Rochester stops serving Benny and starts asserting his new-found black manhood, and *A Black Mass* is a lyrical evocation of a misguided black man's creation of the white race. While some later black nationalist plays by Baraka – *Arm Yrself or Harm Yrself*, for instance – are simple didactic dramas with lines which preach the point, others make considerable use of nonverbal techniques and are theatrical in ways Antonin Artaud would have appreciated. *Slave Ship*, for instance, forces its spectators to feel they themselves are manacled in the hold of that ship, and it employs Swahili and moans and groans quite as much as English dialogue. The play's spectacle of human suffering is marvelously powerful drama. Some other plays of the late 1960's are cinematic or surreal, and some experiment with language in ways outside the tradition of mainstream American drama.

A recent resurgence of the polemical in Baraka's dramaturgy has followed another political change. The creator of and foremost writer in the black arts movement by 1973 had become a Communist leader and had rejected his nationalist rage and rancor toward whites as racist. Therefore, *S-1* and *The Motion of History* employ agit-prop techniques, in the former to attack the proposed Senate Bill 1, the Federal Criminal Code reform bill which opponents feel would abridge freedom of speech and assembly, and in the latter to urge the solidarity of blacks and whites in a revolution to overthrow their oppressors. *The Motion of History* dramatizes instances from the past four centuries in which the ruling class has pitted poor blacks and whites against each other so as to obscure their common interests in ending exploitation. This play even ridicules the black militant, who is represented as a mindless robot chanting "the white man is the devil."

In 1961, LeRoi Jones was president of the Fair Play for Cuba Committee. He strayed far afield from such politics, but has returned now to a Marxist-Leninist-Maoist stance. Whatever his particular affiliation, he continues to be one of the foremost of contemporary committed writers.

—Tish Dace

JONSON, Ben(jamin). English. Born in Westminster, London, probably 11 June 1572. Educated at Westminster School, London, under William Camden. Fought for the Dutch against the Spanish in the Low Countries. Married Anne Lewis c. 1593; had several children. Actor, then playwright, from 1595; acted for Philip Henslowe, 1597; killed a fellow actor in a duel, 1598, but escaped the gallows by pleading benefit of clergy; enjoyed the patronage of Lord Albany and Aurelian Townshend; appointed Poet Laureate, and given royal pension, 1616, and wrote and presented masques at court, 1616–25; gained a reputation as the "literary dictator" of London and in later life attracted a circle of young writers who styled themselves the "Sons of Ben"; visited Scotland, and William Drummond of Hawthornden, 1618–19: elected a Burgess of Edinburgh, 1619; appointed City Chronologer of London, 1628. M.A.: Oxford University, 1619. *Died 6 August 1637.*

Collections

Works, edited by C. H. Herford and P. and E. M. Simpson.   11 vols., 1925–52.
Complete Masques, edited by S. Orgel.   1969.
Complete Poems, edited by Ian Donaldson.   1975.

Plays

The Case Is Altered (produced 1597–98?).   1609.
Every Man in His Humour (produced 1598).   1601; edited by G. B. Jackson, 1969.
Every Man Out of His Humour (produced 1599).   1600.
The Fountain of Self-Love; or, Cynthia's Revels (produced 1600).   1601.
Poetaster; or, The Arraignment (produced 1601).   1602.
Sejanus His Fall (produced 1603).   1605; edited by W. Bolton, 1966.
Entertainment of the Queen and Prince at Althorp (produced 1603).   1604.
King James His Royal and Magnificent Entertainment, with Dekker (produced 1604).
   With *Entertainment of the Queen and Prince at Althorp.*   1604.
A Private Entertainment of the King and Queen at Highgate (produced 1604).   In
   Works, 1616.
Eastward Ho, with Chapman and Marston (produced 1605).   1605; edited by C. G.
   Petter, 1973.
Volpone; or, The Fox (produced 1605).   1607; edited by J. Creaser, 1978.
The Masque of Blackness (produced 1605).   In *The Characters of Two Royal Masques,*
   1608.
Hymenaei (produced 1606).   1606.
The Entertainment of the Two Kings of Great Britain and Denmark at Theobalds
   (produced 1606).   In *Works, 1616.*
An Entertainment of King James and Queen Anne at Theobalds (produced 1607).   In
   Works, 1616.
The Masque of Beauty (produced 1608).   In *The Characters of Two Royal Masques,*
   1608.
The Hue and Cry after Cupid (produced 1608).   In *Works, 1616.*
*The Description of the Masque Celebrating the Marriage of John, Lord Ramsey, Viscount
   Haddington* (produced 1608).   In *Works, 1616.*
The Masque of Queens (produced 1609).   1609.
Epicoene; or, The Silent Woman (produced 1609).   In *Works,* 1616; edited by L. A.
   Beaurline, 1966.
The Speeches at Prince Henry's Barriers (produced 1610).   In *Works, 1616.*
The Alchemist (produced 1610).   1612; edited by Alvin B. Kernan, 1974.
Oberon, The Faery Prince (produced 1611).   In *Works, 1616.*
Love Freed from Ignorance and Folly (produced 1611).   In *Works, 1616.*
Catiline His Conspiracy (produced 1611).   1611; edited by W. Bolton and J. F.
   Gardner, 1972.
Love Restored (produced 1612).   In *Works, 1616.*
The Irish Masque (produced 1613).   In *Works, 1616.*
A Challenge at Tilt (produced 1614).   In *Works, 1616.*
Bartholomew Fair (produced 1614).   1631; edited by Edward B. Partridge, 1964.
The Golden Age Restored (produced 1616).   In *Works, 1616.*
Mercury Vindicated from the Alchemists (produced 1616).   In *Works, 1616.*
The Devil Is an Ass (produced 1616).   1631; edited by M. Hussey, 1967.

Christmas His Masque (produced 1616).   In *Works*, 1640.
The Vision of Delight (produced 1617).   In *Works*, 1640.
Lovers Made Men (produced 1617).   1617.
Pleasure Reconciled to Virtue (produced 1618).   In *Works*, 1640; revised version, as
   For the Honour of Wales (produced 1618), in *Works*, 1640.
News from the New World Discovered in the Moon (produced 1620).   In *Works*, 1640.
An Entertainment at the Blackfriars (produced 1620).   In *The Monthly Magazine; or,
   British Register*, 1816.
Pan's Anniversary; or, The Shepherd's Holiday (produced 1620).   In *Works*, 1640.
The Gypsies Metamorphosed (propoduced 1621).   In *Works*, 1640; edited by W. W.
   Greg, 1952.
The Masque of Augurs (produced 1622).   1622.
Time Vindicated to Himself and to His Honours (produced 1623).   1623.
Neptune's Triumph for the Return of Albion.   1624; revised version, as *The Fortunate
   Isles and Their Union* (produced 1625), 1625.
The Masque of Owls (produced 1624).   In *Works*, 1640.
The Staple of News (produced 1625).   1631; edited by Devra Rowland Kifer, 1976.
The New Inn; or, The Light Heart (produced 1629).   1631.
Love's Triumph Through Callipolis (produced 1631).   1631.
Chloridia (produced 1631).   1631.
The Magnetic Lady; or, Humours Reconciled (produced 1632).   In *Works*, 1640.
A Tale of a Tub (produced 1633).   In *Works*, 1640.
The King's Entertainment at Welbeck (produced 1633).   In *Works*, 1640.
Love's Welcome at Bolsover (produced 1634).   In *Works*, 1640.
The Sad Shepherd; or, A Tale of Robin Hood (incomplete), in *Works*.   1640; edited and
   completed by Alan Porter, 1944.

Other

Works (plays and verse).   1616; revised edition, 2 vols., 1640.
Timber; or, Discoveries Made upon Men and Matter, in *Works*.   1640; edited by R. S.
   Walker, 1953.
The English Grammar, in *Works*.   1640; edited by S. Gibson, 1928.
Leges Convivales.   1692.
Literary Criticism, edited by J. D. Redwine.   1970.

Translator, *Horace His Art of Poetry*, in *Works*.   1640; edited by E. H. Blakeney, 1928.

Bibliography: *Jonson: A Concise Bibliography* by S. A. Tannenbaum, 1938; supplement
1947; supplement in *Elizabethan Bibliographies Supplements 3* by G. R. Guffey, 1968.

Reading List: *Jonson, Poet* by George B. Johnston, 1945; *The Satiric and Didactic in Jonson's
Comedies* by Helena W. Baum, 1947; *Apologie for Bartholomew Fayre: The Art of Jonson's
Comedies* by Freda L. Townsend, 1947; *Jonson of Westminster* (biography) by Marchette
Chute, 1953; *The Accidence of Jonson's Plays, Masques, and Entertainments* by Astley C.
Partridge, 1953; *Jonson and the Comic Truth* by John J. Enck, 1957; *The Broken Compass: A
Study of the Major Comedies of Jonson* by Edward B. Partridge, 1958; *Jonson and the
Language of Prose Comedy* by Jonas A. Barish, 1960; *Jonson: Studies in the Plays* by Calvin
G. Thayer, 1963; *Jonson's Plays: An Introduction* by Robert E. Knoll, 1965; *Jonson's
Dotages: A Reconsideration of the Late Plays* by L. S. Champion, 1967; *Jonson's Romish Plot:
A Study of Catiline and Its Historical Context* by B. N. De Luna, 1967; *Vision and Judgment
in Jonson's Drama* by Gabriele B. Jackson, 1968; *The Aristophanic Comedies of Jonson* by

Coburn Gum, 1969; *Jonson* by John B. Bamborough, 1970; *Jonson's Moral Comedy* by A. C. Dessen, 1971; *Jonson, Public Poet and Private Man* by George Parfitt, 1976.

*   *   *

The opening lines of T. S. Eliot's famous essay on Ben Jonson are now nearly sixty years old, yet they are almost as applicable today as when they were first written: "The reputation of Jonson," Eliot wrote, "has been of the most deadly kind that can be compelled upon the memory of a great poet. To be universally accepted; to be damned by the praise that quenches all desire to read the book; to be afflicted by the imputation of the virtues which excite the least pleasure; and to be read only by historians and antiquaries – this is the most perfect conspiracy of approval." Substitute "academics and students" for "antiquaries" and you have a fair summary of Jonson's current reputation. That this state of affairs is partly of Jonson's own making is certainly true but hardly sufficient justification. In his own day Jonson saw himself as the self-appointed arbiter of true critical taste, the upholder of classical standards of decorum, construction, and moral didacticism against the undiscriminating popular appetite for sensation and extravagant spectacle, and the champion of high erudition against barbarous ignorance. So successful was he in imposing this version of himself on his own age and those that followed that it was not long before the contrast was drawn by which Jonson's reputation is still largely defined – the contrast between the warm, spontaneous, generous-hearted inclusiveness of the "romantic" Shakespeare and the chilly learning and cold perfection of the "classical" Jonson. Like all such sweeping contrasts, this one has enough plausibility to survive as the received truth, though it is as misleading about Shakespeare as it is about Jonson.

By way of building up a fairer picture of the nature of Jonson's achievement we may begin by recalling one of Drummond's remarks about him: "He hath consumed a whole night in lying looking to his great toe, about which he hath seen Tartars and Turks, Romans and Cartheginians, fight in his imagination." Such a detail serves to draw attention to an element in Jonson's work which meets us at every turn and which is at least as important as his undoubted learning and his emphasis on classical precept and precedent. It is a facet of his imagination at once childlike, romantic, and grotesque, and one which clearly contributed to some of his finest comic creations as well as to his tenderest lyrics and his most savage satirical epigrams.

The exuberance of Jonson's imagination is already apparent in his first great stage success, *Every Man in His Humour*, first performed in 1598 by the Lord Chamberlain's Men, the most famous theatrical company of the time. (The tradition that Shakespeare himself arranged for his company to present the play is attractive, though it cannot be traced beyond the eighteenth century.) In terms of plot and setting there is nothing to distinguish Jonson's play from many others deriving from classical Roman Comedy, with its conflict of generations and the convoluted manoeuvrings of wily servants. Jonson's distinctive contribution appears in his conception of the "humorous man," a dramatic character whose personality is shaped by some leading trait (or "humour") in his temperament which was itself, according to prevailing medical notions, based on the predominance of one of the four bodily fluids, blood, choler, melancholy, and phlegm. Jonson's contemporary George Chapman had been the first to put "humorous" characters on the stage (in *A Humorous Day's Mirth* performed a year before Jonson's comedy), but the vigour and extravagance of Jonson's presentation set it apart. The sharp distinction he draws between true "humour" as an element of character and mere affectation is typical of the energy and inventiveness of Jonson's imagination:

> As when some one peculiar quality
> Doth so possess a man, that it doth draw
> All his affects, his spirits, and his powers,
> In their confluctions, all to run one way,
> This may be truly said to be a Humour.

> But that a rook, in wearing a pied feather,
> The cable hat-band, or the three-piled ruff,
> A yard of shoe-tie, or the Switzer's knot
> On his French garters, should affect a Humour!
> Oh, 'tis more than most ridiculous.

Like most sequels, Jonson's attempt to capitalize on the success of this play with *Every Man Out of His Humour* was a comprehensive failure and appears to have led to the Chamberlain's Men dispensing with his services. The Children of the Queen's Chapel, one of the companies of boy actors which sprouted up towards the end of the century, were his new theatrical patrons and for them he wrote the satiric comedies which involved him in the "war of the theatres" with his contemporaries John Marston and Thomas Dekker. In spite of occasional passages of great satirical energy and some beautiful lyrics such as "Queen and huntress, chaste and fair," Jonson's contributions to this "war" are not by any means among his best plays. *Cynthia's Revels* deserves to be remembered for its portrait of Jonson himself as Crites, the impartial and well-informed judge of society and the arts; and in *Poetaster* Jonson as Horace feeds Marston (Crispianus) an emetic that makes the latter spew great quantities of words in his typically turgid style. But Jonson's greatest achievements in drama were yet to come.

This achievement is certainly not to be found in Jonson's two classical tragedies *Sejanus His Fall* and *Catiline His Conspiracy*; though the latter especially has some magnificent speeches as well as dramatic moments of great intensity, both suffer by comparison with Shakespeare's excursions into Roman history, especially *Julius Caesar*. Jonson's enduring reputation as a dramatist rests squarely on three great comedies, *Volpone; or, The Fox*, *The Alchemist*, and *Bartholomew Fair*. Each of them exemplifies Jonson's enormous capacity to dramatize the grotesque aberrations of human appetite, his zest for the variety of life, and his unfailing delight in the villain as artist. *Volpone* is scrupulously classical in its didactic import, yet what delights us is chiefly the artistry of Volpone and his henchman Mosca. *The Alchemist* is a model of the observance of the Aristotelian unities, but its dramatic appeal lies in the breakneck momentum of its plot and the almost unbearable comic tension created by it. And in *Bartholomew Fair* Jonson abandoned even the pretence of being the classical moralist in favour of the unbuttoned enjoyment of Jacobean London in all its colour and richness.

The opening years of the seventeenth century witnessed Jonson's finest dramatic productions, not only for the public stage, but in the sphere of royal entertainment, when Jonson's collaboration with the scene designer and architect Inigo Jones led to a splendid flowering of that most ephemeral of theatrical forms, the court masque. Rooted as it was in time, place, and occasion, the masque can give us little sense of its splendour through the text alone, though Jonson's scripts for such works as *Pleasure Reconciled to Virtue* and *The Gypsies Metamorphosed* are eloquent enough even in the reading. It was precisely the disagreement between Jonson and Jones as to the relative importance of words versus spectacle in masque which led to the dissolution of this brilliant partnership in 1631.

Jonson's last years present a sad picture of commercial failure, declining creative powers, and increasing bodily decrepitude. Apart from the comedies already mentioned, *The Silent Woman*, *The Devil Is an Ass*, and *The Staple of News* deserve to be remembered for their occasional inventiveness and keen-eyed observation of London life and manners. But if Jonson's principal claim to fame lies in his three great comedies, his achievements as lyric and epigrammatic poet are not inconsiderable. Contemporary practitioners of verse esteemed him so highly that a group of them, which included Herrick, Suckling, and Carew styled themselves the Sons of Ben and produced a commemorative volume *Jonsonus Virbius* after his death in 1637. As a critic, too, Jonson was of the first rank, forthright, well-informed, and catholic in taste by the standards of the time. All these qualities are well illustrated in the splendid commendatory verses which he contributed to the Folio edition of Shakespeare's works published in 1623.

That Jonson was a classicist and an erudite one need not be disputed, though he was by no means the most learned classical scholar of his day (his mentor Camden and his contemporary John Selden were far better versed in the classics). But the emphasis should finally fall on the originality of his imagination, his roots in the popular idiom he affected to despise, and his enormous sense of theatre which is illustrated by the continued success on the stage of his great comedies.

—Gāmini Salgādo

KAUFMAN, George S(imon). American. Born in Pittsburgh, Pennsylvania, 16 November 1889. Educated at Liberty School, New Castle School, and Central High School, Pittsburgh, graduated 1907; Western University of Pennsylvania Law School, 1907. Married 1) Beatrice Bakrow in 1917 (died, 1945), one adopted daughter; 2) the writer Leueen MacGrath in 1949 (divorced, 1957). Worked as a surveyor, clerk in the Allegheny County Tax Office, and stenographer in the Pittsburgh Coal Company; travelling salesman for the Columbia Ribbon Company, Paterson, New Jersey; Jornalist: Columnist, *Washington Times*, 1912–13; Drama Critic, New York *Tribune*, 1914–15; Columnist, New York *Evening Mail*, 1915; Drama Critic, *New York Times*, 1917–30. Writer for the stage from 1918, often in collaboration; stage director from 1928. Chairman of the Board, Dramatists' Guild 1927. Recipient: Megrue Prize, 1931; Pulitzer Prize, 1932, 1937. *Died 2 June 1961.*

PUBLICATIONS

Plays

  Among Those Present, with Larry Evans and Walter C. Percival (produced 1918; as *Someone in the House*, produced 1918).
  Jacques Duval, with Hans Mueller (produced 1919).
  Dulcy, with Marc Connelly (produced 1921).   1921.
  To the Ladies!, with Marc Connelly (produced 1922).   1923.
  No, Sirree!, with Marc Connelly (produced 1922).
  A Christmas Carol, with Marc Connelly, from the story by Dickens, in *Bookman*, December 1922.
  The 49ers, with Marc Connelly (produced 1922).
  West of Pittsburgh, with Marc Connelly (produced 1922); revised version, as *The Deep Tangled Wildwood* (produced 1923).
  Merton of the Movies, with Marc Connelly, from the story by Harry Leon Wilson (produced 1922).   1925.
  Helen of Troy, N.Y., with Marc Connelly, music and lyrics by Harry Ruby and Bert Kalmar (produced 1923).
  Beggar on Horseback, with Marc Connelly, music by Deems Taylor, from a play by Paul Apel (produced 1924).   1925.
  Sketches, in *'Round the Town* (produced 1924).
  Be Yourself, with Marc Connelly (produced 1924).
  Minick, with Edna Ferber, from the story "Old Man Minick" by Ferber (produced 1924).   1925.
  The Butter and Egg Man (produced 1925).   1925.
  The Cocoanuts, music by Irving Berlin (produced 1925).   1925.
  If Men Played Cards Like Women Do.   1926.
  The Good Fellow, with Herman J. Mankiewicz (produced 1926).   1931.
  The Royal Family, with Edna Ferber (produced 1927).   1928; as *Theatre Royal* (produced 1935), 1936.
  Animal Crackers, with Morrie Ryskind, music and lyrics by Harry Ruby and Bert Kalmar (produced 1928).
  The Still Alarm (sketch), in *The Little Show* (produced 1929).   1930.
  June Moon, with Ring Lardner, from the story "Some Like Them Cold" by Lardner (produced 1929).   1931.
  The Channel Road, with Alexander Woollcott (produced 1929).
  Strike Up the Band, book by Morrie Ryskind from a libretto by Kaufman, music by George Gershwin, lyrics by Ira Gershwin (produced 1930).

Once in a Lifetime, with Moss Hart (produced 1930).   1930.
The Band Wagon, with Howard Dietz, music by Arthur Schwartz (produced 1931).
Eldorado, with Laurence Stallings (produced 1931).
Of Thee I Sing, with Morrie Ryskind, music by George Gershwin, lyrics by Ira
     Gershwin (produced 1931).   1932.
Dinner at Eight, with Edna Ferber (produced 1932).   1932.
Let 'em Eat Cake, with Morrie Ryskind, music by George Gershwin, lyrics by Ira
     Gershwin (produced 1933).   1933.
The Dark Tower, with Alexander Woollcott (produced 1933).   1934.
Merrily We Roll Along, with Moss Hart (produced 1934).   1934.
Bring on the Girls, with Morrie Ryskind (produced 1934).
Prom Night.   1934.
Cheating the Kidnappers.   1935.
The Paperhanger, with Moss Hart.   1935(?).
First Lady, with Katharine Dayton (produced 1935).   1935.
Stage Door, with Edna Ferber (produced 1936).   1939.
You Can't Take It with You, with Moss Hart (produced 1936).   1937.
I'd Rather Be Right, with Moss Hart, music by Richard Rodgers, lyrics by Lorenz Hart
     (produced 1937).   1937.
The Fabulous Invalid, with Moss Hart (produced 1938).   1938.
The American Way, with Moss Hart, music by Oscar Levant (produced 1939).   1939.
The Man Who Came to Dinner, with Moss Hart (produced 1939).   1939.
George Washington Slept Here, with Moss Hart (produced 1940).   1940.
The Land Is Bright, with Edna Ferber (produced 1941).   1946.
Six Plays, with Moss Hart.   1942.
The Late George Apley, with John P. Marquand, from the novel by Marquand (produced
     1944).   1946.
Hollywood Pinafore (produced 1945).
Park Avenue, with Nunnally Johnson, music by Arthur Schwartz, lyrics by Ira
     Gershwin (produced 1946).
Bravo!, with Edna Ferber (produced 1948).   1949.
The Small Hours, with Leueen MacGrath (produced 1951).   1951.
Fancy Meeting You Again, with Leueen MacGrath (produced 1952).   1952.
The Solid Gold Cadillac, with Howard Teichmann (produced 1953).   1954.
Silk Stockings, with Leueen MacGrath and Abe Burrows, music by Cole Porter,
     suggested by Melchior Lengyel (produced 1955).   1955.
Amicable Parting, with Leueen MacGrath (produced 1957).   1957.

Screenplays: *Business Is Business*, with Dorothy Parker, 1925; *If Men Played Cards As
Women Do*, 1929; *Roman Scandals*, with others, 1933; *A Night at the Opera*, with
Morrie Ryskind, 1935; *Star Spangled Rhythm*, with others, 1943.

Reading List: *Kaufman: An Intimate Portrait*, by Howard Teichmann, 1972; *Kaufman and
His Friends* by Scott Meredith, 1974, abridged version, as *Kaufman and the Algonquin Round
Table*, 1977.

*   *   *

George S. Kaufman was a devastating wit and a serious satirist who worked, almost
always in collaboration, on successful plays, musicals, and films. He was especially effective
with Moss Hart, a productive blend of talents much studied and much admired: "Their most

distinguished works, *You Can't Take It with You* and *The Man Who Came to Dinner*, reveal Kaufman and Hart," says Milton Levin (in *The Reader's Encyclopedia of World Drama*), "as the best satirists in American drama."

Kaufman's first play was with the team of Larry Evans and Walter Percival. Then he and Marc Connelly (another newspaperman from Pennsylvania active in New York) entered on a series of collaborations: *Dulcy, To the Ladies, Merton of the Movies, The Deep Tangled Wildwood*, and *Beggar on Horseback*. Of these only *The Deep Tangled Wildwood* (a satire "upon the Winchell-Smith type of play") was a failure. *Merton of the Movies*, the story of a movie-struck clerk who achieves success because he, unconsciously, burlesques serious roles, was a delight. The dream sequence of *Beggar on Horseback* (a penniless composer, Neil McRae, is given a sedative and has nightmares about having to work in a "widget" factory and then a Consolidated Art Factory, where he has to write music for songs like: "You've broken my heart like you broke my heart/So why should you break it again?") was considered "a fine expression of the resentment of the artist" for those who are "contemptuous of those who show originality" (A. H. Quinn). *Beggar on Horseback* is considered a milestone in American expressionism. The team broke up and Kaufman wrote his one unaided work, *The Butter and Egg Man* (1925), and Connelly tried an original also, *The Wisdom Tooth* (1926). Neither was much good, for Kaufman's farce and Connelly's fantasy did not seem to work separately.

"I have always been smart enough to attach myself to the most promising lad that came along in the theater," said Kaufman, and he joined forces with a number of burgeoning, bright talents. With Edna Ferber he wrote *Minick, The Royal Family, Dinner at Eight, Stage Door*, and *The Land is Bright*. With Herman J. Mankiewicz, another journalist and wit, he wrote *The Good Fellow*, which flopped (Mankiewicz went on to success as a screenwriter, probably writing most of *Citizen Kane*, though that is still argued), but the same year Kaufman had a hit with Ring Lardner, that "wonderful man" with such a great ear for American speech, in an hilarious take-off of Tin-Pan Alley, *June Moon*. About the same time Kaufman began to work with one of the madcap writers behind the Marx Brothers, the too-little-acknowledged zany genius, Morrie Ryskind. With Ryskind Kaufman entered the world of Broadway musicals, starting with *Animal Crackers*. Their collaboration was later to produce *Of Thee I Sing* (with the Gershwins; Pulitzer Prize 1932) and *Let 'em Eat Cake* (with the Gershwins), satires of politics and revolutionaries. With Alexander Woollcott, Kaufman wrote *The Channel Road* and, not much better, *The Dark Tower*. With Katharine Dayton he did a comedy of Washington politics and social life, *First Lady*. In the 1930's he was at his best with Moss Hart. *Once in a Lifetime* was a facile but funny satire on Hollywood. *Merrily We Roll Along* cleverly told its story backwards, taking the middle-aged failure back to the promise of his youth. *I'd Rather Be Right* took its title from a Henry Clay speech of 1850 ("I would rather be right than be President"), but attacked the administration of Franklin Delano Roosevelt. *You Can't Take It with You* well deserved its Pulitzer Prize for 1936, for the crazy Sycamore family creates one of the fastest, most furious, funniest farces ever and manages to effect a sweet, sentimental ending as well. The musicals *Strike Up the Band* and *The Band Wagon* (with Howard Dietz) were fun – but *The Man Who Came to Dinner*, with Hart, was fabulous. At the center of the chaos stands (or sits, in a wheelchair) Sheridan Whiteside, described by Monty Woolley in the film biography of Cole Porter as "an intolerable ass." As Woolley played him on stage and screen, this caricature of Alexander Woollcott was irresistible and, though the play is cluttered with other matters (such as cartoons of Noël Coward, one of the Marx Brothers, and a Lizzie Borden character), he delightfully dominates the action as he dominates the poor family who were unlucky enough to have him break a hip on their premises. The play contains some of the best single lines in American comedy.

The Man Who Came to Dinner may be the highspot of Kaufman's career. *George Washington Slept Here* was accurately reviewed as "George Kaufman slipped here" and later work such as *The Late George Apley* (with novelist J. P. Marquand) and *The Solid Gold Cadillac* (with Howard Teichmann) were a part of Kaufman's long career as a play doctor, though much of their success was no doubt due to his expertise. He also worked with other play doctors (such as Abe Burrows) and with Nunnally Johnson, Leueen MacGrath, and others.

Kaufman gained various strengths from various collaborators – farce, fantasy, satire, structure – but, to put it briefly, he can best be understood if one thinks of him as a Jewish comedian. He was a leader among the "Broadway intellectuals" (with Hart, Dorothy Parker, S. N. Behrman, George Jean Nathan) and a master of the wisecrack. His is the *echt* Jewish humor that plays with language (as in Goodman Ace); often sees the world as *ash und porukh* (ashes and dust) but will hang on to see what happens ("You might as well live" – Dorothy Parker); deals in insult; sometimes takes off into nonsense, intoxicated by words (S. J. Perelman), and sometimes into sentimentality (Sam Levine), attracted to nostalgia for better times; is repelled by pretension and more than a little attracted to cyncism (though not at Kaufman's time going as far as the Shock Schlock of Lenny Bruce) and always loves to tinker with logic until it explodes (you had best read Leo Rosten's *The Joys of Yiddish* rather than Freud on humor). In *World of Our Fathers* (1977), Irving Howe dissects this Jewish humor which chooses laughter as the alternative to tears and often uses satire as both a defensive and an offensive weapon. Professor Howe quotes Gilbert Seldes, who claimed that the Jewish entertainers' "daemonic" approach was traceable to "their fine carelessness about our superstitions of politeness and gentility ... contempt for artificial notions of propriety."

Kaufman was businessman enough to know that an all-out assault on The Establishment would not pay off. His pose was that of the hero of *The Butter and Egg Man*, the naïf in the big city. His targets were the obvious, safe ones that are best suited to musical comedy and farce. When he tried something "positive," like *The American Way* (a patriotic panorama), he was at his weakest. A wisecrack has to be a *zinger*, not a compliment. He never let himself get bitter: *that* was the kind of satire, as he said, which "closes on Saturday night." He wasn't a *kvetch* or a nag or a moralist, just a very funny wisecracking wit, one of the best.

—Leonard R. N. Ashley

KELLY, George (Edward). American. Born in Philadelphia, Pennsylvania, 16 January 1887. Educated privately. Actor as a young man: debut, 1908; subsequently played in touring companies and vaudeville; playwright from 1916. Recipient: Pulitzer Prize, 1926; Brandeis University Creative Arts Award, 1959. D.F.A.: LaSalle College, Philadelphia, 1962. *Died 18 June 1974.*

PUBLICATIONS

Plays

> *Mrs. Ritter Appears* (produced 1917); revised version, as *The Torchbearers: A Satirical Comedy* (produced 1922). 1923; revised version of Act III, as *Mrs. Ritter Appears*, 1964.
> *Poor Aubrey* (produced 1922). In *The Flattering Word and Other One-Act Plays*, 1925; revised version, as *The Show-Off: A Transcript of Life* (produced 1924), 1924.
> *Mrs. Wellington's Surprise* (produced 1922).
> *Finders-Keepers*. 1923.

The Flattering Word and Other One-Act Plays (includes Smarty's Party, The Weak Spot, Poor Aubrey). 1925.
Craig's Wife (produced 1925). 1926.
Daisy Mayme (produced 1926). 1927.
One of Those Things, in One-Act Plays for Stage and Study, Third Series. 1927.
Behold the Bridegroom (produced 1927). 1928.
A La Carte (sketches and lyrics only; produced 1927).
Maggie the Magnificent (produced 1929).
Philip Goes Forth (produced 1931). 1931.
Reflected Glory (produced 1936). 1937.
The Deep Mrs. Sykes (produced 1945). 1946.
The Fatal Weakness (produced 1946). 1947.

Screenplay: Old Hutch, 1936.

Bibliography: "Kelly: An Eclectic Bibliography" by Paul A. Doyle, in Bulletin of Bibliography, September-December 1965.

Reading List: Kelly by Foster Hirsch, 1975.

*   *   *

George Kelly had a lot of brothers and sisters and he followed his older brother Walter ("The Virginia Judge" of vaudeville) into the theatre. In those days it was not quite so unusual a place to find a moralist, even an anti-romantic, deeply-puritanical one.

Kelly played juveniles in the Keith and Orpheum circuits and began to write playlets, sketches really, such as One of Those Things, Finders-Keepers, The Flattering Word, and Poor Aubrey. They were light little satires on character flaws such as vanity and bragging. People who overstepped the accepted moral code were given their comeuppance, like the adventuress who outsmarts herself in Smarty's Party. They were popular enough: really trenchant satire (as George S. Kaufman remarked) "closes on Saturday night," but audiences like to see obvious targets hit skilfully and wittily.

But then Kelly expanded Poor Aubrey into the full-length play of The Show-Off, in which Aubrey Piper's bragging and bluffing are exposed and his lies and pretensions exploded. It was Kelly's first success, for The Torchbearers, a rather gentle send-up of the pretensions of Little Theatres with even littler talents in them, did not catch on at first, though it later was to achieve some recognition.

Kelly achieved the height of his career (and the Pulitzer Prize) with Craig's Wife. The vanity of Flattering Word and the manipulator defeated of Smarty's Party combine in the well-constructed but rather grimly determined story of a woman whose concern with appearances and control of her sterile environment give "Good Housekeeping" a bad name. But character study is confused with the problem play and Kelly is no Ibsen. Mrs. Craig (mordantly played by Chrystal Herne) was unforgettable but essentially just revealed, not developed. A revival of the play in the 1970's made the theatrical success of a half century before look too theatrical and the character of Mrs. Craig too static and that of her long-suffering husband too trivial.

After Craig's Wife, Kelly was on the slide. He had four failures in a row: Daisy Mayme was talky; Behold the Bridegroom was worse, preachy; Maggie the Magnificent and Philip Goes Forth convinced the dramatist to give up Broadway, though he returned with Reflected Glory, and The Deep Mrs. Sykes.

After the poor reception of The Fatal Weakness in 1946, he seemed to recognize his own fatal weaknesses as a playwright – getting in the way of the characters, imposing himself and his views on the situation and using the stage as a soapbox without the brilliance of Shaw or the cleverness of Brecht – and retired. Today he is known as the author of *Craig's Wife* and *The Torchbearers*.

—Leonard R. N. Ashley

KELLY, Hugh. Irish. Born in Killarney in 1739. Received very little formal education; apprenticed to a staymaker. Married in 1761; had five children. Moved to London, 1760, and worked as a staymaker and attorney's copying-clerk, and as writer for one of the daily papers; subsequently Editor of the *Court Magazine* and of the *Lady's Museum* from 1761; also wrote political pamphlets for the bookseller Pottinger, contributed series of essays "The Babler" to Owen's *Weekly Chronicle*, edited the *Public Ledger*, and gained a reputation as a theatrical critic; began to write for the theatre, 1768; employed as a writer by the government from c. 1770, and subsequently received a pension from Lord North; studied law, called to the Bar, Middle Temple, London, 1774, and gave up writing to practise law at the Old Bailey and Middlesex sessions. *Died 3 February 1777.*

PUBLICATIONS

Plays

L'Amour A-la-Mode; or, Love-a-la-Mode. 1760.
False Delicacy (produced 1768). 1768.
A Word to the Wise (produced 1770). 1770.
Clementina (produced 1771). 1771.
The School for Wives, with William Addington, from a play by Molière (produced 1773). 1774.
The Romance of an Hour, from a story by J. F. Marmontel (produced 1774). 1774.
The Man of Reason (produced 1776).

Fiction

Memoirs of a Magdalen; or, The History of Louisa Mildmay. 1767.

Verse

An Elegy to the Memory of the Earl of Bath. 1765 (2nd edition).
Thespis; or, A Critical Examination into the Merits of All the Principal Performers Belonging to Drury Lane Theatre. 1766; revised edition, 1766; part 2, 1767.

Other

The Babler. 2 vols., 1767.
Works. 1778.

Reading List: "Kelly: His Place in the Sentimental School" by Mark Schorer, in *Philological Quarterly*, 1933; "Some Remarks on 18th Century Delicacy, with a Note on Kelly's *False Delicacy*" by C. J. Rawson, in *Journal of English and Germanic Philology 61*, 1962.

*   *   *

Hugh Kelly typifies the mid-eighteenth-century Grub-Street hack: he edited two magazines, the *Lady's Museum* and the *Court Magazine*, and contributed essays and poetic ephemerae to others. His sentimental novel, *Memoirs of a Magdalen: or, The History of Louisa Mildmay*, appeared first in Owen's *Weekly Chronicle*, as did his series of essays *The Babler* (1763–1766). He wrote pro-government pieces for, and edited, *The Public Ledger* for which the administration rewarded him with a £200 pension – but he died poor. Imitating Charles Churchill's poetic satire on the theatres, *The Rosciad*, Kelly wrote *Thespis*, the two parts of which delineated the actors and writers of Drury Lane and of Covent Garden. Having criticized the contemporary theatre, Kelly then wrote *False Delicacy* for Drury Lane, a comedy that Johnson characterized as "totally void of character," but which outplayed Covent Garden's offering, Goldsmith's *Good Natur'd Man*. Critics have increasingly suggested that the work is less a sentimantal comedy than a mildly witty reproof of delicacy. At each of the two performances of Kelly's second produced comedy, *A Word to the Wise*, Kelly's friends and supporters of Wilkes, who were paying Kelly back for being a ministry writer, caused near riots. (In 1777, to benefit Kelly's widow and six children, Johnson wrote a prologue to this comedy for a performance at Covent Garden.)

Kelly's next play, the verse tragedy *Clementina*, was brought out anonymously, and though it lasted nine performances it has no merit: a contemporary reported, "A man can't hiss and yawn at the same time." *The School for Wives*, however, at first ascribed for protection to Captain William Addington, received good printed reviews, as did Kelly's afterpiece, *The Romance of an Hour*, adapted from Marmontel's tale *L'Amitié à l'épreuve*. *The Man of Reason*, Kelly's final comedy, lasted one performance.

Essays in *The Babler*, and the comedies *False Delicacy*, *A Word to the Wise*, and *A School for Wives*, offer the Horatian precept that art must morally instruct (and possibly therefore ennoble) as it entertains. *Thespis* is important as a gossip's recounting of Drury Lane and Covent Garden performers. Neither of Kelly's best plays, *False Delicacy* and *A School for Wives*, seems likely to be revived, but they provided good acting roles which sport with the conventions of sentimentality and are graceful theatrical properties.

—Peter A. Tasch

KILLIGREW, Thomas. English. Born in Lothbury, London, 7 February 1612. Married 1) Cecilia Crotts in 1636, one son; 2) Charlotte de Hesse in 1655, four sons and two daughters. Page to Charles I, 1633; imprisoned on taking up arms for the king, 1642–43; followed Prince Charles into exile in Paris, 1647; appointed by Charles Resident in Vienna, 1651–52; after the Restoration appointed groom of the bedchamber to Charles II, and, later, Chamberlain to the queen; also received a patent to erect a playhouse: manager of the King's Servants players; built the Theatre Royal in Drury Lane, 1663; Master of the Revels from 1673. *Died 19 March 1683.*

PUBLICATIONS

Plays

> The Prisoners (produced 1632–35?). With Claracilla, 1641.
> Claracilla (produced 1636). 1641.
> The Princess; or, Love at First Sight (produced 1661). In Comedies and Tragedies, 1664.
> The Parson's Wedding (produced 1664). In Comedies and Tragedies, 1664.
> Cicilia and Clorinda; or, Love in Arms, from a novel by Mme. Scudéry, Thomaso; or, The Wanderer, Bellamira Her Dream; or, The Love of Shadows, and The Pilgrim, in Comedies and Tragedies. 1664.

Reading List: Killigrew, Cavalier Dramatist by Alfred Harbage, 1930.

* * *

Thomas Killigrew was a courtier and man of the world who wrote plays only intermittently. He was willing to jest at his possible insufficiency as an author; a character in his comedy The Parson's Wedding speaks of "the illiterate Courtier that made this Play." But though not a university man he must have read a great deal, he possessed a quick and rather whimsical mind, and from an early age he was in a position to learn whatever the court of Charles and Henrietta Maria could teach, including the arts by which a gentleman without private means might hope to thrive.

His first three plays, tragi-comedies based on popular French romances, present a breathless sequence of surprising events, interspersed with lofty sentiments and occasional moments of comic relief. The Parson's Wedding, written some years later, abandons romance for realistic comedy in its portrayal of a company of wits in the contemporary London of 1639–40. Real persons may have provided models – if not exactly as they were, at least perhaps as they would have liked to appear. Pepys was to declare it "a bawdy loose play," and so it is. But it moves with compelling gusto.

As an exile on the Continent with other Royalists, Killigrew wrote a tragedy, The Pilgrim, which he conceivably intended for production by Prince Charles's short-lived company at Paris. Heavily influenced by Shirley, and with distant echoes of Hamlet, the five acts press to a harrowing outcome in which the princely hero, disguised as a pilgrim, unwittingly kills his evil father and is himself killed unwittingly by his evil mother. Killigrew's three remaining plays, also from this period, are closet dramas, each in two parts so as to extend to ten acts. Two of these long works attest his continuing love of the romances; the third, a comedy called Thomaso; or, The Wanderer, seems meant as romanticised autobiography. In Madrid with other English exiles ("remnants of the broken regiments; royal and loyal fugitives"), the supremely valiant Thomaso ("being bred with the wolf he grew wise enough to thrive in the forest") immediately proves himself by winning the passionate love of a beautiful and elegant courtesan – so elegant, indeed, that her portrait which hangs outside her house is by Van Dyck. Further exploits, mingled with fantastic scrapes involving the other characters, multiply through the seventy-two scenes, and by Act V of Part II the hero has married a beautiful Spanish heiress. At this romantic height Killigrew's career as an author ends. After the Restoration he was more closely concerned with the stage than ever before, thanks to the theatrical monopoly which he shared with Davenant, and he seems to have done some revising, but he attempted nothing new.

He wrote his plays in a mixture of prose and what looks like verse, though many of the lines are not at all metrical. The collection which he published in 1664 prints everything as prose.

—Rhodes Dunlap

KINGSLEY, Sidney. American. Born Sidney Kieschner in New York City, 22 October 1906. Educated at Townsend Harris Hall, New York, 1920–24; Cornell University, Ithaca, New York (state scholarship), 1924–28, B.A. 1928. Served in the United States Army, 1941–43: Lieutenant. Married the actress Madge Evans in 1939. Worked as an actor in the Tremont Stock Company, Bronx, New York, 1928; thereafter worked as a play-reader and scenario-writer for Columbia Pictures; full-time writer and stage director from 1934. Past President, Dramatists Guild. Recipient: Pulitzer Prize, 1934; New York Theatre Club Medal, 1934, 1936, 1943; New York Drama Critics Circle Award, 1943, 1951; New York Newspaper Guild Front Page Award, 1943, and Page One Citation, 1949; Edgar Allan Poe Award, 1949; Donaldson Award, 1951; American Academy of Arts and Letters Award of Merit Medal, 1951. Lives in New Jersey.

PUBLICATIONS

Plays

Men in White (produced 1933). 1933.
Dead End (produced 1935). 1936.
Ten Million Ghosts (produced 1936).
The World We Make, from the novel *The Outward Room* by Millen Brand (produced 1939). 1939.
The Patriots (produced 1943). 1943.
Detective Story (produced 1949). 1949.
Darkness at Noon, from the novel by Arthur Koestler (produced 1951). 1951.
Lunatics and Lovers (produced 1954). Condensed version in *Theater 1955,* 1955.
Night Life (produced 1962). 1966.

Screenplay: *Homecoming,* with Paul Osborn and Jan Lustig, 1948.

*   *   *

Sidney Kingsley was one of "the young radicals our colleges are said to be full of nowadays" (as S. N. Berhman put it in *End of Summer*). His agit-prop approach to theatre was a bit less strident than that of some other proletarian dramatists, but sufficient to endear him to the famous Group Theater, whose financial life he saved early in its career with the success of his first play, *Men in White*.

The story of the Group Theater is brilliantly told by Harold Clurman in *The Fervent Years*. The story of *Men in White* is accurately told by John Mason Brown (*Two on the Aisle,* 1938): it "is a piffling script, mildewed in its hokum, childishly sketchy in its characterization, and so

343

commonplace in its every written word that it in no way justifies its own unpleasantness." Moreover, "the finished result, as Arthur Hopkins once observed when Mr. [David] Belasco converted his stage into a Child's Restaurant, is *only remarkable because it is not real.*" Very just; but just also to add that Kingsley's approach has since been copied, in its dab-hand dramaturgy and somewhat fuzzy concern with ethical standards, in Paddy Chayefsky's *Hospital* and *Network* and in many television soap operas and feature films.

Also seminal was *Dead End*, establishing for the cinema many of the clichés of slum-life sociology, "a raucous tone-poem of the modern city" (Brooks Atkinson), a shaky melodrama set down in a handsome set (by Norman Bel Geddes) with a pier-head jutting right into the orchestra pit. The contrived plot brings the Dead End kids and other poor folk into contact with some rich East Siders in New York: the façade of the wealthy apartment house is under repair, which brings the rich people round to the back and right on stage. Unfortunately for Kingsley, he does not seem to remember poverty without sentimentality and, at least before the considerable success of *Dead End*, seems never to have met anyone rich. His sociology is superficial and his dramaturgy profoundly pedestrian.

Ten Million Ghosts is a confused discussion of munitions magnates. Kingsley was well out of his intellectual depth. *The World We Make* was not much better, although for once in the 1930's the emphasis is upon character rather than upon "The System" and environment. *The Patriots* is about a decade in the life of Thomas Jefferson. In none of these plays did Kingsley have the advantages he had in *Dead End*. He desperately needed stars and set designers and a whole team to "make something" of his scripts. He once half perceived this when he said: "When two people have a baby, the baby is a bit of a surprise. In the theater we have a marriage of many people. I can't really tell how the baby will come out."

Kingsley was once a leading Broadway playwright. He became known to a wider audience through such films as *Men in White*, *Dead End*, and *Detective Story*. He was at his best whenever he had help: the committed cast of *Men in White*, the street arabs and street scene of *Dead End*, Millen Brand's novel *The Outward Room* as a basis for *The World We Make*, Madge Evans to help with *The Patriots*, Arthur Koestler's novel behind *Darkness at Noon*. *Crowell's Handbook of Contemporary Drama* (1971) give as fair an estimate as any: "In most of his work Kingsley relies on a sense of atmosphere generated by realistic re-creation of a particular world – hospitals, slums, police stations, prisons – a vivid milieu that supplies much of the vivid impact of the play and also constitutes its limitation. The plays are frequently melodramatic in plot and sketchy in characterization; timely issues have made them at first appear more substantial than they later are seen to be."

—Leonard R. N. Ashley

KNOWLES, James Sheridan. Irish. Born in Cork, 12 May 1784; son of the lexicographer James Knowles; moved with his family to London, 1793. Educated at his father's school in Cork, 1790–93; studied medicine at the University of Aberdeen, M.D. Married 1) Maria Charteris in 1809 (died, 1841), one son; 2) Miss Elphinstone in 1842. Abandoned medicine for the stage, and appeared as an actor in Bath, Dublin, and Belfast, 1808–11; schoolmaster in his own school in Belfast, which subsequently transferred to Glasgow, 1811–28; also conducted the literary department of the *Free Press*, Glasgow, 1824–25; returned to acting, 1832–43; evangelical preacher from 1844. Awarded Civil List pension, 1848. *Died 30 November 1862.*

PUBLICATIONS

Collections

Various Dramatic Works.   2 vols., 1874.
Dramatic Works.   1883.

Plays

Leo; or, The Gypsy (produced 1810).
Brian Boroihme; or, The Maid of Erin (produced 1812).   1872.
Caius Gracchus (produced 1815).   1823.
Virginius; or, The Liberation of Rome (produced 1820).   1820.
The Fatal Dowry, from the play by Massinger (produced 1825).   1825.
William Tell (produced 1825).   1825.
The Beggar's Daughter of Bethnal Green (produced 1828).   1828; revised version, as
   The Beggar of Bethnal Green (produced 1834), 1834.
Alfred the Great; or, The Patriot King (produced 1831).   1831.
The Hunchback (produced 1832).   1832.
The Vision of the Bard (produced 1832).   1832.
The Wife: A Tale of Mantua (produced 1833).   1833.
The Daughter (produced 1836; also produced as *The Wrecker's Daughter*).   1837.
The Bridal, from the play *The Maid's Tragedy* by Beaumont and Fletcher (produced
   1837).   1837.
The Love-Chase (produced 1837).   1837.
Woman's Wit; or, Love's Disguises (produced 1838).   1838.
The Maid of Mariendorpt (produced 1838).   1838.
Dramatic Works.   1838; revised edition, 2 vols., 1856.
Love (produced 1839).   1840.
John of Procida; or, The Bridals of Messina (produced 1840; also produced as *The Bride
   of Messina*).   1840.
Old Maids (produced 1841).   1841.
The Rose of Arragon (produced 1842).   1842.
The Secretary (produced 1843).   1843.
The Rock of Rome; or, The Arch Heresy.   1849.
Alexina; or, True unto Death (produced 1866).   1866.

Fiction

Fortesque.   1846.
George Lovell.   1847.
Tales and Novelettes, revised and edited by F. Harvey.   1874.

Verse

The Welsh Harper: A Ballad.   1796.
Fugitive Pieces.   1810.

Other

*The Elocutionist: A Collection of Pieces in Prose and Verse, Peculiarly Adapted to Display
the Art of Reading.* 1823(?).
*The Idol Demolished by Its Own Priest: An Answer to Cardinal Newman's Lectures on
Transubstantiation.* 1851.
*The Gospel Attributed to Matthew Is the Record of the Whole Original
Apostlehood.* 1855.
Lectures on Dramatic Literature, edited by S. W. Abbott and F. Harvey. 2 vols., 1873.

Reading List: *Knowles and the Theatre of His Time* by Leslie H. Meeks, 1933.

*   *   *

The plays that brought James Sheridan Knowles his reputation as a modern Shakespeare
are the tragedies and mawkish melodramas properly remembered alongside his uneasy
relationship with the actor William Charles Macready (1793–1873). It was Macready's
decision to propose *Virginius* for performance at Covent Garden in 1820 that transformed
both men's careers. *Virginius* is a five-act tragedy, written, like all Knowles's plays, in blank
verse which pays consistent homage to Shakespeare and the Elizabethans. It tells the story of
Appius and Virginia, but with the focus on Virginius. He is a simple, recognisable father,
whose very familiarity makes more affecting the climactic murder of his own daughter to
save her honour. Fatherhood is as much a nineteenth century theme as motherhood, and
Macready, in private life a passionate and suffering father, was its supreme theatrical
portrayer. Knowles, too, would bluster fondly about the riches of paternity. He wrote for
Macready another success about the arch-father, *William Tell*, and intended Macready for the
title-role of his later paternal tragedy, *John of Procida*. *William Tell* is a melodrama, told
without distinction, certainly with no sense of place. Like all Knowles's serious semi-
historical plays, it celebrates in regular rhetorical verse the over-easy triumph of liberty over
the forces of repression. His villains are of cardboard, and easily torn apart. The patched-up
friendship with Macready reached a new height in a collaboration on *The Bridal*, an
adaptation of *The Maid's Tragedy* (by Beaumont and Fletcher), but petered out again after a
brief run of *The Secretary*, an historical romance in which Macready played the uncle of an
orphan, since the plot, taken from a novel by G. P. R. James, allowed no nearer approach to
fatherhood.

To those who have followed the lead of nineteenth-century opinion by viewing Knowles
as a writer of tragedies, his reputation has seemed laughably inflated. But his real strength is
elsewhere. There are suggestions of it in *The Hunchback*, in which the courting of the two
young couples has a genuine sprightliness. The influence of Fletcherian romance is developed
in *The Beggar of Bethnal Green* and *Woman's Wit*, but the best evidence of a largely
uncelebrated skill in comedy is in *The Love-Chase* and *Old Maids*. In each of them, the
various fortunes of three courtships are adroitly plotted. In the earlier play, the taming of
Wildrake and the marrying of Widow Green to Sir William Fondlove, and in the later, Lady
Anne's teasing love of Sir Philip Brilliant provide scenes of real comic verve. If only Knowles
had been prepared to forego blank verse, he might have written a comedy quite as long-lived
as Boucicault's *London Assurance*. As it is, Lord Lytton's letter of 1838 to Macready makes
fair comment: "I say, when a door is to be shut, 'Shut the door.' Knowles would say, as I
think he has said somewhere, 'Let the room be airless.' "

—Peter Thomson

KOPIT, Arthur (Lee). American. Born in New York City, 10 May 1937. Educated at Lawrence High School, New York, graduated 1955; Harvard University, Cambridge, Massachusetts, B.A. (cum laude) 1959 (Phi Beta Kappa). Married Leslie Ann Garis. Recipient: Vernon Rice Award, 1962; Outer Circle Award, 1962; Guggenheim Fellowship, 1967; Rockefeller grant, 1968; National Institute of Arts and Letters award, 1971; National Endowment for the Arts grant, 1974; Wesleyan University Center for the Humanities Fellowship, 1974. Lives in Connecticut.

PUBLICATIONS

Plays

The Questioning of Nick (produced 1957). In The Day the Whores Came Out to Play Tennis and Other Plays, 1965.
Gemini (produced 1957).
Don Juan in Texas, with Wally Lawrence (produced 1957).
On the Runway of Life, You Never Know What's Coming Off Next (produced 1957).
Across the River and into the Jungle (produced 1958).
To Dwell in a Place of Strangers, Act I published in Harvard Advocate, May 1958.
Aubade (produced 1959).
Sing to Me Through Open Windows (produced 1959; revised version, produced 1965). In The Day the Whores Came Out to Play Tennis and Other Plays, 1965.
Oh Dad, Poor Dad, Mama's Hung You in the Closet and I'm Feelin' So Sad: A Pseudoclassical Tragifarce in a Bastard French Tradition (produced 1960). 1960.
Mhil'daim (produced 1963).
Asylum; or, What the Gentlemen Are Up To, and And As for the Ladies (produced 1963; And As for the Ladies produced, as Chamber Music, 1971). Chamber Music in The Day the Whores Came Out to Play Tennis and Other Plays, 1965.
The Conquest of Everest (produced 1964). In The Day the Whores Came Out to Play Tennis and Other Plays, 1965.
The Hero (produced 1964). In The Day the Whores Came Out to Play Tennis and Other Plays, 1965.
The Day the Whores Came Out to Play Tennis (produced 1965). In The Day the Whores Came Out to Play Tennis and Other Plays, 1965.
The Day the Whores Came Out to Play Tennis and Other Plays. 1965; as Chamber Music and Other Plays, 1969.
Indians (produced 1968). 1969.
An Incident in the Park, in Pardon Me, Sir, But Is My Eye Hurting Your Elbow?, edited by Bob Booker and George Foster. 1968.
What's Happened to the Thorne's House (produced 1972).
Louisiana Territory; or, Lewis and Clark — Lost and Found (produced 1975).
Secrets of the Rich (produced 1976). 1978.
Wings (produced 1978). 1978.

*   *   *

A brilliant satirist with a highly developed sense of the theatrical, Arthur Kopit has been concerned from the time of his earliest plays with America's continuing need to create myth and mythic heroes in order to justify its barbaric cruelty and unlimited greediness. He is deeply disturbed by the power of these myths to shape its actions, to destroy its people's ability to make moral judgements, and to transform its real heroes into garish, bewildered caricatures of human beings.

In his first play, *The Questioning of Nick*, Kopit develops the crude prototype of his later mythic heroes. Nick Carmonatti, a high school basketball player "named in *Sport* as one of the five hun'red leading basketball prospects in the whole country," is so overpowered by the illusion of his importance that he not only admits that he accepted a bribe to throw a game but also brags that he was the only player good enough to be offered one.

In such early farces as *Don Juan in Texas* and *Across the River and into the Jungle*, as well as in *The Conquest of Everest* and *The Day the Whores Came Out to Play Tennis*, Kopit creates outrageously funny characters – "eighteen bare assed" whores who invade the staid atmosphere of the Cherry Valley Country Club; a soap salesman who is mistaken for Billy the Kid; two American barefooted tourists in Florida garb who climb Everest without realizing what they've accomplished, who eat sandwiches and drink cokes, and who then rejoin their tour for dinner. Through these characters he ridicules such minor American flaws as stuffiness, cowardice, provincialism, and prudishness.

In his more serious works, the ridicule is underscored with a strong sense of menace. *Chamber Music*, for example, features eight hilarious madwomen, each of whom believes she is a well-known historical figure. These women convince themselves that they are in danger of being attacked by the inmates of the men's ward. Then, using logic appropriate to the asylum, they decide to protect themselves by a show of strength, by a sign of their ferocity. So they kill Amelia Earhart, one of their own, and are satisfied that they have thus protected themselves from danger. *Oh Dad, Poor Dad*, Kopit's most vicious satire, again combines the ludicrous and the terrifying. Focusing on the myth of Supermom, Kopit creates Madame Rosepettle, a woman who hangs the stuffed corpse of her husband in her closet, locks her adult son Jonathan in her apartment, keeps a piranha in her living room, and grows Venus's-flytraps on her balcony. When Jonathan rebels – kills the piranha, the Venus's-flytraps, and his seductive babysitter, who is herself a potential supermom – Madame Rosepettle is shocked into a state of bewilderment. She cannot understand the meaning of his action.

Kopit carries the bewildered mythic hero a step further in his best work, *Indians*, where the genocide practiced against the American Indians is used as the metaphor for the American violence in Vietnam. William Cody's frantic struggle to live up to the myth of Buffalo Bill and his futile attempt to regain his own identity, once the barbaric cruelty of the conquest of the West and the bizarre sham of the Wild West Show threaten to destroy all sense of his humanity, epitomize for Kopit the continuing struggle of contemporary America. Thus, he demonstrates most powerfully here what he has already said in his earlier plays and what he reiterates in his most recent works: America has created the wrong kinds of heroes in order to justify the wrong kinds of actions, and it is trapped by its need to perpetuate the myth of its glorious past.

—Helen Houser Popovich

KYD, Thomas. English. Born in London, baptized 6 November 1558. Educated at Merchant Taylors' School, London, from 1565. Little is known about his life: perhaps worked in early life as a scrivener; in the service of an unknown lord, 1587–93; arrested for heresy, because of his association with Christopher Marlowe, 1593, but subsequently released. *Died in December 1594.*

Publications

Collections

Works, edited by F. S. Boas. 1901.

Plays

The Spanish Tragedy (produced 1589?).   1592; revised edition, 1602; edited by J. R.
   Mulryne, 1970; edited by Andrew S. Cairncross, with *The First Part of Hieronimo,*
   1967.
Cornelia, from a play by Robert Garnier.   1594; as *Pompey the Great His Fair
   Cornelia's Tragedy,* 1595.

Other

The Truth of the Most Wicked and Secret Murdering of John Brewen.   1592.

Translator, *The Householder's Philosophy,* by Tasso.   1588.

Bibliography: *Kyd: A Concise Bibliography* by S. A. Tannenbaum, 1941; *Kyd: 1940–66* by
R. C. Johnson, 1968.

Reading List: *"The Spanish Tragedy"* by William Empson, in *Nimbus,* 1956; *"Kyd's
Spanish Tragedy:* The play Explains Itself" by E. Jenson, in *Journal of English and Germanic
Philology,* 1965; *Kyd and Early Elizabethan Tragedy* by Philip W. Edwards, 1966; *Kyd:
Facts and Problems* by Arthur Freeman, 1967; *Kyd* by P. B. Murray, 1970.

*   *   *

No single play is more important in the development of English Renaissance drama than
The Spanish Tragedy, yet it is not two hundred years since its authorship was generally
recognized. In 1773, Thomas Hawkins in his *The Origin of the English Drama* mentioned a
reference to Thomas Kyd as the author of *The Spanish Tragedy* made by Thomas Heywood
in *Apology for Actors* (1612). Although ten editions of the play were published between 1592
and 1633 none of them bore the author's name, a fact which tells us something of the relative
unimportance of the author's name as a "selling point" in late 16th- and early 17th-century
publishing.
   Most of the plays now commonly attributed to Kyd were printed anonymously; as a result
we know very little for certain about his dealings with the professional theatre of his day,
though the continuing popularity of *The Spanish Tragedy* in performance is attested not only
by its printing history but the many contemporary allusions to lines, scenes, and characters
from the play. Is is also noteworthy that fifteen years after the play was written that shrewd
theatre manager Philip Henslowe found it worth his while to employ no less a man than Ben
Jonson to revise the play for a revival at the Rose Theatre by the Lord Admiral's Company.
The only publication to bear Kyd's name in his own lifetime is *Pompey the Great His Fair
Cornelia's Tragedy,* a translation of the French Senecan tragedy *Cornélie* by Robert Garnier,
which may have been inspired by the translation in the previous year of another of Garnier's
tragedies, *Marc Antoine,* by the Countess of Pembroke. Also attributed to Kyd with varying
degrees of confidence are *Soliman and Perseda* (1589), which forms the play within the play

in the last act of *The Spanish Tragedy*, *The Rare Triumphs of Love and Fortune* (1589), and all or part of *Arden of Feversham* (1592), a play based on a contemporary murder which began the vogue for "documentary" domestic tragedy. A prose pamphlet, *The Householder's Philosophy*, based on an Italian story by Torquato Tasso, is more confidently attributed to Kyd. He is also widely believed to have been the author of an earlier version of *Hamlet* (sometimes referred to as the *Ur-Hamlet*) on which Shakespeare drew when he came to write his celebrated tragedy.

It is truer of Kyd than of most dramatists that his achievement resides in a single play. As far as is known, the plot of *The Spanish Tragedy* is Kyd's own invention. In adapting the Senecan form of tragedy to the conventions of the Elizabethan theatre, Kyd showed the born playwright's instinct for what to use, what to discard, and what to add. He abandoned Seneca's mythological plot and characters in favour of a contemporary setting. He also rejected the Senecan device of the *nuntius* or messenger who reports crucial phases of the action. The theatrical tradition of the miracle plays, with their emphasis on violence and spectacle, had equipped the Elizabethan inheritors of that tradition to show rather than tell, and, in leaving out the messenger, Kyd offered them ample scope for their resources and expertise. With these exceptions Kyd took over virtually all the paraphernalia of Senecan tragedy. These included the theme of revenge (soon to spawn a long line of descendants among which *Hamlet* is the most famous), the ghost, the dumb-show and the play within the play, the soliloquy, and the interest in madness and violent action. Though Kyd's debt to Seneca is thus fairly obvious, it is perhaps worth noting that some of the features mentioned are to be found in the popular miracle plays.

To this Senecan stock, Kyd grafted a character, Lorenzo, who embodied the contemporary interest in Machiavelli (as the Elizabethans understood him) and the amoralism associated with his ideas. Lorenzo is thus the ancestor of the unscrupulous figure whose only goal is success and whose only criterion is expediency, though he wears the mask of moral virtue. It is a tribe to which belong some of the most dazzling dramatic creations of the period — Flamineo, De Flores, Edmund, and Iago among a host of others.

If Kyd had merely adapted Senecan conventions for the popular English stage, he would still have a place in any history of the drama, but it would be grossly unjust to imply that *The Spanish Tragedy* is a play whose importance is solely or mainly historical. It is one of the most powerful plays of its time, and modern revivals have shown that it is still full of life. It draws this life from two sources, Kyd's masterly dramatic construction and the richness of his dramatic style. In terms of sheer stagecraft, *The Spanish Tragedy* is one of the most successful English plays of any period. The entire action is presided over by the ghost seeking vengeance and the spirit of Revenge itself, giving effects of resonant irony, while such scenes as the discovery by Hieronimo of his murdered son's body and the climactic moment where the pretended killings of the play within the play erupt into "real life" are unforgettable. Kyd's linguistic virtuosity is fully equal to his constructional skill. He uses all the elaborate rhetorical devices of Elizabethan English — stichomythia, sententiae, and the rest — with confident zest, and the more mannered his verse the more powerful it sounds on the stage:

> Oh eyes, no eyes, but fountains fraught with tears;
> Oh life, no life, but lively form of death;
> Oh world, no world, but mass of public wrongs,
> Confused and filled with murder and misdeeds.

The most convincing evidence of the impact of Kyd's play is the fact that it was parodied and imitated for decades afterwards, but independent of all influence it remains a great tragedy in its own right.

—Gāmini Salgādo

LAURENTS, Arthur. American. Born in Brooklyn, New York, 14 July 1918. Educated at Cornell University, Ithaca, New York, B.A. 1937. Served in the United States Army, rising to the rank of Sergeant, 1940–45: Radio Playwright, 1943–45 (Citation, Secretary of War, 1945). Director, Dramatists Play Service, New York, 1961–66. Since 1955, Member of the Council of the Dramatists Guild. Recipient: National Institute of Arts and Letters grant, 1946; Sidney Howard Memorial Award, 1946; Antoinette Perry Award, 1967. Lives on Long Island, New York.

PUBLICATIONS

Plays

Now Playing Tomorrow (broadcast 1939). In *Short Plays for Stage and Radio,* edited by Carless Jones, 1939.
Western Electric Communicade (broadcast 1944). In *The Best One-Act Plays of 1944,* edited by Margaret Mayorga, 1944.
The Last Day of the War (broadcast 1945). In *Radio Drama in Action,* edited by Erik Barnouw, 1945.
The Face (broadcast 1945). In *The Best One-Act Plays of 1945,* edited by 'Margaret Mayorga, 1945.
Home of the Brave (produced 1945; as *The Way Back,* produced 1946). 1946.
Heartsong (produced 1947).
The Bird Cage (produced 1950). 1950.
The Time of the Cuckoo (produced 1952). 1953.
A Clearing in the Woods (produced 1957). 1957.
West Side Story, music by Leonard Bernstein (produced 1957). 1958.
Gypsy, music by Jule Styne, lyrics by Stephen Sondheim, from a book by Gypsy Rose Lee (produced 1959). 1960.
Invitation to a March (produced 1960). 1961.
Anyone Can Whistle, music by Stephen Sondheim (produced 1964). 1965.
Do I Hear a Waltz?, music by Richard Rodgers, lyrics by Stephen Sondheim (produced 1965). 1966.
Hallelujah, Baby!, music and lyrics by Jule Styne, Betty Comden and Adolph Green (produced 1967). 1967.
The Enclave (produced 1973). 1974.

Screenplays: *The Snake Pit,* with Frank Partos and Millen Brand, 1948; *Rope,* with Hume Cronyn, 1948; *Anna Lucasta,* with Philip Yordan, 1949; *Caught,* 1949; *Anastasia,* 1956; *Bonjour Tristesse,* 1958; *The Way We Were,* 1973; *The Turning Point,* 1977.

Radio Plays: *Now Playing Tomorrow,* 1939; *Hollywood Playhouse, Dr. Christian, The Thin Man, Manhattan at Midnight,* and other series, 1939–40; *The Last Day of the War, The Face, Western Electric Communicade,* 1944, and other plays for *The Man Behind the Gun, Army Service Force Presents* and *Assignment Home* series, 1943–45; *This Is Your FBI* series, 1945.

Fiction

The Way We Were. 1972.

Brooklyn-born, Hollywood-bred, Arthur Laurents is best known for his work in the two most successful American art forms, the Broadway musical and the Hollywood film.

His films include *Caught* and *The Snake Pit* and versions of two of his stage plays, *Home of the Brave* and *Time of the Cuckoo* (filmed as *Summertime*). All tend to prove Samuel Beckett's thesis: "We are all born mad. Some remain so." Psychology, especially self-realization, is Laurents's major interest and it runs through all of his serious work, even getting into musicals.

His musicals are *West Side Story* (*Romeo and Juliet* updated), *Gypsy* (based on the life of stripper Gypsy Rose Lee), *Do I Hear a Waltz?* and *Hallelujah, Baby!* These musicals show all the inventiveness and commercial savvy one would expect from a writer whose work ranges from adapting Marcel Maurette's TV play *Anastasia* for Ingrid Bergman's return to the screen to a modern version of the Sleeping Beauty legend in which the heroine refuses to tread boring conventional paths and takes off with a plumber (*Invitation to a March*). Laurents attempted to make Broadway musicals in some way more serious. He didn't always succeed. As Walter Kerr put it in *Thirty Plays Hath November*, "if a musical is going to be as serious as *Do I Hear a Waltz?* it has got to be more serious than *Do I Hear a Waltz?* ... Half measures taken toward sobriety tend to leave us all halfhearted, torn between an elusive passion on the one hand and a lost playfulness on the other." Shall we settle for the *ersatz*, typically Broadway idea of the serious (especially in diversions such as *A Chorus Line*) and not strive for reality?

Laurents's plays do make a serious effort at seriousness: in a sense they are religious, if psychology is the New Religion. In *The Bird Cage* downtrodden employees of a dictatorial employer fly their nightclub cage. We sense Symbolism and are tempted to ask, like the psychoanalyst greeted with a "hello" in the street: What Does That *Mean*? In *A Clearing in the Woods* a woman yearns "to rise in the air just a little, to climb, to reach a branch, even the lowest" and this bird learns to accept herself as "an imperfect human being," thus escaping the cage of her past. If Tom Driver is right (in *Romantic Quest and Modern Theory*, 1970) that in *West Side Story* "adult authority does not exist ... [and] there is more 'order' in the improvised life of the young than in public institutions," can it be that Laurents, for all his interest in psychology, is telling us in *A Clearing in the Woods* that we should avoid all the psychiatrists who want to adjust us, and achieve "mental health" just by learning to be happy with our craziness, accepting ourselves as "imperfect human beings"? In *Home of the Brave* (which Kenneth Tynan found pat but promising), an Army shrink copes with Coney, a soldier who learns that though he is Jewish he is just another "imperfect human being" like Mingo and everyone else who is secretly glad that it was The Other Guy who got killed, regardless of race, color, or creed. In *Time of the Cuckoo* the uptight New England spinster Leona Samish has to work out for herself the appropriate reactions to a brief encounter in Venice with a dashing (but married) Italian. Predictably, "those louses/Go back to their spouses" (as *Diamonds Are a Girl's Best Friend* teaches) and Ms. Samish realizes, reviewing her Puritan Code, that he wasn't such a nice man, after all. This psychologizing may not be as broad as a barn door, nor so deep as a well, but it will serve in the theatre, where Thornton Wilder once got away with summing up all of Freud in a single sentence: "We're all just as wicked as we can be." Well, not wicked, imperfect.

In 1960, Henry Hewes introducing *Famous American Plays of the 1940's* wrote about Laurents:

In form it is the sort of play that has become an increasingly popular stereotype for American drama. Someone in trouble reviews the reasons for his trouble to find something he has not been facing up to. Because Mr. Laurents introduced the psychiatrist himself and had the answer up his sleeve all the time, some critics found the play too clinical. However, *Home of the Brave* contains the driving theme which seems to motivate most of this young writer's work. It is the acceptance of our imperfections in a society where everyone expects the ideal.

That is a nice, comforting thought! And we can go to movies and musicals and enjoy ourselves and rest very content with our human, albeit imperfect, selves.

—Leonard R. N. Ashley

LAWLER, Ray(mond Evenor). Australian. Born in Footscray, Melbourne, Victoria, in 1921. Left school at age 13. Married Jacklyn Kelleher; three children. Worked in a factory; then as an actor in variety, Brisbane; as actor and producer, National Theatre Company, Melbourne; and as Director, Melbourne University Repertory Company. Recipient: *Evening Standard* award, 1957.

PUBLICATIONS

Plays

> *Cradle of Thunder* (produced 1949).
> *Summer of the Seventeenth Doll* (produced 1955).   1957.
> *The Piccadilly Bushman* (produced 1959).   1961.
> *The Unshaven Cheek* (produced 1963).
> *A Breach in the Wall* (televised 1967; produced 1970).
> *The Man Who Shot the Albatross* (produced 1972).
> *Kid Stakes* (produced 1975).
> *Other Times* (produced 1976).

Television Plays: *A Breach in the Wall*, 1967; *Cousin Bette* (serialization), from the novel by Balzac, 1971; *The Visitors* (serialization), from the novel by Mary McMinnies, 1972; *Two Women* (serialization), from the novel by Alberto Moravia, 1972; *Mrs. Palfrey at the Claremont*, from the novel by Elizabeth Taylor, 1973; *Seeking the Bubbles*, in *The Love School* series, 1975; *True Patriots All*, 1975; *Husband to Mrs. Fitzherbert*, 1975.

*   *   *

With his first professionally produced play, *Summer of the Seventeenth Doll*, Ray Lawler established a landmark in Australian drama. The play awakened his country's theatre from a prolonged sleep of adolescence through an incisive attack on national myths, stereotypes, and the clichéd language of earlier plays. Although Lawler's later work has not had the same power or effect, Australian drama unquestionably owes him an enormous debt.

The Doll, as it is known, explores the "mateship" of two sugarcane cutters who work half the year, and their carefree life with their women during the "layoff." This idyllic society, symbolized by the kewpie doll brought home each summer, is torn apart on its seventeenth anniversary, when the characters are forced to see the insubstantiality of their relationships. Blinded by the Australian national myths of male friendship, the submissiveness of women, and the superiority of the country over the city, they are helpless before the inexorable advance of their own lives. Lawler's precise use of the understatement inherent in Australian colloquial speech and his relentless exposure of the myths and illusions surrounding the characters, as well as his strong dramatic construction, give the play the ring of authenticity and an intense power.

After *The Doll*, Lawler left Australia, settling ultimately in Ireland, and his next play, *The Piccadilly Bushman*, examined the ambivalent attachment of Australians to their mother country. Although it reflects Lawler's continuing investigation of national myths, it is weakened first by the already-diminished force of the very myth he was attacking, and second by a failure to weld his theme to his characters, who remain at such a distance from one another that the play's resolution seems contrived and unsatisfying.

Although most of Lawler's work has been realistic, he has worked in other styles. *The Unshaven Cheek*, for example, progresses largely through flashbacks, but his most serious experiment with non-realistic drama has been *The Man Who Shot the Albatross*. This study of Captain Bligh (of the *Bounty*), who served as governor of New South Wales from 1806 to 1808, mixes present experience, memory, and fantasy on a stage divided into several performance areas, and provides a fascinating look at this curious man's mind.

Lawler's most recent work, however, *Kid Stakes* and *Other Times* (known with *The Doll* as *The Doll Trilogy*) marks a return, both theatrically and dramatically to his first success. The new plays mirror the realism and the structure of *The Doll*, and deal with the same characters in years previous to that play's action, but neither has the intensity and life of before. Despite his lack of development, Ray Lawler is nonetheless a talented and able dramatist, whose place in Australian drama is secure.

—Walter Bode

LAWSON, John Howard. American. Born in New York City, 25 September 1894. Educated at Yonkers High School, New York; Cutler School, New York, graduated 1910; Williams College, Williamstown, Massachusetts, 1910–14, B.A. 1914. Served in the American Ambulance Service in France and Italy during World War I. Married 1) Kathryn Drain in 1919 (divorced, 1923), one son; 2) Susan Edmond in 1925, one son and one daughter. Cable Editor, Reuters Press, New York, 1914–15; lived in Paris for two years after the war; a Director, New Playwrights Theatre, New York, 1927–28; film writer in Hollywood, 1928–47. Member of the Council of the Authors League of America, 1930–40; Founding President, 1933–34, and Member of the Executive Board, 1933–40, Screen Writers Guild. One of the "Hollywood Ten": served a one-year sentence for contempt of the House Un-American Activities Committee, 1950–51. *Died 11 August 1977.*

PUBLICATIONS

Plays

    Servant-Master-Lover (produced 1916).
    Standards (produced 1916).
    Roger Bloomer (produced 1923). 1923.
    Processional: A Jazz Symphony of American Life (produced 1925). 1925.
    Nirvana (produced 1926).
    Loudspeaker (produced 1927). 1927.
    The International (produced 1928). 1928.
    Success Story (produced 1932). 1932.
    The Pure in Heart (produced 1934). In *With a Reckless Preface,* 1934.
    Gentlewoman (produced 1934). In *With a Reckless Preface,* 1934.
    With a Reckless Preface: Two Plays. 1934.

Marching Song (produced 1937). 1937.
Algiers (screenplay), with James M. Cain, in *Foremost Films of 1938,* edited by Frank
Vreeland. 1939.
Parlor Magic (produced 1963).

Screenplays: *Dream of Love,* with others, 1928; *The Pagan,* with Dorothy Farnum,
1929; *Dynamite,* with Jeanie Macpherson and Gladys Unger, 1929; *The Sea Bat,* with
others, 1930; *Our Blushing Brides,* with Bess Meredyth and Helen Mainard, 1930; *The
Ship from Shanghai,* 1930; *Bachelor Apartment,* 1931; *Success at Any Price,* with
others, 1934; *Blockade,* 1938; *Algiers,* with James M. Cain, 1938; *They Shall Have
Music,* with Irmgard Von Cube, 1939; *Four Sons,* with Milton Sperling, 1940;
Earthbound, with Samuel C. Engel, 1940; *Sahara,* with others, 1943; *Action in the
North Atlantic,* with others, 1943; *Counter-Attack,* 1945; *Smashup – The Story of a
Woman,* with others, 1947.

Other

Theory and Technique of Playwriting. 1936; revised edition, as *Theory and Technique
of Playwriting and Screenwriting,* 1949.
*The Hidden Heritage: A Rediscovery of the Ideas and Forces That Link the Thought of
Our Time with the Culture of the Past.* 1950.
Film in the Battle of Ideas. 1953.
*Film: The Creative Process: The Search for an Audio-Visual Language and
Structure.* 1964; revised edition, 1967.

*   *   *

John Howard Lawson was one of the "Hollywood Ten" who went to jail rather than tell
the House Un-American Activities Committee about their Marxist views. HUAC need not
have asked. They could have read his plays or seen his movies. Whether he belonged to the
Communist Party or not is basically none of our business. That his work is imbued with
Marxism and that he is characteristic of a period in which (as the Garment Workers' musical
Pins and Needles put it) many sang "Sing Me a Song of Social Significance," is abundantly
clear. In his time, it gave him strength. Now it makes all but a few of his film works look
impossibly dated.

Servant-Master-Lover, Standards, and *Roger Bloomer* gave him his start, and with
Processional his left-wing sympathies were expressed in the story of "the West Virginia coal
fields during a strike" told in "this new technique ... essentially vaudevillesque in character."
The theory is adumbrated in a Preface (more of his interesting ideas appear in prefatory
material to *The Pure in Heart* and *Gentlewoman* and in the excellent textbook *Theory and
Technique of Playwriting*) and illustrated in a series of scenes which recall the Living
Newspaper of the depression, the propaganda techniques of agitprop, and other attempts at
"an immediate emotional response across the footlights." All the force and all the faults of the
left-wing theatre tracts of the 1920's and 1930's, "the fervent years" (as Harold Clurman calls
them), are here: the party-line dogmatism and narrow vision; the confusion of tragedy and
pathos; the axe-to-grind earnestness, where comedy (and everything else that relates to a
sense of proportion) perishes; and so on, down to the stereotyped characters: Cohen the
Jewish comedian, Rastus the minstrel clown, the hard-boiled Sheriff, the city-slicker
newspaperman Phillpots, the woman called Mrs. Euphemia Stewart Flimmins, even a Man
in a Silk Hat.

George Abbott played Dynamite Jim in *Processional,* but only in the last act did he soar for
a moment above what Stark Young called "antagonisms, bad taste and crass thinking." The
critics thought it basically an amateur play "conceived with varying degrees of taste,

intelligence, insight and imagination." When it is good it is very, very good – Stark Young risked "streaked with genius" – and when it is bad it's as foolish as Odets without his primitive charm. It is not that the characters are unrealistic – "Mr. Lawson," reported Watson and Pressey in *Contemporary Drama,* "says that he can find vaudeville characters on every street corner, whereas the so-called realistic characters he sees on the stage he never meets in life" – but that the politics distort the truth.

Processional was produced by the Theatre Guild and ran 96 performances in 1925 and 81 more when The Federal Theatre revived it in 1937. Today it would not run any more than would *Nirvana, Loudspeaker, The International* (a musical), *Success Story, Marching Song,* or other Lawson efforts. "All great art and literature," boomed Shaw, "is propaganda," but that does not mean that all propaganda is great art.

Some of Lawson's films have survived better. Very typical are, say, *Blockade* and *Smashup.* The cinema was more congenial to Lawson's talents, though *Theory and Technique of Playwriting* amply demonstrates that, as Théophile Gautier said of drama critics and eunuchs in harems, those who see it done every night may know all about it but be quite unable to do it themselves.

—Leonard R. N. Ashley

LEE, Nathaniel. English. Born in Hatfield, Hertfordshire, probably in 1653. Educated at Westminster School, London; Trinity College, Cambridge, 1665–68, B.A. 1668. Settled in London, and at first attempted to become an actor; abandoned acting for writing for the stage c. 1672; a friend of Rochester and his circle: led a dissolute life, and undermined his health and reason by drinking: confined in Bethlehem Hospital (Bedlam), 1684–89. *Died* (buried) 6 *May 1692.*

PUBLICATIONS

Collections

Works, edited by Thomas B. Stroup and Arthur L. Cooke. 2 vols., 1954–55.

Plays

Nero, Emperor of Rome (produced 1674). 1675.
Sophonisba; or, Hannibal's Overthrow (produced 1675). 1675; edited by Bonamy Dobrée, in *Five Heroic Plays,* 1960.
Gloriana; or, The Court of Augustus Caesar (produced 1676). 1676.
The Rival Queens; or, The Death of Alexander the Great (produced 1677). 1677; edited by Paul F. Vernon, 1970.
Oedipus, with Dryden (produced 1678). 1679.
Mithridates, King of Pontus (produced 1678). 1678.
Caesar Borgia, The Son of Pope Alexander the Sixth (produced 1679). 1679.

    Lucius Junius Brutus, Father of His Country (produced 1680). 1681; edited by John
      Loftis, 1967.
    Theodosius; or, The Force of Love (produced 1680). 1680.
    The Princess of Cleve, from a novel by Mme. de la Fayette (produced 1681). 1689.
    The Duke of Guise, with Dryden (produced 1682). 1683.
    Constantine the Great (produced 1683). 1684.
    The Massacre of Paris (produced 1689). 1689.

Verse

    To the Prince and Princess of Orange upon Their Marriage. 1677.
    To the Duke on His Return. 1682.
    On the Death of Mrs. Behn. 1689.
    On Their Majesties' Coronation. 1689.

Bibliography: by A. L. McLeod, in *Restoration and 18th-Century Theatre Research 1,* 1962.

Reading List: *Otway and Lee* by Roswell G. Ham, 1931; "The Satiric Design of Lee's *The Princess of Cleve*" by Robert D. Hume, in *Journal of English and Germanic Philology,* 1976.

*   *   *

    Nathaniel Lee was the most "poetic" of the tragic dramatists in the Restoration period. His twelve tragedies (on characters drawn chiefly from classical and Renaissance history) exude figurative language. Tropes flowed from his pen, reaching a torrent of passionate utterance, with the result that his prolific imagery became both his strength and his weakness. The following passage from Act 3 of his *Lucius Junius Brutus* will illustrate his fondness for clusters of imagery:

> As in that glass of nature thou shalt view
> Thy swoln drown'd eyes with the inverted banks,
> The tops of Willows and their blossoms turn'd,
> With all the Under Sky ten fathom down,
> Wish that the shaddow of the swimming Globe
> Were so indeed, that thou migh'st leap at Fate.

    All his works are characterized by overcharged emotion and verbal extravagance; furthermore, the hysterical emphasis on passion was rarely balanced by any change of pace or variation of manner. He was fond of spectacle, on-stage tortures, and melodramatic turns. His early plays betray a heavy indebtedness to Elizabethan revenge tragedy and to the bombastic "love and honor" drama of his own time. However, he broke away from these influences to develop his own style, and in *The Rival Queens* he used blank verse and thus abandoned the heroic rhymed couplet before Dryden did.

    His own genius showed itself in the depiction of his heroines – Sophonisba, Rosalinda, Statira, Roxana – and in his return to the high road of English tragedy in emphasising the complex character of the protagonist and presenting interior conflict. In *Caesar Borgia,* produced during the anti-Catholic frenzy of 1679, when one would expect only rant and a stereotyped villain, Lee portrays in Borgia (as Allardyce Nicoll says) a struggle "of manliness and vicious influence, of conscience warring against the pernicious atmosphere." Even more dramatic is Alexander in Lee's masterpiece, *The Rival Queens,* a strong protagonist who is torn by internal conflicts and by flaws in his character. The resultant catastrophe is not predetermined but brought on by his own actions. In *Lucius Junius Brutus,* Lee achieved new heights with a drama of ideas, presenting, as James Sutherland says, "a historical tragedy that had a disquieting relevance to contemporary England." Artistically, Brutus seems as fully realised as Addison's Cato but in 1680 no government official stood ready to give the actor £50, as Bolingbroke rewarded Booth; instead, the government banned the play. We ought no longer accept that political verdict as a critical evaluation of the play and should instead recognize the merits of Lee as a tragic dramatist.

In addition, Lee wrote a remarkable "sex" comedy, *The Princess of Cleve*, in the satiric tradition of Wycherley's *The Plain Dealer*, Dryden's *Mr. Limberham*, and Otway's *Friendship in Fashion*. Montague Summers, many years ago, and Robert Hume, in his recent *Development of English Drama*, both show that in the character of Nemours (a comedy of manners "gallant") Lee offers a hostile, even savage depiction of Lord Rochester. Those critics who deny the existence of satire in Restoration drama should read this play.

—Arthur H. Scouten

LILLO, George. English. Born in Moorfields, London, 4 February 1693. Very little is known about his life: Partner in his father's jewelry business in the City of London; began writing for the theatre c. 1730. *Died 3 September 1739.*

PUBLICATIONS

Collections

Works. 2 vols., 1775.

Plays

Silvia; or, The Country Burial (produced 1730). 1730.
The London Merchant; or, The History of George Barnwell (produced 1731). 1731; edited by William H. McBurney, 1965.
The Christian Hero (produced 1735). 1735.
Fatal Curiosity (produced 1736; as Guilt Its Own Punishment, produced 1736). 1737; edited by William H. McBurney, 1966.
Marina, from the play Pericles by Shakespeare (produced 1738). 1738.
Elmerick; or, Justice Triumphant (produced 1740). 1740.
Britannia and Batavia. 1740.
Arden of Faversham, completed by John Hoadly, from the anonymous play (produced 1759). 1762.

Reading List: Introduction by Adolphus W. Ward to *The London Merchant and Fatal Curiosity*, 1906; *Lillo und Siene Bedeutung für die Geschichte des Englischen Dramas* by G. Loccack, 1939; "Notes for a Biography of Lillo" by D. B. Pallette, and "Further Notes" by C. F. Burgess, in *Philological Quarterly*, 1940, 1967.

George Lillo is a dramatist who was once immensely popular and influential, but who has not held the stage for a long time and is now virtually unactable because of the melodramatic and sentimental qualities of his work. Today his plays are almost unknown except to students of the eighteenth century, yet in his time he was an artistic innovator, although not the revolutionary figure in the history of drama he was once thought to be. The view that Lillo pioneered "bourgeois" tragedy almost single-handed is no longer tenable, but it remains true that in the play with which his name is always linked, *The London Merchant; or, The History of George Barnwell*, he developed a form of domestic tragedy in prose about middle-class life that is the precursor of the social drama of Ibsen and his successors. Lillo inherited a tradition of domestic tragedy descending from the Elizabethan theatre and proceeded to modify it in such a way as to make it conform to the increasingly widespread philosophical and ethical tenets of sentimentalism and benevolism, while at the same time making it reflect the concerns of the merchant class. Judging by the almost ecstatic way it was received at the time of its first production, it is obvious that *The London Merchant*, like Steele's slightly earlier and equally popular and influential "sentimental" comedy *The Conscious Lovers* (1722), responded to an unspoken demand for a new kind of serious drama, radically different from the dominant types of comedy and tragedy, still heavily influenced by late seventeenth-century modes. Subsequently *The London Merchant* was championed by Continental intellectuals, being highly praised by Rousseau and Diderot in France and imitated by Lessing in Germany. Lessing's enthusiasm for Lillo was shared by such prominent members of the next generation of German writers as Goethe and Schiller, and, particularly through his other original domestic tragedy, *Fatal Curiosity*, Lillo exerted a decisive influence on the growth of German *Schicksalstragödie* (tragedy of fate) at the end of the eighteenth century. To modern critics, Lillo's influence seems out of proportion to the instrinsic value of his plays but there is no denying that he is a dramatist of considerable historical significance.

As has been noted, domestic tragedy was by no means new in the 1730's. There are a number of Elizabethan and Jacobean examples, including such fine plays as Heywood's *A Woman Killed with Kindness* and the anonymous *A Yorkshire Tragedy* and *Arden of Feversham*, and certain late seventeenth- and early eighteenth-century dramatists, notably Otway, Banks, Southerne, and Rowe, wrote tragedies much more domestic and pathetic than heroic and classical in conception. Yet these Restoration and Augustan plays do not deal with everyday English life and could not be called "bourgeois." Whereas prose comedy usually dealt with contemporary life and ordinary people, poetic tragedy almost invariably adhered to the neoclassical principle that only characters of high birth and social or political eminence, preferably historically or geographically remote ones, could be tragic protagonists. Following the example of Aaron Hill in *The Fatal Extravagance* (1721), ten years before *The London Merchant*, Lillo shattered this doctrine, but whereas Hill's play is a reworking of *A Yorkshire Tragedy*, Lillo's play, which is based on an old ballad and has no dramatic source, is a more conscious attempt to break new ground. The idea of a London apprentice being a tragic hero would have seemed incongruous or even ludicrous to many people at the time, and it is said that some people went to the theatre to sneer, but Lillo won even the sceptics over and his success established that even humble members of society and their private lives were deserving of tragic treatment. Also indicative of his artistic daring is his choice of the medium of comedy, prose; and even though his prose is heightened and sometimes indistinguishable from blank verse it is a decisive step towards greater naturalism in tragic drama and so towards Büchner and Ibsen.

As a tragedy *The London Merchant* is as didactic as a Morality play, contains propaganda on behalf of the merchant class, is incorrigibly sentimental in its treatment of Barnwell's guilt and remorse, and blurs his responsibility for his actions by making him a victim of a power outside himself, the ruthless woman who has led him astray, Millwood. Consequently he is as much a wronged innocent as a culpable human being, even though he is involved in theft and murders his uncle. Many critics have found Lillo's other important play, *Fatal Curiosity*, superior to *The London Merchant* as a domestic tragedy, even though he reverts to blank verse. The provincial setting of *Fatal Curiosity*, the Cornish port of Penryn, makes it more unconventional for a tragedy of its time than the earlier play. As the title suggests, the role of fate is very pronounced, much more so than in *The London Merchant*, and the characters seem to be the helpless playthings and unfortunate victims of fortune. There are certainly no villains. It is out of desperation and necessity and as an alternative to suicide rather than for any evil motive that a destitute, old couple murder an apparent stranger for his wealth, only to discover that he is their long-lost son, a virtuous man of sensibility who has returned in order to help his parents. From the tragic irony of this situation, Lillo extracts a great deal of sentiment. This kind of tragedy of fate was beginning to become popular in the eighteenth century before Lillo, but with this play he did more than any other single dramatist to consolidate it. Discussion of Lillo's interest in domestic tragedy would be incomplete without mentioning his *Arden of Feversham*, staged posthumously in 1759 and obviously based on the Elizabethan play of the same name. The substantial changes Lillo makes in tone and characterization are symptomatic of the impact of sentimentalism on contemporary tragedy, the result being a softening of the tragic intensity of the original. In particular Arden's wife is transformed, so that instead of being the determined and callous prime mover of her husband's murder she is an essentially compassionate woman dominated by her ruthless lover.

Lillo's five other extant dramatic works are of lesser importance (the manuscript of his unpublished comedy, *The Regulators*, was lost in the eighteenth century). His first play, *Silvia*, is a ballad opera in form, but differs from the general run of such works in its moral seriousness and sentimentalism, being about the victory of virtue over vice and the reformation of a libertine. *The Christian Hero* and *Elmerick; or, Justice Triumphant*, both of which have foreign settings, are more conventional tragedies than *The London Merchant* and *Fatal Curiosity*. The first is true to its title in being heroic in conception and idiom, while the second is more deeply tinged with sentiment and pathos. *Marina* is an adaptation of Shakespeare's *Pericles*, while the short masque, *Britannia and Batavia*, is a political allegory. None of these works attracted much attention at the time, and they add almost nothing to his achievement in developing domestic tragedy.

—Peter Lewis

LONSDALE, Frederick. English. Born Lionel Frederick Leonard in St. Helier, Jersey, Channel Islands, 5 February 1881; adopted the name Lonsdale, 1908. Educated in schools in St. Helier. Served as a private in the South Lancashire Regiment. Married Leslie Brook Hoggan in 1904; three daughters. Worked as a railway clerk in St. Helier; worked passage to Canada as a steward on a liner, then worked at odd jobs on the Southampton docks; wrote for the theatre from 1906; lived in the United States, 1938–45, and in France, 1950 until his death. *Died 4 April 1954.*

PUBLICATIONS

Plays

Who's Hamilton? (produced 1906).
The Early Worm (produced 1908).

The King of Cadonia, music by Sidney Jones (produced 1908).
Aren't We All? (as *The Best People,* produced 1909; revised version, as *Aren't We All?,*
     produced 1923).   1924.
The Balkan Princess, with Frank Curzon, music by P. A. Rubens (produced 1910).
The Woman of It (produced 1913).
Betty, with Gladys Unger, music by P. A. Unger (produced 1914).
The Patriot (produced 1915).
High Jinks, from a play by P. Bilhaud and M. Hennequin (produced 1916).
Waiting at the Church (produced 1916).
The Maid of the Mountains, music by H. Fraser-Simson, lyrics by Harry Graham
     (produced 1916).   1949.
Monsieur Beaucaire, music by André Messager, from the novel by Booth Tarkington
     (produced 1919).
The Lady of the Rose, music by J. Gilbert, from a work by R. Schanzer and E. Welisch
     (produced 1921).
Spring Cleaning (produced 1923).   1925.
Madame Pompadour, with Harry Graham, music by Leo Fall (produced 1923).
The Street Singer, music by H. Fraser-Simson, lyrics by P. Greenbank (produced
     1924).   1929.
The Fake (produced 1924).   1926.
Katja the Dancer, with Harry Graham, music by J. Gilbert, from a play by L. Jacobsohn
     and R. Osterreicher (produced 1924).
The Last of Mrs. Cheyney (produced 1925).   1925.
On Approval (produced 1926).   1927.
The High Road (produced 1927).   1927.
Lady Mary, with J. Hastings Turner, music by A. Sirmay (produced 1928).
Canaries Sometimes Sing (produced 1929).   1929.
Never Come Back (produced 1932).
The Foreigners (produced 1939).   1932.
Once Is Enough (produced 1938).   1939; revised version, as *Let Them Eat Cake*
     (produced 1959), in *Plays of the Year 1958–59,* 1961.
Another Love Story (produced 1934).   1948.
But for the Grace of God (produced 1946).
The Way Things Go (produced 1950).   1951.

Screenplays: *The Devil to Pay,* 1930; *Lovers Courageous,* 1932; *The Private Life of Don
Juan,* with Lajos Biro, 1934; *Forever and a Day,* with others, 1944.

Reading List: *Freddy Lonsdale* (biography) by Frances Donaldson, 1957.

*   *   *

Some might think that Frederick Lonsdale is as dated as the Manchester School of Alan
Monkhouse, Harold Brighouse, Stanley Houghton, but the comedies of the 1920's have
survived better than most of the other plays of the period. He has not weathered as well as
Noël Coward, whose *Private Lives* of 1930 is an interesting comparison with Lonsdale's *On
Approval* of several years earlier, but non-dramatic considerations must be taken into account
there; it is really with W. Somerset Maugham's plays that his work invites consideration. The
"Bright Young Thingery" of Lonsdale's clever *Spring Cleaning* relies not so much on what
we have come to think of as Coward characters as on a Maugham situation, and Lonsdale
lacked not so much Coward's insouciance and wit as the stronger satire and "seriousness" of,
say, Maugham's *For Services Rendered.* In his time he was one of the mainstays of West End

theatre, easily as important as William Douglas Home and similar box-office draws of our own period.

His greatest success was probably with musicals such as the comic opera *The Maid of the Mountains* (1352 performances) and the Ruritanian divertissement of *The Balkan Princess*, but the best-remembered of his hits was the romantic comedy *The Last of Mrs. Cheyney*. That displays an unquestioned technical brilliance and produces an electrifying scene in the reading of Lord Elton's foolish letter, even though the ending is marred by sentimentality. Otherwise, it might well have ranked with *The Circle* and *The Constant Wife*, whose salt of cynicism have preserved them better. *The Last of Mrs. Cheyney*, along with *Aren't We All?*, established Lonsdale in the middle of the 1920's as a popular playwright. From then on it was more or less downhill, for times changed and Lonsdale did not.

It is a combination of talented actors and actresses, familiar themes, and craftsmanship (all too unfamiliar in some plays since the war) that endeared Lonsdale to audiences. More recent writers have tried to copy some of his farce techniques, and some turn up in "serious" comedies such as Tennessee Williams's *A Period of Adjustment*, not to mention inferior works. We recall the story of Walter Scott as a boy lying out on the hillside in a thunderstorm and greeting each flash of lightning with delighted cries of "Bonny, bonny!" So too with unabashed and brilliant *coups de théâtre*.

If the plays of Lonsdale's prime seem less impressive in content than in technique, we must recall that playwrights as talented as Maugham and St. John Ervine were content with the titillations of bright boulevard comedy. Maugham wrote: "Plays will only succeed if they amuse. The drama is just as ephemeral as the newspaper, and must reflect the passions and foibles of the day." In the 1920's the passions were trivial: "We just want to have a good time," said Galsworthy's Fleur, "because we don't believe anything can last." *The Last of Mrs. Cheyney* – the story of a shop girl turned crook turned honorable – was perfect for Terence Rattigan's "Aunt Edna" starting out her theatre-going career as a young embodiment of the middle class. The play was full of glittering make-believe people in the tinsel world of theatre, a world of matinée idols and leading actresses in egret feathers and the very latest fashions, of handsome profiles and good lines.

Frederick Lonsdale flourished. When cataclysm swept it all away, he went with it. Whenever it suits us to recall those carefree if confused years between the wars, we could do worse than to revive one of his light but not necessarily flimsy comedies. They are the brief chronicles of the time. I suggest a sounder play then *The Last of Mrs. Cheyney*, the more astringent *On Approval*. Two couples go away to the wilds of Scotland "on approval," considering marriage. The "two even-tempered experimenters withdraw in dismay," as critic Henry Popkin has put it, "leaving the quarrelsome and utterly impossible man and woman to each other." This might be where a Coward of Maugham play would begin, but it is where Lonsdale's audience was pleased to have the curtain drop.

—Leonard R. N. Ashley

LYLY, John. English. Born in the Weald of Kent c. 1553. Educated at King's School, Canterbury, Kent; Magdalen College, Oxford, B.A. 1573, M.A. 1575; also studied at Cambridge University, M.A. 1579. Married Beatrice Browne in 1583; two sons and one daughter. In the service of Lord Delawarr, 1575–80, and the Earl of Oxford, from 1580; leased Blackfriars Theatre, London, 1584, but subsequently gaoled for debt in the same year; wrote for the children's acting companies of the Chapel Royal and St. Paul's, London, until 1591; Member of Parliament for Hindon, Aylesbury, and Appleby, 1589–1601. *Died* (buried) *30 November 1606.*

Collections

> *Dramatic Works*, edited by F. W. Fairholt. 2 vols., 1858–92.
> *Complete Works*, edited by R. W. Bond. 1902.

Plays

> *Alexander, Campaspe, and Diogenes* (produced 1584). 1584; as *Campaspe*, 1584; edited by W. W. Greg, 1933.
> *Sappho and Phao* (produced 1584). 1584.
> *Galathea* (produced 1584–88?). 1592; edited by A. B. Lancashire, with *Midas*, 1969.
> *Mother Bombie* (produced 1587–90?). 1594; edited by A. Harriette Andreadis, 1975.
> *Endymion, The Man in the Moon* (produced 1588). 1591; edited by W. H. Neilson, 1911.
> *Love's Metamorphosis* (produced 1589–90?). 1601.
> *Midas* (produced 1590?). 1592; edited by A. B. Lancashire, with *Galathea*, 1969.
> *The Woman in the Moon* (produced 1590–95?). 1597.

Fiction

> *Euphues: The Anatomy of Wit*. 1578; augmented edition, 1579; edited by J. Winny, 1957.
> *Euphues and His England*. 1580.
> *Euphues* (both parts). 1617; edited by M. W. Croll and H. Clemons, 1916.

Other

> *Pap with a Hatchet, Alias a Fig for my Godson; or, Crack Me This Nut; or, A Country Cuff, That Is, A Sound Box of the Ear, for the Idiot Martin*. 1589.
> *A Whip for an Ape; or, Martin Displayed*. 1589; as *Rhythms Against Martin Mar-Prelate*, 1589 (possibly by Lyly).

Bibliography: *Lyly: A Concise Bibliography* by S. A. Tannenbaum, 1940; *Lyly 1935–65* by R. C. Johnson, 1968.

Reading List: *Lyly and the Italian Renaissance* by V. M. Jeffery, 1928; *Lyly: The Humanist and Courtier*, 1962, and *Lyly and Peele*, 1968, both by George K. Hunter; *The Court Comedies of Lyly: A Study in Allegorical Dramaturgy* by Peter Saccio, 1969.

*   *   *

John Lyly graduated as Master of Arts from Oxford, where he had enjoyed the patronage of Lord Burleigh, Queen Elizabeth's Lord High Treasurer. He gained a position as secretary to the Earl of Oxford, Burleigh's son-in-law and a supporter of a company of boy actors. Lyly's humanistic education, and his entry as a young man to court circles, determined both his audience and his entire literary output. He first appeared in print with a pastoral prose romance, *Euphues: The Anatomy of Wit*, and followed it up with an even more successful sequel, *Euphues and his England*, both parts continuing during his lifetime to be regularly reprinted.

He was appointed vice-master of Paul's Boys (the cathedral choristers who also acted as boy actors) and later to a position in the Revels Office, which was responsible for mounting the Queen's entertainments. He was (with Nashe) drawn in for a time on the side of the bishops in the theological Marprelate controversy to which he contributed one pamphlet, *Pappe with an Hatchet* in colloquial prose. But unlike Nashe, who found in the pamphlet a new and effective prose style, Lyly preferred the prose style of which he was a master and the audience with which he was familiar. His later work, all theatrical, was written to be acted (and sung) by Paul's Boys for performance before Elizabeth and her court.

Euphues, a love-romance, was directed particularly towards an audience of leisured ladies. "Euphues had rather lie shut in a lady's casket then open in a scholar's study," claims its preface. Lyly drew on the stylistic devices of medieval and renaissance rhetoric to produce a skilled, highly mannered, prose (which has always since Lyly's time been termed Euphuism, the sentence quoted above being a relatively simple example). Euphuism was characterised by (a) a balance of similar parts of speech in successive clauses, the matching words generally reinforced by alliteration or by "like endings," (b) equal-length phrases or clauses used in a parallel series, (c) the repetition of words derived from the same stem, (d) the use of antithesis, and (e) frequent far-fetched similes many of them drawn from the natural world and derived from Pliny's *Natural History*. The style was much admired and was fashionable for a few years. It was brilliantly parodied by Shakespeare in a speech by Falstaff, and echoes of it can be found in mannered prose as late as that of Dr. Johnson.

When Lyly came to write for the theatre, he generally used some variation of his Euphuistic prose style, though he could vary it with a more colloquial (but never vulgar) idiom if the situation demanded. Apart from *Campaspe* (derived from Classical history) and *Mother Bombie* (a Terence-type comedy on an English folk-theme), his plays are fantasies based on themes and characters from Classical mythology. The format encouraged lavish spectacle, allegorical references to current affairs in court (in *Endymion*, Cynthia and Endymion could be readily interpreted as Elizabeth and Leicester), aristocratic comedy to evoke what the preface to *Sapho and Phao* called "soft smiling, not loud laughing"; and it could very easily (as in the close of *Endymion*) be diverted to open praise of the monarch who was present at the performance. All was presented with a high degree of wit and dazzling verbal displays.

With a cast of boy actors and choristers, and an audience who demanded glitter, Lyly made no attempt to present real human feelings. His comedy was pantomimic and non-realistic, and (given the terms in which it was written) extremely effective. He made full use of the resources at his disposal. *Endymion*, for instance, contains several lyrics for his choristers, a dumb-show representing a dream, a dance of fairies for his troop of boy actors, and indications in the stage directions for spectacular costumes, changing scenic effects, and a final transformation in full view ("Bagoa recovers human shape").

The drama of the Elizabethan and Jacobean period ranges over a spectrum. At one end is the "drumming decasyllabon" of Marlowe's *Doctor Faustus* and *Tamburlaine* and the poetry and human insights of Shakespeare. Lyly's plays are at the other end of the spectrum. They are scripts for a kind of extended *commedia dell' arte*, and their real affinities are with the later Court Masque of Inigo Jones and Ben Jonson.

—Ian A. Gordon

MacARTHUR, Charles. American. Born in Scranton, Pennsylvania, 5 November 1895. Educated at the Wilson Memorial Academy, Nyack, New York. Served as a trooper in the 1st Illinois Cavalry, Mexican Border, 1916; Private in the 149th Field Artillery of the United States Army, 1917–19; Assistant to the Chief of the Chemical Warfare Service, Washington, D.C., with rank of Lieutenant Colonel, 1942–45. Married 1) Carol Frink (divorced); 2) the actress Helen Hayes in 1928, one daughter and one son, the actor James MacArthur. Reporter, City News Bureau, Chicago, 1914, *Herald and Examiner*, Chicago, 1915–16, and the *Chicago Tribune*, 1916–17; worked on the New York *American*, 1921–23; Special Writer, *Hearst's International Magazine*, New York, 1924; full-time writer and producer from 1929; screen writer and director from 1930; formed a production company with Ben Hecht, 1934. *Died 21 April 1956.*

PUBLICATIONS

Collections

> *The Stage Works* (includes *Lulu Belle; Salvation; The Front Page; Twentieth Century; Ladies and Gentlemen; Swan Song; Johnny on a Spot; Stag at Bay*, with Nunnally Johnson), edited by Arthur Dorlag and John Irvine. 1974.

Plays

> *My Lulu Belle,* with Edward Sheldon (as *Lulu Belle*, produced 1926). 1925; in *Stage Works*, 1974.
> *Salvation,* with Sidney Howard (produced 1928). In *Stage works*, 1974.
> *The Front Page,* with Ben Hecht (produced 1928). 1928; in *Stage Works*, 1974.
> *Twentieth Century,* with Ben Hecht (produced 1932). 1932; in *Stage Works*, 1974.
> *Jumbo,* with Ben Hecht, music by Richard Rodgers, lyrics by Lorenz Hart (produced 1935). 1935.
> *Ladies and Gentlemen,* with Ben Hecht, from a play by Ladislas Bush-Fekete (produced 1939). 1941; in *Stage Works*, 1974.
> *Fun to Be Free: A Patriotic Pageant,* with Ben Hecht (produced 1941). 1941.
> *Johnny on a Spot,* from a story by Parke Levy and Alan Lipscott (produced 1942). In *Stage Works*, 1974.
> *Wuthering Heights* (screenplay), with Ben Hecht, in *Twenty Best Film Plays*, edited by John Gassner and Dudley Nichols. 1943.
> *Swan Song,* with Ben Hecht, from a story by Ramon Romero and Harriett Hinsdale (produced 1946). In *Stage Works*, 1974.
> *Stag at Bay,* with Nunnally Johnson (produced 1976). In *Stage Works*, 1974.

Screenplays: *Billy the Kid,* with Wanda Tuckock and Laurence Stallings, 1930; *The King of Jazz,* with others, 1930; *Paid,* with Lucien Hubbard, 1930; *Way for a Sailor,* with others, 1930; *The Girl Said No,* with Sarah Y. Mason and A. P. Younger, 1930; *New Adventures of Get-Rich-Quick Wallingford,* 1931; *The Sin of Madelon Claudet,* 1931; *The Front Page,* with Ben Hecht, 1931; *Rasputin and the Empress,* 1933; *Twentieth Century,* with Ben Hecht, 1934; *Crime Without Passion,* with Ben Hecht, 1934; *The Scoundrel,* with Ben Hecht, 1935; *Barbary Coast,* with Ben Hecht, 1935; *Once in a Blue Moon,* with Ben Hecht, 1936; *Soak the Rich,* with Ben Hecht, 1936; *Wuthering Heights,* with Ben Hecht, 1939; *Gunga Din,* with others, 1939; *I Take This*

Woman, with James Kevin McGuinness, 1940; *Until I Die,* with Ben Hecht, 1940; *The Senator Was Indiscreet,* with Edwin Lanham, 1947.

Other

A Bug's-Eye View of the War. 1919.
War Bugs. 1928.

Reading List: *Charlie: The Improbable Life and Times of MacArthur* by Ben Hecht, 1957.

*　　*　　*

The young Charles MacArthur was a reporter for the City News Bureau, the *Herald and Examiner,* and the *Tribune* in Chicago, worked on the *New York American,* and contributed to Hearst's *International Magazine* and other journals. From their Chicago journalism experience, but chiefly from Jed Harris traditions of Broadway melodrama, MacArthur and Ben Hecht created the famous play, *The Front Page.* The *New York Times* (15 August 1928) liked this sensational and sentimental, if somewhat raucous and callous hymn to the antics of the working press. It said the play opened the season "noisily": "By superimposing a breathless melodrama upon a good newspaper play the authors and directors [actually George S. Kaufman] of 'The Front Page' ... have packed an evening with loud, rapid, coarse and unfailing entertainment ... have told a racy story with all the tang of front-page journalism ... [and] convey the rowdy comedy of the pressroom, the whirr of excitement, of nerves on edge ... in the hurly-burly of a big newspaper yarn."

MacArthur's unaided work (such as the forced farce of *Johnny on a Spot*) was undistinguished, but in collaboration he did well. In collaboration he also wrote *Lulu Belle* (with Edward Sheldon), *Salvation* (with Sidney Howard), and *Twentieth Century* (with Ben Hecht, 1932). All were solid Broadway vehicles. With Hecht he also wrote the spectacular *Jumbo, Ladies and Gentlemen, Swan Song,* and several film scripts.

MacArthur married as his second wife Helen Hayes, later to be queen of the legitimate stage, but professionally after 1928 he was more or less married to the movies. He began with several scripts in 1930, but hit the jackpot with a vehicle for Helen Hayes, *The Sin of Madelon Claudet.* Later films include *Rasputin and the Empress* (with the Barrymores), *Crime Without Passion* (writer, producer, director), *The Scoundrel, Gunga Din,* and *Wuthering Heights.* When he died he was working with Anita Loos on a vehicle for Miss Hayes. He was by then one of Hollywood's most respected writers.

His service with the Rainbow Division in France in World War I led to *A Bug's-Eye View of the War* and *War Bugs.* It is too bad he did not do more humorous prose. He brought together a nice combination of sentiment and wit and a touch of irony with a raucous sense of fun and irreverence. All these elements are at their best in *The Front Page.* Brooks Atkinson (in his introduction to *Sixteen Famous American Plays,* 1946) wrote that "*The Front Page* is to journalism what *What Price Glory?* is to the marines – rudely realistic style but romantic in its loyalties, and also audaciously profane." Actually, the "baldest profanity and most slatternly jesting as has ever been heard on the public stage" (as the *New York Times* had it in 1928) today sounds rather tame – and the play is not as realist as it seemed then. But some reporters still at least attempt to sound like MacArthur-Hecht characters (for nature imitates art), and *The Front Page* still has life in it, while *Five Star Final, Press Time, The Squeaker, Freedom of the Press,* and *Kiss the Boys Goodbye* and a host of other newspaper plays are long-dead.

—Leonard R. N. Ashley

MacKAYE, Percy (Wallace). American. Born in New York City, 16 March 1875; son of the dramatist Steele MacKaye. Educated at Harvard University, Cambridge, Massachusetts, A.B. 1897; studied at the University of Leipzig, 1898–1900. Married Marion Homer Morse in 1898 (died, 1939), two daughters and one son. Teacher, Craigie School for Boys, New York, 1900–04; full-time writer from 1904; Fellow in Poetry, Miami University, Ohio, 1920–24; Advisory Editor, *Folk-Say* journal, from 1929; Teacher of poetry and folk backgrounds, Rollins College, Winter Park, Florida, 1929–31; Visiting Professor of the creative aspects of drama, Sweet Briar College, Virginia, 1932–33; Director, White Top Mountain Folk Festival, Virginia, 1933; engaged in research into folklore in the Appalachian Mountains, 1933–35, and in Switzerland and the British Isles, 1936–37. Founder Member, Phi Beta Kappa Associates, 1941; President, Pan American Poets League of North America, 1943; Founder, Marion Morse-Percy MacKaye Collection at Harvard University Library, 1943. Recipient: Shelley Memorial Award, 1943; Academy of American Poets Fellowship, 1948. M.A.: Dartmouth College, Hanover, New Hampshire, 1914; Litt.D.: Miami University, 1924. Member, National Institute of Arts and Letters. *Died 31 August 1956.*

PUBLICATIONS

Plays

Kinfolk of Robin Hood (as *Inhabitants of Carlysle,* produced 1901). 1924.
The Canterbury Pilgrims (produced 1903). 1903; revised version, music by Reginald DeKoven, 1916.
Fenris the Wolf. 1905.
St. Gaudens Masque-Prologue (produced 1905). 1910.
Jeanne d'Arc (produced 1906). 1906.
Sappho and Phaon (produced 1907). 1907.
Mater: An American Study in Comedy (produced 1908). 1908.
The Scarecrow, from the story "Feathertop" by Hawthorne (produced 1908). 1908.
A Garland to Sylvia: A Dramatic Reverie. 1910.
Anti-Matrimony (produced 1910). 1910.
Hannele, with Mary Safford, from a play by Gerhart Hauptmann (produced 1910).
A Masque of Labor. 1912.
Tomorrow (produced 1913). 1912.
Yankee Fantasies (includes *Chuck, Gettysburg, The Antick, The Cat-Boat, Sam Average*). 1912.
Chuck (produced 1912). In *Yankee Fantasies,* 1912.
Sam Average (produced 1912). In *Yankee Fantasies,* 1912.
Gettysburg (produced 1912). In *Yankee Fantasies,* 1912.
The Antick (produced 1915). In *Yankee Fantasies,* 1912.
Sanctuary: A Bird Masque (produced 1913). 1914.
A Thousand Years Ago: A Romance of the Orient (produced 1913). 1914.
St. Louis: A Civic Pageant, with Thomas Wood Stevens (produced 1914). 1914.
The Immigrants, music by Frederick Converse. 1915.
The New Citizenship: A Civic Ritual (produced 1916). 1915.
Caliban, By the Yellow Sands (produced 1916). 1916.
The Evergreen Tree (produced 1917). 1917.
Sinbad the Sailor. 1917.
The Roll Call: A Masque of the Red Cross (produced 1918). 1918.
The Will of Song: A Dramatic Service of Community Singing, music by Harry Barnhart (produced 1919). 1919.

Washington, The Man Who Made Us (produced 1920). 1919; shortened versions
 published, as *George Washington*, 1920, *Washington and Betsy Ross*, 1927, and *Young
 Washington at Mt. Vernon*, 1927.
Rip Van Winkle, music by Reginald DeKoven (produced 1920). 1919.
The Pilgrim and the Book. 1920.
This Fine-Pretty World (produced 1923). 1924.
Kentucky Mountain Fantasies (includes *Napoleon Crossing the Rockies*, *The
 Funeralizing of Crickneck, Timber*). 1928; revised edition, 1932.
The Sphinx. 1929.
Wakefield: A Folk-Masque of America, music by John Tasker Howard (produced
 1932). 1932.
The Mystery of Hamlet, Prince of Denmark; or, What We Will: A Tetralogy (produced
 1949). 1950.

Fiction

Tall Tales of the Kentucky Mountains. 1926.
Weathergoose Woo! 1929.

Verse

Johnny Crimson: A Legend of Hollis Hall. 1895.
Ode on the Centenary of Abraham Lincoln. 1909.
Poems. 1909; as *The Sistine Eve and Other Poems*, 1915.
Uriel and Other Poems. 1912.
The Present Hour. 1914.
Dogtown Common. 1921.
The Skippers of Nancy Gloucester. 1924.
April Fire. 1925.
Winged Victory. 1927.
The Gobbler of God: A Poem of the Southern Appalachians. 1928.
Songs of a Day. 1929.
William Vaughn Moody, Twenty Years After. 1930.
Moments en Voyage: Nine Poems for the Harvard Class of 1897. 1932.
In Another Land, with Albert Steffen. 1937.
The Far Familiar. 1938.
Poem-Leaflets in Remembrance of Marion Morse MacKaye. 1939.
*My Lady Dear, Arise! Songs and Sonnets in Remembrance of Marion Morse
 MacKaye*. 1940.
What Is She? A Sonnet of Sonnets to Marion Morse. 1943.
Rememberings 1895–1945: Four Poems. 1945.
The Sequestered Shrine. 1950.
Discoveries and Inventions: Victories of the American Spirit. 1950.

Other

*The Playhouse and the Play, and Other Addresses Concerning the Theatre and
 Democracy in America*. 1909.
The Civic Theatre in Relation to the Redemption of Leisure. 1912.
The New Citizenship. 1915.
A Substitute for War. 1915.

Poems and Plays.   2 vols., 1916.
Epoch: The Life of Steele MacKaye.   2 vols., 1927.
American Theatre-Poets.   1935.
Poesia Religio.   1940.
Poog's Pasture: The Mythology of a Child: A Vista of Autobiography.   1951.
Poog and the Caboose Man: The Mythology of a Child: A Vista of Autobiography.   1952.

Editor, *Letters to Harriet,* by William Vaughn Moody.   1935.
Editor, *An Arrant Knave and Other Plays,* by Steele MacKaye.   1941.

Translator, *The Canterbury Tales of Chaucer: A Modern Rendering into Prose of the Prologue and Ten Tales.*   1904.
Translator, with John S. P. Tatlock, *The Modern Reader's Chaucer: Complete Poetical Works Now First Put into Modern English.*   1912; selection as *Canterbury Tales,* edited by Carl W. Ziegler, 1923.

Reading List: *MacKaye: A Sketch of His Life with Bibliography of His Works,* 1922; *Dipped in Sky* by Frank A. Doggett, 1930; *Annals of an Era: Percy MacKaye and the MacKaye Family* edited by E. O. Grover, 1932.

*   *   *

As the son of Steele MacKaye, Percy MacKaye might have been expected to show an interest in experimental drama. And he did, beginning with his graduation speech from Harvard in 1897 entitled "The Need of Imagination in the Drama of Today." Early in his career he added his efforts to the work of a small group of poetic dramatists – William Vaughn Moody, Josephine Peabody Marks, George Cabot Lodge – who were attempting to offset the excess of Realism on the American stage with something of the artistry which Yeats and Maeterlinck were creating abroad. MacKaye's poetic dramas, however – *The Canterbury Pilgrims, Jeanne d'Arc, Sappho and Phaon* – were minor contributions to the genre.

It was with pageant drama and community theatre that MacKaye trod most successfully in the steps of his father, generally celebrating America's heritage on the grand scale his father envisioned. As a crusader for community theatre he wrote several books and numerous articles – *The Playhouse and the Play, The Civic Theatre.* One of his most successful pageants – allegorical masques is a more accurate descriptive term: he called his work "poetry for the masses; the drama of democracy" – was *St. Louis: A Civic Pageant* which had a cast of 7,500 and attracted over half a million people to its five performances. *Caliban, By the Yellow Sands,* produced on the 300th anniversary of Shakespeare's death, was an elaborate pageant using various scenes from Shakespeare's plays to humanize Caliban, to suggest, as MacKaye explained, "the slow education of mankind through the influences of cooperative art." His other pageants included *The Roll Call,* requested by the American Red Cross, and *Wakefield,* in which he attempted to dramatize the effect of "the Folk-Spirit of America" on American freedom.

For the historian of American drama one of MacKaye's particular contributions is his definitive two-volume biography of his father, *Epoch,* a man Percy worshipped and with whom he shared the dream of creating drama for the people. As a poet and a dramatist, MacKaye's best and most enduring work was his dramatization of Nathaniel Hawthorne's "Feathertop" which he called *The Scarecrow.* Created before the audience's eyes with a display of imagination and theatrical skill, the scarecrow comes to life as Lord Ravensbane and achieves a considerable sense of humanity before it succumbs to the wiles of mankind and its own artificial construction. It is a fine example of MacKaye's commentary on the "need of imagination" and still retains its theatrical magic for modern audiences.

—Walter J. Meserve

MACKLIN, Charles. Irish. Born in Culdaff, Inishowen, in 1699. Educated in a school at Island Bridge, near Dublin. Married 1) Ann Grace in 1739 (died, 1758), one son and one daughter; 2) Elizabeth Jones in 1759 (died, 1781). Lived in London, working in a public house in the Borough district; Badgeman, or Scout, at Trinity College, Dublin, 1713; subsequently joined a strolling company of actors in Bristol; debut as an actor, London, 1725; played with the Drury Lane Company, 1733, the Haymarket Company, 1734, and again with Drury Lane, 1734–48; accidentally killed a fellow actor, tried for murder and acquitted, 1735; taught acting from 1743; appeared in Dublin for Sheridan, 1748–50, and at Covent Garden, London, 1750 until his retirement from the stage, 1753; proprietor of a tavern and coffee house in Covent Garden, 1754–58; returned to the stage, 1759, and continued to act in London, and occasionally in Dublin, until he again retired, 1789. *Died 11 July 1797.*

PUBLICATIONS

Collections

　Four Comedies (includes *Love A-la-Mode, The True-Born Irishman, The School for Husbands, The Man of the World*), edited by J. O. Bartley.   1968.

Plays

　King Henry VII; or, The Popish Imposter (produced 1746).   1746.
　A Will and No Will; or, A Bone for the Lawyers, from a play by J. F. Regnard (produced 1746).   Edited by Jean B. Kern, with *The New Play Criticized,* 1967.
　The New Play Criticized; or, The Plague of Envy (produced 1747).   Edited by Jean B. Kern, with *A Will and No Will,* 1967.
　The Club of Fortune-Hunters; or, The Widow Bewitched (produced 1748).
　The Lover's Melancholy, from the play by Ford (produced 1748).
　Covent Garden Theatre; or, Pasquin Turned Drawcansir, Censor of Great Britain (produced 1752).   Edited by Jean B. Kern, 1965.
　Love A-la-Mode (produced 1759).   1784; in *Four Comedies,* 1968.
　The School for Husbands; or, The Married Libertine (produced 1761).   In *Four Comedies,* 1968.
　The True-Born Irishman; or, The Irish Fine Lady (produced 1762; revised version, as *The Irish Fine Lady,* produced 1767).   In *Plays,* 1793; in *Four Comedies,* 1968.
　The Man of the World (as *The True Born Scotsman,* produced 1764; revised version, as *The Man of the World,* produced 1781).   1785; in *Four Comedies,* 1968.
　The Whim; or, A Christmas Gambol (produced 1764).
　Plays.   1793.

Other

　The Case of Charles Macklin, Comedian.   1743.
　Mr. Macklin's Reply to Mr. Garrick's Answer.   1743.
　Epistle from Tully in the Shades to Orator M—n in Covent Garden.   1755.
　An Apology for the Conduct of Mr. Charles Macklin, Comedian.   1773.
　The Genuine Arguments for a Conspiracy to Deprive Charles Macklin of His Livelihood.   1774.

Riot and Conspiracy: The Trial of Thomas Leigh and Others for Conspiring to Ruin in His Profession Charles Macklin. 1775.

Reading List: *Macklin: An Actor's Life* by William W. Appleton, 1960; "The Comic Plays of Macklin: Dark Satire at Mid-18th Century" by R. R. Findlay, in *Educational Theatre Journal*, 1968.

*   *   *

Charles Macklin was more important to the eighteenth-century English stage as an actor than as a playwright, and his plays frequently adopt the actor's perspective on the world. All ten of them (nine comedies and the ill-starred *Henry VII*) were composed during a busy theatrical career, either as a vehicle for himself or for someone else in the profession, and all are directed towards audiences, not readers. They keep reverting to the nature of the dramatic illusion – whether the stage presents an imitation of our reality, some other reality, or simply unreality – which was also debated by the critics of the time. *A Will and No Will* begins with a "Prologue by the Pit" in which some "members of the audience" onstage discuss the play to come, concluding that they will now see "a Prologue by the Pit." Similarly, at the end of *The New Play Criticized* Heartly asks Lady Critic to write a farce based on the events of the last hour and called *The New Play Criticized*; it will close with his marriage to her daughter. She agrees, and thus Heartly wins his Harriet. Another Harriet, the heroine of *The School for Husbands*, informs Lord Belville that he has been the victim of an elaborate charade by telling him, "We have all been acting a sort of comedy at your expence." More than half of Macklin's comedies play at confusing, at least momentarily, the boundaries commonly supposed to divide life from dramatic art.

This preoccupation is understandable in a man whose consciousness must have been almost wholly histrionic, whose life was the fixed backdrop of Georgian theatre. His acting career spanned sixty-five years, from the days of Cibber and Quin and *The Beggar's Opera*, fifteen years before Garrick's début, to the dawn of melodrama a dozen years after the latter's death. He worked with Fielding at the Haymarket before the Licensing Act, evolved the naturalistic Shylock that made Pope exclaim, "This is the Jew/That Shakespeare drew," tutored Sam Foote in acting, watched Goldsmith and Sheridan come and go, gave some of the earliest lessons in ensemble playing, and opened as the star of his own last comedy when over eighty. On the whole his influence on eighteenth-century theatre rivals Garrick's.

Macklin's forte as a dramatist was a particular kind of verisimilitude: on occasion he commanded the energy to "bounce" an audience into belief in his illusion, as Forster said a novelist should do. He could take a conventional scene (e.g., social climbing in *The True-Born Irishman*, raking and exposure in *The School for Husbands*) and bring it alive through his mastery of colloquial speech and his eye for realistic detail. Had he been able to do this more often we should have heard and thought more of him.

Macklin's best-known full-scale comedy was and is *The Man of the World*, an interesting if flawed prototype of the Victorian problem play; Sir Pertinax Macsycophant, played by Macklin, remains a powerful character. More successful are his short satiric afterpieces, particularly *Love A-la-Mode*, his most popular and lucrative work. The classic testing of Charlotte's four humorous suitors – the fop, the horsey squire, the Scot, and the Teague – gave Macklin an opportunity for writing some of his best dialogue and provided him with a symmetrical structure. The farce as a whole gives an accurate idea of what Macklin could and could not do. It concludes with Sir Callaghan O'Brallaghan remarking that "the whole business is something like the catastrophe of a stage play": another involuted reminder of Macklin's profession.

—R. W. Bevis

MacLEISH, Archibald. American. Born in Glencoe, Illinois, 7 May 1892. Educated at the Hotchkiss School, Lakeville, Connecticut; Yale University, New Haven, Connecticut, A.B. 1915; Harvard University, Cambridge, Massachusetts, LL.B. 1919. Served in the United States Army, 1917–19: Captain. Married Ada Hitchcock in 1916; three children. Lecturer in Government, Harvard University, 1919–21; Attorney, Choate, Hall, and Stewart, Boston, 1920–23; Editor, *Fortune* magazine, New York, 1929–38; Curator of the Niemann Foundation, Harvard University, 1938; Librarian of Congress, Washington, D.C., 1939–44; Director, United States Office of Facts and Figures, 1941–42, Assistant Director of the Office of War Information, 1942–43, and Assistant Secretary of State, 1944–45, Washington, D.C. Chairman of the United States Delegation to the Unesco drafting conference, London, 1945, and Member of the Executive Board, Unesco, 1946. Rede Lecturer, Cambridge University, 1942; Boylston Professor of Rhetoric and Oratory, Harvard University, 1949–62; Simpson Lecturer, Amherst College, Massachusetts, 1964–67. Recipient: Shelley Memorial Award, 1932; Pulitzer Prize, 1933, 1953, for drama, 1959; New England Poetry Club Golden Rose, 1934; Bollingen Prize, 1952; National Book Award, 1953; Sarah Josepha Hale Award, 1958; Antoinette Perry Award, 1959; National Association of Independent Schools Award, 1959; Academy of American Poets Fellowship, 1965; Academy Award, 1966; National Medal for Literature, 1978. M.A.: Tufts University, Medford, Massachusetts, 1932: Litt.D.: Wesleyan University, Middletown, Connecticut, 1938; Colby College, Waterville, Maine, 1938; Yale University, 1939; University of Pennsylvania, Philadelphia, 1941; University of Illinois, Urbana, 1947; Rockford College, Illinois, 1952; Columbia University, New York, 1954; Harvard University, 1955; Carleton College, Northfield, Minnesota, 1956; Princeton University, New Jersey, 1965; University of Massachusetts, Amherst, 1969; York University, Toronto, 1971; LL.D.: Dartmouth College, Hanover, New Hampshire, 1940; Johns Hopkins University, Baltimore, 1941; University of California, Berkeley, 1943; Queen's University, Kingston, Ontario, 1948; University of Puerto Rico, Rio Piedras, 1953; Amherst College, Massachusetts, 1963; D.C.L.: Union College, Schenectady, New York, 1941; L.H.D.: Williams College, Williamstown, Massachusetts, 1942; University of Washington, Seattle, 1948. Commander, Legion of Honor; Commander, El Sol del Peru. President, American Academy of Arts and Letters, 1953–56. Lives in Massachusetts.

PUBLICATIONS

Plays

> *Nobodaddy.* 1926.
> *Union Pacific* (ballet scenario; produced 1934). In *The Book of Ballets*, 1939.
> *Panic: A Play in Verse* (produced 1935). 1935.
> *The Fall of the City: A Verse Play for Radio* (broadcast 1937). 1937.
> *Air Raid: A Verse Play for Radio* (broadcast 1938). 1938.
> *The States Talking* (broadcast 1941). In *The Free Company Presents,* edited by James Boyd. 1941.
> *The American Story: Ten Radio Scripts* (includes *The Admiral; The American Gods; The American Name; Not Bacon's Bones; Between the Silence and the Surf; Discovered; The Many Dead; The Names for the Rivers; Ripe Strawberries and Gooseberries and Sweet Single Roses; Socorro, When Your Sons Forget*) (broadcast 1944). 1944.
> *The Trojan Horse* (broadcast 1952). 1952.
> *This Music Crept by Me upon the Waters* (broadcast 1953). 1953.
> *J.B.: A Play in Verse* (produced 1958). 1958.
> *The Secret of Freedom* (televised 1959). In *Three Short Plays*, 1961.
> *Three Short Plays: The Secret of Freedom, Air Raid, The Fall of the City.* 1961.

Our Lives, Our Fortunes, and Our Sacred Honor (as *The American Bell*, music by David Amram, produced 1962). In *Think*, July-August 1961.

Herakles: A Play in Verse (produced 1965). 1967.

An Evening's Journey to Conway, Massachusetts: An Outdoor Play (produced 1967). 1967.

Scratch, suggested by *The Devil and Daniel Webster* by Stephen Vincent Benét (produced 1971). 1971.

The Great American Fourth of July Parade (produced 1975). 1975.

Screenplays: *Grandma Moses*, 1950; *The Eleanor Roosevelt Story*, 1965.

Radio Plays: *The Fall of the City*, 1937; *King Lear*, from the play by Shakespeare, 1937; *Air Raid*, 1938; *The States Talking*, 1941; *The American Story* series, 1944; *The Son of Man*, 1947; *The Trojan Horse*, 1952; *This Music Crept by Me upon the Waters*, 1953.

Television Play: *The Secret of Freedom*, 1959.

Verse

Songs for a Summer's Day (A Sonnet-Cycle). 1915.

Tower of Ivory. 1917.

The Happy-Marriage and Other Poems. 1924.

The Pot of Earth. 1925.

Streets in the Moon. 1926.

The Hamlet of A. MacLeish. 1928.

Einstein. 1929.

New Found Land: Fourteen Poems. 1930.

Before March. 1932.

Conquistador. 1932.

Frescoes for Mr. Rockefeller's City. 1933.

Poems 1924–1933. 1933; as *Poems*, 1935.

Public Speech: Poems. 1936.

Land of the Free – U.S.A. 1938.

America Was Promises. 1939.

Actfive and Other Poems. 1948.

Collected Poems 1917–1952. 1952.

Songs for Eve. 1954.

Collected Poems. 1963.

"The Wild Old Wicked Man" and Other Poems. 1968.

The Human Season: Selected Poems 1926–1972. 1972.

New and Collected Poems 1917–1976. 1976.

Other

Housing America, by the Editors of *Fortune*. 1932.

Jews in America, by the Editors of *Fortune*. 1936.

Background of War, by the Editors of *Fortune*. 1937.

The Irresponsibles: A Declaration. 1940.

The Next Harvard, As Seen by MacLeish. 1941.

A Time to Speak: The Selected Prose. 1941.

The American Cause. 1941.

A Time to Act: Selected Addresses. 1943.

Poetry and Opinion: The Pisan Cantos of Ezra Pound: A Dialogue on the Role of Poetry. 1950.
Freedom Is the Right to Choose: An Inquiry into the Battle for the American Future. 1951.
Poetry and Journalism. 1958.
Emily Dickinson: Papers Delivered at Amherst College, with others. 1960.
Poetry and Experience. 1961.
The Dialogues of MacLeish and Mark Van Doren, edited by Warren V. Busch. 1964.
The Eleanor Rossevelt Story. 1965.
A Continuing Journey. 1968.
The Great American Frustration. 1968.
Riders of the Earth: Essays and Reminiscences. 1978.

Editor, *Law and Politics,* by Felix Frankfurter. 1962.

Bibliography: *A Catalogue of the First Editions of MacLeish* by Arthur Mizener, 1938; *MacLeish: A Checklist* by Edward J. Mullahy, 1973.

Reading List: *MacLeish* by Signi Lenea Falk, 1965; *MacLeish* by Grover G. Smith, 1971.

*   *   *

By 1940, Archibald MacLeish had written numerous books of poems, and was a well-known writer. He was also the target of adverse criticism. MacLeish's early work is too derivative. It abounds with the distracting influence of Eliot and Pound, among others. MacLeish writes on the same subjects as Eliot and Pound and from exactly their point of view. MacLeish's early long poems proved very weak. His most famous one is *Conquistador,* which won him the first of three Pulitzer Prizes. It is a verbose, unqualified glorification of Spain's slaughter and enslavement of Mexican natives, and is, at best, unthinkingly adolescent. Other works in this period are marred by the confusing about-face MacLeish executes concerning the role of the poet. In his "Invocation to the Social Muse," MacLeish criticizes those who would urge the poet to concentrate on social issues. These issues, however, soon become central to his own work. MacLeish proceeds to sermonize, harangue – and produced much poor poetry, especially in *Public Speech* and his plays for radio.

Yet, despite the inferior work written in these decades, MacLeish was beginning to compile an outstanding body of lyric poetry. Some of the short poems in *Streets in the Moon* and *New Found Land* hold up very well. "L'an trentiesme de mon eage" is a superior presentation on the subject of the lost generation. Other fine poems include "Eleven," "Immortal Autumn," and "Memorial Rain." "Ars poetica" develops the stimulating idea that "A poem should not mean/But be." Perhaps the best of all is "The End of the World," a dramatization of the belief that the universe is basically meaningless. *Poems 1924–1933* brought together such superior lyrics as "Pony Rock," "Unfinished History," and "Lines for an Interment."

What became increasingly apparent in the 1940's and thereafter is that MacLeish's primary strength as a writer resides in the lyric form. In fact, MacLeish has done most of his best work after the age of fifty.

Even some of MacLeish's later plays and long poems, two genres he never really excels at, rise above the mediocre. The full-length play *J.B.,* despite its bland poetry and tepid main character, effectively dramatizes the tragedies that engulf J.B. and offers a frequently rousing debate between Mr. Zuss (representing orthodox religion) and Nickles (representing a pragmatic outlook). MacLeish's one-act play *This Music Crept by Me upon the Waters* is also successful. The main characters, Peter and Elizabeth, are interesting; the plot builds in suspense; and the poetry and the theme (a preference for the present over the past) are powerful. *Actfive* is MacLeish's best long poem. The first section, which delineates modern man's basic predicament, is quite absorbing.

Still, it is MacLeish's lyric poetry that will be remembered the longest. Starting with the poems collected in 1948, the number of excellent lyrics mounts steadily. For this reason, the critical neglect MacLeish has suffered in recent years is unjust. These later lyrics center on three sometimes overlapping subjects. One presents MacLeish's increasing awareness of the mystery that permeates human experience. Earlier in his life, he wrote several poems that spoke confidently, if not cockily about setting out on explorations; now he writes "Voyage West," a sensitive expression of the uncertainty involved in a journey. Significantly, "Poet's Laughter" and "Crossing" are full of questions, while "The Old Man to the Lizard" and "Hotel Breakfast" end with questions, not answers. MacLeish sums up his sense of the mysterious in "Autobiography" when he says, "What do I know of the mystery of the universe?/Only the mystery."

MacLeish has also written several tender eulogies and epitaphs. Two such poems about his mother are "The Burial" and "For the Anniversary of My Mother's Death." A pair of even finer poems, "Poet" and "Hemingway," have Ernest Hemingway for their subject. Other outstanding poems in this vein include "Edwin Muir," "Cummings," and "The Danger in the Air."

Finally, MacLeish has written a host of fine poems about old age. The difficulty of creativity when one is no longer young is described in "They Come No More, Those Words, Those Finches." Tiredness is poignantly depicted in "Waking" and "Dozing on the Lawn." "Ship's Log" records the narrowing awareness of the old. Here, MacLeish states: "Mostly I have relinquished and forgotten/Or grown accustomed, which is a way of forgetting." Yet " 'The Wild Old Wicked Man' " presents an old person's wisdom and passion. In the two poems concerning "The Old Gray Couple," he offers the reader a moving portrait of the final, deepest stage of human love. Lastly, using Odysseus as narrator, MacLeish chooses human love (symbolized by his aging wife) and mortal life over love for the abstract (symbolized by the goddess Calypso) and the metaphysical in his lovely poem "Calypso's Island." This poem declares, "I long for the cold, salt,/Restless, contending sea and for the island/Where the grass dies and seasons alter."

—Robert K. Johnson

MARLOWE, Christopher. English. Born in Canterbury, Kent, 6 February 1564. Educated at King's School, Canterbury, 1579; Benet College, now Corpus Christi College, Cambridge, matriculated 1581, B.A. 1584, M.A. 1587. Settled in London c. 1587: wrote plays for the Lord Admiral's Company and Lord Strange's Company; charged with heresy, 1593: stabbed to death in a tavern brawl before the case was considered. *Died 30 May 1593.*

PUBLICATIONS

Collections

Works, edited by R. H. Case and others.   6 vols., 1930–33.
Poems, edited by Millar Maclure.   1968.

375

Plays, edited by Roma Gill. 1971.
Complete Works, edited by Fredson Bowers. 2 vols., 1973.
Complete Plays and Poems, edited by E. D. Pendry. 1976.

Plays

Tamburlaine the Great, Divided into Two Tragical Discourses (produced 1587). 1590;
   edited by Irving Ribner, 1974.
Doctor Faustus (produced 1588? or 1592?). 1604; alternative text, 1616; both texts
   edited by W. W. Greg, 1950; edited by Keith Walker, 1973.
The Rich Jew of Malta (produced 1589?). 1633; edited by N. W. Bawcutt, 1977.
Edward the Second (produced 1592?). 1594; edited by Irving Ribner, 1970.
Dido, Queen of Carthage (produced 1593?). 1594.
The Massacre at Paris (produced 1593?). 1594(?).

Verse

Epigrams and Elegies of Ovid, with John Davies. 1595(?); as *All Ovid's Elegies: 3
   Books, with Epigrams by John Davies,* 1598(?).
Hero and Leander, Begun by Marlowe, Completed by Chapman. 1598; edited by Louis
   L. Martz, 1972.
Lucan's First Book Translated Line for Line. 1600.

Bibilography: *Marlowe: A Concise Bibliography* by S. A. Tannenbaum, 1937; supplement,
1947; supplement by R. C. Johnson, 1967.

Reading List: *Marlowe* by M. Poirier, 1951; *The Overreacher: A Study of Marlowe* by Harry
Levin, 1952; *Marlowe and the Early Shakespeare* by F. P. Wilson, 1953; *Suffering and Evil
in the Plays of Marlowe* by D. Cole, 1962; *Marlowe: A Collection of Critical Essays* edited by
Clifford Leech, 1964; *Marlowe: A Critical Study* by J. B. Steane, 1964; *In Search of Marlowe:
A Pictorial Biography* by A. D. Wraight and V. F. Stern, 1965; *Marlowe* by R. E. Knoll,
1968; *Critics on Marlowe* edited by J. O'Neill, 1969; *Marlowe's Agonists* by C. C. Fanta,
1970; *Marlowe, Merlin's Prophet* by Judith Weil, 1977.

                              *   *   *

   A "Coblers eldest son" (as Robert Greene jealously scorned him) Christopher Marlowe
earned for himself the education of a gentleman at the University of Cambridge, and almost
immediately after graduating as Master of Arts startled London with *Tamburlaine.* The play's
"high astounding terms" (Prologue to Part 1) conquered the new world of the theatre with
the same *éclat* as its eponymous hero overcame the Turks and Persians; for many years after
its presumed first production, no dramatist could shake himself free of its cadences.
   The echoes of *Tamburlaine* in other sixteenth-century plays whose dates are more certain
is almost the only objective means of establishing a date for the play; the same is true of all
Marlowe's works. Subjective evidence, from its style, suggests that *Dido, Queen of Carthage*
was his earliest dramatic production, and that it belongs with the translations of Lucan and
Ovid, perhaps accomplished while he was still at Cambridge. Translating the Latin taught
him to handle his native language, and a steady progression can be observed in the facility
with which he treats the classical authors. Book 1 of his version of Lucan's *Pharsalia* is a line-
for-line rendering of the original; the *Elegies* convert Ovid's verse form (hexameter followed

by pentameter) into racy, sometimes witty, English heroic couplets. *Dido* takes the whole of the first part of Virgil's *Aeneid* as its provenance; the plot centres on Book 4, but details of character and episode are snatched up with easy deliberation from Books 1 to 6.

The titlepage presents *Dido* as having been performed by the Children of the Chapel Royal, and it ought to be judged by the criteria obtaining for children's plays written by such authors a Lyly and Marston. Its distinction is unmistakable. Marlowe exploits the delight in costume and effect, making his characters draw attention to what they are wearing or to the efforts of the stage technicians. Children's plays aspired to verisimilitude only in the accidentals of a performance; by no stretch of the imagination could boys with unbroken voices imitate to the life the great heroes of classical mythology who were the protagonists of these plays. But if they could not act, they could recite; they had been chosen for their voices, and they were highly trained in all the Renaissance arts of elocution. In Aeneas's account of the fall of Troy Marlowe writes a stirring "aria" which augurs well for his subsequent career as a dramatist writing for the public theatres.

The Prologue to the first part of *Tamburlaine*, written perhaps in 1585, disdains the "jigging veins of rhyming mother-wits," preferring language more appropriate to its tale of the Scythian shepherd whose personal magnetism and force of arms raised him to imperial status and won the love of his captive Egyptian princess, Zenocrate. The success of Part 1 "made our poet pen his second part" (Prologue to Part 2), and the two parts together show the complete revolution of Fortune's Wheel. Tamburlaine is not vanquished by any human power; mortality itself brings about his overthrow: he falls sick, and dies, lamenting that he must "die, and this unconquered." The play is a tragedy only in the Elizabethan sense; the hero suffers no Aristotelian flaw, and the dramatist does not presume to criticize any of his callous slaughters as errors. The pride with which Tamburlaine identifies himself as "the scourge of God" is no *hubris* but a factual description of the English drama's first superman, larger than life in every sense. In comparison with Tamburlaine, the rest of the *dramatis personae* are two-dimensional, of interest merely as they enhance their conqueror's achievement in Part 1, and show in their deaths the waning of his power in Part 2.

In *Tamburlaine* the famous "mighty line" praised by Ben Jonson (in a poem prefixed to the First Folio of Shakespeare's works), is appropriate to the "aspiring mind" of its great hero. In Marlowe's next play, *The Jew of Malta*, rhetoric is inflated for comic purposes. In this story of a Jew's battle against Christians, neither of the opposing factions is worthy of respect; admiration is compelled only for the skill of unscrupulous dealings, and sentiment is dismissed by cruel laughter. The Jew's daughter is murdered by her father, but calls upon two friars to witness that she dies a Christian; any pathos arising from this situation is dispelled by the friar's response: "Ay, and a virgin too; that grieves me most." The audience's sympathy is with the Jew, Barabas – not because he is virtuous but because he makes no secret of his double-dealings, confiding in elaborate asides his schemes to outwit the no-less villainous, but hypocritical, Christians. Barabas of course overreaches himself and meets an appropriate end in the boiling cauldron that he had prepared for his chief enemy – but not until he has engineered the deaths of his daughter and her two suitors, an entire convent of nuns, the two friars, the army of Turkish soldiers, a prostitute, her pimp, and one of her clients (who happens to be Barabas's blackmailing slave). Like Tamburlaine, Barabas is larger than life; the rest of the characters, in this play too, are insignificant in comparison with the protagonist, and chiefly remarkable as objects or agents of his malevolence.

Marlowe probably wrote *The Massacre at Paris*, which survives only in a mangled, reported text, at much the same time as he wrote *The Jew of Malta*. Both have the same black comedy, in which murder is committed with a jest – and the laugh is the murderer's. *The Massacre at Paris* is a political play, dealing with recent events in the struggle between Catholics and Protestants in France in the late 1580's. The central figure is the Duke of Guise, a professed villain like Barabas but more menacing than him because the crimes are not imagined but historical. In a reported text, which relies on the memory of actors, poetry suffers more damage than plot, but one can still detect in the Guise the note of true Marlovian aspiration:

What glory is there in a common good,
That hangs for every peasant to achieve?
That like I best that flies beyond my reach.

In *The Jew of Malta* and *The Massacre at Paris* Marlowe makes great play with the popular concept of the machiavellian "politician" who parodied the Florentine statesman by putting self before state. In *Edward II* he treats Machiavelli's ideas more seriously, showing in the character of Young Mortimer a hot-headed patriot who, for the first half of the play, is genuinely distressed by the king's weakness and profligacy. But as the play progresses, covering twenty-three years of chronicled history, Mortimer loses principle as he gains power until, when Edward is imprisoned in the dungeon sewers of Kenilworth Castle and he himself is, as he believes, secure as Protector over the prince and lover of the queen, he manifests all the characteristics of the Italianate villain who so appealed to the Elizabethan imagination: "Fear'd am I more than lov'd; let me be fear'd,/And when I frown, make all the court look pale." Mortimer contrasts with Edward, passively homosexual and ambitious for nothing more than "some nook or corner" in which to "frolic with [his] dearest Gaveston."

Marlowe manipulates the sympathies of the audience, turning them away from Edward and his recklessness to support Mortimer and the barons in their care for the realm. But this care is not flawless: pride and ambition vitiate it from the start. Mortimer's regime is hateful, and the treatment meted out to Edward is brutal and obscene. There is no "mighty line" in this play, but the quick cut and thrust of conversations between conspirators and enemies. Isabella, Edward's queen, is allowed a languid romanticism as the despised wife, but when she comes under Mortimer's domination her speeches are at first hollow and hypocritical, and later subdued by fear. In some ways *Edward II* is Marlowe's best play: its structure is shapely, with Mortimer's fortunes rising as Edward's decline; its characterisation is diversified, and for the first time the protagonist has a worthy antagonist and a supporting cast who are characters and not merely names; its verse, though businesslike to the point of drabness, is nevertheless suited to the unheroic action. *Dr. Faustus*, the play that followed *Edward II* and which was Marlowe's last play, has none of these qualities, but while *Edward II* is a good play, *Dr. Faustus* is a great one.

Two texts of *Dr. Faustus* survive, but neither represents the play as Marlowe intended it. The earlier was published in 1604 and seems to be the work of actors who repeated their lines inaccurately, were sometimes vague about meaning, and often confused about which speech came next. The 1616 text is longer and more coherent, being based probably upon some theatrical document such as a prompt-book. But this too is unreliable. An "editor" has been at work, simplifying, censoring, and adding the extra material for which Henslowe, the actor-manager, paid Bird and Rowley four pounds in 1602. A twentieth-century text can only be eclectic in its attempts to approach the play that Marlowe wrote.

The plot of *Dr. Faustus* is simple: a brilliant scholar, frustrated by the limitations imposed on human learning, sells his soul to the devil for four and twenty years of knowledge, power, and voluptuousness. At the end of the play only one hour is left, after which "The devil will come, and Faustus must be damn'd." The play is remarkable for its first two and last acts. In the first, Faustus reviews the whole scope of learning available to Renaissance man in a speech where the names of Aristotle, Galen, and Justinian glitter for a while until they are extinguished by the logic which sees death as the inevitable climax of all human endeavour, and by the perverse will that presents necromancy as the only means of escaping human bondage. An interview with Mephostophilis, one of the "Unhappy spirits that fell with Lucifer," does nothing to shake Faustus's resolution even though the troubled spirit begs him to "leave these frivolous demands/Which strikes a terror to my fainting soul." The play disintegrates in the middle acts, where clownage distracts Faustus's mind from contemplation of his deed. The 1616 text's comic scenes are fully developed, but the rudiments are present in the 1604 text, forcing the conclusion that although Marlowe may not have written them himself, he nevertheless acquiesced to their presence in his play. Parts of 1616's Act V, however, are not to be found anywhere in 1604; among them is the interchange between Faustus and Mephostophilis where Faustus blames the devil for his damnation and Mephostophilis proudly claims responsibility. Eleven lines (V, ii, 80–91) are crucial to an interpretation of the play. If they are included as part of Marlowe's design, then Dr. Faustus is no more than a puppet, manipulated by external forces of good and evil, and in no way responsible for his fate; the play is in that case a Morality Play which lacks the traditional happy ending in which God's mercy prevails over His justice. But if the lines are discarded (as I think they should be), Faustus appears as an independent being who, of his own free will, although with imperfect knowledge, chooses damnation; and the play is a true tragedy.

Plague raged in London during the last year of Marlowe's life. The theatres were closed, to avoid the spread of infection; and there was consequently no demand for new plays. Like Shakespeare, Marlowe spent some of the time writing a long narrative poem. His subject, the love between Hero and Leander, is a tragic one, but the poem stops with the consummation of the love; it is not clear whether Marlowe intended to proceed to the catastrophe. The eight hundred lines that he wrote reveal a marvellously rich invention that combines tenderness with sardonic wit in a form that is, in the best sense, artificial. Describing his two protagonists, Marlowe counterpoises the elaborateness of Hero's garments with the sensuous simplicity of Leander's naked body. Of "Venus' nun" he tells us:

> Buskins of shells all silver'd used she
> And branch'd with blushing coral to the knee,
> Where sparrows perch'd, of hollow pearl and gold,
> Such as the world would wonder to behold.

Sight and sound predominate in the description of Hero, but Marlowe refers to touch and taste when he speaks of Leander:

> Even as delicious meat is to the taste,
> So was his neck in touching, and surpass'd
> The white of Pelops' shoulder. I could tell ye
> How smooth his breast was, and how white his belly.

The ease with which he moves through the polished couplets is assurance enough that Marlowe, when he died in the spring of 1593, had by no means exhausted his genius.

—Roma Gill

MARMION, Shakerley. English. Born at Aynho, near Brackley, Northamptonshire, in January 1603. Educated at the free school at Thame; Wadham College, Oxford, 1620–25, B.A. 1622, M.A. 1624. Served as a soldier in the Netherlands. Settled in London; enjoyed the patronage of Ben Jonson; indicted for murder, 1629, but apparently was not convicted; gained some reputation as a playwright, especially with the court of Charles I; joined Sir John Suckling's expedition to Scotland in 1638 but became ill en route and was removed back to London. *Died in January 1639.*

PUBLICATIONS

Collections

Dramatic Works, edited by James Maidment and W. H. Logan.   1875.

Plays

Holland's Leaguer (produced 1631).   1632.
A Fine Companion (produced 1632–33?).   1633.
The Antiquary (produced 1634–36?).   1641.

Verse

A Moral Poem Entitled the Legend of Cupid and Psyche.   1637; as *Cupid's Courtship*, 1666; edited by A. J. Nearing, 1944.

Reading List: *The Sons of Ben: Jonsonian Comedy in Caroline England* by J. L. Davis, 1967.

*   *   *

During his short career as a dramatist Shakerley Marmion produced three plays, *Hollands Leaguer*, *A Fine Companion*, and *The Antiquary*, a few occasional poems, and a long verse narrative, *Cupid and Psyche*.

Hollands Leaguer was performed at the Salisbury Court Theatre by the newly constituted Prince Charles' Men in December 1631, and it appeared in print in an untidy censored quarto early in 1632. Marmion evidently prepared his text for the press, and the quarto is divided into acts and scenes according to classical criteria, containing a list of actors in the new company. This was one of the first plays to introduce the technique of "place realism" to the Caroline Stage, although the scenes depicting Elizabeth Holland and her notorious Southwark brothel serve primarily as a thematic contrast to the loosely chivalric temper of the main plot. This is an apprenticeship piece rigid in its structure, crude in irony and moral design, and clumsy in its attempts to assimilate material from a variety of dramatic and classical sources. But Marmion's handling of blank verse dialogue demonstrates his undoubted ability to evoke moods of lyrical intensity, and he makes a genuine effort to vary the pace of the dramatic action.

A Fine Companion was performed by the same company, and appeared in quarto in 1633. The play takes its name from a fashionable dance, and is often cited as evidence that Marmion was one of the "Sons of Ben" who frequented the Apollo Room of the Devil Tavern. The influence of Jonson's *The New Inn* (1629) is recognizable, and its apologetic Induction recalls the critical debate following the earlier play's stage failure. *A Fine Companion*, like *Hollands Leaguer*, is a Jonsonian "humours" comedy, although Marmion learned quickly to work within the confines of this form and managed to produced memorable social types like the braggadocio Captain Whibble. Generally, type-characterization is handled more decorously in the later play, the irony is more refined, and the dramatic design more confident. Although these plays lack the satiric venom of Marston or the earlier Jonson, or the exuberant raciness of Middleton, they demonstrate a developing awareness on Marmion's part of the technical requirements of stage comedy.

The Antiquary, acted probably in 1635 by Queen Henrietta's Men at the Phoenix Theatre, but not published in quarto until a year after Marmion's death, is clearly his best play. It shares with the two earlier plays a boldness of scenic design, and manages to exploit parallel dramatic situations for their ironic as well as their comic potentiality. The play deals with the follies of old age, and shows Marmion's eclecticism at its most fertile and inventive, as he assimilates material and plot devices from Petronius, Shakespeare, Middleton, and Jonson. Despite minor technical flaws, which are present in all his plays, *The Antiquary* demonstrates a competent awareness of comic form, and even within the constricting framework of "humours" comedy, manages to move easily and naturally from vigorous prose dialogue to substantial blank verse. Marmion returned to the problems of writing verse in *Cupid and Psyche*, skilfully dramatising his source, Apuleius's *The Golden Ass*, and successfully circumventing the limitations of the rhyming couplet form. In his three plays and in *Cupid and Psyche*, Marmion looks back to the poetry and drama of the Elizabethan period, but his growing confidence in the handling of theme and dialogue point forward to the more refined world of Restoration comedy.

—John Drakakis

MARSTON, John.   English.   Born in Wardington, Oxfordshire, baptized 7 October 1576. Educated at Brasenose College, Oxford, 1592–94, B.A. 1594; Middle Temple, London, 1595–1606. Married Mary Wilkes c. 1605; one son. Wrote for Paul's boys company after 1599, and shareholder in the Queen's Revels company after 1604; imprisoned (for unknown reasons), 1608; ordained deacon, then priest, 1609, and ceased writing for the theatre after taking orders; Rector of Christchurch, Hampshire, 1616 until his resignation, 1631. *Died 25 June 1634.*

PUBLICATIONS

Collections

> *Works*, edited by A. H. Bullen.   3 vols., 1887.
> *Plays*, edited by H. H. Wood.   3 vols., 1934–39.
> *Poems*, edited by Arnold Davenport.   1961.

Plays

> *Antonio and Mellida*, part 1 (produced 1599).   1602; edited by G. K. Hunter, 1965.
> *Antonio's Revenge* (part 2 of *Antonio and Mellida*) (produced 1599).   1602; edited by Reavley Gair, 1977.
> *Histriomastix; or, The Player Whipped*, from an anonymous play (produced 1599).   1610.
> *Jack Drum's Entertainment; or, The Comedy of Pasquill and Katherine* (produced 1600).   1601.
> *What You Will* (produced 1601?).   1607.
> *The Dutch Courtesan* (produced 1603–04?).   1605; edited by Peter Davison, 1968.
> *The Malcontent* (produced 1604).   1604; edited by Bernard Harris, 1967.

Parasitaster; or, The Fawn (produced 1604–05?).   1606; edited by David A. Blostein, 1978.
Eastward Ho, with Chapman and Jonson (produced 1605).   1605; edited by C. G. Petter, 1973.
The Wonder of Women; or, The Tragedy of Sophonisba (produced 1606).   1606.
The Honorable Lord and Lady of Huntingdon's Entertainment at Ashby (produced 1607).   In *Works*, 1887, in *Poems*, 1961.
The Insatiate Countess, completed by William Barksted (produced 1610?).   1613.
Works (tragedies and comedies).   1633.

Verse

The Metamorphosis of Pygmalion's Image, and Certain Satires.   1598; edited by Elizabeth Story Donno, in *Elizabethan Minor Epics*, 1968.
The Scourge of Villainy: Three Books of Satires.   1598; revised edition, 1599.

Bibliography: *Marston: A Concise Bibliography* by S. A. Tannenbaum, 1940; supplement in *Elizabethan Bibliographies Supplements 4* by C. A. Pennel and W. P. Williams, 1968.

Reading List: *Marston: Satirist* by A. Caputi, 1961; *The Satire of Marston* by M. S. Allen, 1965; *Jacobean City Comedy: A Study of Satiric Plays by Jonson, Marston, and Middleton* by B. Gibbons, 1968; *Marston of the Middle Temple: An Elizabethan Dramatist in His Social Setting* by P. J. Finkelpearl, 1969.

*   *   *

John Marston's crabbed and bitter satire quickly established his literary reputation. In the "Parnassus Plays" of 1598–1601 at Cambridge University, Marston's satiric style was parodied in the character of "W. Kinsayder": "What, Monsieur Kinsayder, lifting up your leg and pissing against the world? Put up, man, put up for shame. Methinks he is a ruffian in his style." His literary quarrels with Ben Jonson and Joseph Hall created a furor at the time; Drummond of Hawthornden notes that Jonson "had many quarrels with Marston, beat him and took his pistol from him, wrote his Poetaster on him." Jonson also attacked him in *Every Man Out of His Humour* and *Cynthia's Revels*, since Marston had "represented him on stage." This so-called *Poetomachia* was not enduring, though, and the two eventually became friends.

Marston's tendency to stumble in and out of quarrels, jails and royal favour has marked him for centuries of literary criticism as a railing and often incoherently self-defeating malcontent. This is not entirely justified, however, as in all his works, from the most violent to the most flippant, there is an underlying moral concern. Many details of Marston's life are anomalous, but it is not altogether surprising that at the age of thirty-two he set aside his writing and, like his fellow satirists John Donne and Joseph Hall, took Holy Orders.

Marston's literary career begins with two collections of verse satires: the semi-erotic *Metamorphosis of Pygmalion's Image* and the snarling and snapping *Scourge of Villainy*, in which Marston ridicules the poses and pretenses of the young gallants of the Inns of Court and London. In both volumes, the satire shifts uneasily from a range of effete social pastimes to vulgar depravities; both were considered immoral, and burned in 1599. The harsh and contentious style of the verse satires is carried over to Marston's first play, *Histriomastix*, a pageant-like allegory performed at the Inns of Court, which deals with the function of law in a crumbling society. *Jack Drum's Entertainment* and *What You Will* reflect the lighter side of the verse satires, again attacking the foppish young gallants, though love themes and Shakespearean echoes complement the satire in these romantic comedies.

Antonio and Mellida and *Antonio's Revenge* introduce the dark qualities of Marston's satiric vision. In spite of its tentative comic reconciliation, the first play is largely influenced by evil and unjust characters, and the moral climate of the Venetian court is oppressive and sordid. The second play, however, lurches into perhaps the most violent and painful revenge tragedy in Elizabethan drama. As the protagonist degenerates both psychologically and morally, his "barbarism and blood lust" confirm the play's assertion that men are "vermin bred of putrifacted slime."

The Malcontent is generally considered Marston's greatest play. His tragi-comic satire of the court and of a morally degenerating world is successfully accomplished, while at the same time the play is well-structured and temperate in plot, character, and language. Through the character of Malevole, Marston probes the moral complexities of the human condition by dramatically juxtaposing neo-stoicism with worldy epicureanism. The play's Induction reveals that the King's Men stole it from the Children of Blackfriars in response to their theft of *The First Part of Jeronimo*. While *The Malcontent* was clearly influenced by Shakespeare's *Measure for Measure*, and particularly by *Hamlet*, it was also performed at the Globe, and the title role of Malevole was played by Shakespeare's Hamlet, Richard Burbage.

After *The Malcontent*, *The Dutch Courtesan* is perhaps Marston's next best work. It is a very entertaining comedy dealing again with complex moral values, in particular the relationship of love and lust, set against a colourful city background of prostitutes, rakes, and mountebanks. The satire in *Parasitaster; or, The Fawn* is to a large degree directed against James I and his Court: flattering and deluded courtiers, corrupting and corrupted governors. The Fawn's speeches expose the moral vacuum in this society, but the play ends on a reconciliatory note with a masque that acknowledges both the "Ship of Fools" and the "Parliament of Cupid." These two comedies are more epicurean than Marston's earlier works.

Marston's part in the collaborative *Eastward Ho* with Ben Jonson and George Chapman is generally accepted as the entirety of the first act, as well as various parts throughout the play, though it is difficult to determine his specific authorship beyond this point. The play is a delightful parody of the "citizen comedy" tradition that was so popular on the London stage in the first decade of the seventeenth century. Several references to the Scots proved objectionable enough to James to result in the imprisonment of Chapman and Jonson, though Marston apparently escaped.

In his preface to *The Fawn*, Marston observes that comedies are "writ to be spoken, not read" because they consist solely in action. He wrote *The Wonder of Women; or, The Tragedy of Sophonisba*, however, as a tragedy that "shall boldly abide the most curious perusal." While sensation and spectacle abound, the highminded rhetoric in such an austere Roman tragedy demands our close reading, or "curious perusal." The play is often quite moving, and the moral dichotomy in this classical world is presented in great earnest, though there is little memorable action. Contrasted with the Stoic integrity of Sophonisba is the pathological lust of the heroine in Marston's unfinished play, *The Insatiate Countess*. Marston presumably left the various plots and characters in the play unresolved when he was sent to prison in 1608, though his hand is traceable in the 1613 edition completed by William Barksted.

Recent criticism has begun to acknowledge the considerable range and variety of Marston's dramatic works. His bold experimentation and unique characterization, particularly in the *Antonio* plays and *The Malcontent*, were completely new to Elizabethan audiences. Studies of the individual plays reveal a dramatic craftsmanship and originality that liberate him from his contemporary reputation as Kinsayder, "pissing against the world." There are many aspects of Marston's life and writings that deserve further critical analysis. His greater defects are very apparent, but T. S. Eliot's observation is still true: "for both scholars and critics he remains a territory of unexplored riches and risks."

—Raymond C. Shady

MARTYN, Edward (Joseph).   Irish.   Born in Galway, 31 January 1859. Educated at Christ Church, Oxford, left without taking a degree. Settled in Dublin, and began to write for the theatre, 1899; Co-Founder, with William Butler Yeats and Lady Gregory, Irish Literary Theatre, 1899, which became the Abbey Theatre, Dublin, 1904; Founder, Palestrina Society, Dublin, 1901; left the Irish Literary Theatre after a quarrel with Yeats, 1902, and abandoned the theatre for the next decade; returned to the theatre when he began writing plays for the Independent Theatre Company, from 1912; founded the Irish Theatre, to present plays in Gaelic, 1914. *Died 5 December 1923.*

PUBLICATIONS

Plays

The Heather Field (produced 1899).   In *The Heather Field, and Maeve,* 1899.
Maeve (produced 1900).   1899.
The Tale of a Town, and An Enchanted Sea.   1902.
The Place-Hunters, in *Leader,* 26 July 1902.
Romulus and Remus.   1907.
Grangecolman (produced 1912).   1912.
The Dream Physician (produced 1914).   1918.
Privilege of Place (produced 1915).
Regina Eyre (produced 1919).

Fiction

Morgante the Lesser, His Notorious Life and Wonderful Deeds.   1890.

Reading List: *Martyn and the Irish Revival* by Denis R. Gwynn, 1930; *Martyn and the Irish Theatre* by Marie-T. Courtney, 1956.

*   *   *

Edward Martyn was one of the founders of the Irish Literary Theatre, which performed his *The Heather Field* as its second production in 1899. The declared aim of the Literary Theatre was to break with the crude sensationalism of commercial theatre. By appealing to the intellect and spirit it would furnish a vehicle for the literary expression of the national thought and ideals of Ireland. This was the movement which, under the inspiration of W. B. Yeats and Lady Gregory, was to lead to the foundation of the Abbey Theatre, and to the work of Synge and O'Casey.

Although the theme of *The Heather Field* is Irish (it describes the infatuated attempt of Carden Tyrrel to reclaim waste land for agriculture), the main influence upon Martyn was Ibsen. He follows closely Ibsen's attempts to introduce poetic and symbolic elements within a naturalistic setting. In *Maeve* the heroine proves a reincarnation of an ancient Irish queen, and in *An Enchanted Sea* the sinister deities of the ocean bring tragedy to an old family. Partly because of his concern with the life of the middle and upper classes, Martyn broke from the Abbey Theatre which had become preoccupied with peasant plays and heroic fantasies, and he satirised Yeats and his circle in *Romulus and Remus* and *The Dream Physician.*

Although Martyn associated with figures in the Irish political movement such as Constance Markievicz and Thomas MacDonagh, his national idealism is haunted by the shades of Pater (whose early influence he had felt at Oxford – especially the essay on Winckelmann), and it was the hard gemlike flame of intellectual abstraction his plays seek to kindle. Lord Mask's praise of Ireland in *An Enchanted Sea* may serve an example: "Here in the Insula Sacra – the Ogygia of Homer and our Hellenic ancestors – the genius is here and will soon awaken, and he will revive arts, and trades, and letters in our ancient tongue which all will speak again. Let us be ready to minister." Besides generously patronising theatre in Ireland, Martyn was active also in his support of music, the Catholic Church, and the Gaelic League.

—Malcolm Kelsall

MASON, Bruce (Edward George). New Zealander. Born in Wellington, 28 September 1921. Educated at Takapuna Grammar School, Auckland; Wellington Boys' College; Victoria University College, now Victoria University of Wellington, B.A. 1945. Served in the New Zealand Army, 1941–45; Royal New Zealand Naval Volunteer Reserve, 1943–45: Sub-Lieutenant. Married Dr. Diana Manby Shaw in 1945; one son and two daughters. Research Assistant, War History Branch, Wellington, 1946–48; Assistant Curator of Manuscripts, Alexander Turnbull Library, Wellington, 1948–49; travelled in Europe, 1949–51; Public Relations Officer, New Zealand Forest Service, Wellington, 1951–57; Radio Critic, 1955–61, Record Critic, 1961–62, and Music Critic, 1964–69, *New Zealand Listener*, Wellington; Senior Journalist, *Tourist and Publicity*, Wellington, 1957–58; Drama Critic, *Dominion*, Wellington, 1958–60; Editor, *Te Ao Hou* (Maori Affairs), Wellington, 1960–61; Editor, *Act*, Wellington, 1967–70; Senior Copywriter, Wood and Mitchell Advertising, Wellington, 1969–71. President, Secretary, and Committee Member, Unity Theatre, Wellington, 1948–60. New Zealand Delegate, International Drama Conference, Edinburgh, 1963. Full-time actor, producer and director: has directed first productions of most of his own plays, operas for the New Zealand Opera Company, and revues for the Unity Theatre and Downstage, Wellington; has appeared in his own plays for solo actor, in New Zealand, England, and the United States. Recipient: British Drama League Playwriting Competition Prize, five times; Auckland Festival Society National Playwriting Competition Prize, 1958; State Literary Fund Scholarship in Letters, 1973. Lives in Wellington.

PUBLICATIONS

Plays

The Bonds of Love (produced 1953).
The Evening Paper (produced 1953).
The Verdict (produced 1955).
The Licensed Victualler, music by Mason (produced 1955).
A Case in Point (produced 1956).
Wit's End (revue; produced 1956).
The Light Enlarging (produced 1957).
Birds in the Wilderness (produced 1957).
The Pohutukawa Tree (produced 1957). 1960.

The End of the Golden Weather (produced 1960).   1962.
We Don't Want Your Sort Here, music by Mason (cabaret; produced 1961).
Awatea (broadcast 1964; produced 1968).   1969.
Swan Song (broadcast 1964; produced 1965).
The Hand on the Rail (broadcast 1964; produced 1965).
The Counsels of the Wood (produced 1965).
The Waters of Silence, from a work by Vercors (produced 1965).
Hongi (broadcast 1967; produced 1968).   In *Contemporary New Zealand Plays,* edited
     by Howard McNaughton, 1974.
Zero Inn (produced 1970).   1970.
Not Christmas, But Guy Fawkes (produced 1976).
Courting Blackbird (produced 1976).

Radio Plays: *The Cherry Orchard,* from a play by Chekhov, 1960; *Awatea,* 1964; *Swan Song,* 1964; *The Hand on the Rail,* 1965; *Hongi,* 1967.

Verse

We Don't Want Your Sort Here: A Collection of Light Verse.   1963.

Other

Theatre in Danger, with John Pocock.   1957.
New Zealand Drama: A Parade of Forms and a History.   1972.

Reading List: *Mason* by Howard McNaughton, 1975.

*   *   *

The artistic career of Bruce Mason reflects, in its breadth, the resourcefulness which until recently has been essential to the professional artist in New Zealand. While his earliest short stories were establishing his literary reputation in the late 1940's, he was already gaining the intimate knowledge of all aspects of stage production that was to enable him to write, direct, and act in most of his early plays, in the 1950's. *The Bonds of Love, The Evening Paper,* and *The Verdict* brought a new intensity and severity to New Zealand realistic drama, while *The Light Enlarging* and the full-length *Birds in the Wilderness* educated audiences to subtleties of stylised comedy. The constrictions of domestic drama, however, proved increasingly frustrating to a writer with more epic propensities, and an expansion of professional production resources on both radio and stage stimulated Mason into his most ambitious series of plays, the five dramas on Maori themes.

The Pohutukawa Tree quickly became famous through stage, radio, and television productions, and remains the seminal dramatic portrayal of the corrosion between Maori and European culture. Other plays offer a more optimistic resolution to such an issue, all of them written for radio in 1964–5: the controversial *Awatea,* conceived on a scale as grand as that of *The Pohutukawa Tree, Swan Song,* a more stylised treatment of the cultural impasse, and *The Hand on the Rail,* an intimate study of the tensions within a bicultural family. Reverting to a more pessimistic tone, *Hongi* is a historical drama with a highly resonant core of ethnic pageantry. All of these later Maori plays have also been radically reshaped and rescripted for the stage, but their production has been limited because they were originally written with lead parts for the great Maori bass singer, the late Inia Te Wiata; only *Awatea* is familiar to theatre audiences, and more subtle plays like *The Hand on the Rail* and *Hongi* have been undeservedly neglected.

Mason's most dramatically innovative work, however, lies in his plays for solo actor. Initially inspired by Emlyn Williams's Dickens performances, he wrote and performed *The End of the Golden Weather*, a study of New Zealand boyhood; between 1959 and 1962 he was engaged in extensive internal tours, and after appearances in London, at the Edinburgh Festival, and in the U.S.A., the popularity of the work is unabated. In 1965, he extended his solo repertoire with *The Counsels of the Wood* and *The Waters of Silence* (adapted from Vercors); though the more exotic content of these works has limited their stage popularity, he has combined them under the title of *Men of Soul* and continues to present the programme during his larger seasons. For his two most recent solo works, both premiered in 1976, Mason has returned to New Zealand material; *Not Christmas, But Guy Fawkes* is based on some of his own short stories and autobiographical pieces, while *Courting Blackbird* is a swift-moving, well-integrated, highly comic anecdotal piece about an expatriate eccentric.

Since the Maori works, Mason's output of plays has been limited, with only *Zero Inn* (1970) making an impact on the stage. His solo theatre, however, has flourished, and his tours continue to be among the most remarkable feats of sustained creativity that the New Zealand stage has seen.

—Howard McNaughton

MASSINGER, Philip. English. Born in Salisbury, Wiltshire, baptized 24 November 1583. Educated at St. Alban Hall, Oxford, 1602–06, left without taking a degree. Married; possibly had children. Settled in London, 1606, and quickly gained a reputation as a playwright; collaborated with Field, Daborne, Tourneur, and Dekker, and regularly with Fletcher, 1613–25; wrote for the King's Men, 1613–23, and the Cockpit Company, 1623–25; after Fletcher's death in 1625 rejoined the King's Men as their chief writer and continued to write for them until his death. *Died* (buried) *18 March 1640.*

PUBLICATIONS

Collections

> *Plays and Poems* (excludes those plays written with Beaumont and Fletcher), edited by Philip Edwards and Colin Gibson. 5 vols., 1976; *Selected Plays* (includes *A New Way to Pay Old Debts, The City Madam, The Duke of Milan, The Roman Actor*), edited by Gibson, 1978.

Plays

> *The Queen of Corinth,* with Fletcher and Nathan Field (produced 1616–17?). In *Comedies and Tragedies* by Beaumont and Fletcher, 1647.
> *The Knight of Malta,* with Fletcher and Nathan Field (produced 1616–19?). In *Comedies and Tragedies* by Beaumont and Fletcher, 1647.

The Fatal Dowry, with Nathan Field (produced 1616–19?). 1632.

Sir John Van Olden Barnavelt, with Fletcher (produced 1619). Edited by A. H. Bullen, in *A Collection of Old English Plays 2*, 1883; edited by W. P. Frijlinck, 1922.

The Custom of the Country, with Fletcher (produced 1619–20?). In *Comedies and Tragedies* by Beaumont and Fletcher, 1647.

The Little French Lawyer, with Fletcher (produced 1619–23?). In *Comedies and Tragedies*, by Beaumont and Fletcher, 1647.

The Virgin Martyr, with Dekker (produced 1620?). 1622; edited by Fredson Bowers, in *Dramatic Works of Dekker*, 1958.

The False One, with Fletcher (produced 1620?). In *Comedies and Tragedies* by Beaumont and Fletcher, 1647.

Thierry, King of France, and His Brother Theodoret, with Fletcher (produced ?). 1621; edited by Robert K. Turner, Jr., in *Dramatic Works in the Beaumont and Fletcher Canon 3*, 1976.

The Maid of Honour (produced 1621?). 1632.

The Double Marriage, with Fletcher (produced 1621?). In *Comedies and Tragedies* by Beaumont and Fletcher, 1647.

The Duke of Milan (produced 1621–22?). 1623.

A New Way to Pay Old Debts (produced 1621–22?). 1633.

The Unnatural Combat (produced 1621–25?). 1639.

The Spanish Curate, with Fletcher (produced 1622?). In *Comedies and Tragedies* by Beaumont and Fletcher, 1647.

The Beggars' Bush, with Fletcher (produced 1622). In *Comedies and Tragedies* by Beaumont and Fletcher, 1647; edited by Fredson Bowers, in *Dramatic Works in the Beaumont and Fletcher Canon 3*, 1976.

The Sea Voyage, with Fletcher (produced 1622). In *Comedies and Tragedies* by Beaumont and Fletcher, 1647.

The Prophetess, with Fletcher (produced 1622). In *Comedies and Tragedies* by Beaumont and Fletcher, 1647.

The Bondman: An Ancient Story (produced 1623). 1624.

The Parliament of Love (produced 1624). Edited by William Gifford, 1805.

The Renegado (produced 1624). 1630.

The Elder Brother, with Fletcher (produced 1625?). 1637.

Fair Maid of the Inn, with Fletcher (produced 1625–26?). In *Comedies and Tragedies* by Beaumont and Fletcher, 1647.

The Roman Actor (produced 1626). 1629.

The Great Duke of Florence (produced 1627?). 1636.

The Picture (produced 1629). 1630.

The Emperor of the East (produced 1631). 1632.

Believe As You List (produced 1631). Edited by T. C. Croaker, 1849.

The City Madam (produced 1632?). 1658.

The Guardian (produced 1633). In *Three New Plays*, 1655.

The Bashful Lover (produced 1633–37?). In *Three New Plays*, 1655.

A Very Woman; or, The Prince of Tarent, with Fletcher (produced 1634). In *Three New Plays*, 1655.

Love's Cure; or, The Martial Maid, with Fletcher (produced ?). In *Comedies and Tragedies* by Beaumont and Fletcher, 1647; edited by George Walton Williams, in *Dramatic Works in the Beaumont and Fletcher Canon 3*, 1976.

Bibliography: *Massinger: A Concise Bibliography* by S. A. Tannenbaum, 1938; supplement in *Elizabethan Bibliographies Supplements 8* by C. A. Pennel and W. P. Williams, 1968.

Reading List: *Massinger* by Alfred H. Cruickshank, 1920; *Massinger and Fletcher: A*

Comparison by Henri J. Makkink, 1927; *Massinger, The Man and the Playwright* by Thomas A. Dunn, 1957; *Massinger and His Associates* by Donald S. Lawless. 1967.

*   *   *

Together with his older contemporary Thomas Middleton, Philip Massinger shares the distinction of being the boldest Jacobean dramatist in his dealings with controversial religious and political questions of the day, at a time when such boldness incurred official displeasure which was often expressed in terms more severe than mere censorship. He began his dramatic career as part of a group of playwrights working for Philip Henslowe, and his earliest plays were written in collaboration with John Fletcher and Nathan Field. The first play to carry his name on the title page was *The Virgin Martyr* (1622), of which he was joint author with Thomas Dekker. Already Massinger's unorthodox religious and political attitudes can be seen in his sympathetic portrayal of Catholicism at a time when the general temper was fiercely anti-Catholic. Later, in *The Renegado* he makes a Jesuit priest the most admirable character in the play. In 1630 the censor refused to allow the performance of *Believe As You List* because of its strongly anti-Spanish bias, whereupon Massinger changed the setting from modern Spain and Portugal to ancient Asia and classical Rome, an alteration which fooled the censor but not apparently the audience. In *The Maid of Honour* Charles I's brother-in-law, Frederick V, Elector Palatine, was the object of attack, while *The Bondman* satirized the powerful George Villiers, Duke of Buckingham, an enemy of Massinger's patron Philip Herbert, Earl of Montgomery.

The first play known to be entirely Massinger's work is *The Duke of Milan*, a work which has many resemblances to *Othello*. Massinger's debt to Shakespeare is visible throughout his work, and it has even been suggested that it was Massinger and not John Fletcher who collaborated with Shakespeare in *Henry VIII* and *The Two Noble Kinsmen*.

Massinger himself regarded his tragedy *The Roman Actor* as his finest dramatic work: "I ever held it the most perfit birth of my Minerva." Posterity has not agreed with him. The only two plays by Massinger which have survived into the modern repertory are *A New Way to Pay Old Debts* and *The City Madam*. Both are comedies and the first is undoubtedly a masterpiece. Its plot is based on Middleton's *A Trick to Catch the Old One* written twenty years earlier, but there is nothing in Middleton's play to match the central character Sir Giles Overreach, a usurer, extortioner, and rack-renter of monstrous proportions based on an actual historical figure, Sir Giles Mompesson. The sheer demonic energy of Overreach threatens to swamp the conventional romantic plot through which he blusters his way. It is not surprising that the celebrated nineteenth-century actor Edmund Kean had one of his greatest successes in this role, as did Donald Wolfit in the twentieth century.

The City Madam is also based on an earlier play, *Eastward Ho* by Chapman, Jonson and Marston. Here again Massinger has created a monster of capacity in the character of Luke Frugal. Both plays are savage satires against the pretensions of the new city rich whom Massinger depicted as destroying the traditional virtues which he saw in the hereditary landed aristocracy and which, in his view, kept society ordered and stable.

In addition to the plays already mentioned, Massinger also wrote several romantic tragi-comedies, the best of them *The Beggars' Bush* (1622) in collaboration with Fletcher. His was the finest satirical dramatic talent in the years immediately before the curtain came down on the theatres in 1642.

—Gãmini Salgãdo

MAUGHAM, W(illiam) Somerset. English. Born in Paris, 25 January 1874, of English parents. Educated at King's School, Canterbury, Kent, 1887–91; University of Heidelberg, 1891–92; studied medicine at St. Thomas's Hospital, London, 1892–97; interned in Lambeth London; qualified as a surgeon, L.R.C.P., M.R.C.S., 1897, but never practised. Served with the Red Cross Ambulance Unit, later with the British Intelligence Corps, in World War I. Married Syrie Barnardo Wellcome in 1915 (divorced, 1927); one daughter. Writer from 1896; lived abroad, mainly in Paris, 1897–1907; successful dramatist for the London stage, 1907–33; travelled widely during the 1920's, in the South Seas, Malaya, and China; lived at Cap Ferrat in the south of France from 1928; lived in the United States during World War II; instituted annual prize for promising young British writer, 1947. D.Litt.: Oxford University; University of Toulouse. Fellow, and Companion of Literature, 1961, Royal Society of Literature. Commander, Legion of Honour; Honorary Senator, University of Heidelberg; Honorary Fellow, Library of Congress, Washington, D.C.; Honorary Member, National Institute of Arts and Letters. Companion of Honour, 1954. *Died 16 December 1965.*

PUBLICATIONS

Plays

Marriages Are Made in Heaven (as *Schiffbrüchig*, produced 1902). Published in *Venture*, 1903.
A Man of Honour (produced 1903). 1903.
Mademoiselle Zampa (produced 1904).
Lady Frederick (produced 1907). 1912.
Jack Straw (produced 1908). 1911.
Mrs. Dot (produced 1908). 1912.
The Explorer: A Melodrama (produced 1908). 1912.
Penelope (produced 1909). 1912.
The Noble Spaniard, from a work by Ernest Grenet-Dancourt (produced 1909). 1953.
Smith (produced 1909). 1913.
The Tenth Man (produced 1910). 1913.
Landed Gentry (as *Grace*, produced 1910). 1913.
Loaves and Fishes (produced 1911). 1924.
A Trip to Brighton, from a play by Abel Tarride (produced 1911).
The Perfect Gentleman, from a play by Molière (produced 1913). Published in *Theatre Arts*, November 1955.
The Land of Promise (produced 1913). 1913.
The Unattainable (as *Caroline*, produced 1916). 1923.
Our Betters (produced 1917). 1923.
Love in a Cottage (produced 1918).
Caesar's Wife (produced 1919). 1922.
Home and Beauty (produced 1919; as *Too Many Husbands*, produced 1919). 1923.
The Unknown (produced 1920). 1920.
The Circle (produced 1921). 1921.
East of Suez (produced 1922). 1922.
The Camel's Back (produced 1923).
The Constant Wife (produced 1926). 1927.
The Letter, from his own story (produced 1927). 1927.
The Sacred Flame (produced 1928). 1928.
The Bread-Winner (produced 1930). 1930.
Dramatic Works. 6 vols., 1931–34; as *Collected Plays,* 3 vols., 1952.

For Services Rendered (produced 1932).   1932.
The Mask and the Face: A Satire, from a play by Luigi Chiarelli (produced 1933).
Sheppey (produced 1933).   1933.
Trio: Stories and Screen Adaptations, with R. C. Sherriff and Noel Langley.   1950.

Screenplay: *The Verger,* in *Trio,* 1950.

Fiction

Liza of Lambeth.   1897; revised edition, 1904.
The Making of a Saint.   1898.
Orientations (stories).   1899.
The Hero.   1901.
Mrs. Craddock.   1902.
The Merry-Go-Round.   1904.
The Bishop's Apron: A Study in the Origins of a Great Family.   1906.
The Explorer.   1907.
The Magician.   1908.
Of Human Bondage.   1915.
The Moon and Sixpence.   1919.
The Trembling of the Leaf: Little Stories of the South Sea Islands.   1921; as *Sadie Thompson and Other Stories,* 1928; as *Rain and Other Stories,* 1933.
The Painted Veil.   1925.
The Casuarina Tree: Six Stories.   1926; as *The Letter: Stories of Crime,* 1930.
Ashenden; or, The British Agent.   1928.
Cakes and Ale; or, The Skeleton in the Cupboard.   1930.
Six Stories Written in the First Person Singular.   1931.
The Book-Bag.   1932.
The Narrow Corner.   1932.
Ah King: Six Stories.   1933.
The Judgement Seat (story).   1934.
East and West: The Collected Short Stories.   1934; as *Altogether,* 1934.
Cosmopolitans (stories).   1936.
Favorite Short Stories.   1937.
Theatre.   1937.
Princess September and the Nightingale (juvenile).   1939.
The Round Dozen (stories).   1939.
Christmas Holiday.   1939.
The Mixture as Before: Short Stories.   1940; as *Great Stories of Love and Intrigue,* 1947.
Up at the Villa.   1941.
The Hour Before the Dawn.   1942.
The Unconquered (story).   1944.
The Razor's Edge.   1944.
Then and Now.   1946.
Creatures of Circumstance: Short Stories.   1947.
Catalina: A Romance.   1948.
East of Suez: Great Stories of the Tropics.   1948.
Here and There (stories).   1948.
Complete Short Stories.   3 vols., 1951.
The World Over: Stories of Manifold Places and People.   1952.
Selected Novels.   3 vols., 1953.
Best Short Stories, edited by John Beecroft.   1957.

Malaysian Stories, edited by Anthony Burgess. 1969.
Seventeen Lost Stories, edited by Craig V. Showalter. 1969.

Other

The Land of the Blessed Virgin: Sketches and Impressions of Andalusia. 1905.
On a Chinese Screen. 1922.
The Gentleman in the Parlour: A Record of a Journey from Rangoon to Haiphong. 1930.
Non-Dramatic Works. 28 vols., 1934–69.
Don Fernando; or, Variations on Some Spanish Themes. 1935.
My South Sea Island. 1936.
The Summing Up. 1938.
Books and You. 1940.
France at War. 1940.
Strictly Personal. 1941.
The Somerset Maugham Sampler, edited by Jerome Weidman. 1943; as *The Somerset Maughan Pocket Book*, 1944.
Great Novelists and Their Novels: Essays on the Ten Greatest Novels of the World and the Men and Women Who Wrote Them. 1948; revised edition, as *Ten Novels and Their Authors*, 1954; as *The Art of Fiction*, 1955.
A Writer's Notebook. 1949.
The Maugham Reader, edited by Glenway Wescott. 1950.
The Vagrant Mood: Six Essays. 1952.
Mr. Maugham Himself, edited by John Beecroft. 1954.
The Partial View (includes *The Summing Up* and *A Writer's Notebook*). 1954.
The Travel Books. 1955.
Points of View. 1958.
Purely for Pleasure. 1962.
Selected Prefaces and Introductions. 1963.
Essays on Literature. 1967.

Editor, with Laurence Housman, *Venture: An Annual of Art and Literature.* 2 vols., 1903–05.
Editor, *The Truth at Last*, by Charles Hawtrey. 1924.
Editor, *The Travellers' Library.* 1933; as *Fifty Modern English Writers*, 1933.
Editor, *Tellers of Tales: 100 Short Stories.* 1939; as *The Greatest Stories of All Time*, 1943.
Editor, *A Choice of Kipling's Prose.* 1952; as *Maugham's Choice of Kipling's Best: Sixteen Stories*, 1953.

Bibliography: *A Bibliography of the Works of Maugham* by Raymond Toole Stott, 1956; revised edition, 1973.

Reading List: *The Maugham Enigma*, 1954, and *The World of Maugham*, 1959, both edited by K. W. Jonas; *Maugham* by J. Brophy, revised edition, 1958; *Maugham: A Candid Portrait* by K. G. Pfeiffer, 1959; *Maugham: A Guide* by Laurence Brander, 1963; *The Two Worlds of Maugham* by W. Menard, 1965; *Maugham* by M. K. Naik, 1966; *The Dramatic Comedy of Maugham* by R. E. Barnes, 1968; *Maugham: A Biographical and Critical Study* by R. A. Cordell, revised edition, 1969; *Maugham and the Quest for Freedom* by Robert L. Calder, 1972; *The Pattern of Maugham: A Critical Portrait*, 1974, and *Maugham*, 1977, both by Anthony Curtis; *Maugham and His World* by Frederic Raphael, 1976.

"Every writer who has any sense," said Somerset Maugham in a press interview, "writes about the circumstances in which he himself has lived. What else can he write about with authority?" That statement is well illustrated by the closeness with which a long and varied life is reflected in Maugham's equally versatile achievement as short-story writer, novelist, dramatist, critic, essayist, and autobiographer. Upbringing in Paris and an early familiarity with the work of the French naturalists profoundly influenced his style and method, giving him a classical sense of form, lucidity, and Gallic detachment of attitude to human frailty and the ironies of existence. Later experiences as a medical student in London provided material for a realistic portrayal of slum life in his first novel, *Liza of Lambeth*, and, as a British intelligence agent during the First World War, for the Ashenden stories. Above all Maugham's extensive foreign travels, in search of new backgrounds and ways of life, proved inexhaustibly fruitful. He paints exotic Eastern scenes with economy and exactitude; and observes a wealth of bizarre incident and human idiosyncrasy – on liners, in clubs, in the bungalows of the white man in the tropics, where passions are stripped of the masks of conformity and convention demanded by more civilized communities – with amused tolerance and an unerring eye for the significant detail. Unlike his contemporaries Bennett, Galsworthy, and Wells, Maugham was not interested in fiction as the vehicle of social criticism. Savouring instead the singularity, paradox, and sheer unexpectedness of individual lives, he proclaimed his subject, in his short stories, novels, and plays alike, "the personal drama of human relationships."

Maugham's career as a dramatist spanned three decades, beginning with *A Man of Honour* in 1903 and ending in 1933 with *Sheppey*. His comedies of manners in the tradition of Oscar Wilde were less immediately successful than his fiction. Within a year of the production of *Lady Frederick* in 1907, however, he was rivalling the popularity of Shaw with four plays running in London. Such caustic, wittily satirical portrayals of elegant society as *Home and Beauty*, *The Circle*, *Our Betters*, and *The Bread-Winner*, with their dexterous craftsmanship and sparkling epigrammatic dialogue, continued to enjoy a steady stage success.

Maugham's achievement as a novelist is distinctly uneven. The authenticity of deep feeling in perhaps his most popular work, the long autobiographical *Of Human Bondage*, is vitiated by prolixity and that sentimentality which in many of his short stories masquerades as cynicism. In *The Razor's Edge*, written when he was over seventy, and *Catalina*, he is perceptibly out of his native element in ambitious explorations of uncharacteristic themes. The moral confusions and simplifications, lapses in taste, and overall implausibility in these novels show Maugham less at ease as an anatomist of spiritual struggles and values than in his accustomed role of shrewd and worldy observer of his fellow men. Essentially a master of shorter forms of fiction, he makes far greater impact in *The Moon and Sixpence*, based on the career of Gauguin, and *Cakes and Ale*, his own favourite. This astringent picture of London literary life introduces thinly disguised, maliciously acute portraits of two eminent contemporaries; and the engaging personality of Rosie, the maternal, warm-hearted barmaid, is in a clear line of descent from an earlier Maugham heroine, Liza. In its narrative expertise, perception, and credibility of characterization, *Cakes and Ale* is indisputably Maugham's most completely realized novel.

But it is in the short story form that his individual gifts are most satisfyingly exemplified. Temperamentally and technically out of tune with Chekhov and his methods, Maugham from the first made Maupassant his model. His avowed aim was the "compact, dramatic story," tightly knit, sharply characterized, ending "with a fullstop rather than a straggle of dots," which could hold the attention of listeners over a dinner-table or in a ship's smoking room. To this end he developed with consummate skill the device of the narrator: his own urbane, ubiquitous presence, as ringside spectator rather than active participant, lending his tales the heightened verisimilitude of the conversational eye-witness account. Maugham's factual first-person narratives not only invest with veracity what might otherwise seem incredible (as he cunningly allows at the opening of "The Kite"); the deliberate tone of dry understatement intensifies by contrast the violent, often tragic events related by this suave, unobtrusive commentator. Sometimes, indeed, his "shock" climax seems calculated enough

393

to be over-simplified and superficial. Compared with the psychological penetration and compassion in a story like Maupassant's "Boule de Suif," Maugham's situations and characterization lack subtlety and depth. His ironical revelations can be more effective in such lighter vein as the delectable disclosure of "The Colonel's Lady."

One of Maugham's favourite and most typical themes, in his sardonic clinical diagnoses of human folly in "Before the Party," "The Door of Opportunity," "The Lion's Skin," and many other stories, is the disillusioning disparity between the outward appearances of a relationship and its underlying reality. Not only amorous frailty is relentlessly exposed, but also the humbug of moral conventions and literary pretentiousness. Yet Maugham never explicitly moralizes. He presents life, as he sees it, dispassionately: almost – for his very lack of comment can carry its own acid implication. His cool, fastidious detachment is that of the outsider remote from the complexities and disasters of ordinary living. Disarmingly aware of his own limitations, both personal and literary, he acknowledges in his autobiographies his lack of that emotional warmth and sympathetic involvement which would, as he says, have given his work "intimacy, the broad human touch."

Maugham saw himself primarily as an entertainer; and he was indeed a supremely successful one, with his work broadcast, televised, filmed, and translated into many languages. In the light of his serious lifelong dedication to the writer's craft, he felt he had been consistently undervalued by the "intellectual" critics. Certainly his reputation has always stood higher abroad than in England; but an appreciative world-wide readership has made him possibly the most popular storyteller who has ever lived.

—Margaret Willy

MAY, Thomas. English. Born in Mayfield, Sussex, in 1595. Educated at Sidney Sussex College, Cambridge (fellow-commoner), 1609–12, B.A. 1612; entered Gray's Inn, London, 1615. Settled in London; gave up the law because of a speech defect, and turned to literature; enjoyed patronage of Charles I, but was disappointed in his hopes for preferment and later supported the parliamentary cause during the civil war: served as Secretary of the Parliament, 1646 until his death. *Died 13 November 1650.*

PUBLICATIONS

Plays

> *The Heir* (produced before 1620). 1622; edited by W. C. Hazlitt, in *Dodsley's Old Plays,* 1875.
> *Cleopatra Queen of Egypt* (produced 1626). 1639.
> *Antigone, The Theban Princess* (produced 1627–31?). 1631.
> *Julia Agrippina, Empress of Rome* (produced 1628). 1639; edited by F. Ernst Schmid, in *Bang's Materialen,* 1914.
> *The Old Couple* (produced 1636). 1658; edited by M. Simplicia Fitzgibbons, 1943.

Verse

> *Lucan's Pharsalia.* 1626; with *A Continuation till the Death of Julius Caesar,* by May, 1630.

The Reign of King Henry the Second. 1633.
The Victorious Reign of King Edward the Third. 1635.

Other

A Discourse Concerning the Success of Former Parliaments. 1642.
The Character of a Right Malignant. 1644.
The Lord George Digby's Cabinet and Dr. Goff's Negotiations. 1646.
The History of the Parliament [of] 1640. 1647; edited by F. Maseres, 1812.
The Changeable Covenant. 1650.
A Breviary of the History of the Parliament of England (in Latin and English). 1650.

Translator, *Virgil's Georgics.* 1628.
Translator, *Selected Epigrams of Martial.* 1629.
Translator, *Barclay His Argenis* (verse sections only). 1629.
Translator, *The Mirror of Minds; or, Icon Animorum,* by Barclay. 1631.

Reading List: *May, Man of Letters* by Allan Griffith Chester, 1932.

*   *   *

A solid classicist, and at his best as a translator, Thomas May wrote poetry both English and Latin, comedies, tragedies, and prose history. His most substantial achievement is his translation of Lucan's *Pharsalia* in heroic couplets; Ben Jonson, in verses "To my chosen Friend, the learned Translator," praises Lucan and May as exhibiting "the self-same genius." Subsequently May himself continued Lucan's unfinished poem with seven additional books in both English and Latin versions – an ambitious project carried out with a competence that gained him something of a reputation on the Continent. The successful Lucan, which was admired by Charles I, led directly ("by His Majesty's Command") to two original "historical poems" in English heroic couplets, *The Reign of King Henry the Second* and *The Victorious Reign of King Edward the Third,* in seven books each. Both poems have epic pretensions, with formal invocations and supernatural machinery; there is even a vision of the future which extends to the renowned Charles, "A King in virtue as in Royalty." For all the heroic trappings, May does not succeed in making the action in either poem amount to much more than versified chronicle. In a prose note he suggests that Henry II's life may be looked at as a five-act tragedy, but the suggestion seems stillborn.

May's two comedies take Jonson as their main model, but *The Heir* pays tribute to Shakespeare as well with a comic Watch and a Constable who might as well be named Dogberry – "For your better destruction, I will deride my speech into two parts" – and a pair of lovers whose marriage will reconcile their two warring houses. *The Old Couple,* with less complex a plot but more skilful dramatic writing, draws on a long tradition of usury comedy. Much of the action involves the "old miserly niggard" Earthworm, but the title-roles are those of Sir Argent Scrape and Lady Covet, each eager for marriage in hope of inheriting the other's wealth. Thus touched by Cupid's golden-headed arrow, they court each other from invalid chairs; both are deaf; she is eighty years old, and he ninety-five. A happy ending shows avarice foiled and Earthworm reformed.

May's three tragedies, *Antigone, Cleopatra,* and *Julia Agrippina,* are respectable learned drama which echo both Seneca and the Jonson of the Roman plays. He shows some originality in his manipulation of the three actions, and for the *Cleopatra* draws upon Plutarch quite independently of Shakespeare.

The King had called May "my poet," but during the conflicts of the 1640's it was as "Secretary for the Parliament" that he published his *History* of that body. He professes to

DRAMATISTS

offer a "plain and naked discourse" with truth as its sole object, but in spite of occasional refusal to pass judgment he is hardly even-handed in his reporting of events, in which he incorporates a glowing personal tribute to Oliver Cromwell. The classical bent of his earlier writings is recognisable in the way that he explains his own times by analogy with ancient history: London had no walls "but such as old Sparta used for their guard, the hearts of courageous citizens," and Lucan and Claudian are made to comment on the Earl of Strafford.

—Rhodes Dunlap

MAYNE, Jasper. English. Born in Hatherleigh, Devon, baptized 23 November 1604. Educated at Westminster School, London; Christ Church, Oxford, matriculated 1623, student 1627, B.A. 1628, M.A. 1631, B.D. 1642, D.D. 1646. Ordained: given college living of Cassington, near Woodstock, 1639; because of his Royalist views, deprived of his studentship and living at Cassington, 1648; Rector of Pyrton, Oxfordshire, 1648 until he was ejected, 1656; maintained by the Earl of Devonshire in late 1650's; after the Restoration returned to his benefices, and appointed canon of Christ Church, archdeacon of Chichester, and chaplain-in-ordinary to the king. *Died 6 December 1672.*

PUBLICATIONS

Plays

The City Match (produced 1637–38?). 1639; edited by W. C. Halitt, in *Dodsley's Old Plays,* 1875.
The Amorous War (produced 1628–48?). 1648.

Verse

To the Duke of York on Our Late Sea-Fight. 1665.

Other

Certain Sermons and Letters. 1653.

Translator, *Part of Lucian Made English.* 1664.

Reading List: *The Sons of Ben: Jonsonian Comedy in Caroline England* by J. L. Davis, 1967.

*   *   *

Jasper Mayne's extant works consist of two plays, a handful of poems, and several sermons. The sermons, which reveal him as a reasonable, charitable man, have no literary merit; their only interest for the purposes of this essay lies in the awareness Mayne shows of Puritan linguistic habits and of the part that language was playing in exacerbating the conflicts of the age.

The poems also are mainly of value for the light they throw on contemporary attitudes, in this case cultural ones. Mayne's elegy in Donne's *Poems* (1633), has received attention for its comment on Donne's poetry, "We are thought wits, when 'tis understood"; but its description of Donne in the pulpit is also worth reading. An encomium on Jonson in *Parnassus Biceps* (1656), praises his dramatic art in some detail. A poem lauding Denham (in Bodleian MS. Engl.poet.e.4) also shows Mayne capable of neat couplets very much in Denham's manner. Elsewhere he expresses views on art and gardening. His longest poem, a fulsome address to the Duke of York, is devoid of interest.

Mayne's comedy *The City Match* uses ingredients from Jonson and his successors; the plot is derived from *Epicoene*. The action is unsatisfactory, however, partly because of excessive reliance on the convention that a change of attire makes one's nearest relations instantly unrecognisable, partly because of the inconsistency and uncertainty of the author's moral attitudes. Like Jonson, Middleton, and Massinger, Mayne deals with the duping of a rich uncle by a scheming nephew; unlike his predecessors, he omits to ensure that our sympathies lie with the nephew, and in the unexplained reconciliations of the dénouement moral problems are shelved, not solved. *The Amorous War*, a romantic tragi-comedy, repeats and magnifies the faults of the earlier play; the plot is silly and unconvincing, and Mayne's ethical insensitivity is a serious flaw in a play purporting to deal with the themes of love and faithfulness.

Yet comedy is undoubtedly the genre to which Mayne is best suited. Scenes such as that in which the drunken Timothy, suitably attired, is exhibited as a monstrous fish, or one in which three dandified courtiers are forced to change clothes with their ragged flea-bitten captors, have genuine dramatic potentiality. Mayne possessed a sense of theatre as well as a sense of humour, and in his loosely structured blank verse has achieved much easy, humorous dialogue, particularly in the London setting of *The City Match*. The later play also contains two songs with complex stanza-forms which reveal a lyric gift which one may wish that Mayne had cultivated further. One of these, "Time is a feathered thing," treats with some poignancy the theme of "Gather ye rosebuds," and deserves to be better known.

—Margaret Forey

MEDWALL, Henry.   English.   Lived in the latter part of the 15th century; first positively known English dramatist; served as chaplain to John Morton, Archbishop of Canterbury, 1486–1500.

PUBLICATIONS

Plays

> *Fulgens and Lucrece* (produced 1497).   1515(?); edited by Glynne Wickham, in *English Moral Interludes*, 1976.
> *Nature*.   1530(?); edited by J. S. Farmer, in *"Lost" Tudor Plays*, 1907.

Reading List: *Medwalls Fulgens and Lucres* by Hans Hecht, 1925; *The Tudor Interlude* by T. W. Craik, 1958; *The Staging of Plays Before Shakespeare* by Richard Southern, 1973.

*   *   *

Henry Medwall's two known plays (the story that he wrote a third which wearied Henry VIII is without foundation) are both two-part interludes designed as banquet entertainments at Cardinal Morton's palace. *Nature* is named after the opening speaker, but its central character is Man, and its pattern the typical morality one of temptation, fall, and restoration. Man, given Reason and Sensuality as his two companions, becomes governed by the latter, who introduces him to the seven deadly sins (under false names, Pride becoming Worship and so on). Reason, assisted by Shamefastness, reclaims him at the end of the first part, but in the second he reverts to his bad ways, until (off-stage) Age reconverts him to Reason. The plot is awkwardly managed, nothing being made of the impact of remorse on Man on either occasion; but the dialogue and stage movement are lively, and there are racy accounts of meetings with off-stage characters like Kate and Margery in taverns and brothels, while Nature's opening speech has some grandeur.

Fulgens and Lucres is far superior as drama, besides being more palatable to modern tastes because it employs neither allegory nor religious didacticism. It is a debate as to whether birth or merit constitutes a gentleman, the occasion being the wooing by two suitors of the contrary qualifications of the daughter (Lucretia) of a Roman senator (Fulgentius). The source is the English translation of a Latin prose *controversia* of 1428. To his borrowed plot Medwall has added a sub-plot involving two serving-men (A and B: their lack of proper names fosters the half-illusion that they are members of the audience joining in, which in turn fosters the further half-illusion that the events of the play are true and in the present). These attach themselves to the two rival suitors (carrying messages and making errors) and themselves become rivals for the love of Lucrece's waiting-maid, who makes them ridiculous. As involuntary parodists and foils, and as (often wrong-headed) commentators, they add a great deal to the play's substance as well as to its humour, and point towards later Shakespearean effects. Medwall uses mainly rhyme-royal stanzas for his serious monologues and dialogues, and tail-rhyme for his comic ones, though couplets also occur.

—T. W. Craik

MERCER, David. English. Born in Wakefield, Yorkshire, 27 June 1928. Educated at King's College, Newcastle upon Tyne, University of Durham, B.A. (honours) in fine art 1953. Served as a laboratory technician in the Royal Navy, 1945–48. Two daughters. Worked as a laboratory technician, 1942–45; Supply Teacher, 1955–59; Teacher, Barrett Street Technical College, 1959–61. Full-time writer since 1962. Recipient: Writer's Guild Award, for television play, 1962, 1967, 1968; *Evening Standard* award, 1965; British Film Academy Award, 1966. Lives in London.

PUBLICATIONS

Plays

The Governor's Lady (broadcast 1960; produced 1965). 1968.

The Buried Man (produced 1962).
The Generations: Three Television Plays (includes *Where the Difference Begins, A Climate of Fear, The Birth of a Private Man*). 1964.
Ride a Cock Horse (produced 1965). 1966.
Belcher's Luck (produced 1966). 1967.
Three TV Comedies (includes *A Suitable Case for Treatment, For Tea on Sunday, And Did Those Feet*). 1966.
In Two Minds (televised 1967; produced 1973). In *The Parachute with Two More TV Plays*, 1967.
The Parachute with Two More TV Plays: Let's Murder Vivaldi, In Two Minds. 1967.
Let's Murder Vivaldi (televised 1968; produced 1972). In *The Parachute with Two More TV Plays*, 1967.
On the Eve of Publication and Other Plays (television plays: includes *The Cellar and the Almond Tree* and *Emma's Time*). 1970.
White Poem (produced 1970).
Flint (produced 1970). 1970.
After Haggerty (produced 1970). 1970.
Blood on the Table (produced 1971).
Duck Song (produced 1974). 1974.
The Bankrupt and Other Plays (includes *You and Me and Him, An Afternoon at the Festival, Find Me*). 1974.
Huggy Bear and Other Plays (television plays: includes *The Arcata Promise* and *A Superstition*). 1977.
Shooting the Chandelier (televised, 1977). With *Cousin Vladimir*, 1978.
Cousin Vladimir (produced 1978). 1978.

Screenplays: *Ninety Degrees in the Shade* (English dialogue), 1965; *Morgan! A Suitable Case for Treatment*, 1966; *Family Life*, 1972; *A Doll's House*, 1973; *Providence*, 1977.

Radio Plays: *The Governor's Lady*, 1960; *Folie à Deux*, 1974.

Television Plays: *Where the Difference Begins*, 1961; *A Climate of Fear*, 1962; *A Suitable Case for Treatment*, 1962; *The Birth of a Private Man*, 1963; *For Tea on Sunday*, 1963; *The Buried Man*, 1963; *A Way of Living*, 1963; *And Did Those Feet*, 1965; *In Two Minds*, 1967; *Let's Murder Vivaldi*, 1968; *The Parachute*, 1968; *On the Eve of Publication*, 1968; *The Cellar and the Almond Tree*, 1970; *Emma's Time*, 1970; *The Bankrupt*, 1972; *You and Me and Him*, 1973; *An Afternoon at the Festival*, 1973; *Barbara of the House of Grebe*, from a story by Hardy, 1973; *Find Me*, 1974; *The Arcata Promise*, 1974; *Huggy Bear*, 1976; *A Superstition*, 1977; *Shooting the Chandelier*, 1977; *The Ragazza*, 1978.

Fiction

The Long Crawl Through Time (story) in *New Writers 3*. 1965.

Bibliography: *The Quality of Mercer: Bibliography of Writings by and about the Playwright Mercer*, edited by Francis Jarman, 1974.

Reading List: *The Second Wave* by John Russell Taylor. 1971.

*   *   *

David Mercer's hallmark for many years was his opposition to repression, whether political or psychological. In plays sometimes Marxist in ideology, sometimes in keeping with R. D. Laing's precepts on psychology, he championed the individual in opposition to the political and/or psychiatric establishment's authoritarian pressures to conform. Repeatedly he favored the anarchic or aberrant over the pedestrian and normal. Mercer's plays in the 1960's frequently reflected his socialist allegiance, but they were not simplistic in content or truly social realist in style, and as the years passed, his anti-Stalinism and individualism have more and more alienated those he once called comrades. His interest in psychopathology, which has caused him to examine and re-examine the origin, development, and manifestations of mental illness from a distinctly maverick perspective that virtually denies the existence of abnormality, has always set him apart from the purely politically partisan playwright. His allegiance to personal freedom precluded his becoming a party member or taking a party line.

Mercer began writing plays when he discovered in psychoanalysis that he was fascinated with stateless wanderers because he had strayed from his working class origins and simple upbringing to a sophisticated, intellectual life. So he wrote his television play *Where the Difference Begins*. This play and the subsequent *A Climate of Fear* and *The Birth of a Private Man* examine the conflicts of working-class children educated into the middle class. Like so many of Mercer's subsequent plays, they are domestic dramas, the first probing the dilemma's roots, the second considering family crisis during the campaign for nuclear disarmament, and the third examining a man disillusioned with his communist affiliations.

In the last play of this trilogy, Colin goes mad from his loss of political faith, and what most people would term insanity or neurosis – often involving violence between the sexes or violence turned inward – figured in most of Mercer's plays for more than a decade to come. *The Buried Man* suggested the preoccupation by taking as its protagonist a boilerman judged mad when found crying over his machinery, but *A Suitable Case for Treatment*, established the quintessential Mercer hero. Illustrating his premise that aberrance "may be a necessary, meaningful and creative means by which the personality reveals its relationship to the world, and the 'breakdown' may be on the world's side," Mercer in Morgan fashions a character who has an understanding with the gorilla at the zoo and with animals in general. Though Morgan is in some way's Rousseau's noble savage, his relations with his wife Leonie have deteriorated to the point that he's living in her car. When Leonie divorces Morgan and tries to remarry, he kidnaps her. After his abduction is circumvented, he dresses in a gorilla suit to disrupt the wedding reception and then, costume ablaze, careens on a stolen motorcycle into the Thames. Morgan lies delirious on riverbank garbage till carted off to an institution, where he cheerfully ascertains that he fathered the baby his ex-wife carries. The film's final image – more symbol of rebellion than political statement – is the asylum's flower bed, which Morgan has planted in the shape of hammer and sickle.

Mercer's fascination with animals and their contrast to less genuine, more duplicitous and barbaric people are likewise featured in *The Governor's Lady* and in *And Did Those Feet*. In the latter the twin zoo-keepers even release their animals and then emigrate to the African jungle. In *Belcher's Luck*, the natural and fecund Belcher and his horses are foils to the impotent and rapacious patricians, and in *For Tea on Sunday* the psychotic hero who identifies with animals explains that his body contains a harmless leopard.

Other Mercer plays depict, not animals or the animal-obsessed, but abnormal characters whom he seems to regard as superior to or more sympathetic than the beastly normal folk around them. Even those who suffer total mental collapse – Peter, the regressive paranoid in *Ride a Cock Horse*, for instance, or the schizophrenic Kate of *In Two Minds* – are clearly favored by Mercer over more ordinary mortals. Peter's setting his wife's clothes and paintings and books afire and his eventual donning of an SS uniform bring spectators nearer to tears than to derision. And as for Kate, she is unquestionably more sinned against than sinning, having been driven into psychosis by repressive parents and the insensitive psychiatric establishment. Unable to please both herself and her parents, she succumbs to guilt feelings, and, deprived of the supportive treatment of one renegade therapist, she is drugged into submission and eventual catatonia. In Morgan Mercer admires abnormality, but here he laments the loss of mental health. One of Mercer's major tenets is that psychiatric care must treat, not symptoms, but causes. Kate suffers from unenlightened sedation and a dullard doctor who leaves her a zombie because he thinks her illness bears no relation to her family environment.

Although the outlook for aberrance there is bleak, the obverse to that prognosis comes in *Flint*, where the rapscallion hero, whose name suggests striking sparks to create fire, is a promethean, seventy-year-old Anglican priest who is all libido. As devoid of repression or inhibitions as he is free of religious convictions, Flint is sleeping with a pregnant girl who tried to kill herself in his church. After he has dissuaded Dixie from self-destruction, the adventures of this formidable proponent of the joy of life comprise affirmative but iconoclastic farce far removed from the harrowing documentary treatment of schizophrenia.

For the first decade, Mercer's plays of political and psychological disorientation were life-affirming. When a character suffers, the blame is usually to be laid upon some interference with his or her personal freedom by malicious or misguided social units or institutions or because inhibitions – as with Bernard Link in *After Haggerty* – reduce a character to phlegmatic ineffectuality. During this period, Mercer was a playwright of compassionate optimism, one who believed in the individual if not in the social order. Harold Hobson could write, with some justification, "Mr. Mercer is a dramatist whose generosity of spirit strengthens and breathes life into those who come into contact with it. He writes of the universe as an experiment that is justified, because he instinctively finds in it so much of good."

Recent developments, however, would prevent such an assessment. The disorientation of which he writes is now more frequently metaphysical, as his fear of totalitarianism and repression has receded in the wake of troubling anxieties on the basic human condition. A profoundly Beckettian pessimism about birth, death, the quest for meaning and purpose, and the fear of futility pervade the recent plays and films. Often employing daring dramatic techniques, Mercer does combat with ontological despair in *An Afternoon at the Festival*, *The Bankrupt*, *Find Me*, *Ducksong*, *The Arcata Promise*, *Providence* and *A Superstition*.

Among the recent works, the teleplay *The Arcata Promise*, the film *Providence* (written for Alain Resnais), and the stage work *Ducksong* are especially durable drama. The destructive and self-destructive dissociated actor – actually named John, but called "Gunge" by the Voice with which he pursues interior dialogue – about whom Mercer writes in *The Arcata Promise*, haunted by imagined failures in his distinguished acting career and the real failure of his relations with a woman, suffers a collapse – as much moral as mental – which leads to murder and suicide. Mercer is no longer enjoying eccentricity and condoning aberrance here; Morgan was a charming zany, but Gunge's self indulgence, past and present, prompts sympathy mixed with revulsion.

Resnais has not altogether realised the more whimsical aspects of the surreal comedy *Providence*, in which ageing novelist Clive Langham as creator – a sort of god or providence over his imagination's issue – asserts control in unexpected ways. He thinks up a nubile young thing to be his son's mistress, decides she'd be wasted on priggish Claud, and substitutes a middle-aged, intellectual journalist. The creative process may get out of hand: while imagining a scene between Claud and the fictive mistress, Clive bemusedly watches a rugger jog through towards the shower; to wrench the intruder out of the frame, he instantly resets the scene in another hotel room. Although the film's visual and verbal surprises, as well as the self-importance and bombast of its dream characters, are flippant, serious revulsion at mortality is as fundamental to the screenplay as to *Ducksong*. The sundrenched verdant festivities at the end hardly erase the terminally ill Langham's nightmarish night.

Ducksong dramatizes one family's efforts to come to terms with death, or perhaps with their failures in life, since the title refers to their rather ordinary attempts at swansongs. A cuckoo clock, a sort of *memento mori*, goads a man who dreads dying into hurling walnuts at its bobbing bird. Soon, forced to confront an entropic universe, all the characters' real needs and obsessions emerge. Some are topical issues – class conflicts, women's liberation, red power – but others are the more universal matters of transience, futility, and violence which Mercer summarizes as "the terrible poetry of doom."

In *Where the Difference Begins* Richard worried over the Communist ideal of feeding the body without regard for the soul. Mercer is still, in his latest plays, worried that the consumer society fails to provide spiritual nourishment. And he still sees the fanatical individualist as our last, best hope in a grim cosmos.

—Tish Dace

MIDDLETON, Thomas.   English.   Born in London, baptized 18 April 1580. Educated at Queen's College, Oxford, and possibly at Gray's Inn, London. Married Mary (or Magdalen) Morbeck in 1602; one son. Playwright for Philip Henslowe by 1602, and wrote for Paul's boys company, 1602 to 1606–07; City Chronologer of London, 1620–27. *Died* (buried) *4 July 1627.*

PUBLICATIONS

Collections

> *Works,* edited by A. H. Bullen.   8 vols., 1885–86.
> *Selected Plays* (includes *The Changeling, Women Beware Women, A Chaste Maid in Cheapside, A Mad World, My Masters*), edited by David L. Frost.   1978.

Plays

> *The Phoenix* (produced 1603–04?).   1607.
> *The Honest Whore,* with Dekker (produced 1604).   1604; as *The Converted Courtesan,* 1604; edited by Fredson Bowers, in *Dramatic Works of Dekker,* 1953–62.
> *A Mad World, My Masters* (produced 1604–06?).   1608; in *Selected Plays,* 1978.
> *A Trick to Catch the Old One* (produced 1604–06?).   1608; edited by G. J. Watson, 1968.
> *The Family of Love* (produced 1604–07?).   1608.
> *Michaelmas Term* (produced 1606?).   1607; edited by Richard Levin, 1967.
> *Your Five Gallants* (produced 1607).   1608(?).
> *Sir Robert Shelley, His Royal Entertainment* (produced 1609 ?).   1609.
> *The Roaring Girl; or, Moll Cut-Purse,* with Dekker (produced 1610?).   1611; edited by Andor Gomme, 1976.
> *The Witch* (produced 1610–16?).   1778; edited by W. W. Greg and F. P. Wilson, 1950.
> *A Chaste Maid in Cheapside* (produced 1611).   1630; in *Selected Plays,* 1978.
> *No Wit, No Help Like a Woman's* (produced 1613?).   Revised version published 1657; edited by Lowell E. Johnson, 1976.
> *The Manner of His Lordship's Entertainment on Michaelmas Day Last* (produced 1613).   1613; edited by J. Nichols, in *Progresses of James I,* 1828.
> *The Triumphs of Truth: A Solemnity* (produced 1613).   1613; edited by J. Nichols, in *Progresses of James I,* 1828.

More Dissemblers Besides Women (produced 1615?). In *Two New Plays,* 1657.

A Fair Quarrel, with William Rowley (produced 1615–17?). 1617; edited by George R. Price, 1976.

The Nice Valour; or, The Passionate Woman, with Fletcher (produced before 1616). In *Comedies and Tragedies* by Beaumont and Fletcher, 1647.

The Widow (produced 1616?). 1652; edited by Robert Trager Levine, 1975.

Civitatis Amor, The City's Love: An Entertainment by Water (produced 1616) 1616; edited by J. Nichols, in *Progresses of James I,* 1828.

The Mayor of Quimborough (produced 1616–20?). 1661; edited by R. C. Bald, as *Hengist, King of Kent,* 1938.

The Triumphs of Honour and Industry: A Solemnity (produced 1617). 1617.

The Peace-Maker; or, Great Britain's Blessing (produced 1618?). 1618.

The Old Law; or, A New Way to Please You, with William Rowley (produced 1618?). 1656.

The Inner Temple Masque; or, Masque of Heroes (produced 1619). 1619; edited by R. C. Bald, in *A Book of Masques in Honour of Allardyce Nicoll,* 1967.

The Triumphs of Love and Antiquity: An Honourable Solemnity (produced 1619). 1619; edited by J. Nichols, in *Progresses of James I,* 1828.

The World Tossed at Tennis, with William Rowley (produced 1619–20?). 1620.

The Marriage of the Old and New Testament (produced 1620?). 1620; as *God's Parliament House,* 1627.

Honourable Entertainments, Composed for the Service of This Noble City. 1621; edited by R. C. Bald and F. P. Wilson, 1953.

The Sun in Aries: A Noble Solemnity (produced 1621). 1621.

Any Thing for a Quiet Life, with Webster (produced 1621?). 1662; edited by F. L. Lucas, in *Complete Works of Webster,* 1927.

An Invention Performed for the Service of Edward Barkham, Lord Mayor of London (produced 1622). In *Works,* 1885–86.

The Triumphs of Honour and Virtue: A Noble Solemnity (produced 1622). 1622.

The Changeling, with William Rowley (produced 1622). 1653; in *Selected Plays,* 1978.

The Triumphs of Integrity: A Noble Solemnity (produced 1623). 1623.

The Spanish Gipsy, with William Rowley (produced 1623). 1653; edited by C. M. Hayley, in *Representative English Comedies,* 1914.

A Game at Chess (produced 1624). 1625; edited by J. W. Harper, 1966.

Women Beware Women (produced 1625–27?). In *Two New Plays,* 1657; in *Selected Plays,* 1978.

The Triumphs of Health and Prosperity: A Noble Solemnity (produced 1626). 1626.

Wit at Several Weapons, with Fletcher and William Rowley (produced ?). In *Comedies and Tragedies,* by Beaumont and Fletcher, 1647.

Verse

The Wisdom of Solomon Paraphrased. 1597.
Microcynicon: Six Snarling Satires. 1599.
The Ghost of Lucrece. 1600; edited by Joseph Quincy Adams, 1937.

Other

The Ant and the Nightingale; or, Father Hubbard's Tales. 1604; revised edition, as *Father Hubbard's Tales,* 1604.
The Black Book. 1604.

Bibliography: *Middleton: A Concise Bibliography* by S. A. Tannenbaum, 1940; supplement in *Elizabethan Bibliographies Supplements 1*, by D. G. Donovan, 1967.

Reading List: *Non-Dramatic Sources for the Rogues in Middleton's Plays* by M. G. Christian, 1936; *Middleton's Tragedies* by Samuel Schoenbaum, 1955; *Middleton* by Richard H. Barker, 1958; *The Art of Middleton: A Critical Study* by David M. Holmes, 1970; *Parody and Burlesque in the Tragicomedies of Middleton* by John F. MacElroy, 1972; *Middleton and the Drama of Realism* by Dorothy M. Farr, 1973; *The Lust Motif in the Plays of Middleton* by Barbara J. Baines, 1973; *The Most Unvaluedst Purchase: Women in the Plays of Middleton* by Caroline L. Cherry, 1973; *A Study of Middleton's Tragicomedies* by Carolyn Asp, 1974; *The Canon of Middleton's Plays* by David J. Lake, 1975.

*   *   *

An attempt to narrate the plot of any one of Thomas Middleton's plays could only end in disastrous confusion. Comedies and tragedies alike are composed of multiple actions which, when the dramatist is at his best, intertwine, sharing characters and themes, so that each is enriched by the conjunction. In the comedy *A Chaste Maid in Cheapside* a single character, Sir Walter Whorehound, is common to all the actions, and makes unity out of diversity. He provides Master Allwit with comfort and children, and he schemes to rid himself of a former mistress by presenting her as an heiress, a desirable daughter-in-law for the avaricious Master and Mistress Yellowhammer. They in turn intend Sir Walter as a husband for their daughter, Moll, who is in love with Touchwood Junior. By marrying Moll, Sir Walter could breed legitimate heirs to inherit the wealth of the childless Sir Oliver and Lady Kix. Preoccupations with sex and procreation, wealth and gentility, are shared by all the characters, usually to the total exclusion of any other quality; and yet they are more than personifications, having a vitality which re-creates seventeenth-century Cheapside. They live in a world where everything has its price, and where double-dealing is the normal practice of young and old alike – of Touchwood Junior as much as Master Yellowhammer. Sir Walter is the villain, and at the end of Act V he has been defeated in a duel by Touchwood; disappointed of his hopes because Lady Kix has been made pregnant; and disowned by Mistress Allwit. But the duel is not an assertion of the triumph of good over evil, or innocent youth over unprincipled age. Touchwood wins his Moll, and romance ends the play, but the hero of *A Chaste Maid in Cheapside* is the least romantic and idealistic of the characters, Master Allwit. He has stood by, as door-keeper and bawd to his wife, and thanked Sir Walter for making him a comfortable cuckold:

> I thank him, h'as maintained my house this ten years,
> Not only keeps my wife, but a keeps me,
> And all my family; I am at his table,
> He gets me all my children, and pays the nurse,
> Monthly, or weekly, puts me to nothing,
> Rent, nor church duties, not so much as the scavenger:
> The happiest state that ever man was born to.

But when the ruined knight turns to him for support, Allwit's rejection of him is as unequivocal as Henry V's "I know thee not, old man" to Falstaff. Allwit and his wife have a future to plan together: to set up a bawdy-house in the Strand.

Middleton sees that luxury, in its Elizabethan double sense (both "extravagance" and "lechery"), will continue to thrive. His comedies are moral, but realistic. He examines the vices of contemporary middle-class society, and displays them for laughter; but for the most part he eschews poetic justice in his endings. As a moralist, he is no visionary.

In the tragedy *Women Beware Women* Livia occupies a similar pivotal position to Sir Walter, having a part in both plots as a manipulator, drawing Bianca and Isabella into sin and corruption. Eventually she becomes entangled in her own snares. In the tragic catastrophe the injured revenge themselves on the guilty – but so widespread is the guilt that only two characters, the foolish ones, are left alive at the end of the play, together with the Cardinal whose well-intentioned sermon triggered off the first murder. In this play, and in another late tragedy, *The Changeling*, Middleton is still the moralist, although his emphasis has shifted a little and lust, as a theme, is largely independent of avarice. In the sub-plot of *Women Beware Women* Isabella is a mere commodity, to be sold by her father to the highest bidder. Isabella has been, he tells the Duke, a "dear child" to him: "dear to my purse, I mean,/Beside my person; I nev'r reckoned that." Beatrice-Joanna, however, the heroine of *The Changeling*, is accustomed to having her every want supplied, and she has no hesitation in demanding the removal of one suitor to make place for a new one when her fancy has changed. Both tragedies are set in the exotic "abroad," and Spanish passions are hot in *The Changeling*. But although Middleton is careful to make occasional references to location in *Women Beware Women* these are not strong enough to counter the strong impression that Jacobean England and its mercantile middle classes are once more the object of the moralist's concern.

At the very beginning of his career as a writer, Middleton seized on the extravagances of his affluent society; in *Microcynicon* he sets himself firmly in the tradition of the satirists who regarded sartorial excess as the emblem of prodigality, likely to bring about the ruin both of the individual and of the nation:

> Suit upon suit, satin too, too base;
> Velvet laid on with gold or silver lace
> A mean man doth become; but he must ride
> In cloth of fined gold, and by his side
> Two footmen at the least, with choice of steeds,
> Attired, when he rides, in gorgeous weeds.

He always has criticism, varying in its degree of severity, for the wastrel who has sacrificed property, the legacy of generations, for the transitory splendour of an appearance at Court, or the "poor benefit of a bewitching minute." But he is still more scornful of those who, having (in the words of Henry Peacham) "by Mechanicke and base meanes ... raked up a masse of wealth," seek to acquire gentility. The Yellowhammers in *A Chaste Maid in Cheapside* presume to send their son to Cambridge, and we are encouraged to agree that they get their just deserts when the boy is married to Sir Walter's discarded whore in the mistaken belief that she is a Welsh heiress. Ephestian Quomodo in *Michaelmas Term* is a London woollen-draper who dreams of the respectability which will be his when he has bought an estate from the impecunious gentleman, Easy: "Oh, that sweet, neat, comely, proper, delicate parcel of land, like a fine gentlewoman i'th'waist, not so great as pretty, pretty; the trees in summer whistling, the silver waters by the banks harmoniously gliding...." His vocabulary registers his inability to lay claim to the status of a gentleman: he is very much the draper when he compares the land to a gentlewoman's waist, although he has certainly learned some of the appropriate literary pastoral language. Similarly, Leantio in *Women Beware Women* cannot attain the status to which he has aspired in marrying Bianca, and here again his language betrays his deficiency: employed as a "factor" in buying and selling, he can only appreciate Bianca as a "most unvalued'st purchase."

Middleton's verse never glitters, but it is always taut and smooth, firm in its rhythms, which approximate to speech but never permit slackness. As a dramatic craftsman he is almost impeccable. His early experience was in writing as one of a hard-pressed team of collaborators for Henslowe's two dramatic companies. In this work he so successfully subdued any idiosyncrasies that his voice is not audible in the few surviving collaborated plays. He went on to write for the two children's companies (as did such writers as Jonson and Marston), and then joined the many playwrights who, with Fletcher at their head, supplied the London stage with escapist fiction in tragi-comedies. His play *A Game at Chess* defies categorization. A political play, it describes the struggles between Spain and England,

Catholicism and Protestantism, in terms of a chess game. The Black Knight was immediately recognized by the audiences as the Spanish Ambassador, Count Gondomar, who earned English hatred for his attempts to secure an Anglo-Spanish alliance through the marriage of Prince Charles. The play was an instant success, and it was (as the titlepage says) "Acted *nine days to gether at the Globe on the banks side*" – after which the play was banned, the King's Men forbidden to act, and a warrant issued for the arrest of the dramatist. Once the topicality was gone, of course, the play lost its impact, and today the text is swamped with footnotes. Yet although the meaning is obscure and the characters unrecognizable, the strength of the plot is clear; the action is conducted with the firm sense of direction that marks all Middleton's plays, from the beginning to the end of his career.

Some scholars have also credited Middleton with the authorship of *The Revenger's Tragedy*, which was published anonymously. In the absence of overwhelming evidence to prove Middleton's claim, this play has been discussed together with the work of Cyril Tourneur, to whom it was attributed in 1656.

—Roma Gill

MILLER, Arthur.   American.   Born in New York City, 17 October 1915. Educated at the University of Michigan, Ann Arbor (Hopwood Award, 1936, 1937), 1934–38, A.B. 1938. Married 1) Mary Slattery in 1940 (divorced, 1956), one son and one daughter; 2) the actress Marilyn Monroe in 1956 (divorced, 1961) ; 3) Ingeborg Morath in 1962, one daughter. Member of the Federal Theatre Project, 1938. Wrote for the CBS and NBC Radio Workshops. International President, P.E.N., London and New York, 1965–69. Recipient: Theatre Guild Award, 1938; New York Drama Critics Circle Award, 1947, 1949; Antoinette Perry Award, 1947, 1949, 1953; Pulitzer Prize, 1949; National Association of Independent Schools Award, 1954; American Academy of Arts and Letters Gold Medal, 1959; Brandeis University Creative Arts Award, 1969. D.H.L.: University of Michigan, 1956. Member, American Academy of Arts and Letters, 1971.

PUBLICATIONS

Plays

Honors at Dawn (produced 1936).
No Villains (They Too Arise) (produced 1937).
The Pussycat and the Expert Plumber Who Was a Man and *William Ireland's Confession*, in *100 Non-Royalty Radio Plays*, edited by William Kozlenko.   1941.
The Man Who Had All the Luck (produced 1944).   In *Cross-Section 1944*, edited by Edwin Seaver, 1944.
That They May Win (produced 1944).   In *Best One-Act Plays of 1944*, edited by Margaret Mayorga, 1945.
Grandpa and the Statue, in *Radio Drama in Action*, edited by Erik Barnouw.   1945.
The Story of Gus, in *Radio's Best Plays*, edited by Joseph Liss.   1947.
The Guardsman, radio adaptation of a play by Ferenc Molnar, in *Theatre Guild on the Air*, edited by H. William Fitelson.   1947.

Three Men on a Horse, radio adaptation of the play by George Abbott and John Cecil Holm, in *Theatre Guild on the Air*, edited by H. William Fitelson. 1947.

All My Sons (produced 1947). 1947.

Death of a Salesman: Certain Private Conversations in Two Acts and a Requiem (produced 1949). 1949.

An Enemy of the People, from a play by Ibsen (produced 1950). 1951.

The Crucible (produced 1953). 1953.

A View from the Bridge, and A Memory of Two Mondays: Two One-Act Plays (produced 1955). 1955; revised version of *A View from the Bridge* (produced 1956), 1956.

Collected Plays (includes *All My Sons, Death of a Salesman, The Crucible, A Memory of Two Mondays, A View from the Bridge*). 1957.

After the Fall (produced 1964). 1964.

Incident at Vichy (produced 1964). 1965.

The Price (produced 1968). 1968.

Fame, and The Reason Why (produced 1970). *Fame* in *Yale Literary Magazine*, March 1971.

The Creation of the World and Other Business (produced 1972). 1973.

Up from Paradise (produced 1974).

The Archbishop's Ceiling (produced 1976).

Screenplay: *The Misfits*, 1961.

Radio Plays: *The Pussycat and the Expert Plumber Who Was a Man, William Ireland's Confession, Grandpa and the Statue*, and *The Story of Gus*, in early 1940's.

Fiction

Focus. 1945.

The Misfits (screenplay in novel form). 1961.

I Don't Need You Any More: Stories. 1967.

Other

Situation Normal. 1944.

Jane's Blanket (juvenile). 1963.

In Russia, photographs by Inge Morath. 1969.

The Portable Miller, edited by Harold Clurman. 1971.

In the Country, photographs by Inge Morath. 1977.

The Theatre Essays of Miller, edited by Robert A. Martin. 1978.

Bibliography: "Miller: The Dimension of His Art: A Checklist of His Published Works," in *The Serif*, June 1967, and *Miller Criticism (1930–1967)*, 1969, both by Tetsumaro Hayashi.

Reading List: *Miller*, 1961, and *Miller: A Study of His Plays*, 1979, both by Dennis Welland; *Miller* by Robert G. Hogan, 1964; *Miller: The Burning Glass* by Sheila Huftel, 1965; *Miller* by Leonard Moss, 1967 (includes bibliography); *Miller, Dramatist* by Edward Murray, 1967; *Miller: A Collection of Critical Essays* edited by Robert W. Corrigan, 1969; *Miller: Portrait of a Playwright* by Benjamin Nelson, 1970; *Miller* by Ronald Hayman, 1970.

*   *   *

In "On Social Plays," the introduction to the 1955 edition of *A View from the Bridge*, Arthur Miller expressed his dissatisfaction with the subjective play so popular on Broadway in the 1950's. At the same time, he rejected the customary definition of the social play ("an arraignment of society's evils") and identified his own work as "the drama of the whole man," an inextricable mixture of the social and the psychological. The emphasis on one side or the other varied over the years and his conception of the nature of man underwent a change in the 1960's, but his 1955 sense of his work is a useful description of the whole career of Arthur Miller as a social playwright.

In his student plays, his wartime one-acters, his early radio plays, even his first Broadway offering, *The Man Who Had All the Luck*, Miller can be seen working his way toward the theme that was to dominate his early plays. From *All My Sons* through *A View from the Bridge*, Miller places his protagonist in a setting in which society functions as a creator of images, and the hero-victim is destroyed because, as he says in the essay quoted above, "the individual is doomed to frustration when once he gains a consciousness of his own identity." Ironically, the destruction comes whether a man accepts or rejects the role that society asks or demands that he play. Joe Keller, in *All My Sons*, is a good man, a loving husband and father, a successful business man who believes that his responsibility ends "at the building line"; when his son teaches him that neither the welfare of his family nor the self-protective impulse of conventional business ethics can excuse a shipment of faulty airplane parts, he commits suicide. Willy Loman, in *Death of a Salesman*, embraces the American dream, assumes that success is not only possible, but inevitable, and, faced with his failure, kills himself; the irony of the final suicide and the strength of the play is that Willy goes to his death, his dream still intact, convinced that the elusive success will be visited on his son, Biff, a man already crippled by society's neatly packaged ideas. In *The Crucible*, the victim becomes a romantic hero. John Proctor, guilty of adultery, confuses his accusing wife with an accusing society and admits to practicing witchcraft, but, finally unwilling to sign his name, he rejects society's demand for ritual confession, regains his identity, and dies, purely, in an act of defiance. Eddie Carbone, in *A View from the Bridge*, dies crying out for his name, too, but he wants a lie, the pretense that he has not violated the neighborhood ethic; like Joe Keller and Willy Loman, he accepts his society, but he breaks its rules when his desire for his niece and his attraction to her sweetheart threaten him with labels more frightening than informer. The explicit assumption of all these plays is that, win or lose, in contemporary society you can't win; the implicit assumption is that the individual is at his strongest, philosophically and dramatically, when the tensions between self and society are made manifest by a revealing crisis. The artistic result of the twin assumptions is a group of remarkably effective plays, reflecting Miller's theatrical skill as clearly as they do his moral concerns. In the best of them, *Death of a Salesman*, Miller's social-psychological mix has given birth, in Willy Loman, to one of the richest characters in American drama.

Between 1956, when the revised version of *A View from the Bridge* appeared, and 1964, Miller was inactive in the theater. During those years he published a number of short stories, later collected in *I Don't Need You Any More*, including "The Misfits," which was the basis for the short novel and screenplay, written for his wife Marilyn Monroe. The most startling thing about the work is that in it Miller seems to be accepting the concept of the curative power of love in a way that recalls the prevailing cliché of Broadway in the 1950's; he had already given the idea explicit statement in two essays published a few years before the story-novel-film – the introduction to *Collected Plays* and "Bridge to a Savage World" (*Esquire*, October 1958).

When Miller returned to the theater with *After the Fall* and *Incident at Vichy*, he had put aside the momentary softness of *The Misfits*, but he had also discarded the concept of man as an admirable loser which marked his earlier plays. "The first problem," he wrote in "Our Guilt for the World's Evil" (*New York Times Magazine*, 3 January 1965), "is ... to discover our own relationship to evil, its reflection of ourselves." Quentin in *Fall* learns to live and Von Berg in *Vichy* to die by the process of self-discovery already familiar in Miller's work, but identity is no longer individual. Miller, like the Salem of *The Crucible*, is now forcing an image of guilt on his characters. Finally in 1972, with *The Creation of the World and Other Business*, Miller makes obvious what has already been stated in the title *After the Fall*, that his post-1964 subject is original sin translated into the psychological commonplace that makes everyone responsible for "the World's Evil." Miller does not try to dramatize the corollary, that when everyone is guilty no one is, but it is possible – or so the autobiographical elements in *After the Fall* suggest – that the idea is working on the author if not within the play. One result of Miller's new concept of man is that the later plays have a schematic look to them; the characters lack the vitality of Miller's early protagonists and often appear to be simply figures in an exemplum. *The Price* is the only one of the later plays that escapes the look of drama as demonstration. Ideologically one with the other post-1964 plays, it returns to the domestic setting familiar with Miller as far back as the time of his student work *They Too Arise*. Whether it is the inherent drama of two brothers at odds or the presence of the old furniture dealer, Miller's only successful comic figure, *The Price* escapes Significance with a capital S and finds theatrical validity. In his most recent work, *The Archbishop's Ceiling*, Miller seems to have moved away from the ideological concerns that marked his drama from *After the Fall* to *Creation of the World*, but the play is more intellectual than dramatic and the characters are more complex in conception than in presentation.

Since Miller is a playwright of ideas, it is perhaps fitting that I have largely stuck to his themes in discussing his work, stopping occasionally to suggest that the ideational content of a play can interfere with the dramatic action or dehumanize character. These strictures are valid only to the extent that Miller is a realistic playwright in the American tradition, a dramatist who wants to create psychologically valid characters with whom audiences can identify directly. That is Miller's tradition, although he is one of a number of postwar American playwrights who recognize that that kind of character can exist outside a conventional realistic play. *Death of a Salesman* and *After the Fall* are examples of domesticated American Expressionism in which realistic scenes are played in an anti-realistic context. *The Crucible* is a romantic history play with a consciously artificial language, and Alfieri's stilted speeches in *A View from the Bridge*, which turn into free verse in the original version, are an attempt to impose the label *tragedy* on the play. *The Creation of the World* is an unhappy mixture of philosophical drama and Jewish low comedy. *Incident at Vichy* is a roundtable discussion and *The Price* is a debate of sorts with exits and entrances so artificially conceived that Miller surely means them to be seen as devices. The playwright's nearest approaches to traditional realism are *All My Sons* and the affectionate short play *A Memory of Two Mondays*.

Aside from his plays, Miller's work includes not only the short stories and screenplay mentioned above, but a novel, *Focus*; a report on Americans in training during World War II, *Situation Normal*; a children's book, *Jane's Blanket*; two volumes in which his text shares space with photographs by his wife Inge Morath, *In Russia* and *In the Country*; and a great many articles and essays, most of them about the theater. The chief value of these works lies less in their specific generic virtues than in those analogies – in theme, in method – that heighten our appreciation of the plays. After all, Arthur Miller is pre-eminently a playwright, one of the best the American theater has produced.

—Gerald Weales

MITCHELL, Langdon (Elwyn).   American.   Born in Philadelphia, Pennsylvania, 17 February 1862; son of the novelist S. Weir Mitchell. Educated at St. Paul's School, Concord, New Hampshire; studied abroad for three years in Dresden and Paris, then studied law at the

Harvard Law School, Cambridge, Massachusetts, and Columbia University, New York; admitted to the New York Bar, 1886, but did not practice. Married the actress Marion Lea in 1892; one son and two daughters. Playwright and author from the mid-1880's; Lecturer in English Literature, George Washington University, Washington, D.C., 1918–20; Professor of Playwriting, University\ of Pennsylvania, Philadelphia, 1928–30. Member, National Institute of Arts and Letters. *Died 21 October 1935.*

PUBLICATIONS

Plays

Sylvian, in *Sylvian and Poems.* 1885.
George Cameron (produced 1891).
In the Season (produced 1892). 1898.
Ruth Underwood (produced 1892).
Deborah (produced 1892; as *The Slave Girl,* produced 1893).
Don Pedro (produced 1892).
Becky Sharp, from the novel *Vanity Fair* by Thackeray (produced 1899). Edited by J.
    B. Russak, in *Monte Cristo and Other Plays,* 1940.
The Adventures of Françoise, from a novel by S. Weir Mitchell (produced 1900).
The Kreutzer Sonata, from a work by Jacob Gordin (produced 1906). 1907.
The New York Idea (produced 1906). 1908.
The New Marriage (produced 1911).
Major Pendennis, from the novel by Thackeray (produced 1916).

Fiction

Love in the Backwoods (stories). 1897.

Verse

Sylvian: A Tragedy, and Poems. 1885.
Poems. 1894.

Other

Understanding America. 1897.

*   *   *

Langdon Mitchell's reputation in American theatre rests almost completely on one play – *The New York Idea.* His first published play, *Sylvian,* a tragedy written partly in verse and more for the closet than the stage, appeared in a volume of verse in 1885. Among his ten other plays, *Becky Sharp,* a dramatization of Thackeray's *Vanity Fair,* was a successful vehicle for the American actress Minnie Madden Fiske. But only *The New York Idea* which Arthur Hobson Quinn, the drama historian, termed a "sterling comedy," could be considered a contribution to the developing American drama. It also helped spread the work of American dramatists abroad where it played in London, was produced in Germany as

Jonathans Tochter under the direction of Max Reinhardt, and was translated into other European languages.

Something of a landmark in the progress of social comedy in America, *The New York Idea* – "New York is bounded on the North, South, East and West by the state of Divorce" – mixes farce-comedy with melodrama in delightful portions while Mitchell reveals his rather probing insights into the "state of Divorce" through witty and satirical comments. As a satire on marriage in New York society, the play defines marriage as "three parts love and seven parts forgiveness of sin." The fast-moving plot is determined by two divorced women who plan to marry each other's ex-husband until one of them decides she really loves the man she had just divorced. Most of the characters are one-dimensional foils for the author's quick wit – the stuffy husband, the insipid clergyman, the English fop intriguer. Contrived situations such as the wedding scene and the club-house episode make the play successful and show Mitchell's particular skills as a dramatist. With wit, irony, and carefully created incongruities, the play treats a serious issue with a modern touch that provides some distinction to early twentieth-century American drama.

Mitchell never repeated his success and, in fact, made only two more attempts to write for the theatre, neither one successful. In related work he became, in 1928, the first occupant of the Chair of Playwriting founded by the Mask and Wig Club at the University of Pennsylvania, a position he held for two years. For the student or historian of American drama he remains primarily the author of a single memorable play.

—Walter J. Meserve

MONCRIEFF, William Thomas. English. Born in London, 24 August 1794. Clerk in a solicitor's office, c. 1804, then entered the service of the solicitor Moses Hooper, London; began writing songs and subsequently plays; became manager of the Regency Theatre, subsequently known as the Queen's Theatre, then as the Prince of Wales Theatre; when the theatre close worked as a law stationer, and contributed drama criticism to the *Satirist* and the *Scourge*; Manager of Astley's, then of the Coburg Theatre; wrote for Elliston at Drury Lane, 1820–24; Manager, Vauxhall Gardens, 1827; opened a music shop with John Barnett in Regent Street, London, 1828; lessee of the City Theatre, 1833; wrote for the Strand Theatre, 1837–38; went blind by 1843; brother of the Charterhouse from 1844. *Died 3 December 1857.*

PUBLICATIONS

Plays

   Moscow (produced 1820).
   The Diamond Arrow; or, The Postmaster's Wife and the Mayor's Daughter, music by G. W. Reeve (produced 1815).   1816.
   All at Coventry; or, Love and Laugh (produced 1816).   1816.
   Joconde; or, Le Prince Troubadour (produced 1816).   1816.
   John Adams; or, The Mutineers of the High Seas (produced 1816).
   Giovanni in London; or, The Libertine Reclaimed (produced 1817).   1817.

Rochester; or, King Charles the Second's Merry Days (produced 1818). 1819.
The Dandy Family and the Ascot Jockies (produced 1818).
The Monk's Cowl; or, The Child of Mystery (produced 1818).
Wanted a Wife; or, A Cheque on My Bankers (produced 1819). 1819.
Pigeons and Crows (produced 1819).
The Bride of Lammermuir (produced 1819).
The Green Dragon; or, I've Quite Forgot (produced 1819).
Modern Collegians; or, Over the Bridge (produced 1820). 1820.
Ivanhoe; or, The Jewess (produced 1820). 1820.
The Lear of Private Life; or, Father and Daughter, from the novel *The Father and Daughter* by Mrs. Opie (produced 1820). N.d.
The Shipwreck of the Medusa; or, The Fatal Raft! (produced 1820). N.d.
The Ravens of Orleans; or, The Forest of Cercotte (produced 1820). N.d.
The Vampire (produced 1820). , n.d.
What Are You At? What Are You After? or, There Never Was Such Times (produced 1820).
The Actor in Distress; or, How to Raise Your Salary (produced 1820).
The Smuggler's Dog; or, The Blind Boy's Murder (produced 1820).
Giovanni in Ireland, music by Tom Cooke (produced 1821). 1824.
Tereza Tomkins; or, The Fruits of Geneva (produced 1821). 1821.
The Spectre Bridegroom; or, A Ghost in Spite of Himself (produced 1821). 1821.
Monsieur Tonson (produced 1821). 1821.
The Lost Life (produced 1821).
Tom and Jerry; or, Life in London, from the work by Pierce Egan (produced 1821). 1826.
Adventures of a Ventriloquist; or, The Rogueries of Nicholas (produced 1822). 1822.
Actors al Fresco; or, The Play in the Pleasure Garden, music by Jonathan Blewitt and C. E. Horn (produced 1823). Songs published 1827.
The Party Wall (as *The Secret; or, The Hole in the Wall*, produced 1823). 1823.
Fazio (produced 1823).
The Cataract of the Ganges! or, The Rajah's Daughter (produced 1823). 1823.
Zoroaster; or, The Spirit of the Star (produced 1824). 1824.
The Bashful Man (produced 1824). 1827.
Jack Sheppard the Housebreaker; or, London in 1724 (produced 1825).
The Kiss and the Rose; or, Love in the Nursery Grounds (produced 1827). 1827.
Home for the Holidays (produced 1828).
The Somnambulist; or, The Phantom of the Village, from a play by Scribe (produced 1828). 1828.
The Irresistibles (produced 1828). N.d.
The Hollow Way; or, The Hidden Treasure (produced 1828).
Monsieur Mallet; or, My Daughter's Letter, music by John Barnett (produced 1829). 1851.
Father and Daughter; or, The Victim of Seduction (produced 1829).
The Pestilence of Marseilles; or, The Four Thieves, from a play by Pixérécourt (produced 1829). 1829.
Van Diemen's Land; or, Settlers and Natives (produced 1830). 1888.
The Heart of London; or, A Sharper's Progress (produced 1830). 1839.
The Beggar of Cripplegate; or, The Humours of Bluff King Hal (produced 1830). 1830.
Shakespeare's Festival; or, The New Comedy of Errors (produced 1830). 1830.
Old Heads on Young Shoulders; or, The House in the Forest (produced 1830).
Electioneering; or, Village Politicians (produced 1830).
The Devil's Walk; or, Pluto in London (produced 1830).
The Man-Wolf; or, The Loup-Garçon of the Odenwald (produced 1831).
What a Shocking Bad Hat! (produced 1831).

The Monkey That Has Seen the World (produced 1831).

Courting by Mistake; or, A Trip to the Coronation (produced 1831).

Favourites in Town; or, Stage Arrivals (produced 1831).

Bringing Home the Bride; or, The Husband's First Journey, from a French play (produced 1838).

Reform; or, John Bull Triumphant (produced 1831). 1831.

Gipsy Jack; or, The Napoleon of Humble Life (produced 1831). N.d.

Eugene Aram; or, St. Robert's Cave, from the novel by Bulwer-Lytton (produced 1832). N.d.

The Peer and Peasant (produced 1832). 1832.

Lochinvar; or, The Bridal of Netherby (produced 1832). N.d.

Victor Dene; or, I'll Sleep on It (produced 1832).

The World as It Runs; or, Fancy's Freaks (produced 1832).

One Fault (produced 1833). N.d.

How to Take Up a Bill; or, The Village Vauxhall, from a play by Melesville (produced 1833). 1833.

The Birth Day; or, The Parson's Nose, music by G. B. Chapman, from a play by Désaugiers (produced 1835). 1833; as *The Parson's Nose*, 1837.

The Waggoner of Westmorland (produced 1834).

Mount St. Bernard; or, The Headsman (produced 1834). N.d.

The Revolt of the Seraglio on the Other Side of the Pole (produced 1834).

The Court of Queen Anne; or, The Prince and the Breeches Maker (produced 1834). N.d.

The Smuggler's Haunt; or, The Fireside Story (produced 1835).

What's in a Name; or, Black's White (produced 1835).

Lestocq, music by Tom Cooke, from a play by Scribe, music by Auber (produced 1835). N.d.

The Jewess; or, The Council of Constance, music by Tom Cooke, from an opera by Scribe, music by Halévy (produced 1835). N.d.

The Winterbottoms! or, My Aunt the Dowager (produced 1837). 1837.

Sam Wellers; or, The Pickwickians (produced 1837). 1837.

A Down East Bargain; or, Love in New York (produced 1837).

The Blind Father; or, The Peasant Marchioness (produced 1837).

The Fitzpatricks; or, Lovers from Tipperary (produced 1838).

The Tobit's Dog! (produced 1838). 1838.

Tarnation Strange; or, More Jonathans (produced 1838). 1842.

Sam Weller's Tour; or, The Pickwickians in France (produced 1838).

Shakespeare and Burbage (produced 1838).

Up and Down; or, The Road of Life (produced 1838).

Nicholas Nickleby and Poor Smike; or, The Victim of the Yorkshire School (produced 1839).

Popularity (produced 1839).

Foreign Airs and Native Graces (produced 1839).

The Ballad Singer (produced 1839).

The Devil's in the Room (produced 1840).

Harlequin and Jack of Newberry; or, Baa, Baa, Black Sheep and the Old Woman of Berkeley (produced 1840).

The Queen of a Day, from a play by Scribe and J. N. Verney de St. Georges, music by Alphonse Adam (produced 1840).

Harlequin and My Lady Lee; or, Goosey, Goosey Gander and the Spell-Bound Goslings (produced 1840).

The Tribute of a Hundred Virgins (produced 1840).

Giselle; or, The Phantom Night Dancers, from the ballet with music by Alphonse Adam (produced 1842). 1842.

Love and Laugh; or, The M.P. (produced 1842).
Perourou, The Bellows Mender and the Beauty of Lyons (produced 1842).   N.d.
Far Off; or, The Royal Visit to Edinburgh (produced 1842).
The Red Farm; or, The Well of St. Marie (produced 1842).   1885.
The Wood Wolf of the Black Mountains; or, The Milo of Brittany (produced 1842).
The Scamps of London; or, The Cross Roads of Life, from a novel by Eugène Sue
    (produced 1843).   1851.
Borrowing a Husband; or, Sleeping Out (produced 1843).   With *My Wife's Out* by
    George Rodwell, 1885.
An Armful of Bliss (produced 1843).
The Favourite of the Derby; or, The Life of Man and Horse (produced 1844; as *The Royal
    Foxhunt; or, The Life and Death of Tom Moody,* produced 1847).
Caesar the Watch Dog of the Castle; or, The Sword of My Father (produced
    1844).   1886.
The Mistress of the Mill, from a play by Melesville (produced 1849).   1850.
The Mayor of Rochester, with *The Omnibus* by Isaac Pocock.   1886.
Bonnie Prince Charlie; or, The Gathering of the Clans.   1887.
William's Visits.   N.d.

Verse

Prison Thoughts: Elegy Written in King's Bench, in Imitation of Gray.   1821.
Songs, Duets, and Glees Sung at the Royal Gardens, Vauxhall.   1827.
Poems.   1829.
The March of Intellect.   1830.
Old Booty: A Serio-Comic Sailor's Tale.   1830.
The Triumph of Reform.   1832.
An Original Collection of Songs.   1850.

Other

The New Guide to the Spa or Leamington Priors.   1822.
Excursion to Stratford upon Avon, with a Compendious Life of Shakespeare.   1824.

Editor, *Richardson's New Minor Drama.*   4 vols., 1828–31.

*   *   *

William Thomas Moncrieff wrote according to the requirements of the theatre of his time. His experience as a dramatic critic and theatre manager was inextricably linked with his dramatic work. If the craze was for fairy plays he would write *Giselle*. Since the dramatizing of Scott suited the box-office, he would write a version of *Ivanhoe*. When the vaudeville reached England, Moncrieff wrote an early example, *The Kiss and the Rose*. He was also concerned enough to distinguish vaudeville from burletta as "a dramatic story in verse, rather than prose, illustrated and carried on by means of the songs and melodies of the day rather than original compositions." His most famous play was an adaptation of Pierce Egan's documentary novel, *Life in London*. Moncrieff called his version *Tom and Jerry*, and openly exploited a naive taste for realism by presenting a sequence of scenes set in familiar London places. The characters as written by Egan are already dramatic cameos. It was comparatively easy for a theatrical expert like Moncrieff to exploit such material. He had already shown an ability to anticipate as well as to follow trends. His *Shipwreck of the Medusa* in 1820 was possibly the first nautical melodrama. In the same year his tear-jerking adaptation of a novel by Mrs. Opie, *The Lear of Private Life*, advertised the possible uses of Shakespearean plots in modern settings. Moncrieff was modest enough to accept a place as part of a theatrical team. In *The Cataract of the Ganges* that place was secondary to the scene-designer's. Clarkson Stanfield's real waterfall was the sensation that made this play such a triumph at Drury Lane. The life of a moderately talented working dramatist in the early decades of the nineteenth century is vividly presented in the evidence Moncrieff gave to the Select Committee which met in 1832 under Lord Lytton's chairmanship to enquire into the state of the theatre. His introductions to the plays in Richardson's *New Minor Drama* are also quite useful indicators of contemporary evaluation.

—Peter Thomson

MOODY, William Vaughn. American. Born in Spencer, Indiana, 8 July 1869; grew up in New Albany, Indiana. Educated at New Albany High School; Harvard University, Cambridge, Massachusetts (an editor of the *Harvard Monthly*), 1889–94, B.A. 1893, M.A. 1894. Married Harriet Tilden Brainard in 1909. Taught in a high school in Spencer, 1885–89; Instructor in English, Harvard University and Radcliffe College, Cambridge, Massachusetts, 1894–95; Instructor in English and Rhetoric, 1895–99, and Assistant Professor of English, 1901–07, University of Chicago; full-time writer, 1907 until his death. Litt.D.: Yale University, New Haven, Connecticut, 1908. Member, American Academy of Arts and Letters, 1908. *Died 17 October 1910.*

PUBLICATIONS

Collections

Selected Poems, edited by Robert Morss Lovett.   1931.

Plays

The Masque of Judgment: A Masque-Drama.   1900.
The Fire-Bringer.   1904.
The Great Divide (as *A Sabine Woman*, produced 1906; as *The Great Divide*, produced 1906).   1909.
The Faith Healer.   1909.

Verse

Poems.   1901; as *Gloucester Moors and Other Poems*, 1909.

Other

A History of English Literature, with Robert Morss Lovett.   1902; revised edition,

1918; simplified edition, as *A First View of English Literature,* 1905; as *A First View of English and American Literature,* 1909.

Poems and Plays, edited by John M. Manly.   2 vols., 1912.

Some Letters, edited by Daniel Gregory Mason.   1913.

Letters to Harriet, edited by Percy MacKaye.   1935.

Editor, *The Pilgrim's Progress,* by Bunyan.   1897.

Editor, *The Rime of the Ancient Mariner by Coleridge and The Vision of Sir Launfal by Lowell.*   1898.

Editor, *The Lady of the Lake,* by Scott.   1899.

Editor, with Wilfred Wesley Cressy, *The Iliad of Homer,* books 1, 6, 22, 24.   1899.

Editor, *The Complete Poetical Works of Milton.*   1899.

Editor, with George Cabot Lodge and John Ellerton Lodge, *The Poems of Trumbull Stickney.*   1905.

Editor, *Selections from De Quincey.*   1909.

Reading List: *Moody: A Study* by David D. Henry, 1934; *Moody* by Martin Halpern, 1964; *Estranging Dawn: The Life and Works of Moody* by Maurice F. Brown, 1973.

*   *   *

After William Vaughn Moody's early death, Edwin Arlington Robinson, his close friend and literary ally, wrote Harriet Moody, "Thank God he lived to do his work – or enough of it to place him among the immortals." While that assessment now seems exaggerated, Moody's work, as a scholar, poet, and dramatist, is sufficient to give him a firm place in literary history. As the author of *The Great Divide,* he is considered the first playwright to provide the American stage with a serious, realistic, modern drama, thus ushering in the new age in American theatre. Critics have speculated that had he lived to realize his full potential, his only rival would have been Eugene O'Neill.

Martin Halpern, in his critical biography of Moody, has suggested that his literary career falls into two periods: from 1890 until the publication of *The Masque of Judgment* and *Poems,* in 1900 and 1901 respectively, his primary interest was poetry; from then until his final illness debilitated him in 1909 he worked consciously as a practicing dramatist. Although *The Masque of Judgment* is the first part of a projected dramatic trilogy, it is a closet drama in verse. And while two of the four plays he wrote during the last decade of his life are also verse dramas, they were intended for the stage.

Moody's poems have few admirers today, largely because they seem imitative of the English romantics in inflated diction and archaic subject matter. Some of his poems are innovative, however, notably his poems that involve social commentary or those that are conscious attempts to use the vernacular. "On a Soldier Fallen in the Philippines," for instance, is an ironic attack on American foreign policy. Perhaps his most celebrated poem today is "The Menagerie," a comic soliloquy in which the inebriated speaker speculates on how the animals in the zoo regard the putative fulfillment of the evolutionary process, man. The psychologically honest "The Daguerreotype," a tribute to his mother, and the ambiguous "I Am the Woman" are two disparate treatments of the symbolic and psychic implications of the feminine principle, an interest that informs "The Death of Eve." Generally his poems, like his poetic trilogy, are full of high seriousness, frequently devolving upon theological, especially eschatological, matters.

Moody's two prose plays successfully combine realistic and symbolic dramatic techniques. Originally produced as *A Sabine Woman* in Chicago, *The Great Divide* was a commercial as well as a critical success, playing for two years in New York. The play deals with the conflicting cultures of the eastern and western United States, symbolized by the abduction and eventual marriage of a woman from Massachusetts to a rough but honest man from

Arizona. The less well-received *Faith Healer* deals with the conflict between human and spiritual passions; the conflict is resolved when the protagonist discovers that his religious work is effective only when he has accepted human love.

Although *The Fire-Bringer*, Moody's verse play based on the Prometheus legend, and the fragment, *The Death of Eve*, were not produced commercially, critics have found them to be more artistically interesting than the prose plays. Moody was able to complete only one act of *The Death of Eve*, but the poem by the same title and his recorded plans for the play suggest that with it he might have achieved his dream of making verse drama a viable theatrical experience. Even so, his contribution to American drama and poetry is considerable.

—Nancy C. Joyner

MOORE, Edward. English. Born in Abingdon, Berkshire, 22 March 1712. Educated by his uncle, a schoolmaster in Bridgwater, Somerset, and at a school in East Orchard, Dorset. Married Jenny Hamilton in 1749; one son. Apprenticed to a linendraper in London, then worked as a factor in Ireland, then returned to London to set up as a linendraper on his own: turned to literature when the business failed; enjoyed the patronage of Lord Lyttelton: through Lyttelton's influence appointed Editor of *The World* magazine, 1753–56. *Died 1 March 1757.*

PUBLICATIONS

Collections

Poetical Works, edited by Thomas Park.   1806.

Plays

Solomon: A Serenata, music by William Boyce (produced 1743).   1750.
The Foundling (produced 1748).   1748.
Gil Blas, from the novel by Le Sage (produced 1751).   1751.
The Gamester (produced 1753).   1753.

Verse

Fables for the Female Sex.   1744.
The Trial of Selim the Persian for Divers High Crimes and Misdemeanors.   1748.
An Ode to David Garrick.   1749.

Other

The World, with others.   6 vols., 1755–57.
Poems, Fables, and Plays.   1756.

Reading List: *The Life and Works of Moore* by John H. Caskey, 1927; Introduction by Charles H. Peake to *The Gamester*, 1948.

*   *   *

It is not hard to see how George Lillo's *George Barnwell; or, The London Merchant* (1731) was one of the greatest hits of the eighteenth-century London stage. The most significant of later eighteenth-century dramatists in the line of Lillo was Edward Moore, best-known as the author of the bourgeois prose tragedy *The Gamester*. The *Poems, Fables, and Plays* show he had wider scope, but it is as a dramatist of domestic dolors that he stands out in John H. Caskey's study and in literary history. He is an important link between Lillo and what came after.

True, he has a secure place in the history of the journalistic essay. After Johnson's *Rambler* and Hawksworth's *Adventurer* came over 200 numbers of *The World* (1753–56) which Moore edited. He wrote a lot of it himself and attracted contributors such as Chesterfield, Horace Walpole, Soame Jenyns, Richard Owen Cambridge, and Hanbury Williams.

But it was when he went bankrupt as a London linen-draper that Moore came into the theatre and into his own. *Gil Blas* is a lively comedy of disguise based on an episode of Le Sage in which a young lady dresses up as a student in order to capture a man who has caught her eye. Moore adequately handles the quick changes of the young lady back and forth but lacks the verbal lightness for really effective quick exchanges of dialogue. The borrowed plot remains the redeeming feature.

The Foundling was more in Moore's style, a sentimental and moral excursion along the lines that Cibber had more or less invented and Steele had made more or less popular, an earnest endeavor such as Moore's friend Fielding has his Parson Adams damn with feinting praise like this: "there are some things almost solemn enough for a sermon." The remark may underline for us how far comedy had strayed at that period from corrective laughter. If comedy was full of fine feeling and nearly devoid of fun, just imagine the domestic tragedy between, say, *The London Merchant* and Kelly's *False Delicacy*. *The Foundling* was nominally a comedy but is hardly a laugh riot. I find the work with which Moore started to make money as a writer, *Fables for the Female Sex*, funnier. The play is well constructed, however.

Then when Garrick (who played in it) gave Moore a hand with *The Gamester*, Moore had a first-rate piece of its kind. If you have tears, prepare to shed them now as we note the sad story of Beverley, a victim (like Barnwell) of evil in the vile form of Stukeley (who owes something to Lillo's Millwood, something to Shakespeare's Iago, and something to Fielding's Jonathan Wild). Beverley is sunk in a mire of gambling debts. Under the mercantile ethic (presented in numerous middle-class plays as well as in novels from Defoe and others throughout the century) squandering money was the foulest of crimes. In a comedy, by some stratagem finances as well as love affairs all come right in the end. In this tragedy, Beverley poisons himself in despair just before it transpires that he was to inherit the estate of his rich uncle! The distraught Mrs. Beverley wrings every drop of sentiment out of her husband's fate, though the play is not a "she-tragedy" of the Otway or Rowe variety. It is rather in the Elizabethan tradition of domestic melodrama and a milestone in the "road to ruin" genre which began to concentrate more and more not on the gambler himself but, as in temperance dramas, on the dire effects upon guiltless wives and suffering children.

The weakness in the genre is that the gambler is generally either a villain (in which case he attracts no sympathy) or a sap (like Barnwell or Beverley). It is hard to bring naturalism to the hysteria and histrionics. Moore's dialogue is more "natural" than Lillo's, but what Goldsmith would have called "natural" (as when he spoke of Garrick's "simple, natural, affecting" acting) may look pretty stilted and posturing to us.

Diderot adapted *The Gamester* as a *drame bourgeois* and Thomas Holcroft echoed some aspects of Moore in *The Road to Ruin* (1792). Moore's play has relevance to all the sentimental plays of the latter part of the eighteenth century and all the melodramatic ones of the first half of the nineteenth century; in its confusion of tragic hero and hapless victim, of sentiment and seriousness, of tragedy and melodrama, it is related to such works as Arthur Miller's *Death of a Salesman*. *The Gamester* is a masterpiece of the second-rate and as such of first-rate importance in the history of the theatre.

—Leonard R. N. Ashley

MORTIMER, John (Clifford). English. Born in Hampstead, London, 21 April 1923. Educated at Harrow School, 1937–40; Brasenose College, Oxford, 1940–42, B.A. 1947; called to the Bar, 1948. Served with the Crown Film Unit as a scriptwriter during World War II. Married the writer Penelope Dimont, i.e., Penelope Mortimer, in 1949 (divorced, 1971); Penny Gollop in 1972; three children. Has practised law in London since 1948: noted for his defense in free speech and civil liberties cases; Queen's Counsel, 1966; Master of the Bench, Inner Temple, London, 1975. Drama Critic, *New Statesman*, *Evening Standard*, and *Observer*, 1972, all in London. Chairman, League of Dramatists. Recipient: Italia Prize, for radio play, 1958; Screenwriters Guild Award, for television play, 1970. Lives in Henley on Thames, Oxfordshire.

PUBLICATIONS

Plays

> *The Dock Brief* (broadcast 1957; produced 1958).   In *Three Plays*, 1958.
> *I Spy* (broadcast 1957; produced 1959).   In *Three Plays*, 1958.
> *What Shall We Tell Caroline?* (produced 1958).   In *Three Plays*, 1958.
> *Three Plays*.   1958.
> *Call Me a Liar* (televised 1958; produced 1968).   In *Lunch Hour and Other Plays*, 1960.
> Sketches in *One to Another* (produced 1959).   1960.
> *The Wrong Side of the Park* (produced 1960).   1960.
> *Lunch Hour* (broadcast 1960; produced 1960).   1960.
> *David and Broccoli* (televised 1960).   In *Lunch Hour and Other Plays*, 1960.
> *Lunch Hour and Other Plays*.   1960.
> *Collect Your Hand Baggage* (produced 1963).   In *Lunch Hour and Other Plays*, 1960.
> Sketches in *One over the Eight* (produced 1961).
> *Two Stars for Comfort* (produced 1962).   1962.
> *A Voyage round My Father* (broadcast 1963; produced 1970).   1971.
> Sketches in *Changing Gear* (produced 1965).
> *A Flea in Her Ear*, from a play by Feydeau (produced 1966).   1967.
> *A Choice of Kings* (televised 1966).   In *Playbill Three*, edited by Alan Durband, 1969.
> *The Judge* (produced 1967).   1967.
> *Desmond* (televised 1968).   In *The Best Short Plays 1971*, edited by Stanley Richards, 1971.
> *Cat among the Pigeons*, from a play by Feydeau (produced 1969).   1970.
> *Come As You Are: Four Short Plays* (includes *Mill Hill*, *Bermondsey*, *Gloucester Road*, *Marble Arch*) (produced 1970).   1971.

The Captain of Köpenick, from a play by Carl Zuckmayer (produced 1971). 1971.
Conflicts, with others (produced 1971).
I, Claudius, from the novels *I, Claudius* and *Claudius the God* by Robert Graves (produced 1972).
Knightsbridge (televised 1972). 1973.
Collaborators (produced 1973). 1973.
Heaven and Hell (includes *The Fear of Heaven* and *The Prince of Darkness*) (produced 1976); revised version of *The Prince of Darkness,* as *The Bells of Hell* (produced 1977).
The Lady from Maxim's, from a play by Feydeau (produced 1977). 1978.

Screenplays: *Ferry to Hong Kong,* with Lewis Gilbert and Vernon Harris, 1959; *The Innocents,* with Truman Capote and William Archibald, 1961; *Guns of Darkness,* 1962; *I Thank a Fool,* with others, 1962; *Lunch Hour,* 1962; *The Running Man,* 1963; *Bunny Lake Is Missing,* with Penelope Mortimer, 1964; *A Flea in Her Ear,* 1967; *John and Mary,* 1969.

Radio Plays: *Like Men Betrayed,* 1955; *No Hero,* 1955; *The Dock Brief,* 1957; *I Spy,* 1957; *Three Winters,* 1958; *Call Me a Liar,* 1958; *Lunch Hour,* 1960; *The Encyclopedist,* 1961; *A Voyage round My Father,* 1963; *Personality Split,* 1964; *Education of an Englishman,* 1964; *A Rare Device,* 1965; *Mr. Luby's Fear of Heaven,* 1976.

Television Plays: *Call Me a Liar,* 1958; *David and Broccoli,* 1960; *A Choice of Kings,* 1966; *The Exploding Azalea,* 1966; *The Head Waiter,* 1966; *Hughie,* 1967; *The Other Side,* 1967; *Desmond,* 1968; *Infidelity Took Place,* 1968; *Married Alive,* 1970; *Swiss Cottage,* 1972; *Knightsbridge,* 1972; *Rumpole of the Bailey,* 1975, and series, 1978; *A Little Place off Edgware Road, The Blue Film, The Destructors, The Case for the Defence, Chagrin in Three Parts, The Invisible Japanese Gentlemen, Special Duties,* and *Mortmain,* all from stories by Graham Greene, 1975–76; *Will Shakespeare* series, 1978.

Ballet Scenario: *Home,* 1968.

Son et Lumière script: *Hampton Court,* 1964.

Fiction

Charade. 1947.
Rumming Park. 1948.
Answer Yes or No. 1950; as *The Silver Hook,* 1950.
Like Men Betrayed. 1953.
The Narrowing Stream. 1954.
Three Winters. 1956.
Will Shakespeare: The Untold Story. 1977.

Other

No Moaning at the Bar. 1957.
With Love and Lizards (travel), with Penelope Mortimer. 1957.

Reading List: *Anger and After* by John Russell Taylor, 1962.

Although his first writing was for film, a medium more visual than verbal, John Mortimer then devoted a decade to the novel. This proficiency at prose fiction, taken with a degree of education which for a contemporary British playwright is unusual, may be responsible for the dramatist's felicitous style. If the drama in a Mortimer play is sometimes thin, the language in which it is orchestrated, at its most urbane, boasts cunning cadenzas and playful arabesques; even at its more mundane the Mortimer speech is literate and sensitive to both cerebral quirk and linguistic nuance.

This verbal urbanity is accompanied by a sophistication of viewpoint. Q.C. Mortimer's distinguished career in jurisprudence has found him repeatedly as defense attorney in film and literary prosecutions on grounds of obscenity or blasphemy. As a stalwart champion of freedom of press and speech, he has denied any danger inherent in the magazine *Oz*, the books *Last Exit to Brooklyn* and *Inside Linda Lovelace*, and a poem about Christ published in *Gay News*. As a vocal opponent of stage censorship, his testimony against the Lord Chamberlain's bowdlerizing function was instrumental in bringing an end to that practice. Yet for all his theoretical permissiveness, Mortimer has never written what the censorious could label lewd or profane. He defends hedonism in plays of the utmost civility.

Mortimer's allegiance to the pleasure principle is part of a larger worldview which prefers the joy of life to propriety and requires him to side habitually with the underdog. In the courtroom, he is a defense attorney; in the theatre, he is an advocate for those he describes as "the lonely, the neglected, the unsuccessful," for people engaged "in the war against established rules." He cannot take middle-class conventionality seriously. He delights in pricking the pretensions of the pompous and exposing repression or hypocrisy cloaked though it is in the mantle of respectability, but more often still he's engaged in opening viewers' hearts to sympathy for the simple or the forlorn.

Thus in *The Dock Brief* the life's losers for whom Mortimer wins our sympathy are a woebegone wife murderer and his court-appointed attorney who has long awaited a case. In the first scene the barrister brags of how he'll secure his client's acquittal; in the second we learn the accused has been saved all right – by his counsel's incompetence. In the equally whimsical *What Shall We Tell Caroline?*, an irascible husband seemingly unbearable to his wife reveals his true sympathy for her when he bullies their friend into continuing a pretended flirtation with her so she shan't be hurt. Mortimer's optimism for those willing to leave the shelter of tradition for the risk of independence imbues this study of the eighteen-year-old Caroline's escape from over-protective parents, and his philosophy is nowhere articulated more clearly than in the family friend's admonition "Every day she should collect some small pleasure to keep her warm ... because when she reaches our age, it won't be the things she's done she'll regret, it will be the things she hasn't done."

The zest for life lived fully and the compassion for crippled souls are apparent in other plays. The proprietor of the hotel in *Two Stars for Comfort* – a rating earned for lodging and for the comforts of reassurance and sexual pleasure as well – is a free spirit not treated with the same tolerance and affection which he offers the world. The title character's dour view in *The Judge*, who is as repressed as the law he administers is repressive, contrasts with the acceptance of life practised by his former mistress. In *Mr. Luby's Fear of Heaven*, the pompous old Byron scholar who wakes in a hospital with a ceiling painting of heaven so beautiful he thinks he has died comes to realize he is "sexually underprivileged" when he contrasts his merely literary sensuality with the unrepressed enjoyments of the practicing sensualist in the adjacent bed. *The Bells of Hell* finds the devil is "a gentleman," one who can perform the miracles of putting sin back in sex and otherwise feeding the emotionally malnourished. And the old defense lawyer in *Rumpole of the Bailey* triumphantly secures acquittal for a black teenager accused in a stabbing by proving the lad couldn't have read his signed confession since he is illiterate.

Mortimer usually writes comedy, but within this genre he has permitted himself considerable stylistic latitude. Not surprisingly for a translator of Feydeau, he has mastered the sex farce in a play like *Marble Arch*. Actress Laura is being kept by a married Labor peer who appears to die in her loo. It's not the lines which convulse us but the exits and entrances mere seconds apart of characters who must not meet. Similarly, in *Mill Hill* a husband interrupts an illicit rendezvous but the wife's subterfuge preserves the appearance of decorum.

It's usually the situation, rather than plot or character, which especially takes our fancy in a Mortimer play, and many of them might most fairly be termed situation comedies. In *Bermondsey*, a wife and a homosexual, for their mutual benefit, connive to keep the man in their life out of the arms of a young barmaid. The detective of *I Spy* falls in love with the woman he's observing and conspires with her falsely to impugn her virtue so as to win her for himself following the divorce proceedings. *The Wrong Side of the Park* gives us a decaying family in a crumbling house where a hysterical woman, of the type its originator Margaret Leighton did so well, seeks to bring some glamor into her humdrum life only to discover the real excitement in her own husband. Similar genial fun is had with gentility in *A Voyage round My Father*, a charming ramble down memory lane without pretension to plot. This play includes recollections of Mortimer's boyhood, his early experiences of women, and his film-making during the war, but mostly it is a loving tribute to his father, the barrister whose blindness prompted the program's solicitation for "The Prevention of Blindness Fund." *Collaborators* is a domestic comedy about a barrister and his wife who are collaborating on a film. Both the play by Mortimer and the film his characters are concocting examine another kind of collaboration, modern marriage.

Indeed marriage, love and sex, and failure are Mortimer's repeated subjects, whether the style is relatively representational – as in the early plays – or more presentational, as in *I, Claudius*, *A Voyage round My Father*, *The Judge*, and *Rumpole of the Bailey*. The characteristic Mortimer atmosphere is mildly Chekhovian, and he is more often than not ironic. We expect from Mortimer eloquence in middle-class speech, idiosyncratic character parts, freedom of thought, and humor aimed at evoking grins more often than guffaws. He shares his wry amusement at people lovingly created and brought to life with understated but inventive theatricality.

—Tish Dace

MORTON, Thomas. English. Born in Durham c. 1764. Educated at Soho Square School, London; entered Lincoln's Inn, 1784, but was not subsequently admitted to the bar. Married; one daughter and two sons, including the playwright John Maddison Morton. Full-time playwright from 1792. Senior Member of Lord's, London; Honorary Member, Garrick Club, 1837. *Died 28 March 1838.*

PUBLICATIONS

Plays

    Columbus; or, A World Discovered (produced 1792). 1792.
    The Children in the Wood, music by Samuel Arnold (produced 1793). 1794.
    Zorinski, music by Samuel Arnold (produced 1795). 1795.
    The Way to Get Married (produced 1796). 1796.
    A Cure for the Heart-Ache (produced 1797). 1797.

Secrets Worth Knowing (produced 1798). 1798.

Speed the Plough (produced 1800). 1800; edited by Allardyce Nicoll in *Lesser English Comedies of the Eighteenth Century,* 1931.

The Blind Girl; or, A Receipt for Beauty, music by Joseph Massinghi and William Reeve (produced 1801). Songs published 1801.

Beggar My Neighbour; or, A Rogue's a Fool, from a play by A. W. Iffland (produced 1802; as *How to Tease and How to Please,* produced 1810).

The School of Reform; or, How to Rule a Husband (produced 1805). 1805.

Town and Country (produced 1807). 1807.

The Knight of Snowdoun, music by Henry Bishop, from the poem "The Lady of the Lake" by Scott (produced 1811). 1811.

Education (produced 1813). 1813.

The Slave, music by Henry Bishop (produced 1816). 1816.

Methinks I See My Father; or, Who's My Father? (produced 1818). 1850(?).

A Roland for an Oliver, from a play by Scribe (produced 1819). 1819.

Henri Quatre; or, Paris in the Olden Time, music by Henry Bishop (produced 1820). 1820.

A School for Grown Children (produced 1827). 1827.

The Invincibles, music by A. Lee (produced 1828). 1829.

The Sublime and Beautiful (produced 1828).

Peter the Great; or, The Battle of Pultawa, with James Kenney, music by Tom Cooke and William Carnaby, from a play by Frédéric du Petit-Mère (produced 1829).

Separation and Reparation (produced 1830).

The King's Fireside (produced 1830).

The Writing on the Wall!, with J. M. Morton (produced 1852). N.d.

*   *   *

Thomas Morton's first five-act comedy, *The Way to Get Married,* gave good acting parts to Lewis, Quick, Munden, and Fawcett. It also established his method, which is to embed a pathetic tale of poverty and remorse amid comic episodes and eccentric characters. Scenes of convulsive anguish alternate with amusing encounters and adventures whose general intention is to commend generosity and expose the mercenary motives of a heartless society. Morton was, in effect, writing melodrama before the word had reached the English theatre. He had, generally, the tact to give his comedians more stage time than his "heavies," and to allow one of his comic men to make the crucial discovery that makes all well. *Secrets Worth Knowing* is an exact example of the style. The comedy survives well, but the suffering resists contemporary staging. The same is true of Morton's best play, *Speed the Plough,* in which the real life belongs to the characters least involved in the main plot. Sir Philip Blandford's remorse over a dead wife, lost child, and murdered brother is tediously related in embarrassingly pompous prose. The child (not lost), the brother (not murdered), and the daughter also speak in grandiose archaisms. By extraordinary contrast, the uxorious Sir Abel Handy, his well-intentioned son, his wife, Farmer and Mrs. Ashfield, and their daughter are all finely observed and provided with sprightly dialogue. It is Mrs. Ashfield's obsessive concern with what Mrs. Grundy (who never appears) may say that has provided Morton's best known monument. *The School of Reform* is an attempt to repeat the success of *Speed the Plough,* but the influence of the German dramatists, particularly of Kotzebue's guilt-laden stories of sexual sin, swamps most of Morton's own talent. The character of Robert Tyke, and the final sensation scene in a Gothic chapel, underline the close relations between contemporary comedy and melodrama. *A Cure for the Heart-Ache* is the only one of Morton's comedies to suit the description, though even that play is not without pathetic attitudinising.

—Peter Thomson

MOWATT, Anna Cora (née Ogden).   American.   Born in Bordeaux, France, 5 March 1819, to American parents; lived in or near Bordeaux as a child; settled with her family in New York City, 1826. Educated at Mrs. Okill's School, New York, 1826–28, and at a school in New Rochelle, New York, 1828–31. Married 1) James Mowatt in 1834 (died, 1851), three adopted children; 2) William Foushee Ritchie in 1854. Travelled abroad for her health, 1837–38; returned to New York and began writing for the stage, 1839; appeared in recitals of poetry, New York and Boston, 1841–42, and thereafter wrote under the pseudonym Helen Berkley for *Godey's Lady's Book, Graham's,* and other magazines, and compiled books on cooking, etiquette, etc. for various publishers; made debut as actress, New York, 1845, and appeared, with E. L. Davenport as leading man, in New York and other major American cities, London, and Dublin, 1846 until she retired in 1854; full-time writer from 1854; lived abroad after 1861, mainly in Florence. Active in the campaign to preserve Mount Vernon: Vice-Regent, Mount Vernon Ladies Association of the Union, 1858–66. *Died 21 July 1870.*

PUBLICATIONS

Plays

> *Gulzara; or, The Persian Slave* (produced 1840).   In *The New World,* 1840.
> *Fashion; or, Life in New York* (produced 1845).   1849.
> *Armand; or, The Peer and the Peasant* (produced 1847).   1849.

Fiction

> *The Fortune Hunter; or, The Adventures of a Man about Town: A Novel of New York Society.* 1842.
> *Evelyn; or, A Heart Unmasked.*   1845.
> *Mimic Life; or, Before and Behind the Curtain* (stories).   1856.
> *Twin Roses.*   1857.
> *Fairy Fingers.*   1865.
> *The Mute Singer.*   1866.
> *The Clergyman's Wife and Other Sketches.*   1867.

Verse

> *Pelayo; or, The Cavern of Covadonga.*   1836.
> *Reviewers Reviewed: A Satire.*   1837.

Other

> *Life of Goethe.*   1844.
> *Etiquette of Courtship and Marriage.*   1844.
> *The Management of the Sick Room.*   1844.
> *The Memoirs of Madame d'Arblay.*   1844.
> *Autobiography of an Actress; or, Eight Years on the Stage.*   1853.
> *Italian Life and Legends.*   1870.

Reading List: *Life and Letters* by Marius Blesi, 1952; *Anna Cora: The Life and Theatre of Anna Cora Mowatt* by Eric Wollencott Barnes, 1954, as *The Lady of Fashion*, 1955.

*   *   *

Mid-nineteenth-century American stage history records no more engaging figure than author-actress Anna Cora Mowatt, whose performances in her own and others' plays delighted audiences throughout the United States and Great Britain. Though known today chiefly for her comedy, *Fashion*, an amusing satire on middle-class pretentiousness, Mrs. Mowatt's popularity during the 1850's derived from numerous other writings, but primarily from the many successful roles she brought to life in both English and American theatres. Her dual career marked a turning point, demonstrating that an American woman of genteel birth, given talent, perseverance, family support, and hard work, could achieve professional recognition in theatrical circles without sacrificing social respectability.

As her autobiography reveals, the story of Mrs. Mowatt's dramatic experiences is still fascinating. Born in Bordeaux, the ninth of sixteen children of wealthy Americans, she enjoyed from early childhood such cultural advantages as extensive European travel; entrée into the world of art, literature, and theatre; familial stimulus and encouragement toward creative effort; and, above all, the guidance and support of her husband, James Mowatt, whom she married at fifteen. At sixteen she published a juvenile poetic romance entitled *Pelayo; or, The Cavern of Covadonga*, and then wrote an operetta, "The Gypsy Wanderer." These youthful effusions led to more mature essays, stories, and sketches appearing in leading American periodicals, and to her three plays, *Gulzara; or, The Persian Slave*, *Fashion*, and *Armand*. Other publications included three novels, two romantic tales of theatrical life under the title *Mimic Life; or, Before and Behind the Curtain*, and the detailed account of her experiences in *Autobiography of an Actress* – in all, an impressive collection, written mainly between frequent illnesses and extended theatrical engagements.

Although Anna Mowatt's stage performances were more widely heralded than her writings in the 1850's, throughout ensuing decades her reputation as the author of *Fashion* superseded that of her acting career. For the play not only scored immediate hits and enjoyed repeated, long-run performances in both England and America; it has continued, even within recent times, to attract more attention from producing groups than any other nineteenth century American play except *Uncle Tom's Cabin*. Its enduring appeal is well deserved because no other play of its period captured so accurately or spoofed with such buoyant, satiric humor, characterization, and sprightly dialogue, the bourgeois aspirations of mid-century New York society.

—Eugene Current-Garcia

MUNDAY, Anthony. English. Born in London in 1560. May have travelled, and may have been an actor, prior to being apprenticed to the stationer John Allde, 1576–78. Married; four daughters and one son. Visited Rome, to gather material on the English seminary there, 1578–79; actor with the Earl of Oxford's Company, London, 1579–84; involved in the writing of some 18 plays, 1584–92, and also known for his ballads and songs; served as Messenger to Her Majesty's Chamber, 1584–93; wrote most of the City of London pageants, and was keeper of the pageant properties, 1592–1623; travelled as "pageanter" with the Earl of Pembroke's Men to Holland, 1598–99; may have followed his father's trade of draper in the latter years of his life. *Died* (buried) *10 August 1633*.

Plays

> *Fedele and Fortunio: The Deceits in Love,* with Chapman and Stephen Gosson, from a
> play by L. Pasqualigo (produced 1584?). 1585; edited by P. Simpson, 1909.
> *John a Kent and John a Cumber* (produced 1594). Edited by J. P. Collier, 1851; edited
> by M. St. C. Byrne, 1923.
> *Sir Thomas More,* with Shakespeare (produced 1596?). Edited by A. Dyce, 1844;
> edition of W. W. Greg revised by H. Jenkins, 1961.
> *The Downfall of Robert, Earl of Huntingdon,* with Henry Chettle (produced
> 1598). 1601; edited by J. C. Meagher, 1965.
> *The Death of Robert, Earl of Huntingdon,* with Henry Chettle (produced 1598). 1601;
> edited by J. C. Meagher, 1967.
> *Sir John Oldcastle,* part 1, with others (produced 1599). 1600; edited by P. Simpson,
> 1908.
> *The Triumphs of Re-United Britannia, Performed in Honor of Sir Leonard Holliday, Lord
> Mayor* (produced 1605). 1605.
> *Campbell; or, The Ironmonger's Fair Field* (produced 1609). 1609.
> *London's Love to the Royal Prince Henry, Meeting Him on the River of Thames*
> (produced 1610). 1610.
> *Chruso-Thriambos: The Triumphs of Gold, at the Inauguration of Sir James Pemberton
> in the Dignity of Lord Mayor* (produced 1611). 1611; edited by J. H. P. Pafford,
> 1962.
> *Himatia-Poleoa: The Triumphs of Old Drapery at the Entertainment of Sir Thomas
> Hayes, Lord Major* (produced 1614). 1614.
> *Metropolis Coronata: The Triumphs of Ancient Drapery in a Second Year's
> Entertainment in Honour of Sir John Jolles, Lord Mayor* (produced 1615). 1615.
> *Chrysanaleia: The Golden Fishing, Applauding the Advancement of Mr. John Leman to
> the Dignity of Lord Mayor* (produced 1616). 1616; edited by J. G. Nichols, as *The
> Fishmongers' Pageant,* 1884.
> *Sidero-Thriambos; or, Steel and Iron Triumphing, Applauding the Advancement of Sir
> Sebastian Harvey to the Dignity of Lord Mayor* (produced 1618). 1618.
> *The Triumphs of the Golden Fleece, Performed at the Installment of Sir Martin Lumley in
> the Mayoralty* (produced 1623). 1623.

Fiction

> *Zelauto: The Fountain of Fame.* 1580; edited by Jack Stillinger, 1963.
> *A True and Admirable History of a Maiden of Consolens in Poitiers.* 1603.

Verse

> *The Mirror of Mutability; or, Principal Part of the Mirror of Magistrates, Selected Out of
> the Sacred Scriptures.* 1579.
> *The Pain of Pleasure.* 1580.
> *A Banquet of Dainty Conceits.* 1588.

Other

> *A Second and Third Blast of Retreat from Plays and Theatres,* with Salvianus. 1580.

A View of Sundry Examples, Reporting Many Strange Murders. 1580(?).
An Advertisement and Defense for Truth Against Her Backbiters. 1581.
The True Report of the Prosperous Success Which God Gave unto Our English Soldiers in Ireland. 1581.
A Brief Discourse of the Taking of Edmund Campion. 1581.
A Courtly Controversy Between Love and Learning Between a Lady and a Gentleman of Siena. 1581.
A Discovery of Edmund Campion and His Confederates. 1582.
A Brief Answer Made unto Two Seditious Pamphlets. 1582.
A Brief and True Report of the Execution of Certain Traitors at Tyburn. 1582.
The English Roman Life, Discovering the Lives of the Englishmen at Rome. 1582; edited by G. B. Harrison, 1925.
A Watch-Word to England, to Beware of Traitors. 1584.
The Admirable Deliverance of 166 Christians by J. Reynard, Englishman, from the Turks. 1608.
A Brief Chronicle of the Success of Times from the Creation of the World to This Instant. 1611.
A Survey of London, by John Stow, revised by Munday. 1618; revised edition, with D. Dyson and others, 1633; edited by H. B. Wheatley, 1960.

Translator, *Palmerin D'Oliva.* 2 vols., 1588–97.
Translator, *The Famous, Pleasant, and Variable History of Palladine of England,* by Claude Colet. 1588.
Translator, *The Declaration of the Lord de la Noue, upon His Taking Arms.* 1589.
Translator, *The Honorable, Pleasant, and Rare Conceited History of Palmendos,* by Francisco de Moraes. 1589.
Translator, *Amadis of Gaul.* 3 vols., 1590–1618.
Translator, *The Copy of the Anti-Spaniard.* 1590.
Translator, *The Masque of the League and the Spaniard Discovered.* 1592; as *Falsehood in Friendship,* 1605.
Translator, *Archaioplutos; or, The Riches of Elder Ages,* by Guillaume Thelin. 1592.
Translator, *Gerileon of England,* part 2, by Estienne de Maisonneufve. 1592.
Translator, *The Defense of Contraries: Paradoxes Against Common Opinion,* by Charles Estienne. 1593.
Translator, *Primaleon of Greece.* 3 vols., 1595–1619.
Translator, *Palmerin of England,* by Francisco de Moraes. 3 vols., 1596–1602; edited by Robert Southey, 1807.
Translator, *A Brief Treatise of the Virtue of the Cross.* 1599.
Translator, *The True Knowledge of a Man's Own Life,* by Philippe de Mornay. 1602.
Translator, *The Dumb Divine Speaker,* by Fra. Giacomo Affinati d'Acuto Romano. 1605.
Translator, *The Conversion of a Most Noble Lady of France.* 1608.

Bibliography: *Munday: A Concise Bibliography* by S. A. Tannenbaum, 1942; *Munday 1941–66* by R. C. Johnson, 1968.

Reading List: *Munday, An Elizabethan Man of Letters* by Celeste Turner, 1928; *The Palmerin Romances in Elizabethan Prose Fiction* by Mary Patchell, 1947; *Amadis de Gaul and Its Influence on Elizabethan Literature* by J. J. O'Connor, 1970; *English Civic Pageantry 1558–1642* by D. M. Bergeron, 1971.

*   *   *

Anthony Munday is the most fascinating of all the minor dramatists of his time, and very unusually it was a very long time: he was born in 1560 (not 1553 as used to be thought) and died when the Jacobean period had largely run its course (1633). He was a stationer's apprentice, a failed comedian of the Tarlton and Kemp type, a spy, a translator, a writer of pamphlets, ballads, and city pageants, and − *Histriomastix* calls him Posthaste − an industrious original and collaborative dramatist for Henslowe. Turner's *Life* and Tannenbaum's bibliography have many interesting details of his active career.

He plays an important part in the history of the prose romances that were so popular in the late Elizabethan period, and, though Southey thought them inaccurate, produced influential translations of Palmerin romances: three parts of *Palmerin of England, Palmerin D'Oliva, History of Palmendos, Gerileon of England, Primaleon of Greece*, and *Amadis of Gaul*. This makes him of interest to scholars of the semi-Arthurian romance (of whom there are many) and of the origins of the English novel (of whom there have not been enough).

Like Marlowe, he was a spy against the Jesuit plotters; if ever the whole story of Sir Thomas Walsingham's Elizabethan "CIA" is told (which is unlikely), it could reveal exciting secrets.

Munday was the author of numerous pamphlets about sensational crimes and executions in the days of Deloney, Nashe, and Lodge, and was involved in the much-studied "War of the Theatres" when he followed up Stephen Gosson's *Schoole of Abuse*, which asked the public to "shut up our ears to poets, pipers, and players" in the Puritan tradition, in *A Second and Third Blast of Retrait from Plays and Theatres*, a reformed-Bohemian effort in the style of Robert Greene which earned a resounding riposte from Lodge.

Yet while he on that occasion seemed even more sincere than the Puritans and the parsons in regarding the theatre as the sink of sin, Munday wrote (in addition to a number of adequate civic pageants in the 1600's) many plays himself. Most of the Elizabethan drama is lost, so it should be no surprise that among Munday's probable works now missing are *The Rare Triumphs of Love and Fortune, The Funeral of Richard Coeur de Lion, Chance Medley, Mother Redcap, Valentine and Orson*, the first part of *Fair Constance of Rome, Owen Tudor, The Rising of Cardinal Wolsey, Caesar's Fall (Two Shapes), Jephthah, The Set at Tennis*, and *The Widow's Charm*. It should be remembered, however, that Henslowe was keeping a diary for his own use, not for posterity, and also that The Stationer's Register noted plays it was intended to print and not simply those that were actually published.

Extant works indicate the range and quality of this dramatist whom Francis Meres in *Palladis Tamia* (1598) called "the best for comedy" and "our best plotter" (George Saintsbury sensed a gibe in that). These are a court play of 1584 (or earlier) called *Fedele and Fortunio* derived from Pasquaglio's *Il Fedele*, with the interesting *miles glorioso* Captain Crackstone and connections with Shakespeare's intrigue comedies; *John a Kent and John a Cumber*; a hand in *Sir Thomas More*, a fascinating MS representing collaborative revision of a play of c.1590–1593, itself dating anywhere from about 1593 to 1601 and involving Shakespeare; two Robin Hood plays, *The Downfall of Robert, Earl of Huntingdon* and *The Death of Robert, Earl of Huntingdon*, both with Chettle; a hand in the first part of *Sir John Oldcastle*; and several entertainments and pageants.

Munday's work has still not been fully studied, though his collaborations bring him importantly into examinations of a number of much-discussed playwrights. His work with mythological subjects connects him with Lyly and others, biblical subjects with Peele and others, history and folklore sources with Greene and his followers, while his period inevitably involves him in abstruse discussions of anonymous and lost plays and the apocryphal and actual plays of Shakespeare. Shakespeare is said to have quoted only Marlowe (the "dead shepherd") among his contemporaries, but *Macbeth* in a famous line echoes *The Downfall of Robert, Earl of Huntingdon*'s "made the green sea red" and "the multitudes of seas dyed red with blood" from *The Death of Robert, Earl of Huntingdon*.

Jonson's mention of his pageants in *The Case is Altered* ("Antonio Balladino" is hired, he says, "when a worse cannot be had") is prejudiced and not wholly fair, and I strongly agree with George Sampson (*Cambridge History of English Literature*) that "Munday is one of the minor Elizabethans eminently worthy of sympathetic study."

—Leonard R. N. Ashley

MURPHY, Arthur. Irish. Born in Clomquin, Roscommon, 27 December 1727; lived with his family in Dublin, 1729–35, and in London from 1735. Studied at the English College in St. Omer, France, 1738–44. Clerk to a merchant in Cork, 1747–49; worked in the City banking house of Ironside and Belchier, London, 1749–51; publisher of, and leading contributor to, *Gray's Inn Journal*, 1752–54; appeared as an actor at Covent Garden and Drury Lane, 1754–55, and began writing for the stage, 1756; admitted to Lincoln's Inn, London, 1757, was subsequently called to the bar, and practised in London; also edited the weekly papers, *The Test* and *The Auditor*; retired from the law and the theatre, 1788; appointed a commissioner of bankrupts and granted a pension by George III, 1803. *Died 18 June 1805.*

PUBLICATIONS

Collections

The Way to Keep Him and Five Other Plays (includes *The Apprentice, The Upholsterer, The Old Maid, Three Weeks after Marriage, Know Your Own Mind*), edited by John P. Emery. 1956.

Plays

The Apprentice (produced 1756). 1756; in *The Way to Keep Him and Five Other Plays*, 1956.
The Englishman from Paris (produced 1756).
The Upholsterer; or, What News? (produced 1758). 1758; edited by R. W. Bevis, in *Eighteenth Century Drama: Afterpieces*, 1970.
The Orphan of China, from a play by Voltaire (produced 1759). 1759.
The Tears and Triumphs of Parnassus, with Robert Lloyd, music by John Stanley (produced 1760).
The Way to Keep Him, from a play by Moissy (produced 1760). 1760; revised version (produced 1761), 1761; in *The Way to Keep Him and Five Other Plays*, 1956; 1760 version edited by R. W. Bevis, in *Eighteenth Century Drama: Afterpieces*, 1970.
The Desert Island, from a play by Metastasio (produced 1760). 1760.
All in the Wrong (produced 1761). 1761.
The Old Maid, from a play by Fagan (produced 1761). 1761.
The Citizen, from a play by Destouches (produced 1761). 1763.
No One's Enemy But His Own, from a play by Voltaire (produced 1764). 1764.
What We Must All Come To (produced 1764). 1764; as *Three Weeks after Marriage* (produced 1776), 1776; in *The Way to Keep Him and Five Other Plays*, 1956.

The Choice (produced 1765).   In *Works*, 1786.
The School for Guardians, from a play by Molière (produced 1767).   1767.
Zenobia (produced 1768).   1768.
The Grecian Daughter (produced 1772).   1772.
Alzuma (produced 1773).   1773.
News from Parnassus (produced 1776).   In *Works*, 1786.
Know Your Own Mind, from a play by Destouches (produced 1777).   1778; in *The Way to Keep Him and Five Other Plays*, 1956.
The Rival Sisters (produced 1793).   In *Works*, 1786.
Arminius.   1798.
Hamlet, with Alterations, from the play by Shakespeare, in *Life of Murphy* by J. Foot. 1811; edited by Martin Lehnert, in *Shakespeare Jahrbuch 102*, 1966.

Verse

A Poetical Epistle to Samuel Johnson.   1760.
An Ode to the Naiads of Fleet Ditch.   1761.
The Examiner: A Satire.   1761.
Seventeen Hundred and Ninety-One: A Poem in Imitation of the Thirteenth Satire of Juvenal.   1791.
The Bees: A Poem from the Fourteenth Book of Vaniere's Praedium Rusticum.   1799.
The Game of Chess, from a poem by Vida.   1876.

Other

The Gray's Inn Journal.   2 vols., 1756.
A Letter to Voltaire on The Desert Island.   1760.
Works.   7 vols., 1786.
An Essay on the Life and Genius of Samuel Johnson.   1792.
The Life of David Garrick.   2 vols., 1801.
New Essays, edited by Arthur Sherbo.   1963.

Editor, *Works*, by Fielding.   4 vols., 1762.

Translator, *The Works of Tacitus*.   4 vols., 1793.
Translator, *The Works of Sallust*.   1807.

Reading List: *Murphy: An Eminent English Dramatist of the Eighteenth Century* by John P. Emery, 1946; *The Dramatic Career of Murphy* by Howard Hunter Dunbar, 1946; Introduction by Simon Trefman to *The Englishman from Paris*, 1969.

*   *   *

A man of broad interests and a prolific writer, Arthur Murphy was a journalist, biographer, editor, actor, translator of the classics, lawyer, political writer, and one of the most successful playwrights of the third quarter of the eighteenth century. Of particular interest among Murphy's various non-dramatic writings are his *Gray's Inn Journal* and biographies of Garrick, Fielding, and Johnson. These works contain much perceptive practical criticism, Murphy's generally traditional literary theories, and a great deal of information about the theater and literary life of his age.

About twenty of Murphy's plays were performed during the eighteenth century. These range from short farces and satires used as afterpieces to full-length tragedies and comedies. Although at least minimally successful in all the dramatic genres he attempted, Murphy's greatest skill is evident in his comedies and farces. One of the best of these is *The Way to Keep Him*, which was first performed as a three-act afterpiece and was a miniature comedy, not a farce. After Murphy rewrote it in five acts, the resulting full-fledged comedy of manners remained popular for a century. The play, which deals with various modes of marital behavior, contains some sentimental elements, but generally shares the same spirit as the comedies of Congreve and Sheridan. *All in the Wrong*, *The School for Guardians*, and *Know Your Own Mind* also display Murphy's talent for writing comedies of manners.

Murphy's farces are among the best in an age that is noted for good farces. Whether focusing on satire or outlandish situations, his farces are usually fast-paced and his characters, often "humours" types, well-drawn. *The Apprentice* and *The Upholsterer* satirize stage-struck apprentices and tradesmen who are excessively interested in politics, respectively. The latter contains a character, Mrs. Termagant, who may have been a source for Sheridan's Mrs. Malaprop. Other farces worthy of mention are *The Old Maid*, *No One's Enemy But His Own*, and *Three Weeks after Marriage*. The ingenious situational humor and riotous quarrel scenes make the latter an especially lively theatrical piece.

—James S. Malek

NABBES, Thomas. English. Born in Worcestershire in 1605. Educated at Exeter College, Oxford, matriculated 1621, left without taking a degree. Subsequently employed in the household of a nobleman near Worcester; settled in London, 1630; nothing is recorded about him after 1639.

PUBLICATIONS

Collections

    Works, edited by A. H. Bullen.   1887.

Plays

    Covent Garden (produced 1632–33?).   1638.
    Tottenham Court (produced 1633).   1638.
    Hannibal and Scipio (produced 1635).   1637.
    Microcosmus: A Moral Masque (produced 1637).   1637.
    The Spring's Glory, in a Masque, in *The Spring's Glory, with Other Poems.*   1638;
        edited by J. R. Brown, in *A Book of Masques in Honour of Allardyce Nicoll,* 1967.
    A Presentation Intended for the Prince on His Birthday.   1638.
    The Bride (produced 1638).   In *Plays ...,* 1639.
    The Unfortunate Mother, in *Plays. ...*   1639.

Other

    The Spring's Glory, with Other Poems, Epigrams, Elegies, and Epithalamiums.   1638.
    Plays, Masques, Epigrams, Elegies, and Epithalamiums.   1639.

Reading List: *Nabbes: A Critical Monograph* by A. C. Swinburne, 1914; *The Dramatic Works of Nabbes* by Charlotte Moore, 1918.

*   *   *

In the last half of the 1630's, two generations of playwrights and two monarchs removed from the vigour of the English theatre under Elizabeth, Thomas Nabbes produced his half dozen or so comedies, tragedies, and masques. His dramatic activity may have been cut short by the climate of anxiety preceding the close of the theatres in 1642. Perhaps he found his competence written out in the works he left us and, lacking genius, retired rather than repeat himself. All that we know is that Nabbes's surviving works were published from 1637–39, and then Nabbes disappears from literary history.

His two comedies, *Covent Garden* and *Tottenham Court,* seem to have been written first. Their titles indicate their strength, a palpable realism of locale, as well as their dependence on the London or citizen comedies and the theatre of humours of Ben Jonson. *Covent Garden* is especially lively, filled as it is with the clumsy pretensions of the would-be country gentleman, Dungworth, and the hectic antics of Dasher, the "complementing Vintner" whom Swinburne found a "really humorous and original figure." The plots of both comedies involve the amorous wooing of gentlewomen by gallants or libertines, who ultimately reform their ways, and by "deserving" gentlemen, whose common-sense virtue wins the day.

Nabbes's last comedy, *The Bride*, attempts a religious or moral allegory symbolized in the names of its principals: Goodlove, his son Theophilus, the "villane" Raven, and the object of their interest, a maiden called simply The Bride. Of the three comedies this is the most crammed with humorous characters – the antiquarian Horten, the French cook Kickshaw, Justice and Mrs. Ferret, and the Vintner Squirrel, among others. Its serious moral vision may be shaken out of focus at times by the vitality of the humours, but the earnestness of the author is evident here, as throughout his comedies. The satire is always gentle and accepting in these three "easy" Caroline sentimental comedies.

His two tragedies are less appealing. *Hannibal and Scipio*, modelled on Marston's *Sophonisba*, is at times inflated, at times inane. *The Unfortunate Mother*, a tragedy of intrigue, was never performed: the actors refused to go through with the performance.

His poems are likewise negligible, although the few poems that concern Worcester, its steeple and its beer, have some, if only biographical, interest.

Nabbes wrote three masques, *Microcosmus*, *The Spring's Glory*, and *A Presentation Intended for the Prince on His Birthday*. The first, a fairly substantial production, combines the visual splendour of the masque with the seriousness of an allegorical moral interlude. Physander (the Body) betrothed to Bellanima (the Soul) is tempted by Malus Genius (evil spirit) to jilt his beloved for Sensuality. He ruins his health courting her, but is ultimately cured, tried, acquitted, and reunited with Bellanima. This combination of masque and theatre is important because it represents an attempt to curb the empty extravagance of the Caroline masque; it domesticates the masque from court to private house (*Microcosmus* was the first masque performed on the public stage in England); and it leads toward the redefinition of the masque form that culminates in Milton's *Comus*. Both *The Spring's Glory* and *A Presentation* also have charm. That they were not presented in Nabbes's lifetime may be a consequence of their old-fashioned moral seriousness, out of favour with those who relished the elaborate spectacle of the Caroline court masque.

These masques, as well as the three comedies, are attractive in their gentleness and their lack of pretension. Perhaps the finest compliment, and the most perceptive, payable to Nabbes is Swinburne's: a "modest and good-humoured author."

—Daniel DeMatteis

NORTON, Thomas. English. Born in London in 1532. Nothing is known about his academic career except that he was created M.A. by Cambridge University in 1570; admitted to the Inner Temple, London, 1555, and subsequently practised law in London. Married 1) Margery Cranmer, the daughter of Archbishop Cranmer, in 1555 (died); 2) her cousin Alice Cranmer c. 1568; three sons and two daughters. Secretary to the Protector, the Duke of Somerset, in the early 1550's; elected Member of Parliament for Gatton, 1558, Berwick, 1562, and for the City of London, 1571, 1572, and 1580, and sponsored or strongly supported all measures against Roman Catholics; Standing Counsel to the Stationers' Company, 1562; Remembrancer of the City of London, 1571; Solicitor to the Merchant Taylors' Company, 1581; Official Censor of the Queen's Catholic Subjects from 1581, and conducted examinations of numerous Roman Catholic prisoners under torture: accused of treason because of his extreme Protestant views, imprisoned in the Tower of London, then released, 1584. *Died 10 March 1584.*

Play

> *The Tragedy of Gorboduc,* with Thomas Sackville (produced 1561).   1565; as *The Tragedy of Ferrex and Porrex,* 1570(?); edited by Irby B. Cauthen, 1970.

Verse

> *25 Psalms,* in *The Whole Book of Psalms Collected into English by Sternhold and Hopkins.*   1562.

Other

> *Orations.*   1560(?).
> *To the Queen's Deceived Subjects of the North Country.*   1569.
> *A Warning Against the Dangerous Practices of Papists.*   1570(?).

> Translator, *The Institution of Christian Religion,* by John Calvin.   1561.
> Translator, *A Catechism,* by Alexander Nowell.   1570.

*   *   *

See the essay on Thomas Sackville.

O'CASEY, Sean. Irish. Born in Dublin, 30 March 1880. Attended a school in Dublin for three years; lived in extreme poverty as a child: largely self-educated. Married Eileen Reynolds in 1927; two sons and one daughter. Began working at age 13 in a Dublin chandlery; thereafter worked as a docker, hod carrier, stone breaker on road-building crews, and for a news agency; involved in the Dublin transport strike in 1913, and served in the Irish Citizen Army; associated with the Abbey Theatre, Dublin, from 1923; settled in England, 1926. Recipient: Hawthornden Prize, 1926. *Died 18 September 1964.*

PUBLICATIONS

Collections

The O'Casey Reader, edited by Brooks Atkinson. 1968.
The Letters 1910–41, edited by David Krause. Vol. 1 (of 3), 1975.

Plays

The Shadow of a Gunman (produced 1923). In Two Plays, 1925.
Cathleen Listens In: A Phantasy (produced 1923). In Feathers from the Green Crow, 1962.
Juno and the Paycock (produced 1924). In Two Plays, 1925.
Nannie's Night Out (produced 1924). In Feathers from the Green Crow, 1962.
Two Plays: Juno and the Paycock, The Shadow of a Gunman. 1925.
The Plough and the Stars (produced 1926). 1926.
The Silver Tassie (produced 1929). 1928.
Within the Gates (produced 1934). 1933.
The End of the Beginning (produced 1937). In Windfalls, 1934.
A Pound on Demand (produced 1939). In Windfalls, 1934.
The Star Turns Red (produced 1940). 1940.
Purple Dust: A Wayward Comedy (produced 1943). 1940.
Red Roses for Me (produced 1943). 1942.
Oak Leaves and Lavender; or, A World on Wallpaper (produced 1947). 1946.
Cock-a-Doodle Dandy (produced 1949). 1949.
Collected Plays. 4 vols., 1949–51.
Bedtime Story: An Anatole Burlesque (produced 1952). In Collected Plays 4, 1951.
Hall of Healing: A Sincerious Farce (produced 1952). In Collected Plays 3, 1951.
Time to Go: A Morality Comedy (produced 1952). In Collected Plays 4, 1951.
The Bishop's Bonfire (produced 1955). 1955.
The Drums of Father Ned: A Mickrocosm of Ireland (produced 1959). 1960.
The Moon Shines on Kylenamoe (produced 1961). In Behind the Green Curtains ..., 1961.
Behind the Green Curtains, Figaro in the Night, The Moon Shines on Kylenamoe: Three Plays. 1961.
Behind the Green Curtains (produced 1962). In Behind the Green Curtains ..., 1961.
Figaro in the Night (produced 1962). In Behind the Green Curtains ..., 1961.

Screenplay: Juno and the Paycock (The Shame of Mary Boyle), with Alma Reville and Alfred Hitchcock, 1929.

435

Verse

> *Songs of the Wren.*   2 vols., 1918.
> *More Wren Songs.*   1918.

Other

> *The Sacrifice of Thomas Ashe.*   1918.
> *The Story of Thomas Ashe.*   1918.
> *The Story of the Irish Citizen Army.*   1919.
> *Windfalls: Stories, Poems, and Plays.*   1934.
> *The Flying Wasp* (on theatre).   1937.
> Autobiography:
>> 1. *I Knock at the Door: Swift Glances Back at Things That Made Me.*   1939.
>> 2. *Pictures in the Hallway.*   1942.
>> 3. *Drums under the Window.*   1945.
>> 4. *Inishfallen, Fare Thee Well.*   1949.
>> 5. *Rose and Crown.*   1952.
>> 6. *Sunset and Evening Star.*   1956.
> *The Green Crow* (essays and stories).   1956.
> *Feathers from the Green Crow 1905–15* (miscellany), edited by Robert Hogan.   1962.
> *Under a Colored Cap: Articles Merry and Mournful with Comments and a Song.*   1963.
> *Blasts and Benedictions: Articles and Stories,* edited by Ronald Ayling.   1967.
> *The Sting and the Twinkle: Conversations with O'Casey,* edited by E. H. Mikhail and John O'Riordan.   1974.

Bibliography: *O'Casey: A Bibliography* by Ronald Ayling and Michael J. Durkan, 1977.

Reading List: *The Green and the Red: O'Casey, The Man and His Plays* by Jules Koslow, 1950, revised edition, 1966; *The Experiments of O'Casey* by Robert Hogan, 1960; *O'Casey, The Man and His Work,* 1960, revised edition, 1976, and *O'Casey and His World,* 1976, both by David Krause; *O'Casey, The Man Behind the Plays,* 1963, revised edition, 1965, and *O'Casey,* 1966, both by Saros Cowasjee; *The World of O'Casey* edited by S. McCann, 1966; *O'Casey* by W. A. Armstrong, 1967; *A Self-Portrait of the Artist as a Man: O'Casey's Letters* edited by David Krause, 1968; *The Plays of O'Casey* by Maureen Malone, 1969; *The Early Life of O'Casey* by Martin B. Margulies, 1970; *Sean* by Eileen O'Casey, edited by J. C. Trewin, 1971; *O'Casey: A Collection of Critical Essays* edited by Thomas Kilroy, 1974; *O'Casey* by Doris Darin, 1975; *O'Casey* by C. Desmond Greaves, 1978.

*   *   *

Fame came to Sean O'Casey at the age of forty-three when the Abbey Theatre, after rejecting four of his "apprentice" plays, accepted *The Shadow of a Gunman* in 1923. Set during the Anglo-Irish wars, the play deals with a pseudo-poet Donal Davoren who pretends, with tragic consequences, to be a gunman to win the affections of Minnie Powell – one of the tenement residents. The immediate success of the play paved the way for *Juno and the Paycock* and *The Plough and the Stars.* The former, with the Irish Civil War as its backdrop, is the story of the Boyle family trapped between events they themselves have precipitated and others over which they have no control. While Captain Jack Boyle, the dry-land sailor, struts about the snugs saturating himself on stout with his "butty" Joxer Daly, Juno, his hardworking wife, keeps the home together. But misfortunes move in fast: their son Johnny is shot as a traitor, their daughter Mary is left pregnant by her suitor, and the promise of the expected legacy is not fulfilled. The latter play, to my mind O'Casey's finest work, is about the tenement dwellers caught in the 1916 Easter Rising. While a few idealistic Irishmen strike a blow for freedom, the vast majority of the Dubliners loot, swear, gamble, and applaud the fighters from a safe distance. The result is as one would expect: the Rising fails; the hero, Jack Clitheroe, and his wife, Nora, die, while the braggarts and the good-for-nothings live on. Among them is Fluther Good, a veritable Falstaff, some of whose wildness O'Casey saw in himself and whose name he sprawls all over his autobiographies.

The above three plays have many features in common. They have a war period for background, and O'Casey views the war strictly from the angle of the slum dweller. He condemns all wars, and shows their horrible impact on people who have the least to do with fighting. The evils of tenement life are depicted with frightening realism and accuracy. Characters generally take precedence over plot: in the main his women are brave and earthy, his men are dreamers and braggarts. Through the interaction of his male and female characters (many of them modelled on people from real life), O'Casey offers a juxtaposition of tragedy and comedy rarely rivalled in English dramatic literature. But his main concern is to give an honest and unflinching portrayal of his countrymen and times. It is no exaggeration to say that these plays are a suitable appendix to any political and social history of Ireland between the years 1916 and 1923.

Realism had never strongly appealed to O'Casey in spite of the success it had brought him. His lost play, *The Robe of Rosheen*, was according to him "in the 'first principle' of a fantasy," and his one-actor *Cathleen Listens In* was also a fantasy with symbolic characters. But his first conscious experiment in symbolism and expressionism was *The Silver Tassie*. It is the story of the footballer Harry Heegan who goes unthinkingly to the trenches. He returns an invalid to discover that the man who saved his life has been awarded the Victoria Cross and has won the affection of the girl he loves. Through the agony of the crippled hero, O'Casey voices his hatred of warfare. To show the colossal nightmare war is, O'Casey makes the second act totally expressionistic and juxtaposes it with other acts written in the naturalistic manner. The setting of the act (a ruined monastery), the intoning of the prophecies of doom (parodies from the Book of Ezekiel), the fantastic chanted poetry, the stylisation of characters and dialogue, all go to make the play, in the words of John Gassner, "one of the most trenchant pacifist protests of the generation."

Having seen the possibilities of symbolic drama in *The Silver Tassie*, O'Casey went on to write a completely expressionistic play, *Within the Gates*. The setting is no longer Dublin but Hyde Park, London, and the three principal characters are the Bishop, the Dreamer, and the Young Woman. The Young Woman is torn between conflicting emotions: on the one hand she wishes to live a life of joy, sex, and unrestrained youth; on the other hand she seeks the salvation which her mode of life denies her. The Bishop and the Dreamer, holding views that are diametrically opposite, struggle to win her to their respective beliefs. In a way they both succeed, for O'Casey gets the Bishop to bless her as she dies dancing in the arms of the Dreamer. The message of the play seems to be that God should be approached through joy, not fear.

What is unique about this play is its design. Its four scenes, Morning, Noon, Evening, and Night, correspond to the four seasons, Spring, Summer, Autumn, and Winter. These blend with the changing colours of flowers and trees. Close significance is implicit in chosen moments of bird-song and sunshine; human action in all instances is related to seasonal references. The dialogue is stylised, and the entry and exit of the numerous characters and their positions on the stage are expertly controlled. Music and dance are closely woven into the symbolic pattern of the drama – they do not merely further the theme but contain it as well. The whole play is a triumph of technique and stagecraft.

With a couple of exceptions, O'Casey's remaining plays are less successful. They may conveniently be divided into two groups, plays concerned primarily with Communism and plays expressing his views of life in Ireland. Technique, characterisation, humour, and a strong urge to promote happiness for all are common to these two groups.

In the first group falls *The Star Turns Red*, *Red Roses for Me*, and *Oak Leaves and Lavender*. Of these only *Red Roses for Me* has distinctive merit. The background of the play is the Irish Transport Workers' strike of 1913; the hero is a doomed idealist called Ayamonn Breydon, a Protestant, in love with a Catholic girl, Shiela Moorneen. A strike is organised by the workers for a shilling-a-week increase in wages, and Shiela begs him to take no part in it. But Ayamonn ignores her entreaties, and is killed in a clash with the police. Dying, he sends words to his friend, the parish Rector: "this day's but a day's work done, an' it'll be begun again tomorrow."

In *Red Roses for Me*, O'Casey returns to Dublin for his *milieu*. Slum life is depicted with its accompanying poverty and hunger; there is the same lack of privacy to be found in his Abbey plays. But the most moving thing here is the expressionistic third act. The dull and dismal quays of Dublin are transformed into a vision of beauty as Ayamonn unfolds to the people his dream of the city's hidden splendour. Under the stress of genuine poetry the Party Line disappears, and we have a political play which is no facile propaganda.

The second group comprises *Purple Dust*, *Cock-a-Doodle Dandy*, *The Bishop's Bonfire*, *The Drums of Father Ned*, and *Behind the Green Curtains*. They are all set in "imaginary" Irish villages, and among the things they have in common are O'Casey's attack on the Irish clergy and a vibrant plea for joy, sex, and sanity. Of these, *Purple Dust* is the gayest. It deals with the efforts of two Englishmen to transplant themselves to a Tudor mansion in the west of Ireland to enjoy the pleasures of country life. Their manners, temperaments, and outlook clash with those of the Irish, till the whole house becomes a bedlam. *Cock-a-Doodle Dandy*, the author's favourite, is an uproarious fantasy that most sharply defines O'Casey's view of Ireland in particular and life in general. The all-out battle waged by the priest and his puritanical crew against the indefatigable Cock (symbolic of joy, courage, and sexual ecstasy) is the play's highlight and shows O'Casey at his funniest. *The Bishop's Bonfire* centres on the preparations being made to receive Bishop Bill Mullarkey in his home town of Ballyoonagh. A lesser play that the preceding two, it tackles the problems of Ireland more pointedly by its vigorous condemnation of men and institutions that stand between the individual and his right to happiness.

Among O'Casey's prose works, his six volumes of autobiography are a notable achievement. Each volume covers a 12-year span of his life, beginning with *I Knock at the Door*, and continuing with *Picture in the Hallway*, *Drums under the Window*, *Inishfallen, Fare Thee Well*, *Rose and Crown*, and *Sunset and Evening Star*. Written in the third person, and in a variety of styles, the work is, as one reviewer puts it, "one of the most astonishing and appalling documents of poverty, failure, success, and then the poverty and failure of success itself, written in the last half century." They also throw enormous light on the Dublin of O'Casey's youth and are an indispensable source-book for the study of his plays.

Of the six books, the first four dealing with his hard struggle to survive and become a great dramatist are the best. And of these four, *Inishfallen, Fare Thee Well* is the most impressive. He recalls with great clarity the year immediately following the Easter Rising, his grief at his mother's death and the pauper's funeral that accompanied it, the fight against the Black and Tans, and the heart-rending Civil War. He tells us of his meeting with Yeats and Lady Gregory, and the circumstances that forced him into exile. Any account following those memorable years and events was sure to be an anti-climax, and it is not surprising that the last two volumes are the least successful. But they still make fascinating reading because of the old O'Casey traits: narrative detail, sharp observation, comic invective, incisive humour, and glorious puns and malapropisms.

—Saros Cowasjee

ODETS, Clifford.   American.   Born in Philadelphia, Pennsylvania, 18 July 1906; grew up in the Bronx, New York. Educated at Morris High School, New York, 1921–23. Married 1) the actress Luise Rainer in 1937 (divorced, 1941); 2) Betty Grayson in 1943 (died, 1954), one son and one daughter. Actor on radio and on Broadway, 1923–28, and with Theatre Guild Productions, New York, 1928–30; Co-Founder, Group Theatre, New York, 1930; wrote for the stage from 1933; film writer and director. Recipient: New Theatre League prize, 1935; Yale drama prize, 1935; American Academy of Arts and Letters Award of Merit Medal, 1961. *Died 15 August 1963.*

PUBLICATIONS

Plays

> *Waiting for Lefty* (produced 1935).   In *Three Plays,* 1935.
> *Awake and Sing!* (produced 1935).   In *Three Plays,* 1935.
> *Till the Day I Die* (produced 1935).   In *Three Plays,* 1935.
> *I Can't Sleep: A Monologue* (produced 1935).   1936.
> *Paradise Lost* (produced 1935).   1936.
> *Golden Boy* (produced 1937).   1937.
> *Rocket to the Moon* (produced 1938).   1939.
> *Night Music* (produced 1940).   1940.
> *Clash by Night* (produced 1941).   1942.
> *The Russian People,* from a play by Konstantin Simonov (produced 1942).
> *None But the Lonely Heart* (screenplay), in *Best Film Plays 1945,* edited by John Gassner
> and Dudley Nichols.   1946.
> *The Big Knife* (produced 1949).   1949.
> *The Country Girl* (produced 1950).   1951; as *Winter Journey* (produced 1952), 1953.
> *The Flowering Peach* (produced 1954).   1954.
> *The Silent Partner* (produced 1972).

> Screenplays: *The General Died at Dawn,* 1936; *Black Sea Fighters,* 1943; *None But the Lonely Heart,* 1944; *Deadline at Dawn,* 1946; *Humoresque* with Zachery Gold, 1946; *Sweet Smell of Success,* with Ernest Lehman, 1957; *The Story on Page One,* 1960; *Wild in the Country,* 1961.

> Television Plays: *Big Mitch,* 1963; *The Mafia Man,* 1964.

Other

> *Rifle Rule in Cuba,* with Carleton Beals.   1935.

Reading List: *Odets* by R. Baird Shuman, 1963; *Odets: The Thirties and After* by Edward Murray, 1968; *Odets, Humane Dramatist* by Michael J. Mendelsohn, 1969; *Odets* by Gerald Weales, 1971; *Odets, Playwright-Poet* by Harold Cantor, 1978.

*   *   *

Clifford Odets's first produced play was *Waiting for Lefty,* a one-act agitprop drama based on the New York City taxi strike of 1934. It is uncharacteristic Odets in both form and intention. A group of naturalistic dramatic sketches set within a union meeting, still visible while the more intimate scenes are being played, *Waiting for Lefty* is non-realistic theater that breaks the conventional frame to invite the audience to join in the final call for a strike. Aside from this play, Odets remained within the American realistic tradition even when he attempted to open the form with cinematic techniques (*Golden Boy*), visual and musical devices (*Night Music*) and Yiddish-Biblical fantasy (*The Flowering Peach*). Although most of his plays, particularly the early ones like *Awake and Sing!* and *Paradise Lost*, have the mandatory optimistic ending decreed by the American Left in the 1930's, *Waiting for Lefty* is the only overt propaganda play Odets wrote, except for *Till the Day I Die*, an ineffective anti-fascist piece hastily written to fill out the bill when *Lefty* moved to Broadway. He did do a few sketches, like "I Can't Sleep," for benefit performances and he worked at two political plays, *The Cuban Play* and *The Silent Partner*, which he never got into final form. If *Waiting for Lefty* is uncharacteristic in some ways, it is also unmistakable Odets. Scenes like "Joe and Edna" and "The Young Hack and His Girl" show that Odets's political and social concerns look their best transformed into domestic conflict, and the language of those scenes set the tone for the Odets work to come. When Edna says "Get out of here!" meaning "I love you" and Sid, in affectionate exasperation, calls his brother, "that dumb basketball player," we get a first taste of the Odets obliquity – the wisecrack as lament, slang as lyricism – that, trailing its Yiddish and urban roots, enriches *Awake and Sing!* and *Paradise Lost* before it peters out in the self-parody of some of the lines in the screenplay *Sweet Smell of Success*.

Although *Waiting for Lefty* introduced Odets to audiences and critics, it was not his first play. *Awake and Sing!* was already written and about to open when *Lefty* was produced. *Awake and Sing!*, Odets's most enduring work, is *the* American depression play, a still vital example of the 1930's conviction that, however terrible the situation, it could be rectified by an infusion of idealistic rhetoric administered at the final curtain. Although Odets was a Communist when he wrote it (and the play carries a few verbal indications of that fact), its optimism is more generalized, tied into the historical American penchant for possibility which, battered by the first years of the depression, had begun to revive with the election of Franklin D. Roosevelt in 1932. Not only is Odets hooked into the American ideational mainstream in *Awake and Sing!* but he recalls earlier American drama in his choice of a family setting for his play and in his willing employment of melodramatic commonplaces – the suicide of Jacob, the pregnancy of Hennie. He transcends the structural weaknesses in the play with the creation of a milieu so real that an audience feels it can be touched; this texture – partly verbal, partly emotional – is probably a product not simply of Odets's talent but of the context in which the play was written. Odets was a member of the Group Theatre, an acting company that was a family of sorts, and his Bergers are an echo of the loving, quarreling Group company which was a home for Odets, one that – reacting like Ralph and Hennie to Bessie Berger's Bronx – he sometimes saw as a trap. All of his plays through *Night Music* were written for the Group actors, but *Paradise Lost*, which Odets once correctly described as "a beautiful play, velvety ... gloomy and rich," and *Rocket to the Moon* come closest in texture to *Awake and Sing!*

When the success of *Awake and Sing!* was followed by the failure of *Paradise Lost*, Odets went to Hollywood to work on *The General Died at Dawn*. After that, he vacillated between Hollywood and New York, commerce and art, guilt and regeneration. These terms suit his view of the matter as reflected in *The Big Knife*, in which the Odets surrogate, the actor Charlie Castle, is destroyed as man and artist by the movie business. Despite this gloomy view of Hollywood Odets constantly returned to a suspicion that the movies too were an art, all the more attractive for the size of the audience. Ironically, the movies he worked on were conventional Hollywood products; even the two he directed as well as wrote, *None But the Lonely Heart* and *The Story on Page One*, are interesting primarily for their attempt at poetic verisimilitude, the visual equivalent of the sense of milieu created by other means in *Awake and Sing!* and *Paradise Lost*.

Odets's greatest commercial successes were *Golden Boy*, a parable in boxing gloves about the destructiveness of the American success ethic, and *The Country Girl*, an effective sentimental melodrama about an alcoholic actor's attempt to recover his career and his life. Both plays show Odets's theatrical skill, but his most attractive failures, *Paradise Lost* and *Night Music*, display a bumbling sweetness that is as important a part of Odets's talent as his technical proficiency. Both the staccato dialogue of *Golden Boy* and the rambling non sequiturs of *Paradise Lost* are aspects of the authentic Odets voice which can still be heard at its purest in *Awake and Sing!*

—Gerald Weales

O'KEEFFE, John. Irish. Born in Dublin, 24 June 1747. Educated at a Jesuit school in Saul's Court, Dublin; afterwards studied art in the Dublin School of Design. Married; one daughter and two sons. Originally an actor: member of Henry Mossop's stock company, Dublin, 1762–74; wrote for the stage from 1767; settled in London, c. 1780, and thereafter wrote comic pieces for the Haymarket and Covent Garden theatres; blind from the mid-1780's; received an annuity from Covent Garden, 1803, and a royal pension, 1820. *Died 4 February 1833.*

PUBLICATIONS

Plays

The She Gallant; or, Square-Toes Outwitted (produced 1767). 1767; revised version, as The Positive Man, music by Samuel Arnold and Michael Arne (produced 1782), in Dramatic Works, 1798.
Colin's Welcome (produced 1770).
Tony Lumpkin in Town (produced 1774). 1780.
The Poor Soldier (as The Shamrock, or, St. Patrick's Day, produced 1777; revised version, as The Poor Soldier, music by William Shield, produced 1783). 1785.
The Son-in-Law, music by Samuel Arnold (produced 1779). 1783.
The Dead Alive, music by Samuel Arnold (produced 1781). 1783.
The Agreeable Surprise, music by Samuel Arnold (produced 1781). 1784.
The Banditti; or, Love's Labyrinth, music by Samuel Arnold (produced 1781). Songs published 1781; revised version, as The Castle of Andalusia (produced 1782), 1783; revised version (produced 1788).
Harlequin Teague; or, The Giant's Causeway, music by Samuel Arnold (produced 1782). Songs published 1782.
Lord Mayor's Day; or, A Flight from Lapland, music by William Shield (produced 1782). Songs published 1782.
The Maid the Mistress, from a play by G. A. Federico (produced 1783). Songs published 1783.
The Young Quaker (produced 1783). 1784.
The Birthday; or, The Prince of Arragon, music by Samuel Arnold, from a play by Saint-Foix (produced 1783). 1783.
Gretna Green (lyrics only), play by Charles Stuart, music by Samuel Arnold (produced 1783). 1791.

Friar Bacon; or, Harlequin's Adventures in Lilliput, Brobdignag etc. (lyrics only), play by Charles Bonner, music by William Shield (produced 1783; as *Harlequin Rambler*, produced 1784). Songs published 1784.

Peeping Tom of Coventry, music by Samuel Arnold (produced 1784). 1786.

Fontainbleau; or, Our Way in France, music by William Shield (produced 1784). 1785.

The Blacksmith of Antwerp (produced 1785). In *Dramatic Works*, 1798.

A Beggar on Horseback, music by Samuel Arnold (produced 1785). In *Dramatic Works*, 1798.

Omai; or, A Trip round the World, music by William Shield (produced 1785). Songs published 1785.

Love in a Camp; or, Patrick in Prussia, music by William Shield (produced 1786). 1786.

The Siege of Curzola, music by Samuel Arnold (produced 1786). Songs published 1786.

The Man Milliner (produced 1787). In *Dramatic Works*, 1798.

Love and War, from the play *The Campaign* by Robert Jephson (produced 1787).

The Farmer, music by William Shield (produced 1787). 1788.

Tantara-Rara, Rogues All, from a play by Dumaniant (produced 1788). In *Dramatic Works*, 1798.

The Prisoner at Large (produced 1788). 1788.

The Highland Reel, music by William Shield (produced 1788). 1789.

Aladdin; or, The Wonderful Lamp, music by William Shield (produced 1788). Songs published 1788.

The Lie of the Day (as *The Toy*, produced 1789; revised version, as *The Lie of the Day*, produced 1796). In *Dramatic Works*, 1798.

The Faro Table, from the play *The Gamester* by Mrs. Centlivre (produced 1789).

The Little Hunch-Back; or, A Frolic in Bagdad (produced 1789). 1789.

The Czar Peter, music by William Shield (as *The Czar*, produced 1790; as *The Fugitive*, produced 1790). In *Dramatic Works*, 1798.

The Basket-Maker, music by Samuel Arnold (produced 1790). In *Dramatic Works*, 1798.

Modern Antiques; or, The Merry Mourners (produced 1791). 1792.

Wild Oats; or, The Strolling Gentleman (produced 1791). 1791; edited by Clifford Williams, 1977.

Tony Lumpkin's Ramble to Town (produced 1792).

Sprigs of Laurel, music by William Shield (produced 1793). 1793; revised version, as *The Rival Soldiers* (produced 1797).

The London Hermit; or, Rambles in Dorsetshire (produced 1793). 1793.

The World in a Village (produced 1793). 1793.

Life's Vagaries (produced 1795). 1795.

The Irish Mimic; or, Blunders at Brighton, music by William Shield (produced 1795). 1795.

Merry Sherwood; or, Harlequin Forester (lyrics only), play by Mark Lonsdale and William Pearce, music by William Reeve (produced 1795). Songs published 1795.

The Wicklow Gold Mines; or, The Lad of the Hills, music by William Shield (produced 1796). 1814; revised version, as *The Wicklow Mountains* (produced 1796), 1797.

The Doldrum; or, 1803 (produced 1796). In *Dramatic Works*, 1798.

Alfred; or, The Magic Banner (produced 1796). 1796.

Olympus in an Uproar; or, The Descent of the Deities, from the play *The Golden Pippin* by Kane O'Hara (produced 1796).

Britain's Brave Tars; or, All for St. Paul's, music by Thomas Attwood (produced 1797).

She's Eloped (produced 1798).

The Eleventh of June; or, The Daggerwoods at Dunstable (produced 1798).

A Nosegay of Weeds; or, Old Servants in New Places (produced 1798).
Dramatic Works.   4 vols., 1798.

Verse

Oatlands; or, The Transfer of the Laurel.   1795.
A Father's Legacy to His Daughter, Being the Poetical Works, edited by Adelaide
   O'Keeffe.   1834.

Other

Recollections of the Life of O'Keeffe, Written by Himself.   2 vols., 1826.

*   *   *

John O'Keeffe wrote for a living, and was the slave of a public about which he must
sometimes have grumbled but which he hated to upset. Between 1778, when the elder
Colman bought for the Haymarket his opportunistic afterpiece *Tony Lumpkin in Town,* and
1800, when Thomas Harris awarded him a benefit at Covent Garden, O'Keeffe was a
provider of theatrical pieces for those two theatres. Most of these pieces depend as much on
song as on dialogue. Of the some 60 he admits to in his *Recollections,* over 20 are called
"operas," a way of assuring contemporary audiences that the dialogue would be frequently
interrupted by songs. In the three acts of *The Castle of Andalusia* there are over 20 such
interruptions. The music for this popular piece was arranged by Dr. Arnold, but borrowed
from Italy, Ireland, and the London streets. The plot calls for a noble bandit, a resourceful
rogue, two pairs of lovers, an ageing and covetous widow, and the audience's ready
acceptance of the convention of gullibility without which plays of mistaken identity will
crumble about their ears. In *Fontainbleau* there are fewer songs and a greater dependence on
bright dialogue and quirky characters like Colonel Epaulette, the anglophile Frenchman who
makes his first entrance singing "Rule Britannia, Britannia rule de vay." The Jonsonian
"humour" is close to journey's end in mere risible eccentricity, although there is comic
resource and energy in O'Keeffe's handling of a slender story. He was bound by convention
to attempt the more exacting five-act comedy form. *The Young Quaker* was moderately
successful at the small Haymarket, and *The Toy,* later reduced to three acts as *The Lie of the
Day,* was an effective vehicle for William Lewis, Quick, and Aickin.

But it was *Wild Oats* that made and has preserved O'Keeffe's reputation as a writer of
comedy. The play depends on an alias, a carefully contrived mistaken identity, a sequence of
coincidences, and a lost baby miraculously rediscovered in the person of the leading
character, a strolling player conditionally named Rover. Plot and characters are not original,
but if not of invention, there is a sufficient freshness of deployment to explain the success of
the 1976 revival by the Royal Shakespeare Company. Rover, who has a dramatic quotation
for every emergency, was created by Lewis and has proved the play's main attraction in the
theatre. In a reading, the hostility towards Quaker puritanism and a veiled egalitarianism are
quite as striking. O'Keeffe was proud to boast of Sheridan's calling him "the first that turned
the public taste from the dullness of sentiment ... towards the sprightly channel of comic
humour." He was *not* the first, but *Wild Oats* is a substantial alternative to the sentimental
plays that surrounded it. Of the three other five-act comedies performed in his lifetime, *She's
Eloped* survived only one night while *The World in a Village* and *Life's Vagaries* were
moderately successful.

—Peter Thomson

443

O'NEILL, Eugene (Gladstone). American. Born in New York City, 16 October 1888; son of the actor James O'Neill. Toured with his father as a child, and educated at Catholic boarding schools, and at Betts Academy, Stamford, Connecticut; attended Princeton University, New Jersey, 1906–07, and George Pierce Baker's "47 Workshop" at Harvard University, Cambridge, Massachusetts, 1914–15. Married 1) Kathleen Jenkins in 1909 (divorced, 1912), one son; 2) Agnes Boulton in 1918 (divorced, 1929), one son and one daughter; 3) the actress Carlotta Monterey in 1929. Worked in a mail order firm in New York, 1908; gold prospector in Honduras, 1909; advance agent and box-office man for his father's company, and seaman on a Norwegian freighter to Buenos Aires, 1910–11; Reporter for the *New London Telegraph*, Connecticut, 1912; patient in a tuberculosis sanitarium, where he began to write, 1912–13; full-time writer from 1914; associated with the Provincetown Players, New York, and Provincetown, Massachusetts, as actor and writer, 1914–20; wrote for the Theatre Guild; Manager, with Kenneth Macgowan and Robert Edmond Jones, Greenwich Village Theatre, New York, 1923–27; a Founding Editor, *American Spectator*, 1934; in ill-health from 1934: in later years suffered from Parkinson's Disease. Recipient: Pulitzer Prize, 1920, 1922, 1928, 1957; American Academy of Arts and Letters Gold Medal, 1922; Nobel Prize for Literature, 1936; New York Drama Critics Circle Award, 1957. Litt.D.: Yale University, New Haven, Connecticut, 1926. Member, National Institute of Arts and Letters, and Irish Academy of Letters. *Died 27 November 1953.*

PUBLICATIONS

Plays

> *Thirst and Other One Act Plays* (includes *The Web, Warnings, Fog, Recklessness*). 1914.
> *Thirst* (produced 1916). In *Thirst and Other Plays*, 1914.
> *Fog* (produced 1917). In *Thirst and Other Plays*, 1914.
> *Bound East for Cardiff* (produced 1916). In *The Moon of the Caribbees ...*, 1919.
> *Before Breakfast* (produced 1916). 1916.
> *The Sniper* (produced 1917). In *Lost Plays*, 1950.
> *In the Zone* (produced 1917). In *The Moon of the Caribbees ...*, 1919.
> *The Long Voyage Home* (produced 1917). In *The Moon of the Caribbees ...*, 1919.
> *Ile* (produced 1917). In *The Moon of the Caribbees ...*, 1919.
> *The Rope* (produced 1918). In *The Moon of the Caribbees ...*, 1919.
> *Where The Cross Is Made* (produced 1918). In *The Moon of the Caribbees ...*, 1919.
> *The Moon of the Caribbees* (produced 1918). In *The Moon of the Caribbees...*, 1919.
> *The Moon of the Caribbees and Six Other Plays of the Sea.* 1919.
> *The Dreamy Kid* (produced 1919). In *Complete Works 2*, 1924.
> *Beyond the Horizon* (produced 1920). 1920.
> *Anna Christie* (as *Chris*, produced 1920; revised version, as *Anna Christie*, produced 1921). With *The Hairy Ape, The First Man*, 1922.
> *Exorcism* (produced 1920).
> *The Emperor Jones* (produced 1920). With *Diff'rent, The Straw*, 1921.
> *Diff'rent* (produced 1920). With *The Emperor Jones, The Straw*, 1921.
> *The Straw* (produced 1921). With *The Emperor Jones, Diff'rent*, 1921.
> *Gold* (produced 1921). 1921.
> *The First Man* (produced 1922). With *The Hairy Ape, Anna Christie*, 1922.
> *The Hairy Ape* (produced 1922). With *The First Man, Anna Christie*, 1922.
> *Welded* (produced 1924). With *All God's Chillun Got Wings*, 1924.
> *All God's Chillun Got Wings* (produced 1924). With *Welded*, 1924.

Desire under the Elms (produced 1924).   In *Complete Works 2*, 1924.

Complete Works.   2 vols., 1924.

The Fountain (produced 1925).   With *The Great God Brown, The Moon of the Caribbees*, 1926.

The Great God Brown (produced 1926).   With *The Fountain, The Moon of the Caribbees*, 1926.

Marco Millions (produced 1928).   1927.

Lazarus Laughed (produced 1928).   1927.

Strange Interlude (produced 1928).   1928.

Dynamo (produced 1929).   1929.

Mourning Becomes Electra: A Trilogy (produced 1931).   1931.

Ah, Wilderness! (produced 1933).   1933.

Days Without End (produced 1934).   1934.

The Iceman Cometh (produced 1946).   1946.

Lost Plays (includes *Abortion, The Movie Man, The Sniper, Servitude, Wife for a Life*), edited by Lawrence Gellert.   1950.

A Moon for the Misbegotten (produced 1957).   1952.

Long Day's Journey into Night (produced 1956).   1956.

A Touch of the Poet (produced 1957).   1957.

Hughie (produced 1958).   1959.

More Stately Mansions (produced 1962).   1964.

Ten "Lost" Plays.   1964.

Children of the Sea and Three Other Unpublished Plays (includes *Bread and Butter, Now I Ask You, Shell Shock*), edited by Jennifer McCabe Atkinson.   1972.

Other

Inscriptions: O'Neill to Carlotta Monterey O'Neill, edited by Donald Gallup.   1960.

Bibliography: *O'Neill and the American Critic: A Summary and Bibliographical Checklist* by Jordan Y. Miller, 1973; *O'Neill: A Descriptive Bibliography* by Jennifer McCabe Atkinson, 1974.

Reading List: *The Haunted Heroes of O'Neill* by Edwin A. Engel, 1955; *O'Neill and His Plays: Four Decades of Criticism* edited by Oscar Cargill and other, 1961; *O'Neill* (biography) by Arthur and Barbara Gelb, 1962, revised edition, 1973; *The Tempering of O'Neill* by Doris Alexander, 1962; *O'Neill* by Frederic I. Carpenter, 1964; *O'Neill: A Collection of Critical Essays* edited by John Gassner, 1964; *The Plays of O'Neill* by John Henry Raleigh, 1965; *Playwright's Progress: O'Neill and the Critics* by Jordan Y. Miller, 1965; *O'Neill* by John Gassner, 1965; *O'Neill's Scenic Images* by Timo Tiusanen, 1968; *O'Neill: Son and Playwright*, 1968, and *O'Neill: Son and Artist*, 1973, both by Louis Sheaffer; *A Drama of Souls: Studies in O'Neill's Super-Naturalistic Techniques* by Egil Törnqvist, 1969; *O'Neill* by H. Frenz, 1971; *Contour in Time* by T. M. Bogard, 1972; *O'Neill: A Collection of Criticism* edited by Ernest Griffin, 1976.

*   *   *

Eugene O'Neill, writing dramas comparable to the best available overseas models, brought the American Theater of his actor-father's *Monte Cristo* into the twentieth century. He acknowledged (1936) drawing from the Greeks, Strindberg, and Nietzsche. Nietzsche gave this romantic pessimist a usable theory of classical tragedy: the Apollonian mask with the Dionysian force behind it.

The stage sea caught the real and the poets' seas in 1916 in O'Neill's first production. *Bound East for Cardiff* compresses the international crew of the *S.S. Glencairn* into the wedge of a forecastle. Around Yank's dying, a rusting freighter continues toward Wales, the sea-sounds adding density to the squalid realism. Yet somehow, for the attentive Driscoll and audience, something spacious has been shown through or behind the seaman-life image that contains it. The play opened the Provincetown Players' new Playwrights' Theater in New York that fall, and within the next year three new scripts completed the *S.S. Glencairn* series. In *The Long Voyage Home* deliberate and casual inhumanity (Fate?) allows a shipmate to be shanghaied. Theatricality builds mood in all four *Glencairn* plays, but their author found the tropical night and carousing seamen of *Moon of the Caribbees* more poetic than the war-hysteria of *In the Zone* for conveying "the compelling inscrutable forces behind life."

O'Neill aspired to be a poet – to catch unexpected "rhythms" and to show man's "glorious self-destructive struggle to make the Force express him." A too "acutely conscious," too articulate protagonist or heavy schematization undermines many of the heroic searches in O'Neill's plays during the 1920's. Though thematically prophetic, *Diff'rent* and *Gold* blare out the undeniability of Life and the power of "the hopeless hope." They share with many O'Neill one-acters of 1916–20 a hammering illustrativeness. Still, O'Neill's purposefulness salvages moments in faulty plays like *Lazarus Laughed* and justifies even his overblown experiments. Spectacle and comedy in *Marco Millions* cannot make delightful the overwritten dialectic, as in *Fog* earlier, between Eastern poetry and Western business; yet Marco's epilogue journey from puzzlement to complacency comments expressively on a new function of O'Neill's theater. He insisted on testing forms and tampering with his audience.

The Pulitzer Prizes for *Beyond the Horizon* and *Anna Christie* designated O'Neill the outstanding American dramatist. The former, alternating indoor–outdoor scenes for affecting "rhythm," wrings two brothers and a wife through ironic choices of farm or sea. Still challenging for top actresses, *Anna Christie* sets an ex-prostitute, her barge-skipper father, and a hesitant seaman awash together in the rhythms of that "ole davil sea." *Strange Interlude*, awarded his third Pulitzer Prize of the decade, alternates outer, realistic dialogue with inner monologues to portray the figure of (O'Neill's) Woman. A nostalgic comedy, *Ah, Wilderness!* celebrates the happier side of the autobiographical setting of *Long Day's Journey into Night*, the tragedy which would win O'Neill his fourth Pulitzer Prize, posthumously. With Aeschylus's *Oresteia* lending substance and stature, *Mourning Becomes Electra* is a modern psychological myth placed in New England after the Civil War. His drafts show masks and asides abandoned once they have helped raise the three-play drama to the desired level of formal realism. Though finally unsatisfying to O'Neill in its language and melodrama, it was the basis for his Nobel Prize.

O'Neill's socially angry 1919 portrayals of Black Americans in *The Dreamy Kid* suffer from the lurid extremities of their situation, at the terrifying juncture of religion and criminality in a New York flat. A shared "Lawd Jesus!" signals the approach of the dark God; the all-black cast was another breakthrough. *All God's Chillun Got Wings* welds black Jim and white Ella into a Strindberg marriage; their love-hate festers ever more privately upon the racial violence of their destructive self-images. That the protagonists have O'Neill's parents' names adds another dimension of identification and concern. Watching *The Emperor Jones*, an audience awaiting the irregular firing of the hero's six bullets shares his panic in the increasing pulse-rate of the incessant drums and his dread of his next night vision. The final scene returns the audience to its daily (theatrical) reality, but with emotional overtones making them more aware than those who have not undergone the stripping away of the hero.

The Hairy Ape further dislocates hero and audience in each of eight scenes. Below decks, Yank epitomizes power among the half-naked crew members and identifies himself with steel, coal, and speed. The stokers move with demonic rhythm. When a young lady descends to call Yank a hairy ape, the titanic figure falls out of the rhythm of his own life. Yank's displacements accelerate until his love-death embrace of the gorilla at the zoo satisfies the play's imagery and demand for tragic inevitability, but also looses upon the city another sinister, unthinking force.

When after tiresome grandiloquence the artist Dion(-ysus) dies three-fourths of the way through *The Great God Brown*, the play actually shifts the character beneath the protagonist's mask. Brown, a businessman, puts on Dion's mask, and accepts his wife Margaret and mother-mistress Cybel. Shot as Brown's murderer and unmasked, he speaks his last ecstatic vision in a pietà with Cybel. She croons the eternal recurrence of spring, while upstage Margaret hymns her love to Dion's mask. Reenter the cop with *"grimy notebook"* to ask, "Well, what's his name?" "Man!" answers Cybel. "How d'yuh spell it?" The accumulated rhythms press this joking question into brute fact and poetic theater. Its hard mask distances those who cannot see the tragedy behind, but also drops an audience abruptly back into everyday rhythms. *Desire under the Elms* sets the same pattern more grimly and solidly in the dialect and rock farms of the New England in the gold-fevered 1850's. Ephraim Cabot, 75, returns with "God's message t'me in the spring" – a new wife, Abbie. Finally prisoners for murdering their love-child, she and mother-haunted Eben pause, *"strangely aloof and devout,"* to repeat the play's first line: "Purty, hain't it?" Then, as in *The Great God Brown* and later *The Iceman Cometh* the cop comes in at the normal level of greedy imperception: "Wished I owned it." With an ironic chuckle of recognition, an audience rejects the tragic imperception.

"A Tale of Possessors Self-Dispossessed," O'Neill's name for his 11-play cycle, would have traced an American family from pre-Revolution to 1932. In the fifth (the only one finished), *A Touch of the Poet*, Major Cornelius Melody, an immigrant Irish tavern-keeper near Boston, 1828, remembers heroics, recites Byron, and resents the Irish. His cruel pretensions victimize his wife and embarrass his daughter Sara, who sees a "poet" only in the wealthy Harfords' son. Americanization destroys Con's special dignity and vitality. Historical details and Irish humour enrich the tragic shift of power to a less noble generation. A double-length manuscript intended for destruction, *More Stately Mansions* dandles Simon Harford between his mother's symbolic garden and the realistic world of his mistress-wife Sara, 1832–41. In the edited and produced versions, artistic styles clash more than characters do. Another projected series has left only *Hughie* and the pattern of a dead title character, a talkative central character (Erie Smith), and a listener (the new nightclerk). Night sounds press New York upon the 1928 dialogue with multimedia effect.

The autobiographical plays that interrupted his cycle work have climactic monologues. *The Iceman Cometh* gathered the political, social, and psychological dreams-deferred into a period piece of 1912. All the characters and pipedreams of Harry Hope's flophouse bar had been New York familiars of O'Neill's. Everyone awaits the salesman Theodore Hickman who cometh, like Dionysus, every spring with drinks for Hope's birthday binge. This spring Hickey pushes the inhabitants into testing and destroying their pipedreams. Hickey's own mask of delusion is that he has murdered his wife out of love. The cops lead Hickey away; life returns to the booze and a kind of peace to everyone but Larry Slade, the sensitive O'Neill type. He recognizes death in disillusion but cannot die. *A Moon for the Misbegotten* is an often comic, sometimes lyric tragedy of entropy. On a Connecticut pigfarm soaked in September moonlight and an alcoholic haze, James plays out his 1923 epilogue to the story told in *Long Day's Journey into Night* and receives from huge Josie Hogan an absolution and benediction. O'Neill wrote *Long Day's Journey into Night* with "deep pity and understanding and forgiveness for *all* the four haunted Tyrones." The characters' self-indulgences are objectified as though "the Force behind" had become the playwright's own perspective. An opium-addicted mother, miserly father, alcoholic and tubercular sons use humor and hurting wit to sustain their tragedy. Conventional artistry and deeply felt characters keep the relentless exposition moving for almost five hours. Dope-dreaming Mary Tyrone – behind her, her family – finishes it: "... so happy for a time." Her line is a delicate mask of glass, cracking.

O'Neill thought drama began "in the worship of Dionysus," and critics have generally granted his plays this big, dark, tragic vision along with stage-worthy melodrama. A wild

Celtic humor couches the inevitable destruction in his last tragedies. A period-richness informs them with a sense of history, and a more quietly compassionate understanding cleanses the combatants. Excellent posthumous productions and revivals showed unexpected delicacy in feeling and expression. This secured for the plays, more excruciatingly and less ironically, that massive "Force behind" which a younger playwright had often sought too directly. Outside his grandest schemes, he worked his Apollonian images with a finer, richer sensitivity.

—John G. Kuhn

ORTON, Joe (John Kingsley Orton). English. Born in Leicester, 1 January 1933. Educated at the Royal Academy of Dramatic Art, London (Leicester Council grant), for 2 years. Actor at the Ipswich Repertory Theatre. Recipient: *Evening Standard* award, 1966. *Died 9 August 1967.*

PUBLICATIONS

Collections

The Complete Plays. 1976.

Plays

Entertaining Mr. Sloane (produced 1964). 1964.
The Ruffian on the Stair (broadcast 1964; produced 1966). In *Crimes of Passion*, 1967.
Loot (produced 1965). 1967.
Crimes of Passion: The Ruffian on the Stair, and The Erpingham Camp (produced 1967). 1967.
The Good and Faithful Servant (televised 1967; produced 1971). In *Funeral Games, and The Good and Faithful Servant*, 1970.
Funeral Games (televised 1968; produced 1970). In *Funeral Games, and The Good and Faithful Servant*, 1970.
What the Butler Saw (produced 1969). 1969.
Funeral Games, and The Good and Faithful Servant. 1970.

Radio Play: *The Ruffian on the Stair*, 1964.

Television Plays: *The Good and Faithful Servant*, 1967; *Funeral Games*, 1968.

Other

Head to Toe. 1971.

Reading List: *Prick Up Your Ears: The Biography of Orton* by John Lahr, 1978.

* * *

When Joe Orton rewrote his first play, *The Ruffian on the Stair*, he removed the element of mystification. It was a conscious attempt to restrict the influence of Pinter. Even so, both this play and his first theatrical success, *Entertaining Mr. Sloane*, are centred on the familiar room with its alien visitor. The manifest sexuality and the preparedness to vilify are Orton's emendation of his model. The resolution of *Entertaining Mr. Sloane* is achieved when brother and sister come to an agreement to take turns in sleeping with the smooth-skinned young man who has just murdered their father.

The "combination of elegance and crudity," which Orton observed in Genet, and noted in his diary as "irresistibly funny," became increasingly a characteristic of his own style. The language is polished and the sentence-structure artful, however vulgar the subject. In *Loot*, Hal tips his mother's body out of its coffin in order to conceal in its place the swag from a bank-raid. The corpse becomes a comic property, gleefully exploited in defiance of "good taste." In the decade of the "sick" joke, Orton was the "sick" dramatist. His malice – towards the church, the police force, intellectuals, supporters of routine – gives edge to the carefully planted and highly polished jokes with which his plays are littered. The wild and whirling climax of *The Erpingham Camp* seems almost to endorse anarchic violence as a response to the respectable rituals of the establishment. This short play turns on an incident in a holiday camp in which religion and clean chalets are complementary offshoots of patriotism. The sudden death of the Entertainments Organiser at the beginning of the play, and the emergency substitution of Chief Redcoat Riley, lead through some physically punishing farce-scenes to the climactic death of Erpingham himself. It is a much wittier farce than *Funeral Games*, in which death and religion again provide a framework.

But Orton's talent was not on the decline. *What the Butler Saw*, his last play, is also his finest farce. Set in a private clinic, it describes a lunatic day in which the sexual desires of the proprietary psychiatrist fall foul of his nymphomaniac wife's to the confusion of everything, including sex. Transvestite disguise is the running joke, and the tangle is finally resolved when it is discovered that the twins who resulted from a thoughtless indiscretion in the Station Hotel during a black-out have been reunited before our very eyes. The psychiatrist, then, has been narrowly denied the chance of seducing his daughter, while his wife has succeeded in seducing her son – who took pictures in order to blackmail her. The play's final image is a mischievous parody of a Greek apotheosis, Orton cocking a snook at cultural snobs.

—Peter Thomson

OSBORNE, John (James). English. Born in London, 12 December 1929. Educated at Belmont College, Devon. Married 1) Pamela Lane in 1951 (divorced, 1957); 2) the actress Mary Ure in 1957 (divorced, 1963); 3) the writer Penelope Gilliatt in 1963 (divorced, 1968), one daughter; 4) the actress Jill Bennett in 1968 (divorced, 1977). Journalist, 1947–48; toured as an actor, 1948–49; actor-manager, Ilfracombe Repertory, 1951; also in repertory, as actor and stage manager, in Leicester, Derby, Bridgewater and London. Since 1958, Co-Director, Woodfall Films; since 1960, Director, Oscar Lewenstein Plays Ltd., London. Member of the Council, English Stage Company, London, since 1960. Recipient: *Evening Standard* award, 1956, 1965, 1968; New York Drama Critics Circle Award, 1958, 1965; Antoinette Perry

Award, 1963; Academy Award, 1964. Honorary doctor: Royal College of Art, London, 1970. Lives in Sussex.

PUBLICATIONS

Plays

> *The Devil Inside Him,* with Stella Linden (produced 1950).
> *Personal Enemy,* with Anthony Creighton (produced 1955).
> *Look Back in Anger* (produced 1956). 1957.
> *The Entertainer* (produced 1957). 1957.
> *Epitaph for George Dillon,* with Anthony Creighton (produced 1957). 1958.
> *The World of Paul Slickey,* music by Christopher Whelan (produced 1959). 1959.
> *A Subject of Scandal and Concern* (as *A Matter of Scandal and Concern,* televised 1960; as *A Subject of Scandal and Concern,* produced 1962). 1961.
> *Luther* (produced 1961). 1961.
> *Plays for England: The Blood of the Bambergs, Under Plain Cover* (produced 1963). 1963.
> *Tom Jones: A Film Script.* 1964.
> *Inadmissible Evidence* (produced 1964). 1965.
> *A Bond Honoured,* from a play by Lope de Vega (produced 1966). 1966.
> *A Patriot for Me* (produced 1966). 1966.
> *The Hotel in Amsterdam* (produced 1968). In *Time Present, The Hotel in Amsterdam,* 1968.
> *Time Present* (produced 1968). In *Time Present, The Hotel in Amsterdam,* 1968.
> *The Right Prospectus: A Play for Television* (televised 1969). 1970.
> *Very Like a Whale* (televised 1970). 1971.
> *West of Suez* (produced 1971). 1971.
> *Hedda Gabler,* from the play by Ibsen (produced 1972). 1972.
> *The Gift of Friendship* (televised 1972). 1972.
> *A Sense of Detachment* (produced 1972). 1973.
> *A Place Calling Itself Rome,* from the play *Coriolanus* by Shakespeare. 1973.
> *The Picture of Dorian Gray: A Moral Entertainment,* from the novel by Oscar Wilde (produced 1975). 1973.
> *Jill and Jack* (as *Ms.; or, Jill and Jack,* televised 1974). In *The End of Me Old Cigar, and Jill and Jack,* 1975.
> *The End of Me Old Cigar* (produced 1975). In *The End of Me Old Cigar, and Jill and Jack,* 1975.
> *The End of Me Old Cigar, and Jill and Jack: A Play for Television.* 1975.
> *Watch It Come Down* (produced 1976). 1975.
> *You're Not Watching Me, Mummy, and Try a Little Tenderness* (television plays). 1978.

Screenplays: *Look Back in Anger,* with Nigel Kneale, 1959; *The Entertainer,* with Nigel Kneale, 1960; *Tom Jones,* 1963; *Inadmissible Evidence,* 1968; *The Charge of the Light Brigade,* with Charles Wood, 1968.

Television Plays: *For the Children* series: *Billy Bunter,* 1952, and *Robin Hood,* 1953; *A Matter of Scandal and Concern,* 1960; *The Right Prospectus,* 1969; *Very Like a Whale,* 1970; *The Gift of Friendship,* 1972; *Ms.; or, Jill and Jack,* 1974.

Reading List: *Anger and After* by John Russell Taylor, 1962; *Osborne* by Ronald Hayman, 1968; *Osborne* by Martin Banham, 1969; *Osborne* by Alan Carter, 1969; *The Plays of Osborne* by Simon Trussler, 1969; *Theatre Language: A Study of Arden, Osborne, Pinter, and Wesker* by John Russell Brown, 1972; *Osborne* by Harold Ferrar, 1973; *Anger and Detachment: A Study of Arden, Osborne, and Pinter* by Michael Anderson, 1976.

*   *   *

It is easy to be glib, in retrospect, about John Osborne's decline from spokesmanship for his intellectual generation to his present role as a sniper from the sidelines of disgruntled middle age. Arguably, this is only a sideways shift – from the sympathetic treatment of nostalgic values which informed even his earliest work to an overt declaration of hatred for contemporary values in the later plays. After all, the work by which he is still best known had us *look back* in anger.

Such an interpretation depends, however, on a response that is limited to the social standpoint of his work – and Osborne has always been least assured in that area. Although for many young people of the 1950's *Look Back in Anger* induced a shock of recognition such as most had despaired of ever receiving from a theatrical experience, the effect of that shock, assisted by the other political realignments of that post-war watershed, 1956, was an upsurge of political and social activity. Jimmy Porter, the central character of *Look Back in Anger*, had long since abandoned any such activity, to retreat into his own necessary sexual fantasies – and it is difficult to image Alison and Jimmy Porter trudging the road from Aldermaston with a scruffy toddler in their wake.

Thus, *Look Back in Anger* was only accidentally a clarion call to action: primarily, it was a perceptive (but structurally conventional) psychological drama, in which a couple who found it necessary to tear each other's hearts out for their mutual satisfaction happened also to live in a provincial garret, share their bed-sit with an ironing board, and strew the posh Sunday papers over the floor. Their political disillusion was inward-turning: it was the physical trappings of that disillusion with which the activists could identify.

Osborne's dramatic career has, it is true, witnessed an apparent change of political mind: more important, it has witnessed a failure to achieve maturity of craftsmanship, and this has inevitably made the plays less interesting as the purely imaginative impulse behind them has become ... not necessarily reactionary, but merely commonplace.

Even in the early years of his career, for every work of major theatrical significance there was an equally resounding disappointment. After *The Entertainer* – in which the decline of empire was microcosmically reflected through the prism of the dying music-hall tradition – came the broken-backed *The World of Paul Slickey*, one-third musical, one-third diffuse satire on gossip columnists, one-third rambling comedy about an attempt to evade death duties. Such a wavering of narrative line has often flawed Osborne's writing – just as, in *Luther* and *A Patriot for Me*, his attempts to take his characters through extended time spans were weakened by his showing each stage of their development fully accomplished, rather than dramatically evolved.

Luther is also weakened by a would-be epic structure which is ostensibly appropriate for so public a figure, yet which Osborne's actual concentration on the intensely private person renders unnecessary, and positively distracting. Of the two *Plays for England* which followed, *The Blood of the Bambergs* was an essentially occasional piece (the occasion being the flummery of a royal wedding), while *Under Plain Cover* began as a compassionate cameo study of a shared sexual fantasy, but changed direction half-way with the heavy-footed intrusion of a hack journalist, and thereafter focused on the easier, pock-marked target.

Osborne is not readily able to find the appropriate form for his plays – yet when he does so, by accident or intention, as in *Inadmissible Evidence*, the result is striking. This is a brilliant study of one man's loss of touch with reality, its style increasingly impressionistic as its peripheral characters become more and more enmeshed in the personal endgame being played out by the central character, the solicitor Bill Maitland. This is a bourgeois tragedy of the stature of Miller's *Death of a Salesman* – and the more compelling in that Maitland remains, always, aware of the wasted potential, and of exactly what is happening to him.

In spite of the defeat already noted, *A Patriot for Me*, which followed, is much more successful than *Luther* in its realization of a broad social context – that of the decaying Austro-Hungarian Empire, in the twilight period before the First World War. The play now seems somewhat dated in its (then daring) treatment of homosexuality, and, yet again, changes direction half way, to become virtually a period spy-thriller, complete with an honourable suicide as its climax. *A Bond Honoured* began, interestingly, as a study of incest, but splurged itself over a broad canvas of depravity, reducing its original – Lope de Vega's *La Fianza Satisfecha* – from a masterly portrayal of Christian redemption to an orgy of adolescent existentialism, strong on action, short on philosophic justification.

In many ways Osborne's most mature work, *The Hotel in Amsterdam* is a surely-paced evocation of the satisfaction and insidious dangers of close friendship, spread over a single weekend jaunt to Amsterdam. Its three couples eat, drink, see sights – and, mainly, just talk. Patterns of mutual dependence and affection are traced, and the play is remarkable for allowing unremarkable characters to relate on equal terms to extraordinary ones, rather than to exist (as in many of the earlier plays) in a different dimension.

West of Suez set old imperial against new anarchic values in the location its title suggests, but was fatally flawed by simplistic dialectical short-cuts. The ironically titled *A Sense of Detachment* set about all and sundry in a style half way between Pirandello and the Living Theatre, but carrying the conviction of neither. And an assortment of pieces for television, adaptations, and lightweight stage plays has completed the canon to date. Since Osborne's work has never been technically remarkable, the lack of a redeeming imaginative spark has reduced it recently to little more than run-of-the-mill, though the occasional rhetorical flares remind one of a potential for mature greatness that might yet be realized.

—Simon Trussler

OTWAY, Thomas. English. Born in Trotten, Sussex, 3 March 1652. Educated at Winchester College, Hampshire, 1668; Christ Church, Oxford, 1669–71, left without taking a degree. Served in the Duke of Monmouth's Regiment in the Netherlands, 1678–79. Settled in London, 1671, and worked temporarily as an actor; wrote for the Duke's Company at the Dorset Garden Theatre, London, from 1675. *Died 14 April 1685.*

PUBLICATIONS

Collections

The Works, edited by J. C. Ghosh.   2 vols., 1932.

Plays

Alcibiades (produced 1675).   1675.
Don Carlos, Prince of Spain (produced 1676).   1676.

Titus and Berenice, from a play by Racine (produced 1676).   1677.

The Cheats of Scapin, from a play by Molière (produced 1676).   In *Titus and Berenice*, 1677.

Friendship in Fashion (produced 1678).   1678.

The History and Fall of Caius Marius (produced 1679).   1680.

The Orphan; or, The Unhappy Marriage (produced 1680).   1680; edited by Aline M. Taylor, 1976.

The Soldier's Fortune (produced 1680).   1681.

Venice Preserved; or, A Plot Discovered (produced 1682).   1682; edited by Malcolm Kelsall, 1969.

The Atheist; or, The Second Part of the Soldier's Fortune (produced 1683).   1684.

Verse

The Poet's Complaint of His Muse; or, A Satire Against Libels.   1680.

Windsor Castle in a Monument to Our Late Sovereign Charles II.   1685.

Other

Familiar Letters (by Rochester, Otway, and Katherine Philips), edited by Tom Brown and Charles Gildon.   2 vols., 1697.

Translator, *The History of the Triumvirates*, by Samuel de Broe.   1686.

Reading List: *Otway and Lee* by Roswell G. Ham, 1931; *Next to Shakespeare* by Aline M. Taylor, 1950; *Gestalt und Funktion der Bilder im Otway und Lee* by Gisela Fried, 1965; *Die Künstlerische Entwicklung in der Tragödien Otways* by Helmut Klinger, 1971.

*   *   *

In the eight years between 1675 and 1683 Thomas Otway wrote and had produced at Dorset Garden Theatre ten plays. Two of his six tragedies are of lasting quality; the other four are of varying merit. The four comedies are generally regarded as having little to recommend them, though a farce entitled *The Cheats of Scapin* held the stage for many years. The first two plays, *Alcibiades* and *Don Carlos*, belong to the prevailing genre of Heroic Tragedy, being written in heroic couplets of elevated rhetoric to be spoken by supremely noble characters, and emphasizing the themes of love, honour, and valour. Yet even in these Otway broke out of the stereotype, especially in the latter play, to create scenes of unaffected sincerity, tenderness, and simplicity. The later tragedies are derived, as was becoming the fashion by 1677, more directly in form and substance from Elizabethan and Jacobean antecedents. His comedies likewise follow, though with less success, Elizabethan and Jacobean structure and variety – brought up to date with fashionable cynicism, vulgarity, and attempts at Restoration wit.

For his direct source Otway went to Plutarch (*Alcibiades*), Racine (*Titus and Berenice*), Molière (*The Cheats of Scapin*), Roger Boyle (*The Orphan*), Shakespeare (*Don Carlos* and *Caius Marius*) and Saint Réal (*Don Carlos*). Just as importantly, he drew in his bitter comedies upon the cynical tone and wit of Wycherley, and upon Shakespeare for the same qualities in all his plays, as well as for dramatic situation, structure, and poetry. Out of his own poverty, disappointment in patronage, unhappy army experience, and hopeless love for Mrs. Barry came also much of his fatalism, cynicism, and despair, tones which fit well the popular Hobbesism of the time. His striking this popular mood of the theatre-goers – the nobles, courtiers, and wits – doubtless accounted for his considerable success in his own day. Furthermore, the slightly veiled parallels and references in his plays (in the comedies and in *Caius Marius* and *Venice Preserved*) to current political intrigues, especially the popish plot and attacks upon the Whigs and the Earl of Shaftesbury, brought patrons to Dorset Garden. But his temperament and his attraction to Shakespeare's special brand of satire perhaps account best for Otway's more lasting qualities.

And his success upon the tragic stage has been considerable. For his two powerful tragedies he has been called "Next to Shakespeare," the title of Aline Taylor's full account of the remarkable stage success of *Venice Preserved* and *The Orphan*. Contributing greatly to this success have been the superb actors who have played the chief roles. But other lasting qualities have contributed to their survival and retained a place for them and the rest of Otway's plays in the history of dramatic literature. Otway became an excellent dramatic craftsman, and he also had something important, though quite unflattering, to say about the human condition.

Otway's exposition usually follows an immediate plunge into the midst of the action, such as the opening quarrel of *Venice Preserved*, which creates effective suspense. The suspense is intensified through the complication, and the direct, swift action brings on the powerful climax. The result is a shattering recognition for the principals, especially in the tragedies, which is followed by an unrelieved dénouement of defeat and despair in the tragedies and only cynicism in the comedies. The movement in the tragedies is often, like that of Greek tragedy, direct and inevitable. In *The Orphan* onlooker and reader alike are held horrified in their anxiety: surely Castalio will tell Polydore that he is married to Monimia; surely someone will light a taper! But the light comes too late; the recognition is too great for the principals to bear, as is also true in *Venice Preserved*, *Don Carlos*, and *Caius Marius*. Such inability reflects the basic fault in Otway's main characters. His dramas rise from the weaknesses of his characters: they are strong in emotion, but weak in judgment, more given to blaming fate than recognizing their own crucial errors – which lead to self-destruction.

This same quality of irresponsibility gave rise to a sort of perverse wit, bitter and sardonic, in both his comedies and tragedies. Inherited from Shakespeare and Marston in large part, it is perhaps best exemplified in *Venice Preserved*. Pierre makes his nervous midnight entrance upon the Rialto for his assignation with Jaffeir. Like Bernardo in *Hamlet*, he improperly challenges the one who is already on the scene: "Speak, who goes there?" He gets the reply: "A dog, that comes to howl/At yonder moon: What's he that asks the Question?" Pierre answers "A Friend to Dogs, for they are honest creatures." (In *Julius Caesar* Brutus reproves Cassius with "I'd rather be a dog and bay the moon/Than such a Roman.") The following speeches revile priesthood and condemn prayer and religion.

This same sort of cynicism in Otway's plays gives rise to numerous oaths, curses, and orations, all of which make for intense dramatic effect. Pierre's notable speech before the Senate asks in four ironic rhetorical questions whether the chains that bind him are "the wreaths of triumph ye bestow," for his service to the state. Jaffeir's solemn oath to remain faithful to the conspiracy becomes ironic as he, for love of Belvidera, fails to keep the oath and then denounces his own failure before the Senate. He curses Old Priuli, as might a primitive Irish satirist: "Kind Heav'n! let heavy Curses/Gall his old Age; Cramps, Aches rack his Bones...." Belvidera calls upon heaven to pour down curses with vengeance, despair, danger, etc. upon her; and Jaffeir in a final curse, such as Polydore's in *The Orphan*, asks that a "Final destruction seize the world...." And this is just what happens to his world as he and Belvidera commit suicide. All is left in ruins. Though one may argue that underlying *Venice Preserved* is the affirmation of the integrity of the family (as one may argue for the same in *Coriolanus*), such integrity does not prevail at the end of the play – only the corrupt Senate prevails. The very title is ironic: Venice preserved indeed!

Just such lack of affirmation, just such lack of hope characterize Otway's plays. Fortune, Chance, Fate control – not men or benevolent gods. Even the earlier *Alcibiades, Don Carlos*, and *Caius Marius* lack a just settling of accounts; the comedies, *The Soldier's Fortune* and *The Atheist*, are dissertations upon Fortune and Chance.

The ritualistic use of formal curses, prayers, oaths, and set speeches make Otway's plays dramatically effective. But the sardonic and cynical quality be gives them belong rather to satire than pure comedy or tragedy. As a part of rhetoric, style, and invention this quality reverses the normal processes of expression and appeals both to emotion and intellect. It is inherently dramatic, and Otway uses it with great effect. Yet it cannot rise to affirmation. The conclusions of his plots bring no sense of order or justice having been reasserted. Rather, chaos prevails, and an effective catharsis does not take place. The audience are left to face a meaningless, unintelligible world, anticipating the school of the absurd of the mid-twentieth century.

Otway's dozen poems outside the plays and his half-dozen love letters are useful chiefly in explaining the partisanship, political and historical allusions, and tone of the plays. The love letters reveal in effective, if sometimes maudlin, prose the poet's hopeless passion for Mrs. Barry; hence the character of his tragic heroines. Of the poems, *The Poet's Complaint of His Muse* and *Windsor Castle* seem most significant. The former is autobiographical, consisting of twenty-one strophes shot through with allusions to contemporary events and political affairs. It ends with a tribute to James, Duke of York, as he takes precautionary leave of England because of the Popish Plot. The latter is an extensive panegyric upon the ascension of James II, who "By mighty deeds has earn'd the Crown he wears." Both indicate directly the poet's scornful opposition to the Whigs and his sympathy and admiration for the Royalists – attitudes revealed implicitly in his plays.

—Thomas B. Stroup

PAYNE, John Howard. American. Born in New York City, 9 June 1791. Educated at a school in Boston to 1805, and at Union College, Schenectady, New York, 1806–08. Clerk in the counting house of Grant and Bennet Forbes, New York, 1805–06; Editor, *Thespian Mirror*, 1805–06, and *The Pastime*, 1807–08; began writing for the stage, 1806; made debut as an actor in New York in 1809 and enjoyed an immediate success; settled in England, 1813; acted in the provinces, 1814; thereafter earned his living in London by dramatic hackwork; acted as a secretary at Covent Garden, 1818–19; leased Sadler's Wells Theatre, 1820, but went bankrupt: imprisoned for debt, Fleet Prison, 1820–21; settled in Paris, 1821; wrote the lyrics for "Home Sweet Home" (in his *Clari*, 1823); collaborated with Washington Irving in writing plays, 1823–26; lived in London, 1823–25, and resettled there, 1826; Editor and Publisher of the weekly theatrical paper *Opera Glass*, 1826–27; returned to America, 1832; United States Consul in Tunis, 1842–45, 1851–52. *Died 9 April 1852.*

PUBLICATIONS

Collections

Trial Without Jury and Other Plays (includes *Mount Savage, The Boarding Schools, The Two Sons-in-Law, Mazeppa, The Spanish Husband*), edited by Codman Hislop and W. R. Richardson. 1940.
The Last Duel in Spain and Other Plays (includes *Woman's Revenge, The Italian Bride, Romulus the Shepherd King, The Black Man*), edited by Codman Hislop and W. R. Richardson. 1940.

Plays

Julia; or, The Wanderer (as *The Wanderer*, produced 1806). 1806.
Lover's Vows, from versions by Mrs. Inchbald and Benjamin Thompson of a play by Kotzebue (produced 1809?). 1809.
Trial Without Jury; or, The Magpie and the Maid, from a play by L. C. Caigniez and Théodore Baudouin (as *The Maid and the Magpie*, produced 1815?). In *Trial Without Jury and Other Plays*, 1940.
Accusation; or, The Family of D'Anglade, from a play by Frédéric du Petit-Méré (produced 1816). 1817.
The Tragedy of Brutus; or, The Fall of Tarquin, music by Hayward (produced 1818). 1818.
Thérèse, The Orphan of Geneva, from a play by Victor Ducange (produced 1821). 1821.
Adeline; or, The Victim of Seduction, from a play by Pixérécourt (produced 1822). 1822.
Love in Humble Life, from a play by Scribe and Dupin (produced 1822). 1823(?).
Ali Pacha; or, The Signet-Ring, adapted by J. R. Planché (produced 1822). 1822.
Peter Smink; or, The Armistice (produced 1822; revised version, produced 1826). 1826(?).
The Two Galley Slaves; or, The Mill of St. Aldervon, music by Tom Cooke and C. E. Horn (produced 1822). 1823(?).
Mount Savage, from a play by Pixérécourt (as *The Solitary of Mount Savage; or, The Fate of Charles the Bold*, produced 1822). In *Trial Without Jury and Other Plays*, 1940.
Clari; or, The Maid of Milan, music by Henry Bishop (produced 1823). 1823.

Mrs. Smith; or, The Wife and the Widow (produced 1823). 1823.

Charles the Second; or, The Merry Monarch, with Washington Irving, from a play by A. V. P. Duval (produced 1824). 1824; edited by A. H. Quinn, in *Representative American Plays,* 1917.

'Twas I; or, The Truth a Lie, from a French play (produced 1825). 1827.

The Fall of Algiers, music by Henry Bishop (produced 1825). 1825.

Richelieu: A Domestic Comedy, with Washington Irving, from a play by A. V. P. Duval (produced 1826; as *The French Libertine,* produced 1826). 1826.

The White Maid, from a play by Scribe, music by Adrien Boieldieu (produced 1827; also produced as *The White Lady*).

The Lancers (produced 1827). 1828(?).

Procrastination (produced 1829).

The Spanish Husband; or, First and Last Love, from a play by La Beaumelle (produced 1830). In *Trial Without Jury and Other Plays,* 1940.

Fricandeau; or, The Coronet and the Cook (produced 1831).

Oswali at Athens (produced 1831).

Woman's Revenge (produced 1832). In *The Last Duel in Spain and Other Plays,* 1940.

Virginia (produced 1834).

Fiction

Essays of Howard; or, Tales of the Prison. 1811.

Verse

Juvenile Poems. 1813; selections published as *Lispings of the Muse,* 1815.

Other

Indian Justice: A Cherokee Murder Trial, edited by Grant Foreman. 1934.

Payne to His Countrymen, edited by Clemens de Baillou. 1961.

Bibliography: "Payne: A Bibliography" by Charles F. Heartman and Harry B. Weiss, in *American Book Collector 3* and *4,* 1933.

Reading List: *The Early Life of Payne* by W. T. Hanson, 1913; *Payne* by Rosa P. Chiles, 1930; *America's First Hamlet* by Grace Overmyer, 1957.

*   *   *

During the first half of the nineteenth century, theatre audiences in both England and America enjoyed the strong, romantic rhetoric of poetic drama. In America the earliest dramatist to achieve success in this genre, and the most prolific, was John Howard Payne. A youthful prodigy, he attracted attention as an actor, a critic, and an editor of the *Thespian Mirror,* and a playwright whose first work, *Julia; or, The Wanderer,* was performed at New York's Park Theatre in 1806. When his career as an actor did not reach the success he anticipated, however, he embarked in 1813 for what he felt would be the greener theatrical fields of England. In this he was seriously mistaken for his acting engagements were few and soon relegated to the provinces. But chance and necessity offered him a new career.

In 1809 before going to England Payne had published a version of August von Kotzebue's

Das Kind der Liebe which he had adapted from two English translations. Six years later while in Paris he translated the current French hit, *La Pie Voleuse* by L. C. Caigniez and Théodore Baudouin as *The Maid and the Magpie* for the Drury Lane management. This was the beginning of a career – adapting and translating comedy, melodrama, and romantic tragedy – in which his particular forte was his ability to recognize dramatic material and create a successful play from various sources. Like other prolific dramatists of his time. his talent was not in writing original plays, but he soon became the first American dramatist to enjoy a substantial reputation abroad.

Among his best works is *The Tragedy of Brutus; or, The Fall of Tarquin*. Using five major sources he created a major acting vehicle for Edmund Kean, whereas the subsequent cry of plagiarism was particularly ironic at a time when play pirating was a common sport. Another popular adaptation was *Clari; or, The Maid of Milan*, which contains the song for which most Americans will, if at all, remember Payne – "Home, Sweet Home." They would, however, readily recognize the name of his collaborator in his most successful comedy, *Charles the Second; or, The Merry Monarch* – Washington Irving. Before Irving tired of the drama they worked on six plays together.

Returning to America in 1832 Payne epitomized the plight of the dramatist during America's formative years. With considerable skill and abundant energy, he had created many successful plays and made money for everyone – actors, managers – but himself. Recognized by theatre-goers and critics as a major contributor to American drama, he was never financially secure and became increasingly bitter over the treatment of American dramatists during the final years of his life which were separated from the theatre. His position in the history of American drama is unquestionably secure.

—Walter J. Meserve

PEELE, George. English. Born in London in 1558. Educated at Christ's Hospital School, London, 1565; Broadgates Hall, later Pembroke College, Oxford, 1571–74, and Christ Church, Oxford, matriculated 1574, B.A. 1577, M.A. 1579. Married in 1583. Very little is known about his life: settled in London, 1581, and began to write for the stage; recognized as one of the "university wits"; wrote several of the lord mayor's pageants for the City of London; his later life was spent in poverty and sickness. *Died* (buried) *9 November 1596.*

PUBLICATIONS

Collections

Life and Works, edited by C. T. Prouty.   3 vols., 1952–70.

Plays

The Arraignment of Paris: A Pastoral (produced 1584?).   1584.
The Device of the Pageant Borne Before Wolstan Dixie, Lord Mayor of London (produced 1585).   1585.

The Battle of Alcazar (produced 1589?).   1594.

The Hunting of Cupid (produced before 1591).   Edited by W. W. Greg, 1911.

Descensus Astraeae: The Device of a Pageant Borne Before William Webb, Lord Mayor of London (produced 1591).   1591.

The Old Wives Tale (produced 1591–94?).   1595.

King Edward the First, Surnamed Edward Longshanks (produced 1593?).   1593.

The Love of King David and Fair Bethsabe (produced 1594?).   1599.

Verse

Pareus (in Latin).   1585.

An Eclogue Gratulatory to Robert, Earl of Essex for His Welcome into England from Portugal.   1589.

A Farewell to Sir John Norris and Sir Francis Drake; A Tale of Troy.   1589; revised edition of *A Tale of Troy*, 1604.

Polyhymnia, Describing the Honourable Triumph at Tilt Before Her Majesty.   1590.

The Honour of the Garter.   1593.

Anglorum Feriae: England's Holidays, edited by R. Fitch.   1830(?).

Other

Life and Minor Works of Peele, by D. H. Horne.   1952.

Bibliography: *Peele: A Concise Bibliography* by S. A. Tannenbaum, 1940; *Peele 1939–65* by R. C. Johnson, 1968.

Reading List: *Peele* by P. H. Cheffaud, 1913; *Authorship and Evidence: A Study of Attribution and the Renaissance Drama, Illustrated by the Case of Peele* by Leonard R. N. Ashley, 1968; *Lyly and Peele* by George K. Hunter, 1968.

*   *   *

George Peele was an Oxford graduate who returned to his native London to earn a living by writing occasional poems, occasional pageants, and plays. He was a representative "University Wit," a free-lance author whose range, while confined to poetry and drama, embraced the taste of the court and that of the city and included most of the dramatic types fashionable in his day.

Having at Oxford translated one of Euripides's *Iphigenia* plays and written a digest of the Trojan war in under 500 lines of heroic couplets, he pursued his classical and mythological themes in his first extant original play, *The Arraignment of Paris*, written for the Children of the Chapel Royal to act before Elizabeth I. Paris awards the golden apple to Venus, whose disappointed rivals indict him for partiality before a court of gods and goddesses (hence the title); after his spirited defence the prize is adjudged to be re-awarded by Diana, who delivers a panegyric on the nymph Eliza, "whom some Zabeta call," and actually delivers the apple into the hand of the spectator-Queen. Though Peele celebrated several courtly occasions this seems to have been his only court play. Its slight, complimentary structure is somewhat filled out by introducing Oenone and her desertion by Paris, and, to balance this male infidelity, the constant unrequited lover Colin (drawn from Spenser's recent *Shepherd's Calendar*): but neither of these episodes is developed, and the play's attraction lies chiefly in its lyricism (there is considerable metrical variety, and several songs) and its eloquence.

Peele's next play was *The Battle of Alcazar*, a drama of violent deeds (mostly, however, symbolized by dumbshows or described in speeches) centred upon a recent battle in Morocco where Sebastian of Portugal and the English expatriate adventurer Tom Stukeley were slain. Like all his later ones, this play was written for the public theatre – another of its principal characters, the revengeful Moor, was played by Alleyn – and in its technique it is related to Marlowe's *Tamburlaine* and also to Kyd's *Spanish Tragedy*.

The order of Peele's remaining plays is not certainly known. *Edward I* is a history play insofar as it introduces historical characters and something of their story (the king's wars with the Scots and the Welsh, with the birth of the English Prince of Wales at Caernarvon), but it is a romance insofar as many incidents are apocryphal: from time to time Queen Elinor is portrayed (with anti-Spanish feeling) as a proud and cruel woman; the Welsh prince Lluellen takes to a Robin-Hood life in the woods, where he is joined by the disguised Lord Mortimer (his rival in love) and by a robust Friar who provides most of the comedy in this thoroughly mingled play.

In *David and Bethsabe* Peele dramatizes biblical incidents (from 1 Samuel and 2 Kings) into a play far more unified in structure and in style. It is a moral treatment, unrelieved by comedy, of David's sin and repentance, introducing also the revenge theme in Absalon's slaying of his brother for ravishing their sister, and the military-heroic in the seige of the enemy city and in Absalon's rebellion and death. Peele has here cultivated decorum of style by drawing on biblical language and imagery, without suppressing his characteristic lyricism and eloquence. All Peele's plays discussed so far are notable for the lengthy speeches they contain. They are also all highly spectacular.

His *Old Wives* (i.e. Wife's) *Tale*, though it too has spectacle, eloquence, and lyricism, is unique, not only in Peele's work but in English literature. This romance of an adventurous knight who rescues a princess abducted by a magician suggests Ariosto (from whose *Orlando Furioso* the magician Sacrapant takes his name), but the grateful ghost who is his loyal servant comes from homelier folklore, as do the pair of unlike sisters who go to a magic well to find their allotted husbands, one of whom is a comic braggart who speaks in the "English hexameters" with which poets were then experimenting. All these threads of plot – and others – are supposed to be united in a rambling tale told by an old woman to entertain benighted travellers at her cottage. To regard the play as quite serious would be unjust to Peele's sophistication; to regard it as a burlesque of popular drama would be unjust to his delight (seen in *Edward I*, for example) in simple and abundant storytelling.

It is by this play that Peele is best known. His verses for civic pageants (*Descensus Astraeae*, and Sir Wolstan Dixie's Lord Mayor's Show) and for court ceremonies (*Polyhymnia*; *The Honour of the Garter*; *Anglorum Feriae*) have the stylistic qualities of the verse in his plays: he developed a lucid expressiveness in his blank verse, while some of his lyrics (specially the gravely beautiful valedictory poem for the Royal Champion in *Polyhymnia*, "His golden locks Time hath to silver turned") have the literal memorability which is one of the marks of true poetry.

—T. W. Craik

PHILLIPS, Stephen. English. Born in Summertown, near Oxford, 28 July 1864. Educated at Trinity College School, Stratford upon Avon; King's School, Peterborough; Oundle School, 1878–83; also read for the civil service examinations. Married May Lidyard in 1892; one son. Settled in London; actor with Sir Frank Benson's Company, 1885–92; lectured on history at an army tutor's, 1892–98; full-time writer from 1898, especially successful as a dramatic poet in the period 1898–1908; Editor, *Poetry Review*, 1913 until his death. *Died 9 December 1915.*

PUBLICATIONS

Plays

Herod (produced 1900). 1901.
Paolo and Francesca (produced 1902). 1900.
Ulysses (produced 1902). 1902.
The Sin of David (produced 1905). 1904; revised edition, 1912.
Aylmer's Secret (produced 1905).
Nero (produced 1906). 1906.
Faust, with J. Comyns Carr, from the play by Goethe (produced 1908). 1908.
The Bride of Lammermoor, from the novel by Scott (produced 1908; as *The Last Heir*, produced 1908).
Iole (produced 1913). In *New Poems*, 1908.
Pietro of Siena (produced 1911). 1910.
The King. 1912.
Everywoman: Her Pilgrimage in Quest of Love, from the play by Walter Browne (produced 1912). 1912.
Lyrics and Dramas (includes *Nero's Mother*, *The King*, *The Adversary*, *Armageddon*). 1913.
Armageddon (produced 1915). In *Lyrics and Dramas*, 1913.
Harold: A Chronicle Play, edited by Arthur Symons. 1927.

Verse

Orestes and Other Poems. 1884.
Eremus. 1894.
Christ in Hades. 1896; edited by C. L. Hind, 1917.
Poems. 1897; revised edition, 1898.
Marpessa. 1900.
New Poems. 1908.
The New Inferno. 1911.
Panama and Other Poems, Narrative and Occasional. 1915.

*　　　*　　　*

The extravagant adulation which greeted the arrival of Stephen Phillips's poems and verse dramas was symptomatic of an age desperately anxious for literature in the grand manner of the past but uncertain how to assess current writing. In the apparent vacuum left by the death of Tennyson, Phillips, with his evident facility, plangent diction, expansive gestures, and confident handling of metrical forms, seemed to possess all the qualifications of a new Shelley or Swinburne: comparisons were drawn not only with Rossetti and Marlowe, but with Dante, Milton, Shakespeare, and Sophocles, even such normally shrewd critics as William Archer and Max Beerbohm joining the chorus of praise. Triteness of sentiment, slackness of rhythm, archaic encrustations, and a complete absence of poetic individuality were overlooked in the belief that here was an authentic word-master who would restore to English poetry its Elizabethan or Romantic glory.

The impact made by such poems as *Christ in Hades* or *Marpessa* seemed confirmed by Phillips's plays, which, when opulently staged by Tree and Alexander, won incredulous approbation from playgoers and readers of poetry alike. In the best of the group, *Paolo and Francesca*, Phillips dramatized with some skill and an ex-actor's keen instinct for stage effect the onset of fatal adulterous passion between the reluctant Paolo and his brother's child-bride, but the style is anaemic sub-Shakespearean pastiche, which the felicity of half-a-dozen isolated lines cannot redeem from fustian. All the plays abound in echoes, both verbal and theatrical, from greater tragedies, and these serve ultimately to expose the thin texture and empty eloquence of the imitations, where the poet's observations and language prove sadly insufficient in originality and resonance to match the strong emotions and heroic actions presented. In *Herod* family intrigue and political faction in the Jewish palace at least culminate in an effective scene where the court conspires to keep the fact of Mariamne's death from the king, but *Ulysses* is a loosely-constructed and somewhat frigid adaptation of parts of Homer's *Odyssey*, and *Nero* merely a spectacular chronicle-play devoid of both plausibility and psychological interest.

It has long been common to dismiss Phillips's work as contemptible, but he was as much the victim of his age as its deceiver; in a period when poetry was required to follow outmoded romantic traditions, he can be blamed for little more than pandering to conservative tastes by supplying the public with the derivative cadences and tone his admirers identified as the genuine hallmarks of genius. In so doing he became the hero of the right wing in English poetic politics, and, with its rout by the Georgians, the Imagists, and the school of Pound and Eliot, was inevitably doomed to ignominy. The most damaging charge against Phillips's verse is that its content and style were massively irrelevant to the age in which it was created; its triple inspiration was Hellenic, Jacobean, and Romantic, but on such grounds it is legitimate to indict almost all Phillips's poetic contemporaries.

—William M. Tydeman

PINERO, Sir Arthur Wing. English. Born in Islington, London, 24 May 1855. Educated in day schools, and in evening classes at Birkbeck Institute, London; also worked and studied in his father's law office, London, 1865–74. Chairman of the United Artists' Rifles during World War I. Married Myra Emily Wood (the actress Myra Holme) in 1883 (died, 1919); one step-daughter. Actor with the Theatre Royal, Edinburgh, 1874, in Liverpool, 1875, and in London, 1876; actor with Irving's Lyceum Company, 1876–81; joined the Haymarket Theatre Company, London, 1881; began to write for the theatre, 1877, and retired from acting to devote himself full-time to playwriting, 1884. Member, Academic Committee, Royal Society of Literature. Knighted, 1909. *Died 23 November 1934.*

PUBLICATIONS

Collections

Collected Letters, edited by J. P. Wearing. 1974.

Plays

£200 a Year (produced 1877).
La Comète; or, Two Hearts (produced 1880). N.d.
Daisy's Escape (produced 1879).

Hester's Mystery (produced 1880).   N.d.

The Money Spinner (produced 1880).   1900.

Bygones (produced 1880).

Imprudence (produced 1881).

The Squire (produced 1881).   1881.

Girls and Boys: A Nursery Tale (produced 1882).

The Rector: The Story of Four Friends (produced 1883).

Lords and Commons (produced 1883).

The Rocket (produced 1883).   1905.

Low Water (produced 1884).

The Iron Master (produced 1884).

In Chancery (produced 1884).   1905.

Mayfair, from a play by Sardou (produced 1885).

The Magistrate (produced 1885).   1892; edited by Eric Bentley, in *From the Modern Repertory 3,* 1956.

The Schoolmistress (produced 1886).   1894.

The Hobby-Horse (produced 1886).   1892.

Dandy Dick (produced 1887).   1893.

Sweet Lavender (produced 1888).   1893.

The Weaker Sex (produced 1888; revised version, produced 1889).   1894.

The Profligate (produced 1889).   1892.

The Cabinet Minister (produced 1890).   1892.

Lady Bountiful: A Story of Years (produced 1891).   1892.

The Times (produced 1891).   1891.

The Amazons (produced 1893).   1895.

The Second Mrs. Tanqueray (produced 1893).   1895; edited by George Rowell, in *Late Victorian Plays,* 1968.

The Notorious Mrs. Ebbsmith (produced 1895).   1895; edited by C. M. Selle, in *The New Drama,* 1963.

The Benefit of the Doubt (produced 1895).   1895.

The Princess and the Butterfly; or, The Fantastics (produced 1897).   1896.

Trelawny of the "Wells" (produced 1898).   1897.

The Beauty Stone, with J. Comyns Carr, music by Arthur Sullivan (produced 1898).   1898.

The Gay Lord Quex (produced 1899).   1899.

Iris (produced 1901).   1901.

Letty (produced 1903).   1903.

A Wife Without a Smile: A Comedy in Disguise (produced 1904).   1904.

His House in Order (produced 1906).   1905.

The Thunderbolt (produced 1908).   1908.

Mid-Channel (produced 1909).   1909; edited by Gerald Weales, in *Edwardian Plays,* 1962.

Preserving Mr. Panmure (produced 1911).   1910.

The "Mind the Paint" Girl (produced 1912).   1912.

The Widow of Wasdale Head: A Fantasy (produced 1912).   1912.

Playgoers (produced 1913).   1913.

The Big Drum (produced 1915).   1915.

Mr. Livermore's Dream (produced 1917).   1916.

The Freaks: An Idyll of Suburbia (produced 1918).   1917.

Social Plays, edited by Clayton Hamilton.   4 vols., 1917–22.

Monica's Blue Boy, music by Frederic Cowen (produced 1918).

Quick Work (produced 1919).   1918.

A Seat in the Park (produced 1922).   1922.

The Enchanted Cottage (produced 1922).   1922.

A *Private Room* (produced 1928).   1928.
Two Plays (includes *Dr. Harmer's Holidays* and *Child Man*).   1930.
Dr. Harmer's Holidays (produced 1931).   In *Two Plays*, 1930.
A Cold June (produced 1932).

Bibliography: *Pinero's Plays and Players* by H. H. Fyfe, 1930.

Reading List: *Pinero und Sein Verhältnis zu Ibsen* by H. Küther, 1937; *Pinero: A Critical Biography with Letters* by Wilbur D. Dunkel, 1941; *Pinero* by Walter Lazenby, 1972.

*   *   *

Arthur Wing Pinero was the cleverest dramatist of his day in two distinct styles. It is in the first of these, the farce style best represented by *The Magistrate*, *The Schoolmistress*, and *Dandy Dick*, that he more easily survives in the modern theatre; but it was in the second, the genre that came to be known as the "problem play," that he earned his formidable contemporary reputation.

The farces are well-constructed, and the dialogue outstandingly easy. Pinero may ask us to accept initially a gross improbability, but there is a persuasive likelihood about the consequent events. The achievement is to have created characters whose self-regard invites the very disaster that is imminent. In *The Magistrate*, for example, we must accept that a mother might conceal her son's real age not only from her second husband but also from the son himself. It would be impossible to persuade any nineteen-year-old that he is only fourteen – except Cis Farringdon, who is so easy-going, and so inane, so peculiar a mixture of the ingenuous and the knowing, that he would never wish to disagree. The second act, in the Hotel des Princes, is as ingenious as the characteristic Feydeau scenes of confrontation in public places of ill repute, but the achievement is less purely mechanical than it is in the French models. Pinero's characters remain themselves throughout.

After the success of the three Court Theatre farces and the even greater success of the sentimental comedy *Sweet Lavender*, it was bold of Pinero to risk his reputation in *The Profligate*, a moral tale of seduction and eventual suicide (though not in the first production, for which Pinero was persuaded to provide a softer ending). It reads now as a posturing, pompous, and thoroughly contrived play, but its reception opened Pinero's eyes to the theatrical advantages of controversy, and to the extraordinarily low level of public honesty on sexual relations. His next farce for the Court Theatre, *The Cabinet Minister*, is without the social innocence of its predecessors. It sports with the grand pretensions that threaten the sympathetic Lady Twombly with an agony quite outside the world of farce, and, like *The Times*, it exposes the shams of ostentation in a dangerously humourless way.

The Ibsen debate was raging in theatrical London, and Pinero was ready to present himself as an English alternative. When *The Second Mrs. Tanqueray* opened at the St. James's, most people heard in it the voice of a master. Shaw was an exception. "I find little except a scaffold for the situation of a step-daughter and step-mother finding themselves in the positions respectively of affianced wife and discarded mistress of the same man. Obviously, the only necessary conditions of this situation are that the persons concerned shall be respectable enough to be shocked by it, and that the step-mother shall be an improper person." What irritated Shaw, and may disappoint a modern reader, was Pinero's supposition that Paula Tanqueray must aspire to the respectability she has forfeited. Her suicide is a surrender to the world of Victorian "respectability," simultaneously an unhappy ending to the play and a happy conclusion for society. The compromise is even more marked in Pinero's next attempt at the "higher" drama, *The Notorious Mrs. Ebbsmith*. Once again he succeeds in creating a woman too complex to submit, as she does, to the pressures of conventional morality. It is not until *The Benefit of the Doubt* that Pinero allows some hope to a woman with a past; and that is made easier for him because Theophila Fraser is innocent, whatever people may think and despite her discovery of desire.

The plight of women in an unforgiving sector of society is the main theme of these three plays as well as of the intermittently powerful *Iris*, *Letty*, the accomplished *His House in Order*, *The Thunderbolt*, and *Mid-Channel*; and there are lighter reflections of it in *The Princess and the Butterfly* and *The Gay Lord Quex*. Of these plays, *His House in Order* is the best controlled and written. It tells the touching story of an underrated second wife who refuses to take her revenge when the opportunity arises. Reduced to its outline the plot would sound melodramatic, and it is evidence of Pinero's skill in the dramatic handling of narrative that the play seems notably restrained.

Trelawny of the "Wells," perhaps his best play, lies slightly outside the two styles with which Pinero is most frequently associated. It displays his unashamed love of the theatre, and his sympathy with its traditions. For Shaw, it was a relief to find Pinero writing about the year 1860 rather than about the present, and he recognised the charm and delicacy of the piece. The reuniting of the lovers in the final act is a contrivance, but the theatrical setting goes a long way to excuse it. It is probably fair to look to this play for many of Pinero's own theatrical and social ideals. If so, they have the kind of old-world benevolence that can easily harden into the rigidity of conformism. We should not expect modernity in Pinero, however the case for innovation in later plays like *Playgoers*, *Monica's Blue Boy*, *The Freaks*, and *Dr. Harmer's Holidays* may be argued. The surface turbulence leaves the central values undisturbed.

—Peter Thomson

PINTER, Harold. English.   Born in Hackney, London, 10 October 1930. Educated at Hackney Downs Grammar School, 1943–47; Royal Academy of Dramatic Art, London, 1948. Married the actress Vivien Merchant in 1956 (divorced, 1976); one son. Professional actor since 1949; writer for the stage since 1957. Since 1973, Associate Director of the National Theatre, London. Member, Drama Panel, Arts Council of Great Britain. Recipient: *Evening Standard* award, 1960; Newspaper Guild of New York Award, 1962; Italia Prize, for television play, 1962; Screenwriters Guild Award, for television play, 1963, for screenplay, 1963; Guild of Televison Producers and Directors Award, 1963; New York Film Critics Award, 1964; British Film Academy Award, 1965, 1971; Antoinette Perry Award, 1967; Whitbread Award, 1967; New York Drama Critics Circle Award, 1967; Shakespeare Prize, Hamburg, 1970; Writers Guild Award, 1971. C.B.E. (Commander, Order of the British Empire), 1966. Lives In London.

PUBLICATIONS

Plays

> *The Room* (produced 1957).   In *The Birthday Party and Other Plays*, 1960.
> *The Birthday Party* (produced 1958).   1959; revised version, 1965.
> Sketches in *One to Another* (produced 1959).   1960.
> Sketches in *Pieces of Eight* (produced 1959).   In *A Slight Ache and Other Plays*, 1961.

A Slight Ache (broadcast 1959; produced 1961).   In *A Slight Ache and Other Plays*, 1961.

The Dwarfs (broadcast 1960; produced 1963; revised version, produced 1966).   In *A Slight Ache and Other Plays*, 1961.

The Dumb Waiter (produced 1960).   In *The Birthday Party and Other Plays*, 1960.

The Birthday Party and Other Plays.   1960; as *The Birthday Party and The Room* (includes *The Dumb Waiter*), 1961.

The Caretaker (produced 1960).   1960.

Night School (televised 1960).   In *Tea Party and Other Plays*, 1967.

A Night Out (broadcast 1960; produced 1961).   1961.

The Collection (televised 1961; produced 1962).   1962.

The Lover (televised 1963; produced 1963).   1965.

Tea Party (televised 1965; produced 1968).   1965; revised version, 1968.

The Homecoming (produced 1965).   1965; revised version, 1968.

The Dwarfs and Eight Revue Sketches.   1965.

The Collection and The Lover (includes the prose piece *The Examination*).   1966.

The Basement (televised 1967; produced 1968).   In *Tea Party and Other Plays*, 1967.

Tea Party and Other Plays.   1967.

Early Plays: A Night Out, Night School, Revue Sketches.   1968.

Sketches by Pinter (produced 1969).   In *Early Plays*, 1968.

Landscape (broadcast 1968; produced 1969).   1968.

Silence (produced 1969).   In *Landscape and Silence*, 1969.

Landscape and Silence.   1969.

Night, in *Mixed Doubles* (produced 1969).   In *Landscape and Silence*, 1969.

Five Screenplays (includes *The Caretaker, The Servant, The Pumpkin Eater, Accident, The Quiller Memorandum*).   1971; modified version, omitting *The Caretaker* and including *The Go-Between*, 1973.

Old Times (produced 1971).   1971.

Monologue (televised 1973; produced 1973).   1973.

No Man's Land (produced 1975).   1975.

Pinter Plays 1-3.   3 vols., 1975-78.

Complete Works 1 and *2*.   2 vols., 1977.

The Proust Screenplay: A la Recherche du Temps Perdu.   1977.

Betrayal (produced 1978).   1978.

Screenplays: *The Servant*, 1963; *The Guest (The Caretaker)*, 1964; *The Pumpkin Eater*, 1964; *The Quiller Memorandum*, 1966; *Accident*, 1967; *The Birthday Party*, 1968; *The Go-Between*, 1971; *The Homecoming*, 1971.

Radio Plays: *A Slight Ache*, 1959; *The Dwarfs*, 1960; *A Night Out*, 1960; *Landscape*, 1968.

Television Plays: *Night School*, 1960; The Collection, 1961, revised version, 1978; *The Lover*, 1963; *Tea Party*, 1965; *The Basement*, 1967; *Monologue*, 1973; *Langrishe, Go Down*, from the novel by Aidan Higgins, 1978.

Verse

Poems, edited by Alan Clodd.   1968; revised edition, 1970.

Other

Mac (on Anew McMaster).   1968.

Poems and Prose 1949–1977.   1978.

Editor, with others, *New Poems 1967.*   1968.

Bibliography: *Pinter: A Bibliography: His Works and Occasional Writings with a Comprehensive Checklist of Criticism and Reviews of the London Productions* by Rudiger Imhof, 1975.

Reading List: *Pinter* by Ronald Hayman, 1968; *Pinter* by John Russell Taylor, 1969; *The Peopled Wound: The Work of Pinter* by Martin Esslin, 1970, as *Pinter: A Study of His Plays,* 1973; *Strategems to Uncover Nakedness: The Dramas of Pinter* by Lois Gordon, 1970; *Pinter* by Alrene Sykes, 1970; *Pinter: A Study of His Reputation, 1956–1969* by Herman T. Schroll, 1971; *Pinter: A Collection of Critical Essays* edited by Arthur Ganz, 1972; *The Plays of Pinter: An Assessment* by Simon Trussler, 1973; *Pinter* by William Baker and Stephen E. Tabachnick, 1973; *The Pinter Problem* by Austin E. Quigley, 1975.

*   *   *

Harold Pinter's plays at first acquaintance bear a deceptive resemblance to conventional realistic fare: almost all are set in a room, the dialogue appears uncannily close to actual desultory chit-chat, and the characters seem simple slice-of-life folks drawn from Pinter's observation of his own associates of the working classes and, eventually, the upper-middle class.

Yet so rich are his plays with inscrutable motivations and latent or ambiguous import that a whole industry has arisen in the explication of his art, and his name has entered the critical lexicon in order to deal with those derivative dramas now termed "Pinteresque."

Most writers of realistic drama feel obliged to explain their characters' behavior. Even the first few minutes of a Pinter play, however, suggest that further exposure to the situation will merely compound the conundrum, heighten the obscurity, elaborate the elusive hints at the sources of his characters' anxiety or bereavement. Early in his career, Pinter defended the seemingly impenetrable nature of his work by asserting "The assumption that to verify what has happened and what is happening presents few problems I take to be inaccurate. A character on the stage who can present no convincing argument or information as to his past experience, his present behaviour or his aspirations, nor give a comprehensive analysis of his motives is as legitimate and as worthy of attention as one who, alarmingly, can do all these things. The more acute the experience the less articulate its expression."

Where most other playwrights set out to bring clarity, shape, and order to what they dramatize, Pinter may seem to delight in slyly selecting exactly what will appear most cryptic, vague or even contradictory. His substitution of hints for exposition and intangible menace for explicit confrontation has set directors to worrying over how to convey the "subtext" and critics to contriving exegeses which more often than not reveal more about themselves than about their subjects.

Symbol hunters enter a nirvana where they can deduce ever more ingenious significance. Pinter's eponymous dwarfs have been identified in the quest for allegory as tycoons, dictators, poetic genius, the tensions of friendship, or projection of the protagonists' anxieties or sense of inadequacy. All the titles have been subjected to such scrutiny. *The Dumb Waiter,* literally the restaurant lift to transport food between floors, is seen figuratively as mute service expected by a hired killer, or a description of the psyche's operation, or even a frightened child who wakes in the night needing to go to the toilet. Critics have labored over the nature of the slight ache, debated whose homecoming is intended, examined the landscape of the mind, the no man's land of the soul, and the old times recalled or imagined or fabricated.

Religion, philosophy, and psychology have been scavanged for evidence that Teddy is the prodigal son, Riley a messenger from the dead, Edward and Flora gods of the dying year and of fertility, and the lift in *Tea Party* a rising into consciousness of repressed desires. One critic has devoted an entire book to identifying Freudian symbolic content just as though the plays were dreams. Anal and oedipal imagery are deemed ubiquitous: the most innocuous exchanges perform sexual service here, the "sit down-stand up" dialogue in *The Room* for example, demonstrating penis envy. Even playwright Terence Rattigan propounded an allegorical interpretation, opining *The Caretaker* was about the God of the Old Testament, the God of the New Testament, and Humanity.

Pinter, who insisted to Rattigan that his subject was simply a caretaker and two brothers, has resisted the imposition of the unduly arcane abstraction on what can be accounted for on an immediate human level. On the other hand, frugality in supplying us with details in the text, his acknowledgment of such obscure references as the naming of everyone in *No Man's Land* after Edwardian cricketers, and his flippancy with critics, to one of whom he suggested he was writing about "the weasel under the cocktail cabinet," have encouraged a probing for clues to withheld information or keys to unspecified puzzles.

Instead of supplying us with the neat solutions usually contrived for plays, Pinter artfully deploys menace (in the early plays) and mystery (in the later work) to tantalize our attention. He creates myths of the modern psyche which seem to touch universal responses in men and women reared to repress violence, rage, fear, and sexuality and to substitute guilt for joy. A sort of poet laureate to the age of anxiety, Pinter substitutes indefinable dread for more routine dramatic action.

Dialogue in such drama takes on the character of combat, with words the weapons. No ordinary debate this, but power struggles in which even seeming non-sequiturs, delivered with sufficient conviction, can best an adversary. Stanley in *The Birthday Party* succumbs to an assault of this sort by McCann and Goldberg. Conversations which defy the analysis appropriate to ordinary discursive prose but which have the suggestive value and the rhythmic force of poetry orchestrate each Pinter play. Moving quickly from giggles to gasps, veering off into digression, repetition, and the most halting or elliptical approach to what must really most concern the speaker, Pinter's dialogue suggests that we often chatter without any intention of conveying an idea.

The degree to which Pinter sees people as inarticulate, either unable to communicate or unwilling to chance it, is exemplified by the amount of silence his plays require. Moments in which speech stalls he indicates by three of four dots, and these ellipses run into the thousands in a single play. Longer periods when no sound is uttered number, in *The Caretaker* alone, 17 long silences and 170 or so extended pauses. And Pinter insists that speech itself, as a "strategem to cover nakedness," is a kind of silence. He has even named one play about three loquacious though isolated characters (on the pattern of Beckett's *Play*) simply *Silence*. Whether his characters are using language to evade others or to manipulate them, what they speak of is often only indirectly indicative of the real subject of the scene. Thus Ruth and Lennie ostensibly discuss a glass of water and Ben and Gus quibble over the terminology of the tea kettle when control of the relationship is the real issue of both scenes.

In the early plays this struggle is rather more overt than in the later work. The proportion of physical violence and other threats to security likewise diminishes. In *The Room*, Rose fears the loss of her womb-like retreat even though her curiosity about outsiders leaves her ambivalent towards those who visit her. Ironically, it is the blind Riley, not Rose, who is victimized and Rose's husband Bert, rather than a stranger, who proves the real danger. In *The Birthday Party*, Stanley's haven is violated by mysterious intruders who reduce the poor fellow (often regarded as a symbol of individual creative talent) to catatonia. *The Dumb Waiter* works still another variation on the inhabitants-of-a-room-threatened-by-menace formula by turning the tables on a hired killer who suddenly finds that he is a menacer himself menaced, the target he and his partner were engaged to kill.

The work grows more subtle. Although most of Pinter's stage plays are set in a room which is visited by an alien spirit, mere menace is rejected in favor of less simple sources of dramatic tension. Thus in *The Caretaker* and *The Homecoming* visitors Davies and Teddy, having lost much of their dignity and status, are pathetic by play's end, and in *Landscape*, *Silence*, *Old Times*, and *No Man's Land*, the characters' past anxieties have long since given way to loneliness, sterility, even despair.

By the late 1960's Pinter was using a form almost as spare as that of Beckett. The womb room is now more of a tomb for the living dead, and characters are more likely to fear, not what is outside the room, but what's inside it or inside themselves. The considerable activity of the earlier plays has been reduced to a mere hint of change or conflict glossing a substance so static, indeed so private, that the terrain is nearly inaccessible. The danger of writing about people who are numb is that of leaving the audience also in that state, and late Pinter may touch the heart less than do his masterpieces *The Caretaker* and *The Homecoming*.

Although on the printed page this is not always evident, in the theatre even the serious plays prompt some laughter, and lighter work such as *The Collection* and *The Lover* amuse for long stretches. The humor of *No Man's Land* is one of the factors which renders its stasis an artistic success. And one of the theatre's finest comic scenes is the opening of *The Basement*, in which Law, the bewildered host, makes polite small talk while his guests strip and have sexual relations.

Critics fascinated by the puzzles in Pinter often advance hypotheses which neglect the broader human issues. Pinter is above all a playwright fascinated by man's metaphysical isolation, evanescence, futility, hostility, and narcissism. Frequently the characters suffer from a sort of ontological hysteria. Unsure of who or what they are, they seek to learn this by examining their reflections in others' eyes or by confirming their roles as these relate to their companions' functions. Rose plays "wife" to Bert's reluctant "husband" and Duff babbles to Beth in much the same spirit. Because Edward operates on the premise "You hear me, therefore I am," his failure to elicit a response from the Matchseller costs him his whole personality and his position in the house.

The derelict Davies uses an assumed name, reminds Mick of three other men, has no papers proving his identity. This ineffectual nonentity has no firm grasp on his place in the universe. He mistrusts those who are trustworthy and attempts to manipulate those who can best him at that game. The insight into aggression's source in insecurity, into the ways in which we might be our brother's keeper, and into the compulsion to undermine relationships, is much more important than some rigidly allegorical reading. Ungrateful, self-seeking Davies, by betraying Aston's friendship, does precisely what is contrary to his best interests. The universality of this experience is expressed in the old saw about the dog that bites the hand that feeds it and also that of doing unto others what you would have them do unto you. Eugene O'Neill's title for his abandoned cycle, *Dispossessors Self-Dispossessed*, would express one of the play's archetypical aspects.

Likewise, in *The Homecoming* just who comes home – Teddy to a house, Ruth to a past profession in another kind of house, or Max and his other sons to their need of dominance by a madonna-whore – is less significant than the universal elements of impotence, frustration, and the territorial disputes which are also waged in *The Basement* and *Night School*, among others. Repressed Disson in *Tea Party*, superfluous Deeley in *Old Times*, and sodden Hirst in *No Man's Land* are particularly poignant variations on the financially successful men who are nevertheless among life's losers.

Pinter's vision is archetypically male. He epitomizes the view of woman as the Other, a figure to be desired and feared, venerated, reviled and, often, lost. The maternal figures – Rose, Meg, Flora, Mrs. Stokes, Wally's aunts, even Ruth as a substitute for Jessie – are emasculating or suffocating or both. The younger women often are disguised mother-figures, and they disconcert their men by withholding information (Stella or Sally) or sexual favors (Ruth) or affection (Beth, Ellen, Kate). Women are objects invested with unfathomable allure, danger, and mystery who evade all male attempts to comprehend or control them, whether, like Kate or Diana, they prompt the repression of eroticism, or, as in *No Man's Land*, the effort to confront them and the whole matter of sensuality has been dropped, as forever unprofitable, in favor of acquiescence to alcohol. Pinter's recent women tend to be unresponsive to their men or arouse a compulsion to debase them as well as a feeling of guilt over the sensuality they inspire.

For Pinter, the world may be unstable, uncertain, unpredictable, and inhospitable. At best, memory surpasses present experience and mutability is our inescapable lot. Verification, communication, cooperation, satisfaction are equally unlikely. The pleasantries and amenities of civilisation provide only temporary buffers against a terror of both death and life itself.

—Tish Dace

PLANCHÉ, James Robinson.   English.   Born in Piccadilly, London, 27 February 1796. Studied at the Reverend Farrer's school, then at Monsieur de Court's school, London; articled to a bookseller, 1810. Married Elizabeth St. George in 1821 (died, 1846); two daughters. Began acting, as an amateur, at various private theatres in London, and began writing for the theatre in 1818; wrote for the Adelphi Theatre, 1820–21; wrote first opera, 1822, and designed costumes and supervised the production of the revival of Shakespeare's *King John* at Drury Lane, 1823; manager of the musical arrangements at the Vauxhall Gardens, 1826–27; wrote regularly for Covent Garden from 1828; managed the Adelphi Theatre, 1830; in partnership with the actress/manager Madame Vestris, first at the Olympic Theatre, then at Covent Garden, and then at the Lyceum, as resident writer and director of costumes, 1831–56; continued to write for other managements until 1872; also gained a reputation as an antiquary and scholar of heraldry and costume: Rouge Croix Pursuivant of Arms at the College of Heralds, 1854–66; Somerset Herald, 1866 until his death. Fellow, Society of Antiquaries, 1829; helped to found the British Archaeological Association, 1843. Granted Civil List pension, 1871. *Died 30 May 1880.*

PUBLICATIONS

Collections

> *Extravaganzas 1825–71,* edited by T. F. Dillon Croker and Stephen Tucker.   5 vols., 1879.

Plays

> *Amoroso, King of Little Britain,* music by Tom Cooke (produced 1818).   1818.
> *Rodolph the Wolf; or, Columbine Red Riding Hood* (produced 1818).   1819.
> *The Troubadours; or, Jealousy Out-Witted* (produced 1819).
> *Abudah; or, The Talisman of Oromanes,* music by Michael Kelly (produced 1819).
> *The Czar; or, A Day in the Dockyards,* from a French play (produced 1819).
> *The Caliph and the Cadi; or, Rambles in Bagdad* (produced 1819).
> *Fancy's Sketch; or, Look Before You Leap* (produced 1819).
> *Odds and Ends; or, Which Is the Manager?* (produced 1819).
> *The Vampyre; or, The Bride of the Isles,* from a French play (produced 1820).   1820.

A Burletta of Errors; or, Jupiter and Alcmena (produced 1820).   Songs published 1820.

Who's to Marry Her? or, What's Bred in the Bone Won't Come Out of the Flesh (produced 1820).

The Deuce Is in Her! or, Two Nights in Madrid (produced 1820).

Zamoski; or, The Fortress and the Mine (produced 1820).

Dr. Syntax; or, Harlequin in London (produced 1820).

Giovanni the Vampire; or, How Shall We Get Rid of Him? (produced 1821).

Kenilworth Castle; or, The Days of Queen Bess, from the novel by Scott (produced 1821).

Lodgings to Let (produced 1821).

Half an Hour's Courtship; or, Le Chambre à Coucher (produced 1821).

Sherwood Forest; or, The Merry Archers (produced 1821).

The Mountain Hut; or, The Tinker's Son (produced 1821).

Peter and Paul; or, Love in the Vineyards (produced 1821).   1887.

The Witch of Derncleuch, music by William Reeve, from the novel *Guy Mannering* by Scott (produced 1821).

Capers at Canterbury (produced 1821).

The Corsair's Bride; or, The Valley of Mount Etna (produced 1821).

Love's Alarum (produced 1821).

Le Solitaire; or, The Unknown of the Mountains (produced 1821).

Marplot in Spain, music by William Reeve, from the play by Mrs. Centlivre (produced 1821; as *Too Curious by Half*, produced 1823).

The Pirate (produced 1822).   1822.

All in the Dark; or, The Banks of the Elbe, music by B. Livius, from a play by H. J. B. D. Victor (produced 1822).   1822.

The Fair Gabrielle, music by B. Livius (produced 1822).   1822.

Ali Pacha; or, The Signet-Ring, from a play by John Howard Payne (produced 1822).   1822.

Maid Marian; or, The Huntress of Arlingford, music by Henry Bishop, from the novel by Peacock (produced 1822).   1822.

Clari; or, The Maid of Milan (songs only), play by John Howard Payne, music by Henry Bishop (produced 1823).   1823.

I Will Have a Wife!, music by William Reeve (produced 1823).

Cortez; or, The Conquest of Mexico, music by William Reeve (produced 1823).   1823.

St. Ronan's Well, from the novel by Scott (produced 1824).

Military Tactics, music by William Reeve, from a French play (produced 1824).

The Frozen Lake, music by William Reeve, from a play by Scribe (produced 1824).   Songs published 1824.

Der Freischutz; or, The Black Huntsman of Bohemia, music by B. Livius, from the opera by J. F. Kind, music by Weber (produced 1824).   1825.

A Woman Never Vext; or, The Widow of Cornhill, from the play by William Rowley (produced 1824).   1824.

The Coronation of Charles X of France (produced 1825).

Lilla (produced 1825).

Jocko; or, The Brazilian Monkey (produced 1825).

Success; or, A Hit If You Like It (produced 1825).   In *Extravaganzas 1*, 1879.

Oberon; or, The Elf-King's Oath, from a poem by Wieland, music by Weber (produced ;826).   1826.

Returned Killed, from a French play (produced 1826).   1826.

All's Right; or, The Old School-Fellow (produced 1827).

Pay to My Order; or, A Chaste Salute (produced 1827).

The Recontre; or, Love Will Fine Out the Way (produced 1827).

You Must Be Buried, from a French play (produced 1827).

Paris and London; or, A Trip Across the Herring Pond (produced 1828).   1829.

The Merchant's Wedding; or, London Frolics in 1638, from the plays *The City Match* by

Jasper Mayne and *Match Me at Midnight* by William Rowley (produced 1828). 1828.

Carron Side; or, Fête Champêtre (produced 1828).

My Daughter, Sir; or, A Daughter to Marry, from a French play (as *A Daughter to Marry,* produced 1828; as *My Daughter, Sir,* produced 1832). 1830(?).

The Green-Eyed Monster, from a French play (produced 1828). 1830(?).

The Mason of Buda, music by George Rodwell (produced 1828). 1828.

Charles XII; or, The Siege of Stralsund (produced 1828). 1830(?).

Thierna-na-Oge; or, The Prince of the Lakes, music by Tom Cooke (produced 1829).

The Partisans; or, The War of Paris in 1649, from a French play (produced 1829).

Manoeuvring, with Charles Dance, from a French play (produced 1829). 1829.

Der Vampyr, music by William Hawes, from an opera by W. A. Wohlbrück, music by Heinrich Marschner (produced 1829).

The Brigand (produced 1829). 1830(?).

Hofer; or, The Tell of the Tyrol, from an opera by Jouy, Bis, and Marrast, music by Rossini (produced 1830). 1830.

The National Guard; or, Bride and No Bride, from an opera by Scribe, music by Auber (produced 1830). Songs published 1830.

The Dragon's Gift; or, The Scarf of Flight and the Mirror of Light, music by Tom Cooke (produced 1830).

The Jenkinses; or, Boarded and Done For (produced 1830). 1853.

Olympic Revels; or, Prometheus and Pandora, with Charles Dance (produced 1831). 1834; in *Extravaganzas 1,* 1879.

The Romance of a Day, music by Henry Bishop (produced 1831). 1831.

My Great Aunt; or, Relations and Friends (produced 1831). 1846.

The Legion of Honour, from a French play (produced 1831).

A Friend at Court (produced 1831).

The Army of the North; or, The Spaniard's Secret (produced 1831).

The Love Charm; or, The Village Coquette, from an opera by Scribe, music by Auber (produced 1831).

Olympic Devils; or, Orpheus and Eurydice, with Charles Dance (produced 1831). 1831; in *Extravaganzas 1,* 1879.

The Compact (produced 1832).

His First Campaign (produced 1832).

The Paphian Bower; or, Venus and Adonis, with Charles Dance (produced 1832). In *Extravaganzas 1,* 1879.

Little Red Riding Hood; or, The Fairy of the Silver Lake (produced 1832).

Promotion; or, A Morning at Versailles (produced 1833). 1852.

Reputation; or, The Court Secret (produced 1833). 1833.

The Students of Jena; or, The Family Concert, from a German opera, music by Hippolyte Chelard (produced 1833).

The Court Masque; or, Richmond in the Olden Time, music by William Hawes, from an opera by F. A. F. de Planard, music by Hérold (produced 1833).

High, Low, Jack, and the Game; or, The Card Party, with Charles Dance (produced 1833). 1833; in *Extravaganzas 1,* 1879.

Gustave III; or, The Masked Ball, music by Tom Cooke, from an opera by Scribe, music by Auber (produced 1833). 1833.

The Deep Deep Sea; or, Perseus and Andromeda, with Charles Dance (produced 1833). 1834; in *Extravaganzas 1,* 1879.

The Challenge (songs only), libretto by H. M. Milner, music by Tom Cooke, from a French play (produced 1834).

Secret Service, from a play by Mélesville and Duveyrier (produced 1834). 1834.

The Loan of a Lover (produced 1834). 1834; revised version, as *Peter Spyk* (produced 1870).

My Friend the Governor (produced 1834). 1834.

The Regent, from a play by Scribe and Mélesville (produced 1834). 1834.

The Red Mask; or, The Council of Three, music by John Templeton, from an opera by A. Berrettoni, music by Marliani (produced 1834). Songs published 1834.

Telemachus; or, The Island of Calypso, with Charles Dance (produced 1834). In *Extravaganzas I,* 1879.

The Court Beauties (produced 1835). 1835.

The Travelling Carriage (produced 1835).

The Jewess, music by Tom Cooke, from an opera by Scribe, music by Halévy (produced 1835). 1835.

Chevy Chase, music by George Macfarren (produced 1836). Songs published 1836.

Court Favour; or, Private and Confidential (produced 1836). 1838.

The Siege of Corinth, music by Tom Cooke, from an opera by C. della Valle, music by Rossini (produced 1836). Songs published 1836.

The Two Figaros (produced 1836). 1837.

Riquet with the Tuft, with Charles Dance, from a French play (produced 1836). 1837; in *Extravaganzas 1,* 1879.

A Peculiar Position (produced 1837). 1837(?).

Norma (produced 1837). 1848.

The New Servant (produced 1837).

The Child of the Wreck, music by Tom Cooke (produced 1837). 1859.

Caractacus, music by Michael Balfe, from the play *Bonduca* by Fletcher (produced 1837).

Puss in Boots, with Charles Dance (produced 1837). 1837; in *Extravaganzas 1,* 1879.

The Magic Flute, from an opera by Emanuel Schikaneder, music by Mozart (produced 1838). Songs published 1838.

The Drama's Levée; or, A Peep at the Past (produced 1838). In *Extravaganzas 2,* 1879.

The Printer's Devil (produced 1838). 1838(?).

The Queen's Horse; or, The Brewer of Preston, with M. B. Honan (produced 1838). 1839.

Blue Beard, with Charles Dance (produced 1839). 1839; in *Extravaganzas 2,* 1879.

Faint Heart Ne'er Won Fair Lady, from a French play (produced 1839). N.d.

The Garrick Fever (produced 1839). 1855.

The Fortunate Isles; or, The Triumphs of Britannia, music by Henry Bishop (produced 1840). 1840.

The Sleeping Beauty in the Wood (produced 1840). 1840; in *Extravaganzas 2,* 1879.

The Spanish Curate, from the play by Fletcher and Massinger (produced 1840). 1887.

Harlequin and the Giant Helmet; or, The Castle of Otranto (produced 1840).

The Captain of the Watch, from a play by Lockroy (produced 1841). 1841.

The Embassy (produced 1841).

Beauty and the Beast (produced 1841). 1841; in *Extravaganzas 2,* 1879.

The Marriage of Figaro, from an opera by Lorenzo da Ponte, music by Mozart (produced 1842). Songs published 1842.

The White Cat, music by J. H. Tully (produced 1842). 1842; in *Extravaganzas 2,* 1879.

The Follies of a Night (produced 1842). 1842.

The Way of the World, from the play by Congreve (produced 1842).

Fortunio; or, The Seven Gifted Servants (produced 1843). 1843; edited by Michael Booth, in *English Plays of the Nineteenth Century 5,* 1976.

Who's Your Friend? or, The Queensberry Fête (produced 1843). 1843.

The Fair One with the Golden Locks (produced 1843). 1844; in *Extravaganzas 2,* 1879.

Grist to the Mill (produced 1844). 1844.

The Drama at Home; or, An Evening with Puff (produced 1844). 1844; in *Extravaganzas 2,* 1879.

Somebody Else (produced 1844).   1845.

Graciosa and Percinet (produced 1844).   1845; in *Extravaganzas 2*, 1879.

The Golden Fleece; or, Jason in Colchis and Medea in Corinth (produced 1845).   1845; in *Extravaganzas 3*, 1879.

A Cabinet Question (produced 1845).   1845.

The Bee and the Orange Tree; or, The Four Wishes (produced 1845).   1846; in *Extravaganzas 3*, 1879.

The Irish Post (produced 1846).   1846.

The Birds of Aristophanes (produced 1846).   1846; in *Extravaganzas 3*, 1879.

Queen Mary's Bower (produced 1846).   1847.

Spring Gardens (produced 1846).   1846.

Story-Telling; or, "Novel" Effects (produced 1846).

The Invisible Prince; or, The Island of Tranquil Delights (produced 1846).   1846; in *Extravaganzas 3*, 1879.

The New Planet; or, Harlequin Out of Place (produced 1847).   1847; in *Extravaganzas 3*, 1879.

The Jacobite (produced 1847).   1847.

The Pride of the Market (produced 1847).   1847.

The Golden Branch (produced 1847).   1848; in *Extravaganzas 3*, 1879.

Not a Bad Judge (produced 1848).   1848.

Theseus and Ariadne; or, The Marriage of Bacchus (produced 1848).   1848; in *Extravaganzas 3*, 1879.

The King of the Peacocks (produced 1848).   1849; in *Extravaganzas 3*, 1879.

A Romantic Idea (produced 1849).   1849.

Hold Your Tongue (produced 1849).   1849.

The Seven Champions of Christendom (produced 1849).   1849; in *Extravaganzas 3*, 1879.

A Lady in Difficulties (produced 1849).   1849.

The Island of Jewels (produced 1849).   1850; edited by Michael Booth, in *English Plays of the Nineteenth Century 5*, 1976.

Fiesco; or, The Revolt of Genoa (produced 1850).

Cymon and Iphigenia, from the play *Cymon* by Garrick (produced 1850).   1850; in *Extravaganzas 4*, 1879.

My Heart's Idol; or, A Desperate Remedy (produced 1850).

The White Hood (produced 1850).

The Day of Reckoning (produced 1850).   1852.

King Charming; or, The Blue Bird of Paradise (produced 1850).   In *Extravaganzas 4*, 1879.

The Queen of the Frogs (produced 1851).   In *Extravaganzas 4*, 1879.

The Prince of Happy Land; or, The Fawn in the Forest (produced 1851).   1851; in *Extravaganzas 4*, 1879.

The Mysterious Lady (produced 1852).   1853.

The Good Woman in the Wood (produced 1852).   In *Extravaganzas 4*, 1879.

Mr. Buckstone's Ascent of Mount Parnassus (produced 1853).   1853(?); in *Extravaganzas 4*, 1879.

The Camp at the Olympic (produced 1853).   1854.

Harlequin King Nutcracker, with J. Halford (produced 1853).   1853.

Once upon a Time There Were Two Kings (produced 1853).   1853; in *Extravaganzas 4*, 1879.

Mr. Buckstone's Voyage round the Globe (in Leicester Square) (produced 1854).   In *Extravaganzas 5*, 1879.

The Knights of the Round Table (produced 1854).   N.d.

The Yellow Dwarf and the King of the Gold Mines (produced 1854).   In *Extravaganzas 5*, 1879.

The New Haymarket Spring Meeting (produced 1855). In *Extravaganzas 5*, 1879.
The Discreet Princess; or, The Three Glass Distaffs (produced 1855). In *Extravaganzas 5*, 1879.
Young and Handsome (produced 1856). In *Extravaganzas 5*, 1879.
An Old Offender (produced 1859).
Love and Fortune (produced 1859). In *Extravaganzas 5*, 1879.
My Lord and My Lady; or, It Might Have Been Worse (produced 1861). 1862.
Love's Triumph, music by W. V. Wallace (produced 1862). 1862.
Orpheus in the Haymarket, from an opera by H. Cremieux and L. Halévy, music by Offenbach (produced 1865). In *Extravaganzas 5*, 1879.
Queen Lucidora, The Fair One with the Golden Locks, and Harlequin Prince Graceful; or, The Carp, The Crow, and the Owl (produced 1868).
Pieces of Pleasantry for Private Performance During the Christmas Holidays. 1868.
King Christmas (produced 1871). In *Extravaganzas 5*, 1879.
Babil and Bijou; or, The Lost Regalia (songs only), play by Dion Boucicault (produced 1872).

Verse

Shere Afkun, The First Husband of Nourmahal: A Legend of Hindoostan. 2 vols., 1823.
William with the Ring: A Romance in Rhyme. 1873.
Songs and Poems from 1819 to 1879. 1881.

Other

Costumes of Shakespeare's King John (and other plays). 5 vols., 1823–25.
Lays and Legends of the Rhine. 2 vols., 1827; as *The Rhenisch Keepsake,* 1837.
Descent of the Danube from Ratisbon to Vienna During the Autumn of 1827. 1828; as *The Danube from Ulm to Vienna,* 1836.
History of British Costume. 1834.
Regal Records; or, A Chronicle of the Coronation of the Queens Regnant of England. 1838.
The Pursuivant of Arms; or, Heraldry Founded upon Facts. 1852; revised edition, 1858.
A Corner of Kent; or, Some Account of the Parish of Ash-Next-Sandwich. 1864.
Recollections and Reflections: A Professional Autobiography. 2 vols., 1872; revised edition, 1901.
The Conqueror and His Companions. 2 vols., 1874.
A Cyclopaedia of Costume; or, Dictionary of Dress. 2 vols., 1876–79.
Suggestions for Establishing an English Art Theatre. 1879.

Editor, *A Complete View of the Dress and Habits of the People of England,* by J. Strutt. 1842.
Editor, *The Regal and Ecclesiastical Antiquities of England,* by J. Strutt. 1842.

Translator, *King Nut-Cracker: A Fairy Tale.* 1853.
Translator, *Fairy Tales,* by Mme. de Aulnoy. 1855.
Translator, *Four and Twenty Fairy Tales.* 1858.

Reading List: "Planché's Classical Burlesques" by D. MacMillan, in *Studies in Philology 25*, 1928; "Exit Planché – Enter Gilbert" by Harley Granville-Barker, in *The Eighteen-Sixties,* edited by John Drinkwater, 1932; *The Rise of English Opera* by Eric Walter White, 1951; *The Burlesque Tradition* by V. C. Clinton Baddeley, 1952; "Shakespeare in Planché's Extravaganzas" by Stanley Wells, in *Shakespeare Survey 16*, 1963; "Planché and the English Burletta Tradition" by P. T. Dircks, in *Theatre Survey 17*, 1976.

*   *   *

James Robinson Planché is best known today for his crucial role in the development of Christmas pantomime. He wrote a "speaking opening" for the harlequinade *Rodolph the Wolf; or Columbine Red Riding Hood* in 1818 and, in the 1830's and following decades, produced an abundance of fairy burlettas and extravaganzas, in effect extended openings without the harlequinade. His sources were eighteenth-century French *contes féeries*. Writing mainly for Madame Vestris, who excelled in "breeches parts," he helped establish the convention of the Principal Boy in combination with the Fairy Godmother and the peculiarly human, even courtly, pantomime animal. He exercised a happy sense of balance between the familiar and fantastic, dialogue, music and spectacle, French wit and English humour; and he was never prolix. In his *Recollections and Reflections* he complained that he was increasingly "painted out" from *The Island of Jewels* (1849) onwards, and attention drawn from his skill to elaborate artistic "transformations."

Although he wrote melodramas and comedies in prose, mostly of the school of Scribe and often with settings that must have appealed to the serious historian of costume and manners in him, it is in light verse and as a librettist that Planché sparkles. *Olympic Devils* gives a fair idea of his quality. "Mythology had always possessed a peculiar fascination for me," he declared, and he brings even the darker elements of the Orpheus legend within the range of this brief piece: a choric lament from the depths ("Singing, oh! that a pool of punch had we, Instead of a flaming sulphur sea"); the Fates ("A never-ceasing game of 'snip-snap-snorum.' For help, alas, man pleads to her in vain – *Her* motto's 'Cut and *never* come again.' "); Pluto's imperiousness ("Forward, my Furies! do your work, ye Fates! And thrust the Thracian thrummer through the gates!"); and the dismemberment of Orpheus ("He seems to have a singing in his head"). The *jeux d'esprit* are organised into episodes and arias unified by some dominant trick sustained just as long as Planché can ring changes on it: so 25 lines of punning dialogue with Cerberus culminate in a musical quartet ("You mean you've howled some doggerel to the moon./No sir; I say I sing – and sing in tune!/A *bark*-a-role of course./No sir, a glee./You take the *treble* then?/I take all three. My voice is tenor – counter-tenor – bass").

He insisted that his nonsense should be played with gravity and restraint in pleasing settings and costumes. With an abundance of graceful gestures (e.g., Paragon's *envoi* in *The White Cat*, "Here ends the tale, – *Finis coronat, O-puss!*") he offered light entertainment to cultivated audiences. His fairy world is an urbane one, his fairy princes recognisably descended from the disguised Rosalind and Viola; and it hardly requires the naming of Pope, in *High, Low, Jack, and the Game*, to identify *The Rape of the Lock* as a model from which he learnt much. His revues and his version of Aristophanes's *The Birds* reveal a limited satiric impulse, and the success of his work led to a temporary decline in the critical function of burlesque. Later writers of more critical bent who drew on the Planché tradition were W. S. Gilbert, Bernard Shaw, and Oscar Wilde.

—Margery Morgan

POOLE, John.   English.   Born in England in 1786. Very little is known about his family, background, or education; the dedications to his printed works suggest that he held a position in society; successful as a dramatist early in life, writing comedies and farces for the London theatres, 1811–29; an active contributor to the *New Monthly Magazine* for many years; lived in Windsor, 1831; and subsequently lived in Paris for many years; appointed a brother of the Charterhouse, London, but later gave up the position; obtained a pension through the influence of Dickens; lived in obscurity during the last 20 years of his life. *Died* (buried) *10 February 1872.*

PUBLICATIONS

Plays

    Hamlet Travestie (produced 1811).   1810.
    The Earls of Hammersmith; or, Infant Maturity, with Dennis Lawler (produced 1811).   N.d.
    Rumfuskin, King of the North Pole; or, Treason Rewarded (produced 1813).   In *Bentley's Miscellany,* 1841.
    The Hole in the Wall (produced 1813).   1813.
    Intrigue (produced 1814).   1814.
    Who's Who; or, The Double Imposture (produced 1815).   1815.
    A Short Reign and a Merry One (produced 1819).   1819.
    Past and Present; or, The Hidden Treasure, from a French play (as *The Hidden Treasure,* produced 1820; as *Past and Present,* produced 1830).   N.d.
    Match Making, from a French play (produced 1821).   1844.
    The Two Pages of Frederick the Great, from a play by Nicolas Dezède (produced 1821).   1821.
    Old and Young (produced 1822).   1822.
    Simpson and Co. (produced 1823).   1823.
    Augusta; or, The Blind Girl (produced 1823).
    Deaf as a Post (produced 1823).   1823.
    A Year in an Hour; or, The Cock of the Walk (produced 1824).   1824.
    Married and Single; or, Belles and Bailiffs, from a French play (produced 1824).   1824.
    'Twould Puzzle a Conjuror (produced 1824).   N.d.
    Tribulation; or, Unwelcome Visitors, from a play by A. J. M. Wafflard and J. D. F. de Bury (produced 1825).   1825.
    Paul Pry (produced 1825).   1825.
    The Scape-Goat (produced 1825).   1826.
    'Twixt the Cup and the Lip (produced 1826).
    The Wife's Strategem; or, More Frightened Than Hurt, from the play *The Gamester* by James Shirley (produced 1827).   1827.
    Gudgeons and Sharks; or, Piecrust Promises (produced 1827).
    The Wealthy Widow; or, They're Both to Blame, from a French play (produced 1827).   1827.
    Ups and Downs; or, The Ladder of Life (produced 1828).
    My Wife! What Wife? (produced 1829).   N.d.
    Lodgings for Single Gentlemen (produced 1829).   N.d.
    Turning the Tables (produced 1830).   1834(?); as *Quite the Reverse* (produced 1839).
    The Bath Road (produced 1830).
    Madame du Barry; or, A Glance at a Court (produced 1831).
    A Nabob for an Hour, from a play by Scribe (produced 1833).   1832; as *Uncle Sam,* n.d.

A Soldier's Courtship (produced 1833). 1833.
Patrician and Parvenu; or, Confusion Worse Confounded (produced 1835). 1835.
Atonement; or, The God-Daughter, from a French play (produced 1836). 1836.
Delicate Attentions (produced 1836). 1837.
Scan Mag; or, The Village Gossip. 1840(?).
The Swedish Ferryman (produced 1843).

Fiction

Sketches and Recollections. 1835; as *The Comic Sketch-Book,* 1836.
Paul Pry's Journal of a Residence at Little Pedlington. 1836.
Paul Pry's Delicate Attentions and Other Tales. 1837.
Little Pedlington and the Pedlingtonians. 1839.
Phineas Quiddy; or, Sheer Industry. 1842.
Christmas Festivities: Tales, Sketches, and Characters. 4 vols., 1845–48.

Verse

Byzantium: A Dramatic Poem. N.d.

Other

Crotchets in the Air; or, An (Un)Scientific Account of a Balloon-Trip. 1838.

Editor, *The Comic Miscellany for 1845.* 1845.

*   *   *

Two works distinguish John Poole from the mass of minor dramatists active in the English theatre during the early decades of the nineteeth century. The first is his *Hamlet Travestie,* and the second *Paul Pry.* This is not to deny merit to certain other pieces – *Tribulation,* for example, a comedy derived from a French original, or the two farces *Deaf as a Post* and *'Twixt the Cup and the Lip.* But these pieces neither initiated a literary fashion, as did the *Hamlet Travestie,* nor added a household name to the English language, as did *Paul Pry.* The credit for the phenomenal success of *Paul Pry* has to be shared between the author and John Liston, who played the title role. The play has a fairly conventional double-plot, but its comic centre is the interfering nosy parker Paul Pry, whose catchphrase "I hope I don't intrude?" convulsed audiences at the Haymarket for an unprecedented 114 nights in its first season. The credit for the success of *Hamlet Travestie* is Poole's alone. It was his first dramatic piece, and it was published and already into three editions before it received any performance. Much of the fun of a reading is to be gained from the "burlesque annotations, after the manner of Dr. Johnson and Geo. Steevens, Esq. and the various commentators," but the text has charms for anyone prepared to enjoy a prolonged exercise in bathos. The flavour can be judged by almost any extract, this of the King's at the opening of the first act, for example:

> Cheer up, my hearty: tho' you've lost your dad,
> Consider that your case is not so bad:
> Your father lost a father; and 'tis certain
> Death o'er your great-grandfather drew the curtain.
> You've mourned enough: 'tis time your grief to smother;
> Don't cry; you shall be king some time or other.

Most of the play's best known lines turn up, only to be pulled down to the level of colloquial, rhyming doggerel. The soliloquies are rewritten as songs, as is some of the dialogue. The extraordinary thing is that Poole sticks very close to Shakespeare's plot; and he writes with more wit than many of those who followed his lead.

—Peter Thomson

PRIESTLEY, J(ohn) B(oynton). English. Born in Bradford, Yorkshire, 13 September 1894. Educated in Bradford schools, and at Trinity Hall, Cambridge, M.A. Served with the Duke of Wellington's and the Devon Regiments, 1914–19. Married 1) Patricia Tempest (died, 1925), two daughters; 2) Mary Wyndham Lewis (divorced, 1952), two daughters and one son; 3) the writer Jacquetta Hawkes in 1953. Writer from 1925; Director of the Mask Theatre, London, 1938–39; radio lecturer on the BBC programme "Postscripts" during World War II; regular contributor to the *New Statesman*, London. President, P.E.N., London, 1936–37; United Kingdom Delegate, and Chairman, UNESCO International Theatre Conference, Paris, 1947, and Prague, 1948; Chairman, British Theatre Conference, 1948; President, International Theatre Institute, 1949; Member, National Theatre Board, London, 1966–67. Recipient: Black Memorial Prize, 1930; Ellen Terry Award, 1948. LL.D.: University of St. Andrews; D.Litt.: University of Birmingham; University of Bradford. Honorary Freeman of the City of Bradford, 1973. Order of Merit, 1977. Lives in Alveston, Warwickshire.

PUBLICATIONS

Plays

> *The Good Companions*, with Edward Knoblock, from the novel by Priestley (produced 1931). 1935.
> *Dangerous Corner* (produced 1932). 1932.
> *The Roundabout* (produced 1932). 1933.
> *Laburnum Grove: An Immoral Comedy* (produced 1933). 1934.
> *Eden End* (produced 1934). 1934.
> *Cornelius: A Business Affair in Three Transactions* (produced 1935). 1935.
> *Duet in Floodlight* (produced 1935). 1935.
> *Bees on the Boat Deck: A Farcical Tragedy* (produced 1936). 1936.
> *Spring Tide*, with George Billam (produced 1936). 1936.
> *The Bad Samaritan* (produced 1937).
> *Time and the Conways* (produced 1937). 1937.
> *I Have Been Here Before* (produced 1937). 1937.
> *I'm a Stranger Here* (produced 1937).
> *People at Sea* (produced 1937). 1937.
> *Mystery at Greenfingers: A Comedy of Detection* (produced 1938). 1937.
> *When We Are Married: A Yorkshire Farcical Comedy* (produced 1938). 1938.
> *Music at Night* (produced 1938). In *Three Plays*, 1943.

Johnson over Jordan (produced 1939).   Published as *Johnson over Jordan: The Play, And All about It (An Essay)*, 1939.

The Long Mirror (produced 1940).   In *Three Plays*, 1943.

Good Night Children: A Comedy of Broadcasting (produced 1942).   In *Three Comedies*, 1945.

Desert Highway (produced 1943).   1944.

They Came to a City (produced 1943).   In *Three Plays*, 1943.

Three Plays.   1943.

How Are They at Home? A Topical Comedy (produced 1944).   In *Three Comedies*, 1945.

The Golden Fleece (as *The Bull Market*, produced 1944).   In *Three Comedies*, 1945.

Three Comedies.   1945.

An Inspector Calls (produced 1945).   1945.

Jenny Villiers (produced 1946).

The Rose and Crown (televised 1946).   1947.

Ever Since Paradise: An Entertainment, Chiefly Referring to Love and Marriage (produced 1946).   1949.

The Linden Tree (produced 1947).   1948.

The Plays of J. B. Priestley.   3 vols., 1948–50; vol. 1 as *Seven Plays*, 1950.

Home Is Tomorrow (produced 1948).   1949.

The High Toby: A Play for the Toy Theatre (produced 1954).   1948.

Summer Day's Dream (produced 1949).   In *Plays III*, 1950.

The Olympians, music by Arthur Bliss (produced 1949).   1949.

Bright Shadow: A Play of Detection (produced 1950).   1950.

Treasure on Pelican (as *Treasure on Pelican Island*, televised 1951; as *Treasure on Pelican*, produced 1952).   1953.

Dragon's Mouth: A Dramatic Quartet, with Jacquetta Hawkes (produced 1952).   1952.

Private Rooms: A One-Act Comedy in the Viennese Style.   1953.

Mother's Day.   1953.

Try It Again (produced 1965).   1953.

A Glass of Bitter.   1954.

The White Countess, with Jacquetta Hawkes (produced 1954).

The Scandalous Affair of Mr. Kettle and Mrs. Moon (produced 1955).   1956.

These Our Actors (produced 1956).

Take the Fool Away (produced 1956).

The Glass Cage (produced 1957).   1958.

The Thirty-First of June (produced 1957).

The Pavilion of Masks (produced 1963).   1958.

A Severed Head, with Iris Murdoch, from the novel by Murdoch (produced 1963).   1964.

Screenplays: *Sing As We Go*, 1934; *We Live in Two Worlds*, 1937; *Jamaica Inn*, with Sidney Gilliat and Joan Harrison, 1939; *Britain at Bay*, 1940; *Our Russian Allies*, 1941; *The Foreman Went to France (Somewhere in France)*, with others, 1942; *Last Holiday*, 1950.

Radio Plays: *The Return of Jess Oakroyd*, 1941; *The Golden Entry*, 1955; *End Game at the Dolphin*, 1956; *An Arabian Night in Park Lane*, 1965.

Television Plays: *The Rose and Crown*, 1946; *Treasure on Pelican Island*, 1951; *The Stone Face*, 1957; *The Rack*, 1958; *Doomsday for Dyson*, 1958; *The Fortrose Incident*, 1959; *Level Seven*, 1966; *The Lost Peace* series, 1966; *Anyone for Tennis*, 1968; *Linda at Pulteneys*, 1969.

Fiction

Adam in Moonlight. 1927.
Benighted. 1927; as *The Old Dark House,* 1928.
Farthing Hall, with Hugh Walpole. 1929.
The Good Companions. 1929.
The Town Major of Miraucourt (story). 1930.
Angel Pavement. 1930.
Faraway. 1932.
Albert Goes Through (story). 1933.
I'll Tell You Everthing: A Frolic, with Gerald Bullett. 1933.
Wonder Hero. 1933.
They Walk in the City: The Lovers in the Stone Forest. 1936.
The Domesday Men: An Adventure. 1938.
Let the People Sing. 1939.
Black-Out in Gretley: A Story of – and for – Wartime. 1942.
Daylight on Saturday: A Novel about an Aircraft Factory. 1943.
Three Men in New Suits. 1945.
Bright Day. 1946.
Jenny Villiers: A Story of the Theatre. 1947.
Going Up: Stories and Sketches. 1950.
Festival at Farbridge. 1951; as *Festival,* 1951.
The Other Place and Other Stories of the Same Sort. 1953.
The Magicians. 1954.
Low Notes on a High Level: A Frolic. 1954.
Saturn over the Water: An Account of His Adventures in London, South America and Australia by Tim Bedford, Painter; Edited, with Some Preliminary and Concluding Remarks, By Henry Sulgrave and Here Presented to the Reading Public. 1961.
The Thirty-First of June: A Tale of True Love, Enterprise and Progress in the Arthurian and ad-Atomic Ages. 1961.
The Shapes of Sleep: A Topical Tale. 1962.
Sir Michael and Sir George: A Tale of COMSA and DISCUS and the New Elizabethans. 1964; as *Sir Michael and Sir George: A Comedy of the New Elizabethans,* 1965(?).
Lost Empires, Being Richard Herncastle's Account of His Life on the Variety Stage from November 1913 to August 1914, Together with a Prologue and Epilogue. 1965.
Salt Is Leaving. 1966.
It's an Old Country. 1967.
The Image Men: Out of Town, and London End. 2 vols., 1968.
The Carfitt Crisis and Two Other Stories. 1975.
Found, Lost, Found; or, The English Way of Life. 1976.

Verse

The Chapman of Rhymes (juvenilia). 1918.

Other

Brief Diversions, Being Tales, Travesties, and Epigrams. 1922.
Papers from Lilliput. 1922.
I for One. 1923.
Figures in Modern Literature. 1924.

Fools and Philosophers: A Gallery of Comic Figures from English Literature. 1925; as *The English Comic Characters,* 1925.

George Meredith. 1926.

Talking: An Essay. 1926.

(Essays). 1926.

Open House: A Book of Essays. 1927.

Thomas Love Peacock. 1927.

The English Novel. 1927; revised edition, 1935.

Too Many People and Other Reflections. 1928.

Apes and Angels: A Book of Essays. 1928.

The Balconinny and Other Essays. 1929; as *The Balconinny,* 1930.

English Humour. 1929.

Self-Selected Essays. 1932.

Four-in-Hand (miscellany). 1934.

English Journey, Being a Rambling But Truthful Account of What One Man Saw and Heard and Felt and Thought During a Journey Through England During the Autumn of the Year 1933. 1934.

Midnight on the Desert: A Chapter of Autobiography. 1937; as *Midnight on the Desert, Being an Excursion into Autobiography During a Winter in America, 1935–36.* 1937.

Rain upon Godshill: A Further Chapter of Autobiography. 1939.

Britain Speaks (radio talks). 1940.

Postscripts (radio talks). 1940.

Out of the People. 1941.

Britain at War. 1942.

British Women Go to War. 1943.

Here Are Your Answers. 1944.

Letter to a Returning Serviceman. 1945.

The Secret Dream: An Essay on Britain, America and Russia. 1946.

Russian Journey. 1946.

Theatre Outlook. 1947.

Delight. 1949.

A Priestley Companion: A Selection from the Writings. 1951.

Journey down a Rainbow, with Jacquetta Hawkes (travel). 1955.

All about Ourselves and Other Essays, edited by Eric Gillett. 1956.

Thoughts in the Wilderness (essays). 1957.

Topside; or, The Future of England: A Dialogue. 1958.

The Story of Theatre (juvenile). 1959; as *The Wonderful World of the Theatre,* 1959; revised edition, 1969.

Literature and Western Man. 1960.

William Hazlitt. 1960.

Charles Dickens: A Pictorial Biography. 1961; as *Dickens and His World,* 1969.

Margin Released: A Writer's Reminiscences and Reflections. 1962.

Man and Time. 1964.

The Moments and Other Pieces. 1966.

The World of Priestley, edited by D. G. MacRae. 1967.

All England Listened: Priestley's Wartime Broadcasts. 1968.

Essays of Five Decades, edited by Susan Cooper. 1968.

Trumpets over the Sea, Being a Rambling and Egotistical Account of the London Symphony Orchestra's Engagement at Daytona Beach, Florida, in July–August 1967. 1968.

The Prince of Pleasure and His Regency, 1811–1820. 1969.

The Edwardians. 1970.

Snoggle (juvenile). 1971.

Victoria's Heyday. 1972.
Over the Long High Wall: Some Reflections and Speculations on Life, Death and Time. 1972.
The English. 1973.
Outcries and Asides. 1974.
A Visit to New Zealand. 1974.
Particular Pleasures, Being a Personal Record of Some Varied Arts and Many Different Artists. 1975.
The Happy Dream (biography). 1976.
English Humour. 1976.
Instead of the Trees (autobiography). 1977.

Editor, *Essayists Past and Present: A Selection of English Essays.* 1925.
Editor, *Tom Moore's Diary: A Selection.* 1925.
Editor, *The Book of Bodley Head Verse.* 1926.
Editor, *The Female Spectator: Selections from Mrs. Eliza Haywood's Periodical, 1744–1746.* 1929.
Editor, *Our Nation's Heritage.* 1939.
Editor, *Scenes of London Life, From Sketches by Boz by Charles Dickens.* 1947.
Editor, *The Best of Leacock.* 1957; as *The Bodley Head Leacock*, 1957.
Editor, with O. B. Davis, *Four English Novels.* 1960.
Editor, with O. B. Davis, *Four English Biographies.* 1961.
Editor, *Adventures in English Literature.* 1963.
Editor, *An Everyman Anthology.* 1966.

Reading List: *Priestley* by Ivor Brown, 1957, revised edition, 1964; *Priestley: An Informal Study of His Work* by David Hughes, 1958; *Mensch und Gesellschaft bei Priestley* by L. Löb, 1962 (includes bibliography); *Priestley the Dramatist* by G. L. Evans, 1964; *Priestley: Portrait of an Author* by Susan Cooper, 1970.

*   *   *

J. B. Priestley, born as long ago as 1894, is not only jack of most literary trades but master of quite a few: novels, plays, essays both historical and literary. He fully deserved his Order of Merit in 1977. During the second world war he became a skilled broadcaster with a large following.

After the first world war he was a widely appreciated essayist and reviewer. More recently he completed a remarkably readable autobiography. He was a superb journalist as he showed in the now classic *English Journey.*

But it is probably as a novelist, translated into almost every known language and in the best-seller class, that he is best known. *The Good Companions*, a picaresque novel without a real picaro (rogue), describes on a broad Victorian-style canvas the adventures of a travelling concert party and those who attach themselves to it. It has a not quite happy ending. No less successful a year or two later was *Angel Pavement* which had no happy ending at all and concerned the disasters brought upon a group of lower middle-class clerical workers in a City of London veneer firm by a predatory "sharp Alec" from the Baltic. There are a dozen or more pieces of fiction he wrote in the ensuing years, notably the superbly, though gently satirical, study of the new universities and the advertising business in *The Image Men* and *Bright Day*, which some regard as his best post-war novel. It harks back, as so often in his work, to the experiences of a family and others the narrator has known before the overwhelming and shattering experience of the First World War (in which Priestley fought) and which changed so many lives in many countries. Almost all his novels continue to be readable and are often stimulating, for example, *Let the People Sing, Daylight on Saturday*, and *Festival at Farbridge*. He discovered a fluent and often witty narrative style. He was obscure neither in subject matter nor character portrayal; yet he did not lack psychological penetration.

It is, however, for certain of his plays that he would claim real originality. Some, excellent though they are – and continually performed all over the world – are conventional in format: *Eden End*, *Laburnum Grove*, and the moving *The Linden Tree*. But he carried out such stage experiments as *Ever Since Paradise*, a comedy about love and marriage where each set of three couples are both actors and soliloquising commentators. The most powerful of the experimental plays is *Johnson over Jordan*, a sort of dramatic obituary of a recently-deceased business man which has moments of great insight and moving intensity. It is full of Johnson's hopes and fears and, now, vain regrets. Difficult, indeed, to stage but as moving as any mid-20th century drama.

Priestley's plays and other works were often centred on the theories popularized by J. W. M. Dunne, Carl Jung, and others about the nature of time, on which Priestley wrote with intelligence and imagination. Priestley has also always been sensitive to, as he would regard it, the untoward interference of politics in men's lives. He is not a party man, though until latter years he would have regarded himself as anti-Conservative. From 1950 or so, his essays became more and more polemical and anti-authoritarian Socialism. He may be summed up as a centre radical if that is not a contradiction in terms. Radical, however, he certainly is in the sense that he believes changes may quickly be made to improve matters rather than having to wait for the slow processes of evolution. He has invented words which became part and parcel of the common talk of his time; one such word was "admass" which conveyed the idea of the mindless majorities of "civilised" mankind helplessly persuaded by subtle advertising schemes to buy more and more goods they did not require.

By some of his contemporaries he was reputed to be of a contumacious nature. Certainly he was not, either as a man or writer, one to be over-ruled or to allow his views to go unheard – and he had views and preferences on pictures (he himself painted) and on music as well as, of course, on the arts he himself practised. But despite his bluntness of speech he was not – as he himself repeatedly declared – quarrelsome. Most who knew him enjoyed his company; and to his millions of devoted followers he was a source of delight on the page and stage, a superb entertainer full of talent, and here and there something of genius.

—Kenneth Young

RANDOLPH, Thomas. English. Born in Newnham-cum-Badby, near Daventry, Northamptonshire, baptized 15 June 1605. Educated at Westminster School, London (King's Scholar); Trinity College, Cambridge, matriculated 1624, B.A. 1628, minor fellow 1629, major fellow 1632, M.A. 1632; also incorporated M.A. at Oxford, 1632. Became famous at Cambridge as a writer of verse; visited London frequently from 1628, and became acquainted with the writers and patrons surrounding Ben Jonson; settled in London, 1632, and lived an increasingly dissipated life which undermined his health. *Died* (buried) *17 March 1635.*

PUBLICATIONS

Collections

    Poetical and Dramatic Works, edited by W. C. Hazlitt.   2 vols., 1875.
    Poems and Amyntas, edited by John Jay Parry.   1917.
    Poems, edited by G. Thorn-Drury.   1929.

Plays

    Aristippus; or, The Jovial Philosopher (produced 1625–26?).   1630.
    The Drinking Academy (produced 1626?).   Edited by Hyder Rollins, in *Publications of the Modern Language Association*, 1924; edited by Rollins and S. A. Tannenbaum, 1930.
    The Conceited Pedlar (produced 1627).   With *Aristippus*, 1630.
    The Muses' Looking-Glass (produced 1630).   In *Poems ...*, 1638.
    Amyntas; or, The Impossible Dowry (produced 1630).   In *Poems ...*, 1638.
    Praeludium (produced 1630?).   In *Poems and Amyntas*, 1917.
    The Jealous Lovers (produced 1632).   1632.
    The Constant Lovers (produced 1634).   Edited by B. H. Newdigate, in *Times Literary Supplement*, 18 and 25 April 1942.
    Hey for Honesty, Down with Knavery, from a play by Aristophanes.   1651.

Other

    Poems, with The Muses' Looking-Glass and Amyntas.   1638; revised edition, 1640.

Bibliography: *Randolph: A Concise Bibliography* by S. A. and D. R. Tannenbaum, 1946.

Reading List: *Randolph* (lecture) by G. C. Moore Smith, 1927; *Pastoral Poetry and Pastoral Drama* by W. W. Greg, 1959; *The Poetry of Randolph* by Ila Mullick, 1974.

*   *   *

For reasons which it is now hardly possible to discern, Thomas Randolph's contemporary popularity was very great. Adopted by Jonson as a "son of Ben," he impressed his acquaintance as his great mentor's most worthy successor, and his early death was seen as a disaster for English letters. Precocity and facility may account for the effect Randolph had on those who knew him, for nothing that survives in his poetry or his plays justifies this high estimate of his work.

"An Ode to Master Anthony Stafford" is Randolph's main poetic achievement. It is his own version of the classical encomium of country life, "where old simplicity,/Though hid in gray,/Doth look more gay/Than foppery in plush and scarlet clad," and abandons his usual easy couplets for a swinging 12-lined stanza, where alternating short and long lines allow the rush of impatience or exuberance into the verse ("More of my days/I will not spend to gain an idiot's praise"; "The thrush and blackbird lend their throats/Warbling melodious notes;/We will all sports enjoy, which others but desire"). The ode is only faintly tinged with the stale pastoral vocabulary in which so many of Randolph's poems are phrased, and gives fresh and lively treatment to a theme which he also dealt with several times in neat and competent translations from classical authors. Of his other pastorals, the "Eclogue ... upon Predestination" achieves an unexpectedly powerful close, but the rest are undistinguished. The wit of such poems as those on "his well-timbered mistress" or "a very deformed gentlewoman" is now tedious, but rueful poems to his empty purse, his creditors, and his lost finger show something of the gaiety and charm that delighted his contemporaries.

Randolph's dramatic works give the impression that, had the age allowed it, he would have found his vocation as a writer of sketches for reviews. The lively monologue *The Conceited Pedlar* is in effect cabaret material; the opportunities it offered a performer in the Cambridge setting for which it was designed are still evident. *Aristippus*, a longer but equally topical sketch, burlesques university life by adding the philosophy of drinking to the syllabus; its wit was well calculated to appeal to an undergraduate audience. *The Drinking Academy*, a similar piece, is less academic and shows Jonson's influence. *The Muses' Looking-Glass* is likewise more a sketch than a play; its demonstration of comedy's power to purge excesses by ridicule is hardly amusing today, except for the presentation of the Puritans whose prejudices are overcome. Randolph's two full-length plays are written in nondescript verse and show little power of dramatic construction on a larger scale. His pastoral drama, *Amyntas*, though admired by W. W. Greg, comes to life only in the comic scenes which Randolph added to the genre; while *The Jealous Lovers*, in which an improbable plot is unconvincingly resolved by a *deus ex machina*, shows Randolph deficient in the ability to portray plausible serious action or genuine feeling.

—Margaret Forey

RASTELL, John. English. Born in London c. 1475. Trained as a lawyer; entered Lincoln's Inn, London, 1502, and subsequently had a successful practice in London. Married Elizabeth More, sister of Sir Thomas More; one son. Printer in London, printing mainly legal books, from 1513; also served as Member of Parliament for Dunheved, Cornwall, 1529–36; involved in the religious controversies of the time from c. 1530: a convert to Protestantism; claimed in later life that his conversion had been the cause of the ruin of his legal practice and printing business. *Died in June 1536.*

PUBLICATIONS

Plays

The Nature of the Four Elements. 1517–27(?); edited by Roger Coleman, 1971.

Terence in English (translation of *Andria* by Terence).   1520(?).
Calisto and Melibea.   1527(?); edited by H. W. Allen, 1908.
Gentleness and Nobility.   1527(?); edited by K. W. Cameron, 1941.

Other

The Pastime of People.   1529; edited by T. F. Dibdin, 1811.
A New Book of Purgatory.   1530.

Editor and Translator, *The Exposition of the Terms of the Laws of England.*   1526 (and
    later versions in English and French).
Editor and Translator, *The Statutes.*   1527 (and later versions in English and French).

*   *   *

John Rastell's celebrity arises partly from his distinction as an early London publisher and
humanist associate of Thomas More, his brother-in-law. As lawyer, Catholic turned
Lutheran, member of the Reformation Parliament, and man of wide interests (contemporary
science, social and legal reform, colonial exploration, the infant printing industry, amateur
dramatics), he epitomizes the vigorous spirit of Henrician England. However, it is now
customary also to credit him with an impressive group of original works, products of an
independent and versatile mind. The disputative *New Boke of Purgatory*, if lacking the
intellectual command, or the wit, range, and flexibility of More's religious polemics,
attractively illuminates a theological controversy, while the discriminating spirit of modern
historical criticism already informs Rastell's highly readable chronicle *Pastyme of People*,
which as a model of fluent narrative prose deserves more respectful attention than it has
usually received.
    His three plays form a distinctive contribution to Tudor drama, in which field Rastell was
probably something of an innovator, although essentially forensic motives led him to employ
characters and situations to present information or advance debating-points rather than create
intrinsically effective stage-images. In the incompletely preserved interlude *The Nature of the
Four Elements* he adapts the form and techniques of the medieval religious morality to
illustrate the principles and content of contemporary humanistic education: thus Nature,
subjecting the student-hero Humanity to a course of instruction in Renaissance science and
geography, is assisted by Studious Desire and Experience but hampered by the boastful vice
Ignorance and the cheerfully disreputable Sensual Appetite who lures Humanity from his
studies to the tavern. Although the lengthy didactic speeches and tame comic digressions
compare unfavourably with those of Henry Medwall's earlier *Fulgens and Lucres*, and a
dearth of psychological interest is also apparent, the piece remains a commendable attempt to
extend the scope of the homiletic morality.
    Gentylnes and Nobylyte depicts three "estates of the realm" (knight, merchant, and
ploughman) engaging in debate over the relative importance of birth and behaviour in
establishing social worth, but the argument becomes diffuse and characterization is thin,
"discussion drama" being exploited more successfully by Rastell's son-in-law, John
Heywood. More promising is *A new commodye in English*, adapted from the Spanish
dialogue-romance *Celestina* and usually known as *Calisto and Meliboea*, which, in telling of
the bawd Celestina's furtherance of the lovers' passionate liaison, breaks free from formal
and ideological constraints to recount a human story. But Rastell evades the original's
retributive dénouement in which the parties suffer violent deaths and substitutes a typical
moral lecture; indeed, he rarely resists the opportunity to instruct or improve his auditors.
Even when a genuinely dramatic development seems inevitable, artistic considerations are
sacrificed to provide social or educational lessons void of theatrical vitality. Yet if Rastell
failed to attain the invention, coherence, and finish of livelier playwrights of his age, his

experiments are historically important, not least his *Terens in Englysh*, a pioneering version of Terence's romantic comedy, *Andria*.

—William M. Tydeman

RATTIGAN, Sir Terence (Mervyn). English. Born in London, 10 June 1911. Educated at Harrow School (scholar), 1925–30; Trinity College, Oxford (history scholar), B.A. 1933. Served as a Flight Lieutenant in the Coastal Command of the Royal Air Force, 1940–45. Full-time playwright, 1934 until his death. Recipient: Ellen Terry Award, 1947; New York Drama Critics Circle Award, 1948. C.B.E. (Commander, Order of the British Empire), 1958. Knighted, 1971. *Died 30 November 1977.*

PUBLICATIONS

Plays

First Episode, with Philip Heimann (produced 1933).
French Without Tears (produced 1936). 1937; revised version, music by Robert Stolz, lyrics by Paul Dehn, as *Joie de Vivre* (produced 1960).
After the Dance (produced 1939). 1939.
Follow My Leader, with Anthony Maurice (produced 1940).
Grey Farm, with Hector Bolitho (produced 1940).
Flare Path (produced 1942). 1942.
While the Sun Shines (produced 1943). 1945.
Love in Idleness (produced 1944). 1945; as *O Mistress Mine* (produced 1946), 1949.
The Winslow Boy (produced 1946). 1946.
Playbill: The Browning Version and Harlequinade (produced 1948). 1949.
Adventure Story (produced 1949). 1950.
Who Is Sylvia? (produced 1950). 1951.
The Deep Blue Sea (produced 1952). 1952.
The Sleeping Prince (produced 1953). 1954.
Collected Plays 1–4. 4 vols., 1953–78.
Separate Tables: Two Plays (produced 1954). 1955.
The Prince and the Showgirl: The Script for the Film. 1957.
Variation on a Theme (produced 1958). 1958.
Ross: A Dramatic Portrait (produced 1960). 1960.
Heart to Heart (televised 1962). In *Collected Plays 3*, 1964.
Man and Boy (produced 1963). 1963.
A Bequest to the Nation (as *Nelson*, televised 1966; revised version, as *A Bequest to the Nation*, produced 1970). 1970.
All on Her Own (televised 1968; produced 1974; as *Duologue*, produced 1976). In *The Best Short Plays 1970*, edited by Stanley Richards, 1970.
High Summer (televised 1972). In *The Best Short Plays 1973*, edited by Stanley Richards, 1973.

In Praise of Love: Before Dawn, and After Lydia (produced 1973).   1973; (*After Lydia* produced, as *In Praise of Love*, 1974), 1975.
Cause Célèbre (broadcast 1975; produced 1977).   1978.

Screenplays: *The Belles of St. Clement's*, 1936; *Gypsy*, with Brock Williams, 1937; *French Without Tears*, with Anatole de Grunwald and Ian Dalrymple, 1939; *Quiet Wedding*, with Anatole de Grunwald, 1941; *The Day Will Dawn* (*The Avengers*), with Anatole de Grunwald and Patrick Kirwan, 1942; *Uncensored*, with Rodney Ackland and Wolfgang Wilhelm, 1942; *English Without Tears* (*Her Man Gilbey*), with Anatole de Grunwald, 1944; *The Way to the Stars* (*Johnny in the Clouds*), with Anatole de Grunwald, 1945; *Journey Together*, with John Boulting, 1946; *Brighton Rock* (*Young Scarface*), with Graham Greene, 1947; *While the Sun Shines*, with Anatole de Grunwald, 1947; *The Winslow Boy*, with Anatole de Grunwald and Anthony Asquith, 1948; *Bond Street*, with Rodney Ackland and Anatole de Grunwald, 1948; *The Browning Version*, 1951; *The Sound Barrier* (*Breaking the Sound Barrier*), 1952; *The Final Test*, 1953; *The Deep Blue Sea*, 1955; *The Man Who Loved Redheads*, 1955; *The Prince and the Showgirl*, 1957; *Separate Tables*, 1958; *The VIPs*, 1963; *The Yellow Rolls-Royce*, 1964; *Goodbye Mr. Chips*, 1969; *A Bequest to the Nation* (*The Nelson Affair*), 1973.

Radio Plays: *A Tale of Two Cities*, from the novel by Dickens, 1950; *Cause Célèbre*, 1975.

Television Plays: *The Final Test*, 1951; *Heart to Heart*, 1962; *Ninety Years On*, 1964; *Nelson*, 1966; *All on Her Own*, 1968; *High Summer*, 1972.

Reading List: *Rattigan: The Man and His Work* by Michael Darlow and Gillian Hodson, 1978.

*   *   *

Few playwrights (or critics) would agree with American dramatist Eugene Walter's statement that "in essence, play writing is a trade," but if it is, one would be hard pressed to name a more craftsmanlike and artistic artisan than Terence Rattigan.

His career began inauspiciously with a collaboration with Philip Heimann (*First Episode*) and five unproduced plays in which Rattigan learned his craft slowly but thoroughly. Then with *French Without Tears* he began an unusually long and successful career of "sheer theatre" which Kenneth Tynan in *Curtains* (1961) translates as "How well these old craftsmen knew their jobs!" Rattigan is the professional playwright supreme. His brilliant introduction to his collected plays stresses the ideal of "good theatre," and it is true that he has appealed to many more than merely the middle-class theatre-goer, and that without sensationalism or "the 'gilded phrase.' "

Along the way Rattigan has given us several first-rate plays, standards of the modern theatre, among them *The Deep Blue Sea*, with a full-length portrait of a woman even better than that of the Grand Duchess in his *The Sleeping Prince*, and *Separate Tables*, which contrives to educate the audience in emotion without attempting, as Rattigan says, "to 'instruct' it in taste"). His *Ross* was better than his play about Alexander (*Adventure Story*) and typically Rattigan in its treatment of humiliation, an episodic and rather Freudian dramatic portrait of the enigmatic Lawrence of Arabia that almost explained that entertaining enigma (and, perhaps, fascinating fraud). *Man and Boy* was a perceptive study of an absconding financier and his son. *Variation on a Theme* a clever discussion of a boy living off an older woman, and these and other plays (even including *Cause Célèbre*) amply demonstrate Rattigan's rare ability to please the public without ever falling into a rut or repeating himself. Nor does he ever stoop to shocking the audience with fake "revolution" aimed at the Establishment or trying to bore or baffle them. In an age when art involves John Cage's music, minimalist art and Pinter (characterized by Bernard Levin as "seeking answers to questions that were never asked, and the questions to answers that were found"), not to mention the shrill or shoddy or senseless works of artists far less talented than Pinter, Rattigan went sincerely and solidly on with good, solid plays, plays with dialogue that may not be eminently quotable but is invariably effective, plays with themes and characters and beginnings, middles, and ends.

This put Rattigan somewhat out of favor in the 1950's but the public has loved him (on and off) from the start. His "power of implication," as he would say, makes his message clear without frills, and the audience always loves a good story or a decent laugh. James Agate thundered against *French Without Tears*: "Nothing. It has no wit, no plot, no characterization, nothing."

But Agate was off the mark on almost every count. Rattigan is not without wit, though his is not a show-off kind of verbal skill: he makes his points with great economy. He is one of the great masters of exposition. His plots are deftly crafted, even those of *The Deep Blue Sea* and *The Browning Version* which he admits are "unsatisfactory to an audience because of their inconclusiveness." He is a genius at weaving together stray characters (as in *Separate Tables*) or disconnected episodes (as in *Ross*). His forte is character and plot rather than ideas, which in the long run will probably keep his plays from dating as fast as the pieces of his colleagues of the 1950's and 1960's. He can handle a sentimental story without getting soppy and he can dish up "a soufflé" of a farce like *Harlequinade* (designed as a dessert after *The Browning Version*) with dazzling ease. He can be as effective on television or in the cinema.

His best works will long be studied as models of playwriting and also as mirrors of the times. Rattigan can capture the social outlook of a whole period in a *Cause Célèbre* (or the *cause célèbre* of *The Winslow Boy*). He can plumb the depths of obsessions rampant in a sedate residential hotel near Bournemouth, a crummy North London flat, a Public School, the active lives of Alexander the Great or T. E. Lawrence or Lord Nelson, the twisted lives of a financier with a charming but weak son or a rapacious woman out to snare her fifth and richest man who falls prey (willingly, self-destructively) to an ambiguous little ballet dancer. *Variation on a Theme* (whose plot is the last of those situations mentioned) is closely based on Dumas *fils' La Dame aux Camélias* – but it is based on a steady and shrewd observation of English life in Rattigan's own time.

Undoubtedly, Rattigan can capture the surface of life; many critics would add that he is all surface, that his works lack profundity. I do not think this charge of superficiality can be made to stick. What is true is that Rattigan's scope is narrow, but where he touches he goes very deep. What he does delve into he will not abandon until he has explored the very depths, and what he finds there he brings to the audience with some reticence but unalloyed honesty. He can make folly funny and pathos poignant and what some would dismiss as "a purely theatrical experience" deeply moving and quite unforgettable.

—Leonard R. N. Ashley

RAVENSCROFT, Edward. English. Born in England c. 1650. Very little is known about his life: descended from an ancient Flintshire family; member of the Middle Temple, London, 1671; career as a playwright extended over a quarter century, but he is thought to have died comparatively young: nothing is recorded about him after 1697.

PUBLICATIONS

Plays

The Citizen Turned Gentleman, from a play by Molière (produced 1672). 1672; as
  Mamamouchi, 1675.
The Careless Lovers (produced 1673). 1673.
The Wrangling Lovers; or, The Invisible Mistress (produced 1676). 1677.
Scaramouche a Philosopher, Harlequin a School-Boy, Bravo, Merchant and Magician
  (produced 1677). 1677.
The English Lawyer, from a Latin play by George Ruggle (produced 1677). 1678.
King Edgar and Alfreda (produced 1677). 1677.
The London Cuckolds (produced 1681). 1682; edited by A. Norman Jeffares, in
  Restoration Comedy, 1974.
Dame Dobson; or, The Cunning Woman, from a play by Thomas Corneille (produced
  1683). 1684.
Titus Andronicus; or, The Rape of Lavinia, from the play by Shakespeare (produced
  1686). 1687.
The Canterbury Guests; or, A Bargain Broken (produced 1694). 1695.
The Anatomist; or, The Sham Doctor (produced 1696). 1697; edited by Leo Hughes
  and Arthur H. Scouten, in Ten English Farces, 1948.
The Italian Husband (produced 1697). 1698.

*   *   *

In the prologue to his *Assignation* Dryden jeered at his rival Edward Ravenscroft for
pleasing the crowd but being condemned by the critics for his very first play, *The Citizen
Turn'd Gentleman*. The Laureate's judgment proved prophetic. In an age which insisted on
interpreting Horace as requiring *edification*, Ravenscroft found his success in *entertainment*.

His early comedies, all following a common Restoration pattern of combining scenes from
as many as three plays by Molière, were generally successful. His serious attempts, a play
borrowed from early English history, *King Edgar and Alfreda*, an adaptation of
Shakespeare's *Titus Andronicus*, and an equally macabre borrowing from the Italian called
The Italian Husband, won no lasting acclaim. *Scaramouche*, borrowed from both Molière
and his *commedia dell'arte* neighbors, anticipates in many ways the vastly popular
pantomimes of the next century and provides something of a pattern for his two most
successful pieces: *The London Cuckolds*, which lasted 102 years but eventually proved too
bawdy for an increasingly squeamish age, and *The Anatomist*, an even livelier but less risqué
piece which proved more fortunate in its long theatrical history. *The London Cuckolds*
borrows only its theme, the absurdity of attempting by contrivance to avoid even the risk of
cuckoldry, from *The School for Wives*, but Ravenscroft multiplies Molière's Arnolphe by
three, adds several farce turns wholly unconnected with the French play, and succeeds in
being shocking and amusing at one and the same time. Borrowed from Hauteroche but much
improved by some additional farce turns of his own, *The Anatomist* was turned into a one-act
afterpiece at Goodman's Fields just a few months before David Garrick began his illustrious
career at that theatre. *The Anatomist* was a favorite of Garrick's. He repeatedly attached it to
his own pieces or to his own performances throughout his career. Beyond Garrick's time it
waned somewhat in popularity but lasted until the mid-nineteenth century, well beyond the
term of a hundred years which, according to Dr. Johnson's dictum, is "commonly fixed as
the test of literary merit." In Ravenscroft's case perhaps *theatrical* merit would be the more
appropriate term.

—Leo Hughes

REANEY, James (Crerar). Canadian. Born near Stratford, Ontario, 1 September 1926. Educated at Elmhurst Public School, Easthope Township, Perth County; Stratford High School; University College, University of Toronto (Epstein Award, 1948), B.A. in English 1948, M.A. 1949, Ph.D. 1956. Married Colleen Thibaudeau in 1951; one son and one daughter. Member of the English faculty, 1949–57, and Assistant Professor of English, 1957–60, University of Manitoba, Winnipeg. Associate Professor, 1960–63, and since 1964 Professor of English, Middlesex College, University of Western Ontario, London. Founding Editor, *Alphabet* magazine, London, Ontario, 1960–71. Active in little theatre groups in Winnipeg and London. Recipient: Governor-General's Award, 1950, 1959, 1963; President's Medal, University of Western Ontario, 1955, 1958; Chalmers Award, 1975, 1976. Lives in Ontario.

Publications

Plays

> *Night-Blooming Cereus* (broadcast 1959; produced 1960). In *The Killdeer and Other Plays*, 1962.
> *The Killdeer* (produced 1960). In *The Killdeer and Other Plays*, 1962; revised version (produced 1970), in *Masks of Childhood*, 1972.
> *One-Man Masque* (produced 1960). In *The Killdeer and Other Plays*, 1962.
> *The Easter Egg* (produced 1962). In *Masks of Childhood*, 1972.
> *The Killdeer and Other Plays.* 1962.
> *Sun and Moon* (produced 1972). In *The Killdeer and Other Plays*, 1962.
> *Names and Nicknames* (produced 1963). In *Apple Butter and Other Plays*, 1973.
> *Apple Butter* (puppet play; produced 1965). In *Apple Butter and Other Plays*, 1973.
> *Let's Make a Carol: A Play with Music for Children*, music by John Beckwith. 1965.
> *Listen to the Wind* (produced 1965). 1972.
> *Colours in the Dark* (produced 1967). 1970.
> *Three Desks* (produced 1967). In *Masks of Childhood*, 1972.
> *Masks of Childhood* (includes *The Killdeer, Three Desks, The Easter Egg*), edited by Brian Parker. 1972.
> *Apple Butter and Other Plays for Children* (includes *Names and Nicknames, Ignoramus, Geography Match*). 1973.
> *The Donnellys: A Trilogy:*
>   1. *Sticks and Stones* (produced 1973). 1975.
>   2. *The Saint Nicholas Hotel* (produced 1974). 1976.
>   3. *Handcuffs* (produced 1975). 1977.
> *All the Bees and All the Keys* (for children), music by John Beckwith. 1976.
> *The Dismissal.* 1978.

Radio Play: *Night-Blooming Cereus*, 1959.

Verse

> *The Red Heart.* 1949.
> *A Suit of Nettles.* 1958.
> *Twelve Letters to a Small Town.* 1962.
> *The Dance of Death at London, Ontario.* 1963.
> *Poems*, edited by Germaine Warkentin. 1972.

Selected Longer Poems, edited by Germaine Warkentin.   1976.
Selected Shorter Poems, edited by Germaine Warkentin.   1976.

Other

The Boy with an "R" in His Hand (juvenile).   1965.
Twenty Barrels.   1976.

Reading List: *Reaney* by Alvin A. Lee, 1968; *Reaney* by Ross G. Woodman, 1971; *Reaney* by James Stewart Reaney, 1976.

*   *   *

James Reaney is probably the best Canadian playwright writing today, yet, paradoxically, his plays are less performed than those of many other dramatists. This is so largely because the conception that Reaney has of the theatre does not accord well with the taste for either naturalism – the theatre of social comment – or surrealism – the theatre of the absurd. Not only do his plays have many and rapidly shifting scenes, but his characters inhabit a world of fragile Proustian nostalgic fantasy that is almost operatic.

It is easy to see Reaney as outside the mainstream not only of Canadian playwriting and literature, but of modern English literature generally. (This may in part account for his former neglect among the fashionable theatrical circles of Toronto – a city he long ago came to think of as Blake's City of Destruction.) But his debt is to a tradition of fantasy that is pre-eminently late nineteenth century. This influence comes strongly from the early Yeats, but it is also indebted to the Brontës (Reaney takes the name Branwell in his long poem *A Suit of Nettles*), and, one can't help feeling, to the Henry James of *The Turn of the Screw* and *Owen Wingrave*. Indeed, in *Listen to the Wind*, the protagonist is called Owen and proceeds to stage within the play another play called *The Saga of Caresfoot Court*. Reaney based this on his own childhood experience of reading Rider Haggard's *Dawn*, but it owes a good deal also to the tradition of the Gothic tale out of *Wuthering Heights*.

Indeed, it is in Reaney's taste for melodrama – the sudden reversals in the last acts, for instance – that he is weakest. His attempt to justify melodrama by claiming for it another and truer world – "the patterns in it are not only sensational but deadly accurate" – is only partly succesful. The "strong pattern" of melodrama can easily obscure the significant moral exploration of the play, as the exterior story of *Listen to the Wind* very nearly does.

But if the theatre of fantasy works against naturalism, it also, allied with strong lexical whimsy, works against the excesses of melodrama. The playbox of *Colours in the Dark* is not only a way of explaining the longing to get back home to childhood's Eden; it is also an outward and visible sign of those wordlists that Reaney loves – the inventory of the world. The naming of things is as important to him as it is for Eliot in *Old Possum's Book of Practical Cats*, and shares something of that whimsical attitude to the serious matter of language. "What did the Indians call you?/For you do not flow/With English accents," asks Reaney addressing the Avon River in his set of poems *Twelve Letters to a Small Town*. And this concern with names is uppermost in *Names and Nicknames* especially. But it is a characteristic concern of all his plays and poetry. We never forget Reaney the classicist by training. "Most of those words you've no idea of their meaning, but we're sowing them in your mind anyhow," says Polly in *Easter Egg*; and elsewhere, in *Masks of Childhood*, we have a fantasia on the street names of Winnipeg, ending in a whoop – "I Winnipeg ... She Winnipeggied ... They Winnipugged."

Reaney's language spars with his imagery and by its whimsy prevents the apocalyptic metaphors from becoming bombastic. The verse many be Blakean but it is spoken in the dialect of John Clare. Reaney's debt to Blake, via Frye's *Fearful Symmetry*, is a stated one, but Walt Disney and Mother Goose are there as well. This is most obvious in his poem sequence, *A Suit of Nettles* in which barnyard animals become part of a complex allegory that owes something to Spenser and mediaeval flyting. Reaney has a sense of the landscape that reminds us more of Palmer than of Blake, though it is the voice of the *Prophetic Books* that speaks in *Colours in the Dark*:

> We sit by the fire and hear the rushing sound
> Of the wind that comes from Temiskaming
> Algoma, Patricia
> Down from the north over the wilderness.

But for Reaney there is none of Blake's sense of contraries or great loss and fall. Innocence is accessible if we can but find the way, or rather listen to the children who, like the children in *Burnt Norton*, know it. Their music has the apocalyptic quality of the poetry of Leonard Cohen: "I saw the sundogs barking/On either side of the sun." This surrealist strain in him combines with his other theme, death, in a sequence of poems, *The Dance of Death at London, Ontario*, illustrated by the well-known Canadian painter Jack Chambers. In the same year that *Nettles* was published, a critic said of Chambers that he too had captured in his paintings "The Life of Death in London Ontario." Chambers insisted that he was not a surrealist or even a hyper-realist but a "perceptual realist," and doubtless this is a more accurate term for Reaney's work as well.

In that world objects have a life that is almost Dickensian (again the connection to Victorian fantasy). "I'll be the orange devil waiting in the stove/I'll be the chimney trumpeting the night," says Madam Fay in *The Killdeer*. And it is the cry of the killdeer – plaintive (like Reaney's search for the ancestors and the past that will make sense of the present) and deceiving (as Eli in that play recognizes, "It's another clock in another time") – that is a paradigm of Reaney's work. In that sense he speaks for the English Canada that he knows and loves – one of great farmhouses surrounded by large trees on summer afternoons among musty books where "long, long ago" is as real as here and now, the world of Blake and Spenser, Yeats and Rider Haggard, as immediate as the killdeer and the barnyard geese.

Reaney's major achievement has been his recently completed Donnellys trilogy. In those plays he has managed to capture a myth that is both poetic and destructive, universal and local – and for the first time in English Canadian culture. For Reaney James Donnelly is still there in Biddulph Township, not a ghost but a myth. The shifts through time and game and song achieve this in the plays.

The drift from real to fantasy in most of his plays (*The Dismissal* is an exception) is encouraged by the elements – the wind to which the children listen or the detailed catalogues of flowers and animals. It shares something with O'Neill and Miller, but its closest analogy is the late Shakespearean romances where Illyria is a pattern of England as Caresfoot Court becomes a way of understanding Ontario, and Pericles goes searching for the lost child, Marina, that is himself.

—D.D.C. Chambers

RICE, Elmer. American. Born Elmer Leopold Reizenstein in New York City, 28 September 1892. Educated at a high school in New York; studied law in night school, LL.B. (cum laude), New York Law School, 1912; admitted to the New York Bar, 1913, but never practiced. Married 1) Hazel Levy in 1915 (divorced, 1942), one son and one daughter; 2) the actress Betty Field in 1942 (divorced, 1956), two sons and one daughter; 3) Barbara A. Marshall in 1966. Claims Clerk, Samstag and Hilder Brothers, New York 1907; Law Clerk, 1908–12; began writing and producing for the theatre, 1914, as Dramatic Director, University Settlement, and Chairman, Inter-Settlement Dramatic Society, New York; Scenarist, Samuel Goldwyn Pictures Corporation, Hollywood, 1918–20; freelance writer for Famous Players, the Lasky Corporation, and Real Art Films, Hollywood, 1920; returned to New York and organized the Morningside Players, with Hatcher Hughes; purchased and operated the Belasco Theatre, New York, 1934–37; Regional Director, Works Progress Administration Federal Theatre Project, New York, 1935–36; Founder, with Robert E. Sherwood, Maxwell Anderson, S. N. Behrman, Sidney Howard, and John F. Wharton, Playwrights Company, 1938; Lecturer in English, University of Michigan, Ann Arbor, 1954; Adjunct Professor of English, New York University, 1957–58. President, Dramatists Guild, 1939–43; President, Author's League of America, 1945–46; International Vice-President, and Vice-President of the New York Center, P.E.N., 1945–46. Recipient: Pulitzer Prize, 1929. Litt.D.: University of Michigan, 1961. Member, National Institute of Arts and Letters. *Died 8 May 1967.*

PUBLICATIONS

Plays

> *On Trial* (produced 1914). 1919.
> *The Iron Cross* (produced 1917). 1965.
> *The Home of the Free* (produced 1917). 1934.
> *For the Defense* (produced 1919).
> *Wake Up, Jonathan*, with Hatcher Hughes (produced 1921). 1928.
> *It Is the Law*, from a novel by Hayden Talbot (produced 1922).
> *The Adding Machine* (produced 1923). 1923.
> *The Mongrel*, from a play by Hermann Bahr (produced 1924).
> *Close Harmony; or, The Lady Next Door*, with Dorothy Parker (produced 1924). 1929.
> *The Blue Hawaii*, from a play by Rudolph Lothar (produced 1927).
> *Cock Robin*, with Philip Barry (produced 1928). 1929.
> *Street Scene* (produced 1929). 1929; revised version, music by Kurt Weill, lyrics by
>   Langston Hughes (produced 1947). 1948.
> *The Subway* (produced 1929). 1929.
> *A Diadem of Snow*, in *One-Act Plays for Stage and Study 5.* 1929.
> *See Naples and Die* (produced 1929). 1930.
> *The Left Bank* (produced 1931). 1931.
> *Counsellor-at-Law* (produced 1931). 1931.
> *The House in Blind Alley.* 1932.
> *Blacksheep* (produced 1932). 1938.
> *We, The People* (produced 1933). 1933.
> *The Gay White Way*, in *One-Act Plays for Stage and Study 8.* 1934.
> *Judgment Day* (produced 1934). 1934.
> *The Passing of Chow-Chow* (produced 1934). 1934.
> *Three Plays Without Words* (includes *Landscape with Figures, Rus in Urbe,*
>   *Exterior*). 1934.
> *Between Two Worlds* (produced 1934). In *Two Plays*, 1935.
> *Two Plays: Not for Children, and Between Two Worlds.* 1935.
> *Not for Children* (as *Life Is Real*, produced 1937; revised version, as *Not for Children*,
>   produced 1951). In *Two Plays*, 1935.

American Language (produced 1938).   1939.
Two on an Island (produced 1940).   1940.
Flight to the West (produced 1940).   1941.
A New Life (produced 1943).   1944.
Dream Girl (produced 1945).   1946.
The Grand Tour (produced 1951).   1952.
The Winner (produced 1954).   1954.
Cue for Passion (produced 1958).   1959.
Love among the Ruins (produced 1963).   1963.

Screenplays: *Help Yourself*, with others, 1920; *Rent Free*, with Izola Forrester and Mann Page, 1922; *Doubling for Romeo*, with Bernard McConville, 1922; *Street Scene*, 1931; *Counsellor-at-Law*, 1933; *Holiday Inn*, with Claude Binyon and Irving Berlin, 1942.

Fiction

A Voyage to Purilia.   1930.
Imperial City.   1937.
The Show Must Go On.   1949.

Other

The Supreme Freedom.   1949.
The Living Theatre.   1959.
Minority Report: An Autobiography.   1963.

Bibliography: "Rice: A Bibliography" by Robert Hogan, in *Modern Drama*, February 1966.

Reading List: *The Independence of Rice* by Robert Hogan, 1965; *Rice* by Frank Durham, 1970.

*   *   *

Elmer Rice was one of the most prolific and technically proficient of modern American dramatists, as well as, in many of his plays, an eclectic experimenter and an outspoken social spokesman. Although he graduated from law school *cum laude* and was admitted to the New York Bar, he gave up law to write plays; and one of his early pieces, a deftly constructed thriller entitled *On Trial*, achieved a rather spectacular success in 1914. For the next nine years, Rice wrote two kinds of plays – commercial potboilers, some of which were produced, and experimental plays with social themes, which were generally not produced. In 1923, however, he had a critical success when the Theatre Guild staged his Expressionistic satire about the automated modern world, *The Adding Machine*. This play is one of Rice's few to retain its popularity and effectiveness over the years, and is considered one of the significant modern American plays. A companion piece, *The Subway*, did not receive a production until 1929; although somewhat dated, it has some remarkable strengths and has been unfairly neglected. Rice's other plays until 1929 were either adaptations or collaborations (one with Dorothy Parker and one with Philip Barry) of little importance.

In 1929, after much difficulty in finding a producer, Rice's *Street Scene* opened in New York, ran for 602 performances, and won the Pulitzer Prize. The play is a realistic depiction of life on a segment of a New York street, with something of a melodramatic plot to tie its many diverse strands together. Its powerful impact was that of a "shock of recognition"; and only a huge cast requirement (more than eighty characters) has prevented its more frequent revival. Rice also directed this play, and was thereafter to direct all of his New York productions, as well as some by Behrman and Sherwood. Also in 1929 Rice produced a trivial light comedy, *See Naples and Die*, and, in 1931, a somewhat more substantial study of American expatriates in Paris, *The Left Bank*. The same year saw one of Rice's most durable pieces, *Counsellor-at-Law*. Somewhat akin in tone and pace to *The Front Page*, the play is full of hectic activity and a vehicle for a strong actor.

Three other plays of the 1930's show Rice's pre-occupation with social issues. *We, The People* is a sprawling "panoramic presentation" of American life, specifically critical but generally affirmative. Its large cast and many issues make it thin in characterisation and rather more akin to a movie scenario than to a play. In novel form, such as his novels *Imperial City* and *The Show Must Go On*, Rice was able to be fuller and more effective. In 1934 Rice acquired the Belasco Theatre in New York, intending to produce a season of his own work. The first play, *Judgment Day*, a serious melodrama based somewhat on the Reichstag fire trial, was an indictment of Fascism; it was a failure in New York, but a distinct success in London. Rice's second play at the Belasco, *Between Two Worlds*, was even less successful with the New York critics, though a better play. It is a thickly drawn Chekhovian drama of ideas, containing some of the playwright's best work. Set on an ocean liner and with the usual large cast, the play contrasts the values of capitalistic and communistic societies, and suggests that the best of two worlds must somehow be welded together. Rice was to have produced a third play, *Not for Children*, at the Belasco, but, disheartened by the critical response to the first two plays, he announced his disenchantment with the commercial stage and turned to travel and to writing a novel. The unproduced play (done some years later in an inferior revised version) is a richly droll, technically dazzling attack on the inadequacies and superficialities of the drama as an artistic form. Successful really only in its Dublin production at the Gate Theatre, the play remains a seriously neglected tour de force.

In 1938 Rice returned to the theatre as a partner in the Playwrights Company. Most of the plays he wrote for the company were patriotic social commentaries, such as *American Landscape* and *Flight to the West*, and thin work compared to the Belasco plays. One comedy, *Dream Girl*, which starred his second wife, Betty Field, was successful theatre; and his panoramic paean to New York City, *Two on an Island*, contains some excellent satiric writing in a rather trite plot.

Rice's last commercially produced plays were less ambitious in scope, but more thoughtful in content. *The Grand Tour* and *The Winner* were about the relation of morality to money, and, although not his most memorable work and set on a much smaller scale, both were quite craftsmanlike. *Cue for Passion* was a psychoanalytic version of the Hamlet story, set in California, and is really too weak in characterization to be successful. *Love among the Ruins* is a thoughtful contemplation of the contemporary world, in which a group of American tourists in Lebanon look back on America. Rather more ambitious than *The Winner*, the play is also somewhat dull.

When Rice died in 1967, he had written over fifty plays (of which about forty were published or produced), two long novels, a satire on the early movies, a knowledgeable book about the professional theatre, and a long autobiography. He will, however, be remembered primarily as a playwright, as one of the men who transformed the American theatre from the gentility of Clyde Fitch and the entertainment of David Belasco into a form for the serious depiction of life, the critical social statement, and the broadening of technique. Not as powerful as Eugene O'Neill, sometimes deficient in character drawing, and often simplistic in statement, Rice nevertheless left a handful of plays which must be considered part of the permanent American repertory.

—Robert Hogan

ROBERTSON, Thomas William. English. Born in Newark, Nottinghamshire, 9 January 1829; the son of professional actors. Appeared on the stage as a child, 1834–36; educated at Henry Young's Academy, Spalding, Lincolnshire, 1836–41, and at Moore's school, Whittlesea, 1841–43. Married 1) the actress Elizabeth Burton in 1856 (died, 1865), one son and two daughters; 2) Rosetta Feist in 1867, one daughter. Worked for his father's Lincoln company as stagehand, prompter, songwriter, and subsequently as actor, 1843–48; on break-up of the company settled in London, 1848; worked as a gentleman-usher in a school in Utrecht for a few months in 1848, then returned to London: worked as a writer for various obscure newspapers, and as a stagehand, as prompter for Madame Vestris, and later as an actor, in the smaller London theatres and in the provinces, 1848–60, touring with his wife, 1856–60; began writing for the stage, 1850; retired as an actor in 1860, and worked as an editor, free-lance writer, and translator for the publisher Lacy, until 1864 when his first theatrical success allowed him to devote himself entirely to writing for the stage: associated with Marie Wilton and Squire Bancroft at the Prince of Wales's Theatre. *Died 3 February 1871.*

PUBLICATIONS

Collections

Principal Dramatic Works. 2 vols., 1889.

Plays

The Battle of Life, from the story by Dickens (produced 1843–47?).

The Haunted Man, from the story by Dickens (produced 1843–47?).

The Chevalier de St. George, from a play by M. Melesville and Roger de Beauvoir (produced 1845). 1870.

Noémie, from a play by A. Dennery and Clement (as *Ernestine*, produced 1846; as *Clarisse*, produced 1855; as *The Foster Sisters*, produced 1855). 1855.

A Night's Adventures; or, Highways and Byways, from the novel *Paul Clifford* by Bulwer-Lytton (produced 1851).

The Ladies' Battle, from a play by Scribe and Legouvé (produced 1851). 1867.

Faust and Marguerite, from a play by M. Carré (produced 1854). 1854.

Castles in the Air (produced 1854).

My Wife's Diary, from a play by A. Dennery and Clairville (as *A Wife's Journal*, produced 1854). 1855.

The Star of the North, from a play by Scribe (as *The Northern Star*, produced 1855). 1871.

The Clockmaker's Hat (produced 1855; as *Betty Martin*, produced 1865). 1855(?).

Peace at Any Price (produced 1856). 1872.

The Muleteer of Toledo (produced 1856).

The Half-Caste; or, The Poisoned Pearl (produced 1856). 1872.

Two Gay Deceivers; or, Black, White, and Grey, with T. H. Lacy, from a play by Labiche (produced 1858). N.d.

An Evening's Entertainment (includes *Our Private Theatricals, Robinson Crusoe, The Cantab*). 1860.

The Cantab (produced 1861). In *An Evening's Entertainment*, 1860.

Jocrisse the Juggler, from a play by A. Dennery and Jules Brésil (produced 1861). 1861.

David Garrick, from a play by Anne H. J. Duveyrier (produced 1864). 1864; as
  Sullivan (produced 1873), 1873.
Constance, music by Fred Clay (produced 1865).
Society (produced 1865). 1866.
Ours (produced 1866). 1866(?).
Shadow-Tree Shaft (produced 1867).
A Rapid Thaw, from a play by Sardou (produced 1867).
A Dream in Venice (produced 1867).
Caste, from his own story "The Poor Rate Unfolds a Tale" (produced 1867). 1868;
  edited by J. O. Bailey, in *British Plays of the Nineteenth Century,* 1966.
For Love (produced 1867).
The Sea of Ice; or, The Prayer of the Wrecked (produced 1867).
Play (produced 1868). 1868(?).
Passion Flowers (produced 1868).
Home, from a play by G. V. E. Augier (produced 1869). 1869.
School, from a play by Roderick Benedix (produced 1869). 1879.
Dreams (as *My Lady Clara,* produced 1869; as *Dreams,* produced 1869). 1879.
A Breach of Promise (produced 1869). 1888.
Dublin Bay (produced 1869).
Progress, from a play by Sardou (produced 1869). 1891.
The Nightingale (produced 1870). In *Principal Dramatic Works,* 1889.
M.P. (produced 1870). In *Principal Dramatic Works* 1889.
Birth (produced 1870). In *Principal Dramatic Works,* 1889.
War (produced 1871). 1871.
Policy (produced 1871).
Not at All Jealous (produced 1871). 1872.
Which Is It? (produced 1881).
Birds of Prey; or, A Duel in the Dark. 1872.
Other Days (produced 1883).
A Row in the House (produced 1883). 1888.
Cinderella (produced 1892).
Over the Way (produced 1893).

Fiction

David Garrick. 1865.

Other

Editor, with E. P. Hingston, *Artemus Ward's Panorama.* 1869.

Reading List: *The Life and Writings of Robertson* by T. Edgar Pemberton, 1893; *Robertson, His Plays and Stagecraft* by Maynard Savin, 1950 (includes bibliography); *The Victorian Theatre* by George Rowell, 1956.

*   *   *

Thomas William Robertson was a popular dramatist of the mid-Victorian era. He was born into a theatrical family, and his early experience in the theater and his young adult exposure to intellectual and bohemian writers combined to shape his entire career as an essayist and dramatist. The central question to ask about this playwright is whether he is, in fact, a transitional figure or a revolutionary influence upon the theater.

Robertson's early plays included several translations of French plays and adaptations from Dickens. His early plays usually worked within the conventions of set speeches, rodomontade, stock characterizations, and melodramatic presentations. But Robertson's increasing attention to realistic stage settings and props developed along with increasing subtlety of characterization. The best way to imagine this interaction between staging and characterization is to realize that it is difficult for an actor to rant and storm about the stage while trying to balance a real teacup and saucer. By the middle of his career Robertson was writing meticulous stage directions for realistic productions. His audience was defined as a largely upper-middle-class group capable of noticing the dramatic importance of an actor's small gesture, such as an uplifted eyebrow. The productions also developed a troupe of skilled ensemble performers, instead of the traditional declamatory stars.

Robertson heightened his dramatic effects by including numerous meta-theatrical remarks, commenting upon the art of the drama within the context of his plays. Another characteristic is his use of a deliberate clear dramatic counterpoint between two or more simultaneous speeches or actions.

Robertson's sympathies were certainly orthodox. His values supported class distinctions, benevolent aristocrats, patriotism, and obedient womanhood. The titles of his most famous plays indicate the thematic nature of his mind: *Society*, *Ours* (about a regiment in the Crimean War), *Caste*, *School*, *M.P.*

Robertson earned the respect of commentators as diverse as Shaw, Wilde, and W. S. Gilbert. The dramatist is also portrayed as Tom Wrench in Pinero's *Trelawny of the "Wells"* (1898).

—Victor A. Doyno

ROWE, Nicholas. English. Born in Little Barford, Bedfordshire, baptized 30 June 1674. Educated at Westminster School, London (King's Scholar); entered the Middle Temple, London, 1691. Married Antonia Parons in 1698. Inherited the family estate, 1692, and gave up the law for playwriting; also held various official appointments: Under-Secretary to the Duke of Queensbury, Secretary of State for Scotland, 1709–11. First modern editor of Shakespeare, 1709. Poet Laureate, 1715 until his death. *Died 6 December 1718.*

PUBLICATIONS

Collections

> *Plays* edited by Anne D. Devenish. 2 vols., 1747.
> *Works*. 2 vols., 1764.
> *Three Plays* (includes *Tamerlane*, *The Fair Penitent*, *Jane Shore*), edited by James R. Sutherland. 1929.

Plays

> *The Ambitious Step-Mother* (produced 1700). 1701.

Tamerlane (produced 1701).   1701; edited by Landon C. Burns, 1966.
The Fair Penitent, from the play *The Fatal Dowry* by Massinger and Nathan Field
   (produced 1703).   1703; edited by Malcolm Goldstein, 1969.
The Biter (produced 1704).   1705.
Ulysses (produced 1705).   1706.
The Royal Convert (produced 1707).   1708; as *Ethelinda* (produced 1776).
The Tragedy of Jane Shore (produced 1714).   1714; edited by Harry William Pedicord,
   1974.
Tragedies.   2 vols., 1714.
Lady Jane Gray (produced 1715).   1715.

Verse

A Poem upon the Late Glorious Successes of Her Majesty's Arms.   1707.
Poems on Several Occasions.   1714.
Poetical Works.   1715.
Ode for the New Year 1716.   1716.
Ode for the Year 1717.   1717.
Ode to the Thames for the Year 1719.   1719.

Other

Editor, with J. Tonson, *Poetical Miscellanies 5–6*, by Dryden.   2 vols., 1704–09.
Editor, *Works of Shakespeare.*   6 vols., 1709.

Translator, *The Life of Pythagoras* (verse only).   1707.
Translator, with others, *Callipaedia*, by Claudius Quillet.   1712.
Translator, with others, *Ovid's Metamorphoses.*   1717.
Translator, *Lucan's Pharsalia.*   1718.

Reading List: *Pity and Tears: The Tragedies of Rowe* by Landon C. Burns, 1974; *Rowe and
Christian Tragedy* by J. Douglas Canfield, 1977.

*   *   *

Nicholas Rowe, a lawyer-turned-playwright, wrote some of the best and most frequently
acted tragedies between 1700 and 1740: *Tamerlane, Jane Shore*, and *The Fair Penitent*. He
knew Addison and Pope, and honored the theory of tragedy Pope described in his Prologue to
Addison's *Cato.*

Rowe, as Shakespeare's first modern editor (1709), compared copies of the texts available
to him instead of merely reprinting the First Folio, improving many obscure passages,
discovering a missing scene in *Hamlet*, and adding for the first time consistent act and scene
divisions, exits and entrances, and other stage directions. He demonstrated, as Alan S.
Downer explains (*The British Drama: A Handbook and Brief Chronicle*), how inaccurately
the Elizabethan tradition was understood 100 years later. His Preface preserves facts and
traditions about Shakespeare plus observations on the way he handled various types of plays,
many typical of his time, though others transcend it.

Rowe was sentimental and melodramatic in his own plays, achieving his greatest effects in
pathos, though with power, in *The Fair Penitent, Jane Shore*, and *Lady Jane Gray*. These
looked back chiefly to Thomas Otway's tender love scenes in *Venice Preserved* and *The
Orphan*, and provided powerful emotional roles for actresses such as Mrs. Siddons.

Dr. Johnson, in his life of Rowe, commended Rowe's plays for interesting fables, delightful language, easily imagined domestic stories of common life, and exquisitely harmonious and appropriate diction. He declared that Lothario in *The Fair Penitent*, however, retained too much of the spectator's kindness. Rowe, borrowing *The Fair Penitent*'s plot from Massinger's *The Fatal Dowry*, has Calista seduced and abandoned by the gay Lothario (whom she really loved), married to the noble Altamount to save her honor, and reduced to utter despair when Altamount bursts in upon a love tryst and kills Lothario. Crushed by grief, she kills herself beside Lothario's coffin with her father's dagger, at his suggestion, but is tearfully received again as his daughter before she expires, thus lacing the play with Otway's pathos from a middle-class viewpoint and in the manner soon to dominate the sentimental novel.

Tamerlane, which demonstrated political tragedy's potential but failed to express, according to John Loftis (*The Politics of Drama in Augustan England*), the "lively conflicts embodying rival political philosophies," praised the amiable William III (Tamerlane) and attacked Louis XIV (Bajazet), and was produced annually on November 4 (William's birthday) and November 5 (the anniversary of his landing in England in 1688). Gone, however, was Marlowe's amoral Herculean superman with his boundless aspiration, love, cruelty, and wrath.

Jane Shore, "written in imitation of Shakespeare's style" plus much pathos, was typical of that phase of English drama (stimulated by Dryden's *All for Love*, with its love versus duty theme) when dramatists selected Shakespearean stories but developed different themes. Purportedly a Restoration heroic tragedy, the play shows political scheming as applicable to Queen Anne's time as to Elizabeth's, especially concerning Gloster, the civil war, and the uncertain succession. Richard of Gloster throws Jane, mistress to Edward IV, out into the street to starve, forbidding anyone to feed or shelter her under penalty of death. Her disguised husband saves her from rape by Lord Hastings, but the insanely jealous Alicia, Hastings's lover and Jane's close friend, pretending to appeal for Jane's banishment, substitutes a letter damning both Jane and Hastings as the crown's enemies. This prompts Gloster to execute Hastings, but drives the love-mad Alicia wild when she cannot embrace him one last time. Ironically, only Jane's still loving husband helps her, and he is taken to prison after she dies. Alicia's concluding madness recalls Otway's ending to *Venice Preserved* when Pierre and Jaffeir die on the scaffold and their ghosts appear to Belvidera, who then goes mad and dies. Rowe's handling of the Jane Shore story, the best since Shakespeare's day, advocated and applauded domestic virtue in the context of Richard of Gloster's ruthless tyranny, presenting Jane caught by as fierce a royal decree as that which tormented Sophocles' Antigone.

Rowe's last play, *Lady Jane Gray*, again focuses on a lady in distress. Though superior to the other "she-tragedies" in dramatic technique (interest is concentrated on Jane rather than being dispersed), it was never as popular. Jane, a defiant Protestant martyr, forfeits her pardon from Mary and prays from the scaffold for a monarch "To save the altars from the rage of Rome."

Nicholas Rowe helped to define a new sort of tragedy, where sympathy for love in distress and admiration for the hero's struggles against impossible odds replaced Aristotelian catharsis with its pity and terror. Characters were wept out of their evil ways; pity for the poor fallen sinners, and the implicit grim warning to others to avoid their errors, purposefully create a chasm between the tragic hero and the audience. In his best work, Rowe avoided the excesses of crass sentimentality which mars the tragedies of dramatists such as George Lillo, thus establishing his modest claim to success in tragedy.

—Louis Charles Stagg

ROWLEY, William. English. Born in England c. 1585. Actor: with the Duke of York's Company, later Prince Charles's Company, 1609–17; with the King's Men from 1623; noted for his portrayals in comic parts; collaborated with several other dramatists in writing for the stage, and may have assisted with as many as 50 plays. *Died in February 1626.*

PUBLICATIONS

Plays

Fortune by Land and Sea, with Thomas Heywood (produced 1607?). 1655; edited by J. E. Walker, 1899.

The Travels of the Three English Brothers, Sir Thomas, Sir Anthony, Mr. Robert Shirley, with John Day and George Wilkins (produced 1607). 1607; edited by A. H. Bullen, in *Works* by Day, 1881.

A Shoemaker a Gentleman (produced 1608?). 1638; edited by Charles Wharton Stork, with *All's Lost by Lust*, 1910.

A Fair Quarrel, with Middleton (produced 1615–17?). 1617; edited by George R. Price, 1976.

The Old Law; or, A New Way to Please You, with Middleton (produced 1618?). 1656; edited by A. H. Bullen, in *Works* by Middleton, 1885–86.

The World Tossed at Tennis, with Middleton (produced 1619–20?). 1620.

All's Lost by Lust (produced 1619–20?). 1633; edited by Charles Wharton Stork, with *A Shoemaker a Gentleman*, 1910.

The Birth of Merlin; or, The Child Hath Found His Father (produced 1620?). 1662; edited by C. F. Tucker Brooke, in *Shakespeare Apocrypha*, 1908.

The Witch of Edmonton, with Dekker and Ford (produced 1621). 1658; edited by Fredson Bowers, in *Dramatic Works of Dekker*, 1953–61.

The Changeling, with Middleton (produced 1622). 1653; edited by Kenneth Muir, in *Three Plays* by Middleton, 1975.

The Maid in the Mill, with Fletcher (produced 1623). In *Comedies and Tragedies* by Beaumont and Fletcher, 1647.

The Spanish Gipsy, with Middleton (produced 1623). 1653; edited by C. M. Hayley, in *Representative English Comedies*, 1914.

A Cure for a Cuckold, with Webster (produced 1624–25?). 1661; edited by F. L. Lucas, in *Works* by Webster, 1927.

A New Wonder: A Woman Never Vexed (produced ?). 1632; edited by W. C. Hazlitt, in *Dodsley's Old Plays*, 1875.

A Match at Midnight (produced ?). 1633; edited by W. C. Hazlitt, in *Dodsley's Old Plays*, 1875.

Wit at Several Weapons, with Fletcher and Middleton (produced ?). In *Comedies and Tragedies* by Beaumont and Fletcher, 1647.

Fiction

A Search for Money; or, The Lamentable Complaint for the Loss of the Wandering Knight M. l'Argent; or, Come Along with Me, I Know Thou Lovest Money. 1609.

Reading List: *An Inquiry into the Authorship of the Middleton-Rowley Plays* by P. G. Wiggin, 1897; "The Canon of Rowley's Plays" by D. M. Robb, in *Modern Language Review 45*, 1950; *Middleton's Tragedies* by Samuel Schoenbaum, 1955.

William Rowley was at his best as a dramatist when writing in collaboration, especially with Thomas Middleton. In their finest work, *The Changeling*, Rowley's sub-plot moves quickly and satisfyingly on its own account and, by ironic connections with the main plot, it powerfully reinforces the play's themes of lust, deceit, and corruption. In his early work, Rowley's dialogue is stilted and choppy, but his verse style developed a strength and natural flexibility, seen at their finest in the opening and closing scenes of *The Changeling*. His command of characterization is weak as a whole, but from about 1616 onward his clowns are markedly individual, probably because he played these roles himself. Compass of *A Cure for a Cuckold* and the justly praised Cuddy Banks of *The Witch of Edmonton,* for example, are both credibly human in the Shakespearian mould. Of his unaided plays, *A Woman Never Vexed* and *A Match at Midnight* are citizen comedies which owe something of their tone and setting, if little of their artlessness, to Middleton's influence. His one tragedy, *All's Lost by Lust*, is complex in plot, and though the verse is generally rough it occasionally rises to a melodramatic eloquence; the characterization is unsubtle and the structure crude. It was, however, acted "divers times" and "with great applause," according to the title page of its only early edition. Rowley's prose pamphlet, *A Search for Money*, is a goodhumoured satire which incidentally throws light on the topography and society of contemporary London. He also wrote commendatory verses for Webster's *Duchess of Malfi* (1623) and John Taylor's *Nipping and Snipping of Abuses* (1614) and verses on the death of Prince Henry for Taylor's *Great Britain All in Black* (1612) and William Drummond's *Mausoleum* (1613). Although Rowley has been neglected by modern critics, according to the late seventeenth-century stage historian Gerard Langbaine he was "beloved by those Great Men, Shakespear, Fletcher and Johnson."

—Alan Brissenden

SACKVILLE, Thomas; 1st Earl of Dorset; Baron Buckhurst. English. Born in Buckhurst, Withyham, Sussex, in 1536. Educated at the grammar school in Sullington, Sussex; possibly at Hart Hall, Oxford, or St. John's College, Cambridge; entered the Middle Temple, London; called to the bar. Married Cecily Baker in 1554; four sons and three daughters. Elected Member of Parliament for Westmorland, 1558, for East Grinstead, Sussex, 1559, and for Aylesbury, Buckinghamshire, 1563; toured France and Italy, 1563–66; inherited family estates and returned to England, 1566; served in the House of Lords from 1567; on diplomatic missions for the crown to France, 1568, 1571; Privy Councillor, from 1571, and served as Commissioner at State Trials; sent to the Low Countries by the queen to survey political affairs after Leicester's return to England, incurred her displeasure, was recalled, confined to his house, then restored to favour, 1587–88; appointed Commissioner for Ecclesiastical Causes, 1588; again sent on an embassy to the Low Countries, 1589; commissioner to sign treaty with France on behalf of the queen, 1591; with Burghley unsuccessfully attempted to negotiate peace with France, 1598; appointed Lord Treasurer, 1599, and confirmed in the position for life by James I, 1603; Lord High Steward, presiding at the trial of the Earl of Essex, 1601; a commissioner in the successful negotiation of a new peace treaty with Spain, and pensioned for his services by the king, 1604. Grand Master of the Order of the Freemasons, 1561–67; Chancellor of Oxford University, 1591. M.A.: Cambridge University, 1571; Oxford University, 1592. Knighted, and created Baron Buckhurst, 1567; Knight of the Garter, 1589; Earl of Dorset, 1604. *Died 19 April 1608.*

PUBLICATIONS

Collections

> *Works,* edited by R. W. Sackville-West. 1859.
> *Poems,* edited by M. Hearsey. 1936.

Play

> *The Tragedy of Gorboduc,* with Thomas Norton (produced 1561). 1565; as *The Tragedy of Ferrex and Porrex,* 1570(?); edited by Irby B. Cauthen, 1970.

Verse

> *Induction,* and *Complaint of Henry, Duke of Buckingham,* in *Mirror for Magistrates.* 1563; edited by L. B. Campbell, 1938.

Reading List: *Sackville* by Normand Berlin, 1974.

*   *   *

In the first edition of *Gorboduc,* the first three acts are attributed to Norton and the last two to Sackville, but some current opinion also ascribes the play's first scene to Sackville and its final one to Norton. *Gorboduc,* the first English tragedy properly so called, is based on a story from the British pseudo-history written by Geoffrey of Monmouth. The authors have altered this story (of brother-princes' rivalry, leading to the death of one of them in battle and their mother's murder of the survivor, after which the nobles fall to civil war) by making it begin with the king's abdication of rule in favour of both his sons, by causing the king and queen to be slain in a popular rebellion which is then put down by the nobles, and by introducing in the last act an ambitious nobleman who covets the vacant throne. Their play is therefore concerned both with tragic passions (which destroy a fated royal house) and with political lessons (particularly the dangers of civil war and the importance of a settled succession): it partakes both of the world of Senecan tragedy and of that of the *Mirror for Magistrates*. In form it resembles classical tragedy, though actually defective in all three unities of time, place, and (finally, when the chief characters are dead) action. It is divided into acts and scenes, with choruses between the acts; there are long speeches containing many *sententiae*; physical action, instead of being shown, is narrated by messengers. From non-classical tradition come the symbolic dumb-shows between the acts. The speeches are in blank verse, the choruses in quatrains (sometimes double) rounded off with couplets.

Sackville also contributed to the 1563 edition of the *Mirror for Magistrates*, supplying one of the tragic narratives (the "complaint" of the Duke of Buckingham, Richard III's right-hand-man) and a long 76-stanza "induction" to the whole work. In the induction, the poet, musing in a dreary winter landscape, encounters Sorrow personified, who escorts him to the underworld, where he sees various other appropriate personifications – Remorse of Conscience, Dread, Revenge, Misery, Care, Sleep, Age, Malady, Famine, Death, War, and Debate – before crossing in Charon's boat to interview the great men whose falls are the subject of the *Mirror*. Written in rhyme-royal pentameter, this induction powerfully evokes the sombre mood of the collection of "tragedies" by drawing partly on Virgilian and partly on medieval artistic conventions; it looks forward towards Spenser in this mingling, as also in its deliberate use of archaic words for their emotional associations.

—T. W. Craik

SAROYAN, William. American. Born in Fresno, California, 31 August 1908. Educated in Fresno public schools. Served in the United States Army, 1942–45. Married Carol Marcus in 1943 (divorced, 1949; remarried, 1951; divorced, 1952); one daughter and one son, the poet Aram Saroyan. Past occupations include grocery clerk, vineyard worker, post office employee; Clerk, Telegraph Operator, then Office Manager of the Postal Telegraph Company, San Francisco, 1926–28; Co-Founder, Conference Press, Los Angeles, 1936; Founder and Director, Saroyan Theatre, New York, 1942; Writer-in-Residence, Purdue University, Lafayette, Indiana, 1961. Recipient: New York Drama Critics Circle Award, 1940; Pulitzer Prize, 1940 (refused). Member, National Institute of Arts and Letters. Lives in Fresno, California.

PUBLICATIONS

Plays

> *The Man with the Heart in the Highlands*, in *Contemporary One-Act Plays*, edited by William Kozlenko. 1938; revised version, as *My Heart's in the Highlands* (produced 1939), 1939.

The Time of Your Life (produced 1939).   1939.

The Hungerers (produced 1945).   1939.

A Special Announcement (broadcast 1940).   1940.

Love's Old Sweet Song (produced 1940).   In *Three Plays*, 1940.

Three Plays: My Heart's in the Highlands, The Time of Your Life, Love's Old Sweet Song.   1940.

Subway Circus.   1940.

Something about a Soldier (produced 1940).

Hero of the World (produced 1940).

The Great American Goof (ballet scenario; produced 1940).   In *Razzle Dazzle*, 1942.

Radio Play (broadcast 1940).   In *Razzle Dazzle*, 1942.

The Ping Pong Game (produced 1945).   1940.

Sweeney in the Trees (produced 1940).   In *Three Plays*, 1941.

The Beautiful People (produced 1941).   In *Three Plays*, 1941.

Three Plays: The Beautiful People, Sweeney in the Trees, Across the Board on Tomorrow Morning.   1941.

Across the Board on Tomorrow Morning (produced 1941).   In *Three Plays*, 1941.

The People with Light Coming Out of Them (broadcast 1941).   In *The Free Company Presents*, edited by James Boyd, 1941.

There's Something I Got To Tell You (broadcast 1941).   In *Razzle Dazzle*, 1942.

Hello, Out There (produced 1941).   In *Razzle Dazzle*, 1942.

Jim Dandy (produced 1941).   1941; as *Jim Dandy: Fat Man in a Famine*, 1947.

Talking to You (produced 1942).   In *Razzle Dazzle*, 1942.

Razzle Dazzle; or, The Human Opera, Ballet, and Circus; or, There's Something I Got to Tell You: Being Many Kinds of Short Plays As Well As the Story of the Writing of Them (includes *Hello, Out There, Coming Through the Rye, Talking to You, The Great American Goof, The Poetic Situation in America, Opera, Opera, Bad Men in the West, The Agony of Little Nations, A Special Announcement, Radio Play, The People with Light Coming Out of Them, There's Something I Got to Tell You, The Hungerers, Elmer and Lily, Subway Circus, The Ping Pong Players*).   1942.

Opera, Opera (produced 1955).   In *Razzle Dazzle*, 1942.

Get Away Old Man (produced 1943).   1944.

Sam Ego's House (produced 1947–48?).   In *Don't Go Away Mad and Two Other Plays*, 1949.

Don't Go Away Mad (produced 1949).   In *Don't Go Away Mad and Two Other Plays*, 1949.

Don't Go Away Mad and Two Other Plays: Sam Ego's House; A Decent Birth, A Happy Funeral.   1949.

The Son (produced 1950).

The Slaughter of the Innocents (produced 1957).   1952.

The Oyster and the Pearl: A Play for Television (televised 1953).   In *Perspectives USA*, Summer 1953.

Once Around the Block (produced 1956).   1959.

The Cave Dwellers (produced 1957).   1958.

Ever Been in Love with a Midget (produced 1957).

Cat, Mouse, Man, Woman; and The Accident, in *Contact I*, 1958.

Settled Out of Court, with Henry Cecil, from the novel by Henry Cecil (produced 1960).   1962.

The Dogs; or, The Paris Comedy (as *Lily Dafon*, produced 1960).   In *The Dogs; or, The Paris Comedy and Two Other Plays*, 1969.

Sam, The Highest Jumper of Them All; or, The London Comedy (produced 1960).   1961.

High Time along the Wabash (produced 1961).

Ah Man, music by Peter Fricker (produced 1962).

Four Plays: The Playwright and the Public, The Handshakers, The Doctor and the
   Patient, This I Believe, in Atlantic, April 1963.
Dentist and Patient, and Husband and Wife, in The Best Short Plays 1968, edited by
   Stanley Richards.   1968.
The Dogs; or, The Paris Comedy and Two Other Plays: Chris Sick; or, Happy New Year
   Anyway, Making Money, and Ninteen Other Very Short Plays.   1969.
The New Play, in The Best Short Plays 1970, edited by Stanley Richards.   1970.
Armenians (produced 1974).
The Rebirth Celebration of the Human Race at Artie Zabala's Off-Broadway Theatre
   (produced 1975).

Screenplay: The Good Job, 1942.

Radio Plays: Radio Play, 1940; A Special Announcement, 1940; There's Something I Got
to Tell You, 1941; The People with Light Coming Out of Them, 1941.

Television Plays: The Oyster and the Pearl, 1953; Ah Sweet Mystery of Mrs. Murphy,
1959; The Unstoppable Gray Fox, 1962.

Ballet Scenario: The Great American Goof, 1940.

Fiction

The Daring Young Man on the Flying Trapeze and Other Stories.   1934.
Inhale and Exhale (stories).   1936.
Three Times Three (stories).   1936.
Little Children (stories).   1937.
A Gay and Melancholy Flux: Short Stories.   1937.
Love, Here Is My Hat (stories).   1938.
A Native American (stories).   1938.
The Trouble with Tigers (stories).   1938.
Peace, It's Wonderful (stories).   1939.
3 Fragments and a Story.   1939.
My Name Is Aram (stories).   1940.
Saroyan's Fables.   1941.
The Insurance Salesman and Other Stories.   1941.
48 Saroyan Stories.   1942.
31 Selected Stories.   1943.
Some Day I'll Be a Millionaire: 34 More Great Stories.   1943.
The Human Comedy.   1943.
Dear Baby (stories).   1944.
The Adventures of Wesley Jackson.   1946.
The Saroyan Special: Selected Short Stories.   1948.
The Fiscal Hoboes (stories).   1949.
The Twin Adventures: The Adventures of Saroyan: A Diary; The Adventures of Wesley
   Jackson: A Novel.   1950.
The Assyrian and Other Stories.   1950.
Rock Wagram.   1951.
Tracy's Tiger..   1951.
The Laughing Matter.   1953; as The Secret Story, 1954.
The Whole Voyald and Other Stories.   1956.
Mama, I Love You.   1956.
Papa, You're Crazy.   1957.

Love (stories).   1959.
Boys and Girls Together.   1963.
One Day in the Afternoon of the World.   1964.
After Thirty Years: The Daring Young Man on the Flying Trapeze (includes essays).   1964.
Best Stories of Saroyan.   1964.
My Kind of Crazy Wonderful People: 17 Stories and a Play.   1966.

Other

The Time of Your Life (miscellany).   1939.
Harlem as Seen by Hirschfeld.   1941.
Hilltop Russians in San Francisco.   1941.
Why Abstract?, with Henry Miller and Hilaire Hiler.   1945.
The Bicycle Rider in Beverly Hills (autobiography).   1952.
Saroyan Reader.   1958.
Here Comes, There Goes, You Know Who (autobiography).   1961.
A Note on Hilaire Hiler.   1962.
Me (juvenile).   1963.
Not Dying (autobiography).   1963.
Short Drive, Sweet Chariot (autobiography).   1966.
Look at Us: Let's See: Here We Are: Look Hard: Speak Soft: I See, You See, We All See; Stop, Look, Listen; Beholder's Eye; Don't Look Now But Isn't That You? (us? U.S.?).   1967.
Horsey Gorsey and the Frog (juvenile).   1968.
I Used to Believe I Had Forever; Now I'm Not So Sure.   1968.
Letters from 74 rue Taitbout; or, Don't Go But if You Must Say Hello to Everybody.   1969; as *Don't Go But If You Must Say Hello to Everybody*, 1970.
Days of Life and Death and Escape to the Moon.   1970.
Places Where I've Done Time.   1972.
The Tooth and My Father (juvenile).   1974.
Famous Faces and Other Friends: A Personal Memoir.   1976.
Morris Hirshfield.   1976.
Sons Come and Go, Mothers Hang In Forever (memoirs).   1976.
Chance Meetings.   1978.

Editor, *Hairenik 1934–1939: An Anthology of Short Stories and Poems.*   1939.

Bibliography: *A Bibliography of Saroyan 1934–1963* by David Kherdian, 1965.

Reading List: *Saroyan* by Howard R. Floan, 1966.

*   *   *

Hailed by some as the greatest writer to come out of San Francisco since Frank Norris, William Saroyan is one of the striking paradoxes in 20th-century literary writing in America. If he has been dismissed for being non-literary, a critic of the eminence of Edmund Wilson has lauded him for his uncanny gift for creating atmosphere in his books: "Saroyan takes you to the bar, and he creates for you there a world which is the way the world would be if it conformed to the feeling instilled by drinks. In a word, he achieves the feat of making and keeping us boozy without the use of alcohol and purely by the action of art."

Saroyan never went beyond high school and thus exemplifies the successful homespun writer. *The Daring Young Man on the Flying Trapeze, and Other Stories* was his first collection of short fiction, and many still consider it to be among his finest writing. A breathtakingly prolific writer (he produced about five hundred stories between 1934 and 1940), Saroyan is a short story writer, playwright, and novelist, but his claim to greatness rests essentially on plays like *My Heart's in the Highlands* and *The Time of Your Life* and on his short stories. He has been criticized for his pervasive sentimentality, but his retort to the charge is that it is a very sentimental thing to be a human being. And to the charge that his style is careless and sloppy, he responded: "I do not know a great deal about what the words come to, but the presence says, Now don't get funny; just sit down and say something: it'll be all right. Say it wrong; It'll be all right anyway. Half the time I *do* say it wrong, but somehow or other, just as the presence says, it's right anyway. I am always pleased about this."

One of his best stories, "A Daring Young Man on the Flying Trapeze," is an interior monologue revealing the recollections of a poor writer who lives in the troubled present while achieving distance from it by reaching back into the past centuries. Unperturbed on the conscious level by his problems, occasionally the young writer is embittered by such experiences as the need to sell his books to buy food. Finally, on returning to his room in the afternoon from his wanderings he dies a sudden and painless death. Saroyan's identification with his young protagonist is evident, despite the author's disclaimers. The story is suffused with pathos, though there is clearly an attempt to hold the sentimentality in check. The story would also appear to be a plea for sympathy and support for deprived writers. Among his plays, *The Time of Your Life* is the one that probably most fully reflects Saroyan the artist. It received both the Drama Critics Circle Award and the Pulitzer Prize, but Saroyan refused the latter as an expression of his contempt for commercial patronage of art. Despite its melodramatic plot the play, as Howard R. Floan admirably sums up, is "about a state of mind, illusive but real, whose readily recognizable components are, first, an awareness of America's youth – its undisciplined swaggering, unregulated early life – and, secondly, a pervasive sense of America in crisis: an America of big business, of labor strife, of depersonalized government, and, above all, of imminent war."

At seventy, Saroyan's interest in the comedy-tragedy of life remains undiminished: "Living is the only thing. It is an awful pain most of the time, but this compels comedy and dignity." What makes Saroyan stand out in American literary writing is his optimism about life despite the evidence to the contrary in the world around, especially as perceived by most American writers; and his buoyancy seems to work with his considerable reading public. But the major appeal of his writing comes from his characters, who are common people like gas station attendants, and from his heavily romantic emphasis on the individuality of man. With charming candour Saroyan not too long ago declared that his main purpose was to earn as much money as possible – a confession that has been used by adverse criticism to exaggerate the casualness of his writing and to withhold due recognition from him.

—J. N. Sharma

SETTLE, Elkanah. English. Born in Dunstable, Bedfordshire, 1 February 1648. Educated at Westminster School, London; Trinity College, Oxford, matriculated 1666, but left without taking a degree. Married Mary Warner in 1673. Settled in London, 1666, and was immediately successful as a playwright; enjoyed the patronage of Rochester; involved in a literary feud with Dryden; appointed Official Poet to the City of London, 1691, and wrote the Lord Mayor's Pageants until 1708; wrote drolls for Bartholomew Fair in his old age; poor brother of the Charterhouse from 1718. *Died 12 February 1724.*

PUBLICATIONS

Plays

Cambyses, King of Persia (produced 1667?).   1671; revised version, 1675.

The Empress of Morocco (produced 1671?).   1673; edited by Bonamy Dobrée, in *Five Heroic Plays*, 1960.

Love and Revenge, from the play *The Fatal Contract* by William Hemmings (produced 1674).   1675.

The Conquest of China by the Tartars (produced 1675).   1676.

Ibrahim the Illustrious Bassa, from the novel by Mme. de Scudéry (produced 1676).   1677.

Pastor Fido; or, The Faithful Shepherd, from a play by Guarini (produced 1676).   1677.

The Female Prelate, Pope Joan (produced 1680).   1680.

Fatal Love: or, The Forced Inconstancy (produced 1680).   1680.

The Heir of Morocco (produced 1682).   1682.

Distressed Innocence; or, The Princess of Persia (produced 1690).   1691.

The Triumphs of London (produced 1691).   1691 (later pageants performed and published in 1692–95, 1698–1702, 1708).

The Fairy Queen, music by Henry Purcell, from the play *A Midsummer Night's Dream* by Shakespeare (produced 1692).   1692.

The New Athenian Comedy.   1693.

The Ambitious Slave; or, A Generous Revenge (produced 1694).   1694.

Philaster; or, Love Lies A-Bleeding, from the play by Beaumont and Fletcher (produced 1695).   1695.

The World in the Moon, music by Daniel Purcell and Jeremiah Clarke (produced 1697).   1697.

The Virgin Prophetess; or, The Fate of Troy, music by Gottfried Finger (produced 1701).   1701; as *Cassandra,* 1702.

The Siege of Troy (Bartholomew and Southwark fairs droll).   1707.

The City-Ramble; or, A Play-House Wedding (produced 1711).   1711.

The Lady's Triumph, with Lewis Theobald (produced 1718).   1718.

Fiction

Diego Redivivus.   1692; edited by Spiro Peterson, in *The Counterfeit Lady Unveiled,* 1961.

The Notorious Impostor.   2 vols., 1692; revised edition, as *The Complete Memoirs of That Notorious Impostor Will Morrell,* 1694; edited by Spiro Peterson, in *The Counterfeit Lady Unveiled,* 1961.

Verse

Mare Clausam; or, A Ransack for the Dutch.   1666.

Absalom Senior; or, Achitophel Transprosed: A Poem.   1682; edited by Harold W. Jones, in *Anti-Achitophel,* 1961.

Some 80 complimentary poems are cited in the bibliography by Frank C. Brown, below.

Other

Notes and Observations on The Empress of Morocco Revised.   1674.
The Character of a Popish Successor.   1681.
A Defence of Dramatic Poetry.   1698.

Editor, *Herod and Mariamne*, by Samuel Pordage.   1673.

Reading List: *Settle: His Life and Works* by Frank C. Brown, 1910 (includes bibliography).

*   *   *

Faustus solicited Helen of Troy to make him immortal with a kiss. Dryden made Elkanah Settle immortal with a gibe. This very minor writer is embedded in the amber of *Absalom and Achitophel* as a fly which once buzzed around the laureate.

The facts of Settle's life are quickly told and help to explain Dryden's antagonism. Settle attended Westminster School and Trinity College, Oxford, but took no degree, setting off to seek fame and fortune in London and within a year having his first, rodomontade tragedy produced. It was pompous "in King Cambyses' vein" and indeed was called *Cambyses, King of Persia.* Its "bombastic grandiloquence" echoed Thomas Preston's tragedy of the same name (1569) and was calculated to appeal to the self-important young lawyers of Lincoln's Inn, then much impressed with the fad of heroic drama. Full of sound and fury, Settle's tyro effort threatened to eclipse Dryden and Sir Robert Howard's *Indian Emperor.*

Dryden was in the ascendant. Soon he was to become Poet Laureate and Historiographer Royal. He was to score in the theatre with *Tyrannic Love; or, The Royal Martyr* (1669) and *The Conquest of Granada* (1670). But he was doing it on his own. Settle was set up as his rival by John Wilmot, Earl of Rochester. Settle's *Empress of Morocco* was played at Whitehall by lords and ladies and was a resounding success. The Duke of Buckingham and some of his smart friends pilloried Dryden as Bayes in *The Rehearsal*, a satiric swipe at the "heroic" plays of Davenant and Dryden which must have hurt Dryden. Settle's public success was used as another club with which to beat Dryden.

After 1675 Settle lost some of his backers but little of his public. Recruited to the Whig faction by the Earl of Shaftesbury, Settle entered the pamphlet wars and attacked Dryden's interests from many angles; when Dryden turned Catholic, Settle was hired by Shaftesbury to write a "pope-burning" pageant. Settle's career stretched from 1673 into the next century and ended with his writing and performing drolls for Bartholomew Fair. Meanwhile, Dryden ticked him off as Og, while Thomas Shadwell was Doeg and held up to ridicule in *Absalom and Achitophel* and *Mac Flecknoe.*

Honestly speaking, the whole "heroic drama" was a bore and Settle's pieces are not much less bombastic than Dryden's or anyone else's. Only in *The Female Prelate*, dealing with Pope Joan, does he step really far beyond the bounds of taste in this rather tasteless period. He may have ended up in the Charterhouse while Dryden ended up in the literary Pantheon, but it was not "heroic drama" that basically explained these two extreme fates. Thomas Duffett's burlesque of *The Empress of Morocco*, clever as it is, cannot really make it sound worse than the inflated junk so cruelly pricked in *The Rehearsal*. Settle never got really much better than *The Empress of Morocco* in that unpromising genre and his operatic *Fairy Queen* (based on *A Midsummer Night's Dream*) is still remembered, albeit chiefly for the music by Henry Purcell. Settle had none of the collaborators of Dryden, nor does Settle enjoy or deserve Dryden's fame. His work was done at a time when too many plays were actually what Davenant called his 1656 entertainments at Rutland House, *Declamations and Musick*. The whole "heroic drama" was a mistake – and Settle was not even the best of that lot.

—Leonard R. N. Ashley

SHADWELL, Thomas. English. Born in Broomhill, Norfolk, c. 1642. Educated at home for five years, then at King Edward VI Grammar School, Bury St. Edmunds, Suffolk, 1654–56; admitted as a pensioner to Caius College, Cambridge, 1656, but left without taking a degree; entered the Middle Temple, London, 1658, and studied there for some time. Married the actress Anne Gibbs c. 1665; three sons and one daughter. Travelled abroad, then returned to London and began writing for the theatre and the opera c. 1668; involved in a feud with Dryden from 1682; succeeded Dryden as Poet Laureate and Historiographer Royal, 1689. *Died 19 November 1692.*

Publications

Collections

Complete Works, edited by Montague Summers. 5 vols., 1927.

Plays

The Sullen Lovers; or, The Impertinents (produced 1668). 1668.
The Royal Shepherdess, from the play *The Rewards of Virtue* by John Fountain (produced 1669). 1669.
The Humorists (produced 1670). 1671.
Epsom Wells (produced 1672). 1673; edited by Dorothy M. Walmsley, with *The Volunteers,* 1930.
The Miser (produced 1672). 1672.
The Tempest; or, The Enchanted Island, from the play by Shakespeare (produced 1674). 1674; edited by Christopher Spencer, in *Five Restoration Adaptations of Shakespeare,* 1965.
The Triumphant Widow; or, The Medley of Humours, with William Cavendish (produced 1674). 1677.
Psyche, music by Matthew Locke (produced 1675). 1675.
The Libertine (produced 1675). 1676; edited by Oscar Mandel, in *The Theatre of Don Juan,* 1963.
The Virtuoso (produced 1676). 1676; edited by Marjorie Hope Nicolson and David Stuart Rodes, 1966.
A True Widow (produced 1678). 1679.
Timon of Athens, The Man-Hater, from the play by Shakespeare (produced 1678). 1678.
The Woman Captain (produced 1679). 1680.
The Lancashire Witches and Tegue o Divelly the Irish Priest (produced 1681). 1682.
The Squire of Alsatia (produced 1688). 1688; edited by A. Norman Jeffares, in *Restoration Comedy,* 1974.
Bury Fair (produced 1689). 1689.
The Amorous Bigot, with the Second Part of Tegue o Divelly (produced 1690). 1690.
The Scourers (produced 1690). 1691.
The Volunteers; or, The Stock Jobbers (produced 1692). 1693; edited by Dorothy M. Walmsley, with *Epsom Wells,* 1930.

Verse

The Medal of John Bayes: A Satire Against Folly and Knavery. 1682.

A Lenten Prologue. 1683.

The Tenth Satire of Juvenal. 1687.

A Congratulatory Poem on His Highness the Prince of Orange His Coming into England. 1689.

A Congratulatory Poem to the Most Illustrious Queen Mary upon Her Arrival in England. 1689.

Ode on the Anniversary of the King's Birth. 1690.

Ode to the King, on His Return from Ireland. 1690(?).

Votum Perenne: A Poem to the King on New Year's Day. 1692.

Ode on the King's Birthday. 1692.

Other

Notes and Observations on The Empress of Morocco by Settle, with Dryden and John Crowne. 1674.

Some Reflections upon the Pretended Parallel in the Play The Duke of Guise. 1683.

Reading List: *Shadwell: His Life and Comedies* by Albert S. Borgman, 1928; *Shadwell* by Michael W. Alssid, 1967; *The Drama of Shadwell* by Don Kunz, 1972.

*   *   *

Thomas Shadwell is best known today as the target of John Dryden's satiric poem *Mac Flecknoe* (1678). Reading this cunning, exquisitely amusing lampoon, one is utterly convinced that Shadwell was no more than a clumsy, dull, nonsensical dramatist who repeated the same formula in play after play like one of his own comic humours. But reading Shadwell's drama beside Dryden's, one make a fairer assessment: while Shadwell was not nearly as accomplished a poet as his rival Dryden, he was a skillful and successful playwright. Actually, Dryden was able to enjoy a dramatic triumph over Shadwell only in the extravagantly imaginative fiction of his own poetic satire. The facts are that Shadwell was a very prolific, shrewdly professional, and highly popular Restoration dramatist.

Shadwell wrote during a literary epoch familiar to most of us either through Dryden's poetry or through some dozen outstanding plays written by a handful of gentlemen amateurs and companions to Charles II – men like the Second Duke of Buckingham, Sir Charles Sedley, Sir George Etherege, and William Wycherley. Like Dryden, Shadwell consorted with this group of witty courtiers, but he was a middle-class writer whose living depended increasingly more on box-office receipts than on their patronage. As a professional writer Shadwell was compelled to engage in nearly constant experimentation with a variety of dramatic kinds in order to appeal to an audience hungry for novelty. For example, his first play, *The Sullen Lovers,* was clearly a comedy of humours written in imitation of Ben Jonson, who along with Shakespeare had undergone a successful revival in the newly reopened theatres after Charles II's restoration to the throne. However, by the time he wrote *Epsom Wells,* Shadwell had already mastered the more modern, sophisticated comedy of wit made popular by Sedley and Etherege. Similarly, as spectacular operatic performances came into vogue, Shadwell adapted *The Tempest* and the story of Psyche; when his audience clamored for bombastic heroic tragedy, for which Dryden had created a following, Shadwell produced *The Libertine* and *Timon of Athens.* Later when political turmoil made it impossible to stage anything but farce and propaganda, Shadwell obliged with *The Woman Captain* and *The Lancashire Witches.* And when the taste was for sentimental comedy, he offered *The Squire of Alsatia* and *Bury Fair.*

Altogether between 1668 and 1692 Shadwell wrote at least eighteen plays. According to his editor, Montague Summers, some of these, like *Epsom Wells,* merited command performances at court; others, like *The Tempest*, set records for box-office receipts; fifteen of his plays continued to be performed after 1700 and six of them compiled distinguished stage histories, remaining in repertory for forty to eighty years. It was a living.

The remarkable variety in the canon of a professional playwright like Shadwell does much to dispel the common notion that Restoration drama consists essentially of heroic plays and comedies of wit. Similarly, reading Shadwell results in further correction of the gradually waning Victorian hypothesis that Restoration drama is noteworthy principally for its licentiousness and trivial frivolity. Despite their sometimes irreverent tone and frothy surface Shadwell's plays have a consistently orthodox Christian moral core; and, although they may go to extravagant lengths to entertain, invariably some socially utilitarian message is worked out in the dramatic action. His artistic credo is stated succinctly in his prologue to *The Lancashire Witches*: "Instruction is an honest Poet's aim,/And not a large or wide, but a good Fame." Among his contemporaries Shadwell enjoyed both. And sometimes envy as well.

Most of Shadwell's poetry was written in connection with his drama. He composed satiric prologues and epilogues notable for their wit and verve, their rapidly shifting tone and perspective, and their ingenious metaphors defining the playwright's relationship to his audience and plays – conceits which ranged anywhere from depicting the author as a warrior on a battlefield to a procurer in a bawdy-house. His songs typically treat of love or drinking, hunting or war; ensconced in the plays, they work to develop character or amplify theme in addition to providing a seemingly impromptu entertainment. His best poetry displays his natural ability as a dramatist: amusing characterizations, a swiftly developing argument, and clever turns of phrase.

The remainder of Shadwell's poetry consists of vituperative, Juvenalian invective like *The Medal of John Bayes* or lavish panegyrics on public figures. His most conventional and unimaginative poetry was written in fulfillment of his duty as Poet Laureate – a post in which he succeeded Dryden in 1689 and served until his death in 1692. These official birthday odes, celebrations of monarchical arrivals, and congratulations for battlefield victories are frankly dull enough to have been written by Mac Flecknoe. But once again in poetry as well as drama Shadwell is notable for his range from the crude and scurrilous to the elegant and highly stylized.

Unquestionably Shadwell's real talent was for dramatic satire and comedy – pieces like *Epsom Wells*, *The Virtuoso*, and *The Squire of Alsatia*. These seem to have been inspired by a volatile combination of mischief, social purpose, and exuberant delight at the folly surrounding him. Quite likely the rest was composed because a patron or playhouse wanted it or because a reputation needed living up to or because he needed the money. This is to say that such hack work was a practical necessity, making possible that drama which is the principal justification of Shadwell's career.

—Don Kunz

SHAFFER, Peter (Levin). English. Born in Liverpool, Lancashire, 15 May 1926; twin brother of the playwright Anthony Shaffer. Educated at St. Paul's School, London; Trinity College, Cambridge, 1947–50, B.A. 1950. Served as a conscript in coal mines in England, 1944–47. Worked in the acquisitions department of the New York Public Library, 1951–54; worked for Boosey and Hawkes, music publishers, London, 1954–55; Literary Critic, *Truth*, London, 1956–57; Music Critic, *Time and Tide*, London, 1961–62. Recipient: *Evening Standard* award, 1958; New York Drama Critics Circle Award, 1960, 1975; Antoinette Perry Award, 1975. Lives in London.

PUBLICATIONS

Plays

Five Finger Exercise (produced 1958). 1958.
The Private Ear and The Public Eye (produced 1962). 1962.
The Merry Roosters Panto, with the Theatre Workshop (produced 1963).
Sketch in *The Establishment* (produced 1963).
The Royal Hunt of the Sun: A Play Concerning the Conquest of Peru (produced 1964). 1965.
Black Comedy (produced 1965). In *Black Comedy, Including White Lies,* 1967.
A Warning Game (produced 1967).
White Lies (produced 1967). In *Black Comedy, Including White Lies,* 1967; as *The White Liars* (produced 1968), 1967; (revised version, produced 1976).
Black Comedy, Including White Lies: Two Plays. 1967; as *The White Liars, Black Comedy: Two Plays,* 1968.
It's about Cinderella (produced 1969).
Shrivings (as *The Battle of Shrivings,* produced 1970). 1974.
Equus (produced 1973). 1973.

Screenplays: *Lord of the Flies,* with Peter Brook, 1963; *The Public Eye (Follow Me!),* 1972.

Radio Play: *The Prodigal Father,* 1957.

Television Plays: *The Salt Land,* 1955; *Balance of Terror,* 1957.

Fiction

How Doth the Little Crocodile?, with Anthony Shaffer. 1951.
Woman in the Wardrobe, with Anthony Shaffer. 1952.
Withered Murder, with Anthony Shaffer. 1955.

Reading List: *Shaffer* by John Russell Taylor, 1974.

*   *   *

Four of Peter Shaffer's plays have had considerable success in the theatre and have given him a misleading reputation for versatility without personal commitment. Furthermore, comparisons with Brecht and Rattigan have obscured deeper affinities with the "total theatre" of Paul Claudel and the intimate savagery of O'Neill's or Albee's drama. Certainly his work ranges from farce to tragedy, but it is criss-crossed with recurrent images, and the same basic structures emerge in secular and religious transformations. A line from *Shrivings,* "The most anyone can say in the end to God or Man is 'Let us see!' " is crucially pertinent to all the plays, both one-act and full-length. An allusion to self-blinded Oedipus, planted early in *Five Finger Exercise,* anticipates the blackened sun of *The Royal Hunt of the Sun* and the blinded horses of *Equus;* there seems to be a connection with the owl image of dim-sighted innocence in *Five Finger Exercise* and *Shrivings* with the unilluminating crystal ball in *White Liars* and, in reversal, the casting of stage light on what the characters of *Black Comedy* get up to in the dark. The Oedipal family situation which is exposed in *Five Finger Exercise* and *Equus,* and resides as a phantasm in the background of *Shrivings,* has its maturer variant in the situation of the sceptic who is faced by an impossible choice between a Christianity he loathes and a humaner faith he cannot trust: Pizarro, in *Royal Hunt of the Sun*, caught between the greed and cruelty of the Church and a sixteenth-century equivalent of the Marxist dream; Mark Askelon, in *Shrivings* (the re-written, published text of the theatrical failure, *The Battle of Shrivings*), who plays the Devil to Gideon Petrie's humanist saint in longing for a defeat that will save him from taking hopeless refuge in traditional religion; the psychiatrist, Dysart, in *Equus*, who sees the issues but evades battle and makes do with a nostalgia for the Greek world at the price of self-contempt. The visionary dream of faith takes alternative form as music in some of the plays (*Five Finger Exercise*, *The Private Ear*), and the apparent conflict between culture and philistinism seems to be an obscurer enactment of the alternatives of belief or destructive nihilism.

Shaffer has declared his aesthetic predilection for "the cold which burns," and the emotions that give power and intensity to the verbal battles and the pursuit of ultimates in his plays are the cold ones of guilt, envy, disgust, despondency, hatred. (The author's loathing is most consistently projected on the adult female characters in the plays, who range from tiresome and stupid to nauseating, though Shaffer can also be arraigned for some degree of contempt for the lower middle class.) Pizarro's cry, "Where can a man live, between two hates?" defines the quest of a playwright whose recognition of man's spiritual nature springs from an agonised consciousness of original sin. This has been an unfashionable viewpoint in the 1960's and 1970's, and in technique also Peter Shaffer stands apart from any school or group of contemporary dramatists.

The plays are firmly and ingeniously structured and ask to be met by creative collaboration from designers and choreographers, as well as directors and actors. The result has been a degree of physical stage action unusual in modern drama. Shaffer has a liking for multiple sets, or at least two acting areas, which allow for the counterpointing of different lines of dialogue, or of dialogue and action, and set up a convention in which long rhetorical speeches, and even soliloquies, are acceptable. The action is deftly farcical in *Black Comedy* and grandly spectacular in *Royal Hunt of the Sun* — but not epic in the Brechtian sense, as Shaffer maintains theatrical illusion and does not use his period setting to give a provocatively estranged view of modern issues. Indeed it may be a weakness of both *Royal Hunt of the Sun* and *Equus* that there is some muffling of the contemporary and personal anguish by elements that have led to the work's success with the general public. In *Equus*, the elucidation of the mystery which gives the play its plot is a more unfortunate reminder than the comic fantasy of a detective in *The Public Eye* that Peter and Anthony Shaffer had collaborated on several detective novels; for this interferes with the proper relation of the play's lyrical core to its true protagonist, Dysart. Perhaps significantly, it is in passages of the least-liked major play, *Shrivings*, that the emotional urgency is strongest.

Shaffer is never a meticulous naturalist; he is not concerned to make it credible that the parents in *Five Finger Exercise* should have such a wise and happy child as Pamela, or that the ex-teacher and the left-wing printer of *Equus* have an illiterate son; more obviously deliberate is the morality-play element in *Shrivings*, and this, apart from the embarrassing way in which the characters take theatrically ineffective symbols out of parcels, may account for the hostile reception given to the original staged version of this work. He has an unreliable ear for colloquial speech. But this weakness is venial in a writer whose concern with society is indirect and secondary. Even the undistinguished prose of his more formal dialogue does not cancel out the genuine dramatic gift, the courage and ability to tackle large subjects, and the force of conviction.

—Margery Morgan

SHAKESPEARE, William. English. Born in Stratford upon Avon, Warwickshire, baptized 26 April 1564. Probably educated at the King's New School, Stratford, 1571–77. Married Anne Hathaway in 1582; two daughters, one son. May have taught school in or near Stratford; settled in London c. 1588, and was well-known as an actor and had begun to write for the stage by 1592; Shareholder in the Lord Chamberlain's Company (after James I's accession, called the King's Men) by 1594, performing at the Globe Theatre from 1599, and, after 1609, at the Blackfriars Theatre; bought New Place in Stratford, 1597, and acquired land in Stratford; retired to Stratford in 1611. *Died 23 April 1616.*

PUBLICATIONS

Collections

> *Comedies, Histories, and Tragedies* (First Folio), edited by John Heming and Henry Condell. 1623.
> *Works* (New Variorum Edition), edited by H. H. Furness and H. H. Furness, Jr. 27 vols., 1871–
> *Works* (New Cambridge Edition), edited by J. Dover Wilson and A. H. Quiller-Couch. 1921–66.
> *The New Arden Shakespeare,* edited by Una Ellis-Fermor and others. 1951–
> *The New Penguin Shakespeare.* 1967–

Plays

> *King John* (produced 1589). In First Folio, 1623.
> *1 Henry VI* (produced 1591?). In First Folio, 1623.
> *2 Henry VI* (produced 1592?). 1594 (bad quarto).
> *3 Henry VI* (produced 1592?). 1595 (bad quarto).
> *Richard III* (produced 1592?). 1597.
> *The Comedy of Errors* (produced 1593?). In First Folio, 1623.
> *Titus Andronicus* (produced 1594). 1594.
> *The Taming of the Shrew* (produced 1594). In First Folio, 1623.
> *Love's Labour's Lost* (produced 1594?). 1598.
> *Romeo and Juliet* (produced 1594–95?). 1597 (bad quarto); 1599.
> *Two Gentlemen of Verona* (produced 1595?). In First Folio, 1623.
> *A Midsummer Night's Dream* (produced 1595). 1600.
> *Richard II* (produced 1595–96?). 1597.
> *Sir Thomas More,* with Munday (produced 1596?). Edited by A. Dyce, 1844; edition of W. W. Greg revised by H. Jenkins, 1961.
> *The Merchant of Venice* (produced 1596?). 1600.
> *Henry IV,* part 1 (produced 1596–97?). 1598.
> *Henry IV,* part 2 (produced 1597–98?). 1600.
> *Much Ado about Nothing* (produced 1598?). 1600.
> *Henry V* (produced 1599). 1600 (bad quarto).
> *Julius Caesar* (produced 1599). In First Folio, 1623.
> *The Merry Wives of Windsor* (produced 1599–1600?). 1602 (bad quarto).
> *As You Like It* (produced 1600?). In First Folio, 1623.
> *Hamlet* (produced 1601?). 1603 (bad quarto); 1604.
> *Twelfth Night; or, What You Will* (produced 1601–02?). In First Folio, 1623.
> *Troilus and Cressida* (produced 1602?). 1609.

All's Well That Ends Well (produced 1602?).   In First Folio, 1623.
Measure for Measure (produced 1604?).   In First Folio, 1623.
Othello (produced 1604?).   1622.
King Lear (produced 1605).   1608 (bad quarto).
Macbeth (produced 1606).   In First Folio, 1623.
Antony and Cleopatra (produced 1606?).   In First Folio, 1623.
Coriolanus (produced 1606?).   In First Folio, 1623.
Timon of Athens (produced 1607?).   In First Folio, 1623.
Pericles, with George Wilkins (produced 1608?).   1609.
Cymbeline (produced 1609?).   In First Folio, 1623.
The Winter's Tale (produced 1610?).   In First Folio, 1623.
The Tempest (produced 1611).   In First Folio, 1623.
Henry VIII, with Fletcher(?) (produced 1613).   In First Folio, 1623.
The Two Noble Kinsmen, with Fletcher (produced 1613).   1634; edited by G. R.
   Proudfoot, 1970.

Verse

Venus and Adonis.   1593.
The Rape of Lucrece.   1594.
Sonnets.   1609.
Poems.   1640.

Bibliography: *A Shakespeare Bibliography* by Walther Ebisch and Levin L. Schücking, 1931,
supplement, 1937; *A Classified Shakespeare Bibliography 1936–1958* by Gordon Ross Smith,
1963.

Reading List: *Shakespeare: A Study of the Facts and Problems* by E. K. Chambers, 2 vols.,
1930; *Narrative and Dramatic Sources of Shakespeare* edited by Geoffrey Bullough, 8 vols.,
1957–75; *The Printing and Proof-Reading of the First Folio of Shakespeare* by C. Hinman, 2
vols., 1963; *Four Centuries of Shakespeare Criticism* edited by Frank Kermode, 1965; *A
Shakespeare Encyclopaedia* edited by O. J. Campbell and E. G. Quinn, 1966; *A New and
Systematic Concordance to the Works of Shakespeare* by M. Spevack, 6 vols., 1968–70; *A
New Companion of Shakespeare Studies* edited by Kenneth Muir and Samuel Schoenbaum,
1971; *Shakespeare: The Critical Heritage* edited by Brian Vickers, 6 vols., 1973–74;
Shakespeare: A Documentary Life by Samuel Schoenbaum, 1975, compact edition, 1977.

*   *   *

Shakespeare, "of all modern, and perhaps ancient poets, had the largest and most
comprehensive soul." Dryden's tribute, the more generous for coming from an age that
prided itself on a superior standard of polish and "politeness," sums up what students of
Shakespeare have at all times sought to express. No writer of comparable greatness is more
elusive to final definition. None has exercised a more diverse appeal or shown a greater
capacity for continual and fruitful renewal in the minds of succeeding generations.
   This protean genius came only gradually to full expression. Shakespeare's earliest work is
that of a man engaged in exploring, and in some measure creating, the possibilities of his art.
The earliest work attributed to him, the three plays on *Henry VI*, show him engaged in
shaping chronicle material to dramatic ends. They lead, in *Richard III*, to the creation of a
character who stands out by his passionate dedication to the achievement of power against
the world of short-sighted time-servers, ambitious politicians, and helpless moralists in which
he moves.

Side by side with these early chronicle dramas we find Shakespeare, in a series of plays running from *The Comedy of Errors* through *The Taming of the Shrew* to *Love's Labour's Lost*, shaping the conventions of comedy into an instrument for expressing the finished statements about life – and more especially about love and marriage as central aspects of it – that he was already concerned to make.

In the 1590's Shakespeare also wrote two narrative poems, *Venus and Adonis* and *The Rape of Lucrece*, possibly stimulated by the success of Marlowe's *Hero and Leander* of 1593, and he was also at work on his sonnets, though the 1609 *Sonnets* is now generally thought to contain poems from virtually all the periods of his development. Many of the sonnets are exercises in the conventions of the period, addressed to a patron or to an imaginary mistress. But Shakespeare was able to use the thematic conventions in a fresh way, investigating – as he would do in his later plays – the relation of individual experience (in particular the heightened emotions of friendship and love) to time. At the same time Shakespeare developed a distinctively intense and immediate language to meet the strict formal limitations of the sonnet. The stress of feeling informing the language and the exploration of shifting attitudes to a particular emotion are essentially *dramatic*, and mark out linguistic and thematic areas that Shakespeare was to explore in his "problem" plays and later.

His early works led, approximately from 1595 to 1596, to a first remarkable explosion of creative energy. Within a brief period of time, Shakespeare produced his first great tragedy, *Romeo and Juliet*, a comedy of outstanding brilliance, *A Midsummer Night's Dream*, and a historical play, *Richard II*, which gives the chronicle type of drama an entirely new dimension. In *Romeo and Juliet* a pair of young lovers seek to affirm the truth of their mutual dedication in the face of an intolerably hostile world. Their attempt ends, inevitably, in separation and death; but because it is a true emotion, involving an intuition of *value*, of life and generosity, it achieves, even in the doom which overtakes it, a measure of triumph over external circumstance. *A Midsummer Night's Dream* could be regarded as a comic counterpoise to the "romantic" tragedy. Within the framework of a rational and social attitude to marriage, it transports two pairs of youthful lovers to the mysterious woods, where the irrational but potent impulses which men ignore at their peril are released and their capacity to master them tested. By the end of their misadventures, and when the central theme of the play has been presented in the infatuation of Titania, the queen of the fairies, for Bottom the weaver with his ass's head, there is a return to daylight reality and, with it, a resolution of the issues raised by the play in terms of creative paradox. Love is seen at once to be a folly and to contain within itself, absurd indeed but not the less real, a glimpse of the divine element by which human life is imaginatively transformed in terms of "wonder."

The third play of this period, *Richard II*, is the starting-point for a series, continued in *Henry IV*, Parts I and II and *Henry V*, which traces the downfall of a traditional conception of royalty and its replacement by a political force at once more competent, more truly self-aware, and more precariously built on the foundation of its own desire for power. The Lancastrian Bolingbroke, having achieved the crown by deposing and murdering his predecessor, is seen striving to impose unity upon his realm, but foiled in his efforts by the consequences of his original crime. The success which eludes him is finally attained, in *Henry V*, by his son, but in a way which underlines the cost as well as the necessity of his triumph. The presence of Shakespeare's greatest comic creation, Falstaff, and his final rejection, underline the human complexity involved in the new king's necessary choices. As King, he can hardly do otherwise than banish the companion of his youth, and it would surely be wrong to sentimentalize Falstaff in any way; but we are required, in a manner that is very essentially Shakespearean, to weigh the *cost* against the success, and perhaps to conclude that the human and the political orders – both necessary aspects of human life – are in the real world barely to be reconciled.

At about the time that he was writing this second series of history plays, Shakespeare was engaged in developing further his concept of comedy to cover other aspects of human behaviour. In *Much Ado about Nothing* he produced a highly formal comedy which works, through strict conventions and largely in prose, to illuminate facets of truth and illusion in the reality of love. In *As You Like It* the consideration of the basic realities of love and friendship is extended to cover a concept of sociability, of true civilization. The central part of the play, which displaces the action to the Forest of Arden where human relationships are taken temporarily into the state of nature (itself presented in conventional terms) and set in contrast to the corrupt sophistication which prevails at Duke Frederick's court, presents a set of variations on the theme of love. When the various amorous combinations have been sorted out, leading into the concluding "dance" of married harmonies which is a reflection of the universal order of things, the reconciliation at which comedy aims is finally consummated.

The last of these great comedies, *Twelfth Night*, deals in its "serious" part with two characters, Orsino and Olivia, whose lives are initially a blend of sentiment and artifice, and who learn, largely through their relationship with the self-reliant Viola, that the compulsive force of their passions is such as to draw them finally beyond themselves, demanding from each the acceptance of a fuller, more natural and spontaneous way of living. The "lesson" is reinforced by the comic underplot, and more particularly by the exposure of Olivia's steward Malvolio, who is – and remains to the last – "imprisoned" in a darkness which reflects his self-infatuation. Feste, too, the most individual thus far of Shakespeare's clowns, stands rather outside the prevailing mood, answering to the constant tendency of Shakespearean comedy to qualify its imaginative harmonies with a profound sense of relativity, of a final uniqueness and autonomy in human experience.

The period which produced these great comedies was followed by a turning of the dramatist's interest towards tragedy. Two plays of obscure intention and uneven execution – *Troilus and Cressida* and *Measure for Measure* – form the background to *Hamlet* in which many of the same issues were raised to the consistent level of tragedy. The play presents a central figure of unique complexity whose motives penetrate the action at every point, seeking clarification through contact with it and illuminating it in turn by his central presence. In pursuing his duty to avenge his father's death, Hamlet brings to light a state of disease in "Denmark" – the "world" of the play – which affects the entire field presented to his consciousness; and, in the various stages through which the ramifications of this infection are exposed, he finds himself exploring progressively the depths of his own disaffection.

In the great tragedies that followed *Hamlet*, the conflicts there presented are polarized, on an ever-increasing scale, into more clearly defined contrasts. In the earliest of them, *Othello*, the heroic figure of the Moor, tragically compounded of nobility and weakness, is exposed to the critical scepticism of Iago which operates upon his simplicity with the effect of an anarchic and sinister dissolvent. "Perplexed" to the last, betrayed by emotions which he has never really understood in their true nature, Othello makes a last attempt to return, through suicide, to his original simplicity of nature. By then, however, the critical acid supplied by Iago has undermined the structure of his greatness.

In his next tragedy, *King Lear*, Shakespeare embarked upon what is probably the most universal of his conceptions. Lear is at once father and king, head of a family and ruler of a state. As father he produces in his daughters contrasted reactions which reflect contradictions in his own nature; as king, his wilful impulses release in society destructive forces which nothing less than their utter exhaustion can contain. In the central storm scenes, the action of the elements becomes a reflection of Lear's own condition. Man and his environment are seen as organically related in the conflicts of a universe poetically conceived. Human relationships are shattered, and the state of "unaccomodated man" is seen in terms of subjection to the beast of prey in his own nature. Through these overwhelming events we are led step by step to Lear's awakening and recognition of his returned daughter Cordelia. This is the central reconciliation, the restoration of the natural "bond" between father and child, which is seen – while it lasts – as the resolution of the ruin caused by passion and egoism in the most intimate of human relationships. It is not, however, lasting. Since we are engaged in an exploration of the human condition under its tragic aspect, not elaborating the supposedly beneficial effects of suffering in promoting moral understanding, the armies of France are defeated by the "Machiavellian" realist Edmund; and though he dies in meeting the challenge of his disguised half-brother Edgar, his death cannot reverse the hanging of

Cordelia by his orders. As the play ends, Lear returns with her dead body in his arms and, in a world dominated by returning darkness, the curtain falls.

The next great tragedy, *Macbeth*, deals with the overthrow of harmony not merely in an individual of tragic stature, but in an ordered realm. Macbeth murders, not only a man and a kinsman, but order, sanity, life itself. From the moment of the execution of his deed his character and that of his wife develop on lines of rigid determinism. One crime leads logically, by a dreadful and pre-determined process, to another; and the career that began by following the illusion of "freedom," mastery of circumstance, ends by an inexorable development in a complete enslavement from which defeat and death provide the only conceivable release.

Close in time to the writing of these great tragedies, a series of plays on Roman themes represents Shakespeare's final effort in this kind. The earliest, *Julius Caesar*, is one of his most effective studies of public behaviour. The central character, Brutus, the nearest approach to a truly consistent figure which the play offers, is flawed by the self-consciousness of his determination to be true to his ideals. His need to live up to an acceptable image of himself makes him the victim of those who appeal to him in the name of friendship and devotion to freedom, but who are moved in no small part by resentment and envy. The other principal agent in the tragedy, Mark Antony, combines genuine feeling with the ability to exploit mob emotion, and ends by disclaiming responsibility for the destruction and brutality he has unleashed. Finally, after Caesar's death, the world which survives him is shown separating into its component elements of selfish "realism" and disillusionment.

The next Roman play, *Antony and Cleopatra*, is among Shakespeare's greatest masterpieces. His Cleopatra is at once the Egyptian queen of history and something more: a woman experienced in the ways of a corrupt and cynical world and ready to use her fascination over men in order to survive in it. Antony's love for her is, at least in part, the fascination of a man no longer young, who has chosen to give up his public responsibilities to become the dupe of an emotion that he knows to be unworthy. Side by side with the moral judgment that is unrelentingly pressed throughout the tragedy, the implication remains that the measure of the passion which has led this pair to accept death and ruin may be correspondingly universal in its value. It is the play's achievement to convey that *both* judgments contain a measure of truth, that neither can be suppressed without distorting our sense of the complete human reality which the play offers.

After *Coriolanus*, the disconcerting study of a gauche and inflexible hero whose unnatural desire for revenge upon his city leaves him at the last disoriented and ruined in a world that he is incapable of understanding, the last stage of Shakespeare's development consists of a series of "romances," written from 1607 onwards, which represent an effort to give dramatic form to a new "symbolic" intuition. After two plays – *Pericles* and *Cymbeline* – which can be thought of as experiments, *The Winter's Tale* presents the story of two kings whose life-long friendship is broken up by the jealous conviction of one of them – Leontes – that his friend Polixenes has replaced him in the affection of his wife Hermione. By the end of an action in which the passage of time has an essential part to play, the estranged monarchs are reconciled through the spontaneous love of their children, the divisions introduced by disordered and self-consuming passion into the harmony of life have been healed, and winter has passed through spring into the summer of gracious fulfilment.

The Tempest, which some have seen, perhaps a little over-schematically, as Shakespeare's farewell to the stage, takes us to an island in which the normal laws of nature are magically suspended. Prospero can be seen as a figure of the imaginative artist, bringing together on his island stage the men who, in another world, have wronged him and whom he now subjects to a process of judgment and reconciliation. He is accompanied by his servants Ariel and Caliban, the former of whom may represent the imaginative, creative side of his nature, the latter the passionate instincts which, as a human being, he keeps uneasily under control. By the end of the play, as in *The Winter's Tale*, a measure of reconciliation has been born out of the exposure to tragic experience. Prospero's daughter Miranda marries Ferdinand, the son of his former enemy, whom she first saw in her inexperience as a vision proceeding from a "brave new world," but whom she has learned to love as a man. The "brave new world" is seen as an ennobling vision of love in the light of an enriched experience, and upon it the "gods" are invited to bestow the "crown" which raises a new-born vision of humanity into a symbol of royalty. The "crown" they bestow is a sign of the "second," the redeemed and "reasonable" life which Prospero's action has made accessible. At this point, if anywhere, and always within the limits of the imaginative action which has created a *play*, the design presented by Shakespeare's work is substantially complete.

—Derek A. Traversi

SHAW, George Bernard. Irish. Born in Dublin, 26 July 1856. Educated privately and at the Wesleyan Connexional School and elsewhere in Dublin. Married Charlotte Payne-Townshend in 1898 (died, 1943). Office boy and cashier for Charles Townshend, estate agent, Dublin, 1871–76; settled in London, 1876; worked briefly for the Edison Telephone Company, 1879; wrote novels and literary and art criticism for various newspapers, 1879–83; became a socialist in 1882: speaker for the Social Democratic Federation: joined the Fabian Society in 1884: Member of the Executive Committee for many years; Music Critic (as "Corno di Bassetto"), *The Star*, 1888–1890, and *The World*, 1890–94; began writing for the stage in the 1890's; Drama Critic, *The Saturday Review*, 1895–98; Member of the Borough Council of St. Pancras, London, 1900–03; Founder, with Sidney and Beatrice Webb, *The New Statesman*, 1913, and helped establish the London School of Economics; drafted his last manifesto for the Fabian Society in 1929; lifelong advocate of spelling reform. Recipient: Nobel Prize for Literature, 1925; Irish Academy of Letters medal, 1934. Declined a peerage and the Order of Merit. *Died 2 November 1950.*

PUBLICATIONS

Collections

    Collected Letters, edited by Dan H. Laurence.　2 vols. only, 1965–72.
    The Bodley Head Shaw (plays and prefaces).　7 vols., 1970–74.
    The Portable Shaw, edited by Stanley Weintraub.　1977.

Plays

    Widowers' Houses: A Didactic Realistic Play (produced 1892).　1893; revised version, in *Plays Unpleasant*, 1898.
    Arms and the Man (produced 1894).　In *Plays Pleasant*, 1898.
    Candida (produced 1897).　In *Plays Pleasant*, 1898.
    The Devil's Disciple (produced 1897).　In *Three Plays for Puritans*, 1901.
    The Man of Destiny (produced 1897).　In *Plays Pleasant*, 1898.
    The Gadfly; or, The Son of the Cardinal, from the novel by Ethel Voynich (produced 1898).　In *Bodley Head Shaw 7*, 1974.
    You Never Can Tell (produced 1899).　In *Plays Pleasant*, 1898.

Mrs. Warren's Profession (produced 1902). In *Plays Unpleasant*, 1898.

The Philanderer (produced 1905). In *Plays Unpleasant*, 1898.

Captain Brassbound's Conversion (produced 1900). In *Three Plays for Puritans*, 1901.

Caesar and Cleopatra (produced 1907). In *Three Plays for Puritans*, 1901.

The Admirable Bashville; or, Constancy Rewarded, from his novel *Cashel Byron's Profession* (produced 1902). In *Cashel Byron's Profession*, 1901.

Man and Superman: A Comedy and a Philosophy (produced 1905). 1903; excerpt, as *Don Juan in Hell: A Dream* (produced 1907).

How He Lied to Her Husband (produced 1904). With *John Bull's Other Island, Major Barbara*, 1907.

John Bull's Other Island (produced 1904). With *How He Lied to Her Husband, Major Barbara*, 1907.

Passion, Poison, and Petrification; or, The Fatal Gazogene (produced 1905). 1905.

Major Barbara (produced 1905). With *How He Lied to Her Husband, John Bull's Other Island*, 1907; revised version (screenplay), 1945.

The Doctor's Dilemma (produced 1906). With *Getting Married, The Shewing Up of Blanco Posnet*, 1911.

The Interlude at the Playhouse (produced 1907). In *Behind the Scenes with Cyril Maude*, 1927.

Getting Married (produced 1908). With *The Doctor's Dilemma, The Shewing Up of Blanco Posnet*, 1911.

The Shewing Up of Blanco Posnet (produced 1909). With *The Doctor's Dilemma, Getting Married*, 1911.

Press Cuttings (produced 1909). 1909.

Misalliance (produced 1910). With *The Dark Lady of the Sonnets, Fanny's First Play*, 1914.

The Dark Lady of the Sonnets (produced 1910). With *Misalliance, Fanny's First Play*, 1914.

Fanny's First Play (produced 1911). With *Misalliance, The Dark Lady of the Sonnets*, 1914.

Overruled (produced 1912). With *Androcles and the Lion, Pygmalion*, 1916.

Androcles and the Lion (produced 1913). With *Overruled, Pgymalion*, 1916.

Pygmalion (produced 1913). With *Overruled, Androcles and the Lion*, 1916; revised version (screenplay), 1941.

Great Catherine (produced 1913). With *Heartbreak House, Playlets of the War*, 1919.

The Music Cure (produced 1914). In *Translations and Tomfooleries*, 1926.

The Inca of Perusalem (produced 1916). With *Great Catherine, Heartbreak House, Playlets of the War*, 1919.

Augustus Does His Bit (produced 1917). With *Great Catherine, Heartbreak House, Playlets of the War*, 1919.

O'Flaherty, V.C. (produced 1917). With *Great Catherine, Heartbreak House, Playlets of the War*, 1919.

Annajanska, The Bolshevik Empress (produced 1918). With *Great Catherine, Heartbreak House, Playlets of the War*, 1919.

Heartbreak House (produced 1920). With *Great Catherine, Playlets of the War*, 1919.

Back to Methuselah (produced 1922). 1921.

Jitta's Atonement, from a work by Siegfried Trebitsch (produced 1923). In *Translations and Tomfooleries*, 1926.

Saint Joan (produced 1923). 1924; revised version (screenplay), 1968.

The Glimpse of Reality (produced 1927). In *Translations and Tomfooleries*, 1926.

Translations and Tomfooleries. 1926.

The Fascinating Foundling (produced 1928). In *Translations and Tomfooleries*, 1926.

The Apple Cart (produced 1929). 1930.

Complete Plays. 1931; revised edition, 1934, 1938, 1950, 1952, 1965.

Too True to Be Good (produced 1932).   With *Village Wooing, On the Rocks*, 1934.
On the Rocks (produced 1933).   With *Village Wooing, Too True to Be Good*, 1934.
Village Wooing (produced 1934).   With *Too True to Be Good, On the Rocks*, 1934.
The Six of Calais (produced 1934).   With *The Simpleton of the Unexpected Isles, The Millionairess*, 1936.
The Simpleton of the Unexpected Isles (produced 1935).   With *The Six of Calais, The Millionairess*, 1936.
The Millionairess (produced 1936).   With *The Six of Calais, The Simpleton of the Unexpected Isles*, 1936.
Cymbeline Refinished (produced 1937).   With *Geneva, In Good King Charles's Golden Days*, 1946.
Geneva (produced 1938).   1939.
In Good King Charles's Golden Days (produced 1939).   1939.
Buoyant Billions (produced 1948).   1949.
Shakes Versus Shav: A Puppet Play (produced 1949).   With *Buoyant Billions, Far-Fetched Fables*, 1950.
Far-Fetched Fables (produced 1950).   With *Buoyant Billions, Shakes Versus Shav*, 1950.
Why She Would Not (produced 1957).   In *Ten Short Plays*, 1960.
Ten Short Plays.   1960.
Passion Play: A Dramatic Fragment, 1878, edited by Jerald E. Bringle.   1971.

Screenplays: *Pygmalion*, with others, 1938; *Major Barbara*, with Anatole de Grunwald, 1941; *Caesar and Cleopatra*, with Marjorie Deans and W. P. Lipscomb, 1946.

Fiction

Cashel Byron's Profession.   1886; revised edition, 1889, 1901.
An Unsocial Socialist.   1887.
Love among the Artists.   1900.
The Irrational Knot.   1905.
Immaturity, in *Works*.   1930.
The Adventures of the Black Girl in Her Search for God.   1932.
My Dear Dorothea: A Practical Guide of Moral Education for Females, edited by Stephen Winsten.   1956.
An Unfinished Novel, edited by Stanley Weintraub.   1958.

Other

The Quintessence of Ibsenism.   1891; revised edition, 1913.
The Perfect Wagnerite: A Commentary on the Ring of the Niblungs.   1898; revised edition, 1907.
Dramatic Opinions and Essays.   2 vols., 1906.
The Sanity of Art.   1908.
Common Sense about the War.   1914.
How to Settle the Irish Question.   1917.
Ruskin's Politics.   1921.
Letters to Miss Alma Murray.   1927; *More Letters*, 1932.
The Intelligent Woman's Guide to Socialism and Capitalism.   1928; revised edition, 1937.
Works.   33 vols., 1930–38.
Ellen Terry and Shaw: A Correspondence.   1931.

Works (Standard Edition). 34 vols., 1931–51.
What I Really Wrote about the War. 1931.
Doctors' Delusions, Crude Criminology, Sham Education, in *Works* (Standard Edition). 1931.
Pen Portraits and Reviews, in *Works* (Standard Edition). 1931.
Our Theatre in the Nineties, in *Works* (Standard Edition). 3 vols., 1932.
Essays in Fabian Socialism, in *Works* (Standard Edition). 1932.
The Political Madhouse in America and Nearer Home, in *Works* (Standard Edition). 1933.
Prefaces. 1934; revised edition, 1938, 1965.
Short Stories, Scraps, and Shavings, in *Works* (Standard Edition). 1934.
London Music in 1888–89 as Heard by Corno di Bassetto, in *Works* (Standard Edition. 1937.
Shaw Gives Himself Away: An Autobiographical Miscellany. 1939.
Florence Farr, Shaw, and W. B. Yeats Letters, edited by Clifford Bax. 1941.
Everybody's Political What's What. 1944.
Sixteen Self Sketches, in *Works* (Standard Edition). 1949.
Shaw on Vivisection, edited by G. H. Bowker. 1949.
Rhyming Picture Guide to Ayot Saint Lawrence. 1950.
Correspondence Between Shaw and Mrs. Patrick Campbell, edited by A. Dent. 1952.
Advice to a Young Critic and Other Letters, edited by E. J. West. 1955.
Letters to Granville Barker, edited by C. B. Purdom. 1957.
To a Young Actress: Letters to Molly Tompkins, edited by P. Tompkins. 1960.
The Matter with Ireland, edited by Dan H. Laurence and D. H. Greene. 1962.
The Rationalization of Russia, edited by H. M. Geduld. 1964.
Non-Dramatic Literary Criticism, edited by Stanley Weintraub. 1972.
Shaw 1914–1918: Journey to Heartbreak (from Shaw's journals), edited by Stanley Weintraub. 1973.

Editor, *Fabian Essays on Socialism.* 1889; revised edition, 1908, 1931, 1948.
Editor, *Fabianism and the Empire: A Manifesto.* 1900.

Bibliography: *A Bibliography of the Books and Pamphlets of Shaw* by G. H. Wells, 1925, supplements in *Bookman's Journal,* 1925, 1928; *The Rehearsal Copies of Shaw's Plays* by F. E. Loewenstein, 1950; *Shaw: An Exhibit, A Catalogue* by Dan H. Laurence, 1977.

Reading List: *Shaw, Playboy and Prophet,* 1932, and *Shaw, Man of the Century,* 1956, both by Archibald Henderson; *Shaw: A Reconsideration* by Eric Bentley, 1947, revised edition, 1957; *A Good Man Fallen among Fabians* by Alick West, 1950; *Shaw: A Critical Survey* edited by Louis Kronenberger, 1955; *Shaw: The Style and the Man* by Richard M. Ohmann, 1962; *Shaw and the Nineteenth Century* by Martin Meisel, 1963; *Shaw of Dublin: The Formative Years* by B. C. Rosset, 1964; *Twentieth Century Views of Shaw* edited by R. J. Kaufmann, 1965; *Shaw and the Charlatan Genius* by John O'Donovan, 1965; *Shaw and the Art of Destroying Ideals* by Charles A. Carpenter, 1969; *The Shavian Background* by Margery Morgan, 1972; *Shaw, Playwright* by Bernard F. Dukore, 1973; *Shaw and the Art of Drama* by Charles A. Berst, 1973; *The Cart and the Trumpet* by Maurice Valency, 1973; *Shaw's Moral Vision: The Self and Salvation* by Alfred Turco, Jr., 1976; *Shaw: The Critical Heritage* edited by T. F. Evans, 1976.

*   *   *

George Bernard Shaw achieved the status of a classic dramatist in his life-time, yet the question of how good he is still perplexes criticism. One reason for this is undoubtedly the suspicion that attaches to commercial success in the arts. Another is the idiosyncratic nature of his comic genius: on his own admission, childhood experience of a drunken father and a coolly indifferent mother blocked his capacity for feeling as other men do, and a long virginity followed by deliberate entry on a sexless yet happy marriage mark him out as further removed from the apotheosis of the normal which is the least disturbing form of greatness. His unflagging sense of the ridiculous, his gift of the gab, even the rationality that brought opprobrium on him amid the mass hysteria of the First World War (see *Common Sense about the War*), can be seen as grotesque over-developments of particular faculties in an unbalanced personality. His love of horseplay may strike grown men and women as juvenile. It seems easier to acknowledge a supreme clown if he is inarticulate and his art seems largely instinctive, and if he stays in the "primitive" ambience of circus or music hall. The clown as political theorist, intellectual leader, and religious visionary, invading the realms of literature and the serious, "legitimate" stage, throws all civilised activities anarchically into doubt. It is not even as though Shaw's satire had the savagery of Swift's; at his most vituperative he has an air of only playing and enjoying his own jokes. When turned by others, against his intentions, into a librettist of musical comedy (*The Chocolate Soldier* and *My Fair Lady*), he has provided smash hits easier to categorise and assimilate.

He first made his reputation as a journalist, writing music criticism under the name of "Corno di Bassetto," and he went on to become theatre critic to *The Saturday Review*, writing plays at the same time. His reviews combine technical knowledge with acute judgment and an extremely lively, exaggerative style, and his example did much to raise the standard of criticism in both fields. He had already written five novels, which have been most fully and sympathetically discussed by Alick West in *A Good Man Fallen among Fabians*. In these he attempts a panoramic view of society and tackles some of the large themes that are to occupy him in his plays, among them marriage (*The Irrational Knot*), genius and class distinctions (*Immaturity* and *Cashel Byron's Profession*), the politician as Don Juan (*An Unsocial Socialist*). In all, he presents the independent professional woman in contrast to the conventionally domesticated type, and studies (especially in *Love among the Artists*) examples of men and women on whom the impersonal claims of work, art, or science are stronger than those of personal relationships. These novels are brimming with current ideas and abound in entertaining passages, but the sense of direction is usually uncertain and the impulse to break into self-parody is strongly marked, appearing most oddly in the antics of Trefusis *alias* Smilash, the self-ironical clown of a hero in *An Unsocial Socialist*. *Cashel Byron's Profession* stands apart as the briefest and most evenly sustained, and here Shaw first tries out the satiric formula to be used as a basis for *Mrs. Warren's Profession* and *Major Barbara*. Here his hero is an innocent who speaks out the literal truth of his experience as a prize-fighter and is heard as a philosopher spinning metaphors of the competitive society and its economic system. Shaw later drew on this novel for his burlesque in heroic couplets, *The Admirable Bashville*.

Interest in the less intellectual forms of nineteenth-century theatre surfaces in *Immaturity* and in *The Irrational Knot*, where one of the principal characters is a star of burletta, admired by an upper-class, amateur comedian who plays the banjo. This strain in his work is kept relatively subdued in Shaw's earliest published plays: the blue-book themes of slum landlordism (*Widowers' Houses*) and prostitution (*Mrs. Warren's Profession*) advertised the Fabian socialist's reforming purpose and were associated with his lecture to the Fabian Society, later expanded into *The Quintessence of Ibsenism*, introducing the Norwegian dramatist as a social iconoclast. Structural features of the Ibsen social play are imitated in several early Shavian dramas: the retrospective action, involving interpretation and re-interpretation of the past, is clear in *Mrs. Warren's Profession*; the extended *raisonnement* with which Ibsen ended *A Doll's House* also marks the end of *Candida* (which Shaw described as an English version of the same situation, but with the man as the doll); the Dickensian caricature-figure that intrudes into Act I and reappears, perhaps transformed, towards the end of the play (Lickcheese in *Widowers' Houses* and later Doolittle in *Pygmalion*, recalling Ibsen's Engstrand and Brendel). But it is for a strictly philosophical, not stylistic, naturalism that Shaw declares himself in the Preface to *Plays Pleasant*: "To me the tragedy and comedy of life lie in the consequences ... of our persistent attempts to found our institutions on the ideals suggested to our imaginations by our half-satisfied passions, instead of on a genuinely scientific natural history." Indeed Ibsen as author of *Peer Gynt* offered a major precedent for the blending of fantasy with moral allegory which is characteristic of so much of Shaw's later work.

Failure to secure more than a few private performances of his "Unpleasant" plays led Shaw to change his tactics and strengthen the comic element in his work. He turned to the mock-heroic variety of burlesque in *Arms and the Man*, and the piece calls for an evidently artificial, exaggerated style of acting in most of its roles. *You Never Can Tell* has taken a hint from the phase in the development of pantomime when the characters of the opening story doubled with those of the attached harlequinade, and both action and dialogue are devised to suggest the stock situations and sprightly stock types of the *commedia dell'arte* tradition. Not until *The Apple Cart* and *Geneva* did Shaw describe his work as "political extravaganza," but already in the 1890's he was establishing a continuity with the theatrical entertainments most skilfully devised in the middle of the nineteenth century by J. R. Planché. *Androcles and the Lion* includes the simplest Shavian variation on the extravaganza mode; *Caesar and Cleopatra* manages to combine historical and Shakespearian burlesque; the early scenes, the epilogue, and some of the characters in *Saint Joan*, including the Dauphin and intermittently Joan herself, belong to the same theatrical category. The capacity of parody to retain some distillation of mood from the original it travesties is already realised in the anti-romanticism of *Arms and the Man*; it is outstandingly illustrated, in a more limited instance, in Bloomfield-Bonnington's muddled and misapplied quotations from Shakespeare, in *The Doctor's Dilemma*. This seems to give Shaw the medium in which he is best able to convey the often poignant human emotions at the heart of his plays, and stage presentations of his drama succeed to the measure that they realise the pure grain of truthful feeling among the absurdities.

A substratum of burlesque may be concealed under the superficial naturalism of contemporary situations and characters. The secret is revealed in the detachable hell scene of *Man and Superman*, in which Tanner dreams of himself as Don Juan. *Candida* guards its secret in an almost obscurantist way, linked with Shaw's personal ambivalence towards mother figures which emerges in play after play. The subcategory of burlesque which embodies classical myth in familiar domestic form serves him as a means of portraying the hold of the domestic ideal, with its virtual worship of virgin-mother goddesses, on late Victorian society. In *Pygmalion* he uses classical myth as a form of metaphor, in combination with a fairy extravaganza of Cinderella. When he came to write *Heartbreak House*, mythological burlesque emerged in a more grandiose form under the influence of Wagnerian music-drama. Then in *Back to Methuselah*, the "metabiological pentateuch," parody almost returns to its matrix, becoming the thing it travesties.

It was through the movement to establish a National Theatre that Shaw eventually, in 1904, gained command of a theatre public. With the first of his "national" plays put on by the Court Theatre management of Vedrenne and Granville-Barker, *John Bull's Other Island*, he set about using the stage more blatantly as a forum for public debate, debate, in this instance on the Irish Question. The fluid form, in which comic episodes, character turns, and set discussions were loosely strung together, ensured a mood of relaxation in which ideas could be exploded most forcefully on the governing classes. *Major Barbara*, with a much tighter dialectical structure reinforcing the mythic element, is Shaw's most impressive examination of the theme of political power, and its complex system of ironies makes doubtful the critical reading, not confined to Marxists, which represents it as the author's abandonment of socialism. Playing devil's advocate is a recurrent Shavian intellectual trick which led to unsubtle charges of Fascism against *On the Rocks*. This raises the question of how politically influential Shaw's drama has been, and whether doctrine has been sacrificed to entertainment, or confused in overloaded, overcomplex imaginative structures. The problem has to be considered play by play; but it can be said, as of his nearest European analogue,

Brecht, that Shaw's comedic brilliance and his geniality tend to enliven the mind and break down prejudice.

The First World War and Granville-Barker's withdrawal from the theatre left Shaw for a time without access to the stage. One effect of this was the turning of *Back to Methuselah*, in the course of writing, into non-theatrical literature, though even this has managed to hold the stage in a few productions. Barry Jackson, founder of the Malvern Shaw Festival, came to the rescue, but a number of Shaw's later plays have still had little theatrical testing and exploration.

—Margery Morgan

SHEPARD, Sam. American. Born in Fort Sheridan, Illinois, 5 November 1943. Educated at Duarte High School, California; Mount San Antonio Junior College, Walnut, California, 1961–62. Married O-Lan Johnson Dark in 1969; one son. Worked as a "hot walker" at Santa Anita Race Track, a stable hand, sheep shearer, herdsman and orange picker, all in California; car wrecker, Charlemont, Massachusetts; busboy at the Village Gate, a waiter at Marie's Crisis Cafe, and musician with the Holy Modal Rounders, all in New York. Recipient: Obie Award, 1967, 1977; Guggenheim Fellowship, 1968, 1971; National Institute of Arts and Letters award, 1974; Brandeis University Creative Arts Award, 1975.

PUBLICATIONS

Plays

> *Cowboys* (produced 1964).
> *Rock Garden* (produced 1964; excerpt produced in *Oh! Calcutta!*, 1969). In *The Unseen Hand and Other Plays*, 1971.
> *Up to Thursday* (produced 1964).
> *Dog* (produced 1964).
> *Rocking Chair* (produced 1964).
> *Chicago* (produced 1965). In *Five Plays*, 1967.
> *Icarus's Mother* (produced 1965). In *Five Plays*, 1967.
> *4-H Club* (produced 1965). In *Mad Dog Blues and Other Plays*, 1967.
> *Fourteen Hundred Thousand* (produced). In *Five Plays*, 1967.
> *Red Cross* (produced 1966). In *Five Plays*, 1967.
> *La Turista* (produced 1966). 1968.
> *Forensic and the Navigators* (produced 1967). In *The Unseen Hand and Other Plays*, 1971.
> *Melodrama Play* (produced 1967). In *Five Plays*, 1967.
> *Five Plays*. 1967.
> *Cowboys No. 2* (produced 1967). In *Mad Dog Blues and Other Plays*, 1971.
> *Shaved Splits* (produced 1969). In *The Unseen Hand and Other Plays*, 1971.
> *The Unseen Hand* (produced 1970). In *The Unseen Hand and Other Plays*, 1971.
> *Operation Sidewinder* (produced 1970). 1970.

529

Holy Ghostly (produced 1970). In *The Unseen Hand and Other Plays*, 1971.
Back Bog Beast Bait (produced 1971). In *The Unseen Hand and Other Plays*, 1971.
Mad Dog Blues (produced 1971). In *Mad Dog Blues and and Other Plays*, 1971.
Cowboy Mouth (produced 1971). In *Mad Dog Blues and Other Plays*, 1971.
The Unseen Hand and Other Plays. 1971.
Mad Dog Blues and Other Plays. 1971.
The Tooth of Crime (produced 1972). In *The Tooth of Crime, and Geography of a Horse Dreamer*, 1974.
Nightwalk, with Megan Terry and Jean-Claude van Itallie (produced 1973).
Blue Bitch (produced 1973).
Little Ocean (produced 1974).
Geography of a Horse Dreamer (produced 1974). In *The Tooth of Crime, and Geography of a Horse Dreamer*, 1974.
The Tooth of Crime, and Geography of a Horse Dreamer. 1974.
Action (produced 1974). In *Action, and The Unseen Hand*, 1975.
Action, and The Unseen Hand. 1975.
Killer's Head (produced 1975). In *Angel City ...*, 1976.
Angel City (produced 1976). In *Angel City ...*, 1976.
Angel City, Curse of the Starving Class, and Other Plays (includes *Killer's Head, Action, Mad Dog Blues, Cowboy Mouth, Rock Garden, Cowboys No. 2)*. 1976.
Curse of the Starving Class (produced 1977). In *Angel City ...*, 1976.
Suicide in B-flat (produced 1976).

Screenplays: *Me and My Brother*, with Robert Frank, 1967; *Zabriskie Point*, with others, 1970; *Ringaleevio*, with Murray Mednick, 1971.

Fiction

Hawk Moon (stories). 1972.

Other

Rolling Thunder Logbook. 1977.

*   *   *

Sam Shepard shapes the intellectual, physical, and temporal spaces where improvisational chance must happen for actors and audience. *Action*'s two couples seek through standard improvisations to re-create lost group or individual identities that would enable them to combat fear and cold and perhaps to act. The dramatic event characteristically witholds any genuine resolution and focuses on the procession of images within an occasioning action-celebration.

Most of Shepard's over thirty tragi-comedies, like *Action*, are set on a down-slope, "highs" during the decline of a revolution (*Shaved Splits*), a literacy-based civilization (*Fourteen Hundred Thousand*), or even Fourth-of-July celebrations (*Icarus's Mother*). Haunting power plays arise from striking theatrical exercises. Three characters demand attention as relationships deteriorate in *Red Cross*. Jim uses role-playing to dominate, until each woman glides off through her compelling sexual/death aria, down a ski-slope or undersea, to a private place. Returning to everyday hysteria and complacency, they leave their parasitic victim-tormentor bleeding and empty. Despite established orders of fundamentalism, Mariology, and gunslingers in *Back Bog Beast Bait*, a new beast slouches toward the stage to be born – with the aid of poisonous mushrooms, totem animals, and a bewitching Cajun fiddler.

Language is a probe, a veil, an incantation, a mystery of voices. Diction and syntax catch and flow directly from the styles of different contemporary subcultures. The verbal vitality of a young man in an electric chair (*Killer's Head*) ignores and postpones the inevitable with talk of trucks, rodeos, distances, racing, breeding. Disorganizing-discovering voices often surprise the speaker. The seventh son of "Holy Ghostly" leads his father through ancient-modern myths and shamanisms to embrace his own dying. Their languages slip one to another, and roles slide and erode identities.

In the brilliant, extended battle of words and musical movement of *The Tooth of Crime*, Hoss's original, characterizing virtuosity falls to the power-stealing dazzle of Crow's mimicry. The art-and-power theme – begun in *Cowboy Mouth* and *Melodrama Play*, toyed with in *Mad Dog Blues* – finally bleeds through its images. *Angel City* explores the same theme with movies, instead of pop-rock. Indian magic reinforces its artists' mystery (intuition-inspiration) until the ultimate disaster film engulfs the audience too: "Even chaos has a form!" *Geography of a Horse Dreamer* charts the broken flow of inspiration through race-track and criminal images, until brothers' shotguns save the dreamer's magic neckbone from falling into a medicine bundle. Primitive magic that decorates the matched panels of punning *La Turista* is the overwhelming ground of power in *Operation Sidewinder*, *Holy Ghostly*, and *Back Bog Beast*, but it becomes a dangerous net-below in these later, and better, plays. Rituals cannot prevent the sale and destruction of a California family and farm in *Curse of the Starving Class*. Man is caught but falls through the magic charts or totems. Keeping Shepard's special coherence, *Action* and *Curse* somehow make his notoriously bizarre images, arias, and rituals feel inevitable as Russian realism.

This prolific young playwright knowingly freshens the conventions, terror, and pleasure essential to theatre.

—John G. Kuhn

SHERIDAN, Richard Brinsley (Butler). Irish. Born in Dublin, 30 October 1751; moved with his family to Bath, 1770. Educated at Harrow School, Middlesex, 1762–68; Waltham Abbey School, 1772–73; Middle Temple, London, 1773. Married 1) Elizabeth Ann Linley in 1773 (died, 1792), one son; 2) Esther Jane Ogle in 1795, one son. Part-owner and Director of the Drury Lane Theatre, London, 1776; served in Parliament, first as Member for Stafford, then Westminster, then Ilchester, 1780–1812: Under-Secretary of State for Foreign Affairs in the Rockingham Administration, 1782, and Secretary of the Treasury in the coalition ministry, 1783; manager of the Warren Hastings trial by Parliament, 1788–94; Treasurer of the Navy, 1806; Member of the Privy Council. *Died 7 July 1816.*

PUBLICATIONS

Collections

Works, edited by F. Stainworth. 1874.
Plays and Poems, edited by R. Crompton Rhodes. 3 vols., 1928.
Letters, edited by Cecil Price. 3 vols., 1966.
Dramatic Works, edited by Cecil Price. 2 vols., 1973.

Plays

> *The Rivals* (produced 1775).   1775; edited by R. L. Purdy, 1935.
> *St. Patrick's Day; or, The Scheming Lieutenant* (produced 1775).   1788.
> *The Duenna*, music by Thomas Linley and others (produced 1775).   1775.
> *A Trip to Scarborough*, from the play *The Relapse* by Vanbrugh (produced 1777).   1781.
> *The School for Scandal* (produced 1777).   1780.
> *The Camp*, music by Thomas Linley (produced 1778).   1795.
> *The Critic; or, A Tragedy Rehearsed* (produced 1779).   1781.
> *The Storming of Fort Omoa* (interlude in *Harlequin Fortunatus* by Henry Woodward; produced 1780).
> *Robinson Crusoe; or, Harlequin Friday*, music by Thomas Linley (produced 1781).   Songs published 1781.
> *The Glorious First of June*, with James Cobb (benefit entertainment, produced 1794).   Songs published 1794; revised version, as *Cape St. Vincent* (produced 1797), songs published 1797.
> *The Stranger*, from a translation by Benjamin Thompson of a play by Kotzebue (produced 1798).
> *Pizarro*, from a play by Kotzebue (produced 1799).   1799.
> *The Forty Thieves*, with Charles Ward and Colman the Younger, music by Michael Kelly (produced 1806).   1808; as *Ali Baba*, 1814.

Verse

> *The Ridotto of Bath: A Panegyric.*   1771.
> *The Love Epistle of Aristaenetus*, with Nathaniel Halhed.   1771.
> *The Rival Beauties*, with Miles Peter Andrews(?).   1772.
> *Verses to the Memory of Garrick.*   1779; as *The Tears of Genius*, 1780.

Other

> *A Familiar Epistle to the Author of the Epistle to William Chambers.*   1774.
> *Speeches.*   5 vols., 1816.

Bibliography: in *Plays and Poems*, 1928.

Reading List: *Sheridan* (biography) by Walter S. Sichel, 2 vols., 1909; *Harlequin Sheridan: The Man and the Legends* by R. Crompton Rhodes, 1933; *Sheridan of Drury Lane* by Alice Glasgow, 1940; *Sheridan* by Lewis Gibbs, 1947; *Sheridan and Kotzebue: A Comparative Essay* by G. Sinko, 1949; *Sheridan: The Track of a Comet* by Madeleine Bingham, 1972; *Sheridan's Comedies: Their Contexts and Achievements* by Mark S. Auburn, 1977; *Sheridan and the Drama of Georgian England* by John Loftis, 1977.

*   *   *

   Sheridan's first comedy, *The Rivals*, was produced in 1775, as were *St. Patrick's Day; or, The Scheming Lieutenant*, a farce, and *The Duenna*, a comic opera. *The Duenna* made his name. Then he adapted Vanbrugh's *The Relapse* (1696) to suit the greater refinement of his own age and called it *A Trip to Scarborough*; it was staged in February 1777, and followed in the same year by *The School for Scandal*; two years later came *The Critic*. With the exception of *Pizarro*, which he adapted from the German of Kotzebue in 1799, and some minor work, his dramatic career was compressed into four years.

The Rivals is characterized by liveliness and vitality. The plot is skilfully devised, the dialogue is fresh, and the characters, though types, are well differentiated and probably created with particular actors and actresses in mind, for Sheridan knew about the theatre from an early age: his father was an actor and the author of a successful farce as well as a teacher of elocution, and his mother had written successful comedies. Sheridan set the action of *The Rivals* in Bath, where his father had set up his school of elocution in 1770, and where his own youth had been socially successful. He danced and flirted and observed the fashionable life of this elegant spa, with its concerts, plays, and balls, its circulating libraries, cards, and scandal occupying the time of the people of distinction who frequented it. He captured its ethos well in *The Rivals*. One heroine, Lydia Languish, headlong and romantic, derives much of her silliness from her diet of light reading, and the other, Julia Melville, is sentimental in the eighteenth-century manner. Jack Absolute refuses his father's plans for him until he finds that the girl chosen is Lydia whom he loves – but there is the complication that he has pretended to be Ensign Beverley, to cater to Lydia's romantic nature. Jack's relationship with his autocratic father adds to the play's liveliness, but the other hero, Faulkland, who suffers from jealousy, can seem sickly to a modern audience in his fashionably sentimental speeches to Julia. But Sir Lucius O'Trigger, the fire-eating Irishman, and Mrs. Malaprop, vulgar, ambitious, a magnificent mishandler of language, give the play its own particular comic – and farcical – flavour. Vitality and speed of action have kept this play successful on the stage.

The School for Scandal is more serious, for Sheridan was satirising the excesses of contemporary journalism and scandal-mongering. But what he created in his mockery of the polite world of his own day was lasting comedy. He used proven ingredients, lovers kept apart and finally rewarded, mistaken identity, the country girl out of her depth in the life of the town, the reassessment of an apparent rake, and, above all, the exposure – and, significantly, the explanation – of hypocrisy. It is all done very effectively, with sparkling conversation, a clever, indeed complex, plot of intrigue, a comedy of manners which exposes the soulful sentimentality of contemporary drama, the slandering, the malice, selfishness, and hypocrisy of contemporary society. Sheridan's ironies are clear: he distinguished between appearance and reality brilliantly, without the coarseness or indeed the immorality of Restoration comedy; he supplied suspense, the ludicrous situation, the unexpected reversal; he knew what kept – and still keeps – an audience amused. And so the contrast between the Surface brothers, the effect of the screen's falling upon the main characters, the reconciliation of Sir Peter and Lady Teazle, the marriage of Charles and Maria are all timeless in achievement.

Sheridan's views of comedy emerge not only in the second prologue to *The Rivals* but in *The Critic*, which was inspired by Buckingham's *The Rehearsal*. In it he mocked his contemporary Cumberland in the character of Sir Fretful Plagiary, and contemporary critics in the characters Puff and Sneer. This play is an amusing parody of contemporary dramatic techniques, which were often fairly crude – and so there are often references which are obscure to modern audiences or readers. *The Critic* is in effect a series of sketches, designed as an after-play to *Hamlet* – hence when Tilburina burlesques Ophelia's speech the audiences would have had the original in mind. Sheridan is exposing dull dialogue, artificial devices and asides, the melodrama inherent in plots which were unsophisticatedly resolved, the insistence upon fashion in dress, stereotyped delivery of lines, and crude acting in badly illuminated auditoriums. In fact, he is giving us a somewhat exasperated manager's view of the unsatisfactory elements of the stage in his own day: but he does it, as usual, with the light touch and sense of absurdity which illuminate all his own drama.

—A. Norman Jeffares

SHERRIFF, R(obert) C(harles).   English.   Born in Kingston upon Thames, Surrey, 6 June
1896. Educated at Kingston Grammar School; New College, Oxford, 1931–34. Served as a
Captain in the East Surrey Regiment, 1917. Entered the Sun Insurance Company, 1914.
Fellow, Society of Antiquaries; Fellow, Royal Society of Literature. *Died 13 November 1975.*

PUBLICATIONS

Plays

    Profit and Loss (produced 1923).
    Cornlow-in-the-Downs (produced 1923).
    Badger's Green (as *Mr. Birdie's Finger,* produced 1926; revised version, as *Badger's
       Green,* produced 1930).   1930.
    Journey's End (produced 1928).   1929.
    Windfall (produced 1934).
    St. Helena, with Jeanne de Casalis (produced 1936).   1934.
    Two Hearts Doubled: A Playlet.   1934.
    Goodbye Mr. Chips (screenplay), with Claudine West and Eric Maschwitz, in *The Best
       Pictures 1939–1940,* edited by Jerry Wald and Richard Macaulay.   1940.
    Mrs. Miniver (screenplay), with others, in *Twenty Best Film Plays,* edited by John
       Gassner and Dudley Nichols.   1943.
    Miss Mabel (produced 1948).   1949.
    Quartet: Stories by W. Somerset Maugham, Screenplays by Sherriff.   1948.
    Trio: Stories and Screen Adaptations, with W. Somerset Maugham and Noel
       Langley.   1950.
    Odd Man Out (screenplay) with F. L. Green, in *Three British Screen Plays,* edited by
       Roger Manvell.   1950.
    Home at Seven (produced 1950).   1950.
    The Kite, in *Action: Beacon Lights of Literature,* edited by Georgia G. Winn and
       others.   1952.
    The White Carnation (produced 1953).   1953.
    The Long Sunset (broadcast 1955; produced 1955).   In *Plays of the Year 12,* 1956.
    The Telescope (broadcast 1956; produced 1957).   1957.
    A Shred of Evidence (produced 1960).   1961.

Screenplays: *The Invisible Man,* 1933; *The Road Back,* with Charles Kenyon, 1937;
Goodbye Mr. Chips, with Claudine West and Eric Maschwitz, 1939; *The Four Feathers,*
with Arthur Wimperis and Lajos Biro, 1939; *That Hamilton Woman* (*Lady Hamilton*),
with Walter Reisch, 1941; *Unholy Partners,* with others, 1941; *This Above All,* 1942;
Mrs. Miniver, with others, 1942; *Stand By for Action,* with others, 1943; *Forever and a
Day,* with others, 1944; *Odd Man Out,* with F. L. Green, 1947; *Quartet,* 1948; *Mr.
Know-All* (in *Trio*), 1950; *No Highway* (*No Highway in the Sky*), with Alec Coppel and
Oscar Millard, 1951; *The Dam Busters,* 1955; *The Night My Number Came Up,* 1955;
Storm over the Nile, with Lajos Biro and Arthur Wimperis, 1955.

Radio Plays: *The Long Sunset,* 1955; *The Night My Number Came Up,* 1956; *The
Telescope,* 1956; *Cards with Uncle Tom,* 1958.

Television Play: *The Ogburn Story,* 1963.

Fiction

>*Journey's End,* with Vernon Bartlett. 1930.
>*The Fortnight in September.* 1931.
>*Greengates.* 1936.
>*The Hopkins Manuscript.* 1939; revised edition, as *The Cataclysm,* 1958.
>*Chedworth.* 1944.
>*Another Year.* 1948.
>*The Wells of St. Mary's.* 1962.

Other

>*King John's Treasure: An Adventure Story* (juvenile). 1954.
>*No Leading Lady: An Autobiography.* 1968.
>*The Siege of Swayne Castle* (juvenile). 1973.

*　　*　　*

R. C. Sherriff has been an excellent and prolific screenwriter. Among his first-rate or even classic films have been *The Invisible Man, Goodbye Mr. Chips, Lady Hamilton* (*That Hamilton Woman*), *Odd Man Out, Quartet,* and *The Dam Busters.* These and many other cinema achievements and his fiction are all discussed in his readable autobiography, *No Leading Lady.* But Sherriff is chiefly known as a playwright, and that for only one of his plays, the first that took him from amateur theatricals (*Profit and Loss, Mr. Birdie's Finger*) to London. That is the war drama set in a dugout under fire at St. Quentin in World War I, *Journey's End.*

Journey's End is a very sentimental play, more sentimental than *What Price Glory?, Sergeant York,* or *All Quiet on the Western Front,* so (since men tend to be more sentimental than women, at least when it comes to war) let us quote a couple of women on the subject of the play's rather unthinking acceptance of sentiment and slaughter. First, Anita Block in *The Changing World in Plays and Theatre* (1939): "I freely admit all its fine qualities, but it is important for us to understand that *Journey's End* is an old-fashioned play exhibiting the time-honored ambivalent emotions of loathing war's cruelty while glorifying its victims as heroes.... The audience leaves the theatre weeping for dead heroes, but without a single clarifying or provocative idea on the subject of war." Albert Hunt (*Encore,* December 1959) is only one of the many who have noted in *Journey's End* "an acceptance of the values that make war possible."

Dame Rebecca West (in *Ending in Earnest,* 1931) finds *Journey's End* "enormously impressive and stirring" but also "neurotic" in its inspiration:

>To begin with, it is one more expression of the desperate infantilism characteristic of the modern young Englishman. I do not mean by that to quarrel with his emphasis on the tragedy of murdered youth which was the war's foulest offence, for that is legitimate and most beautifully contrived ... but one is disquieted by Mr. Sherriff's assumption that immaturity is the most important phase of existence. The older men in the play are represented as being not only protective to the boys, but deferential to them, as to people of obviously greater importance....
>
>The significance of this can be seen when one considers that there have been three first-rate plays written by young Englishmen since the war – *Prisoners of War,* by J. R. Ackerley; *Young Woodley,* by John Van Druten; and this *Journey's End;* and they all have this obsession with immaturity....

Chambers' Biographical Dictionary puts it succinctly when it notes that Sherriff "achieved an international reputation" with his first play, *Journey's End* but "later plays did not match up to his first." Still, one play as famous as *Journey's End* is no mean achievement and perhaps someday Sherriff's considerable gifts as a screenwriter will be studied.

—Leonard R. N. Ashley

SHERWOOD, Robert E(mmet). American. Born in New Rochelle, New York, 4 April 1896. Educated at Milton Academy, Massachusetts, 1909–14; Harvard University, Cambridge, Massachusetts, 1914–17, B.A. 1918. Served in the Canadian Black Watch, 1917–19; wounded in action, 1918; served as Special Assistant to the Secretary of War, Washington, D.C., 1939–42; Director, Overseas Branch, Office of War Information, 1942–44; Special Assistant to the Secretary of the Navy, Washington, D.C., 1945. Married 1) Mary Brandon in 1922 (divorced, 1934), one daughter; 2) Madeline Hurlock Connelly in 1935. Dramatic Editor, *Vanity Fair*, New York, 1919–20; Film Reviewer and Associate Editor, 1920–24, and Editor, 1924–28, *Life* magazine, New York; Literary Editor of *Scribner's Magazine*, New York, 1928–30; full-time playwright from 1930; Founder, with Elmer Rice, Sidney Howard, Maxwell Anderson, S. N. Behrman, and John F. Wharton, Playwrights Company, 1938. Secretary, 1935, and President, 1937–40, Dramatists Guild; President, American National Theatre and Academy, 1940. Recipient: Megrue Prize, 1932; Pulitzer Prize, 1936, 1939, 1941, and, for biography, 1949; American Academy of Arts and Letters Gold Medal, 1941; Academy Award, 1946; Bancroft Prize, for history, 1949; Gutenberg Award, 1949. D.Litt.: Dartmouth College, Hanover, New Hampshire, 1940; Yale University, New Haven, Connecticut, 1941; Harvard University, 1949; D.C.L.: Bishop's University, Lennoxville, Quebec, 1950. *Died 14 November 1955.*

PUBLICATIONS

Plays

> *The Road to Rome* (produced 1926). 1927.
> *The Love Nest* (produced 1927).
> *The Queen's Husband* (produced 1928). 1928.
> *Waterloo Bridge* (produced 1929). 1930.
> *This Is New York* (produced 1930). 1931.
> *Reunion in Vienna* (produced 1931). 1932.
> *Acropolis* (produced 1933).
> *The Petrified Forest* (produced 1935). 1935.
> *Idiot's Delight* (produced 1936). 1936.
> *The Ghost Goes West* (screenplay), with Geoffrey Kerr, in *Successful Film Writing* by
>   Seton Margrave. 1936.
> *Tovarich*, from a play by Jacques Deval (produced 1936). 1937.
> *The Adventures of Marco Polo* (screenplay), in *How to Write and Sell Film Stories* by
>   Frances Marion. 1937.
> *Abe Lincoln in Illinois* (produced 1938). 1939.
> *There Shall Be No Night* (produced 1940). 1940.

An American Crusader (broadcast 1941).   In The Free Company Presents, edited by
James Boyd, 1941.
Rebecca (screenplay), with others, in Twenty Best Film Plays, edited by John Gassner
and Dudley Nichols.   1943.
The Rugged Path (produced 1945).   Shortened version in The Best Plays of 1945–46,
edited by Burns Mantle, 1946.
Miss Liberty, music by Irving Berlin (produced 1949).   1949.
Second Threshold, from a play by Philip Barry (produced 1951).
Small War on Murray Hill (produced 1957).   1957.

Screenplays: The Lucky Lady, with James T. O'Donohoe and Bertram Bloch, 1926; Oh,
What a Nurse!, with Bertram Bloch and Daryl F. Zanuck, 1926; Age for Love, 1931;
Around the World in Eighty Minutes with Douglas Fairbanks, 1931; Cock of the Air, with
Charles Lederer, 1932; Roman Scandal, with George S. Kaufman, 1933; The Scarlet
Pimpernel, with others, 1935; The Ghost Goes West, with Geoffrey Kerr, 1936; Over the
Moon, with others, 1937; Thunder in the City, with others, 1937; The Adventures of
Marco Polo, 1938; The Divorce of Lady X, with Lajos Biro, 1938; Idiot's Delight, 1939;
Abe Lincoln in Illinois, 1940; Rebecca, with others, 1940; The Best Years of Our Lives,
1946; The Bishop's Wife, with Leonardo Bercovici, 1947; Man on a Tightrope, 1953;
Main Street to Broadway, with Samson Raphaelson, 1953.

Radio Play: An American Crusader, 1941.

Television Writing: The Backbone of America, 1954.

Fiction

The Virtuous Knight.   1931; as Unending Crusade, 1932.

Other

Roosevelt and Hopkins: An Intimate History.   1948; revised edition, 1950; as The White
House Papers of Harry L. Hopkins, 2 vols., 1948–49.

Editor, The Best Moving Pictures of 1922–23.   1923.

Reading List: Sherwood by R. Baird Shuman, 1964; The Worlds of Sherwood: Mirror to His
Times 1896–1939, 1965, and The Ordeal of a Playwright: Sherwood and the Challenge of
War, edited by Norman Cousins, 1970, both by John Mason Brown; Sherwood: Reluctant
Moralist by Walter J. Meserve, 1970.

*   *   *

Though of a generation very often described as "rootless" and "lost," Robert Sherwood
was a romantic idealist with a liberal outlook whose plays closely corroborated the
assumptions underlying the political philosophy of the Roosevelt administration and gave
them powerful artistic expression. Alive to the need of creating an art imbued with a social
and moral fervour, he believed that the one determining consideration for the future of the
theatre was "its ability to give its audiences something they can't obtain, more cheaply and
conveniently, in the neighbouring cinema palaces." The artist's lack of social purpose, he

pointed out in his address to the P.E.N. International Congress in 1950, gave him a guilty sense of inadequacy – the uneasy knowledge that reform, though needed, was not taking place. The supreme task of "all writers, young and old" was, therefore, to achieve a reconciliation of the "problems of the human heart with a world state of mind that appears to become increasingly inhuman."

Sherwood's anxious apprehension of the insidious threats posed by a world situation indifferent to finer human sentiments constitutes a dominant resonance of his dramatic art. His realistic problem plays – whether set in Finland under Russian attack (*There Shall Be No Night*), or in a hotel in the Alps (*Idiot's Delight*) or in a gasoline station and lunch room in the Arizona desert (*The Petrified Forest*) – often relied on an extreme situation, a background of war or violence, to highlight his protagonists' search for viable ethical values and their eventual affirmation of freedom and peace. Sherwood's pacifism, though closely attuned to the feeling of liberals during the Roosevelt era, was never parochial or chauvinistic and displayed dynamic, even militant, modulations of growth over the years. If his first play, *The Road to Rome*, dealing comically with Hannibal's decision to defer his march on Rome, represents a plea for absolute peace, his last important play, *There Shall Be No Night*, is characterised by the realisation that freedom has to be defended even at the cost of endangering peace temporarily. In fighting the Russians in Finland, the scientist-protagonist of *There Shall Be No Night*, therefore, fights for the emancipation of all men from oppression and unfreedom. Likewise, *The Rugged Path* can be read, at one level, as an idealist's resolve to join the war in defence of peace and human dignity.

Several of Sherwood's plays exemplify his belief that the ability to make personal sacrifice is an index of moral refinement. Sacrifice appears, in *The Petrified Forest*, as a necessary means of preventing Nature from "taking the world away from the intellectuals and giving it back to the apes." On the other hand, *Abe Lincoln in Illinois*, chronicling Lincoln's struggling years before his election to the presidency, sensitively focuses on the relationship between an individual's sacrifice and national interest. Returning to the same moral issue, *There Shall Be No Night* implies through the fate of its protagonist that "There is no coming to consciousness without pain."

Sherwood's moral bias often made him vulnerable to the charge of overt didacticism – and not without some justification. As one who always had his fingertips on the pulse of his age and depended securely on its grammar of assent, Sherwood, in a literary career spanning nearly three decades, rarely suggested new and daring departures from the opinions current in his milieu. As a result, the moralistic intentions of his plays tended to be so static that their appeal rarely extended beyond their topical issues. But it must also be recognized that his didacticism very often went beyond direct statements to become an integral aspect of dramatic form. In *Abe Lincoln in Illinois*, for example, the curtain is meant to drop just as the farewell crowd, which has been singing "John Brown's Body," reaches the line "His soul goes marching on." Also, his frequent use of comedy, as in *The Road to Rome* and *The Queen's Husband*, helped substantially in relieving the solemnity of potentially moralistic themes. Moreover, one sign of "health" that critics always detected in Sherwood was that his ironic consciousness did not overlook the flaws in his own plays and made him record them with rare candour and precision. To cite one instance, he found *The Road to Rome* defective, because it employed "the cheapest sort of device – making historical characters use modern slang."

Sherwood also experimented with several other kinds of writing, achieving mixed results. *The Virtuous Knight*, his early historic novel about the Third Crusade, was generally regarded as a failure, though its perusal in retrospect does provide useful insights into his treatment of the themes and techniques of character-delineation that were to be employed later in his plays. His scenario *The Best Years of Our Lives* won an Academy Award in 1946, but his TV show, *The Backbone of America*, produced a year before his death, turned out to be a dismal flop. The crowning success of his non-dramatic writing was his biography *Roosevelt and Hopkins*, based on his experience as special assistant to the Secretary of War, director of the Overseas Branch of the Office of War Information, and, more important, as Roosevelt's favourite speechwriter and unofficial adviser. The book, ranked among the finest histories of World War II written in the United States, received several awards.

In spite of his immense popular appeal in his own lifetime, Sherwood does not belong to the same class of playwrights as Eugene O'Neill, Arthur Miller, and Tennessee Williams. For this reason, as time passes, his plays are unlikely to be received with the same immediacy they once elicited. Still, there can be no denying that his realistic problem plays, inspirited as they were by his passion for freedom and peace, faithfully reflected the urges and anxieties of the American people and, in the attempt, made a significant contribution to American drama in the 1920's and 1930's.

—Chirantan Kulshrestha

SHIRLEY, James.   English.   Born in Walbrook, London, 18 September 1596. Educated at Merchant Taylors' School, London, 1608–12; St. John's College, Oxford, 1612, subsequently St. Catharine's College, Cambridge, B.A. c. 1618. Married Elizabeth Gilmet in 1618; three sons and two daughters. Ordained: parish priest in or near St. Albans, and Headmaster at Edward VI Grammar School in St. Albans, 1623 until he was converted to Roman Catholicism and resigned his positions c. 1625; settled in London, 1625, and began writing plays: became a favourite of the court; wrote for Ogilby's theatre in Dublin, after plague closed the London theatres, 1636–40; returned to London and continued to produce plays until Parliament closed the theatres in 1642; fought for the Royalists, under his patron, the Earl of Newcastle, 1642–44, then returned to London: taught school during the Commonwealth. *Died* (buried) *29 October 1666.*

PUBLICATIONS

Collections

   Dramatic Works and Poems, edited by William Gifford and Alexander Dyce.   6 vols., 1833.

Plays

   The School of Compliment (produced 1625).   1631; as *Love Tricks,* 1667.
   The Wedding (produced 1626?).   1629; edited by A. S. Knowland, in *Six Caroline Plays,* 1962.
   The Maid's Revenge (produced 1626).   1639.
   The Witty Fair One (produced 1628).   1633; edited by Edmund Gosse, in *Plays,* 1888.
   The Grateful Servant (produced 1629).   1630.
   The Traitor (produced 1631).   1635; edited by J. S. Carter, 1965.
   Love's Cruelty (produced 1631).   1640.
   The Humorous Courtier (as *The Duke,* produced 1631).   1640.
   The Arcadia, from the work by Sidney (produced before 1632).   1640.
   Changes; or, Love in a Maze (produced 1632).   1632.

The Ball (produced 1632).   1639; edited by Thomas Marc Parrott, in *Plays and Poems of Chapman*, 1914.

Hyde Park (produced 1632).   1637; edited by Edmund Gosse, in *Plays*, 1888.

The Bird in a Cage (produced 1632–33?).   1633.

A Contention for Honour and Riches.   1633; revised version, as *Honoria and Mammon*, 1658.

The Gamester (produced 1633).   1637.

The Young Admiral (produced 1633).   1637.

The Example (produced 1634).   1637.

The Triumph of Peace (produced 1634).   1634; edited by Edmund Gosse, in *Plays*, 1888.

The Opportunity (produced 1634).   1640.

The Night-Walker; or, The Little Thief, from a play by Fletcher (produced 1634).   1661.

The Lady of Pleasure (produced 1635).   1637; edited by A. S. Knowland, in *Six Caroline Plays*, 1962.

The Coronation (produced 1635).   1640.

Chabot, Admiral of France, from the play by Chapman (produced 1635).   1639; edited by Ezra Lehman, 1906.

The Duke's Mistress (produced 1636).   1638.

The Constant Maid (produced 1636–40?).   1640; as *Love Will Find Out the Way*, 1661.

The Royal Master (produced 1637).   1638; edited by A. W. Ward, in *Representative English Comedies*, 1914.

The Doubtful Heir (produced 1638?).   In *Six New Plays*, 1653.

The Country Captain, with William Cavendish (produced 1639?).   With *The Variety*, 1649; edited by A. H. Bullen, as *Captain Underwit*, in *Old English Plays 2*, 1883.

St. Patrick of Ireland (produced 1639?).   1640.

The Politician (produced 1639?).   1655.

The Gentleman of Venice (produced 1639).   1655.

The Imposture (produced 1640).   In *Six New Plays*, 1653.

The Brothers (produced 1641?).   In *Six New Plays*, 1653.

The Cardinal (produced 1641).   In *Six New Plays*, 1653; edited by Charles R. Forker, 1964.

The Court Secret (produced 1642).   In *Six New Plays*, 1653.

The Sisters (produced 1642).   In *Six New Plays*, 1653.

The Contention of Ajax and Ulysses for the Armour of Achilles (produced 1645–58?).   With *Honoria and Mammon*, 1658.

The Triumph of Beauty (produced ?).   In *Poems*, 1646.

Six New Plays.   1653.

Cupid and Death, music by Matthew Locke (produced 1653).   1653; edited by B. A. Harris, in *A Book of Masques in Honour of Allardyce Nicoll*, 1967.

Verse

Poems.   1646; edited by R. L. Armstrong, 1941; *Narcissus* edited by Elizabeth Story Donno, in *Elizabethan Minor Epics*, 1963.

The Rudiments of Grammar: The Rules Composed in Verse for the Greater Benefit and Delight of Young Beginners.   1656; revised edition, as *Manductio*, 1660.

Other

Via ad Latinam Linguam Complanata, The Way Made Plain to the Latin Tongue.   1649; as *Grammatica Anglo-Latina*, 1651.

The True Impartial History and Wars of the Kingdom of Ireland. 1693.

Bibliography: *Shirley: A Concise Bibliography* by S. A. and D. R. Tannenbaum, 1946; supplement in *Elizabethan Bibliographies Supplements 8* by C. A. Pennel and W. P. Williams, 1968.

Reading List: *The Relation of Shirley's Plays to the Elizabethan Drama* by R. S. Forsythe, 1914; *Shirley, Dramatist: A Biographical and Critical Study* by Arthur H. Nason, 1915; *Shirley: His Catholic Philosophy of Life* by S. J. Radtke, 1929.

*   *   *

James Shirley wrote as many plays as Shakespeare, and his work displays a quality and range which make him easily the most important dramatist for more than a decade before the closing of the theatres in 1642. Though never an actor, he was a thorough man of the theatre, and he built very successfully on the main dramatic patterns popular with Stuart playwrights, among whom Beaumont and Fletcher were for him supreme; their work, he declares in an Address to the Reader which he wrote for the 1647 Beaumont and Fletcher folio, is "the greatest monument of the scene that time and humanity have produced."

He is probably at his best in his comedies, which usually employ romantic multiple plots, with thin but dramatically effective characters and, especially when the setting is London, many realistic touches. In *Hyde Park* the high-spirited Mistress Carol (a simplified version of Shakespeare's Beatrice) had rather hear "the tedious tales of Holinshed" than lovers' speeches but is conquered by a suitor cleverer than she; the out-of-door scenes in the same play are enlivened by offstage sounds of racing in the Park and (for both realism and romance) the voices of cuckoo and nightingale to presage lovers' fortunes. Shirley is also capable of good epigrammatic wit, as in *The Lady of Pleasure*, where French is "one of the finest tongues for ladies to show their teeth in."

The tragi-comedies are typically noble and rhetorical, though lightened by occasional comic episodes. In *The Young Admiral*, which owes something to Lope de Vega, the brave hero and his sweetheart are captured by enemy forces who threaten to kill her unless he will lead them against his native Naples, but if he does this his father will be put to death in Naples. The characters are appealing enough to carry the contrived plot, and the skill of the playwright resolves all problems happily at the end.

The tragedies show a starker confrontation of good and evil. In *The Politician* the black-souled Gotharus attempts to usurp power in Norway from a weak king and a virtuous prince; ultimately he is poisoned by his hellish paramour the queen, who then poisons herself and dies with an anguished "forgive, forgive." Shirley's most famous tragedy, *The Cardinal*, which he himself called "the best of my flock," has a relatively simple plot, with an atmosphere of brooding evil which twice breaks into terrifying violence. The language is generally restrained, the blank verse admirably fluent.

Shirley also wrote the showiest of the Stuart masques (*The Triumph of Peace*) and many lyrics which compare well with those of his best contemporaries, to whom they were sometimes misascribed. One of his songs, "The glories of our blood and state," achieves a sombre dignity which has made it better remembered than the rest. It occurs as a dirge at the end of a short piece dramatised from Ovid, *The Contention of Ajax and Ulysses for the Armour of Achilles*, which Shirley perhaps intended, after Parliament had closed the theatres, for production by schoolboys.

—Rhodes Dunlap

SIMPSON, N(orman) F(rederick). English. Born in London, 29 January 1919. Educated at Emanuel School, London, 1930–37; Birkbeck College, University of London, 1950–54, B.A. (honours) 1954. Served in the Royal Artillery, 1941–43, and the Intelligence Corps, 1943–46. Married Joyce Bartlett in 1944; one child. Teacher, City of Westminster College, London, and extra-mural lecturer, 1946–62. Full-time playwright since 1963. Since 1976, Literary Manager of the Royal Court Theatre, London. Lives in London.

PUBLICATIONS

Plays

A Resounding Tinkle (produced 1957). In The Observer Plays, 1958; shortened version included in The Hole and Other Plays and Sketches, 1964.
The Hole (produced 1958). 1958.
One Way Pendulum (produced 1959). 1960.
Sketches in One to Another (produced 1959). 1960.
Sketches in You, Me and the Gatepost (produced 1960).
Sketches in On the Avenue (produced 1961).
Sketches in One over the Eight (produced 1961).
The Form (produced 1961). 1961.
Oh (produced 1961). In The Hole and Other Plays and Sketches, 1964.
The Hole and Other Plays and Sketches (includes shortened version of A Resounding Tinkle, The Form, Gladly Otherwise, Oh, One Blast and Have Done). 1964.
The Cresta Run (produced 1965). 1966.
We're Due in Eastbourne in Ten Minutes (televised, 1967; produced 1971). In Some Tall Tinkles, 1968.
Some Tall Tinkles: Television Plays (includes We're Due in Eastbourne in Ten Minutes, The Best I Can Do by Way of a Gate-Leg Table Is a Hundredweight of Coal, At Least It's a Precaution Against Fire). 1968.
Playback 625, with Leopoldo Maler (produced 1970).
How Are Your Handles? (includes Gladly Otherwise, Oh, The Other Side of London) (produced 1971).
Was He Anyone? (produced 1972). 1973.
In Reasonable Shape (produced 1977). In Play Ten: Ten Short Plays, edited by Robin Rook, 1977.
Anyone's Gums Can Listen to Reason, in Play Ten: Ten Short Plays, edited by Robin Rook. 1977.

Screenplays: One Way Pendulum, 1964; Diamonds for Breakfast, with Pierre Rouve and Ronald Harwood, 1968.

Radio Plays: Something Rather Effective, 1972; Sketches for Radio, 1974.

Television Plays: Make a Man, 1966; Three Rousing Tinkles series: The Father by Adoption of One of the Former Marquis of Rangoon's Natural Granddaughters, If Those Are Mr. Heckmondwick's Own Personal Pipes They've Been Lagged Once Already, and The Best I Can Do by Way of a Gate-Leg Table Is a Hundredweight of Coal, 1966; Four Tall Tinkles series: We're Due in Eastbourne in Ten Minutes, In a Punt with Friends Under a Haystack on the River Mersey, A Row of Potted Plants, and At Least It's a Precaution Against Fire, 1967; World in Ferment series, 1969; Charley's Grants series, 1970; Thank You Very Much, 1971; Elementary, My Dear Watson, 1973; Silver Wedding, 1974; An Upward Fall (Crown Court series), 1977.

Fiction

> *Harry Bleachbaker.* 1976; as *Man Overboard: A Testimonial to the High Art of Incompetence,* 1976.

Reading List: *Curtains* by Kenneth Tynan, 1961; *The Theatre of the Absurd* by Martin Esslin, 1961; *Dramatic Essays* by Nigel Dennis, 1962.

*   *   *

Although a coincidence of chronology tempted critics to pigeonhole N. F. Simpson alongside the dramatists of the absurd, his is a very English style of humour. His sense of man's sublime dependence on the inanimate owes more to Jerome K. Jerome and the early Paul Jennings than to Ionesco, and his plays keep company with Lewis Carroll in their plunges along the Möbius slopes of language, when language gets slightly out of phase with conventional logic.

Simpson's is a world in which effects tend to anticipate their causes. In *One Way Pendulum*, Kirby Groomkirby is thus a multiple murderer because he has a passion for wearing black, and so craves the instant kick of attending funerals. Indeed, he only finds himself on trial because his father has built a courtroom from a do-it-yourself kit in his front parlour, and its presence calls irresistibly for a trial. But this is no Kafkaesque affair: in spite of the damning evidence that not one of Kirby's victims is willing to speak in his defence, he is discharged, and his choir of speak-your-weight machines celebrates the event with a renewed attempt at the Hallelujah Chorus.

One Way Pendulum is the most successful of Simpson's stage plays because it never stretches its ideas too thin. *The Cresta Run* has moments of sublime lunacy, but the tenuous consistency of its "plot" actually weakens its impact − as if a throwaway comic were to attempt an extended monologue. For Simpson has been at his happiest at his most episodic − notably, in the succession of parodic sketches (including a climactic gathering of "The Critics") which added up to *A Resounding Tinkle*. In recent years he has thus tended to concentrate on work for television, and has succeeded in finding visual equivalents to those deftly deflected verbal transitions for which he was surely indebted to that vintage radio comedy, *The Goon Show*.

Thus, critics who have noted a certain pedantry in his humour may only be discerning the inherently more mechanical nature of anarchic comedy in live performance, the resources of the tape and video recorder perhaps offering fuller scope for Simpson's genius. So little comic innovation is there in the broadcasting media that it has to be stressed that this judgement is an attempt to define his art, not to diminish it: the relative infrequency of new work from him in recent years would certainly suggest a writer not quite certain that he has yet found his true medium.

—Simon Trussler

SOUTHERNE, Thomas. Irish. Born in Oxmantown, near Dublin, in Autumn 1660. Educated at Trinity College, Dublin (pensioner), 1676–78, M.A. 1696; entered the Middle Temple, London, 1678. Served as an Ensign in Princess Anne's Regiment, and rose to the command of a company, 1685–88. Thereafter devoted himself entirely to writing for the stage, at first as a protégé and disciple of Dryden; retired in 1726. *Died 22 May 1746.*

PUBLICATIONS

Collections

Plays, edited by T. Evans.   3 vols., 1774.

Plays

The Loyal Brother; or The Persian Prince (produced 1682).   1682; edited by P.
   Hamelius, 1911.
The Disappointment; or, The Mother in Fashion (produced 1684).   1684.
Sir Anthony Love; or, The Rambling Lady (produced 1690).   1691.
The Wives' Excuse; or, Cuckolds Make Themselves (produced 1691).   1692; edited by
   Ralph R. Thornton, 1973.
The Maid's Last Prayer; or, Any, Rather Than Fail (produced 1693).   1693; edited by
   Ralph R. Thornton, 1978.
The Fatal Marriage; or, The Innocent Adultery, from the story "The Nun" by Aphra
   Behn (produced 1694).   1694.
Oroonoko, from the story by Aphra Behn (produced 1695).   1696; edited by
   Maximillian E. Novak and David Stuart Rodes, 1976.
The Fate of Capua (produced 1700).   1700.
The Spartan Dame (produced 1719).   1719.
Money the Mistress (produced 1726).   1726.

Reading List: *Southerne, Dramatist* by John W. Dobbs, 1933; *The Comedy of Manners* by
Kenneth Muir, 1970.

*   *   *

Thomas Southerne's career as a dramatist was, like his life's span, a lengthy one. His first
play, *The Loyal Brother,* a panegyric to the Duke of York, appeared in the troubled year
1682; his last, *Money the Mistress,* a failed comedy, in 1726. His major works came apace
between 1690 and 1696: three comedies in the manners genre and two extraordinarily
popular tragedies in the pathetic vein.
    Of the comedies, *Sir Anthony Love* was best received; its success gave rise to a new
practice, the author's sixth-night benefit. The action is conventionally vigorous, the intrigues
multiplex; Southerne's twist lies in representing his rake-hero, Sir Anthony, by "the female
Montford bare above the knee." The next comedy, *The Wives' Excuse,* a flat failure,
paradoxically excites critical interest today as the link between the older plays of Etherege and
Wycherley and the revival of the manners genre by Congreve and Vanbrugh. The foibles of
fashionable Londoners are exhaustively chronicled, but the play devolves into a "problem
play" with its distressed heroine consciously choosing not to take the usual revenge on an
impertinent coxcomb of a husband. Stung by the failure, Southerne reverted to the sure-fire
formula of gallantry and intrigue in *The Maid's Last Prayer,* adding genuinely comic (nigh
farcical) scenes of amateur "musick-meetings," Lady Susan's dogged pursuit of men, any
man, rather than fail, and, curiously, one of the darkest senes of sexual revenge in dramatic
literature.
    The success of *The Fatal Marriage* and *Oroonoko* confirmed Southerne's popular
reputation in his own generation. Adapting both plots from the works of Aphra Behn,
Southerne commingled new action and characters, as well as counterpoint comic sub-plots,
to accentuate the pathos and distressed nobility of his sentimentalized tragic protagonists.

Each play remained an actor's vehicle well into the nineteenth century, Garrick having altered *The Fatal Marriage* in 1757 to *Isabella*.

Of the remaining plays, *The Disappointment* is an olio of dramatic elements; it points, however, to an interest in the distressed-heroine problem play. *The Fate of Capua*, a neo-classical tragedy set in the Second Punic War, was unsuccessful, despite moving individual scenes. *The Spartan Dame* was Southerne's true valedictory to the theatre, though it was really an old play, having been largely completed in 1687 but denied production because of its fable (from Plutarch) – usurpation by a daughter.

In a partisan age, Southerne managed to maintain widespread and abiding friendships: Dryden, Wycherley, Congreve, Dennis, Gildon, the Earls of Orrery; later Pope and his circle regarded him with affection; his literary mid-wifery to unproduced dramatists was legendary; and his dedications to Whigs or Tories were made with an eye to profit, not politics. In the theatre, Southerne's astute eye caught the changes in the audiences' taste and composition; he learned early to supply these new arbiters of the box and pit with drama of pathos – she-tragedies – not the out-of-style realistic, satiric comedy. Therein his popularity lay.

—Ralph R. Thornton

SOYINKA, Wole (Akinwande Oluwole Soyinka).   Nigerian.   Born in Abeokuta, Western Nigeria, 13 July 1934. Educated at the Government College, Ibadan; University of Leeds, Yorkshire, 1954–57, B.A. (honours) in English. Married; one son and three daughters. Play Reader, Royal Court Theatre, London, 1958–59; Research Fellow in Drama, University of Ibadan, 1960–61; Lecturer in English, University of Ife, 1962–63; Senior Lecturer in English, University of Lagos, 1964–67; Political Prisoner, for alleged pro-Biafra activities, Kaduna Prison, 1967–69; Director of the School of Drama, University of Ibadan, 1969–72. Research Professor in Drama, 1972–75, and since 1975 Professor of Comparative Literature, University of Ife. Founding Director of the Orisun Theatre and The 1960 Masks Theatre, Lagos and Ibadan. Recipient: Dakar Negro Arts Festival award, 1966; John Whiting Award, 1966. D.Litt.: University of Leeds, 1973. Lives in Nigeria.

PUBLICATIONS

Plays

   The Swamp Dwellers (produced 1958).   In *Three Plays*, 1963.
   The Lion and the Jewel (produced 1959).   1963.
   The Invention (produced 1959).
   A Dance of the Forests (produced 1960).   1963.
   The Trial of Brother Jero (produced 1960).   In *Three Plays*, 1963.
   Camwood on the Leaves (broadcast 1960).   1973.
   Three Plays.   1963.
   The Strong Breed (produced 1964).   In *Three Plays*, 1963.
   Kongi's Harvest (produced 1964).   1967.
   Before the Blackout (produced 1964).   N.d. (1965?).
   The Road (produced 1965).   1965.
   Madmen and Specialists (produced 1970; revised version, produced 1971).   1971.

The Jero Plays: The Trials of Brother Jero and Jero's Metamorphosis.   1973.
The Bacchae: A Communion Rite, from the play by Euripides (produced 1973).   1973.
Collected Plays:
  I. A Dance of the Forests, The Swamp Dwellers, The Strong Breed, The Road,
     The Bacchae.   1973.
  II. The Lion and the Jewel, Kongi's Harvest, The Trials of Brother Jero, Jero's
     Metamorphosis, Madmen and Specialists.   1974.
Death and the King's Horseman.   1975.

Screenplay: Kongi's Harvest, 1970.

Radio Play: Camwood on the Leaves, 1960.

Television Documentaries: Joshua: A Nigerian Portrait, 1962; Culture in Transition,
1963.

Fiction

The Interpreters.   1965.
Season of Anomy.   1973.

Verse

Idanre and Other Poems.   1967.
Poems from Prison.   1969.
A Shuttle in the Crypt.   1972.
Ogun Abibiman.   1977.

Other

The Man Died: Prison Notes.   1972.
In Person: Achebe, Awooner, and Soyinka at the University of Washington.   1975.
Myth, Literature, and the African World.   1976.

Editor, Poems of Black Africa.   1975.

Translator, The Forest of a Thousand Daemons: A Hunter's Saga, by D. A.
   Fagunwa.   1968.

Reading List: Mother Is Gold: A Study in West African Literature by A. Roscoe, 1971;
Soyinka by Gerald H. Moore, 1971, revised edition, 1978; The Writing of Soyinka by Eldred
D. Jones, 1973; The Movement of Transition: A Study of the Plays of Soyinka by Oyin
Ogunba, 1975.

                          *   *   *

Wole Soyinka is not only Nigeria's leading playwright but possibly the most versatile
writer at work in Africa today, having also excelled as a poet, novelist, essayist, critic, editor,
and translator. Born in 1934, Soyinka was educated in Ibadan and Leeds. On his return to
Nigeria in 1960, after nearly six years in Europe (one result of which was the much-

anthologised poem "Telephone Conversation," in which he wittily sums up on the racial prejudice of English landladies), Soyinka was appointed to a number of university posts. These afforded him, particularly at Ibadan and Ife, the chance to produce his own plays, sometimes acting in them himself. He also worked for Nigerian radio and television, and formed an acting company in Lagos called The 1960 Masks. Soyinka was arrested by the Federal Government in 1967 for alleged pro-Biafran activity. The result of his experiences in solitary confinement at Kaduna Prison are recorded with great bitterness in *The Man Died*, a set of prison notes which make little attempt to enter the fashionable spirit of magnanimity which followed the Federal victory.

Soyinka's early work as a dramatist showed his skill as a comic writer. In both *The Swamp Dwellers* and *The Lion and the Jewel* he deals with traditional village life, but in the second he is already experimenting with mime and dance elements as an integral part of the comedy.

Soyinka's plays have subsequently become more technically daring. In *A Dance of the Forests*, his highly ambiguous celebration of Nigerian independence, the mortal world and the divine are brought into conjunction in a half-satirical, half-fantastic blend of traditional Yoruba imagery, dance motifs, and masque. Soyinka has written ironic comedies like his Jero plays, where the main character is a charlatan preacher all too easily exploiting the gullibility of his fellow countrymen, but his most significant dramatic work in recent years is probably *Madmen and Specialists*. This play arises from the mood of war, and the aftermath of war, but the form it takes shows the influence of experimental drama in America (where an early version was first staged) and Europe. Recent work, such as *Death and the King's Horseman* and his new version of *The Bacchae* of Euripides, commissioned for performance by the National Theatre in London, show a growing concern to relate African experience with European.

Soyinka has always tried to express a broad humanity in his work which will not be narrowly nationalistic. Many of his cultural principals are set out in an illuminating critical book, *Myth, Literature, and the African World*. Here he admits a recognizable distinction between African and European aesthetics but believes that they should not operate in isolation from each other.

As a novelist Soyinka has been the subject of some controversy. *The Interpreters* has probably gained in reputation in recent years as African fiction in English has faced up to more contemporaneous themes and more complex relationships. The book concerns a group of young Nigerian intellectuals, capturing, largely through dialogue, their idealism and anticipation about the development of the new Africa. *Season of Anomy* may seem to possess a Joycean difficulty of presentation, but it corresponds to *Madmen and Specialists* in its attempts to make sense of the recent devastations of war. The publisher's description is apt – "an expression of the affirmative, humane response to chaos and blind social forces." Soyinka has also translated *The Forest of a Thousand Daemons*, a Yoruba novel by D. O. Fagunwa. The folk and fantasy material with which it deals has often been reflected in Soyinka's plays.

Idanre and *A Shuttle in the Crypt* are two collections of verse, written over several years. The tone of the second collection is even bleaker than the first, distilling not just the horror and pity of war but the sterility of modern politics:

> They do not bleed
> On whom the dunghill falls, nor they
> Whose bones are sucked of marrow
> In noon perversions of inhuman tongues.
> They do not bleed whose breaths are stilled
> In sludges or sewers, who slither down
> To death on the burst tumour of hate's
> Inventive mind, through chasms of the flight
> Of earth from rites of defilement,
> Dark of abomination. They do not bleed
> Whose wombs are bared to leprous lust

This extract from the long poem "Conversation at Night with a Cockroach" captures the morbid pessimism out of which Soyinka is only just beginning to emerge through the affirmative quality of works like *Season of Anomy*.

—Alastair Niven

STEELE, Sir Richard. Irish. Born in Dublin, baptized 12 March 1672. Educated at Charterhouse, London, where he met Joseph Addison, 1684–89; matriculated at Christ Church, Oxford, 1690; postmaster at Merton College, Oxford, 1691–94, but left without taking a degree. Enlisted as a cadet in the Duke of Ormonde's guards, 1694; Ensign in Lord Cutts's Regiment, 1695, and served as Cutts's confidential secretary, 1696–97; Captain, stationed at the Tower of London, by 1700; transferred as Captain to Lord Lucas's Regiment in 1702. Married 1) Margaret Ford Stretch in 1705 (died, 1706); 2) Mary Scurlock in 1707 (died, 1718), two sons and two daughters. Wrote extensively for the theatre, 1701–05; Gentleman-Writer to Prince George of Denmark, 1706–08; Gazetteer (i.e., Manager of the *Gazette*, the official government publication), 1707–10; Commissioner of Stamps, 1710–13; Founding Editor, *The Tatler*, to which Addison was the major contributor, 1709–11; Founder, and Editor with Addison, *The Spectator*, 1711–12; Founding Editor, *The Guardian*, 1713; elected Member of Parliament for Stockbridge, Hampshire, 1713, but expelled for anti-government views; Founding Editor, *The Englishman*, 1713–14, *The Lover*, 1714, and *The Reader*, 1714; on accession of George I, 1714, appointed Justice of the Peace, Deputy Lieutenant for the County of Middlesex, Surveyor of the Royal Stables at Hampton Court, and Supervisor of the Drury Lane Theatre, London: granted life patent of Drury Lane, 1715; Member of Parliament for Boroughbridge, Yorkshire, 1715; Founding Editor, *Town Talk*, 1715–16, *The Tea-Table*, and *Chit-Chat*, 1716; appointed Commissioner for Forfeited Estates in Scotland, 1716; quarrelled with Addison, 1719; Founding Editor, *The Plebeian*, 1719, and *The Theatre*, 1720; Member of Parliament for Wendover, Buckinghamshire, 1722; retired to Wales, 1724. Knighted, 1715. *Died 1 September 1729*.

Publications

Collections

    Correspondence, edited by R. Blanchard. 1941; revised edition, 1968.
    Plays, edited by Shirley S. Kenny. 1971.

Plays

    The Funeral; or, Grief a-la-Mode (produced 1701). 1702.
    The Lying Lover; or, The Ladies' Friendship (produced 1703). 1704.
    The Tender Husband; or, The Accomplished Fools (produced 1703). 1705.
    The Conscious Lovers (produced 1722). 1723.

Verse

The Procession: A Poem on Her Majesty's Funeral.   1695.
Occasional Verse, edited by R. Blanchard.   1952.

Other

The Christian Hero, An Argument Proving That No Principles But Those of Religion Are
    Sufficient to Make a Great Man.   1701; edited by R. Blanchard, 1932.
The Tatler, with Addison.   4 vols., 1710–11; edited by G. A. Aitken, 4 vols., 1898–99;
    selections edited by L. Gibbs, 1953.
The Spectator, with Addison.   8 vols., 1712–15; edited by D. F. Bond, 5 vols., 1965;
    selections edited by R. J. Allen, 1957.
An Englishman's Thanks to the Duke of Marlborough.   1712.
A Letter to Sir M. W[arton] Concerning Occasional Peers.   1713.
The Importance of Dunkirk.   1713.
The Guardian, with others.   2 vols., 1714; edited by Alexander Chalmers, 1802.
The Englishman (2 series, and an epistle).   3 vols., 1714–16; edited by R. Blanchard,
    1955.
The Crisis, with Some Seasonable Remarks on the Danger of a Popish Successor.   1714.
The French Faith Represented in the Present State of Dunkirk.   1714.
A Letter Concerning the Bill for Preventing the Growth of Schism.   1714.
Mr. Steele's Apology for Himself and His Writings.   1714.
A Letter from the Earl of Mar to the King.   1715.
A Letter Concerning the Condemned Lords.   1716.
Account of Mr. Desagulier's New-Invented Chimneys.   1716.
An Account of the Fish Pool, with Joseph Gillmore.   1718.
The Joint and Humble Address to the Tories and Whigs Concerning the Intended Bill of
    Peerage.   1719.
A Letter to the Earl of O—d Concerning the Bill of Peerage.   1719.
The Plebeian.   1719; edited by R. Hurd, in Addison's Works, 1856.
The Spinster, in Defence of the Woollen Manufactures.   1719.
The Crisis of Property.   1720.
A Nation a Family; or, A Plan for the Improvement of the South-Sea Proposal.   1720.
The State of the Case Between the Lord Chamberlain and the Governor of the Royal
    Company of Comedians.   1720.
The Theatre.   1720; edited by John Loftis, 1962.
Tracts and Pamphlets, edited by R. Blanchard.   1944.
Steele's Periodical Journalism 1714–16: The Lover, The Reader, Town Talk, Chit-Chat,
    edited by R. Blanchard.   1959.

Editor, The Ladies Library.   3 vols., 1714.
Editor, Poetical Miscellanies.   1714.

Reading List: Steele by Willard Connely, 1934; Steele at Drury Lane by John Loftis, 1952;
Steele, Addison, and Their Periodical Essays by Arthur R. Humphreys, 1959; Steele: The
Early Career, 1964, and The Later Career, 1970, both by Calhoun Winton.

*   *   *

Though best remembered as a periodical essayist, Sir Richard Steele began his literary
career in the theatre – if, that is, one forgets and forgives his moralizing tract The Christian

Hero, an unsuccessful attempt at self-admonition. His plays were frank attempts to make piety more palatable, while avoiding the sexual excesses for which Collier had condemned the stage, and which increasingly middle-class audiences were also finding offensive.

The first, *The Funeral*, has several touches of originality, notably in its satire on the undertaking business, its sprightly yet sympathetic treatment of its female characters, and its liveliness of plotting. Indeed, two of the participants in Gildon's *A Comparison Between the Two Stages* allege that in this latter respect the play resembles a farce more than it does a comedy, and it may be regretted that Steele never successfully evaded formal considerations of this kind – though two fragments, *The School of Action* and *The Gentleman*, do begin to assert the kind of freedom from the rules that Gay and Fielding more happily achieved.

The Lying Lover was unalleviated by realism, displayed less comic spirit, and was, as Steele ruefully admitted, "damn'd for its piety." Loosely derived from Corneille's *Le Menteur*, it features a pathetic repentance scene, in which its hero, Young Bookwit, awakens in prison to find that he has killed a rival in a drunken duel. For this he is duly contrite in blank verse, to the extent of putting forgiveness before honour. There is some wit in the quixotic Bookwit's romancing in the earlier scenes, and his respectful welcome to Newgate by his fellow inmates hints at the inverted morality of *The Beggar's Opera*: yet, just a few scenes later, Steele perpetrates a double shift in the plot, lacking any sense of its own fatal absurdity.

The Tender Husband, Steele's third play, also proved to be his last to reach the stage for nearly eighteen years. It has a female Quixote, or prototype Lydia Languish, as its heroine – and, indeed, the original of Tony Lumpkin in that heroine's cousin, Humphry Gubbin. Unfortunately, the sub-plot featuring the titular husband, who devises an unlikely test of his wife's faithfulness by disguising his own mistress as a suitor, disrupts the comic flow, and complicates the conclusion with a sentimental reconciliation.

In the following years, Steele was increasingly active as a Whig politician, his major literary achievement being, of course, the succession of periodicals he created, some written in collaboration with Joseph Addison. Of these, the best remembered are *The Tatler*, *The Spectator*, and *The Guardian*, with the irrelevantly titled *The Theatre* probably the most important of the later series. Whether or not Steele succeeded in his aim "to make the pulpit, the bar, and the stage all act in concert in the cause of piety, justice, and virtue" is arguable: but he certainly perfected a distinctive new form of clubable *belles lettres*, incidentally exploring techniques of characterization for his recurrent *personae* which were to be of significance to the early novelists, and publishing some first-rate dramatic criticism.

Although *The Conscious Lovers*, which did not reach the stage until 1722, was influential in the development of the *comédie larmoyante* in France, to the modern mind it merely demonstrates that, at its most sentimental, eighteenth-century comedy was no laughing matter. With the exception of its scenes below stairs – their purpose all too evidently to sugar a didactic pill – it is a distinctly unfunny play: yet, according to Steele, an audience's pleasure might be "too exquisite for laughter," and thus better expressed in the tears evoked by the inexpressibly virtuous behaviour of his hero, Young Bevil, and by the convenient reshufflings of the characters in the closing scene.

The mercantile morality of the play is at once over-explicit and interruptive, and its characters are in neither the humours nor the manners tradition, but mere ethical absolutes. No wonder that Fielding's Parson Adams considered it the first play fit for a Christian to read since the pagan tragedies – but then good Parson Adams lacked both irony and a sense of incongruity, as does *The Conscious Lovers*. Steele is better remembered by the feeling for both irony *and* incongruity in his earlier plays, and, of course, by his largeness of heart as a periodical essayist.

—Simon Trussler

STEWART, Douglas (Alexander).   Australian.   Born in Eltham, New Zealand, 6 May 1913.   Educated at New Plymouth Boys High School; Victoria University College, Wellington. Married Margaret Coen in 1946; one daughter. Literary Editor, *The Bulletin*, Sydney, 1940–61; Literary Advisor, Angus and Robertson Ltd., publishers, Sydney, 1961–73. Recipient: *Encyclopaedia Britannica* Award, 1968; Wilke Award, for non-fiction, 1975. O.B.E. (Officer, Order of the British Empire). Lives in Sydney.

PUBLICATIONS

Plays

Ned Kelly (produced 1944).   1943.
The Fire on the Snow and The Golden Lover: Two Plays for Radio.   1944.
Shipwreck (produced 1948).   1947.
Four Plays (includes *The Fire on the Snow, The Golden Lover, Ned Kelly, Shipwreck*).   1958.
Fisher's Ghost: The Historical Comedy (produced 1961).   1960.

Radio Plays: *The Fire on the Snow,* 1941; *The Golden Lover,* 1943; *The Earthquake Shakes the Land,* 1944.

Fiction

A Girl with Red Hair and Other Stories.   1944.

Verse

Green Lions.   1937.
The White Cry.   1939.
Elegy for an Airman.   1940.
Sonnets to the Unknown Soldier.   1941.
The Dosser in Springtime.   1946.
Glencoe.   1947.
Sun Orchids.   1952.
The Birdsville Track and Other Poems.   1955.
Rutherford and Other Poems.   1962.
The Garden of Ships: A Poem.   1962.
(Poems).   1963; as *Selected Poems,* 1969, 1973.
Collected Poems, 1936–1967.   1967.

Other

The Flesh and the Spirit: An Outlook on Literature.   1948.
The Seven Rivers (on angling).   1966.
The Broad Stream (criticism).   1975.
Norman Lindsay: A Personal Memoir.   1975.

Editor, *Coast to Coast: Australian Stories.*   1945.

Editor, with Nancy Keesing, *Australian Bush Ballads*.   1955.
Editor, with Nancy Keesing, *Old Bush Songs and Rhymes of Colonial Times, Enlarged and Revised from the Collection by A. B. Paterson*.   1957.
Editor, *Voyager Poems*.   1960.
Editor, *The Book of Bellerive*, by Joseph Tischler.   1961.
Editor, *(Poems)*, by A. D. Hope.   1963.
Editor, *Modern Australian Verse: Poetry in Australia II*.   1964.
Editor, *Selected Poems*, by Hugh McCrae.   1966.
Editor, *Short Stories of Australia: The Lawson Tradition*.   1967.
Editor, with Nancy Keesing, *The Pacific Book of Bush Ballads*.   1967.
Editor, with Nancy Keesing, *Bush Songs, Ballads, and Other Verse*.   1968.
Editor, with Beatrice Davis, *Best Australian Short Stories*.   1971.
Editor, *The Wide Brown Land: A New Selection of Australian Verse*.   1971.
Editor, *Australia Fair*.   1976.

Reading List: *Stewart* by Nancy Keesing, 1965; *Stewart* by Clement Semmler, 1975.

*   *   *

Douglas Stewart is one of the most prolific and versatile of Australian writers. Well-known as a poet and radio playwright, he has also written short stories, essays, and biography. His account of the Sydney *Bulletin*, whose Red Page he edited from 1940 to 1960, is lively, informative, and graceful, and an important contribution to local literary history.

Stewart's *Collected Poems* assembled the best of his verse from 1936 onwards, and included some not before published in book-form. Though he is a New Zealander by birth, few native Australians have developed Stewart's feeling for Australian landscape and animal life. His relationship with the natural world has been in turns egocentric, anthropomorphic, even animistic, but in the later poems it has become fraternal and non-attached. Where once he would have wished an insect to look at the world as a man would, he now tries to see the world, not merely as an insect would see it, which would be affectation, but through the eyes of an insect without surrendering the vision of a man. Courtesy is what distinguishes Stewart's atttitude to the non-human world, and the reserve which is part of his own nature is scrupulously respected in other creatures, as the volume *Sun Orchids* makes clear. The mood of his verse is primarily one of good humour and well-being, and, in a darkening world living on the edge of a balance of terror, such a mood strikes many readers as superficial and evasive. The long narrative poem *Rutherford* wrongly attributes to Rutherford misgivings about the outcome of his researches, and in spite of some fine passages, it never really comes to grip with the central moral problem of post-Baconian science, while the weight of the verse suggests that the author shares the fuzzy optimism of his hero. Against this, however, should be set the magnificent ballad-sequence, *Glencoe*, with its fine structural coherence, its dramatic appropriateness and the timeless urgency of its theme: the wanton spirit of senseless faction in mankind which guarantees the suffering of the innocent. The main part of the sequence ends with one of Stewart's finest lyrics, the lament "Sigh, wind in the pine," with its grim warning:

> Oh life is fierce and wild
> And the heart of the earth is stone,
> And the hand of a murdered child
> Will not bear thinking on.
>
> Sigh, wind in the pine,
> Cover it over with snow;
> But terrible things were done
> Long, long ago.

The poem was written not long after another massacre: Hiroshima.

Those who deny Stewart the capacity for reflection must take *Glencoe* into account. They must also consider that his reflective exercises are as a rule conducted far below the surface of his poems, as the early poem "The River" makes plain: what he sees he has no objection to sharing, what he really thinks or feels, he seems to regard as largely his own business. His principal gift as a poet is the ability to transfigure the commonplace, to catch a moment of heightened experience and endow it with a history. The facility with which he seizes the poetic moment has sometimes led him into verbosity through over-exercise, and in some of his occasional verse there is a sense of strain. At times indeed he can degenerate into producing a kind of poetic "chirruping." Stewart's preoccupation with an immediate moment of intense awareness has tended to obscure the metaphysical base from which he works, expressed in paradoxical images of fire and snow, heat and cold, which perhaps hint at a struggle between the rational and the irrational in his own nature. Flame and snow come together in his earliest poem "Day and Night with Snow" and in the latest piece in *Collected Poems*, "Flowering Place," while variants of the same image crop up throughout the work, in "Spider Gums," from *The Birdsville Track*; in "The River," from *The Dosser in Springtime*; and in "Flower of Winter," from *Sun Orchids*. There is nothing static about this symbolism: fire is as much an image of destruction as it is of the continuity of life; snow, cold, as much an image of potentiality, of steadfastness, as of death. His grasp of this archetypal imagery seems to be intuitional rather than intellectual, but for a lyrist, this is hardly a disadvantage. The lack of intellectual rigour however becomes something of an obstacle in his prose work, especially in the literary criticism, in spite of its general good sense. His criticism, in *The Flesh and the Spirit* and *The Broad Stream*, belongs to the same impressionistic genre, without being as captious or exhibitionist, as that of his more famous predecessor on the *Bulletin* A. G. Stephens. It is intuitional, idiosyncratic, intensely subjective, capable of crystallising the essentials of a work under scrutiny, but liable to the temptations of the large, arresting generalisation, which will not stand up to close analysis because it takes little account of what is extra-literary. It is never dull, always stimulating, often prejudiced, on occasions brilliant, and like much of the verse, often humorous.

Stewart's plays, written mainly for radio and all in verse, are strangely static: there is a much more genuinely dramatic element in the *Glencoe* ballads, or the poem "Terra Australis" than in *Fire on the Snow* or *Ned Kelly*. It is odd, for instance, that a dramatist should always choose situations which involve the characters in so much merely waiting around and talking. *Fire on the Snow*, about Scott's last expedition, unlike *Ned Kelly* and *Shipwreck*, is in addition devoid of human conflict; the enemy is nature, and endurance the only possible response. Written for radio, it is not a play for theatre at all; and even *Ned Kelly*, which lends itself more easily to the stage, almost founders from excessive verbalisation. *Shipwreck* is a more shapely drama, in which the tendency to lyric expansion is kept under control. Even so, there is too much reliance at certain points on clumsy reporting of off-stage events. This play, however, is securely founded on a real moral conflict: whether a captain is justified in making a dangerous journey to bring help to his shipwrecked crew and passengers, when he must leave them on the verge of mutiny under precarious control. *Shipwreck* is perhaps the strongest and most interesting of Stewart's plays, though not the most endearing. *The Golden Lover*, on a New Zealand theme, is that. It dramatises the difficulty of choosing between dream and reality, between unearthly, intense love, and domestic security; and in the Maori girl Tawhai, her lumpish husband Ruarangi, and Whana, the "golden lover" from the People of the Mist, Stewart has succeeded in creating three of his most convincing characters. As with *Ned Kelly*, however, the ending is left ambiguous, or rather it seems to be ambiguous, until we reflect that the voices of commonsense have been given all the best tunes. It is difficult to avoid the conclusion, when one considers all the plays together, that the one value Stewart unequivocally endorses is sheer survival.

It is in the prose, finally, especially the biographical writing on Kenneth Slessor and Norman Lindsay, that doubts make themselves felt about Stewart's ultimate seriousness. The weight given to the superficial picturesqueness of some of the figures he admires, the flavour of old boy nostalgia for Bohemia, seem to sort ill with the realities of the life the world has known since Hiroshima. Nevertheless, it is possible that the generally light-hearted and circumspect temper of Stewart's writing may conceal a deep ineradicable pessimism, even disgust, about human nature, and that having a conviction of irremediable original sin, he has turned away to the natural world, content only with the surface pleasures of human society. Two passages in *Shipwreck* may crystallise his view of humanity; when Heynorick, the "observing" butler says suddenly, echoing Hamlet – "The appalling things that happen between sky and earth/Where the beast called man walks upright!" – and when Pelsart tells the condemned sailor: "I cannot pity you, prisoner; but, sometimes, my friends,/I am sorry for the race of men, trapped on this planet."

—Dorothy Green

STOPPARD, Tom. English.   Born in Zlin, Czechoslovakia, 3 July 1937; emigrated to Singapore in 1938, and to England in 1946. Educated abroad, and at the Dolphin School, Nottinghamshire, and Pocklington School, Yorkshire. Married 1) Jose Ingle in 1965 (divorced, 1972), two sons; 2) Dr. Miriam Moore-Robinson in 1972, one son. Journalist, *Western Daily Press*, Bristol, 1954–58, and *Bristol Evening World*, 1958–60; free-lance journalist in London, 1960–63. Recipient: John Whiting Award, 1967; *Evening Standard* award, 1967, 1972, 1974; Prix Italia, 1968; Antoinette Perry Award, 1968, 1976; New York Drama Critics Circle Award, 1968, 1976. Lives in Buckinghamshire.

PUBLICATIONS

Plays

A Walk on the Water (televised 1963; produced 1964); revised version, as *The Preservation of George Riley* (televised 1964); as *Enter a Free Man* (produced 1968).   1968.
M Is for Moon among Other Things (broadcast 1964; produced 1977).
The Gamblers (produced 1965).
Tango, from a play by Slawomir Mrozek, translated by Nicholas Bethell (produced 1966).   1968.
A Separate Peace (televised 1966).   1978.
Rosencrantz and Guildenstern Are Dead (produced 1966; revised version, produced 1967).   1967.
Albert's Bridge (broadcast 1967; produced 1975).   In *Albert's Bridge and If You're Glad I'll Be Frank,* 1969.
The Real Inspector Hound (produced 1968).   1968.
Albert's Bridge and If You're Glad I'll Be Frank: Two Plays for Radio.   1969.
After Magritte (produced 1970).   1971.
Dogg's Our Pet (produced 1971).   In *Six of the Best,* 1976.
Jumpers (produced 1972).   1972.
The House of Bernarda Alba, from a play by Lorca (produced 1973).

Artist Descending a Staircase, and Where Are They Now? Two Plays for Radio. 1973.
Travesties (produced 1974). 1975.
Dirty Linen, and New-found-land (produced 1976). 1976.
Albert's Bridge and Other Plays. 1977.
Professional Foul (televised 1977). With *Every Good Boy Deserves Favour*, 1978.
Every Good Boy Deserves Favour, music by André Previn (produced 1977). 1978.
Night and Day (produced 1978). 1978.

Screenplays: *The Engagement*, 1969; *The Romantic Englishwoman*, 1975; *Despair*, 1978.

Radio Plays: *The Dissolution of Dominic Boot*, 1964; *M Is for Moon among Other Things*, 1964; *If You're Glad I'll Be Frank*, 1965; *Albert's Bridge*, 1967; *Where Are They Now?*, 1970; *Artist Descending a Staircase*, 1972.

Television Plays: *A Walk on the Water*, 1963 (as *The Preservation of George Riley*, 1964); *A Separate Peace*, 1966; *Teeth*, 1967; *Another Moon Called Earth*, 1967; *Neutral Ground*, 1968; *One Pair of Eyes* (documentary), 1972; *Boundaries*, with Clive Exton, 1975; *Three Men in a Boat*, from the novel by Jerome K. Jerome, 1975; *Professional Foul*, 1977.

Fiction

Lord Malquist and Mr. Moon. 1966.

Reading List: *Stoppard* by C. W. E. Bigsby, 1976; *Stoppard* by Ronald Hayman, 1977.

*   *   *

In Tom Stoppard's early and greatly successful play, *Rosencrantz and Guildenstern Are Dead*, occur examples of the habits of dramatic composition and ways of thinking that appear in all of his plays; habits of thought and dramatic conventions that are taken seriously in many quarters undergo exaggeration, with results that are disconcerting or delightful according to taste. Thus, in *Rosencrantz and Guildenstern Are Dead*, the center of the stage is occupied by Hamlet's two undependable friends, and they watch – but without much comprehension – the Elsinor events. Their paths keep making farcical contact with Hamlet's until he deserts them for their fate in England. Stoppard fashions his drama out of the contrasts between the high-flown language of Hamlet and the groping comment and search for meaning manifest in the speech of Rosencrantz and Guildenstern. For they as well as Hamlet take up the great questions. But they reduce them to triviality, and their failure suggests that Shakespeare's successes with the same questions are more apparent than real.

In other plays, Stoppard mounts dramas that are his non-involved meditations on selected pretensions from the more recent past. Characters better endowed with language than are Stoppard's Rosencrantz and Guildenstern (their language is as restricted as that of Beckett's two who wait for Godot) are harried along very complicated courses. At many points in the chase, Stoppard allows his creatures to define – to themselves and to the audience – the meaning of their flights. But the definition is always one that reaches ridiculous extremes.

The parody of *Hamlet* frees us from *Hamlet*. *The Real Inspector Hound* frees us from a lesser mistress, Agatha Christie. With amusing variations on Rosencrantz and Guildenstern watching a chain of events they can hardly understand, the watchers of the action in *The Real Inspector Hound* observe a play that *they* cannot grasp. The two doltish, pretentious drama critics earnestly discuss a vacuous modern thriller and, by its conclusion, are as much

555

involved in its conventions as were Hamlet's two friends in his tragedy. It is as though Stoppard were saying, "A curse on all your serious dramatic intents."

Elsewhere, Stoppard's entertaining maledictions move outside the theatre itself and reject many of the serious pretensions of this century. In *Jumpers*, a grotesque plot concerning the murder of a modern philosopher unites his survivors not so much in the investigation of the crime as in extreme displays of twentieth-century British philosophical themes: proofs of the existence (or non-existence) of God; the authority (or nullity) of standards of morality and taste; the power of words themselves to represent (or misrepresent) reality. The events that precipitate such discourse are preposterous, and the characters are incredible. But the parodies and the neatly managed distortions of serious modern concerns are not. A retired musical-comedy star, her erudite husband, her sexually active analyst, and the police inspector swing like puppets in the intellectual gusts that Stoppard creates.

Two other examples will indicate how pervasive is Stoppard's habit of mind. In a play written for radio, *Artist Descending a Staircase*, the event is the probable murder of an artist by one of two old friends. But the substance of the play is the wonderfully dextrous reproduction of talk by artists about art during the last half-century. Knowing hearers – and hearers who are not well-informed are given enough buffoonery to make them content – will recognize windy versions of the arguments that have carried painters through several of the currents and counter-currents of modern art: cubism, surrealism, and other tendencies that were first discussed and then only later illustrated by brush.

And in *Travesties* Stoppard mixes up a stew which contains several of the most serious and transforming aspirations of the present era. The years are the war-years of 1914–18, and the scene is Zurich. In that city Joyce was writing *Ulysses*, Tristan Tzara was initiating Dadaism, and Lenin was waiting to bring his kind of revolution to Russia. Responsive to all kinds of pretension (and Stoppard's Zurich is full of pretension's cross-purpose and inconsequence), the mocking dramatist does both justice and injustice to all the artistic and political propaganda. The ridiculous plot is but an ornament to the bravura display of Stoppard's power to hear other voices and to mock them as they pass through the baffle chamber of his own mind.

Some criticism judges that Stoppard is a latter-day G. B. Shaw. This perception occurs because both dramatists are primarily celebrators of ideas. The ideas that Shaw displayed are, roughly speaking, all his own. With Stoppard, the case is altered; the ideas are, without exception, those of others. Shaw delighted the receptive with a display of ideas that were "better"; the cumulative effect of Stoppard's theatre is that there simply are no "better" ideas. One and all, they commit us to imbecility. Perhaps this is a desponding message. But it is one that Stoppard executes with unhalting zest and brilliance.

—Harold H. Watts

STOREY, David (Malcolm). English. Born in Wakefield, Yorkshire, 13 July 1933; brother of the novelist Anthony Storey. Educated at Queen Elizabeth Grammar School, Wakefield, 1943–51; Wakefield College of Art, 1951–53; Slade School of Fine Art, London, 1953–56, diploma in fine arts. Married Barbara Rudd Hamilton in 1956; two sons and two daughters. Played professionally for the Leeds Rugby League Club, 1952–56. Fellow, University College, London, 1974. Recipient: Rhys Memorial Award, for fiction, 1961; Maugham Award, 1963; *Evening Standard* award, 1967, 1970; Variety Club of Great Britain Writer of the Year Award, 1971; New York Drama Critics Circle Award, 1971, 1973, 1974; Faber Memorial Prize, 1973; Obie Award, 1974; Booker Prize, for fiction, 1976. Lives in London.

PUBLICATIONS

Plays

The Restoration of Arnold Middleton (produced 1966). 1967.
In Celebration (produced 1969). 1969.
The Contractor (produced 1969). 1970.
Home (produced 1970). 1970.
The Changing Room (produced 1971). 1972.
The Farm (produced 1973). 1973.
Cromwell (produced 1973). 1973.
Life Class (produced 1974). 1975.
Mother's Day (produced 1976). 1977.

Screenplays: *This Sporting Life*, 1963; *In Celebration*, 1974.

Television Play: *Grace*, from the story by James Joyce, 1974.

Fiction

This Sporting Life. 1960.
Flight into Camden. 1961.
Radcliffe. 1963.
Pasmore. 1972.
A Temporary Life. 1973.
Saville. 1976.

Other

Writers on Themselves, with others. 1964.
Edward, drawings by Donald Parker. 1973.

Reading List: *Revolutions in Modern English Drama* by Katharine J. Worth, 1972; *Storey* by John Russell Taylor, 1974; *Playwrights' Theatre* by Terry Browne, 1975.

* * *

It is rare for a writer to claim attention equally as a dramatist and a novelist, but it is impossible to say that David Storey is primarily one or the other. He had already published an accomplished novel of working-class experience, *This Sporting Life*, in 1960, when a group of plays, all presented at the Royal Court Theatre and directed by Lindsay Anderson, established him as one of the two leading figures (Edward Bond, the other) in the "second wave" of contemporary British drama. More recently he has produced a series of further, prize-winning novels. There is considerable variation of tone across his work from the sombreness of *Radcliffe* or *Cromwell* to the sardonic persiflage of *Life Class* or *A Temporary Life*; but reticence and subjectivity complement each other in his writing in both genres.

His undeniable concern with social class has a moral and cultural rather than political focus. *In Celebration* most straightforwardly exposes the strains that social mobility has set up in a family of working-class origins. The influence of D. H. Lawrence shows clearly here, but Storey marks out his individual territory in the expression of bitter and painful feelings and extreme mental turmoil on the edge of breakdown. Though he can recreate social detail precisely, as in *This Sporting Life* and *Saville*, his avoidance of explicit general comment contributes to the impression that the major characters in his novels move somnambulistically through a pattern of events unconsciously chosen. They themselves are manifestations of tradition, or deep-rooted class experience – of manual labour, poverty, and deprivation (Mrs. Hammond, in *This Sporting Life*, an unappeasable figure of suffering and defeat, is an impressive early example). If they find themselves in comfortable middle-class circumstances, they compulsively reject and destroy the conformist role and drift into more fundamentally determined alignments and confrontations. In *Radcliffe*, the strength of the labouring class is seen with fascination from the point-of-view of the opposed and dependent high culture. The titles of the novels, *Radcliffe* and *Saville*, and of the play, *Cromwell*, denote the hold of tradition on individual life: *Saville* presents its main figure living out the experience of a family identified with a particular place in social history; *Radcliffe* is a Gothic novel in which an old house haunts and dominates the minds of a family; *Cromwell* stands for a complex of moral qualities and social ideals.

Though the plots of all Storey's novels and plays are quite distinct from each other, the reader is struck by the reworking of particular episodes (including a beating-up) again and again, in variant order and associated with different characters. The analogy that comes to mind is that of the painter (which Storey also is) who includes a number of motifs idiosyncratically in picture after picture. The play *Life Class* and the novel *A Temporary Life* draw specifically on his familiarity with art schools, and the latter is interestingly structured so that stages of the narrative are linked with current ideas (and practices) of the nature and status of visual art.

If Storey's interest in continuity is reminiscent of Raymond Williams's, his most distinguished plays suggest a structuralist model in the kind of integration they achieve. *The Contractor* and *The Changing Room* dispense with star parts and a conventional narrative plot in favour of theatrical teamwork to create a new version of the ancient notion of the theatre as microcosm. Stage business takes on the status of dramatic action and the dialogue is spare, laconic, half-articulate, close to being a neutral element from which no line can be abstracted and quoted to significant effect. It approximates to "writing degree zero" and serves a drama that has a more than usually tenuous existence as a literary work. In the theatre, the actors create the form of the play and, in *The Contractor*, it is their achievement that stands clear at the climax: the wedding marquee, an image of art and the play itself, not as an individual production, but emerging out of the communal work process. *The Changing Room* excludes the separate achievement, the sacred ritual of the Rugby League game, to trace the emergence – and later dissolution – of the team out of disparate individuals. *Home* moves closer to absurdist drama (though Ewbank is no more the Contractor of the earlier play's title than Pozzo is Godot); but the idea of "home" from which the sense of alienation arises is here replaced by the reality which the characters (the actors in rehearsal and performance) make for themselves: the relationships they build, the communications they effect. The strict observance of the unities works both ways: preserving the effect of extreme naturalism and defining the plays as symbols. The richness of meaning arising from this inexplicit drama recalls Chekhov, as does the degree and quality of theatrical collaboration required.

—Margery Morgan

SUTRO, Alfred. English. Born in London, 7 August 1863. Educated at the City of London School, and in Brussels. Served in the Artists' Rifles, and on the staff of the War

Trade Intelligence Department, during World War I: O.B.E. (Officer, Order of the British Empire), 1918. Married Esther Stella Isaacs in 1894. Worked in the City of London for 14 years, first as a clerk, 1880–83, then in partnership with his brother as wholesale merchants, 1883–94; also active in the direction of working men's clubs in London during this period; lived in Paris, 1894, met Maeterlinck and became his translator: devoted himself to the translations, as well as to occasional journalism and to writing plays, 1895–1904; full-time playwright from 1904. *Died 11 September 1933.*

PUBLICATIONS

Plays

The Chili Widow, with Arthur Bourchier, from a play by Alexandre Busson (produced 1895).

Aglavaine and Selysette, from a play by Maeterlinck (produced 1904). 1897.

Alladine and Palomides, Interior, The Death of Tintagiles: Three Little Dramas for Marionettes, from plays by Maeterlinck. 1899.

The Death of Tintagiles, from a play by Maeterlinck (produced 1902). In *Alladine and Palomides ...,* 1899.

Carrots, from a play by J. Renard (produced 1900). 1904.

The Cave of Illusion. 1900.

A Marriage Has Been Arranged (produced 1902). 1904.

Women in Love: Eight Studies in Sentiment (includes *The Correct Thing, The Gutter of Time, Ella's Apology, A Game of Chess, The Salt of Life, Mr. Steinmann's Corner, Maggie, A Maker of Men).* 1902.

A Maker of Men (produced 1905). In *Women in Love,* 1902.

The Correct Thing (produced 1905). In *Women in Love,* 1902.

Ella's Apology (produced 1906). In *Women in Love,* 1902.

Mr. Steinmann's Corner (produced 1907). In *Women in Love,* 1902.

The Gutter of Time (produced 1908). In *Women in Love,* 1902.

A Lonely Life (produced 1907). 1903.

Arethusa (produced 1903).

The Walls of Jericho (produced 1904). 1906.

Monna Vanna, from a play by Maeterlinck (produced 1911). 1904.

Mollentrave on Women (produced 1905). 1905.

The Perfect Lover (produced 1905). 1905.

The Fascinating Mr. Vanderveldt (produced 1906). 1906.

The Open Door. 1906.

The Price of Money (produced 1906). 1906.

The Desperate Duke; or, The Culpable Countess, with R. Marshall (produced 1907).

John Glayde's Honour (produced 1907). 1907.

The Barrier (produced 1907). 1908.

The Romantic Barber (produced 1908).

The Man on the Kerb (produced 1908). 1908.

The Builder of Bridges (produced 1908). 1908.

Making a Gentleman (produced 1909).

The Perplexed Husband (produced 1911). 1913.

The Man in the Stalls (produced 1911). 1911.

The Firescreen (produced 1912). 1912.

The Bracelet (produced 1912). 1912.

Five Little Plays (includes *The Man in the Stalls, A Marriage Has Been Arranged, The Man on the Kerb, The Open Door, The Bracelet*). 1912.
The Two Virtues (produced 1914). 1914.
The Clever Ones (produced 1914).
Rude Min and Christine. 1915; as *Uncle Anyhow* (as *The Two Miss Farndons*, produced 1917, as *Uncle Anyhow*, produced 1918), 1919.
Freedom. 1916.
The Great Redding Street Burglary (produced 1916).
The Marriage Will Not Take Place (produced 1917). 1917.
The Trap (produced 1918).
The Egoist, from the novel by Meredith. 1919.
The Choice (produced 1919). 1920.
The Laughing Lady (produced 1922). 1922.
The Great Well (produced 1922). 1922.
Far above Rubies (produced 1924). 1924.
The Man with a Heart (produced 1925). 1925.
The Desperate Lovers (produced 1927). 1927.
Living Together (produced 1929). 1928.
The Blackmailing Lady. 1929.

Fiction

The Foolish Virgins (stories). 1904.
About Women. 1931.
Which. 1932.

Other

Celebrities and Simple Souls (autobiography). 1933.

Translator, *The Treasure of the Humble*, by Maeterlinck. 1897.
Translator, *Wisdom and Destiny*, by Maeterlinck. 1898.
Translator, *The Life of the Bee*, by Maeterlinck. 1901.
Translator, *Buried Temple*, by Maeterlinck. 1902.
Translator, *Ancient Egypt*, by Maeterlinck. 1925.
Translator, *The Life of the White Ant*, by Maeterlinck. 1927.
Translator, *The Magic of the Stars*, by Maeterlinck. 1930.

Reading List: *Some Modern Authors* by S. P. B. Mais, 1923; "Some Plays by Sutro" by G. Sutton, in *Bookman 63*, 1923.

                              *   *   *

Alfred Sutro is most well-known for his Maeterlinck translations. But it was his plays that for a time established him as a leading English popular dramatist, though he is now little remembered.

At the time that Henry Arthur Jones was describing *The Renascence of the English Drama* and calling for more serious work, Sutro succeeded with commercial glitter. His earliest plays went unproduced (a collaboration with George Meredith on a dramatization of *The Egoist*) or were tepidly received. A collaboration with actor Arthur Bourchier on *The Chili Widow* (cleaning up Alexandre Busson's *Monsieur le Directeur* as a vehicle) starred Bourchier and

Violet Vanbrugh. "Almost sixty years afterwards," wrote Ernest Short in *Sixty Years of Theatre* (1951), "one can remember her play with a parasol and a prospective lover," but that was Miss Vanbrugh's charm, not Sutro's dramaturgy. Sutro did make a splash with *The Walls of Jericho*, though Jones was to employ similar material even better in *The Ogre*. Thereafter Sutro held the boards in the West End year after year with trivial plays. "He has nothing to say that matters," wrote S. P. B. Mais, "but his stagecraft is good. He entertains, but leaves no permanent impression on the mind."

His *coups de théâtre* and starring players kept him going for some time. *John Glayde's Honour* was good enough for the matinée crowd and *The Builder of Bridges* was better, though less popular. Clayton Hamilton found *The Builder of Bridges* "the best of all his plays – better even than that powerful and popular work, *The Walls of Jericho*," but he had to admit (*Forum*, December 1909) that "it was reviewed adversely by nearly all the newspapers of New York, and has also failed to make money with the public."

Commercial failure must have hurt Sutro more than critical gibes. He said in a lecture that "the dramatist should keep one eye raised to heaven and the other on the box-office," and his gaze at the latter was the more steadfast. Throughout his career, charmingly reported in *Celebrities and Simple Souls*, he looked not upward and inward but forward and outward, like a commercial hack. He repackaged some imported tricks (Scribe, Sardou, etc.) and was clever in adapting, solid in construction, deft in dialogue, always innocuous and also inconsequential. By the 1920's he was old-hat: *The Laughing Lady*, *The Man with a Heart*, *The Desperate Lovers* increasingly depend upon an old-fashioned though facile manipulation of "inconsequential and wholly artificial themes" (Mais). His last play, *Living Together* (1929), was "given away with a pound of tea," said Francis Birrell, because it was too contrived, put "too much new wine into old bottles ... tried to sing songs of Cowardice in the tempo of Sardou," too – *theatrical*. "All the brilliant old men have dubbed him out of date."

By the year of Sutro's death the critics were saying frankly that "his plays are uniformly worthless" and that his "method was to produce, merely from the box-office standpoint, more failures than successes." The trick is to be bad but to get *very* old and be revived, like Ben Travers. But *The Walls of Jericho* (with the Australian backwoodsman taking on Lady Alethea and Mayfair society) and *The Laughing Lady* might play now. After all, William Douglas Home is in the West End. *Five Little Plays* and *Carrots* might give those few people who stage one-acters some ideas. *The Perplexed Husband* would be fun: it brings an unwonted (unwanted?) humor to the grimness of Women's Liberation. But do not expect a Sutro revival. Clark and Freedley in their pedestrian *History of the Modern Theatre* (1947) are strolling in the right direction: "Alfred Sutro was a serious writer of the well-made play who moved from drama to light comedy with that expert efficiency which is the hallmark of the second- or third-rate talent. In his more than thirty years of play writing he was one of the most popular dramatists of his day." Since he lacks Jones's craftsmanship, Shaw's genius, Maugham's wit, Pinero's effectiveness with a stagey idea (or even Barrie's with a fuzzy one), perhaps "second- or third-rate" had best be reserved for those admirable Edwardians St. John Hankin and Harley Granville-Barker, and that leaves Alfred Sutro considerably lower in the ranks.

—Leonard R. N. Ashley

SYNGE, (Edmund) J(ohn) M(illington).   Irish.   Born in Newtown Villas, Rathfarnham, near Dublin, 16 April 1871. Educated at private schools until age 14, then with a private tutor for three years, and at Trinity College, Dublin, 1888–92, B.A. 1892; studied piano and violin at the Royal Irish Academy, Dublin, and thereafter studied music and travelled in Germany, Italy, and France; settled in Paris and studied intermittently at the Sorbonne, 1895–97. Met William Butler Yeats, who encouraged him to write, 1896; returned to Ireland, 1897, and summers 1898–1902; with Yeats and Lady Gregory, involved in the initial planning of the Irish Literary Theatre, which became the Abbey Theatre, Dublin; wrote for the stage from 1901; Director, with Yeats and Lady Gregory, of the Abbey Theatre, from 1904. Suffered from Hodgkin's disease: *Died 24 March 1909.*

PUBLICATIONS

Collections

> *Poems,* edited by Robin Skelton.   1962.
> *Prose,* edited by Alan Price.   1966.
> *Plays,* edited by Ann Saddlemyer.   2 vols., 1968.

Plays

> *In the Shadow of the Glen* (produced 1903).   1904.
> *Riders to the Sea* (produced 1904).   With *In the Shadow of the Glen,* 1905; edited by Robin Skelton, 1969.
> *The Well of the Saints* (produced 1905).   1905.
> *The Playboy of the Western World* (produced 1907).   1907; edited by Malcolm Kelsall, 1974.
> *The Tinker's Wedding* (produced 1909).   1907.
> *Deirdre of the Sorrows* (produced 1910).   1910.

Verse

> *Poems and Translations.*   1909.

Other

> *The Aran Islands.*   1907.
> *In Wicklow, West Kerry, and Connemara.*   1911.
> *Some Unpublished Letters and Documents.*   1959.
> *The Autobiography, Constructed from the Manuscripts,* edited by Alan Price.   1965.
> *Letters to Molly: Synge to Maire O'Neill,* edited by Ann Saddlemyer.   1971.
> *Some Letters to Lady Gregory and Yeats,* edited by Ann Saddlemyer.   1971.

Bibliography: "Bibliographies of Irish Authors: Synge" by M. MacManus, in *Dublin Magazine,* October-December 1930; *Synge: A Bibliography of Criticism* by E. H. Mikhail, 1974.

Reading List: *Synge and Anglo-Irish Literature* by Daniel Corkery, 1931; *Synge* by David H. Greene and Edward Stephens, 1959; *Synge and Anglo-Irish Drama* by Alan Price, 1961; *Synge and Lady Gregory* by Elizabeth Coxhead, 1962; *Synge* by Denis Johnston, 1965;

Synge by Donna L. Gerstenberger, 1965; *Synge and Modern Comedy* by Ann Saddlemyer, 1968; *The Writings of Synge* by Robin Skelton, 1971; *Synge Centenary Papers* edited by Maurice Harmon, 1972; *Synge: A Critical Study of the Plays* by Nicholas Greene, 1976; *Interviews and Recollections* edited by E. H. Mikhail, 1977.

*   *   *

Although the bulk of his work was written during the last six years of his life when he was involved in the creation of Dublin's Abbey Theatre, J. M. Synge's preparation as a writer was deliberate, intensive, and lengthy. The poems, plays, travel writings, even his critical essays and translations, were shaped by his early training in music and languages, while his nature mysticism dictated choice and handling of subject matter and formed his aesthetic theory. All his experience was conscientiously woven into his developing philosophy, eventually reappearing in the fabric of his art. Thus, his bitter private struggle as a young adolescent with his mother's evangelical teaching, all the more painful because of his admiration for her strong moral commitment, surfaces in the poignant portrayal of mother and son in *Riders to the Sea*, in the strong simplicity of "Prayer of the Old Woman" after Villon, and in old Mary Byrne's indomitable embrace of life in *The Tinker's Wedding*. Similarly, his fascination for the manufacture of words, which led him to create in any language he studied, is responsible not only for the extraordinary richness and vitality of his dialogue but the conscious conjunction, sometimes harmonic, sometimes contrapuntal, of vivid imagery, exaggerated action, and sweeping rhythmical patterns.

Synge's musical training and correspondingly close study of art and natural history are the foundation also of his attempt to bring into harmony in his writing not only the sound, meaning, colour, and rhythm of language ("every speech should be as fully flavoured as a nut or apple") but a harmony of nature, myth, and passion. Thus the characters of his plays honour the moods of both nature and man and celebrate sounds and senses, while his travel essays evoke the peculiar clarity and intensity of Wicklow's light and atmosphere, Aran's majestic harmony of the supranatural and natural, the exotic grandeur and innate power of Mayo and Kerry. The extraordinary plot of *The Playboy of the Western World*, he insisted to his close friend the translator and journalist Stephen MacKenna, "in its *essence* – is probable given the psychic state of the locality."

Against this background of cosmic orchestration the passions, actions, and dreams of characters in his plays are etched with simple precision. His people experience intensely the incidents of everyday life, while longing equally vividly for the excitement and fulfilment of the unusual or the ideal. In both dream and reality they remain true to themselves; in the resolution of the play we perceive a greater truth to the universe without losing sight of the disparate parts. Thus in *The Tinker's Wedding*, Sarah Casey dreams of acquiring the respectability of marriage, while at the same time refusing to turn her back on the rich joys of the vagrant's unconventional ways; in *The Playboy of the Western World* Pegeen Mike is tempted to "go sailing the seas till I'd marry a Jew-man with ten kegs of gold," but the horror of Christy Mahon's potentially dirty deed is too great for her to face despite her love of the playboy; blind Martin and Mary Doul in *The Well of the Saints* choose certain death and the preservation of their deliberately fostered illusions to the well-meaning Saint's gift of participation in the working world of the sighted; and, in his last play, Deirdre and Naisi embrace both myth and reality by electing a vibrant seven years and an equally resounding death. "On the stage one must have reality, and one must have joy," he wrote in his preface to *The Playboy*, and rejoiced that "in Ireland, for a few years more, we have a popular imagination that is fiery and magnificent, and tender." In Synge's own life, Yeats's famous advice to seek for subject matter in the Aran Islands met with a temperament and personality long prepared for the event.

Synge's travel writings, in particular *The Aran Islands* and his Wicklow essays, reflect these values in a more personal, less artificial style. Where he deliberately objectified feelings and responses in his plays, his essays and poems use his own personal reactions as touchstone. Centering himself in a particular time and place, his descriptions take in the full sweep of horizon and history until the reader shares the flash of illumination achieved at a moment of intense awareness, and is then led, usually through an ironic device, back to the natural and the mundane. In these writings he aligns himself with the wanderer, the vagrant, who views all life and action through the eyes of the self-imposed semi-exile; frequently he signed his love letters to the actress Maire O'Neill (Molly Allgood) "your old Tramp," recognizing not only his affinity with the Stranger in *In the Shadow of the Glen* but with the tinkers, playboys, and beggers celebrated in his other plays.

Constantly striving to distil the essence of experience in his art, he filled thousands of pages with dialogue, critical commentary, made or overheard phrases, lists, analyses, and readings. But his few critical essays and notebook entries are of value primarily to the student of his evolving aesthetic. His experimental scenarios and prose translations, on the other hand, indicate the restlessness with which he approached form and language. Always the student, his method remained one of selectivity and a distant appreciation of other writers. Absorbed in his own vision, sensitive to his private responses, striving towards the perfection of a unique ambition, he preserved to an almost unique extent an individual voice throughout all his work. For Synge, the only arbiter conceivable was the art itself.

—Ann Saddlemyer

TATE, Nahum. Irish. Born Nahum Teate in Dublin in 1652. Educated at Trinity College, Dublin, 1668–72, B.A. 1672. Settled in London, 1672; began writing for the theatre, 1678; also subsequently involved in extensive work as editor and translator of various authors; Editor, with M. Smith, *The Monitor*, 1713; appointed Poet Laureate, 1692, and Historiographer Royal, 1702. *Died 30 July 1715.*

PUBLICATIONS

Plays

> *Brutus of Alba; or, The Enchanted Lovers* (produced 1678).   1678.
> *The Loyal General* (produced 1679).   1680.
> *King Richard the Second,* from the play by Shakespeare.   1681; as *The Sicilian Usurper* (produced 1680), 1691; as *The Tyrant of Sicily* (produced 1681).
> *King Lear,* from the play by Shakespeare (produced 1681).   1681; edited by James Black, 1975.
> *The Ingratitude of a Commonwealth; or, The Fall of Caius Martius Coriolanus,* from the play by Shakespeare (produced 1681).   1682.
> *A Duke and No Duke,* from the play *Trappolin Supposed a Prince* by Aston Cokayne (produced 1684).   1685; edited by Leo A. Hughes and Arthur H. Scouten, in *Ten English Farces,* 1948.
> *Cuckold's Haven; or, An Alderman No Conjuror,* from the play *Eastward Ho* by Jonson, Chapman, and Marston (produced 1685).   1685.
> *The Island Princess,* from the play by Fletcher (produced 1687).   1687.
> *Dido and Aeneas,* music by Henry Purcell (produced 1689).   1690; edited by G. A. Macfarren, 1841.
> *Injured Love; or, The Cruel Husband.*   1707.

Verse

> *Poems.*   1677; revised edition, 1684.
> *The Second Part of Absalom and Achitophel,* with Dryden.   1682.
> *On the Sacred Memory of Our Late Sovereign.*   1685.
> *A Pastoral in Memory of the Duke of Ormonde.*   1688.
> *A Poem Occasioned by His Majesty's Voyage to Holland.*   1691.
> *A Poem Occasioned by the Late Discontents.*   1691.
> *Characters of Virtue and Vice, Attempted in Verse from a Treatise by Joseph Hall.*   1691.
> *An Ode upon Her Majesty's Birthday.*   1693.
> *A Present for the Ladies.*   1693.
> *A Poem upon the Late Promotion of Several Eminent Persons.*   1694.
> *In Memory of Joseph Washington: An Elegy.*   1694.
> *An Ode upon the University of Dublin's Foundation.*   1694.
> *Mausolaeum: A Funeral Poem on Our Late Queen.*   1695.
> *An Elegy on the Late Archbishop of Canterbury.*   1695.
> *The Anniversary Ode for His Majesty's Birthday.*   1698.
> *A Consolatory Poem to Lord Cutts.*   1698.
> *Elegies.*   1699.
> *An Essay of a Character of Sir George Treby.*   1700.
> *Funeral Poems.*   1700.

Panacea: A Poem upon Tea. 1700; as *A Poem upon Tea,* 1702.
An Elegy in Memory of Ralph Marshall. 1700.
A Congratulatory Poem on the New Parliament. 1701.
The Kentish Worthies. 1701.
A Monumental Poem in Memory of Sir George Treby. 1702.
Portrait-Royal: A Poem upon Her Majesty's Picture. 1703.
The Song for New Year's Day. 1703.
The Triumph: A Poem on the Glorious Successes of the Last Year. 1705.
Britannia's Prayer for the Queen. 1706.
The Triumph of Union. 1707.
A Congratulatory Poem to Prince George of Denmark. 1708.
The Muse's Memorial to the Earl of Oxford. 1712.
The Muses Bower. 1713.
The Triumph of Peace. 1713.
A Poem Sacred to the Memory of Queen Anne. 1714.

Other

An Essay for Promoting of Psalmody. 1710.

Editor, *Poems by Several Hands.* 1685.
Editor, *A Memorial for the Learned,* by J. D. 1686.
Editor, *The Life of Alexander the Great,* by Quintus Curtius Rufius. 1690.
Editor, *The Political Anatomy of Ireland,* by Sir William Petty. 1691.
Editor, *Guzman,* by Roger Boyle. 1693.
Editor, *The Four Epistles of A. G. Bushbequius.* 1694.
Editor, *Miscellanea Sacra; or, Poems on Divine and Moral Subjects.* 1696; revised
   edition, 1698.
Editor, *An Essay on Poetry,* by John Sheffield, Duke of Buckingham. 1697.
Editor, *The Original of the Soul* (Nosce Teipsum), by Sir John Davies. 1697.
Editor, *The Innocent Epicure; or, The Art of Angling,* by J. S. 1697.

Translator, with others, *Ovid's Epistles.* 1680.
Translator, *Syphilus: A Poetical History of the French Disease,* by Fracastoro. 1686.
Translator, with "a person of quality," *The Aethiopian History,* by Heliodorus. 1686;
   as *The Triumphs of Love and Constancy,* 1687.
Translator, with others, *Cowley's Six Books of Plants.* 1689.
Translator, *The Life of the Prince of Condé.* 2 vols., 1693.
Translator, with others, *The Satires of Juvenal,* with *The Satires of Persius* translated by
   Dryden. 1693.
Translator, with Nicholas Brady, *An Essay of a New Version of the Psalms of
   David.* 1695; revised edition, 1695, 1696; *Supplement,* 1700.
Translator, *Majesta Imperii Britannici, The Glories of Great Britain,* by Mr.
   Maidwell. 1706.
Translator, with Aaron Hill, *The Celebrated Speeches of Ajax and Ulysses,* by
   Ovid. 1708.
Translator, with others, *The Works of Lucian.* 4 vols., 1710–11.
Translator, with others, *Ovid's Art of Love and His Remedy of Love.* 1712.

Reading List: *Tate* by Christopher Spencer, 1972.

*   *   *

Nahum Tate is best known for his scaled-down version of *King Lear* with its love story between Cordelia and Edgar and its happy ending in which Lear retires and leaves his kingdom to the lovers. After Tate's version was finally replaced in the theatre by Shakespeare's in 1838, the word "Tatefication" was coined to refer to the debasement of great literary works; however, the term ignores the ingenuity with which the adaptation was fitted to the Restoration theatre and its long success. The farce *A Duke and No Duke* (based on Aston Cokayne's *Trappolin Supposed a Prince*, 1633) also continued to please audiences until well into the 19th century; for the second edition (1693) Tate wrote an extended defence of farce. Tate's libretto for Henry Purcell's operatic masterpiece *Dido and Aeneas* contains verse that, though undistinguished as poetry, is well designed for setting to music.

Tate was not a vigorous or original writer, and his best work was done in adaptation, translation, or collaboration. He joined successfully with Dryden in Ovid's *Epistles* and Juvenal's *Satires*, as well as *The Second Part of Absalom and Achitophel* (1682). With a clerical family background and experience in translation and in writing for music, Tate was well-qualified to collaborate with Nicholas Brady in versifying the Psalms. Their *New Version of the Psalms of David* was more polished and elegant than the old Sternhold and Hopkins version of 1562, and was generally used in Anglican churches for more than a century. Some of the Tate-Brady renderings are included as hymns in modern hymnals, e.g., "Thro' All the Changing Scenes of Life" (Psalm 34) and "As Pants the Hart for Cooling Streams" (Psalm 62). The carol "While Shepherds Watched Their Flocks by Night" first appeared in the *Supplement to the New Version*.

Of the 102 poems in Tate's two collections (1677, 1684), many are on melancholy themes but some suggest Cavalier or Metaphysical models or echo Shakespeare or Milton. The odes, elegies, and other occasional poems that Tate felt were a laureate's duty generally do an adequate job of expressing (sometimes to musical accompaniment by Purcell or John Blow) the grand thoughts that are appropriate for the public occasion. A more relaxed poem (perhaps his best original work) is the amusing, mock-heroic *Panacea: A Poem upon Tea*.

—Christopher Spencer

TATHAM, John. English. Born in England c. 1610. Nothing is known about his background, family, or education. Probably served in the Army under Lord Carnarvon in 1642. Settled in London, and began writing for the stage in 1632; appointed Laureate of the Lord Mayor's Show, and wrote the City pageants, 1657–64. Nothing is known about him after 1664.

PUBLICATIONS

Collections

Dramatic Works, edited by James Maidment and W. H. Logan. 1879.

Plays

Love Crowns the End: A Pastoral (produced 1632). In *The Fancy's Theatre,* 1640.

The Distracted State (produced 1641–50?).   1651.
The Scots Figgaries; or, A Knot of Knaves.   1652.
London's Triumphs (produced 1657).   1657; other pageants produced and published
   1658–64.
The Rump; or, The Mirror of the Late Times (produced 1660).   1660.
The Royal Oak (produced 1660).   1660.
Neptune's Address to Charles the Second (produced 1661).   1661.
Aqua Triumphalis (produced 1662).   1662.

Verse

The Fancy's Theatre. 1640.
Ostella; or, The Faction of Love and Beauty Reconciled.   1650.

Reading List: "English Street Theatre 1655–1708" by L. J. Morrissey, in *Costerus 4*, 1972.

*   *   *

John Tatham, one of those minor talents who observes all of the outward forms of the art
he would imitate, must have been puzzled when he did not succeed. His two books of poetry,
The Fancies Theatre and *Ostella*, include most of the poetic types of the 17th century –
acrostic odes, epithalamiums, elegies, epigrams, dialogues, as well as a poem of 110 quatrains
called "Daphnes" and a poem on "A Wart on a Gentlewomans Arme." His several poems
"To a Coy Mistress" touch on conventional themes (time, decay, reversed compliments), and
he can write lyrics of sustained personification, as he does in "The Letter." At his best he can
rise to a minor metaphysical conceit when he ends "The Nut to Ostella" with "[our hearts]
may knit and seem to be/Two Kirnels in one shell." At his worst he sinks to anti-petrarchan
bathos when he tells a lady that "Grape or Gooseberry/yield a juyce more savoury" than her
breasts. The masque *Love Crownes the End* illustrates the elements that made him a
successful writer of pageants for the City of London from 1657 to 1664. In this masque
Tatham mixes the low comedy of a country bumpkin, a heavenly messenger, violent action
(an attempted murder), and both Christian and overtly sexual language with the usual
pastoral romance of the masque. Thus, his masques and pageants have many of the elements
of the primitive mummings from which the Jacobean masque evolved. He wrote both Lord
Mayors pageants – most, like *The Royal Oake*, "staged" on 29 October 1660, call for loyalty
and unity – and the water fete *Aqua Triumphalis* staged by the City to welcome Charles II
and his new Queen from Hampton Court to Whitehall in 1662.

Tatham wrote three regular plays. All three were political. Both *The Scots Figgaries*, a
comedy partly in Scottish stage dialect, and *The Distracted State*, a tragedy set in Sicily, attack
the Scots, religious extremism, and disunity in household and state. *The Distracted State*
illustrates Tatham's weakness as a playwright. He cannot find a means of enacting his ideas,
and so this "revenge" tragedy is full of scenes of static intrigue followed by outbursts of
violence. After two static acts, the third begins with the head of a decapitated man thrown on
stage, a man shot, another killed in a sword battle, and a suicide by falling on a sword.
Twelve of the nineteen characters die violently on stage in the play, including the heroine
Harmonia. The language of the play, which deserves to be memorialized in Fielding's
Tragedy of Tragedies, is nearly as excessive: "I have a soul as big/with grief as you, that fain
would be deliver'd/If reason would turn midwife." Despite its excesses, this play is part of a
tradition, which continues into the 18th century, of thinly disguising contemporary politics as
remote tragedy. *The Rump*, a broad comedy written after General Monk forced the
dissolution of the Rump parliament, is the best of Tatham's plays. It brings real
Commonwealth leaders, and their wives, on stage, and ends with the elder Mrs. Cromwell

hawking kitchen stuff, Stoneware (Warestone) selling ballads, and Lockwhite (Whitelock) returning to his practice as a cheating lawyer. Again Tatham fails to find an appropriate action for his play, and he can only solve this problem by staging riots of apprentices. The strength of the play lies in its dialogue which is a compendium of cliché language ("trust them no farther than I can fling 'um") and folk sayings ("soft fire makes sweet malt") that reveal the "simplicity" of the Commonwealth leaders. With scenes of the male world balanced by scenes of the female world, it anticipates the witty comedies of Etherege and Congreve, and was revised by Aphra Behn in 1681 as *The Roundheads*.

—L. J. Morrissey

TAYLOR, Tom. English. Born in Bishop Wearmouth, Sunderland, 19 October 1817. Educated at the Grange School, Sunderland; University of Glasgow (gold medallist, three times); Trinity College, Cambridge, matriculated 1837, B.A. (first-class honours) 1840, Fellow 1842, M.A. 1843; entered the Middle Temple, London: called to the Bar, 1846. Married Laura Barker in 1855. Tutor at Cambridge, 1843–44; settled in London, 1844, and began immediately successful career as a playwright and occasional actor: associated with the Olympic Theatre, 1853–60, and the Haymarket Theatre, 1857–70; also worked as a journalist: became leader writer for the *Morning Chronicle* and *Daily News*, began life-long association with *Punch*, and subsequently, for many years, served as Art Critic of *The Times* and *Graphic*; Professor of English Literature and English Language, University of London, 1845–47; practised law on the northern circuit, 1847–50; Assistant Secretary, Board of Health, London, 1850–54, and Secretary from 1854 (the Board of Health was thereafter absorbed in the Local Government Board, and his post became that of Secretary to the Sanitary Department) until he retired on a pension in 1871; Editor of *Punch*, 1874 until his death. *Died 12 July 1880.*

PUBLICATIONS

Plays

    A Trip to Kissingen (produced 1844). With *The Garrick Fever*, by Planché, 1881.
    Valentine and Orson, with Albert R. Smith and James Kenney (produced 1844). 1844(?).
    Cinderella, with Albert R. Smith and James Kenney (produced 1845).
    Friends at Court (produced 1845).
    The Enchanted Horse (produced 1845?).
    To Parents and Guardians (produced 1846). N.d.
    The Bottle (produced 1847). 1847.
    Wanted a Hermit (produced 1847).
    Diogenes and His Lantern; or, The Hue and Cry after Honesty (produced 1849).
    The Vicar of Wakefield; or, The Pastor's Fireside (produced 1850). 1851.
    The Philosopher's Stone (produced 1850). 1850(?).
    Novelty Fair; or, Hints for 1851, with Albert R. Smith (produced 1850). N.d.
    Prince Dorus; or, The Romance of the Nose (produced 1850). 1850.

Sir Roger de Coverley; or, The Widow and Her Wooers (produced 1851).   1851.

Little Red Riding Hood (produced 1851).

Our Clerks; or, No. 3, Fig Tree Court, Temple (produced 1852).   N.d.

Wittikind and His Brothers; or, The Seven Swan Princes and the Fair Melusine (produced 1852).   N.d.

Masks and Faces; or, Before and Behind the Curtain, with Charles Reade (produced 1852).   1854; edited by George Rowell, in *Nineteenth-Century Plays,* 1953.

Slave Life; or, Uncle Tom's Cabin, with Mark Lemon (produced 1852).   1852.

Plot and Passion, with John Lang (produced 1853).   1869.

A Nice Firm (produced 1853).   N.d.

Harlequin Columbus; or, The Old World and the New (produced 1853).

To Oblige Benson (produced 1854).   N.d.

Two Loves and a Life, with Charles Reade (produced 1854).   1854.

Barefaced Imposters (produced 1854).   1854.

The King's Rival, with Charles Reade (produced 1854).   1854.

A Blighted Being (produced 1854).   1857(?).

Guy Fawkes; or, A Match for a King, with others (produced 1855).   1855.

Still Waters Run Deep (produced 1855).   1856(?).

Helping Hands (produced 1855).   N.d.

The First Printer, with Charles Reade (produced 1856).

Retribution (produced 1856).   1856(?).

William Tell, with others (produced 1856).

A Sheep in Wolf's Clothing (produced 1857).   1870(?).

Victims (produced 1857).   1860(?).

An Unequal Match (produced 1857).   1874.

Going to the Bad (produced 1858).   N.d.

Our American Cousin (produced 1858).   1869; edited by J. O. Bailey, in *British Plays of the Nineteenth Century,* 1966.

Nine Points of the Law (produced 1859).   N.d.

The House or the Home? (produced 1859).   N.d.

The Contested Election (produced 1859).   1868.

Payable on Demand (produced 1859).   N.d.

Garibaldi (produced 1859).

The Fool's Revenge, from a play by Hugo (produced 1859).   1877.

The Late Lamented (produced 1859).

A Tale of Two Cities (produced 1860).   1868.

The Overland Route (produced 1860).   1866.

The Seasons (produced 1860).

A Christmas Dinner (produced 1860).

A Lesson for Life (produced 1860).   1867.

The Brigand and His Banker (produced 1860).

Up at the Hills (produced 1860).   N.d.

The Babes in the Wood (produced 1860; also produced as *Eloped*).   N.d.

A Duke in Difficulties (produced 1861).

Court and Cottage, music by Fred Clay (produced 1861).

The Ticket-of-Leave Man (produced 1863).   1863; edited by Michael Booth, in *English Plays of the Nineteenth Century 2,* 1969.

An Awful Rise in Spirits (produced 1863).

Sense and Sensation; or, The Seven Saints of Thule (produced 1864).   N.d.

The Hidden Hand, from a play by J. Dennery and C. Edmond (produced 1864).   1870(?).

Settling Day (produced 1865).   N.d.

Hearts and Hands (produced 1865).

The Serf; or, Love Levels All (produced 1865).   N.d.

Henry Dunbar; or, A Daughter's Trial (produced 1865).   N.d.
The White Boy (produced 1866).
A Sister's Penance, with Augustus W. Dubourg (produced 1866).   N.d.
The Antipodes; or, The Ups and Downs of Life (produced 1867).
Narcisse (produced 1868).
Won by a Head; or, Forewarned Is Forearmed (produced 1869).
Mary Warner; or, Tried in the Fire (produced 1869).
New Men and Old Acres; or, A Managing Mama, with Augustus W. Dubourg (produced
    1869).   Edited by Michael Booth, in *English Plays of the Nineteenth Century 3*, 1973.
'Twixt Axe and Crown; or, The Lady Elizabeth (produced 1870; revised version,
    produced 1889).   1877.
Handsome Is That Handsome Does: A Story of the Lake Country (produced 1870).
Joan of Arc (produced 1871).   1877.
Dead or Alive (produced 1872).
Arkwright's Wife, with John Saunders (produced 1873).   1877.
Lady Clancarty; or, Wedded and Wooed (produced 1874).   N.d.
The White Cockade (produced 1874).
Abel Drake, with John Saunders (produced 1874).
Anne Boleyn (produced 1876).   1877.
Historical Dramas.   1877.
Such Is the Law, with Paul Merritt (produced 1878).
Love and Life, with Paul Merritt (produced 1878).

Verse

Storm at Midnight and Other Poems, edited by J. H. Burn.   1893.

Other

Birket Foster's Pictures of English Landscape, with Pictures in Words by Taylor.   1853.
Handbook of the Pictures in the International Exhibition of 1862.   1862.
The Railway Station, Painted by W. P. Frith, Described.   1862.
*A Marriage Memorial: Verse and Prose, Commemorative of the Wedding of the Prince
    and Princess of Wales.*   1863.
Life and Times of Sir Joshua Reynolds, by C. R. Leslie, completed by Taylor.   2 vols.,
    1865.
English Painters of the Present Day: Essays, with J. B. Atkinson.   1871.
The Theatre in England: Some of Its Shortcomings and Possibilities.   1871.
Leicester Square: Its Associations and Its Worthies, with *A Sketch of Hunters' Scientific
    Character and Works*, by Richard Owen.   1874.

Editor, *Life of B. R. Haydon.*   1853.
Editor, *Autobiographical Recollections*, by C. R. Leslie.   1860.
Editor, *Pen Sketches by a Vanished Hand*, by Mortimer Collins.   2 vols., 1879.

Translator, *Ballads and Songs of Brittany*, by Vicomte Hersart de la
    Villemarqué.   1865.

Reading List: *Taylor and the Victorian Drama* by Winton Tolles, 1940 (includes
bibliography).

                              *   *   *

Tom Taylor is perhaps most memorable as the author of *Our American Cousin*, the play at a performance of which Abraham Lincoln was assassinated, and *The Ticket-of-Leave Man*, which introduced the stage figure of Hawkshaw the Detective. Yet the first owed its enormous popularity to the eccentric character of Lord Dundreary as re-written and expanded by the actor E. A. Sothern, while the second was an adaptation from the French.

A prolific playwright, a contributor to and eventually editor of *Punch*, a professor of language and literature, Taylor was theatrically derivative and generally rather heavy-handed. Nathaniel Hawthorne found him sensible but unimaginative. He had little wit, but much humour, kindly and often pedantic. As an editor, he liked academic jokes; as an art critic, he supported Ruskin against Whistler; as a dramatist, he owed much to the well-made plays of Scribe and his followers. Like most of his contemporaries, Taylor habitually adapted French plays and French and English fiction to the English stage, the practical possibilities of which he knew thoroughly. The *Athenaeum* critic once remarked that Taylor "never exhibits the originality of intellect," yet he was very skilful at Anglicising his borrowed personages, plots, and places. In *The Ticket-of-Leave Man*, for example, Mrs. Willoughby the landlady, Melter Moss the confidence man, and the theatrical Joneses seem much more Dickensian than Gallic.

Taylor worked in every genre of mid-Victorian drama, not excluding burlesque (e.g., *Diogenes and His Lantern*) and hippodrome, or play on horseback (*Garibaldi*). His best works, however, were well-constructed, "taylor-made" comedies and dramas, such as *To Oblige Benson*, a comedy of marital suspicions, and *Still Waters Run Deep*, a drawing-room drama in which "dull" John Mildmay outmanoeuvres a criminal cad, Captain Hawksley, and asserts himself as master of his own household. Both these plays were produced at the Olympic Theatre, with which Taylor was associated from 1853 to 1860. Another very popular Olympic play, *Plot and Passion*, was largely original with Taylor, although he used Scribe's techniques for an exciting historical drama.

Like other Victorian dramatists, Taylor hoped to improve the stage in general. His article "The Theatre in England: Its Shortcomings and Possibilities" (*The Dark Blue*, August 1871) made a number of practical suggestions, drawn in part from the Comédie Française, including pensions for actors, schools to be attached to theatres, the abolition of the star system and of long runs. In *Masks and Faces*, a play about Peg Woffington, which he wrote with Charles Reade, Taylor also urged more social toleration of actresses.

Although Taylor was neither iconoclastic nor innovative, his plays often contained a mild social message. The title of *The Serf; or, Love Levels All*, for instance, indicates a libertarian and egalitarian moral, even though its aristocratic heroine is saved from the consequences of marrying beneath her when her beloved serf is revealed to be a prince in disguise. The satiric comedy *Victims* caricatured female enthusiasts, pseudo-poets, feminists, and political economists, while approving of good-natured businessmen. In *The Overland Route*, another very popular play, Taylor anticipated J. M. Barrie's *The Admirable Crichton*, with a cast of shipwrecked passengers whose characters improve while they lead an ingeniously Crusoe-esque existence on a desert island. Like *Victims*, *The Overland Route* was written for the Haymarket Theatre while Taylor was house dramatist (1857–70).

Like most serious nineteenth-century playwrights, Taylor aspired to serious blank verse dramas, the best of which is his adaptation of Victor Hugo's *Le Roi s'Amuse*, *The Fool's Revenge*. Taylor's version deals with the complicated intrigue by which Bertuccio, a hunch-backed jester, intends to avenge himself of his wife's abduction and death upon "her wronger and his order." In doing so, he unintentionally exposes his own daughter to the lust of a dissolute duke. Fortunately, the jealous duchess poisons her husband in time to preserve his victim's purity and to return her to her father and the noble poet who loves her. Bertuccio realizes that vengeance should be left to Heaven. This kind of ending, which took its characters to the edge of tragedy but not beyond, exactly suited advanced mid-Victorian taste, and *The Fool's Revenge* had a great success both in England and America, where the critic William Winter described Edwin Booth's performance of Bertuccio as "one of the finest things ever done by an actor."

Several of Taylor's plays were repeatedly revived, for his clear if not complex characters and theatrically exciting situations provided effective opportunities for actors. His casts included many of the best players of his day, among them Frederick Robson, Joseph Jefferson, Kate and Ellen Terry, and the Bancrofts.

—Jane W. Stedman

THOMAS, Augustus. American. Born in St. Louis, Missouri, 8 January 1857. Educated in local elementary and high schools. Married Lisle Colby in 1890; one son and one daughter. Page boy in the Missouri Legislature, 1868, and in the United States House of Representatives, Washington, D.C., 1870–71; worked in the freight department of a railway company in St. Louis from 1871; Reporter on the *St. Louis Post-Dispatch*, 1885; worked for the *Kansas City Mirror*, 1887–88; began acting and writing for the stage from 1875; moved to New York, 1888, and worked as a theatrical assistant and press agent; full-time playwright after 1891. President, American Dramatists Association, 1906–11; President, National Institute of Arts and Letters, 1914–15; Executive Chairman, Producing Managers Association, and campaigned unsuccessfully for the establishment of a national theatre, 1922–25. Recipient: American Academy of Arts and Letters Gold Medal, 1913. M.A.: Williams College, Williamstown, Massachusetts, 1914; Litt.D.: Columbia University, New York, 1921; LL.D.: University of Missouri, Columbia, 1923. Member, American Academy of Arts and Letters. *Died 16 August 1934.*

PUBLICATIONS

Plays

Alone (produced 1875).
The Big Rise (produced 1882).
A Leaf from the Woods (produced 1883).
A New Year's Call (produced 1883).
Editha's Burglar, from the story by Frances Hodgson Burnett (produced 1883).   1932.
A Man of the World (produced 1883).
Combustion (produced 1884).
The Burglar (produced 1889).
A Proper Impropriety (produced 1889).   1932.
Tit for Tat, with Helen Barry, from a German play (produced 1890; as *A Night's Frolic*, produced 1891).
A Woman of the World (produced 1890).
For Money, with Clay M. Greene (produced 1890).
Afterthoughts (produced 1890).
Reckless Temple (produced 1890).
Alabama (produced 1891).   1898.
Colonel Carter of Cartersville, from the novel by F. Hopkinson Smith (produced 1892).
The Holly-Tree Inn (produced 1892).
Surrender (produced 1892).

In Mizzoura (produced 1893).   1916.

New Blood (produced 1894).

The Music Box (produced 1894).

The Man Upstairs (produced 1895).   1918.

The Capitol, from a story by Opie Read (produced 1895).

Chimmie Fadden, from a story by E. W. Townsend (produced 1896).

The Jucklins (produced 1896).

The Hoosier Doctor (produced 1897).

That Overcoat (produced 1898).

Don't Tell Her Husband (produced 1898; as *The Meddler*, produced 1898).

Colonel George of Mount Vernon (produced 1898).   1931.

Arizona (produced 1899).   1899.

Oliver Goldsmith (produced 1900).   1916.

On the Quiet (produced 1901).

Champagne Charley (produced 1901).

Colorado (produced 1901).

Soldiers of Fortune, from the play by R. H. Davies, from the novel by F. Marion
     Crawford (produced 1902).

The Earl of Pawtucket (produced 1903).   1917.

The Other Girl (produced 1903).   1917.

Mrs. Leffingwell's Boots (produced 1905).   1916.

Beside the Bonnie Briar Bush, with James MacArthur, from a novel by Ian Maclaren
     (produced 1905).

The Education of Mr. Pipp, from pictures by Charles Dana Gibson (produced 1905).

Delancey (produced 1905).

The Embassy Ball (produced 1905).

A Constitutional Point (produced 1906).   1932.

The Ranger (produced 1907).

The Member from Ozark (produced 1907).

The Witching Hour (produced 1907).   1916.

The Harvest Moon (produced 1909).   1922.

The Matinee Idol, from the play *His Last Legs* by Bernard (produced 1909).

As a Man Thinks (produced 1911).   1911.

The Model (produced 1912; also produced as *When It Comes Home*).

Mere Man (produced 1912).

At Liberty (produced 1912).

At Bay, with George Scarborough (produced 1913).

Indian Summer (produced 1913).

Three of Hearts (produced 1913).

The Battle Cry, from a novel by Charles N. Buck (produced 1914).   1914.

The Nightingale (produced 1914).   1914.

Rio Grande (produced 1916).

The Copperhead, from the work *The Glory of His Country* by Frederick Landis
     (produced 1918).   1922.

David's Adventures, from a novel (produced 1918).

The Cricket of Palmy Days (as *Palmy Days*, produced 1919).   1929.

Under the Bough (produced 1920; also called *The Blue Devil* and *Speak of the Devil*).

The Tent of Pompey (produced 1920).

Nemesis (produced 1921).   1921.

Still Waters (produced 1925).   1926.

Other plays (for amateurs): *Love Will Find a Way; The Dress Suit.*

Other

The Print of My Remembrance (autobiography).   1922.
Commemorative Tribute to Francis Hopkinson Smith.   1922.

Reading List: *The Wallet of Time* by William Winter, 1913.

*   *   *

Considered by contemporary critics as one of the half-dozen major American dramatists at the turn of the century, Augustus Thomas achieved some success by dramatizing American subjects that would catch the public interest. Like his contemporaries he was a good craftsman who wrote exciting melodramas and farces, generally with a particular actor or actress in mind. During his long career he wrote some 60 plays (including one-act plays and adaptations), organized and managed a professional theatre company, served as Executive Chairman of the Producing Managers Association and tried to develop a sense of self-censorship in the theatre world, was decorated by the French government, and wrote an autobiography, *The Print of My Remembrance*, which remains a useful if biased source for an appreciation of his plays and his theory of playwriting.

Thomas's playwriting took advantage of such topics of national interest as western regionalism, the labor movement, Washington politics, and new social fads. In *Alabama, In Mizzoura, Arizona*, and *Colorado* he used local scenery and atmosphere to enhance melodramatic plots. Only *Arizona* had any real success on stage. *New Blood* was sympathetic to the problems of laborers in a large manufacturing company. *The Capitol* revealed the influence of financiers on Washington politics and the lobbying practices of the Catholic Church but in a manner that would offend no one. *As a Man Thinks*, an average play on the double moral standard in marriage that interested playwrights and social reformers of this period, is distinguished by one of Thomas's best characters, the Jewish Dr. Seelig, who functions as a raisonneur in the play. *The Copperhead* achieved reasonable success on stage as a realistic picture of the effect of the Civil War on a midwestern town.

Thomas's best known play and probably his most significant work is *The Witching Hour*. Although a conventional melodrama of sentiment and morality, it exploits a popular interest by dramatizing the story of a young man who, under the influence of hypnotism, has killed a man. Beneath the mystery-laden plot there is the deeper idea of the effect of suggestion upon the human mind, but Thomas was seldom thought-provoking. Mainly he entertained with farces such as *The Earl of Pawtucket* and the thrills of the well-made melodrama.

—Walter J. Meserve

TOURNEUR, Cyril.   English.   Born in England c. 1575. Very little is known about his life: served the Cecils, the Veres, and the Earl of Essex at various times during his career, much of which was spent in military or diplomatic service: government courier in 1613; campaign soldier, probably in the Low Countries, 1614; accompanied Sir Edward Cecil, Lord Marshall of the Fleet, on expedition to Spain, 1625–26, having been appointed by Cecil Secretary to the Council of War and Secretary to the Marshall's Court: died from wounds incurred in the expedition. *Died 28 February 1626.*

Collections

Works, edited by Allardyce Nicoll.   1930.

Plays

The Revenger's Tragedy (produced 1606–07?).   1607; edited by R. A. Foakes, 1966.
The Atheist's Tragedy; or, The Honest Man's Fortune (produced 1607–11?).   1611;
   edited by Brian Morris and Roma Gill, 1974.

Verse

The Transformed Metamorphosis.   1600.
A Funeral Poem upon the Death of Sir Francis Vere, Knight.   1609.
A Grief on the Death of Prince Henry, in *Three Elegies.*   1613.

Bibliography: *Tourneur: A Bibliography* by S. A. and D. R. Tannenbaum, 1937.

Reading List: *A Study of Tourneur* by Peter B. Murray, 1964; *The Language of "The Revenger's Tragedy"* by Daniel J. Jacobson, 1974.

*   *   *

The name of Cyril Tourneur would be virtually unknown were it not for its association with *The Revenger's Tragedy*, one of the most impressive dramatic productions of the seventeenth century. Yet the association may be no more than conventional, the acceptance of an arbitrary assignment made by Edward Archer in 1656, thirty years after Tourneur died in Ireland, having been put ashore there when he was taken ill on Cecil's unhappy Cadiz expedition.

Born probably in the decade 1570–1580, Tourneur seems to have spent much of his life in the service of the Vere and Cecil families, and he occasionally celebrated their members in verses that testify more to his sense of duty than to any poetic ability. In 1600 he published a long and obscure satiric poem, *The Transformed Metamorphosis*, which shows the influence of Spenser and Marston but ultimately yields up no very clear meaning. A short spell of dramatic activity is vouched for by the publication of *The Atheist's Tragedy*, said on its title-page to have been "written by Cyril Tourneur." There is also an entry in the Stationers' Register, February 1611/12, for "a Tragecomedy called, the Noble man, written by Cyrill Tourneur," and a letter of 1613 in which Robert Daborne tells Henslowe that he has "given Cyrill Tourneur an act of ye Arreignment of london to write." These two plays were never printed, but Warburton claimed to have possessed the manuscript of "The Nobleman T. C." by "Cyrill Turnuer," until his cook used it underneath her pies, and burnt it.

The Atheist's Tragedy stands as an epitaph to the revenge tradition, incorporating all the salient features, but not the life. The "atheist" is D'Amville, convinced that "death casts up Our total sum of joy and happiness." He resolves to provide for his posterity (in whom he sees his only immortality) by murdering and robbing those from whom he will inherit. Having killed his brother and reported his nephew, Charlemont, to be dead in the wars, D'Amville secures the marriage of Castabella, Charlemont's betrothed, to his own son Rousard. But the union is not consummated: Rousard confesses that "A general weakness did surprise my health/The very day I married Castabella." To compensate for his son's impotence, D'Amville proposes that he should himself supply Rousard's place, to beget the desired heir. The proposition is made in the churchyard, D'Amville assuring Castabella that "These dead men's bones lie here of purpose to/Invite us to supply the number of/The living." The living, however, are already present in the graveyard. A puritan chaplain and his wench are bent on fornication; Borachio (D'Amville's servant) is intending murder; and his victim is Charlemont, supposed dead but in secret returned from the wars and now brooding over mortality among the tombs. The scene is a hilarious mixture of melancholy and murder, bawdy farce, and the melodrama of attempted incestuous rape. Charlemont kills Borachio and rescues Castabella, then a stage direction (probably authorial) indicates that the two lovers "*lie down with either of them a death's head for a pillow.*" This edifying spectacle, *de contemptu mortis*, is immediately disturbed by the arrival of the puritan, who mistakes the corpse of Borachio for his paramour, kisses with anticipation, then recoils in precise horror: "Now purity defend me from the sin of Sodom."

The scene ends with D'Amville's distracted vision of his brother's ghost (really the chaplain in a sheet) seeking revenge for his murder; and the last act of the play shows how the revenge is exacted with true Senecan excess. D'Amville's own death is comically appropriate. He attends the execution of Charlemont (condemned for his killing of Borachio), and offers his services as headsman; the author's stage direction indicates the course of justice: "*As he raises up the axe [he] strikes out his own brains.*" Charlemont, the most inactive of heroes, pronounces the moral that "patience is the honest man's revenge."

Shifting from solemn philosophizing to melodrama, heightened by supernatural interjections in the thunder, and relieved by the lascivious caperings of a tallow-chandler turned chaplain, *The Atheist's Tragedy* could hardly hope for success in the theatre, where it must bewilder audiences with the instability of its mood. This is the first point of contrast with *The Revenger's Tragedy*, a magnificently sombre play published anonymously. Here, only flashes of the blackest comedy light up skeletal figures, whose personalities reside in their names alone, pursuing a *danse macabre* where gold and lust lead to death and revenge.

For nine years Vindice has waited for the right opportunity to avenge the death of his betrothed lady, Gloriana. She was poisoned by the lustful Duke, a seventeenth-century stereotype of "royal lust ... grey-hair'd adultery." Vindice's constant companion, his "study's ornament," throughout these years has been Gloriana's skull; and now, concealed in a mask but with poison in its mouth, the skull becomes a weapon. Lured by the promise of a "country lady ... [who] has somewhat a grave look with her," the Duke kisses his destruction. Diversifying the action, but not dissipating the mood, are parallel plots of lust and its rewards. The Duchess commits incestuous adultery with Spurio, the Duke's bastard son. Her own youngest son rapes a virtuous lady, while his two brothers plot against Lussurioso, their step-brother and the Duke's heir, to have him disinherited. Their plot fails, and Lussurioso inherits his father's throne – and also Vindice's hatred, which finds a new focus in Lussurioso's attempt on the honour of Castiza, Vindice's sister.

The catastrophe comes in a masque, the traditional vehicle for vengeance ever since *The Spanish Tragedy*: "A masque is treason's licence, that build upon:/'Tis murder's best face, when a vizard's on." Vindice stabs Lussurioso; suspecting a rival for the throne, Ambitioso (the Duchess's son) stabs his brother; he himself is stabbed by the Duke's bastard. Momentarily Vindice is triumphant, and boasts of his victory. Then he is condemned to death by Antonio, the play's survivor, who cares little for the justice or appropriateness of Vindice's revenge but looks (wisely) to his own safety: "You that would murder him would murder me."

The exaggerations and contrivances of character and plot are supported in *The Revenger's Tragedy* (as they never are in *The Atheist's Tragedy*) by a poetry of distinction and intensity. Sharpened by the verse, the plot develops into a keenly pointed attack on the corruptions of court life, where "lordships [are] sold to maintain ladyships." From being a personal "ornament" to Vindice's study, and the petard with which the Duke's lust is hoist, Gloriana's skull becomes a *memento mori*. The emblematic cliché is brought to new life by the poetry, felt at its most powerful in Vindice's unanswerable rhetoric:

> Does the silkworm expend her yellow labours
> For thee? for thee does she undo herself?
> Are lordships sold to maintain ladyships
> For the poor benefit of a bewitching minute?

The Revenger's Tragedy has been discussed along with the known works of Cyril Tourneur because, as yet, there is no overwhelming evidence to disprove Archer's 1656 attribution. Many critics react instinctively that this cannot be the work of the author of *The Atheist's Tragedy*, and Thomas Middleton continues to be proposed as a strong claimant.

—Roma Gill

TRAVERS, Ben. English. Born in Hendon, London, 12 November 1886. Educated at the Abbey School, Beckenham, Surrey; Charterhouse, Surrey. Served in the Royal Navy Air Service, 1914–17: Squadron Commander; transferred to the Royal Air Force as Major, 1918: Air Force Cross, 1920; rejoined the Royal Air Force in 1939: Squadron Leader, 1940. Married Violet Mouncey in 1916 (died, 1951); two sons and one daughter. Prime Warden of the Fishmongers Company, London, 1946. President, Dramatists Club, 1956–60. Recipient: *Evening Standard* award, 1975. C.B.E. (Commander, Order of the British Empire), 1976. Lives in London.

PUBLICATIONS

Plays

The Dippers, from his own novel (produced 1922).
The Three Graces, from the play by Carl Lombardi and A. M. Willner, music by Franz Lehar (produced 1924).
A Cuckoo in the Nest, from his own novel (produced 1925). 1938.
Rookery Nook, from his own novel (produced 1926). 1930.
Thark (produced 1927). 1932.
Plunder (produced 1928). 1931.
Mischief, from his own novel (produced 1928).
A Cup of Kindness (produced 1929). 1934.
A Night Like This (produced 1930).
Turkey Time (produced 1931). 1934.
Dirty Work (produced 1932).
A Bit of a Test (produced 1933).
Chastity, My Brother (produced 1936).
Nun's Veiling (as *O Mistress Mine*, produced 1936; revised version, as *Nun's Veiling*, produced 1953). 1956.
Banana Ridge (produced 1938). 1939.

Spotted Dick (produced 1939).
She Follows Me About (produced 1943).   1945.
Outrageous Fortune (produced 1947).   1948.
Runaway Victory (produced 1949).
Wild Horses (produced 1952).   1953.
Corker's End (produced 1968).
The Bed Before Yesterday (produced 1975).   In *Five Plays*, 1977.
Five Plays (includes *A Cuckoo in the Nest, Rookery Nook, Thark, Plunder, The Bed Before Yesterday*).   1977.

Screenplays: *A Little Bit of Fluff (Skirts),* with Ralph Spence and Wheeler Dryden, 1928; *Rookery Nook (One Embarrassing Night),* with W. P. Lipscomb, 1930; *Thark,* 1932; *A Night Like This,* 1932; *Just My Luck,* 1933; *Turkey Time,* 1933; *A Cuckoo in the Nest,* with A. R. Rawlinson, 1933; *Up to the Neck,* 1933; *Dirty Work,* 1934; *Lady in Danger,* 1934; *A Cup of Kindness,* 1934; *Fighting Stock,* 1935; *Stormy Weather,* 1935; *Foreign Affaires,* 1935; *Pot Luck,* 1936; *Dishonour Bright,* 1936; *For Valour,* 1937; *Second Best Bed,* 1938; *Old Iron,* 1938; *So This Is London,* with others, 1939; *Banana Ridge,* with Walter C. Mycroft and Lesley Storm, 1941; *Uncle Silas (The Inheritance),* 1947; *Fast and Loose,* with A. R. Rawlinson, 1954.

Television Plays: *Potter,* 1948; *Picture Page,* 1949.

Fiction

The Dippers.   1920.
A Cuckoo in the Nest.   1922.
Rookery Nook.   1923.
Mischief.   1925.
The Collection Today (stories).   1929.
The Dippers, Together with Game and Rubber and The Dunkum Jane.   1932.
Hyde Side Up.   1933.

Other

Vale of Laughter (autobiography).   1957.
A-Sitting on a Gate (autobiography).   1978.

Editor, *The Leacock Book.*   1930.
Editor, *Pretty Pictures, Being a Selection of the Best American Pictorial Humour.*   1932.

*   *   *

Educated at Charterhouse, where he showed no particular promise of any sort, Ben Travers, though he spent his early years in London and the Far East in the family firm, had an early passion for the theatre. He was not able to indulge this till he had completed his years with the Royal Naval Air Service during World War I, and big success did not come his way till Tom Walls, who had leased the Aldwych Theatre, took up his early farce *A Cuckoo in the Nest.* From 1922 till 1933, he wrote for the Aldwych company, and his plays were more or less adapted to the cast: the horsy, cunning Tom Walls; the silly ass Ralph Lynn, always dropping his monocle; the bald, clerkish, bespectacled Robertson Hare, always liable at some point in the play to have his trousers removed for perfectly logical reasons; the slim pretty Winifred Shotter, equally liable to dash across the stage in her underclothes; and Mary

Brough, the gruff, suspicious landlady. Tom Walls was very much the boss of the show and once made Travers spend fifty-two hours revising, and much improving, a weak third act.

Travers's plays, which were essentially farces of suspense in which the most extravagant pains, lies, deceptions, and assumed identities were used to conceal improprieties that had not taken place, became very popular both with amateur theatrical companies and in their film versions in the 1930's. There was a long silence after 1952, but Travers produced *Corker's End* in 1968 and a serious farce, *The Bed Before Yesterday*, in 1975. In this last play he dealt (setting the scene in 1930) with the predicament of an essentially likable woman who had been put off sex for life by her utter ignorance on her marriage night. Not quite too late, she discovers its delights, but at the end realises that with a new husband of sixty she will have to rely more on affection. The play is more touching than funny (and the younger characters do not really belong to the 1930's), but it shows Travers's good heart. The cult of panic-stricken propriety in the 1920's gives his early work, however, in its very improbability, a more genuinely farcical flavour. There cannot be true farce without taboos.

—G. S. Fraser

TYLER, Royall. American. Born in Boston, Massachusetts, 18 July 1757. Educated at Harvard University, Cambridge, Massachusetts, 1772–76, B.A. 1776; also received an honorary B.A. from Yale University, New Haven, Connecticut, 1776; studied law in the office of Francis Dana in Cambridge; admitted to the Massachusetts Bar, 1780. Commanding Major, Independent Company of Boston, in the Continental Army, serving as aide to General Sullivan in the Battle of Rhode Island, 1778; later served as aide to General Benjamin Lincoln and participated in the suppression of Shay's Rebellion, 1787. Married Mary Hunt Palmer in 1794; had at least one son. Practised law in Falmouth, Massachusetts, Portland, Maine, and Braintree, Massachusetts, 1780–85, Boston, 1785–91, and Putney, Vermont, 1791–1801; began writing in 1787; entered literary partnership with Joseph Dennie, as Colon and Spondee, 1794, and contributed satirical verse and prose to various periodicals; served as State's Attorney for Windham County, Vermont, 1794–1801; Assistant Judge, 1801–07, and Chief Justice, 1807–13, of the Supreme Court of Vermont; Professor of Jurisprudence, University of Vermont, 1811–14. Trustee of the University of Vermont, 1802–13. *Died 26 August 1826.*

PUBLICATIONS

Collections

    Verse and *Prose*, edited by Marius B. Péladeau. 2 vols., 1968–72.

Plays

    The Contrast (produced 1787). 1790; edited by James B. Wilbur, 1920.
    May Day in Town; or, New York in an Uproar (produced 1787).
    The Georgia Spec; or, Land in the Moon (produced 1797; as *A Good Spec*, produced 1797).

Four Plays (includes *The Island of Barrataria, The Origin of the Feast of Purim, Joseph and His Brethren, The Judgement of Solomon*), edited by Arthur Wallace Peach and George Floyd Newbrough. 1941.

Fiction

The Algerine Captive. 1797.

Verse

The Origin of Evil. 1793.
The Chestnut Tree; or, A Sketch of Brattleboro at the Close of the Twentieth Century. 1824.

Other

The Trial of Cyrus B. Dean. 1808.
The Yankey in London. 1809.
Reports of Cases Argued and Determined in the Supreme Court of Vermont (for 1800–03). 2 vols., 1809–10.
A Book of Forms (law forms). 1845.

Reading List: *Tyler* by G. Thomas Tanselle, 1967.

*   *   *

With the presentation of *The Contrast* in New York City on 16 April 1787, Royall Tyler, identified by the evening's drama critics as "a man of genius," entered the history of American drama, becoming the first known native American writer of comedy to be professionally produced. At a time when the new nation was struggling for identity, Tyler showed his particular genius in his choice of material and the manner of his expression. Creating a typical Yankee character, and generally fostering the "just pride of patriotism" which Washington would later emphasize in his Farewell Address, Tyler wrote a popular play for his time. He was never able to do it again, and perhaps once was enough. He also had other interests to pursue.

Royall Tyler was that inspired person who could combine the joys of literary creation with a professional career, and as a lawyer he eventually rose in his profession to serve as a justice of Vermont's Supreme Court. As a writer, however, he was attracted by all genres. With Joseph Dennie, essayist, critic and editor of the *Port Folio*, he wrote a large number of amusing and satiric essays, sketches, and verses. Signing themselves as "Colon & Spondee" they provided light and topical commentary on society, literature, and politics until 1811. Poetry, particularly in a light and satiric vein, interested Tyler throughout his life. His only novel, an episodic work stimulated by the activity of the Barbary Coast pirates, was *The Algerine Captive*. Other than *The Contrast*, however, he was at his best in the essay or short sketch. The collection called *The Yankey in London* best illustrates his work: a sprightly style, a reverence for America, and a varied subject matter.

It was with *The Contrast* that he gained his reputation as a writer. Although it lacks much of a plot and is a talky play imitative of eighteenth-century British sentimental comedy, it is clearly distinguished by an originality in thought and character. From the prologue – "Exult each patriot heart!" – to the climax all aspects of the play emphasize the new nationalism.

Although they may be caricatures, the characters' distinctive qualities delight the reader and viewer. And everywhere there is satire – on fashion, theatre, the English, gossip – superimposed on the *contrast* – a contrast between the people of England and those of America, between affectation and straightforwardness, between city and country, between hypocrisy and sincerity, between foreign fraud and native worth. It was a play well designed to meet the demands and tastes of the new country.

Tyler continued to write more plays, but without great success. *May Day in Town; or, New York in an Uproar* appeared in a New York theatre a month after *The Contrast* but was not repeated. Four of Tyler's plays are published in the *America's Lost Plays* series. *The Island of Barrataria* is based on an episode in *Don Quixote*; the others have biblical sources. Only *The Island of Barrataria* deserves more critical attention than it has received. All, as might be expected of a lawyer, treat concepts of law, government, and justice. For Tyler, however, playwriting was only an avocation, though a pleasant one; he earned his living as a lawyer and justice. For the historian of American letters he is remembered mainly as the author of a single play.

—Walter J. Meserve

UDALL, Nicholas. English. Born in Hampshire in 1505. Educated at Winchester College (scholar), 1517–20; Corpus Christi College, Oxford, admitted a scholar 1520, B.A. 1524, probationer-fellow 1524, M.A. 1534. Tutor at Corpus Christi College from 1524; Headmaster of Eton College, 1534–41; Vicar of Braintree, Essex, 1537–44; Prebend at Windsor, 1551, and Rector of Calborne, Isle of Wight, 1553; appointed playwriter to Queen Mary, 1554; Headmaster of Westminster School, London, 1554–56. *Died* (buried) *23 December 1556.*

PUBLICATIONS

Plays

Ralph Roister Doister (produced 1553?). 1566(?); edited by G. Scheurwegh, 1939.
Respublica (produced 1553). Edited by J. P. Collier, in *Illustrations of English Literature*, 1866; edited by W. W. Greg, 1952.
Jack Juggler (produced ?). 1563; edited by E. L. Smart and W. W. Greg, 1937.
Jacob and Esau (produced ?). 1568; edited by J. Crow and F. P. Wilson, 1956.

Other

Flowers for Latin Speaking, from Terence. 1533.
Apothegms, from Erasmus. 1542.
The Paraphrase of Erasmus upon the New Testament. 1548.
A Discourse Concerning the Lord's Supper, from P. M. Vermigh. 1550(?).

Translator, *Compendiosa Totius Anatomie Delineatio* (in English), by Thomas Geminus. 1553; revised edition, 1559.

Reading List: Introduction by C. D. O'Malley to *Compendiosa*, 1959.

*   *   *

Nicholas Udall is the known author of only one extant play, *Ralph Roister Doister*, and of one lost one, *Ezechias* (acted 1564, but possibly Henrician in date and polemical in matter). He has been credited with *Thersites, Jack Juggler, Respublica*, and *Jacob and Esau*; of these the last three are more likely to be his than the first both for their Terentian structure and for their versification and diction (especially the last two). Writing for boy actors, he reflects the new interest in classical comedy (he published a Terentian Latin-English phrase-book, *Flowers for Latin Speaking*) as studied in schools. The models of *Ralph Roister Doister*, Terence's *Eunuchus* and *Miles Gloriosus*, gave Udall his comic duo of braggart lover and flattering parasite, here called Ralph Roister-Doister and Matthew Merrygreek (nearly all the names alliterate). The braggart's wooing proceeds from one disaster to another: his love-tokens are refused, his commissioned love-letter ruined by his own mispunctuation, his assault on his intended wife's house repulsed by her and her servants with kitchen armaments – to the barely concealed enjoyment of Merrygreek, who at one point reads a mock-requiem over his despairing patron. After a brief misunderstanding between the lady and her accepted suitor, the latter is convinced that Roister-Doister's courtship was without her encouragement, and a general feast ends the play.

Respublica (which survives in a manuscript stating that it was played by boys before Mary

I) is a political morality in Terentian technique, showing how Avarice and his subordinate vices Insolence, Oppression, and Adulation take false names in order to exploit Respublica and oppress her rustic servant People under the guise of reforming their estate until Nemesis (identified with the Queen) exposes them. *Jacob and Esau* treats the biblical story in the manner of the humanist religious drama, equipping the main characters with neighbours and with household servants who would be at home in *Ralph Roister Doister*. All three plays are divided into acts and scenes, introduce their characters by Terentian techniques, and develop the action systematically to a crisis and catastrophe. They are written in freely rhythmical couplets and all contain songs. The dialogue is idiomatic and there is plenty of English local colour, even in the biblical play. This last point also applies to *Jack Juggler*, but its plot is from Plautus (his *Amphitryon*), not from Terence, it is undivided into acts and scenes, and it contains no songs. (*Thersites*, loosely based on a neo-classical dialogue, is closer akin to the style of earlier than middle sixteenth-century drama.)

—T. W. Craik

USTINOV, Peter (Alexander).   English.   Born in London, 16 April 1921. Educated at Westminster School, London, 1934–37; London Theatre Studio, 1937–39. Served in the Royal Sussex Regiment and the Royal Army Ordnance Corps, 1942–46; Army Kinetograph Service, 1943. Married 1) Isolde Denham in 1940 (divorced, 1950), one daughter; 2) Susanne Cloutier in 1953 (divorced, 1971), two daughters and one son; 3) Helene du Laud-Allemans in 1972. Entered the theatre as an actor, 1939; first appearance in films, 1940. Co-Director of the Nottingham Playhouse, 1963. Rector, University of Dundee, 1968–73; Member, British U.S.A. Bicentennial Liaison Committee, 1973. Goodwill Ambassador for Unicef since 1969. Recipient: Golden Globe Award, 1952; New York Drama Critics Circle Award, 1953; *Evening Standard* award, 1956; Benjamin Franklin Medal, 1957; Emmy Award, for acting, three times; Academy Award, for acting, 1961, 1965. D.L.: University of Dundee, 1969; D.F.A.: LaSalle University, Philadelphia, 1971; D.Litt.: University of Lancaster, 1972. Fellow, Royal Society of Arts. C.B.E. (Commander, Order of the British Empire), 1975. Lives in Switzerland.

PUBLICATIONS

Plays

> *The Bishop of Limpopoland* (sketch; produced 1939).
> Sketches in *Diversion* and *Diversion 2* (produced 1940, 1941).
> *Fishing for Shadows*, from a play by Jean Sarment (produced 1940).
> *House of Regrets* (produced 1942).   1943.
> *Beyond* (produced 1943).   1944.
> *Blow Your Own Trumpet* (produced 1943).   In *Plays about People*, 1950.
> *The Banbury Nose* (produced 1944).   1945.
> *The Tragedy of Good Intentions* (produced 1945).   In *Plays about People*, 1950.
> *The Indifferent Shepherd* (produced 1948).   In *Plays about People*, 1950.
> *Frenzy*, from a play by Ingmar Bergman (produced 1948).

The Man in the Raincoat (produced 1949).
Plays about People. 1950.
The Love of Four Colonels (produced 1951). 1951.
The Moment of Truth (produced 1951). 1953.
High Balcony (produced 1952).
No Sign of the Dove (produced 1953). In *Five Plays*, 1965.
Romanoff and Juliet (produced 1956). 1957; revised version, as *R Loves J*, music by
    Alexander Faris, lyrics by Julian More (produced 1973).
The Empty Chair (produced 1956).
Paris Not So Gay (produced 1958).
Photo Finish: An Adventure in Biography (produced 1962). 1962.
The Life in My Hands (produced 1963).
Five Plays: Romanoff and Juliet, The Moment of Truth, The Love of Four Colonels,
    Beyond, No Sign of the Dove. 1965.
The Unknown Soldier and His Wife: Two Acts of War Separated by a Truce for
    Refreshment (produced 1967). 1967.
Halfway up the Tree (produced 1967). 1968.
Who's Who in Hell (produced 1974).

Screenplays: *The New Lot* (documentary), 1943; *The Way Ahead*, with Eric Ambler,
1944; *The True Glory*, 1944; *Carnival*, with others, 1946; *School for Secrets*, 1946; *Vice
Versa*, 1948; *Private Angelo*, with Michael Anderson, 1949; *The Secret Flight*, 1952;
School for Scoundrels, with others, 1960; *Romanoff and Juliet*, 1961; *Billy Budd*, with
Robert Rossen and DeWitt Bodeen, 1962; *Lady L.*, 1965; *Hot Millions*, with Ira
Wallach, 1968; *Hammersmith Is Out*, 1972.

Radio Plays: *In All Directions* series.

Television Play: *Ustinov ad lib*, 1969.

Fiction

Add a Dash of Pity: Short Stories. 1959.
The Loser. 1961.
The Frontiers of the Sea (stories). 1966.
Krumnagel. 1971.

Other

Ustinov's Diplomats: A Book of Photographs. 1961.
We Were Only Human (caricatures). 1961.
The Wit of Ustinov, edited by Dick Richards. 1969.
Dear Me (autobiography). 1977.

Reading List: *Ustinov* by Geoffrey Willans, 1957; *Ustinov in Focus* by Tony Thomas, 1971.

*   *   *

The delightful comic vision of Peter Ustinov has been most significantly shaped by his
cosmopolitan heritage, his talent for mimicry, his buffeting by the British educational system,
his wide reading, and especially by his service in the British army. The son of a Russian

journalist-spy-diplomat, who worked for the Germans until he defected to the British, and of a French artist, Ustinov was conceived in Holland and born in London. He claimed in the introduction to *Five Plays* to feel "more emotionally involved in the United Nations than in any individual country." This perspective is reflected throughout his works. The characters in his plays typically represent at least three different countries; their stereotypical provincialism, their jingoistic patriotism, and their pompous posings are major objects of Ustinov's satire. In *Romanoff and Juliet*, for instance, the Russians and the Americans badger each other in the main square of the capital city of the smallest country in the world. And although the families of the two lovers are ideological enemies, their quarrels are reduced to lilliputian insignificance as they crumble in the face of adolescent love.

In *The Love of Four Colonels* an American, an Englishman, a Frenchman, and a Russian are spirited away from their Allied Headquarters in a disputed section of Germany to an enchanted castle where each, in turn, tries to awaken Sleeping Beauty, acting out a fantasy in which he envisions her as his own conception of the ideal woman. The discrepancy between these fantasies and the moralistic proclamations of the four men provide much of the play's best comedy.

In *The Unknown Soldier and His Wife* the central characters repeatedly change their nationalities as Ustinov follows the course of battle from Greece and Rome through England of the Middle Ages to the eighteenth century and finally to the present. In *No Sign of the Dove*, a reworking of the Noah myth, the central characters are Russian and English; the setting is a cosmopolitan mansion whose rooms are designated as the Venetian, the Roman, and the Chinese Regency. Such a mixture of nationalities, such ready combination of the realistic and the supernatural, and such disregard for chronology enable Ustinov to satirize the pettiness and prejudice of people everywhere. No one ideology, he seems to say, has a corner on idiocy.

If there is one particular idiocy that people everywhere cling to, it is, in Ustinov's view, the supposition that a country can benefit from the actions of its government and its army. An undistinguished private in the British army during World War II, Ustinov learned that the military was the seat of stupidity, confusion, and waste. His writing consistently reflects this opinion. Military figures appear and play significant roles in virtually every work that he has written. They are usually bumbling incompetents, like the four colonels who seek to maintain the honor of their countries by quibbling over which language will be spoken on which weeks in their shared headquarters; or they are impotent, like Colonel Radley in *Beyond*, who wishes he could have made general, wishes he could have stayed in Africa, wishes he had not been forced to retire, and finally dies because there are no more worlds for him to conquer. When the military figures are perceptive, like General Sir Mallalieu in *Halfway up the Tree*, they perceive that death and bloodshed have done nothing to improve the human condition and that in any war the good and the bad are equally shared by each of the contending forces.

In the military establishment, with its rigid hierarchies, Ustinov found an apt metaphor for all the structured social systems and institutions which stifle creativity and make human beings more uniform and predictable. His belief that such systems should be ridiculed began as early as his grammar school days, when one of his masters reported, "He shows great originality, which must be curbed at all cost." This great originality, which led Ustinov to create brilliant vignettes rather than plays with conventionally unified and carefully developed plots and which caused him to try constantly to dramatize "the comic side of things tragic and the melancholy of things ribald," has accounted for much of the criticism he has received from reviewers who wish his satires were curbed by closer attention to proper form. But the battle against rigidity and preconceptions continues to affect the style as well as the substance of Ustinov's works.

—Helen Houser Popovich

VANBRUGH, Sir John. English. Born in London, baptized 24 January 1664. Educated at the King's School, Chester, to age 19; also studied in France, 1683–85. Commissioned ensign in the 13th foot regiment of Lord Huntingdon, 1686; arrested in Calais for espionage, and imprisoned in France, 1688–92; Captain in Lord Berkeley's Marine Regiment, 1696; Captain in Lord Huntingdon's Regiment, 1702. Married Henrietta Maria Yarborough in 1719; one son. Architect: designed Castle Howard, 1701, Haymarket Theatre, 1703, Blenheim Palace, 1705, Fleurs (Floors Castle), 1716, Seaton Delavel, 1720, etc.; Comptroller to the Public Works, 1702–13, 1715; Manager, with Congreve, Haymarket Theatre, London, 1705–06; appointed Carlisle Herald, 1703, and Clarenceux King-at-Arms, 1704–26, in the College of Heralds; Surveyor of Greenwich Hospital, 1715. Knighted, 1723. *Died 26 March 1726.*

PUBLICATIONS

Collections

Complete Works, edited by Bonamy Dobrée and Geoffrey Webb. 4 vols., 1927–28.

Play

The Relapse; or, Virtue in Danger (produced 1696). 1697; edited by Bernard Harris, 1971.
Aesop, 2 parts, from a play by Boursault (produced 1696–97). 2 vols., 1697.
The Provoked Wife (produced 1697). 1697; edited by Peter Dixon, 1975.
The Country House, from a play by Dancourt (produced 1698). 1715.
The Pilgrim, from the play by Fletcher (produced 1700). 1700.
The False Friend, from a play by Le Sage (produced 1702). 1702.
Squire Trelooby, with Congreve and William Walsh, from a play by Molière (produced 1704). Revised version by James Ralph published as *The Cornish Squire,* 1734.
The Confederacy, from a play by Dancourt (produced 1705; also produced as *The City Wives' Confederacy).* 1705.
The Mistake, from a play by Molière (produced 1705). 1706.
The Cuckold in Conceit (produced 1707).
Plays. 2 vols., 1719.
A Journey to London, completed by Cibber (as *The Provoked Husband,* produced 1728). 1728.

Other

A Short Vindication of The Relapse and The Provoked Wife from Immorality and Profaneness. 1698.
Vanbrugh's Justification of What He Deposed in the Duchess of Marlborough's Late Trial. 1718.

Reading List: *Vanbrugh, Architect and Dramatist,* 1938, and *The Imagination of Vanbrugh and His Fellow Artists,* 1954, both by Laurence Whistler; *Vanbrugh* by Bernard Harris, 1967; "Vanbrugh and the Conventions of Restoration Comedy" by Gerald M. Berkowitz, in *Genre*

6, 1973; *Masks and Façades: Vanbrugh: The Man in His Setting* by Madeleine Bingham, 1974; *Vanbrugh* by Kerry Downes, 1977.

*   *   *

Vanbrugh's reputation as a major comic dramatist rests on two plays produced within six months of each other at the end of the seventeenth century, *The Relapse* and *The Provok'd Wife*. Like Etherege and Wycherley, the two finest comic playwrights of the previous generation, Vanbrugh was not a professional writer and devoted only a fairly short period of his life to the theatre, so that his output, like theirs, is relatively small. Indeed he is at least as renowned for his architecture, especially Castle Howard and Blenheim Palace, as for his plays. Belonging to the generation of dramatists that includes Congreve, Farquhar, Steele, and Colley Cibber, Vanbrugh was writing after the Glorious Revolution of 1688 when the theatre was again coming under moralistic attacks because of its alleged licentiousness and obscenity. Vanbrugh himself was criticized in the most influential of these, Jeremy Collier's comprehensive *A Short View of the Immorality and Profaneness of the English Stage* (1698), and published a reply in the same year, *A Short Vindication,* in which he defends *The Relapse* and *The Provok'd Wife* against Collier's strictures. At a time when comic drama was beginning to undergo the transformation that led to the homiletic "exemplary" or "sentimental" comedy of the eighteenth century, which concentrated on providing models of virtue and examples of moral reformation to be emulated rather than on comedy's traditional function of ridiculing vice, folly, and affectation, Vanbrugh was intent on keeping alive the satirical mainstream of seventeenth-century comedy descending from Ben Jonson. Like Congreve, he was greatly indebted to the dramatists of Charles II's reign who developed the so-called "wit" or "manners" comedy of the Restoration, but because of his originality in handling its conventions he made a distinctive contribution to this kind of comedy. This is partly because of his essentially serious preoccupation with the subject of marriage, especially the tensions between husband and wife in ill-matched and unhappy relationships, and partly because of the robust energy of his plays that manifests itself in his rich characterization and his inventiveness in creating comic situations. Vanbrugh does in fact cross Shadwell's comedy of "humours" with Etherege's and Congreve's comedy of "wit." Although less caustically satirical than Wycherley, less stylistically refined than Congreve, and less genial than Farquhar, he is undoubtedly one of the wittiest of Restoration writers and for sheer vitality he has few equals among his contemporaries and eighteenth-century successors.

Vanbrugh wrote *The Relapse*, his first play to be staged, in response to Cibber's *Love's Last Shift* (1696), in which Amanda employs subterfuge and deception, including seduction, to win back her rakish husband Loveless who has deserted her. Cibber presents Amanda's reprehensible conduct as admirable, and Loveless, overwhelmed by her display of wifely love, is instantly reconciled to her and morally reformed. Vanbrugh clearly found this sentimental and sententious dénouement facile, dishonest, and unconvincing, and in *The Relapse* wrote a sequel that is also a reply to *Love's Last Shift*. *The Relapse* does, however, stand as a completely independent work that can be appreciated without reference to Cibber's considerably inferior play. Vanbrugh's main plot continues the story of Amanda and Loveless after the penitent's apparent rehabilitation and shows how temporary such reformations usually are. Loveless soon reverts to his promiscuous ways when temptation arrives in the form of Amanda's widowed cousin Berinthia, whereas the virtuous Amanda resists Worthy's offer of adulterous love. At the end of the play Vanbrugh presents no solution to the problem of Amanda and Loveless's marriage, which is left unresolved. Interesting and unusual as this part of the play is, it almost takes second place to the sub-plot concerning Lord Foppington. Vanbrugh again draws on *Love's Last Shift*, since Lord Foppington is Cibber's Sir Novelty Fashion elevated to the peerage, but Vanbrugh also transforms Cibber's amusing portrait of a fop into not only the most rounded presentation of a fashionable beau in contemporary drama but one of the great comic characters of the English stage. Almost as unforgettable is Sir Tunbelly Clumsey, Vanbrugh's version of another stereotype of Restoration comedy, the boorish country knight. Structurally *The Relapse* may be faulty, and Vanbrugh, a fundamentally moral writer, is unable to eschew completely the sentimentality that mars Cibber's play so badly, but its sustained comic brilliance more than compensates for its defects.

The Provok'd Wife, a better organised play than its predecessor, also contains one of the best comic characters of the period, Sir John Brute, the most memorable of the numerous husbands in Restoration comedy who are heartily sick of marriage and their wives and who try, not very successfully, to devote themselves to a life of debauchery. The surly, rude, and stubborn Sir John has ruined his marriage, and Vanbrugh explores sympathetically the predicament of Lady Brute who is maltreated by her husband but who is too virtuous to give herself to her admirer Constant. Vanbrugh deals with the issue of marital incompatibility, at a time when divorce was virtually impossible, in a sensitive and humane way, not in the flippant and jokey manner typical of contemporary comedy, and is too realistic to offer an easy theatrical solution producing a happy ending for Lady Brute. As in *The Relapse*, there is no tidy resolution of the main plot.

Apart from the unfinished *A Journey to London*, which reached the stage in 1728 in a version revised, completed, and sentimentalized by Colley Cibber entitled *The Provok'd Husband*, Vanbrugh's other dramatic works are either adaptations or translations of earlier plays. His one attempt to revamp an English play, a prose version of Fletcher's *The Pilgrim*, impoverishes rather than enriches the original, but the opposite occurs in the case of some of his translations. As a translator of recent French plays, including some of Molière's, Vanbrugh was far from slavish and felt free to alter and add to his sources, the result being that he imbued them with some of his typical vigour and broad humour. The outstanding example is *The Confederacy*, a superb adaptation of Dancourt's *Les Bourgeoises à la Mode*, itself a lively and witty comedy that Vanbrugh, by transferring the action from Paris to London, nevertheless succeeds in enhancing from beginning to end. Also worthy of note is *Aesop*, based on Boursault's *Les Fables d'Ésope*, in which Vanbrugh characteristically tones down the sentiment of the original in favour of comic action. Vanbrugh's two masterpieces still hold the stage and *The Confederacy* has been revived in recent years, but they are not produced as frequently as they deserve.

—Peter Lewis

---

van DRUTEN, John (William).   American.   Born in London, England, 1 June 1901; emigrated to the United States. 1926; naturalized, 1944. Educated at University College School, London, 1911–17; subsequently studied law: awarded LL.B., University of London, 1922; Solicitor of the Supreme Court of Judicature, 1923. Special Lecturer in English Law and Legal History, University College of Wales, Aberystwyth, 1923–26; full-time writer from 1928. Recipient: American Academy of Arts and Letters Award of Merit Medal, 1946; New York Drama Critics Circle Award, 1952. *Died 19 December 1957.*

PUBLICATIONS

Plays

The Return Half (produced 1924).

Chance Acquaintance (produced 1927).
Diversion (produced 1928).   1928.
Young Woodley (produced 1928).   1928.
The Return of the Soldier, from the novel by Rebecca West (produced 1928).   1928.
After All (produced 1929).   1929.
London Wall (produced 1931).   1931.
Sea Fever, with Auriol Lee, from a play by Marcel Pagnol (produced 1931).
There's Always Juliet (produced 1931).   1931.
Hollywood Holiday, with Benn Levy (produced 1931).   1931.
Somebody Knows (produced 1932).   1932.
Behold We Live (produced 1932).   1932.
The Distaff Side (produced 1933).   1933.
Flowers of the Forest (produced 1934).   1934.
Most of the Game (produced 1935).   1936.
Gertie Maude (produced 1937).   1937.
Leave Her to Heaven (produced 1940).   1941.
Old Acquaintance (produced 1940).   1941.
Solitaire, from the novel by E. Corle (produced 1942).
The Damask Cheek, with Lloyd R. Morris (produced 1942).   1943.
The Voice of the Turtle (produced 1943).   1944.
I Remember Mama, from the novel *Mama's Bank Account* by Kathryn Forbes (produced 1944).   1945.
The Mermaids Singing (produced 1945).   1946.
The Druid Circle (produced 1947).   1948.
Make Way for Lucia, from novels by E. F. Benson (produced 1948).   1949.
Bell, Book, and Candle (produced 1950).   1951.
I Am a Camera, from *The Berlin Stories* by Christopher Isherwood (produced 1951).   1954.
I've Got Sixpence (produced 1952).   1953.
Dancing in the Chequered Shade (produced 1955).

Screenplays: *Young Woodley*, with Victor Kendall, 1930; *I Loved a Soldier*, 1936; *Parnell*, with S. N. Behrman, 1937; *Night Must Fall*, 1937; *The Citadel*, with others, 1938; *Raffles*, with Sidney Howard, 1939; *Lucky Partner*, with Allen Scott, 1940; *My Life with Caroline*, with Arnold Belgard, 1941; *Johnny Come Lately*, 1943; *Old Acquaintance*, with Lenore Coffee, 1943; *Forever and a Day*, with others, 1944; *Gaslight*, with Walter Reisch and John L. Balderston, 1944; *The Voice of the Turtle*, 1948.

Fiction

Young Woodley.   1929.
A Woman on Her Way.   1930.
And Then You Wish.   1936.
The Vicarious Years.   1955.

Other

The Way to the Present: A Personal Record.   1938.
Playwright at Work.   1953.
Widening Circle (autobiography).   1957.

*   *   *

A prolific writer – best known for his plays but also recognized as a novelist, screenwriter, and autobiographer – John van Druten delighted audiences for more than thirty years with his polished, urbane comedies. The persistent tone in his works is warm and gentle; his style has been praised for its convincing naturalness and controlled simplicity.

Van Druten's plots are often loosely structured, imitative, and readily forgettable. *I Remember Mama*, one of his most popular works, for example, is structured as a series of vignettes linked together by tone and characters, but scarcely more unified than the collection of Kathryn Forbes's short stories on which it was based.

When there is a developed plot in either his original works or his adaptations, it is usually one of two variations on the same basic action: two people meet, have or contemplate having an affair, discover that they love each other, and then joyfully renounce wantonness and move toward a thoroughly conventional marriage (as in *There's Always Juliet*; *The Distaff Side*; *Bell, Book, and Candle*; *The Damask Cheek*; and *The Voice of the Turtle*); or, sadly, discover that their age, circumstance, or character prevents such a marriage (as in *Young Woodley*, *Old Acquaintance*, *The Mermaids Singing*, and *I Am a Camera*). In developing these plots, van Druten moves perilously close to the brink of sentimentality and heavy-handed moralism; but his wit and determination to master "the difficult art of sincerity" keep him, with rare exceptions, from plunging headlong into the abyss.

Indeed, van Druten's plays were consistently praised for their fresh dialogue, their unforced cleverness, and their sophisticated repartée. His fiction and autobiographies, too, are natural and eminently readable.

His awareness of the importance of style and his concern that his works be well-written are reflected both in his commentary on his own works and in his evaluation of the works of others. For example, he criticizes bad writing, which he describes as that which is filled with bathos, facetiousness, and an endless flow of shop-worn phrases that "produce no effect save that of total weariness." He states that only the immature taste can appreciate great sweetness or a "mustard and vinegar sharpness," which the experienced palate would disdain. And in his own works, from the beginning, he attempted to avoid these excesses.

Van Druten's artistry in writing dialogue brings his characters to life. They are unforgettable. Sally Bowles, the complex, misguided, comical, pathetic American ex-patriate in *I Am a Camera*, who leads the life of the grasshopper as the deadly threat of the Third Reich moves forward; Marta, the warm, clever, protective, stable foundation of her family in *I Remember Mama*; Gillian Holroyd, the thoroughly human witch in *Bell, Book, and Candle* – these are only three who clearly rise above the ordinary to the distinctive.

This ability to create memorable characters, and thus major roles, was early recognized by Hollywood, where van Druten wrote dialogue, adapted his own works and those of others, and collaborated on screen plays for major actors from virtually every important studio. He was largely responsible, for instance, for creating the role of Paula Alquist in *Gaslight*, a role for which Ingrid Bergman won the Academy Award in 1944. It is on such success that his reputation rests.

—Helen Houser Popovich

VILLIERS, George.   See BUCKINGHAM, 2nd Duke of.

WAKEFIELD MASTER.

PUBLICATIONS

Plays

The Wakefield Pageants in the Towneley Cycle, edited by A. C. Cawley. 1958.

Reading List: "The Craftsmanship of the Wakefield Master" by H-J. Diller, in *Anglia 83,* 1965; Introduction by M. Rose to *The Wakefield Mystery Plays,* 1961; *The English Mystery Plays* by R. Woolf, 1972; *The Construction of the Wakefield Cycle* by John Gardner, 1974.

*   *   *

The Wakefield Master was a man of exceptional dramatic skill who wrote and revised parts of the Towneley Cycle of mystery plays in the first half of the fifteenth century. His highly original style is characterised by a) local allusions, referring to places in the neighbourhood of Wakefield, Yorkshire; b) vivid language, utilising proverbs, colloquialisms, vulgarisms, and sometimes blasphemy; c) frequent anachronism; d) a fondness for developing non-biblical material, particularly folktales; e) extensive use of a unique nine-line stanza of varying line length, rhyming aaaabcccb with internal rhyme in the first four. A. C. Cawley in *The Wakefield Pageants* further adds "a lively use of gesture and action, an outspoken criticism of contemporary abuses, a bold rehandling of secular material for comic purposes, and an unusual skill in characterization."

The extent of his work has to be inferred on stylistic grounds. Of the thirty-two plays in the Towneley manuscript, five complete plays – *Noah* (3), *First Shepherds' Play* (12), *Second Shepherds' Play* (13), *Herod* (16), and *The Buffeting* (21) – can with conviction be assigned to him as they are written entirely in the nine-line stanza. Plays 2, 20, 22, 23, 24, 27, 29, and 30 make some use of this stanza, and probably reflect a reworking of older material. This second group has verbal and thematic parallels with the first, particularly in play 2 (*The Killing of Abel*), which is reckoned to be largely, if not entirely, the Wakefield Master's work, despite the fact that it contains only one stanza of characteristic Wakefield form.

The Wakefield Master's technique is most clearly demonstrated by comparison with the York, Chester, and *Ludus Coventriae* plays on the same subjects (see H-J. Diller). Noah's building of the ark, for instance, clearly presented a problem and a challenge to the mystery play authors. In the York *Building of the Ark* Noah simply describes his actions; in the Chester *Deluge* the speeches and the actions are stylised; in *Ludus Coventriae* Noah goes offstage and returns with the ark fully constructed; but the Wakefield Master's technique is to intersperse Noah's commentary on his solitary work with frequent pleas to the Almighty ("Unless God help ..."), physical reactions ("Now I'll throw off my gown and work in my tunic ..."), complaints ("My back will break, I think ..."), and psychological reactions ("It is better made than I could have thought ..."). The dramatic potential is thus more fully realised.

Whereas in many of the mystery plays characters simply enact the facts of a well-established narrative, the *dramatis personae* of the Master's plays have motivation and psychological realism, so that we often witness the evolution of an idea in the context of external events. We recognise in Cain, for example, a brooding and irrational grievance developing against Abel; we recognise in Herod a dangerous combination of temporal power and spiritual weakness through which he is steered towards his desperate plan to slaughter the Innocents; we see in Caiaphas the flame of anger growing fiercer as Jesus maintains his rigid silence in the face of his accusers.

The Wakefield Master's dramatic skill is nowhere more clearly shown than in his best-known work, *The Second Shepherds' Play*, apparently an alternative to *The First Shepherds' Play* which is different in all but the formal biblical features and in the general characterisation of the Shepherds themselves. Mak's elaborate scheme to steal a sheep provides a good plot, and the hiding of the animal in a cradle is clearly a bold parody of the birth of Christ, "the lamb of God." The audience is involved by reference to contemporary conditions, local places, and possibly local personages: there is good balance between scenes, with subtle movement from one to the next; there are humour and tension, as when the Third Shepherd's tenderness in presenting a gift to the supposed "child" in its cradle results in the discovery of the stolen sheep. All the same, the visit of the Shepherds to the Christ Child in the stable is simple and dignified.

Praise of the Wakefield Master, though extensive, has been tempered by some adverse criticism. The charge to which he is most susceptible is that his extensive use of secular material obscures the essential doctrinal themes of his plays; however, it is possible that the subjects on which he wrote (especially Noah, the Shepherds, and Herod) had already become established points of farce and light relief in the cycles as a whole.

—G. A. Lester

WALCOTT, Derek (Alton). Jamaican. Born in Castries, St. Lucia, West Indies, 23 January 1930. Educated at St. Mary's College, St. Lucia; University of the West Indies, Kingston, Jamaica, B.A. 1953. Married; three children. Taught at St. Mary's College and Jamaica College. Formerly, Feature Writer, *Public Opinion*, Kingston, and *Trinidad Guardian*, Port-of-Spain. Since 1959, Founding Director, Trinidad Theatre Workshop. Recipient: Rockefeller Fellowship, 1957; Guinness Award, 1961; Heinemann Award, 1966; Cholmondeley Award, 1969; Order of the Humming Bird, Trinidad and Tobago, 1969; Obie Award, 1971. Lives in Trinidad.

Publications

Plays

    Henri Christophe: A Chronicle (produced 1950). 1950.
    Henri Dernier: A Play for Radio Production. 1951.
    Sea at Dauphin (produced 1954). 1954.
    Ione: A Play with Music (produced 1957). 1954.
    Drums and Colours (produced 1958). In *Caribbean Quarterly 1* and *2*, 1961.
    Ti-Jean and His Brothers, music by André Tanker (produced 1958). In *The Dream on Monkey Mountain and Other Plays*, 1971.
    Malcochon; or, Six in the Rain (produced 1959; as *Six in the Rain*, produced 1960; as *Malcochon*, produced 1969). In *The Dream on Monkey Mountain and Other Plays*, 1971.

The Dream on Monkey Mountain (produced 1967).   In *The Dream on Monkey Mountain and Other Plays*, 1971.
In a Fine Castle (produced 1970).
The Dream on Monkey Mountain and Other Plays (includes *Ti-Jean and His Brothers, Malcochon, Sea at Dauphin*, and the essay "What the Twilight Says").   1971.
The Charlatan, music by Galt MacDermot (produced 1974).
The Joker of Seville, and O Babylon!   1978.

Verse

Twenty-Five Poems.   1948.
Epitaph for the Young.   1949.
Poems.   1953.
In a Green Night: Poems 1948–1960.   1962.
Selected Poems.   1964.
The Castaway and Other Poems.   1965.
The Gulf and Other Poems.   1969.
Another Life.   1973.
Sea Grapes.   1976.
Selected Verse.   1976.
Selected Poems, edited by O. R. Dathorne.   1977.

Reading List: *Walcott: "Another Life"* by Edward Baugh, 1978.

*   *   *

The first and simplest pleasure offered by Derek Walcott's poetry is the sense of being alive and out-of-doors in the West Indies: sand and salt on the skin, sunlight and space and the open beach, sea-grapes and sea-almonds, liners and islands, where always "The starved eye devours the seascape for the morsel of a sail,/The horizon threads it infinitely."

Walcott was a painter before he was a poet, and as a youth set off with a friend around his native island of St. Lucia to put it on canvas and thus create it in the imagination. Later he found he could do the work of creation better with words and metaphor, and that this too was needed:

> For no-one had yet written of this landscape
> that it was possible, though there were sounds
> given to its varieties of wood.

Walcott has kept his painter's eye, and is especially aware of effects of light. He often compares life with art ("Tables in the trees, like entering Renoir"), as indeed he often quotes or echoes lines from the English Metaphysicals, Tennyson, Eliot, Dylan Thomas, and others. These things, taken together with the high polish of his verse, have sometimes led to accusations of virtuoso artificiality and preciosity. But, though there may be some lapses which deserve such strictures, it is precisely the successful transmuting of life into art which makes Walcott's achievement so important.

At his best he fuses the outward scene with inward experience and with a form of English words, resonant within the tradition of literature in English but also appropriate to the particular occasion, all in one single act of perception. In so doing he enhances and illustrates (in the Renaissance sense of that word) the landscape and the human lives that are found on the islands. It is not surprising, perhaps, that he should be such a good love poet, for the experience of love has this same quality of enhancing places: "But islands can only exist/If we have loved in them."

Love, the creation of a centre of consciousness and a relationship of security with the place one lives are particularly important in societies where a history of slavery, cultural deprivation, colonial dependency, and, latterly, tourism have combined to reinforce the more generalized modern feelings of alienation and contingency. Walcott's work may therefore be quite as socially important as that of more obsessively socially-orientated West Indian writers.

Walcott by no means ignores the well-known dilemmas of the West Indian situation. In "Ruins of a Great House" he works out in a complex fashion his relationship with men like Ralegh, "ancestral murderers and poets," with England and the English language, and with the earlier history of a ruined plantation house. Here and elsewhere he is aware that he has one white grandfather, who like many others "drunkenly seeded their archipelago." When the Mau Mau insurrection in Kenya occurs, he cannot give murderers on either side his blessing though "poisoned with the blood of both," and when he sees television film of the Biafran war he notes "The soldiers' helmeted shadows could have been white." In general his aim seems to be not to make rhetoric out of the past, but to transcend it: "All in compassion ends/So differently from what the heart arranged."

Walcott is also a successful and prolific playwright, the founder-director of the Trinidad Theatre Workshop, a travelling group of players who move around the Caribbean. Whereas the poetry is almost entirely in standard English, the plays are largely in the creole idiom of the West Indies. A further linguistic complication is that the popular language of Walcott's home island is a Creole French (as on Jean Rhys's home island of Dominica) and the French phrases and songs of the islands also find their way in quotation, and, with their special intonations, into his work.

In his best-known play, *Dream on Monkey Mountain*, Makak the charcoal-burner lives in utter degradation, dreams he is king of a united Africa, yet has to go on living in the everyday world. "The problem," Walcott said in an interview (*New Yorker*, 26 June 1971), "is to recognize our African origins but not to romanticize them." Generally, one feels that Walcott has little sympathy for exploitation of the past by modern ideologists, even if they are negro ideologists, and some of his bitterest lines are reserved for post-independence politicians. Against their power and rhetoric he sets out on a subtler and more revolutionary course:

> I sought more power than you, more fame than yours,
> I was more hermetic, I knew the commonweal,
> I pretended subtly to lose myself in crowds
> knowing my passage would alter their reflection

and at the same time to redeem the past

> Its racial quarrels blown like smoke to sea.
> From all that sorrow, beauty is our gain
> Though it may not seem so
> To an old fisherman rowing home in the rain.

—Ned Thomas

WARREN, Mercy (née Otis). American. Born in Barnstable, Massachusetts, 14 September 1728; sister of the American political activist James Otis. Educated privately. Married James Warren in 1754; five sons. Settled in Plymouth, Massachusetts, 1754; became active poet and historical apologist for the American cause in the pamphlet war preceding the War of Independence; a friend of John Adams and other American patriots. *Died 19 October 1814.*

PUBLICATIONS

Plays

The Adulator. 1773.
The Defeat, in Boston *Gazette*, 1773.
The Group. 1775.
The Sack of Rome and The Ladies of Castille, in *Poems*. 1790.

Verse

Poems, Dramatic and Miscellaneous. 1790.

Other

Observations on the New Constitution. 1788.
History of the Rise, Progress, and Termination of the American Revolution. 3 vols., 1805.
A Study in Dissent: The Warren-Gerry Correspondence, edited by C. Harvey Gardiner. 1968.

Reading List: *Warren* by Alice Brown, 1896; *First Lady of the Revolution: The Life of Warren* by Katharine S. Anthony, 1958.

*   *   *

Under normal circumstances, Mercy Warren would probably have restrained her literary impulse to private correspondence, elegant letters with, now and then, a poem enclosed. By birth and by marriage, however, she was allied to the anti-Tory faction in Massachusetts and, as a matron in her forties, she emerged as a voice in the pamphlet war which preceded America's Revolutionary War for Independence. Unlike her brother, James Otis, whose passionate but closely reasoned pamphlets were so influential in the 1760's, Mrs. Warren chose to write satirical dramatic sketches. In *The Adulateur*, to which some other hand added a high-rhetoric account of the Boston Massacre, *The Defeat*, and *The Group*, she introduced caricatures of her political opponents who, in waspish blank verse, condemned themselves and their colleagues. However interesting as eighteenth-century agitprops, Mrs. Warren's satires are minimally dramatic and have no characters in the complex sense of the word. Since the plays were published anonymously, as so much of the pamphlet literature was, later scholars decided that Mrs. Warren was the author of a number of unsigned satirical plays. *The Blockheads; or, The Affrighted Officers* (1776) and *The Motley Assembly* (1779), are still assigned to her by some editors, but they are so different in tone and style from anything else that she published that it is highly unlikely that she wrote them. One anonymous work, the pamphlet *Observations on the New Constitution*, a vigorous statement of the anti-federalist position in the ratification fight of 1787–88, is now rightly recognized as her work.

Aside from her political writings, Mrs. Warren wrote occasional verse, sometimes satirical, more often philosophic. Written in rhymed couplets, her poems were conventional in sentiment, vocabulary, and imagery, although they often embodied the austere, anti-deist, Christian morality that was so important to Mrs. Warren's life and thought. She wrote two verse tragedies, *The Ladies of Castile* and *The Sack of Rome*, which used historical material with contemporary overtones; like so many minor British plays of the eighteenth century, they substituted declamation for dramatic action. Her *History of the Rise, Progress, and Termination of the American Revolution*, thirty years in the making, is her most lasting work, although it is interesting today not as an objective history but for the "Biographical, Political, and Moral Observations" the title page promises. Her work as a whole is less important as a literary *oeuvre* than as a vehicle which gives the reader a glimpse of a tough-minded American woman who reflected and in some ways transcended the political and social context in which she wrote.

—Gerald Weales

WEBSTER, John.   English.   Born in England, probably in London, c. 1580. Very little is known of his life: he was married and had several children; possibly a member of the Merchant Taylors' Company; clerk of the parish of St. Andrews, Holborn; writer for Henslowe c. 1602. *Died in the 1630's.*

PUBLICATIONS

Collections

Works, edited by F. L. Lucas.   4 vols., 1927; revised edition, 1966.

Plays

Sir Thomas Wyatt, with Thomas Heywood and Dekker (produced 1602–07?).   1607; edited by Fredson Bowers, in *Dramatic Works of Dekker*, 1953–61.
Westward Ho, with Dekker (produced 1604).   1607; edited by Fredson Bowers, in *Dramatic Works of Dekker*, 1953–61.
Northward Ho, with Dekker (produced 1605).   1607; edited by Fredson Bowers, in *Dramatic Works of Dekker*, 1953–61.
Appius and Virginia, with Thomas Heywood (produced 1608?).   1654.
The Devil's Law Case; or, When Women Go to Law the Devil Is Full of Business (produced 1610?).   1623; edited by Elizabeth M. Brennan, 1974.
The White Devil (produced 1612?).   1612; edited by J. R. Mulryne, 1970.
The Duchess of Malfi (produced 1613–14?).   1623; edited by Clive Hart, 1972.
Any Thing for a Quiet Life, with Middleton (produced 1621?).   1662.

Monuments of Honour (produced 1624). 1624; edited by R. T. D. Sayle, in *Lord Mayors' Pageants of the Merchant Taylors' Company*, 1931.
A Cure for a Cuckold, with William Rowley (produced 1624–25?). 1661.

Verse

A Monumental Column, in *Three Elegies on the Most Lamented Death of Prince Henry*. 1613.

Bibliography: *Webster: A Classified Bibliography* by William E. Mahaney, 1973.

Reading List: *Webster: A Critical Study*, 1951, and *Webster: The Duchess of Malfi*, 1963, both by Clifford Leech; *The Tragic Satire of Webster* by Travis Bogard, 1955; *Webster's Borrowings* by Robert W. Dent, 1960; *Webster* by Ian Scott-Kilvert, 1964; *Webster and His Critics 1617–1964* by Don D. Moore, 1966; *A Study of Webster* by Peter B. Murray, 1969; *Webster* edited by Brian Morris, 1970; *The Art of Webster* by Ralph Berry, 1972; *Tragedy and the Jacobean Temper: The Major Plays of Webster* by Richard Bodtke, 1972; *Webster: Politics and Tragedy* by Robert P. Griffin, 1972.

*   *   *

John Webster is among the shadowiest figures of the Elizabethan age; even the dates of his birth and death are not known for certain. We first hear of him in May 1602 when Philip Henslowe records a payment of £5 to Drayton, Webster, Middleton, and others as advance fees on a play called *Caesar's Fall*; the play, however, is lost. In the preface to his play *The Devil's Law Case* Webster himself refers to another of his plays, *The Guise*; this too is lost. In his pageant *Monuments of Honour* he describes himself as "born free of the Merchant Taylers' Company." This may mean that he was the son of John Webster, a freeman of that guild. Webster may also be the actor of that name who toured Germany in 1596.

In 1604 Webster wrote an induction to Marston's *The Malcontent* when the King's Men first performed the play, which was originally written for a boys' company. The induction ingeniously frames the play within a discussion of its merits by the actors about to perform it. In the same year he collaborated with Thomas Dekker in writing *Westward Ho* and the following year they wrote *Northward Ho*. The same pair also contributed verses to a volume illustrating the allegorical arches erected to welcome King James to London. In 1613 Webster published *A Monumental Column* commemorating Prince Henry who had died the year before.

Many plays or parts of plays have been assigned to Webster but only four are generally recognized as being by him alone. Of these *The Devil's Law Case* is the least impressive, being a meagre and loosely structured tragi-comedy. Swinburne wrote that "the author of *Appius and Virginia* would have earned an honourable and enduring place in the history of English letters," and the play, in various adaptations, held the stage for a century or so after Webster's death. But it does not bear sustained comparison with his two great achievements in tragedy, *The White Devil* and *The Duchess of Malfi*.

Both plays are based on actual events in the recent past as transmitted through popular Italian novellas. The appetite for scenes of blood and violence and for lavish spectacle, and the audience's delight in elaborate stage apparatus are amply catered for in both plays. Ghosts, poisoned paintings, disembodied hands as well as murder by strangulation and breaking the victim's neck are a few of the many such occurrences in the plays. Incest, adultery, lycanthropy, to say nothing of mere murder, form the ingredients of both plots. But what gives them their tragic intensity is the atmosphere of brooding darkness which pervades them and the eloquent dignity with which Webster's central figures face their impending death.

Vittoria, Flamineo, and the Duchess of Malfi find in their last moments epitaphs for themselves of such compelling power that, in the case of the two former figures at least, we forget how corrupt the course of their lives has been: "My soul like to a ship in a black storm,/Is driven, I know not whither," cries Vittoria, the "White Devil," and her brother responds with "While we look up to heaven we confound/Knowledge with knowledge. Oh, I am in a mist!" The intense melancholy, haunting disillusionment, and pervasive sense of corruption in high places, which are so marked a feature of Jacobean tragedy, found in these two plays their most striking expression. Encountering them we understand, if we cannot altogether share, the feeling which moved Swinburne to write: "Except in Aeschylus, in Dante and in Shakespeare, I at least know not where to seek for passages which in sheer force of tragic and noble horror ... may be set against the subtlest, the deepest, the sublimest passages of Webster."

—Gāmini Salgādo

WESKER, Arnold.   English.   Born in Stepney, London, 24 May 1932. Educated at Upton House School, Hackney, London, 1943–48; London School of Film Technique, 1956. Served in the Royal Air Force, 1950–52. Married Doreen (Dusty) Bicker in 1958; two sons and one daughter. Worked as a furniture-maker's apprentice and carpenter's mate, 1948, bookseller's assistant, 1949, 1952, plumber's mate, 1952, farm labourer and seed sorter, 1953, kitchen porter, 1953–54, and pastry cook, 1954–58. Founder-Director, Centre 42, London, 1961–70. Former Member, Youth Service Council. Recipient: Arts Council grant, 1958; *Evening Standard* award, 1959; *Encyclopaedia Britannica* Award, 1959; Marzotto Prize, 1964. Lives in London.

PUBLICATIONS

Plays

    The Wesker Trilogy.   1960.
        Chicken Soup with Barley (produced 1958).   In *New English Dramatists*, 1959.
        Roots (produced 1959).   1959.
        I'm Talking about Jerusalem (produced 1960).   1960.
    The Kitchen (produced 1959).   In *New English Dramatists 2*, 1960; expanded version, 1962.
    Chips with Everything (produced 1962).   1962.
    The Nottingham Captain: A Moral for Narrator, Voices and Orchestra, music by Wilfred Josephs and Dave Lee (produced 1962).   In *Six Sundays in January*, 1971.
    Menace (televised 1963).   In *Six Sundays in January*, 1971.
    Their Very Own and Golden City (produced 1965).   1966; revised version (produced 1974).
    The Four Seasons (produced 1965).   1966.
    The Friends (produced 1970).   1970.
    The Old Ones (produced 1972).   1973; revised version, edited by Michael Marland, 1974.

The Wedding Feast, from a story by Dostoevsky (produced 1974).
The Journalists. 1975.
The Plays. 2 vols., 1976–77.
Love Letters on Blue Paper, from his own story (televised 1976; revised version, produced 1978).
The Merchant, from the play *The Merchant of Venice* by Shakespeare (produced 1977).

Screenplay: *The Kitchen*, 1961.

Television Plays: *Menace*, 1963; *Love Letters on Blue Paper*, from his own story, 1976.

Fiction

Love Letters on Blue Paper (stories). 1974.
Said the Old Man to the Young Man: Three Stories. 1978.

Other

Labour and the Arts: II; or, What, Then Is to Be Done? 1960.
The Modern Playwright; or, "O Mother, Is It Worth It?" 1961.
Fears of Fragmentation (essays). 1970.
Six Sundays in January (miscellany). 1971.
Say Goodbye – You May Never See Them Again: Scenes from Two East-End Backgrounds, paintings by John Allin. 1974.
Journey into Journalism. 1977.
Fatlips (juvenile). 1978.

Reading List: *Anger and After* by John Russell Taylor, 1962; *Wesker* by Ronald Hayman, 1970; *The Plays of Wesker* by Glenda Leeming and Simon Trussler, 1971; *Theatre Language: A Study of Arden, Osborne, Pinter, and Wesker* by John Russell Brown, 1972.

*   *   *

Arnold Wesker has suffered from instant critical acclaim for early works which appeared to conform to a fashion for working-class drama – and, conversely, from what he has himself called the "casual condemnation" of later plays which have sought new directions and themes, and so upset critical preconceptions. He is a writer much-hated and much-loved, and it is not difficult to identify the ingredients which his detractors have found superficially irritating: an assumption that answers *may* be there for the seeking, in a theatre where middle-brow nihilism is a dominant force; an unfashionably sincere faith in the power of the written word and, indeed, of literacy itself, at a time when the McLuhanite heresy remains widespread; and a refusal to conceal what is serious beneath a compromising veneer of comedy, where it is modish to argue that existential anguish can only be made bearable by laughter.

Wesker is an autobiographical writer, not (at least, since the early plays) in his choice of plots, but in the sources of the characters from which they spring. He is a skilled but largely instinctive craftsman, with a wide stylistic range, and an expository skill appropriate to all formal requirements. He has a quick, responsive ear for racial or regional idioms. And he is an independent though not entirely an original thinker: thus, while other dramatists were drawing inspiration from Marcuse or R. D. Laing, he was writing *The Merchant* saturated in the works of Ruskin and George Eliot.

He has often been accused of naivety and a simplistic reading of complex social and political issues: yet a closer look at the plays indicts his critics of the very same charges. Alike in *The Kitchen* and the plays which came to comprise *The Wesker Trilogy*, his conclusions show the failure of revolutionary hopes, or, as in *Roots*, reveal a very tiny and particular success which only serves to highlight pervasive apathy and incomprehension. In *The Friends* and *Love Letters on Blue Paper*, a perverse optimism is achieved only through full acceptance of the fact of death. And *The Merchant* rewrites Shakespeare to show Shylock and Antonio intensely individualised, yet trapped by a bond that is a product of the law regulating the relationship between gentile and Jew, and so was intended as a surety for friendship rather than a symptom of hatred.

Why, then, has Wesker found his work since *The Friends* so difficult to get staged in the English-speaking theatre, although in parts of the world as different as Scandinavia, Latin America, and Japan he remains highly regarded and regularly produced? Perhaps it is in part a consequence of his characters' very openness – their lack of decent, British reticence. There is little that remains unspoken in Wesker's plays – and when a character does find an overt expression of feelings difficult, as in *Love Letters on Blue Paper*, an alternative but equally direct mode of expression (as the title here suggests) is found.

This was somehow acceptable in the East End Jewish setting of *Chicken Soup with Barley*, or in the working-class worlds of *The Kitchen*, *Roots*, or *Chips with Everything*, for English middle-class audiences do not expect the lower orders to preserve stiff upper lips (and Wesker's own valiant attempt to broaden the audience for the arts in Britain, through trades-union sponsorship and the Centre 42 movement, was an honourable failure). Although the later plays were written in a period when so many taboos have allegedly been overcome, their themes have nonetheless offended in direct proportion to their unsuitability for a liberal dinner table. Thus, *The Friends* is concerned not only with an awareness of mortality (the ultimate contemporary taboo), but the nature of friendship itself. And *The Journalists* similarly touched raw radical nerves: all very well to question the role of a capitalist-dominated press, but not the ethics of even *being* a journalist, in a society which probably gets the journalism it deserves.

Wesker is an unconscious craftsman, yet has ranged from the almost expressionist dominance of setting over characters in *The Kitchen*, to the "straightforward" naturalism of the Trilogy, to the impressionism of *Their Very Own and Golden City*, to the poetic feeling for *caesurae* in *The Four Seasons*, to the entirely logical yet un-pin-downable narrative flow of *The Wedding Feast*. His other plays are even harder to define stylistically, for he moulds each so closely to its subject that it would take a latter-day Polonius adequately to categorise the barrack-square realism combined with comic-strip caricature in *Chips with Everything*, or the extraordinary blending of minutely researched historical detail with acceptable Shakespearian "givens" in *The Merchant*.

As surely as Wesker has gone out of fashion, yet persevered to produce such master works as *The Friends* and *The Merchant*, almost as surely will he return to critical acclaim, and, one hopes, ignore it, the better to weather the next swing of fashion. He has staying power, stylistic range, and an entirely personal vocabulary and vision. For the discerning, his plays will survive so long as the insidious newspeak of the trendy and the trivial does not entirely overwhelm the English-speaking theatre.

—Simon Trussler

WHITE, Patrick (Victor Martindale). Australian. Born in London, England, 28 May 1912. Educated at schools in Australia, 1919–25; Cheltenham College, 1925–29; King's College, Cambridge, 1932–35, B.A. in modern languages 1935. Served in the Royal Air Force as an Intelligence Officer, in the Middle East, 1940–45. Travelled in Europe and the United States, and lived in London, before World War II; returned to Australia after the war. Recipient: Australian Literary Society Gold Medal, 1956; Miles Franklin Award, 1958, 1962; Smith Literary Award, 1959; National Conference of Christians and Jews' Brotherhood Award, 1962; Nobel Prize for Literature, 1973. A.C. (Companion, Order of Australia), 1975. Lives in Sydney.

PUBLICATIONS

Plays

> *Return to Abyssinia* (produced 1947).
> *The Ham Funeral* (produced 1961). In *Four Plays*, 1965.
> *The Season at Sarsaparilla* (produced 1962). In *Four Plays*, 1965.
> *A Cheery Soul* (produced 1963). In *Four Plays*, 1965.
> *Night on Bald Mountain* (produced 1964). In *Four Plays*, 1965.
> *Four Plays*. 1965.
> *Big Toys* (produced 1977).

Fiction

> *Happy Valley*. 1939.
> *The Living and the Dead*. 1941.
> *The Aunt's Story*. 1948.
> *The Tree of Man*. 1955.
> *Voss*. 1957.
> *Riders in the Chariot*. 1961.
> *The Burnt Ones* (stories). 1964.
> *The Solid Mandala*. 1966.
> *The Vivisector*. 1970.
> *The Eye of the Storm*. 1973.
> *The Cockatoos: Shorter Novels and Stories*. 1974.
> *A Fringe of Leaves*. 1976.

Verse

> *The Ploughman and Other Poems*. 1935.

Bibliography: *A Bibliography of White* by Janette Finch, 1966.

Reading List: *White* by Geoffrey Dutton, 1961; *White* by Robert F. Brissenden, 1966; *White* by Barry Argyle, 1967; *The Mystery of Unity: Theme and Technique in the Novels of White* by Patricia A. Morley, 1972; *The Eye in the Mandala: White, A Vision of Man and God* by Peter Beatson, 1976.

*   *   *

Patrick White comes from a pioneering Australian family, although he was born in London. He was educated in New South Wales and England, travelled widely in Europe and the U.S.A. before World War II, and also lived in London where he was much involved with the theatre, a life-long passion. Part of the depth and intensity of his view of the world comes from his experience of its newer and older civilizations.

His first novel, *Happy Valley* (which he will not allow to be reprinted), was highly praised by some of the most eminent contemporary English critics and writers. It is an uneven but powerful work, set in the high, cold country of southern New South Wales, where he had worked as a jackeroo (an Australian term for a young man learning the skills of managing sheep or cattle). Its immaturity shows in the strong stylistic influence of Joyce, its maturity in its characteristic searching assessment of the causes of human failure.

The Living and the Dead is set in the England of the second and third decades of the twentieth century, and is a harsh judgement of a society more dead than living, softened by the refusal of some of the characters, especially female, to "behave in the convention of a clever age that encouraged corrosiveness, destruction." It is also the first of White's many onslaughts on "the disgusting, the nauseating aspect of the human ego." White's deepest and most consistent purpose in all his work is the offering of signposts on the road to humility. He is a profoundly religious writer, not bound to any creed.

White's original genius appears unmistakably in his next novel, *The Aunt's Story*. The aunt is a spinster, Theodora Goodman, who although lonely and "leathery" has an extraordinarily rich understanding of life and people. Her story moves from reality to illusion, in Australia, Europe and the U.S.A.; she is broken by her longing, but inability, to reconcile the two.

White's next novel, *The Tree of Man*, is the result of his decision to return to Australia after the War, where he settled on a farm near Castle Hill, on the edge of Sydney, with a Greek friend and partner, Manoly Lascaris. All his subsequent books are, in a sense, his attempts to populate what he once called "The Great Australian Emptiness." His love-hate relationship with his own country (for some years now he has lived in Sydney) has in recent years extended to an active involvement in public issues, especially over the Constitutional crisis of 1975, surprising perhaps in someone who guards his privacy so fiercely. *The Tree of Man* is White's tribute to the ability of ordinary men and women to survive against the elemental and inhuman forces of nature in Australia; ironically, the action takes place on the outskirts of Sydney, and not in the immensities of the outback.

Into these surroundings White plunged his next hero. *Voss* is a novel about a German explorer in New South Wales, Queensland, and the Northern Territory, some of the inspiration for which came from White's reading of the journals of the explorers E. J. Eyre and Ludwig Leichhardt. With *The Tree of Man* and *Voss* White secured his international reputation; both have been translated into many languages. In *The Tree of Man* he attempted to explain the ordinary. In *Voss* he took an extraordinary hero into an extraordinary country, with the Aborigines leading Voss on to further mysteries of magic and death. But the explorer's real journey is in the purification of his soul through torments of both agony and joy, understood only by the partner of his spiritual life, Laura Trevelyan, who remains in Sydney.

However, no discussion of White's work should be involved exclusively with the spiritual. White is also a master of social comedy, with a classical eye and ear for pretension and vulgarity, and an equally classical, if perhaps surprising, love of knockabout farce and bawdry.

White's next novel, *Riders in the Chariot*, brings a European experience of war and racial persecution into the stifling bourgeois normality of White's mythical Sydney suburb, Sarsaparilla. But, as the title indicates, understanding is only achieved by those who see that life is "streaming with implications," those with the vision of the Chariot. The range of the book may be hinted at by the individuality of the "Riders": Himmelfarb, the Jewish migrant; Miss Hare, a slightly dotty old lady; Mrs. Godbold, a working-class woman (and one of White's great gallery of women without whom the world would collapse); and Alf Dubbo, an Aboriginal artist who is also familiar with booze and the brothel.

In the early 1960's White's energies shifted temporarily to the theatre and the short story. An early (1947) play, *The Ham Funeral*, was produced in Adelaide for the first time in 1961, followed in rapid succession by *The Season at Sarsaparilla* (successfully revived in 1977), *A Cheery Soul* (adapted from a short story), and *Night on Bald Mountain*. These plays came from a deep and long-felt passion for the theatre, but White, disillusioned with the intrigues of theatrical life, turned his back on the stage until 1976, when spurred on by contemporary Australian social and political corruption, he wrote *Big Toys*, which had a long run in various Australian capital cities in 1977.

The Solid Mandala, set in Sydney, is perhaps the most tightly knit, difficult, yet rewarding of White's novels. The twin brothers, Waldo and Arthur Brown, are in many ways the two halves of human nature, knowledge and intuition, fancy and imagination.

The Vivisector, a novel about an artist and the nature of art itself, is the most unsparing and uncompromising of White's works. As the title suggests, no compromise is possible for a true artist, doomed to loneliness, uncomforted by love or sex because both are in competition with art. It is a bleak philosophy, but, as so often with White, it must be emphasized that there is always comedy, from wit to bawdry, from irony to hilarity, which is present not for light relief but because White is always conscious of the human comedy beyond the individual tragedy.

White's recent novel *A Fringe of Leaves* is immediately accessible, with an unexpected tenderness considering the violence of the action: 19th-century shipwreck and murder, and the ordeal of a white woman, naked except for a fringe of leaves, among wild Aborigines, who may be "wild" but in fact have plenty to teach her.

White's genius shows no sign of slackening in its attack or invention. He has more novels on the way, and a film (based on a short story), *The Night the Prowler*, was made in 1977. His intense individuality comes in life from his depth and clarity of vision, and in literature from his unmistakable style, which is based on the widest expansion of metaphor; to adapt De Quincey's words, his style "cannot be regarded as a *dress* or alien covering, but it becomes the *incarnation* of his thoughts."

—Geoffrey Dutton

WHITEHEAD, William. English. Born in Cambridge, baptized 12 February 1715. Educated at Winchester College, 1729–35; Clare Hall, Cambridge (sizar), matriculated 1735, B.A. 1739, M.A. 1743. Fellow of Clare Hall from 1742; tutor to the future Earl of Jersey and Lord Villiers, 1745; gave up his fellowship, and settled in London, to devote himself to writing: quickly became known as poet and playwright; accompanied Villiers and Lord Nuneham on a tour of Germany and Italy, 1754–56; appointed Secretary and Registrar of the Order of Bath, 1756, and Poet Laureate, 1757; Reader of Plays for David Garrick, at Drury Lane, London, from 1762. *Died 14 April 1785.*

PUBLICATIONS

Collections

Plays and Poems. 2 vols., 1774; revised edition, 3 vols., 1788.

Plays

> *The Roman Father,* from a play by Corneille (produced 1750).   1750.
> *Fatal Constancy,* in *Poems on Several Occasions.*   1754.
> *Creusa, Queen of Athens* (produced 1754).   1754.
> *The School for Lovers,* from a play by Fontenelle (produced 1762).   1762.
> *A Trip to Scotland* (produced 1770).   1770.

Verse

> *The Danger of Writing Verse.*   1741.
> *Anne Boleyn to Henry the Eighth: An Epistle.*   1743.
> *An Essay on Ridicule.*   1743.
> *Atys and Adrastus: A Tale, in the Manner of Dryden's Fables.*   1744.
> *On Nobility: An Epistle.*   1744.
> *An Hymn to the Nymph of Bristol Spring.*   1751.
> *Poems on Several Occasions.*   1754.
> *Elegies, with an Ode to the Tiber.*   1757.
> *Verses to the People of England.*   1758.
> *A Charge to the Poets.*   1762.
> *Variety: A Tale for Married People.*   1776.
> *The Goat's Beard: A Fable.*   1777.

Reading List: *Whitehead, Poeta Laureatus* (in German) by August Bitter, 1933.

*   *   *

William Whitehead began to write poetry during Pope's later years, but lived and wrote through the era variously known as the age of Pre-Romanticism, Reason, or Johnson. Most of the qualities implied by those associations can be found somewhere in his work. "The Enthusiast," for example, whose deism and nature description have been considered pre-romantic, is deeply indebted to the *Essay on Man*; the enthusiast for nature is finally taught that "man was made for man," and drawn from solitude to society. Many of his early poems pay their respects to Pope – verbally, ideologically, or both – and supply us with bad examples of late Augustan "definite-article verse" ("the vacant mind," "the social bosom," "the mutual morning task they ply"). Generally they are light, occasional, often epistolary, and gently satirical, when not congratulating the Royal Family on a marriage or birth. His commonest mood is mild, free-floating mockery, directed both at self and at a rather amusing environment. Whitehead publishes twelve quarto pages of heroic couplets under the title "The Danger of Writing Verse"; playfully emulates Spenser and the early Milton in the freely enjambed blank verse of *An Hymn to the Nymph of Bristol Spring*; and begins "The Sweepers" like a Johnson and Boswell joke: "I sing of Sweepers, frequent in thy streets,/ Augusta." Passion is seldom indulged and never intense, and Reason is often praised. The recurrent Tory patriotism was duly rewarded: as Laureate from 1757 to 1785, Whitehead had to compose birthday odes to George III throughout the American Revolution, a task he performed unflinchingly amid the customary howls of poets and critics.

Whitehead's interest in theatre began while he was a schoolboy at Winchester, where he played Marcia in a production of *Cato*, but reached new heights when the leading actor of the day took over Drury Lane in 1747. In "To Mr. Garrick" he warned the new manager – a nervous man anyway – that "A nation's taste depends on you/– Perhaps a nation's virtue too." The poem inaugurated a long association: Whitehead served as both playwright and play-reader for Drury Lane, and Garrick took leading roles in three of the poet's plays, all fairly successful. *The Roman Father*, a blank-verse tragedy based on Corneille's *Horace*, is distinctly reminiscent of *Cato*; the title-character Horatius (Garrick) is honoured to donate his sons' lives to Rome, and the closing paean to patriotism as the "first, best passion" was a sure clap-trap. Certain scenes, indeed, could be played as *parodies* of Addison, an idea which seems less far-fetched in view of *Fatal Constancy*, a fragmentary "sketch of a tragedy ... in the heroic taste." Though Whitehead gives only the hero's speeches and the scene directions, they are enough to suggest why he wrote no more tragedies after 1754. "My starting eyeballs hang/Upon her parting steps" cries the protagonist as his lover departs, after which they "Exeunt severally, languishing at each other." (Significantly, the play's forte is ingenious exits.) Unlike his plays designed for the stage, *Fatal Constancy* has the lightness of most of his verse, and a keen eye for theatrical absurdities. *Creusa, Queen of Athens*, with Garrick as Alestes, was produced to "great applause" and the approbation of Horace Walpole the same year.

Whitehead's only full-length comedy, *The School for Lovers*, caught and perpetuated the vogue of genteel or "sentimental" drama, though it also included stock bits of comic business that turn up in Goldsmith and Sheridan. The rhetoric of the prologue ("with strokes refin'd .../Formed on the classic scale his structures rise") conveys Whitehead's pure and reformist intentions as a playwright. *The Dramatic Censor* (1770) complained that "a dreadful soporific languor drowses over the whole, throwing both auditors and readers into a poppean lethargy," but the play, with Garrick as Dorilant, had a good first run and several revivals. Likewise *A Trip to Scotland*, Whitehead's only farce, pleased audiences for several seasons despite an unimpressive text. None of his plays reads well today, yet none failed, and *The Roman Father* and *The School for Lovers* were still being revived at the end of the eighteenth century.

—R. W. Bevis

WHITING, John (Robert). English. Born in Salisbury, Wiltshire, 15 November 1917. Educated at Taunton School, Somerset; Royal Academy of Dramatic Art, London, 1934–36. Served in the Royal Artillery, 1939–44. Married Asthore Lloyd Mawson in 1940; two sons and two daughters. Actor in repertory and in London, 1936–52; Drama Critic, *London Magazine*, 1961–62. Member, Drama Panel, Arts Council of Great Britain, 1954–63. *Died 16 June 1963.*

PUBLICATIONS

Collections

The Collected Plays, edited by Ronald Hayman. 2 vols., 1969.

Plays

Paul Southman (broadcast 1946; produced 1965).
A Penny for a Song (produced 1951). In *The Plays*, 1957; revised version (produced 1962), 1964.

Saint's Day (produced 1951).   In *The Plays,* 1957.

Marching Song (produced 1954).   1954.

Sacrifice to the Wind, from a play by André Obey (televised, 1954; produced 1955).   In
     Plays for Radio and Television, edited by Nigel Samuels, 1959.

The Gates of Summer (produced 1956).   In *The Collected Plays,* 1969.

The Plays (includes *Saint's Day, A Penny for a Song, Marching Song*).   1957.

Madame de ... , and *Traveller Without Luggage,* from plays by Jean Anouilh (produced
     1959).   1959.

A Walk in the Desert (televised 1960).   In *The Collected Plays,* 1969.

The Devils, from the book *The Devils of Loudun* by Aldous Huxley (produced
     1961).   1961.

No Why (produced 1964).   1961.

Conditions of Agreement (produced 1964).   In *The Collected Plays,* 1969.

The Nomads (produced 1965).   In *The Collected Plays,* 1969.

No More A-Roving.   1975.

Screenplays: *The Ship That Died of Shame,* with Michael Relph and Basil Dearden,
1955; *The Good Companions,* with T. J. Morrison and J. L. Hodgson, 1957; *The
Captain's Table,* with Bryan Forbes and Nicholas Phipps, 1959; *Young Cassidy,* 1965.

Radio Plays: *Paul Southman,* 1946; *Eye Witness,* 1949; *The Stairway,* 1949; *Love's Old
Sweet Song,* 1950.

Television Plays: *A Walk in the Desert,* 1960; *Sacrifice to the Wind,* 1964.

Other

Whiting on Theatre.   1966.

The Art of the Dramatist and Other Pieces, edited by Ronald Hayman.   1969.

Reading List: *Whiting* by Ronald Hayman, 1969; *The Plays of Whiting: An Assessment* by
Simon Trussler, 1972; *The Dark Journey: A Critical Survey of Whiting's Plays* by Eric
Salmon, 1979.

                              *   *   *

"I may have been meant for the Drama – God knows! – but I certainly wasn't meant for
the theatre." Whiting scribbled this remark in his *Notebook* for 1960. Like Henry James, from
whom the remark comes, Whiting saw himself doomed to write plays that would get at best a
lukewarm response from an audience – always supposing that they were accepted for
production in the first place. And, also like James, he had a deeply ingrained distrust for that
popularity which he yet desired. The distrust comes out in a lecture he gave at the Old Vic in
1957, "The Art of the Dramatist." Whiting there prophesies, with stylish gloom, a time
shortly to come when the individual voice will have to give way to the voice of the collective,
the group, demos: what you will. For Kenneth Tynan, who was present on that very odd
occasion, Whiting "seemed to anticipate, even to embrace, defeat. He stood before us like one
lately descended from an ivory tower, blinking in the glare and bustle of the day."

It is a perceptive comment. For Whiting was something of an ivory-tower artist. He
scorned the naturalism, the kitchen-sink drama, which he saw as the major disease of
contemporary British drama; and he took much of his inspiration from the verse dramas of
T. S. Eliot. Not that he himself wrote verse drama. But his language, heightened and
supercharged as it is, is very clearly not the language of naturalism, his themes are large ones

– he had an essentially tragic vision of life – and he never bothered to invent characters with whom an audience could identify or at least sympathise. Now of course all this can be true of writers and plays which find a wide measure of acceptance. How then shall we explain Whiting's unpopularity? In terms of a deficiency in his dramatic art, perhaps?

"I may have been meant for the drama...." But was he really so meant? The question is worth asking, if only because it draws attention to the following facts: that Whiting began his career by writing a novel, *Not a Foot of Land*, which is "a strange and remarkable first work," according to Eric Salmon, but which was never published; that he continued to write and broadcast short stories; that he made most of his money by writing film scripts, for which he seems to have had a real gift; that in November 1956, he began to make notes for a novel called *Noman* which he then tried to turn into a play (he made in all four abortive attempts to finish this play, whose title he changed to *The Nomads*); that in a career spanning the best part of twenty years he completed only nine plays. Does this suggest an uncertainty of direction? Did Whiting know *that* he wanted to write, but not *how*, not what medium would best suit his talents? "I may have been meant for the Drama" includes the possibility that "I may *not* have been meant for the Drama."

At this point it is necessary to quote Ronald Hayman, writing in praise of Whiting: "The turning points in *Saint's Day*, *Marching Song*, *The Gates of Summer* and *The Devils* involve personality changes which are so basic it's no exaggeration to call them conversions. The characters fall in and out of love not with each other but with life and death. But these moments of conversion are not directly dramatised." This seems to me more of a flaw than Hayman recognises, or is willing to admit. And indeed he himself appears to be not totally happy with what he has said, for he quickly adds that "we do see how and we do see why these moments of conversion occur. To dramatise them too directly would be to write melodrama." One problem with *The Devils*, for example, is that it *is* often merely melodramatic. Grandier's conversion to a course of self-destruction isn't sufficiently explained to make it at all convincing, though I don't deny that it can be theatrically effective.

Yet having said this much, we must reconsider; after all, Whiting's plays are regarded by a small but constant number as undeniably the work of a major writer. Certainly, the best of them – *Saint's Day* and *Marching Song* – couldn't have been written by anyone else, and have about them a queer, compelling authority. Hayman notes, very shrewdly, that Whiting's work is "characterised by its sensitivity to the violence of unreason and the impossibility of reasoning about violence"; and this is particularly true of *Saint's Day* and *Marching Song*. What is odd about Whiting, of course, and what makes it unlikely that his plays will ever attract a wide audience, is that he seems much more interested in ideas than the people who express them. They are vehicles rather than embodiments. In this, he is perhaps like Ben Jonson: he has something of Jonson's steely integrity, and he shares a measure of Jonson's scornful contempt at the muddle and compromise for which most people settle.

Perhaps a better point of comparison, however, is with Byron. Eric Salmon has remarked that after Whiting's death fifty-four volumes relating to the poet were found on his shelves. "It is easy," Salmon says, "to see why Whiting would feel an instinctive sympathy for Byron and the Byronic hero: many of his own characters have that savage self-disgust, the same contempt for the shoddiness of human society coupled paradoxically with an intuitive belief in what they feel ought to be the nobility of life and man." Given this, and given also Whiting's passion for a system that will somehow permit the nobility to come through – it amounts to a kind of political metaphysic – it is not surprising that his plays shouldn't address themselves to present concerns, shouldn't even *try* to do so, should in a word, lack popular appeal. But this isn't to say that they lack durability.

—John Lucas

WILDE, Oscar (Fingal O'Flahertie Wills). Irish. Born in Dublin, 16 October 1854. Educated at Portora Royal School; Trinity College, Dublin; Magdalen College, Oxford (Newdigate Prize for poetry), 1874–78, B.A. (honours) in moderations and greats 1878. Married Constance Lloyd in 1884 (separated, 1895; died, 1898); two sons. Travelled in Italy and Greece, then settled in London, 1878; Editor, *Woman's World*, London, 1887–89; sued the Marquess of Queensberry for slander, 1895, but revelations at the trial about his relations with the Marquess's son Lord Alfred Douglas caused him to be prosecuted for homosexual practices and sentenced to two years in Reading Gaol, 1895–97; after release settled in Paris; converted to Roman Catholicism. *Died 30 November 1900.*

PUBLICATIONS

Collections

> *Selected Essays and Poems.* 1954; as *De Profundis and Other Writings,* 1973.
> *Letters,* edited by Rupert Hart-Davis. 1962; selection, 1978.
> *Complete Works,* edited by P. Drake. 1966.
> *Poems,* edited by Denys Thompson. 1972.

Plays

> *Vera; or, The Nihilists* (produced 1883). 1880.
> *The Duchess of Padua: A Tragedy of the XVI Century* (as *Guido Ferrandi,* produced 1891). 1883.
> *Lady Windermere's Fan: A Play about a Good Woman* (produced 1892). 1893.
> *A Woman of No Importance* (produced 1893). 1894.
> *An Ideal Husband* (produced 1895). 1899.
> *The Importance of Being Earnest: A Trivial Comedy for Serious People* (produced 1895). 1899; 2 versions of the play edited by Vyvyan Holland, 2 vols., 1957.
> *Salome* (in French; produced 1896). 1893.
> *A Florentine Tragedy* (produced 1906). In *Works,* 1908.
> *For Love of the King: A Burmese Masque.* 1922.

Fiction

> *The Happy Prince and Other Tales.* 1888.
> *Lord Arthur Savile's Crime and Other Stories.* 1891.
> *A House of Pomegranates.* 1891.
> *The Picture of Dorian Gray.* 1891; edited by Isobel Murray, 1974.
> *The Portrait of Mr. W.H.* 1921.

Verse

> *Ravenna.* 1878.
> *Poems.* 1881.
> *The Sphinx.* 1894.
> *The Ballad of Reading Gaol.* 1898.

Other

Intentions. 1891.
Oscariana: Epigrams. 1895; revised edition, 1910.
The Soul of Man. 1895; as *The Soul of Man under Socialism,* 1912.
Sebastian Melmoth (miscellany). 1904.
De Profundis. 1905; revised edition, 1909; *Suppressed Portion,* 1913; *The Complete Text,* edited by Vyvyan Holland, 1949; complete version, in *Letters,* 1962.
Decorative Art in America, Together with Letters, Reviews, and Interviews, edited by R. B. Glaenzer. 1906.
A Critic in Pall Mall, Being Extracts from Reviews and Miscellanies. 1919.
Literary Criticism, edited by Stanley Weintraub. 1968.

Bibliography: *Bibliography of Wilde* by Stuart Mason, 1908; *Wilde: An Annotated Bibliography* by E. H. Mikhail, 1978.

Reading List: *The Paradox of Wilde* by George Woodcock, 1950; *Wilde* by St. John Ervine, 1951; *The Fate of Wilde* by Vivien Mercier, 1955; *The Three Trials of Wilde,* 1956, and *Wilde: The Aftermath,* 1963, both by H. Montgomery Hyde; *Wilde: The Critical Heritage* edited by Karl Beckson, 1970; *The Plays of Wilde* by Alan Bird, 1977.

*   *   *

Oscar Wilde's writings have always been overwhelmed by his biography: a career consciously shaped as drama, begun as farce and concluding in tragedy. The work has seemed merely the detritus of the life. His history has been conveniently appropriable by Germans in search of English "decadence" as opposed to German "kultur," a decadence either embodied in Wilde himself or in the English who vindictively punished one who had indicted them for their lack of "kultur," and who in an unpropitious English context struggled unavailingly to achieve unity of being. The French both blessed and dismissed Wilde as a provincial version of Parisian culture, while the English middle-classes and their critics floundered in the notion of "sincerity." The English press had conducted a collusively profitable relation with Wilde for years, but played the major part in his crucifixion none the less. Wilde's complex "afterlife" has also affected the capacity to respond committedly to the works. He was gradually transformed (his faithful friends began the process) into what W. H. Auden called "St. Oscar, the Homintern Martyr" – the scapegoat of sexual deviance whose first fruits were the Wolfenden Report.

Wilde's reputation as a talker, the best since Dr. Johnson, has also diverted attention from his texts. The reputation seems deserved: no monologist, he had wit, humour, pathos, and analysis under his control, and about his best writing there is an obvious flavour of heightened conversation. He tended not untypically either to use talk as a substitute for writing or to expend in talk what should have been written – to "talk things out of himself" – and when he came to write the colloquial spontaneities and directness were often lost, particularly in the florid prose-poems which were originally spoken. Just as his appetites were coarse, so his style sometimes tended to the flashy, loaded with sing-song bric-a-brac. Yeats described him half truthfully as a failed man of action, whose action had dissolved in talk, or rather whose talk was a mode of action: the paradox was not merely a truth seen from the other side demanding a higher reconciliation; it was also intended irreconcilably.

A talker may justifiably transpose the ideas of others; Wilde wrote down his transpositions. In essence a synthesiser, he rejoiced in edging ideas to their extremes. His several roles in late nineteenth-century England were complex: at the simplest level he was a familiar type of Anglo-Irish literary adventurer who stuns the Saxon with his wit and charm; he enjoyed the company of cultivated, sometimes aristocratic, women, but was also attracted to humanitarian ideals; he believed in the superiority of art to life, and the dandy in him attempted to make an art of life, yet, rather than keeping to the ivory tower, he feasted with panthers. So long as he merely touted dangerous ideas, he was tolerated by English society, but as soon as he was proved to have acted them out he was destroyed. Others had been guilty of the same vice, but had kept quiet about it: Wilde's crime was actually to have frightened the horses.

Pater was his main master, and from Pater he derived two opposed philosophical traditions: one Darwinist, empirical and sceptical, the other Platonist, idealist and finally Hegelian. Pater, who was essentially a reconciler, married the two; but Wilde had no wish to do so. It was his mode of deviating from and indeed distorting Pater, the creative "swerve" by which the disciple transfigures himself into a master. From Pater, he took the notion of the instability of the self; but he had no wish to create "a general" best self, preferring to multiply selves as masks; and from hints in Pater, he developed the identification of the artist with the criminal, the importance of sin, the centrality of the "secret," perhaps homosexuality, the urge to confession.

Pater also allowed him to despoil the past, whether French farce and comedy or Dion Boucicault for his own comedies or Flaubert, Heine, and Maeterlinck for his *Salome*. *Poems* was an extended deliberate homage to a gallery of masters, while *The Ballad of Reading Gaol* invoked Coleridge, Poe, and Housman; *The Picture of Dorian Gray*, besides parodying Dickens and realism, summons Huysmans, Maturin, and Poe. The end of the aesthete, according to Pater, is to focus, embody, and reduce to its burning element the chaotic culture of one's own time, hence Wilde's half-truth of the critic being more artist than the artist and the half-belief that the magic of his paradoxes could renew society.

In his earlier comedies, a void opens between high life conceived as melodrama and the dandy commentator who cannot act; in *An Ideal Husband* the dandy invades but also succumbs to the fashionable world, while in *The Importance of Being Earnest* Wilde creates a masterpiece by presenting a world in which only the dandy exists. *The Soul of Man* is acute and all too dismally prophetic, and "The Decay of Lying" rich in insights, but most of Wilde's other work is flawed. In *The Ballad of Reading Gaol*, moving though it is, realism and the ornate jostle uneasily; "The Critic as Artist" is stimulating but mixes too much purple with its prose; *The Sphinx* is jolly but little more; and *Salome*, though the first symbolist drama in English, wastes too many words. The *Letters*, including those to *The Daily Chronicle* on prison reform, are undeniably impressive and in the "Epistola" the purple prose is in tension with the fascinating financial underpinning (or lack of it) in Wilde's relationship with Douglas.

Much of the work, indeed, has an obscure vitality that cannot be attributed to the fascination of Wilde's "legend," or to the way in which the biography and the works can be so readily used in the service of quite disparate parties. Wilde is now part of popular culture.

—Ian Fletcher

WILDER, Thornton (Niven). American. Born in Madison, Wisconsin, 17 April 1897. Educated at Oberlin College, Ohio, 1915–17; Yale University, New Haven, Connecticut, A.B. 1920; American Academy in Rome, 1920–21; Princeton University, New Jersey, A.M. 1926. Served in the United States Coast Artillery Corps, 1918–19; in the United States Army Air Intelligence, rising to the rank of Lieutenant-Colonel, 1942–45: honorary M.B.E. (Member, Order of the British Empire), 1945. Teacher, 1921–28, and House Master, 1927–28, Lawrenceville School, New Jersey. Full-time writer from 1928. Lecturer in

Comparative Literature, University of Chicago, 1930-36; Visiting Professor, University of Hawaii, Honolulu, 1935; Charles Eliot Norton Professor of Poetry, Harvard University, Cambridge, Massachusetts, 1950–51. United States Delegate: Institut de Cooperation Intellectuelle, Paris, 1937; with John Dos Passos, International P.E.N. Club Congress, England, 1941; UNESCO Conference of the Arts, Venice, 1952. Recipient: Pulitzer Prize, for fiction, 1928, for drama, 1938, 1943; National Institute of Arts and Letters Gold Medal, 1952; Friedenpreis des Deutschen Buchhandels, 1957; Austrian Ehrenmedaille, 1959; Goethe-Plakette, 1959; Brandeis University Creative Arts Award, 1959; Edward MacDowell Medal, 1960; Presidential Medal of Freedom, 1963; National Book Committee's National Medal for Literature, 1965; Century Association Art Medal; National Book Award, for fiction, 1968. D.Litt.: New York University, 1930; Yale University, 1947; Kenyon College, Gambier, Ohio, 1948; College of Wooster, Ohio, 1950; Northeastern University, Boston, 1951; Oberlin College, 1952; University of New Hampshire, Durham, 1953; Goethe University, Frankfurt, 1957; University of Zurich, 1961; LL.D.: Harvard University, 1951. Chevalier, Legion of Honor, 1951; Member, Order of Merit, Peru; Order of Merit, Bonn, 1957; Honorary Member, Bavarian Academy of Fine Arts; Mainz Academy of Science and Literature. Member, American Academy of Arts and Letters. *Died 7 December 1975.*

PUBLICATIONS

Plays

The Trumpet Shall Sound (produced 1927).
The Angel That Troubled the Waters and Other Plays (includes Nascuntur Poetae, Proserpina and the Devil, Fanny Otcott, Brother Fire, The Penny That Beauty Spent, The Angel on the Ship, The Message and Jehanne, Childe Roland to the Dark Tower Came, Centaurs, Leviathan, And the Sea Shall Give Up Its Dead, Now the Servant's Name was Malchus, Mozart and the Gray Steward, Hast Thou Considered My Servant Job?, The Flight into Egypt). 1928.
The Long Christmas Dinner (produced 1931). In The Long Christmas Dinner and Other Plays, 1931; libretto, music by Paul Hindemith (produced 1961), libretto published, 1961.
The Happy Journey to Trenton and Camden (produced 1931). In The Long Christmas Dinner and Other Plays, 1931; revised version, as The Happy Journey, 1934.
Such Things Only Happen in Books (produced 1931). In The Long Christmas Dinner and Other Plays, 1931.
Love and How to Cure It (produced 1931). In The Long Christmas Dinner and Other Plays. 1931.
The Long Christmas Dinner and Other Plays in One Act. 1931.
Queens of France (produced 1932). In The Long Christmas Dinner and Other Plays, 1931.
Pullman Car Hiawatha (produced 1962). In The Long Christmas Dinner and Other Plays, 1931.
Lucrece, from a play by André Obey (produced 1932). 1933.
A Doll's House, from a play by Ibsen (produced 1937).
Our Town (produced 1938). 1938.
The Merchant of Yonkers, from a play by Johann Nostroy, based on A Well-Spent Day by John Oxenford (produced 1938). 1939; revised version, as The Matchmaker (produced 1954), 1955.
The Skin of Our Teeth (produced 1942). 1942.
Our Century. 1947.

The Victors, from a play by Sartre (produced 1949).
A Life in the Sun (produced 1955); as *The Alcestiad,* music by L. Talma (produced 1962). Published as *Die Alkestiade,* 1958; as *The Alcestiad; or, A Life in the Sun, and The Drunken Sisters: A Satyr Play,* 1977.
The Drunken Sisters. 1957.
Bernice (produced 1957).
The Wreck of the 5:25 (produced 1957).
Plays for Bleecker Street (includes *Infancy, Childhood,* and *Someone from Assisi*) (produced 1962). 3 vols., 1960–61.

Screenplays: *Our Town,* 1940; *Shadow of a Doubt,* 1943.

Fiction

The Cabala. 1926.
The Bridge of San Luis Rey. 1927.
The Woman of Andros. 1930.
Heaven's My Destination. 1934.
The Ides of March. 1948.
The Eighth Day. 1967.
Theophilus North. 1973.

Other

The Intent of the Artist, with others. 1941.
Kultur in einer Demokratie. 1957.
Goethe und die Weltliteratur. 1958.

Bibliography: *A Bibliographical Checklist of the Writings of Wilder* by J. M. Edelstein, 1959.

Reading List: *Wilder* by Rex Burbank, 1961; *Wilder* by Helmut Papajewski, 1961, translated by John Conway, 1968; *Wilder* by Bernard Grebanier, 1964; *The Art of Wilder* by Malcolm Goldstein, 1965; *The Plays of Wilder: A Critical Study* by Donald Haberman, 1967.

*   *   *

Many recent American writers have written both plays and fiction, but no other has achieved such a distinguished reputation for both as Thornton Wilder. He is distinguished also for the uniqueness of his works: each is a fresh formal experiment that contributes to his persistent conception of the artist's re-inventing the world by revivifying our perceptions of the universal elements of human experience.

Wilder's earliest published plays in *The Angel That Troubled the Waters and Other Plays* are short pieces presenting usually fantastic situations in an arch, cryptic style employed by such favored writers of the 1920's as Elinor Wylie. A number of the plays deal with the special burden that falls upon persons who discover that they possess artistic gifts, and most of them demand staging too complex for actual performance.

Before he became a successful playwright, Wilder was a novelist. His first novel *The Cabala,* displays much the same preciosity as the early plays. It describes through loosely linked episodes the effort of an aspiring young American writer to be accepted by the Cabala, "members of a circle so powerful and exclusive that ... Romans refer to them with bated breath." These elegant figures turn out to be contemporary embodiments of the ancient

Roman gods, and the veiled point of the work is that the United States is to succeed a decaying Rome as the next abiding place of these gods.

This fantasy did not attract many readers, but Wilder achieved an astonishing success with his next short novel, *The Bridge of San Luis Rey*, which became a surprise best seller. This episodic story about the perishability of material things and the endurance of love is exquisitely structured. It tells the stories of the five persons who die in the collapse of a famous Peruvian bridge with a framework provided by the narrative of a Brother Juniper, who investigates the accident to learn whether "we live by accident and die by accident, or live by plan and die by plan." For his efforts, both he and his book are publicly burned. The last sentence stresses that the only bridge that survives is love.

Wilder's third novel, *The Woman of Andros*, was attacked by social-minded critics of the 1930's for evading present realities and retreating to the classical world; but this subtle fictionalization of Terence's *Andria* actually relates closely to Wilder's own seemingly dying world through its presentation of the death of the Greek world at the time of the coming of Christ because its commercial and artistic communities had become alienated. With his next novel, *Heaven's My Destination*, Wilder returned to contemporary America to create one of his most beguiling characters, George Brush, a high-school textbook salesmen in the midwest, who fails comically and pathetically in his constant efforts to uplift other people and who recovers his faith only when he realizes that he must remain an isolated wanderer, happy only in the world that he makes for himself.

The world that we make for ourselves is the subject again of one of Wilder's most admired works and one of his major contributions to a myth of American community, the play *Our Town*. Wilder explained in *The Intent of the Artist* that he turned from the novel to the stage in the 1930's because "the theater carries the art of narration to a higher power than the novel or the epic poem." He was impatient, however, with the elaborate stage settings of the naturalistic theater, and he had already sought in short plays like *The Long Christmas Dinner* to tell a fundamental human story with only the simplest of props. His culminating experiment with this technique was *Our Town*, a chronicle of the value of "the smallest events in our daily life" in a traditional New England village.

Wilder next experimented with updating a nineteenth-century farce that had been popular in both English and German versions as *The Merchant of Yonkers*. Unsuccessful when first ponderously presented by Max Reinhardt, the play in a revised version entitled *The Matchmaker* was a popular success that subsequently provided the basis for the enormously popular musical comedy, *Hello, Dolly!* Wilder did enjoy enormous immediate success with his third major play, *The Skin of Our Teeth*, an expressionist fantasy about man's struggles for survival through the Ice Age, the Flood, and the Napoleonic Wars as symbolized by the travails of the Antrobus family. Again Wilder's timing was superb. A world reduced to doubt and despair by World War II responded enthusiastically to this affirmative vision of man's possible survival despite his destructive propensities.

Wilder served with American Intelligence units in Italy during World War II, and for his first post-war work returned to the novel and to a classical Roman setting for *The Ides of March*. This pseudo-history, which Malcolm Goldstein compares to "a set of bowls placed one within another," centers on the assassination of Julius Caesar, but traces through four overlapping sections an ever widening circle of events in order to present "the tragic difference between Caesar's idealistic visions and the sordid events for which they are finally responsible" – a subject fraught with implications for the mid-twentieth century.

After the comparatively cool reception of this work, Wilder published little for twenty years. Although his plays remained popular, he was generally too lightly regarded after World War II when existential *angst* dominated in literary criticism. His writings were felt to be too affirmative and optimistic, and his long silence caused him to be regarded as an artist whose time had passed. Literary mandarins were startled, therefore, by the appearance in 1967 of his longest and most complex work, *The Eighth Day*. This novel jumps back and forth in time as it resurrects the events relating to a murder in a southern Illinois coal town early in the twentieth century, the false conviction of a man who escapes, and the eventual solution of the cunning crime. This mystery plot, however, provides only a backdrop for Wilder's observation that all history is one "enormous tapestry" and that "there are no Golden Ages and no Dark Ages. There is the oceanlike monotony of the generations of men under the alternations of fair and foul weather." At the center of the work stands falsely accused John Ashley, who avoids succumbing to despair over this inescapable cycle by "inventing" afresh such fossilized institutions as marriage and fatherhood as he also invents small practical objects to make man's work easier. An old woman whom he meets sums up the sensibility that informs the novel, "The human race gets no better. Mankind is vicious, slothful, quarrelsome, and self-centered....[But] you and I have a certain quality that is rare as teeth in a hen. We work. And we forget ourselves in our work."

The Eighth Day triumphantly capped Wilder's "re-invention" of mankind, but he had one final delight for readers. Perhaps to complement James Joyce's and others' portraits of the artist as a young man *by* a young man, Wilder presented in his last published work, *Theophilus North*, an episodic novel about the artist as a young man *by* an old man. The seemingly loosely connected tales are actually – as in his other works – parts of an intricate mosaic that discloses against a background of the "nine cities" of Newport, Rhode Island, the nine career possibilities that a young man explores before discovering that being a writer will encompass all of them.

—Warren French

WILLIAMS, (George) Emlyn.   Welsh.   Born in Mostyn, Flintshire, 26 November 1905. Educated at Holywell County School, Flintshire; Christ Church, Oxford, M.A. 1927. Married Molly O'Shann in 1935 (died, 1971); two sons. Actor and director: debut as actor, 1927. Recipient: New York Drama Critics Circle Award, 1941. LL.D.: University College of North Wales, Bangor, 1949. C.B.E. (Commander, Order of the British Empire), 1962. Lives in London.

PUBLICATIONS

Plays

    Vigil (produced 1925).   In *The Second Book of One-Act Plays,* 1954.
    Full Moon (produced 1927).
    Glamour (produced 1928).
    A Murder Has Been Arranged: A Ghost Story (produced 1930).   1930.
    Port Said (produced 1931; revised version, as *Vessels Departing,* produced 1933).
    The Late Christopher Bean, from the play by Sidney Howard, based on a play by René
        Fauchois (produced 1933).   1933.
    Josephine, from a work by Hermann Bahr (produced 1934).
    Spring 1600 (produced 1934; revised version, produced 1945).   1946.
    Night Must Fall (produced 1935).   1935.
    He Was Born Gay: A Romance (produced 1937).   1937.
    The Corn Is Green (produced 1938).   1938.
    The Citadel (screenplay), with others, in *Foremost Films of 1938,* edited by Frank
        Vreeland.   1939.

The Light of Heart (produced 1940). 1940.
The Morning Star (produced 1941). 1942.
Yesterday's Magic (produced 1942).
Pen Don (produced 1943).
A Month in the Country, from a play by Turgenev (produced 1943). 1943; revised version (produced 1956), 1957.
The Druid's Rest (produced 1944). 1944.
The Wind of Heaven (produced 1945). 1945.
Thinking Aloud: A Dramatic Sketch (produced 1945). 1946.
Trespass: A Ghost Story (produced 1947). 1947.
Pepper and Sand: A Duologue (broadcast 1947). 1948.
Dear Evelyn, from a play by Hagar Wilde and Dale Eunson (produced 1948). N.d.
Accolade (produced 1950). 1951.
Emlyn Williams as Charles Dickens, based on writings by Dickens (produced 1951). Published as *Readings from Dickens,* 1953.
Bleak House, dramatic reading based on the novel by Dickens (produced 1952).
Someone Waiting (produced 1953). 1954.
A Boy Growing Up, dramatic reading based on works by Dylan Thomas (produced 1955; as *Dylan Thomas Growing Up,* produced 1977).
Beth (produced 1958). 1959.
The Master Builder, from a play by Ibsen (produced 1964). 1967.
Saki, dramatic reading based on works by Saki (produced 1977).

Screenplays: *Friday the Thirteenth,* 1933; *Evergreen,* with Marjorie Gaffney, 1934; *The Man Who Knew Too Much,* with A. R. Rawlinson and Edwin Greenwood, 1934; *The Divine Spark,* with Richard Benson, 1935; *Broken Blossoms,* 1936; *Dead Men Tell No Tales,* with others, 1938; *The Citadel,* with others, 1938; *This England,* 1941; *The Last Days of Dolwyn,* 1949.

Radio Play: *Pepper and Sand,* 1947.

Television Plays: *Every Picture Tells a Story,* 1949; *In Town Tonight,* 1954; *A Blue Movie of My Own True Love,* 1968; *The Power of Dawn,* 1975.

Other

George: An Early Autobiography. 1961.
Beyond Belief: A Chronicle of Murder and Its Detection. 1967.
Emlyn: An Early Autobiography 1927–1935. 1973.

Editor, *Short Stories,* by Saki. 1978.

Reading List: *Williams: An Illustrated Study of His Work with a List of His Appearances on Stage and Screen* by Richard Findlater, 1957 (includes bibliography).

*   *   *

Night Must Fall is probably Emlyn Williams's most famous work and has earned him a reputation as a writer of suspense drama, though suspense elements may be traced back to his earliest plays such as *Vigil* and *A Murder Has Been Arranged.* Although he reacted against Strindberg's *Ghost Sonata* as being "too obscurely symbolic," Williams allowed most of his early suspense dramas to pivot on supernatural causation; in *Night Must Fall,* he was able to generate the whole action through plausibly realistic motivation, but later plays such as *The Wind of Heaven* and *Trespass* achieve their resolution only at the convenience of ghosts, mediums, or heavenly intervention. This aspect of Williams's drama has dated fast, and his plays which are dependent on such mechanics generally trivialise his more substantial dramatic talents.

Though a minor, unsuccessful work, *Glamour* anticipated Williams's greatest dramatic achievements. With this play, he decided that his most apposite material was "Wales and the theatre," subjects to which he has returned often. The theatre had already provided the context of *A Murder Has Been Arranged* and was to be dominant in *Spring 1600*, a play about Burbage's company rehearsing *Twelfth Night* for the opening of the Globe Theatre. In most of Williams's other plays, the theatre has a slighter, though significant, function: *The Light of Heart*, in which the main character is an aging alcoholic actor, typifies his effective exploitation of theatricality as a dramatic energy source.

A related issue, basic to Williams's dramaturgy, was that in *Glamour* he first wrote a lead part specifically for himself, and he has continued to act central roles in most of his major plays. This habit has inevitably resulted in a certain typification: the flamboyant, assertive character is glimpsed on the brink of spectacular success, and, although he tends to have an extraordinary capacity for initiating a central action, an extraneous complicating factor deprives him of the likely consummation. Such is the position of the murderer in *Night Must Fall*, the actor in *The Light of Heart*, the surgeon in *The Morning Star*, the circus owner in *The Wind of Heaven*, the medium in *Trespass*, and the Nobel prize winner in *Accolade*; similar characters appear in the costume drama *He Was Born Gay* and the psychological thriller *Someone Waiting*. Sometimes, this pattern dissolves into sentiment, but it can also work its way out in terms of powerful comedy or irony. A logical extension of Williams's interest in the writer-actor persona may be seen in his Dickens solo performances in the 1950's, virtuoso acting achievements which emphasise a basic propensity in his work.

It is the Welsh content of Williams's plays which may well prove their most lasting element. Almost all of them include a Welsh character, several have Welsh settings, and two are obviously based on Williams's boyhood in Wales: *The Corn Is Green* (about an old schoolmistress), and *The Druid's Rest*. This latter, much-underrated play, with its determinedly English perspective of a doggedly Celtic subject, activates many of the comic ironies to be found in the plays O'Casey wrote in England; if Williams's originative influence on both Welsh and English drama has been slight, he has at least written several plays which deserve to be read as long as O'Casey's *Purple Dust*.

—Howard McNaughton

WILLIAMS, Tennessee (Thomas Lanier Williams). American. Born in Columbus, Mississippi, 26 March 1911. Educated at the University of Missouri, Columbia, 1930–32; Washington University, St. Louis, 1936–37; University of Iowa, Iowa City, 1938, A.B. 1938. Clerical Worker and Manual Laborer, International Shoe Company, St. Louis, 1934–36; held various jobs, including waiter and elevator operator, New Orleans, 1939; teletype operator, Jacksonville, Florida, 1940; worked at odd jobs, New York, 1942, and as a screenwriter for MGM, 1943. Full-time writer since 1944. Recipient: Rockefeller Fellowship, 1940; National Institute of Arts and Letters grant, 1944, and Gold Medal, 1969; New York Drama Critics Circle Award, 1945, 1948, 1955, 1962; Pulitzer Prize, 1948, 1955; *Evening Standard* award, 1958; Brandeis University Creative Arts Award, 1964. Member, American Academy of Arts and Letters, 1976. Lives in Key West, Florida, and New York City.

PUBLICATIONS

Plays

Cairo! Shanghai! Bombay! (produced 1936).
The Magic Tower (produced 1936).
Headlines (produced 1936).
Candles in the Sun (produced 1936).
Fugitive Kind (produced 1937).
Spring Song (produced 1938).
The Long Goodbye (produced 1940).   In *27 Wagons Full of Cotton*, 1946.
Battle of Angels (produced 1940).   1945; revised version, as *Orpheus Descending* (produced 1957), published as *Orpheus Descending, with Battle of Angels*, 1958.
At Liberty (produced 1968).   In *American Scenes*, edited by William Kozlenko, 1941.
Stairs to the Roof (produced 1944).
You Touched Me, with Donald Windham, suggested by the story by D. H. Lawrnece (produced 1944).   1947.
The Glass Menagerie (produced 1944).   1945.
27 Wagons Full of Cotton and Other One-Act Plays (includes *The Purification, The Lady of Larkspur Lotion, The Last of My Solid Gold Watches, Portrait of a Madonna, Auto-da-Fé, Lord Byron's Love Letter, The Strangest Kind of Romance, The Long Goodbye, Hello from Bertha*, and *This Property Is Condemned*).   1946; augmented edition (includes *Talk to Me Like the Rain and Let Me Listen* and *Something Unspoken*), 1953.
This Property Is Condemned (produced 1946).   In *27 Wagons Full of Cotton*, 1946.
Portrait of a Madonna (produced 1946).   In *27 Wagons Full of Cotton*, 1946.
The Last of My Solid Gold Watches (produced 1946).   In *27 Wagons Full of Cotton*, 1946.
Lord Byron's Love Letter (produced 1947).   In *27 Wagons Full of Cotton*, 1946; revised version, music by Raffaello de Banfield (produced 1964); libretto published, 1955.
Auto-da-Fé (produced 1947).   In *27 Wagons Full of Cotton*, 1946.
The Lady of Larkspur Lotion (produced 1947).   In *27 Wagons Full of Cotton*, 1946.
The Purification (produced 1954).   In *27 Wagons Full of Cotton*, 1946.
27 Wagons Full of Cotton (produced 1955).   In *27 Wagons Full of Cotton*, 1946.
Hello from Bertha (produced 1961).   In *27 Wagons Full of Cotton*, 1946.
The Strangest Kind of Romance (produced 1969).   In *27 Wagons Full of Cotton*, 1946.
Mooney's Kid Don't Cry (produced 1946).   In *American Blues*, 1948.
A Streetcar Named Desire (produced 1947).   1947.
Summer and Smoke (produced 1947).   1948; revised version, as *The Eccentricities of a Nightingale* (produced 1964), published as *The Eccentricities of a Nightingale, and Summer and Smoke*, 1965; revised version (produced 1976).
American Blues: Five Short Plays.   1948.
Ten Blocks on the Camino Real, in *American Blues*.   1948; revised version, as *Camino Real* (produced 1953), 1953.
The Case of the Crushed Petunias (produced 1957).   In *American Blues*, 1948.
The Dark Room (produced 1966).   In *American Blues*, 1948.
The Long Stay Cut Short; or, The Unsatisfactory Supper (produced 1971).   In *American Blues*, 1948.
The Rose Tattoo (produced 1951).   1951.
I Rise in Flame, Cried the Phoenix: A Play about D. H. Lawrence (produced 1953).   1951.
Talk to Me Like the Rain and Let Me Listen (produced 1958).   In *27 Wagons Full of Cotton*, 1953.
Something Unspoken (produced 1958).   In *27 Wagons Full of Cotton*, 1953.

Cat on a Hot Tin Roof (produced 1955).   1955; revised version (produced 1973), 1975.
Three Players of a Summer Game (produced 1955).
Sweet Bird of Youth (produced 1956).   1959.
Baby Doll: The Script for the Film, Incorporating the Two One-Act Plays Which Suggested It: 27 Wagons Full of Cotton and The Long Stay Cut Short; or, The Unsatisfactory Supper.   1956.
Garden District: Something Unspoken, Suddenly Last Summer (produced 1958).   1958.
The Fugitive Kind: Original Play Title: Orpheus Descending (screenplay).   1958.
A Perfect Analysis Given by a Parrot (produced 1976).   1958.
The Enemy: Time, in *Theatre,* March 1959.
The Night of the Iguana (produced 1959; revised version, produced 1961).   1962.
Period of Adjustment: High Point over a Cavern: A Serious Comedy (produced 1959).   1960.
To Heaven in a Golden Coach (produced 1961).
The Milk Train Doesn't Stop Here Anymore (produced 1962; revised versions, produced 1962, 1963, 1964, 1968).   1964.
Slapstick Tragedy (The Mutilated and *The Gnädiges Fräulein)* (produced 1966).   2 vols., 1967; revised version of *The Gnädiges Fräulein,* as *The Latter Days of a Celebrated Soubrette* (produced 1974).
Kingdom of Earth, in *Esquire,* February 1967; revised version, as *Kingdom of Earth: The Seven Descents of Myrtle* (produced 1968).   1968.
The Two Character Play (produced 1967; revised version, produced 1969).   1969; revised version, as *Out Cry* (produced 1971), 1973; revised version (produced 1974).
In the Bar of a Tokyo Hotel (produced 1969).   1969.
I Can't Imagine Tomorrow (televised 1970; produced 1976).   In *Dragon Country,* 1970.
Dragon Country: A Book of Plays (includes *In the Bar of a Tokyo Hotel, I Rise in Flame, Cried the Phoenix, The Mutilated, I Can't Imagine Tomorrow, Confessional, The Frosted Glass Coffin, The Gnädiges Fräulein, A Perfect Analysis Given by a Parrot).*   1970.
Senso, with Paul Bowles, in *Two Screenplays,* by Luigi Visconti.   1970.
A Streetcar Named Desire (screenplay), in *Film Scripts One,* edited by George P. Garrett, O. B. Harrison, Jr., and Jane Gelfann.   1971.
Small Craft Warnings (produced 1972).   1972.
The Theatre of Williams I–V.   5 vols., 1972–76.
The Red Devil Battery Sign (produced 1974; revised version, produced 1976; revised version, produced 1977).
Demolition Downtown: Count Ten in Arabic – Then Run (produced 1976).
This Is an Entertainment (produced 1976).
Vieux Carré (produced 1977).

Screenplays: *Senso (The Wanton Countess,* English dialogue, with Paul Bowles), 1949; *The Glass Menagerie,* with Peter Berneis, 1950; *A Streetcar Named Desire,* with Oscar Saul, 1951; *The Rose Tattoo,* with Hal Kanter, 1955; *Baby Doll,* 1956; *Suddenly Last Summer,* with Gore Vidal, 1960; *The Fugitive Kind,* with Meade Roberts, 1960; *Boom,* 1968.

Television Play: *I Can't Imagine Tomorrow,* 1970.

Fiction

One Arm and Other Stories.   1948.
The Roman Spring of Mrs. Stone.   1950.
Hard Candy: A Book of Stories.   1954.

Three Players of a Summer Game and Other Stories.   1960.
Grand (stories).   1964.
The Knightly Quest: A Novella and Four Short Stories.   1967; augmented edition, as
   The Knightly Quest: A Novella and Twelve Short Stories, 1968.
Eight Mortal Ladies Possessed: A Book of Stories.   1974.
Moise and the World of Reason.   1975.

Verse

Five Young American Poets, with others.   1944.
In the Winter of Cities: Poems.   1956.
Androgyne, Mon Amour.   1977.

Other

Memoirs.   1975.
Letters to Donald Windham 1940–1965, edited by Windham.   1976.
Where I Live (essays).   1978.

Reading List: *Williams* by Signi Lenea Falk, 1961 (includes bibliography); *Williams: Rebellious Puritan* by Nancy M. Tischler, 1961; *Williams: The Man and His Work* by Benjamin Nelson, 1961; *The Dramatic World of Williams* by Francis Donahue, 1964; *The Broken World of Williams* by Esther M. Jackson, 1965; *Williams* by Gerald Weales, 1965; *Williams: A Tribute* edited by Jac Tharpe, 1977; *Williams: A Collection of Critical Essays* edited by Stephen S. Stanton, 1977; *The World of Williams* by Richard Freeman Leavitt, 1978.

                                   *   *   *

   Shortly before *Vieux Carré* opened on Broadway in 1977, Tennessee Williams wrote an article for the New York *Times* which began, "Of course no one is more acutely aware than I that I am widely regarded as the ghost of a writer." So he is. The name Tennessee Williams still conjures up the flamboyant plays of the 1940's and 1950's – *A Streetcar Named Desire, Cat on a Hot Tin Roof, Suddenly Last Summer.* Except for a period in the mid-sixties when he suffered mental and physical collapse, Williams has been a remarkably busy ghost. Since 1974, he has seen new plays staged in London, San Francisco, and New York, and he has published a novel (*Moise and the World of Reason*), a book of short stories (*Eight Mortal Ladies Possessed*), a book of poems (*Androgyne, Mon Amour*) and *Memoirs.* Artistically and personally, he has become an advertisement for the theme that has obsessed him since Amanda Wingfield tried to hold her disintegrating family together in *The Glass Menagerie* – survival.
   When *Vieux Carré* opened, the critics did treat it as a ghost play, a nostalgic look at the New Orleans of Williams's youth, full of echoes of characters, situations, themes relentlessly familiar to Williams admirers. In the *Times* article, in *Memoirs,* in any number of interviews, Williams has attempted to explain how he was transformed from America's most popular serious playwright into an historical figure, inexplicably still active in the real world. His plays through *The Night of the Iguana,* he suggests, shared a similarity of style – "poetic naturalism" he calls it – which became so identified with him that when he made a shift into new styles, his audiences could not or would not follow him. It is true that there are great stylistic similarities among the Williams plays through *Iguana* and it is also true that he has

lost the large audiences that once flocked to his work, but the new styles have their roots in his earlier work.

He has never been a realistic playwright, which may be what the phrase *poetic naturalism* is supposed to suggest, but he has always been capable of writing a psychologically valid scene in the American realistic tradition – the breakfast scene in *The Glass Menagerie*, for instance, or the birthday dinner in *A Streetcar Named Desire*. His characters are able to claim the allegiance of audiences who continue to identify with them even after they become larger than life (Big Daddy in *Cat on a Hot Tin Roof*, Alexandra Del Lago in *Sweet Bird of Youth*) or when the use of significant names (Val Xavier in *Orpheus Descending*, Alma in *Summer and Smoke*) turn them into myth or symbol. However grounded in realistic surface, the events in Williams's plays, particularly the violent events, take on meaning that transcends psychological realism ("Here is your God, Mr. Shannon," says Hannah when the storm breaks in *Night of the Iguana*), and when the violence moves off stage – the cannibalism in *Suddenly Last Summer*, the castration in *Sweet Bird of Youth* – the nonrealistic implications of event are heightened by its transformation into narrative (*Summer and Smoke*) or promise (*Sweet Bird of Youth*). From the glass menagerie through the dressmaker's dummies in *The Rose Tattoo* to the costumes, ritually donned by Shannon and Hannah in *Night of the Iguana*, Williams has always used sets, props, dress as devices whose significance runs deeper than the verisimilitude required by realism. When Williams deserted old forms – or thought he did – he brought two decades of nonrealistic theater with him. *Slapstick Tragedy* may have suggested absurdist drama to some of its viewers, but Polly and Molly, the grotesque comedy team whose voices sustain *The Gnädiges Fräulein*, are variations on Dolly and Beulah, who introduce *Orpheus Descending*, and Flora and Bessie, the "female clowns" of *The Rose Tattoo* and *A Perfect Analysis Given by a Parrot*. When each of the characters in *Small Craft Warnings* takes his place in the spotlight to sound his sorrow – a mechanism which suggests that the title of an earlier version of the play, *Confessional*, is more apt – we have at most an intensification of the device Williams used extensively in his earlier plays, most notably in Maggie's opening speech in *Cat on a Hot Tin Roof* and the soliloquies of Chance and Alexandra in *Sweet Bird of Youth*.

Stylistically, then, the later Williams plays grow out of the early ones. Nor are there surprising shifts in theme. The similarities between the pre- and post-*Night of the Iguana* plays can best be seen in the recurrence of characters. The Blanche of *Streetcar Named Desire*, whose variants people *Summer and Smoke*, *Camino Real*, *Sweet Bird of Youth*, and *Night of the Iguana*, is still visible in Isabel in *Period of Adjustment*, Miriam in *In the Bar of a Tokyo Hotel*, and, bizarrely, in the fish-trapping heroine of *The Gnädiges Fräulein*. Amanda – or at least her comic toughness – is apparent in Flora Goforth in *The Milk Train Doesn't Stop Here Anymore*, Myrtle in *Kingdom of Earth*, and Leona in *Small Craft Warnings*, and Laura, the frightened daughter of *The Glass Menagerie*, is present in characters as different as One in *I Can't Imagine Tomorrow* and Clare in *Out Cry*. Blanche, Amanda, Laura, three aspects of the perennial Williams character, the fugitive kind, who, male and female, has been the playwright's concern from his very early one-act plays to *Vieux Carré*. At first, his characters were simply outsiders, set off from the rest of society by a recognizable difference of one kind or another – Laura's limp, Blanche's defensive sexuality, Alma's pseudo-artistic sensitivity. It became increasingly clear – even as the forces that opposed his protagonists became more violent – that all men are outsiders. The murderous Jabe in *Orpheus Descending* is set apart by the disease that is killing him as obviously as Val is by his priapic aura, his guitar, and his snakeskin jacket, as Lady is by being Italian, as Carol Cutrere is by her unconsoling wealth and self-lacerating sex, as Vee Talbot is by her painting and her religious visions. Chance calls Alexandra "nice monster" in *Sweet Bird of Youth*, and she calls him "pitiful monster," and both are "Lost in the beanstalk country ... the country of the flesh-hungry, blood-thirsty ogre," but the play's ogre, Boss Finley, is supposed to be monster-ridden too and Williams keeps revising the play in the hopes that that point will emerge. The enemy is no longer the ugly other, but a surrogate self, or time (note all those age-obsessed Williams characters, like Mrs. Stone who wanted a Roman spring), or a godless universe. This last is presented most clearly in two plays, *Suddenly Last Summer* and *Night of the Iguana*, which come closest to making specific theological statements. Man, as Tennessee Williams sees him – as Tennessee Williams embodies him – is a temporary resident in a frightening world in an indifferent universe. The best he can hope is the transitory consolation of touching and the best he can do is hang on for dear (and only) life.

In the *Times* article quoted above Williams mentions his "private panic," his dreams "full of alarm and wild suspicion" that he wants to "cry ... out to all who will listen," and his continued revision of *Out Cry* emphasized his urgency. But that cry has always echoed through his work – his novels, his short stories, his poetry, his autobiography and all his plays. In the hope that the cry will come through more clearly, he has always revised and rewritten, turning short stories into plays, short plays into long ones, full-length plays into other full-length plays, as *Battle of Angels* became *Orpheus Descending*, and *Summer and Smoke* became *The Eccentricities of a Nightingale*. Audiences have withdrawn from Williams, I suspect, not because his style has changed or his concerns altered, but because in his desperate need to cry out he has turned away from the sturdy dramatic containers which once gave the cry resonance and has settled for pale imitations of familiar stage images; he has built on the direct address of the early soliloquies and the discursiveness of plays like *Night of the Iguana* and substituted lyric argument for dramatic language. It is a measure of his stature as a playwright and the importance of his central theme that each new play bears the promise of old vigor in new disguise. The promise has not been fulfilled for some years now, but while we wait, we can always turn back to those other Williams plays, elevated now to contemporary classics, which remind us that this ghost just may produce something worth waiting for.

—Gerald Weales

WILSON, John. English. Born in London, baptized 27 December 1626; lived with his family in Plymouth, 1634–44. Educated at Exeter College, Oxford, matriculated 1644, but left without taking a degree; entered Lincoln's Inn, London, 1646: called to the Bar, 1652. Courtier and royalist: chairman of a board of sequestration after the Restoration; may have accompanied the Duke of Ormonde to Ireland, 1677; Recorder of Londonderry, 1681–89; possibly served as Secretary to the Viceroy of Ireland, 1687; lived in Dublin, 1689–90; returned to London, 1690. *Died c. 1695.*

PUBLICATIONS

Collections

Dramatic Works, edited by James Maidment and W. H. Logan.   1874.

Plays

The Cheats (produced 1663).   1664; edited by Milton C. Nahm, 1935.
Andronicus Comnenius.   1664.

The Protectors. 1665.
Belphegor; or, The Marriage of the Devil (produced 1675). 1691.

Verse

To His Grace James, Duke of Ormonde. 1677.
To His Excellence Richard, Earl of Arran. 1682.
A Pindaric to Their Sacred Majesties James II and Queen Mary on Their Joint Coronation. 1685.

Other

A Discourse of Monarchy. 1684.
Jus Regium Coronae. 1688.

Translator, *Moriae Encomium; or, The Praise of Folly,* by Erasmus. 1668.

Reading List: *Wilsons Dramen* by K. Faber, 1904; "John Wilson and 'Some Few Plays' " by Milton C. Nahm, in *Review of English Studies,* 1938.

*   *   *

Like many of the more important Restoration dramatists, John Wilson devoted only a small part of his life to writing. In his case the crucial years were those immediately following the Restoration of the monarchy in 1660, when he wrote two prose comedies, *The Cheats* and *The Projectors,* a blank-verse tragedy, *Andronicus Comnenius,* and made his well-known translation of Erasmus's *Moriae Encomium* (*The Praise of Folly*). After the 1660's he wrote only one play, the tragi-comic *Belphegor* (performed in Dublin in 1675 and in London in 1690), and a few poems and tracts.

His reputation as a dramatist rests mainly on his first play, *The Cheats,* which was revived and reprinted from time to time during the rest of the seventeenth century and the first quarter of the eighteenth century. Wilson, a lawyer and a man of considerable learning, knew the work of Ben Jonson and his pre-Commonwealth followers intimately, and his two comedies belong to the Jonsonian comic tradition, especially to the "low" city comedy that Middleton specialized in; they therefore illustrate the element of continuity in seventeenth-century drama despite the closure of the theatres between 1642 and 1660. As comedies of "humours," both *The Cheats* and *The Projectors* contain numerous satirical portraits of the type found in the plays of Jonson and his "sons," as the names of the characters indicate; the cast of *The Projectors,* for example, includes Suckdry (a relative of Jonson's Volpone), Sir Gudgeon Credulous (very similar to Fitzdottrel in Jonson's *The Devil Is an Ass*), Jocose, Squeeze, and Leanchops. The world of Wilson's comedies is the familiar Jonsonian one of knaves and gulls, deceivers and deceived, cheats and cheated, and many of Wilson's targets, such as hypocrites, casuists, usurers, and misers, are identical to Jonson's. Derivative and backward-looking as Wilson's comedies are, they are lively and varied, and contain some memorable "humour" figures. Although *Belphegor* is a tragi-comedy set in Italy, it too shows Jonson's influence, being partly modelled on *The Devil Is an Ass;* Wilson's main source, however, is Machiavelli's version of a legend about a devil taking human form in order to discover the truth about women and marriage. In his one attempt at tragedy, *Andronicus Comnenius,* a study of a revengeful tyrant who indulges in wholesale slaughter to become Emperor of Constantinople, Wilson observes many of the neo-classical proprieties and rules, but is influenced by Shakespeare as well as Jonson, one scene being closely based on

Richard's wooing of Anne in *Richard III*. Despite the abundance of off-stage action and murder, *Andronicus Comnenius* is a static play lacking in subtlety, and is much less interesting than Shakespeare's relatively immature history play about a similar character. Wilson's talent was for satirical comedy.

—Peter Lewis

WILSON, Robert. English. Nothing is known about his background or education. Married; the playwright Robert Wilson, The Younger, is probably his son. Joined the Earl of Leicester's Company at its establishment, 1574, and quickly gained a reputation as a comic actor; chosen as one of twelve actors to form Queen Elizabeth's Company, 1583, and remained with the company until 1588 when he joined Lord Strange's Company, which subsequently became the Lord Chamberlain's Men. *Died* (buried) *20 November 1600*.

PUBLICATIONS

Plays

The Three Ladies of London (produced 1581?). 1584; edited by J. S. Farmer, 1911.
The Three Lords and Three Ladies of London (produced 1589?). 1590; edited by J. S. Farmer, 1912.
The Cobbler's Prophecy (produced 1594?). 1594; edited by A. C. Wood, 1914.

Reading List: "The Two-Wilsons Controversy" by H. S. H. Mithal, in *Notes and Queries*, March 1959.

*   *   *

In his extant plays Robert Wilson is seen adapting the morality play to the changing theatrical taste of the time of Marlowe and the early Shakespeare. *The Three Ladies of London* is centred on social criticism, employing mid-century techniques in a lively manner. Four knaves, Dissimulation, Fraud, Simony, and Usury, seek employment with the three ladies. Refused by Conscience and by Love (who instead engages Simplicity, a clown having a leading role), they are entertained by the already corrupt Lucre, in whose service they do much social harm. Conscience and Love are dispossessed of their house; the former is deluded into being Lucre's bawd and the latter into marrying Dissimulation. Finally all three ladies are arraigned before Judge Nemo who condemns them. Though the play's moral view is pessimistic, its technique is lively, a number of minor characters providing concrete examples of London's corruption, and the clown being frequently involved. Two striking episodes are the unscrupulous Mercatore's abuse of an honest Jew's trust, and the cutting of Hospitality's throat by Usury. There is vivid stage symbolism when corrupt Conscience is given a spotted face and corrupt Love a double one. The style is homely; as for the versification, though some regular "fourteener" passages are found, long irregular couplets predominate.

The sequel, *The Three Lords and Three Ladies of London*, takes an optimistic view. Though the knaves reappear, they vainly solicit the reformed ladies, who are claimed in marriage by the three lords, Policy, Pomp, and Pleasure. Before the wedding, the lords must outbrave Pride, Ambition, and Tyranny, three Spanish lords bent on conquest, and, these defeated, encounter (in a short, abstract, and superfluous episode) three further rival lords of Lincoln. Much use is made of moral-heraldic spectacle. The clown Simplicity is again prominent, having some scenes with the knaves and another with the lords' witty pages. The style is more elevated; the verse is mostly now iambic pentameter, either unrhymed or (occasionally) rhyming in couplets and quatrains; there is also some prose and some use of irregular couplets tighter than those of the earlier play.

In *The Cobbler's Prophecy*, which has more elaborate stage requirements suggesting performance at court, Wilson continues in this later style. Any social criticism is embodied in, and secondary to, a part-mythological allegory whereby the effete Mars's mistress Venus is seduced by Contempt and bears a child Ruina – events which Mercury causes the once-again-prominent clown, this time Ralph Cobbler, to foretell; finally military and civic virtue prevails and disaster is averted.

Wilson's classical pretensions appear in all three plays alongside his English vivacity: there are Latin speeches and mottoes in his second play, and allusions (Nemo, St. Nihil, Brifrons) even in his first.

—T. W. Craik

WYCHERLEY, William. English. Born in Clive, near Shrewsbury, Shropshire, in 1640. Lived in Paris, 1655–60; spent a short time at Queen's College, Oxford (gentleman commoner), 1660; entered the Inner Temple, London, 1660, but never practised law. Married 1) the Countess of Drogheda in 1679 (died, 1681); 2) Elizabeth Jackson in 1715. Served in the Army, and may have been both an actor and theatre manager before he began to write for the theatre in 1671; enjoyed the patronage of Charles II until 1680 when the king banished him from court because of his marriage; gaoled for debt on his wife's estate, 1682; released and given a pension by James II, 1686; retired to Clive and devoted himself to writing poetry. *Died 31 December 1715.*

PUBLICATIONS

Collections

    Complete Works, edited by Montague Summers. 4 vols., 1924.
    Complete Plays, edited by Gerald Weales. 1967.

Plays

    Love in a Wood; or, St. James's Park (produced 1671). 1672.
    The Gentleman Dancing-Master (produced 1672). 1673.

The Country-Wife (produced 1675).   1675; edited by David Cook and John Swannell, 1975.
The Plain-Dealer (produced 1676).   1677.

Verse

Hero and Leander in Burlesque.   1669.
Epistles to the King and Duke.   1683.
Miscellany Poems.   1704.
The Idleness of Business: A Satire.   1705.
On His Grace the Duke of Marlborough.   1707.

Other

Posthumous Works, edited by Lewis Theobald and Alexander Pope.   2 vols., 1729.

Reading List: *Wycherley: Sa Vie, Son Oeuvre* by Charles Perromat, 1921 (includes bibliography); *Brawny Wycherley* by Willard Connely, 1930; *Wycherley's Drama: A Link in the Development of English Satire* by Rose A. Zimbardo, 1965; *Wycherley* by P. F. Vernon, 1965; *Wycherley* by Katharine M. Rogers, 1972.

*   *   *

Like so many literary gentlemen of the Restoration, William Wycherley fancied himself a poet, but it was not until he was in his sixties and the Restoration had begun to turn into the eighteenth century, spiritually as well as chronologically, that his *Miscellany Poems* appeared. The collection, in which long, tedious philosophic poems share space with love-and-seduction verses, is, as Macaulay said, "beneath criticism." Its publication did attract Alexander Pope, then a bright teen-ager on the literary make, who became a friend of the aging Wycherley. Pope's promise to polish the old man's verse was not kept during Wycherley's life, but it did lead to a volume, *Posthumous Works,* in which it is impossible to separate standard Wycherley from bad Pope. Wycherley occasionally dipped to prurience in his poems, as in "The Answer," a verse reply to "A Letter from Mr. Shadwell to Mr. Wycherley," but he seldom rose to the kind of wit that can be found on almost any page of *The Country-Wife.*

From the little we know about Wycherley, he was ambitious for social position and greedy for money but finally inept in his attempts to get what he wanted; he was also an urban snob as only a transplanted country boy can be. How so conventional a Restoration figure and so dull a poet could have written the comedies that mark him as one of the major English playwrights is still one of the mysteries of English literary history. We do not even know why he wrote them. He may have needed money; he may have wanted to impress the Restoration Wits – Rochester, Dorset, Sedley, Etherege – with whom he had become friends; he may have been overcome by a temporary artistic afflatus. For whatever reason, between 1671 and 1676, he wrote three good plays and one fine one, comedies that provide the theater's best and harshest view of Restoration society, and then, after the publication of *The Plain-Dealer* in 1677, he turned his back on the theater. He did return once, in 1696, to write a pedestrian prologue which was probably never performed for Catharine Trotter's preposterous *Agnes de Castro.* Strange company for the creator of Horner and Mrs. Pinchwife!

Wycherley's plays, like most of the Restoration comedies, are about the endless quest for sex and money, in and out of marriage, and the central theme is enriched by the playwright's marvelous sense for social pretension and polite hypocrisy. Whether he sends Alderman Gripe (*Love in a Wood*) into an old bawd's house, a pious prayer on his lips, or allows Lady Fidget (*The Country-Wife*) to reach from behind her prim exterior for the ever available Horner, he raises laughter at surface behavior which is the child of mendacious society by deep-seated lubricity. Except when a voice of pure delight, like that of the titular country wife, is needed to set off the shady machinations of most of the characters, there is no place for healthy sexuality in Wycherley's plays. Even Mrs. Pinchwife has to learn to deceive, but to her credit and to the play's advantage she remains a child trickster, the happy side of corruption. For the most part sex is a game (and often a brutal one) or a commodity (and often a shoddy one). From bawds and pimps to courting couples, Wycherley's characters know that sex is money, that whatever other entry marriage supplies, it opens purses. When Manly in *The Plain-Dealer* loses his jewels to the scheming Olivia, he is not simply robbed, he is unmanned.

Because Wycherley has always seemed so much a part of the world he depicts, some critics have taken Horner as an author surrogate and read the plays as a celebration of a society in which the true wits are successful manipulators, properly winning sex or money from the imperfect pretenders who deserve being used. Because that depicted world is essentially an ugly one, some critics have taken Manly as Wycherley (the playwright's later pseudonymous use of The Plain-Dealer in letters and in the preface to *Miscellany Poems* helped feed the notion) and taken Manly's abusive attacks on society as the playwright's true voice. There are obvious satiric elements in Wycherley's plays – conventional portraits of literary poseurs, bumbling cuckolds, overeager importers of foreign dress and manners – and they help prove the case for the concerned critic whether he sees Wycherley as Horner or Manly. On a deeper level, however, neither approach really works. On closer look, the clever Horner becomes a sex machine, servicing his clientele with all the efficiency and false gaiety of a fast-food shop, and Manly, who so hates hypocrisy, can be seen as a man for whom plain-dealing is a mask, a self-righteous, self-absorbed individual who uses the falseness of society as an excuse to act dishonestly. The strength of Wycherley's plays is that they are not ordinary period satires. He is the most modern of the Restoration writers because he refuses to provide a place for the audience to stand. His good characters, like Christina in *Love in a Wood*, turn fool through overstatement; his clever characters become butts; his fools refuse to remain skewered. John Dennis, praising Wycherley, once said " 'tis the Business of a Comick Poet to paint the Age in which he lives," and that Wycherley has done superbly, but without providing an ideational frame to fence in his presentation.

In emphasizing the ugliness of the world in which Wycherley's characters play their dead-serious games, I am in danger of falsifying the quality of the playwright's work, as have a number of recent revivals in which plain-dealing directors have displayed a chic fondness for sordid detail. Although the plays are harshly realistic in their approach to life, they are artificial in a theatrical sense. The characters are stereotypical and the exchanges between them are as set as vaudeville comic routines. Take, as an instance, the scene in *Love in a Wood* in which Dapperwit is about to introduce Ranger to his mistress, for whom he is pimping. The realistic content of the scene – the need to get the money in hand – need not interfere with the theatrical effect of a comic turn in which Dapperwit's loquacity, established in an earlier scene, becomes a hesitation device, enticing Ranger and then putting verbal obstacles in his path. Like so much that goes on in Wycherley's plays, this is overtly funny aside from any satirical implications; yet, unlike so much popular comedy, the theatrical fun of the scene does not disguise or weaken the essential nastiness of the situation. As though to emphasize the theatricality of his plays, Wycherley introduces in-jokes – references to his own work (*The Plain-Dealer*), to his actors (*The Gentleman Dancing-Master*), to the fact that the audience is in a theater. "She's come, as if she came expresly to sing the new Song she sung last night," says Hippolita in *The Gentleman Dancing-Master*, and a character who has no other function in the play walks on stage to perform a number. This kind of playfulness not only underscores the conscious artifice in Wycherley's work, it reminds the audience that there is a distance between the action and its referent, that these very funny plays are about a world in which the comic stereotypes have painful counterparts. Only occasionally, as when the brutality of Manly threatens the comic surface of *The Plain-Dealer*, does the real world come dragging its unpleasantness onto the stage. For the most part, Wycherley invokes laughter haunted by a suspicion which, a beat or two beyond the laugh, asks what was so funny. At his best, which means at almost any point in *The Country-Wife*, the laughter and the questioning come at the same time, the play's artistry and its documentary integrity go hand-in-hand.

—Gerald Weales

YEATS, William Butler.   Irish.   Born in Sandymount, County Dublin, 13 June 1865; son of the artist John Butler Yeats, and brother of the artist Jack Butler Yeats; lived in London, 1874–83. Educated at Godolphin School, Hammersmith, London; Erasmus Smith School, Dublin; studied art in Dublin, 1883–86; left art school to concentrate on poetry. Married Georgie Hyde-Lees in 1917; one son and one daughter. Lived mainly in London, spending part of each year in Ireland, 1890–1921: a Founder of the Rhymers Club, London, and member of the *Yellow Book* group; met Lady Gregory, 1896, and thereafter spent many of his summer holidays at her home in Sligo; Co-Founder, with Lady Gregory and Edward Martyn, Irish Literary Theatre, 1899, which became the Abbey Theatre, Dublin, 1904: Director, with Lady Gregory (to 1932), until his death; Editor of *Beltaine*, 1899–1900, *Samhain*, 1901–08, and *The Arrow*, 1906–09; settled with his family in Ireland, 1922: Senator of the Irish Free State, 1922–28. Recipient: Nobel Prize, 1923. D.Litt.: Oxford University, 1931; Cambridge University; University of Dublin. *Died 28 January 1939.*

PUBLICATIONS

Collections

> *Letters*, edited by Allan Wade.   1954.
> *Poems, Prose, Plays*, and *Criticism* (selections), edited by A. Norman Jeffares.   4 vols., 1963–64.
> *Variorum Edition of the Plays*, edited by Russell and C. C. Alspach.   1966.
> *Variorum Edition of the Poems*, edited by Peter Allt and Russell Alspach.   1967.

Plays

> *The Countess Kathleen* (produced 1899).   In *The Countess Kathleen and Various Legends and Lyrics*, 1892; revised version, as *The Countess Cathleen*, 1912.
> *The Land of Heart's Desire* (produced 1894).
> *The Shadowy Waters* (produced 1904).   1900; revised version, in *Poems*, 1906.
> *Diarmuid and Grania*, with George Moore (produced 1901).   1951; edited by Anthony Farrow, 1974.
> *Cathleen ni Hoolihan* (produced 1902).   1902.
> *The Pot of Broth* (produced 1902).   In *The Hour Glass and Other Plays*, 1904.
> *Where There Is Nothing* (produced 1904).   1902; revised version, with Lady Gregory, as *The Unicorn from the Stars* (produced 1907), 1908.
> *The Hour Glass: A Morality* (produced 1903).   1903; revised version (produced 1913), in *The Mask*, April 1913.
> *The King's Threshold* (produced 1903).   1904; revised version (produced 1913), in *Poems*, 1906.
> *The Hour Glass and Other Plays, Being Volume 2 of Plays for an Irish Theatre* (includes *Cathleen ni Houlihan* and *The Pot of Broth*).   1904.
> *On Baile's Strand* (produced 1904).   In *Plays for an Irish Theatre 3*, 1904; revised version, in *Poems*, 1906.
> *Deirdre* (produced 1906).   In *Plays for an Irish Theatre 5*,1907.
> *The Golden Helmet* (produced 1908).   1908; revised version, as *The Green Helmet* (produced 1910), 1910.
> *At the Hawk's Well; or, Waters of Immortality* (produced 1916).   In *The Wild Swans at Coole*, 1917.
> *The Dreaming of the Bones* (produced 1931).   In *Two Plays for Dancers*, 1919.

Two Plays for Dancers (includes *The Dreaming of the Bones* and *The Only Jealousy of Emer*). 1919.

The Player Queen (produced 1919). 1922.

Four Plays for Dancers (includes *At the Hawk's Well, The Only Jealousy of Emer, The Dreaming of the Bones, Calvary*). 1921.

Plays in Prose and Verse (Collected Works 2). 1922.

Plays and Controversies (Collected Works 3). 1923.

King Oedipus, from the play by Sophocles (produced 1926). 1928.

The Resurrection (produced 1934). 1927.

Oedipus at Colonus, from the play by Sophocles (produced 1927). In *Collected Plays*, 1934.

Fighting the Waves (produced 1929). In *Wheels and Butterflies*, 1934.

The Words upon the Window Pane. 1934.

Collected Plays. 1934; revised edition, 1952.

Nine One-Act Plays. 1937.

The Herne's Egg. 1938.

The Herne's Egg and Other Plays (includes *A Full Moon in March* and *The King of the Great Clock Tower*). 1938.

Purgatory and *The Death of Cuchulain*, in *Last Poems and Two Plays.* 1939.

Verse

Mosada: A Dramatic Poem. 1886.

The Wanderings of Oisin and Other Poems. 1889.

The Countess Kathleen and Various Legends and Lyrics. 1892.

Poems. 1895; revised edition, 1899, 1901, 1904, 1908, 1912, 1913, 1927, 1929.

The Wind among the Reeds. 1899.

In the Seven Woods, Being Poems Chiefly of the Irish Heroic Age. 1903.

Poems 1899–1905. 1906.

Poetical Works: Lyrical Poems, Dramatic Poems. 2 vols., 1906–07.

Poems, Second Series. 1909.

The Green Helmet and Other Poems. 1910; revised edition, 1912.

A Selection from the Poetry. 1913.

A Selection from the Love Poetry. 1913.

Poems Written in Discouragement 1912–13. 1913.

Nine Poems. 1914.

Responsibilities: Poems and a Play. 1914.

Responsibilities and Other Poems. 1916.

The Wild Swans at Coole, Other Verses, and a Play in Verse. 1917; revised edition, 1919.

Nine Poems. 1918.

Michael Robartes and the Dancer. 1921.

Selected Poems. 1921.

Later Poems (Collected Works 1). 1922.

Seven Poems and a Fragment. 1922.

The Cat and the Moon and Certain Poems. 1924.

October Blast. 1927.

The Tower. 1928.

Selected Poems, Lyrical and Narrative. 1929.

The Winding Stair. 1929.

Words for Music Perhaps and Other Poems. 1932.

The Winding Stair and Other Poems. 1933.

Collected Poems. 1933; revised edition, 1950.

Wheels and Butterflies. 1934.
The King of the Great Clock Tower: Commentaries and Poems. 1934.
A Full Moon in March. 1935.
Poems. 1935.
New Poems. 1938.
Last Poems and Two Plays. 1939.
Selected Poems, edited by A. Holst. 1939.
Last Poems and Plays. 1940.
The Poems. 2 vols., 1949.

Fiction

John Sherman and Dhoya. 1891.
The Secret Rose (stories). 1897.
The Tables of the Law; The Adoration of the Magi. 1897.
Stories of Red Hanrahan. 1905.

Other

The Celtic Twilight: Men and Women, Dhouls and Fairies. 1893; revised edition, 1902.
Literary Ideals in Ireland, with AE and John Eglinton. 1899.
Is the Order of R.R. and A.C. to Remain a Magical Order? 1901.
Ideas of Good and Evil. 1903.
Discoveries: A Volume of Essays. 1907.
Collected Works. 8 vols., 1908.
Poetry and Ireland: Essays, with Lionel Johnson. 1908.
Synge and the Ireland of His Time. 1911.
The Cutting of an Agate. 1912; revised edition, 1919.
Reveries over Childhood and Youth. 1915.
Per Amica Silentia Lunae. 1918.
Four Years. 1921.
The Trembling of the Veil. 1922.
Essays (Collected Works 4). 1924.
A Vision. 1925; revised edition, 1937; edited by George Mills Harper and W. K. Hood, 1978.
Early Poems and Stories (Collected Works 5). 1925.
Estrangement, Being Some Fifty Thoughts from a Diary Kept in 1909. 1926.
Autobiographies (Collected Works 6). 1926.
The Death of Synge and Other Passages from an Old Diary. 1928.
A Packet for Ezra Pound. 1929.
Stories of Michael Robartes and His Friends. 1932.
Letters to the New Islands, edited by Horace Reynolds. 1934.
Dramatis Personae. 1935.
Dramatis Personae 1896–1902. 1936.
Essays 1931 to 1936. 1937.
The Autobiography. 1938; revised edition, as *Autobiographies,* 1955.
On the Boiler (essays, includes verse). 1939.
If I Were Four-and-Twenty. 1940.
Pages from a Diary Written in 1930. 1940.
The Senate Speeches, edited by Donald Pearce. 1960.
Reflections, edited by Curtis Bradford. 1970.
Ah, Sweet Dancer: Yeats and Margaret Ruddock: A Correspondence, edited by Roger McHugh. 1970.

Uncollected Prose, edited by John F. Frayne and Colton Johnson. 2 vols., 1970–74.
Interviews and Recollections, edited by E. H. Mikhail. 1977.
The Correspondence of Robert Bridges and Yeats, edited by J. Finneran. 1977.

Editor, *Fairy and Folk Tales of the Irish Peasantry*. 1888; as *Irish Fairy and Folk Tales*, 1893.
Editor, *Stories from Carleton*. 1889.
Editor, *Representative Irish Tales*. 1891.
Editor, *Irish Fairy Tales*. 1892.
Editor, with E. Ellis, *The Works of Blake*. 3 vols., 1893.
Editor, *The Poems of Blake*. 1893.
Editor, *A Book of Irish Verse*. 1895; revised edition, 1900.
Editor, *A Book of Images Drawn by W. Horton*. 1898.
Editor, *Twenty-One Poems*, by Lionel Johnson. 1905.
Editor, *Some Essays and Passages*, by John Eglinton. 1905.
Editor, *Sixteen Poems*, by William Allingham. 1905.
Editor, *Poems of Spenser*. 1906.
Editor, *Twenty-One Poems*, by Katharine Tynan. 1907.
Editor, *Poems and Translations*, by J. M. Synge. 1909.
Editor, *Selections from the Writings of Lord Dunsany*. 1912.
Editor, with F. Higgins, *Broadsides: A Collection of Old and New Songs*. 2 vols., 1935–37.
Editor, *The Oxford Book of Modern Verse 1892–1935*. 1936.
Editor, *The Ten Principal Upanishads*, translated by Shree Purohit Swami and Yeats. 1937.

Bibliography: *A Bibliography of the Writings of Yeats* by Allan Wade, 1951, revised edition, 1958, additions by Russell Alspach, in *Irish Book 2*, 1963; *Yeats: A Classified Bibliography of Criticism* by K. P. S. Jochum, 1978.

Reading List: *The Poetry of Yeats* by Louis MacNeice, 1941; *Yeats: The Man and the Masks*, 1948, and *The Identity of Yeats*, 1954, revised edition, 1964, both by Richard Ellmann; *The Golden Nightingale: Essays on Some Principles of Poetry in the Lyrics of Yeats* by Donald Stauffer, 1949; *Yeats: The Tragic Phase: A Study of the Last Poems* by V. Koch, 1951; *Prolegomena to the Study of Yeats's Poems* and *Plays* by G. B. Saul, 2 vols., 1957–58; *Yeats the Playwright: A Commentary on Character and Design in the Major Plays* by Peter Ure, 1963; *Between the Lines: Yeats's Poetry in the Making* by Jon Stallworthy, 1963; *Yeats's Vision and the Later Poems* by Helen Vendler, 1963; *Yeats: A Collection of Critical Essays* edited by John Unterecker, 1963; *Yeats's Golden Dawn* by George Mills Harper, 1974; *A Commentary on the Collected Plays of Yeats* by A. Norman Jeffares and A. S. Knowland, 1974; *Yeats's Early Poetry: The Quest for Reconciliation* by Frank Murphy, 1975; *Yeats: The Critical Heritage* edited by A. Norman Jeffares, 1976.

*   *   *

William Butler Yeats wrote his early poetry out of a love of a particular place, Sligo, in the West of Ireland, with its folklore, its belief in the supernatural, and its legends. He found material for his own mythology in translations of the Gaelic tales into English. These tales of the Red Branch cycle and the Fenian cycle became tinged in his handling with *fin de siècle* melancholy, with what was called the Celtic twilight. His first long poem, "The Wanderings of Oisin," was founded upon Gaelic pagan legends and gave an account of Oisin visiting three islands in the other-world. In "The Rose" his poems developed this use of Gaelic material, and his Rose symbolism showed the effect of his editing Blake and his interest in the occult tradition, as well as the effect of his love for Maud Gonne. *The Wind among the Reeds* contains more elaborate poetry, intense, at times obscurely allusive, drawing upon Gaelic mythology and Rosicrucian images ("The Secret Rose"), defeatist in its romantic poems (the devotion of "He wishes for the Cloths of Heaven"), and filled with a delicate melancholic beauty.

He began to change this style; *In the Seven Woods* contains more personal, realistic poems ("The Folly of Being Comforted," "Adam's Curse"). *The Green Helmet* records the emptiness of love, now Maud Gonne had married (there is exalted celebration of her beauty in "No Second Troy" and "Words"). He reflects on how he seemed to have lost spontaneity ("All Things can tempt me from this craft of verse"). His *Collected Works* had appeared in 1908; but he found a new kind of poetic voice in *Responsibilities*; this is the antithesis of his early work; stripped of decoration and mystery it is savagely satiric in its defence of art against the philistines. He draws images of aristocratic patronage from Renaissance Italy, he contrasts contemporary Ireland with the past, filled with brave leaders ("September 1913"), he reflects on Irish ingratitude ("To a Shade"), and in his poems on beggars and hermits transmits enjoyment of coarse vitality. And yet there is still the magnificence of vision in "The Cold Heaven." "A Coat" repudiates the celtic "embroideries out of old mythologies"; now he is walking naked. *The Wild Swans at Coole* continues his praise of Maud Gonne ("The People" and "Broken Dreams"); his elegy on Major Robert Gregory and "An Irish Airman Foresees His Death" mark a new capacity for elevating the personal into heroic stature; and his three poems "Ego Dominus Tuus," "The Phases of the Moon," and "The Double Vision of Michael Robartes" reflect his interest in putting his thoughts into order, into some kind of system. This found its best poetic expression in "The Second Coming" of *Michael Robartes and the Dancer* which also contained his poems (notably "Easter 1916") on the Rising. Other poems record his marriage, and "A Prayer for My Daughter" attacks the intellectual hatred of Maud Gonne.

These two volumes showed Yeats emerging from the wintry rages of *Responsibilities* into a new appreciation of beauty balanced against tragedy. His own life had blossomed: marriage, children, his tower in the west of Ireland, the Nobel Prize for poetry, membership of the Irish Senate – and, above all, the writing of *A Vision* which gave him a "system of symbolism," a structure for his thought, and the confidence to write fully of his interests – he was now a sufficient subject for his poetry. And how superbly he wrote in *The Tower* of his ideas on life, on death. "Sailing to Byzantium," "The Tower," "Meditations in Time of Civil War," "Nineteen Hundred and Nineteen," "Leda and the Swan," "Among School Children," and "All Soul's Night" have a lofty but passionate authority about them. He was discovering his own intellectual ancestry among the eighteenth-century Anglo-Irish, expressed in "Blood and the Man" and "The Seven Sages" of *The Winding Stair*. Here, too, are the extremes of "vacillation," the contemplation of death after life in "Byzantium," and the noble poems on his friends Eva Gore-Booth and Con Markiewicz, and on Lady Gregory at Coole Park in 1929 and again in 1931 – "we were the last romantics," he cried, realising "all is changed." This note is there in *A Full Moon in March*, where "An age is the reversal of an age"; and, as Yeats grows older, the brilliant metaphysical compression of "The Four Ages of Man" strikes a note which runs through *Last Poems*, which records heroic stances in the face of coming death – of civilization and the self. There are, of course, as ever, the poems on love, the celebration of his friends ("The Municipal Galley Revisited" and "Beautiful Lofty Things"), the despairing recognition of the foul rag and bone shop of the heart, the recording of his own views on Ireland, on poetry, and on himself in "Under Ben Bulben" and, most movingly, in "The Man and the Echo."

Yeats began writing plays in his teens – heroic plays with little dramatic content. But he left conventional modes behind with *The Countess Cathleen*, written for Maud Gonne, and with the aim of blending pagan legend with Christian belief. Yeats revised this play extensively, as he did *The Shadowy Waters*, a study of the heroic gesture, carried by somewhat cryptic symbolism. He also wrote some short plays for the Irish National Dramatic Society, notably the revolutionary *Cathleen ni Houlihan*. *The King's Threshold* marks a change in Yeats's heroes from passivity to more active roles – Seanchan the poet hero in this play (founded upon a middle-Irish story) asserts the place of poetry in public life. Yeats was also deeply interested in Cuchulain, the hero of the Red Branch cycle of stories, and in *On Baile's Strand* he used the story of Cuchulain unwittingly killing his own son. In *Deirdre* he conferred a lofty dignity upon Deirdre's suicide after the heroic gesture made by her and Naoise when they realise they are doomed. In *The Golden Helmet*, rewritten in verse as *The Green Helmet*, Yeats used an old Irish tale as basis for an ironical farce, another "moment of intense life." The strangeness of Yeats's imagination and his very real capacity for farce emerged in *The Player Queen*, which is most effective on stage and extends the theories which were first elaborated in the prose work *Per Amica Silentia Lunae.*

Yeats found the Abbey Theatre was not suitable for the plays he wanted to write: his *Four Plays for Dancers* arose in part out of his interest in the Japanese Noh drama to which Ezra Pound had introduced him. He wanted to do without an orthodox theatre, and so the ritual of music and dancing aided the mysterious art he sought. *At the Hawk's Well* and *The Only Jealousy of Emer* develop the Cuchulain mythology, while *The Dreaming of the Bones* blends supernatural with political themes. *Calvary* is more complex, and depends upon *A Vision*'s ideas. A later play, *Resurrection*, is far more effective, being intense and economic in its presentation of abstract ideas against a turbulent background. His versions of *King Oedipus* and *Oedipus at Colonus* capture the essence of the Greek tragedies with success, and his sense of dialogue and neat construction make *The Words upon the Window Pane* a *tour de force*, communicating via a glance the agony in Swift's spirit. After *The King of the Great Clock Tower*, *A Full Moon in March*, and *The Herne's Egg*, another examination of the limitations of the hero's role, came *Purgatory*, a brilliant evocation of the history of a ruined house and its family, bound in a murderous cycle. *The Death of Cuchulain* written just before Yeats's death in 1939 examines the proud disdain of his hero for death.

Yeats wrote a large number of articles and reviews up to the end of the century; these were mainly on Irish writing. His first extended prose work was *John Sherman and Dhoya*, fiction which gave his youthful impressions of Sligo. The essays in *The Celtic Twilight* portrayed the traditional beliefs and scenery of the West of Ireland in limpid prose, but *The Secret Rose* contained more complex stories, a mixture of symbolism and mysticism written in that "artificial elaborate English" which was popular in the 1890's. His mannered prose appeared in *The Tables of the Law* and *The Adoration of the Magi*. By the turn of the century he changed his prose style, revised *The Celtic Twilight* and some of the stories in *The Secret Rose*. *Ideas of Good and Evil* contained essays written earlier in his complex style. The need for propaganda for the Abbey Theatre further simplified his style, and he was influenced by Lady Gregory's use of the idiomatic language of country people in her translations from the Irish.

In his autobiographical writings Yeats created an evocative, richly patterned record of his own unique experience, and of his family and his friends. His diaries, some of which were published in *Estrangement*, show his attempts to achieve unity. And his thought, based on most diverse sources, appeared in *A Vision* which contains many witty as well as profound passages as he got "it all in order." His prose became more flexible, ranging between complexity and simplicity – "The Bounty of Sweden" is a good example. Some of his senate speeches are excellent pieces of rhetoric. His introduction to *The Words upon the Window Pane* (1934) shows his capacity for imaginative meditation and creative criticism. The many introductions he wrote to the work of writers he admired contain a lofty generosity. On the other hand, his airing of opinions – and prejudices – in *On the Boiler* has an engaging touch of the outrageous. His intellectual curiosity, his originality, and his ability to convey his ideas attractively appears in his correspondence, notably in his youthful letters to Katharine Tynan and his later unreserved, lively letters to Mrs. Shakespeare. His criticism is beginning to be appreciated more fully as the complexity and strength of his mind are understood.

—A. Norman Jeffares

NOTES
ON
ADVISERS
AND
CONTRIBUTORS

ALLEN, Walter.   Novelist and Literary Critic. Author of six novels (the most recent being *All in a Lifetime*, 1959); several critical works, including *Arnold Bennett*, 1948; *Reading a Novel*, 1949 (revised, 1956); *Joyce Cary*, 1953 (revised, 1971); *The English Novel*, 1954; *Six Great Novelists*, 1955; *The Novel Today*, 1955 (revised, 1966); *George Eliot*, 1964; and *The Modern Novel in Britain and the United States*, 1964; and of travel books, social history, and books for children. Editor of *Writers on Writing*, 1948, and of *The Roaring Queen* by Wyndham Lewis, 1973. Has taught at several universities in Britain, the United States, and Canada, and been an editor of the *New Statesman*.

ASHLEY, Leonard R. N.   Professor of English, Brooklyn College, City University of New York. Author of *Colley Cibber*, 1965; *19th-Century British Drama*, 1967; *Authorship and Evidence: A Study of Attribution and the Renaissance Drama*, 1968; *History of the Short Story*, 1968; *George Peele: The Man and His Work*, 1970. Editor of the *Enriched Classics* series, several anthologies of fiction and drama, and a number of facsimile editions. **Essays:** S. N. Behrman; Henry Brooke; John Baldwin Buckstone; Paddy Chayefsky; Henry Chettle; Colley Cibber; George M. Cohan; Noël Coward; Nathan Field; Edward Fitzball; Moss Hart; Aaron Hill; George S. Kaufman; George Kelly; Sidney Kingsley; Arthur Laurents; John Howard Lawson; Frederick Lonsdale; Charles MacArthur; Edward Moore; Anthony Munday; Sir Terence Rattigan; Elkanah Settle; R. C. Sherriff; Alfred Sutro.

BACKSCHEIDER, Paula R.   Associate Professor of English, University of Rochester, New York. Author of "Defoe's Women: Snares and Prey" in *Studies in Eighteenth Century Culture*, 1977, and "Home's *Douglas* and the Theme of the Unfulfilled Life" in *Studies in Scottish Literature*, 1978. Editor of the Garland series *Eighteenth-Century Drama* (60 vols.) and of *Probability, Time, and Space in Eighteenth Century Literature*, 1978. **Essay:** John Crowne.

BATESON, F. W.   Emeritus Fellow and Tutor in English Literature, Corpus Christi College, Oxford. Formerly, Founding-Editor of *Essays in Criticism*. Author of many books, including *English Comic Drama 1700–1750*, 1929; *English Poetry and the English Language*, 1934 (revised, 1973); *English Poetry: A Critical Introduction*, 1950 (revised, 1966); *Wordsworth: A Re-interpretation*, 1954; *A Guide to English Literature*, 1965 (revised, 1976); *Essays in Critical Dissent*, 1972; *The Scholar Critic*, 1972. Editor of *Pope's Epistles to Several Persons*, 1951 (revised, 1961), and *Selected Poems of Blake*, 1957.

BATTESTIN, Martin C.   William R. Kenan, Jr., Professor of English, University of Virginia, Charlottesville. Author of *The Moral Basis of Fielding's Art*, 1959, *The Providence of Wit: Aspects of Form in Augustan Literature and the Arts*, 1974, and a forthcoming biography of Fielding. Editor of the Wesleyan Edition of Fielding's works, and of *Joseph Andrews*, *Tom Jones*, and *Amelia*. **Essay:** Henry Fielding.

BERGONZI, Bernard.   Senior Lecturer in English, University of Warwick, Coventry. Author of *Descartes and the Animals*, 1954; *The Early H.G. Wells*, 1961; *Heroes' Twilight*, 1965; *The Situation of the Novel*, 1970; *T. S. Eliot*, 1971; *Gerard Manley Hopkins*, 1977; *Reading the Thirties*, 1978. Contributor to *The Observer*, *Times Literary Supplement*, and other periodicals.

BEVIS, R. W.   Member of the Department of English, University of British Columbia, Vancouver. Editor, *Eighteenth Century Drama: Afterpieces*, 1970. **Essays:** George Colman, the Elder; John Dennis; Samuel Foote; Charles Macklin; William Whitehead.

BIRNEY, Earle.   Free-lance Writer and Lecturer. Formerly, Professor of English at the University of British Columbia, Vancouver. Author of many volumes of verse (*Collected*

Poems, 2 vols., 1974), two novels, and a play. Editor of several anthologies of verse and of works by Malcolm Lowry.

BODE, Walter. Editor in the Chemistry Department, University of California, Berkeley; Assistant Editor of *San Francisco Theatre Magazine*, and free-lance theatre and film critic. **Essay:** Ray Lawler.

BRAKE, Laurel. Member of the Department of English, University College of Wales, Aberystwyth. **Essay:** John Arden.

BRISSENDEN, Alan. Senior Lecturer in English, University of Adelaide, Australia; Joint General Editor, Tudor and Stuart Text series. Author of *Rolf Boldrewood*, 1972. Editor of *A Chaste Maid in Cheapside* by Thomas Middleton, 1968; *Shakespeare and Some Others* (contributing editor), 1976; *The Portable Boldrewood*, 1978. **Essay:** William Rowley.

CAMPBELL, Ian. Lecturer in English Literature, University of Edinburgh. Author of *Thomas Carlyle*, 1974, and of articles on Scottish literature since 1750. Associate Editor of the Duke-Edinburgh edition of *Carlyle Letters*, and editor of Carlyle's *Reminiscences* and *Selected Essays*. **Essay:** James Bridie.

CHAMBERS, D. D. C. Associate Professor of English, Trinity College, Toronto. **Essay:** James Reaney.

COHN, Ruby. Professor of Comparative Drama, University of California, Davis; Editor of *Modern Drama*, and Associate Editor of *Educational Theatre Journal*. Author of *Samuel Beckett: The Comic Gamut*, 1962; *Currents in Contemporary Drama*, 1969; *Edward Albee*, 1970; *Dialogue in American Drama*, 1971; *Back to Beckett*, 1973; *Modern Shakespeare Offshoots*, 1976. **Essays:** Edward Albee; Samuel Beckett; Ed Bullins.

COWASJEE, Saros. Professor of English, University of Regina, Saskatchewan. Author of *Sean O'Casey: The Man Behind the Plays*, 1963; *O'Casey*, 1966; *Stories and Sketches*, 1970; *Goodbye to Elsa*, 1974; *Coolie: An Assessment*, 1976; *So Many Freedoms*, 1977; *The Last of the Maharajas*, 1978. Editor of the novels of Mulk Raj Anand. **Essay:** Sean O'Casey.

CRAIK, T. W. Professor of English, University of Durham. Author of *The Tudor Interlude*, 1958, and *The Comic Tales of Chaucer*, 1964. Joint General Editor of *The Revels History of Drama in the English Language*, and editor of plays by Massinger, Marlowe, and Shakespeare. **Essays:** Henry Medwall; George Peele; Thomas Sackville and Thomas Norton; Nicholas Udall; Robert Wilson.

CURNOW, Allen. Associate Professor of English, University of Auckland, New Zealand. Author of many volumes of verse (*Collected Poems 1933–1973*, 1974), and six plays. Editor of two anthologies of New Zealand verse.

CURRENT-GARCIA, Eugene. Professor of American Literature, Auburn University, Alabama; Editor of *Southern Humanities Review*. Author of *American Short Stories*, 1952, *What Is the Short Story?*, 1962, and *Realism and Romanticism in Fiction*, 1962 (all with W. R. Patrick), and of *O. Henry: A Critical Study*, 1965, and *Shem, Ham, and Japheth: The Papers of W.O. Tuggle*, 1973. **Essay:** Anna Cora Mowatt.

DACE, Tish. Associate Professor of Speech, Drama, and English, John Jay College of Criminal Justice, City University of New York; Theatre Critic, *Soho Weekly News*, and contributor to the *Village Voice*, the *New York Times*, and other newspapers. Author of *LeRoi Jones (Imamu Amiri Baraka): A Checklist of Works by and about Him*, 1971, *The Theatre*

Student: Modern Theatre and Drama, 1973, and the article on Baraka in *Black American Writers*, 1978. **Essays:** LeRoi Jones; David Mercer; John Mortimer; Harold Pinter.

DeMATTEIS, Daniel. Visiting Assistant Professor, Scarborough College, University of Toronto. **Essays:** Henry Glapthorne; Thomas Nabbes.

DOYLE, Charles. Professor of English, and Director of the Division of American and Commonwealth Literature, University of British Columbia. Author (as Mike Doyle) of several books of poetry, the most recent being *Going On*, 1974, and of critical studies of New Zealand poetry, R. A. K. Mason, and James K. Baxter. Editor of *Recent Poetry in New Zealand*, 1965. **Essay:** James K. Baxter.

DOYNO, Victor A. Associate Professor of English, State University of New York, Buffalo. Editor of *Parthenophil and Parthenophe*, by Barnabe Barnes, 1971. **Essay:** Thomas William Robertson.

DRAKAKIS, John. Member of the Department of English Studies, University of Stirling, Scotland. **Essay:** Shakerley Marmion.

DUNLAP, Rhodes. Member of the Department of English, University of Iowa, Iowa City. Editor of *The Poems of Thomas Carew*, 1949. **Essays:** William Cartwright; Thomas Killigrew; Thomas May; James Shirley.

DUTTON, Geoffrey. Author of more than 25 books, including verse (most recently *New Poems to 1972*, 1972), novels (most recently *Queen Emma of the South Seas*, 1977), travel books, biographies, art criticism, and critical works, including *Patrick White*, 1961, and *Walt Whitman*, 1961. Editor of anthologies of Australian writing and translator of works by Yevtushenko and Bella Akhmadulina. **Essay:** Patrick White.

FLETCHER, Ian. Reader in English Literature, University of Reading, Berkshire. Author of plays and verse, and of *Walter Pater*, 1959 (revised, 1970); *A Catalogue of Imagist Poets*, 1966; *Beaumont and Fletcher*, 1967; *Meredith Now*, 1971; *Swinburne*, 1972. Editor of anthologies of verse and drama, and of works by Lionel Johnson, Victor Plarr, and John Gray. **Essays:** Henry Arthur Jones; Oscar Wilde.

FLORA, Joseph M. Professor of English, University of North Carolina, Chapel Hill. Author of *Vardis Fisher*, 1965; *William Ernest Henley*, 1974; *Frederick Manfred*, 1974. Editor of *The Cream of the Jest* by James Branch Cabell, 1975, and *A Biographical Guide to Southern Literature* (with R. A. Bain and Louis D. Rubin, Jr.), 1978. **Essay:** Marc Connelly.

FOREY, Margaret. Examiner and part-time teacher; currently editing a work by William Strode. Formerly lecturer at the University of Durham. Author of "Cleveland's 'Square Cap': Some Questions of Structure and Date" in *Durham University Journal*, 1974. **Essays:** Jasper Mayne; Thomas Randolph.

FRASER, G. S. Reader in Modern English Literature, University of Leicester. Author of several books of verse, the most recent being *Conditions*, 1969; travel books; critical studies of Yeats, Dylan Thomas, Pound, Durrell, and Pope; and of *The Modern Writer and His World*, 1953, *Vision and Rhetoric*, 1959, and *Metre, Rhythm, and Free Verse*, 1970. Editor of works by Keith Douglas and Robert Burns, and of verse anthologies. **Essay:** Ben Travers.

FRENCH, Warren. Professor of English and Director of the Center for American Studies, Indiana University-Purdue University, Indianapolis; Member of the Editorial Board, *American Literature* and *Twentieth-Century Literature*; series editor for Twayne publishers.

Author of *John Steinbeck*, 1961; *Frank Norris*, 1962; *J.D. Salinger*, 1963; *A Companion to "The Grapes of Wrath,"* 1963; *The Social Novel at the End of an Era*, 1966; and a series on American fiction, poetry, and drama, *The Thirties*, 1967, *The Forties*, 1968, *The Fifties*, 1971, and *The Twenties*, 1975. **Essay:** Thornton Wilder.

GERBER, John C. Chairman of the Department of English, State University of New York, Albany; Member of the Editorial Board, *Resources for American Literary Study*. Formerly Chairman of the Department of English, University of Iowa. Author of *Factual Prose* (with Walter Blair), 1945, *Literature*, 1948, *Writers Resource Book*, 1953, and other works on writing and speaking. Editor of *Twentieth-Century Interpretations of "The Scarlet Letter,"* 1968, and *Studies in Huckleberry Finn*, 1971; General Editor of the Iowa-California edition of the works of Mark Twain.

GIBBS, A. M. Professor, School of English and Linguistics, Macquarie University, New South Wales. Author of *G.B. Shaw*, 1969. Editor of *The Shorter Poems, and Songs from the Plays and Masques* by Sir William Davenant, 1972. **Essay:** Sir William Davenant.

GILL, Roma. Member of the English Department, University of Sheffield, Yorkshire. Editor of *The Plays of Christopher Marlowe*, 1971, *William Empson: The Man and His Work*, 1974, and of works by Middleton and Tourneur. **Essays:** John Bale; Sir Aston Cokayne; Christopher Marlowe; Thomas Middleton; Cyril Tourneur.

GORDON, Ian A. Professor of English, University of Wellington, 1936–74. Has taught at the University of Leeds and the University of Edinburgh. Author of *John Skelton*, 1943; *The Teaching of English*, 1947; *Katherine Mansfield*, 1954; *The Movement of English Prose*, 1966; *John Galt*, 1972. Editor of *English Prose Technique*, 1948, and of works by William Shenstone, John Galt, and Katherine Mansfield. **Essay:** John Lyly.

GREEN, Dorothy. Member of the Faculty, Humanities Research Centre, Australian National University, Canberra. Author of books of verse, including *The Dolphin*, 1967, and of articles on Australian literature. **Essay:** Douglas Stewart.

GREEN, Roger Lancelyn. Author of more than 50 books including fiction and verse for children and adults, retellings of folk and fairy tales, and critical studies of Andrew Lang, A. E. W. Mason, Lewis Carroll, J. M. Barrie, Mrs. Molesworth, C. S. Lewis, and Rudyard Kipling; also editor of works by these authors and others, and translator of plays by Sophocles. **Essay:** J. M. Barrie.

GURR, Andrew. Professor of English Language and Literature, University of Reading, Berkshire. Author of *The Shakespearean Stage*, 1970. Editor of several plays by Beaumont and Fletcher. **Essay:** Francis Beaumont.

HOFFMAN, Daniel. Professor of English, University of Pennsylvania, Philadelphia. Author of several books of verse, the most recent being *Able Was I Ere I Saw Elba*, 1977, and of critical works including *The Poetry of Stephen Crane*, 1957, *Form and Fable in American Fiction*, 1961, *Poe Poe Poe Poe Poe Poe Poe*, 1972, and *Barbarous Knowledge: Myth in the Poetry of Yeats, Graves, and Muir*, 1973. Editor of anthologies and of works by Crane and Robert Frost.

HOGAN, Robert. Free-lance Writer. Former Professor of English, University of Delaware, Newark. Author of *The Experiments of Sean O'Casey*, 1960; *Arthur Miller*, 1964; *The Independence of Elmer Rice*, 1965; *The Plain Style* (with H. Bogart), 1967; *After the Irish Renaissance*, 1967; *Dion Boucicault*, 1969; *The Fan Club*, 1969; *Lost Plays of the Irish Renaissance* (with James Kilroy), 1970; *Eimar O'Duffy*, 1972; *Mervyn Wall*, 1972; *Conor*

Cruise O'Brien (with E. Young-Bruehl), 1974; *The Irish Literary Theatre* (vol. 1 of *A History of the Modern Irish Drama*, with James Kilroy), 1975. Editor of several collections of plays and of anthologies of drama criticism. **Essays:** Dion Boucicault; George Fitzmaurice; Denis Johnston; Elmer Rice.

HOLMAN, C. Hugh. Kenan Professor of English, Chairman of the Division of Humanities, and Special Assistant to the Chancellor, University of North Carolina, Chapel Hill; Editor of *Southern Literary Journal*. Author or co-author of several books, including five detective novels; *The Development of American Criticism*, 1955; *The Southerner as American*, 1960; *Thomas Wolfe*, 1960; *Seven Modern American Novelists*, 1964; *The American Novel Through Henry James: A Bibliography*, 1966; *Three Modes of Modern Southern Fiction*, 1966; *Roots of Southern Writing*, 1972; *The Loneliness at the Core*, 1975. Editor of works by Wolfe, William Gilmore Simms, and others.

HUGHES, Leo. Professor of English, University of Texas, Austin. Author of *A Century of English Farce*, 1956, and *The Drama's Patrons*, 1971. Editor of *Ten English Farces* (with Arthur H. Scouten), 1948, and *The Plain Dealer* by William Wycherley, 1967. **Essay:** Edward Ravenscroft.

JAMES, Louis. Senior Lecturer in English and American Literature, University of Kent, Canterbury. Author of *The Islands in Between*, 1968, and *Fiction for the Working Class Man 1830–1850*, 1974.

JEFFARES, A. Norman. Professor of English Studies, University of Stirling, Scotland; Editor of *Ariel: A Review of International English Literature*, and General Editor of the Writers and Critics series and the New Oxford English series. Past Editor of *A Review of English Studies*. Author of *Yeats: Man and Poet*, 1949; *Seven Centuries of Poetry*, 1956; *A Commentary on the Collected Poems* (1958) and *Collected Plays* (1975) *of Yeats*. Editor of *Restoration Comedy*, 1974, and *Yeats: The Critical Heritage*, 1977. **Essays:** William Congreve; Richard Brinsley Sheridan; William Butler Yeats.

JOHNSON, Robert K. Professor of English, Suffolk University, Boston. Author of articles on Richard Wilbur, Wallace Stevens, T. S. Eliot, and William Carlos Williams. **Essay:** Archibald MacLeish.

JOYNER, Nancy C. Member of the Department of English, Western Carolina University, Cullowhee, North Carolina. **Essay:** William Vaughn Moody.

KAPLAN, Zoë Coralnik. Adjunct Assistant Professor of Speech and Theatre, John Jay College of Criminal Justice, City University of New York. **Essay:** Rachel Crothers.

KELLY, Richard. Professor of English, University of Tennessee, Knoxville. Editor of *Tennessee Studies in Literature*, 1970–76. Author of *Douglas Jerrold*, 1970; *Lewis Carroll*, 1970; *Great Cartoonists of Nineteenth-Century Punch*, 1978. Editor of *The Best of Mr. Punch: The Humorous Writings of Douglas Jerrold*, 1970. **Essay:** Douglas William Jerrold.

KELSALL, Malcolm. Professor of English, University College, Cardiff; Advisory Editor of *Byron Journal*. Editor of *The Adventures of David Simple* by Sarah Fielding, 1969, *Venice Preserved* by Thomas Otway, 1969, and *Love for Love* by William Congreve, 1970. **Essay:** Edward Martyn.

KENDLE, Burton. Associate Professor of English, Roosevelt University, Chicago. Author of articles on D. H. Lawrence, John Cheever, and Chekhov. **Essay:** Simon Gray.

KING, Kimball. Member of the Department of English, University of North Carolina, Chapel Hill. **Essay:** Lillian Hellman.

KUHN, John G. Professor of English and Director of Theatre, Rosemont College, Pennsylvania. Author of an article in *Walt Whitman Review*, 1962, poems in *Denver Quarterly*, 1973, and a play, *Statu(t)es Like Cartoons*, produced 1976. **Essays:** James Nelson Barker; William Dunlap; Eugene O'Neill; Sam Shepard.

KULSHRESTHA, Chirantan. Reader in English, University of Hyderabad, India. Author of *The Saul Bellow Estate*, 1976; *Bellow: The Problem of Affirmation*, 1978; chapters in *Considerations*, edited by Meenakshi Mukherjee, 1977, and *Through the Eyes of the World: International Essays in American Literature*, edited by Bruce A. Lohof, 1978; and articles in *Chicago Review, American Review, Quest, Indian Literature*, and other periodicals. Editor of *Not by Politics Alone!* (with V. V. John), 1978. **Essay:** Robert E. Sherwood.

KUNZ, Don. Associate Professor of English, University of Rhode Island, Kingston. Author of *The Drama of Thomas Shadwell*, 1972, and of articles on Shadwell in *Restoration and Eighteenth Century Theatre Research*. **Essay:** Thomas Shadwell.

LEARY, Lewis. Kenan Professor Emeritus of English, University of North Carolina, Chapel Hill. Author of *Idiomatic Mistakes in English*, 1932; *That Rascal Freneau: A Study in Literary Failure*, 1941; *The Literary Career of Nathaniel Tucker*, 1951; *Mark Twain*, 1960; *Twain's Letters to Mary*, 1961; *John Greenleaf Whittier*, 1962; *Washington Irving*, 1963; *Norman Douglas*, 1967; *Southern Excursions*, 1971; *Faulkner of Yoknapatawpha County*, 1973; *Soundings: Some Early American Writers*, 1975; *American Literature: A Study and Research Guide*, 1976. Editor of works by Freneau and Twain, and several collections of essays.

LESTER, G. A. Lecturer in English Language and Medieval Literature, University of Sheffield. Author of *The Anglo-Saxons*, 1976. **Essays:** John Heywood; Wakefield Master.

LEWIS, Peter. Lecturer in English, University of Durham. Author of *The Beggar's Opera* (critical study), 1976, and of articles on Restoration and Augustan drama and modern poetry. Editor of *The Beggar's Opera* by John Gay, 1973, and *Poems '74* (anthology of Anglo-Welsh poetry), 1974. **Essays:** George Farquhar; John Gay; George Lillo; Sir John Vanbrugh; John Wilson.

LINDSAY, Maurice. Director of the Scottish Civic Trust, Glasgow, and Managing Editor of *The Scottish Review*. Author of several books of verse, the most recent being *Walking Without an Overcoat*, 1977; plays; travel and historical works; and critical studies including *Burns: The Man, His Work, The Legend*, 1954 (revised, 1968), *The Burns Encyclopedia*, 1959 (revised, 1970), and *A History of Scottish Literature*, 1977. Editor of the Saltire Modern Poets series, several anthologies of Scottish writing, and works by Sir Alexander Gray, Sir David Lyndsay, Marion Angus, and John Davidson. **Essay:** Joanna Baillie.

LINK, Frederick M. Professor of English, University of Nebraska, Lincoln. Author of *Aphra Behn*, 1968, and *English Drama 1660–1800: A Guide to Information Sources*, 1976. Editor of *The Rover* by Behn, 1967, and *Aureng-Zebe* by John Dryden, 1971. **Essays:** Aphra Behn; Henry Carey; Hannah Cowley.

LODGE, David. Reader in English, University of Birmingham. Author of five novels (the most recent being *Changing Places*, 1975), *Language of Fiction*, 1966, *The Novelist at the Crossroads*, 1971, and studies of Graham Greene and Evelyn Waugh. Editor of novels by

642

Jane Austen, George Eliot, and Hardy, and *Twentieth Century Literary Criticism: A Reader*, 1972.

LOHOF, Bruce A. Associate Professor and Chairman of the Department of History, University of Miami; Joint Editor of the *Indian Journal of American Studies*, and member of the editorial board of *Journal of Popular Culture*. Former Senior Fulbright-Hays Scholar and Director of the American Studies Research Centre, Hyderabad, India. Author of articles for *Social Studies Bulletin, Industrial Archaeology, Centennial Review*, and other periodicals, and of papers for the American Studies Association and the Popular Culture Association. **Essay:** George Henry Boker.

LUCAS, John. Professor of English and Drama, Loughborough University, Leicestershire; Editor of *Victorian Studies, Literature and History*, and *Journal of European Studies*. Author of *Tradition and Tolerance in 19th-Century Fiction*, 1966; *The Melancholy Man: A Study of Dickens*, 1970; *Arnold Bennett*, 1975; *Egilssaga: The Poems*, 1975; *The Literature of Change*, 1977; *The 1930's: Challenge to Orthodoxy*, 1978. Editor of *Literature and Politics in the 19th Century*, 1971, and of works by George Crabbe and Jane Austen. **Essay:** John Whiting.

MACKERNESS, E. D. Member of the Department of English Literature, University of Sheffield. Author of *The Heeded Voice: Studies in the Literary Status of the Anglican Sermon 1830–1900*, 1959, *A Social History of English Music*, 1964, and *Somewhere Further North: A History of Music in Sheffield*, 1974. Editor of *The Journals of George Sturt 1890–1927*, 1967. **Essay:** John Hughes.

MALEK, James S. Professor of English and Associate Graduate Dean, University of Idaho, Moscow. Author of *The Arts Compared: An Aspect of Eighteenth-Century British Aesthetics*, 1974, and of articles in *Modern Philology, The Journal of Aesthetics and Art Criticism, Neuphilologische Mitteilungen, Texas Studies in Literature and Language*, and other periodicals. **Essays:** Sir George Etherege; John Home; Arthur Murphy.

McCORMACK, W. J. Member of the Faculty, School of English, University of Leeds. Editor of *A Festschrift for Francis Stuart on His Seventieth Birthday*, 1972. **Essay:** Brendan Behan.

McNAUGHTON, Howard. Senior Lecturer in English, University of Canterbury, Christchurch, New Zealand; Theatre Critic, *The Press* since 1968; Advisory Editor, *Act* since 1976. Author of *New Zealand Drama: A Bibliographical Guide*, 1974, and *Bruce Mason*, 1976. Editor of *Contemporary New Zealand Plays*, 1976. **Essays:** Enid Bagnold; Ben Hecht; Bruce Mason; Emlyn Williams.

MESERVE, Walter J. Professor of Theatre and Drama, Indiana University, Bloomington. Author of *An Outline of American Drama*, 1965, *Robert Sherwood: Reluctant Moralist*, 1970, and *An Emerging Entertainment: The Drama of the American People to 1828*, 1977. Editor of *The Complete Plays of W.D. Howells*, 1960; *Discussions of Modern American Drama*, 1966; *American Satiric Comedies*, 1969; *Modern Dramas from Communist China*, 1970; *The Rise of Silas Lapham* by W. D. Howells, 1971; *Studies in "Death of a Salesman,"* 1972; *Modern Literature from China*, 1974. **Essays:** Robert Montgomery Bird; Augustin Daly; Clyde Fitch; Susan Glaspell; Edward Harrigan; Bronson Howard; Sidney Howard; Percy MacKaye; Langdon Mitchell; John Howard Payne; Augustus Thomas; Royall Tyler.

MILLER, Jordan Y. Chairman of the Department of English, University of Rhode Island, Kingston. Exchange Professor, University of East Anglia, Norwich, 1977. Author of *Eugene O'Neill and the American Critic*, 1962; *Maxwell Anderson: Gifted Technician*, 1967; *Eugene*

O'Neill, 1968; *The War Play Comes of Age*, 1969; *Expressionism: The Wasteland Enacted*, 1974; *The Other O'Neill*, 1974. Editor of *American Dramatic Literature*, 1961, *Playwright's Progress*, 1965, and *Twentieth-Century Interpretations of "A Streetcar Named Desire,"* 1971. **Essays:** Lorraine Hansberry; James A. Herne; William Inge.

MINER, Earl. Townsend Martin Professor of English and Comparative Literature, Princeton University, New Jersey. Author of *Dryden's Poetry*, 1967; *An Introduction to Japanese Court Poetry*, 1968; *The Metaphysical Mode from Donne to Cowley*, 1969; *The Cavalier Mode from Jonson to Cotton*, 1971; *Seventeenth-Century Imagery*, 1971; *The Restoration Mode from Milton to Dryden*, 1974; *Japanese Linked Poetry*, 1978. **Essay:** John Dryden.

MORGAN, Margery. Reader in English, University of Lancaster. Author of *A Drama of Political Man: A Study of the Plays of Harley Granville-Barker*, 1961, and *The Shavian Playground: An Exploration of the Art of G.B. Shaw*, 1972. Editor of *You Never Can Tell* by Shaw, 1967, and *The Madras House* by Granville-Barker, 1977. **Essays:** Harley Granville-Barker; Laurence Housman; James Robinson Planché; Peter Shaffer; George Bernard Shaw; David Storey.

MORPURGO, J. E. Professor of American Literature, University of Leeds. Author and editor of many books, including the *Pelican History of the United States*, 1955 (third edition, 1970), and volumes on Cooper, Lamb, Trelawny, Barnes Wallis, and on Venice, Athens, and rugby football. **Essay:** John Burgoyne.

MORRISSEY, L. J. Member of the Department of English, University of Saskatchewan, Saskatoon. Author of articles on English street theatre and the theatrical records of the London Guilds, and of a forthcoming book on Swift. **Essay:** John Tatham.

NEW, W. H. Associate Professor of English, University of British Columbia, Vancouver; Associate Editor of *Canadian Literature* and *World Literature Written in English*. Author of *Four Hemispheres*, 1971, and *Malcolm Lowry*, 1971.

NIVEN, Alastair. Member of the Department of English Studies, University of Stirling, Scotland. Author of *D.H. Lawrence: The Novels*, 1978. **Essay:** Wole Soyinka.

OLIVER-MORDEN, B. C. Teacher at the Open University and the University of Keele. Editor of the 18th-Century section of *The Year's Work in English 1973*. **Essay:** Oliver Goldsmith.

PEARCE, Roy Harvey. Professor of English, University of California at San Diego. Author of *Colonial American Writing*, 1951, *The Savages of America*, 1953 (revised, 1965), and *The Continuity of American Poetry*, 1961. Co-Editor of the Centennial Edition of the Writings of Hawthorne, and of anthologies of essays on Hawthorne and Whitham.

PERKINS, Barbara M. Director of Writing Improvement, Humanities Program, Eastern Michigan University, Ypsilanti. **Essay:** Maxwell Anderson.

PERKINS, George. Professor of English, Eastern Michigan University, Ypsilanti. Author or editor of *Writing Clear Prose*, 1964; *Varieties of Prose*, 1966; *The Theory of the American Novel*, 1970; *Realistic American Short Fiction*, 1972; *American Poetic Theory*, 1972; *The American Tradition in Literature* (with others), fourth edition, 1974.

PETERSEN, Kirsten Holst. Member of the Commonwealth Literature Division of the

English Department, University of Aarhus, Denmark; reviewer for *Danida*. Editor of *Enigma of Values* (with Anna Rutherford), 1975. **Essay:** Athol Fugard.

POPOVICH, Helen Houser. Associate Dean of the College of Arts and Sciences and Associate Professor of English, University of South Florida, Tampa. Author of articles on Samuel Beckett in *South Atlantic Bulletin 37*, 1972, and composition in *College Composition and Communication 27*, 1976. **Essays:** Arthur Kopit; Peter Ustinov; John van Druten.

REILLY, John M. Associate Professor of English, State University of New York, Albany; Advisory Editor, *Obsidian: Black Literature in Review*, and *Melus*. Author of the bibliographical essay on Richard Wright in *Black American Writers* and of articles on Wright and other Afro-American writers, and on detective fiction, in *Colorado Quarterly, Phylon, CLA Journal, Journal of Black Studies, Armchair Detective, Journal of Popular Culture*, and other periodicals. Editor of *Twentieth-Century Interpretations of "Invisible Man,"* 1970, *Richard Wright: The Critical Reception*, 1978, and of the reference book *Detective and Crime Writers*, 1980.

RHODES, H. Winston. Professor of English (retired), University of Canterbury, Christchurch. Past Editor of *New Zealand Monthly Review*. His books include *New Zealand Fiction since 1945*, 1968, *Frank Sargeson*, 1969, and six edited volumes of Rewi Alley's prose and verse.

ROGERS, Pat. Professor of English, University of Bristol. Author of *Grub Street: Studies in a Subculture*, 1972, and *The Augustan Vision*, 1974. Editor of *A Tour Through Great Britain* by Daniel Defoe, 1971, *Defoe: The Critical Heritage*, 1972, and *The Eighteenth Century*, 1978. **Essay:** Susanna Centlivre.

RUOFF, James E. Associate Professor of English, City College of New York. Author of *Elizabethan Poetry and Prose*, 1972, *Crowell Handbook of Elizabethan and Stuart Literature*, 1973, and *Major Shakespearean Tragedies* (with Edward G. Quinn), 1973. **Essays:** Thomas Dekker; John Fletcher.

SADDLEMYER, Ann. Professor of English and Drama, University of Toronto. Author of *The World of W.B. Yeats*, 1965, and *In Defence of Lady Gregory, Playwright*, 1966. Editor of *The Plays of J.M. Synge*, 1968; *The Plays of Lady Gregory*, 1971; *Letters to Molly: Synge to Maire O'Neill*, 1971; *Some Letters of Synge to Lady Gregory and Yeats*, 1971. **Essays:** Lady Gregory; J. M. Synge.

SALGĀDO, Gāmini. Professor of English, University of Exeter, Devon. Author of *Eyewitnesses of Shakespeare: Firsthand Accounts of Performances, 1590–1890*, 1975, and *The Elizabethan Underworld*, 1977. Editor of *Sons and Lovers: A Collection of Critical Essays*, 1969, *Cony Catchers and Bawdy Baskets*, 1973, works by D. H. Lawrence and Shakespeare, and collections of Jacobean and Restoration plays. **Essays:** Richard Brome; John Ford; Ben Jonson; Thomas Kyd; Philip Massinger; John Webster.

SCOUTEN, Arthur H. Professor of English, University of Pennsylvania, Philadelphia. Author of articles on Swift, Defoe, and the London theatre in periodicals. Editor of *Ten English Farces* (with Leo Hughes), 1948, *The London Stage 3*, 2 vols., 1961, and *1*, 1965, and *A Bibliography of the Writings of Swift* by Teerink Herman, second edition, 1963. **Essays:** John Banks; Thomas D'Urfey; Sir Robert Howard; Nathaniel Lee.

SHADY, Raymond C. Member of the English Department, St. John Fisher College, Rochester, New York. Editor of *Love's Mistress* by Thomas Heywood, 1977. **Essays:** John Day; John Marston.

SHARMA, J. N. Academic Associate, American Studies Research Centre, Hyderabad. **Essay:** William Saroyan.

SMITH, Stan. Lecturer in English, University of Dundee, Scotland. Author of the forthcoming book *A Superfluous Man* (on Edward Thomas), and of articles on modern literature for *Critical Quarterly, Literature and History, Irish University Review, Scottish International Review*, and other periodicals. **Essay:** W. H. Auden.

SOLOMON, Harry M. Associate Professor of English, Auburn University, Alabama. Author of *Sir Richard Blackmore* (forthcoming), and of articles on Shaftesbury, Swift, and others in *Southern Humanities Review, Keats-Shelley Journal, Studies in English Literature*, and other periodicals. **Essay:** Robert Dodsley.

SPENCER, Christopher. Professor of English, University of North Carolina, Greensboro. Author of *Nahum Tate*, 1972. Editor of *Davenant's Macbeth from the Yale Manuscript*, 1961, and *Five Restoration Adaptations of Shakespeare*, 1965. **Essay:** Nahum Tate.

STAGG, Louis Charles. Professor of English, Memphis State University, Tennessee; Member of the Executive Committee, Tennessee Philological Association. Author of *Index to Poe's Critical Vocabulary*, 1966; *Index to the Figurative Language in the Tragedies of Webster, Jonson, Heywood, Chapman, Marston, Tourneur*, and *Middleton*, 7 vols., 1967–70, revised edition, as *Index to the Figurative Language of the Tragedies of Shakespeare's Chief 17th-Century Contemporaries*, 1977. **Essays:** Lord Dunsany; Christopher Fry; William Gillette; Thomas Heywood; Nicholas Rowe.

STEAD, C. K. Professor of English, University of Auckland, New Zealand. Author of three volumes of verse – *Whether the Will Is Free*, 1964, *Crossing the Bar*, 1972, and *Quesada*, 1975 – a novel, *Smith's Dream*, 1971, and *The New Poetic: Yeats to Eliot*, 1964. Editor of *New Zealand Short Stories: Second Series*, 1966, a casebook on Shakespeare's *Measure for Measure*, 1971, and *The Letters and Journals of Katherine Mansfield: A Selection*, 1977.

STEDMAN, Jane W. Professor of English, Roosevelt University, Chicago. Author of *Gilbert Before Sullivan*, 1967, and of articles on Gilbert, Dickens, and the Brontës. Regular contributor to *Opera News*. **Essays:** David Belasco; W. S. Gilbert; Tom Taylor.

STROUP, Thomas B. Professor Emeritus, University of Kentucky, Lexington. Author of a book on composition, and of *Microcosmos: The Shape of the Elizabethan Play*, 1965, and *Religious Rite and Ceremony in Milton's Poetry*, 1968. Editor or Joint Editor of *Humanistic Scholarship in the South*, 1948; *South Atlantic Studies for Sturgis E. Leavitt*, 1953; *The Works of Nathaniel Lee*, 2 vols., 1954–55; *The Selected Poems of George Daniel of Beswick*, 1959; *The Cestus: A Mask*, 1962; *The University and the American Future*, 1965; *The Humanities and the Understanding of Reality*, 1966. **Essay:** Thomas Otway.

SUTHERLAND, James. Emeritus Professor of Modern English Literature, University College, London. Formerly, Editor of *Review of English Studies*. Author of many books, including *Leucocholy* (poems), 1926; *The Medium of Poetry*, 1934; *Defoe*, 1937; *A Preface to Eighteenth Century Poetry*, 1948; *The English Critic*, 1952; *On English Prose*, 1957; *English Satire*, 1958; *English Literature in the Late Seventeenth Century*, 1969; *Daniel Defoe: A Critical Study*, 1971. Editor of plays by Rowe, Dekker, Shakespeare, and Dryden, *The Dunciad* by Pope, 1943, and *The Oxford Book of Literary Anecdotes*, 1975.

TASCH, Peter A. Associate Professor of English, Temple University, Philadelphia; Co-Editor of *The Scriblerian*. Author of *The Dramatic Cobbler: The Life and Works of Isaac*

Bickerstaff, 1971. Editor of *Fables by the Late Mr. Gay*, 1970. **Essays:** Isaac Bickerstaff; Charles Dibdin; David Garrick; Hugh Kelly.

THOMAS, Ned. Lecturer in English, University College of Wales, Aberystwyth; Founding Editor of *Planet* magazine. Author of *George Orwell*, 1965, and *The Welsh Extremist: Essays on Modern Welsh Literature and Society*, 1971. **Essay:** Derek Walcott.

THOMSON, Peter. Professor of Drama, University of Exeter, Devon; Author of *Ideas in Action*, 1977. Editor of *Julius Caesar* by Shakespeare, 1970; *Essays on Nineteenth-Century British Theatre* (with Kenneth Richards), 1971; *The Eighteenth-Century English Stage*, 1973; *Lord Byron's Family*, 1975. **Essays:** H. J. Byron; George Colman, the Younger; James Sheridan Knowles; William Thomas Moncrieff; Thomas Morton; John O'Keeffe; Joe Orton; Arthur Wing Pinero; John Poole.

THORNTON, Ralph R. Associate Professor of English, La Salle College, Philadelphia. Editor of *The Wive's Excuse*, 1973, and *The Maid's Last Prayer*, 1978, both by Thomas Southerne. **Essay:** Thomas Southerne.

TOMLIN, E. W. F. Free-lance Writer, Broadcaster, and Lecturer. Author of *The Approach to Metaphysics*, 1947; *The Western Philosophers*, 1950; *The Eastern Philosophers*, 1952; *Simone Weil*, 1954; *Living and Knowing*, 1955; *Wyndham Lewis*, 1955; *R.G. Collingwood*, 1956; *Tokyo Essays*, 1967; and books on Turkey and Japan. Editor of *Wyndham Lewis: An Anthology*, 1969, *Dickens: A Centenary Volume*, 1970, and *Arnold Toynbee: A Selection from His Works*, 1978. **Essay:** Ronald Duncan.

TRAVERSI, Derek A. Professor of English, Swarthmore College, Pennsylvania. Author of *An Approach to Shakespeare*, 1938 (revised, 1968); *Shakespeare: The Last Phase*, 1954; *Shakespeare: From Richard II to Henry V*, 1957; *Shakespeare: The Roman Plays*, 1963; *T.S. Eliot: The Longer Poems*, 1976. **Essays:** T. S. Eliot; William Shakespeare.

TRUSSLER, Simon. Editor of *Theatre Quarterly*. Theatre Critic, *Tribune*, 1969–76. Author of several books on theatre and drama, including studies of John Osborne, Arnold Wesker, John Whiting, Harold Pinter, and Edward Bond, and of articles on theatre bibliography and classification. Editor of two collections of eighteenth-century plays and of *The Oxford Companion to the Theatre*, 1969. **Essays:** Edward Bond; Richard Cumberland; John Osborne; N. F. Simpson; Sir Richard Steele; George Villiers, Duke of Buckingham; Arnold Wesker.

TYDEMAN, William M. Senior Lecturer in English, University College of North Wales, Bangor. Author of *The Theatre in the Middle Ages*, 1978, and of the chapter on the earlier 16th century in *Year's Work in English Studies*, 1971–74. Editor of *English Poetry 1400–1800*, 1970, and of casebooks on Wordsworth and Coleridge. **Essays:** Clifford Bax; Gordon Bottomley; Harold Brighouse; Clemence Dane; John Drinkwater; St. John Ervine; St. John Hankin; Stanley Houghton; N. C. Hunter; Stephen Phillips; John Rastell.

WADDINGTON, Raymond B. Professor of English Literature, University of Wisconsin, Madison; Member of the editorial boards of *Sixteenth Century Journal* and *Literary Monographs*. Author of *The Mind's Empire: Myth and Form in George Chapman's Narrative Poems*, 1974, and of articles on Shakespeare, Chapman, Milton, and others. Co-Editor of *The Rhetoric of Renaissance Poetry*, 1974. **Essay:** George Chapman.

WALSER, Richard. Professor Emeritus of English, North Carolina State University, Raleigh. Author of *North Carolina Drama*, 1956; *Thomas Wolfe: An Introduction and*

Interpretation, 1961; *Literary North Carolina*, 1970; *Thomas Wolfe, Undergraduate*, 1977. **Essay:** Paul Green.

WATTS, Harold H.   Professor of English, Purdue University, Lafayette, Indiana. Author of *The Modern Reader's Guide to the Bible*, 1949; *Ezra Pound and the Cantos*, 1951; *Hound and Quarry*, 1953; *The Modern Reader's Guide to Religions*, 1964; *Aldous Huxley*, 1969. **Essays:** William Douglas Home; Tom Stoppard.

WEALES, Gerald.   Professor of English, University of Pennsylvania, Philadelphia; Drama Critic for *The Reporter* and *Commonweal*. Author of *Religion in Modern English Drama*, 1961; *American Drama since World War II*, 1962; *A Play and Its Parts*, 1964; *The Jumping-Off Place: American Drama in the 1960's*, 1969; *Clifford Odets*, 1971. Editor of *The Complete Plays of William Wycherley*, 1966, and with Robert J. Nelson, of the collections *Enclosure*, 1975, and *Revolution*, 1975. Recipient of the George Jean Nathan Award for Dramatic Criticism, 1965. **Essays:** Philip Barry; Arthur Miller; Clifford Odets; Mercy Warren; Tennessee Williams; William Wycherley.

WILLY, Margaret.   Free-lance Writer and Lecturer. Author of two books of verse – *The Invisible Sun*, 1946, and *Every Star a Tongue*, 1951 – and of several critical works, including *Life Was Their Cry*, 1950; *Three Metaphysical Poets: Crashaw, Vaughan, Traherne*, 1961; *Three Women Diarists: Celia Fiennes, Dorothy Wordsworth, Katherine Mansfield*, 1964; *A Critical Commentary on "Wuthering Heights,"* 1966; *A Critical Commentary on Browning's "Men and Women,"* 1968. Editor of two anthologies and of works by Goldsmith. **Essay:** W. Somerset Maugham.

WOODRESS, James.   Professor of English, University of California, Davis; Editor of *American Literary Scholarship*. Author of *Howells and Italy*, 1952; *Booth Tarkington*, 1955; *A Yankee's Odyssey: The Life of Joel Barlow*, 1958; *Willa Cather: Her Life and Art*, 1970; *American Fiction 1900–1950*, 1974. Editor of *Voices from America's Past* (with Richard Morris), 1961, and *Eight American Authors*, 1971.

WRIGHT, Judith.   Honours Tutor in English, University of Queensland, Brisbane. Author of a dozen books of verse – including *Collected Poems 1942–1970*, 1971, and *The Double Tree: Selected Poems*, 1978 – a novel, *The Nature of Love*, 1966; several juveniles; and books on Australian poetry, Shaw Neilson, Charles Harpur, and Henry Lawson. Editor of several anthologies of Australian verse and verse by Neilson.

YOUNG, Kenneth.   Literary and Political Adviser, Beaverbrook Newspapers. Author of *John Dryden*, 1954; *A.J. Balfour*, 1963; *Churchill and Beaverbrook*, 1966; *The Greek Passion*, 1969; *Stanley Baldwin*, 1976; and other biographies and works on political and social history. Editor of the diaries of Sir R. Bruce Lochart. **Essays:** John Galsworthy; J. B. Priestley.